RACE *and* EMPLOYMENT *in* AMERICA 2013

REFERENCE Library Use Only

RACE and EMPLOYMENT in AMERICA 2013

EDITED BY **DEIRDRE A. GAQUIN**
AND **GWENAVERE W. DUNN**

JUNG-KELLOGG LIBRARY
MO. BAPTIST UNIVERSITY
ONE COLLEGE PARK DR.
ST. LOUIS, MO 63141-8698

Lanham • Boulder • New York • Toronto
• Plymouth, UK

REF
HD
8081
.A5
R234
2013

Published by Bernan Press
A wholly owned subsidiary of Rowman & Littlefield
4501 Forbes Boulevard, Suite 200, Lanham, Maryland 20706

www.rowman.com
800-865-3457; info@bernan.com
10 Thornbury Road, Plymouth PL6 7PP, United Kingdom

Copyright © 2013 by Bernan Press

All rights reserved. No part of this publication may be reproduced, stored in a retrieval system, or transmitted in any form or by any means, electronic, mechanical, photocopying, recording, or otherwise, without the prior permission of the copyright holder. Bernan Press does not claim copyright in U.S. government information.

ISBN: 978-1-59888-680-1
e-ISBN: 978-1-59888-681-8

∞ ™ The paper used in this publication meets the minimum requirements of American National Standard for Information Sciences—Permanence of Paper for Printed Library Materials, ANSI/NISO Z39.48-1992.
Manufactured in the United States of America.

Contents

	Page
Preface	viii
Highlights	xi
Fifty Metropolitan Statistical Areas, Ranked by Proportion in Each Occupation Group	xix

Part A. National, 2006–2010

Tables

		Page
A-1.	EEO Occupation Groups, by Sex, Race, and Hispanic or Latino Origin	2
A-2.	Detailed Occupations in the Management, Business, and Financial Workers Occupation Group, by Sex, Race, and Hispanic Origin	6
A-3.	Detailed Occupations in the Science, Engineering, and Computer Professionals Occupation Group, by Sex, Race, and Hispanic Origin	10
A-4.	Detailed Occupations in the Health Care Practitioner Professionals Occupation Group, by Sex, Race, and Hispanic Origin	13
A-5.	Detailed Occupations in the Other Professional Workers Occupation Group, by Sex, Race, and Hispanic Origin	15
A-6.	Detailed Occupations in the Technicians Occupation Group, by Sex, Race, and Hispanic Origin	18
A-7.	Detailed Occupations in the Sales Workers Occupation Group, by Sex, Race, and Hispanic Origin	21
A-8.	Detailed Occupations in the Administrative Support Workers Occupation Group, by Sex, Race, and Hispanic Origin	23
A-9.	Detailed Occupations in the Construction and Extractive Craft Workers Occupation Group, by Sex, Race, and Hispanic Origin	27
A-10.	Detailed Occupations in the Installation, Maintenance, and Repair Craft Workers Occupation Group, by Sex, Race, and Hispanic Origin	30
A-11.	Detailed Occupations in the Production Operative Workers Occupation Group, by Sex, Race, and Hispanic Origin	35
A-12.	Detailed Occupations in the Transportation and Material Moving Operative Workers Occupation Group, by Sex, Race, and Hispanic Origin	40
A-13.	Detailed Occupations in the Laborers and Helpers Occupation Group, by Sex, Race, and Hispanic Origin	43
A-14.	Detailed Occupations in the Protective Service Workers Occupation Group, by Sex, Race, and Hispanic Origin	45
A-15.	Detailed Occupations in the Service Workers, except Protective Occupation Group, by Sex, Race, and Hispanic Origin	48
A-16.	Educational Attainment by Selected Age Groups, Sex, and Race/Ethnicity for the Civilian Labor Force 20 Years Old and Older, EEO Tabulation	50
A-17.	Detailed Occupations, by Educational Attainment for Persons Age 16 and Older (worksite geography)	52
A-18.	Workers Who are Not High School Graduates: Detailed Occupations, by Sex, Race, and Hispanic Origin	72
A-19.	Workers With High School Diploma or Equivalency: Detailed Occupations, by Sex, Race, and Hispanic Origin	100

A-20.	Workers With Some College or Associate's Degree: Detailed Occupations, by Sex, Race, and Hispanic Origin	130
A-21.	Workers With Bachelor's Degree: Detailed Occupations, by Sex, Race, and Hispanic Origin	156
A-22.	Workers With Graduate or Professional Degree: Detailed Occupations, by Sex, Race, and Hispanic Origin	182

Figures

A-2.1; 2.2	Management, Business, and Financial Workers Occupation Group, by Race and Hispanic Origin, and Sex	5
A-3.1; 3.2	Science, Engineering, and Computer Professionals Occupation Group, by Race and Hispanic Origin, and Sex	9
A-4.1; 4.2	Health Care Practitioner Professionals Occupation Group, by Race and Hispanic Origin, and Sex	12
A-5.1; 5.2	Other Professional Workers Occupation Group, by Race and Hispanic Origin, and Sex	14
A-6.1; 6.2	Technicians Occupation Group, by Race and Hispanic Origin, and Sex	17
A-7.1; 7.2	Sales Workers Occupation Group, by Race and Hispanic Origin, and Sex	20
A-8.1; 8.2	Administrative Support Workers Occupation Group, by Race and Hispanic Origin, and Sex	22
A-9.1; 9.2	Construction and Extractive Craft Workers Occupation Group, by Race and Hispanic Origin, and Sex	26
A-10.1; 10.2	Installation, Maintenance, and Repair Craft Workers Occupation Group, by Race, and Hispanic Origin, and Sex	29
A-11.1; 11.2	Production Operative Workers Occupation Group, by Race and Hispanic Origin, and Sex	34
A-12.1; 12.2	Transportation and Material Moving Operative Workers Occupation Group, by Race and Hispanic Origin, and Sex	39
A-13.1; 13.2	Laborers and Helpers Occupation Group, by Race and Hispanic Origin, and Sex	42
A-14.1; 14.2	Protective Service Workers Occupation Group, by Race and Hispanic Origin, and Sex	44
A-15.1; 15.2	Service Workers, except Protective Occupation Group, by Race and Hispanic Origin, and Sex	47

Part B. State Tables, 2006–2010

B-1.	All Workers, by State and Occupation Group	211
B-2.	All Workers, by State, Sex, Race, and Hispanic or Latino Origin	214
B-3.	Management, Business, and Financial Workers, by State, Sex, Race, and Hispanic or Latino Origin	216
B-4.	Science, Engineering, and Computer Professionals, by State, Sex, Race, and Hispanic or Latino Origin	218
B-5.	Health Care Practitioner Professionals, by State, Sex, Race, and Hispanic or Latino Origin	220
B-6.	Other Professional Workers, by State, Sex, Race, and Hispanic or Latino Origin	222
B-7.	Technicians, by State, Sex, Race, and Hispanic or Latino Origin	224
B-8.	Sales Workers, by State, Sex, Race, and Hispanic or Latino Origin	226
B-9.	Administrative Support Workers, by State, Sex, Race, and Hispanic or Latino Origin	228
B-10.	Construction and Extractive Craft Workers, by State, Sex, Race, and Hispanic or Latino Origin	230
B-11.	Installation, Maintenance, and Repair Craft Workers, by State, Sex, Race, and Hispanic or Latino Origin	232

B-12.	Production Operative Workers, by State, Sex, Race, and Hispanic or Latino Origin	234
B-13.	Transportation and Material Moving Operative Workers, by State, Sex, Race, and Hispanic or Latino Origin	236
B-14.	Laborers and Helpers, by State, Sex, Race, and Hispanic or Latino Origin	238
B-15.	Protective Service Workers, by State, Sex, Race, and Hispanic or Latino Origin	240
B-16.	Service Workers, except Protective, by State, Sex, Race, and Hispanic or Latino Origin	242

Part C. Metropolitan Statistical Area Tables, 2006–2010

C-1.	All Workers, by Metropolitan Statistical Area and Occupation Group	246
C-2.	All Workers, by Metropolitan Statistical Area, Sex, Race, and Hispanic or Latino Origin	267
C-3.	Management, Business, and Financial Workers, by Metropolitan Statistical Area, Sex, Race, and Hispanic or Latino Origin	281
C-4.	Science, Engineering, and Computer Professionals, by Metropolitan Statistical Area, Sex, Race, and Hispanic or Latino Origin	295
C-5.	Health Care Practitioner Professionals, by Metropolitan Statistical Area, Sex, Race, and Hispanic or Latino Origin	309
C-6.	Other Professional Workers, by Metropolitan Statistical Area, Sex, Race, and Hispanic or Latino Origin	323
C-7.	Technicians, by Metropolitan Statistical Area, Sex, Race, and Hispanic or Latino Origin	337
C-8.	Sales Workers, by Metropolitan Statistical Area, Sex, Race, and Hispanic or Latino Origin	351
C-9.	Administrative Support Workers, by Metropolitan Statistical Area, Sex, Race, and Hispanic or Latino Origin	365
C-10.	Construction and Extractive Craft Workers, by Metropolitan Statistical Area, Sex, Race, and Hispanic or Latino Origin	379
C-11.	Installation, Maintenance, and Repair Craft Workers, by Metropolitan Statistical Area, Sex, Race, and Hispanic or Latino Origin	393
C-12.	Production Operative Workers, by Metropolitan Statistical Area, Sex, Race, and Hispanic or Latino Origin	407
C-13.	Transportation and Material Moving Operative Workers, by Metropolitan Statistical Area, Sex, Race, and Hispanic or Latino Origin	421
C-14.	Laborers and Helpers, by Metropolitan Statistical Area, Sex, Race, and Hispanic or Latino Origin	435
C-15.	Protective Service Workers, by Metropolitan Statistical Area, Sex, Race, and Hispanic or Latino Origin	449
C-16.	Service Workers, except Protective, by Metropolitan Statistical Area, Sex, Race, and Hispanic or Latino Origin	463

Appendix A. Notes and Definitions 479

Appendix B. Detailed Occupations, by EEO Occupation Groups, 2006–2010 483

Appendix C. Metropolitan Areas 555

Index 571

PREFACE

Race and Employment in America contains a selection of information from the Census Bureau's Equal Employment Opportunity (EEO) tabulation. Based on the 2006–2010 American Community Survey (ACS), the EEO tabulation provides detailed data on employment in nearly 500 occupations, classified by sex, race, and Hispanic origin. The Census Bureau produces this tabulation for four sponsoring federal agencies: the Equal Employment Opportunity Commission (EEOC), the Department of Justice (DOJ), the Office of Federal Contract Compliance Programs (OFCCP) at the Department of Labor (DOL), and the Office of Personnel Management (OPM). Characteristics in the EEO file include citizenship, industry, age, educational attainment, earnings, and unemployment status, providing a benchmark for comparing the race, ethnicity, and sex composition of an organization's internal workforce, and the analogous external labor market, within a specified geography and job category.

The EEO Tabulation 2006–2010 (five-year ACS data) contains information similar to comparable tabulations from the 1970, 1980, 1990, and 2000 censuses. The 2010 Census occupation categories used in this file are based on the 2010 Standard Occupational Classification (SOC) categories. Due to the U.S. Census Bureau's Disclosure Review Board requirements, any occupational category containing fewer than 10,000 people employed nationwide cannot be shown separately and must be combined with related occupational categories to create aggregates containing 10,000 or more people. As a result, the tables in this book include 487 detailed occupations, including some combinations within the 539 detailed occupations in the SOC categories.

The ACS is a sample survey and a margin of error is provided for all numbers in the online tables. Because of space limitations, the margins of error are not included in this book. All users are urged to refer to the online tables, especially when working with smaller numbers. The ACS is an ongoing survey, with one-year, three-year, and five-year data sets. Because of the very detailed nature of the EEO data, the five-year file is used so that the larger sample results in the most accurate estimates possible, with the least margin of error.

The focus of this book is on occupations. Occupation refers to the type of work that a person does on the job, regardless of the industry or class of worker of the employee. Industry refers to the kind of business conducted by a person's employing organization, while class of worker categorizes people according to the type of ownership of the employing organization. The online EEO tabulations include a large set of tables detailing industry by occupation, but they are not included in this book.

The ACS occupation data may differ from other sources for several reasons. The ACS is a household survey, while some of the occupation data from the Bureau of Labor Statistics are based on establishment surveys—samples of workers from employer establishments. Some sources include only employees of private organizations, while the ACS estimates include all civilian workers, including the self-employed.

The ACS contains two specific questions about each individual's occupation:

- What kind of work was this person doing? (for example, registered nurse, personnel manager, supervisor of order department, secretary, accountant)
- What were this person's most important activities or duties? (for example, patient care, directing hiring policies, supervising order clerks, typing and filing, reconciling financial records)

These write-in responses, together with other responses about the person's industry and class of worker, are evaluated by Census Bureau coders and assigned one of the detailed occupation codes.

Appendix A includes descriptions of all 487 detailed occupations organized into the 14 occupation groups. Most tables represent the civilian labor force of 154,037,475 persons who were employed or looking for work at the time they were interviewed. All persons were assigned an occupation based on their current or most recent job. An "unemployed" category includes only those unemployed persons who were looking for work and who had not worked in the past five years or whose most recent job was in a military occupation not included in the occupations of the civilian labor force.

PREFACE

Table 1. Occupation Groups Ranked by Number of Workers, United States, 2006–2010

Rank	Group	Civilian labor force Number	Percent
	Total in civilian labor force	154,037,475	100.0
1	Administrative Support Workers	23,586,105	15.3
2	Service Workers, except Protective	21,572,140	14.0
3	Management, Business, and Financial workers	18,514,755	12.0
4	Sales Workers	17,256,510	11.2
5	Other Professional Workers	16,723,700	10.9
6	Construction and Extractive Craft Workers	9,205,480	6.0
7	Production Operative Workers	7,769,340	5.0
8	Transportation and Material Moving Operative Workers	6,984,985	4.5
9	Installation, Maintenance, and Repair Craft Workers	6,316,335	4.1
10	Laborers and Helpers	5,991,240	3.9
11	Science, Engineering, and Computer Professionals	5,907,405	3.8
12	Health Care Practitioner Professionals	5,041,270	3.3
13	Technicians	4,244,165	2.8
14	Protective Service Workers	3,257,310	2.1
15	Unemployed, no work experience in the last 5 years or most recent job was in a military-specific occupation	1,666,735	1.1

Many tables include 14 EEO Occupation Groups, aggregations of detailed occupations based on the general type of work:

1. Management, Business, and Financial Workers
2. Science, Engineering, and Computer Professionals
3. Health Care Practitioner Professionals
4. Other Professional Workers
5. Technicians
6. Sales Workers
7. Administrative Support Workers
8. Construction and Extractive Craft Workers
9. Installation, Maintenance, and Repair Craft Workers
10. Production Operative Workers
11. Transportation and Material Moving Operative Workers
12. Laborers and Helpers
13. Protective Service Workers
14. Service Workers, except Protective

Some of the tables in this book are based on "worksite geography," tallying persons at their workplaces. Those tables represent a civilian workforce of only 138,049,895 persons who were employed at the time of their interviews. Of that total, there are 10 of the 487 detailed occupations in which more than 2 million employees work.

Table 2. Employees in the Top Ten Detailed Occupations, United States, 2006–2010

Occupations	Number of employees
Secretaries and administrative assistants	3,698,890
Retail salespersons	3,318,785
Elementary and middle school teachers	3,154,520
Cashiers	3,067,255
Drivers/sales workers and truck drivers	3,058,960
Miscellaneous managers, including funeral service managers and postmasters and mail superintendents (does not include most managers who are listed in about 25 other specific categories)	3,020,000
First-line supervisors of retail sales workers	2,985,505
Registered nurses	2,522,995
Janitors and building cleaners	2,316,220
Customer service representatives	2,149,510

The EEO Tabulation includes 15 race and ethnicity categories, derived from the ACS questions about race and Hispanic origin.

Table 3. Civilian labor force by detailed race and Hispanic origin, United States, 2006–2010

Race or Hispanic Origin	Number
Total	154,037,475
Hispanic or Latino	
White alone Hispanic or Latino	13,249,220
All other Hispanic or Latino	9,207,890
Not Hispanic or Latino	
White alone	103,278,400
Black or African American alone	17,469,155
American Indian and Alaska native alone	894,060
Asian alone	7,426,015
Native Hawaiian and other Pacific Islander alone	234,430
White and Black	330,740
White and AIAN	633,080
White and Asian	416,885
Black and AIAN	116,800
Balance of two or more races	780,775

Note: Three additional groupings are available for Hawaii.

Due to space constraints, the tables in this book include only the following seven categories:

Hispanic or Latino
Not Hispanic or Latino:
   White alone
   Black or African American alone
   American Indian and Alaska Native alone
   Asian alone
   Native Hawaiian and Other Pacific Islander alone
   Two or more races

Part A presents 22 tables for the United States as a whole, beginning with the 14 major occupation groups and showing the detailed occupations in each of the groups. Tables 16 through 22 provide information about educational attainment and include only employed workers.

Part B consists of 15 tables showing age, race, and Hispanic origin in the 14 occupation groups for each state, while Part C shows the same information for each metropolitan area.

To access the full set of EEO Tabulation 2006–2010 (five-year ACS data) tables, go to www.census.gov/people/eeotabulation/data/eeotables20062010.html. Additional data is available online, including detailed occupations at the state and metropolitan area levels and also for counties and places.

A great deal of information about occupations is available online. The Census Bureau's "Industry and Occupation" page (www.census.gov/people/io/) and several pages on the website of the Bureau of Labor Statistics (including www.bls.gov/oes/) provide links to many reference sources. Of particular note is the *Occupational Outlook Handbook*, which provides comprehensive and up-to-date information on most occupations, including work environment, job prospects, and education requirements. The *Occupational Outlook Handbook* is available in print from Bernan Press at www.bernan.com or online at www.bls.gov/ooh/.

Deirdre A. Gaquin has been a data use consultant to private organizations, government agencies, and universities for more than 30 years. Prior to that, she was Director of Data Access Services at Data Use and Access Laboratories, a pioneer in private sector distribution of federal statistical data. A former President of the Association of Public Data Users, Ms. Gaquin has served on numerous boards, panels, and task forces concerned with federal statistical data and she has worked on five decennial censuses. She holds a Master of Urban Planning (MUP) degree from Hunter College. Ms. Gaquin is also an editor of Bernan Press's *State and Metropolitan Area Data Book, Almanac of American Education; the Congressional District Atlas; The Who, What, and Where of America: Understanding the American Community Survey; Places, Towns and Townships; and County and City Extra.*

Gwenavere W. Dunn is a research editor with Bernan Press. She holds a Master of Science degree in Human Resource Management from Trinity Washington University. She is a former senior editor with the Board of Governors of the Federal Reserve System and was managing editor of the Board's *Federal Reserve Bulletin*. At Bernan, she is the editor of *Crime in the United States and Employment, Hours, and Earnings*; and assistant editor of the *State and Metropolitan Area Data Book; Almanac of American Education*; and *The Who, What, and Where of America: Understanding the American Community Survey.*

HIGHLIGHTS

The EEO tabulations used in this book were derived from the 2006–2010 five-year file from the American Community Survey. They provide an overview of workers' occupations during a volatile time. The national unemployment rate rose from a 4.6 percent annual average in 2006 to 9.6 percent in 2010.[1] But this book is not about unemployment. If a person was unemployed at the time of their ACS interview, their most recent occupation was listed.

Among the resident population of the United States, 154 million persons were active in the labor force. In 14 aggregated occupation groups, the largest groups of workers were Administrative Support Workers and Service Workers, except Protective Services, each representing more than 20 million persons. In both of those groups, however, the majority of workers were women. Among men, the largest number—11 million—reported working as Management, Business, and Financial Workers, while 9 million men worked as Construction and Extractive Craft Workers, and another 8.5 million worked as Sales Workers.

Among the detailed occupations, Secretaries and Administrative Assistants constituted the largest group, nearly 4 million (3.8 million were women). For men, the largest detailed occupation was Driver/Sales Workers and Truck Drivers, with 3.4 million workers (3.2 million were men).

Race and Hispanic Origin

White workers were more likely to work as Administrative Support Workers, while among African-American, Latino, Asian, and American Indian workers, the largest occupation group was Service Workers, except Protective. The highest numbers of White workers were in the detailed occupations, Secretaries and Administrative Assistants and Elementary and Middle School Teachers, both with very large majorities of women. For African-Americans, the dominant detailed occupation was Nursing, Psychiatric, and Home Health Aides, while Latino workers were more likely to be Construction Laborers. The largest single detailed occupation among Asian workers was Software Developers, Applications and Systems Software.

Metropolitan Areas

The New York metropolitan area has 9.7 million workers, 6.3 percent of the entire labor force of the United States, followed by the Los Angeles area, with 6.5 million workers. The top ten metropolitan areas (by population size) provide jobs for 27 percent of the labor force of the United States. More than half of all workers live in the 50 largest metropolitan areas (with populations more than 500,000 people), and 85 percent of workers live in metropolitan areas.

In six metropolitan areas, more than 15 percent of residents work in the Management, Business, and Financial Occupations. The Washington, DC metropolitan area leads this list with 17.9 percent, followed closely by Bridgeport–Stamford–Norwalk, Connecticut, the residence of many workers in financial industries. Boulder, Colorado; San Francisco, California; Raleigh–Cary, North Carolina; and San Jose, California, are the four other metropolitan areas where more than 15 percent of the workers are in these occupations.

San Jose, California; Boulder, Colorado; and Huntsville, Alabama, top the list of Science, Engineering, and Computer Professionals, with more than 10 percent of their residents in these occupations. Other metropolitan areas with high employment in these fields include Washington, DC; Ann Arbor, Michigan; Corvallis, Oregon; Raleigh–Cary, North Carolina; and Seattle–Tacoma, Washington.

In Rochester, Minnesota, home of the Mayo Clinic, 10 percent of the residents are Health Care Practitioner Professionals, the highest level of all metropolitan areas. There are nine other metropolitan areas in which more than 5 percent of the residents are Health Care Practitioner Professionals, including Iowa City, Iowa; Gainesville, Florida; Ann Arbor, Michigan; and Greenville and Durham–Chapel Hill, North Carolina.

Ithaca, New York, tops the list of metropolitan areas with 22 percent of its residents classified as Other Professional Workers, the category that includes teachers. Five other university areas have more than 17 percent of their residents in this group: Lawrence, Kansas; Ames, Iowa; State College, Pennsylvania; Ann Arbor, Michigan; and Champaign–Urbana, Illinois.

Rochester, Minnesota, again tops the list of metropolitan areas for its Technicians—6.2 percent of its residents. Ten other metropolitan areas reported 4 percent or more of the workers are technicians, led by Corvallis, Oregon, and Johnson City, Tennessee, both reporting 4.4 percent.

Myrtle Beach, South Carolina, has the highest proportion of Sales Workers—16.3 percent of its labor force. Eight additional metropolitan areas have Sales Worker levels of 13.8 percent or higher, seven of them in Florida.

Administrative Support Workers constitute 18 percent or more of the labor force in six metropolitan areas, topped by Springfield, Illinois, and Laredo, Texas, both higher than 19 percent.

In nine metropolitan areas, the proportion of Construction and Extractive Craft Workers tops 10 percent. Led by Farmington, New Mexico, and Pascagoula, Mississippi, half of these are Gulf Coast areas in Texas, Louisiana, and Mississippi.

Two small metropolitan areas with large military facilities top the list for Installation, Maintenance, and Repair Craft Workers: Hinesville–Fort Stewart, Georgia, and Anniston–Oxford, Alabama. This probably reflects the presence of civilian defense contractors. Other metropolitan areas with high employment in this category include Odessa, Texas; Farmington, New Mexico; Texarkana, Texas–Arkansas; and Casper, Wyoming.

---

[1] Bureau of Labor Statistics. Labor Force Statistics from the Current Population Survey. www.bls.gov/cps/cpsaat01.htm .

In Elkhart–Goshen, Indiana—often cited as the center of recreational vehicle manufacturing—20 percent of residents work as Production Operative Workers. Similarly, in Dalton, Georgia—a center of carpet and flooring manufacturing—the level in these occupations is 19.9 percent. Twenty-five additional metropolitan areas have 10 percent or more of their residents working as Production Operative Workers. These are mostly small metropolitan areas in the Midwest and the South.

Dalton, Georgia, again tops the list for having 10 percent of its population employed as Transportation and Material Moving Operative Workers. Another 12 metropolitan areas have levels higher than 7 percent in this category, led by Rocky Mount, North Carolina, and Merced, California, both higher than 8 percent.

Employment as Laborers and Helpers is highest in two metropolitan areas in California's agricultural Central Valley: Visalia–Porterville and Madera–Chowchilla, California, where more than 17 percent of workers are in the Laborer and Worker occupation. Eight more metropolitan areas, five of them in California, have levels of 10 percent or more.

El Centro, California, tops the list for having 5.5 percent of its residents working in Protective Service. On the Mexican border, El Centro has many border patrol employees and two prisons. Other metropolitan areas with high levels of employment in this occupation include Hanford–Corcoran, California; and Pine Bluff, Arkansas—both sites of correctional institutions—and Laredo, Texas, on the Mexican border.

The top metropolitan areas for employment as Service Workers (except Protective) are two major casino gambling destinations: Atlantic City, New Jersey, with 25.9 percent of its residents, and Las Vegas, Nevada, with 23.1 percent. Three other metropolitan areas count more than 19 percent of their residents as Service Workers: Brownsville–Harlingen, Texas; Lake Havasu City–Kingman, Arizona; and Muncie, Indiana.

HIGHLIGHTS

Occupation Profiles by Sex, Race, and Hispanic Origin, United States, 2006–2010

1. Total Civilian Labor Force, Resident Population

Rank	Occupation group	Number of workers
	Total civilian labor force	154,037,475
1	Administrative Support Workers	23,586,105
2	Service Workers, except Protective	21,572,140
3	Management, Business, and Financial Workers	18,514,755
4	Sales Workers	17,256,510
5	Other Professional Workers	16,723,700
6	Construction and Extractive Craft Workers	9,205,480
7	Production Operative Workers	7,769,340
8	Transportation and Material Moving Operative Workers	6,984,985
9	Installation, Maintenance, and Repair Craft Workers	6,316,335
10	Laborers and Helpers	5,991,240
11	Science, Engineering, and Computer Professionals	5,907,405
12	Health Care Practitioner Professionals	5,041,270
13	Technicians	4,244,165
14	Protective Service Workers	3,257,310
15	Unemployed[1]	1,666,735
	Top Ten Detailed Occupations Held by Total Civilian Labor Force	
1	Secretaries and administrative assistants	3,991,485
2	Retail salespersons	3,747,080
3	Cashiers	3,703,420
4	Elementary and middle school teachers	3,452,545
5	Driver/sales workers and truck drivers	3,410,730
6	Miscellaneous managers[2]	3,183,835
7	First-line supervisors of retail sales workers	3,182,300
8	Registered nurses	2,639,750
9	Janitors and building cleaners	2,607,880
10	Customer service representatives	2,415,235

2. Males in the Civilian Labor Force, Resident Population

Rank	Occupation group	Number of workers
	Total males	81,323,090
1	Management, Business, and Financial Workers	11,000,315
2	Construction and Extractive Craft Workers	8,951,330
3	Sales Workers	8,552,900
4	Service Workers, except Protective	7,477,890
5	Other Professional Workers	6,345,860
6	Administrative Support Workers	5,990,085
7	Installation, Maintenance, and Repair Craft Workers	5,871,165
8	Transportation and Material Moving Operative Workers	5,695,450
9	Production Operative Workers	5,340,305
10	Laborers and Helpers	4,999,790
11	Science, Engineering, and Computer Professionals	4,528,390
12	Protective Service Workers	2,514,290
13	Technicians	1,861,185
14	Health Care Practitioner Professionals	1,359,170
15	Unemployed[1]	834,965
	Top Ten Detailed Occupations Held by Males	
1	Driver/sales workers and truck drivers	3,230,810
2	Miscellaneous managers[2]	2,074,525
3	Laborers and freight, stock, and material movers, hand	1,882,770
4	Construction laborers	1,872,555
5	Retail salespersons	1,821,005
6	Janitors and building cleaners	1,781,815
7	First-line supervisors of retail sales workers	1,765,580
8	Carpenters	1,590,715
9	Cooks	1,342,460
10	Grounds maintenance workers	1,294,995

[1] No work experience in the last 5 years or most recent job was in a military-specific occupation.
[2] Includes funeral service managers; postmasters and mail superintendents; and managers who are not listed separately. Does not include most managers who are listed in about 25 other specific categories, such as General and Operations Managers, Marketing and Sales Managers, and so on.

Occupation Profiles by Sex, Race, and Hispanic Origin, United States, 2006–2010—*Continued*

3. Females in the Civilian Labor Force, Resident Population

Rank	Occupation group	Number of workers
	Total females..	72,714,390
1	Administrative Support Workers..	17,596,020
2	Service Workers, except Protective...	14,094,250
3	Other Professional Workers...	10,377,840
4	Sales Workers..	8,703,610
5	Management, Business, and Financial Workers.....................	7,514,440
6	Health Care Practitioner Professionals....................................	3,682,105
7	Production Operative Workers...	2,429,035
8	Technicians..	2,382,975
9	Science, Engineering, and Computer Professionals...............	1,379,015
10	Transportation and Material Moving Operative Workers...	1,289,535
11	Laborers and Helpers..	991,450
12	Unemployed[1]...	831,770
13	Protective Service Workers...	743,020
14	Installation, Maintenance, and Repair Craft Workers........	445,170
15	Construction and Extractive Craft Workers........................	254,155
	Top Ten Detailed Occupations Held by Females	
1	Secretaries and administrative assistants..............................	3,828,290
2	Cashiers...	2,766,555
3	Elementary and middle school teachers................................	2,737,785
4	Registered nurses..	2,408,225
5	Nursing, psychiatric, and home health aides.......................	1,941,620
6	Retail salespersons...	1,926,075
7	Waiters and waitresses...	1,652,155
8	Customer service representatives...	1,640,965
9	First-line supervisors of retail sales workers........................	1,416,725
10	Maids and housekeeping cleaners...	1,382,430

4. White Alone, not Hispanic or Latino, Persons in the Civilian Labor Force, Resident Population

Rank	Occupation group	Number of workers
	Total White alone, not Hispanic or Latino................	103,278,400
1	Administrative Support Workers..	15,972,595
2	Management, Business, and Financial workers.....................	14,425,760
3	Other Professional Workers...	12,680,020
4	Sales Workers..	12,163,980
5	Service Workers, except Protective...	11,868,285
6	Construction and Extractive Craft Workers........................	5,811,335
7	Installation, Maintenance, and Repair Craft Workers........	4,590,455
8	Production Operative Workers...	4,484,160
9	Science, Engineering, and Computer Professionals...............	4,246,640
10	Transportation and Material Moving Operative Workers...	4,211,875
11	Health Care Practitioner Professionals....................................	3,806,800
12	Laborers and Helpers..	3,217,175
13	Technicians..	3,000,415
14	Protective Service Workers...	2,090,840
15	Unemployed[1]...	708,065
	Top Ten Detailed Occupations Held by White Alone	
1	Secretaries and administrative assistants..............................	3,049,700
2	Elementary and middle school teachers................................	2,766,040
3	Retail salespersons...	2,580,665
4	Miscellaneous managers[2]...	2,494,480
5	First-line supervisors of retail sales workers........................	2,350,140
6	Driver/sales workers and truck drivers..................................	2,251,200
7	Cashiers...	2,050,995
8	Registered nurses..	1,997,830
9	Waiters and waitresses...	1,552,220
10	Accountants and auditors...	1,537,555

[1] No work experience in the last 5 years or most recent job was in a military-specific occupation.
[2] Includes funeral service managers; postmasters and mail superintendents; and managers who are not listed separately. Does not include most managers who are listed in about 25 other specific categories, such as General and Operations Managers, Marketing and Sales Managers, and so on.

HIGHLIGHTS

Occupation Profiles by Sex, Race, and Hispanic Origin, United States, 2006–2010—*Continued*

5. Black Alone, not Hispanic or Latino, Persons in the Civilian Labor Force, Resident Population

Rank	Occupation group	Number of workers
	Total Black alone, not Hispanic or Latino	17,469,155
1	Service Workers, except Protective	3,485,605
2	Administrative Support Workers	3,079,780
3	Sales Workers	1,746,595
4	Other Professional Workers	1,584,760
5	Management, Business, and Financial Workers	1,372,180
6	Transportation and Material Moving Operative Workers	1,121,360
7	Production Operative Workers	1,003,295
8	Laborers and Helpers	703,955
9	Protective Service Workers	615,010
10	Construction and Extractive Craft Workers	593,195
11	Installation, Maintenance, and Repair Craft Workers	492,785
12	Technicians	484,455
13	Unemployed[1]	434,665
14	Health Care Practitioner Professionals	399,915
15	Science, Engineering, and Computer Professionals	351,600
	Top Ten Detailed Occupations Held by Black Alone	
1	Nursing, psychiatric, and home health aides	730,795
2	Cashiers	652,615
3	Janitors and building cleaners	458,795
4	Driver/sales workers and truck drivers	455,230
5	Unemployed[1]	434,665
6	Customer service representatives	412,615
7	Retail salespersons	411,275
8	Cooks	393,790
9	Laborers and freight, stock, and material movers, hand	387,030
10	Secretaries and administrative assistants	360,895

6. Hispanic or Latino Persons in the Civilian Labor Force, Resident Population

Rank	Occupation group	Number of workers
	Total Hispanic or Latino	22,457,110
1	Service Workers, except Protective	4,523,995
2	Administrative Support Workers	3,075,280
3	Construction and Extractive Craft Workers	2,481,855
4	Sales Workers	2,154,145
5	Laborers and Helpers	1,817,710
6	Production Operative Workers	1,742,115
7	Management, Business, and Financial workers	1,466,850
8	Other Professional Workers	1,299,960
9	Transportation and Material Moving Operative Workers	1,297,050
10	Installation, Maintenance, and Repair Craft Workers	899,470
11	Protective Service Workers	388,655
12	Unemployed[1]	368,025
13	Technicians	360,235
14	Science, Engineering, and Computer Professionals	326,755
15	Health Care Practitioner Professionals	255,010
	Top Ten Detailed Occupations Held by Hispanic or Latino Persons in the Civilian Labor Force	
1	Construction laborers	721,920
2	Janitors and building cleaners	691,690
3	Cashiers	668,725
4	Cooks	666,215
5	Maids and housekeeping cleaners	647,245
6	Driver/sales workers and truck drivers	580,800
7	Grounds maintenance workers	547,115
8	Retail salespersons	497,675
9	Miscellaneous agricultural workers	483,295
10	Laborers and freight, stock, and material movers, hand	451,910

[1] No work experience in the last 5 years or most recent job was in a military-specific occupation.

Occupation Profiles by Sex, Race, and Hispanic Origin, United States, 2006–2010—*Continued*

7. Asian Alone, not Hispanic or Latino, Persons in the Civilian Labor Force, Resident Population

Rank	Occupation group	Number of workers
	Total Asian alone, not Hispanic or Latino	7,426,015
1	Service Workers, except Protective	1,100,785
2	Management, Business, and Financial Workers	920,515
3	Administrative Support Workers	908,890
4	Science, Engineering, and Computer Professionals	867,955
5	Other Professional Workers	826,590
6	Sales Workers	809,545
7	Health Care Practitioner Professionals	498,670
8	Production Operative Workers	397,465
9	Technicians	307,115
10	Transportation and Material Moving Operative Workers	207,095
11	Installation, Maintenance, and Repair Craft Workers	202,305
12	Laborers and Helpers	111,940
13	Construction and Extractive Craft Workers	106,950
14	Unemployed[1]	93,100
15	Protective Service Workers	67,095
	Top Ten Detailed Occupations Held by Asian Alone	
1	Software developers, applications and systems software	247,000
2	Accountants and auditors	218,470
3	Registered nurses	212,815
4	Cashiers	212,035
5	Retail salespersons	167,415
6	First-line supervisors of retail sales workers	165,210
7	Miscellaneous managers[2]	162,745
8	Postsecondary teachers	158,150
9	Physicians and surgeons	154,970
10	Waiters and waitresses	124,415

8. American Indian and Alaska Native Alone, not Hispanic or Latino, Persons in the Civilian Labor Force, Resident Population

Rank	Occupation group	Number of workers
	Total American Indian and Alaska Native alone, not Hispanic or Latino	894,060
1	Service Workers, except Protective	168,060
2	Administrative Support Workers	139,440
3	Sales Workers	81,310
4	Construction and Extractive Craft Workers	77,485
5	Management, Business, and Financial Workers	77,300
6	Other Professional Workers	74,070
7	Laborers and Helpers	45,120
8	Production Operative Workers	45,105
9	Transportation and Material Moving Operative Workers	42,095
10	Installation, Maintenance, and Repair Craft Workers	40,315
11	Protective Service Workers	29,220
12	Technicians	23,050
13	Unemployed[1]	18,110
14	Science, Engineering, and Computer Professionals	17,045
15	Health Care Practitioner Professionals	16,335
	Top Ten Detailed Occupations Held by American Indian and Alaska Native Alone	
1	Cashiers	30,745
2	Janitors and building cleaners	23,820
3	Secretaries and administrative assistants	22,915
4	Cooks	20,020
5	Nursing, psychiatric, and home health aides	19,805
6	Driver/sales workers and truck drivers	19,755
7	Laborers and freight, stock, and material movers, hand	18,520
8	Unemployed[1]	18,110
9	Retail salespersons	16,770
10	Construction laborers	16,410

[1] No work experience in the last 5 years or most recent job was in a military-specific occupation.
[2] Includes funeral service managers; postmasters and mail superintendents; and managers who are not listed separately. Does not include most managers who are listed in about 25 other specific categories, such as General and Operations Managers, Marketing and Sales Managers, and so on.

HIGHLIGHTS

Occupation Profiles by Sex, Race, and Hispanic Origin, United States, 2006–2010—*Continued*

9. Native Hawaiian and Other Pacific Islander Alone, not Hispanic or Latino, Persons in the Civilian Labor Force, Resident Population

Rank	Occupation group	Number of workers
	Total Native Hawaiian and Other Pacific Islander alone, not Hispanic or Latino	234,430
1	Administrative Support Workers	44,440
2	Service Workers, except Protective	41,760
3	Sales Workers	23,455
4	Management, Business, and Financial workers	19,115
5	Other Professional Workers	15,995
6	Construction and Extractive Craft Workers	15,845
7	Transportation and Material Moving Operative Workers	13,920
8	Laborers and Helpers	12,490
9	Production Operative Workers	10,445
10	Installation, Maintenance, and Repair Craft Workers	9,395
11	Protective Service Workers	9,190
12	Science, Engineering, and Computer Professionals	6,045
13	Technicians	4,845
14	Unemployed[1]	4,130
15	Health Care Practitioner Professionals	3,360
	Top Ten Detailed Occupations Held by Native Hawaiian and Other Pacific Islander Alone	
1	Cashiers	8,700
2	Laborers and freight, stock, and material movers, hand	6,035
3	Driver/sales workers and truck drivers	5,725
4	Secretaries and administrative assistants	5,000
5	Security guards and gaming surveillance officers	4,925
6	Customer service representatives	4,855
7	Cooks	4,825
8	Stock clerks and order fillers	4,665
9	Janitors and building cleaners	4,520
10	Nursing, psychiatric, and home health aides	4,495

10. Two or More Races, not Hispanic or Latino, Persons in the Civilian Labor Force, Resident Population

Rank	Occupation group	Number of workers
	Total two or more races, not Hispanic or Latino	2,278,280
1	Service Workers, except Protective	383,650
2	Administrative Support Workers	365,670
3	Sales Workers	277,475
4	Other Professional Workers	242,305
5	Management, Business, and Financial Workers	233,045
6	Construction and Extractive Craft Workers	118,815
7	Transportation and Material Moving Operative Workers	91,585
8	Science, Engineering, and Computer Professionals	91,370
9	Production Operative Workers	86,760
10	Laborers and Helpers	82,845
11	Installation, Maintenance, and Repair Craft Workers	81,610
12	Technicians	64,040
13	Health Care Practitioner Professionals	61,175
14	Protective Service Workers	57,295
15	Unemployed[1]	40,640
	Top Ten Detailed Occupations Held by Two or More Races	
1	Cashiers	79,595
2	Retail salespersons	69,020
3	Secretaries and administrative assistants	52,160
4	First-line supervisors of retail sales workers	48,335
5	Waiters and waitresses	48,190
6	Customer service representatives	45,210
7	Driver/sales workers and truck drivers	41,680
8	Miscellaneous managers[2]	40,720
9	Unemployed[1]	40,640
10	Nursing, psychiatric, and home health aides	39,290

[1] No work experience in the last 5 years or most recent job was in a military-specific occupation.
[2] Includes funeral service managers; postmasters and mail superintendents; and managers who are not listed separately. Does not include most managers who are listed in about 25 other specific categories, such as General and Operations Managers, Marketing and Sales Managers, and so on.

Top Fifty Metropolitan Statistical Areas, by Proportion in Each EEO Occupation Group

Total Labor Force			Management, Business, and Financial Workers				Science, Engineering, and Computer Professionals			
Rank by size of labor force	Metropolitan Statistical Area	Total who worked in the last 5 years	Rank by size of labor force	Rank in occupation group	Metropolitan Statistical Area	Percent	Rank by size of labor force	Rank in occupation group	Metropolitan Statistical Area	Percent
	United States	154,037,475			**United States**	12.0			**United States**	3.8
1	New York-Northern New Jersey-Long Island, NY-NJ-PA	9,654,290	6	1	Washington-Arlington-Alexandria, DC-VA-MD-WV	17.9	32	1	San Jose-Sunnyvale-Santa Clara, CA	13.4
2	Los Angeles-Long Beach-Santa Ana, CA	6,510,485	52	2	Bridgeport-Stamford-Norwalk, CT	16.9	148	2	Boulder, CO	10.8
3	Chicago-Joliet-Naperville, IL-IN-WI	4,936,190	148	3	Boulder, CO	16.3	120	3	Huntsville, AL	10.2
4	Dallas-Fort Worth-Arlington, TX	3,240,180	11	4	San Francisco-Oakland-Fremont, CA	15.8	6	4	Washington-Arlington-Alexandria, DC-VA-MD-WV	9.0
5	Philadelphia-Camden-Wilmington, PA-NJ-DE-MD	3,073,915	46	5	Raleigh-Cary, NC	15.6	136	5	Ann Arbor, MI	8.3
6	Washington-Arlington-Alexandria, DC-VA-MD-WV	3,067,930	32	6	San Jose-Sunnyvale-Santa Clara, CA	15.5	355	6	Corvallis, OR	8.2
7	Houston-Sugar Land-Baytown, TX	2,915,695	35	7	Austin-Round Rock-San Marcos, TX	14.9	46	7	Raleigh-Cary, NC	8.1
8	Miami-Fort Lauderdale-Pompano Beach, FL	2,809,665	10	7	Boston-Cambridge-Quincy, MA-NH	14.9	16	8	Seattle-Tacoma-Bellevue, WA	7.6
9	Atlanta-Sandy Springs-Marietta, GA	2,730,620	21	9	Denver-Aurora-Broomfield, CO	14.8	11	9	San Francisco-Oakland-Fremont, CA	7.3
10	Boston-Cambridge-Quincy, MA-NH	2,498,630	15	9	Minneapolis-St. Paul-Bloomington, MN-WI	14.8	110	10	Manchester-Nashua, NH	7.2
11	San Francisco-Oakland-Fremont, CA	2,306,445					98	10	Palm Bay-Melbourne-Titusville, FL	7.2
12	Detroit-Warren-Livonia, MI	2,166,755	16	9	Seattle-Tacoma-Bellevue, WA	14.8	35	12	Austin-Round Rock-San Marcos, TX	7.0
13	Phoenix-Mesa-Glendale, AZ	2,009,550	9	12	Atlanta-Sandy Springs-Marietta, GA	14.7	146	12	Fort Collins-Loveland, CO	7.0
14	Riverside-San Bernardino-Ontario, CA	1,901,430	19	13	Baltimore-Towson, MD	14.5	359	14	Columbus, IN	6.9
15	Minneapolis-St. Paul-Bloomington, MN-WI	1,840,260	82	13	Des Moines-West Des Moines, IA	14.5	220	15	Bloomington-Normal, IL	6.8
16	Seattle-Tacoma-Bellevue, WA	1,833,705	110	15	Manchester-Nashua, NH	14.4	10	16	Boston-Cambridge-Quincy, MA-NH	6.7
17	San Diego-Carlsbad-San Marcos, CA	1,497,805	183	16	Olympia, WA	14.3	84	16	Colorado Springs, CO	6.7
18	St. Louis, MO-IL	1,464,850	64	17	Oxnard-Thousand Oaks-Ventura, CA	14.2	78	18	Madison, WI	6.5
19	Baltimore-Towson, MD	1,438,090	268	18	Napa, CA	14.1	129	19	Trenton-Ewing, NJ	6.4
20	Tampa-St. Petersburg-Clearwater, FL	1,372,115	33	19	Charlotte-Gastonia-Rock Hill, NC-SC	14.0	19	20	Baltimore-Towson, MD	6.3
							21	20	Denver-Aurora-Broomfield, CO	6.3
21	Denver-Aurora-Broomfield, CO	1,371,265	84	19	Colorado Springs, CO	14.0	338	22	Ames, IA	6.2
22	Pittsburgh, PA	1,200,920	146	19	Fort Collins-Loveland, CO	14.0	336	22	Ithaca, NY	6.2
23	Portland-Vancouver-Hillsboro, OR-WA	1,169,465	362	22	Palm Coast, FL	13.9	17	22	San Diego-Carlsbad-San Marcos, CA	6.2
24	Orlando-Kissimmee-Sanford, FL	1,109,310	129	22	Trenton-Ewing, NJ	13.9	97	25	Durham-Chapel Hill, NC	6.1
25	Cincinnati-Middletown, OH-KY-IN	1,100,965	44	24	Richmond, VA	13.7	188	26	Kennewick-Pasco-Richland, WA	6.0
26	Cleveland-Elyria-Mentor, OH	1,081,565	283	24	Warner Robins, GA	13.7	158	26	Norwich-New London, CT	6.0
27	Kansas City, MO-KS	1,074,060	31	26	Columbus, OH	13.6	61	28	Worcester, MA	5.9
28	Sacramento-Arden-Arcade-Roseville, CA	1,056,940	4	26	Dallas-Fort Worth-Arlington, TX	13.6	187	29	Bremerton-Silverdale, WA	5.8
29	Las Vegas-Paradise, NV	997,625	78	26	Madison, WI	13.6	202	30	Rochester, MN	5.7
			28	26	Sacramento-Arden-Arcade-Roseville, CA	13.6	15	31	Minneapolis-St. Paul-Bloomington, MN-WI	5.6
							246	31	State College, PA	5.6
30	San Antonio-New Braunfels, TX	993,330	17	26	San Diego-Carlsbad-San Marcos, CA	13.6	23	33	Portland-Vancouver-Hillsboro, OR-WA	5.5
31	Columbus, OH	962,935		26	Santa Fe, NM	13.6	206	34	Charlottesville, VA	5.4
32	San Jose-Sunnyvale-Santa Clara, CA	942,880	248	32	Bloomington-Normal, IL	13.5	166	34	Santa Cruz-Watsonville, CA	5.4
33	Charlotte-Gastonia-Rock Hill, NC-SC	914,240	220	32	Charlottesville, VA	13.5	240	36	Blacksburg-Christiansburg-Radford, VA	5.3
34	Indianapolis-Carmel, IN	910,210	206	32	Hartford-West Hartford-East Hartford, CT	13.5	59	37	Albuquerque, NM	5.2
35	Austin-Round Rock-San Marcos, TX	897,255	43				162	37	Cedar Rapids, IA	5.2
36	Providence-New Bedford-Fall River, RI-MA	856,225	27	32	Kansas City, MO-KS	13.5	183	37	Olympia, WA	5.2
37	Milwaukee-Waukesha-West Allis, WI	826,530	13	36	Phoenix-Mesa-Glendale, AZ	13.4	28	37	Sacramento-Arden-Arcade-Roseville, CA	5.2
38	Virginia Beach-Norfolk-Newport News, VA-NC	824,655	23	36	Portland-Vancouver-Hillsboro, OR-WA	13.4	248	37	Santa Fe, NM	5.2
39	Nashville-Davidson--Murfreesboro--Franklin, TN	819,770	166	36	Santa Cruz-Watsonville, CA	13.4	86	42	Boise City-Nampa, ID	5.1
			40	39	Jacksonville, FL	13.3	185	42	Burlington-South Burlington, VT	5.1
			90	39	Portland-South Portland-Biddeford, ME	13.3	12	42	Detroit-Warren-Livonia, MI	5.1
40	Jacksonville, FL	678,960					43	42	Hartford-West Hartford-East Hartford, CT	5.1
41	Memphis, TN-MS-AR	655,310	136	41	Ann Arbor, MI	13.2	109	42	Provo-Orem, UT	5.1
42	Louisville/Jefferson County, KY-IN	653,945	185	41	Burlington-South Burlington, VT	13.2	125	47	Anchorage, AK	5.0
43	Hartford-West Hartford-East Hartford, CT	653,940	5	41	Philadelphia-Camden-Wilmington, PA-NJ-DE-MD	13.2	305	47	Idaho Falls, ID	5.0
44	Richmond, VA	647,365	61	41	Worcester, MA	13.2	51	47	Rochester, NY	5.0
45	Oklahoma City, OK	624,140	193	45	Barnstable Town, MA	13.1	283	47	Warner Robins, GA	5.0
46	Raleigh-Cary, NC	580,680	359	45	Columbus, IN	13.1				
47	Salt Lake City, UT	577,550	99	45	Ogden-Clearfield, UT	13.1				
48	Buffalo-Niagara Falls, NY	575,645	3	48	Chicago-Joliet-Naperville, IL-IN-WI	13.0				
49	New Orleans-Metairie-Kenner, LA	558,690	86	49	Boise City-Nampa, ID	12.9				
50	Birmingham-Hoover, AL	555,515	34	49	Indianapolis-Carmel, IN	12.9				
			253	49	Jefferson City, MO	12.9				
			1	49	New York-Northern New Jersey-Long Island, NY-NJ-PA	12.9				
			100	49	Santa Rosa-Petaluma, CA	12.9				

# Top Fifty Metropolitan Statistical Areas, by Proportion in Each EEO Occupation Group—Continued

Health Care Practitioner Professionals

Rank by size of labor force	Rank in occupation group	Metropolitan Statistical Area	Percent
		United States..............................	3.3
202	1	Rochester, MN..............................	10.0
229	2	Iowa City, IA.................................	6.8
172	3	Gainesville, FL..............................	6.1
136	4	Ann Arbor, MI...............................	6.0
215	5	Greenville, NC..............................	5.9
97	6	Durham-Chapel Hill, NC................	5.8
206	7	Charlottesville, VA........................	5.7
266	8	Wheeling, WV-OH........................	5.2
216	9	Columbia, MO...............................	5.1
101	10	Lexington-Fayette, KY..................	5.0
193	11	Barnstable Town, MA....................	4.8
361	11	Great Falls, MT.............................	4.8
96	11	Jackson, MS.................................	4.8
279	11	Johnstown, PA..............................	4.8
174	11	Sioux Falls, SD.............................	4.8
190	11	Springfield, IL...............................	4.8
161	17	Charleston, WV.............................	4.7
356	17	Elmira, NY....................................	4.7
276	17	Hattiesburg, MS............................	4.7
181	17	Huntington-Ashland, WV-KY-OH....	4.7
72	17	Little Rock-North Little Rock-Conway, AR...................................	4.7
219	22	Johnson City, TN..........................	4.6
22	22	Pittsburgh, PA...............................	4.6
207	22	Tyler, TX.......................................	4.6
118	25	Asheville, NC................................	4.5
357	25	Hot Springs, AR............................	4.5
301	25	Morgantown, WV...........................	4.5
268	25	Napa, CA......................................	4.5
314	25	Steubenville-Weirton, OH-WV.......	4.5
271	30	Alexandria, LA..............................	4.4
239	30	Bangor, ME...................................	4.4
263	30	Pueblo, CO...................................	4.4
302	33	Bismarck, ND................................	4.3
156	33	Duluth, MN-WI..............................	4.3
260	33	Grand Junction, CO......................	4.3
318	33	Jackson, TN..................................	4.3
344	33	Ocean City, NJ.............................	4.3
54	33	Omaha-Council Bluffs, NE-IA.......	4.3
108	33	Spokane, WA................................	4.3
102	40	Augusta-Richmond County, GA-SC	4.2
10	40	Boston-Cambridge-Quincy, MA-NH	4.2
358	40	Casper, WY...................................	4.2
256	40	La Crosse, WI-MN........................	4.2
130	40	Peoria, IL......................................	4.2
5	40	Philadelphia-Camden-Wilmington, PA-NJ-DE-MD	4.2
131	40	Shreveport-Bossier City, LA.........	4.2
105	40	Winston-Salem, NC......................	4.2
296	48	Altoona, PA...................................	4.1
26	48	Cleveland-Elyria-Mentor, OH........	4.1
281	48	Dothan, AL....................................	4.1
165	48	Erie, PA...	4.1
351	48	Gadsden, AL.................................	4.1
78	48	Madison, WI..................................	4.1
309	48	Missoula, MT.................................	4.1
55	48	New Haven-Milford, CT................	4.1
270	48	Pittsfield, MA.................................	4.1
90	48	Portland-South Portland-Biddeford, ME	4.1
151	48	Roanoke, VA.................................	4.1
298	48	Salisbury, MD...............................	4.1
91	48	Scranton-Wilkes-Barre, PA...........	4.1

Other Professional Workers

Rank by size of labor force	Rank in occupation group	Metropolitan Statistical Area	Percent
		United States..............................	10.9
336	1	Ithaca, NY.....................................	22.1
291	2	Lawrence, KS...............................	17.9
338	3	Ames, IA.......................................	17.8
246	4	State College, PA.........................	17.7
136	5	Ann Arbor, MI...............................	17.1
182	6	Champaign-Urbana, IL.................	17.0
355	7	Corvallis, OR................................	16.4
148	8	Boulder, CO..................................	16.1
216	9	Columbia, MO...............................	15.9
206	10	Charlottesville, VA........................	15.7
217	11	Bloomington, IN............................	15.5
6	12	Washington-Arlington-Alexandria, DC-VA-MD-WV	15.3
223	13	Athens-Clarke County, GA............	15.2
172	13	Gainesville, FL..............................	15.2
196	15	College Station-Bryan, TX............	15.1
97	15	Durham-Chapel Hill, NC................	15.1
315	17	Manhattan, KS..............................	15.0
133	17	Tallahassee, FL............................	15.0
229	19	Iowa City, IA.................................	14.9
248	20	Santa Fe, NM...............................	14.7
200	21	Lafayette, IN.................................	14.4
213	22	Kingston, NY.................................	14.3
78	22	Madison, WI..................................	14.3
240	24	Blacksburg-Christiansburg-Radford, VA	14.1
52	24	Bridgeport-Stamford-Norwalk, CT..	14.1
10	26	Boston-Cambridge-Quincy, MA-NH	14.0
1	27	New York-Northern New Jersey-Long Island, NY-NJ-PA	13.9
166	28	Santa Cruz-Watsonville, CA.........	13.6
275	29	Auburn-Opelika, AL......................	13.5
185	29	Burlington-South Burlington, VT....	13.5
11	29	San Francisco-Oakland-Fremont, CA	13.5
129	29	Trenton-Ewing, NJ........................	13.5
70	33	Springfield, MA.............................	13.1
35	34	Austin-Round Rock-San Marcos, TX	13.0
109	34	Provo-Orem, UT............................	13.0
301	36	Morgantown, WV...........................	12.9
103	37	Lansing-East Lansing, MI.............	12.8
55	38	New Haven-Milford, CT................	12.7
51	38	Rochester, NY..............................	12.7
143	40	Lincoln, NE...................................	12.6
56	41	Albany-Schenectady-Troy, NY......	12.5
221	41	Las Cruces, NM............................	12.5
101	41	Lexington-Fayette, KY..................	12.5
303	41	Logan, UT-ID................................	12.5
309	41	Missoula, MT.................................	12.5
46	41	Raleigh-Cary, NC..........................	12.5
43	47	Hartford-West Hartford-East Hartford, CT	12.4
2	47	Los Angeles-Long Beach-Santa Ana, CA	12.4
76	47	Syracuse, NY...............................	12.4
19	50	Baltimore-Towson, MD.................	12.3
267	50	Flagstaff, AZ.................................	12.3

Technicians

Rank by size of labor force	Rank in occupation group	Metropolitan Statistical Area	Percent
		United States..............................	2.8
202	1	Rochester, MN..............................	6.2
355	2	Corvallis, OR................................	4.4
219	2	Johnson City, TN..........................	4.4
216	4	Columbia, MO...............................	4.3
336	4	Ithaca, NY.....................................	4.3
301	4	Morgantown, WV...........................	4.3
341	7	Lawton, OK...................................	4.2
320	7	Victoria, TX...................................	4.2
240	9	Blacksburg-Christiansburg-Radford, VA	4.0
181	9	Huntington-Ashland, WV-KY-OH....	4.0
157	9	Kingsport-Bristol-Bristol, TN-VA.....	4.0
338	12	Ames, IA.......................................	3.9
97	12	Durham-Chapel Hill, NC................	3.9
229	14	Iowa City, IA.................................	3.8
291	14	Lawrence, KS...............................	3.8
246	14	State College, PA.........................	3.8
259	17	Decatur, AL...................................	3.7
186	17	Fargo, ND-MN..............................	3.7
78	17	Madison, WI..................................	3.7
238	17	Monroe, LA...................................	3.7
311	17	Sherman-Denison, TX..................	3.7
265	17	Wichita Falls, TX..........................	3.7
251	23	Abilene, TX...................................	3.6
264	23	Albany, GA...................................	3.6
228	23	Anderson, SC...............................	3.6
245	23	Burlington, NC..............................	3.6
175	23	Columbus, GA-AL.........................	3.6
345	23	Fairbanks, AK...............................	3.6
351	23	Gadsden, AL.................................	3.6
256	23	La Crosse, WI-MN........................	3.6
98	23	Palm Bay-Melbourne-Titusville, FL	3.6
190	23	Springfield, IL...............................	3.6
297	23	St. Joseph, MO-KS.......................	3.6
314	23	Steubenville-Weirton, OH-WV.......	3.6
204	23	Tuscaloosa, AL.............................	3.6
283	23	Warner Robins, GA.......................	3.6
310	23	Williamsport, PA...........................	3.6
275	38	Auburn-Opelika, AL......................	3.5
142	38	Beaumont-Port Arthur, TX............	3.5
182	38	Champaign-Urbana, IL.................	3.5
161	38	Charleston, WV.............................	3.5
356	38	Elmira, NY....................................	3.5
211	38	Florence, SC................................	3.5
172	38	Gainesville, FL..............................	3.5
323	38	Goldsboro, NC..............................	3.5
279	38	Johnstown, PA..............................	3.5
313	38	Jonesboro, AR..............................	3.5
200	38	Lafayette, IN.................................	3.5
163	38	Lafayette, LA................................	3.5
273	38	Lebanon, PA.................................	3.5
274	38	Midland, TX...................................	3.5
362	38	Palm Coast, FL.............................	3.5
249	38	Parkersburg-Marietta-Vienna, WV-OH	3.5
116	38	Pensacola-Ferry Pass-Brent, FL....	3.5
290	38	Punta Gorda, FL...........................	3.5
360	38	Sandusky, OH...............................	3.5
349	38	Sumter, SC...................................	3.5
237	38	Terre Haute, IN.............................	3.5

Top Fifty Metropolitan Statistical Areas, by Proportion in Each EEO Occupation Group–*Continued*

Sales Workers					Administrative Support Workers					Construction and Extractive Craft Workers			
Rank by size of labor force	Rank in occupation group	Metropolitan Statistical Area	Percent		Rank by size of labor force	Rank in occupation group	Metropolitan Statistical Area	Percent		Rank by size of labor force	Rank in occupation group	Metropolitan Statistical Area	Percent
		United States	11.2				**United States**	15.3				**United States**	6.0
171	1	Myrtle Beach-North Myrtle Beach-Conway, SC	16.3		190	1	Springfield, IL	19.5		325	1	Farmington, NM	11.4
290	2	Punta Gorda, FL	14.9		199	2	Laredo, TX	19.0		255	1	Pascagoula, MS	11.4
89	3	Cape Coral-Fort Myers, FL	14.5		88	3	Harrisburg-Carlisle, PA	18.5		286	3	Odessa, TX	10.5
80	4	North Port-Bradenton-Sarasota, FL	14.1		253	3	Jefferson City, MO	18.5		269	4	Coeur d'Alene, ID	10.3
155	5	Naples-Marco Island, FL	13.9		56	5	Albany-Schenectady-Troy, NY	18.3		345	5	Fairbanks, AK	10.2
107	6	Deltona-Daytona Beach-Ormond Beach, FL	13.8		184	6	Topeka, KS	18.0		214	5	Lake Charles, LA	10.2
357	6	Hot Springs, AR	13.8		40	7	Jacksonville, FL	17.9		212	7	Houma-Bayou Cane-Thibodaux, LA	10.1
8	6	Miami-Fort Lauderdale-Pompano Beach, FL	13.8		47	7	Salt Lake City, UT	17.9		142	8	Beaumont-Port Arthur, TX	10.0
24	6	Orlando-Kissimmee-Sanford, FL	13.8		361	9	Great Falls, MT	17.8		260	8	Grand Junction, CO	10.0
20	10	Tampa-St. Petersburg-Clearwater, FL	13.6		174	9	Sioux Falls, SD	17.8		189	10	Gulfport-Biloxi, MS	9.9
128	11	Port St. Lucie, FL	13.5		48	11	Buffalo-Niagara Falls, NY	17.6		274	10	Midland, TX	9.9
210	12	Medford, OR	13.4		82	12	Des Moines-West Des Moines, IA	17.5		316	10	St. George, UT	9.9
277	13	Florence-Muscle Shoals, AL	13.3		319	12	Lewiston-Auburn, ME	17.5		300	13	Sebastian-Vero Beach, FL	9.7
220	14	Bloomington-Normal, IL	13.2		183	12	Olympia, WA	17.5		155	14	Naples-Marco Island, FL	9.5
233	14	Lake Havasu City-Kingman, AZ	13.2		154	12	Utica-Rome, NY	17.5		89	15	Cape Coral-Fort Myers, FL	9.2
218	14	Prescott, AZ	13.2		161	16	Charleston, WV	17.4		301	15	Morgantown, WV	9.2
316	14	St. George, UT	13.2		133	16	Tallahassee, FL	17.4		241	17	Bend, OR	9.0
281	18	Dothan, AL	13.1		129	18	Trenton-Ewing, NJ	17.2		358	17	Casper, WY	9.0
137	18	Wilmington, NC	13.1		121	18	Vallejo-Fairfield, CA	17.2		232	17	Gainesville, GA	9.0
276	20	Hattiesburg, MS	13.0		125	20	Anchorage, AK	17.1		320	20	Victoria, TX	8.6
309	20	Missoula, MT	13.0		91	20	Scranton-Wilkes-Barre, PA	17.1		177	21	Greeley, CO	8.5
242	20	Redding, CA	13.0		220	22	Bloomington-Normal, IL	17.0		218	21	Prescott, AZ	8.5
33	23	Charlotte-Gastonia-Rock Hill, NC-SC	12.9		254	22	Dover, DE	17.0		266	21	Wheeling, WV-OH	8.5
100	23	Santa Rosa-Petaluma, CA	12.9		54	22	Omaha-Council Bluffs, NE-IA	17.0		137	21	Wilmington, NC	8.5
9	25	Atlanta-Sandy Springs-Marietta, GA	12.8		20	22	Tampa-St. Petersburg-Clearwater, FL	17.0		209	25	Longview, TX	8.4
241	25	Bend, OR	12.8		175	26	Columbus, GA-AL	16.9		87	25	McAllen-Edinburg-Mission, TX	8.4
199	25	Laredo, TX	12.8		31	26	Columbus, OH	16.9		171	25	Myrtle Beach-North Myrtle Beach-Conway, SC	8.4
87	25	McAllen-Edinburg-Mission, TX	12.8		356	26	Elmira, NY	16.9		128	25	Port St. Lucie, FL	8.4
167	25	Ocala, FL	12.8		238	26	Monroe, LA	16.9		333	29	Brunswick, GA	8.3
50	30	Birmingham-Hoover, AL	12.7		30	26	San Antonio-New Braunfels, TX	16.9		299	29	Jacksonville, NC	8.3
52	30	Bridgeport-Stamford-Norwalk, CT	12.7		348	31	Cheyenne, WY	16.8		49	31	New Orleans-Metairie-Kenner, LA	8.2
73	32	Knoxville, TN	12.6		345	31	Fairbanks, AK	16.8		193	32	Barnstable Town, MA	8.0
163	32	Lafayette, LA	12.6		143	31	Lincoln, NE	16.8		277	32	Florence-Muscle Shoals, AL	8.0
235	32	Panama City-Lynn Haven-Panama City Beach, FL	12.6		160	31	Lubbock, TX	16.8		344	32	Ocean City, NJ	8.0
116	32	Pensacola-Ferry Pass-Brent, FL	12.6		5	31	Philadelphia-Camden-Wilmington, PA-NJ-DE-MD	16.8		235	32	Panama City-Lynn Haven-Panama City Beach, FL	8.0
13	32	Phoenix-Mesa-Glendale, AZ	12.6		109	31	Provo-Orem, UT	16.8		352	32	Rome, GA	8.0
147	32	Savannah, GA	12.6		76	31	Syracuse, NY	16.8		337	32	San Angelo, TX	8.0
300	32	Sebastian-Vero Beach, FL	12.6		178	38	Binghamton, NY	16.7		287	32	Winchester, VA-WV	8.0
113	32	Springfield, MO	12.6		181	38	Huntington-Ashland, WV-KY-OH	16.7		7	39	Houston-Sugar Land-Baytown, TX	7.9
295	32	Texarkana, TX-Texarkana, AR	12.6		45	38	Oklahoma City, OK	16.7		29	39	Las Vegas-Paradise, NV	7.9
313	41	Jonesboro, AR	12.5		151	38	Roanoke, VA	16.7		258	39	Yuba City, CA	7.9
79	42	El Paso, TX	12.4		337	38	San Angelo, TX	16.7		66	42	Baton Rouge, LA	7.8
40	42	Jacksonville, FL	12.4		57	43	Honolulu, HI	16.6		122	42	Corpus Christi, TX	7.8
109	42	Provo-Orem, UT	12.4		27	43	Kansas City, MO-KS	16.6		127	42	Mobile, AL	7.8
173	42	San Luis Obispo-Paso Robles, CA	12.4		150	43	Killeen-Temple-Fort Hood, TX	16.6		290	42	Punta Gorda, FL	7.8
288	42	Valdosta, GA	12.4		315	43	Manhattan, KS	16.6		305	46	Idaho Falls, ID	7.7
193	47	Barnstable Town, MA	12.3		99	43	Ogden-Clearfield, UT	16.6		233	46	Lake Havasu City-Kingman, AZ	7.7
77	47	Charleston-North Charleston-Summerville, SC	12.3		290	43	Punta Gorda, FL	16.6		92	46	Lakeland-Winter Haven, FL	7.7
29	47	Las Vegas-Paradise, NV	12.3		28	43	Sacramento-Arden-Arcade-Roseville, CA	16.6		363	49	Danville, IL	7.6
160	47	Lubbock, TX	12.3		358	50	Casper, WY	16.5		259	49	Decatur, AL	7.6
					364	50	Hinesville-Fort Stewart, GA	16.5		168	49	Hagerstown-Martinsburg, MD-WV	7.6
					233	50	Lake Havasu City-Kingman, AZ	16.5		249	49	Parkersburg-Marietta-Vienna, WV-OH	7.6
					103	50	Lansing-East Lansing, MI	16.5					
					108	50	Spokane, WA	16.5					

HIGHLIGHTS

Top Fifty Metropolitan Statistical Areas, by Proportion in Each EEO Occupation Group—*Continued*

Installation, Maintenance, and Repair Craft Workers

Rank by size of labor force	Rank in occupation group	Metropolitan Statistical Area	Percent
		United States............................	4.1
364	1	Hinesville-Fort Stewart, GA...........	9.3
330	2	Anniston-Oxford, AL	7.4
286	3	Odessa, TX.....................................	7.1
325	4	Farmington, NM	6.9
295	5	Texarkana, TX-Texarkana, AR.......	6.7
358	6	Casper, WY	6.6
138	7	Hickory-Lenoir-Morganton, NC.......	6.5
281	8	Dothan, AL.....................................	6.4
244	9	Monroe, MI	6.3
346	10	Longview, WA.................................	6.2
345	11	Fairbanks, AK.................................	6.0
328	11	Michigan City-La Porte, IN	6.0
314	11	Steubenville-Weirton, OH-WV	6.0
228	14	Anderson, SC	5.9
192	14	Clarksville, TN-KY	5.9
320	14	Victoria, TX.....................................	5.9
122	17	Corpus Christi, TX.........................	5.8
321	17	Fond du Lac, WI	5.8
252	17	Jackson, MI	5.8
299	17	Jacksonville, NC	5.8
209	17	Longview, TX..................................	5.8
349	17	Sumter, SC	5.8
245	23	Burlington, NC	5.7
306	23	Hanford-Corcoran, CA....................	5.7
212	23	Houma-Bayou Cane-Thibodaux, LA	5.7
163	23	Lafayette, LA	5.7
273	23	Lebanon, PA	5.7
208	23	Racine, WI	5.7
53	23	Tulsa, OK..	5.7
168	30	Hagerstown-Martinsburg, MD-WV..	5.6
230	30	Joplin, MO	5.6
277	32	Florence-Muscle Shoals, AL	5.5
323	32	Goldsboro, NC................................	5.5
157	32	Kingsport-Bristol-Bristol, TN-VA	5.5
265	32	Wichita Falls, TX	5.5
81	32	Wichita, KS.....................................	5.5
106	32	York-Hanover, PA...........................	5.5
247	32	Yuma, AZ..	5.5
296	39	Altoona, PA.....................................	5.4
329	39	Bay City, MI	5.4
259	39	Decatur, AL....................................	5.4
165	39	Erie, PA	5.4
350	39	Kokomo, IN.....................................	5.4
233	39	Lake Havasu City-Kingman, AZ	5.4
236	39	Muskegon-Norton Shores, MI	5.4
283	39	Warner Robins, GA........................	5.4
251	47	Abilene, TX.....................................	5.3
176	47	Amarillo, TX....................................	5.3
356	47	Elmira, NY	5.3
150	47	Killeen-Temple-Fort Hood, TX........	5.3
289	47	Morristown, TN	5.3
331	47	Owensboro, KY	5.3
272	47	Springfield, OH	5.3

Production Operative Workers

Rank by size of labor force	Rank in occupation group	Metropolitan Statistical Area	Percent
		United States............................	5.0
203	1	Elkhart-Goshen, IN	20.0
280	2	Dalton, GA......................................	19.9
293	3	Sheboygan, WI...............................	13.6
138	4	Hickory-Lenoir-Morganton, NC.......	13.5
236	5	Muskegon-Norton Shores, MI	12.6
282	6	Battle Creek, MI.............................	12.5
169	7	Fort Smith, AR-OK.........................	12.2
307	7	Mansfield, OH.................................	12.2
289	7	Morristown, TN	12.2
350	10	Kokomo, IN.....................................	11.9
321	11	Fond du Lac, WI	11.5
231	11	Janesville, WI.................................	11.5
359	13	Columbus, IN..................................	11.4
259	13	Decatur, AL....................................	11.4
257	13	Wausau, WI....................................	11.4
250	16	Sioux City, IA-NE-SD.....................	11.0
164	17	Holland-Grand Haven, MI...............	10.9
327	18	Cleveland, TN.................................	10.8
340	18	Danville, VA....................................	10.8
232	20	Gainesville, GA...............................	10.6
330	21	Anniston-Oxford, AL	10.4
228	22	Anderson, SC	10.3
180	22	Appleton, WI...................................	10.3
141	22	Rockford, IL....................................	10.3
224	25	Oshkosh-Neenah, WI.....................	10.2
349	25	Sumter, SC	10.2
331	27	Owensboro, KY	10.0
170	28	Spartanburg, SC.............................	9.9
363	29	Danville, IL......................................	9.7
208	29	Racine, WI	9.7
334	31	Lima, OH...	9.6
262	32	Rocky Mount, NC	9.5
328	33	Michigan City-La Porte, IN	9.4
292	34	Bowling Green, KY.........................	9.3
135	34	Evansville, IN-KY............................	9.3
318	34	Sandusky, OH.................................	9.3
114	37	Fort Wayne, IN	9.1
351	37	Gadsden, AL...................................	9.1
157	39	Kingsport-Bristol-Bristol, TN-VA	9.0
244	39	Monroe, MI	9.0
115	39	Reading, PA	9.0
272	39	Springfield, OH	9.0
252	43	Jackson, MI	8.9
360	43	Jackson, OH...................................	8.9
65	45	Grand Rapids-Wyoming, MI...........	8.8
230	45	Joplin, MO	8.8
149	45	South Bend-Mishawaka, IN-MI.......	8.8
353	48	Pine Bluff, AR.................................	8.7
237	48	Terre Haute, IN...............................	8.7
245	50	Burlington, NC	8.6
226	50	Waterloo-Cedar Falls, IA	8.6
310	50	Williamsport, PA	8.6

Transportation and Material Moving Operative Workers

Rank by size of labor force	Rank in occupation group	Metropolitan Statistical Area	Percent
		United States............................	4.5
280	1	Dalton, GA......................................	10.0
262	2	Rocky Mount, NC	8.1
194	3	Merced, CA.....................................	8.0
322	4	Kankakee-Bradley, IL.....................	7.7
195	4	Yakima, WA....................................	7.7
199	6	Laredo, TX......................................	7.6
306	7	Hanford-Corcoran, CA....................	7.4
363	8	Danville, IL......................................	7.3
212	8	Houma-Bayou Cane-Thibodaux, LA	7.3
261	8	Vineland-Millville-Bridgeton, NJ......	7.3
364	11	Hinesville-Fort Stewart, GA...........	7.1
289	11	Morristown, TN	7.1
264	13	Albany, GA......................................	7.0
169	14	Fort Smith, AR-OK.........................	6.8
273	14	Lebanon, PA	6.8
104	14	Modesto, CA...................................	6.8
349	17	Sumter, SC	6.7
327	18	Cleveland, TN.................................	6.6
340	18	Danville, VA....................................	6.6
138	18	Hickory-Lenoir-Morganton, NC.......	6.6
170	18	Spartanburg, SC.............................	6.6
85	18	Stockton, CA...................................	6.6
79	23	El Paso, TX	6.5
203	23	Elkhart-Goshen, IN	6.5
351	23	Gadsden, AL...................................	6.5
325	26	Farmington, NM	6.4
231	26	Janesville, WI.................................	6.4
286	26	Odessa, TX.....................................	6.4
353	26	Pine Bluff, AR.................................	6.4
132	26	Visalia-Porterville, CA....................	6.4
321	31	Fond du Lac, WI	6.3
232	31	Gainesville, GA...............................	6.3
244	31	Monroe, MI	6.3
296	34	Altoona, PA.....................................	6.2
230	34	Joplin, MO	6.2
334	34	Lima, OH...	6.2
41	34	Memphis, TN-MS-AR......................	6.2
328	34	Michigan City-La Porte, IN	6.2
259	39	Decatur, AL....................................	6.1
307	39	Mansfield, OH.................................	6.1
141	39	Rockford, IL....................................	6.1
91	39	Scranton-Wilkes-Barre, PA.............	6.1
168	43	Hagerstown-Martinsburg, MD-WV..	6.0
14	43	Riverside-San Bernardino-Ontario, CA	6.0
272	43	Springfield, OH	6.0
74	43	Toledo, OH......................................	6.0
288	43	Valdosta, GA...................................	6.0
294	48	Anderson, IN...................................	5.9
71	48	Bakersfield-Delano, CA..................	5.9
126	48	Davenport-Moline-Rock Island, IA-IL	5.9
323	48	Goldsboro, NC................................	5.9
249	48	Parkersburg-Marietta-Vienna, WV-OH	5.9
247	48	Yuma, AZ..	5.9

xxi

Top Fifty Metropolitan Statistical Areas, by Proportion in Each EEO Occupation Group–*Continued*

Laborers and Helpers					Protective Service Workers					Service Workers, except Protective			
Rank by size of labor force	Rank in occupation group	Metropolitan Statistical Area	Percent		Rank by size of labor force	Rank in occupation group	Metropolitan Statistical Area	Percent		Rank by size of labor force	Rank in occupation group	Metropolitan Statistical Area	Percent
		United States.................	3.9				United States.................	2.1				United States.................	14.0
132	1	Visalia-Porterville, CA................	17.6		278	1	El Centro, CA................	5.5		159	1	Atlantic City-Hammonton, NJ........	25.9
308	2	Madera-Chowchilla, CA................	17.0		306	2	Hanford-Corcoran, CA................	4.8		29	2	Las Vegas-Paradise, NV................	23.1
306	3	Hanford-Corcoran, CA................	15.9		353	2	Pine Bluff, AR................	4.8		152	3	Brownsville-Harlingen, TX................	19.2
124	4	Salinas, CA................	15.7		199	4	Laredo, TX................	4.4		233	4	Lake Havasu City-Kingman, AZ.....	19.1
195	5	Yakima, WA................	15.2		261	4	Vineland-Millville-Bridgeton, NJ.....	4.4		312	5	Muncie, IN................	19.0
194	6	Merced, CA................	12.6		247	4	Yuma, AZ................	4.4		189	6	Gulfport-Biloxi, MS................	18.5
71	7	Bakersfield-Delano, CA................	12.2		364	7	Hinesville-Fort Stewart, GA........	4.1		326	6	Grand Forks, ND-MN................	18.5
63	8	Fresno, CA................	11.1		150	7	Killeen-Temple-Fort Hood, TX.......	4.1		87	8	McAllen-Edinburg-Mission, TX.......	18.3
335	8	Wenatchee-East Wenatchee, WA..	11.1		75	9	Poughkeepsie-Newburgh-Middletown, NY................	4.0		156	8	Duluth, MN-WI................	18.3
247	10	Yuma, AZ................	10.6		159	10	Atlantic City-Hammonton, NJ........	3.9		158	10	Norwich-New London, CT................	18.1
278	11	El Centro, CA................	9.9						171	10	Myrtle Beach-North Myrtle Beach-Conway, SC................	18.1
117	11	Santa Barbara-Santa Maria-Goleta, CA................	9.9		356	10	Elmira, NY................	3.9		222	10	Saginaw-Saginaw Township North, MI................	18.1
268	13	Napa, CA................	9.3		79	12	El Paso, TX................	3.7					
258	14	Yuba City, CA................	8.8		263	13	Pueblo, CO................	3.6		299	10	Jacksonville, NC................	18.1
188	15	Kennewick-Pasco-Richland, WA....	8.6		341	14	Lawton, OK................	3.4		270	14	Pittsfield, MA................	18.0
134	16	Salem, OR................	7.9		152	15	Brownsville-Harlingen, TX................	3.3		329	15	Bay City, MI................	17.7
304	17	Harrisonburg, VA................	7.4		288	15	Valdosta, GA................	3.3		314	16	Steubenville-Weirton, OH-WV........	17.6
346	17	Longview, WA................	7.4		294	17	Anderson, IN................	3.2		267	17	Flagstaff, AZ................	17.5
166	19	Santa Cruz-Watsonville, CA..........	7.3		71	17	Bakersfield-Delano, CA................	3.2		155	18	Naples-Marco Island, FL................	17.4
					366	17	Carson City, NV................	3.2		205	18	Chico, CA................	17.4
85	20	Stockton, CA................	7.2 || 173	17	San Luis Obispo-Paso Robles, CA	3.2						
104	21	Modesto, CA................	7.1		154	17	Utica-Rome, NY................	3.2		344	18	Ocean City, NJ................	17.4
155	22	Naples-Marco Island, FL................	7.0		265	17	Wichita Falls, TX................	3.2		221	21	Las Cruces, NM................	17.3
300	22	Sebastian-Vero Beach, FL............	7.0		271	23	Alexandria, LA................	3.1		309	21	Missoula, MT................	17.3
324	24	Mount Vernon-Anacortes, WA.......	6.7		29	23	Las Vegas-Paradise, NV................	3.1		365	23	Lewiston, ID-WA................	17.2
87	25	McAllen-Edinburg-Mission, TX.......	6.6		128	23	Port St. Lucie, FL................	3.1		337	24	San Angelo, TX................	17.1
92	26	Lakeland-Winter Haven, FL...........	6.4		121	23	Vallejo-Fairfield, CA................	3.1		347	24	Cumberland, MD-WV................	17.1
64	26	Oxnard-Thousand Oaks-Ventura, CA................	6.4		132	23	Visalia-Porterville, CA................	3.1		266	26	Wheeling, WV-OH................	17.0
					254	28	Dover, DE................	3.0		334	26	Lima, OH................	17.0
287	26	Winchester, VA-WV................	6.4		168	28	Hagerstown-Martinsburg, MD-WV..	3.0		131	28	Shreveport-Bossier City, LA............	16.8
313	29	Jonesboro, AR................	6.2		57	28	Honolulu, HI................	3.0		333	28	Brunswick, GA................	16.8
310	29	Williamsport, PA................	6.2		344	28	Ocean City, NJ................	3.0		357	28	Hot Springs, AR................	16.8
353	31	Pine Bluff, AR................	6.1		298	28	Salisbury, MD................	3.0		160	31	Lubbock, TX................	16.6
363	32	Danville, IL................	5.8		349	28	Sumter, SC................	3.0		279	31	Johnstown, PA................	16.6
232	33	Gainesville, GA................	5.7		237	28	Terre Haute, IN................	3.0		57	33	Honolulu, HI................	16.5
293	33	Sheboygan, WI................	5.7		251	35	Abilene, TX................	2.9		153	33	Fayetteville, NC................	16.5
261	33	Vineland-Millville-Bridgeton, NJ......	5.7		176	35	Amarillo, TX................	2.9		227	33	Crestview-Fort Walton Beach-Destin, FL................	16.5
323	36	Goldsboro, NC................	5.6 || 347	35	Cumberland, MD-WV................	2.9						
210	36	Medford, OR................	5.6		189	35	Gulfport-Biloxi, MS................	2.9		123	36	Flint, MI................	16.4
205	38	Chico, CA................	5.5		214	35	Lake Charles, LA................	2.9		215	36	Greenville, NC................	16.4
167	39	Ocala, FL................	5.4								229	36	Iowa City, IA................	16.4
					171	35	Myrtle Beach-North Myrtle Beach-Conway, SC................	2.9		339	36	Dubuque, IA................	16.4
100	39	Santa Rosa-Petaluma, CA............	5.4										
250	39	Sioux City, IA-NE-SD................	5.4		218	35	Prescott, AZ................	2.9		108	40	Spokane, WA................	16.3
355	42	Corvallis, OR................	5.3		290	35	Punta Gorda, FL................	2.9		181	40	Huntington-Ashland, WV-KY-OH....	16.3
307	42	Mansfield, OH................	5.3		58	35	Tucson, AZ................	2.9		217	40	Bloomington, IN................	16.3
257	42	Wausau, WI................	5.3		19	44	Baltimore-Towson, MD................	2.8		218	40	Prescott, AZ................	16.3
321	45	Fond du Lac, WI................	5.2		142	44	Beaumont-Port Arthur, TX............	2.8		251	40	Abilene, TX................	16.3
322	45	Kankakee-Bradley, IL................	5.2		267	44	Flagstaff, AZ................	2.8		111	45	Reno-Sparks, NV................	16.2
354	45	Pocatello, ID................	5.2		253	44	Jefferson City, MO................	2.8		226	45	Waterloo-Cedar Falls, IA................	16.2
128	45	Port St. Lucie, FL................	5.2		233	44	Lake Havasu City-Kingman, AZ.....	2.8		360	45	Sandusky, OH................	16.2
264	49	Albany, GA................	5.1		221	44	Las Cruces, NM................	2.8		366	45	Carson City, NV................	16.2
330	49	Anniston-Oxford, AL................	5.1		158	44	Norwich-New London, CT............	2.8		201	49	Bellingham, WA................	16.1
											341	49	Lawton, OK................	16.1
201	49	Bellingham, WA................	5.1 || 167	44	Ocala, FL................	2.8						
152	49	Brownsville-Harlingen, TX............	5.1 || 255	44	Pascagoula, MS................	2.8						
169	49	Fort Smith, AR-OK................	5.1 || 133	44	Tallahassee, FL................	2.8						

PART A

National Data

A-1 EEO Occupation Groups, by Sex, Race, and Hispanic or Latino Origin, 2006–2010

EEO Occupation Group	Total	Male	Female	Hispanic or Latino	White alone, not Hispanic or Latino
Population in the civilian labor force					
Total civilian labor force	154,037,475	81,323,090	72,714,390	22,457,110	103,278,400
Management, business, and financial workers	18,514,755	11,000,315	7,514,440	1,466,850	14,425,760
Science, engineering and computer professionals	5,907,405	4,528,390	1,379,015	326,755	4,246,640
Health care practitioner professionals	5,041,270	1,359,170	3,682,105	255,010	3,806,800
Other professional workers	16,723,700	6,345,860	10,377,840	1,299,960	12,680,020
Technicians	4,244,165	1,861,185	2,382,975	360,235	3,000,415
Sales workers	17,256,510	8,552,900	8,703,610	2,154,145	12,163,980
Administrative support workers	23,586,105	5,990,085	17,596,020	3,075,280	15,972,595
Construction and extractive craft workers	9,205,480	8,951,330	254,155	2,481,855	5,811,335
Installation, maintenance, and repair craft workers	6,316,335	5,871,165	445,170	899,470	4,590,455
Production operative workers	7,769,340	5,340,305	2,429,035	1,742,115	4,484,160
Transportation and material moving operative workers	6,984,985	5,695,450	1,289,535	1,297,050	4,211,875
Laborers and helpers	5,991,240	4,999,790	991,450	1,817,710	3,217,175
Protective service workers	3,257,310	2,514,290	743,020	388,655	2,090,840
Service workers, except protective	21,572,140	7,477,890	14,094,250	4,523,995	11,868,285
Unemployed	1,666,735	834,965	831,770	368,025	708,065
Sex, race, and Hispanic origin as a percent of each occupation group					
Total civilian labor force	100	52.8	47.2	14.6	67.0
Management, business, and financial workers	100	59.4	40.6	7.9	77.9
Science, engineering and computer professionals	100	76.7	23.3	5.5	71.9
Health care practitioner professionals	100	27.0	73.0	5.1	75.5
Other professional workers	100	37.9	62.1	7.8	75.8
Technicians	100	43.9	56.1	8.5	70.7
Sales workers	100	49.6	50.4	12.5	70.5
Administrative support workers	100	25.4	74.6	13.0	67.7
Construction and extractive craft workers	100	97.2	2.8	27.0	63.1
Installation, maintenance, and repair craft workers	100	93.0	7.0	14.2	72.7
Production operative workers	100	68.7	31.3	22.4	57.7
Transportation and material moving operative workers	100	81.5	18.5	18.6	60.3
Laborers and helpers	100	83.5	16.5	30.3	53.7
Protective service workers	100	77.2	22.8	11.9	64.2
Service workers, except protective	100	34.7	65.3	21.0	55.0
Unemployed	100	50.1	49.9	22.1	42.5
Occupation groups as a percent of workers in each sex, race, and Hispanic origin group					
Total civilian labor force	100	100	100	100	100
Management, business, and financial workers	12.0	13.5	10.3	6.5	14.0
Science, engineering and computer professionals	3.8	5.6	1.9	1.5	4.1
Health care practitioner professionals	3.3	1.7	5.1	1.1	3.7
Other professional workers	10.9	7.8	14.3	5.8	12.3
Technicians	2.8	2.3	3.3	1.6	2.9
Sales workers	11.2	10.5	12.0	9.6	11.8
Administrative support workers	15.3	7.4	24.2	13.7	15.5
Construction and extractive craft workers	6.0	11.0	0.3	11.1	5.6
Installation, maintenance, and repair craft workers	4.1	7.2	0.6	4.0	4.4
Production operative workers	5.0	6.6	3.3	7.8	4.3
Transportation and material moving operative workers	4.5	7.0	1.8	5.8	4.1
Laborers and helpers	3.9	6.1	1.4	8.1	3.1
Protective service workers	2.1	3.1	1.0	1.7	2.0
Service workers, except protective	14.0	9.2	19.4	20.1	11.5
Unemployed	1.1	1.0	1.1	1.6	0.7

PART A—NATIONAL DATA

A-1 EEO Occupation Groups, by Sex, Race, and Hispanic or Latino Origin, 2006–2010—Continued

EEO Occupation Group	Black alone, not Hispanic or Latino	American Indian and Alaska Native alone, not Hispanic or Latino	Asian alone, not Hispanic or Latino	Native Hawaiian and Other Pacific Islander alone, Not Hispanic or Latino	Two or more races, not Hispanic or Latino
Population in the civilian labor force					
Total civilian labor force	17,469,155	894,060	7,426,015	234,430	2,278,280
Management, business, and financial workers	1,372,180	77,300	920,515	19,115	233,045
Science, engineering, and computer professionals	351,600	17,045	867,955	6,045	91,370
Health care practitioner professionals	399,915	16,335	498,670	3,360	61,175
Other professional workers	1,584,760	74,070	826,590	15,995	242,305
Technicians	484,455	23,050	307,115	4,845	64,040
Sales workers	1,746,595	81,310	809,545	23,455	277,475
Administrative support workers	3,079,780	139,440	908,890	44,440	365,670
Construction and extractive craft workers	593,195	77,485	106,950	15,845	118,815
Installation, maintenance, and repair craft workers	492,785	40,315	202,305	9,395	81,610
Production operative workers	1,003,295	45,105	397,465	10,445	86,760
Transportation and material moving operative workers	1,121,360	42,095	207,095	13,920	91,585
Laborers and helpers	703,955	45,120	111,940	12,490	82,845
Protective service workers	615,010	29,220	67,095	9,190	57,295
Service workers, except protective	3,485,605	168,060	1,100,785	41,760	383,650
Unemployed	434,665	18,110	93,100	4,130	40,640
Sex, race, and Hispanic origin as a percent of each occupation group					
Total civilian labor force	11.3	0.6	4.8	0.2	1.5
Management, business, and financial workers	7.4	0.4	5.0	0.1	1.3
Science, engineering, and computer professionals	6.0	0.3	14.7	0.1	1.5
Health care practitioner professionals	7.9	0.3	9.9	0.1	1.2
Other professional workers	9.5	0.4	4.9	9.6	1.4
Technicians	11.4	0.5	7.2	0.1	1.5
Sales workers	10.1	0.5	4.7	0.1	1.6
Administrative support workers	13.1	0.6	3.9	0.2	1.6
Construction and extractive craft workers	6.4	0.8	1.2	0.2	1.3
Installation, maintenance, and repair craft workers	7.8	0.6	3.2	0.1	1.3
Production operative workers	12.9	0.6	5.1	0.1	1.1
Transportation and material moving operative workers	16.1	0.6	3.0	0.2	1.3
Laborers and helpers	11.7	0.8	1.9	0.2	1.4
Protective service workers	18.9	0.9	2.1	0.3	1.8
Service workers, except protective	16.2	0.8	5.1	0.2	1.8
Unemployed	26.1	1.1	5.6	0.2	2.4
Occupation groups as a percent of workers in each sex, race, and Hispanic origin group					
Total civilian labor force	100	100	100	100	100
Management, business, and financial workers	7.9	8.6	12.4	8.2	10.2
Science, engineering, and computer professionals	2.0	1.9	11.7	2.6	4.0
Health care practitioner professionals	2.3	1.8	6.7	1.4	2.7
Other professional workers	9.1	8.3	11.1	6.8	10.6
Technicians	2.8	2.6	4.1	2.1	2.8
Sales workers	10.0	9.1	10.9	10.0	12.2
Administrative support workers	17.6	15.6	12.2	19.0	16.1
Construction and extractive craft workers	3.4	8.7	1.4	6.8	5.2
Installation, maintenance, and repair craft workers	2.8	4.5	2.7	4.0	3.6
Production operative workers	5.7	5.0	5.4	4.5	3.8
Transportation and material moving operative workers	6.4	4.7	2.8	5.9	4.0
Laborers and helpers	4.0	5.0	1.5	5.3	3.6
Protective service workers	3.5	3.3	0.9	3.9	2.5
Service workers, except protective	20.0	18.8	14.8	17.8	16.8
Unemployed	2.5	2.0	1.3	1.8	1.8

PART A—NATIONAL DATA

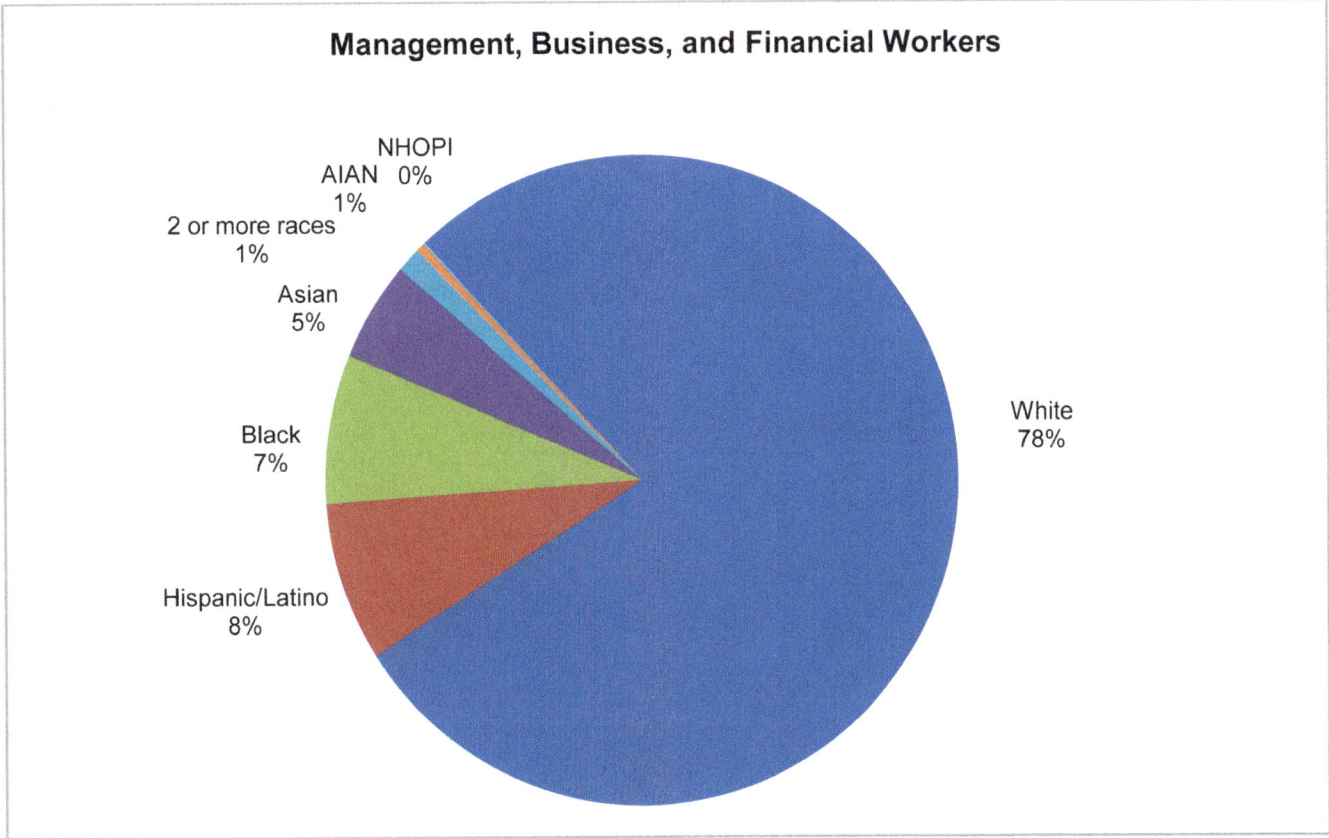

Figure A-2.1

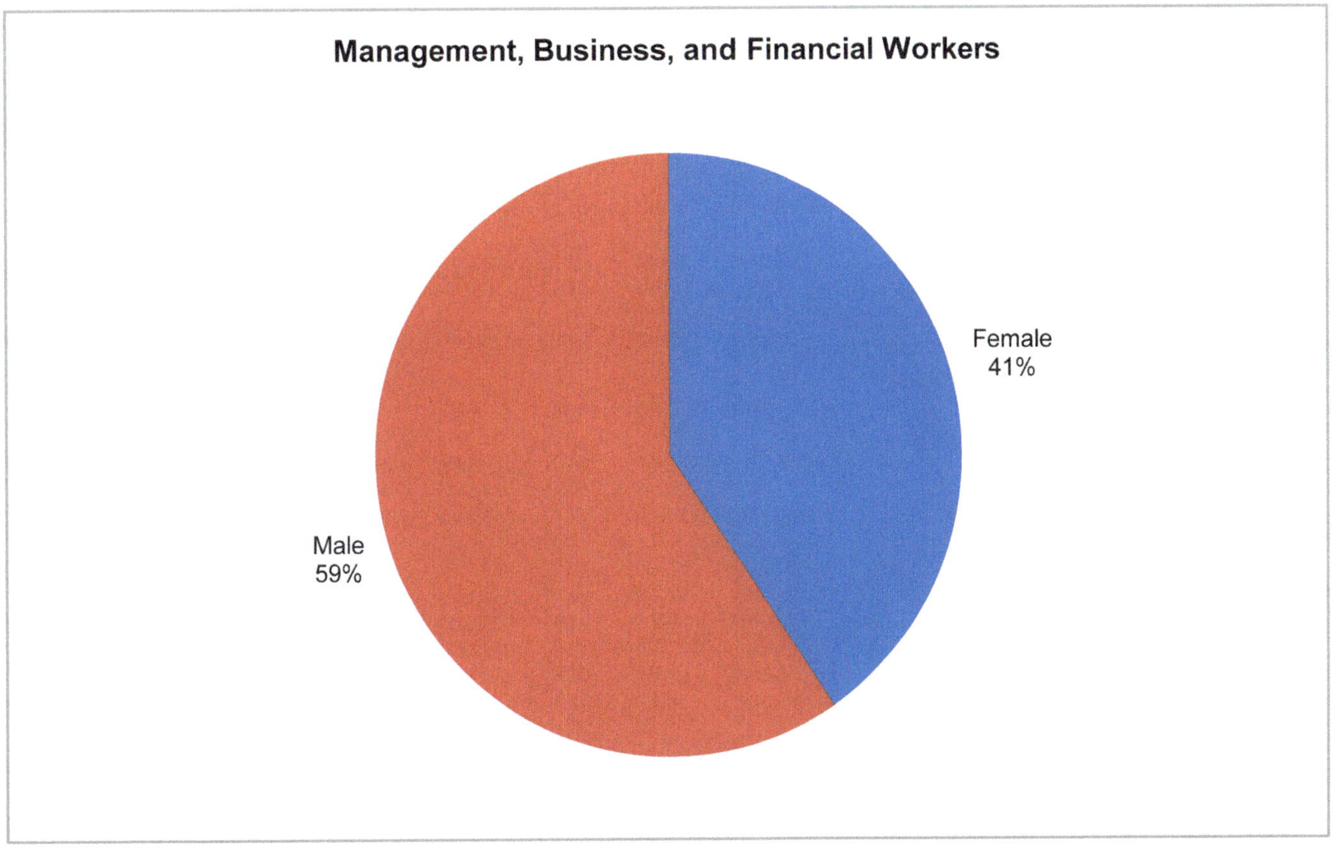

Figure A-2.2

A-2 Detailed Occupations in the Management, Business, and Financial Workers Occupation Group, by Sex, Race, and Hispanic Origin, 2006–2010

Census occupation code	Management, Business, and Financial Workers Occupation Group	Total who worked in the last 5 years	Male Number	Male Percent	Female Number	Female Percent	Hispanic or Latino Number	Hispanic or Latino Percent	White alone, not Hispanic or Latino Number	White alone, not Hispanic or Latino Percent
0010	Chief executives and legislators	1,158,885	901,735	77.8	257,150	22.2	52,320	4.5	1,001,235	86.4
0020	General and operations managers	969,820	686,620	70.8	283,200	29.2	71,220	7.3	785,520	81.0
0040	Advertising and promotions managers	61,375	27,745	45.2	33,630	54.8	3,960	6.5	50,840	82.8
0050	Marketing and sales managers	871,120	488,260	56.0	382,860	44.0	58,670	6.7	715,055	82.1
0060	Public relations and fundraising managers	57,405	22,880	39.9	34,525	60.1	3,140	5.5	47,590	82.9
0100	Administrative services managers	111,065	72,410	65.2	38,660	34.8	8,725	7.9	85,845	77.3
0110	Computer and information systems managers	482,515	338,130	70.1	144,385	29.9	24,285	5.0	369,540	76.6
0120	Financial managers	1,108,810	512,305	46.2	596,500	53.8	97,395	8.8	842,550	76.0
0135	Compensation and benefits managers	28,010	6,115	21.8	21,895	78.2	1,675	6.0	22,665	80.9
0136	Human resources managers	331,125	134,365	40.6	196,760	59.4	36,950	11.2	239,120	72.2
0137	Training and development managers	43,755	20,940	47.9	22,810	52.1	2,615	6.0	34,945	79.9
0140	Industrial production managers	242,520	198,415	81.8	44,105	18.2	20,170	8.3	198,630	81.9
0150	Purchasing managers	191,400	106,150	55.5	85,250	44.5	12,430	6.5	151,395	79.1
0160	Transportation, storage, and distribution managers	230,320	188,740	81.9	41,580	18.1	27,205	11.8	171,210	74.3
0205	Farmers, ranchers, and other agricultural managers	671,560	571,345	85.1	100,215	14.9	32,430	4.8	617,105	91.9
0220	Construction managers	893,930	830,040	92.9	63,895	7.1	81,260	9.1	749,580	83.9
0230	Education administrators	848,645	307,480	36.2	541,165	63.8	62,560	7.4	635,685	74.9
0300	Architectural and engineering managers	146,595	134,670	91.9	11,920	8.1	5,980	4.1	120,975	82.5
0310	Food service managers	958,745	509,395	53.1	449,355	46.9	138,265	14.4	630,060	65.7
0330	Gaming managers	19,195	11,720	61.1	7,475	38.9	1,580	8.2	14,025	73.1
0340	Lodging managers	143,375	70,085	48.9	73,295	51.1	13,045	9.1	98,850	68.9
0350	Medical and health services managers	533,925	161,075	30.2	372,850	69.8	39,345	7.4	400,545	75.0
0360	Natural sciences managers	19,480	11,915	61.2	7,565	38.8	895	4.6	15,425	79.2
0410	Property, real estate, and community association managers	559,240	274,700	49.1	284,540	50.9	60,795	10.9	424,685	75.9
0420	Social and community service managers	325,710	107,455	33.0	218,255	67.0	23,150	7.1	241,630	74.2
0425	Emergency management directors	3,295	2,140	64.9	1,155	35.1	180	5.5	2,645	80.3
0430	Miscellaneous managers, including funeral service managers, postmasters, and mail superintendents	3,183,835	2,074,525	65.2	1,109,305	34.8	243,520	7.6	2,494,480	78.3
0500	Agents and business managers of artists, performers, and athletes	47,010	25,965	55.2	21,040	44.8	5,040	10.7	33,905	72.1
0510	Buyers and purchasing agents, farm products	11,860	8,785	74.1	3,075	25.9	1,515	12.8	9,285	78.3
0520	Wholesale and retail buyers, except farm products	232,065	108,980	47.0	123,085	53.0	22,540	9.7	180,220	77.7
0530	Purchasing agents, except wholesale, retail, and farm products	271,240	125,735	46.4	145,500	53.6	21,430	7.9	212,635	78.4
0540	Claims adjusters, appraisers, examiners, and investigators	296,325	113,190	38.2	183,135	61.8	25,645	8.7	210,700	71.1
0565	Compliance officers	179,290	95,745	53.4	83,545	46.6	16,430	9.2	129,325	72.1
0600	Cost estimators	130,470	113,860	87.3	16,610	12.7	8,690	6.7	114,620	87.9
0640	Compensation, benefits, and job analysis specialists	100,935	17,360	17.2	83,575	82.8	8,825	8.7	73,355	72.7
0650	Training and development specialists	130,910	56,120	42.9	74,790	57.1	11,300	8.6	94,210	72.0
0700	Logisticians	73,640	47,805	64.9	25,835	35.1	6,820	9.3	50,185	68.1
0710	Management analysts	690,680	407,820	59.0	282,860	41.0	34,590	5.0	542,035	78.5
0725	Meeting, convention, and event planners	60,660	13,810	22.8	46,850	77.2	5,310	8.8	45,860	75.6
0726	Fundraisers	85,835	24,080	28.1	61,760	72.0	3,605	4.2	73,495	85.6

PART A—NATIONAL DATA

A-2 Detailed Occupations in the Management, Business, and Financial Workers Occupation Group, by Sex, Race, and Hispanic Origin, 2006–2010—*Continued*

Census occupation code	Management, Business, and Financial Workers Occupation Group	Black alone, not Hispanic or Latino Number	Percent	American Indian and Alaska Native alone, not Hispanic or Latino Number	Percent	Asian alone, not Hispanic or Latino Number	Percent	Native Hawaiian and Other Pacific Islander alone, not Hispanic or Latino Number	Percent	Two or more races, not Hispanic or Latino Number	Percent
0010	Chief executives and legislators	38,695	3.3	4,825	0.4	50,490	4.4	465	0.0	10,865	0.9
0020	General and operations managers	56,755	5.9	4,210	0.4	38,880	4.0	1,070	0.1	12,160	1.3
0040	Advertising and promotions managers	2,610	4.3	90	0.1	2,830	4.6	90	0.1	960	1.6
0050	Marketing and sales managers	40,635	4.7	2,425	0.3	41,985	4.8	615	0.1	11,735	1.3
0060	Public relations and fundraising managers	3,905	6.8	300	0.5	1,625	2.8	4	0.0	840	1.5
0100	Administrative services managers	10,430	9.4	685	0.6	3,500	3.2	230	0.2	1,650	1.5
0110	Computer and information systems managers	28,760	6.0	1,205	0.2	52,270	10.8	395	0.1	6,055	1.3
0120	Financial managers	85,905	7.7	3,300	0.3	65,010	5.9	990	0.1	13,655	1.2
0135	Compensation and benefits managers	2,305	8.2	125	0.4	835	3.0	0	0.0	405	1.4
0136	Human resources managers	33,525	10.1	1,485	0.4	15,610	4.7	435	0.1	3,995	1.2
0137	Training and development managers	4,360	10.0	180	0.4	1,085	2.5	100	0.2	470	1.1
0140	Industrial production managers	9,510	3.9	785	0.3	10,890	4.5	180	0.1	2,355	1.0
0150	Purchasing managers	16,150	8.4	920	0.5	8,215	4.3	150	0.1	2,145	1.1
0160	Transportation, storage, and distribution managers	20,295	8.8	1,220	0.5	7,325	3.2	650	0.3	2,415	1.0
0205	Farmers, ranchers, and other agricultural managers	6,110	0.9	3,010	0.4	7,600	1.1	245	0.0	5,055	0.8
0220	Construction managers	31,495	3.5	4,035	0.5	16,895	1.9	770	0.1	9,900	1.1
0230	Education administrators	113,070	13.3	4,570	0.5	21,575	2.5	690	0.1	10,485	1.2
0300	Architectural and engineering managers	4,125	2.8	350	0.2	13,495	9.2	20	0.0	1,650	1.1
0310	Food service managers	80,870	8.4	4,040	0.4	90,080	9.4	1,525	0.2	13,910	1.5
0330	Gaming managers	1,400	7.3	1,220	6.4	585	3.0	20	0.1	365	1.9
0340	Lodging managers	10,945	7.6	960	0.7	16,480	11.5	435	0.3	2,670	1.9
0350	Medical and health services managers	60,385	11.3	2,555	0.5	24,545	4.6	520	0.1	6,040	1.1
0360	Natural sciences managers	410	2.1	15	0.1	2,235	11.5	45	0.2	450	2.3
0410	Property, real estate, and community association managers	44,235	7.9	3,120	0.6	17,665	3.2	865	0.2	7,870	1.4
0420	Social and community service managers	43,440	13.3	2,670	0.8	9,355	2.9	300	0.1	5,170	1.6
0425	Emergency management directors	340	10.3	15	0.5	35	1.1	0	0.0	84	2.5
0430	Miscellaneous managers, including funeral service managers, postmasters, and mail superintendents	225,570	7.1	13,515	0.4	162,745	5.1	3,285	0.1	40,720	1.3
0500	Agents and business managers of artists, performers, and athletes	5,115	10.9	220	0.5	1,680	3.6	100	0.2	940	2.0
0510	Buyers and purchasing agents, farm products	360	3.0	45	0.4	450	3.8	110	0.9	105	0.9
0520	Wholesale and retail buyers, except farm products	13,215	5.7	650	0.3	11,600	5.0	405	0.2	3,440	1.5
0530	Purchasing agents, except wholesale, retail, and farm products	22,455	8.3	1,210	0.4	10,175	3.8	360	0.1	2,970	1.1
0540	Claims adjusters, appraisers, examiners, and investigators	43,900	14.8	765	0.3	11,085	3.7	305	0.1	3,925	1.3
0565	Compliance officers	19,905	11.1	1,390	0.8	9,395	5.2	310	0.2	2,530	1.4
0600	Cost estimators	1,910	1.5	405	0.3	3,440	2.6	50	0.0	1,350	1.0
0640	Compensation, benefits, and job analysis specialists	13,330	13.2	495	0.5	3,640	3.6	160	0.2	1,125	1.1
0650	Training and development specialists	18,395	14.1	735	0.6	3,795	2.9	100	0.1	2,380	1.8
0700	Logisticians	11,220	15.2	485	0.7	3,290	4.5	295	0.4	1,330	1.8
0710	Management analysts	45,075	6.5	2,135	0.3	57,040	8.3	410	0.1	9,395	1.4
0725	Meeting, convention, and event planners	5,640	9.3	160	0.3	2,440	4.0	10	0.0	1,235	2.0
0726	Fundraisers	4,950	5.8	130	0.2	2,285	2.7	65	0.1	1,305	1.5

A-2 Detailed Occupations in the Management, Business, and Financial Workers Occupation Group, by Sex, Race, and Hispanic Origin, 2006–2010—*Continued*

Census occupation code	Management, Business, and Financial Workers Occupation Group	Total who worked in the last 5 years	Male Number	Male Percent	Female Number	Female Percent	Hispanic or Latino Number	Hispanic or Latino Percent	White alone, not Hispanic or Latino Number	White alone, not Hispanic or Latino Percent
0735	Market research analysts and marketing specialists	184,360	82,815	44.9	101,545	55.1	11,930	6.5	143,525	77.9
0740	Business operations specialists, all other	231,255	86,840	37.6	144,415	62.4	22,830	9.9	158,375	68.5
0810	Appraisers and assessors of real estate	112,895	74,545	66.0	38,345	34.0	5,700	5.0	98,590	87.3
0820	Budget analysts	52,945	19,425	36.7	33,525	63.3	3,720	7.0	35,560	67.2
0830	Credit analysts	30,200	12,750	42.2	17,450	57.8	2,935	9.7	21,040	69.7
0840	Financial analysts	84,900	56,645	66.7	28,255	33.3	4,725	5.6	61,550	72.5
0850	Personal financial advisors	353,120	245,655	69.6	107,465	30.4	21,025	6.0	283,590	80.3
0860	Insurance underwriters	102,170	32,825	32.1	69,345	67.9	6,420	6.3	79,090	77.4
0900	Financial examiners	12,920	7,075	54.8	5,845	45.2	895	6.9	9,260	71.7
0910	Credit counselors and loan officers	386,045	180,140	46.7	205,905	53.3	43,465	11.3	278,410	72.1
0930	Tax examiners and collectors, and revenue agents	65,105	23,350	35.9	41,755	64.1	7,200	11.1	40,760	62.6
0940	Tax preparers	107,865	37,200	34.5	70,665	65.5	12,295	11.4	73,150	67.8
0950	Financial specialists, all other	65,370	28,725	43.9	36,645	56.1	6,905	10.6	45,025	68.9
4465	Morticians, undertakers, and funeral directors	40,280	31,185	77.4	9,095	22.6	1,945	4.8	33,245	82.5
6010	Agricultural inspectors	17,815	10,250	57.5	7,560	42.4	2,760	15.5	11,105	62.3
6660	Construction and building inspectors	108,345	96,430	89.0	11,915	11.0	9,070	8.4	85,170	78.6
9410	Transportation inspectors	52,585	43,855	83.4	8,730	16.6	7,505	14.3	36,660	69.7

Census occupation code	Management, Business, and Financial Workers Occupation Group	Black alone, not Hispanic or Latino Number	Black alone, not Hispanic or Latino Percent	American Indian and Alaska Native alone, not Hispanic or Latino Number	American Indian and Alaska Native alone, not Hispanic or Latino Percent	Asian alone, not Hispanic or Latino Number	Asian alone, not Hispanic or Latino Percent	Native Hawaiian and Other Pacific Islander alone, not Hispanic or Latino Number	Native Hawaiian and Other Pacific Islander alone, not Hispanic or Latino Percent	Two or more races, not Hispanic or Latino Number	Two or more races, not Hispanic or Latino Percent
0735	Market research analysts and marketing specialists	9,825	5.3	375	0.2	15,640	8.5	70	0.0	2,995	1.6
0740	Business operations specialists, all other	27,990	12.1	1,230	0.5	16,555	7.2	165	0.1	4,105	1.8
0810	Appraisers and assessors of real estate	4,110	3.6	415	0.4	2,870	2.5	75	0.1	1,135	1.0
0820	Budget analysts	8,340	15.8	230	0.4	3,780	7.1	130	0.2	1,185	2.2
0830	Credit analysts	3,545	11.7	130	0.4	2,280	7.5	35	0.1	235	0.8
0840	Financial analysts	6,050	7.1	120	0.1	10,910	12.9	55	0.1	1,490	1.8
0850	Personal financial advisors	22,015	6.2	675	0.2	21,505	6.1	300	0.1	4,010	1.1
0860	Insurance underwriters	10,380	10.2	200	0.2	4,810	4.7	95	0.1	1,170	1.1
0900	Financial examiners	1,515	11.7	35	0.3	1,020	7.9	0	0.0	195	1.5
0910	Credit counselors and loan officers	37,715	9.8	835	0.2	19,480	5.0	805	0.2	5,340	1.4
0930	Tax examiners and collectors, and revenue agents	12,645	19.4	275	0.4	3,085	4.7	105	0.2	1,035	1.6
0940	Tax preparers	15,585	14.4	370	0.3	5,250	4.9	120	0.1	1,100	1.0
0950	Financial specialists, all other	8,060	12.3	370	0.6	3,930	6.0	40	0.1	1,045	1.6
4465	Morticians, undertakers, and funeral directors	4,550	11.3	95	0.2	195	0.5	15	0.0	235	0.6
6010	Agricultural inspectors	2,700	15.2	230	1.3	740	4.2	55	0.3	225	1.3
6660	Construction and building inspectors	9,270	8.6	820	0.8	2,790	2.6	195	0.2	1,030	1.0
9410	Transportation inspectors	6,170	11.7	250	0.5	1,525	2.9	80	0.2	385	0.7

PART A—NATIONAL DATA 9

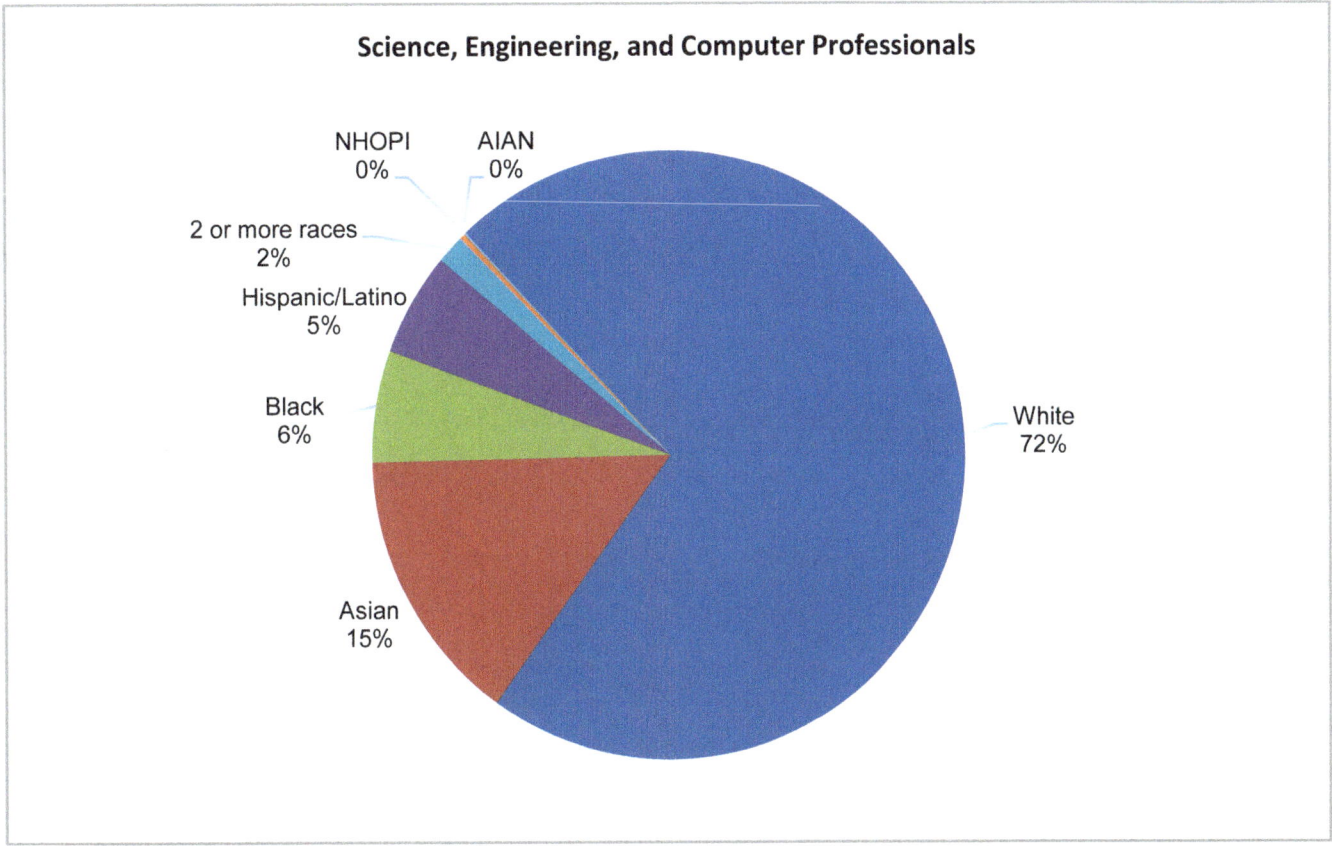

Figure A-3.1

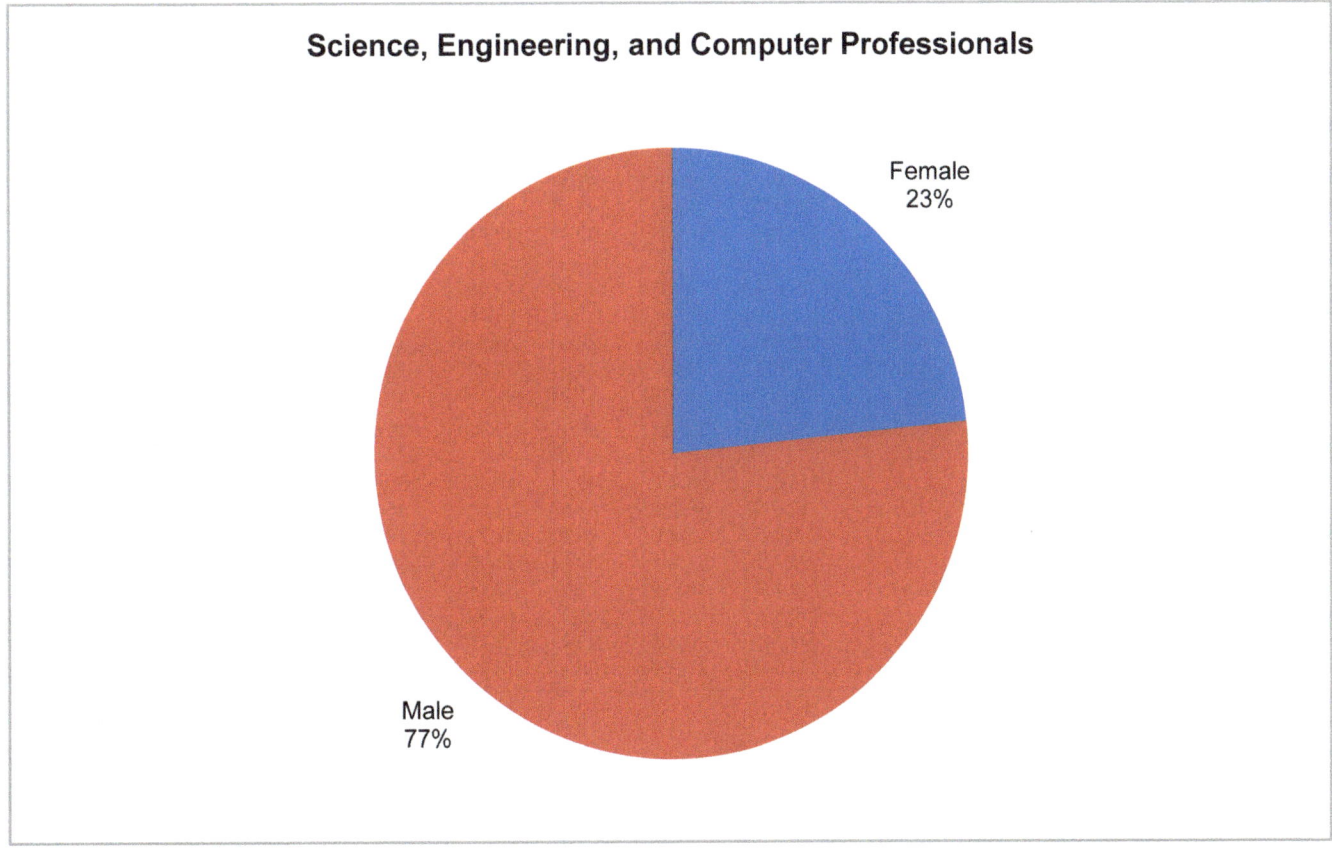

Figure A-3.2

A-3 Detailed Occupations in the Science, Engineering, and Computer Professionals Occupation Group, by Sex, Race, and Hispanic Origin, 2006–2010

Census occupation code	Science, Engineering, and Computer Professionals Occupation Group	Total who worked in the last 5 years	Male Number	Male Percent	Female Number	Female Percent	Hispanic or Latino Number	Hispanic or Latino Percent	White alone, not Hispanic or Latino Number	White alone, not Hispanic or Latino Percent
1005	Computer and information research scientists	16,090	11,260	70.0	4,830	30.0	875	5.4	10,540	65.5
1006	Computer systems analysts	486,535	314,990	64.7	171,545	35.3	24,820	5.1	330,725	68.0
1007	Information security analysts	42,010	31,330	74.6	10,685	25.4	2,700	6.4	31,215	74.3
1020	Software developers, applications and systems software	860,790	673,485	78.2	187,305	21.8	33,230	3.9	525,150	61.0
1030	Web developers	162,325	104,545	64.4	57,780	35.6	9,475	5.8	125,235	77.2
1050	Computer support specialists	519,840	367,120	70.6	152,720	29.4	42,035	8.1	367,800	70.8
1060	Database administrators	107,585	67,085	62.4	40,500	37.6	5,255	4.9	75,880	70.5
1105	Network and computer systems administrators	269,780	214,530	79.5	55,250	20.5	18,535	6.9	197,265	73.1
1106	Computer network architects	109,325	97,220	88.9	12,105	11.1	6,500	5.9	77,340	70.7
1107	Computer occupations, all other	287,425	217,285	75.6	70,135	24.4	22,260	7.7	194,675	67.7
1200	Actuaries	24,310	16,110	66.3	8,200	33.7	540	2.2	20,105	82.7
1220	Operations research analysts	120,780	62,465	51.7	58,315	48.3	8,240	6.8	87,305	72.3
1240	Miscellaneous mathematical science occupations, including mathematicians and statisticians	40,775	21,325	52.3	19,450	47.7	2,105	5.2	27,925	68.5
1300	Architects, except naval	198,105	148,095	74.8	50,010	25.2	14,540	7.3	157,820	79.7
1310	Surveyors, cartographers, and photogrammetrists	40,140	32,695	81.5	7,445	18.5	2,110	5.3	34,730	86.5
1320	Aerospace engineers	139,665	123,200	88.2	16,460	11.8	8,035	5.8	105,405	75.5
1340	Biomedical and agricultural engineers	13,860	11,575	83.5	2,285	16.5	725	5.2	10,660	76.9
1350	Chemical engineers	60,555	51,375	84.8	9,185	15.2	3,095	5.1	46,320	76.5
1360	Civil engineers	322,820	281,770	87.3	41,050	12.7	17,650	5.5	251,915	78.0
1400	Computer hardware engineers	65,755	55,415	84.3	10,345	15.7	3,845	5.8	41,305	62.8
1410	Electrical and electronics engineers	242,135	220,100	90.9	22,040	9.1	13,985	5.8	172,435	71.2
1420	Environmental engineers	34,200	25,790	75.4	8,405	24.6	1,455	4.3	26,690	78.0
1430	Industrial engineers, including health and safety	178,055	144,700	81.3	33,355	18.7	9,960	5.6	140,720	79.0
1440	Marine engineers and naval architects	11,910	10,995	92.3	920	7.7	215	1.8	9,825	82.5
1450	Materials engineers	32,820	28,865	87.9	3,955	12.1	1,600	4.9	24,655	75.1
1460	Mechanical engineers	237,395	219,865	92.6	17,530	7.4	11,475	4.8	189,330	79.8
1520	Petroleum, mining and geological engineers, including mining safety engineers	29,665	26,585	89.6	3,080	10.4	2,040	6.9	23,430	79.0
1530	Miscellaneous engineers, including nuclear engineers	461,335	405,810	88.0	55,520	12.0	24,400	5.3	342,685	74.3
1600	Agricultural and food scientists	30,685	22,860	74.5	7,825	25.5	1,465	4.8	25,670	83.7
1610	Biological scientists	86,130	44,630	51.8	41,500	48.2	4,500	5.2	67,530	78.4
1640	Conservation scientists and foresters	25,325	20,485	80.9	4,840	19.1	610	2.4	23,185	91.5
1650	Medical scientists, and life scientists, all other	118,875	58,470	49.2	60,405	50.8	5,305	4.5	69,430	58.4
1700	Astronomers and physicists	12,875	10,750	83.5	2,125	16.5	520	4.0	10,525	81.7
1710	Atmospheric and space scientists	9,245	7,470	80.8	1,775	19.2	280	3.0	8,100	87.6
1720	Chemists and materials scientists	92,325	57,335	62.1	34,990	37.9	4,285	4.6	63,275	68.5
1740	Environmental scientists and geoscientists	79,130	56,990	72.0	22,140	28.0	3,205	4.1	68,410	86.5
1760	Physical scientists, all other	170,850	106,250	62.2	64,600	37.8	7,650	4.5	112,945	66.1
4930	Sales engineers	32,345	30,205	93.4	2,135	6.6	1,805	5.6	27,450	84.9
9030	Aircraft pilots and flight engineers	133,640	127,360	95.3	6,280	4.7	5,420	4.1	121,020	90.6

A-3 Detailed Occupations in the Science, Engineering, and Computer Professionals Occupation Group, by Sex, Race, and Hispanic Origin, 2006–2010—Continued

Census occupation code	Science, Engineering, and Computer Professionals Occupation Group	Black alone, not Hispanic or Latino Number	Percent	American Indian and Alaska Native alone, not Hispanic or Latino Number	Percent	Asian alone, not Hispanic or Latino Number	Percent	Native Hawaiian and Other Pacific Islander alone, not Hispanic or Latino Number	Percent	Two or more races, not Hispanic or Latino Number	Percent
1005	Computer and information research scientists	1,055	6.6	25	0.2	3,405	21.2	40	0.2	155	1.0
1006	Computer systems analysts	41,405	8.5	1,225	0.3	80,165	16.5	390	0.1	7,810	1.6
1007	Information security analysts	4,410	10.5	75	0.2	2,770	6.6	75	0.2	770	1.8
1020	Software developers, applications and systems software	37,710	4.4	1,505	0.2	247,000	28.7	670	0.1	15,525	1.8
1030	Web developers	7,530	4.6	550	0.3	15,225	9.4	205	0.1	4,105	2.5
1050	Computer support specialists	56,390	10.8	1,975	0.4	41,550	8.0	855	0.2	9,230	1.8
1060	Database administrators	7,905	7.3	190	0.2	16,645	15.5	85	0.1	1,635	1.5
1105	Network and computer systems administrators	22,500	8.3	940	0.3	25,670	9.5	285	0.1	4,595	1.7
1106	Computer network architects	9,345	8.5	295	0.3	13,500	12.3	200	0.2	2,150	2.0
1107	Computer occupations, all other	29,020	10.1	1,430	0.5	34,315	11.9	480	0.2	5,250	1.8
1200	Actuaries	645	2.7	10	0.0	2,675	11.0	20	0.1	310	1.3
1220	Operations research analysts	13,510	11.2	285	0.2	9,390	7.8	190	0.2	1,855	1.5
1240	Miscellaneous mathematical science occupations, including mathematicians and statisticians	2,820	6.9	165	0.4	6,990	17.1	110	0.3	660	1.6
1300	Architects, except naval	5,165	2.6	345	0.2	17,550	8.9	195	0.1	2,485	1.3
1310	Surveyors, cartographers, and photogrammetrists	1,490	3.7	245	0.6	1,030	2.6	0	0.0	535	1.3
1320	Aerospace engineers	5,545	4.0	395	0.3	17,990	12.9	140	0.1	2,150	1.5
1340	Biomedical and agricultural engineers	720	5.2	35	0.3	1,550	11.2	0	0.0	175	1.3
1350	Chemical engineers	3,270	5.4	75	0.1	7,145	11.8	4	0.0	640	1.1
1360	Civil engineers	14,410	4.5	855	0.3	33,230	10.3	375	0.1	4,380	1.4
1400	Computer hardware engineers	4,310	6.6	310	0.5	14,860	22.6	20	0.0	1,100	1.7
1410	Electrical and electronics engineers	12,365	5.1	605	0.2	39,635	16.4	145	0.1	2,960	1.2
1420	Environmental engineers	2,220	6.5	155	0.5	3,245	9.5	45	0.1	390	1.1
1430	Industrial engineers, including health and safety	8,110	4.6	370	0.2	16,460	9.2	205	0.1	2,230	1.3
1440	Marine engineers and naval architects	790	6.6	60	0.5	895	7.5	4	0.0	125	1.0
1450	Materials engineers	1,170	3.6	100	0.3	4,795	14.6	50	0.2	459	1.4
1460	Mechanical engineers	9,265	3.9	495	0.2	23,905	10.1	185	0.1	2,745	1.2
1520	Petroleum, mining and geological engineers, including mining safety engineers	1,470	5.0	105	0.4	2,105	7.1	0	0.0	520	1.8
1530	Miscellaneous engineers, including nuclear engineers	19,350	4.2	1,445	0.3	67,330	14.6	320	0.1	5,805	1.3
1600	Agricultural and food scientists	765	2.5	175	0.6	2,050	6.7	35	0.1	519	1.7
1610	Biological scientists	2,615	3.0	305	0.4	9,765	11.3	80	0.1	1,335	1.5
1640	Conservation scientists and foresters	510	2.0	365	1.4	275	1.1	4	0.0	370	1.5
1650	Medical scientists, and life scientists, all other	4,910	4.1	125	0.1	37,305	31.4	115	0.1	1,680	1.4
1700	Astronomers and physicists	255	2.0	20	0.2	1,315	10.2	10	0.1	225	1.7
1710	Atmospheric and space scientists	365	3.9	60	0.6	340	3.7	0	0.0	110	1.2
1720	Chemists and materials scientists	5,880	6.4	240	0.3	17,395	18.8	120	0.1	1,135	1.2
1740	Environmental scientists and geoscientists	3,065	3.9	445	0.6	3,165	4.0	85	0.1	750	0.9
1760	Physical scientists, all other	5,685	3.3	450	0.3	41,255	24.1	45	0.0	2,815	1.6
4930	Sales engineers	735	2.3	105	0.3	2,030	6.3	0	0.0	224	0.7
9030	Aircraft pilots and flight engineers	2,920	2.2	500	0.4	2,045	1.5	250	0.2	1,485	1.1

Health Care Practitioner Professionals

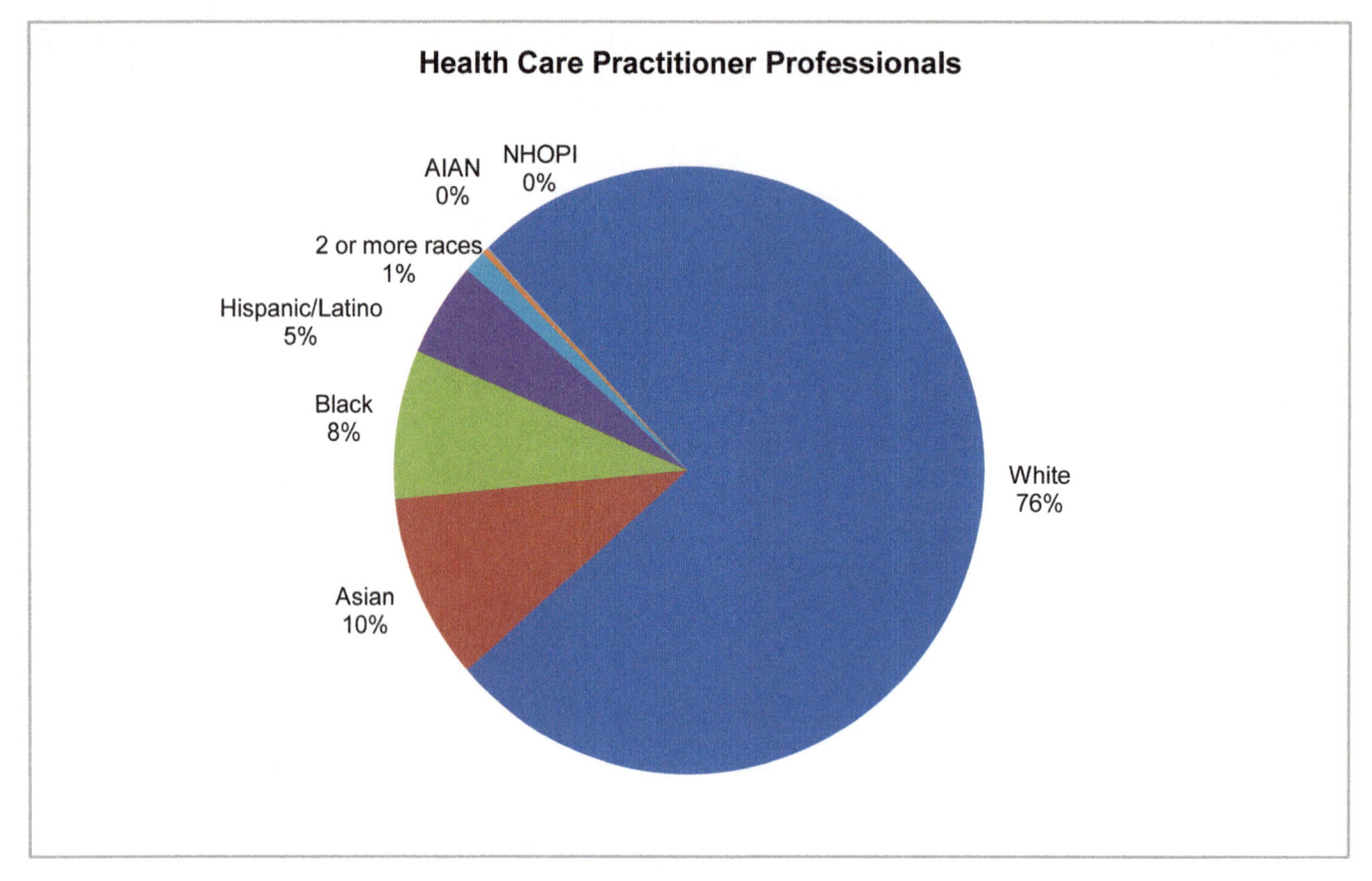

- White 76%
- Asian 10%
- Black 8%
- Hispanic/Latino 5%
- 2 or more races 1%
- AIAN 0%
- NHOPI 0%

Figure A-4.1

Health Care Practitioner Professionals

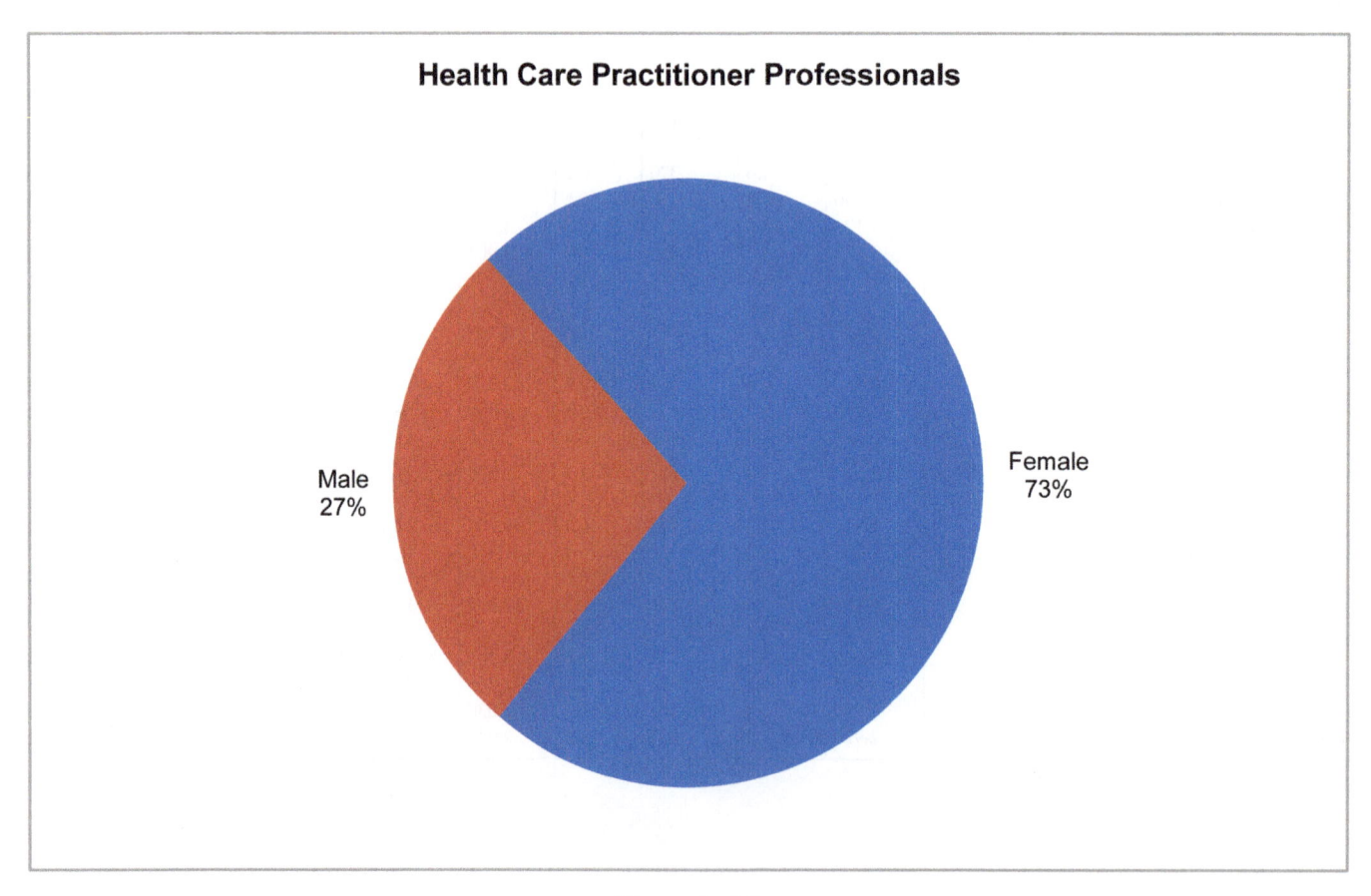

- Female 73%
- Male 27%

Figure A-4.2

A-4 Detailed Occupations in the Health Care Practitioner Professionals Occupation Group, by Sex, Race, and Hispanic Origin, 2006–2010

Census occupation code	Health Care Practitioner Professionals Occupation Group	Total who worked in the last 5 years	Male Number	Male Percent	Female Number	Female Percent	Hispanic or Latino Number	Hispanic or Latino Percent	White alone, not Hispanic or Latino Number	White alone, not Hispanic or Latino Percent
3000	Chiropractors	56,755	42,335	74.6	14,420	25.4	2,025	3.6	50,530	89.0
3010	Dentists	165,835	127,595	76.9	38,240	23.1	9,275	5.6	126,200	76.1
3030	Dietitians and nutritionists	90,140	8,830	9.8	81,310	90.2	7,520	8.3	62,630	69.5
3040	Optometrists	35,155	22,680	64.5	12,475	35.5	1,040	3.0	28,720	81.7
3050	Pharmacists	253,925	120,245	47.4	133,680	52.6	9,380	3.7	186,115	73.3
3060	Physicians and surgeons	834,265	563,595	67.6	270,670	32.4	48,775	5.8	575,355	69.0
3110	Physician assistants	103,945	34,485	33.2	69,460	66.8	10,075	9.7	75,365	72.5
3120	Podiatrists	9,840	7,920	80.5	1,920	19.5	470	4.8	8,160	82.9
3140	Audiologists	13,920	2,860	20.5	11,060	79.5	450	3.2	12,550	90.2
3150	Occupational therapists	84,920	8,685	10.2	76,235	89.8	3,760	4.4	71,010	83.6
3160	Physical therapists	185,185	55,405	29.9	129,780	70.1	8,415	4.5	149,795	80.9
3200	Radiation therapists	13,565	3,600	26.5	9,965	73.5	690	5.1	11,455	84.4
3210	Recreational therapists	14,510	3,160	21.8	11,350	78.2	700	4.8	10,670	73.5
3220	Respiratory therapists	100,170	36,030	36.0	64,140	64.0	7,050	7.0	73,880	73.8
3230	Speech-language pathologists	117,190	4,970	4.2	112,220	95.8	5,700	4.9	102,355	87.3
3245	Other therapists, including exercise physiologists	125,855	26,930	21.4	98,930	78.6	9,525	7.6	95,065	75.5
3250	Veterinarians	72,680	36,355	50.0	36,325	50.0	2,445	3.4	66,250	91.2
3255	Registered nurses	2,639,750	231,525	8.8	2,408,225	91.2	122,940	4.7	1,997,830	75.7
3256	Nurse anesthetists	23,095	9,760	42.3	13,335	57.7	755	3.3	20,430	88.5
3258	Nurse practitioners and nurse midwives	81,805	5,940	7.3	75,865	92.7	3,190	3.9	70,150	85.8
3260	Health diagnosing and treating practitioners, all other	18,770	6,255	33.3	12,515	66.7	825	4.4	12,285	65.5

Census occupation code	Health Care Practitioner Professionals Occupation Group	Black alone, not Hispanic or Latino Number	Black alone, not Hispanic or Latino Percent	American Indian and Alaska Native alone, not Hispanic or Latino Number	American Indian and Alaska Native alone, not Hispanic or Latino Percent	Asian alone, not Hispanic or Latino Number	Asian alone, not Hispanic or Latino Percent	Native Hawaiian and Other Pacific Islander alone, not Hispanic or Latino Number	Native Hawaiian and Other Pacific Islander alone, not Hispanic or Latino Percent	Two or more races, not Hispanic or Latino Number	Two or more races, not Hispanic or Latino Percent
3000	Chiropractors	1,150	2.0	120	0.2	2,230	3.9	35	0.1	660	1.2
3010	Dentists	5,425	3.3	190	0.1	22,850	13.8	70	0.0	1,820	1.1
3030	Dietitians and nutritionists	13,350	14.8	625	0.7	4,975	5.5	50	0.1	990	1.1
3040	Optometrists	460	1.3	100	0.3	4,550	12.9	45	0.1	240	0.7
3050	Pharmacists	14,370	5.7	645	0.3	40,695	16.0	175	0.1	2,545	1.0
3060	Physicians and surgeons	40,940	4.9	1,585	0.2	154,970	18.6	315	0.0	12,330	1.5
3110	Physician assistants	8,735	8.4	490	0.5	7,500	7.2	25	0.0	1,755	1.7
3120	Podiatrists	465	4.7	0	0.0	690	7.0	15	0.2	40	0.4
3140	Audiologists	515	3.7	10	0.1	270	1.9	0	0.0	129	0.9
3150	Occupational therapists	4,170	4.9	160	0.2	4,885	5.8	35	0.0	895	1.1
3160	Physical therapists	7,150	3.9	490	0.3	17,415	9.4	155	0.1	1,765	1.0
3200	Radiation therapists	515	3.8	35	0.3	740	5.5	0	0.0	129	1.0
3210	Recreational therapists	2,445	16.9	105	0.7	490	3.4	0	0.0	100	0.7
3220	Respiratory therapists	11,785	11.8	310	0.3	5,615	5.6	65	0.1	1,465	1.5
3230	Speech-language pathologists	5,515	4.7	305	0.3	2,380	2.0	25	0.0	905	0.8
3245	Other therapists, including exercise physiologists	13,670	10.9	525	0.4	4,600	3.7	130	0.1	2,345	1.9
3250	Veterinarians	1,290	1.8	130	0.2	1,935	2.7	15	0.0	615	0.8
3255	Registered nurses	262,965	10.0	10,305	0.4	212,815	8.1	2,195	0.1	30,700	1.2
3256	Nurse anesthetists	790	3.4	30	0.1	775	3.4	0	0.0	315	1.4
3258	Nurse practitioners and nurse midwives	3,830	4.7	75	0.1	3,545	4.3	10	0.0	1,010	1.2
3260	Health diagnosing and treating practitioners, all other	385	2.1	115	0.6	4,740	25.3	10	0.1	410	2.2

Other Professional Workers

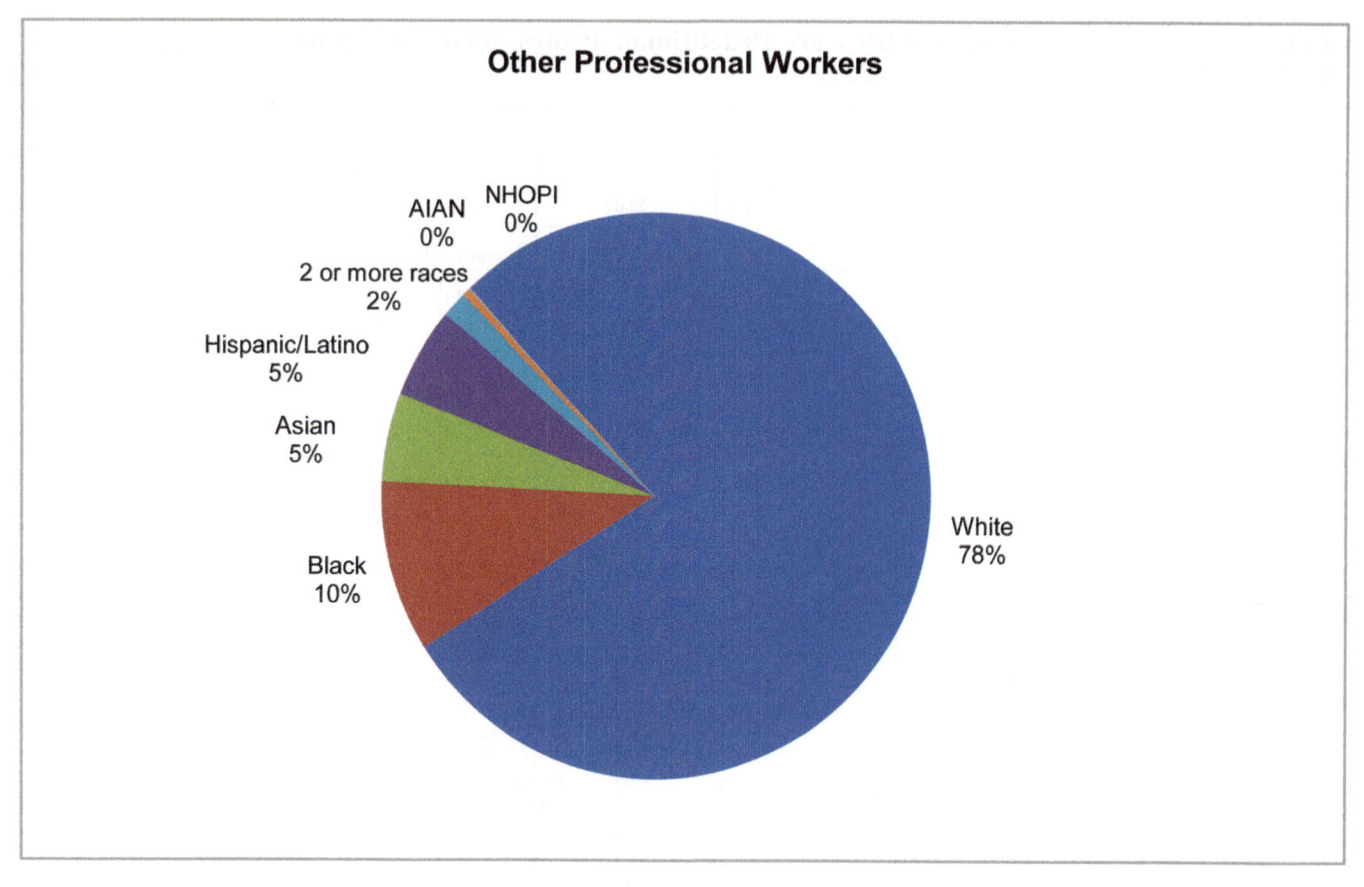

- White 78%
- Black 10%
- Asian 5%
- Hispanic/Latino 5%
- 2 or more races 2%
- AIAN 0%
- NHOPI 0%

Figure A-5.1

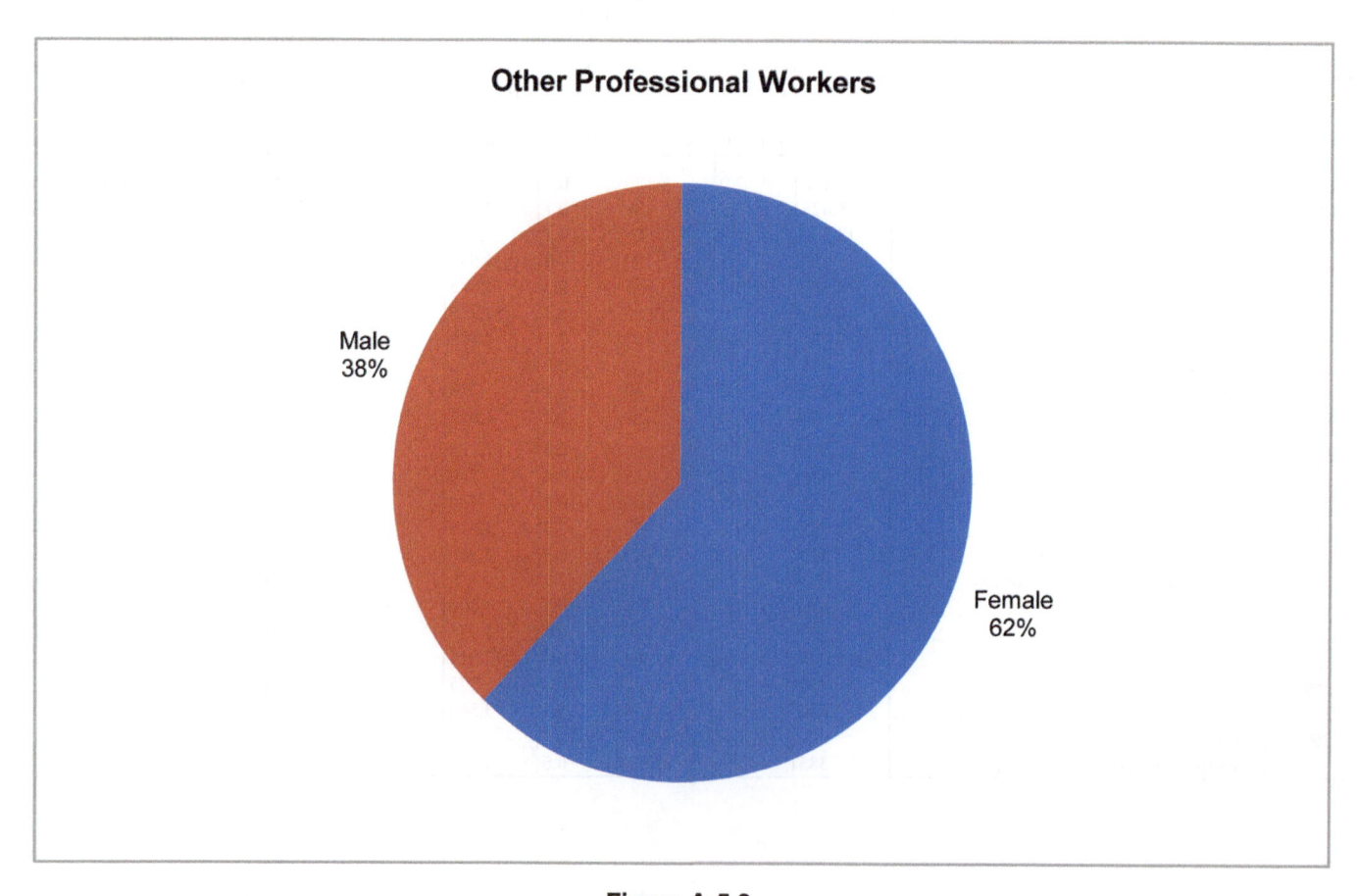

Other Professional Workers

- Female 62%
- Male 38%

Figure A-5.2

PART A—NATIONAL DATA

A-5 Detailed Occupations in the Other Professional Workers Occupation Group, by Sex, Race, and Hispanic Origin, 2006–2010

Census occupation code	Other Professional Workers Occupation Group	Total who worked in the last 5 years	Male Number	Male Percent	Female Number	Female Percent	Hispanic or Latino Number	Hispanic or Latino Percent	White alone, not Hispanic or Latino Number	White alone, not Hispanic or Latino Percent
630	Human resources workers	651,090	191,270	29.4	459,815	70.6	67,480	10.4	450,200	69.1
800	Accountants and auditors	2,100,705	840,595	40.0	1,260,110	60.0	139,540	6.6	1,537,555	73.2
1800	Economists	24,635	16,405	66.6	8,230	33.4	2,160	8.8	18,020	73.1
1820	Psychologists	182,635	59,685	32.7	122,950	67.3	10,235	5.6	156,755	85.8
1840	Urban and regional planners	24,165	14,340	59.3	9,825	40.7	1,340	5.5	19,460	80.5
1860	Miscellaneous social scientists, including survey researchers and sociologists	49,085	23,640	48.2	25,445	51.8	3,205	6.5	38,060	77.5
2000	Counselors	689,195	213,765	31.0	475,430	69.0	64,715	9.4	447,890	65.0
2010	Social workers	779,175	159,540	20.5	619,640	79.5	85,650	11.0	482,675	61.9
2015	Probation officers and correctional treatment specialists	98,525	48,070	48.8	50,455	51.2	12,495	12.7	58,355	59.2
2025	Miscellaneous community and social service specialists, including health educators and community health workers	82,475	27,345	33.2	55,130	66.8	10,450	12.7	50,760	61.5
2040	Clergy	444,045	365,825	82.4	78,220	17.6	24,600	5.5	350,490	78.9
2050	Directors, religious activities and education	53,625	20,600	38.4	33,030	61.6	3,065	5.7	44,265	82.5
2060	Religious workers, all other	90,285	35,100	38.9	55,185	61.1	6,305	7.0	71,380	79.1
2100	Lawyers, and judges, magistrates, and other judicial workers	1,038,895	691,600	66.6	347,300	33.4	47,480	4.6	890,815	85.7
2105	Judicial law clerks	11,830	5,330	45.1	6,500	54.9	800	6.8	9,660	81.7
2200	Postsecondary teachers	1,351,005	702,405	52.0	648,605	48.0	73,290	5.4	1,010,055	74.8
2300	Preschool and kindergarten teachers	591,935	15,180	2.6	576,760	97.4	70,295	11.9	396,465	67.0
2310	Elementary and middle school teachers	3,452,545	714,765	20.7	2,737,785	79.3	255,445	7.4	2,766,040	80.1
2320	Secondary school teachers	812,130	335,740	41.3	476,390	58.7	62,230	7.7	649,520	80.0
2330	Special education teachers	227,105	32,555	14.3	194,550	85.7	16,240	7.2	179,100	78.9
2340	Other teachers and instructors	854,840	317,900	37.2	536,940	62.8	77,055	9.0	614,170	71.8
2400	Archivists, curators, and museum technicians	44,480	17,825	40.1	26,650	59.9	1,800	4.0	37,805	85.0
2430	Librarians	181,670	29,795	16.4	151,875	83.6	8,025	4.4	153,065	84.3
2550	Other education, training, and library workers	91,460	25,575	28.0	65,885	72.0	7,895	8.6	67,345	73.6
2600	Artists and related workers	207,590	115,165	55.5	92,420	44.5	15,475	7.5	169,970	81.9
2630	Designers	820,855	377,915	46.0	442,940	54.0	76,060	9.3	640,880	78.1
2700	Actors	47,455	27,035	57.0	20,420	43.0	3,785	8.0	34,815	73.4
2710	Producers and directors	146,165	91,410	62.5	54,755	37.5	12,170	8.3	113,810	77.9
2720	Athletes, coaches, umpires, and related workers	268,000	174,745	65.2	93,260	34.8	20,450	7.6	208,900	77.9
2740	Dancers and choreographers	24,415	4,495	18.4	19,920	81.6	4,135	16.9	14,720	60.3
2750	Musicians, singers, and related workers	189,510	124,360	65.6	65,150	34.4	16,030	8.5	140,200	74.0
2760	Entertainers and performers, sports and related workers, all other	45,080	23,810	52.8	21,270	47.2	5,225	11.6	32,040	71.1
2800	Announcers	54,380	42,335	77.9	12,045	22.1	7,010	12.9	38,540	70.9
2810	News analysts, reporters and correspondents	86,045	46,695	54.3	39,350	45.7	6,755	7.9	68,765	79.9
2825	Public relations specialists	138,955	49,825	35.9	89,130	64.1	9,730	7.0	111,250	80.1
2830	Editors	180,915	81,625	45.1	99,290	54.9	9,665	5.3	152,635	84.4
2840	Technical writers	64,080	28,400	44.3	35,680	55.7	2,180	3.4	54,130	84.5
2850	Writers and authors	194,250	83,845	43.2	110,405	56.8	7,300	3.8	166,370	85.6
2860	Miscellaneous media and communication workers	85,660	26,310	30.7	59,350	69.3	29,930	34.9	40,000	46.7
2910	Photographers	153,930	84,310	54.8	69,620	45.2	14,205	9.2	121,530	79.0
2920	Television, video, and motion picture camera operators and editors	48,400	39,435	81.5	8,965	18.5	4,495	9.3	37,185	76.8
4340	Animal trainers	40,480	19,305	47.7	21,170	52.3	3,575	8.8	34,385	84.9

A-5 Detailed Occupations in the Other Professional Workers Occupation Group, by Sex, Race, and Hispanic Origin, 2006–2010—*Continued*

Census occupation code	Other Professional Workers Occupation Group	Black alone, not Hispanic or Latino Number	Percent	American Indian and Alaska Native alone, not Hispanic or Latino Number	Percent	Asian alone, not Hispanic or Latino Number	Percent	Native Hawaiian and Other Pacific Islander alone, not Hispanic or Latino Number	Percent	Two or more races, not Hispanic or Latino Number	Percent
630	Human resources workers	91,105	14.0	3,930	0.6	26,730	4.1	1,030	0.2	10,610	1.6
800	Accountants and auditors	170,610	8.1	7,450	0.4	218,470	10.4	2,050	0.1	25,040	1.2
1800	Economists	1,350	5.5	50	0.2	2,840	11.5	15	0.1	199	0.8
1820	Psychologists	8,715	4.8	395	0.2	4,555	2.5	80	0.0	1,905	1.0
1840	Urban and regional planners	1,640	6.8	105	0.4	1,195	4.9	0	0.0	430	1.8
1860	Miscellaneous social scientists, including survey researchers and sociologists	4,235	8.6	235	0.5	2,395	4.9	30	0.1	925	1.9
2000	Counselors	139,145	20.2	6,130	0.9	17,400	2.5	1,310	0.2	12,600	1.8
2010	Social workers	170,860	21.9	5,675	0.7	20,660	2.7	885	0.1	12,775	1.6
2015	Probation officers and correctional treatment specialists	23,015	23.4	850	0.9	1,620	1.6	270	0.3	1,930	2.0
2025	Miscellaneous community and social service specialists, including health educators and community health workers	15,840	19.2	1,235	1.5	2,410	2.9	145	0.2	1,635	2.0
2040	Clergy	42,810	9.6	1,710	0.4	19,260	4.3	515	0.1	4,655	1.0
2050	Directors, religious activities and education	3,830	7.1	135	0.3	1,665	3.1	95	0.2	570	1.1
2060	Religious workers, all other	6,945	7.7	270	0.3	4,110	4.6	95	0.1	1,180	1.3
2100	Lawyers, and judges, magistrates, and other judicial workers	48,185	4.6	2,640	0.3	36,945	3.6	315	0.0	12,520	1.2
2105	Judicial law clerks	615	5.2	55	0.5	575	4.9	0	0.0	130	1.1
2200	Postsecondary teachers	82,185	6.1	3,780	0.3	158,150	11.7	765	0.1	22,785	1.7
2300	Preschool and kindergarten teachers	95,150	16.1	4,550	0.8	17,010	2.9	755	0.1	7,715	1.3
2310	Elementary and middle school teachers	303,080	8.8	13,385	0.4	73,825	2.1	2,145	0.1	38,625	1.1
2320	Secondary school teachers	67,415	8.3	3,430	0.4	18,340	2.3	770	0.1	10,435	1.3
2330	Special education teachers	22,455	9.9	1,290	0.6	4,670	2.1	240	0.1	3,105	1.4
2340	Other teachers and instructors	91,915	10.8	4,895	0.6	48,910	5.7	1,445	0.2	16,445	1.9
2400	Archivists, curators, and museum technicians	2,505	5.6	245	0.6	1,440	3.2	0	0.0	690	1.6
2430	Librarians	10,425	5.7	795	0.4	6,815	3.8	55	0.0	2,485	1.4
2550	Other education, training, and library workers	10,750	11.8	795	0.9	3,015	3.3	180	0.2	1,490	1.6
2600	Artists and related workers	6,490	3.1	1,565	0.8	10,285	5.0	180	0.1	3,625	1.7
2630	Designers	32,845	4.0	1,845	0.2	56,065	6.8	635	0.1	12,525	1.5
2700	Actors	5,260	11.1	210	0.4	1,350	2.8	40	0.1	2,000	4.2
2710	Producers and directors	11,085	7.6	330	0.2	5,950	4.1	80	0.1	2,740	1.9
2720	Athletes, coaches, umpires, and related workers	23,775	8.9	1,175	0.4	7,310	2.7	395	0.1	6,005	2.2
2740	Dancers and choreographers	3,005	12.3	120	0.5	895	3.7	305	1.2	1,245	5.1
2750	Musicians, singers, and related workers	22,520	11.9	495	0.3	6,045	3.2	285	0.2	3,945	2.1
2760	Entertainers and performers, sports and related workers, all other	4,615	10.2	290	0.6	1,120	2.5	165	0.4	1,620	3.6
2800	Announcers	5,865	10.8	265	0.5	1,515	2.8	60	0.1	1,130	2.1
2810	News analysts, reporters and correspondents	5,040	5.9	285	0.3	3,425	4.0	25	0.0	1,750	2.0
2825	Public relations specialists	10,665	7.7	605	0.4	4,770	3.4	80	0.1	1,865	1.3
2830	Editors	7,720	4.3	420	0.2	7,445	4.1	140	0.1	2,890	1.6
2840	Technical writers	3,780	5.9	235	0.4	2,645	4.1	10	0.0	1,095	1.7
2850	Writers and authors	9,875	5.1	870	0.4	6,420	3.3	85	0.0	3,335	1.7
2860	Miscellaneous media and communication workers	4,375	5.1	455	0.5	9,620	11.2	50	0.1	1,230	1.4
2910	Photographers	8,760	5.7	470	0.3	5,985	3.9	145	0.1	2,830	1.8
2920	Television, video, and motion picture camera operators and editors	3,330	6.9	100	0.2	2,115	4.4	80	0.2	1,095	2.3
4340	Animal trainers	985	2.4	315	0.8	620	1.5	45	0.1	555	1.4

PART A—NATIONAL DATA 17

Technicians

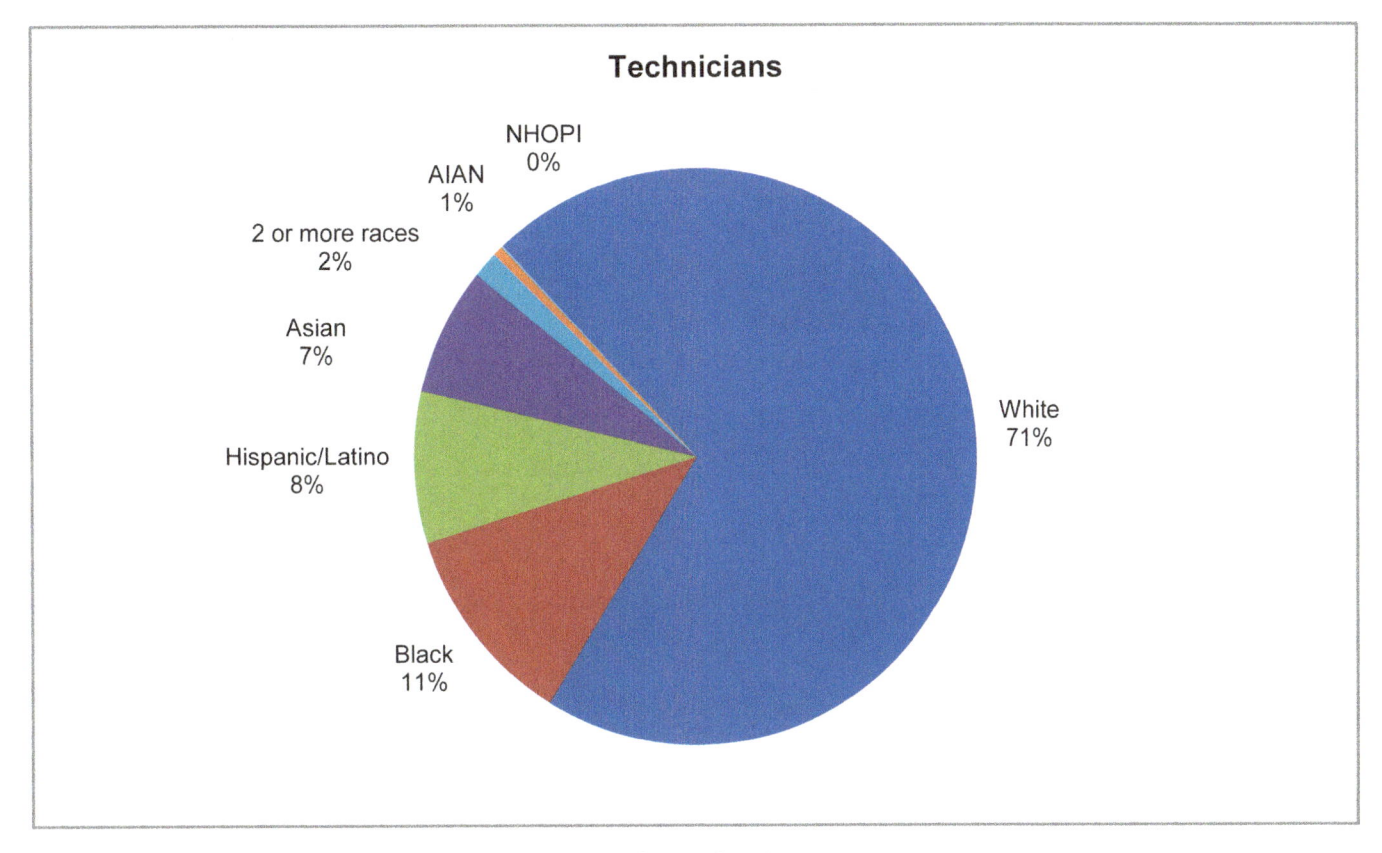

- White 71%
- Black 11%
- Hispanic/Latino 8%
- Asian 7%
- 2 or more races 2%
- AIAN 1%
- NHOPI 0%

Figure A-6.1

Technicians

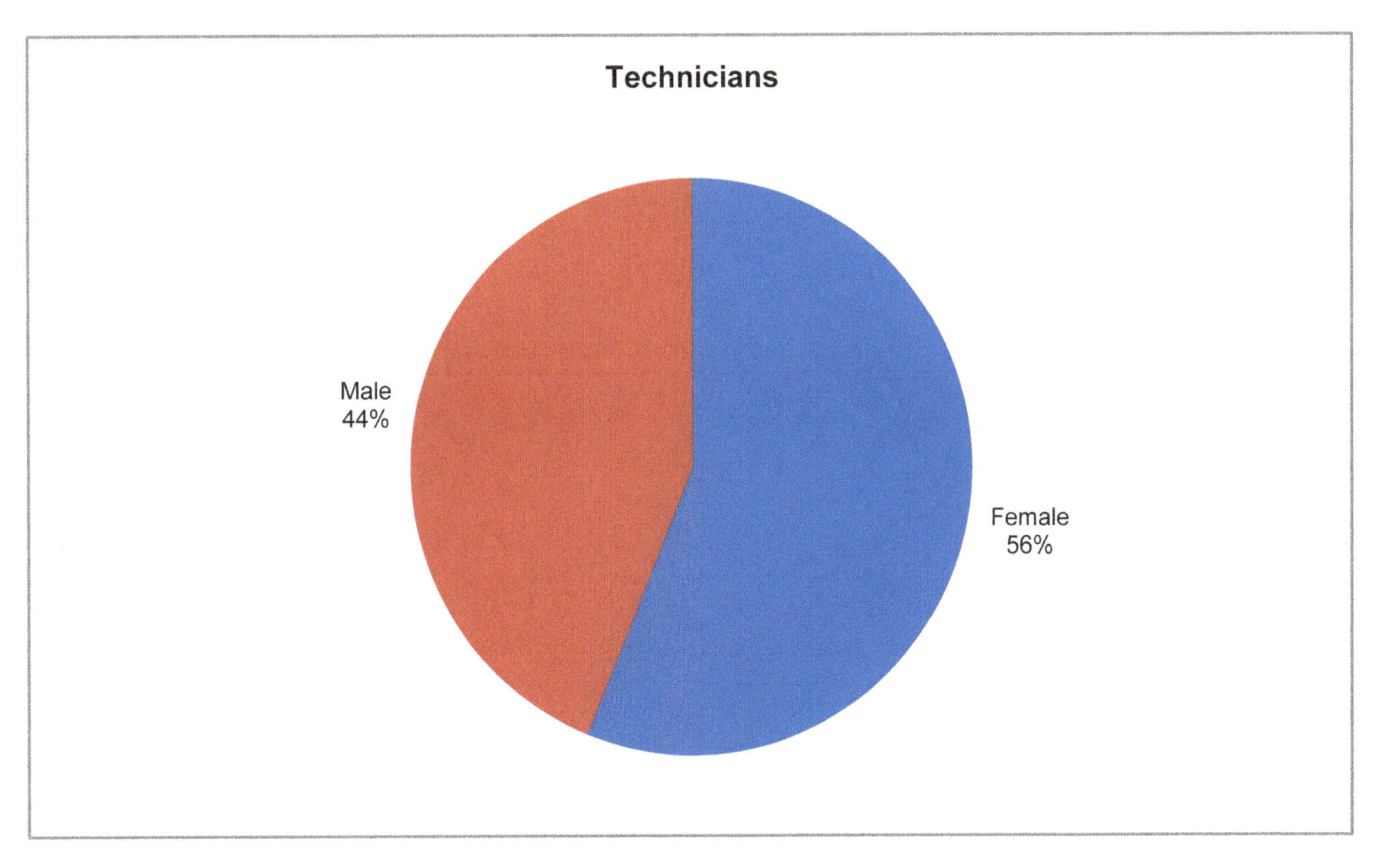

- Female 56%
- Male 44%

Figure A-6.2

A-6 Detailed Occupations in the Technicians Occupation Group, by Sex, Race, and Hispanic Origin, 2006–2010

Census occupation code	Technicians Occupation Group	Total who worked in the last 5 years	Male Number	Male Percent	Female Number	Female Percent	Hispanic or Latino Number	Hispanic or Latino Percent	White alone, not Hispanic or Latino Number	White alone, not Hispanic or Latino Percent
1010	Computer programmers	522,290	394,745	75.6	127,545	24.4	24,565	4.7	374,965	71.8
1540	Drafters	212,205	170,365	80.3	41,840	19.7	20,360	9.6	167,475	78.9
1550	Engineering technicians, except drafters	438,830	353,240	80.5	85,590	19.5	43,155	9.8	311,520	71.0
1560	Surveying and mapping technicians	87,510	79,320	90.6	8,190	9.4	7,195	8.2	73,935	84.5
1900	Agricultural and food science technicians	31,295	18,250	58.3	13,045	41.7	4,255	13.6	22,360	71.4
1910	Biological technicians	24,170	12,625	52.2	11,545	47.8	2,400	9.9	15,780	65.3
1920	Chemical technicians	76,095	48,875	64.2	27,220	35.8	7,190	9.4	52,975	69.6
1930	Geological and petroleum technicians, and nuclear technicians	19,935	14,775	74.1	5,160	25.9	1,920	9.6	15,845	79.5
1965	Miscellaneous life, physical, and social science technicians, including social science research assistants	179,335	93,950	52.4	85,380	47.6	15,555	8.7	123,825	69.0
2900	Broadcast and sound engineering technicians and radio operators, and media and communication equipment workers, all other	94,080	83,070	88.3	11,010	11.7	9,105	9.7	70,265	74.7
3300	Clinical laboratory technologists and technicians	345,965	89,700	25.9	256,265	74.1	30,200	8.7	217,910	63.0
3310	Dental hygienists	148,390	4,905	3.3	143,485	96.7	9,105	6.1	128,285	86.5
3320	Diagnostic related technologists and technicians	306,190	86,265	28.2	219,925	71.8	26,525	8.7	234,955	76.7
3400	Emergency medical technicians and paramedics	172,115	117,760	68.4	54,355	31.6	16,110	9.4	140,100	81.4
3420	Health practitioner support technologists and technicians	509,925	102,675	20.1	407,245	79.9	53,225	10.4	348,960	68.4
3500	Licensed practical and licensed vocational nurses	680,945	50,330	7.4	630,615	92.6	49,330	7.2	434,975	63.9
3510	Medical records and health information technicians	110,065	11,415	10.4	98,650	89.6	14,085	12.8	68,155	61.9
3520	Opticians, dispensing	52,960	15,820	29.9	37,140	70.1	5,805	11.0	40,875	77.2
3535	Miscellaneous health technologists and technicians	123,560	41,955	34.0	81,605	66.0	11,490	9.3	74,855	60.6
3540	Other health care practitioners and technical occupations	73,480	42,730	58.2	30,750	41.8	6,025	8.2	55,270	75.2
9040	Air traffic controllers and airfield operations specialists	34,835	28,415	81.6	6,420	18.4	2,640	7.6	27,125	77.9

PART A—NATIONAL DATA

A-6 Detailed Occupations in the Technicians Occupation Group, by Sex, Race, and Hispanic Origin, 2006–2010—Continued

Census occupation code	Technicians Occupation Group	Black alone, not Hispanic or Latino Number	Percent	American Indian and Alaska Native alone, not Hispanic or Latino Number	Percent	Asian alone, not Hispanic or Latino Number	Percent	Native Hawaiian and Other Pacific Islander alone, not Hispanic or Latino Number	Percent	Two or more races, not Hispanic or Latino Number	Percent
1010	Computer programmers	25,105	4.8	1,060	0.2	88,335	16.9	360	0.1	7,895	1.5
1540	Drafters	8,310	3.9	900	0.4	12,345	5.8	150	0.1	2,670	1.3
1550	Engineering technicians, except drafters	40,250	9.2	2,245	0.5	34,100	7.8	655	0.1	6,900	1.6
1560	Surveying and mapping technicians	3,055	3.5	930	1.1	1,060	1.2	200	0.2	1,135	1.3
1900	Agricultural and food science technicians	2,240	7.2	230	0.7	1,720	5.5	115	0.4	375	1.2
1910	Biological technicians	1,635	6.8	260	1.1	3,470	14.4	25	0.1	585	2.4
1920	Chemical technicians	8,745	11.5	400	0.5	5,710	7.5	65	0.1	1,010	1.3
1930	Geological and petroleum technicians, and nuclear technicians	1,175	5.9	155	0.8	635	3.2	15	0.1	185	0.9
1965	Miscellaneous life, physical, and social science technicians, including social science research assistants	14,520	8.1	1,650	0.9	19,660	11.0	320	0.2	3,800	2.1
2900	Broadcast and sound engineering technicians and radio operators, and media and communication equipment workers, all other	9,280	9.9	475	0.5	2,995	3.2	105	0.1	1,860	2.0
3300	Clinical laboratory technologists and technicians	48,580	14.0	1,525	0.4	41,365	12.0	500	0.1	5,890	1.7
3310	Dental hygienists	3,860	2.6	365	0.2	4,745	3.2	70	0.0	1,960	1.3
3320	Diagnostic related technologists and technicians	25,780	8.4	900	0.3	13,890	4.5	290	0.1	3,850	1.3
3400	Emergency medical technicians and paramedics	9,800	5.7	1,385	0.8	2,505	1.5	45	0.0	2,170	1.3
3420	Health practitioner support technologists and technicians	64,140	12.6	2,990	0.6	31,115	6.1	825	0.2	8,660	1.7
3500	Licensed practical and licensed vocational nurses	158,990	23.3	4,035	0.6	24,295	3.6	530	0.1	8,780	1.3
3510	Medical records and health information technicians	19,135	17.4	1,700	1.5	5,475	5.0	160	0.1	1,355	1.2
3520	Opticians, dispensing	3,250	6.1	270	0.5	1,690	3.2	30	0.1	1,035	2.0
3535	Miscellaneous health technologists and technicians	25,545	20.7	925	0.7	8,515	6.9	135	0.1	2,090	1.7
3540	Other health care practitioners and technical occupations	7,775	10.6	590	0.8	2,575	3.5	55	0.1	1,180	1.6
9040	Air traffic controllers and airfield operations specialists	3,285	9.4	60	0.2	905	2.6	190	0.5	640	1.8

Sales Workers

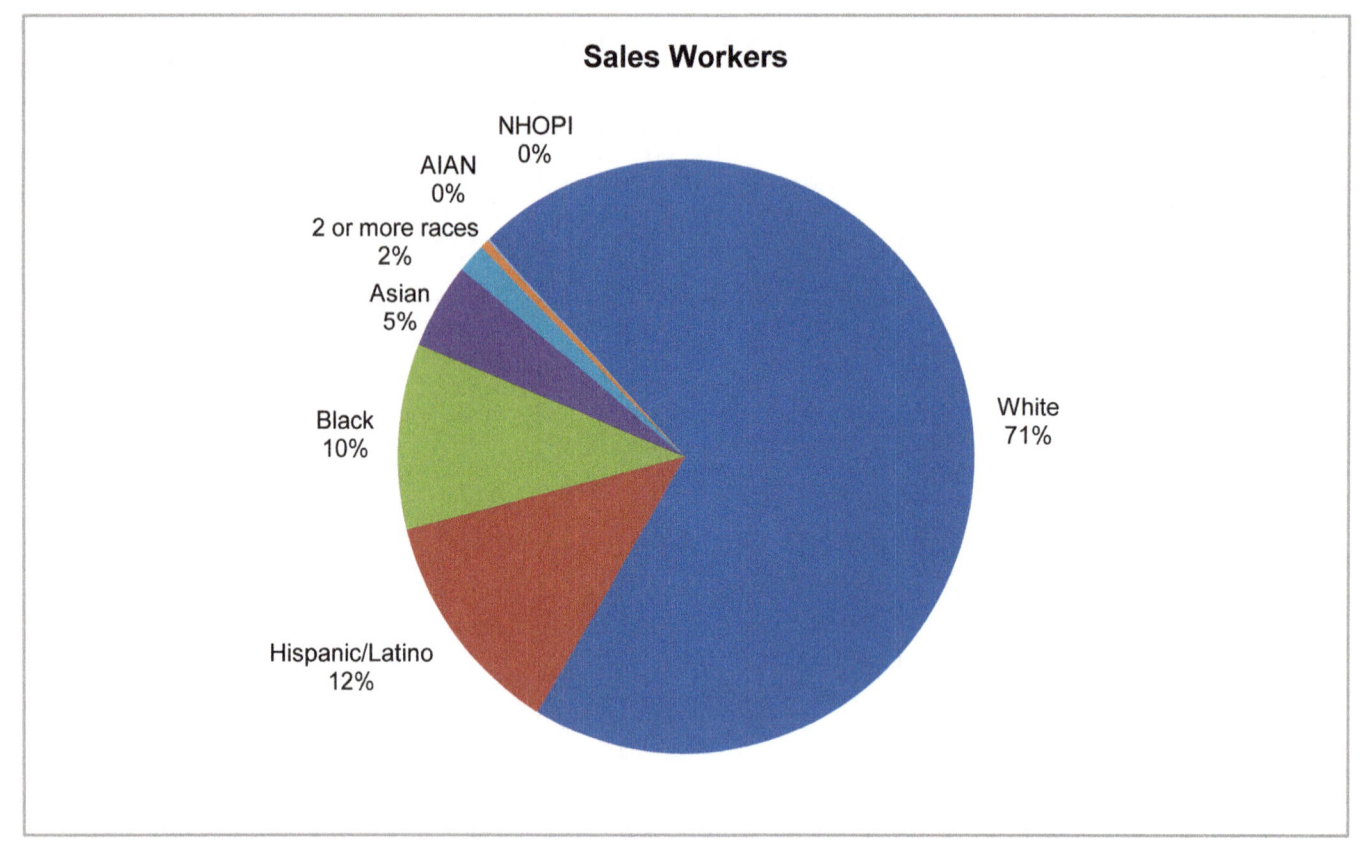

- NHOPI 0%
- AIAN 0%
- 2 or more races 2%
- Asian 5%
- Black 10%
- Hispanic/Latino 12%
- White 71%

Figure A-7.1

Sales Workers

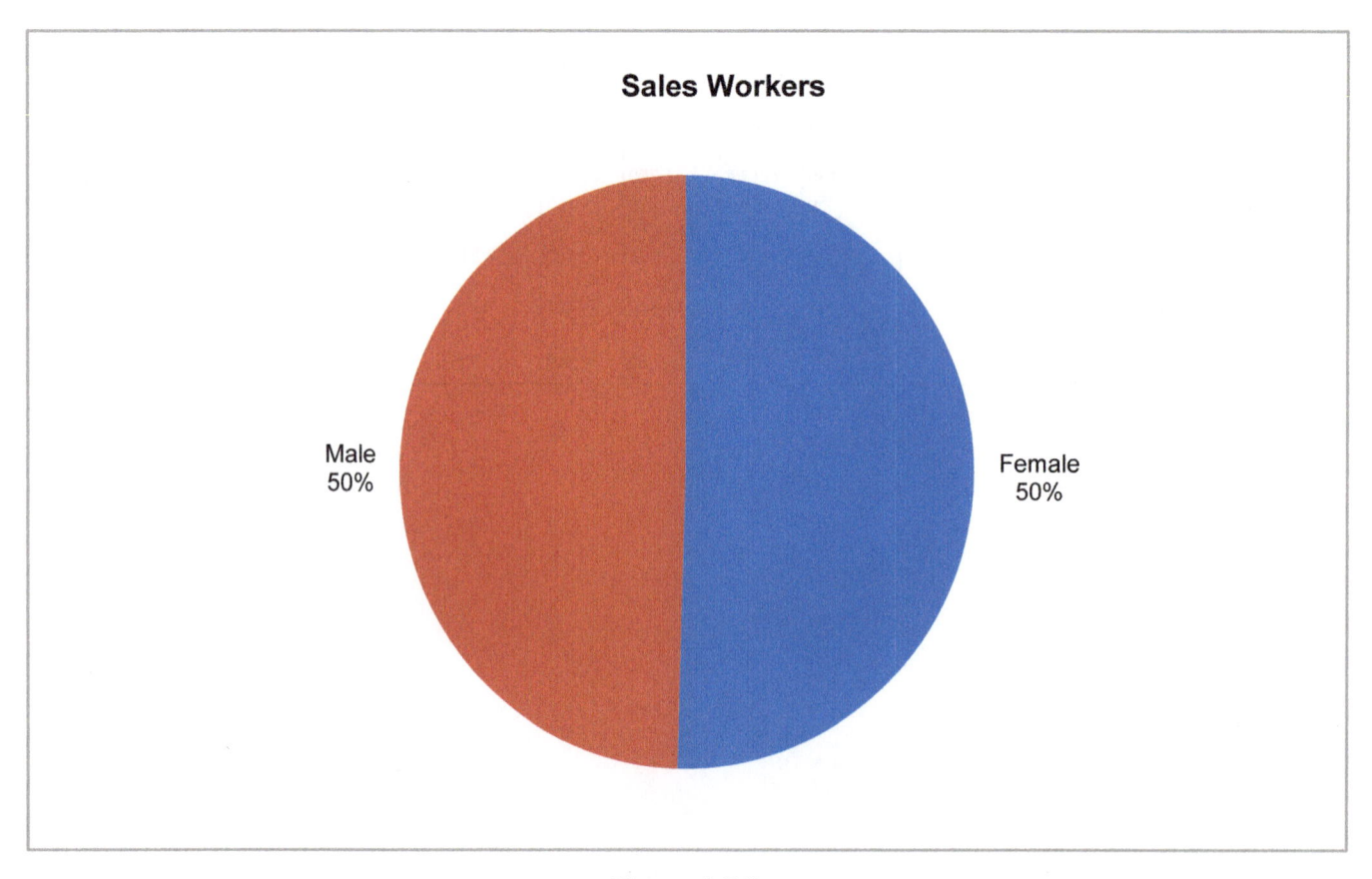

- Male 50%
- Female 50%

Figure A-7.2

PART A—NATIONAL DATA

A-7 Detailed Occupations in the Sales Workers Occupation Group, by Sex, Race, and Hispanic Origin, 2006–2010

Census occupation code	Sales Workers Occupation Group	Total who worked in the last 5 years	Male Number	Male Percent	Female Number	Female Percent	Hispanic or Latino Number	Hispanic or Latino Percent	White alone, not Hispanic or Latino Number	White alone, not Hispanic or Latino Percent
4700	First-line supervisors of retail sales workers	3,182,300	1,765,580	55.5	1,416,725	44.5	352,090	11.1	2,350,140	73.9
4710	First-line supervisors of non-retail sales workers	1,267,795	896,935	70.7	370,855	29.3	132,575	10.5	967,525	76.3
4720	Cashiers	3,703,420	936,865	25.3	2,766,555	74.7	668,725	18.1	2,050,995	55.4
4740	Counter and rental clerks	139,590	61,515	44.1	78,075	55.9	20,555	14.7	91,790	65.8
4750	Parts salespersons	118,355	104,540	88.3	13,820	11.7	16,390	13.8	92,805	78.4
4760	Retail salespersons	3,747,080	1,821,005	48.6	1,926,075	51.4	497,675	13.3	2,580,665	68.9
4800	Advertising sales agents	242,985	115,555	47.6	127,430	52.4	20,545	8.5	194,355	80.0
4810	Insurance sales agents	561,510	305,270	54.4	256,240	45.6	48,320	8.6	448,765	79.9
4820	Securities, commodities, and financial services sales agents	375,110	258,140	68.8	116,970	31.2	29,600	7.9	293,530	78.3
4830	Travel agents	86,860	17,155	19.8	69,705	80.2	7,955	9.2	64,635	74.4
4840	Sales representatives, services, all other	672,815	444,230	66.0	228,580	34.0	60,580	9.0	529,150	78.6
4850	Sales representatives, wholesale and manufacturing	1,541,725	1,121,975	72.8	419,745	27.2	129,150	8.4	1,283,585	83.3
4900	Models, demonstrators, and product promoters	70,935	17,715	25.0	53,220	75.0	9,075	12.8	49,760	70.1
4920	Real estate brokers and sales agents	899,480	402,545	44.8	496,935	55.2	78,050	8.7	717,600	79.8
4940	Telemarketers	183,185	68,750	37.5	114,435	62.5	24,965	13.6	107,075	58.5
4950	Door-to-door sales workers, news and street vendors, and related workers	211,790	90,210	42.6	121,580	57.4	36,450	17.2	145,205	68.6
4965	Sales and related workers, all other	251,580	124,920	49.7	126,660	50.3	21,450	8.5	196,395	78.1

Census occupation code	Sales Workers Occupation Group	Black alone, not Hispanic or Latino Number	Black alone, not Hispanic or Latino Percent	American Indian and Alaska Native alone, not Hispanic or Latino Number	American Indian and Alaska Native alone, not Hispanic or Latino Percent	Asian alone, not Hispanic or Latino Number	Asian alone, not Hispanic or Latino Percent	Native Hawaiian and Other Pacific Islander alone, not Hispanic or Latino Number	Native Hawaiian and Other Pacific Islander alone, not Hispanic or Latino Percent	Two or more races, not Hispanic or Latino Number	Two or more races, not Hispanic or Latino Percent
4700	First-line supervisors of retail sales workers	248,755	7.8	13,955	0.4	165,210	5.2	3,815	0.1	48,335	1.5
4710	First-line supervisors of non-retail sales workers	79,360	6.3	4,045	0.3	68,395	5.4	1,495	0.1	14,395	1.1
4720	Cashiers	652,615	17.6	30,745	0.8	212,035	5.7	8,700	0.2	79,595	2.1
4740	Counter and rental clerks	15,935	11.4	1,025	0.7	7,325	5.2	335	0.2	2,620	1.9
4750	Parts salespersons	4,870	4.1	545	0.5	2,420	2.0	40	0.0	1,280	1.1
4760	Retail salespersons	411,275	11.0	16,770	0.4	167,415	4.5	4,265	0.1	69,020	1.8
4800	Advertising sales agents	17,615	7.2	595	0.2	6,650	2.7	270	0.1	2,950	1.2
4810	Insurance sales agents	40,020	7.1	1,440	0.3	16,890	3.0	300	0.1	5,775	1.0
4820	Securities, commodities, and financial services sales agents	23,450	6.3	525	0.1	23,095	6.2	245	0.1	4,670	1.2
4830	Travel agents	5,670	6.5	300	0.3	6,910	8.0	145	0.2	1,240	1.4
4840	Sales representatives, services, all other	49,545	7.4	2,125	0.3	22,455	3.3	580	0.1	8,380	1.2
4850	Sales representatives, wholesale and manufacturing	56,185	3.6	3,475	0.2	52,175	3.4	1,400	0.1	15,745	1.0
4900	Models, demonstrators, and product promoters	7,445	10.5	365	0.5	2,575	3.6	135	0.2	1,580	2.2
4920	Real estate brokers and sales agents	51,120	5.7	2,145	0.2	39,160	4.4	670	0.1	10,730	1.2
4940	Telemarketers	42,050	23.0	1,100	0.6	3,190	1.7	455	0.2	4,355	2.4
4950	Door-to-door sales workers, news and street vendors, and related workers	19,790	9.3	1,115	0.5	5,075	2.4	305	0.1	3,845	1.8
4965	Sales and related workers, all other	20,895	8.3	1,030	0.4	8,570	3.4	300	0.1	2,950	1.2

Administrative Support Workers

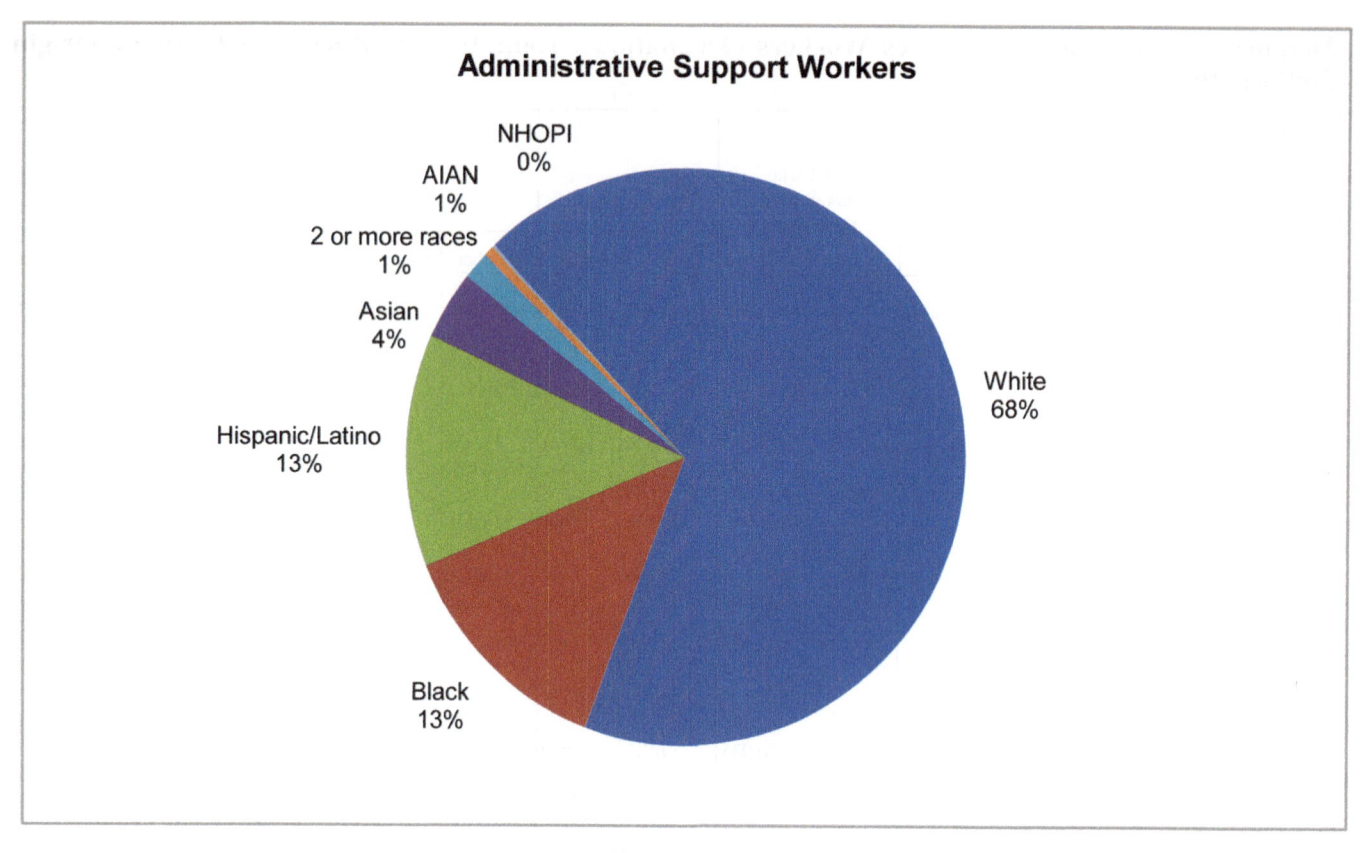

- White 68%
- Black 13%
- Hispanic/Latino 13%
- Asian 4%
- 2 or more races 1%
- AIAN 1%
- NHOPI 0%

Figure A-8.1

Administrative Support Workers

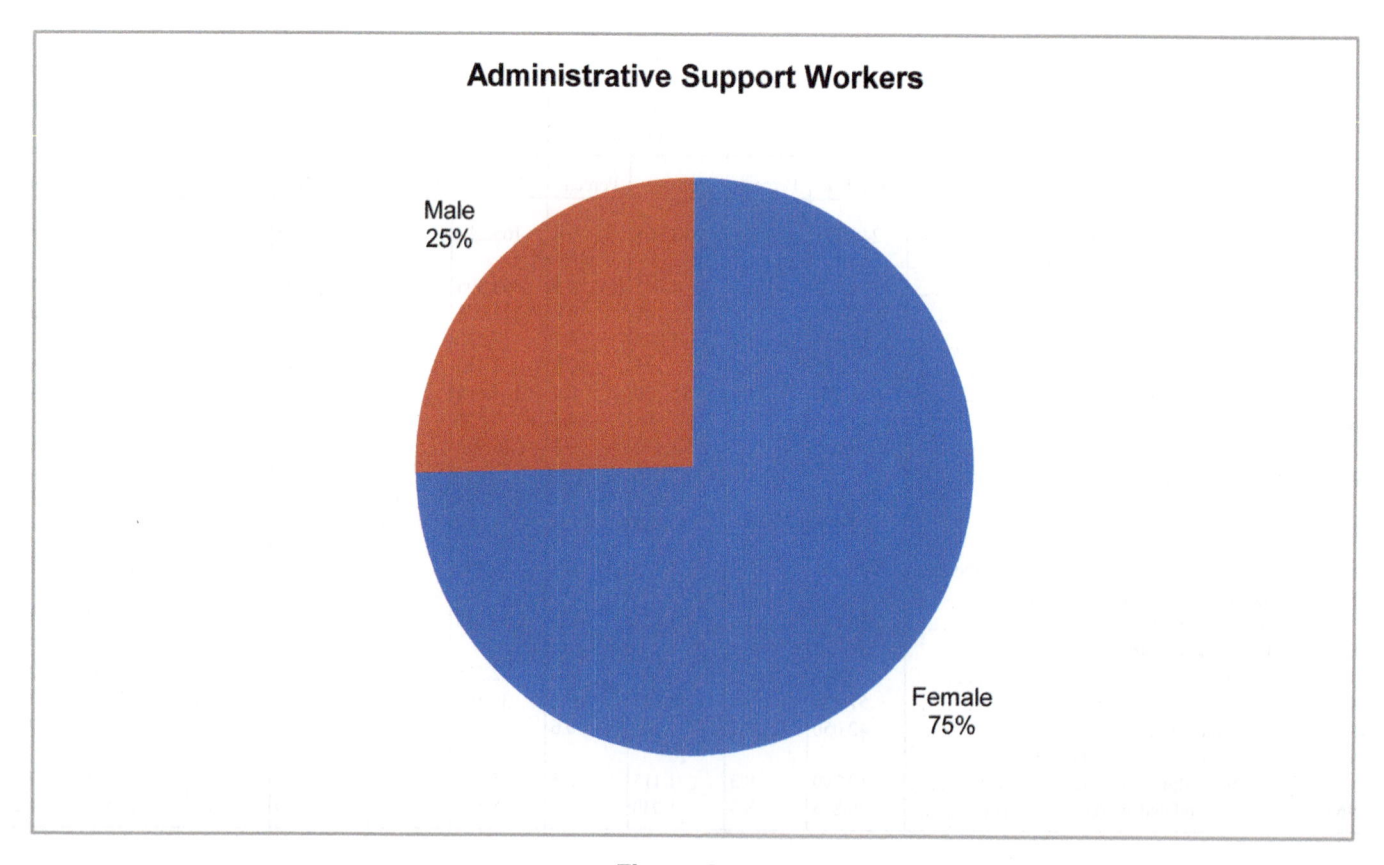

- Female 75%
- Male 25%

Figure A-8.2

PART A—NATIONAL DATA

A-8 Detailed Occupations in the Administrative Support Workers Occupation Group, by Sex, Race, and Hispanic Origin, 2006–2010

Census occupation code	Administrative Support Workers Occupation Group	Total who worked in the last 5 years	Male Number	Male Percent	Female Number	Female Percent	Hispanic or Latino Number	Hispanic or Latino Percent	White alone, not Hispanic or Latino Number	White alone, not Hispanic or Latino Percent
2016	Social and human service assistant	153,535	34,600	22.5	118,935	77.5	22,940	14.9	83,860	54.6
2145	Paralegals and legal assistants	395,210	64,615	16.3	330,595	83.7	44,310	11.2	291,570	73.8
2160	Miscellaneous legal support workers	245,905	64,580	26.3	181,325	73.7	24,670	10.0	181,140	73.7
2440	Library technicians	60,375	14,450	23.9	45,920	76.1	5,260	8.7	44,340	73.4
2540	Teacher assistants	1,051,485	100,025	9.5	951,460	90.5	162,605	15.5	683,295	65.0
3646	Medical transcriptionists	78,065	1,830	2.3	76,230	97.6	3,535	4.5	68,980	88.4
5000	First-line supervisors of office and administrative support workers	1,615,235	558,590	34.6	1,056,645	65.4	178,290	11.0	1,171,120	72.5
5010	Switchboard operators, including answering service	47,655	7,450	15.6	40,205	84.4	5,070	10.6	31,655	66.4
5020	Telephone operators	56,475	11,530	20.4	44,945	79.6	8,820	15.6	30,960	54.8
5030	Communications equipment operators, all other	11,220	4,990	44.5	6,230	55.5	1,215	10.8	7,725	68.9
5100	Bill and account collectors	245,240	72,845	29.7	172,395	70.3	37,285	15.2	145,640	59.4
5110	Billing and posting clerks	497,360	52,835	10.6	444,525	89.4	62,710	12.6	343,295	69.0
5120	Bookkeeping, accounting, and auditing clerks	1,548,285	176,925	11.4	1,371,360	88.6	143,485	9.3	1,188,730	76.8
5130	Gaming cage workers	13,970	3,715	26.6	10,260	73.4	2,070	14.8	6,920	49.5
5140	Payroll and timekeeping clerks	185,035	18,690	10.1	166,345	89.9	20,375	11.0	133,720	72.3
5150	Procurement clerks	31,070	11,650	37.5	19,415	62.5	2,490	8.0	22,565	72.6
5160	Tellers	450,300	63,885	14.2	386,415	85.8	69,660	15.5	294,740	65.5
5165	Financial clerks, all other	69,330	23,300	33.6	46,030	66.4	7,325	10.6	46,295	66.8
5200	Brokerage clerks	10,460	3,435	32.8	7,025	67.2	1,020	9.8	7,860	75.1
5220	Court, municipal, and license clerks	95,185	19,580	20.6	75,600	79.4	11,120	11.7	66,085	69.4
5230	Credit authorizers, checkers, and clerks	58,065	14,930	25.7	43,135	74.3	7,270	12.5	38,670	66.6
5240	Customer service representatives	2,415,235	774,270	32.1	1,640,965	67.9	363,440	15.0	1,487,060	61.6
5250	Eligibility interviewers, government programs	70,355	12,790	18.2	57,565	81.8	14,045	20.0	35,910	51.0
5260	File clerks	415,360	92,150	22.2	323,210	77.8	52,775	12.7	266,770	64.2
5300	Hotel, motel, and resort desk clerks	150,670	48,295	32.1	102,375	67.9	22,300	14.8	89,965	59.7
5310	Interviewers, except eligibility and loan	171,645	42,530	24.8	129,115	75.2	23,455	13.7	106,260	61.9
5320	Library assistants, clerical	129,145	24,130	18.7	105,015	81.3	10,570	8.2	94,860	73.5
5330	Loan interviewers and clerks	154,570	30,055	19.4	124,515	80.6	21,330	13.8	103,250	66.8
5340	New accounts clerks	24,860	5,075	20.4	19,785	79.6	3,925	15.8	16,165	65.0
5350	Correspondence clerks and order clerks	164,135	61,185	37.3	102,945	62.7	26,850	16.4	106,700	65.0
5360	Human resources assistants, except payroll and timekeeping	55,440	9,545	17.2	45,895	82.8	7,750	14.0	34,145	61.6
5400	Receptionists and information clerks	1,318,740	122,115	9.3	1,196,625	90.7	214,240	16.2	875,920	66.4
5410	Reservation and transportation ticket agents and travel clerks	151,640	57,265	37.8	94,375	62.2	21,830	14.4	90,625	59.8
5420	Information and record clerks, all other	102,660	16,230	15.8	86,425	84.2	12,060	11.7	68,380	66.6
5500	Cargo and freight agents	20,465	13,885	67.8	6,580	32.2	3,720	18.2	11,975	58.5
5510	Couriers and messengers	323,105	267,500	82.8	55,605	17.2	49,135	15.2	204,650	63.3
5520	Dispatchers	290,115	126,355	43.6	163,760	56.4	35,105	12.1	207,900	71.7
5530	Meter readers, utilities	39,485	33,395	84.6	6,090	15.4	4,915	12.4	26,475	67.1
5540	Postal service clerks	150,885	74,540	49.4	76,345	50.6	12,525	8.3	77,810	51.6
5550	Postal service mail carriers	341,080	212,935	62.4	128,145	37.6	31,620	9.3	232,995	68.3
5560	Postal service mail sorters, processors, and processing machine operators	97,050	49,265	50.8	47,780	49.2	9,175	9.5	45,850	47.2
5600	Production, planning, and expediting clerks	297,550	129,690	43.6	167,860	56.4	28,745	9.7	224,985	75.6
5610	Shipping, receiving, and traffic clerks	631,960	439,185	69.5	192,775	30.5	138,715	21.9	365,705	57.9
5620	Stock clerks and order fillers	1,690,045	1,075,835	63.7	614,210	36.3	299,315	17.7	994,180	58.8
5630	Weighers, measurers, checkers, and samplers, recordkeeping	80,515	41,280	51.3	39,235	48.7	15,590	19.4	50,045	62.2

A-8 **Detailed Occupations in the Administrative Support Workers Occupation Group, by Sex, Race, and Hispanic Origin, 2006–2010**—*Continued*

Census occupation code	Administrative Support Workers Occupation Group	Black alone, not Hispanic or Latino Number	Black alone, not Hispanic or Latino Percent	American Indian and Alaska Native alone, not Hispanic or Latino Number	American Indian and Alaska Native alone, not Hispanic or Latino Percent	Asian alone, not Hispanic or Latino Number	Asian alone, not Hispanic or Latino Percent	Native Hawaiian and Other Pacific Islander alone, not Hispanic or Latino Number	Native Hawaiian and Other Pacific Islander alone, not Hispanic or Latino Percent	Two or more races, not Hispanic or Latino Number	Two or more races, not Hispanic or Latino Percent
2016	Social and human service assistant...............	37,565	24.5	1,960	1.3	4,475	2.9	295	0.2	2,435	1.6
2145	Paralegals and legal assistants	36,795	9.3	1,510	0.4	14,245	3.6	495	0.1	6,285	1.6
2160	Miscellaneous legal support workers............	24,435	9.9	1,840	0.7	9,850	4.0	260	0.1	3,715	1.5
2440	Library technicians..	5,505	9.1	350	0.6	3,630	6.0	100	0.2	1,185	2.0
2540	Teacher assistants..	150,470	14.3	9,225	0.9	29,565	2.8	1,745	0.2	14,590	1.4
3646	Medical transcriptionists	3,305	4.2	180	0.2	995	1.3	85	0.1	980	1.3
5000	First-line supervisors of office and administrative support workers...................	175,185	10.8	7,675	0.5	57,895	3.6	2,815	0.2	22,255	1.4
5010	Switchboard operators, including answering service..	8,565	18.0	405	0.8	1,240	2.6	130	0.3	590	1.2
5020	Telephone operators......................................	13,470	23.9	390	0.7	1,590	2.8	75	0.1	1,165	2.1
5030	Communications equipment operators, all other..	1,665	14.8	55	0.5	400	3.6	30	0.3	130	1.2
5100	Bill and account collectors............................	51,225	20.9	1,095	0.4	5,580	2.3	450	0.2	3,965	1.6
5110	Billing and posting clerks	58,965	11.9	2,890	0.6	21,300	4.3	1,000	0.2	7,195	1.4
5120	Bookkeeping, accounting, and auditing clerks..	119,985	7.7	8,860	0.6	65,750	4.2	2,150	0.1	19,325	1.2
5130	Gaming cage workers....................................	1,915	13.7	1,080	7.7	1,450	10.4	30	0.2	510	3.7
5140	Payroll and timekeeping clerks.....................	20,675	11.2	1,035	0.6	6,420	3.5	195	0.1	2,610	1.4
5150	Procurement clerks..	3,805	12.2	275	0.9	1,360	4.4	10	0.0	565	1.8
5160	Tellers...	49,060	10.9	1,710	0.4	26,675	5.9	940	0.2	7,520	1.7
5165	Financial clerks, all other..............................	8,445	12.2	310	0.4	5,695	8.2	75	0.1	1,185	1.7
5200	Brokerage clerks..	970	9.3	30	0.3	485	4.6	25	0.2	70	0.7
5220	Court, municipal, and license clerks.............	13,380	14.1	965	1.0	2,465	2.6	135	0.1	1,030	1.1
5230	Credit authorizers, checkers, and clerks.......	8,325	14.3	260	0.4	2,410	4.2	180	0.3	950	1.6
5240	Customer service representatives..................	412,615	17.1	11,935	0.5	90,125	3.7	4,855	0.2	45,210	1.9
5250	Eligibility interviewers, government programs...	15,040	21.4	805	1.1	3,455	4.9	75	0.1	1,025	1.5
5260	File clerks	61,570	14.8	3,330	0.8	22,545	5.4	800	0.2	7,575	1.8
5300	Hotel, motel, and resort desk clerks..............	21,860	14.5	1,620	1.1	10,270	6.8	780	0.5	3,870	2.6
5310	Interviewers, except eligibility and loan	31,215	18.2	1,790	1.0	5,385	3.1	315	0.2	3,220	1.9
5320	Library assistants, clerical.............................	12,710	9.8	620	0.5	7,860	6.1	65	0.1	2,465	1.9
5330	Loan interviewers and clerks........................	18,670	12.1	690	0.4	7,715	5.0	385	0.2	2,540	1.6
5340	New accounts clerks......................................	2,715	10.9	40	0.2	1,570	6.3	30	0.1	420	1.7
5350	Correspondence clerks and order clerks.......	20,340	12.4	895	0.5	6,860	4.2	270	0.2	2,220	1.4
5360	Human resources assistants, except payroll and timekeeping...	9,925	17.9	595	1.1	2,055	3.7	45	0.1	925	1.7
5400	Receptionists and information clerks............	153,180	11.6	8,365	0.6	42,140	3.2	2,095	0.2	22,805	1.7
5410	Reservation and transportation ticket agents and travel clerks...	24,505	16.2	825	0.5	8,830	5.8	1,655	1.1	3,375	2.2
5420	Information and record clerks, all other.......	14,835	14.5	1,150	1.1	4,315	4.2	295	0.3	1,620	1.6
5500	Cargo and freight agents...............................	2,520	12.3	55	0.3	1,705	8.3	225	1.1	265	1.3
5510	Couriers and messengers...............................	51,750	16.0	1,355	0.4	10,820	3.3	575	0.2	4,825	1.5
5520	Dispatchers..	35,575	12.3	2,205	0.8	4,335	1.5	460	0.2	4,535	1.6
5530	Meter readers, utilities..................................	6,410	16.2	335	0.8	635	1.6	80	0.2	630	1.6
5540	Postal service clerks......................................	40,955	27.1	855	0.6	16,500	10.9	265	0.2	1,980	1.3
5550	Postal service mail carriers...........................	48,910	14.3	1,250	0.4	21,475	6.3	695	0.2	4,130	1.2
5560	Postal service mail sorters, processors, and processing machine operators.......................	29,115	30.0	345	0.4	11,180	11.5	210	0.2	1,170	1.2
5600	Production, planning, and expediting clerks	25,895	8.7	1,215	0.4	11,240	3.8	480	0.2	4,985	1.7
5610	Shipping, receiving, and traffic clerks.........	93,595	14.8	2,195	0.3	21,415	3.4	1,710	0.3	8,630	1.4
5620	Stock clerks and order fillers........................	286,170	16.9	12,410	0.7	62,005	3.7	4,665	0.3	31,295	1.9
5630	Weighers, measurers, checkers, and samplers, recordkeeping................................	9,960	12.4	485	0.6	3,175	3.9	85	0.1	1,175	1.5

A-8 Detailed Occupations in the Administrative Support Workers Occupation Group, by Sex, Race, and Hispanic Origin, 2006–2010—Continued

Census occupation code	Administrative Support Workers Occupation Group	Total who worked in the last 5 years	Male Number	Male Percent	Female Number	Female Percent	Hispanic or Latino Number	Hispanic or Latino Percent	White alone, not Hispanic or Latino Number	White alone, not Hispanic or Latino Percent
5700	Secretaries and administrative assistants	3,991,485	163,195	4.1	3,828,290	95.9	399,615	10.0	3,049,700	76.4
5800	Computer operators	151,215	76,705	50.7	74,510	49.3	16,245	10.7	102,845	68.0
5810	Data entry keyers	493,815	102,610	20.8	391,205	79.2	64,840	13.1	313,030	63.4
5820	Word processors and typists	352,460	39,835	11.3	312,620	88.7	39,410	11.2	237,665	67.4
5840	Insurance claims and policy processing clerks	325,030	52,505	16.2	272,530	83.8	36,815	11.3	221,365	68.1
5850	Mail clerks and mail machine operators, except postal service	131,890	64,355	48.8	67,535	51.2	18,585	14.1	71,845	54.5
5860	Office clerks, general	1,282,130	230,885	18.0	1,051,245	82.0	181,540	14.2	827,975	64.6
5900	Office machine operators, except computer	55,825	23,125	41.4	32,700	58.6	7,785	13.9	31,420	56.3
5910	Proofreaders and copy markers	16,395	4,655	28.4	11,740	71.6	815	5.0	13,455	82.1
5920	Statistical assistants	27,600	10,165	36.8	17,435	63.2	2,330	8.4	19,450	70.5
5940	Miscellaneous office and administrative support workers, including desktop publishers	552,105	138,085	25.0	414,015	75.0	62,655	11.3	376,090	68.1

Census occupation code	Administrative Support Workers Occupation Group	Black alone, not Hispanic or Latino Number	Black alone, not Hispanic or Latino Percent	American Indian and Alaska Native alone, not Hispanic or Latino Number	American Indian and Alaska Native alone, not Hispanic or Latino Percent	Asian alone, not Hispanic or Latino Number	Asian alone, not Hispanic or Latino Percent	Native Hawaiian and Other Pacific Islander alone, not Hispanic or Latino Number	Native Hawaiian and Other Pacific Islander alone, not Hispanic or Latino Percent	Two or more races, not Hispanic or Latino Number	Two or more races, not Hispanic or Latino Percent
5700	Secretaries and administrative assistants	360,895	9.0	22,915	0.6	101,205	2.5	5,000	0.1	52,160	1.3
5800	Computer operators	20,440	13.5	975	0.6	8,800	5.8	170	0.1	1,740	1.2
5810	Data entry keyers	76,765	15.5	2,765	0.6	27,180	5.5	1,080	0.2	8,160	1.7
5820	Word processors and typists	50,645	14.4	1,345	0.4	17,725	5.0	575	0.2	5,090	1.4
5840	Insurance claims and policy processing clerks	52,280	16.1	970	0.3	8,460	2.6	455	0.1	4,690	1.4
5850	Mail clerks and mail machine operators, except postal service	30,860	23.4	870	0.7	7,575	5.7	260	0.2	1,885	1.4
5860	Office clerks, general	172,955	13.5	7,680	0.6	67,605	5.3	3,190	0.2	21,185	1.7
5900	Office machine operators, except computer	9,890	17.7	335	0.6	4,865	8.7	65	0.1	1,460	2.6
5910	Proofreaders and copy markers	1,215	7.4	35	0.2	550	3.4	25	0.2	295	1.8
5920	Statistical assistants	3,315	12.0	215	0.8	1,650	6.0	25	0.1	625	2.3
5940	Miscellaneous office and administrative support workers, including desktop publishers	76,765	13.9	3,880	0.7	22,205	4.0	1,260	0.2	9,245	1.7

Construction and Extractive Craft Workers

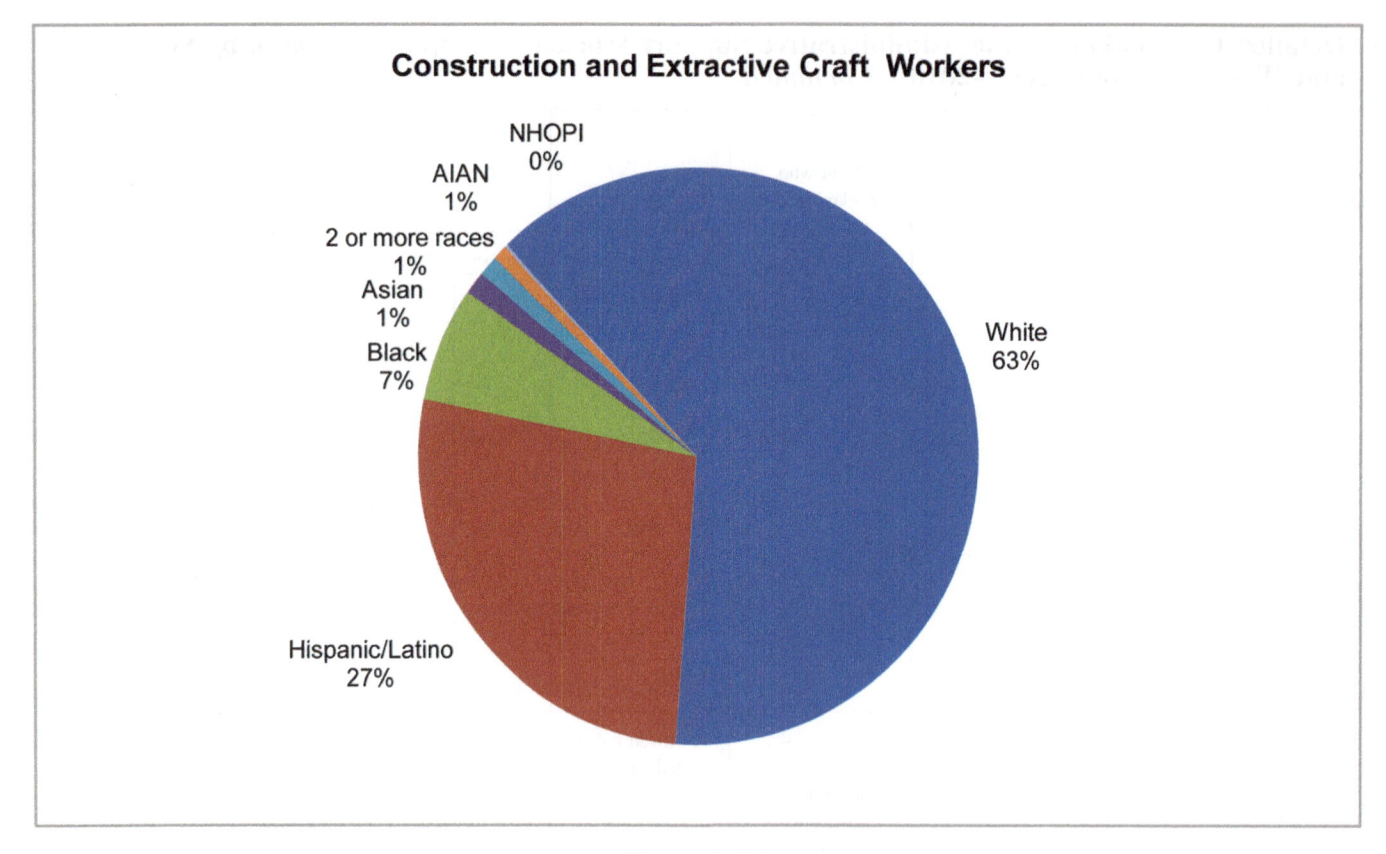

- NHOPI 0%
- AIAN 1%
- 2 or more races 1%
- Asian 1%
- Black 7%
- Hispanic/Latino 27%
- White 63%

Figure A-9.1

Construction and Extractive Craft Workers

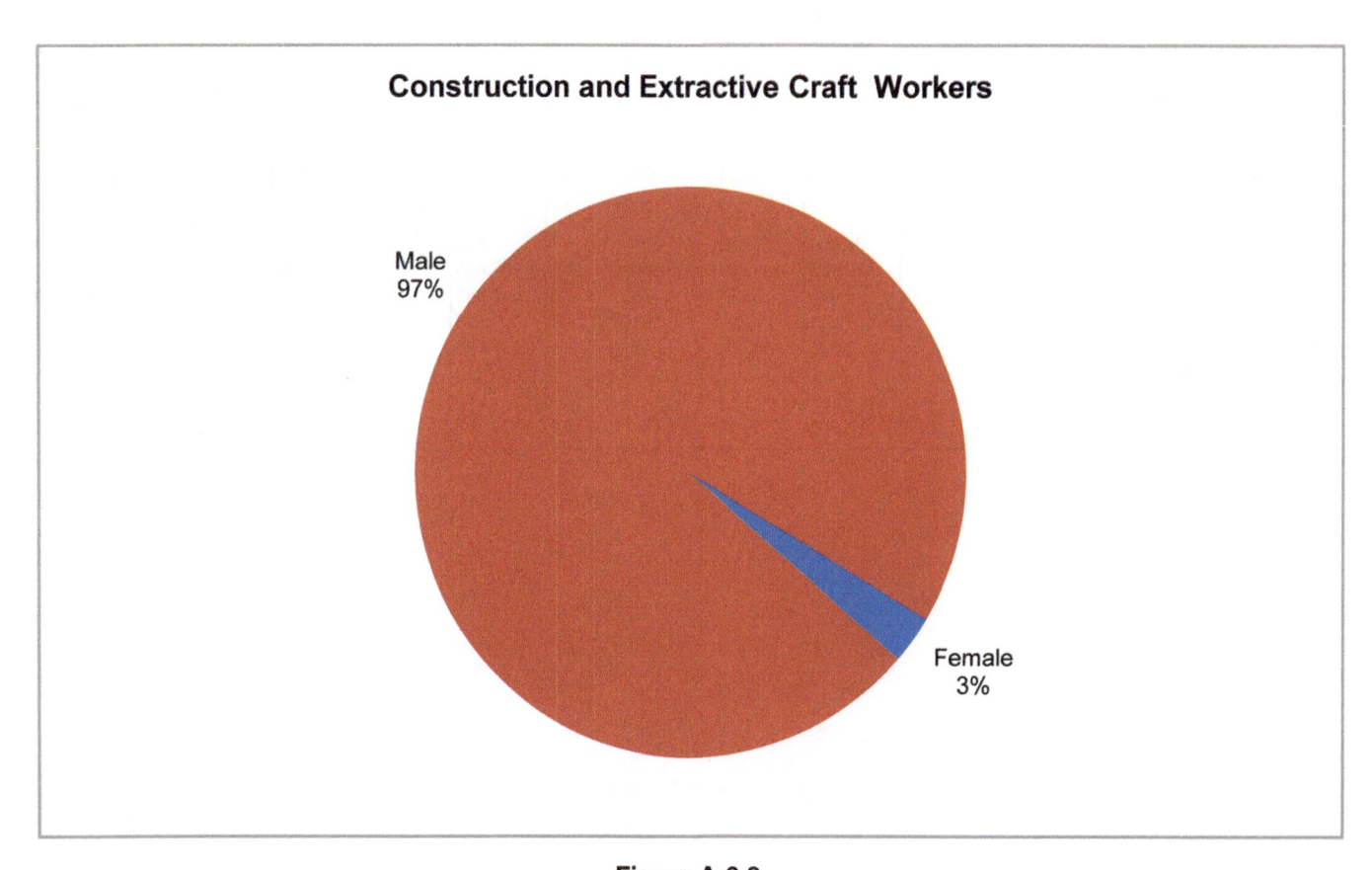

- Male 97%
- Female 3%

Figure A-9.2

PART A—NATIONAL DATA

A-9 Detailed Occupations in the Construction and Extractive Craft Workers Occupation Group, by Sex, Race, and Hispanic Origin, 2006–2010

Census occupation code	Construction and Extractive Craft Workers Occupation Group	Total who worked in the last 5 years	Male Number	Male Percent	Female Number	Female Percent	Hispanic or Latino Number	Hispanic or Latino Percent	White alone, not Hispanic or Latino Number	White alone, not Hispanic or Latino Percent
6200	First-line supervisors of construction trades and extraction workers	1,033,845	1,003,545	97.1	30,300	2.9	147,430	14.3	815,140	78.8
6210	Boilermakers	22,165	21,655	97.7	510	2.3	2,685	12.1	17,260	77.9
6220	Brickmasons, blockmasons, and stonemasons	225,620	223,455	99.0	2,165	1.0	76,755	34.0	120,710	53.5
6230	Carpenters	1,619,895	1,590,715	98.2	29,180	1.8	415,540	25.7	1,066,245	65.8
6240	Carpet, floor, and tile installers and finishers	235,185	229,835	97.7	5,350	2.3	92,045	39.1	125,130	53.2
6250	Cement masons, concrete finishers, and terrazzo workers	95,685	94,535	98.8	1,150	1.2	41,030	42.9	40,855	42.7
6260	Construction laborers	1,932,325	1,872,555	96.9	59,770	3.1	721,920	37.4	982,095	50.8
6300	Paving, surfacing, and tamping equipment operators	21,530	20,865	96.9	660	3.1	4,545	21.1	14,570	67.7
6320	Construction equipment operators except paving, surfacing, and tamping equipment operators	417,390	407,660	97.7	9,730	2.3	55,390	13.3	321,700	77.1
6330	Drywall installers, ceiling tile installers, and tapers	213,410	208,520	97.7	4,895	2.3	112,940	52.9	83,925	39.3
6355	Electricians	830,730	813,400	97.9	17,330	2.1	119,340	14.4	620,675	74.7
6360	Glaziers	47,900	47,000	98.1	900	1.9	9,335	19.5	34,500	72.0
6400	Insulation workers	49,660	47,695	96.0	1,960	3.9	17,905	36.1	26,640	53.6
6420	Painters, construction and maintenance	676,715	629,400	93.0	47,315	7.0	260,960	38.6	347,110	51.3
6430	Paperhangers	8,985	6,880	76.6	2,105	23.4	1,310	14.6	7,010	78.0
6440	Pipelayers, plumbers, pipefitters, and steamfitters	623,165	614,125	98.5	9,045	1.5	121,510	19.5	437,930	70.3
6460	Plasterers and stucco masons	49,780	49,050	98.5	735	1.5	29,545	59.4	15,325	30.8
6500	Reinforcing iron and rebar workers	10,670	10,525	98.6	145	1.4	3,560	33.4	5,795	54.3
6515	Roofers	255,565	252,500	98.8	3,065	1.2	113,610	44.5	119,665	46.8
6520	Sheet metal workers	147,415	141,580	96.0	5,830	4.0	21,415	14.5	112,220	76.1
6530	Structural iron and steel workers	75,900	74,015	97.5	1,885	2.5	13,100	17.3	53,905	71.0
6700	Elevator installers and repairers	29,510	28,980	98.2	535	1.8	3,000	10.2	23,935	81.1
6710	Fence erectors	35,570	35,035	98.5	535	1.5	11,165	31.4	21,575	60.7
6720	Hazardous materials removal workers	35,395	29,260	82.7	6,135	17.3	9,250	26.1	18,535	52.4
6730	Highway maintenance workers	109,780	105,875	96.4	3,905	3.6	12,960	11.8	82,245	74.9
6740	Rail-track laying and maintenance equipment operators	12,090	11,895	98.4	190	1.6	1,570	13.0	7,990	66.1
6765	Miscellaneous construction workers, including solar photovoltaic installers, septic tank servicers and sewer pipe cleaners	53,095	51,055	96.2	2,035	3.8	12,515	23.6	33,740	63.5
6800	Derrick, rotary drill, and service unit operators, and roustabouts, oil, gas, and mining	41,935	41,495	99.0	445	1.1	9,350	22.3	28,675	68.4
6820	Earth drillers, except oil and gas	28,535	28,215	98.9	320	1.1	2,970	10.4	23,845	83.6
6830	Explosives workers, ordnance handling experts, and blasters	11,245	10,525	93.6	720	6.4	1,200	10.7	8,635	76.8
6840	Mining machine operators	60,695	59,280	97.7	1,415	2.3	7,300	12.0	49,825	82.1
6940	Miscellaneous extraction workers, including roof bolters and helpers	68,595	67,245	98.0	1,355	2.0	13,470	19.6	49,030	71.5
9510	Crane and tower operators	72,165	70,250	97.3	1,915	2.7	7,970	11.0	52,470	72.7
9520	Dredge, excavating, and loading machine operators	53,335	52,710	98.8	625	1.2	7,260	13.6	42,420	79.5

A-9 Detailed Occupations in the Construction and Extractive Craft Workers Occupation Group, by Sex, Race, and Hispanic Origin, 2006–2010—*Continued*

Census occupation code	Construction and Extractive Craft Workers Occupation Group	Black alone, not Hispanic or Latino Number	Percent	American Indian and Alaska Native alone, not Hispanic or Latino Number	Percent	Asian alone, not Hispanic or Latino Number	Percent	Native Hawaiian and Other Pacific Islander alone, not Hispanic or Latino Number	Percent	Two or more races, not Hispanic or Latino Number	Percent
6200	First-line supervisors of construction trades and extraction workers	41,445	4.0	7,400	0.7	10,080	1.0	1,395	0.1	10,960	1.1
6210	Boilermakers	1,415	6.4	345	1.6	155	0.7	35	0.2	270	1.2
6220	Brickmasons, blockmasons, and stonemasons	21,510	9.5	2,005	0.9	1,470	0.7	635	0.3	2,540	1.1
6230	Carpenters	77,795	4.8	14,730	0.9	20,420	1.3	2,965	0.2	22,195	1.4
6240	Carpet, floor, and tile installers and finishers	10,535	4.5	1,110	0.5	2,790	1.2	245	0.1	3,320	1.4
6250	Cement masons, concrete finishers, and terrazzo workers	11,155	11.7	970	1.0	245	0.3	295	0.3	1,135	1.2
6260	Construction laborers	154,495	8.0	16,410	0.8	26,855	1.4	3,855	0.2	26,700	1.4
6300	Paving, surfacing, and tamping equipment operators	2,015	9.4	110	0.5	30	0.1	20	0.1	239	1.1
6320	Construction equipment operators except paving, surfacing, and tamping equipment operators	25,785	6.2	5,880	1.4	1,565	0.4	915	0.2	6,150	1.5
6330	Drywall installers, ceiling tile installers, and tapers	10,135	4.7	2,475	1.2	1,245	0.6	210	0.1	2,480	1.2
6355	Electricians	58,190	7.0	5,640	0.7	15,210	1.8	1,425	0.2	10,245	1.2
6360	Glaziers	2,100	4.4	410	0.9	710	1.5	115	0.2	730	1.5
6400	Insulation workers	3,800	7.7	360	0.7	230	0.5	70	0.1	650	1.3
6420	Painters, construction and maintenance	44,275	6.5	3,505	0.5	10,845	1.6	880	0.1	9,135	1.3
6430	Paperhangers	270	3.0	30	0.3	275	3.1	0	0.0	85	0.9
6440	Pipelayers, plumbers, pipefitters, and steamfitters	43,380	7.0	5,075	0.8	6,520	1.0	975	0.2	7,775	1.2
6460	Plasterers and stucco masons	4,270	8.6	160	0.3	75	0.2	45	0.1	369	0.7
6500	Reinforcing iron and rebar workers	785	7.4	230	2.2	105	1.0	30	0.3	160	1.5
6515	Roofers	15,315	6.0	2,225	0.9	1,235	0.5	470	0.2	3,040	1.2
6520	Sheet metal workers	8,530	5.8	720	0.5	2,495	1.7	205	0.1	1,830	1.2
6530	Structural iron and steel workers	5,555	7.3	1,195	1.6	850	1.1	255	0.3	1,045	1.4
6700	Elevator installers and repairers	1,715	5.8	45	0.2	395	1.3	75	0.3	350	1.2
6710	Fence erectors	1,755	4.9	345	1.0	150	0.4	90	0.3	494	1.4
6720	Hazardous materials removal workers	6,005	17.0	425	1.2	690	1.9	55	0.2	440	1.2
6730	Highway maintenance workers	11,615	10.6	1,260	1.1	405	0.4	90	0.1	1,200	1.1
6740	Rail-track laying and maintenance equipment operators	2,115	17.5	150	1.2	160	1.3	0	0.0	105	0.9
6765	Miscellaneous construction workers, including solar photovoltaic installers, septic tank servicers and sewer pipe cleaners	4,850	9.1	290	0.5	640	1.2	110	0.2	945	1.8
6800	Derrick, rotary drill, and service unit operators, and roustabouts, oil, gas, and mining	2,320	5.5	845	2.0	55	0.1	4	0.0	690	1.6
6820	Earth drillers, except oil and gas	885	3.1	320	1.1	115	0.4	50	0.2	345	1.2
6830	Explosives workers, ordnance handling experts, and blasters	1,085	9.6	90	0.8	65	0.6	20	0.2	150	1.3
6840	Mining machine operators	2,215	3.6	575	0.9	245	0.4	30	0.0	500	0.8
6940	Miscellaneous extraction workers, including roof bolters and helpers	3,800	5.5	1,180	1.7	305	0.4	120	0.2	690	1.0
9510	Crane and tower operators	9,665	13.4	570	0.8	175	0.2	155	0.2	1,165	1.6
9520	Dredge, excavating, and loading machine operators	2,415	4.5	410	0.8	140	0.3	0	0.0	690	1.3

PART A—NATIONAL DATA

Installation, Maintenance, and Repair Craft Workers

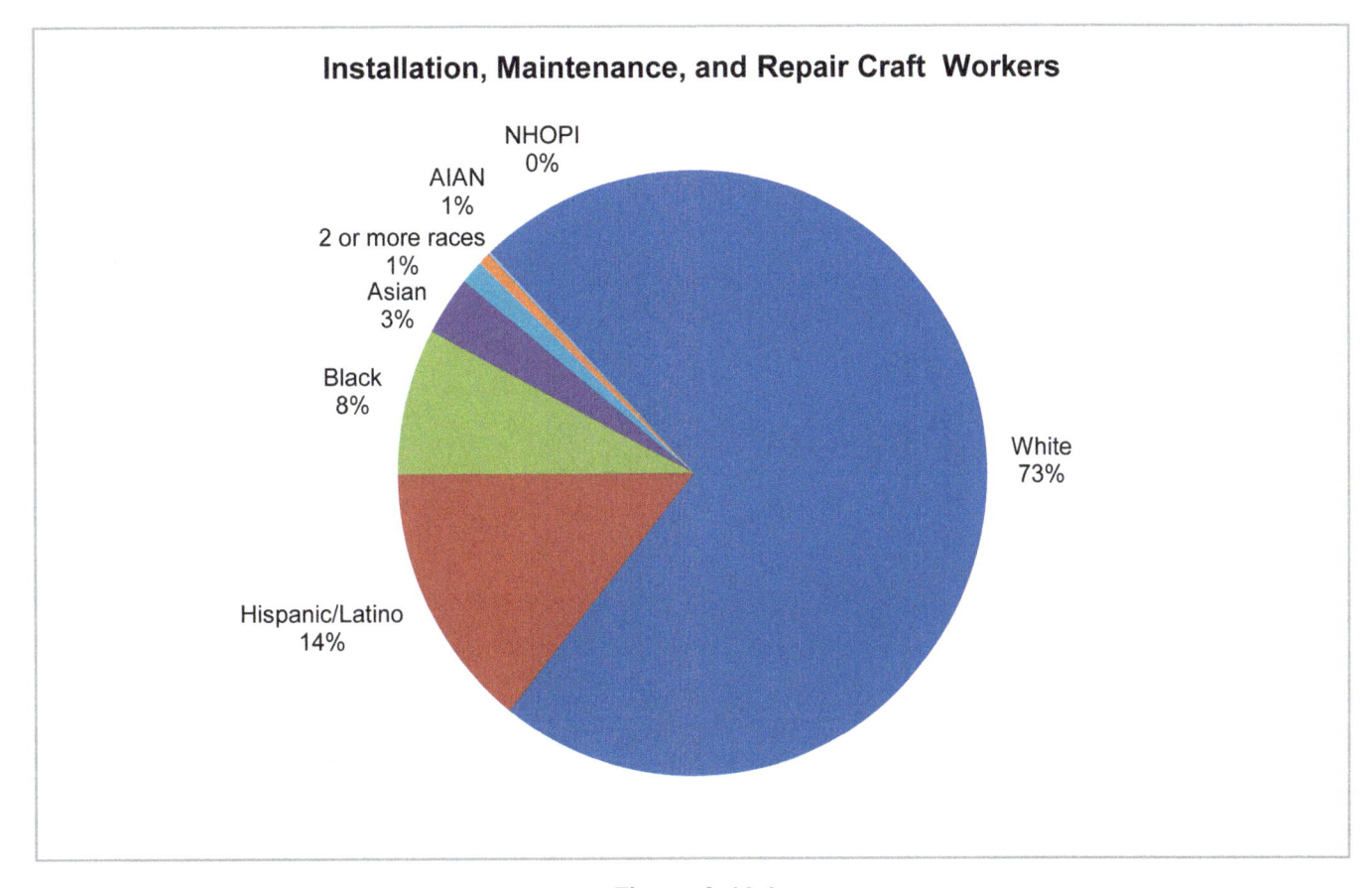

- NHOPI: 0%
- AIAN: 1%
- 2 or more races: 1%
- Asian: 3%
- Black: 8%
- Hispanic/Latino: 14%
- White: 73%

Figure A-10.1

Installation, Maintenance, and Repair Craft Workers

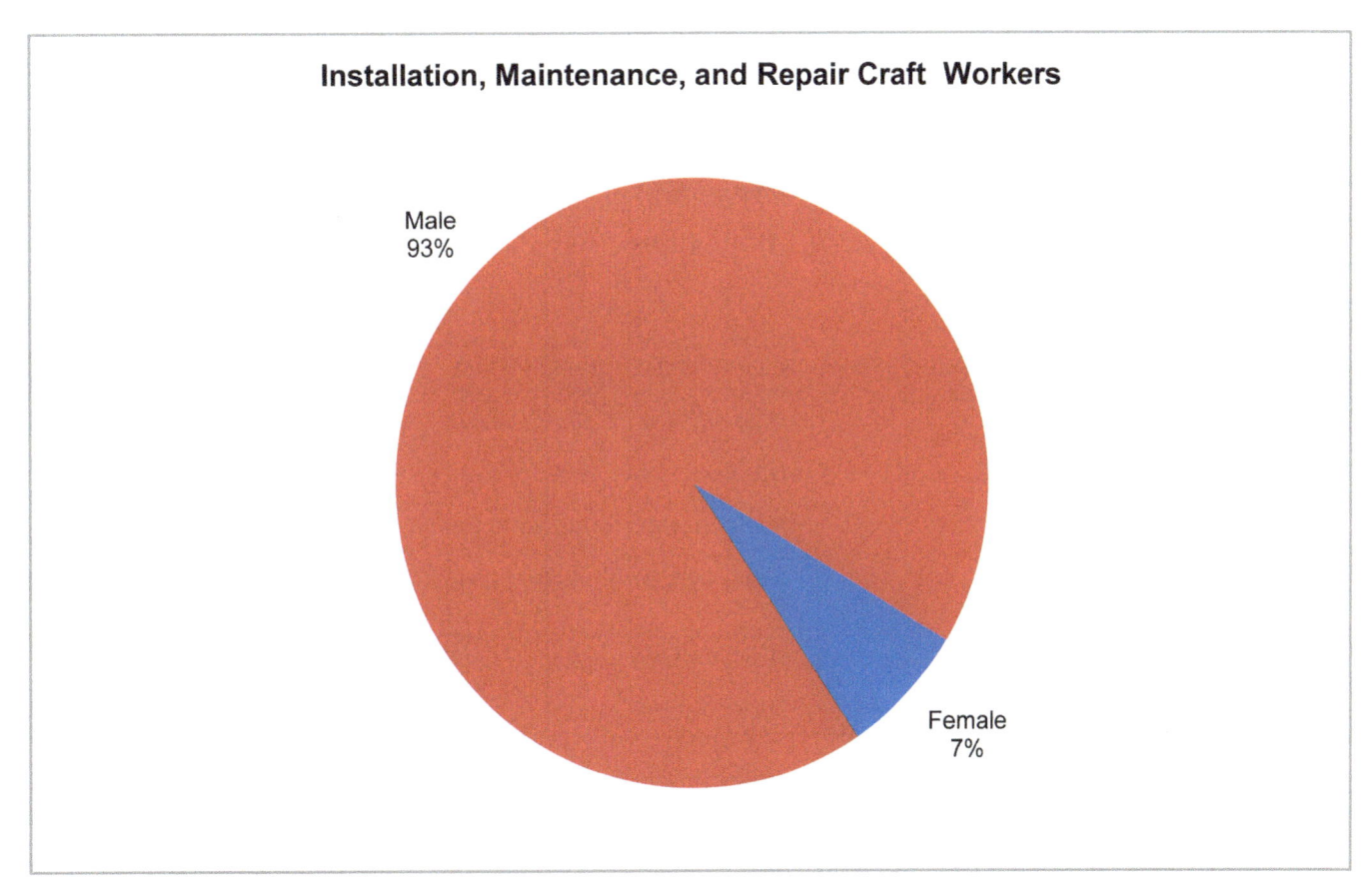

- Male: 93%
- Female: 7%

Figure A-10.2

A-10 **Detailed Occupations in the Installation, Maintenance and Repair Craft Workers Occupation Group, by Sex, Race, and Hispanic Origin, 2006–2010**

Census occupation code	Installation, Maintenance, and Repair Craft Workers Occupation Group	Total who worked in the last 5 years	Male Number	Male Percent	Female Number	Female Percent	Hispanic or Latino Number	Hispanic or Latino Percent	White alone, not Hispanic or Latino Number	White alone, not Hispanic or Latino Percent
7000	First-line supervisors of mechanics, installers, and repairers	314,875	292,195	92.8	22,680	7.2	30,300	9.6	248,720	79.0
7010	Computer, automated teller, and office machine repairers	287,155	251,305	87.5	35,850	12.5	29,510	10.3	201,145	70.0
7020	Radio and telecommunications equipment installers and repairers	196,005	171,990	87.7	24,010	12.2	22,660	11.6	139,285	71.1
7030	Avionics technicians	17,865	16,370	91.6	1,495	8.4	2,320	13.0	13,165	73.7
7040	Electric motor, power tool, and related repairers	30,330	28,865	95.2	1,465	4.8	4,620	15.2	21,895	72.2
7100	Electrical and electronics repairers, transportation equipment, and industrial and utility	17,310	16,715	96.6	595	3.4	1,000	5.8	14,225	82.2
7110	Electronic equipment installers and repairers, motor vehicles	20,215	18,880	93.4	1,335	6.6	3,095	15.3	14,350	71.0
7120	Electronic home entertainment equipment installers and repairers	64,255	62,115	96.7	2,140	3.3	10,780	16.8	43,540	67.8
7130	Security and fire alarm systems installers	60,470	58,815	97.3	1,660	2.7	10,030	16.6	42,325	70.0
7140	Aircraft mechanics and service technicians	156,600	149,245	95.3	7,355	4.7	20,225	12.9	112,285	71.7
7150	Automotive body and related repairers	171,190	168,200	98.3	2,990	1.7	38,575	22.5	116,030	67.8
7160	Automotive glass installers and repairers	20,510	19,830	96.7	675	3.3	4,470	21.8	14,400	70.2
7200	Automotive service technicians and mechanics	884,675	871,350	98.5	13,325	1.5	168,070	19.0	601,520	68.0
7210	Bus and truck mechanics and diesel engine specialists	312,055	308,555	98.9	3,500	1.1	39,810	12.8	236,955	75.9
7220	Heavy vehicle and mobile equipment service technicians and mechanics	220,610	217,940	98.8	2,665	1.2	28,150	12.8	175,180	79.4
7240	Small engine mechanics	52,710	51,895	98.5	815	1.5	4,240	8.0	45,115	85.6
7260	Miscellaneous vehicle and mobile equipment mechanics, installers, and repairers	88,705	87,075	98.2	1,630	1.8	20,045	22.6	56,745	64.0
7300	Control and valve installers and repairers	21,835	20,805	95.3	1,035	4.7	2,805	12.8	15,945	73.0
7315	Heating, air conditioning, and refrigeration mechanics and installers	377,555	372,705	98.7	4,855	1.3	58,170	15.4	281,645	74.6
7320	Home appliance repairers	44,385	42,925	96.7	1,460	3.3	6,660	15.0	31,910	71.9
7330	Industrial and refractory machinery mechanics	421,245	406,155	96.4	15,095	3.6	52,045	12.4	320,685	76.1
7340	Maintenance and repair workers, general	497,610	480,145	96.5	17,465	3.5	75,335	15.1	350,925	70.5
7350	Maintenance workers, machinery	38,810	37,230	95.9	1,580	4.1	5,165	13.3	28,945	74.6
7360	Millwrights	58,295	56,665	97.2	1,630	2.8	2,635	4.5	51,940	89.1
7410	Electrical power-line installers and repairers	119,210	117,480	98.5	1,730	1.5	12,490	10.5	93,575	78.5
7420	Telecommunications line installers and repairers	174,590	164,460	94.2	10,130	5.8	25,935	14.9	116,070	66.5
7430	Precision instrument and equipment repairers	64,940	57,580	88.7	7,360	11.3	6,590	10.1	49,505	76.2
7510	Coin, vending, and amusement machine servicers and repairers	50,185	41,045	81.8	9,140	18.2	5,950	11.9	37,095	73.9
7540	Locksmiths and safe repairers	27,630	25,805	93.4	1,825	6.6	2,930	10.6	21,935	79.4
7550	Manufactured building and mobile home installers	10,925	10,235	93.7	690	6.3	1,725	15.8	8,060	73.8

PART A—NATIONAL DATA

A-10 Detailed Occupations in the Installation, Maintenance and Repair Craft Workers Occupation Group, by Sex, Race, and Hispanic Origin, 2006–2010—Continued

Census occupation code	Installation, Maintenance, and Repair Craft Workers Occupation Group	Black alone, not Hispanic or Latino Number	Black alone, not Hispanic or Latino Percent	American Indian and Alaska Native alone, not Hispanic or Latino Number	American Indian and Alaska Native alone, not Hispanic or Latino Percent	Asian alone, not Hispanic or Latino Number	Asian alone, not Hispanic or Latino Percent	Native Hawaiian and Other Pacific Islander alone, not Hispanic or Latino Number	Native Hawaiian and Other Pacific Islander alone, not Hispanic or Latino Percent	Two or more races, not Hispanic or Latino Number	Two or more races, not Hispanic or Latino Percent
7000	First-line supervisors of mechanics, installers, and repairers	23,825	7.6	1,590	0.5	6,070	1.9	535	0.2	3,830	1.2
7010	Computer, automated teller, and office machine repairers	30,870	10.8	1,190	0.4	18,825	6.6	570	0.2	5,050	1.8
7020	Radio and telecommunications equipment installers and repairers	24,245	12.4	795	0.4	6,610	3.4	195	0.1	2,205	1.1
7030	Avionics technicians	1,345	7.5	95	0.5	585	3.3	35	0.2	315	1.8
7040	Electric motor, power tool, and related repairers	2,195	7.2	270	0.9	1,000	3.3	50	0.2	300	1.0
7100	Electrical and electronics repairers, transportation equipment, and industrial and utility	1,295	7.5	140	0.8	440	2.5	15	0.1	199	1.1
7110	Electronic equipment installers and repairers, motor vehicles	1,810	9.0	120	0.6	490	2.4	20	0.1	340	1.7
7120	Electronic home entertainment equipment installers and repairers	6,000	9.3	320	0.5	2,555	4.0	80	0.1	985	1.5
7130	Security and fire alarm systems installers	5,050	8.4	315	0.5	1,505	2.5	165	0.3	1,080	1.8
7140	Aircraft mechanics and service technicians	12,630	8.1	860	0.5	7,070	4.5	680	0.4	2,855	1.8
7150	Automotive body and related repairers	9,320	5.4	1,080	0.6	4,125	2.4	75	0.0	1,990	1.2
7160	Automotive glass installers and repairers	940	4.6	75	0.4	320	1.6	0	0.0	300	1.5
7200	Automotive service technicians and mechanics	65,860	7.4	5,195	0.6	30,175	3.4	1,415	0.2	12,435	1.4
7210	Bus and truck mechanics and diesel engine specialists	23,805	7.6	1,950	0.6	5,155	1.7	615	0.2	3,770	1.2
7220	Heavy vehicle and mobile equipment service technicians and mechanics	10,675	4.8	1,820	0.8	2,220	1.0	350	0.2	2,215	1.0
7240	Small engine mechanics	1,825	3.5	280	0.5	540	1.0	65	0.1	650	1.2
7260	Miscellaneous vehicle and mobile equipment mechanics, installers, and repairers	8,630	9.7	675	0.8	1,200	1.4	100	0.1	1,300	1.5
7300	Control and valve installers and repairers	2,440	11.2	115	0.5	235	1.1	15	0.1	280	1.3
7315	Heating, air conditioning, and refrigeration mechanics and installers	23,980	6.4	1,975	0.5	6,680	1.8	245	0.1	4,860	1.3
7320	Home appliance repairers	3,630	8.2	310	0.7	1,300	2.9	35	0.1	540	1.2
7330	Industrial and refractory machinery mechanics	30,730	7.3	2,205	0.5	10,550	2.5	450	0.1	4,585	1.1
7340	Maintenance and repair workers, general	47,375	9.5	4,065	0.8	12,975	2.6	1,245	0.3	5,690	1.1
7350	Maintenance workers, machinery	3,120	8.0	290	0.7	810	2.1	85	0.2	389	1.0
7360	Millwrights	2,315	4.0	375	0.6	470	0.8	45	0.1	520	0.9
7410	Electrical power-line installers and repairers	9,750	8.2	800	0.7	905	0.8	170	0.1	1,525	1.3
7420	Telecommunications line installers and repairers	23,740	13.6	795	0.5	4,885	2.8	410	0.2	2,760	1.6
7430	Precision instrument and equipment repairers	4,195	6.5	195	0.3	3,345	5.2	90	0.1	1,015	1.6
7510	Coin, vending, and amusement machine servicers and repairers	4,205	8.4	795	1.6	1,395	2.8	45	0.1	700	1.4
7540	Locksmiths and safe repairers	1,605	5.8	145	0.5	455	1.6	0	0.0	560	2.0
7550	Manufactured building and mobile home installers	820	7.5	110	1.0	70	0.6	4	0.0	134	1.2

A-10 Detailed Occupations in the Installation, Maintenance and Repair Craft Workers Occupation Group, by Sex, Race, and Hispanic Origin, 2006–2010—*Continued*

Census occupation code	Installation, Maintenance, and Repair Craft Workers Occupation Group	Total who worked in the last 5 years	Male Number	Male Percent	Female Number	Female Percent	Hispanic or Latino Number	Hispanic or Latino Percent	White alone, not Hispanic or Latino Number	White alone, not Hispanic or Latino Percent
7560	Riggers	13,050	12,780	97.9	270	2.1	1,610	12.3	9,110	69.8
7630	Other installation, maintenance, and repair workers, including wind turbine service technicians, and commercial divers, and signal and track switch repairers	238,015	223,680	94.0	14,335	6.0	39,945	16.8	169,160	71.1
7740	Structural metal fabricators and fitters	29,340	28,175	96.0	1,165	4.0	2,770	9.4	23,035	78.5
8030	Machinists	394,735	376,520	95.4	18,215	4.6	41,600	10.5	306,205	77.6
8060	Model makers and patternmakers, metal and plastic	7,950	6,690	84.2	1,260	15.8	900	11.3	6,495	81.7
8130	Tool and die makers	76,410	74,230	97.1	2,180	2.9	4,370	5.7	67,795	88.7
8250	Prepress technicians and workers	48,120	23,540	48.9	24,580	51.1	6,070	12.6	33,490	69.6
8256	Print binding and finishing workers	36,810	19,085	51.8	17,725	48.2	5,000	13.6	26,315	71.5
8330	Shoe and leather workers and repairers	11,040	8,635	78.2	2,410	21.8	3,235	29.3	6,125	55.5
8350	Tailors, dressmakers, and sewers	90,355	20,690	22.9	69,665	77.1	19,985	22.1	45,740	50.6
8450	Upholsterers	44,105	36,470	82.7	7,635	17.3	12,300	27.9	26,765	60.7
8500	Cabinetmakers and bench carpenters	75,220	70,525	93.8	4,690	6.2	13,265	17.6	56,515	75.1
8510	Furniture finishers	21,585	17,175	79.6	4,410	20.4	5,260	24.4	14,075	65.2
8550	Miscellaneous woodworkers, including model makers and patternmakers	32,525	29,560	90.9	2,965	9.1	3,420	10.5	25,675	78.9
8600	Power plant operators, distributors, and dispatchers	47,660	44,335	93.0	3,325	7.0	2,575	5.4	39,790	83.5
8610	Stationary engineers and boiler operators	101,025	97,710	96.7	3,315	3.3	10,770	10.7	71,715	71.0
8620	Water and wastewater treatment plant and system operators	80,770	76,815	95.1	3,955	4.9	6,825	8.4	63,025	78.0
8750	Jewelers and precious stone and metal workers	43,730	28,100	64.3	15,630	35.7	9,200	21.0	24,455	55.9
8760	Medical, dental, and ophthalmic laboratory technicians	89,835	44,780	49.8	45,055	50.2	12,710	14.1	61,250	68.2
8910	Etchers and engravers	11,295	7,095	62.8	4,200	37.2	1,325	11.7	8,620	76.3

PART A—NATIONAL DATA

A-10 Detailed Occupations in the Installation, Maintenance and Repair Craft Workers Occupation Group, by Sex, Race, and Hispanic Origin, 2006–2010—*Continued*

Census occupation code	Installation, Maintenance, and Repair Craft Workers Occupation Group	Black alone, not Hispanic or Latino Number	Black alone, not Hispanic or Latino Percent	American Indian and Alaska Native alone, not Hispanic or Latino Number	American Indian and Alaska Native alone, not Hispanic or Latino Percent	Asian alone, not Hispanic or Latino Number	Asian alone, not Hispanic or Latino Percent	Native Hawaiian and Other Pacific Islander alone, not Hispanic or Latino Number	Native Hawaiian and Other Pacific Islander alone, not Hispanic or Latino Percent	Two or more races, not Hispanic or Latino Number	Two or more races, not Hispanic or Latino Percent
7560	Riggers..	1,795	13.8	50	0.4	140	1.1	40	0.3	295	2.3
7630	Other installation, maintenance, and repair workers, including wind turbine service technicians, and commercial divers, and signal and track switch repairers.............	17,425	7.3	1,615	0.7	5,985	2.5	345	0.1	3,540	1.5
7740	Structural metal fabricators and fitters.........	2,460	8.4	195	0.7	510	1.7	10	0.0	360	1.2
8030	Machinists.......................................	23,630	6.0	2,120	0.5	16,170	4.1	580	0.1	4,420	1.1
8060	Model makers and patternmakers, metal and plastic......................................	260	3.3	10	0.1	165	2.1	4	0.1	119	1.5
8130	Tool and die makers...............................	2,380	3.1	115	0.2	1,145	1.5	35	0.0	570	0.7
8250	Prepress technicians and workers................	5,510	11.5	140	0.3	2,170	4.5	70	0.1	670	1.4
8256	Print binding and finishing workers.............	3,375	9.2	150	0.4	1,465	4.0	60	0.2	450	1.2
8330	Shoe and leather workers and repairers......	695	6.3	60	0.5	750	6.8	0	0.0	180	1.6
8350	Tailors, dressmakers, and sewers................	6,300	7.0	205	0.2	17,450	19.3	80	0.1	590	0.7
8450	Upholsterers.....................................	3,475	7.9	275	0.6	855	1.9	20	0.0	415	0.9
8500	Cabinetmakers and bench carpenters............	3,030	4.0	290	0.4	1,415	1.9	40	0.1	665	0.9
8510	Furniture finishers..............................	1,395	6.5	75	0.3	385	1.8	0	0.0	395	1.8
8550	Miscellaneous woodworkers, including model makers and patternmakers..............	1,535	4.7	505	1.6	675	2.1	35	0.1	680	2.1
8600	Power plant operators, distributors, and dispatchers....................................	3,300	6.9	790	1.7	460	1.0	0	0.0	745	1.6
8610	Stationary engineers and boiler operators.....	12,895	12.8	780	0.8	3,740	3.7	60	0.1	1,070	1.1
8620	Water and wastewater treatment plant and system operators............................	7,565	9.4	1,135	1.4	1,020	1.3	55	0.1	1,145	1.4
8750	Jewelers and precious stone and metal workers..	1,505	3.4	2,420	5.5	5,570	12.7	30	0.1	550	1.3
8760	Medical, dental, and ophthalmic laboratory technicians....................................	5,415	6.0	260	0.3	8,860	9.9	135	0.2	1,210	1.3
8910	Etchers and engravers..........................	620	5.5	180	1.6	385	3.4	0	0.0	170	1.5

Production Operative Workers

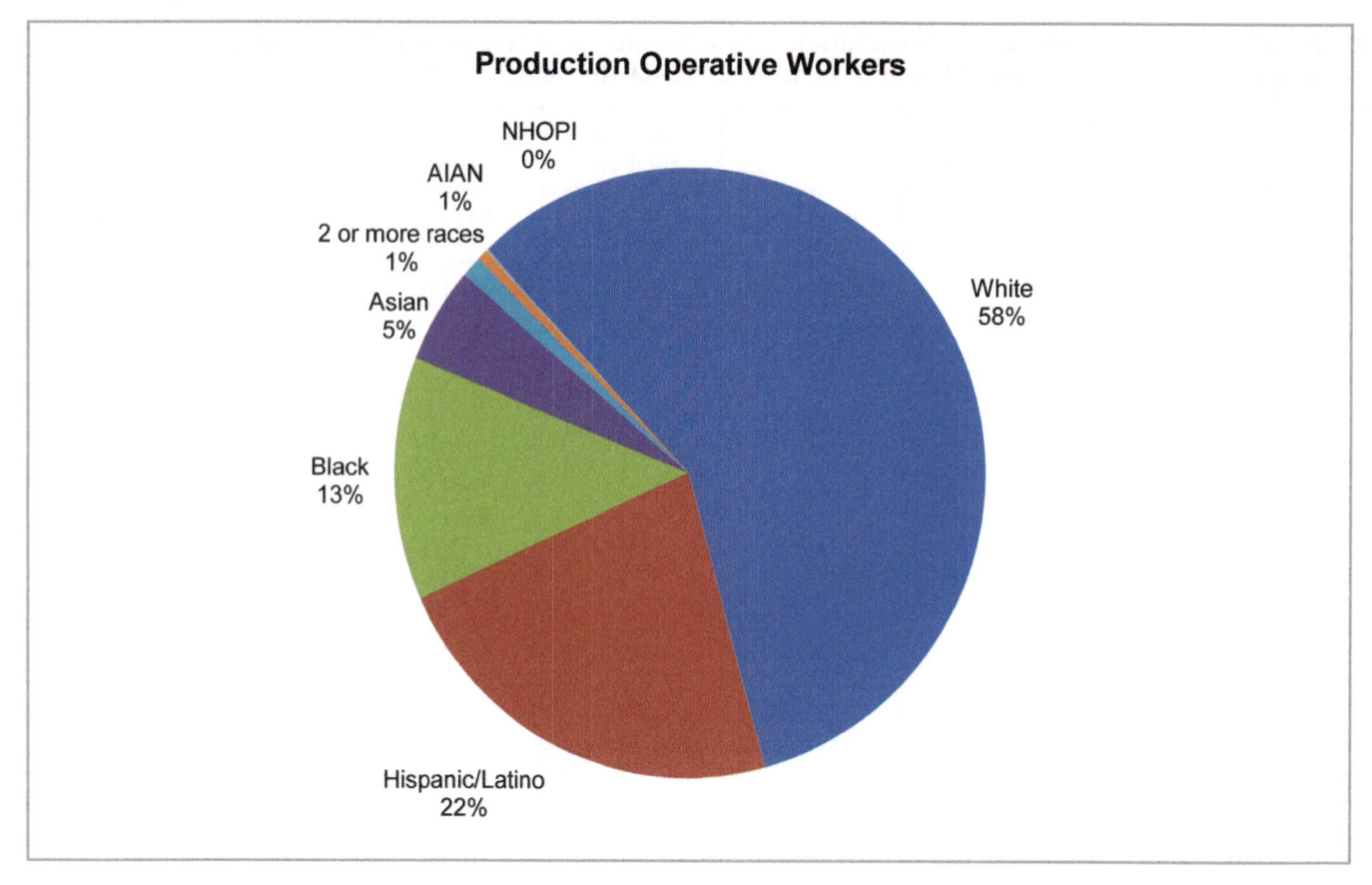

- NHOPI 0%
- AIAN 1%
- 2 or more races 1%
- Asian 5%
- Black 13%
- Hispanic/Latino 22%
- White 58%

Figure A-11.1

Production Operative Workers

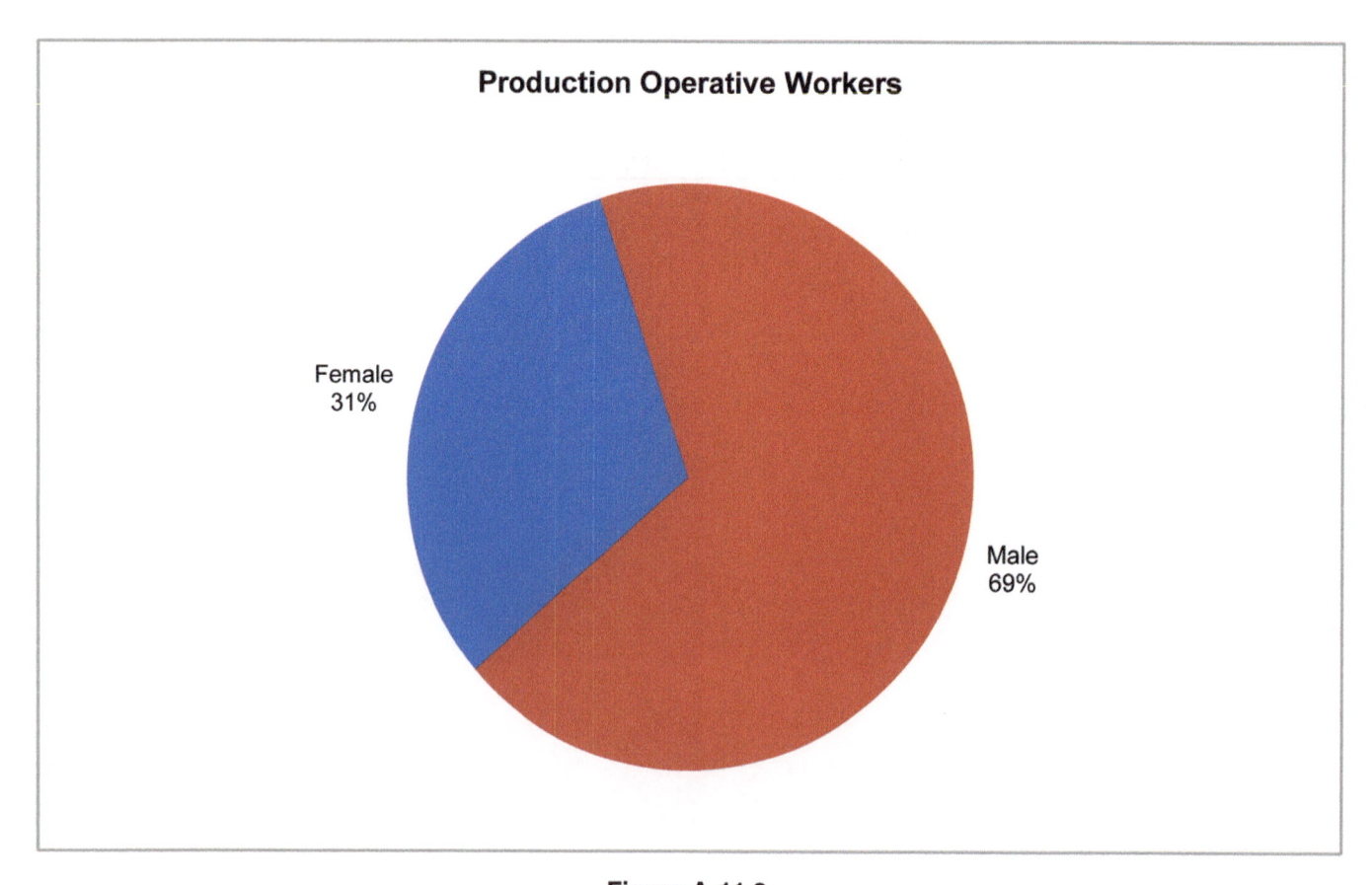

- Female 31%
- Male 69%

Figure A-11.2

PART A—NATIONAL DATA

A-11 Detailed Occupations in the Production Operative Workers Occupation Group, by Sex, Race, and Hispanic Origin, 2006–2010

Census occupation code	Production Operative Workers Occupation Group	Total who worked in the last 5 years	Male Number	Male Percent	Female Number	Female Percent	Hispanic or Latino Number	Hispanic or Latino Percent	White alone, not Hispanic or Latino Number	White alone, not Hispanic or Latino Percent
6040	Graders and sorters, agricultural products....	56,665	18,070	31.9	38,595	68.1	36,635	64.7	11,655	20.6
7700	First-line supervisors of production and operating workers........................	996,450	804,615	80.7	191,835	19.3	137,135	13.8	716,370	71.9
7710	Aircraft structure, surfaces, rigging, and systems assemblers	11,320	7,355	65.0	3,965	35.0	2,835	25.0	6,155	54.4
7720	Electrical, electronics, and electromechanical assemblers......................	192,270	86,110	44.8	106,165	55.2	37,580	19.5	92,435	48.1
7730	Engine and other machine assemblers..........	19,195	15,575	81.1	3,620	18.9	1,935	10.1	14,465	75.4
7750	Miscellaneous assemblers and fabricators....	1,117,435	671,125	60.1	446,310	39.9	211,295	18.9	637,270	57.0
7800	Bakers	189,835	87,400	46.0	102,435	54.0	54,665	28.8	99,335	52.3
7810	Butchers and other meat, poultry, and fish processing workers........................	272,910	205,650	75.4	67,260	24.6	102,155	37.4	116,620	42.7
7830	Food and tobacco roasting, baking, and drying machine operators and tenders	12,190	8,145	66.8	4,040	33.1	2,925	24.0	6,315	51.8
7840	Food batchmakers...	90,760	36,995	40.8	53,765	59.2	24,395	26.9	49,460	54.5
7850	Food cooking machine operators and tenders	13,090	7,620	58.2	5,470	41.8	3,720	28.4	6,250	47.7
7855	Food processing workers, all other...............	134,320	84,080	62.6	50,240	37.4	44,840	33.4	55,610	41.4
7900	Computer control programmers and operators......................	74,025	67,005	90.5	7,020	9.5	6,740	9.1	58,500	79.0
7920	Extruding and drawing machine setters, operators, and tenders, metal and plastic...	13,915	11,585	83.3	2,335	16.8	1,345	9.7	10,950	78.7
7930	Forging machine setters, operators, and tenders, metal and plastic	8,890	8,575	96.5	320	3.6	815	9.2	6,915	77.8
7940	Rolling machine setters, operators, and tenders, metal and plastic	12,455	9,260	74.3	3,195	25.7	1,815	14.6	8,520	68.4
7950	Cutting, punching, and press machine setters, operators, and tenders, metal and plastic............	113,175	89,625	79.2	23,555	20.8	17,140	15.1	78,405	69.3
7960	Drilling and boring machine tool setters, operators, and tenders, metal and plastic...	5,775	4,925	85.3	850	14.7	675	11.7	4,410	76.4
8000	Grinding, lapping, polishing, and buffing machine tool setters, operators, and tenders, metal and plastic	59,575	52,300	87.8	7,280	12.2	13,450	22.6	37,045	62.2
8010	Lathe and turning machine tool setters, operators, and tenders, metal and plastic...	14,420	12,775	88.6	1,645	11.4	2,080	14.4	11,030	76.5
8040	Metal furnace operators, tenders, pourers, and casters....................	27,030	24,835	91.9	2,195	8.1	3,155	11.7	19,180	71.0
8100	Molders and molding machine setters, operators, and tenders, metal and plastic...	53,865	43,445	80.7	10,420	19.3	8,070	15.0	37,065	68.8
8140	Welding, soldering, and brazing workers.....	648,205	611,145	94.3	37,055	5.7	133,830	20.6	430,635	66.4
8150	Heat treating equipment setters, operators, and tenders, metal and plastic	8,660	7,735	89.3	925	10.7	955	11.0	6,420	74.1
8200	Plating and coating machine setters, operators, and tenders, metal and plastic...	18,855	16,870	89.5	1,985	10.5	3,890	20.6	12,210	64.8
8210	Tool grinders, filers, and sharpeners.............	8,760	8,340	95.2	420	4.8	510	5.8	7,340	83.8

A-11. Detailed Occupations in the Production Operative Workers Occupation Group, by Sex, Race, and Hispanic Origin, 2006–2010—Continued

Census occupation code	Production Operative Workers Occupation Group	Black alone, not Hispanic or Latino Number	Black alone, not Hispanic or Latino Percent	American Indian and Alaska Native alone, not Hispanic or Latino Number	American Indian and Alaska Native alone, not Hispanic or Latino Percent	Asian alone, not Hispanic or Latino Number	Asian alone, not Hispanic or Latino Percent	Native Hawaiian and Other Pacific Islander alone, not Hispanic or Latino Number	Native Hawaiian and Other Pacific Islander alone, not Hispanic or Latino Percent	Two or more races, not Hispanic or Latino Number	Two or more races, not Hispanic or Latino Percent
6040	Graders and sorters, agricultural products	5,345	9.4	380	0.7	2,140	3.8	125	0.2	385	0.7
7700	First-line supervisors of production and operating workers	92,410	9.3	4,220	0.4	34,970	3.5	1,100	0.1	10,245	1.0
7710	Aircraft structure, surfaces, rigging, and systems assemblers	1,215	10.7	110	1.0	875	7.7	0	0.0	130	1.1
7720	Electrical, electronics, and electromechanical assemblers	25,120	13.1	1,215	0.6	33,585	17.5	265	0.1	2,080	1.1
7730	Engine and other machine assemblers	1,875	9.8	115	0.6	635	3.3	20	0.1	145	0.8
7750	Miscellaneous assemblers and fabricators	174,015	15.6	5,655	0.5	75,860	6.8	1,250	0.1	12,080	1.1
7800	Bakers	20,965	11.0	1,010	0.5	11,025	5.8	485	0.3	2,350	1.2
7810	Butchers and other meat, poultry, and fish processing workers	38,365	14.1	1,570	0.6	10,825	4.0	505	0.2	2,875	1.1
7830	Food and tobacco roasting, baking, and drying machine operators and tenders	2,040	16.7	150	1.2	580	4.8	20	0.2	160	1.3
7840	Food batchmakers	11,395	12.6	585	0.6	3,385	3.7	60	0.1	1,485	1.6
7850	Food cooking machine operators and tenders	1,905	14.6	95	0.7	810	6.2	25	0.2	295	2.3
7855	Food processing workers, all other	23,660	17.6	855	0.6	7,355	5.5	465	0.3	1,540	1.1
7900	Computer control programmers and operators	4,230	5.7	225	0.3	3,605	4.9	60	0.1	670	0.9
7920	Extruding and drawing machine setters, operators, and tenders, metal and plastic	1,100	7.9	80	0.6	275	2.0	10	0.1	160	1.1
7930	Forging machine setters, operators, and tenders, metal and plastic	860	9.7	55	0.6	185	2.1	4	0.0	60	0.7
7940	Rolling machine setters, operators, and tenders, metal and plastic	1,450	11.6	135	1.1	325	2.6	15	0.1	195	1.6
7950	Cutting, punching, and press machine setters, operators, and tenders, metal and plastic	13,440	11.9	645	0.6	2,220	2.0	10	0.0	1,305	1.2
7960	Drilling and boring machine tool setters, operators, and tenders, metal and plastic	480	8.3	90	1.6	55	1.0	20	0.3	39	0.7
8000	Grinding, lapping, polishing, and buffing machine tool setters, operators, and tenders, metal and plastic	6,625	11.1	360	0.6	1,480	2.5	60	0.1	565	0.9
8010	Lathe and turning machine tool setters, operators, and tenders, metal and plastic	765	5.3	80	0.6	320	2.2	0	0.0	148	1.0
8040	Metal furnace operators, tenders, pourers, and casters	3,965	14.7	185	0.7	310	1.1	10	0.0	230	0.9
8100	Molders and molding machine setters, operators, and tenders, metal and plastic	6,365	11.8	200	0.4	1,455	2.7	105	0.2	615	1.1
8140	Welding, soldering, and brazing workers	52,875	8.2	7,295	1.1	15,590	2.4	830	0.1	7,150	1.1
8150	Heat treating equipment setters, operators, and tenders, metal and plastic	1,010	11.7	90	1.0	120	1.4	15	0.2	55	0.6
8200	Plating and coating machine setters, operators, and tenders, metal and plastic	1,845	9.8	55	0.3	590	3.1	4	0.0	260	1.4
8210	Tool grinders, filers, and sharpeners	510	5.8	30	0.3	250	2.9	0	0.0	125	1.4

A-11 Detailed Occupations in the Production Operative Workers Occupation Group, by Sex, Race, and Hispanic Origin, 2006–2010—*Continued*

Census occupation code	Production Operative Workers Occupation Group	Total who worked in the last 5 years	Male Number	Male Percent	Female Number	Female Percent	Hispanic or Latino Number	Hispanic or Latino Percent	White alone, not Hispanic or Latino Number	White alone, not Hispanic or Latino Percent
8220	Miscellaneous metal workers and plastic workers, including milling and planing machine setters, and multiple machine tool setters, and layout workers..................	463,790	353,705	76.3	110,080	23.7	104,025	22.4	258,185	55.7
8255	Printing press operators.................................	244,330	196,240	80.3	48,090	19.7	38,860	15.9	166,885	68.3
8256	Print binding and finishing workers.............	36,810	19,085	51.8	17,725	48.2	5,000	13.6	26,315	71.5
8300	Laundry and dry-cleaning workers................	217,680	88,725	40.8	128,955	59.2	67,905	31.2	90,820	41.7
8310	Pressers, textile, garment, and related materials..	63,480	19,085	30.1	44,400	69.9	27,990	44.1	18,240	28.7
8320	Sewing machine operators..............................	252,005	56,765	22.5	195,240	77.5	92,650	36.8	94,350	37.4
8340	Shoe machine operators and tenders............	4,910	2,255	45.9	2,655	54.1	1,315	26.8	2,625	53.5
8400	Textile bleaching and dyeing, and cutting machine setters, operators, and tenders......	14,660	8,805	60.1	5,860	40.0	4,230	28.9	7,565	51.6
8410	Textile knitting and weaving machine setters, operators, and tenders......................	13,535	4,950	36.6	8,585	63.4	1,940	14.3	7,880	58.2
8420	Textile winding, twisting, and drawing out machine setters, operators, and tenders......	18,420	6,305	34.2	12,120	65.8	2,960	16.1	9,860	53.5
8460	Miscellaneous textile, apparel, and furnishings workers, except upholsterers...	29,665	15,930	53.7	13,735	46.3	6,500	21.9	15,170	51.1
8530	Sawing machine setters, operators, and tenders..	43,895	38,710	88.2	5,185	11.8	7,890	18.0	30,705	70.0
8540	Woodworking machine setters, operators, and tenders, except sawing........................	33,120	26,065	78.7	7,055	21.3	7,015	21.2	21,500	64.9
8630	Miscellaneous plant and system operators...	41,950	39,520	94.2	2,435	5.8	4,680	11.2	31,515	75.1
8640	Chemical processing machine setters, operators, and tenders.....................................	58,015	50,525	87.1	7,490	12.9	7,535	13.0	39,195	67.6
8650	Crushing, grinding, polishing, mixing, and blending workers...	102,845	91,030	88.5	11,815	11.5	22,730	22.1	61,320	59.6
8710	Cutting workers..	85,155	63,905	75.0	21,250	25.0	21,695	25.5	48,975	57.5
8720	Extruding, forming, pressing, and compacting machine setters, operators, and tenders..	38,045	30,900	81.2	7,145	18.8	5,380	14.1	26,025	68.4
8730	Furnace, kiln, oven, drier, and kettle operators and tenders......................................	13,080	11,075	84.7	2,005	15.3	1,265	9.7	9,475	72.4
8800	Packaging and filling machine operators and tenders..	300,120	127,765	42.6	172,355	57.4	116,990	39.0	106,400	35.5
8810	Painting workers..	176,495	153,610	87.0	22,890	13.0	49,850	28.2	101,850	57.7
8830	Photographic process workers and processing machine operators.....................	66,460	27,040	40.7	39,415	59.3	8,915	13.4	43,050	64.8
8850	Adhesive bonding machine operators and tenders..	15,150	8,715	57.5	6,435	42.5	3,450	22.8	8,635	57.0
8860	Cleaning, washing, and metal pickling equipment operators and tenders................	10,385	7,540	72.6	2,845	27.4	3,385	32.6	5,360	51.6
8920	Molders, shapers, and casters, except metal and plastic...	37,610	32,155	85.5	5,455	14.5	8,890	23.6	24,700	65.7
8930	Paper goods machine setters, operators, and tenders..	38,230	27,330	71.5	10,900	28.5	7,170	18.8	22,470	58.8
8940	Tire builders..	17,100	15,365	89.9	1,735	10.1	1,285	7.5	11,215	65.6
8965	Other production workers, including semiconductor processors and cooling and freezing equipment operators	1,195,140	835,125	69.9	360,015	30.1	261,045	21.8	679,620	56.9

A-11. **Detailed Occupations in the Production Operative Workers Occupation Group, by Sex, Race, and Hispanic Origin, 2006–2010**—*Continued*

Census occupation code	Production Operative Workers Occupation Group	Black alone, not Hispanic or Latino Number	Black alone, not Hispanic or Latino Percent	American Indian and Alaska Native alone, not Hispanic or Latino Number	American Indian and Alaska Native alone, not Hispanic or Latino Percent	Asian alone, not Hispanic or Latino Number	Asian alone, not Hispanic or Latino Percent	Native Hawaiian and Other Pacific Islander alone, not Hispanic or Latino Number	Native Hawaiian and Other Pacific Islander alone, not Hispanic or Latino Percent	Two or more races, not Hispanic or Latino Number	Two or more races, not Hispanic or Latino Percent
8220	Miscellaneous metal workers and plastic workers, including milling and planing machine setters, and multiple machine tool setters, and layout workers..................	61,580	13.3	2,225	0.5	32,640	7.0	415	0.1	4,710	1.0
8255	Printing press operators..............................	24,050	9.8	935	0.4	10,055	4.1	265	0.1	3,275	1.3
8256	Print binding and finishing workers	3,375	9.2	150	0.4	1,465	4.0	60	0.2	450	1.2
8300	Laundry and dry-cleaning workers	38,550	17.7	1,550	0.7	15,505	7.1	545	0.3	2,805	1.3
8310	Pressers, textile, garment, and related materials	12,185	19.2	265	0.4	4,135	6.5	50	0.1	610	1.0
8320	Sewing machine operators	27,415	10.9	1,005	0.4	34,500	13.7	280	0.1	1,805	0.7
8340	Shoe machine operators and tenders	585	11.9	0	0.0	325	6.6	4	0.1	55	1.1
8400	Textile bleaching and dyeing, and cutting machine setters, operators, and tenders......	1,835	12.5	85	0.6	720	4.9	25	0.2	199	1.4
8410	Textile knitting and weaving machine setters, operators, and tenders....................	2,555	18.9	245	1.8	735	5.4	0	0.0	175	1.3
8420	Textile winding, twisting, and drawing out machine setters, operators, and tenders......	4,865	26.4	95	0.5	465	2.5	0	0.0	175	1.0
8460	Miscellaneous textile, apparel, and furnishings workers, except upholsterers ...	5,195	17.5	95	0.3	2,390	8.1	50	0.2	264	0.9
8530	Sawing machine setters, operators, and tenders	3,915	8.9	470	1.1	550	1.3	0	0.0	359	0.8
8540	Woodworking machine setters, operators, and tenders, except sawing........................	3,110	9.4	260	0.8	470	1.4	40	0.1	720	2.2
8630	Miscellaneous plant and system operators ...	4,305	10.3	295	0.7	510	1.2	120	0.3	525	1.3
8640	Chemical processing machine setters, operators, and tenders................................	8,550	14.7	245	0.4	1,545	2.7	70	0.1	880	1.5
8650	Crushing, grinding, polishing, mixing, and blending workers..	13,865	13.5	880	0.9	2,815	2.7	60	0.1	1,180	1.1
8710	Cutting workers	10,375	12.2	630	0.7	2,365	2.8	105	0.1	1,025	1.2
8720	Extruding, forming, pressing, and compacting machine setters, operators, and tenders	5,425	14.3	205	0.5	685	1.8	4	0.0	325	0.9
8730	Furnace, kiln, oven, drier, and kettle operators and tenders................................	1,795	13.7	175	1.3	150	1.1	10	0.1	215	1.6
8800	Packaging and filling machine operators and tenders	56,495	18.8	1,545	0.5	14,545	4.8	625	0.2	3,525	1.2
8810	Painting workers...	16,830	9.5	825	0.5	4,140	2.3	105	0.1	2,895	1.6
8830	Photographic process workers and processing machine operators......................	8,615	13.0	190	0.3	4,145	6.2	100	0.2	1,440	2.2
8850	Adhesive bonding machine operators and tenders	2,135	14.1	85	0.6	625	4.1	40	0.3	184	1.2
8860	Cleaning, washing, and metal pickling equipment operators and tenders................	1,315	12.7	20	0.2	185	1.8	60	0.6	60	0.6
8920	Molders, shapers, and casters, except metal and plastic	2,190	5.8	250	0.7	1,015	2.7	10	0.0	560	1.5
8930	Paper goods machine setters, operators, and tenders	6,715	17.6	345	0.9	1,010	2.6	75	0.2	440	1.2
8940	Tire builders..	3,755	22.0	145	0.8	315	1.8	110	0.6	275	1.6
8965	Other production workers, including semiconductor processors and cooling and freezing equipment operators	181,255	15.2	6,560	0.5	52,105	4.4	1,815	0.2	12,735	1.1

PART A—NATIONAL DATA

Transportation and Material Moving Operative Workers

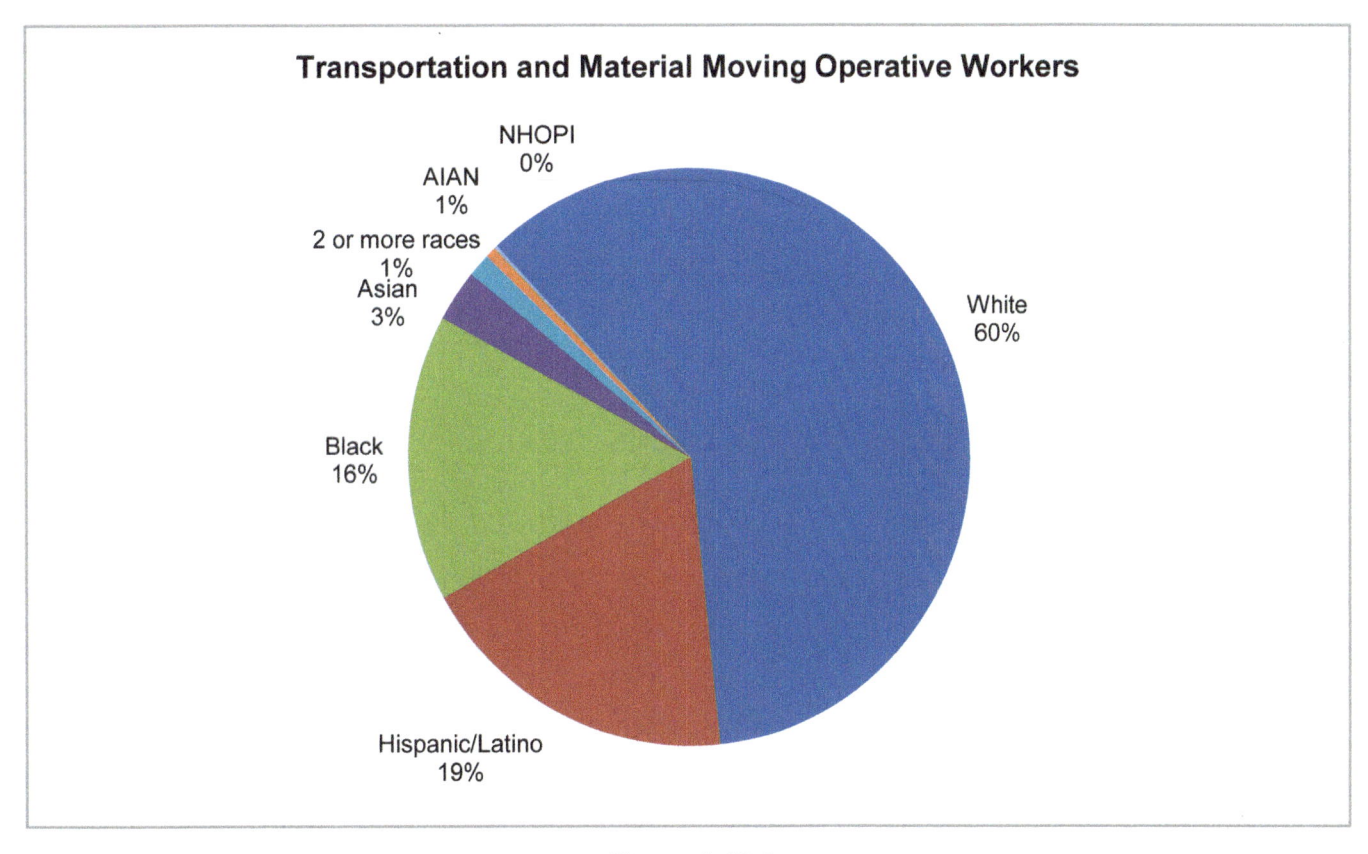

- White: 60%
- Hispanic/Latino: 19%
- Black: 16%
- Asian: 3%
- 2 or more races: 1%
- AIAN: 1%
- NHOPI: 0%

Figure A-12.1

Transportation and Material Moving Operative Workers

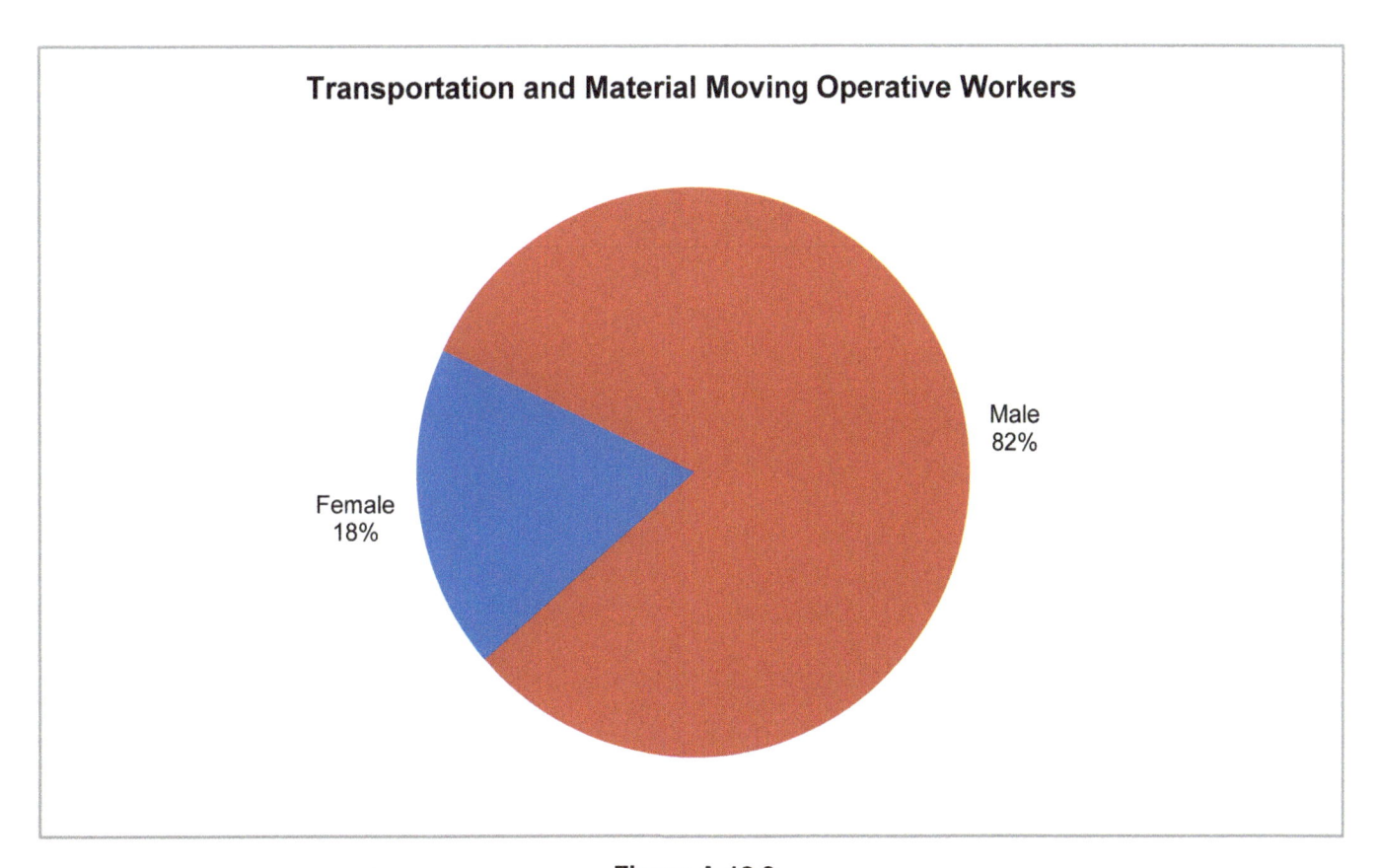

- Male: 82%
- Female: 18%

Figure A-12.2

A-12 Detailed Occupations in the Transportation and Material Moving Operative Workers Occupation Group, by Sex, Race, and Hispanic Origin, 2006–2010

Census occupation code	Transportation and Material Moving Operative Workers Occupation Group	Total who worked in the last 5 years	Male Number	Male Percent	Female Number	Female Percent	Hispanic or Latino Number	Hispanic or Latino Percent	White alone, not Hispanic or Latino Number	White alone, not Hispanic or Latino Percent
8740	Inspectors, testers, sorters, samplers, and weighers	826,110	491,880	59.5	334,230	40.5	129,310	15.7	528,875	64.0
9000	Supervisors of transportation and material moving workers	248,415	197,365	79.4	51,055	20.6	35,420	14.3	164,210	66.1
9110	Ambulance drivers and attendants, except emergency medical technicians	13,140	10,090	76.8	3,050	23.2	2,185	16.6	7,495	57.0
9120	Bus drivers	608,595	319,235	52.5	289,360	47.5	71,705	11.8	349,750	57.5
9130	Driver/sales workers and truck drivers	3,410,730	3,230,810	94.7	179,920	5.3	580,800	17.0	2,251,200	66.0
9140	Taxi drivers and chauffeurs	335,255	287,280	85.7	47,975	14.3	54,975	16.4	151,525	45.2
9150	Motor vehicle operators, all other	58,885	51,900	88.1	6,990	11.9	8,695	14.8	40,605	69.0
9200	Locomotive engineers and operators	52,870	50,235	95.0	2,635	5.0	3,535	6.7	39,465	74.6
9230	Railroad brake, signal, and switch operators	8,000	7,660	95.8	335	4.2	1,275	15.9	5,735	71.7
9240	Railroad conductors and yardmasters	50,725	47,195	93.0	3,535	7.0	3,125	6.2	38,940	76.8
9260	Subway, streetcar, and other rail transportation workers	11,210	9,665	86.2	1,545	13.8	1,100	9.8	6,885	61.4
9300	Sailors and marine oilers, and ship engineers	29,475	28,195	95.7	1,280	4.3	2,515	8.5	21,335	72.4
9310	Ship and boat captains and operators	39,595	38,110	96.2	1,485	3.8	2,000	5.1	34,490	87.1
9350	Parking lot attendants	83,380	72,480	86.9	10,900	13.1	21,675	26.0	36,720	44.0
9420	Miscellaneous transportation workers, including bridge and lock tenders and traffic technicians	23,635	20,540	86.9	3,095	13.1	3,005	12.7	14,525	61.5
9560	Conveyor operators and tenders, and hoist and winch operators	14,420	12,890	89.4	1,535	10.6	2,145	14.9	9,950	69.0
9600	Industrial truck and tractor operators	584,370	538,320	92.1	46,050	7.9	146,490	25.1	283,885	48.6
640	Packers and packagers, hand	501,795	207,250	41.3	294,540	58.7	213,930	42.6	171,125	34.1
9650	Pumping station operators	22,210	21,410	96.4	795	3.6	2,355	10.6	18,280	82.3
9750	Miscellaneous material moving workers, including mine shuttle car operators, and tank car, truck, and ship loaders	62,175	52,945	85.2	9,230	14.8	10,805	17.4	36,890	59.3

PART A—NATIONAL DATA

A-12. Detailed Occupations in the Transportation and Material Moving Operative Workers Occupation Group, by Sex, Race, and Hispanic Origin, 2006–2010—*Continued*

Census occupation code	Transportation and Material Moving Operative Workers Occupation Group	Black alone, not Hispanic or Latino Number	Black alone, not Hispanic or Latino Percent	American Indian and Alaska Native alone, not Hispanic or Latino Number	American Indian and Alaska Native alone, not Hispanic or Latino Percent	Asian alone, not Hispanic or Latino Number	Asian alone, not Hispanic or Latino Percent	Native Hawaiian and Other Pacific Islander alone, not Hispanic or Latino Number	Native Hawaiian and Other Pacific Islander alone, not Hispanic or Latino Percent	Two or more races, not Hispanic or Latino Number	Two or more races, not Hispanic or Latino Percent
8740	Inspectors, testers, sorters, samplers, and weighers	100,270	12.1	3,855	0.5	51,130	64.0	1,530	0.2	11,140	1.3
9000	Supervisors of transportation and material moving workers	33,960	13.7	1,540	0.6	8,905	66.1	915	0.4	3,465	1.4
9110	Ambulance drivers and attendants, except emergency medical technicians	2,785	21.2	375	2.9	195	57.0	0	0.0	114	0.9
9120	Bus drivers	161,280	26.5	5,095	0.8	10,875	57.5	1,370	0.2	8,515	1.4
9130	Driver/sales workers and truck drivers	455,230	13.3	19,755	0.6	56,335	66.0	5,725	0.2	41,680	1.2
9140	Taxi drivers and chauffeurs	84,215	25.1	2,160	0.6	36,000	45.2	485	0.1	5,895	1.8
9150	Motor vehicle operators, all other	7,825	13.3	215	0.4	850	69.0	45	0.1	655	1.1
9200	Locomotive engineers and operators	8,125	15.4	465	0.9	550	74.6	20	0.0	710	1.3
9230	Railroad brake, signal, and switch operators	775	9.7	75	0.9	10	71.7	0	0.0	129	1.6
9240	Railroad conductors and yardmasters	7,350	14.5	285	0.6	345	76.8	75	0.1	610	1.2
9260	Subway, streetcar, and other rail transportation workers	2,625	23.4	130	1.2	215	61.4	15	0.1	235	2.1
9300	Sailors and marine oilers, and ship engineers	3,815	12.9	275	0.9	710	72.4	65	0.2	755	2.6
9310	Ship and boat captains and operators	1,350	3.4	700	1.8	440	87.1	55	0.1	565	1.4
9350	Parking lot attendants	18,630	22.3	410	0.5	3,965	44.0	360	0.4	1,620	1.9
9420	Miscellaneous transportation workers, including bridge and lock tenders and traffic technicians	4,070	17.2	255	1.1	955	61.5	315	1.3	510	2.2
9560	Conveyor operators and tenders, and hoist and winch operators	1,815	12.6	180	1.2	150	69.0	50	0.3	129	0.9
9600	Industrial truck and tractor operators	132,250	22.6	3,335	0.6	8,780	48.6	1,515	0.3	8,115	1.4
640	Packers and packagers, hand	82,005	16.3	2,355	0.5	25,750	34.1	1,190	0.2	5,435	1.1
9650	Pumping station operators	910	4.1	190	0.9	150	82.3	15	0.1	320	1.4
9750	Miscellaneous material moving workers, including mine shuttle car operators, and tank car, truck, and ship loaders	12,075	19.4	450	0.7	790	59.3	175	0.3	995	1.6

Laborers and Helpers

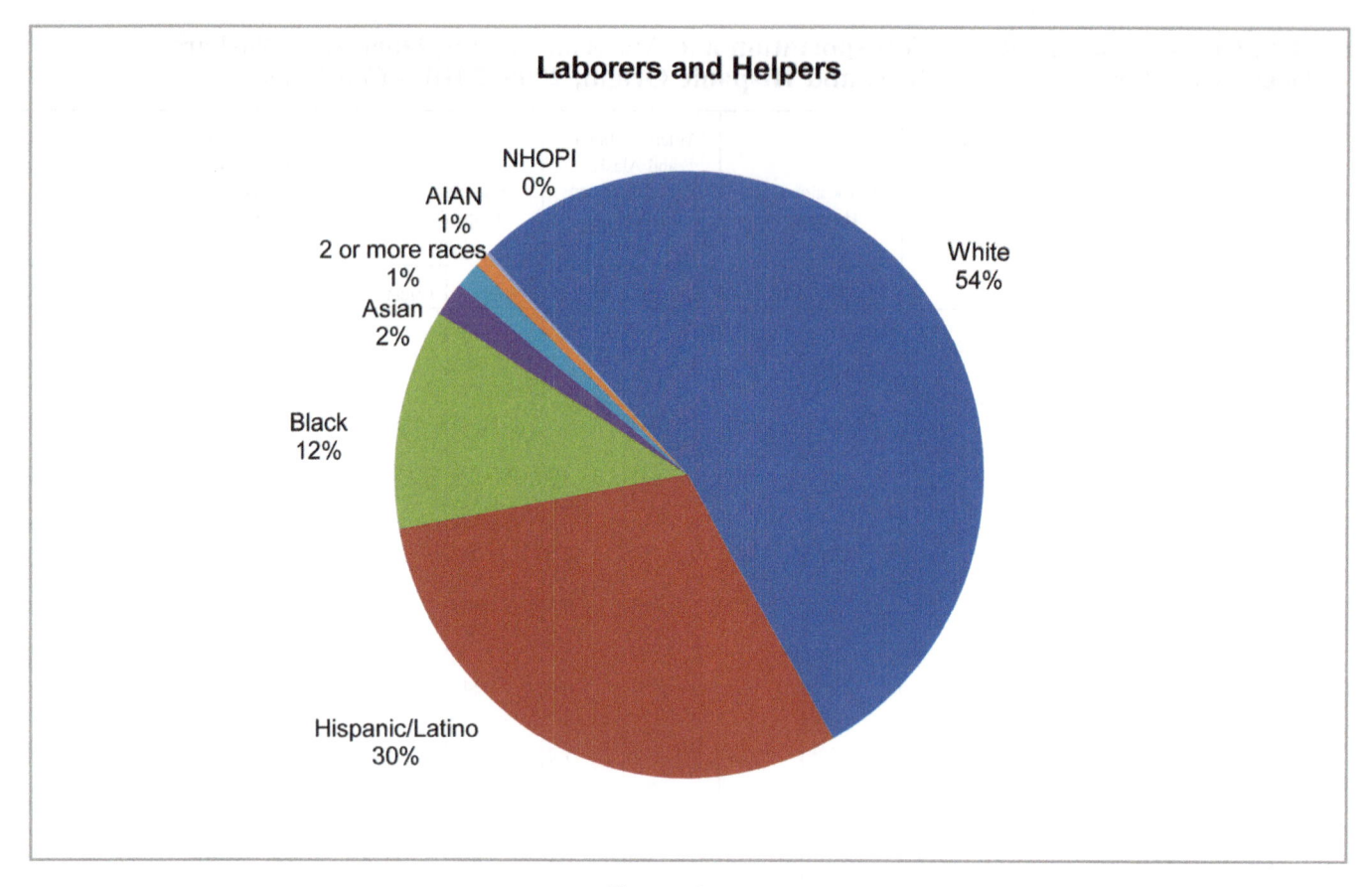

- White: 54%
- Hispanic/Latino: 30%
- Black: 12%
- Asian: 2%
- 2 or more races: 1%
- AIAN: 1%
- NHOPI: 0%

Figure A-13.1

Laborers and Helpers

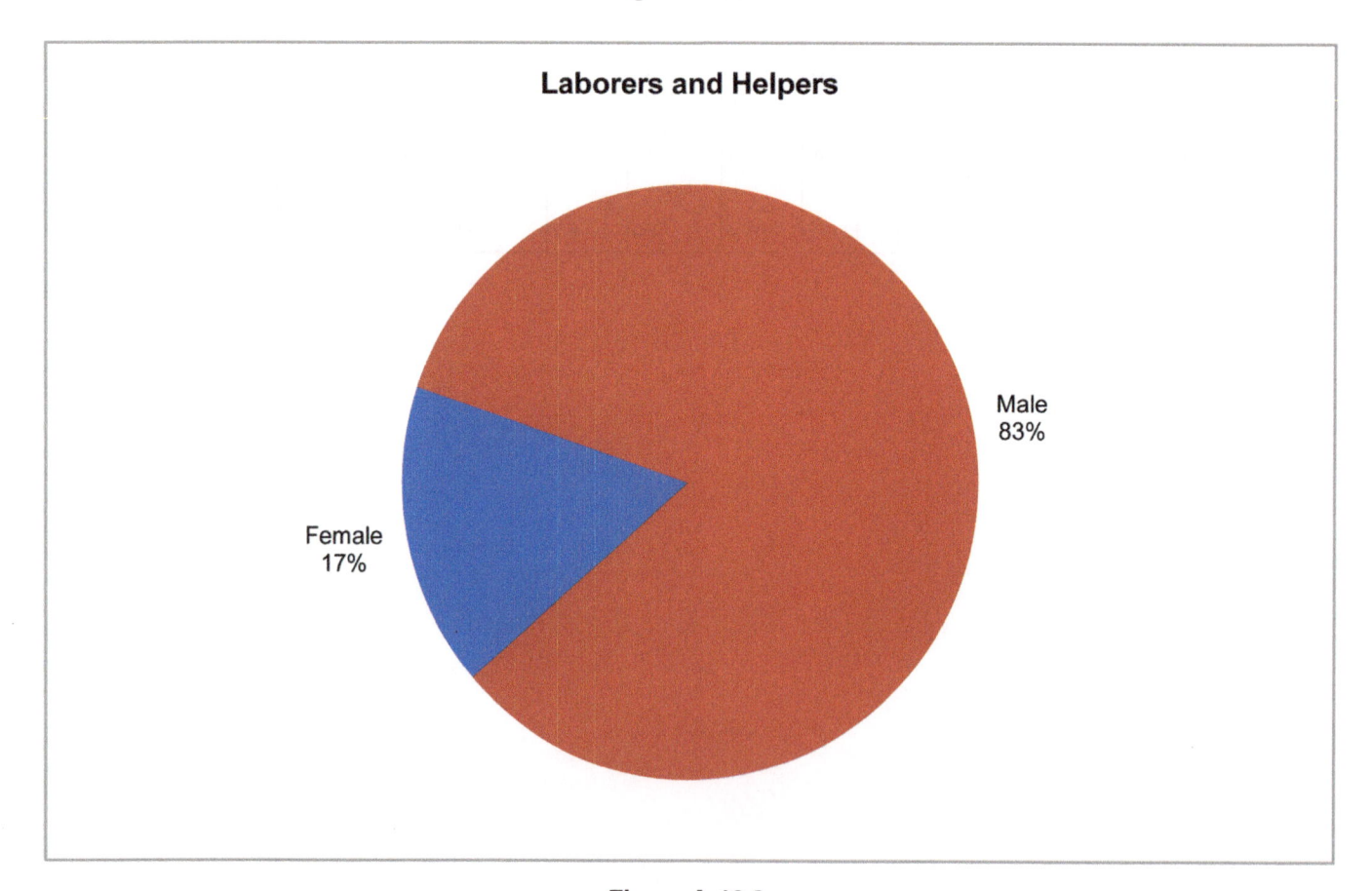

- Male: 83%
- Female: 17%

Figure A-13.2

PART A—NATIONAL DATA

A-13. Detailed Occupations in the Laborers and Helpers Occupation Group, by Sex, Race, and Hispanic Origin, 2006–2010

Census occupation code	Laborers and Helpers Occupation Group	Total who worked in the last 5 years	Male Number	Male Percent	Female Number	Female Percent	Hispanic or Latino Number	Hispanic or Latino Percent	White alone, not Hispanic or Latino Number	White alone, not Hispanic or Latino Percent
4210	First-line supervisors of landscaping, lawn service, and groundskeeping workers	200,480	187,500	93.5	12,980	6.5	39,945	19.9	144,970	72.3
4250	Grounds maintenance workers	1,384,225	1,294,995	93.6	89,235	6.4	547,115	39.5	672,500	48.6
4350	Nonfarm animal caretakers	183,055	52,845	28.9	130,210	71.1	19,235	10.5	150,150	82.0
6005	First-line supervisors of farming, fishing, and forestry workers	61,480	52,345	85.1	9,130	14.9	21,510	35.0	35,745	58.1
6050	Miscellaneous agricultural workers, including animal breeders	871,090	682,060	78.3	189,030	21.7	483,295	55.5	333,180	38.2
6100	Fishing and hunting workers	42,200	40,070	95.0	2,130	5.0	3,230	7.7	32,705	77.5
6120	Forest and conservation workers	16,935	14,110	83.3	2,825	16.7	3,475	20.5	11,695	69.1
6130	Logging workers	85,905	83,750	97.5	2,155	2.5	7,500	8.7	66,225	77.1
6600	Helpers, construction trades	98,490	94,220	95.7	4,265	4.3	39,690	40.3	46,315	47.0
7610	Helpers\installation, maintenance, and repair workers	28,345	26,225	92.5	2,120	7.5	9,665	34.1	14,330	50.6
8950	Helpers\production workers	57,025	43,145	75.7	13,885	24.3	19,880	34.9	25,520	44.8
9360	Automotive and watercraft service attendants	133,050	100,765	75.7	32,285	24.3	15,455	11.6	91,575	68.8
7061	Cleaners of vehicles and equipment	390,400	331,545	84.9	58,855	15.1	124,755	32.0	176,975	45.3
9620	Laborers and freight, stock, and material movers, hand	2,297,785	1,882,770	81.9	415,015	18.1	451,910	19.7	1,342,505	58.4
7063	Machine feeders and offbearers	39,695	21,690	54.6	18,010	45.4	7,835	19.7	22,595	56.9
9720	Refuse and recyclable material collectors	101,085	91,760	90.8	9,325	9.2	23,205	23.0	50,185	49.6

Census occupation code	Laborers and Helpers Occupation Group	Black alone, not Hispanic or Latino Number	Black alone, not Hispanic or Latino Percent	American Indian and Alaska Native alone, not Hispanic or Latino Number	American Indian and Alaska Native alone, not Hispanic or Latino Percent	Asian alone, not Hispanic or Latino Number	Asian alone, not Hispanic or Latino Percent	Native Hawaiian and Other Pacific Islander alone, not Hispanic or Latino Number	Native Hawaiian and Other Pacific Islander alone, not Hispanic or Latino Percent	Two or more races, not Hispanic or Latino Number	Two or more races, not Hispanic or Latino Percent
4210	First-line supervisors of landscaping, lawn service, and groundskeeping workers	10,500	5.2	835	0.4	1,670	0.8	435	0.2	2,120	1.1
4250	Grounds maintenance workers	119,290	8.6	9,390	0.7	16,480	1.2	2,560	0.2	16,885	1.2
4350	Nonfarm animal caretakers	6,770	3.7	780	0.4	2,320	1.3	75	0.0	3,725	2.0
6005	First-line supervisors of farming, fishing, and forestry workers	2,175	3.5	560	0.9	825	1.3	15	0.0	645	1.0
6050	Miscellaneous agricultural workers, including animal breeders	32,830	3.8	4,370	0.5	9,265	1.1	1,055	0.1	7,100	0.8
6100	Fishing and hunting workers	1,085	2.6	1,610	3.8	2,530	6.0	145	0.3	894	2.1
6120	Forest and conservation workers	1,095	6.5	310	1.8	125	0.7	20	0.1	219	1.3
6130	Logging workers	9,095	10.6	1,850	2.2	215	0.3	85	0.1	940	1.1
6600	Helpers, construction trades	8,965	9.1	915	0.9	1,185	1.2	100	0.1	1,320	1.3
7610	Helpers\installation, maintenance, and repair workers	2,705	9.5	175	0.6	985	3.5	65	0.2	425	1.5
8950	Helpers\production workers	7,010	12.3	570	1.0	3,160	5.5	105	0.2	775	1.4
9360	Automotive and watercraft service attendants	13,890	10.4	1,780	1.3	7,445	5.6	195	0.1	2,705	2.0
7061	Cleaners of vehicles and equipment	70,545	18.1	2,250	0.6	8,370	2.1	1,280	0.3	6,225	1.6
9620	Laborers and freight, stock, and material movers, hand	387,030	16.8	18,520	0.8	55,175	2.4	6,035	0.3	36,620	1.6
7063	Machine feeders and offbearers	7,305	18.4	150	0.4	1,120	2.8	130	0.3	565	1.4
9720	Refuse and recyclable material collectors	23,680	23.4	1,055	1.0	1,070	1.1	195	0.2	1,695	1.7

Protective Service Workers

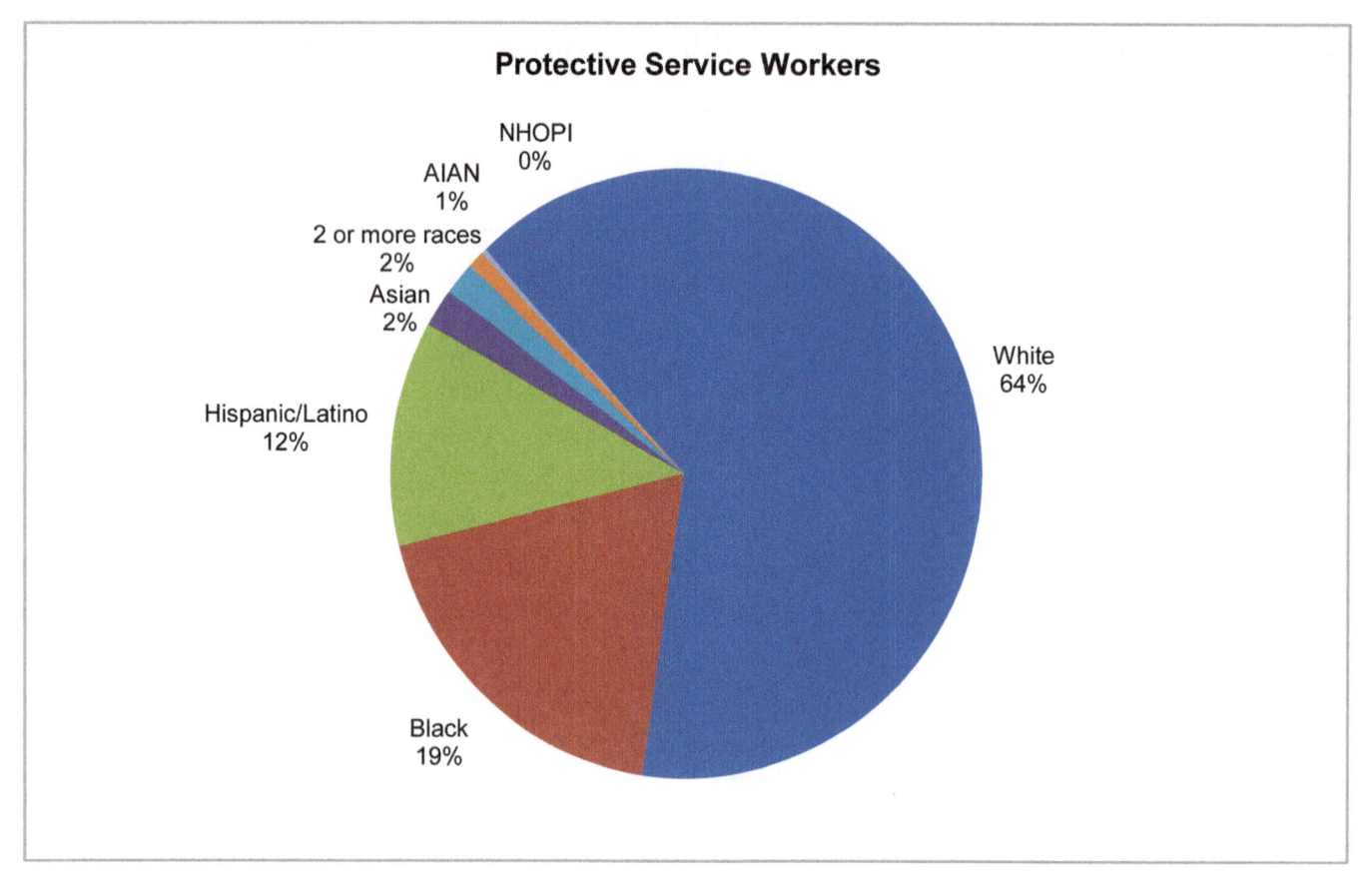

- White 64%
- Black 19%
- Hispanic/Latino 12%
- Asian 2%
- 2 or more races 2%
- AIAN 1%
- NHOPI 0%

Figure A-14.1

Protective Service Workers

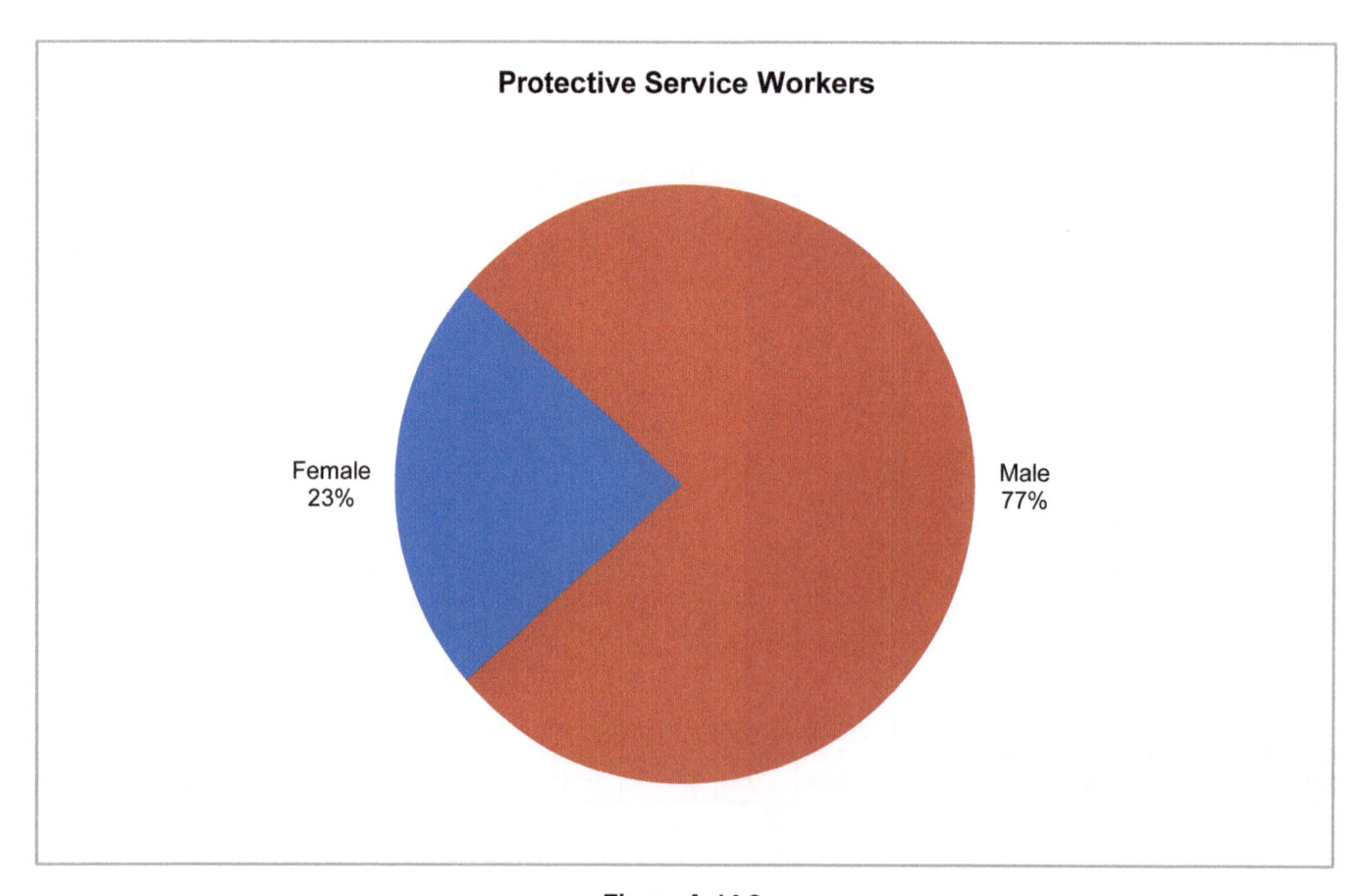

- Male 77%
- Female 23%

Figure A-14.2

A-14. Detailed Occupations in the Protective Service Workers Occupation Group, by Sex, Race, and Hispanic Origin, 2006–2010

Census occupation code	Protective Service Workers Occupation Group	Total who worked in the last 5 years	Male Number	Male Percent	Female Number	Female Percent	Hispanic or Latino Number	Hispanic or Latino Percent	White alone, not Hispanic or Latino Number	White alone, not Hispanic or Latino Percent
3700	First-line supervisors of correctional officers	58,265	42,685	73.3	15,580	26.7	4,915	8.4	37,670	64.7
3710	First-line supervisors of police and detectives	119,270	100,530	84.3	18,740	15.7	9,340	7.8	92,620	77.7
3720	First-line supervisors of fire fighting and prevention workers	53,010	51,035	96.3	1,975	3.7	2,605	4.9	44,965	84.8
3730	First-line supervisors of protective service workers, all other	94,325	71,355	75.6	22,970	24.4	9,775	10.4	61,085	64.8
3740	Firefighters	276,860	265,545	95.9	11,315	4.1	23,415	8.5	219,550	79.3
3750	Fire inspectors	20,025	17,935	89.6	2,090	10.4	1,585	7.9	16,120	80.5
3800	Bailiffs, correctional officers, and jailers	441,185	316,085	71.6	125,100	28.4	50,370	11.4	272,285	61.7
3820	Detectives and criminal investigators	131,215	100,170	76.3	31,045	23.7	14,845	11.3	95,830	73.0
3840	Miscellaneous law enforcement workers	11,530	8,005	69.4	3,525	30.6	1,385	12.0	7,105	61.6
3850	Police officers	663,600	565,100	85.2	98,500	14.8	82,690	12.5	469,535	70.8
3900	Animal control workers	10,770	6,545	60.8	4,225	39.2	1,125	10.4	8,705	80.8
3910	Private detectives and investigators	86,635	52,175	60.2	34,455	39.8	10,370	12.0	60,520	69.9
3930	Security guards and gaming surveillance officers	1,014,210	787,525	77.6	226,685	22.4	146,255	14.4	508,560	50.1
3940	Crossing guards	60,090	24,170	40.2	35,920	59.8	8,685	14.5	36,580	60.9
3945	Transportation security screeners	27,210	17,215	63.3	9,995	36.7	4,180	15.4	13,700	50.3
3955	Lifeguards and other recreational, and all other protective service workers	189,105	88,210	46.6	100,895	53.4	17,110	9.0	146,010	77.2

A-14. **Detailed Occupations in the Protective Service Workers Occupation Group, by Sex, Race, and Hispanic Origin, 2006–2010**—*Continued*

Census occupation code	Protective Service Workers Occupation Group	Black alone, not Hispanic or Latino Number	Black alone, not Hispanic or Latino Percent	American Indian and Alaska Native alone, not Hispanic or Latino Number	American Indian and Alaska Native alone, not Hispanic or Latino Percent	Asian alone, not Hispanic or Latino Number	Asian alone, not Hispanic or Latino Percent	Native Hawaiian and Other Pacific Islander alone, not Hispanic or Latino Number	Native Hawaiian and Other Pacific Islander alone, not Hispanic or Latino Percent	Two or more races, not Hispanic or Latino Number	Two or more races, not Hispanic or Latino Percent
3700	First-line supervisors of correctional officers	13,890	23.8	485	0.8	470	0.8	35	0.1	800	1.4
3710	First-line supervisors of police and detectives	13,565	11.4	790	0.7	1,275	1.1	135	0.1	1,540	1.3
3720	First-line supervisors of fire fighting and prevention workers	3,575	6.7	645	1.2	360	0.7	140	0.3	715	1.3
3730	First-line supervisors of protective service workers, all other	18,950	20.1	815	0.9	1,940	2.1	300	0.3	1,460	1.5
3740	Firefighters	22,600	8.2	3,590	1.3	3,120	1.1	335	0.1	4,255	1.5
3750	Fire inspectors	1,520	7.6	225	1.1	240	1.2	10	0.0	314	1.6
3800	Bailiffs, correctional officers, and jailers	103,730	23.5	3,895	0.9	4,150	0.9	910	0.2	5,840	1.3
3820	Detectives and criminal investigators	15,355	11.7	1,000	0.8	2,250	1.7	140	0.1	1,795	1.4
3840	Miscellaneous law enforcement workers	2,075	18.0	235	2.0	420	3.6	4	0.0	305	2.6
3850	Police officers	81,985	12.4	4,315	0.7	13,260	2.0	1,415	0.2	10,405	1.6
3900	Animal control workers	645	6.0	110	1.0	35	0.3	0	0.0	150	1.4
3910	Private detectives and investigators	11,185	12.9	675	0.8	2,020	2.3	230	0.3	1,635	1.9
3930	Security guards and gaming surveillance officers	290,495	28.6	10,610	1.0	31,825	3.1	4,925	0.5	21,530	2.1
3940	Crossing guards	12,580	20.9	675	1.1	720	1.2	35	0.1	820	1.4
3945	Transportation security screeners	6,900	25.4	150	0.6	1,515	5.6	170	0.6	590	2.2
3955	Lifeguards and other recreational, and all other protective service workers	15,960	8.4	1,000	0.5	3,495	1.8	405	0.2	5,125	2.7

PART A—NATIONAL DATA

Service Workers, except Protective

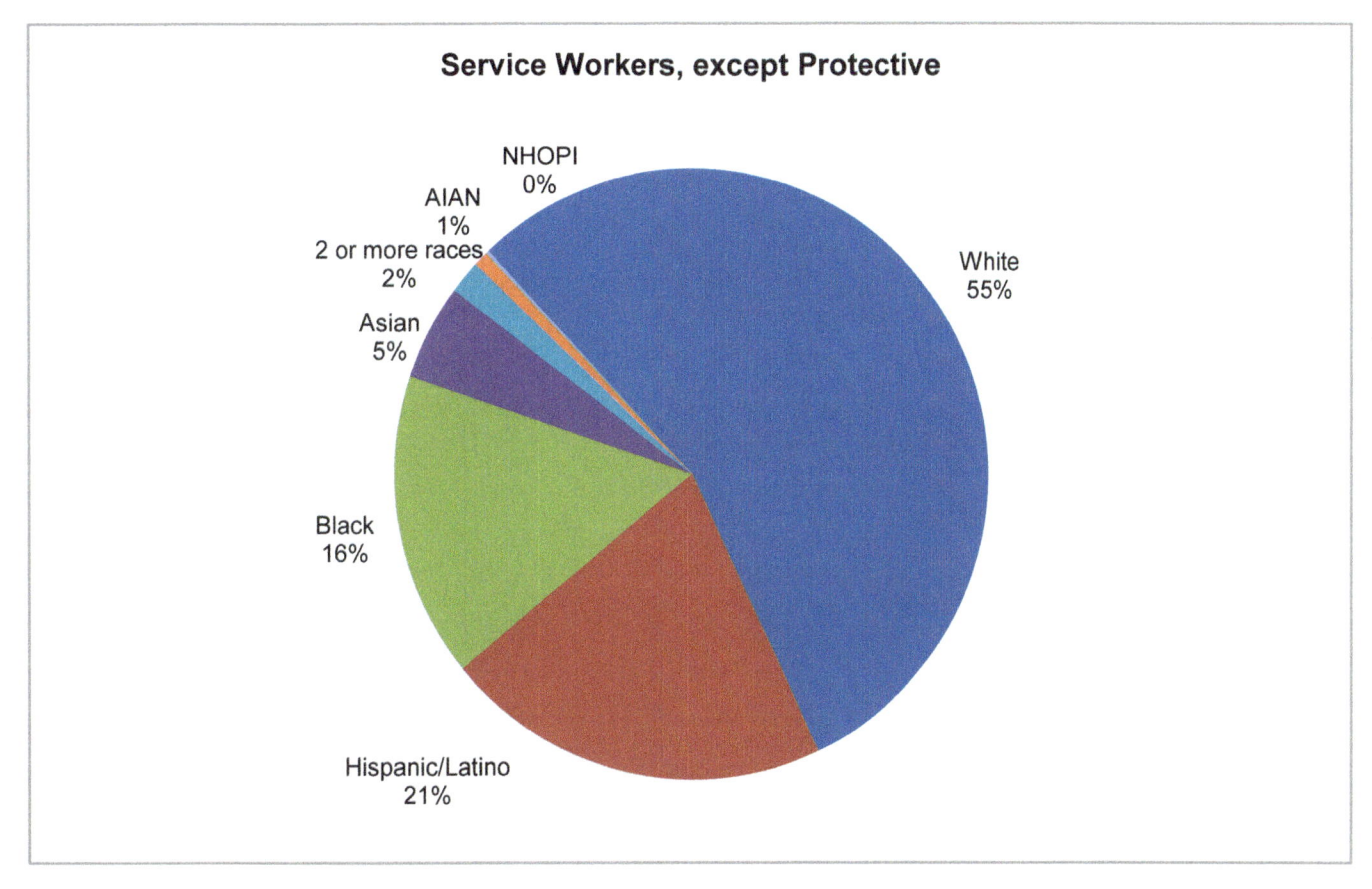

- White: 55%
- Hispanic/Latino: 21%
- Black: 16%
- Asian: 5%
- 2 or more races: 2%
- AIAN: 1%
- NHOPI: 0%

Figure A-15.1

Service Workers, except Protective

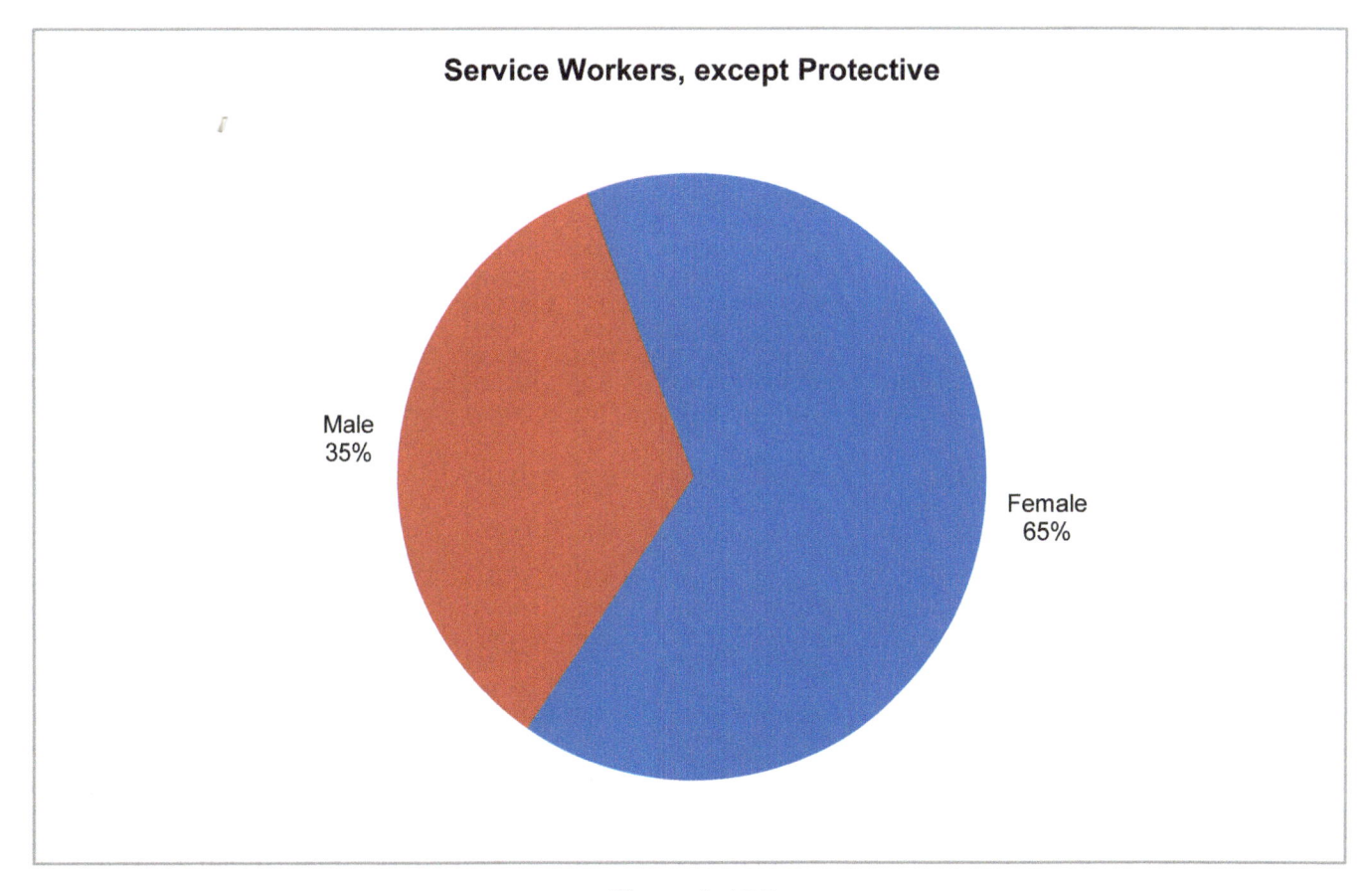

- Female: 65%
- Male: 35%

Figure A-15.2

A-15. **Detailed Occupations in the Service Workers, except Protective Occupation Group, by Sex, Race, and Hispanic Origin, 2006–2010**

Census occupation code	Service Workers, except Protective Occupation Group	Total who worked in the last 5 years	Male Number	Male Percent	Female Number	Female Percent	Hispanic or Latino Number	Hispanic or Latino Percent	White alone, not Hispanic or Latino Number	White alone, not Hispanic or Latino Percent
3600	Nursing, psychiatric, and home health aides	2,207,375	265,755	12.0	1,941,620	88.0	281,835	12.8	1,040,750	47.1
3610	Occupational therapy assistants and aides	13,580	1,175	8.7	12,405	91.3	1,060	7.8	10,515	77.4
3620	Physical therapist assistants and aides	67,410	17,200	25.5	50,215	74.5	6,660	9.9	49,845	73.9
3630	Massage therapists	133,790	22,300	16.7	111,490	83.3	11,720	8.8	105,140	78.6
3640	Dental assistants	275,095	10,140	3.7	264,960	96.3	52,805	19.2	185,685	67.5
3645	Medical assistants	393,055	23,845	6.1	369,210	93.9	91,330	23.2	222,760	56.7
3647	Pharmacy aides	43,825	10,155	23.2	33,665	76.8	7,425	16.9	25,795	58.9
3648	Veterinary assistants and laboratory animal caretakers	43,690	8,745	20.0	34,945	80.0	3,935	9.0	35,835	82.0
3649	Phlebotomists	88,335	11,680	13.2	76,650	86.8	13,035	14.8	51,600	58.4
3655	Health care support workers, all other, including medical equipment preparers	154,475	36,300	23.5	118,170	76.5	17,330	11.2	87,650	56.7
4000	Chefs and head cooks	336,595	267,920	79.6	68,670	20.4	66,005	19.6	167,540	49.8
4010	First-line supervisors of food preparation and serving workers	593,090	245,265	41.4	347,825	58.6	100,145	16.9	365,025	61.5
4020	Cooks	2,300,210	1,342,460	58.4	957,750	41.6	666,215	29.0	1,059,905	46.1
4030	Food preparation workers	865,550	356,210	41.2	509,340	58.8	209,370	24.2	470,530	54.4
4040	Bartenders	423,135	180,090	42.6	243,045	57.4	46,095	10.9	337,315	79.7
4050	Combined food preparation and serving workers, including fast food	353,535	117,825	33.3	235,715	66.7	57,640	16.3	218,490	61.8
4060	Counter attendants, cafeteria, food concession, and coffee shop	275,630	91,005	33.0	184,625	67.0	41,485	15.1	180,770	65.6
4110	Waiters and waitresses	2,275,425	623,275	27.4	1,652,155	72.6	371,825	16.3	1,552,220	68.2
4120	Food servers, nonrestaurant	209,140	67,460	32.3	141,680	67.7	36,595	17.5	106,445	50.9
4130	Miscellaneous food preparation and serving related workers, including dining room and cafeteria attendants and bartender helpers	385,195	216,275	56.1	168,920	43.9	120,075	31.2	191,050	49.6
4140	Dishwashers	333,210	260,000	78.0	73,205	22.0	112,050	33.6	151,975	45.6
4150	Hosts and hostesses, restaurant, lounge, and coffee shop	296,970	38,980	13.1	257,995	86.9	46,220	15.6	203,835	68.6
4200	First-line supervisors of housekeeping and janitorial workers	268,370	163,215	60.8	105,155	39.2	58,445	21.8	151,500	56.5
4220	Janitors and building cleaners	2,607,880	1,781,815	68.3	826,065	31.7	691,690	26.5	1,321,200	50.7
4230	Maids and housekeeping cleaners	1,566,300	183,870	11.7	1,382,430	88.3	647,245	41.3	549,045	35.1
4240	Pest control workers	69,515	65,960	94.9	3,550	5.1	9,890	14.2	50,960	73.3
4300	First-line supervisors of gaming workers	80,390	44,870	55.8	35,520	44.2	6,725	8.4	59,935	74.6
4320	First-line supervisors of personal service workers	188,200	72,035	38.3	116,165	61.7	17,625	9.4	133,345	70.9
4400	Gaming services workers	112,340	58,110	51.7	54,230	48.3	11,855	10.6	58,450	52.0
4410	Motion picture projectionists	9,260	7,700	83.2	1,555	16.8	800	8.6	7,380	79.7
4420	Ushers, lobby attendants, and ticket takers	51,950	29,340	56.5	22,610	43.5	7,075	13.6	32,885	63.3
4430	Miscellaneous entertainment attendants and related workers	196,765	115,745	58.8	81,020	41.2	24,020	12.2	136,775	69.5
4460	Embalmers and funeral attendants	15,315	11,605	75.8	3,710	24.2	1,105	7.2	12,325	80.5
4500	Barbers	94,910	72,475	76.4	22,435	23.6	15,325	16.1	45,905	48.4
4510	Hairdressers, hairstylists, and cosmetologists	779,220	64,580	8.3	714,640	91.7	104,080	13.4	535,000	68.7
4520	Miscellaneous personal appearance workers	242,260	32,210	13.3	210,050	86.7	23,355	9.6	86,660	35.8
4530	Baggage porters, bellhops, and concierges	79,655	63,505	79.7	16,150	20.3	19,455	24.4	32,580	40.9
4540	Tour and travel guides	49,330	25,535	51.8	23,795	48.2	3,170	6.4	38,230	77.5
4600	Childcare workers	1,462,075	86,280	5.9	1,375,795	94.1	282,370	19.3	857,555	58.7
4610	Personal care aides	927,270	133,510	14.4	793,765	85.6	168,275	18.1	447,245	48.2
4620	Recreation and fitness workers	400,220	143,280	35.8	256,940	64.2	36,625	9.2	295,895	73.9
4640	Residential advisors	73,260	26,780	36.6	46,475	63.4	4,375	6.0	44,950	61.4
4650	Personal care and service workers, all other	95,890	49,830	52.0	46,065	48.0	14,480	15.1	63,905	66.6
9050	Flight attendants	97,660	19,950	20.4	77,710	79.6	9,120	9.3	70,550	72.2
9415	Transportation attendants, except flight attendants	35,790	11,630	32.5	24,160	67.5	6,045	16.9	15,330	42.8

PART A—NATIONAL DATA

A-15. Detailed Occupations in the Service Workers, except Protective Occupation Group, by Sex, Race, and Hispanic Origin, 2006–2010—Continued

Census occupation code	Service Workers, except Protective Occupation Group	Black alone, not Hispanic or Latino Number	Percent	American Indian and Alaska Native alone, not Hispanic or Latino Number	Percent	Asian alone, not Hispanic or Latino Number	Percent	Native Hawaiian and Other Pacific Islander alone, not Hispanic or Latino Number	Percent	Two or more races, not Hispanic or Latino Number	Percent
3600	Nursing, psychiatric, and home health aides	730,795	33.1	19,805	0.9	90,410	4.1	4,495	0.2	39,290	1.8
3610	Occupational therapy assistants and aides	1,295	9.5	55	0.4	480	3.5	20	0.1	155	1.1
3620	Physical therapist assistants and aides	6,255	9.3	285	0.4	3,350	5.0	205	0.3	800	1.2
3630	Massage therapists	5,445	4.1	655	0.5	7,150	5.3	175	0.1	3,505	2.6
3640	Dental assistants	16,695	6.1	2,125	0.8	13,205	4.8	530	0.2	4,050	1.5
3645	Medical assistants	53,510	13.6	2,035	0.5	16,000	4.1	1,265	0.3	6,155	1.6
3647	Pharmacy aides	5,490	12.5	200	0.5	4,250	9.7	90	0.2	585	1.3
3648	Veterinary assistants and laboratory animal caretakers	2,220	5.1	150	0.3	745	1.7	20	0.0	785	1.8
3649	Phlebotomists	17,575	19.9	550	0.6	3,845	4.4	165	0.2	1,560	1.8
3655	Health care support workers, all other, including medical equipment preparers	38,695	25.0	980	0.6	6,865	4.4	355	0.2	2,600	1.7
4000	Chefs and head cooks	39,000	11.6	1,210	0.4	56,435	16.8	635	0.2	5,770	1.7
4010	First-line supervisors of food preparation and serving workers	87,240	14.7	4,410	0.7	24,645	4.2	1,065	0.2	10,550	1.8
4020	Cooks	393,790	17.1	20,020	0.9	117,535	5.1	4,825	0.2	37,920	1.6
4030	Food preparation workers	107,645	12.4	5,940	0.7	52,045	6.0	2,040	0.2	17,990	2.1
4040	Bartenders	17,870	4.2	2,810	0.7	9,925	2.3	765	0.2	8,355	2.0
4050	Combined food preparation and serving workers, including fast food	55,220	15.6	2,580	0.7	11,225	3.2	670	0.2	7,715	2.2
4060	Counter attendants, cafeteria, food concession, and coffee shop	33,440	12.1	1,655	0.6	10,375	3.8	560	0.2	7,345	2.7
4110	Waiters and waitresses	162,930	7.2	13,005	0.6	124,415	5.5	2,850	0.1	48,190	2.1
4120	Food servers, nonrestaurant	48,170	23.0	1,320	0.6	12,210	5.8	510	0.2	3,895	1.9
4130	Miscellaneous food preparation and serving related workers, including dining room and cafeteria attendants and bartender helpers	43,105	11.2	3,060	0.8	20,060	5.2	930	0.2	6,915	1.8
4140	Dishwashers	49,235	14.8	3,075	0.9	9,945	3.0	720	0.2	6,210	1.9
4150	Hosts and hostesses, restaurant, lounge, and coffee shop	25,255	8.5	1,565	0.5	11,490	3.9	395	0.1	8,220	2.8
4200	First-line supervisors of housekeeping and janitorial workers	45,305	16.9	2,085	0.8	6,670	2.5	610	0.2	3,755	1.4
4220	Janitors and building cleaners	458,795	17.6	23,820	0.9	73,075	2.8	4,520	0.2	34,790	1.3
4230	Maids and housekeeping cleaners	270,320	17.3	13,985	0.9	57,935	3.7	2,720	0.2	25,055	1.6
4240	Pest control workers	6,310	9.1	235	0.3	880	1.3	135	0.2	1,105	1.6
4300	First-line supervisors of gaming workers	5,080	6.3	2,350	2.9	4,800	6.0	160	0.2	1,340	1.7
4320	First-line supervisors of personal service workers	14,995	8.0	875	0.5	18,305	9.7	190	0.1	2,870	1.5
4400	Gaming services workers	10,610	9.4	3,745	3.3	25,015	22.3	280	0.2	2,385	2.1
4410	Motion picture projectionists	530	5.7	35	0.4	325	3.5	0	0.0	190	2.1
4420	Ushers, lobby attendants, and ticket takers	9,140	17.6	245	0.5	1,385	2.7	45	0.1	1,180	2.3
4430	Miscellaneous entertainment attendants and related workers	21,605	11.0	2,190	1.1	6,990	3.6	455	0.2	4,735	2.4
4460	Embalmers and funeral attendants	1,595	10.4	0	0.0	155	1.0	0	0.0	135	0.9
4500	Barbers	27,835	29.3	370	0.4	4,045	4.3	40	0.0	1,390	1.5
4510	Hairdressers, hairstylists, and cosmetologists	86,685	11.1	2,965	0.4	39,365	5.1	390	0.1	10,730	1.4
4520	Miscellaneous personal appearance workers	9,775	4.0	345	0.1	118,460	48.9	135	0.1	3,530	1.5
4530	Baggage porters, bellhops, and concierges	18,750	23.5	475	0.6	5,900	7.4	540	0.7	1,955	2.5
4540	Tour and travel guides	3,150	6.4	505	1.0	2,705	5.5	210	0.4	1,360	2.8
4600	Childcare workers	241,290	16.5	10,250	0.7	42,750	2.9	2,010	0.1	25,840	1.8
4610	Personal care aides	217,370	23.4	10,680	1.2	62,100	6.7	4,190	0.5	17,410	1.9
4620	Recreation and fitness workers	44,765	11.2	3,025	0.8	10,790	2.7	710	0.2	8,405	2.1
4640	Residential advisors	18,385	25.1	1,110	1.5	2,390	3.3	75	0.1	1,970	2.7
4650	Personal care and service workers, all other	10,115	10.5	760	0.8	3,965	4.1	385	0.4	2,285	2.4
9050	Flight attendants	10,115	10.4	330	0.3	4,775	4.9	565	0.6	2,205	2.3
9415	Transportation attendants, except flight attendants	12,205	34.1	180	0.5	1,410	3.9	115	0.3	505	1.4

A-16. **Educational Attainment by Selected Age Groups, Sex, and Race/Ethnicity for the Civilian Labor Force 20 Years Old and Older, EEO Tabulation, 2006–2010**

Educational attainment and age group	Total who worked in the last 5 years	Male Number	Male Percent	Female Number	Female Percent	Hispanic or Latino Number	Hispanic or Latino Percent	White alone, not Hispanic or Latino Number	White alone, not Hispanic or Latino Percent
Total, All Education Levels									
Total, all ages	146,623,635	77,602,685	52.9	69,020,945	47.1	21,123,280	14.4	98,637,100	67.3
20 to 24 years	15,537,930	8,055,965	51.8	7,481,965	48.2	3,066,875	19.7	9,351,420	60.2
25 to 29 years	16,803,350	8,881,155	52.9	7,922,195	47.1	3,273,230	19.5	10,121,040	60.2
30 to 34 years	15,906,240	8,590,895	54.0	7,315,345	46.0	3,124,590	19.6	9,471,425	59.5
35 to 39 years	16,926,595	9,109,760	53.8	7,816,835	46.2	2,951,735	17.4	10,528,845	62.2
40 years and over	81,449,525	42,964,915	52.8	38,484,610	47.2	8,706,845	10.7	59,164,375	72.6
Not High School Graduate									
Total, all ages	15,106,300	9,507,520	62.9	5,598,780	37.1	6,823,700	45.2	5,515,145	36.5
20 to 24 years	1,728,145	1,150,070	66.5	578,075	33.5	799,425	46.3	603,480	34.9
25 to 29 years	1,807,225	1,214,310	67.2	592,915	32.8	965,580	53.4	556,795	30.8
30 to 34 years	1,754,150	1,151,835	65.7	602,320	34.3	1,019,040	58.1	477,020	27.2
35 to 39 years	1,802,370	1,153,235	64.0	649,135	36.0	1,003,480	55.7	526,610	29.2
40 years and over	8,014,410	4,838,070	60.4	3,176,335	39.6	3,036,175	37.9	3,351,235	41.8
High School Graduate (including Equivalency)									
Total, all ages	39,573,075	22,097,015	55.8	17,476,060	44.2	6,004,745	15.2	26,337,315	66.6
20 to 24 years	4,571,935	2,696,535	59.0	1,875,395	41.0	1,041,155	22.8	2,573,070	56.3
25 to 29 years	4,164,440	2,539,905	61.0	1,624,530	39.0	1,002,395	24.1	2,315,720	55.6
30 to 34 years	3,838,935	2,329,770	60.7	1,509,165	39.3	885,235	23.1	2,168,795	56.5
35 to 39 years	4,254,090	2,489,225	58.5	1,764,865	41.5	812,925	19.1	2,563,935	60.3
40 years and over	22,743,675	12,041,575	52.9	10,702,100	47.1	2,263,035	10.0	16,715,800	73.5
Some College or Associate Degree									
Total, all ages	46,902,415	22,908,965	48.8	23,993,450	51.2	5,377,715	11.5	32,725,700	69.8
20 to 24 years	6,958,705	3,283,530	47.2	3,675,175	52.8	1,043,750	15.0	4,500,320	64.7
25 to 29 years	5,314,690	2,660,550	50.1	2,654,140	49.9	862,580	16.2	3,310,305	62.3
30 to 34 years	4,856,305	2,451,435	50.5	2,404,870	49.5	757,510	15.6	3,052,945	62.9
35 to 39 years	5,129,715	2,547,905	49.7	2,581,810	50.3	684,880	13.4	3,364,495	65.6
40 years and over	24,642,995	11,965,545	48.6	12,677,450	51.4	2,028,995	8.2	18,497,635	75.1
Bachelor's Degree									
Total, all ages	29,026,545	14,771,400	50.9	14,255,145	49.1	2,033,815	7.0	21,887,205	75.4
20 to 24 years	2,127,115	868,830	40.8	1,258,285	59.2	169,605	8.0	1,571,920	73.9
25 to 29 years	4,196,335	1,938,170	46.2	2,258,165	53.8	356,920	8.5	3,029,015	72.2
30 to 34 years	3,568,355	1,797,785	50.4	1,770,570	49.6	326,125	9.1	2,504,915	70.2
35 to 39 years	3,655,810	1,887,955	51.6	1,767,855	48.4	304,365	8.3	2,627,290	71.9
40 years and over	15,478,930	8,278,660	53.5	7,200,270	46.5	876,800	5.7	12,154,070	78.5
Master's Degree									
Total, all ages	11,060,135	5,233,275	47.3	5,826,860	52.7	595,060	5.4	8,413,250	76.1
20 to 24 years	127,380	48,295	37.9	79,085	62.1	9,745	7.7	87,055	68.3
25 to 29 years	1,004,530	386,155	38.4	618,375	61.6	63,275	6.3	691,340	68.8
30 to 34 years	1,352,330	579,970	42.9	772,360	57.1	96,570	7.1	914,715	67.6
35 to 39 years	1,470,965	689,195	46.9	781,765	53.1	102,390	7.0	1,026,565	69.8
40 years and over	7,104,930	3,529,660	49.7	3,575,275	50.3	323,075	4.5	5,693,575	80.1
Doctoral Degree or Professional Degree									
Total, all ages	4,955,170	3,084,515	62.2	1,870,655	37.8	288,245	5.8	3,758,485	75.8
20 to 24 years	24,645	8,705	35.3	15,945	64.7	3,195	13.0	15,575	63.2
25 to 29 years	316,135	142,065	44.9	174,075	55.1	22,485	7.1	217,865	68.9
30 to 34 years	536,160	280,100	52.2	256,060	47.8	40,105	7.5	353,035	65.8
35 to 39 years	613,640	342,245	55.8	271,400	44.2	43,700	7.1	419,950	68.4
40 years and over	3,464,585	2,311,405	66.7	1,153,180	33.3	178,765	5.2	2,752,060	79.4

A-16. Educational Attainment by Selected Age Groups, Sex, and Race/Ethnicity for the Civilian Labor Force 20 Years Old and Older, EEO Tabulation, 2006–2010—Continued

Educational attainment and age group	Black alone, not Hispanic or Latino Number	Percent	American Indian and Alaska Native alone, not Hispanic or Latino Number	Percent	Asian alone, not Hispanic or Latino Number	Percent	Native Hawaiian and Other Pacific Islander alone, not Hispanic or Latino Number	Percent	Two or more races, not Hispanic or Latino Number	Percent
Total, All Education Levels										
Total, all ages	16,503,650	11.3	841,485	0.6	7,221,350	4.9	222,610	0.2	2,074,160	1.4
20 to 24 years	2,007,575	12.9	105,945	0.7	630,720	4.1	32,240	0.2	343,155	2.2
25 to 29 years	2,028,475	12.1	101,070	0.6	926,920	5.5	33,445	0.2	319,165	1.9
30 to 34 years	1,930,885	12.1	95,605	0.6	984,855	6.2	28,505	0.2	270,385	1.7
35 to 39 years	2,049,455	12.1	103,970	0.6	1,013,150	6.0	29,410	0.2	250,025	1.5
40 years and over	8,487,265	10.4	434,895	0.5	3,665,710	4.5	99,010	0.1	891,435	1.1
Not High School Graduate										
Total, all ages	1,802,000	11.9	108,350	0.7	659,410	4.4	20,890	0.1	176,810	1.2
20 to 24 years	243,505	14.1	17,440	1.0	30,180	1.7	3,280	0.2	30,835	1.8
25 to 29 years	207,550	11.5	13,120	0.7	36,740	2.0	2,745	0.2	24,690	1.4
30 to 34 years	176,980	10.1	11,310	0.6	48,665	2.8	2,205	0.1	18,930	1.1
35 to 39 years	164,405	9.1	11,720	0.7	74,840	4.2	2,400	0.1	18,915	1.0
40 years and over	1,009,565	12.6	54,760	0.7	468,985	5.9	10,260	0.1	83,425	1.0
High School Graduate (including Equivalency)										
Total, all ages	5,277,760	13.3	285,255	0.7	1,069,400	2.7	83,025	0.2	515,575	1.3
20 to 24 years	690,190	15.1	42,715	0.9	111,665	2.4	12,815	0.3	100,320	2.2
25 to 29 years	618,010	14.8	36,290	0.9	104,080	2.5	13,460	0.3	74,480	1.8
30 to 34 years	580,605	15.1	31,105	0.8	102,780	2.7	10,700	0.3	59,715	1.6
35 to 39 years	640,405	15.1	34,240	0.8	131,165	3.1	11,625	0.3	59,800	1.4
40 years and over	2,748,545	12.1	140,905	0.6	619,705	2.7	34,420	0.2	221,270	1.0
Some College or Associate Degree										
Total, all ages	6,022,820	12.8	315,435	0.7	1,597,880	3.4	84,670	0.2	778,195	1.7
20 to 24 years	905,810	13.0	39,800	0.6	291,320	4.2	13,765	0.2	163,940	2.4
25 to 29 years	772,480	14.5	37,805	0.7	202,870	3.8	12,180	0.2	116,465	2.2
30 to 34 years	725,160	14.9	36,690	0.8	176,150	3.6	10,760	0.2	97,100	2.0
35 to 39 years	758,435	14.8	40,570	0.8	184,480	3.6	10,070	0.2	86,780	1.7
40 years and over	2,860,935	11.6	160,565	0.7	743,060	3.0	37,895	0.2	313,910	1.3
Bachelor's Degree										
Total, all ages	2,293,570	7.9	88,945	0.3	2,301,100	7.9	25,180	0.1	396,725	1.4
20 to 24 years	157,755	7.4	5,540	0.3	175,155	8.2	2,175	0.1	44,965	2.1
25 to 29 years	341,280	8.1	10,855	0.3	375,890	9.0	4,120	0.1	78,260	1.9
30 to 34 years	307,550	8.6	12,145	0.3	352,515	9.9	3,650	0.1	61,465	1.7
35 to 39 years	324,280	8.9	12,470	0.3	332,270	9.1	3,735	0.1	51,400	1.4
40 years and over	1,162,710	7.5	47,940	0.3	1,065,270	6.9	11,500	0.1	160,640	1.0
Master's Degree										
Total, all ages	852,980	7.7	31,855	0.3	1,018,715	9.2	6,425	0.1	141,855	1.3
20 to 24 years	8,850	6.9	310	0.2	18,755	14.7	155	0.1	2510	2.0
25 to 29 years	72,130	7.2	2,400	0.2	156,155	15.5	710	0.1	18520	1.8
30 to 34 years	111,260	8.2	3,175	0.2	203,125	15.0	760	0.1	22715	1.7
35 to 39 years	125,875	8.6	3,750	0.3	188,680	12.8	1,140	0.1	22,565	1.5
40 years and over	534,860	7.5	22,220	0.3	451,995	6.4	3,660	0.1	75,545	1.1
Doctoral Degree or Professional Degree										
Total, all ages	254,520	5.1	11,645	0.2	574,840	11.6	2,425	0.0	65,010	1.3
20 to 24 years	1,460	5.9	140	0.6	3,640	14.8	45	0.2	590	2.4
25 to 29 years	17,025	5.4	595	0.2	51,185	16.2	235	0.1	6750	2.1
30 to 34 years	29,330	5.5	1,180	0.2	101,615	19.0	430	0.1	10460	2.0
35 to 39 years	36,060	5.9	1,220	0.2	101,710	16.6	440	0.1	10565	1.7
40 years and over	170,645	4.9	8,510	0.2	316,690	9.1	1,275	0.0	36,635	1.1

A-17 **Detailed Occupation, by Educational Attainment for Persons Age 16 and Older (worksite geography), 2006–2010**

Census occupation code	Occupation by educational attainment for persons age 16 and older	Total workers	Not high school graduate Number	Not high school graduate Percent	High school graduate (including equivalency) Number	High school graduate (including equivalency) Percent
	Total, all occupations	138,049,890	15,163,025	11.0	36,711,835	26.6
0010	Chief executives and legislators	1,109,770	19,585	1.8	124,240	11.2
0020	General and operations managers	918,860	20,385	2.2	149,855	16.3
0040	Advertising and promotions managers	57,365	335	0.6	4,340	7.6
0050	Marketing and sales managers	816,290	8,290	1.0	70,840	8.7
0060	Public relations and fundraising managers	54,395	245	0.5	3,280	6.0
0100	Administrative services managers	105,235	1,965	1.9	19,700	18.7
0110	Computer and information systems managers	459,680	2,045	0.4	20,075	4.4
0120	Financial managers	1,053,615	10,055	1.0	125,670	11.9
0135	Compensation and benefits managers	26,320	235	0.9	2,695	10.2
0136	Human resources managers	312,885	8,575	2.7	41,840	13.4
0137	Training and development managers	41,090	615	1.5	3,955	9.6
0140	Industrial production managers	228,540	8,440	3.7	49,515	21.7
0150	Purchasing managers	181,460	2,005	1.1	21,880	12.1
0160	Transportation, storage, and distribution managers	214,680	11,775	5.5	67,845	31.6
0205	Farmers, ranchers, and other agricultural managers	645,785	76,405	11.8	249,805	38.7
0220	Construction managers	823,405	61,960	7.5	243,225	29.5
0230	Education administrators	812,775	5,880	0.7	42,500	5.2
0300	Architectural and engineering managers	141,350	770	0.5	5,155	3.6
0310	Food service managers	890,555	88,440	9.9	272,865	30.6
0330	Gaming managers	17,735	1,100	6.2	4,850	27.3
0340	Lodging managers	132,305	6,330	4.8	26,290	19.9
0350	Medical and health services managers	512,680	5,850	1.1	49,320	9.6
0360	Natural sciences managers	18,690	90	0.5	265	1.4
0410	Property, real estate, and community association managers	526,035	26,365	5.0	110,190	20.9
0410	Social and community service managers	308,715	5,115	1.7	26,480	8.6
0425	Emergency management directors	3,019	4	0.1	195	6.5
0430	Miscellaneous managers, including funeral service managers and postmasters and mail superintendents	3,020,000	87,060	2.9	465,060	15.4
0500	Agents and business managers of artists, performers, and athletes	42,705	1,310	3.1	5,565	13.0
0510	Buyers and purchasing agents, farm products	10,900	1,135	10.4	3,415	31.3
0520	Wholesale and retail buyers, except farm products	216,325	8,730	4.0	54,795	25.3
0530	Purchasing agents, except wholesale, retail, and farm products	255,245	5,380	2.1	49,870	19.5
0540	Claims adjusters, appraisers, examiners, and investigators	280,415	2,770	1.0	48,740	17.4
0565	Compliance officers	170,560	2,230	1.3	19,710	11.6
0600	Cost estimators	122,050	4,120	3.4	28,515	23.4
0630	Human resources workers	604,755	9,025	1.5	73,480	12.2
0640	Compensation, benefits, and job analysis specialists	95,825	1,075	1.1	13,905	14.5
0650	Training and development specialists	122,630	2,705	2.2	17,995	14.7
0700	Logisticians	68,655	1,120	1.6	10,915	15.9
0710	Management analysts	643,655	4,130	0.6	32,970	5.1
0725	Meeting, convention, and event planners	55,505	735	1.3	5,405	9.7
0726	Fundraisers	79,510	590	0.7	4,070	5.1
0735	Market research analysts and marketing specialists	172,635	950	0.6	8,035	4.7
0740	Business operations specialists, all other	215,775	4,645	2.2	31,260	14.5
0800	Accountants and auditors	1,999,480	2,620	0.1	90,765	4.5
0810	Appraisers and assessors of real estate	108,125	875	0.8	13,805	12.8
0820	Budget analysts	51,165	300	0.6	3,525	6.9
0830	Credit analysts	28,495	205	0.7	3,320	11.7
0840	Financial analysts	80,645	345	0.4	2,695	3.3

PART A—NATIONAL DATA

A-17 Detailed Occupation, by Educational Attainment for Persons Age 16 and Older (worksite geography), 2006–2010—Continued

Census occupation code	Occupation by educational attainment for persons age 16 and older	Some college or associate degree Number	Some college or associate degree Percent	Bachelor's degree Number	Bachelor's degree Percent	Graduate or professional degree Number	Graduate or professional degree Percent
	Total, all occupations	43,914,705	31.8	27,140,875	19.7	15,119,450	11.0
0010	Chief executives and legislators	252,560	22.8	429,005	38.7	284,380	25.6
0020	General and operations managers	303,405	33.0	309,815	33.7	135,400	14.7
0040	Advertising and promotions managers	10,790	18.8	35,245	61.4	6,655	11.6
0050	Marketing and sales managers	198,840	24.4	396,940	48.6	141,380	17.3
0060	Public relations and fundraising managers	10,440	19.2	27,265	50.1	13,165	24.2
0100	Administrative services managers	43,375	41.2	28,760	27.3	11,435	10.9
0110	Computer and information systems managers	113,535	24.7	211,945	46.1	112,080	24.4
0120	Financial managers	295,130	28.0	423,055	40.2	199,705	19.0
0135	Compensation and benefits managers	8,025	30.5	10,535	40.0	4,830	18.4
0136	Human resources managers	91,480	29.2	111,865	35.8	59,125	18.9
0137	Training and development managers	11,795	28.7	14,425	35.1	10,300	25.1
0140	Industrial production managers	72,380	31.7	70,425	30.8	27,780	12.2
0150	Purchasing managers	55,850	30.8	69,320	38.2	32,405	17.9
0160	Transportation, storage, and distribution managers	79,345	37.0	43,445	20.2	12,270	5.7
0205	Farmers, ranchers, and other agricultural managers	182,855	28.3	111,920	17.3	24,800	3.8
0220	Construction managers	272,575	33.1	200,555	24.4	45,090	5.5
0230	Education administrators	123,855	15.2	181,835	22.4	458,705	56.4
0300	Architectural and engineering managers	17,305	12.2	66,605	47.1	51,515	36.4
0310	Food service managers	333,110	37.4	166,795	18.7	29,345	3.3
0330	Gaming managers	7,410	41.8	3,675	20.7	700	3.9
0340	Lodging managers	48,520	36.7	39,830	30.1	11,335	8.6
0350	Medical and health services managers	150,225	29.3	156,255	30.5	151,030	29.5
0360	Natural sciences managers	1,305	7.0	5,960	31.9	11,070	59.2
0410	Property, real estate, and community association managers	191,020	36.3	147,050	28.0	51,410	9.8
0410	Social and community service managers	68,080	22.1	115,905	37.5	93,135	30.2
0425	Emergency management directors	895	29.6	1,210	40.1	715	23.7
0430	Miscellaneous managers, including funeral service managers and postmasters and mail superintendents	864,065	28.6	1,029,930	34.1	573,885	19.0
0500	Agents and business managers of artists, performers, and athletes	12,690	29.7	17,790	41.7	5,350	12.5
0510	Buyers and purchasing agents, farm products	3,240	29.7	2,710	24.9	400	3.7
0520	Wholesale and retail buyers, except farm products	82,005	37.9	62,385	28.8	8,410	3.9
0530	Purchasing agents, except wholesale, retail, and farm products	96,630	37.9	82,700	32.4	20,665	8.1
0540	Claims adjusters, appraisers, examiners, and investigators	101,535	36.2	109,225	39.0	18,145	6.5
0565	Compliance officers	51,705	30.3	64,870	38.0	32,045	18.8
0600	Cost estimators	50,465	41.3	34,305	28.1	4,645	3.8
0630	Human resources workers	187,360	31.0	243,010	40.2	91,880	15.2
0640	Compensation, benefits, and job analysis specialists	35,980	37.5	35,675	37.2	9,190	9.6
0650	Training and development specialists	42,480	34.6	40,750	33.2	18,700	15.2
0700	Logisticians	27,080	39.4	22,865	33.3	6,675	9.7
0710	Management analysts	112,075	17.4	272,545	42.3	221,935	34.5
0725	Meeting, convention, and event planners	15,825	28.5	27,885	50.2	5,655	10.2
0726	Fundraisers	14,625	18.4	38,795	48.8	21,430	27.0
0735	Market research analysts and marketing specialists	30,840	17.9	87,275	50.6	45,535	26.4
0740	Business operations specialists, all other	73,775	34.2	73,210	33.9	32,885	15.2
0800	Accountants and auditors	373,220	18.7	1,140,160	57.0	392,715	19.6
0810	Appraisers and assessors of real estate	40,045	37.0	43,255	40.0	10,145	9.4
0820	Budget analysts	12,375	24.2	21,950	42.9	13,015	25.4
0830	Credit analysts	7,860	27.6	12,945	45.4	4,165	14.6
0840	Financial analysts	8,950	11.1	39,830	49.4	28,825	35.7

A-17 **Detailed Occupation, by Educational Attainment for Persons Age 16 and Older (worksite geography), 2006–2010**—*Continued*

Census occupation code	Occupation by educational attainment for persons age 16 and older	Total workers	Not high school graduate Number	Not high school graduate Percent	High school graduate (including equivalency) Number	High school graduate (including equivalency) Percent
0850	Personal financial advisors	339,440	1,320	0.4	14,735	4.3
0860	Insurance underwriters	98,180	635	0.6	16,470	16.8
0900	Financial examiners	12,590	60	0.5	795	6.3
0910	Credit counselors and loan officers	356,545	4,250	1.2	53,145	14.9
0930	Tax examiners and collectors, and revenue agents	61,470	440	0.7	11,935	19.4
0940	Tax preparers	87,325	1,690	1.9	13,215	15.1
0950	Financial specialists, all other	61,580	1,015	1.6	8,615	14.0
1005	Computer and information research scientists	15,305	65	0.4	390	2.5
1006	Computer systems analysts	460,805	1,955	0.4	23,375	5.1
1007	Information security analysts	40,345	335	0.8	2,900	7.2
1010	Computer programmers	494,865	3,110	0.6	26,035	5.3
1020	Software developers, applications and systems software	822,755	2,445	0.3	20,255	2.5
1030	Web developers	151,115	1,875	1.2	9,745	6.4
1050	Computer support specialists	483,450	5,235	1.1	58,725	12.1
1060	Database administrators	102,310	560	0.5	5,290	5.2
1105	Network and computer systems administrators	256,755	1,680	0.7	21,625	8.4
1106	Computer network architects	105,090	580	0.6	6,485	6.2
1107	Computer occupations, all other	271,400	2,900	1.1	23,655	8.7
1200	Actuaries	23,630	55	0.2	45	0.2
1220	Operations research analysts	115,575	495	0.4	7,640	6.6
1240	Miscellaneous mathematical science occupations, including mathematicians and statisticians	38,670	155	0.4	190	0.5
1300	Architects, except naval	186,015	125	0.1	2,970	1.6
1310	Surveyors, cartographers, and photogrammetrists	37,555	40	0.1	30	0.1
1320	Aerospace engineers	135,060	320	0.2	3,195	2.4
1340	Biomedical and agricultural engineers	13,305	0	0.0	415	3.1
1350	Chemical engineers	58,280	130	0.2	1,485	2.5
1360	Civil engineers	309,490	310	0.1	9,580	3.1
1400	Computer hardware engineers	62,145	40	0.1	3,470	5.6
1410	Electrical and electronics engineers	230,650	165	0.1	8,240	3.6
1420	Environmental engineers	33,115	50	0.2	1,270	3.8
1430	Industrial engineers, including health and safety	168,050	135	0.1	11,290	6.7
1440	Marine engineers and naval architects	10,920	0	0.0	1,005	9.2
1450	Materials engineers	31,115	30	0.1	2,055	6.6
1460	Mechanical engineers	225,240	170	0.1	10,965	4.9
1520	Petroleum, mining and geological engineers, including mining safety engineers	28,045	50	0.2	1,360	4.8
1530	Miscellaneous engineers, including nuclear engineers	442,630	600	0.1	14,400	3.3
1540	Drafters	192,470	3,730	1.9	23,860	12.4
1550	Engineering technicians, except drafters	407,510	15,470	3.8	92,910	22.8
1560	Surveying and mapping technicians	78,775	5,085	6.5	24,045	30.5
1600	Agricultural and food scientists	29,450	20	0.1	50	0.2
1610	Biological scientists	82,620	40	0.0	70	0.1
1640	Conservation scientists and foresters	24,625	20	0.1	15	0.1
1650	Medical scientists, and life scientists, all other	114,850	175	0.2	115	0.1
1700	Astronomers and physicists	12,429	20	0.2	4	0.0
1710	Atmospheric and space scientists	8,865	0	0.0	0	0.0
1720	Chemists and materials scientists	87,245	115	0.1	65	0.1
1740	Environmental scientists and geoscientists	75,945	80	0.1	105	0.1
1760	Physical scientists, all other	163,655	110	0.1	175	0.1
1800	Economists	23,560	0	0.0	60	0.3
1820	Psychologists	175,365	160	0.1	105	0.1
1840	Urban and regional planners	23,419	4	0.0	100	0.4
1860	Miscellaneous social scientists, including survey researchers and sociologists	45,660	140	0.3	420	0.9
1900	Agricultural and food science technicians	29,070	2,190	7.5	8,950	30.8

PART A—NATIONAL DATA

A-17 Detailed Occupation, by Educational Attainment for Persons Age 16 and Older (worksite geography), 2006–2010—Continued

Census occupation code	Occupation by educational attainment for persons age 16 and older	Some college or associate degree Number	Some college or associate degree Percent	Bachelor's degree Number	Bachelor's degree Percent	Graduate or professional degree Number	Graduate or professional degree Percent
0850	Personal financial advisors	56,505	16.6	179,880	53.0	87,000	25.6
0860	Insurance underwriters	30,310	30.9	43,020	43.8	7,745	7.9
0900	Financial examiners	1,785	14.2	7,510	59.7	2,440	19.4
0910	Credit counselors and loan officers	127,695	35.8	141,470	39.7	29,985	8.4
0930	Tax examiners and collectors, and revenue agents	20,560	33.4	22,440	36.5	6,095	9.9
0940	Tax preparers	30,910	35.4	26,795	30.7	14,715	16.9
0950	Financial specialists, all other	18,625	30.2	22,715	36.9	10,610	17.2
1005	Computer and information research scientists	1,720	11.2	5,625	36.8	7,505	49.0
1006	Computer systems analysts	111,630	24.2	219,480	47.6	104,365	22.6
1007	Information security analysts	13,820	34.3	15,820	39.2	7,470	18.5
1010	Computer programmers	123,650	25.0	246,240	49.8	95,830	19.4
1020	Software developers, applications and systems software	121,230	14.7	413,505	50.3	265,320	32.2
1030	Web developers	45,135	29.9	74,340	49.2	20,020	13.2
1050	Computer support specialists	227,955	47.2	154,235	31.9	37,300	7.7
1060	Database administrators	28,205	27.6	47,000	45.9	21,255	20.8
1105	Network and computer systems administrators	107,265	41.8	99,025	38.6	27,160	10.6
1106	Computer network architects	39,550	37.6	42,415	40.4	16,060	15.3
1107	Computer occupations, all other	103,005	38.0	104,710	38.6	37,130	13.7
1200	Actuaries	695	2.9	15,155	64.1	7,680	32.5
1220	Operations research analysts	28,775	24.9	47,200	40.8	31,465	27.2
1240	Miscellaneous mathematical science occupations, including mathematicians and statisticians	3,605	9.3	12,135	31.4	22,585	58.4
1300	Architects, except naval	17,635	9.5	98,125	52.8	67,160	36.1
1310	Surveyors, cartographers, and photogrammetrists	8,830	23.5	23,020	61.3	5,635	15.0
1320	Aerospace engineers	18,610	13.8	68,170	50.5	44,765	33.1
1340	Biomedical and agricultural engineers	2,970	22.3	6,180	46.4	3,740	28.1
1350	Chemical engineers	4,850	8.3	34,600	59.4	17,215	29.5
1360	Civil engineers	36,240	11.7	179,245	57.9	84,115	27.2
1400	Computer hardware engineers	13,970	22.5	27,705	44.6	16,960	27.3
1410	Electrical and electronics engineers	41,260	17.9	117,165	50.8	63,820	27.7
1420	Environmental engineers	2,685	8.1	16,055	48.5	13,055	39.4
1430	Industrial engineers, including health and safety	39,035	23.2	85,290	50.8	32,300	19.2
1440	Marine engineers and naval architects	2,170	19.9	5,825	53.3	1,920	17.6
1450	Materials engineers	6,970	22.4	14,670	47.1	7,390	23.8
1460	Mechanical engineers	47,395	21.0	117,810	52.3	48,900	21.7
1520	Petroleum, mining and geological engineers, including mining safety engineers	3,555	12.7	16,410	58.5	6,670	23.8
1530	Miscellaneous engineers, including nuclear engineers	69,310	15.7	219,825	49.7	138,495	31.3
1540	Drafters	118,710	61.7	38,535	20.0	7,635	4.0
1550	Engineering technicians, except drafters	230,200	56.5	58,575	14.4	10,355	2.5
1560	Surveying and mapping technicians	43,995	55.8	5,025	6.4	625	0.8
1600	Agricultural and food scientists	5,880	20.0	12,945	44.0	10,555	35.8
1610	Biological scientists	4,610	5.6	38,250	46.3	39,650	48.0
1640	Conservation scientists and foresters	3,525	14.3	15,930	64.7	5,135	20.9
1650	Medical scientists, and life scientists, all other	1,385	1.2	7,280	6.3	105,895	92.2
1700	Astronomers and physicists	820	6.6	2,450	19.7	9,135	73.5
1710	Atmospheric and space scientists	1,245	14.0	4,310	48.6	3,310	37.3
1720	Chemists and materials scientists	5,990	6.9	47,380	54.3	33,695	38.6
1740	Environmental scientists and geoscientists	4,400	5.8	37,760	49.7	33,600	44.2
1760	Physical scientists, all other	2,970	1.8	43,915	26.8	116,485	71.2
1800	Economists	50	0.2	6,375	27.1	17,075	72.5
1820	Psychologists	1,030	0.6	8,900	5.1	165,170	94.2
1840	Urban and regional planners	1,495	6.4	9,230	39.4	12,590	53.8
1860	Miscellaneous social scientists, including survey researchers and sociologists	5,075	11.1	18,655	40.9	21,370	46.8
1900	Agricultural and food science technicians	29,070	2,190	7.5	8,950	30.8	

A-17 Detailed Occupation, by Educational Attainment for Persons Age 16 and Older (worksite geography), 2006–2010—*Continued*

Census occupation code	Occupation by educational attainment for persons age 16 and older	Total workers	Not high school graduate Number	Not high school graduate Percent	High school graduate (including equivalency) Number	High school graduate (including equivalency) Percent
1910	Biological technicians	21,965	640	2.9	3,945	18.0
1920	Chemical technicians	70,710	2,755	3.9	17,675	25.0
1930	Geological and petroleum technicians, and nuclear technicians	18,165	1,070	5.9	4,070	22.4
1965	Miscellaneous life, physical, and social science technicians, including social science research assistants	164,585	4,330	2.6	26,410	16.0
2000	Counselors	639,020	10,540	1.6	43,365	6.8
2010	Social workers	737,170	8,045	1.1	43,850	5.9
2015	Probation officers and correctional treatment specialists	94,365	595	0.6	5,995	6.4
2016	Social and human service assistants	140,840	5,260	3.7	27,745	19.7
2025	Miscellaneous community and social service specialists, including health educators and community health workers	75,480	2,430	3.2	9,885	13.1
2040	Clergy	432,325	10,025	2.3	29,395	6.8
2050	Directors, religious activities and education	51,925	660	1.3	4,670	9.0
2060	Religious workers, all other	84,840	3,940	4.6	11,150	13.1
2100	Lawyers, and judges, magistrates, and other judicial workers	1,007,385	300	0.0	2,835	0.3
2105	Judicial law clerks	10,750	75	0.7	320	3.0
2145	Paralegals and legal assistants	368,915	3,900	1.1	43,495	11.8
2160	Miscellaneous legal support workers	228,510	4,625	2.0	41,920	18.3
2200	Postsecondary teachers	1,263,490	1,380	0.1	1,385	0.1
2300	Preschool and kindergarten teachers	532,555	12,080	2.3	84,620	15.9
2310	Elementary and middle school teachers	3,154,520	4,625	0.1	5,325	0.2
2320	Secondary school teachers	740,955	1,165	0.2	1,490	0.2
2330	Special education teachers	204,820	1,195	0.6	7,880	3.8
2340	Other teachers and instructors	771,875	31,780	4.1	99,935	12.9
2400	Archivists, curators, and museum technicians	42,030	570	1.4	2,490	5.9
2430	Librarians	171,560	130	0.1	315	0.2
2440	Library technicians	55,700	6,535	11.7	17,280	31.0
2540	Teacher assistants	920,445	34,370	3.7	287,805	31.3
2550	Other education, training, and library workers	85,430	565	0.7	4,130	4.8
2600	Artists and related workers	186,990	5,950	3.2	21,425	11.5
2630	Designers	752,205	20,595	2.7	90,260	12.0
2700	Actors	30,315	1,390	4.6	4,115	13.6
2710	Producers and directors	132,215	1,265	1.0	8,320	6.3
2720	Athletes, coaches, umpires, and related workers	237,485	24,185	10.2	28,525	12.0
2740	Dancers and choreographers	20,250	3,175	15.7	6,625	32.7
2750	Musicians, singers, and related workers	171,500	9,565	5.6	26,130	15.2
2760	Entertainers and performers, sports and related workers, all other	38,125	3,925	10.3	7,770	20.4
2800	Announcers	49,495	2,995	6.1	9,685	19.6
2810	News analysts, reporters and correspondents	80,170	395	0.5	2,605	3.2
2825	Public relations specialists	130,940	910	0.7	6,885	5.3
2830	Editors	168,740	1,085	0.6	6,500	3.9
2840	Technical writers	59,265	380	0.6	3,090	5.2
2850	Writers and authors	177,570	980	0.6	5,765	3.2
2860	Miscellaneous media and communication workers	75,925	2,735	3.6	8,955	11.8
2900	Broadcast and sound engineering technicians and radio operators, and media and communication equipment workers, all other	85,505	2,730	3.2	15,500	18.1
2910	Photographers	135,700	4,835	3.6	21,135	15.6
2920	Television, video, and motion picture camera operators and editors	42,080	1,110	2.6	4,180	9.9
3000	Chiropractors	55,005	40	0.1	570	1.0
3010	Dentists	161,300	180	0.1	110	0.1
3030	Dietitians and nutritionists	85,140	4,080	4.8	11,535	13.5
3040	Optometrists	34,375	0	0.0	20	0.1
3050	Pharmacists	244,525	250	0.1	360	0.1
3060	Physicians and surgeons	812,555	1,030	0.1	730	0.1

PART A—NATIONAL DATA

A-17 Detailed Occupation, by Educational Attainment for Persons Age 16 and Older (worksite geography), 2006–2010—*Continued*

Census occupation code	Occupation by educational attainment for persons age 16 and older	Some college or associate degree Number	Some college or associate degree Percent	Bachelor's degree Number	Bachelor's degree Percent	Graduate or professional degree Number	Graduate or professional degree Percent
1910	Biological technicians	6,150	28.0	7,940	36.1	3,290	15.0
1920	Chemical technicians	27,070	38.3	18,465	26.1	4,745	6.7
1930	Geological and petroleum technicians, and nuclear technicians	7,445	41.0	4,450	24.5	1,130	6.2
1965	Miscellaneous life, physical, and social science technicians, including social science research assistants	70,535	42.9	47,315	28.7	15,995	9.7
2000	Counselors	120,310	18.8	166,430	26.0	298,375	46.7
2010	Social workers	121,055	16.4	318,005	43.1	246,215	33.4
2015	Probation officers and correctional treatment specialists	18,850	20.0	53,495	56.7	15,430	16.4
2016	Social and human service assistants	56,960	40.4	37,570	26.7	13,305	9.4
2025	Miscellaneous community and social service specialists, including health educators and community health workers	24,030	31.8	24,865	32.9	14,270	18.9
2040	Clergy	71,155	16.5	106,260	24.6	215,490	49.8
2050	Directors, religious activities and education	12,745	24.5	20,005	38.5	13,845	26.7
2060	Religious workers, all other	23,580	27.8	26,125	30.8	20,045	23.6
2100	Lawyers, and judges, magistrates, and other judicial workers	8,700	0.9	19,210	1.9	976,340	96.9
2105	Judicial law clerks	475	4.4	765	7.1	9,115	84.8
2145	Paralegals and legal assistants	157,945	42.8	136,805	37.1	26,770	7.3
2160	Miscellaneous legal support workers	92,520	40.5	64,835	28.4	24,610	10.8
2200	Postsecondary teachers	89,140	7.1	248,870	19.7	922,715	73.0
2300	Preschool and kindergarten teachers	214,220	40.2	165,280	31.0	56,355	10.6
2310	Elementary and middle school teachers	163,560	5.2	1,496,045	47.4	1,484,965	47.1
2320	Secondary school teachers	32,095	4.3	343,045	46.3	363,160	49.0
2330	Special education teachers	19,900	9.7	79,435	38.8	96,410	47.1
2340	Other teachers and instructors	252,120	32.7	240,915	31.2	147,125	19.1
2400	Archivists, curators, and museum technicians	6,390	15.2	14,035	33.4	18,545	44.1
2430	Librarians	29,110	17.0	39,210	22.9	102,795	59.9
2440	Library technicians	18,975	34.1	8,430	15.1	4,480	8.0
2540	Teacher assistants	418,255	45.4	148,960	16.2	31,055	3.4
2550	Other education, training, and library workers	15,495	18.1	23,415	27.4	41,825	49.0
2600	Artists and related workers	56,115	30.0	79,300	42.4	24,200	12.9
2630	Designers	255,445	34.0	328,030	43.6	57,875	7.7
2700	Actors	8,855	29.2	12,705	41.9	3,250	10.7
2710	Producers and directors	28,855	21.8	73,775	55.8	20,000	15.1
2720	Athletes, coaches, umpires, and related workers	80,305	33.8	76,185	32.1	28,285	11.9
2740	Dancers and choreographers	7,170	35.4	2,855	14.1	425	2.1
2750	Musicians, singers, and related workers	50,700	29.6	50,660	29.5	34,445	20.1
2760	Entertainers and performers, sports and related workers, all other	14,025	36.8	9,635	25.3	2,770	7.3
2800	Announcers	19,420	39.2	14,785	29.9	2,610	5.3
2810	News analysts, reporters and correspondents	13,450	16.8	48,520	60.5	15,200	19.0
2825	Public relations specialists	22,030	16.8	74,325	56.8	26,790	20.5
2830	Editors	28,475	16.9	94,690	56.1	37,990	22.5
2840	Technical writers	12,470	21.0	28,355	47.8	14,970	25.3
2850	Writers and authors	24,810	14.0	88,535	49.9	57,480	32.4
2860	Miscellaneous media and communication workers	29,275	38.6	22,495	29.6	12,465	16.4
2900	Broadcast and sound engineering technicians and radio operators, and media and communication equipment workers, all other	39,400	46.1	24,290	28.4	3,585	4.2
2910	Photographers	52,835	38.9	48,740	35.9	8,155	6.0
2920	Television, video, and motion picture camera operators and editors	14,670	34.9	19,430	46.2	2,690	6.4
3000	Chiropractors	925	1.7	1,500	2.7	51,970	94.5
3010	Dentists	95	0.1	1,460	0.9	159,455	98.9
3030	Dietitians and nutritionists	11,605	13.6	32,645	38.3	25,275	29.7
3040	Optometrists	155	0.5	295	0.9	33,905	98.6
3050	Pharmacists	9,585	3.9	107,300	43.9	127,030	51.9
3060	Physicians and surgeons	1,555	0.2	7,920	1.0	801,320	98.6

A-17 **Detailed Occupation, by Educational Attainment for Persons Age 16 and Older (worksite geography), 2006–2010**—*Continued*

Census occupation code	Occupation by educational attainment for persons age 16 and older	Total workers	Not high school graduate Number	Not high school graduate Percent	High school graduate (including equivalency) Number	High school graduate (including equivalency) Percent
3110	Physician assistants	99,105	1,355	1.4	5,475	5.5
3120	Podiatrists	9,704	10	0.1	4	0.0
3140	Audiologists	13,445	0	0.0	180	1.3
3150	Occupational therapists	80,905	165	0.2	295	0.4
3160	Physical therapists	178,575	610	0.3	2,385	1.3
3200	Radiation therapists	13,090	30	0.2	345	2.6
3210	Recreational therapists	13,735	335	2.4	1,295	9.4
3220	Respiratory therapists	96,120	205	0.2	2,160	2.2
3230	Speech-language pathologists	109,550	165	0.2	530	0.5
3245	Other therapists, including exercise physiologists	119,350	830	0.7	4,525	3.8
3250	Veterinarians	71,075	120	0.2	165	0.2
3255	Registered nurses	2,522,995	3,635	0.1	26,165	1.0
3256	Nurse anesthetists	22,340	0	0.0	145	0.6
3258	Nurse practitioners and nurse midwives	79,215	80	0.1	175	0.2
3260	Health diagnosing and treating practitioners, all other	17,680	115	0.7	590	3.3
3300	Clinical laboratory technologists and technicians	329,155	4,185	1.3	35,500	10.8
3310	Dental hygienists	141,315	765	0.5	3,895	2.8
3320	Diagnostic related technologists and technicians	292,195	1,785	0.6	25,805	8.8
3400	Emergency medical technicians and paramedics	162,390	1,545	1.0	25,110	15.5
3420	Health practitioner support technologists and technicians	477,800	12,400	2.6	119,460	25.0
3500	Licensed practical and licensed vocational nurses	637,385	7,010	1.1	127,635	20.0
3510	Medical records and health information technicians	102,360	3,695	3.6	32,305	31.6
3520	Opticians, dispensing	50,635	1,480	2.9	14,340	28.3
3535	Miscellaneous health technologists and technicians	115,620	2,890	2.5	24,845	21.5
3540	Other health care practitioners and technical occupations	69,800	1,245	1.8	7,415	10.6
3600	Nursing, psychiatric, and home health aides	1,974,465	290,720	14.7	753,440	38.2
3610	Occupational therapy assistants and aides	13,100	80	0.6	320	2.4
3620	Physical therapist assistants and aides	63,650	1,490	2.3	7,500	11.8
3630	Massage therapists	123,715	2,405	1.9	22,170	17.9
3640	Dental assistants	255,470	9,730	3.8	78,945	30.9
3645	Medical assistants	359,955	11,400	3.2	90,450	25.1
3646	Medical transcriptionists	74,145	780	1.1	15,520	20.9
3647	Pharmacy aides	40,430	2,495	6.2	11,970	29.6
3648	Veterinary assistants and laboratory animal caretakers	40,370	3,915	9.7	12,220	30.3
3649	Phlebotomists	80,940	1,425	1.8	19,785	24.4
3655	Health care support workers, all other, including medical equipment preparers	140,540	22,005	15.7	56,310	40.1
3700	First-line supervisors of correctional officers	56,085	615	1.1	14,170	25.3
3710	First-line supervisors of police and detectives	115,370	625	0.5	15,520	13.5
3720	First-line supervisors of fire fighting and prevention workers	51,235	365	0.7	8,160	15.9
3730	First-line supervisors of protective service workers, all other	89,460	2,710	3.0	19,945	22.3
3740	Firefighters	263,130	2,125	0.8	51,315	19.5
3750	Fire inspectors	18,670	370	2.0	4,280	22.9
3800	Bailiffs, correctional officers, and jailers	418,200	5,775	1.4	146,245	35.0
3820	Detectives and criminal investigators	127,160	460	0.4	11,785	9.3
3840	Miscellaneous law enforcement workers	10,620	330	3.1	2,915	27.4
3850	Police officers	640,700	4,985	0.8	94,245	14.7
3900	Animal control workers	10,040	725	7.2	3,715	37.0
3910	Private detectives and investigators	81,420	905	1.1	10,930	13.4
3930	Security guards and gaming surveillance officers	896,570	79,820	8.9	324,605	36.2
3940	Crossing guards	49,895	11,420	22.9	21,690	43.5
3945	Transportation security screeners	25,315	700	2.8	6,805	26.9

PART A—NATIONAL DATA

A-17 Detailed Occupation, by Educational Attainment for Persons Age 16 and Older (worksite geography), 2006–2010—Continued

Census occupation code	Occupation by educational attainment for persons age 16 and older	Some college or associate degree Number	Some college or associate degree Percent	Bachelor's degree Number	Bachelor's degree Percent	Graduate or professional degree Number	Graduate or professional degree Percent
3110	Physician assistants	24,660	24.9	30,165	30.4	37,450	37.8
3120	Podiatrists	0	0.0	155	1.6	9,535	98.3
3140	Audiologists	385	2.9	670	5.0	12,210	90.8
3150	Occupational therapists	7,650	9.5	43,070	53.2	29,725	36.7
3160	Physical therapists	16,045	9.0	71,340	39.9	88,195	49.4
3200	Radiation therapists	6,740	51.5	5,290	40.4	685	5.2
3210	Recreational therapists	2,730	19.9	7,455	54.3	1,920	14.0
3220	Respiratory therapists	66,730	69.4	22,820	23.7	4,205	4.4
3230	Speech-language pathologists	1,060	1.0	10,000	9.1	97,795	89.3
3245	Other therapists, including exercise physiologists	16,555	13.9	30,645	25.7	66,795	56.0
3250	Veterinarians	185	0.3	550	0.8	70,055	98.6
3255	Registered nurses	1,114,155	44.2	1,131,400	44.8	247,640	9.8
3256	Nurse anesthetists	1,705	7.6	3,550	15.9	16,940	75.8
3258	Nurse practitioners and nurse midwives	3,050	3.9	4,610	5.8	71,300	90.0
3260	Health diagnosing and treating practitioners, all other	1,835	10.4	2,700	15.3	12,440	70.4
3300	Clinical laboratory technologists and technicians	118,155	35.9	146,665	44.6	24,650	7.5
3310	Dental hygienists	88,265	62.5	41,870	29.6	6,520	4.6
3320	Diagnostic related technologists and technicians	195,715	67.0	56,940	19.5	11,950	4.1
3400	Emergency medical technicians and paramedics	112,945	69.6	19,180	11.8	3,610	2.2
3420	Health practitioner support technologists and technicians	269,130	56.3	66,665	14.0	10,145	2.1
3500	Licensed practical and licensed vocational nurses	463,630	72.7	25,615	4.0	13,495	2.1
3510	Medical records and health information technicians	52,040	50.8	11,765	11.5	2,555	2.5
3520	Opticians, dispensing	26,875	53.1	6,855	13.5	1,085	2.1
3535	Miscellaneous health technologists and technicians	56,345	48.7	20,765	18.0	10,775	9.3
3540	Other health care practitioners and technical occupations	18,205	26.1	27,570	39.5	15,365	22.0
3600	Nursing, psychiatric, and home health aides	780,115	39.5	114,495	5.8	35,695	1.8
3610	Occupational therapy assistants and aides	10,905	83.2	1,500	11.5	295	2.3
3620	Physical therapist assistants and aides	41,185	64.7	11,380	17.9	2,095	3.3
3630	Massage therapists	66,235	53.5	24,415	19.7	8,490	6.9
3640	Dental assistants	144,995	56.8	15,440	6.0	6,360	2.5
3645	Medical assistants	224,985	62.5	24,590	6.8	8,530	2.4
3646	Medical transcriptionists	46,465	62.7	9,435	12.7	1,945	2.6
3647	Pharmacy aides	18,920	46.8	5,555	13.7	1,490	3.7
3648	Veterinary assistants and laboratory animal caretakers	17,650	43.7	5,690	14.1	895	2.2
3649	Phlebotomists	51,615	63.8	6,910	8.5	1,205	1.5
3655	Health care support workers, all other, including medical equipment preparers	49,215	35.0	10,850	7.7	2,160	1.5
3700	First-line supervisors of correctional officers	26,960	48.1	10,915	19.5	3,425	6.1
3710	First-line supervisors of police and detectives	54,320	47.1	33,325	28.9	11,580	10.0
3720	First-line supervisors of fire fighting and prevention workers	31,295	61.1	9,315	18.2	2,100	4.1
3730	First-line supervisors of protective service workers, all other	40,550	45.3	18,805	21.0	7,450	8.3
3740	Firefighters	163,835	62.3	41,470	15.8	4,385	1.7
3750	Fire inspectors	9,355	50.1	3,900	20.9	765	4.1
3800	Bailiffs, correctional officers, and jailers	214,280	51.2	46,265	11.1	5,635	1.3
3820	Detectives and criminal investigators	48,565	38.2	51,275	40.3	15,075	11.9
3840	Miscellaneous law enforcement workers	4,435	41.8	2,530	23.8	410	3.9
3850	Police officers	335,960	52.4	175,280	27.4	30,230	4.7
3900	Animal control workers	4,285	42.7	1,155	11.5	160	1.6
3910	Private detectives and investigators	29,505	36.2	30,120	37.0	9,960	12.2
3930	Security guards and gaming surveillance officers	374,115	41.7	97,805	10.9	20,225	2.3
3940	Crossing guards	14,135	28.3	1,915	3.8	735	1.5
3945	Transportation security screeners	12,410	49.0	4,625	18.3	775	3.1

A-17 Detailed Occupation, by Educational Attainment for Persons Age 16 and Older (worksite geography), 2006–2010—*Continued*

Census occupation code	Occupation by educational attainment for persons age 16 and older	Total workers	Not high school graduate Number	Not high school graduate Percent	High school graduate (including equivalency) Number	High school graduate (including equivalency) Percent
3955	Lifeguards and other recreational, and all other protective service workers	159,450	48,075	30.2	36,430	22.8
4000	Chefs and head cooks	305,770	56,320	18.4	92,405	30.2
4010	First-line supervisors of food preparation and serving workers	538,340	76,370	14.2	198,385	36.9
4020	Cooks	1,971,430	695,750	35.3	768,055	39.0
4030	Food preparation workers	735,740	245,640	33.4	248,520	33.8
4040	Bartenders	376,875	31,335	8.3	107,580	28.5
4050	Combined food preparation and serving workers, including fast food	297,885	85,565	28.7	119,200	40.0
4060	Counter attendants, cafeteria, food concession, and coffee shop	222,050	99,120	44.6	63,265	28.5
4110	Waiters and waitresses	1,970,690	360,430	18.3	584,130	29.6
4120	Food servers, nonrestaurant	185,330	43,485	23.5	71,520	38.6
4130	Miscellaneous food preparation and serving related workers, including dining room and cafeteria attendants and bartender helpers	326,930	128,615	39.3	114,985	35.2
4140	Dishwashers	270,080	138,530	51.3	88,550	32.8
4150	Hosts and hostesses, restaurant, lounge, and coffee shop	254,165	83,740	32.9	66,745	26.3
4200	First-line supervisors of housekeeping and janitorial workers	250,580	43,685	17.4	100,940	40.3
4210	First-line supervisors of landscaping, lawn service, and groundskeeping workers	184,275	35,460	19.2	58,890	32.0
4220	Janitors and building cleaners	2,316,220	678,575	29.3	1,003,840	43.3
4230	Maids and housekeeping cleaners	1,364,365	556,600	40.8	536,960	39.4
4240	Pest control workers	63,680	6,850	10.8	27,445	43.1
4250	Grounds maintenance workers	1,163,575	469,110	40.3	396,100	34.0
4300	First-line supervisors of gaming workers	74,750	3,555	4.8	19,710	26.4
4320	First-line supervisors of personal service workers	176,800	10,805	6.1	53,955	30.5
4340	Animal trainers	37,555	4,140	11.0	11,130	29.6
4350	Nonfarm animal caretakers	165,410	26,080	15.8	56,515	34.2
4400	Gaming services workers	102,215	11,215	11.0	35,440	34.7
4410	Motion picture projectionists	8,215	895	10.9	2,080	25.3
4420	Ushers, lobby attendants, and ticket takers	42,480	11,155	26.3	11,210	26.4
4430	Miscellaneous entertainment attendants and related workers	162,255	31,715	19.5	42,385	26.1
4460	Embalmers and funeral attendants	14,110	1,040	7.4	4,630	32.8
4465	Morticians, undertakers, and funeral directors	38,775	430	1.1	3,530	9.1
4500	Barbers	89,735	13,365	14.9	40,875	45.6
4510	Hairdressers, hairstylists, and cosmetologists	736,395	54,130	7.4	349,710	47.5
4520	Miscellaneous personal appearance workers	224,745	47,905	21.3	84,490	37.6
4530	Baggage porters, bellhops, and concierges	71,935	9,665	13.4	24,360	33.9
4540	Tour and travel guides	42,605	2,750	6.5	8,650	20.3
4600	Childcare workers	1,288,595	227,995	17.7	418,930	32.5
4610	Personal care aides	821,805	166,265	20.2	292,605	35.6
4620	Recreation and fitness workers	356,035	21,630	6.1	67,255	18.9
4640	Residential advisors	68,415	1,650	2.4	12,410	18.1
4650	Personal care and service workers, all other	85,125	12,380	14.5	26,790	31.5
4700	First-line supervisors of retail sales workers	2,985,505	192,785	6.5	937,710	31.4
4710	First-line supervisors of non-retail sales workers	1,205,250	65,310	5.4	286,200	23.7
4720	Cashiers	3,067,255	758,370	24.7	1,109,390	36.2
4740	Counter and rental clerks	122,080	20,980	17.2	43,460	35.6
4750	Parts salespersons	109,905	10,585	9.6	52,835	48.1
4760	Retail salespersons	3,318,785	330,430	10.0	995,680	30.0
4800	Advertising sales agents	221,500	4,175	1.9	29,995	13.5
4810	Insurance sales agents	532,705	6,615	1.2	89,350	16.8
4820	Securities, commodities, and financial services sales agents	349,005	3,620	1.0	30,650	8.8
4830	Travel agents	80,510	1,580	2.0	15,980	19.8
4840	Sales representatives, services, all other	616,205	18,035	2.9	104,395	16.9
4850	Sales representatives, wholesale and manufacturing	1,452,830	47,725	3.3	266,600	18.4

A-17 Detailed Occupation, by Educational Attainment for Persons Age 16 and Older (worksite geography), 2006–2010—Continued

Census occupation code	Occupation by educational attainment for persons age 16 and older	Some college or associate degree Number	Some college or associate degree Percent	Bachelor's degree Number	Bachelor's degree Percent	Graduate or professional degree Number	Graduate or professional degree Percent
3955	Lifeguards and other recreational, and all other protective service workers................	58,945	37.0	13,480	8.5	2,520	1.6
4000	Chefs and head cooks................	119,645	39.1	32,435	10.6	4,965	1.6
4010	First-line supervisors of food preparation and serving workers................	199,045	37.0	56,520	10.5	8,020	1.5
4020	Cooks................	432,510	21.9	65,290	3.3	9,825	0.5
4030	Food preparation workers................	202,880	27.6	34,035	4.6	4,665	0.6
4040	Bartenders................	175,650	46.6	56,695	15.0	5,615	1.5
4050	Combined food preparation and serving workers, including fast food.....	81,255	27.3	10,490	3.5	1,375	0.5
4060	Counter attendants, cafeteria, food concession, and coffee shop................	52,385	23.6	6,120	2.8	1,160	0.5
4110	Waiters and waitresses................	827,015	42.0	180,320	9.2	18,795	1.0
4120	Food servers, nonrestaurant................	59,135	31.9	9,765	5.3	1,425	0.8
4130	Miscellaneous food preparation and serving related workers, including dining room and cafeteria attendants and bartender helpers................	71,020	21.7	10,900	3.3	1,410	0.4
4140	Dishwashers................	37,065	13.7	5,210	1.9	725	0.3
4150	Hosts and hostesses, restaurant, lounge, and coffee shop................	88,285	34.7	13,580	5.3	1,815	0.7
4200	First-line supervisors of housekeeping and janitorial workers................	78,100	31.2	22,965	9.2	4,890	2.0
4210	First-line supervisors of landscaping, lawn service, and groundskeeping workers................	58,730	31.9	27,800	15.1	3,395	1.8
4220	Janitors and building cleaners................	526,080	22.7	89,620	3.9	18,105	0.8
4230	Maids and housekeeping cleaners................	213,335	15.6	48,365	3.5	9,105	0.7
4240	Pest control workers................	23,395	36.7	5,065	8.0	925	1.5
4250	Grounds maintenance workers................	229,745	19.7	58,490	5.0	10,130	0.9
4300	First-line supervisors of gaming workers................	29,955	40.1	17,735	23.7	3,795	5.1
4320	First-line supervisors of personal service workers................	71,160	40.2	32,970	18.6	7,910	4.5
4340	Animal trainers................	13,380	35.6	7,540	20.1	1,365	3.6
4350	Nonfarm animal caretakers................	60,495	36.6	19,375	11.7	2,945	1.8
4400	Gaming services workers................	42,165	41.3	11,680	11.4	1,715	1.7
4410	Motion picture projectionists................	4,145	50.5	865	10.5	230	2.8
4420	Ushers, lobby attendants, and ticket takers................	15,885	37.4	3,260	7.7	970	2.3
4430	Miscellaneous entertainment attendants and related workers................	64,420	39.7	19,105	11.8	4,630	2.9
4460	Embalmers and funeral attendants................	5,855	41.5	1,750	12.4	835	5.9
4465	Morticians, undertakers, and funeral directors................	20,625	53.2	11,195	28.9	2,995	7.7
4500	Barbers................	31,480	35.1	3,030	3.4	985	1.1
4510	Hairdressers, hairstylists, and cosmetologists................	293,745	39.9	29,190	4.0	9,620	1.3
4520	Miscellaneous personal appearance workers................	70,205	31.2	18,885	8.4	3,260	1.5
4530	Baggage porters, bellhops, and concierges................	26,725	37.2	9,830	13.7	1,355	1.9
4540	Tour and travel guides................	18,565	43.6	9,295	21.8	3,345	7.9
4600	Childcare workers................	489,275	38.0	129,570	10.1	22,825	1.8
4610	Personal care aides................	279,260	34.0	67,470	8.2	16,205	2.0
4620	Recreation and fitness workers................	140,825	39.6	101,260	28.4	25,065	7.0
4640	Residential advisors................	42,855	62.6	9,305	13.6	2,195	3.2
4650	Personal care and service workers, all other................	31,070	36.5	12,225	14.4	2,660	3.1
4700	First-line supervisors of retail sales workers................	1,146,060	38.4	601,590	20.2	107,360	3.6
4710	First-line supervisors of non-retail sales workers................	395,320	32.8	354,610	29.4	103,810	8.6
4720	Cashiers................	997,865	32.5	172,845	5.6	28,785	0.9
4740	Counter and rental clerks................	42,620	34.9	13,030	10.7	1,990	1.6
4750	Parts salespersons................	39,740	36.2	6,135	5.6	610	0.6
4760	Retail salespersons................	1,353,755	40.8	543,625	16.4	95,295	2.9
4800	Advertising sales agents................	67,975	30.7	104,840	47.3	14,515	6.6
4810	Insurance sales agents................	193,425	36.3	203,305	38.2	40,010	7.5
4820	Securities, commodities, and financial services sales agents................	81,325	23.3	175,975	50.4	57,435	16.5
4830	Travel agents................	36,170	44.9	22,115	27.5	4,665	5.8
4840	Sales representatives, services, all other................	219,530	35.6	229,310	37.2	44,935	7.3
4850	Sales representatives, wholesale and manufacturing................	466,635	32.1	571,575	39.3	100,295	6.9

A-17 **Detailed Occupation, by Educational Attainment for Persons Age 16 and Older (worksite geography), 2006–2010**—*Continued*

Census occupation code	Occupation by educational attainment for persons age 16 and older	Total workers	Not high school graduate Number	Not high school graduate Percent	High school graduate (including equivalency) Number	High school graduate (including equivalency) Percent
4900	Models, demonstrators, and product promoters	58,155	8,235	14.2	20,305	34.9
4920	Real estate brokers and sales agents	838,415	12,885	1.5	124,115	14.8
4930	Sales engineers	30,960	195	0.6	1,430	4.6
4940	Telemarketers	133,225	15,505	11.6	45,450	34.1
4950	Door-to-door sales workers, news and street vendors, and related workers	187,160	33,285	17.8	61,100	32.6
4965	Sales and related workers, all other	228,765	17,915	7.8	50,945	22.3
5000	First-line supervisors of office and administrative support workers	1,519,815	43,635	2.9	382,700	25.2
5010	Switchboard operators, including answering service	42,555	2,520	5.9	18,860	44.3
5020	Telephone operators	49,205	2,985	6.1	16,935	34.4
5030	Communications equipment operators, all other	10,365	290	2.8	2,530	24.4
5100	Bill and account collectors	219,305	9,810	4.5	72,430	33.0
5110	Billing and posting clerks	462,920	15,740	3.4	152,235	32.9
5120	Bookkeeping, accounting, and auditing clerks	1,444,120	47,290	3.3	457,250	31.7
5130	Gaming cage workers	12,670	1,065	8.4	5,115	40.4
5140	Payroll and timekeeping clerks	172,260	4,210	2.4	52,995	30.8
5150	Procurement clerks	28,980	615	2.1	7,610	26.3
5160	Tellers	418,430	12,560	3.0	141,215	33.7
5165	Financial clerks, all other	65,035	1,350	2.1	15,085	23.2
5200	Brokerage clerks	9,685	205	2.1	1,895	19.6
5220	Court, municipal, and license clerks	90,520	1,675	1.9	27,715	30.6
5230	Credit authorizers, checkers, and clerks	53,985	1,490	2.8	17,745	32.9
5240	Customer service representatives	2,149,510	144,325	6.7	630,500	29.3
5250	Eligibility interviewers, government programs	66,510	660	1.0	10,835	16.3
5260	File clerks	367,120	30,025	8.2	109,925	29.9
5300	Hotel, motel, and resort desk clerks	132,855	10,330	7.8	42,840	32.2
5310	Interviewers, except eligibility and loan	140,830	5,375	3.8	36,040	25.6
5320	Library assistants, clerical	119,285	3,420	2.9	23,280	19.5
5330	Loan interviewers and clerks	138,215	2,730	2.0	40,000	28.9
5340	New accounts clerks	23,610	550	2.3	7,080	30.0
5350	Correspondence clerks and order clerks	146,915	14,995	10.2	53,915	36.7
5360	Human resources assistants, except payroll and timekeeping	51,150	1,575	3.1	11,875	23.2
5400	Receptionists and information clerks	1,168,245	74,590	6.4	414,195	35.5
5410	Reservation and transportation ticket agents and travel clerks	138,280	4,775	3.5	37,175	26.9
5420	Information and record clerks, all other	94,285	2,420	2.6	22,345	23.7
5500	Cargo and freight agents	18,980	1,025	5.4	6,375	33.6
5510	Couriers and messengers	291,495	27,630	9.5	108,230	37.1
5520	Dispatchers	268,390	14,950	5.6	96,340	35.9
5530	Meter readers, utilities	37,060	2,220	6.0	16,600	44.8
5540	Postal service clerks	141,170	3,725	2.6	49,700	35.2
5550	Postal service mail carriers	325,825	8,060	2.5	119,665	36.7
5560	Postal service mail sorters, processors, and processing machine operators	88,840	2,760	3.1	31,500	35.5
5600	Production, planning, and expediting clerks	276,975	8,885	3.2	72,420	26.1
5610	Shipping, receiving, and traffic clerks	561,285	81,580	14.5	262,685	46.8
5620	Stock clerks and order fillers	1,443,330	260,890	18.1	613,985	42.5
5630	Weighers, measurers, checkers, and samplers, recordkeeping	70,365	11,350	16.1	27,535	39.1
5700	Secretaries and administrative assistants	3,698,890	100,960	2.7	1,147,115	31.0
5800	Computer operators	138,220	4,345	3.1	37,935	27.4
5810	Data entry keyers	434,210	17,135	3.9	136,250	31.4
5820	Word processors and typists	318,880	9,985	3.1	99,675	31.3
5840	Insurance claims and policy processing clerks	303,265	5,390	1.8	91,070	30.0
5850	Mail clerks and mail machine operators, except postal service	116,240	11,990	10.3	49,370	42.5
5860	Office clerks, general	1,161,240	55,150	4.7	362,830	31.2

A-17 Detailed Occupation, by Educational Attainment for Persons Age 16 and Older (worksite geography), 2006–2010—*Continued*

Census occupation code	Occupation by educational attainment for persons age 16 and older	Some college or associate degree Number	Some college or associate degree Percent	Bachelor's degree Number	Bachelor's degree Percent	Graduate or professional degree Number	Graduate or professional degree Percent
4900	Models, demonstrators, and product promoters	20,110	34.6	7,530	12.9	1,975	3.4
4920	Real estate brokers and sales agents	323,675	38.6	295,135	35.2	82,605	9.9
4930	Sales engineers	7,565	24.4	16,805	54.3	4,965	16.0
4940	Telemarketers	55,555	41.7	13,920	10.4	2,795	2.1
4950	Door-to-door sales workers, news and street vendors, and related workers	60,570	32.4	25,870	13.8	6,335	3.4
4965	Sales and related workers, all other	71,465	31.2	71,545	31.3	16,895	7.4
5000	First-line supervisors of office and administrative support workers	645,845	42.5	349,460	23.0	98,175	6.5
5010	Switchboard operators, including answering service	17,495	41.1	3,020	7.1	660	1.6
5020	Telephone operators	23,855	48.5	4,735	9.6	695	1.4
5030	Communications equipment operators, all other	4,720	45.5	2,275	21.9	550	5.3
5100	Bill and account collectors	104,400	47.6	27,895	12.7	4,770	2.2
5110	Billing and posting clerks	224,580	48.5	60,025	13.0	10,340	2.2
5120	Bookkeeping, accounting, and auditing clerks	721,020	49.9	186,255	12.9	32,305	2.2
5130	Gaming cage workers	5,160	40.7	1,160	9.2	170	1.3
5140	Payroll and timekeeping clerks	87,280	50.7	24,660	14.3	3,115	1.8
5150	Procurement clerks	13,465	46.5	5,630	19.4	1,660	5.7
5160	Tellers	208,310	49.8	51,290	12.3	5,055	1.2
5165	Financial clerks, all other	26,640	41.0	15,580	24.0	6,380	9.8
5200	Brokerage clerks	4,310	44.5	2,845	29.4	430	4.4
5220	Court, municipal, and license clerks	43,715	48.3	14,105	15.6	3,310	3.7
5230	Credit authorizers, checkers, and clerks	23,465	43.5	9,085	16.8	2,200	4.1
5240	Customer service representatives	964,665	44.9	356,540	16.6	53,480	2.5
5250	Eligibility interviewers, government programs	28,520	42.9	22,530	33.9	3,965	6.0
5260	File clerks	167,810	45.7	49,035	13.4	10,325	2.8
5300	Hotel, motel, and resort desk clerks	60,825	45.8	16,735	12.6	2,125	1.6
5310	Interviewers, except eligibility and loan	67,210	47.7	25,075	17.8	7,130	5.1
5320	Library assistants, clerical	56,660	47.5	28,290	23.7	7,635	6.4
5330	Loan interviewers and clerks	65,530	47.4	26,895	19.5	3,060	2.2
5340	New accounts clerks	11,105	47.0	4,305	18.2	570	2.4
5350	Correspondence clerks and order clerks	56,365	38.4	18,790	12.8	2,850	1.9
5360	Human resources assistants, except payroll and timekeeping	24,755	48.4	10,730	21.0	2,215	4.3
5400	Receptionists and information clerks	542,365	46.4	117,480	10.1	19,615	1.7
5410	Reservation and transportation ticket agents and travel clerks	61,690	44.6	29,955	21.7	4,685	3.4
5420	Information and record clerks, all other	51,025	54.1	14,770	15.7	3,725	4.0
5500	Cargo and freight agents	7,955	41.9	3,045	16.0	580	3.1
5510	Couriers and messengers	119,435	41.0	30,900	10.6	5,300	1.8
5520	Dispatchers	127,430	47.5	26,515	9.9	3,155	1.2
5530	Meter readers, utilities	15,305	41.3	2,630	7.1	305	0.8
5540	Postal service clerks	66,710	47.3	18,725	13.3	2,310	1.6
5550	Postal service mail carriers	154,905	47.5	39,085	12.0	4,110	1.3
5560	Postal service mail sorters, processors, and processing machine operators	40,265	45.3	12,475	14.0	1,840	2.1
5600	Production, planning, and expediting clerks	114,795	41.4	64,990	23.5	15,885	5.7
5610	Shipping, receiving, and traffic clerks	179,195	31.9	33,310	5.9	4,515	0.8
5620	Stock clerks and order fillers	470,815	32.6	84,695	5.9	12,945	0.9
5630	Weighers, measurers, checkers, and samplers, recordkeeping	24,105	34.3	6,215	8.8	1,160	1.6
5700	Secretaries and administrative assistants	1,812,030	49.0	548,925	14.8	89,860	2.4
5800	Computer operators	63,615	46.0	27,065	19.6	5,260	3.8
5810	Data entry keyers	209,150	48.2	61,790	14.2	9,885	2.3
5820	Word processors and typists	157,790	49.5	43,810	13.7	7,620	2.4
5840	Insurance claims and policy processing clerks	143,185	47.2	56,135	18.5	7,485	2.5
5850	Mail clerks and mail machine operators, except postal service	44,765	38.5	8,620	7.4	1,495	1.3
5860	Office clerks, general	550,935	47.4	161,155	13.9	31,170	2.7

A-17 Detailed Occupation, by Educational Attainment for Persons Age 16 and Older (worksite geography), 2006–2010—Continued

Census occupation code	Occupation by educational attainment for persons age 16 and older	Total workers	Not high school graduate Number	Not high school graduate Percent	High school graduate (including equivalency) Number	High school graduate (including equivalency) Percent
5900	Office machine operators, except computer	50,345	4,430	8.8	17,835	35.4
5910	Proofreaders and copy markers	14,550	455	3.1	2,565	17.6
5920	Statistical assistants	25,570	475	1.9	5,285	20.7
5940	Miscellaneous office and administrative support workers, including desktop publishers	511,850	16,215	3.2	121,290	23.7
6005	First-line supervisors of farming, fishing, and forestry workers	56,685	16,515	29.1	19,425	34.3
6010	Agricultural inspectors	16,505	1,415	8.6	4,355	26.4
6040	Graders and sorters, agricultural products	42,290	23,765	56.2	11,785	27.9
6050	Miscellaneous agricultural workers, including animal breeders	740,240	410,240	55.4	198,425	26.8
6100	Fishing and hunting workers	33,175	9,145	27.6	13,825	41.7
6120	Forest and conservation workers	14,050	3,820	27.2	4,395	31.3
6130	Logging workers	72,905	25,890	35.5	33,520	46.0
6200	First-line supervisors of construction trades and extraction workers	939,190	139,845	14.9	399,825	42.6
6210	Boilermakers	17,515	2,125	12.1	9,330	53.3
6220	Brickmasons, blockmasons, and stonemasons	182,170	65,870	36.2	79,085	43.4
6230	Carpenters	1,361,845	340,495	25.0	592,960	43.5
6240	Carpet, floor, and tile installers and finishers	200,175	69,685	34.8	85,580	42.8
6250	Cement masons, concrete finishers, and terrazzo workers	76,150	31,655	41.6	32,675	42.9
6260	Construction laborers	1,564,255	554,450	35.4	632,905	40.5
6300	Paving, surfacing, and tamping equipment operators	16,885	5,815	34.4	8,080	47.9
6320	Construction equipment operators except paving, surfacing, and tamping equipment operators	356,985	83,095	23.3	187,920	52.6
6330	Drywall installers, ceiling tile installers, and tapers	176,080	82,305	46.7	68,065	38.7
6355	Electricians	736,130	63,940	8.7	296,280	40.2
6360	Glaziers	41,965	8,675	20.7	22,065	52.6
6400	Insulation workers	42,130	13,225	31.4	18,430	43.7
6420	Painters, construction and maintenance	563,450	191,550	34.0	223,490	39.7
6430	Paperhangers	7,730	1,240	16.0	3,275	42.4
6440	Pipelayers, plumbers, pipefitters, and steamfitters	544,950	99,275	18.2	259,895	47.7
6460	Plasterers and stucco masons	41,080	21,085	51.3	14,620	35.6
6500	Reinforcing iron and rebar workers	8,865	2,375	26.8	4,440	50.1
6515	Roofers	206,575	95,475	46.2	79,040	38.3
6520	Sheet metal workers	128,430	21,145	16.5	61,795	48.1
6530	Structural iron and steel workers	62,015	10,940	17.6	30,470	49.1
6600	Helpers, construction trades	75,810	31,220	41.2	29,225	38.6
6660	Construction and building inspectors	101,195	2,955	2.9	27,105	26.8
6700	Elevator installers and repairers	27,320	1,000	3.7	12,735	46.6
6710	Fence erectors	29,330	10,835	36.9	11,585	39.5
6720	Hazardous materials removal workers	29,325	5,630	19.2	11,750	40.1
6730	Highway maintenance workers	99,605	15,720	15.8	53,375	53.6
6740	Rail-track laying and maintenance equipment operators	11,055	1,170	10.6	6,150	55.6
6765	Miscellaneous construction workers, including solar photovoltaic installers, septic tank servicers and sewer pipe cleaners	45,715	12,050	26.4	19,905	43.5
6800	Derrick, rotary drill, and service unit operators, and roustabouts, oil, gas, and mining	35,735	9,050	25.3	17,080	47.8
6820	Earth drillers, except oil and gas	25,440	4,385	17.2	13,845	54.4
6830	Explosives workers, ordnance handling experts, and blasters	9,900	1,015	10.3	4,235	42.8
6840	Mining machine operators	55,905	9,005	16.1	30,390	54.4
6940	Miscellaneous extraction workers, including roof bolters and helpers	58,390	13,915	23.8	28,850	49.4
7000	First-line supervisors of mechanics, installers, and repairers	298,545	22,520	7.5	109,840	36.8
7010	Computer, automated teller, and office machine repairers	262,905	7,970	3.0	53,810	20.5
7020	Radio and telecommunications equipment installers and repairers	180,600	6,550	3.6	57,850	32.0
7030	Avionics technicians	16,780	345	2.1	4,510	26.9
7040	Electric motor, power tool, and related repairers	28,045	3,120	11.1	10,915	38.9

A-17 Detailed Occupation, by Educational Attainment for Persons Age 16 and Older (worksite geography), 2006–2010—Continued

Census occupation code	Occupation by educational attainment for persons age 16 and older	Some college or associate degree Number	Some college or associate degree Percent	Bachelor's degree Number	Bachelor's degree Percent	Graduate or professional degree Number	Graduate or professional degree Percent
5900	Office machine operators, except computer	22,350	44.4	5,095	10.1	635	1.3
5910	Proofreaders and copy markers	4,410	30.3	5,525	38.0	1,595	11.0
5920	Statistical assistants	12,025	47.0	6,360	24.9	1,425	5.6
5940	Miscellaneous office and administrative support workers, including desktop publishers	219,890	43.0	121,360	23.7	33,095	6.5
6005	First-line supervisors of farming, fishing, and forestry workers	12,395	21.9	6,930	12.2	1,420	2.5
6010	Agricultural inspectors	5,470	33.1	4,195	25.4	1,070	6.5
6040	Graders and sorters, agricultural products	5,175	12.2	1,340	3.2	225	0.5
6050	Miscellaneous agricultural workers, including animal breeders	100,395	13.6	26,345	3.6	4,835	0.7
6100	Fishing and hunting workers	7,055	21.3	2,530	7.6	620	1.9
6120	Forest and conservation workers	3,460	24.6	1,955	13.9	420	3.0
6130	Logging workers	11,400	15.6	1,760	2.4	335	0.5
6200	First-line supervisors of construction trades and extraction workers	300,490	32.0	83,780	8.9	15,250	1.6
6210	Boilermakers	5,465	31.2	580	3.3	15	0.1
6220	Brickmasons, blockmasons, and stonemasons	30,855	16.9	5,525	3.0	835	0.5
6230	Carpenters	338,430	24.9	76,540	5.6	13,420	1.0
6240	Carpet, floor, and tile installers and finishers	36,510	18.2	7,360	3.7	1,040	0.5
6250	Cement masons, concrete finishers, and terrazzo workers	10,240	13.4	1,355	1.8	225	0.3
6260	Construction laborers	301,090	19.2	64,230	4.1	11,580	0.7
6300	Paving, surfacing, and tamping equipment operators	2,665	15.8	235	1.4	90	0.5
6320	Construction equipment operators except paving, surfacing, and tamping equipment operators	75,855	21.2	9,025	2.5	1,090	0.3
6330	Drywall installers, ceiling tile installers, and tapers	22,250	12.6	3,010	1.7	450	0.3
6355	Electricians	326,710	44.4	41,535	5.6	7,665	1.0
6360	Glaziers	9,965	23.7	1,115	2.7	145	0.3
6400	Insulation workers	8,905	21.1	1,365	3.2	205	0.5
6420	Painters, construction and maintenance	110,530	19.6	31,825	5.6	6,055	1.1
6430	Paperhangers	2,500	32.3	635	8.2	80	1.0
6440	Pipelayers, plumbers, pipefitters, and steamfitters	162,965	29.9	18,940	3.5	3,875	0.7
6460	Plasterers and stucco masons	4,230	10.3	1,010	2.5	135	0.3
6500	Reinforcing iron and rebar workers	1,840	20.8	195	2.2	15	0.2
6515	Roofers	26,350	12.8	4,835	2.3	875	0.4
6520	Sheet metal workers	41,015	31.9	3,975	3.1	500	0.4
6530	Structural iron and steel workers	18,370	29.6	2,080	3.4	155	0.2
6600	Helpers, construction trades	13,405	17.7	1,620	2.1	340	0.4
6660	Construction and building inspectors	47,065	46.5	20,640	20.4	3,430	3.4
6700	Elevator installers and repairers	11,595	42.4	1,690	6.2	300	1.1
6710	Fence erectors	5,715	19.5	1,070	3.6	125	0.4
6720	Hazardous materials removal workers	9,185	31.3	2,170	7.4	590	2.0
6730	Highway maintenance workers	27,405	27.5	2,770	2.8	335	0.3
6740	Rail-track laying and maintenance equipment operators	3,460	31.3	265	2.4	10	0.1
6765	Miscellaneous construction workers, including solar photovoltaic installers, septic tank servicers and sewer pipe cleaners	11,610	25.4	1,725	3.8	425	0.9
6800	Derrick, rotary drill, and service unit operators, and roustabouts, oil, gas, and mining	8,010	22.4	1,405	3.9	190	0.5
6820	Earth drillers, except oil and gas	6,175	24.3	1,010	4.0	25	0.1
6830	Explosives workers, ordnance handling experts, and blasters	3,910	39.5	600	6.1	140	1.4
6840	Mining machine operators	14,580	26.1	1,715	3.1	215	0.4
6940	Miscellaneous extraction workers, including roof bolters and helpers	13,830	23.7	1,620	2.8	175	0.3
7000	First-line supervisors of mechanics, installers, and repairers	128,655	43.1	30,490	10.2	7,040	2.4
7010	Computer, automated teller, and office machine repairers	144,990	55.1	48,015	18.3	8,120	3.1
7020	Radio and telecommunications equipment installers and repairers	93,750	51.9	19,600	10.9	2,850	1.6
7030	Avionics technicians	9,820	58.5	1,880	11.2	225	1.3
7040	Electric motor, power tool, and related repairers	11,990	42.8	1,690	6.0	330	1.2

A-17 Detailed Occupation, by Educational Attainment for Persons Age 16 and Older (worksite geography), 2006–2010—*Continued*

Census occupation code	Occupation by educational attainment for persons age 16 and older	Total workers	Not high school graduate Number	Not high school graduate Percent	High school graduate (including equivalency) Number	High school graduate (including equivalency) Percent
7100	Electrical and electronics repairers, transportation equipment, and industrial and utility	16,300	330	2.0	5,395	33.1
7110	Electronic equipment installers and repairers, motor vehicles	18,035	2,290	12.7	5,940	32.9
7120	Electronic home entertainment equipment installers and repairers	57,720	4,595	8.0	20,325	35.2
7130	Security and fire alarm systems installers	54,790	4,655	8.5	21,165	38.6
7140	Aircraft mechanics and service technicians	145,905	4,200	2.9	43,250	29.6
7150	Automotive body and related repairers	156,645	38,155	24.4	77,640	49.6
7160	Automotive glass installers and repairers	18,605	3,700	19.9	9,505	51.1
7200	Automotive service technicians and mechanics	811,835	151,590	18.7	363,790	44.8
7210	Bus and truck mechanics and diesel engine specialists	290,450	45,860	15.8	140,795	48.5
7220	Heavy vehicle and mobile equipment service technicians and mechanics	203,230	30,465	15.0	96,155	47.3
7240	Small engine mechanics	47,665	7,530	15.8	23,095	48.5
7260	Miscellaneous vehicle and mobile equipment mechanics, installers, and repairers	78,045	20,815	26.7	34,815	44.6
7300	Control and valve installers and repairers	19,920	1,595	8.0	8,845	44.4
7315	Heating, air conditioning, and refrigeration mechanics and installers	344,045	42,835	12.5	147,880	43.0
7320	Home appliance repairers	41,420	5,550	13.4	18,280	44.1
7330	Industrial and refractory machinery mechanics	388,175	44,975	11.6	168,020	43.3
7340	Maintenance and repair workers, general	459,560	64,980	14.1	196,805	42.8
7350	Maintenance workers, machinery	35,840	4,805	13.4	15,535	43.3
7360	Millwrights	50,270	4,640	9.2	23,300	46.3
7410	Electrical power-line installers and repairers	110,970	7,595	6.8	50,960	45.9
7420	Telecommunications line installers and repairers	157,430	9,755	6.2	61,360	39.0
7430	Precision instrument and equipment repairers	60,455	2,915	4.8	13,710	22.7
7510	Coin, vending, and amusement machine servicers and repairers	45,950	5,470	11.9	19,385	42.2
7540	Locksmiths and safe repairers	26,295	2,700	10.3	11,475	43.6
7550	Manufactured building and mobile home installers	9,150	3,180	34.8	4,135	45.2
7560	Riggers	11,060	1,855	16.8	5,355	48.4
7610	Helpers—installation, maintenance, and repair workers	23,275	8,300	35.7	9,520	40.9
7630	Other installation, maintenance, and repair workers, including wind turbine service technicians, and commercial divers, and signal and track switch repairers	216,170	33,715	15.6	87,190	40.3
7700	First-line supervisors of production and operating workers	930,550	102,045	11.0	373,560	40.1
7710	Aircraft structure, surfaces, rigging, and systems assemblers	10,365	1,610	15.5	4,350	42.0
7720	Electrical, electronics, and electromechanical assemblers	163,865	34,830	21.3	77,945	47.6
7730	Engine and other machine assemblers	16,405	1,970	12.0	8,440	51.4
7740	Structural metal fabricators and fitters	26,350	3,570	13.5	13,075	49.6
7750	Miscellaneous assemblers and fabricators	937,035	197,960	21.1	454,580	48.5
7800	Bakers	170,330	47,350	27.8	66,685	39.2
7810	Butchers and other meat, poultry, and fish processing workers	246,630	88,855	36.0	104,625	42.4
7830	Food and tobacco roasting, baking, and drying machine operators and tenders	10,560	2,940	27.8	4,495	42.6
7840	Food batchmakers	80,900	19,735	24.4	35,590	44.0
7850	Food cooking machine operators and tenders	11,364	3,295	29.0	5,110	45.0
7855	Food processing workers, all other	119,230	37,765	31.7	54,090	45.4
7900	Computer control programmers and operators	65,700	5,670	8.6	29,985	45.6
7920	Extruding and drawing machine setters, operators, and tenders, metal and plastic	12,195	1,995	16.4	6,505	53.3
7930	Forging machine setters, operators, and tenders, metal and plastic	7,925	1,325	16.7	5,005	63.2
7940	Rolling machine setters, operators, and tenders, metal and plastic	10,895	2,160	19.8	6,150	56.4
7950	Cutting, punching, and press machine setters, operators, and tenders, metal and plastic	95,425	21,295	22.3	51,355	53.8
7960	Drilling and boring machine tool setters, operators, and tenders, metal and plastic	4,895	1,095	22.4	2,635	53.8

PART A—NATIONAL DATA

A-17 Detailed Occupation, by Educational Attainment for Persons Age 16 and Older (worksite geography), 2006–2010—Continued

Census occupation code	Occupation by educational attainment for persons age 16 and older	Some college or associate degree Number	Some college or associate degree Percent	Bachelor's degree Number	Bachelor's degree Percent	Graduate or professional degree Number	Graduate or professional degree Percent
7100	Electrical and electronics repairers, transportation equipment, and industrial and utility	8,685	53.3	1,585	9.7	305	1.9
7110	Electronic equipment installers and repairers, motor vehicles	8,705	48.3	900	5.0	200	1.1
7120	Electronic home entertainment equipment installers and repairers	26,810	46.4	5,310	9.2	680	1.2
7130	Security and fire alarm systems installers	24,280	44.3	4,085	7.5	605	1.1
7140	Aircraft mechanics and service technicians	83,260	57.1	13,335	9.1	1,860	1.3
7150	Automotive body and related repairers	36,975	23.6	3,285	2.1	590	0.4
7160	Automotive glass installers and repairers	4,565	24.5	800	4.3	35	0.2
7200	Automotive service technicians and mechanics	267,805	33.0	24,480	3.0	4,170	0.5
7210	Bus and truck mechanics and diesel engine specialists	96,230	33.1	6,490	2.2	1,075	0.4
7220	Heavy vehicle and mobile equipment service technicians and mechanics	69,665	34.3	6,005	3.0	940	0.5
7240	Small engine mechanics	15,265	32.0	1,450	3.0	325	0.7
7260	Miscellaneous vehicle and mobile equipment mechanics, installers, and repairers	19,445	24.9	2,710	3.5	260	0.3
7300	Control and valve installers and repairers	8,460	42.5	930	4.7	90	0.5
7315	Heating, air conditioning, and refrigeration mechanics and installers	137,875	40.1	12,920	3.8	2,535	0.7
7320	Home appliance repairers	14,775	35.7	2,245	5.4	570	1.4
7330	Industrial and refractory machinery mechanics	154,660	39.8	18,320	4.7	2,200	0.6
7340	Maintenance and repair workers, general	168,940	36.8	24,845	5.4	3,990	0.9
7350	Maintenance workers, machinery	13,760	38.4	1,530	4.3	210	0.6
7360	Millwrights	20,690	41.2	1,340	2.7	300	0.6
7410	Electrical power-line installers and repairers	47,175	42.5	4,665	4.2	575	0.5
7420	Telecommunications line installers and repairers	72,805	46.2	12,025	7.6	1,485	0.9
7430	Precision instrument and equipment repairers	32,410	53.6	9,175	15.2	2,245	3.7
7510	Coin, vending, and amusement machine servicers and repairers	17,000	37.0	3,445	7.5	650	1.4
7540	Locksmiths and safe repairers	9,540	36.3	2,195	8.3	385	1.5
7550	Manufactured building and mobile home installers	1,590	17.4	205	2.2	40	0.4
7560	Riggers	3,185	28.8	595	5.4	70	0.6
7610	Helpers—installation, maintenance, and repair workers	4,795	20.6	560	2.4	100	0.4
7630	Other installation, maintenance, and repair workers, including wind turbine service technicians, and commercial divers, and signal and track switch repairers	76,280	35.3	16,050	7.4	2,935	1.4
7700	First-line supervisors of production and operating workers	313,250	33.7	111,905	12.0	29,790	3.2
7710	Aircraft structure, surfaces, rigging, and systems assemblers	3,875	37.4	465	4.5	65	0.6
7720	Electrical, electronics, and electromechanical assemblers	42,460	25.9	7,495	4.6	1,135	0.7
7730	Engine and other machine assemblers	5,425	33.1	510	3.1	60	0.4
7740	Structural metal fabricators and fitters	8,285	31.4	1,240	4.7	180	0.7
7750	Miscellaneous assemblers and fabricators	238,300	25.4	40,555	4.3	5,640	0.6
7800	Bakers	42,845	25.2	11,500	6.8	1,950	1.1
7810	Butchers and other meat, poultry, and fish processing workers	46,215	18.7	6,040	2.4	895	0.4
7830	Food and tobacco roasting, baking, and drying machine operators and tenders	2,405	22.8	645	6.1	75	0.7
7840	Food batchmakers	21,330	26.4	3,790	4.7	455	0.6
7850	Food cooking machine operators and tenders	2,430	21.4	525	4.6	4	0.0
7855	Food processing workers, all other	23,290	19.5	3,415	2.9	670	0.6
7900	Computer control programmers and operators	26,025	39.6	3,375	5.1	645	1.0
7920	Extruding and drawing machine setters, operators, and tenders, metal and plastic	3,215	26.4	445	3.6	35	0.3
7930	Forging machine setters, operators, and tenders, metal and plastic	1,500	18.9	85	1.1	10	0.1
7940	Rolling machine setters, operators, and tenders, metal and plastic	2,260	20.7	275	2.5	50	0.5
7950	Cutting, punching, and press machine setters, operators, and tenders, metal and plastic	20,100	21.1	2,340	2.5	335	0.4
7960	Drilling and boring machine tool setters, operators, and tenders, metal and plastic	1,110	22.7	55	1.1	0	0.0

A-17 **Detailed Occupation, by Educational Attainment for Persons Age 16 and Older (worksite geography), 2006–2010**—*Continued*

Census occupation code	Occupation by educational attainment for persons age 16 and older	Total workers	Not high school graduate Number	Not high school graduate Percent	High school graduate (including equivalency) Number	High school graduate (including equivalency) Percent
8000	Grinding, lapping, polishing, and buffing machine tool setters, operators, and tenders, metal and plastic	50,665	14,290	28.2	25,400	50.1
8010	Lathe and turning machine tool setters, operators, and tenders, metal and plastic	12,345	2,280	18.5	6,865	55.6
8030	Machinists	359,720	39,880	11.1	172,820	48.0
8040	Metal furnace operators, tenders, pourers, and casters	23,455	3,590	15.3	13,425	57.2
8060	Model makers and patternmakers, metal and plastic	7,035	830	11.8	2,380	33.8
8100	Molders and molding machine setters, operators, and tenders, metal and plastic	46,135	9,985	21.6	23,215	50.3
8130	Tool and die makers	69,770	4,465	6.4	27,710	39.7
8140	Welding, soldering, and brazing workers	563,405	128,055	22.7	281,315	49.9
8150	Heat treating equipment setters, operators, and tenders, metal and plastic	7,835	1,195	15.3	3,970	50.7
8200	Plating and coating machine setters, operators, and tenders, metal and plastic	16,915	3,645	21.5	8,650	51.1
8210	Tool grinders, filers, and sharpeners	8,200	1,175	14.3	4,005	48.8
8220	Miscellaneous metal workers and plastic workers, including milling and planing machine setters, and multiple machine tool setters, and layout workers	407,345	92,750	22.8	204,055	50.1
8250	Prepress technicians and workers	42,790	3,655	8.5	15,405	36.0
8255	Printing press operators	220,880	29,675	13.4	107,780	48.8
8256	Print binding and finishing workers	32,010	5,675	17.7	15,945	49.8
8300	Laundry and dry-cleaning workers	192,805	70,955	36.8	79,805	41.4
8310	Pressers, textile, garment, and related materials	54,605	25,700	47.1	20,740	38.0
8320	Sewing machine operators	217,880	93,875	43.1	82,975	38.1
8330	Shoe and leather workers and repairers	10,095	3,115	30.9	3,845	38.1
8340	Shoe machine operators and tenders	4,255	1,385	32.5	1,920	45.1
8350	Tailors, dressmakers, and sewers	82,270	21,720	26.4	29,350	35.7
8400	Textile bleaching and dyeing, and cutting machine setters, operators, and tenders	13,000	4,525	34.8	5,655	43.5
8410	Textile knitting and weaving machine setters, operators, and tenders	11,580	3,330	28.8	5,870	50.7
8420	Textile winding, twisting, and drawing out machine setters, operators, and tenders	15,430	5,775	37.4	7,580	49.1
8450	Upholsterers	39,940	12,415	31.1	17,980	45.0
8460	Miscellaneous textile, apparel, and furnishings workers except upholsterers	25,495	7,030	27.6	11,265	44.2
8500	Cabinetmakers and bench carpenters	66,520	14,285	21.5	29,520	44.4
8510	Furniture finishers	19,215	5,090	26.5	7,880	41.0
8530	Sawing machine setters, operators, and tenders, wood	37,720	12,930	34.3	18,015	47.8
8540	Woodworking machine setters, operators, and tenders, except sawing	28,100	9,020	32.1	13,175	46.9
8550	Miscellaneous woodworkers, including model makers and patternmakers	29,160	5,665	19.4	12,195	41.8
8600	Power plant operators, distributors, and dispatchers	45,350	1,065	2.3	15,490	34.2
8610	Stationary engineers and boiler operators	94,880	6,665	7.0	39,135	41.2
8620	Water and wastewater treatment plant and system operators	77,635	3,195	4.1	33,170	42.7
8630	Miscellaneous plant and system operators	39,450	2,830	7.2	16,275	41.3
8640	Chemical processing machine setters, operators, and tenders	53,215	5,055	9.5	20,790	39.1
8650	Crushing, grinding, polishing, mixing, and blending workers	89,965	20,905	23.2	42,975	47.8
8710	Cutting workers	73,860	24,475	33.1	33,630	45.5
8720	Extruding, forming, pressing, and compacting machine setters, operators, and tenders	32,810	6,820	20.8	17,135	52.2
8730	Furnace, kiln, oven, drier, and kettle operators and tenders	11,710	1,415	12.1	5,675	48.5
8740	Inspectors, testers, sorters, samplers, and weighers	732,215	92,055	12.6	281,865	38.5
8750	Jewelers and precious stone and metal workers	39,880	7,565	19.0	12,275	30.8
8760	Medical, dental, and ophthalmic laboratory technicians	84,440	5,970	7.1	27,625	32.7

PART A—NATIONAL DATA

A-17 Detailed Occupation, by Educational Attainment for Persons Age 16 and Older (worksite geography), 2006–2010—Continued

Census occupation code	Occupation by educational attainment for persons age 16 and older	Some college or associate degree Number	Some college or associate degree Percent	Bachelor's degree Number	Bachelor's degree Percent	Graduate or professional degree Number	Graduate or professional degree Percent
8000	Grinding, lapping, polishing, and buffing machine tool setters, operators, and tenders, metal and plastic	9,705	19.2	1,025	2.0	245	0.5
8010	Lathe and turning machine tool setters, operators, and tenders, metal and plastic	2,880	23.3	270	2.2	50	0.4
8030	Machinists	135,155	37.6	10,125	2.8	1,740	0.5
8040	Metal furnace operators, tenders, pourers, and casters	5,710	24.3	635	2.7	95	0.4
8060	Model makers and patternmakers, metal and plastic	2,955	42.0	660	9.4	210	3.0
8100	Molders and molding machine setters, operators, and tenders, metal and plastic	11,545	25.0	1,270	2.8	120	0.3
8130	Tool and die makers	34,700	49.7	2,425	3.5	470	0.7
8140	Welding, soldering, and brazing workers	142,230	25.2	10,280	1.8	1,525	0.3
8150	Heat treating equipment setters, operators, and tenders, metal and plastic	2,415	30.8	235	3.0	20	0.3
8200	Plating and coating machine setters, operators, and tenders, metal and plastic	4,110	24.3	330	2.0	180	1.1
8210	Tool grinders, filers, and sharpeners	2,595	31.6	375	4.6	50	0.6
8220	Miscellaneous metal workers and plastic workers, including milling and planing machine setters, and multiple machine tool setters, and layout workers	94,695	23.2	13,865	3.4	1,980	0.5
8250	Prepress technicians and workers	16,650	38.9	6,215	14.5	865	2.0
8255	Printing press operators	67,805	30.7	13,655	6.2	1,965	0.9
8256	Print binding and finishing workers	7,995	25.0	1,845	5.8	550	1.7
8300	Laundry and dry-cleaning workers	32,730	17.0	7,875	4.1	1,440	0.7
8310	Pressers, textile, garment, and related materials	6,745	12.4	1,170	2.1	250	0.5
8320	Sewing machine operators	31,160	14.3	8,215	3.8	1,655	0.8
8330	Shoe and leather workers and repairers	2,345	23.2	655	6.5	135	1.3
8340	Shoe machine operators and tenders	640	15.0	275	6.5	35	0.8
8350	Tailors, dressmakers, and sewers	19,550	23.8	9,435	11.5	2,215	2.7
8400	Textile bleaching and dyeing, and cutting machine setters, operators, and tenders	2,380	18.3	375	2.9	65	0.5
8410	Textile knitting and weaving machine setters, operators, and tenders	1,975	17.1	315	2.7	90	0.8
8420	Textile winding, twisting, and drawing out machine setters, operators, and tenders	1,945	12.6	105	0.7	25	0.2
8450	Upholsterers	7,780	19.5	1,445	3.6	320	0.8
8460	Miscellaneous textile, apparel, and furnishings workers except upholsterers	4,575	17.9	2,195	8.6	430	1.7
8500	Cabinetmakers and bench carpenters	17,295	26.0	4,535	6.8	885	1.3
8510	Furniture finishers	4,485	23.3	1,460	7.6	300	1.6
8530	Sawing machine setters, operators, and tenders, wood	5,850	15.5	700	1.9	225	0.6
8540	Woodworking machine setters, operators, and tenders, except sawing	4,970	17.7	615	2.2	320	1.1
8550	Miscellaneous woodworkers, including model makers and patternmakers	7,455	25.6	3,220	11.0	625	2.1
8600	Power plant operators, distributors, and dispatchers	21,850	48.2	6,010	13.3	935	2.1
8610	Stationary engineers and boiler operators	38,490	40.6	8,515	9.0	2,075	2.2
8620	Water and wastewater treatment plant and system operators	33,785	43.5	6,525	8.4	960	1.2
8630	Miscellaneous plant and system operators	16,820	42.6	3,085	7.8	440	1.1
8640	Chemical processing machine setters, operators, and tenders	19,135	36.0	6,725	12.6	1,510	2.8
8650	Crushing, grinding, polishing, mixing, and blending workers	21,935	24.4	3,460	3.8	690	0.8
8710	Cutting workers	13,365	18.1	2,090	2.8	300	0.4
8720	Extruding, forming, pressing, and compacting machine setters, operators, and tenders	7,935	24.2	855	2.6	65	0.2
8730	Furnace, kiln, oven, drier, and kettle operators and tenders	3,975	33.9	610	5.2	35	0.3
8740	Inspectors, testers, sorters, samplers, and weighers	257,480	35.2	79,645	10.9	21,170	2.9
8750	Jewelers and precious stone and metal workers	12,240	30.7	6,150	15.4	1,650	4.1
8760	Medical, dental, and ophthalmic laboratory technicians	39,610	46.9	9,070	10.7	2,165	2.6

A-17 **Detailed Occupation, by Educational Attainment for Persons Age 16 and Older (worksite geography), 2006–2010**—*Continued*

Census occupation code	Occupation by educational attainment for persons age 16 and older	Total workers	Not high school graduate Number	Not high school graduate Percent	High school graduate (including equivalency) Number	High school graduate (including equivalency) Percent
8800	Packaging and filling machine operators and tenders	251,825	90,850	36.1	108,490	43.1
8810	Painting workers	155,160	41,940	27.0	72,900	47.0
8830	Photographic process workers and processing machine operators	59,165	4,880	8.2	20,945	35.4
8850	Adhesive bonding machine operators and tenders	12,955	3,525	27.2	6,230	48.1
8860	Cleaning, washing, and metal pickling equipment operators and tenders	8,945	2,740	30.6	4,285	47.9
8910	Etchers and engravers	10,460	1,255	12.0	4,145	39.6
8920	Molders, shapers, and casters, except metal and plastic	33,870	8,260	24.4	13,160	38.9
8930	Paper goods machine setters, operators, and tenders	33,740	6,325	18.7	18,190	53.9
8940	Tire builders	15,150	1,875	12.4	8,430	55.6
8950	Helpers—production workers	46,125	15,755	34.2	18,950	41.1
8965	Other production workers, including semiconductor processors and cooling and freezing equipment operators	1,040,180	234,355	22.5	496,780	47.8
9000	Supervisors of transportation and material moving workers	234,845	19,605	8.3	83,140	35.4
9030	Aircraft pilots and flight engineers	123,890	460	0.4	6,230	5.0
9040	Air traffic controllers and airfield operations specialists	33,100	195	0.6	4,935	14.9
9050	Flight attendants	86,615	830	1.0	13,180	15.2
9110	Ambulance drivers and attendants, except emergency medical technicians	12,070	1,540	12.8	4,900	40.6
9120	Bus drivers	548,270	59,100	10.8	255,160	46.5
9130	Driver/sales workers and truck drivers	3,058,960	595,410	19.5	1,490,730	48.7
9140	Taxi drivers and chauffeurs	303,095	50,100	16.5	117,310	38.7
9150	Motor vehicle operators, all other	52,430	9,720	18.5	22,080	42.1
9200	Locomotive engineers and operators	49,710	1,400	2.8	20,770	41.8
9230	Railroad brake, signal, and switch operators	7,335	680	9.3	3,665	50.0
9240	Railroad conductors and yardmasters	47,100	1,470	3.1	18,615	39.5
9260	Subway, streetcar, and other rail transportation workers	10,370	690	6.7	4,180	40.3
9300	Sailors and marine oilers, and ship engineers	23,530	3,295	14.0	10,320	43.9
9310	Ship and boat captains and operators	33,630	3,985	11.8	13,640	40.6
9350	Parking lot attendants	71,675	12,455	17.4	26,200	36.6
9360	Automotive and watercraft service attendants	111,570	25,530	22.9	49,045	44.0
9410	Transportation inspectors	48,890	3,070	6.3	16,990	34.8
9415	Transportation attendants, except flight attendants	30,750	5,115	16.6	14,525	47.2
9420	Miscellaneous transportation workers, including bridge and lock tenders and traffic technicians	21,680	1,385	6.4	8,050	37.1
9510	Crane and tower operators	62,950	11,055	17.6	35,560	56.5
9520	Dredge, excavating, and loading machine operators	47,015	12,690	27.0	24,395	51.9
9560	Conveyor operators and tenders, and hoist and winch operators	12,510	2,140	17.1	6,375	51.0
9600	Industrial truck and tractor operators	501,775	122,990	24.5	260,695	52.0
9610	Cleaners of vehicles and equipment	328,125	117,785	35.9	135,065	41.2
9620	Laborers and freight, stock, and material movers, hand	1,919,685	469,075	24.4	878,595	45.8
9630	Machine feeders and offbearers	33,195	8,850	26.7	15,680	47.2
9640	Packers and packagers, hand	405,075	157,815	39.0	165,115	40.8
9650	Pumping station operators	21,200	2,715	12.8	10,615	50.1
9720	Refuse and recyclable material collectors	87,910	28,345	32.2	39,670	45.1
9750	Miscellaneous material moving workers, including mine shuttle car operators, and tank car, truck, and ship loaders	53,720	10,985	20.4	26,860	50.0

PART A—NATIONAL DATA

A-17 Detailed Occupation, by Educational Attainment for Persons Age 16 and Older (worksite geography), 2006–2010—Continued

Census occupation code	Occupation by educational attainment for persons age 16 and older	Some college or associate degree Number	Some college or associate degree Percent	Bachelor's degree Number	Bachelor's degree Percent	Graduate or professional degree Number	Graduate or professional degree Percent
8800	Packaging and filling machine operators and tenders	43,200	17.2	7,890	3.1	1,395	0.6
8810	Painting workers	35,550	22.9	3,985	2.6	785	0.5
8830	Photographic process workers and processing machine operators	23,405	39.6	8,255	14.0	1,680	2.8
8850	Adhesive bonding machine operators and tenders	2,945	22.7	200	1.5	55	0.4
8860	Cleaning, washing, and metal pickling equipment operators and tenders	1,680	18.8	230	2.6	10	0.1
8910	Etchers and engravers	3,825	36.6	1,025	9.8	210	2.0
8920	Molders, shapers, and casters, except metal and plastic	8,195	24.2	2,985	8.8	1,270	3.7
8930	Paper goods machine setters, operators, and tenders	8,015	23.8	1,100	3.3	110	0.3
8940	Tire builders	4,400	29.0	390	2.6	55	0.4
8950	Helpers—production workers	9,525	20.7	1,660	3.6	235	0.5
8965	Other production workers, including semiconductor processors and cooling and freezing equipment operators	254,930	24.5	45,680	4.4	8,435	0.8
9000	Supervisors of transportation and material moving workers	93,195	39.7	33,135	14.1	5,770	2.5
9030	Aircraft pilots and flight engineers	27,655	22.3	73,885	59.6	15,660	12.6
9040	Air traffic controllers and airfield operations specialists	16,875	51.0	9,840	29.7	1,255	3.8
9050	Flight attendants	41,540	48.0	28,020	32.4	3,045	3.5
9110	Ambulance drivers and attendants, except emergency medical technicians	4,315	35.7	1,035	8.6	280	2.3
9120	Bus drivers	193,070	35.2	32,600	5.9	8,340	1.5
9130	Driver/sales workers and truck drivers	824,285	26.9	125,890	4.1	22,645	0.7
9140	Taxi drivers and chauffeurs	89,975	29.7	36,175	11.9	9,535	3.1
9150	Motor vehicle operators, all other	15,510	29.6	4,150	7.9	970	1.9
9200	Locomotive engineers and operators	21,965	44.2	4,875	9.8	700	1.4
9230	Railroad brake, signal, and switch operators	2,615	35.7	350	4.8	25	0.3
9240	Railroad conductors and yardmasters	21,500	45.6	5,040	10.7	475	1.0
9260	Subway, streetcar, and other rail transportation workers	4,510	43.5	805	7.8	185	1.8
9300	Sailors and marine oilers, and ship engineers	7,295	31.0	2,150	9.1	470	2.0
9310	Ship and boat captains and operators	9,690	28.8	5,285	15.7	1,030	3.1
9350	Parking lot attendants	25,970	36.2	5,960	8.3	1,090	1.5
9360	Automotive and watercraft service attendants	31,275	28.0	4,950	4.4	770	0.7
9410	Transportation inspectors	21,750	44.5	5,965	12.2	1,115	2.3
9415	Transportation attendants, except flight attendants	8,535	27.8	2,075	6.7	500	1.6
9420	Miscellaneous transportation workers, including bridge and lock tenders and traffic technicians	9,430	43.5	2,270	10.5	545	2.5
9510	Crane and tower operators	15,095	24.0	1,070	1.7	170	0.3
9520	Dredge, excavating, and loading machine operators	8,305	17.7	1,380	2.9	245	0.5
9560	Conveyor operators and tenders, and hoist and winch operators	3,425	27.4	455	3.6	115	0.9
9600	Industrial truck and tractor operators	106,235	21.2	10,445	2.1	1,410	0.3
9610	Cleaners of vehicles and equipment	65,055	19.8	8,975	2.7	1,245	0.4
9620	Laborers and freight, stock, and material movers, hand	490,455	25.5	70,055	3.6	11,505	0.6
9630	Machine feeders and offbearers	7,565	22.8	935	2.8	165	0.5
9640	Packers and packagers, hand	67,400	16.6	12,535	3.1	2,210	0.5
9650	Pumping station operators	6,430	30.3	1,325	6.3	115	0.5
9720	Refuse and recyclable material collectors	16,665	19.0	2,695	3.1	535	0.6
9750	Miscellaneous material moving workers, including mine shuttle car operators, and tank car, truck, and ship loaders	13,850	25.8	1,750	3.3	275	0.5

A-18 **Workers Who are Not High School Graduates: Detailed Occupation, by Sex, Race, and Hispanic Origin, 2006–2010**

Census occupation code	Detailed Occupation	Total	Not high school graduate					Not Hispanic or Latino, one race	
			Male		Female		Hispanic or Latino		White alone	
			Number	Percent	Number	Percent	Number	Percent	Number	Percent
	Total, all occupations............................	15,163,025	9,361,770	61.7	5,801,260	38.3	6,387,865	42.1	6,259,895	41.3
0010	Chief executives and legislators	19,585	16,305	83.3	3,280	16.7	2,680	13.7	14,610	74.6
0020	General and operations managers	20,385	14,325	70.3	6,060	29.7	4,280	21.0	13,365	65.6
0040	Advertising and promotions managers ...	335	175	52.2	160	47.8	80	23.9	255	76.1
0050	Marketing and sales managers	8,290	4,650	56.1	3,640	43.9	1,875	22.6	5,420	65.4
0060	Public relations and fundraising managers...	245	100	40.8	145	59.2	30	12.2	175	71.4
0100	Administrative services managers..........	1,965	1,515	77.1	450	22.9	455	23.2	1,050	53.4
0110	Computer and information systems managers...	2,045	1,460	71.4	585	28.6	395	19.3	1,170	57.2
0120	Financial managers.................................	10,055	3,735	37.1	6,320	62.9	2,755	27.4	5,950	59.2
0135	Compensation and benefits managers.....	235	55	23.4	180	76.6	55	23.4	160	68.1
0136	Human resources managers....................	8,575	5,100	59.5	3,475	40.5	3,150	36.7	3,785	44.1
0137	Training and development managers......	615	315	51.2	295	48.0	95	15.4	480	78.0
0140	Industrial production managers...............	8,440	7,360	87.2	1,080	12.8	2,525	29.9	5,210	61.7
0150	Purchasing managers..............................	2,005	1,175	58.6	830	41.4	470	23.4	1,385	69.1
0160	Transportation, storage, and distribution managers...	11,775	10,410	88.4	1,365	11.6	3,810	32.4	6,625	56.3
0205	Farmers, ranchers, and other agricultural managers............................	76,405	67,820	88.8	8,585	11.2	16,260	21.3	56,200	73.6
0220	Construction managers	61,960	60,400	97.5	1,560	2.5	17,050	27.5	40,055	64.6
0230	Education administrators	5,880	2,155	36.6	3,725	63.4	1,680	28.6	2,665	45.3
0300	Architectural and engineering managers	770	715	92.9	55	7.1	140	18.2	550	71.4
0310	Food service managers	88,440	44,020	49.8	44,420	50.2	31,565	35.7	38,075	43.1
0330	Gaming managers...................................	1,100	510	46.4	590	53.6	135	12.3	810	73.6
0340	Lodging managers	6,330	2,900	45.8	3,430	54.2	1,300	20.5	3,250	51.3
0350	Medical and health services managers ...	5,850	1,330	22.7	4,520	77.3	1,495	25.6	2,970	50.8
0360	Natural sciences managers	90	20	22.2	75	83.3	25	27.8	45	50.0
0410	Property, real estate, and community association managers.........................	26,365	13,265	50.3	13,100	49.7	8,985	34.1	14,405	54.6
0410	Social and community service managers..	5,115	1,595	31.2	3,520	68.8	680	13.3	2,975	58.2
0425	Emergency management directors	4	0	0.0	4	####	0	0.0	4	100.0
0430	Miscellaneous managers, including funeral service managers and postmasters and mail superintendents..	87,060	66,330	76.2	20,730	23.8	25,325	29.1	51,715	59.4
0500	Agents and business managers of artists, performers, and athletes............	1,310	920	70.2	390	29.8	390	29.8	490	37.4
0510	Buyers and purchasing agents, farm products..	1,135	1,025	90.3	110	9.7	510	44.9	570	50.2
0520	Wholesale and retail buyers, except farm products	8,730	5,050	57.8	3,680	42.2	2,605	29.8	5,285	60.5
0530	Purchasing agents, except wholesale, retail, and farm products.....................	5,380	2,730	50.7	2,650	49.3	1,285	23.9	3,545	65.9
0540	Claims adjusters, appraisers, examiners, and investigators	2,770	780	28.2	1,985	71.7	660	23.8	1,785	64.4
0565	Compliance officers................................	2,230	1,025	46.0	1,205	54.0	640	28.7	1,100	49.3

PART A—NATIONAL DATA

A-18 **Workers Who are Not High School Graduates: Detailed Occupation, by Sex, Race, and Hispanic Origin, 2006–2010**—Continued

Census occupation code	Detailed Occupation	Not high school graduate									
		Not Hispanic or Latino, one race								Not Hispanic or Latino, two or more races	
		Black or African American alone		American Indian and Alaska Native alone		Asian alone		Native Hawaiian and Other Pacific Islander alone			
		Number	Percent	Number	Percent	Number	Percent	Number	Percent	Number	Percent
	Total, all occupations..........	1,566,125	10.3	96,140	0.6	632,330	4.2	19,470	0.1	201,200	1.3
0010	Chief executives and legislators.............	1,055	5.4	220	1.1	745	3.8	25	0.1	255	1.3
0020	General and operations managers...........	1,525	7.5	235	1.2	605	3.0	10	0.0	364	1.8
0040	Advertising and promotions managers ...	0	0.0	0	0.0	0	0.0	0	0.0	0	0.0
0050	Marketing and sales managers................	505	6.1	55	0.7	270	3.3	35	0.4	120	1.4
0060	Public relations and fundraising managers..................	25	10.2	4	1.6	10	4.1	0	0.0	0	0.0
0100	Administrative services managers..........	285	14.5	4	0.2	115	5.9	0	0.0	55	2.8
0110	Computer and information systems managers...................	275	13.4	25	1.2	140	6.8	0	0.0	40	2.0
0120	Financial managers.................	850	8.5	50	0.5	320	3.2	0	0.0	125	1.2
0135	Compensation and benefits managers.....	20	8.5	0	0.0	0	0.0	0	0.0	0	0.0
0136	Human resources managers.....................	670	7.8	35	0.4	750	8.7	50	0.6	134	1.6
0137	Training and development managers......	40	6.5	0	0.0	0	0.0	0	0.0	0	0.0
0140	Industrial production managers..............	245	2.9	70	0.8	350	4.1	10	0.1	35	0.4
0150	Purchasing managers.............	30	1.5	25	1.2	85	4.2	0	0.0	4	0.2
0160	Transportation, storage, and distribution managers...................	870	7.4	35	0.3	290	2.5	45	0.4	105	0.9
0205	Farmers, ranchers, and other agricultural managers............	1,545	2.0	395	0.5	1,520	2.0	15	0.0	465	0.6
0220	Construction managers................	2,285	3.7	385	0.6	1,050	1.7	170	0.3	955	1.5
0230	Education administrators............	1,165	19.8	85	1.4	170	2.9	10	0.2	98	1.7
0300	Architectural and engineering managers	0	0.0	4	0.5	75	9.7	0	0.0	0	0.0
0310	Food service managers...............	6,720	7.6	375	0.4	10,300	11.6	130	0.1	1,285	1.5
0330	Gaming managers...............	80	7.3	60	5.5	15	1.4	0	0.0	0	0.0
0340	Lodging managers..................	290	4.6	35	0.6	1,280	20.2	25	0.4	149	2.4
0350	Medical and health services managers ...	1,060	18.1	95	1.6	150	2.6	4	0.1	69	1.2
0360	Natural sciences managers.............	0	0.0	0	0.0	20	22.2	0	0.0	0	0.0
0410	Property, real estate, and community association managers............	1,935	7.3	225	0.9	540	2.0	10	0.0	265	1.0
0410	Social and community service managers.................	1,110	21.7	75	1.5	150	2.9	0	0.0	127	2.5
0425	Emergency management directors..........	0	0.0	0	0.0	0	0.0	0	0.0	0	0.0
0430	Miscellaneous managers, including funeral service managers and postmasters and mail superintendents..	5,500	6.3	490	0.6	3,015	3.5	40	0.0	975	1.1
0500	Agents and business managers of artists, performers, and athletes............	375	28.6	4	0.3	45	3.4	0	0.0	10	0.8
0510	Buyers and purchasing agents, farm products	15	1.3	0	0.0	40	3.5	0	0.0	0	0.0
0520	Wholesale and retail buyers, except farm products	370	4.2	25	0.3	300	3.4	70	0.8	75	0.9
0530	Purchasing agents, except wholesale, retail, and farm products...............	335	6.2	25	0.5	145	2.7	20	0.4	34	0.6
0540	Claims adjusters, appraisers, examiners, and investigators	225	8.1	25	0.9	70	2.5	0	0.0	0	0.0
0565	Compliance officers..............	360	16.1	20	0.9	75	3.4	0	0.0	34	1.5

A-18 **Workers Who are Not High School Graduates: Detailed Occupation, by Sex, Race, and Hispanic Origin, 2006–2010**—Continued

Census occupation code	Detailed Occupation	Total	Not high school graduate						Not Hispanic or Latino, one race	
			Male		Female		Hispanic or Latino		White alone	
			Number	Percent	Number	Percent	Number	Percent	Number	Percent
0600	Cost estimators	4,120	3,800	92.2	320	7.8	570	13.8	3,415	82.9
0630	Human resources workers	9,025	3,605	39.9	5,420	60.1	3,165	35.1	3,925	43.5
0640	Compensation, benefits, and job analysis specialists	1,075	130	12.1	945	87.9	355	33.0	470	43.7
0650	Training and development specialists	2,705	1,505	55.6	1,200	44.4	875	32.3	1,310	48.4
0700	Logisticians	1,120	605	54.0	515	46.0	225	20.1	590	52.7
0710	Management analysts	4,130	2,430	58.8	1,700	41.2	700	16.9	2,700	65.4
0725	Meeting, convention, and event planners	735	465	63.3	270	36.7	250	34.0	195	26.5
0726	Fundraisers	590	145	24.6	445	75.4	90	15.3	435	73.7
0735	Market research analysts and marketing specialists	950	400	42.1	555	58.4	235	24.7	530	55.8
0740	Business operations specialists, all other	4,645	2,175	46.8	2,465	53.1	1,670	36.0	2,015	43.4
0800	Accountants and auditors	2,620	855	32.6	1,765	67.4	755	28.8	635	24.2
0810	Appraisers and assessors of real estate	875	490	56.0	385	44.0	200	22.9	630	72.0
0820	Budget analysts	300	115	38.3	185	61.7	130	43.3	115	38.3
0830	Credit analysts	205	115	56.1	85	41.5	75	36.6	30	14.6
0840	Financial analysts	345	215	62.3	130	37.7	155	44.9	120	34.8
0850	Personal financial advisors	1,320	635	48.1	685	51.9	295	22.3	755	57.2
0860	Insurance underwriters	635	155	24.4	480	75.6	155	24.4	310	48.8
0900	Financial examiners	60	15	25.0	45	75.0	0	0.0	30	50.0
0910	Credit counselors and loan officers	4,250	1,475	34.7	2,780	65.4	1,420	33.4	2,115	49.8
0930	Tax examiners and collectors, and revenue agents	440	95	21.6	345	78.4	75	17.0	225	51.1
0940	Tax preparers	1,690	295	17.5	1,390	82.2	585	34.6	660	39.1
0950	Financial specialists, all other	1,015	525	51.7	490	48.3	195	19.2	495	48.8
1005	Computer and information research scientists	65	50	76.9	15	23.1	0	0.0	4	6.2
1006	Computer systems analysts	1,955	1,095	56.0	860	44.0	430	22.0	885	45.3
1007	Information security analysts	335	295	88.1	45	13.4	50	14.9	230	68.7
1010	Computer programmers	3,110	2,315	74.4	795	25.6	730	23.5	1,655	53.2
1020	Software developers, applications and systems software	2,445	2,005	82.0	440	18.0	460	18.8	1,305	53.4
1030	Web developers	1,875	1,440	76.8	435	23.2	205	10.9	1,365	72.8
1050	Computer support specialists	5,235	3,875	74.0	1,360	26.0	950	18.1	2,955	56.4
1060	Database administrators	560	280	50.0	280	50.0	130	23.2	345	61.6
1105	Network and computer systems administrators	1,680	1,280	76.2	400	23.8	285	17.0	1,005	59.8
1106	Computer network architects	580	535	92.2	45	7.8	85	14.7	365	62.9
1107	Computer occupations, all other	2,900	2,455	84.7	445	15.3	730	25.2	1,570	54.1
1200	Actuaries	55	20	36.4	35	63.6	0	0.0	25	45.5
1220	Operations research analysts	495	250	50.5	245	49.5	65	13.1	310	62.6
1240	Miscellaneous mathematical science occupations, including mathematicians and statisticians	155	55	35.5	100	64.5	50	32.3	0	0.0
1300	Architects, except naval	125	30	24.0	95	76.0	10	8.0	15	12.0

PART A—NATIONAL DATA

A-18 Workers Who are Not High School Graduates: Detailed Occupation, by Sex, Race, and Hispanic Origin, 2006–2010—Continued

Census occupation code	Detailed Occupation	Not high school graduate									
		Not Hispanic or Latino, one race								Not Hispanic or Latino, two or more races	
		Black or African American alone		American Indian and Alaska Native alone		Asian alone		Native Hawaiian and Other Pacific Islander alone			
		Number	Percent	Number	Percent	Number	Percent	Number	Percent	Number	Percent
0600	Cost estimators	65	1.6	35	0.8	20	0.5	0	0.0	15	0.4
0630	Human resources workers	1,390	15.4	155	1.7	230	2.5	4	0.0	164	1.8
0640	Compensation, benefits, and job analysis specialists	160	14.9	10	0.9	50	4.7	0	0.0	25	2.3
0650	Training and development specialists	425	15.7	35	1.3	55	2.0	0	0.0	8	0.3
0700	Logisticians	220	19.6	0	0.0	25	2.2	0	0.0	55	4.9
0710	Management analysts	350	8.5	95	2.3	215	5.2	0	0.0	70	1.7
0725	Meeting, convention, and event planners	215	29.3	0	0.0	65	8.8	0	0.0	10	1.4
0726	Fundraisers	40	6.8	0	0.0	20	3.4	0	0.0	10	1.7
0735	Market research analysts and marketing specialists	150	15.8	0	0.0	15	1.6	0	0.0	25	2.6
0740	Business operations specialists, all other	620	13.3	4	0.1	250	5.4	10	0.2	75	1.6
0800	Accountants and auditors	765	29.2	70	2.7	265	10.1	15	0.6	114	4.4
0810	Appraisers and assessors of real estate	10	1.1	0	0.0	30	3.4	0	0.0	10	1.1
0820	Budget analysts	55	18.3	0	0.0	0	0.0	0	0.0	0	0.0
0830	Credit analysts	40	19.5	0	0.0	55	26.8	0	0.0	0	0.0
0840	Financial analysts	15	4.3	0	0.0	50	14.5	0	0.0	0	0.0
0850	Personal financial advisors	120	9.1	4	0.3	85	6.4	0	0.0	55	4.2
0860	Insurance underwriters	115	18.1	0	0.0	35	5.5	0	0.0	15	2.4
0900	Financial examiners	30	50.0	0	0.0	0	0.0	0	0.0	0	0.0
0910	Credit counselors and loan officers	495	11.6	0	0.0	155	3.6	0	0.0	65	1.5
0930	Tax examiners and collectors, and revenue agents	40	9.1	25	5.7	60	13.6	0	0.0	10	2.3
0940	Tax preparers	300	17.8	35	2.1	30	1.8	0	0.0	75	4.4
0950	Financial specialists, all other	185	18.2	20	2.0	20	2.0	0	0.0	100	9.9
1005	Computer and information research scientists	35	53.8	0	0.0	10	15.4	0	0.0	15	23.1
1006	Computer systems analysts	385	19.7	10	0.5	145	7.4	0	0.0	100	5.1
1007	Information security analysts	35	10.4	0	0.0	0	0.0	0	0.0	25	7.5
1010	Computer programmers	275	8.8	10	0.3	360	11.6	0	0.0	85	2.7
1020	Software developers, applications and systems software	175	7.2	60	2.5	360	14.7	20	0.8	65	2.7
1030	Web developers	70	3.7	25	1.3	75	4.0	0	0.0	130	6.9
1050	Computer support specialists	755	14.4	110	2.1	340	6.5	0	0.0	120	2.3
1060	Database administrators	20	3.6	0	0.0	65	11.6	0	0.0	0	0.0
1105	Network and computer systems administrators	170	10.1	0	0.0	135	8.0	4	0.2	85	5.1
1106	Computer network architects	110	19.0	0	0.0	20	3.4	0	0.0	4	0.7
1107	Computer occupations, all other	300	10.3	10	0.3	260	9.0	0	0.0	25	0.9
1200	Actuaries	10	18.2	0	0.0	0	0.0	20	36.4	0	0.0
1220	Operations research analysts	125	25.3	0	0.0	0	0.0	0	0.0	0	0.0
1240	Miscellaneous mathematical science occupations, including mathematicians and statisticians	50	32.3	0	0.0	50	32.3	0	0.0	0	0.0
1300	Architects, except naval	20	16.0	0	0.0	80	64.0	0	0.0	4	3.2

A-18 **Workers Who are Not High School Graduates: Detailed Occupation, by Sex, Race, and Hispanic Origin, 2006–2010**—*Continued*

Census occupation code	Detailed Occupation	Total	Not high school graduate							
			Male		Female		Hispanic or Latino		Not Hispanic or Latino, one race — White alone	
			Number	Percent	Number	Percent	Number	Percent	Number	Percent
1310	Surveyors, cartographers, and photogrammetrists	40	40	100.0	0	0.0	0	0.0	40	100.0
1320	Aerospace engineers	320	285	89.1	35	10.9	85	26.6	85	26.6
1340	Biomedical and agricultural engineers	0	0	0.0	0	0.0	0	0.0	0	0.0
1350	Chemical engineers	130	110	84.6	20	15.4	30	23.1	10	7.7
1360	Civil engineers	310	255	82.3	60	19.4	60	19.4	40	12.9
1400	Computer hardware engineers	40	25	62.5	15	37.5	15	37.5	0	0.0
1410	Electrical and electronics engineers	165	155	93.9	15	9.1	55	33.3	60	36.4
1420	Environmental engineers	50	50	100.0	0	0.0	0	0.0	0	0.0
1430	Industrial engineers, including health and safety	135	80	59.3	55	40.7	25	18.5	60	44.4
1440	Marine engineers and naval architects	0	0	0.0	0	0.0	0	0.0	0	0.0
1450	Materials engineers	30	30	100.0	0	0.0	25	83.3	4	13.3
1460	Mechanical engineers	170	150	88.2	20	11.8	15	8.8	95	55.9
1520	Petroleum, mining and geological engineers, including mining safety engineers	50	50	100.0	0	0.0	35	70.0	4	8.0
1530	Miscellaneous engineers, including nuclear engineers	600	500	83.3	95	15.8	195	32.5	125	20.8
1540	Drafters	3,730	3,315	88.9	415	11.1	985	26.4	2,295	61.5
1550	Engineering technicians, except drafters	15,470	11,660	75.4	3,810	24.6	4,340	28.1	7,730	50.0
1560	Surveying and mapping technicians	5,085	4,545	89.4	540	10.6	1,045	20.6	3,660	72.0
1600	Agricultural and food scientists	20	20	100.0	0	0.0	0	0.0	10	50.0
1610	Biological scientists	40	0	0.0	40	####	0	0.0	25	62.5
1640	Conservation scientists and foresters	20	20	100.0	0	0.0	0	0.0	20	100.0
1650	Medical scientists, and life scientists, all other	175	45	25.7	130	74.3	55	31.4	20	11.4
1700	Astronomers and physicists	20	0	0.0	20	####	0	0.0	20	100.0
1710	Atmospheric and space scientists	0	0	0.0	0	0.0	0	0.0	0	0.0
1720	Chemists and materials scientists	115	40	34.8	75	65.2	80	69.6	10	8.7
1740	Environmental scientists and geoscientists	80	40	50.0	40	50.0	0	0.0	70	87.5
1760	Physical scientists, all other	110	85	77.3	20	18.2	10	9.1	0	0.0
1800	Economists	0	0	0.0	0	0.0	0	0.0	0	0.0
1820	Psychologists	160	60	37.5	100	62.5	80	50.0	20	12.5
1840	Urban and regional planners	4	4	100.0	0	0.0	0	0.0	4	100.0
1860	Miscellaneous social scientists, including survey researchers and sociologists	140	45	32.1	90	64.3	65	46.4	45	32.1
1900	Agricultural and food science technicians	2,190	1,270	58.0	920	42.0	965	44.1	1,030	47.0
1910	Biological technicians	640	265	41.4	375	58.6	175	27.3	300	46.9
1920	Chemical technicians	2,755	1,565	56.8	1,190	43.2	955	34.7	1,215	44.1
1930	Geological and petroleum technicians, and nuclear technicians	1,070	820	76.6	250	23.4	335	31.3	660	61.7
1965	Miscellaneous life, physical, and social science technicians, including social science research assistants	4,330	2,575	59.5	1,755	40.5	1,320	30.5	2,065	47.7

A-18 Workers Who are Not High School Graduates: Detailed Occupation, by Sex, Race, and Hispanic Origin, 2006–2010—Continued

Census occupation code	Detailed Occupation	Black or African American alone Number	Percent	American Indian and Alaska Native alone Number	Percent	Asian alone Number	Percent	Native Hawaiian and Other Pacific Islander alone Number	Percent	Not Hispanic or Latino, two or more races Number	Percent
1310	Surveyors, cartographers, and photogrammetrists	0	0.0	0	0.0	0	0.0	0	0.0	0	0.0
1320	Aerospace engineers	95	29.7	10	3.1	45	14.1	0	0.0	0	0.0
1340	Biomedical and agricultural engineers	0	0.0	0	0.0	0	0.0	0	0.0	0	0.0
1350	Chemical engineers	45	34.6	0	0.0	40	30.8	0	0.0	0	0.0
1360	Civil engineers	75	24.2	15	4.8	100	32.3	0	0.0	20	6.5
1400	Computer hardware engineers	0	0.0	0	0.0	25	62.5	0	0.0	0	0.0
1410	Electrical and electronics engineers	25	15.2	0	0.0	30	18.2	0	0.0	0	0.0
1420	Environmental engineers	35	70.0	0	0.0	0	0.0	0	0.0	15	30.0
1430	Industrial engineers, including health and safety	25	18.5	0	0.0	25	18.5	0	0.0	0	0.0
1440	Marine engineers and naval architects	0	0.0	0	0.0	0	0.0	0	0.0	0	0.0
1450	Materials engineers	0	0.0	0	0.0	0	0.0	0	0.0	0	0.0
1460	Mechanical engineers	40	23.5	0	0.0	10	5.9	10	5.9	0	0.0
1520	Petroleum, mining and geological engineers, including mining safety engineers	10	20.0	0	0.0	0	0.0	0	0.0	0	0.0
1530	Miscellaneous engineers, including nuclear engineers	155	25.8	0	0.0	120	20.0	4	0.7	0	0.0
1540	Drafters	205	5.5	85	2.3	125	3.4	0	0.0	30	0.8
1550	Engineering technicians, except drafters	1,105	7.1	155	1.0	1,820	11.8	25	0.2	290	1.9
1560	Surveying and mapping technicians	135	2.7	45	0.9	30	0.6	30	0.6	135	2.7
1600	Agricultural and food scientists	10	50.0	0	0.0	0	0.0	0	0.0	0	0.0
1610	Biological scientists	15	37.5	0	0.0	0	0.0	0	0.0	0	0.0
1640	Conservation scientists and foresters	0	0.0	0	0.0	0	0.0	0	0.0	0	0.0
1650	Medical scientists, and life scientists, all other	45	25.7	0	0.0	40	22.9	10	5.7	4	2.3
1700	Astronomers and physicists	0	0.0	0	0.0	0	0.0	0	0.0	0	0.0
1710	Atmospheric and space scientists	0	0.0	0	0.0	0	0.0	0	0.0	0	0.0
1720	Chemists and materials scientists	15	13.0	0	0.0	15	13.0	0	0.0	0	0.0
1740	Environmental scientists and geoscientists	0	0.0	0	0.0	10	12.5	0	0.0	0	0.0
1760	Physical scientists, all other	15	13.6	0	0.0	80	72.7	0	0.0	0	0.0
1800	Economists	0	0.0	0	0.0	0	0.0	0	0.0	0	0.0
1820	Psychologists	40	25.0	0	0.0	20	12.5	0	0.0	0	0.0
1840	Urban and regional planners	0	0.0	0	0.0	0	0.0	0	0.0	0	0.0
1860	Miscellaneous social scientists, including survey researchers and sociologists	15	10.7	0	0.0	15	10.7	0	0.0	0	0.0
1900	Agricultural and food science technicians	95	4.3	4	0.2	60	2.7	10	0.5	25	1.1
1910	Biological technicians	85	13.3	15	2.3	35	5.5	0	0.0	29	4.5
1920	Chemical technicians	460	16.7	0	0.0	115	4.2	0	0.0	10	0.4
1930	Geological and petroleum technicians, and nuclear technicians	20	1.9	4	0.4	45	4.2	0	0.0	4	0.4
1965	Miscellaneous life, physical, and social science technicians, including social science research assistants	495	11.4	150	3.5	250	5.8	0	0.0	44	1.0

A-18 **Workers Who are Not High School Graduates: Detailed Occupation, by Sex, Race, and Hispanic Origin, 2006–2010**—Continued

Census occupation code	Detailed Occupation	Total	Not high school graduate							
			Male		Female		Hispanic or Latino		Not Hispanic or Latino, one race — White alone	
			Number	Percent	Number	Percent	Number	Percent	Number	Percent
2000	Counselors	10,540	4,480	42.5	6,055	57.4	2,130	20.2	3,875	36.8
2010	Social workers	8,045	1,865	23.2	6,180	76.8	2,160	26.8	3,000	37.3
2015	Probation officers and correctional treatment specialists	595	380	63.9	215	36.1	130	21.8	160	26.9
2016	Social and human service assistants	5,260	1,600	30.4	3,655	69.5	1,455	27.7	2,155	41.0
2025	Miscellaneous community and social service specialists, including health educators and community health workers	2,430	980	40.3	1,455	59.9	675	27.8	975	40.1
2040	Clergy	10,025	8,595	85.7	1,430	14.3	3,600	35.9	4,080	40.7
2050	Directors, religious activities and education	660	225	34.1	435	65.9	100	15.2	425	64.4
2060	Religious workers, all other	3,940	2,105	53.4	1,830	46.4	900	22.8	2,415	61.3
2100	Lawyers, and judges, magistrates, and other judicial workers	300	115	38.3	185	61.7	125	41.7	125	41.7
2105	Judicial law clerks	75	40	53.3	40	53.3	60	80.0	15	20.0
2145	Paralegals and legal assistants	3,900	820	21.0	3,080	79.0	1,570	40.3	1,570	40.3
2160	Miscellaneous legal support workers	4,625	1,100	23.8	3,525	76.2	1,355	29.3	2,375	51.4
2200	Postsecondary teachers	1,380	700	50.7	675	48.9	510	37.0	165	12.0
2300	Preschool and kindergarten teachers	12,080	385	3.2	11,695	96.8	3,210	26.6	5,535	45.8
2310	Elementary and middle school teachers	4,625	915	19.8	3,710	80.2	1,230	26.6	1,535	33.2
2320	Secondary school teachers	1,165	505	43.3	660	56.7	285	24.5	310	26.6
2330	Special education teachers	1,195	160	13.4	1,035	86.6	250	20.9	640	53.6
2340	Other teachers and instructors	31,780	12,475	39.3	19,310	60.8	5,645	17.8	17,880	56.3
2400	Archivists, curators, and museum technicians	570	230	40.4	340	59.6	85	14.9	355	62.3
2430	Librarians	130	45	34.6	85	65.4	10	7.7	40	30.8
2440	Library technicians	6,535	1,965	30.1	4,570	69.9	755	11.6	4,650	71.2
2540	Teacher assistants	34,370	5,445	15.8	28,925	84.2	9,045	26.3	17,515	51.0
2550	Other education, training, and library workers	565	270	47.8	295	52.2	180	31.9	225	39.8
2600	Artists and related workers	5,950	3,870	65.0	2,080	35.0	1,335	22.4	3,650	61.3
2630	Designers	20,595	8,550	41.5	12,045	58.5	7,830	38.0	10,330	50.2
2700	Actors	1,390	700	50.4	690	49.6	150	10.8	995	71.6
2710	Producers and directors	1,265	990	78.3	270	21.3	225	17.8	670	53.0
2720	Athletes, coaches, umpires, and related workers	24,185	13,955	57.7	10,230	42.3	2,645	10.9	19,205	79.4
2740	Dancers and choreographers	3,175	220	6.9	2,955	93.1	690	21.7	1,810	57.0
2750	Musicians, singers, and related workers	9,565	8,225	86.0	1,340	14.0	3,840	40.1	3,365	35.2
2760	Entertainers and performers, sports and related workers, all other	3,925	1,420	36.2	2,505	63.8	690	17.6	2,570	65.5
2800	Announcers	2,995	2,430	81.1	565	18.9	1,145	38.2	1,385	46.2
2810	News analysts, reporters, and correspondents	395	205	51.9	190	48.1	165	41.8	155	39.2
2825	Public relations specialists	910	470	51.6	440	48.4	140	15.4	625	68.7
2830	Editors	1,085	360	33.2	730	67.3	200	18.4	540	49.8
2840	Technical writers	380	205	53.9	175	46.1	90	23.7	210	55.3
2850	Writers and authors	980	495	50.5	490	50.0	130	13.3	695	70.9
2860	Miscellaneous media and communication workers	2,735	825	30.2	1,910	69.8	1,880	68.7	475	17.4

PART A—NATIONAL DATA

A-18 Workers Who are Not High School Graduates: Detailed Occupation, by Sex, Race, and Hispanic Origin, 2006–2010—Continued

Census occupation code	Detailed Occupation	Not high school graduate									
		Not Hispanic or Latino, one race										Not Hispanic or Latino, two or more races	
		Black or African American alone		American Indian and Alaska Native alone		Asian alone		Native Hawaiian and Other Pacific Islander alone			
		Number	Percent	Number	Percent	Number	Percent	Number	Percent	Number	Percent
2000	Counselors	3,880	36.8	240	2.3	165	1.6	0	0.0	260	2.5
2010	Social workers	2,420	30.1	100	1.2	195	2.4	30	0.4	140	1.7
2015	Probation officers and correctional treatment specialists	290	48.7	0	0.0	0	0.0	0	0.0	15	2.5
2016	Social and human service assistants	1,340	25.5	40	0.8	210	4.0	0	0.0	60	1.1
2025	Miscellaneous community and social service specialists, including health educators and community health workers	665	27.4	40	1.6	25	1.0	0	0.0	44	1.8
2040	Clergy	1,605	16.0	130	1.3	360	3.6	65	0.6	189	1.9
2050	Directors, religious activities and education	115	17.4	0	0.0	10	1.5	0	0.0	15	2.3
2060	Religious workers, all other	280	7.1	15	0.4	190	4.8	0	0.0	140	3.6
2100	Lawyers, and judges, magistrates, and other judicial workers	25	8.3	15	5.0	10	3.3	0	0.0	0	0.0
2105	Judicial law clerks	0	0.0	0	0.0	0	0.0	0	0.0	0	0.0
2145	Paralegals and legal assistants	590	15.1	50	1.3	75	1.9	30	0.8	24	0.6
2160	Miscellaneous legal support workers	505	10.9	35	0.8	220	4.8	0	0.0	130	2.8
2200	Postsecondary teachers	390	28.3	10	0.7	225	16.3	0	0.0	80	5.8
2300	Preschool and kindergarten teachers	2,710	22.4	110	0.9	295	2.4	15	0.1	200	1.7
2310	Elementary and middle school teachers	1,345	29.1	125	2.7	295	6.4	30	0.6	65	1.4
2320	Secondary school teachers	400	34.3	4	0.3	105	9.0	0	0.0	55	4.7
2330	Special education teachers	280	23.4	0	0.0	20	1.7	0	0.0	4	0.3
2340	Other teachers and instructors	4,410	13.9	475	1.5	2,600	8.2	90	0.3	680	2.1
2400	Archivists, curators, and museum technicians	80	14.0	0	0.0	20	3.5	0	0.0	30	5.3
2430	Librarians	55	42.3	0	0.0	10	7.7	0	0.0	15	11.5
2440	Library technicians	575	8.8	45	0.7	285	4.4	0	0.0	220	3.4
2540	Teacher assistants	5,420	15.8	575	1.7	1,085	3.2	65	0.2	670	1.9
2550	Other education, training, and library workers	90	15.9	4	0.7	70	12.4	0	0.0	0	0.0
2600	Artists and related workers	290	4.9	265	4.5	270	4.5	15	0.3	130	2.2
2630	Designers	1,105	5.4	15	0.1	1,020	5.0	30	0.1	255	1.2
2700	Actors	125	9.0	0	0.0	45	3.2	0	0.0	70	5.0
2710	Producers and directors	320	25.3	0	0.0	0	0.0	0	0.0	49	3.9
2720	Athletes, coaches, umpires, and related workers	990	4.1	140	0.6	605	2.5	15	0.1	595	2.5
2740	Dancers and choreographers	310	9.8	25	0.8	85	2.7	85	2.7	180	5.7
2750	Musicians, singers, and related workers	1,960	20.5	50	0.5	225	2.4	0	0.0	125	1.3
2760	Entertainers and performers, sports and related workers, all other	270	6.9	75	1.9	155	3.9	0	0.0	170	4.3
2800	Announcers	350	11.7	15	0.5	35	1.2	0	0.0	65	2.2
2810	News analysts, reporters, and correspondents	45	11.4	0	0.0	0	0.0	15	3.8	15	3.8
2825	Public relations specialists	115	12.6	10	1.1	10	1.1	0	0.0	4	0.4
2830	Editors	130	12.0	4	0.4	135	12.4	0	0.0	75	6.9
2840	Technical writers	60	15.8	0	0.0	15	3.9	0	0.0	4	1.1
2850	Writers and authors	120	12.2	4	0.4	35	3.6	0	0.0	0	0.0
2860	Miscellaneous media and communication workers	60	2.2	35	1.3	185	6.8	10	0.4	85	3.1

A-18 **Workers Who are Not High School Graduates: Detailed Occupation, by Sex, Race, and Hispanic Origin, 2006–2010**—Continued

Census occupation code	Detailed Occupation	Total	Not high school graduate							
			Male		Female		Hispanic or Latino		Not Hispanic or Latino, one race — White alone	
			Number	Percent	Number	Percent	Number	Percent	Number	Percent
2900	Broadcast and sound engineering technicians and radio operators, and media and communication equipment workers, all other	2,730	2,415	88.5	315	11.5	520	19.0	1,770	64.8
2910	Photographers	4,835	2,245	46.4	2,585	53.5	1,155	23.9	2,785	57.6
2920	Television, video, and motion picture camera operators and editors	1,110	930	83.8	175	15.8	375	33.8	605	54.5
3000	Chiropractors	40	20	50.0	20	50.0	0	0.0	30	75.0
3010	Dentists	180	180	100.0	0	0.0	10	5.6	135	75.0
3030	Dietitians and nutritionists	4,080	655	16.1	3,425	83.9	1,310	32.1	1,410	34.6
3040	Optometrists	0	0	0.0	0	0.0	0	0.0	0	0.0
3050	Pharmacists	250	100	40.0	145	58.0	20	8.0	95	38.0
3060	Physicians and surgeons	1,030	740	71.8	290	28.2	255	24.8	160	15.5
3110	Physician assistants	1,355	450	33.2	905	66.8	420	31.0	475	35.1
3120	Podiatrists	10	0	0.0	10	####	0	0.0	0	0.0
3140	Audiologists	0	0	0.0	0	0.0	0	0.0	0	0.0
3150	Occupational therapists	165	40	24.2	125	75.8	60	36.4	20	12.1
3160	Physical therapists	610	55	9.0	550	90.2	170	27.9	225	36.9
3200	Radiation therapists	30	20	66.7	10	33.3	20	66.7	0	0.0
3210	Recreational therapists	335	60	17.9	275	82.1	20	6.0	200	59.7
3220	Respiratory therapists	205	115	56.1	85	41.5	10	4.9	50	24.4
3230	Speech-language pathologists	165	30	18.2	135	81.8	45	27.3	65	39.4
3245	Other therapists, including exercise physiologists	830	140	16.9	690	83.1	295	35.5	310	37.3
3250	Veterinarians	120	4	3.3	115	95.8	10	8.3	10	8.3
3255	Registered nurses	3,635	695	19.1	2,940	80.9	970	26.7	1,010	27.8
3256	Nurse anesthetists	0	0	0.0	0	0.0	0	0.0	0	0.0
3258	Nurse practitioners and nurse midwives	80	0	0.0	80	####	75	93.8	10	12.5
3260	Health diagnosing and treating practitioners, all other	115	15	13.0	95	82.6	25	21.7	60	52.2
3300	Clinical laboratory technologists and technicians	4,185	995	23.8	3,190	76.2	1,010	24.1	1,790	42.8
3310	Dental hygienists	765	240	31.4	525	68.6	225	29.4	345	45.1
3320	Diagnostic related technologists and technicians	1,785	695	38.9	1,095	61.3	685	38.4	615	34.5
3400	Emergency medical technicians and paramedics	1,545	1,025	66.3	515	33.3	220	14.2	1,210	78.3
3420	Health practitioner support technologists and technicians	12,400	2,535	20.4	9,860	79.5	2,055	16.6	7,800	62.9
3500	Licensed practical and licensed vocational nurses	7,010	360	5.1	6,650	94.9	1,275	18.2	3,005	42.9
3510	Medical records and health information technicians	3,695	375	10.1	3,325	90.0	1,070	29.0	1,940	52.5
3520	Opticians, dispensing	1,480	485	32.8	995	67.2	420	28.4	905	61.1
3535	Miscellaneous health technologists and technicians	2,890	670	23.2	2,220	76.8	630	21.8	1,200	41.5
3540	Other health care practitioners and technical occupations	1,245	805	64.7	440	35.3	420	33.7	540	43.4

PART A—NATIONAL DATA

A-18 Workers Who are Not High School Graduates: Detailed Occupation, by Sex, Race, and Hispanic Origin, 2006–2010—Continued

Census occupation code	Detailed Occupation	Not high school graduate								
		Not Hispanic or Latino, one race							
		Black or African American alone		American Indian and Alaska Native alone		Asian alone		Native Hawaiian and Other Pacific Islander alone		Not Hispanic or Latino, two or more races	
		Number	Percent	Number	Percent	Number	Percent	Number	Percent	Number	Percent
2900	Broadcast and sound engineering technicians and radio operators, and media and communication equipment workers, all other	135	4.9	60	2.2	105	3.8	0	0.0	145	5.3
2910	Photographers	565	11.7	60	1.2	115	2.4	0	0.0	150	3.1
2920	Television, video, and motion picture camera operators and editors	65	5.9	0	0.0	4	0.4	10	0.9	45	4.1
3000	Chiropractors	0	0.0	10	25.0	0	0.0	0	0.0	0	0.0
3010	Dentists	25	13.9	0	0.0	10	5.6	0	0.0	0	0.0
3030	Dietitians and nutritionists	1,065	26.1	55	1.3	215	5.3	0	0.0	30	0.7
3040	Optometrists	0	0.0	0	0.0	0	0.0	0	0.0	0	0.0
3050	Pharmacists	45	18.0	10	4.0	70	28.0	0	0.0	10	4.0
3060	Physicians and surgeons	250	24.3	30	2.9	290	28.2	15	1.5	34	3.3
3110	Physician assistants	240	17.7	0	0.0	110	8.1	4	0.3	100	7.4
3120	Podiatrists	10	100.0	0	0.0	0	0.0	0	0.0	0	0.0
3140	Audiologists	0	0.0	0	0.0	0	0.0	0	0.0	0	0.0
3150	Occupational therapists	90	54.5	0	0.0	0	0.0	0	0.0	0	0.0
3160	Physical therapists	115	18.9	0	0.0	100	16.4	0	0.0	0	0.0
3200	Radiation therapists	0	0.0	0	0.0	10	33.3	0	0.0	0	0.0
3210	Recreational therapists	100	29.9	0	0.0	10	3.0	0	0.0	0	0.0
3220	Respiratory therapists	120	58.5	0	0.0	4	2.0	0	0.0	20	9.8
3230	Speech-language pathologists	40	24.2	0	0.0	10	6.1	0	0.0	4	2.4
3245	Other therapists, including exercise physiologists	145	17.5	0	0.0	50	6.0	0	0.0	25	3.0
3250	Veterinarians	100	83.3	0	0.0	0	0.0	0	0.0	0	0.0
3255	Registered nurses	930	25.6	50	1.4	600	16.5	20	0.6	60	1.7
3256	Nurse anesthetists	0	0.0	0	0.0	0	0.0	0	0.0	0	0.0
3258	Nurse practitioners and nurse midwives	0	0.0	0	0.0	0	0.0	0	0.0	0	0.0
3260	Health diagnosing and treating practitioners, all other	10	8.7	4	3.5	15	13.0	0	0.0	0	0.0
3300	Clinical laboratory technologists and technicians	985	23.5	20	0.5	325	7.8	4	0.1	50	1.2
3310	Dental hygienists	65	8.5	0	0.0	110	14.4	15	2.0	4	0.5
3320	Diagnostic related technologists and technicians	405	22.7	20	1.1	45	2.5	0	0.0	20	1.1
3400	Emergency medical technicians and paramedics	110	7.1	0	0.0	0	0.0	0	0.0	0	0.0
3420	Health practitioner support technologists and technicians	1,555	12.5	105	0.8	495	4.0	70	0.6	310	2.5
3500	Licensed practical and licensed vocational nurses	2,255	32.2	80	1.1	305	4.4	0	0.0	88	1.3
3510	Medical records and health information technicians	445	12.0	40	1.1	110	3.0	0	0.0	90	2.4
3520	Opticians, dispensing	105	7.1	10	0.7	20	1.4	0	0.0	20	1.4
3535	Miscellaneous health technologists and technicians	780	27.0	80	2.8	165	5.7	0	0.0	35	1.2
3540	Other health care practitioners and technical occupations	55	4.4	165	13.3	25	2.0	0	0.0	40	3.2

A-18 **Workers Who are Not High School Graduates: Detailed Occupation, by Sex, Race, and Hispanic Origin, 2006–2010**—*Continued*

Census occupation code	Detailed Occupation	Total	Not high school graduate							
			Male		Female		Hispanic or Latino		Not Hispanic or Latino, one race — White alone	
			Number	Percent	Number	Percent	Number	Percent	Number	Percent
3600	Nursing, psychiatric, and home health aides............	290,720	21,620	7.4	269,100	92.6	74,990	25.8	97,860	33.7
3610	Occupational therapy assistants and aides............	80	0	0.0	80	100.0	14	17.5	20	25.0
3620	Physical therapist assistants and aides....	1,490	310	20.8	1,180	79.2	370	24.8	805	54.0
3630	Massage therapists............	2,405	570	23.7	1,830	76.1	470	19.5	940	39.1
3640	Dental assistants............	9,730	775	8.0	8,955	92.0	4,380	45.0	3,880	39.9
3645	Medical assistants............	11,400	590	5.2	10,810	94.8	5,210	45.7	4,190	36.8
3646	Medical transcriptionists............	780	10	1.3	770	98.7	135	17.3	465	59.6
3647	Pharmacy aides............	2,495	265	10.6	2,230	89.4	500	20.0	1,530	61.3
3648	Veterinary assistants and laboratory animal caretakers............	3,915	1,080	27.6	2,840	72.5	615	15.7	2,930	74.8
3649	Phlebotomists............	1,425	260	18.2	1,165	81.8	435	30.5	430	30.2
3655	Health care support workers, all other, including medical equipment preparers............	22,005	4,630	21.0	17,375	79.0	3,740	17.0	11,665	53.0
3700	First-line supervisors of correctional officers............	615	430	69.9	180	29.3	125	20.3	355	57.7
3710	First-line supervisors of police and detectives............	625	505	80.8	115	18.4	80	12.8	290	46.4
3720	First-line supervisors of fire fighting and prevention workers............	365	360	98.6	4	1.1	15	4.1	260	71.2
3730	First-line supervisors of protective service workers, all other............	2,710	2,115	78.0	595	22.0	805	29.7	1,000	36.9
3740	Firefighters............	2,125	1,965	92.5	160	7.5	535	25.2	1,090	51.3
3750	Fire inspectors............	370	335	90.5	35	9.5	85	23.0	235	63.5
3800	Bailiffs, correctional officers, and jailers............	5,775	4,230	73.2	1,540	26.7	770	13.3	3,340	57.8
3820	Detectives and criminal investigators.....	460	365	79.3	95	20.7	115	25.0	280	60.9
3840	Miscellaneous law enforcement workers	330	240	72.7	95	28.8	35	10.6	205	62.1
3850	Police officers............	4,985	3,890	78.0	1,095	22.0	955	19.2	2,650	53.2
3900	Animal control workers............	725	545	75.2	180	24.8	80	11.0	600	82.8
3910	Private detectives and investigators........	905	465	51.4	440	48.6	265	29.3	520	57.5
3930	Security guards and gaming surveillance officers............	79,820	62,290	78.0	17,530	22.0	21,565	27.0	30,270	37.9
3940	Crossing guards............	11,420	5,335	46.7	6,085	53.3	3,465	30.3	5,105	44.7
3945	Transportation security screeners............	700	265	37.9	430	61.4	235	33.6	240	34.3
3955	Lifeguards and other recreational, and all other protective service workers.....	48,075	22,700	47.2	25,375	52.8	4,045	8.4	39,085	81.3
4000	Chefs and head cooks............	56,320	47,895	85.0	8,425	15.0	22,640	40.2	10,055	17.9
4010	First-line supervisors of food preparation and serving workers..........	76,370	29,725	38.9	46,650	61.1	26,335	34.5	34,005	44.5
4020	Cooks............	695,750	427,735	61.5	268,015	38.5	332,050	47.7	221,150	31.8
4030	Food preparation workers............	245,640	111,345	45.3	134,295	54.7	95,455	38.9	103,395	42.1
4040	Bartenders............	31,335	10,995	35.1	20,345	64.9	7,515	24.0	20,980	67.0
4050	Combined food preparation and serving workers, including fast food............	85,565	31,280	36.6	54,285	63.4	21,310	24.9	46,190	54.0
4060	Counter attendants, cafeteria, food concession, and coffee shop............	99,120	32,670	33.0	66,445	67.0	16,730	16.9	66,380	67.0

PART A—NATIONAL DATA

A-18 **Workers Who are Not High School Graduates: Detailed Occupation, by Sex, Race, and Hispanic Origin, 2006–2010**—*Continued*

Census occupation code	Detailed Occupation	Not high school graduate									
		Not Hispanic or Latino, one race									Not Hispanic or Latino, two or more races	
		Black or African American alone		American Indian and Alaska Native alone		Asian alone		Native Hawaiian and Other Pacific Islander alone			
		Number	Percent	Number	Percent	Number	Percent	Number	Percent	Number	Percent
3600	Nursing, psychiatric, and home health aides	99,095	34.1	2,600	0.9	11,165	3.8	545	0.2	4,465	1.5
3610	Occupational therapy assistants and aides	40	50.0	0	0.0	0	0.0	0	0.0	0	0.0
3620	Physical therapist assistants and aides	190	12.8	0	0.0	75	5.0	0	0.0	55	3.7
3630	Massage therapists	65	2.7	30	1.2	815	33.9	10	0.4	75	3.1
3640	Dental assistants	520	5.3	55	0.6	725	7.5	20	0.2	150	1.5
3645	Medical assistants	1,280	11.2	145	1.3	420	3.7	40	0.4	114	1.0
3646	Medical transcriptionists	160	20.5	0	0.0	0	0.0	0	0.0	19	2.4
3647	Pharmacy aides	245	9.8	45	1.8	170	6.8	0	0.0	0	0.0
3648	Veterinary assistants and laboratory animal caretakers	185	4.7	40	1.0	20	0.5	0	0.0	120	3.1
3649	Phlebotomists	445	31.2	10	0.7	75	5.3	0	0.0	35	2.5
3655	Health care support workers, all other, including medical equipment preparers	5,530	25.1	150	0.7	550	2.5	0	0.0	375	1.7
3700	First-line supervisors of correctional officers	125	20.3	0	0.0	0	0.0	0	0.0	15	2.4
3710	First-line supervisors of police and detectives	240	38.4	15	2.4	0	0.0	0	0.0	0	0.0
3720	First-line supervisors of fire fighting and prevention workers	0	0.0	75	20.5	0	0.0	0	0.0	15	4.1
3730	First-line supervisors of protective service workers, all other	730	26.9	15	0.6	100	3.7	0	0.0	55	2.0
3740	Firefighters	255	12.0	150	7.1	45	2.1	0	0.0	54	2.5
3750	Fire inspectors	20	5.4	4	1.1	20	5.4	0	0.0	0	0.0
3800	Bailiffs, correctional officers, and jailers	1,490	25.8	50	0.9	45	0.8	25	0.4	60	1.0
3820	Detectives and criminal investigators	45	9.8	0	0.0	10	2.2	0	0.0	4	0.9
3840	Miscellaneous law enforcement workers	55	16.7	10	3.0	10	3.0	0	0.0	10	3.0
3850	Police officers	875	17.6	110	2.2	125	2.5	0	0.0	265	5.3
3900	Animal control workers	25	3.4	20	2.8	0	0.0	0	0.0	0	0.0
3910	Private detectives and investigators	85	9.4	10	1.1	20	2.2	0	0.0	0	0.0
3930	Security guards and gaming surveillance officers	22,630	28.4	1,145	1.4	2,435	3.1	420	0.5	1,350	1.7
3940	Crossing guards	2,580	22.6	120	1.1	40	0.4	20	0.2	89	0.8
3945	Transportation security screeners	165	23.6	0	0.0	15	2.1	0	0.0	45	6.4
3955	Lifeguards and other recreational, and all other protective service workers	2,680	5.6	170	0.4	805	1.7	40	0.1	1,245	2.6
4000	Chefs and head cooks	4,870	8.6	75	0.1	18,205	32.3	80	0.1	390	0.7
4010	First-line supervisors of food preparation and serving workers	11,520	15.1	640	0.8	2,695	3.5	195	0.3	990	1.3
4020	Cooks	90,165	13.0	4,820	0.7	37,035	5.3	890	0.1	9,645	1.4
4030	Food preparation workers	24,740	10.1	1,275	0.5	16,255	6.6	290	0.1	4,235	1.7
4040	Bartenders	1,475	4.7	310	1.0	585	1.9	10	0.0	460	1.5
4050	Combined food preparation and serving workers, including fast food	12,780	14.9	625	0.7	2,675	3.1	265	0.3	1,725	2.0
4060	Counter attendants, cafeteria, food concession, and coffee shop	9,675	9.8	590	0.6	2,955	3.0	155	0.2	2,635	2.7

A-18 **Workers Who are Not High School Graduates: Detailed Occupation, by Sex, Race, and Hispanic Origin, 2006–2010**—*Continued*

Census occupation code	Detailed Occupation	Total	Not high school graduate							
			Male		Female		Hispanic or Latino		Not Hispanic or Latino, one race: White alone	
			Number	Percent	Number	Percent	Number	Percent	Number	Percent
4110	Waiters and waitresses	360,430	90,235	25.0	270,195	75.0	98,000	27.2	205,130	56.9
4120	Food servers, nonrestaurant	43,485	13,930	32.0	29,560	68.0	11,430	26.3	19,380	44.6
4130	Miscellaneous food preparation and serving related workers, including dining room and cafeteria attendants and bartender helpers	128,615	81,570	63.4	47,045	36.6	54,890	42.7	55,395	43.1
4140	Dishwashers	138,530	109,105	78.8	29,425	21.2	67,235	48.5	50,410	36.4
4150	Hosts and hostesses, restaurant, lounge, and coffee shop	83,740	10,245	12.2	73,500	87.8	13,110	15.7	59,990	71.6
4200	First-line supervisors of housekeeping and janitorial workers	43,685	21,240	48.6	22,445	51.4	18,895	43.3	15,750	36.1
4210	First-line supervisors of landscaping, lawn service, and groundskeeping workers	35,460	34,385	97.0	1,075	3.0	19,565	55.2	13,285	37.5
4220	Janitors and building cleaners	678,575	421,225	62.1	257,345	37.9	323,470	47.7	221,590	32.7
4230	Maids and housekeeping cleaners	556,600	52,950	9.5	503,650	90.5	329,635	59.2	116,480	20.9
4240	Pest control workers	6,850	6,460	94.3	390	5.7	1,870	27.3	4,315	63.0
4250	Grounds maintenance workers	469,110	451,520	96.3	17,585	3.7	322,695	68.8	107,775	23.0
4300	First-line supervisors of gaming workers	3,555	2,155	60.6	1,405	39.5	765	21.5	2,065	58.1
4320	First-line supervisors of personal service workers	10,805	4,275	39.6	6,535	60.5	2,445	22.6	5,040	46.6
4340	Animal trainers	4,140	3,060	73.9	1,080	26.1	1,110	26.8	2,655	64.1
4350	Nonfarm animal caretakers	26,080	10,870	41.7	15,210	58.3	5,900	22.6	18,115	69.5
4400	Gaming services workers	11,215	5,350	47.7	5,870	52.3	1,965	17.5	3,705	33.0
4410	Motion picture projectionists	895	675	75.4	220	24.6	90	10.1	710	79.3
4420	Ushers, lobby attendants, and ticket takers	11,155	7,030	63.0	4,125	37.0	1,870	16.8	6,800	61.0
4430	Miscellaneous entertainment attendants and related workers	31,715	19,195	60.5	12,520	39.5	4,895	15.4	21,400	67.5
4460	Embalmers and funeral attendants	1,040	825	79.3	210	20.2	195	18.8	640	61.5
4465	Morticians, undertakers, and funeral directors	430	355	82.6	75	17.4	24	5.6	295	68.6
4500	Barbers	13,365	10,825	81.0	2,540	19.0	4,380	32.8	5,265	39.4
4510	Hairdressers, hairstylists, and cosmetologists	54,130	5,890	10.9	48,240	89.1	18,610	34.4	22,105	40.8
4520	Miscellaneous personal appearance workers	47,905	9,105	19.0	38,800	81.0	4,770	10.0	3,955	8.3
4530	Baggage porters, bellhops, and concierges	9,665	8,265	85.5	1,400	14.5	4,290	44.4	2,070	21.4
4540	Tour and travel guides	2,750	1,460	53.1	1,295	47.1	450	16.4	1,730	62.9
4600	Childcare workers	227,995	14,620	6.4	213,375	93.6	87,295	38.3	94,645	41.5
4610	Personal care aides	166,265	18,055	10.9	148,210	89.1	64,210	38.6	51,425	30.9
4620	Recreation and fitness workers	21,630	8,740	40.4	12,890	59.6	3,415	15.8	14,315	66.2
4640	Residential advisors	1,650	350	21.2	1,305	79.1	170	10.3	540	32.7
4650	Personal care and service workers, all other	12,380	6,785	54.8	5,590	45.2	3,215	26.0	7,110	57.4

PART A—NATIONAL DATA

A-18 Workers Who are Not High School Graduates: Detailed Occupation, by Sex, Race, and Hispanic Origin, 2006–2010—Continued

Census occupation code	Detailed Occupation	Black or African American alone Number	Black or African American alone Percent	American Indian and Alaska Native alone Number	American Indian and Alaska Native alone Percent	Asian alone Number	Asian alone Percent	Native Hawaiian and Other Pacific Islander alone Number	Native Hawaiian and Other Pacific Islander alone Percent	Not Hispanic or Latino, two or more races Number	Not Hispanic or Latino, two or more races Percent
4110	Waiters and waitresses	25,915	7.2	2,240	0.6	22,550	6.3	350	0.1	6,240	1.7
4120	Food servers, nonrestaurant	9,505	21.9	145	0.3	2,045	4.7	105	0.2	885	2.0
4130	Miscellaneous food preparation and serving related workers, including dining room and cafeteria attendants and bartender helpers	9,835	7.6	985	0.8	5,415	4.2	115	0.1	1,975	1.5
4140	Dishwashers	13,955	10.1	800	0.6	3,925	2.8	180	0.1	2,030	1.5
4150	Hosts and hostesses, restaurant, lounge, and coffee shop	5,855	7.0	360	0.4	2,180	2.6	80	0.1	2,160	2.6
4200	First-line supervisors of housekeeping and janitorial workers	7,500	17.2	310	0.7	735	1.7	75	0.2	420	1.0
4210	First-line supervisors of landscaping, lawn service, and groundskeeping workers	1,680	4.7	225	0.6	340	1.0	15	0.0	344	1.0
4220	Janitors and building cleaners	100,635	14.8	4,270	0.6	19,915	2.9	875	0.1	7,815	1.2
4230	Maids and housekeeping cleaners	81,110	14.6	3,495	0.6	18,305	3.3	650	0.1	6,920	1.2
4240	Pest control workers	405	5.9	30	0.4	65	0.9	65	0.9	99	1.4
4250	Grounds maintenance workers	27,585	5.9	2,070	0.4	4,485	1.0	500	0.1	4,000	0.9
4300	First-line supervisors of gaming workers	230	6.5	140	3.9	280	7.9	4	0.1	75	2.1
4320	First-line supervisors of personal service workers	520	4.8	40	0.4	2,550	23.6	15	0.1	195	1.8
4340	Animal trainers	235	5.7	35	0.8	35	0.8	0	0.0	75	1.8
4350	Nonfarm animal caretakers	1,105	4.2	120	0.5	375	1.4	60	0.2	405	1.6
4400	Gaming services workers	710	6.3	425	3.8	4,290	38.3	10	0.1	110	1.0
4410	Motion picture projectionists	0	0.0	4	0.4	10	1.1	0	0.0	75	8.4
4420	Ushers, lobby attendants, and ticket takers	1,830	16.4	80	0.7	210	1.9	10	0.1	360	3.2
4430	Miscellaneous entertainment attendants and related workers	3,570	11.3	310	1.0	780	2.5	70	0.2	690	2.2
4460	Embalmers and funeral attendants	165	15.9	0	0.0	30	2.9	0	0.0	4	0.4
4465	Morticians, undertakers, and funeral directors	95	22.1	20	4.7	0	0.0	0	0.0	0	0.0
4500	Barbers	2,450	18.3	0	0.0	1,070	8.0	4	0.0	200	1.5
4510	Hairdressers, hairstylists, and cosmetologists	6,540	12.1	190	0.4	5,850	10.8	80	0.1	760	1.4
4520	Miscellaneous personal appearance workers	745	1.6	15	0.0	37,960	79.2	0	0.0	460	1.0
4530	Baggage porters, bellhops, and concierges	2,550	26.4	50	0.5	535	5.5	30	0.3	135	1.4
4540	Tour and travel guides	285	10.4	4	0.1	190	6.9	15	0.5	79	2.9
4600	Childcare workers	32,680	14.3	1,800	0.8	7,260	3.2	115	0.1	4,195	1.8
4610	Personal care aides	33,255	20.0	1,940	1.2	12,150	7.3	565	0.3	2,725	1.6
4620	Recreation and fitness workers	2,670	12.3	130	0.6	405	1.9	45	0.2	645	3.0
4640	Residential advisors	820	49.7	70	4.2	15	0.9	0	0.0	40	2.4
4650	Personal care and service workers, all other	1,215	9.8	80	0.6	385	3.1	30	0.2	345	2.8

A-18 Workers Who are Not High School Graduates: Detailed Occupation, by Sex, Race, and Hispanic Origin, 2006–2010—Continued

Census occupation code	Detailed Occupation	Total	Not high school graduate							
			Male		Female		Hispanic or Latino		Not Hispanic or Latino, one race — White alone	
			Number	Percent	Number	Percent	Number	Percent	Number	Percent
4700	First-line supervisors of retail sales workers	192,785	101,020	52.4	91,765	47.6	53,635	27.8	111,085	57.6
4710	First-line supervisors of non-retail sales workers	65,310	51,045	78.2	14,260	21.8	22,640	34.7	34,575	52.9
4720	Cashiers	758,370	201,295	26.5	557,075	73.5	184,095	24.3	391,830	51.7
4740	Counter and rental clerks	20,980	7,365	35.1	13,615	64.9	5,400	25.7	12,255	58.4
4750	Parts salespersons	10,585	9,510	89.8	1,075	10.2	2,675	25.3	7,160	67.6
4760	Retail salespersons	330,430	141,365	42.8	189,065	57.2	86,085	26.1	186,315	56.4
4800	Advertising sales agents	4,175	2,060	49.3	2,115	50.7	1,145	27.4	2,395	57.4
4810	Insurance sales agents	6,615	2,505	37.9	4,110	62.1	1,845	27.9	4,140	62.6
4820	Securities, commodities, and financial services sales agents	3,620	2,175	60.1	1,445	39.9	1,165	32.2	1,930	53.3
4830	Travel agents	1,580	470	29.7	1,110	70.3	310	19.6	950	60.1
4840	Sales representatives, services, all other	18,035	11,600	64.3	6,435	35.7	4,370	24.2	11,350	62.9
4850	Sales representatives, wholesale and manufacturing	47,725	32,090	67.2	15,635	32.8	17,125	35.9	25,055	52.5
4900	Models, demonstrators, and product promoters	8,235	2,090	25.4	6,145	74.6	2,215	26.9	4,760	57.8
4920	Real estate brokers and sales agents	12,885	5,320	41.3	7,560	58.7	3,485	27.0	7,940	61.6
4930	Sales engineers	195	195	100.0	0	0.0	0	0.0	175	89.7
4940	Telemarketers	15,505	5,500	35.5	10,005	64.5	3,230	20.8	8,525	55.0
4950	Door-to-door sales workers, news and street vendors, and related workers	33,285	18,185	54.6	15,100	45.4	12,025	36.1	17,490	52.5
4965	Sales and related workers, all other	17,915	8,420	47.0	9,495	53.0	3,715	20.7	10,580	59.1
5000	First-line supervisors of office and administrative support workers	43,635	21,015	48.2	22,620	51.8	12,895	29.6	23,580	54.0
5010	Switchboard operators, including answering service	2,520	410	16.3	2,110	83.7	480	19.0	1,695	67.3
5020	Telephone operators	2,985	545	18.3	2,440	81.7	530	17.8	1,735	58.1
5030	Communications equipment operators, all other	290	145	50.0	145	50.0	80	27.6	55	19.0
5100	Bill and account collectors	9,810	3,420	34.9	6,395	65.2	2,720	27.7	4,645	47.3
5110	Billing and posting clerks	15,740	1,565	9.9	14,175	90.1	5,040	32.0	8,375	53.2
5120	Bookkeeping, accounting, and auditing clerks	47,290	5,505	11.6	41,790	88.4	10,120	21.4	29,585	62.6
5130	Gaming cage workers	1,065	185	17.4	880	82.6	385	36.2	280	26.3
5140	Payroll and timekeeping clerks	4,210	355	8.4	3,855	91.6	910	21.6	2,795	66.4
5150	Procurement clerks	615	150	24.4	465	75.6	145	23.6	345	56.1
5160	Tellers	12,560	2,130	17.0	10,430	83.0	3,220	25.6	6,990	55.7
5165	Financial clerks, all other	1,350	245	18.1	1,105	81.9	415	30.7	590	43.7
5200	Brokerage clerks	205	35	17.1	175	85.4	75	36.6	105	51.2
5220	Court, municipal, and license clerks	1,675	390	23.3	1,285	76.7	435	26.0	985	58.8
5230	Credit authorizers, checkers, and clerks	1,490	80	5.4	1,410	94.6	445	29.9	875	58.7
5240	Customer service representatives	144,325	50,855	35.2	93,470	64.8	41,445	28.7	74,450	51.6
5250	Eligibility interviewers, government programs	660	180	27.3	480	72.7	275	41.7	140	21.2
5260	File clerks	30,025	7,100	23.6	22,925	76.4	6,240	20.8	17,485	58.2

PART A—NATIONAL DATA

A-18 **Workers Who are Not High School Graduates: Detailed Occupation, by Sex, Race, and Hispanic Origin, 2006–2010**—*Continued*

Census occupation code	Detailed Occupation	Not high school graduate									
		Not Hispanic or Latino, one race								Not Hispanic or Latino, two or more races	
		Black or African American alone		American Indian and Alaska Native alone		Asian alone		Native Hawaiian and Other Pacific Islander alone			
		Number	Percent	Number	Percent	Number	Percent	Number	Percent	Number	Percent
4700	First-line supervisors of retail sales workers	12,105	6.3	1,395	0.7	11,730	6.1	185	0.1	2,645	1.4
4710	First-line supervisors of non-retail sales workers	3,475	5.3	330	0.5	3,580	5.5	95	0.1	620	0.9
4720	Cashiers	120,085	15.8	6,160	0.8	38,280	5.0	1,225	0.2	16,695	2.2
4740	Counter and rental clerks	1,670	8.0	170	0.8	1,010	4.8	20	0.1	455	2.2
4750	Parts salespersons	295	2.8	130	1.2	235	2.2	0	0.0	90	0.9
4760	Retail salespersons	33,755	10.2	1,585	0.5	15,340	4.6	440	0.1	6,910	2.1
4800	Advertising sales agents	435	10.4	4	0.1	110	2.6	4	0.1	84	2.0
4810	Insurance sales agents	315	4.8	30	0.5	220	3.3	0	0.0	65	1.0
4820	Securities, commodities, and financial services sales agents	200	5.5	4	0.1	275	7.6	15	0.4	30	0.8
4830	Travel agents	130	8.2	20	1.3	135	8.5	10	0.6	30	1.9
4840	Sales representatives, services, all other	1,410	7.8	50	0.3	685	3.8	15	0.1	155	0.9
4850	Sales representatives, wholesale and manufacturing	2,185	4.6	175	0.4	2,640	5.5	75	0.2	475	1.0
4900	Models, demonstrators, and product promoters	710	8.6	50	0.6	325	3.9	0	0.0	175	2.1
4920	Real estate brokers and sales agents	710	5.5	20	0.2	495	3.8	55	0.4	180	1.4
4930	Sales engineers	0	0.0	0	0.0	15	7.7	0	0.0	4	2.1
4940	Telemarketers	2,855	18.4	55	0.4	320	2.1	60	0.4	450	2.9
4950	Door-to-door sales workers, news and street vendors, and related workers	2,185	6.6	105	0.3	860	2.6	20	0.1	610	1.8
4965	Sales and related workers, all other	2,445	13.6	85	0.5	845	4.7	0	0.0	245	1.4
5000	First-line supervisors of office and administrative support workers	4,190	9.6	290	0.7	1,750	4.0	125	0.3	805	1.8
5010	Switchboard operators, including answering service	255	10.1	55	2.2	30	1.2	0	0.0	4	0.2
5020	Telephone operators	585	19.6	0	0.0	80	2.7	0	0.0	49	1.6
5030	Communications equipment operators, all other	125	43.1	0	0.0	30	10.3	0	0.0	0	0.0
5100	Bill and account collectors	1,995	20.3	50	0.5	220	2.2	25	0.3	155	1.6
5110	Billing and posting clerks	1,575	10.0	65	0.4	465	3.0	4	0.0	215	1.4
5120	Bookkeeping, accounting, and auditing clerks	3,935	8.3	510	1.1	2,620	5.5	60	0.1	465	1.0
5130	Gaming cage workers	185	17.4	120	11.3	25	2.3	0	0.0	65	6.1
5140	Payroll and timekeeping clerks	350	8.3	25	0.6	70	1.7	0	0.0	55	1.3
5150	Procurement clerks	55	8.9	20	3.3	30	4.9	0	0.0	15	2.4
5160	Tellers	1,120	8.9	210	1.7	770	6.1	15	0.1	240	1.9
5165	Financial clerks, all other	225	16.7	10	0.7	95	7.0	0	0.0	15	1.1
5200	Brokerage clerks	0	0.0	0	0.0	25	12.2	4	2.0	0	0.0
5220	Court, municipal, and license clerks	190	11.3	20	1.2	10	0.6	0	0.0	30	1.8
5230	Credit authorizers, checkers, and clerks	135	9.1	15	1.0	25	1.7	0	0.0	0	0.0
5240	Customer service representatives	19,365	13.4	835	0.6	4,990	3.5	185	0.1	3,055	2.1
5250	Eligibility interviewers, government programs	200	30.3	0	0.0	40	6.1	0	0.0	4	0.6
5260	File clerks	3,390	11.3	355	1.2	1,905	6.3	30	0.1	625	2.1

A-18 **Workers Who are Not High School Graduates: Detailed Occupation, by Sex, Race, and Hispanic Origin, 2006–2010**—*Continued*

Census occupation code	Detailed Occupation	Total	Not high school graduate							
			Male		Female		Hispanic or Latino		Not Hispanic or Latino, one race — White alone	
			Number	Percent	Number	Percent	Number	Percent	Number	Percent
5300	Hotel, motel, and resort desk clerks	10,330	2,980	28.8	7,355	71.2	2,575	24.9	5,235	50.7
5310	Interviewers, except eligibility and loan	5,375	1,305	24.3	4,070	75.7	1,210	22.5	2,870	53.4
5320	Library assistants, clerical	3,420	815	23.8	2,605	76.2	455	13.3	2,135	62.4
5330	Loan interviewers and clerks	2,730	430	15.8	2,300	84.2	830	30.4	1,325	48.5
5340	New accounts clerks	550	30	5.5	520	94.5	150	27.3	220	40.0
5350	Correspondence clerks and order clerks	14,995	7,295	48.6	7,700	51.4	6,610	44.1	5,845	39.0
5360	Human resources assistants, except payroll and timekeeping	1,575	225	14.3	1,350	85.7	530	33.7	690	43.8
5400	Receptionists and information clerks	74,590	8,075	10.8	66,515	89.2	20,865	28.0	42,525	57.0
5410	Reservation and transportation ticket agents and travel clerks	4,775	1,960	41.0	2,810	58.8	1,405	29.4	1,925	40.3
5420	Information and record clerks, all other	2,420	560	23.1	1,855	76.7	845	34.9	1,055	43.6
5500	Cargo and freight agents	1,025	710	69.3	315	30.7	420	41.0	405	39.5
5510	Couriers and messengers	27,630	22,755	82.4	4,875	17.6	9,540	34.5	12,285	44.5
5520	Dispatchers	14,950	8,260	55.3	6,690	44.7	4,045	27.1	8,870	59.3
5530	Meter readers, utilities	2,220	1,915	86.3	305	13.7	335	15.1	1,440	64.9
5540	Postal service clerks	3,725	1,685	45.2	2,040	54.8	715	19.2	1,255	33.7
5550	Postal service mail carriers	8,060	4,240	52.6	3,820	47.4	1,865	23.1	4,110	51.0
5560	Postal service mail sorters, processors, and processing machine operators	2,760	965	35.0	1,795	65.0	825	29.9	595	21.6
5600	Production, planning, and expediting clerks	8,885	4,135	46.5	4,750	53.5	3,095	34.8	4,620	52.0
5610	Shipping, receiving, and traffic clerks	81,580	59,675	73.1	21,905	26.9	38,195	46.8	31,145	38.2
5620	Stock clerks and order fillers	260,890	170,565	65.4	90,325	34.6	86,035	33.0	125,585	48.1
5630	Weighers, measurers, checkers, and samplers, recordkeeping	11,350	5,585	49.2	5,765	50.8	5,210	45.9	4,090	36.0
5700	Secretaries and administrative assistants	100,960	5,650	5.6	95,310	94.4	23,270	23.0	65,165	64.5
5800	Computer operators	4,345	1,910	44.0	2,435	56.0	1,280	29.5	2,375	54.7
5810	Data entry keyers	17,135	4,390	25.6	12,745	74.4	4,320	25.2	9,170	53.5
5820	Word processors and typists	9,985	1,425	14.3	8,560	85.7	2,245	22.5	5,540	55.5
5840	Insurance claims and policy processing clerks	5,390	545	10.1	4,845	89.9	1,770	32.8	2,665	49.4
5850	Mail clerks and mail machine operators, except postal service	11,990	5,435	45.3	6,555	54.7	3,625	30.2	4,770	39.8
5860	Office clerks, general	55,150	12,575	22.8	42,575	77.2	14,755	26.8	29,840	54.1
5900	Office machine operators, except computer	4,430	2,000	45.1	2,430	54.9	1,545	34.9	1,530	34.5
5910	Proofreaders and copy markers	455	105	23.1	350	76.9	40	8.8	355	78.0
5920	Statistical assistants	475	180	37.9	295	62.1	80	16.8	270	56.8
5940	Miscellaneous office and administrative support workers, including desktop publishers	16,215	6,325	39.0	9,890	61.0	4,325	26.7	8,605	53.1
6005	First-line supervisors of farming, fishing, and forestry workers	16,515	14,670	88.8	1,850	11.2	11,865	71.8	3,825	23.2
6010	Agricultural inspectors	1,415	530	37.5	880	62.2	670	47.3	465	32.9
6040	Graders and sorters, agricultural products	23,765	6,485	27.3	17,280	72.7	19,540	82.2	1,675	7.0
6050	Miscellaneous agricultural workers, including animal breeders	410,240	332,390	81.0	77,850	19.0	315,840	77.0	74,630	18.2

PART A—NATIONAL DATA

A-18 Workers Who are Not High School Graduates: Detailed Occupation, by Sex, Race, and Hispanic Origin, 2006–2010—Continued

Census occupation code	Detailed Occupation	Black or African American alone Number	Black or African American alone Percent	American Indian and Alaska Native alone Number	American Indian and Alaska Native alone Percent	Asian alone Number	Asian alone Percent	Native Hawaiian and Other Pacific Islander alone Number	Native Hawaiian and Other Pacific Islander alone Percent	Not Hispanic or Latino, two or more races Number	Not Hispanic or Latino, two or more races Percent
5300	Hotel, motel, and resort desk clerks	1,375	13.3	95	0.9	695	6.7	70	0.7	290	2.8
5310	Interviewers, except eligibility and loan	1,000	18.6	30	0.6	150	2.8	0	0.0	119	2.2
5320	Library assistants, clerical	450	13.2	30	0.9	255	7.5	10	0.3	85	2.5
5330	Loan interviewers and clerks	395	14.5	0	0.0	150	5.5	0	0.0	25	0.9
5340	New accounts clerks	130	23.6	0	0.0	45	8.2	0	0.0	0	0.0
5350	Correspondence clerks and order clerks	1,705	11.4	75	0.5	665	4.4	0	0.0	89	0.6
5360	Human resources assistants, except payroll and timekeeping	315	20.0	4	0.3	20	1.3	0	0.0	19	1.2
5400	Receptionists and information clerks	6,745	9.0	560	0.8	2,215	3.0	150	0.2	1,525	2.0
5410	Reservation and transportation ticket agents and travel clerks	840	17.6	80	1.7	275	5.8	60	1.3	195	4.1
5420	Information and record clerks, all other	305	12.6	10	0.4	125	5.2	35	1.4	43	1.8
5500	Cargo and freight agents	80	7.8	4	0.4	60	5.9	35	3.4	20	2.0
5510	Couriers and messengers	3,950	14.3	255	0.9	1,180	4.3	0	0.0	420	1.5
5520	Dispatchers	1,455	9.7	105	0.7	225	1.5	20	0.1	235	1.6
5530	Meter readers, utilities	395	17.8	20	0.9	10	0.5	0	0.0	25	1.1
5540	Postal service clerks	830	22.3	4	0.1	780	20.9	30	0.8	110	3.0
5550	Postal service mail carriers	1,000	12.4	10	0.1	995	12.3	0	0.0	74	0.9
5560	Postal service mail sorters, processors, and processing machine operators	885	32.1	0	0.0	405	14.7	10	0.4	40	1.4
5600	Production, planning, and expediting clerks	665	7.5	60	0.7	325	3.7	35	0.4	85	1.0
5610	Shipping, receiving, and traffic clerks	8,170	10.0	240	0.3	2,675	3.3	255	0.3	900	1.1
5620	Stock clerks and order fillers	33,700	12.9	1,855	0.7	9,420	3.6	355	0.1	3,945	1.5
5630	Weighers, measurers, checkers, and samplers, recordkeeping	1,155	10.2	40	0.4	580	5.1	0	0.0	280	2.5
5700	Secretaries and administrative assistants	7,315	7.2	995	1.0	2,515	2.5	50	0.0	1,640	1.6
5800	Computer operators	445	10.2	15	0.3	125	2.9	0	0.0	99	2.3
5810	Data entry keyers	1,880	11.0	125	0.7	1,345	7.8	30	0.2	260	1.5
5820	Word processors and typists	1,375	13.8	40	0.4	595	6.0	25	0.3	170	1.7
5840	Insurance claims and policy processing clerks	615	11.4	4	0.1	240	4.5	4	0.1	90	1.7
5850	Mail clerks and mail machine operators, except postal service	2,175	18.1	80	0.7	1,190	9.9	30	0.3	119	1.0
5860	Office clerks, general	6,070	11.0	410	0.7	2,995	5.4	45	0.1	1,035	1.9
5900	Office machine operators, except computer	785	17.7	40	0.9	420	9.5	35	0.8	75	1.7
5910	Proofreaders and copy markers	40	8.8	0	0.0	4	0.9	0	0.0	10	2.2
5920	Statistical assistants	85	17.9	0	0.0	40	8.4	0	0.0	0	0.0
5940	Miscellaneous office and administrative support workers, including desktop publishers	2,215	13.7	70	0.4	575	3.5	0	0.0	430	2.7
6005	First-line supervisors of farming, fishing, and forestry workers	550	3.3	140	0.8	90	0.5	0	0.0	50	0.3
6010	Agricultural inspectors	240	17.0	0	0.0	30	2.1	0	0.0	8	0.6
6040	Graders and sorters, agricultural products	1,345	5.7	150	0.6	895	3.8	40	0.2	115	0.5
6050	Miscellaneous agricultural workers, including animal breeders	12,545	3.1	1,250	0.3	3,425	0.8	375	0.1	2,170	0.5

A-18 Workers Who are Not High School Graduates: Detailed Occupation, by Sex, Race, and Hispanic Origin, 2006–2010—*Continued*

Census occupation code	Detailed Occupation	Total	Not high school graduate							
			Male		Female		Hispanic or Latino		Not Hispanic or Latino, one race — White alone	
			Number	Percent	Number	Percent	Number	Percent	Number	Percent
6100	Fishing and hunting workers	9,145	8,755	95.7	390	4.3	1,565	17.1	5,950	65.1
6120	Forest and conservation workers	3,820	3,355	87.8	460	12.0	1,980	51.8	1,390	36.4
6130	Logging workers	25,890	25,320	97.8	570	2.2	4,475	17.3	17,335	67.0
6200	First-line supervisors of construction trades and extraction workers	139,845	137,575	98.4	2,270	1.6	49,990	35.7	81,055	58.0
6210	Boilermakers	2,125	2,075	97.6	50	2.4	790	37.2	1,140	53.6
6220	Brickmasons, blockmasons, and stonemasons	65,870	65,430	99.3	435	0.7	41,655	63.2	18,610	28.3
6230	Carpenters	340,495	336,690	98.9	3,805	1.1	186,725	54.8	131,795	38.7
6240	Carpet, floor, and tile installers and finishers	69,685	68,305	98.0	1,380	2.0	45,065	64.7	20,900	30.0
6250	Cement masons, concrete finishers, and terrazzo workers	31,655	31,420	99.3	235	0.7	22,400	70.8	6,510	20.6
6260	Construction laborers	554,450	542,945	97.9	11,510	2.1	371,620	67.0	141,255	25.5
6300	Paving, surfacing, and tamping equipment operators	5,815	5,730	98.5	80	1.4	2,300	39.6	2,830	48.7
6320	Construction equipment operators, except paving, surfacing, and tamping equipment operators	83,095	81,790	98.4	1,300	1.6	25,215	30.3	50,325	60.6
6330	Drywall installers, ceiling tile installers, and tapers	82,305	80,980	98.4	1,325	1.6	60,465	73.5	17,940	21.8
6355	Electricians	63,940	62,875	98.3	1,065	1.7	25,895	40.5	32,085	50.2
6360	Glaziers	8,675	8,525	98.3	150	1.7	2,970	34.2	5,045	58.2
6400	Insulation workers	13,225	12,950	97.9	275	2.1	8,800	66.5	3,665	27.7
6420	Painters, construction and maintenance	191,550	184,110	96.1	7,440	3.9	125,160	65.3	54,105	28.2
6430	Paperhangers	1,240	1,010	81.5	230	18.5	675	54.4	470	37.9
6440	Pipelayers, plumbers, pipefitters, and steamfitters	99,275	98,085	98.8	1,195	1.2	47,700	48.0	43,865	44.2
6460	Plasterers and stucco masons	21,085	20,915	99.2	170	0.8	17,075	81.0	2,660	12.6
6500	Reinforcing iron and rebar workers	2,375	2,375	100.0	4	0.2	1,580	66.5	650	27.4
6515	Roofers	95,475	94,855	99.4	620	0.6	63,840	66.9	26,720	28.0
6520	Sheet metal workers	21,145	20,245	95.7	900	4.3	7,235	34.2	12,480	59.0
6530	Structural iron and steel workers	10,940	10,615	97.0	325	3.0	4,275	39.1	5,430	49.6
6600	Helpers, construction trades	31,220	30,375	97.3	845	2.7	20,075	64.3	8,810	28.2
6660	Construction and building inspectors	2,955	2,710	91.7	245	8.3	600	20.3	1,940	65.7
6700	Elevator installers and repairers	1,000	995	99.5	4	0.4	240	24.0	520	52.0
6710	Fence erectors	10,835	10,780	99.5	55	0.5	5,710	52.7	4,425	40.8
6720	Hazardous materials removal workers	5,630	4,430	78.7	1,200	21.3	2,895	51.4	1,805	32.1
6730	Highway maintenance workers	15,720	15,320	97.5	400	2.5	4,610	29.3	8,740	55.6
6740	Rail-track laying and maintenance equipment operators	1,170	1,170	100.0	0	0.0	445	38.0	540	46.2
6765	Miscellaneous construction workers, including solar photovoltaic installers, septic tank servicers, and sewer pipe cleaners	12,050	11,595	96.2	460	3.8	5,270	43.7	5,440	45.1
6800	Derrick, rotary drill, and service unit operators, and roustabouts, oil, gas, and mining	9,050	9,010	99.6	40	0.4	3,830	42.3	4,735	52.3
6820	Earth drillers, except oil and gas	4,385	4,355	99.3	35	0.8	1,010	23.0	3,150	71.8
6830	Explosives workers, ordnance handling experts, and blasters	1,015	935	92.1	85	8.4	290	28.6	700	69.0
6840	Mining machine operators	9,005	8,895	98.8	110	1.2	2,345	26.0	6,105	67.8
6940	Miscellaneous extraction workers, including roof bolters and helpers	13,915	13,740	98.7	175	1.3	5,360	38.5	7,875	56.6

A-18 **Workers Who are Not High School Graduates: Detailed Occupation, by Sex, Race, and Hispanic Origin, 2006–2010**—*Continued*

| Census occupation code | Detailed Occupation | Not Hispanic or Latino, one race ||||||||| Not Hispanic or Latino, two or more races ||
| | | Black or African American alone || American Indian and Alaska Native alone || Asian alone || Native Hawaiian and Other Pacific Islander alone || ||
		Number	Percent	Number	Percent	Number	Percent	Number	Percent	Number	Percent
6100	Fishing and hunting workers	210	2.3	255	2.8	990	10.8	15	0.2	165	1.8
6120	Forest and conservation workers	325	8.5	55	1.4	10	0.3	4	0.1	48	1.3
6130	Logging workers	3,355	13.0	395	1.5	65	0.3	0	0.0	265	1.0
6200	First-line supervisors of construction trades and extraction workers	5,155	3.7	1,035	0.7	1,270	0.9	100	0.1	1,235	0.9
6210	Boilermakers	125	5.9	4	0.2	20	0.9	0	0.0	45	2.1
6220	Brickmasons, blockmasons, and stonemasons	4,195	6.4	380	0.6	390	0.6	95	0.1	545	0.8
6230	Carpenters	11,925	3.5	2,230	0.7	3,950	1.2	225	0.1	3,645	1.1
6240	Carpet, floor, and tile installers and finishers	1,790	2.6	190	0.3	820	1.2	20	0.0	910	1.3
6250	Cement masons, concrete finishers, and terrazzo workers	2,265	7.2	235	0.7	15	0.0	45	0.1	190	0.6
6260	Construction laborers	25,865	4.7	2,675	0.5	6,955	1.3	400	0.1	5,685	1.0
6300	Paving, surfacing, and tamping equipment operators	605	10.4	30	0.5	0	0.0	10	0.2	35	0.6
6320	Construction equipment operators except paving, surfacing, and tamping equipment operators	5,320	6.4	905	1.1	230	0.3	90	0.1	1,015	1.2
6330	Drywall installers, ceiling tile installers, and tapers	2,020	2.5	625	0.8	320	0.4	75	0.1	860	1.0
6355	Electricians	3,500	5.5	550	0.9	1,150	1.8	110	0.2	644	1.0
6360	Glaziers	325	3.7	45	0.5	130	1.5	40	0.5	115	1.3
6400	Insulation workers	610	4.6	55	0.4	15	0.1	45	0.3	34	0.3
6420	Painters, construction and maintenance	7,520	3.9	555	0.3	2,005	1.0	215	0.1	1,995	1.0
6430	Paperhangers	15	1.2	10	0.8	40	3.2	0	0.0	25	2.0
6440	Pipelayers, plumbers, pipefitters, and steamfitters	5,265	5.3	705	0.7	960	1.0	40	0.0	739	0.7
6460	Plasterers and stucco masons	1,200	5.7	25	0.1	15	0.1	0	0.0	110	0.5
6500	Reinforcing iron and rebar workers	125	5.3	0	0.0	20	0.8	0	0.0	0	0.0
6515	Roofers	3,220	3.4	745	0.8	300	0.3	40	0.0	610	0.6
6520	Sheet metal workers	820	3.9	15	0.1	320	1.5	20	0.1	265	1.3
6530	Structural iron and steel workers	680	6.2	220	2.0	185	1.7	35	0.3	114	1.0
6600	Helpers, construction trades	1,845	5.9	80	0.3	270	0.9	0	0.0	135	0.4
6660	Construction and building inspectors	185	6.3	0	0.0	110	3.7	45	1.5	75	2.5
6700	Elevator installers and repairers	160	16.0	0	0.0	30	3.0	0	0.0	50	5.0
6710	Fence erectors	475	4.4	105	1.0	0	0.0	0	0.0	114	1.1
6720	Hazardous materials removal workers	785	13.9	30	0.5	75	1.3	0	0.0	40	0.7
6730	Highway maintenance workers	1,995	12.7	175	1.1	55	0.3	4	0.0	139	0.9
6740	Rail-track laying and maintenance equipment operators	160	13.7	20	1.7	0	0.0	0	0.0	0	0.0
6765	Miscellaneous construction workers, including solar photovoltaic installers, septic tank servicers and sewer pipe cleaners	970	8.0	70	0.6	155	1.3	15	0.1	130	1.1
6800	Derrick, rotary drill, and service unit operators, and roustabouts, oil, gas, and mining	140	1.5	195	2.2	10	0.1	4	0.0	134	1.5
6820	Earth drillers, except oil and gas	155	3.5	70	1.6	0	0.0	0	0.0	4	0.1
6830	Explosives workers, ordnance handling experts, and blasters	20	2.0	0	0.0	0	0.0	0	0.0	14	1.4
6840	Mining machine operators	410	4.6	40	0.4	10	0.1	0	0.0	95	1.1
6940	Miscellaneous extraction workers, including roof bolters and helpers	430	3.1	145	1.0	55	0.4	0	0.0	50	0.4

A-18 **Workers Who are Not High School Graduates: Detailed Occupation, by Sex, Race, and Hispanic Origin, 2006–2010**—*Continued*

Census occupation code	Detailed Occupation	Total	Not high school graduate							
			Male		Female		Hispanic or Latino		Not Hispanic or Latino, one race — White alone	
			Number	Percent	Number	Percent	Number	Percent	Number	Percent
7000	First-line supervisors of mechanics, installers, and repairers...	22,520	21,585	95.8	935	4.2	5,125	22.8	14,735	65.4
7010	Computer, automated teller, and office machine repairers...	7,970	6,940	87.1	1,030	12.9	2,225	27.9	4,315	54.1
7020	Radio and telecommunications equipment installers and repairers...	6,550	5,830	89.0	720	11.0	2,720	41.5	3,015	46.0
7030	Avionics technicians...	345	265	76.8	75	21.7	30	8.7	280	81.2
7040	Electric motor, power tool, and related repairers...	3,120	2,970	95.2	150	4.8	1,090	34.9	1,760	56.4
7100	Electrical and electronics repairers, transportation equipment, and industrial and utility...	330	315	95.5	15	4.5	55	16.7	270	81.8
7110	Electronic equipment installers and repairers, motor vehicles...	2,290	2,010	87.8	275	12.0	955	41.7	1,085	47.4
7120	Electronic home entertainment equipment installers and repairers...	4,595	4,415	96.1	180	3.9	1,495	32.5	2,625	57.1
7130	Security and fire alarm systems installers...	4,655	4,615	99.1	40	0.9	2,040	43.8	2,250	48.3
7140	Aircraft mechanics and service technicians...	4,200	3,900	92.9	300	7.1	1,500	35.7	1,945	46.3
7150	Automotive body and related repairers...	38,155	37,480	98.2	670	1.8	16,350	42.9	18,425	48.3
7160	Automotive glass installers and repairers...	3,700	3,600	97.3	100	2.7	1,675	45.3	1,895	51.2
7200	Automotive service technicians and mechanics...	151,590	149,825	98.8	1,765	1.2	56,700	37.4	78,315	51.7
7210	Bus and truck mechanics and diesel engine specialists...	45,860	45,470	99.1	390	0.9	11,985	26.1	29,805	65.0
7220	Heavy vehicle and mobile equipment service technicians and mechanics...	30,465	30,005	98.5	460	1.5	9,905	32.5	18,955	62.2
7240	Small engine mechanics...	7,530	7,520	99.9	10	0.1	1,180	15.7	5,945	79.0
7260	Miscellaneous vehicle and mobile equipment mechanics, installers, and repairers...	20,815	20,665	99.3	150	0.7	8,130	39.1	10,355	49.7
7300	Control and valve installers and repairers...	1,595	1,590	99.7	4	0.3	500	31.3	905	56.7
7315	Heating, air conditioning, and refrigeration mechanics and installers...	42,835	42,100	98.3	735	1.7	15,710	36.7	24,390	56.9
7320	Home appliance repairers...	5,550	5,350	96.4	200	3.6	1,935	34.9	3,030	54.6
7330	Industrial and refractory machinery mechanics...	44,975	42,955	95.5	2,020	4.5	15,375	34.2	24,620	54.7
7340	Maintenance and repair workers, general...	64,980	63,120	97.1	1,860	2.9	24,770	38.1	32,200	49.6
7350	Maintenance workers, machinery...	4,805	4,510	93.9	295	6.1	1,675	34.9	2,865	59.6
7360	Millwrights...	4,640	4,380	94.4	260	5.6	680	14.7	3,770	81.3
7410	Electrical power-line installers and repairers...	7,595	7,520	99.0	75	1.0	2,920	38.4	3,870	51.0
7420	Telecommunications line installers and repairers...	9,755	9,135	93.6	620	6.4	3,685	37.8	4,445	45.6
7430	Precision instrument and equipment repairers...	2,915	2,350	80.6	560	19.2	930	31.9	1,555	53.3
7510	Coin, vending, and amusement machine servicers and repairers...	5,470	4,045	73.9	1,425	26.1	1,465	26.8	3,450	63.1
7540	Locksmiths and safe repairers...	2,700	2,465	91.3	230	8.5	695	25.7	1,805	66.9
7550	Manufactured building and mobile home installers...	3,180	3,065	96.4	120	3.8	795	25.0	1,965	61.8
7560	Riggers...	1,855	1,850	99.7	4	0.2	350	18.9	1,280	69.0
7610	Helpers—installation, maintenance, and repair workers...	8,300	7,710	92.9	590	7.1	4,145	49.9	3,085	37.2
7630	Other installation, maintenance, and repair workers, including wind turbine service technicians, and commercial divers, and signal and track switch repairers...	33,715	31,890	94.6	1,825	5.4	14,390	42.7	15,865	47.1

A-18 Workers Who are Not High School Graduates: Detailed Occupation, by Sex, Race, and Hispanic Origin, 2006–2010—*Continued*

Census occupation code	Detailed Occupation	\multicolumn{10}{c}{Not high school graduate}
		\multicolumn{8}{c}{Not Hispanic or Latino, one race}	\multicolumn{2}{c}{Not Hispanic or Latino, two or more races}
		Black or African American alone		American Indian and Alaska Native alone		Asian alone		Native Hawaiian and Other Pacific Islander alone			
		Number	Percent	Number	Percent	Number	Percent	Number	Percent	Number	Percent
7000	First-line supervisors of mechanics, installers, and repairers...	1,850	8.2	170	0.8	285	1.3	35	0.2	315	1.4
7010	Computer, automated teller, and office machine repairers...	530	6.6	65	0.8	680	8.5	0	0.0	155	1.9
7020	Radio and telecommunications equipment installers and repairers...	535	8.2	0	0.0	220	3.4	0	0.0	60	0.9
7030	Avionics technicians...	35	10.1	0	0.0	0	0.0	0	0.0	0	0.0
7040	Electric motor, power tool, and related repairers...	140	4.5	10	0.3	90	2.9	0	0.0	29	0.9
7100	Electrical and electronics repairers, transportation equipment, and industrial and utility...	4	1.2	0	0.0	0	0.0	0	0.0	0	0.0
7110	Electronic equipment installers and repairers, motor vehicles...	165	7.2	0	0.0	35	1.5	0	0.0	45	2.0
7120	Electronic home entertainment equipment installers and repairers...	155	3.4	4	0.1	270	5.9	0	0.0	55	1.2
7130	Security and fire alarm systems installers...	95	2.0	55	1.2	170	3.7	0	0.0	45	1.0
7140	Aircraft mechanics and service technicians...	255	6.1	15	0.4	345	8.2	0	0.0	140	3.3
7150	Automotive body and related repairers...	1,565	4.1	280	0.7	1,115	2.9	25	0.1	399	1.0
7160	Automotive glass installers and repairers...	50	1.4	0	0.0	75	2.0	0	0.0	4	0.1
7200	Automotive service technicians and mechanics...	9,815	6.5	745	0.5	4,325	2.9	125	0.1	1,565	1.0
7210	Bus and truck mechanics and diesel engine specialists...	2,485	5.4	360	0.8	655	1.4	55	0.1	510	1.1
7220	Heavy vehicle and mobile equipment service technicians and mechanics...	1,085	3.6	220	0.7	115	0.4	20	0.1	170	0.6
7240	Small engine mechanics...	195	2.6	4	0.1	130	1.7	15	0.2	55	0.7
7260	Miscellaneous vehicle and mobile equipment mechanics, installers, and repairers...	1,915	9.2	45	0.2	120	0.6	60	0.3	180	0.9
7300	Control and valve installers and repairers...	165	10.3	0	0.0	20	1.3	0	0.0	4	0.3
7315	Heating, air conditioning, and refrigeration mechanics and installers...	1,380	3.2	155	0.4	680	1.6	15	0.0	505	1.2
7320	Home appliance repairers...	315	5.7	4	0.1	235	4.2	15	0.3	10	0.2
7330	Industrial and refractory machinery mechanics...	3,005	6.7	130	0.3	1,360	3.0	45	0.1	445	1.0
7340	Maintenance and repair workers, general...	5,380	8.3	590	0.9	1,330	2.0	135	0.2	570	0.9
7350	Maintenance workers, machinery...	260	5.4	4	0.1	0	0.0	0	0.0	4	0.1
7360	Millwrights...	55	1.2	75	1.6	15	0.3	0	0.0	50	1.1
7410	Electrical power-line installers and repairers...	575	7.6	85	1.1	20	0.3	0	0.0	125	1.6
7420	Telecommunications line installers and repairers...	885	9.1	15	0.2	455	4.7	50	0.5	230	2.4
7430	Precision instrument and equipment repairers...	155	5.3	4	0.1	265	9.1	0	0.0	0	0.0
7510	Coin, vending, and amusement machine servicers and repairers...	330	6.0	125	2.3	65	1.2	0	0.0	34	0.6
7540	Locksmiths and safe repairers...	85	3.1	45	1.7	25	0.9	0	0.0	50	1.9
7550	Manufactured building and mobile home installers...	335	10.5	15	0.5	25	0.8	0	0.0	45	1.4
7560	Riggers...	175	9.4	10	0.5	10	0.5	0	0.0	35	1.9
7610	Helpers—installation, maintenance, and repair workers...	570	6.9	45	0.5	300	3.6	0	0.0	150	1.8
7630	Other installation, maintenance, and repair workers, including wind turbine service technicians, and commercial divers, and signal and track switch repairers...	1,955	5.8	220	0.7	725	2.2	50	0.1	515	1.5

A-18 **Workers Who are Not High School Graduates: Detailed Occupation, by Sex, Race, and Hispanic Origin, 2006–2010**—*Continued*

Census occupation code	Detailed Occupation	Total	Not high school graduate					Not Hispanic or Latino, one race	
			Male		Female		Hispanic or Latino		White alone	
			Number	Percent	Number	Percent	Number	Percent	Number	Percent
7700	First-line supervisors of production and operating workers.................	102,045	79,040	77.5	23,005	22.5	41,105	40.3	48,955	48.0
7710	Aircraft structure, surfaces, rigging, and systems assemblers.................	1,610	925	57.5	680	42.2	915	56.8	330	20.5
7720	Electrical, electronics, and electromechanical assemblers.................	34,830	12,505	35.9	22,325	64.1	14,420	41.4	8,380	24.1
7730	Engine and other machine assemblers..............	1,970	1,720	87.3	250	12.7	590	29.9	1,125	57.1
7740	Structural metal fabricators and fitters.............	3,570	3,465	97.1	105	2.9	1,000	28.0	2,085	58.4
7750	Miscellaneous assemblers and fabricators...........	197,960	110,915	56.0	87,045	44.0	87,315	44.1	70,930	35.8
7800	Bakers.................	47,350	26,450	55.9	20,905	44.1	26,215	55.4	13,490	28.5
7810	Butchers and other meat, poultry, and fish processing workers.................	88,855	61,265	68.9	27,590	31.1	59,035	66.4	15,535	17.5
7830	Food and tobacco roasting, baking, and drying machine operators and tenders............	2,940	2,005	68.2	935	31.8	1,335	45.4	930	31.6
7840	Food batchmakers.................	19,735	8,945	45.3	10,785	54.6	10,785	54.6	6,365	32.3
7850	Food cooking machine operators and tenders........	3,295	1,810	54.9	1,485	45.1	1,575	47.8	970	29.4
7855	Food processing workers, all other.................	37,765	22,780	60.3	14,990	39.7	23,545	62.3	6,695	17.7
7900	Computer control programmers and operators.......	5,670	4,995	88.1	675	11.9	1,535	27.1	3,155	55.6
7920	Extruding and drawing machine setters, operators, and tenders, metal and plastic.............	1,995	1,655	83.0	345	17.3	460	23.1	1,330	66.7
7930	Forging machine setters, operators, and tenders, metal and plastic.................	1,325	1,295	97.7	30	2.3	230	17.4	880	66.4
7940	Rolling machine setters, operators, and tenders, metal and plastic.................	2,160	1,585	73.4	580	26.9	790	36.6	865	40.0
7950	Cutting, punching, and press machine setters, operators, and tenders, metal and plastic.........	21,295	16,950	79.6	4,350	20.4	7,770	36.5	10,810	50.8
7960	Drilling and boring machine tool setters, operators, and tenders, metal and plastic........	1,095	980	89.5	115	10.5	225	20.5	750	68.5
8000	Grinding, lapping, polishing, and buffing machine tool setters, operators, and tenders, metal and plastic.................	14,290	12,500	87.5	1,790	12.5	7,060	49.4	5,265	36.8
8010	Lathe and turning machine tool setters, operators, and tenders, metal and plastic.................	2,280	2,040	89.5	240	10.5	790	34.6	1,270	55.7
8030	Machinists.................	39,880	37,140	93.1	2,740	6.9	13,035	32.7	21,580	54.1
8040	Metal furnace operators, tenders, pourers, and casters.................	3,590	3,315	92.3	270	7.5	1,300	36.2	1,845	51.4
8060	Model makers and patternmakers, metal and plastic.................	830	695	83.7	135	16.3	405	48.8	395	47.6
8100	Molders and molding machine setters, operators, and tenders, metal and plastic.................	9,985	7,930	79.4	2,050	20.5	4,170	41.8	4,380	43.9
8130	Tool and die makers.................	4,465	4,150	92.9	315	7.1	1,150	25.8	2,910	65.2
8140	Welding, soldering, and brazing workers............	128,055	121,765	95.1	6,290	4.9	60,530	47.3	53,000	41.4
8150	Heat treating equipment setters, operators, and tenders, metal and plastic.................	1,195	1,090	91.2	105	8.8	365	30.5	755	63.2
8200	Plating and coating machine setters, operators, and tenders, metal and plastic.................	3,645	3,375	92.6	270	7.4	1,775	48.7	1,515	41.6
8210	Tool grinders, filers, and sharpeners...............	1,175	1,085	92.3	95	8.1	175	14.9	830	70.6
8220	Miscellaneous metal workers and plastic workers, including milling and planing machine setters, and multiple machine tool setters, and layout workers.................	92,750	68,655	74.0	24,095	26.0	49,220	53.1	27,830	30.0
8250	Prepress technicians and workers.................	3,655	1,630	44.6	2,025	55.4	1,610	44.0	1,435	39.3
8255	Printing press operators.................	29,675	22,610	76.2	7,065	23.8	12,240	41.2	12,955	43.7
8256	Print binding and finishing workers.................	5,675	2,300	40.5	3,375	59.5	1,510	26.6	2,935	51.7

A-18 **Workers Who are Not High School Graduates: Detailed Occupation, by Sex, Race, and Hispanic Origin, 2006–2010**—Continued

Census occupation code	Detailed Occupation	Not high school graduate								
		Not Hispanic or Latino, one race								Not Hispanic or Latino, two or more races	
		Black or African American alone		American Indian and Alaska Native alone		Asian alone		Native Hawaiian and Other Pacific Islander alone			
		Number	Percent	Number	Percent	Number	Percent	Number	Percent	Number	Percent
7700	First-line supervisors of production and operating workers............	6,690	6.6	440	0.4	3,610	3.5	50	0.0	1,195	1.2
7710	Aircraft structure, surfaces, rigging, and systems assemblers............	40	2.5	30	1.9	290	18.0	0	0.0	0	0.0
7720	Electrical, electronics, and electromechanical assemblers............	2,380	6.8	75	0.2	9,235	26.5	50	0.1	290	0.8
7730	Engine and other machine assemblers............	185	9.4	15	0.8	50	2.5	0	0.0	4	0.2
7740	Structural metal fabricators and fitters............	260	7.3	4	0.1	220	6.2	0	0.0	0	0.0
7750	Miscellaneous assemblers and fabricators............	15,910	8.0	795	0.4	20,975	10.6	140	0.1	1,895	1.0
7800	Bakers............	3,480	7.3	190	0.4	3,350	7.1	25	0.1	604	1.3
7810	Butchers and other meat, poultry, and fish processing workers............	8,540	9.6	255	0.3	4,855	5.5	105	0.1	535	0.6
7830	Food and tobacco roasting, baking, and drying machine operators and tenders............	400	13.6	20	0.7	225	7.7	0	0.0	25	0.9
7840	Food batchmakers............	1,360	6.9	75	0.4	950	4.8	0	0.0	195	1.0
7850	Food cooking machine operators and tenders............	385	11.7	0	0.0	340	10.3	0	0.0	23	0.7
7855	Food processing workers, all other............	4,030	10.7	130	0.3	2,725	7.2	220	0.6	415	1.1
7900	Computer control programmers and operators............	215	3.8	15	0.3	695	12.3	0	0.0	59	1.0
7920	Extruding and drawing machine setters, operators, and tenders, metal and plastic............	150	7.5	20	1.0	40	2.0	0	0.0	0	0.0
7930	Forging machine setters, operators, and tenders, metal and plastic............	145	10.9	0	0.0	70	5.3	0	0.0	0	0.0
7940	Rolling machine setters, operators, and tenders, metal and plastic............	385	17.8	25	1.2	75	3.5	10	0.5	15	0.7
7950	Cutting, punching, and press machine setters, operators, and tenders, metal and plastic............	1,900	8.9	90	0.4	455	2.1	0	0.0	275	1.3
7960	Drilling and boring machine tool setters, operators, and tenders, metal and plastic............	110	10.0	10	0.9	0	0.0	0	0.0	4	0.4
8000	Grinding, lapping, polishing, and buffing machine tool setters, operators, and tenders, metal and plastic............	980	6.9	100	0.7	690	4.8	0	0.0	195	1.4
8010	Lathe and turning machine tool setters, operators, and tenders, metal and plastic............	85	3.7	35	1.5	95	4.2	0	0.0	4	0.2
8030	Machinists............	1,820	4.6	110	0.3	2,885	7.2	35	0.1	400	1.0
8040	Metal furnace operators, tenders, pourers, and casters............	280	7.8	30	0.8	60	1.7	0	0.0	80	2.2
8060	Model makers and patternmakers, metal and plastic............	0	0.0	0	0.0	25	3.0	0	0.0	10	1.2
8100	Molders and molding machine setters, operators, and tenders, metal and plastic............	870	8.7	90	0.9	380	3.8	10	0.1	90	0.9
8130	Tool and die makers............	250	5.6	0	0.0	130	2.9	0	0.0	23	0.5
8140	Welding, soldering, and brazing workers............	7,325	5.7	850	0.7	5,060	4.0	75	0.1	1,220	1.0
8150	Heat treating equipment setters, operators, and tenders, metal and plastic............	55	4.6	4	0.3	20	1.7	0	0.0	0	0.0
8200	Plating and coating machine setters, operators, and tenders, metal and plastic............	130	3.6	0	0.0	170	4.7	0	0.0	60	1.6
8210	Tool grinders, filers, and sharpeners............	110	9.4	0	0.0	40	3.4	0	0.0	25	2.1
8220	Miscellaneous metal workers and plastic workers, including milling and planing machine setters, and multiple machine tool setters, and layout workers............	7,030	7.6	320	0.3	7,585	8.2	65	0.1	690	0.7
8250	Prepress technicians and workers............	240	6.6	15	0.4	290	7.9	10	0.3	53	1.5
8255	Printing press operators............	2,210	7.4	85	0.3	1,870	6.3	30	0.1	285	1.0
8256	Print binding and finishing workers............	825	14.5	10	0.2	340	6.0	0	0.0	49	0.9

A-18 Workers Who are Not High School Graduates: Detailed Occupation, by Sex, Race, and Hispanic Origin, 2006–2010—Continued

Census occupation code	Detailed Occupation	Total	Not high school graduate							
			Male		Female		Hispanic or Latino		Not Hispanic or Latino, one race — White alone	
			Number	Percent	Number	Percent	Number	Percent	Number	Percent
8300	Laundry and dry-cleaning workers	70,955	22,765	32.1	48,190	67.9	36,270	51.1	18,530	26.1
8310	Pressers, textile, garment, and related materials	25,700	6,255	24.3	19,440	75.6	16,505	64.2	3,775	14.7
8320	Sewing machine operators	93,875	25,125	26.8	68,750	73.2	54,250	57.8	17,870	19.0
8330	Shoe and leather workers and repairers	3,115	2,510	80.6	605	19.4	1,640	52.6	1,205	38.7
8340	Shoe machine operators and tenders	1,385	655	47.3	735	53.1	765	55.2	355	25.6
8350	Tailors, dressmakers, and sewers	21,720	6,590	30.3	15,125	69.6	8,990	41.4	6,420	29.6
8400	Textile bleaching and dyeing, and cutting machine setters, operators, and tenders	4,525	2,785	61.5	1,740	38.5	2,365	52.3	1,715	37.9
8410	Textile knitting and weaving machine setters, operators, and tenders	3,330	1,365	41.0	1,970	59.2	985	29.6	1,610	48.3
8420	Textile winding, twisting, and drawing out machine setters, operators, and tenders	5,775	1,980	34.3	3,795	65.7	1,635	28.3	2,910	50.4
8450	Upholsterers	12,415	11,020	88.8	1,395	11.2	6,070	48.9	5,195	41.8
8460	Miscellaneous textile, apparel, and furnishings workers, except upholsterers	7,030	3,965	56.4	3,065	43.6	2,735	38.9	2,960	42.1
8500	Cabinetmakers and bench carpenters	14,285	13,350	93.5	940	6.6	6,125	42.9	6,950	48.7
8510	Furniture finishers	5,090	4,000	78.6	1,090	21.4	2,090	41.1	2,325	45.7
8530	Sawing machine setters, operators, and tenders, wood	12,930	11,630	89.9	1,305	10.1	4,045	31.3	7,620	58.9
8540	Woodworking machine setters, operators, and tenders, except sawing	9,020	6,960	77.2	2,060	22.8	3,575	39.6	4,360	48.3
8550	Miscellaneous woodworkers, including model makers and patternmakers	5,665	5,120	90.4	540	9.5	1,420	25.1	3,390	59.8
8600	Power plant operators, distributors, and dispatchers	1,065	865	81.2	200	18.8	135	12.7	805	75.6
8610	Stationary engineers and boiler operators	6,665	6,500	97.5	165	2.5	1,635	24.5	3,735	56.0
8620	Water and wastewater treatment plant and system operators	3,195	3,100	97.0	95	3.0	545	17.1	1,945	60.9
8630	Miscellaneous plant and system operators	2,830	2,775	98.1	55	1.9	775	27.4	1,805	63.8
8640	Chemical processing machine setters, operators, and tenders	5,055	4,415	87.3	640	12.7	2,660	52.6	1,540	30.5
8650	Crushing, grinding, polishing, mixing, and blending workers	20,905	18,665	89.3	2,240	10.7	10,325	49.4	7,900	37.8
8710	Cutting workers	24,475	18,095	73.9	6,380	26.1	10,945	44.7	9,805	40.1
8720	Extruding, forming, pressing, and compacting machine setters, operators, and tenders	6,820	5,740	84.2	1,080	15.8	2,645	38.8	3,150	46.2
8730	Furnace, kiln, oven, drier, and kettle operators and tenders	1,415	1,215	85.9	200	14.1	400	28.3	860	60.8
8740	Inspectors, testers, sorters, samplers, and weighers	92,055	40,605	44.1	51,450	55.9	39,850	43.3	36,045	39.2
8750	Jewelers and precious stone and metal workers	7,565	5,095	67.3	2,465	32.6	2,660	35.2	1,870	24.7
8760	Medical, dental, and ophthalmic laboratory technicians	5,970	3,110	52.1	2,860	47.9	1,840	30.8	3,105	52.0
8800	Packaging and filling machine operators and tenders	90,850	35,935	39.6	54,915	60.4	60,145	66.2	15,600	17.2
8810	Painting workers	41,940	37,060	88.4	4,880	11.6	23,410	55.8	14,455	34.5
8830	Photographic process workers and processing machine operators	4,880	1,700	34.8	3,185	65.3	1,100	22.5	2,640	54.1
8850	Adhesive bonding machine operators and tenders	3,525	1,905	54.0	1,620	46.0	1,630	46.2	1,265	35.9
8860	Cleaning, washing, and metal pickling equipment operators and tenders	2,740	1,835	67.0	905	33.0	1,720	62.8	700	25.5

A-18 Workers Who are Not High School Graduates: Detailed Occupation, by Sex, Race, and Hispanic Origin, 2006–2010—Continued

Census occupation code	Detailed Occupation	Black or African American alone Number	Percent	American Indian and Alaska Native alone Number	Percent	Asian alone Number	Percent	Native Hawaiian and Other Pacific Islander alone Number	Percent	Not Hispanic or Latino, two or more races Number	Percent
8300	Laundry and dry-cleaning workers	10,585	14.9	425	0.6	4,435	6.3	40	0.1	670	0.9
8310	Pressers, textile, garment, and related materials	3,625	14.1	55	0.2	1,530	6.0	0	0.0	210	0.8
8320	Sewing machine operators	5,070	5.4	195	0.2	16,010	17.1	70	0.1	405	0.4
8330	Shoe and leather workers and repairers	90	2.9	30	1.0	105	3.4	0	0.0	45	1.4
8340	Shoe machine operators and tenders	170	12.3	0	0.0	105	7.6	0	0.0	0	0.0
8350	Tailors, dressmakers, and sewers	1,025	4.7	35	0.2	5,025	23.1	40	0.2	179	0.8
8400	Textile bleaching and dyeing, and cutting machine setters, operators, and tenders	220	4.9	0	0.0	160	3.5	0	0.0	65	1.4
8410	Textile knitting and weaving machine setters, operators, and tenders	395	11.9	70	2.1	220	6.6	0	0.0	49	1.5
8420	Textile winding, twisting, and drawing out machine setters, operators, and tenders	920	15.9	85	1.5	160	2.8	0	0.0	65	1.1
8450	Upholsterers	835	6.7	45	0.4	170	1.4	20	0.2	75	0.6
8460	Miscellaneous textile, apparel, and furnishings workers except upholsterers	820	11.7	4	0.1	515	7.3	0	0.0	0	0.0
8500	Cabinetmakers and bench carpenters	780	5.5	55	0.4	265	1.9	4	0.0	104	0.7
8510	Furniture finishers	425	8.3	15	0.3	215	4.2	0	0.0	25	0.5
8530	Sawing machine setters, operators, and tenders, wood	810	6.3	165	1.3	195	1.5	0	0.0	94	0.7
8540	Woodworking machine setters, operators, and tenders, except sawing	695	7.7	65	0.7	140	1.6	0	0.0	190	2.1
8550	Miscellaneous woodworkers, including model makers and patternmakers	430	7.6	85	1.5	205	3.6	0	0.0	130	2.3
8600	Power plant operators, distributors, and dispatchers	40	3.8	35	3.3	0	0.0	0	0.0	59	5.5
8610	Stationary engineers and boiler operators	915	13.7	55	0.8	215	3.2	10	0.2	95	1.4
8620	Water and wastewater treatment plant and system operators	550	17.2	110	3.4	20	0.6	0	0.0	25	0.8
8630	Miscellaneous plant and system operators	200	7.1	0	0.0	50	1.8	0	0.0	0	0.0
8640	Chemical processing machine setters, operators, and tenders	625	12.4	4	0.1	125	2.5	0	0.0	95	1.9
8650	Crushing, grinding, polishing, mixing, and blending workers	1,610	7.7	205	1.0	665	3.2	0	0.0	194	0.9
8710	Cutting workers	2,375	9.7	160	0.7	1,025	4.2	10	0.0	160	0.7
8720	Extruding, forming, pressing, and compacting machine setters, operators, and tenders	735	10.8	35	0.5	205	3.0	0	0.0	50	0.7
8730	Furnace, kiln, oven, drier, and kettle operators and tenders	100	7.1	4	0.3	0	0.0	0	0.0	45	3.2
8740	Inspectors, testers, sorters, samplers, and weighers	9,065	9.8	405	0.4	5,715	6.2	75	0.1	910	1.0
8750	Jewelers and precious stone and metal workers	255	3.4	850	11.2	1,805	23.9	15	0.2	105	1.4
8760	Medical, dental, and ophthalmic laboratory technicians	335	5.6	10	0.2	610	10.2	0	0.0	75	1.3
8800	Packaging and filling machine operators and tenders	8,730	9.6	250	0.3	5,110	5.6	150	0.2	875	1.0
8810	Painting workers	2,550	6.1	215	0.5	845	2.0	25	0.1	439	1.0
8830	Photographic process workers and processing machine operators	740	15.2	4	0.1	265	5.4	60	1.2	75	1.5
8850	Adhesive bonding machine operators and tenders	355	10.1	20	0.6	225	6.4	0	0.0	30	0.9
8860	Cleaning, washing, and metal pickling equipment operators and tenders	220	8.0	4	0.1	75	2.7	0	0.0	25	0.9

A-18 **Workers Who are Not High School Graduates: Detailed Occupation, by Sex, Race, and Hispanic Origin, 2006–2010**—Continued

Census occupation code	Detailed Occupation	Total	Not high school graduate							
			Male		Female		Hispanic or Latino		Not Hispanic or Latino, one race — White alone	
			Number	Percent	Number	Percent	Number	Percent	Number	Percent
8910	Etchers and engravers	1,255	860	68.5	395	31.5	475	37.8	640	51.0
8920	Molders, shapers, and casters, except metal and plastic	8,260	7,585	91.8	675	8.2	4,645	56.2	2,520	30.5
8930	Paper goods machine setters, operators, and tenders	6,325	3,600	56.9	2,725	43.1	2,865	45.3	2,185	34.5
8940	Tire builders	1,875	1,715	91.5	160	8.5	450	24.0	1,090	58.1
8950	Helpers—production workers	15,755	12,190	77.4	3,560	22.6	9,620	61.1	4,005	25.4
8965	Other production workers, including semiconductor processors and cooling and freezing equipment operators	234,355	158,400	67.6	75,955	32.4	115,710	49.4	80,495	34.3
9000	Supervisors of transportation and material moving workers	19,605	16,740	85.4	2,870	14.6	6,275	32.0	10,390	53.0
9030	Aircraft pilots and flight engineers	460	440	95.7	20	4.3	50	10.9	280	60.9
9040	Air traffic controllers and airfield operations specialists	195	130	66.7	65	33.3	50	25.6	130	66.7
9050	Flight attendants	830	130	15.7	700	84.3	150	18.1	510	61.4
9110	Ambulance drivers and attendants, except emergency medical technicians	1,540	1,225	79.5	315	20.5	505	32.8	575	37.3
9120	Bus drivers	59,100	31,490	53.3	27,610	46.7	15,195	25.7	26,285	44.5
9130	Driver/sales workers and truck drivers	595,410	571,570	96.0	23,840	4.0	202,665	34.0	316,710	53.2
9140	Taxi drivers and chauffeurs	50,100	43,360	86.5	6,745	13.5	17,320	34.6	14,260	28.5
9150	Motor vehicle operators, all other	9,720	8,335	85.8	1,390	14.3	2,890	29.7	5,430	55.9
9200	Locomotive engineers and operators	1,400	1,320	94.3	80	5.7	155	11.1	900	64.3
9230	Railroad brake, signal, and switch operators	680	650	95.6	30	4.4	310	45.6	230	33.8
9240	Railroad conductors and yardmasters	1,470	1,415	96.3	55	3.7	200	13.6	850	57.8
9260	Subway, streetcar, and other rail transportation workers	690	680	98.6	15	2.2	285	41.3	320	46.4
9300	Sailors and marine oilers, and ship engineers	3,295	3,165	96.1	130	3.9	450	13.7	2,385	72.4
9310	Ship and boat captains and operators	3,985	3,845	96.5	135	3.4	235	5.9	3,315	83.2
9350	Parking lot attendants	12,455	10,915	87.6	1,540	12.4	5,875	47.2	3,500	28.1
9360	Automotive and watercraft service attendants	25,530	20,485	80.2	5,045	19.8	3,960	15.5	16,850	66.0
9410	Transportation inspectors	3,070	2,255	73.5	815	26.5	985	32.1	1,700	55.4
9415	Transportation attendants, except flight attendants	5,115	1,330	26.0	3,785	74.0	1,355	26.5	1,670	32.6
9420	Miscellaneous transportation workers, including bridge and lock tenders and traffic technicians	1,385	1,185	85.6	200	14.4	225	16.2	910	65.7
9510	Crane and tower operators	11,055	10,885	98.5	170	1.5	2,760	25.0	6,800	61.5
9520	Dredge, excavating, and loading machine operators	12,690	12,615	99.4	75	0.6	4,020	31.7	7,580	59.7
9560	Conveyor operators and tenders, and hoist and winch operators	2,140	1,940	90.7	200	9.3	790	36.9	985	46.0
9600	Industrial truck and tractor operators	122,990	116,925	95.1	6,065	4.9	63,015	51.2	39,380	32.0
9610	Cleaners of vehicles and equipment	117,785	100,675	85.5	17,110	14.5	61,415	52.1	38,065	32.3
9620	Laborers and freight, stock, and material movers, hand	469,075	379,915	81.0	89,160	19.0	175,630	37.4	214,470	45.7
9630	Machine feeders and offbearers	8,850	5,085	57.5	3,765	42.5	3,485	39.4	3,865	43.7
9640	Packers and packagers, hand	157,815	60,740	38.5	97,075	61.5	106,155	67.3	28,105	17.8
9650	Pumping station operators	2,715	2,635	97.1	80	2.9	650	23.9	1,940	71.5
9720	Refuse and recyclable material collectors	28,345	25,735	90.8	2,610	9.2	11,810	41.7	10,645	37.6
9750	Miscellaneous material moving workers, including mine shuttle car operators, and tank car, truck, and ship loaders	10,985	9,755	88.8	1,235	11.2	3,870	35.2	5,090	46.3

A-18 Workers Who are Not High School Graduates: Detailed Occupation, by Sex, Race, and Hispanic Origin, 2006–2010—Continued

Census occupation code	Detailed Occupation	Black or African American alone Number	Black or African American alone Percent	American Indian and Alaska Native alone Number	American Indian and Alaska Native alone Percent	Asian alone Number	Asian alone Percent	Native Hawaiian and Other Pacific Islander alone Number	Native Hawaiian and Other Pacific Islander alone Percent	Not Hispanic or Latino, two or more races Number	Not Hispanic or Latino, two or more races Percent
8910	Etchers and engravers	10	0.8	60	4.8	70	5.6	0	0.0	0	0.0
8920	Molders, shapers, and casters, except metal and plastic	630	7.6	50	0.6	260	3.1	0	0.0	155	1.9
8930	Paper goods machine setters, operators, and tenders	940	14.9	45	0.7	255	4.0	0	0.0	35	0.6
8940	Tire builders	220	11.7	25	1.3	90	4.8	0	0.0	0	0.0
8950	Helpers—production workers	850	5.4	150	1.0	1,015	6.4	30	0.2	80	0.5
8965	Other production workers, including semiconductor processors and cooling and freezing equipment operators	22,510	9.6	795	0.3	12,720	5.4	360	0.2	1,760	0.8
9000	Supervisors of transportation and material moving workers	1,880	9.6	180	0.9	655	3.3	25	0.1	199	1.0
9030	Aircraft pilots and flight engineers	45	9.8	0	0.0	60	13.0	0	0.0	25	5.4
9040	Air traffic controllers and airfield operations specialists	0	0.0	0	0.0	10	5.1	0	0.0	10	5.1
9050	Flight attendants	125	15.1	0	0.0	40	4.8	0	0.0	10	1.2
9110	Ambulance drivers and attendants, except emergency medical technicians	385	25.0	55	3.6	0	0.0	0	0.0	20	1.3
9120	Bus drivers	15,020	25.4	555	0.9	1,320	2.2	165	0.3	570	1.0
9130	Driver/sales workers and truck drivers	55,005	9.2	2,740	0.5	11,365	1.9	585	0.1	6,335	1.1
9140	Taxi drivers and chauffeurs	11,375	22.7	215	0.4	6,365	12.7	30	0.1	535	1.1
9150	Motor vehicle operators, all other	1,055	10.9	10	0.1	180	1.9	0	0.0	159	1.6
9200	Locomotive engineers and operators	280	20.0	4	0.3	0	0.0	0	0.0	55	3.9
9230	Railroad brake, signal, and switch operators	70	10.3	55	8.1	0	0.0	0	0.0	20	2.9
9240	Railroad conductors and yardmasters	375	25.5	45	3.1	0	0.0	0	0.0	0	0.0
9260	Subway, streetcar, and other rail transportation workers	65	9.4	0	0.0	4	0.6	0	0.0	15	2.2
9300	Sailors and marine oilers, and ship engineers	270	8.2	95	2.9	20	0.6	0	0.0	75	2.3
9310	Ship and boat captains and operators	105	2.6	320	8.0	4	0.1	0	0.0	4	0.1
9350	Parking lot attendants	2,250	18.1	10	0.1	535	4.3	25	0.2	255	2.0
9360	Automotive and watercraft service attendants	2,430	9.5	320	1.3	1,480	5.8	75	0.3	420	1.6
9410	Transportation inspectors	265	8.6	0	0.0	55	1.8	20	0.7	45	1.5
9415	Transportation attendants, except flight attendants	1,845	36.1	25	0.5	120	2.3	15	0.3	85	1.7
9420	Miscellaneous transportation workers, including bridge and lock tenders and traffic technicians	175	12.6	15	1.1	25	1.8	0	0.0	39	2.8
9510	Crane and tower operators	1,175	10.6	130	1.2	15	0.1	45	0.4	125	1.1
9520	Dredge, excavating, and loading machine operators	725	5.7	75	0.6	80	0.6	0	0.0	210	1.7
9560	Conveyor operators and tenders, and hoist and winch operators	250	11.7	85	4.0	30	1.4	0	0.0	4	0.2
9600	Industrial truck and tractor operators	16,675	13.6	620	0.5	1,945	1.6	300	0.2	1,060	0.9
9610	Cleaners of vehicles and equipment	13,995	11.9	420	0.4	2,080	1.8	325	0.3	1,485	1.3
9620	Laborers and freight, stock, and material movers, hand	55,565	11.8	3,050	0.7	12,705	2.7	615	0.1	7,035	1.5
9630	Machine feeders and offbearers	1,150	13.0	25	0.3	240	2.7	0	0.0	80	0.9
9640	Packers and packagers, hand	13,415	8.5	565	0.4	8,345	5.3	235	0.1	995	0.6
9650	Pumping station operators	35	1.3	10	0.4	60	2.2	10	0.4	8	0.3
9720	Refuse and recyclable material collectors	5,030	17.7	160	0.6	335	1.2	30	0.1	340	1.2
9750	Miscellaneous material moving workers, including mine shuttle car operators, and tank car, truck, and ship loaders	1,600	14.6	150	1.4	140	1.3	0	0.0	135	1.2

A-19 **Workers with High School Diploma or Equivalency: Detailed Occupation, by Sex, Race, and Hispanic Origin, 2006–2010**

Census occupation code	Detailed Occupation	Total	Male Number	Male Percent	Female Number	Female Percent	Hispanic or Latino Number	Hispanic or Latino Percent	Not Hispanic or Latino, one race White alone Number	Not Hispanic or Latino, one race White alone Percent
	Total, all occupations	36,711,835	20,393,130	55.5	16,318,705	44.5	5,634,140	15.3	24,725,235	67.3
0010	Chief executives and legislators	124,240	94,425	76.0	29,815	24.0	7,250	5.8	108,695	87.5
0020	General and operations managers	149,855	106,275	70.9	43,580	29.1	13,810	9.2	123,750	82.6
0040	Advertising and promotions managers	4,340	1,655	38.1	2,680	61.8	530	12.2	3,530	81.3
0050	Marketing and sales managers	70,840	38,165	53.9	32,675	46.1	6,390	9.0	58,375	82.4
0060	Public relations and fundraising managers	3,280	1,060	32.3	2,220	67.7	165	5.0	2,740	83.5
0100	Administrative services managers	19,700	13,575	68.9	6,125	31.1	1,870	9.5	15,185	77.1
0110	Computer and information systems managers	20,075	12,655	63.0	7,415	36.9	1,465	7.3	16,495	82.2
0120	Financial managers	125,670	26,090	20.8	99,580	79.2	16,210	12.9	95,190	75.7
0135	Compensation and benefits managers	2,695	80	3.0	2,615	97.0	205	7.6	2,230	82.7
0136	Human resources managers	41,840	16,270	38.9	25,570	61.1	5,910	14.1	30,370	72.6
0137	Training and development managers	3,955	2,000	50.6	1,955	49.4	280	7.1	3,290	83.2
0140	Industrial production managers	49,515	42,680	86.2	6,835	13.8	4,625	9.3	41,370	83.6
0150	Purchasing managers	21,880	11,065	50.6	10,810	49.4	1,680	7.7	17,990	82.2
0160	Transportation, storage, and distribution managers	67,845	57,660	85.0	10,185	15.0	8,835	13.0	50,865	75.0
0205	Farmers, ranchers, and other agricultural managers	249,805	217,800	87.2	32,010	12.8	6,275	2.5	236,915	94.8
0220	Construction managers	243,225	232,905	95.8	10,320	4.2	22,065	9.1	207,145	85.2
0230	Education administrators	42,500	11,090	26.1	31,410	73.9	5,005	11.8	29,455	69.3
0300	Architectural and engineering managers	5,155	4,955	96.1	205	4.0	515	10.0	4,180	81.1
0310	Food service managers	272,865	128,250	47.0	144,615	53.0	43,300	15.9	176,135	64.6
0330	Gaming managers	4,850	2,805	57.8	2,040	42.1	555	11.4	3,325	68.6
0340	Lodging managers	26,290	10,980	41.8	15,310	58.2	2,750	10.5	18,215	69.3
0350	Medical and health services managers	49,320	10,570	21.4	38,745	78.6	5,970	12.1	34,185	69.3
0360	Natural sciences managers	265	175	66.0	95	35.8	20	7.5	230	86.8
0410	Property, real estate, and community association managers	110,190	44,950	40.8	65,235	59.2	14,950	13.6	83,310	75.6
0410	Social and community service managers	26,480	7,445	28.1	19,035	71.9	2,330	8.8	19,045	71.9
0425	Emergency management directors	195	185	94.9	15	7.7	0	0.0	180	92.3
0430	Miscellaneous managers, including funeral service managers and postmasters and mail superintendents	465,060	305,455	65.7	159,605	34.3	46,075	9.9	370,855	79.7
0500	Agents and business managers of artists, performers, and athletes	5,565	3,175	57.1	2,390	42.9	715	12.8	3,825	68.7
0510	Buyers and purchasing agents, farm products	3,415	2,505	73.4	910	26.6	400	11.7	2,695	78.9
0520	Wholesale and retail buyers, except farm products	54,795	25,660	46.8	29,135	53.2	5,750	10.5	43,595	79.6
0530	Purchasing agents, except wholesale, retail, and farm products	49,870	21,400	42.9	28,470	57.1	4,620	9.3	40,955	82.1
0540	Claims adjusters, appraisers, examiners, and investigators	48,740	11,775	24.2	36,965	75.8	5,620	11.5	35,700	73.2
0565	Compliance officers	19,710	10,980	55.7	8,735	44.3	2,210	11.2	14,440	73.3
0600	Cost estimators	28,515	25,185	88.3	3,335	11.7	1,935	6.8	25,490	89.4
0630	Human resources workers	73,480	18,000	24.5	55,480	75.5	10,320	14.0	51,650	70.3
0640	Compensation, benefits, and job analysis specialists	13,905	1,345	9.7	12,565	90.4	1,380	9.9	10,550	75.9

PART A—NATIONAL DATA

A-19 **Workers with High School Diploma or Equivalency: Detailed Occupation, by Sex, Race, and Hispanic Origin, 2006–2010**—*Continued*

Census occupation code	Detailed Occupation	\multicolumn{8}{c}{High school diploma or equivalency}							
		\multicolumn{8}{c}{Not Hispanic or Latino, one race}	Not Hispanic or Latino, two or more races	
		Black or African American alone		American Indian and Alaska Native alone		Asian alone		Native Hawaiian and Other Pacific Islander alone			
		Number	Percent	Number	Percent	Number	Percent	Number	Percent	Number	Percent
	Total, all occupations	4,545,280	12.4	247,855	0.7	1,006,025	2.7	75,265	0.2	478,050	1.3
0010	Chief executives and legislators	3,330	2.7	990	0.8	2,835	2.3	70	0.1	1,064	0.9
0020	General and operations managers	7,290	4.9	735	0.5	2,220	1.5	370	0.2	1,690	1.1
0040	Advertising and promotions managers	60	1.4	4	0.1	135	3.1	0	0.0	75	1.7
0050	Marketing and sales managers	3,715	5.2	290	0.4	1,015	1.4	70	0.1	990	1.4
0060	Public relations and fundraising managers	250	7.6	80	2.4	20	0.6	0	0.0	25	0.8
0100	Administrative services managers	1,945	9.9	120	0.6	275	1.4	4	0.0	300	1.5
0110	Computer and information systems managers	1,185	5.9	50	0.2	470	2.3	120	0.6	290	1.4
0120	Financial managers	9,790	7.8	435	0.3	2,280	1.8	200	0.2	1,570	1.2
0135	Compensation and benefits managers	195	7.2	4	0.1	35	1.3	0	0.0	14	0.5
0136	Human resources managers	3,545	8.5	275	0.7	1,295	3.1	70	0.2	370	0.9
0137	Training and development managers	265	6.7	20	0.5	15	0.4	0	0.0	80	2.0
0140	Industrial production managers	1,630	3.3	280	0.6	1,125	2.3	70	0.1	415	0.8
0150	Purchasing managers	1,505	6.9	90	0.4	335	1.5	30	0.1	255	1.2
0160	Transportation, storage, and distribution managers	5,360	7.9	490	0.7	1,305	1.9	235	0.3	760	1.1
0205	Farmers, ranchers, and other agricultural managers	1,820	0.7	1,175	0.5	1,750	0.7	110	0.0	1,770	0.7
0220	Construction managers	7,695	3.2	1,395	0.6	2,200	0.9	140	0.1	2,590	1.1
0230	Education administrators	6,795	16.0	225	0.5	595	1.4	45	0.1	380	0.9
0300	Architectural and engineering managers	295	5.7	35	0.7	100	1.9	0	0.0	39	0.8
0310	Food service managers	25,985	9.5	1,215	0.4	22,640	8.3	470	0.2	3,115	1.1
0330	Gaming managers	420	8.7	405	8.4	80	1.6	0	0.0	70	1.4
0340	Lodging managers	2,300	8.7	245	0.9	2,055	7.8	75	0.3	645	2.5
0350	Medical and health services managers	7,720	15.7	260	0.5	635	1.3	50	0.1	495	1.0
0360	Natural sciences managers	0	0.0	4	1.5	10	3.8	0	0.0	0	0.0
0410	Property, real estate, and community association managers	7,855	7.1	520	0.5	1,845	1.7	295	0.3	1,405	1.3
0410	Social and community service managers	3,965	15.0	345	1.3	340	1.3	75	0.3	380	1.4
0425	Emergency management directors	15	7.7	4	2.1	0	0.0	0	0.0	0	0.0
0430	Miscellaneous managers, including funeral service managers and postmasters and mail superintendents	31,495	6.8	3,095	0.7	8,595	1.8	530	0.1	4,420	1.0
0500	Agents and business managers of artists, performers, and athletes	830	14.9	15	0.3	65	1.2	25	0.4	85	1.5
0510	Buyers and purchasing agents, farm products	95	2.8	4	0.1	25	0.7	110	3.2	84	2.5
0520	Wholesale and retail buyers, except farm products	3,080	5.6	260	0.5	1,490	2.7	75	0.1	539	1.0
0530	Purchasing agents, except wholesale, retail, and farm products	3,065	6.1	250	0.5	515	1.0	15	0.0	450	0.9
0540	Claims adjusters, appraisers, examiners, and investigators	6,150	12.6	80	0.2	620	1.3	125	0.3	440	0.9
0565	Compliance officers	2,145	10.9	255	1.3	350	1.8	70	0.4	250	1.3
0600	Cost estimators	340	1.2	60	0.2	325	1.1	35	0.1	335	1.2
0630	Human resources workers	8,375	11.4	555	0.8	1,300	1.8	125	0.2	1,150	1.6
0640	Compensation, benefits, and job analysis specialists	1,670	12.0	80	0.6	80	0.6	30	0.2	115	0.8

A-19 **Workers with High School Diploma or Equivalency: Detailed Occupation, by Sex, Race, and Hispanic Origin, 2006–2010**—*Continued*

Census occupation code	Detailed Occupation	Total	High school diploma or equivalency							
			Male		Female		Hispanic or Latino		Not Hispanic or Latino, one race White alone	
			Number	Percent	Number	Percent	Number	Percent	Number	Percent
0650	Training and development specialists	17,995	7,545	41.9	10,450	58.1	2,110	11.7	12,815	71.2
0700	Logisticians	10,915	6,505	59.6	4,410	40.4	1,325	12.1	7,540	69.1
0710	Management analysts	32,970	15,265	46.3	17,705	53.7	2,670	8.1	26,700	81.0
0725	Meeting, convention, and event planners	5,405	1,610	29.8	3,795	70.2	855	15.8	3,710	68.6
0726	Fundraisers	4,070	1,205	29.6	2,865	70.4	370	9.1	3,140	77.1
0735	Market research analysts and marketing specialists	8,035	3,500	43.6	4,535	56.4	665	8.3	6,530	81.3
0740	Business operations specialists, all other	31,260	9,100	29.1	22,160	70.9	3,835	12.3	22,255	71.2
0800	Accountants and auditors	90,765	13,480	14.9	77,285	85.1	9,790	10.8	66,610	73.4
0810	Appraisers and assessors of real estate	13,805	6,985	50.6	6,820	49.4	800	5.8	12,475	90.4
0820	Budget analysts	3,525	780	22.1	2,745	77.9	215	6.1	2,455	69.6
0830	Credit analysts	3,320	380	11.4	2,940	88.6	425	12.8	2,305	69.4
0840	Financial analysts	2,695	1,135	42.1	1,565	58.1	235	8.7	1,995	74.0
0850	Personal financial advisors	14,735	5,770	39.2	8,965	60.8	1,645	11.2	11,090	75.3
0860	Insurance underwriters	16,470	1,145	7.0	15,330	93.1	1,485	9.0	13,410	81.4
0900	Financial examiners	795	235	29.6	560	70.4	145	18.2	520	65.4
0910	Credit counselors and loan officers	53,145	14,155	26.6	38,985	73.4	7,990	15.0	38,245	72.0
0930	Tax examiners and collectors, and revenue agents	11,935	1,690	14.2	10,245	85.8	1,225	10.3	8,535	71.5
0940	Tax preparers	13,215	2,470	18.7	10,745	81.3	2,065	15.6	8,680	65.7
0950	Financial specialists, all other	8,615	2,620	30.4	5,995	69.6	1,210	14.0	6,195	71.9
1005	Computer and information research scientists	390	230	59.0	160	41.0	70	17.9	300	76.9
1006	Computer systems analysts	23,375	11,500	49.2	11,875	50.8	1,400	6.0	18,400	78.7
1007	Information security analysts	2,900	1,840	63.4	1,060	36.6	195	6.7	2,240	77.2
1010	Computer programmers	26,035	19,645	75.5	6,395	24.6	2,460	9.4	20,865	80.1
1020	Software developers, applications and systems software	20,255	14,345	70.8	5,910	29.2	1,665	8.2	16,215	80.1
1030	Web developers	9,745	6,395	65.6	3,345	34.3	660	6.8	8,040	82.5
1050	Computer support specialists	58,725	38,890	66.2	19,835	33.8	6,455	11.0	43,295	73.7
1060	Database administrators	5,290	2,255	42.6	3,035	57.4	365	6.9	4,265	80.6
1105	Network and computer systems administrators	21,625	16,030	74.1	5,595	25.9	1,735	8.0	16,925	78.3
1106	Computer network architects	6,485	5,805	89.5	685	10.6	500	7.7	5,145	79.3
1107	Computer occupations, all other	23,655	16,975	71.8	6,680	28.2	2,585	10.9	17,265	73.0
1200	Actuaries	45	10	22.2	35	77.8	35	77.8	10	22.2
1220	Operations research analysts	7,640	2,970	38.9	4,670	61.1	835	10.9	5,800	75.9
1240	Miscellaneous mathematical science occupations, including mathematicians and statisticians	190	100	52.6	90	47.4	0	0.0	135	71.1
1300	Architects, except naval	2,970	2,470	83.2	505	17.0	315	10.6	2,320	78.1

PART A—NATIONAL DATA

A-19 Workers with High School Diploma or Equivalency: Detailed Occupation, by Sex, Race, and Hispanic Origin, 2006–2010—*Continued*

Census occupation code	Detailed Occupation	Black or African American alone Number	Percent	American Indian and Alaska Native alone Number	Percent	Asian alone Number	Percent	Native Hawaiian and Other Pacific Islander alone Number	Percent	Not Hispanic or Latino, two or more races Number	Percent
0650	Training and development specialists	2,415	13.4	100	0.6	270	1.5	10	0.1	265	1.5
0700	Logisticians	1,585	14.5	50	0.5	215	2.0	25	0.2	175	1.6
0710	Management analysts	2,455	7.4	170	0.5	570	1.7	10	0.0	400	1.2
0725	Meeting, convention, and event planners	615	11.4	4	0.1	170	3.1	4	0.1	50	0.9
0726	Fundraisers	300	7.4	15	0.4	150	3.7	0	0.0	95	2.3
0735	Market research analysts and marketing specialists	555	6.9	135	1.7	30	0.4	20	0.2	95	1.2
0740	Business operations specialists, all other	3,700	11.8	250	0.8	820	2.6	30	0.1	375	1.2
0800	Accountants and auditors	8,865	9.8	735	0.8	3,640	4.0	130	0.1	995	1.1
0810	Appraisers and assessors of real estate	235	1.7	90	0.7	95	0.7	10	0.1	104	0.8
0820	Budget analysts	640	18.2	10	0.3	165	4.7	0	0.0	45	1.3
0830	Credit analysts	490	14.8	30	0.9	20	0.6	15	0.5	35	1.1
0840	Financial analysts	285	10.6	0	0.0	95	3.5	0	0.0	85	3.2
0850	Personal financial advisors	1,400	9.5	40	0.3	295	2.0	80	0.5	175	1.2
0860	Insurance underwriters	945	5.7	80	0.5	380	2.3	50	0.3	119	0.7
0900	Financial examiners	60	7.5	0	0.0	65	8.2	0	0.0	0	0.0
0910	Credit counselors and loan officers	4,775	9.0	135	0.3	1,095	2.1	190	0.4	710	1.3
0930	Tax examiners and collectors, and revenue agents	1,965	16.5	45	0.4	50	0.4	0	0.0	105	0.9
0940	Tax preparers	2,155	16.3	35	0.3	190	1.4	40	0.3	55	0.4
0950	Financial specialists, all other	850	9.9	40	0.5	95	1.1	0	0.0	220	2.6
1005	Computer and information research scientists	15	3.8	0	0.0	0	0.0	0	0.0	0	0.0
1006	Computer systems analysts	2,575	11.0	90	0.4	590	2.5	60	0.3	275	1.2
1007	Information security analysts	325	11.2	0	0.0	60	2.1	0	0.0	80	2.8
1010	Computer programmers	1,330	5.1	80	0.3	860	3.3	45	0.2	395	1.5
1020	Software developers, applications and systems software	1,300	6.4	105	0.5	710	3.5	10	0.0	245	1.2
1030	Web developers	480	4.9	95	1.0	245	2.5	45	0.5	180	1.8
1050	Computer support specialists	5,995	10.2	330	0.6	1,680	2.9	60	0.1	905	1.5
1060	Database administrators	480	9.1	15	0.3	100	1.9	0	0.0	75	1.4
1105	Network and computer systems administrators	1,800	8.3	60	0.3	720	3.3	15	0.1	370	1.7
1106	Computer network architects	610	9.4	20	0.3	130	2.0	0	0.0	85	1.3
1107	Computer occupations, all other	2,425	10.3	260	1.1	700	3.0	80	0.3	330	1.4
1200	Actuaries	0	0.0	0	0.0	0	0.0	0	0.0	0	0.0
1220	Operations research analysts	690	9.0	15	0.2	205	2.7	30	0.4	69	0.9
1240	Miscellaneous mathematical science occupations, including mathematicians and statisticians	50	26.3	0	0.0	4	2.1	0	0.0	4	2.1
1300	Architects, except naval	175	5.9	35	1.2	75	2.5	45	1.5	0	0.0

A-19 **Workers with High School Diploma or Equivalency: Detailed Occupation, by Sex, Race, and Hispanic Origin, 2006–2010**—*Continued*

Census occupation code	Detailed Occupation	Total	High school diploma or equivalency						Not Hispanic or Latino, one race	
			Male		Female		Hispanic or Latino		White alone	
			Number	Percent	Number	Percent	Number	Percent	Number	Percent
1310	Surveyors, cartographers, and photogrammetrists	30	30	100.0	0	0.0	0	0.0	30	100.0
1320	Aerospace engineers	3,195	2,710	84.8	485	15.2	245	7.7	2,520	78.9
1340	Biomedical and agricultural engineers	415	360	86.7	55	13.3	15	3.6	320	77.1
1350	Chemical engineers	1,485	1,360	91.6	130	8.8	40	2.7	1,025	69.0
1360	Civil engineers	9,580	8,795	91.8	790	8.2	735	7.7	7,530	78.6
1400	Computer hardware engineers	3,470	2,735	78.8	740	21.3	310	8.9	2,870	82.7
1410	Electrical and electronics engineers	8,240	7,245	87.9	995	12.1	570	6.9	6,565	79.7
1420	Environmental engineers	1,270	1,240	97.6	30	2.4	160	12.6	615	48.4
1430	Industrial engineers, including health and safety	11,290	8,815	78.1	2,475	21.9	660	5.8	9,655	85.5
1440	Marine engineers and naval architects	1,005	995	99.0	15	1.5	0	0.0	825	82.1
1450	Materials engineers	2,055	1,730	84.2	325	15.8	115	5.6	1,760	85.6
1460	Mechanical engineers	10,965	10,565	96.4	405	3.7	705	6.4	8,995	82.0
1520	Petroleum, mining and geological engineers, including mining safety engineers	1,360	1,240	91.2	125	9.2	55	4.0	1,180	86.8
1530	Miscellaneous engineers, including nuclear engineers	14,400	12,840	89.2	1,560	10.8	1,235	8.6	11,240	78.1
1540	Drafters	23,860	20,015	83.9	3,845	16.1	1,890	7.9	20,205	84.7
1550	Engineering technicians, except drafters	92,910	72,915	78.5	19,995	21.5	9,515	10.2	68,420	73.6
1560	Surveying and mapping technicians	24,045	21,920	91.2	2,125	8.8	2,380	9.9	19,960	83.0
1600	Agricultural and food scientists	50	45	90.0	4	8.0	35	70.0	15	30.0
1610	Biological scientists	70	50	71.4	20	28.6	45	64.3	20	28.6
1640	Conservation scientists and foresters	15	15	100.0	0	0.0	0	0.0	15	100.0
1650	Medical scientists, and life scientists, all other	115	40	34.8	70	60.9	50	43.5	30	26.1
1700	Astronomers and physicists	4	4	100.0	0	0.0	0	0.0	4	100.0
1710	Atmospheric and space scientists	0	0	0	0	0	0	0	0	0
1720	Chemists and materials scientists	65	35	53.8	30	46.2	0	0.0	10	15.4
1740	Environmental scientists and geoscientists	105	60	57.1	45	42.9	0	0.0	30	28.6
1760	Physical scientists, all other	175	105	60.0	70	40.0	0	0.0	20	11.4
1800	Economists	60	50	83.3	10	16.7	10	16.7	45	75.0
1820	Psychologists	105	25	23.8	80	76.2	40	38.1	40	38.1
1840	Urban and regional planners	100	55	55.0	45	45.0	20	20.0	50	50.0
1860	Miscellaneous social scientists, including survey researchers and sociologists	420	115	27.4	305	72.6	65	15.5	175	41.7
1900	Agricultural and food science technicians	8,950	5,710	63.8	3,240	36.2	1,145	12.8	6,735	75.3
1910	Biological technicians	3,945	1,915	48.5	2,025	51.3	480	12.2	2,640	66.9
1920	Chemical technicians	17,675	12,530	70.9	5,140	29.1	1,605	9.1	13,100	74.1
1930	Geological and petroleum technicians, and nuclear technicians	4,070	3,200	78.6	870	21.4	470	11.5	3,330	81.8
1965	Miscellaneous life, physical, and social science technicians, including social science research assistants	26,410	15,655	59.3	10,755	40.7	3,035	11.5	18,085	68.5

PART A—NATIONAL DATA

A-19 Workers with High School Diploma or Equivalency: Detailed Occupation, by Sex, Race, and Hispanic Origin, 2006–2010—*Continued*

Census occupation code	Detailed Occupation	Black or African American alone Number	Percent	American Indian and Alaska Native alone Number	Percent	Asian alone Number	Percent	Native Hawaiian and Other Pacific Islander alone Number	Percent	Not Hispanic or Latino, two or more races Number	Percent
1310	Surveyors, cartographers, and photogrammetrists	0	0.0	0	0.0	0	0.0	0	0.0	0	0.0
1320	Aerospace engineers	210	6.6	10	0.3	100	3.1	35	1.1	74	2.3
1340	Biomedical and agricultural engineers	25	6.0	30	7.2	10	2.4	0	0.0	15	3.6
1350	Chemical engineers	275	18.5	0	0.0	100	6.7	4	0.3	40	2.7
1360	Civil engineers	800	8.4	55	0.6	225	2.3	4	0.0	240	2.5
1400	Computer hardware engineers	225	6.5	0	0.0	60	1.7	0	0.0	10	0.3
1410	Electrical and electronics engineers	715	8.7	10	0.1	275	3.3	35	0.4	74	0.9
1420	Environmental engineers	485	38.2	10	0.8	0	0.0	0	0.0	0	0.0
1430	Industrial engineers, including health and safety	585	5.2	20	0.2	280	2.5	25	0.2	60	0.5
1440	Marine engineers and naval architects	155	15.4	0	0.0	0	0.0	0	0.0	25	2.5
1450	Materials engineers	65	3.2	4	0.2	30	1.5	40	1.9	44	2.1
1460	Mechanical engineers	820	7.5	85	0.8	275	2.5	15	0.1	65	0.6
1520	Petroleum, mining and geological engineers, including mining safety engineers	75	5.5	40	2.9	10	0.7	0	0.0	0	0.0
1530	Miscellaneous engineers, including nuclear engineers	1,090	7.6	140	1.0	470	3.3	55	0.4	175	1.2
1540	Drafters	870	3.6	55	0.2	610	2.6	15	0.1	215	0.9
1550	Engineering technicians, except drafters	8,855	9.5	490	0.5	4,270	4.6	100	0.1	1,265	1.4
1560	Surveying and mapping technicians	1,100	4.6	230	1.0	45	0.2	45	0.2	280	1.2
1600	Agricultural and food scientists	0	0.0	0	0.0	0	0.0	0	0.0	0	0.0
1610	Biological scientists	4	5.7	0	0.0	0	0.0	0	0.0	0	0.0
1640	Conservation scientists and foresters	0	0.0	0	0.0	0	0.0	0	0.0	0	0.0
1650	Medical scientists, and life scientists, all other	30	26.1	0	0.0	0	0.0	0	0.0	0	0.0
1700	Astronomers and physicists	0	0.0	0	0.0	0	0.0	0	0.0	0	0.0
1710	Atmospheric and space scientists	0	0	0	0	0	0	0	0	0	0
1720	Chemists and materials scientists	0	0.0	0	0.0	35	53.8	20	30.8	0	0.0
1740	Environmental scientists and geoscientists	45	42.9	30	28.6	0	0.0	0	0.0	0	0.0
1760	Physical scientists, all other	85	48.6	0	0.0	55	31.4	15	8.6	0	0.0
1800	Economists	0	0.0	0	0.0	0	0.0	0	0.0	0	0.0
1820	Psychologists	15	14.3	0	0.0	10	9.5	0	0.0	0	0.0
1840	Urban and regional planners	30	30.0	0	0.0	0	0.0	0	0.0	0	0.0
1860	Miscellaneous social scientists, including survey researchers and sociologists	175	41.7	0	0.0	0	0.0	4	1.0	0	0.0
1900	Agricultural and food science technicians	735	8.2	75	0.8	215	2.4	4	0.0	45	0.5
1910	Biological technicians	385	9.8	125	3.2	205	5.2	4	0.1	105	2.7
1920	Chemical technicians	1,990	11.3	105	0.6	585	3.3	35	0.2	250	1.4
1930	Geological and petroleum technicians, and nuclear technicians	170	4.2	45	1.1	0	0.0	0	0.0	50	1.2
1965	Miscellaneous life, physical, and social science technicians, including social science research assistants	2,455	9.3	490	1.9	1,705	6.5	165	0.6	465	1.8

A-19 Workers with High School Diploma or Equivalency: Detailed Occupation, by Sex, Race, and Hispanic Origin, 2006–2010—Continued

Census occupation code	Detailed Occupation	Total	Male Number	Male Percent	Female Number	Female Percent	Hispanic or Latino Number	Hispanic or Latino Percent	Not Hispanic or Latino, one race White alone Number	Not Hispanic or Latino, one race White alone Percent
2000	Counselors	43,365	16,130	37.2	27,240	62.8	4,985	11.5	21,130	48.7
2010	Social workers	43,850	9,810	22.4	34,040	77.6	6,285	14.3	24,105	55.0
2015	Probation officers and correctional treatment specialists	5,995	3,105	51.8	2,890	48.2	805	13.4	2,950	49.2
2016	Social and human service assistants	27,745	5,730	20.7	22,015	79.3	4,290	15.5	14,805	53.4
2025	Miscellaneous community and social service specialists, including health educators and community health workers	9,885	3,955	40.0	5,930	60.0	1,295	13.1	5,930	60.0
2040	Clergy	29,395	23,655	80.5	5,735	19.5	3,215	10.9	19,600	66.7
2050	Directors, religious activities and education	4,670	1,630	34.9	3,040	65.1	400	8.6	3,625	77.6
2060	Religious workers, all other	11,150	2,925	26.2	8,225	73.8	1,035	9.3	8,475	76.0
2100	Lawyers, and judges, magistrates, and other judicial workers	2,835	1,040	36.7	1,790	63.1	245	8.6	2,095	73.9
2105	Judicial law clerks	320	35	10.9	285	89.1	90	28.1	205	64.1
2145	Paralegals and legal assistants	43,495	2,810	6.5	40,685	93.5	5,640	13.0	33,085	76.1
2160	Miscellaneous legal support workers	41,920	5,970	14.2	35,950	85.8	4,710	11.2	32,405	77.3
2200	Postsecondary teachers	1,385	655	47.3	730	52.7	340	24.5	395	28.5
2300	Preschool and kindergarten teachers	84,620	1,760	2.1	82,865	97.9	11,045	13.1	51,475	60.8
2310	Elementary and middle school teachers	5,325	1,225	23.0	4,100	77.0	940	17.7	1,920	36.1
2320	Secondary school teachers	1,490	660	44.3	830	55.7	235	15.8	745	50.0
2330	Special education teachers	7,880	755	9.6	7,125	90.4	1,165	14.8	5,370	68.1
2340	Other teachers and instructors	99,935	39,395	39.4	60,540	60.6	11,700	11.7	67,140	67.2
2400	Archivists, curators, and museum technicians	2,490	1,090	43.8	1,395	56.0	175	7.0	1,980	79.5
2430	Librarians	315	45	14.3	265	84.1	0	0.0	195	61.9
2440	Library technicians	17,280	2,865	16.6	14,415	83.4	1,520	8.8	13,150	76.1
2540	Teacher assistants	287,805	19,465	6.8	268,340	93.2	40,845	14.2	198,335	68.9
2550	Other education, training, and library workers	4,130	1,195	28.9	2,935	71.1	760	18.4	2,650	64.2
2600	Artists and related workers	21,425	13,630	63.6	7,795	36.4	2,335	10.9	17,190	80.2
2630	Designers	90,260	38,505	42.7	51,755	57.3	10,910	12.1	71,445	79.2
2700	Actors	4,115	2,475	60.1	1,640	39.9	345	8.4	3,130	76.1
2710	Producers and directors	8,320	6,495	78.1	1,825	21.9	895	10.8	5,870	70.6
2720	Athletes, coaches, umpires, and related workers	28,525	17,970	63.0	10,550	37.0	3,460	12.1	20,970	73.5
2740	Dancers and choreographers	6,625	985	14.9	5,640	85.1	1,145	17.3	3,915	59.1
2750	Musicians, singers, and related workers	26,130	19,490	74.6	6,640	25.4	3,230	12.4	16,895	64.7
2760	Entertainers and performers, sports and related workers, all other	7,770	3,720	47.9	4,050	52.1	1,185	15.3	5,370	69.1
2800	Announcers	9,685	7,960	82.2	1,730	17.9	1,825	18.8	6,185	63.9
2810	News analysts, reporters, and correspondents	2,605	1,370	52.6	1,230	47.2	180	6.9	2,115	81.2
2825	Public relations specialists	6,885	2,265	32.9	4,620	67.1	965	14.0	4,715	68.5
2830	Editors	6,500	2,905	44.7	3,595	55.3	620	9.5	5,105	78.5
2840	Technical writers	3,090	1,160	37.5	1,930	62.5	50	1.6	2,605	84.3
2850	Writers and authors	5,765	2,675	46.4	3,090	53.6	470	8.2	4,445	77.1
2860	Miscellaneous media and communication workers	8,955	2,665	29.8	6,290	70.2	4,380	48.9	3,030	33.8

A-19 **Workers with High School Diploma or Equivalency: Detailed Occupation, by Sex, Race, and Hispanic Origin, 2006–2010**—Continued

Census occupation code	Detailed Occupation	Black or African American alone Number	Percent	American Indian and Alaska Native alone Number	Percent	Asian alone Number	Percent	Native Hawaiian and Other Pacific Islander alone Number	Percent	Not Hispanic or Latino, two or more races Number	Percent
2000	Counselors	14,730	34.0	540	1.2	585	1.3	205	0.5	1,190	2.7
2010	Social workers	11,550	26.3	525	1.2	540	1.2	75	0.2	775	1.8
2015	Probation officers and correctional treatment specialists	1,910	31.9	110	1.8	40	0.7	4	0.1	174	2.9
2016	Social and human service assistants	7,305	26.3	545	2.0	400	1.4	105	0.4	290	1.0
2025	Miscellaneous community and social service specialists, including health educators and community health workers	2,290	23.2	145	1.5	115	1.2	4	0.0	110	1.1
2040	Clergy	5,575	19.0	195	0.7	495	1.7	75	0.3	235	0.8
2050	Directors, religious activities and education	455	9.7	10	0.2	85	1.8	4	0.1	89	1.9
2060	Religious workers, all other	1,040	9.3	25	0.2	375	3.4	35	0.3	165	1.5
2100	Lawyers, and judges, magistrates, and other judicial workers	400	14.1	15	0.5	55	1.9	0	0.0	23	0.8
2105	Judicial law clerks	25	7.8	0	0.0	0	0.0	0	0.0	0	0.0
2145	Paralegals and legal assistants	3,395	7.8	120	0.3	530	1.2	45	0.1	680	1.6
2160	Miscellaneous legal support workers	3,425	8.2	445	1.1	415	1.0	30	0.1	490	1.2
2200	Postsecondary teachers	355	25.6	60	4.3	115	8.3	0	0.0	120	8.7
2300	Preschool and kindergarten teachers	18,915	22.4	995	1.2	1,115	1.3	210	0.2	865	1.0
2310	Elementary and middle school teachers	1,860	34.9	115	2.2	305	5.7	10	0.2	180	3.4
2320	Secondary school teachers	385	25.8	4	0.3	60	4.0	0	0.0	60	4.0
2330	Special education teachers	965	12.2	225	2.9	65	0.8	15	0.2	80	1.0
2340	Other teachers and instructors	13,340	13.3	870	0.9	4,405	4.4	455	0.5	2,030	2.0
2400	Archivists, curators, and museum technicians	275	11.0	20	0.8	40	1.6	0	0.0	0	0.0
2430	Librarians	90	28.6	4	1.3	25	7.9	0	0.0	0	0.0
2440	Library technicians	1,750	10.1	115	0.7	615	3.6	0	0.0	125	0.7
2540	Teacher assistants	37,925	13.2	2,665	0.9	4,035	1.4	620	0.2	3,380	1.2
2550	Other education, training, and library workers	505	12.2	25	0.6	90	2.2	35	0.8	70	1.7
2600	Artists and related workers	585	2.7	340	1.6	615	2.9	50	0.2	310	1.4
2630	Designers	3,500	3.9	260	0.3	2,915	3.2	40	0.0	1,180	1.3
2700	Actors	430	10.4	50	1.2	40	1.0	0	0.0	119	2.9
2710	Producers and directors	1,110	13.3	15	0.2	215	2.6	0	0.0	209	2.5
2720	Athletes, coaches, umpires, and related workers	2,365	8.3	185	0.6	815	2.9	15	0.1	710	2.5
2740	Dancers and choreographers	825	12.5	25	0.4	205	3.1	150	2.3	360	5.4
2750	Musicians, singers, and related workers	4,920	18.8	105	0.4	335	1.3	75	0.3	575	2.2
2760	Entertainers and performers, sports and related workers, all other	845	10.9	15	0.2	90	1.2	55	0.7	215	2.8
2800	Announcers	1,350	13.9	50	0.5	60	0.6	4	0.0	215	2.2
2810	News analysts, reporters, and correspondents	195	7.5	20	0.8	55	2.1	10	0.4	24	0.9
2825	Public relations specialists	905	13.1	70	1.0	130	1.9	0	0.0	105	1.5
2830	Editors	415	6.4	65	1.0	155	2.4	10	0.2	130	2.0
2840	Technical writers	305	9.9	0	0.0	45	1.5	0	0.0	80	2.6
2850	Writers and authors	435	7.5	70	1.2	200	3.5	0	0.0	145	2.5
2860	Miscellaneous media and communication workers	755	8.4	105	1.2	595	6.6	4	0.0	84	0.9

A-19 **Workers with High School Diploma or Equivalency: Detailed Occupation, by Sex, Race, and Hispanic Origin, 2006–2010**—*Continued*

Census occupation code	Detailed Occupation	Total	Male Number	Male Percent	Female Number	Female Percent	Hispanic or Latino Number	Hispanic or Latino Percent	Not Hispanic or Latino, one race White alone Number	Not Hispanic or Latino, one race White alone Percent
2900	Broadcast and sound engineering technicians and radio operators, and media and communication equipment workers, all other	15,500	13,915	89.8	1,585	10.2	1,855	12.0	11,190	72.2
2910	Photographers	21,135	9,995	47.3	11,140	52.7	2,850	13.5	16,060	76.0
2920	Television, video, and motion picture camera operators and editors	4,180	3,480	83.3	700	16.7	635	15.2	2,795	66.9
3000	Chiropractors	570	130	22.8	440	77.2	75	13.2	395	69.3
3010	Dentists	110	80	72.7	35	31.8	60	54.5	35	31.8
3030	Dietitians and nutritionists	11,535	1,350	11.7	10,185	88.3	1,510	13.1	5,225	45.3
3040	Optometrists	20	4	20.0	15	75.0	0	0.0	20	100.0
3050	Pharmacists	360	65	18.1	295	81.9	0	0.0	105	29.2
3060	Physicians and surgeons	730	430	58.9	305	41.8	250	34.2	135	18.5
3110	Physician assistants	5,475	980	17.9	4,495	82.1	870	15.9	3,420	62.5
3120	Podiatrists	4	0	0.0	4	100.0	0	0.0	0	0.0
3140	Audiologists	180	75	41.7	105	58.3	60	33.3	100	55.6
3150	Occupational therapists	295	35	11.9	265	89.8	25	8.5	180	61.0
3160	Physical therapists	2,385	610	25.6	1,775	74.4	525	22.0	1,000	41.9
3200	Radiation therapists	345	100	29.0	250	72.5	25	7.2	245	71.0
3210	Recreational therapists	1,295	175	13.5	1,120	86.5	80	6.2	755	58.3
3220	Respiratory therapists	2,160	835	38.7	1,325	61.3	195	9.0	1,575	72.9
3230	Speech-language pathologists	530	55	10.4	475	89.6	95	17.9	310	58.5
3245	Other therapists, including exercise physiologists	4,525	895	19.8	3,625	80.1	650	14.4	2,600	57.5
3250	Veterinarians	165	45	27.3	120	72.7	95	57.6	65	39.4
3255	Registered nurses	26,165	1,905	7.3	24,260	92.7	2,430	9.3	15,435	59.0
3256	Nurse anesthetists	145	105	72.4	40	27.6	0	0.0	60	41.4
3258	Nurse practitioners and nurse midwives	175	45	25.7	130	74.3	55	31.4	90	51.4
3260	Health diagnosing and treating practitioners, all other	590	220	37.3	370	62.7	90	15.3	295	50.0
3300	Clinical laboratory technologists and technicians	35,500	8,130	22.9	27,370	77.1	5,040	14.2	19,320	54.4
3310	Dental hygienists	3,895	200	5.1	3,695	94.9	650	16.7	2,785	71.5
3320	Diagnostic related technologists and technicians	25,805	5,995	23.2	19,815	76.8	2,915	11.3	18,140	70.3
3400	Emergency medical technicians and paramedics	25,110	17,165	68.4	7,950	31.7	2,150	8.6	20,490	81.6
3420	Health practitioner support technologists and technicians	119,460	18,180	15.2	101,280	84.8	13,660	11.4	85,895	71.9
3500	Licensed practical and licensed vocational nurses	127,635	6,295	4.9	121,340	95.1	10,530	8.3	73,635	57.7
3510	Medical records and health information technicians	32,305	1,965	6.1	30,335	93.9	4,330	13.4	21,630	67.0
3520	Opticians, dispensing	14,340	2,940	20.5	11,400	79.5	1,565	10.9	11,390	79.4
3535	Miscellaneous health technologists and technicians	24,845	7,115	28.6	17,730	71.4	2,970	12.0	13,820	55.6
3540	Other health care practitioners and technical occupations	7,415	4,635	62.5	2,780	37.5	690	9.3	4,860	65.5
3600	Nursing, psychiatric, and home health aides	753,440	75,880	10.1	677,560	89.9	85,225	11.3	355,585	47.2
3610	Occupational therapy assistants and aides	320	25	7.8	300	93.8	70	21.9	145	45.3
3620	Physical therapist assistants and aides	7,500	1,830	24.4	5,670	75.6	1,065	14.2	4,545	60.6

PART A—NATIONAL DATA

A-19 Workers with High School Diploma or Equivalency: Detailed Occupation, by Sex, Race, and Hispanic Origin, 2006–2010—*Continued*

Census occupation code	Detailed Occupation	Black or African American alone Number	Black or African American alone Percent	American Indian and Alaska Native alone Number	American Indian and Alaska Native alone Percent	Asian alone Number	Asian alone Percent	Native Hawaiian and Other Pacific Islander alone Number	Native Hawaiian and Other Pacific Islander alone Percent	Not Hispanic or Latino, two or more races Number	Not Hispanic or Latino, two or more races Percent
2900	Broadcast and sound engineering technicians and radio operators, and media and communication equipment workers, all other	1,870	12.1	140	0.9	200	1.3	15	0.1	234	1.5
2910	Photographers	1,320	6.2	60	0.3	510	2.4	25	0.1	305	1.4
2920	Television, video, and motion picture camera operators and editors	345	8.3	45	1.1	240	5.7	0	0.0	115	2.8
3000	Chiropractors	100	17.5	0	0.0	0	0.0	0	0.0	0	0.0
3010	Dentists	10	9.1	4	3.6	0	0.0	0	0.0	0	0.0
3030	Dietitians and nutritionists	4,375	37.9	105	0.9	210	1.8	4	0.0	100	0.9
3040	Optometrists	0	0.0	0	0.0	0	0.0	0	0.0	0	0.0
3050	Pharmacists	125	34.7	10	2.8	90	25.0	0	0.0	30	8.3
3060	Physicians and surgeons	190	26.0	35	4.8	120	16.4	0	0.0	0	0.0
3110	Physician assistants	985	18.0	0	0.0	105	1.9	0	0.0	89	1.6
3120	Podiatrists	0	0.0	0	0.0	0	0.0	0	0.0	4	100.0
3140	Audiologists	20	11.1	0	0.0	0	0.0	0	0.0	0	0.0
3150	Occupational therapists	90	30.5	0	0.0	0	0.0	0	0.0	0	0.0
3160	Physical therapists	660	27.7	0	0.0	185	7.8	0	0.0	14	0.6
3200	Radiation therapists	30	8.7	0	0.0	50	14.5	0	0.0	0	0.0
3210	Recreational therapists	390	30.1	40	3.1	15	1.2	0	0.0	10	0.8
3220	Respiratory therapists	330	15.3	35	1.6	30	1.4	0	0.0	0	0.0
3230	Speech-language pathologists	120	22.6	0	0.0	0	0.0	0	0.0	0	0.0
3245	Other therapists, including exercise physiologists	1,065	23.5	25	0.6	115	2.5	0	0.0	75	1.7
3250	Veterinarians	0	0.0	0	0.0	10	6.1	0	0.0	0	0.0
3255	Registered nurses	5,615	21.5	155	0.6	2,165	8.3	70	0.3	299	1.1
3256	Nurse anesthetists	85	58.6	0	0.0	0	0.0	0	0.0	0	0.0
3258	Nurse practitioners and nurse midwives	25	14.3	0	0.0	0	0.0	0	0.0	0	0.0
3260	Health diagnosing and treating practitioners, all other	55	9.3	4	0.7	120	20.3	0	0.0	15	2.5
3300	Clinical laboratory technologists and technicians	8,695	24.5	225	0.6	1,615	4.5	90	0.3	510	1.4
3310	Dental hygienists	285	7.3	25	0.6	90	2.3	0	0.0	65	1.7
3320	Diagnostic related technologists and technicians	3,975	15.4	65	0.3	405	1.6	30	0.1	270	1.0
3400	Emergency medical technicians and paramedics	1,630	6.5	285	1.1	230	0.9	0	0.0	330	1.3
3420	Health practitioner support technologists and technicians	13,850	11.6	765	0.6	3,315	2.8	220	0.2	1,750	1.5
3500	Licensed practical and licensed vocational nurses	38,800	30.4	750	0.6	2,510	2.0	105	0.1	1,300	1.0
3510	Medical records and health information technicians	5,090	15.8	430	1.3	485	1.5	130	0.4	210	0.7
3520	Opticians, dispensing	775	5.4	55	0.4	250	1.7	30	0.2	275	1.9
3535	Miscellaneous health technologists and technicians	6,495	26.1	105	0.4	930	3.7	20	0.1	510	2.1
3540	Other health care practitioners and technical occupations	1,540	20.8	70	0.9	165	2.2	0	0.0	90	1.2
3600	Nursing, psychiatric, and home health aides	274,005	36.4	6,895	0.9	18,325	2.4	1,665	0.2	11,745	1.6
3610	Occupational therapy assistants and aides	30	9.4	0	0.0	20	6.3	0	0.0	55	17.2
3620	Physical therapist assistants and aides	1,555	20.7	40	0.5	280	3.7	4	0.1	8	0.1

A-19 **Workers with High School Diploma or Equivalency: Detailed Occupation, by Sex, Race, and Hispanic Origin, 2006–2010**—*Continued*

Census occupation code	Detailed Occupation	Total	High school diploma or equivalency					Not Hispanic or Latino, one race	
			Male		Female		Hispanic or Latino		White alone	
			Number	Percent	Number	Percent	Number	Percent	Number	Percent
3630	Massage therapists	22,170	3,385	15.3	18,785	84.7	3,055	13.8	15,530	70.0
3640	Dental assistants	78,945	2,070	2.6	76,875	97.4	16,575	21.0	53,755	68.1
3645	Medical assistants	90,450	4,725	5.2	85,725	94.8	24,705	27.3	49,840	55.1
3646	Medical transcriptionists	15,520	140	0.9	15,380	99.1	680	4.4	13,975	90.0
3647	Pharmacy aides	11,970	1,520	12.7	10,450	87.3	2,460	20.6	7,425	62.0
3648	Veterinary assistants and laboratory animal caretakers	12,220	2,820	23.1	9,400	76.9	875	7.2	10,050	82.2
3649	Phlebotomists	19,785	2,245	11.3	17,540	88.7	3,415	17.3	11,775	59.5
3655	Health care support workers, all other, including medical equipment preparers	56,310	10,825	19.2	45,485	80.8	5,810	10.3	32,495	57.7
3700	First-line supervisors of correctional officers	14,170	11,050	78.0	3,120	22.0	1,270	9.0	9,520	67.2
3710	First-line supervisors of police and detectives	15,520	12,270	79.1	3,245	20.9	1,210	7.8	11,790	76.0
3720	First-line supervisors of fire fighting and prevention workers	8,160	7,980	97.8	180	2.2	385	4.7	7,030	86.2
3730	First-line supervisors of protective service workers, all other	19,945	14,915	74.8	5,030	25.2	2,460	12.3	12,730	63.8
3740	Firefighters	51,315	49,560	96.6	1,755	3.4	3,645	7.1	40,955	79.8
3750	Fire inspectors	4,280	3,940	92.1	340	7.9	410	9.6	3,480	81.3
3800	Bailiffs, correctional officers, and jailers	146,245	109,320	74.8	36,925	25.2	15,905	10.9	94,170	64.4
3820	Detectives and criminal investigators	11,785	9,015	76.5	2,765	23.5	1,650	14.0	8,305	70.5
3840	Miscellaneous law enforcement workers	2,915	1,760	60.4	1,155	39.6	315	10.8	1,525	52.3
3850	Police officers	94,245	81,090	86.0	13,150	14.0	10,825	11.5	65,265	69.3
3900	Animal control workers	3,715	2,365	63.7	1,350	36.3	330	8.9	3,010	81.0
3910	Private detectives and investigators	10,930	5,110	46.8	5,820	53.2	1,705	15.6	7,610	69.6
3930	Security guards and gaming surveillance officers	324,605	248,830	76.7	75,775	23.3	48,295	14.9	158,270	48.8
3940	Crossing guards	21,690	7,650	35.3	14,040	64.7	2,180	10.1	14,085	64.9
3945	Transportation security screeners	6,805	3,910	57.5	2,895	42.5	960	14.1	3,490	51.3
3955	Lifeguards and other recreational, and all other protective service workers	36,430	15,330	42.1	21,100	57.9	4,140	11.4	25,890	71.1
4000	Chefs and head cooks	92,405	73,785	79.8	18,615	20.1	19,750	21.4	39,575	42.8
4010	First-line supervisors of food preparation and serving workers	198,385	71,165	35.9	127,220	64.1	31,830	16.0	123,710	62.4
4020	Cooks	768,055	414,525	54.0	353,525	46.0	188,980	24.6	379,240	49.4
4030	Food preparation workers	248,520	93,420	37.6	155,105	62.4	54,685	22.0	138,240	55.6
4040	Bartenders	107,580	40,310	37.5	67,270	62.5	12,310	11.4	85,980	79.9
4050	Combined food preparation and serving workers, including fast food	119,200	33,915	28.5	85,285	71.5	17,310	14.5	77,425	65.0
4060	Counter attendants, cafeteria, food concession, and coffee shop	63,265	19,445	30.7	43,820	69.3	10,250	16.2	40,205	63.6
4110	Waiters and waitresses	584,130	145,540	24.9	438,590	75.1	106,060	18.2	384,010	65.7
4120	Food servers, nonrestaurant	71,520	18,655	26.1	52,870	73.9	11,505	16.1	36,895	51.6
4130	Miscellaneous food preparation and serving related workers, including dining room and cafeteria attendants and bartender helpers	114,985	54,640	47.5	60,345	52.5	34,390	29.9	56,840	49.4
4140	Dishwashers	88,550	67,290	76.0	21,265	24.0	23,450	26.5	45,220	51.1

A-19 Workers with High School Diploma or Equivalency: Detailed Occupation, by Sex, Race, and Hispanic Origin, 2006–2010—Continued

Census occupation code	Detailed Occupation	Black or African American alone Number	Black or African American alone Percent	American Indian and Alaska Native alone Number	American Indian and Alaska Native alone Percent	Asian alone Number	Asian alone Percent	Native Hawaiian and Other Pacific Islander alone Number	Native Hawaiian and Other Pacific Islander alone Percent	Not Hispanic or Latino, two or more races Number	Not Hispanic or Latino, two or more races Percent
3630	Massage therapists	915	4.1	110	0.5	1,815	8.2	75	0.3	675	3.0
3640	Dental assistants	4,560	5.8	765	1.0	1,985	2.5	185	0.2	1,125	1.4
3645	Medical assistants	11,645	12.9	380	0.4	2,585	2.9	340	0.4	965	1.1
3646	Medical transcriptionists	545	3.5	25	0.2	110	0.7	40	0.3	145	0.9
3647	Pharmacy aides	1,460	12.2	45	0.4	400	3.3	35	0.3	140	1.2
3648	Veterinary assistants and laboratory animal caretakers	985	8.1	40	0.3	155	1.3	15	0.1	90	0.7
3649	Phlebotomists	4,010	20.3	125	0.6	250	1.3	0	0.0	205	1.0
3655	Health care support workers, all other, including medical equipment preparers	15,335	27.2	305	0.5	1,600	2.8	170	0.3	600	1.1
3700	First-line supervisors of correctional officers	3,045	21.5	130	0.9	35	0.2	0	0.0	170	1.2
3710	First-line supervisors of police and detectives	2,045	13.2	140	0.9	190	1.2	4	0.0	135	0.9
3720	First-line supervisors of fire fighting and prevention workers	600	7.4	35	0.4	10	0.1	15	0.2	85	1.0
3730	First-line supervisors of protective service workers, all other	4,115	20.6	220	1.1	110	0.6	55	0.3	265	1.3
3740	Firefighters	5,020	9.8	805	1.6	435	0.8	70	0.1	385	0.8
3750	Fire inspectors	295	6.9	15	0.4	25	0.6	0	0.0	55	1.3
3800	Bailiffs, correctional officers, and jailers	32,785	22.4	1,210	0.8	610	0.4	290	0.2	1,280	0.9
3820	Detectives and criminal investigators	1,450	12.3	125	1.1	60	0.5	30	0.3	165	1.4
3840	Miscellaneous law enforcement workers	805	27.6	55	1.9	140	4.8	4	0.1	70	2.4
3850	Police officers	14,480	15.4	1,015	1.1	955	1.0	180	0.2	1,520	1.6
3900	Animal control workers	225	6.1	45	1.2	10	0.3	0	0.0	94	2.5
3910	Private detectives and investigators	1,120	10.2	55	0.5	90	0.8	35	0.3	320	2.9
3930	Security guards and gaming surveillance officers	98,805	30.4	3,545	1.1	7,110	2.2	2,185	0.7	6,390	2.0
3940	Crossing guards	4,795	22.1	225	1.0	155	0.7	4	0.0	245	1.1
3945	Transportation security screeners	1,985	29.2	25	0.4	245	3.6	55	0.8	44	0.6
3955	Lifeguards and other recreational, and all other protective service workers	4,310	11.8	160	0.4	765	2.1	100	0.3	1,070	2.9
4000	Chefs and head cooks	14,185	15.4	350	0.4	16,770	18.1	235	0.3	1,540	1.7
4010	First-line supervisors of food preparation and serving workers	31,955	16.1	1,610	0.8	5,335	2.7	515	0.3	3,440	1.7
4020	Cooks	140,345	18.3	7,130	0.9	39,420	5.1	1,930	0.3	11,000	1.4
4030	Food preparation workers	34,425	13.9	1,895	0.8	13,875	5.6	935	0.4	4,470	1.8
4040	Bartenders	4,350	4.0	775	0.7	2,280	2.1	245	0.2	1,640	1.5
4050	Combined food preparation and serving workers, including fast food	17,855	15.0	765	0.6	3,330	2.8	245	0.2	2,275	1.9
4060	Counter attendants, cafeteria, food concession, and coffee shop	8,055	12.7	425	0.7	2,385	3.8	290	0.5	1,655	2.6
4110	Waiters and waitresses	43,260	7.4	3,510	0.6	34,755	5.9	945	0.2	11,590	2.0
4120	Food servers, nonrestaurant	18,540	25.9	310	0.4	2,980	4.2	230	0.3	1,065	1.5
4130	Miscellaneous food preparation and serving related workers, including dining room and cafeteria attendants and bartender helpers	15,125	13.2	865	0.8	5,645	4.9	250	0.2	1,865	1.6
4140	Dishwashers	14,805	16.7	795	0.9	2,735	3.1	170	0.2	1,375	1.6

A-19 **Workers with High School Diploma or Equivalency: Detailed Occupation, by Sex, Race, and Hispanic Origin, 2006–2010**—*Continued*

Census occupation code	Detailed Occupation	Total	Male Number	Male Percent	Female Number	Female Percent	Hispanic or Latino Number	Hispanic or Latino Percent	Not Hispanic or Latino, one race White alone Number	Not Hispanic or Latino, one race White alone Percent
4150	Hosts and hostesses, restaurant, lounge, and coffee shop	66,745	8,555	12.8	58,185	87.2	11,275	16.9	45,185	67.7
4200	First-line supervisors of housekeeping and janitorial workers	100,940	59,715	59.2	41,225	40.8	18,635	18.5	58,940	58.4
4210	First-line supervisors of landscaping, lawn service, and groundskeeping workers	58,890	55,730	94.6	3,165	5.4	10,540	17.9	42,725	72.6
4220	Janitors and building cleaners	1,003,840	699,520	69.7	304,315	30.3	197,250	19.6	575,595	57.3
4230	Maids and housekeeping cleaners	536,960	69,210	12.9	467,750	87.1	164,715	30.7	235,870	43.9
4240	Pest control workers	27,445	26,245	95.6	1,200	4.4	3,765	13.7	20,460	74.5
4250	Grounds maintenance workers	396,100	373,760	94.4	22,340	5.6	120,505	30.4	221,960	56.0
4300	First-line supervisors of gaming workers	19,710	10,110	51.3	9,600	48.7	1,835	9.3	14,210	72.1
4320	First-line supervisors of personal service workers	53,955	17,160	31.8	36,795	68.2	4,730	8.8	38,190	70.8
4340	Animal trainers	11,130	6,440	57.9	4,690	42.1	870	7.8	9,655	86.7
4350	Nonfarm animal caretakers	56,515	15,645	27.7	40,870	72.3	5,665	10.0	47,065	83.3
4400	Gaming services workers	35,440	16,305	46.0	19,135	54.0	3,790	10.7	18,245	51.5
4410	Motion picture projectionists	2,080	1,885	90.6	195	9.4	255	12.3	1,645	79.1
4420	Ushers, lobby attendants, and ticket takers	11,210	6,360	56.7	4,850	43.3	1,570	14.0	7,090	63.2
4430	Miscellaneous entertainment attendants and related workers	42,385	23,630	55.8	18,755	44.2	5,965	14.1	27,485	64.8
4460	Embalmers and funeral attendants	4,630	3,560	76.9	1,070	23.1	255	5.5	3,775	81.5
4465	Morticians, undertakers, and funeral directors	3,530	2,585	73.2	945	26.8	285	8.1	2,800	79.3
4500	Barbers	40,875	31,080	76.0	9,795	24.0	6,370	15.6	21,625	52.9
4510	Hairdressers, hairstylists, and cosmetologists	349,710	25,965	7.4	323,745	92.6	42,880	12.3	252,570	72.2
4520	Miscellaneous personal appearance workers	84,490	11,185	13.2	73,305	86.8	8,190	9.7	30,200	35.7
4530	Baggage porters, bellhops, and concierges	24,360	20,270	83.2	4,090	16.8	6,640	27.3	8,600	35.3
4540	Tour and travel guides	8,650	4,965	57.4	3,685	42.6	595	6.9	6,370	73.6
4600	Childcare workers	418,930	18,985	4.5	399,945	95.5	72,665	17.3	250,875	59.9
4610	Personal care aides	292,605	37,800	12.9	254,800	87.1	44,240	15.1	152,875	52.2
4620	Recreation and fitness workers	67,255	20,875	31.0	46,380	69.0	7,530	11.2	47,850	71.1
4640	Residential advisors	12,410	3,755	30.3	8,655	69.7	865	7.0	6,290	50.7
4650	Personal care and service workers, all other	26,790	15,735	58.7	11,060	41.3	4,315	16.1	17,510	65.4
4700	First-line supervisors of retail sales workers	937,710	485,270	51.8	452,435	48.2	107,795	11.5	707,300	75.4
4710	First-line supervisors of non-retail sales workers	286,200	206,005	72.0	80,200	28.0	35,350	12.4	219,655	76.7
4720	Cashiers	1,109,390	238,800	21.5	870,590	78.5	195,510	17.6	646,185	58.2
4740	Counter and rental clerks	43,460	17,160	39.5	26,300	60.5	6,470	14.9	28,750	66.2
4750	Parts salespersons	52,835	46,765	88.5	6,070	11.5	7,135	13.5	42,555	80.5
4760	Retail salespersons	995,680	464,715	46.7	530,960	53.3	140,885	14.1	692,755	69.6
4800	Advertising sales agents	29,995	12,000	40.0	17,995	60.0	3,030	10.1	23,595	78.7
4810	Insurance sales agents	89,350	28,435	31.8	60,910	68.2	10,840	12.1	70,735	79.2

A-19 Workers with High School Diploma or Equivalency: Detailed Occupation, by Sex, Race, and Hispanic Origin, 2006–2010—*Continued*

Census occupation code	Detailed Occupation	Black or African American alone Number	Percent	American Indian and Alaska Native alone Number	Percent	Asian alone Number	Percent	Native Hawaiian and Other Pacific Islander alone Number	Percent	Not Hispanic or Latino, two or more races Number	Percent
4150	Hosts and hostesses, restaurant, lounge, and coffee shop	5,475	8.2	500	0.7	2,395	3.6	60	0.1	1,860	2.8
4200	First-line supervisors of housekeeping and janitorial workers	19,075	18.9	815	0.8	1,605	1.6	215	0.2	1,655	1.6
4210	First-line supervisors of landscaping, lawn service, and groundskeeping workers	4,175	7.1	190	0.3	490	0.8	195	0.3	580	1.0
4220	Janitors and building cleaners	184,060	18.3	9,245	0.9	22,930	2.3	2,295	0.2	12,465	1.2
4230	Maids and housekeeping cleaners	102,060	19.0	4,690	0.9	18,845	3.5	1,185	0.2	9,595	1.8
4240	Pest control workers	2,460	9.0	95	0.3	150	0.5	45	0.2	470	1.7
4250	Grounds maintenance workers	40,620	10.3	2,380	0.6	4,680	1.2	930	0.2	5,015	1.3
4300	First-line supervisors of gaming workers	1,195	6.1	770	3.9	1,215	6.2	80	0.4	400	2.0
4320	First-line supervisors of personal service workers	4,410	8.2	190	0.4	5,870	10.9	10	0.0	560	1.0
4340	Animal trainers	240	2.2	115	1.0	85	0.8	0	0.0	160	1.4
4350	Nonfarm animal caretakers	1,740	3.1	220	0.4	485	0.9	0	0.0	1,350	2.4
4400	Gaming services workers	3,190	9.0	1,410	4.0	7,940	22.4	90	0.3	779	2.2
4410	Motion picture projectionists	60	2.9	15	0.7	40	1.9	0	0.0	65	3.1
4420	Ushers, lobby attendants, and ticket takers	2,125	19.0	40	0.4	215	1.9	0	0.0	169	1.5
4430	Miscellaneous entertainment attendants and related workers	5,360	12.6	675	1.6	1,560	3.7	110	0.3	1,230	2.9
4460	Embalmers and funeral attendants	520	11.2	0	0.0	40	0.9	0	0.0	35	0.8
4465	Morticians, undertakers, and funeral directors	375	10.6	10	0.3	35	1.0	4	0.1	25	0.7
4500	Barbers	10,705	26.2	190	0.5	1,400	3.4	0	0.0	585	1.4
4510	Hairdressers, hairstylists, and cosmetologists	33,715	9.6	1,390	0.4	14,750	4.2	170	0.0	4,230	1.2
4520	Miscellaneous personal appearance workers	2,765	3.3	110	0.1	42,145	49.9	70	0.1	1,000	1.2
4530	Baggage porters, bellhops, and concierges	7,000	28.7	100	0.4	1,480	6.1	85	0.3	455	1.9
4540	Tour and travel guides	645	7.5	150	1.7	420	4.9	60	0.7	420	4.9
4600	Childcare workers	75,635	18.1	3,195	0.8	9,705	2.3	875	0.2	5,985	1.4
4610	Personal care aides	73,045	25.0	3,900	1.3	12,540	4.3	1,510	0.5	4,490	1.5
4620	Recreation and fitness workers	8,360	12.4	780	1.2	1,265	1.9	235	0.3	1,235	1.8
4640	Residential advisors	4,475	36.1	255	2.1	255	2.1	25	0.2	240	1.9
4650	Personal care and service workers, all other	3,045	11.4	255	1.0	1,010	3.8	95	0.4	560	2.1
4700	First-line supervisors of retail sales workers	70,490	7.5	4,795	0.5	32,715	3.5	1,525	0.2	13,085	1.4
4710	First-line supervisors of non-retail sales workers	17,960	6.3	1,060	0.4	8,810	3.1	435	0.2	2,930	1.0
4720	Cashiers	181,865	16.4	9,300	0.8	52,520	4.7	3,230	0.3	20,785	1.9
4740	Counter and rental clerks	5,285	12.2	375	0.9	1,970	4.5	90	0.2	515	1.2
4750	Parts salespersons	1,770	3.4	200	0.4	760	1.4	4	0.0	410	0.8
4760	Retail salespersons	105,650	10.6	5,315	0.5	32,910	3.3	1,140	0.1	17,020	1.7
4800	Advertising sales agents	2,335	7.8	110	0.4	605	2.0	25	0.1	285	1.0
4810	Insurance sales agents	5,385	6.0	390	0.4	1,165	1.3	55	0.1	775	0.9

A-19 **Workers with High School Diploma or Equivalency: Detailed Occupation, by Sex, Race, and Hispanic Origin, 2006–2010**—*Continued*

Census occupation code	Detailed Occupation	Total	Male Number	Male Percent	Female Number	Female Percent	Hispanic or Latino Number	Hispanic or Latino Percent	Not Hispanic or Latino, one race White alone Number	Not Hispanic or Latino, one race White alone Percent
4820	Securities, commodities, and financial services sales agents	30,650	14,645	47.8	16,005	52.2	3,755	12.3	23,340	76.2
4830	Travel agents	15,980	1,925	12.0	14,055	88.0	1,600	10.0	12,495	78.2
4840	Sales representatives, services, all other	104,395	64,825	62.1	39,570	37.9	12,760	12.2	80,150	76.8
4850	Sales representatives, wholesale and manufacturing	266,600	191,695	71.9	74,905	28.1	31,825	11.9	213,720	80.2
4900	Models, demonstrators, and product promoters	20,305	4,015	19.8	16,290	80.2	1,875	9.2	15,055	74.1
4920	Real estate brokers and sales agents	124,115	43,670	35.2	80,445	64.8	14,280	11.5	99,610	80.3
4930	Sales engineers	1,430	1,410	98.6	20	1.4	50	3.5	1,370	95.8
4940	Telemarketers	45,450	14,975	32.9	30,475	67.1	6,740	14.8	28,315	62.3
4950	Door-to-door sales workers, news and street vendors, and related workers	61,100	26,525	43.4	34,575	56.6	10,135	16.6	43,850	71.8
4965	Sales and related workers, all other	50,945	22,780	44.7	28,165	55.3	4,805	9.4	39,825	78.2
5000	First-line supervisors of office and administrative support workers	382,700	117,890	30.8	264,810	69.2	46,030	12.0	288,485	75.4
5010	Switchboard operators, including answering service	18,860	2,055	10.9	16,800	89.1	1,885	10.0	13,740	72.9
5020	Telephone operators	16,935	3,040	18.0	13,895	82.0	2,860	16.9	10,235	60.4
5030	Communications equipment operators, all other	2,530	1,085	42.9	1,440	56.9	280	11.1	2,050	81.0
5100	Bill and account collectors	72,430	17,820	24.6	54,610	75.4	12,490	17.2	45,970	63.5
5110	Billing and posting clerks	152,235	11,205	7.4	141,030	92.6	18,915	12.4	113,575	74.6
5120	Bookkeeping, accounting, and auditing clerks	457,250	31,450	6.9	425,800	93.1	40,855	8.9	372,105	81.4
5130	Gaming cage workers	5,115	1,135	22.2	3,985	77.9	845	16.5	2,900	56.7
5140	Payroll and timekeeping clerks	52,995	3,605	6.8	49,390	93.2	5,685	10.7	41,670	78.6
5150	Procurement clerks	7,610	2,330	30.6	5,280	69.4	690	9.1	5,840	76.7
5160	Tellers	141,215	10,420	7.4	130,795	92.6	20,830	14.8	102,430	72.5
5165	Financial clerks, all other	15,085	2,910	19.3	12,175	80.7	1,890	12.5	10,530	69.8
5200	Brokerage clerks	1,895	535	28.2	1,360	71.8	100	5.3	1,570	82.8
5220	Court, municipal, and license clerks	27,715	3,845	13.9	23,870	86.1	3,085	11.1	20,430	73.7
5230	Credit authorizers, checkers, and clerks	17,745	2,470	13.9	15,275	86.1	2,745	15.5	12,025	67.8
5240	Customer service representatives	630,500	169,295	26.9	461,205	73.1	105,140	16.7	404,680	64.2
5250	Eligibility interviewers, government programs	10,835	1,020	9.4	9,815	90.6	2,205	20.4	6,580	60.7
5260	File clerks	109,925	18,355	16.7	91,570	83.3	14,465	13.2	73,940	67.3
5300	Hotel, motel, and resort desk clerks	42,840	11,360	26.5	31,480	73.5	6,840	16.0	25,900	60.5
5310	Interviewers, except eligibility and loan	36,040	5,860	16.3	30,180	83.7	5,290	14.7	23,875	66.2
5320	Library assistants, clerical	23,280	2,960	12.7	20,315	87.3	1,900	8.2	17,970	77.2
5330	Loan interviewers and clerks	40,000	4,805	12.0	35,195	88.0	5,980	15.0	28,375	70.9
5340	New accounts clerks	7,080	885	12.5	6,195	87.5	1,215	17.2	4,905	69.3
5350	Correspondence clerks and order clerks	53,915	18,555	34.4	35,360	65.6	8,520	15.8	36,865	68.4
5360	Human resources assistants, except payroll and timekeeping	11,875	1,305	11.0	10,575	89.1	1,720	14.5	7,785	65.6
5400	Receptionists and information clerks	414,195	26,215	6.3	387,980	93.7	70,410	17.0	287,155	69.3
5410	Reservation and transportation ticket agents and travel clerks	37,175	13,120	35.3	24,055	64.7	6,225	16.7	21,105	56.8
5420	Information and record clerks, all other	22,345	2,690	12.0	19,660	88.0	2,850	12.8	15,120	67.7
5500	Cargo and freight agents	6,375	4,275	67.1	2,100	32.9	1,150	18.0	3,945	61.9
5510	Couriers and messengers	108,230	89,760	82.9	18,470	17.1	18,000	16.6	69,700	64.4

A-19 Workers with High School Diploma or Equivalency: Detailed Occupation, by Sex, Race, and Hispanic Origin, 2006–2010—Continued

Census occupation code	Detailed Occupation	Black or African American alone Number	Black or African American alone Percent	American Indian and Alaska Native alone Number	American Indian and Alaska Native alone Percent	Asian alone Number	Asian alone Percent	Native Hawaiian and Other Pacific Islander alone Number	Native Hawaiian and Other Pacific Islander alone Percent	Not Hispanic or Latino, two or more races Number	Not Hispanic or Latino, two or more races Percent
4820	Securities, commodities, and financial services sales agents	2,515	8.2	100	0.3	615	2.0	10	0.0	310	1.0
4830	Travel agents	930	5.8	70	0.4	655	4.1	35	0.2	190	1.2
4840	Sales representatives, services, all other	7,560	7.2	445	0.4	1,810	1.7	130	0.1	1,545	1.5
4850	Sales representatives, wholesale and manufacturing	11,050	4.1	640	0.2	6,125	2.3	365	0.1	2,875	1.1
4900	Models, demonstrators, and product promoters	2,200	10.8	100	0.5	700	3.4	20	0.1	355	1.7
4920	Real estate brokers and sales agents	6,170	5.0	380	0.3	2,240	1.8	95	0.1	1,339	1.1
4930	Sales engineers	10	0.7	0	0.0	0	0.0	0	0.0	0	0.0
4940	Telemarketers	8,700	19.1	305	0.7	465	1.0	145	0.3	790	1.7
4950	Door-to-door sales workers, news and street vendors, and related workers	4,625	7.6	360	0.6	1,140	1.9	160	0.3	830	1.4
4965	Sales and related workers, all other	4,360	8.6	295	0.6	995	2.0	75	0.1	600	1.2
5000	First-line supervisors of office and administrative support workers	35,750	9.3	1,640	0.4	5,755	1.5	915	0.2	4,125	1.1
5010	Switchboard operators, including answering service	2,595	13.8	130	0.7	350	1.9	60	0.3	100	0.5
5020	Telephone operators	3,165	18.7	70	0.4	365	2.2	10	0.1	235	1.4
5030	Communications equipment operators, all other	95	3.8	20	0.8	0	0.0	30	1.2	50	2.0
5100	Bill and account collectors	11,710	16.2	235	0.3	890	1.2	200	0.3	930	1.3
5110	Billing and posting clerks	14,095	9.3	885	0.6	2,905	1.9	280	0.2	1,580	1.0
5120	Bookkeeping, accounting, and auditing clerks	26,630	5.8	2,145	0.5	9,475	2.1	785	0.2	5,265	1.2
5130	Gaming cage workers	500	9.8	435	8.5	365	7.1	4	0.1	70	1.4
5140	Payroll and timekeeping clerks	3,815	7.2	235	0.4	925	1.7	35	0.1	619	1.2
5150	Procurement clerks	570	7.5	75	1.0	320	4.2	0	0.0	120	1.6
5160	Tellers	11,155	7.9	650	0.5	3,740	2.6	370	0.3	2,035	1.4
5165	Financial clerks, all other	1,770	11.7	75	0.5	545	3.6	25	0.2	255	1.7
5200	Brokerage clerks	170	9.0	0	0.0	45	2.4	0	0.0	4	0.2
5220	Court, municipal, and license clerks	3,280	11.8	300	1.1	410	1.5	30	0.1	185	0.7
5230	Credit authorizers, checkers, and clerks	2,195	12.4	30	0.2	465	2.6	85	0.5	204	1.1
5240	Customer service representatives	91,710	14.5	3,135	0.5	14,250	2.3	1,700	0.3	9,880	1.6
5250	Eligibility interviewers, government programs	1,485	13.7	175	1.6	290	2.7	0	0.0	103	1.0
5260	File clerks	14,980	13.6	1,030	0.9	3,725	3.4	265	0.2	1,520	1.4
5300	Hotel, motel, and resort desk clerks	6,050	14.1	310	0.7	2,230	5.2	255	0.6	1,255	2.9
5310	Interviewers, except eligibility and loan	5,470	15.2	235	0.7	495	1.4	70	0.2	605	1.7
5320	Library assistants, clerical	2,105	9.0	95	0.4	855	3.7	0	0.0	364	1.6
5330	Loan interviewers and clerks	3,835	9.6	195	0.5	1,035	2.6	200	0.5	380	1.0
5340	New accounts clerks	710	10.0	4	0.1	110	1.6	0	0.0	135	1.9
5350	Correspondence clerks and order clerks	6,050	11.2	295	0.5	1,525	2.8	95	0.2	560	1.0
5360	Human resources assistants, except payroll and timekeeping	2,045	17.2	55	0.5	145	1.2	15	0.1	104	0.9
5400	Receptionists and information clerks	40,460	9.8	2,660	0.6	7,365	1.8	720	0.2	5,430	1.3
5410	Reservation and transportation ticket agents and travel clerks	6,430	17.3	275	0.7	1,420	3.8	790	2.1	935	2.5
5420	Information and record clerks, all other	3,025	13.5	275	1.2	670	3.0	200	0.9	205	0.9
5500	Cargo and freight agents	835	13.1	20	0.3	275	4.3	80	1.3	70	1.1
5510	Couriers and messengers	16,235	15.0	345	0.3	2,480	2.3	245	0.2	1,225	1.1

A-19 Workers with High School Diploma or Equivalency: Detailed Occupation, by Sex, Race, and Hispanic Origin, 2006–2010—*Continued*

Census occupation code	Detailed Occupation	Total	Male Number	Male Percent	Female Number	Female Percent	Hispanic or Latino Number	Hispanic or Latino Percent	Not Hispanic or Latino, one race — White alone Number	Percent
5520	Dispatchers	96,340	40,960	42.5	55,375	57.5	12,005	12.5	70,875	73.6
5530	Meter readers, utilities	16,600	14,200	85.5	2,400	14.5	1,985	12.0	11,250	67.8
5540	Postal service clerks	49,700	22,525	45.3	27,170	54.7	4,765	9.6	28,410	57.2
5550	Postal service mail carriers	119,665	65,740	54.9	53,925	45.1	11,400	9.5	86,980	72.7
5560	Postal service mail sorters, processors, and processing machine operators	31,500	15,820	50.2	15,680	49.8	3,215	10.2	16,790	53.3
5600	Production, planning, and expediting clerks	72,420	28,675	39.6	43,745	60.4	7,415	10.2	56,930	78.6
5610	Shipping, receiving, and traffic clerks	262,685	179,475	68.3	83,210	31.7	50,370	19.2	163,730	62.3
5620	Stock clerks and order fillers	613,985	375,455	61.2	238,530	38.8	97,145	15.8	384,880	62.7
5630	Weighers, measurers, checkers, and samplers, recordkeeping	27,535	13,665	49.6	13,875	50.4	4,515	16.4	18,820	68.3
5700	Secretaries and administrative assistants	1,147,115	27,830	2.4	1,119,285	97.6	108,100	9.4	935,065	81.5
5800	Computer operators	37,935	15,680	41.3	22,260	58.7	4,170	11.0	27,245	71.8
5810	Data entry keyers	136,250	19,790	14.5	116,460	85.5	18,625	13.7	92,380	67.8
5820	Word processors and typists	99,675	7,810	7.8	91,865	92.2	10,775	10.8	73,495	73.7
5840	Insurance claims and policy processing clerks	91,070	6,870	7.5	84,200	92.5	11,100	12.2	66,955	73.5
5850	Mail clerks and mail machine operators, except postal service	49,370	22,295	45.2	27,075	54.8	6,635	13.4	28,915	58.6
5860	Office clerks, general	362,830	50,455	13.9	312,375	86.1	52,805	14.6	247,295	68.2
5900	Office machine operators, except computer	17,835	6,820	38.2	11,015	61.8	2,315	13.0	10,565	59.2
5910	Proofreaders and copy markers	2,565	435	17.0	2,130	83.0	95	3.7	1,970	76.8
5920	Statistical assistants	5,285	1,600	30.3	3,685	69.7	470	8.9	3,720	70.4
5940	Miscellaneous office and administrative support workers, including desktop publishers	121,290	26,775	22.1	94,520	77.9	14,600	12.0	86,170	71.0
6005	First-line supervisors of farming, fishing, and forestry workers	19,425	16,840	86.7	2,585	13.3	4,910	25.3	13,125	67.6
6010	Agricultural inspectors	4,355	2,315	53.2	2,045	47.0	605	13.9	2,760	63.4
6040	Graders and sorters, agricultural products	11,785	4,610	39.1	7,175	60.9	4,885	41.5	4,345	36.9
6050	Miscellaneous agricultural workers, including animal breeders	198,425	161,695	81.5	36,730	18.5	70,400	35.5	112,785	56.8
6100	Fishing and hunting workers	13,825	13,160	95.2	665	4.8	630	4.6	11,610	84.0
6120	Forest and conservation workers	4,395	3,880	88.3	515	11.7	630	14.3	3,375	76.8
6130	Logging workers	33,520	32,965	98.3	555	1.7	1,400	4.2	27,795	82.9
6200	First-line supervisors of construction trades and extraction workers	399,825	391,060	97.8	8,760	2.2	47,655	11.9	327,290	81.9
6210	Boilermakers	9,330	9,095	97.5	235	2.5	955	10.2	7,630	81.8
6220	Brickmasons, blockmasons, and stonemasons	79,085	78,180	98.9	905	1.1	19,455	24.6	50,285	63.6

PART A—NATIONAL DATA

A-19 Workers with High School Diploma or Equivalency: Detailed Occupation, by Sex, Race, and Hispanic Origin, 2006–2010—*Continued*

Census occupation code	Detailed Occupation	Black or African American alone Number	Percent	American Indian and Alaska Native alone Number	Percent	Asian alone Number	Percent	Native Hawaiian and Other Pacific Islander alone Number	Percent	Not Hispanic or Latino, two or more races Number	Percent
5520	Dispatchers	10,110	10.5	735	0.8	985	1.0	200	0.2	1,425	1.5
5530	Meter readers, utilities	2,840	17.1	155	0.9	170	1.0	10	0.1	190	1.1
5540	Postal service clerks	12,365	24.9	355	0.7	3,375	6.8	40	0.1	390	0.8
5550	Postal service mail carriers	15,060	12.6	315	0.3	4,595	3.8	335	0.3	980	0.8
5560	Postal service mail sorters, processors, and processing machine operators	8,960	28.4	125	0.4	2,090	6.6	60	0.2	255	0.8
5600	Production, planning, and expediting clerks	5,255	7.3	380	0.5	1,310	1.8	100	0.1	1,019	1.4
5610	Shipping, receiving, and traffic clerks	37,960	14.5	790	0.3	6,560	2.5	555	0.2	2,720	1.0
5620	Stock clerks and order fillers	100,765	16.4	4,315	0.7	15,365	2.5	1,590	0.3	9,930	1.6
5630	Weighers, measurers, checkers, and samplers, recordkeeping	3,195	11.6	150	0.5	510	1.9	85	0.3	260	0.9
5700	Secretaries and administrative assistants	73,070	6.4	6,375	0.6	12,715	1.1	1,495	0.1	10,295	0.9
5800	Computer operators	5,245	13.8	175	0.5	755	2.0	45	0.1	295	0.8
5810	Data entry keyers	18,785	13.8	620	0.5	3,905	2.9	195	0.1	1,740	1.3
5820	Word processors and typists	11,175	11.2	380	0.4	2,555	2.6	205	0.2	1,095	1.1
5840	Insurance claims and policy processing clerks	10,405	11.4	250	0.3	1,160	1.3	90	0.1	1,110	1.2
5850	Mail clerks and mail machine operators, except postal service	11,135	22.6	255	0.5	1,735	3.5	125	0.3	569	1.2
5860	Office clerks, general	44,695	12.3	2,055	0.6	10,105	2.8	1,285	0.4	4,590	1.3
5900	Office machine operators, except computer	3,510	19.7	115	0.6	1,105	6.2	25	0.1	200	1.1
5910	Proofreaders and copy markers	350	13.6	30	1.2	90	3.5	0	0.0	25	1.0
5920	Statistical assistants	760	14.4	70	1.3	220	4.2	0	0.0	45	0.9
5940	Miscellaneous office and administrative support workers, including desktop publishers	15,350	12.7	1,060	0.9	2,270	1.9	425	0.4	1,415	1.2
6005	First-line supervisors of farming, fishing, and forestry workers	765	3.9	225	1.2	195	1.0	4	0.0	200	1.0
6010	Agricultural inspectors	800	18.4	55	1.3	105	2.4	4	0.1	34	0.8
6040	Graders and sorters, agricultural products	1,880	16.0	60	0.5	495	4.2	30	0.3	89	0.8
6050	Miscellaneous agricultural workers, including animal breeders	9,980	5.0	1,135	0.6	2,045	1.0	280	0.1	1,810	0.9
6100	Fishing and hunting workers	415	3.0	410	3.0	425	3.1	65	0.5	270	2.0
6120	Forest and conservation workers	250	5.7	60	1.4	25	0.6	0	0.0	55	1.3
6130	Logging workers	3,220	9.6	700	2.1	115	0.3	25	0.1	259	0.8
6200	First-line supervisors of construction trades and extraction workers	15,500	3.9	2,845	0.7	2,015	0.5	410	0.1	4,100	1.0
6210	Boilermakers	555	5.9	95	1.0	25	0.3	0	0.0	65	0.7
6220	Brickmasons, blockmasons, and stonemasons	7,140	9.0	785	1.0	290	0.4	185	0.2	945	1.2

A-19 **Workers with High School Diploma or Equivalency: Detailed Occupation, by Sex, Race, and Hispanic Origin, 2006–2010**—*Continued*

| Census occupation code | Detailed Occupation | Total | High school diploma or equivalency |||||| Not Hispanic or Latino, one race ||
| | | | Male || Female || Hispanic or Latino || White alone ||
			Number	Percent	Number	Percent	Number	Percent	Number	Percent
6230	Carpenters	592,960	583,685	98.4	9,275	1.6	117,035	19.7	426,395	71.9
6240	Carpet, floor, and tile installers and finishers	85,580	84,090	98.3	1,490	1.7	26,235	30.7	52,905	61.8
6250	Cement masons, concrete finishers, and terrazzo workers	32,675	32,410	99.2	270	0.8	9,570	29.3	17,130	52.4
6260	Construction laborers	632,905	614,740	97.1	18,165	2.9	181,815	28.7	374,820	59.2
6300	Paving, surfacing, and tamping equipment operators	8,080	7,760	96.0	320	4.0	1,110	13.7	6,215	76.9
6320	Construction equipment operators, except paving, surfacing, and tamping equipment operators	187,920	184,395	98.1	3,525	1.9	16,770	8.9	154,060	82.0
6330	Drywall installers, ceiling tile installers, and tapers	68,065	66,750	98.1	1,315	1.9	27,870	40.9	34,715	51.0
6355	Electricians	296,280	291,485	98.4	4,800	1.6	40,610	13.7	227,220	76.7
6360	Glaziers	22,065	21,575	97.8	490	2.2	4,080	18.5	16,205	73.4
6400	Insulation workers	18,430	17,735	96.2	695	3.8	4,390	23.8	11,810	64.1
6420	Painters, construction and maintenance	223,490	210,145	94.0	13,345	6.0	73,255	32.8	125,380	56.1
6430	Paperhangers	3,275	2,595	79.2	680	20.8	200	6.1	2,845	86.9
6440	Pipelayers, plumbers, pipefitters, and steamfitters	259,895	256,835	98.8	3,060	1.2	37,175	14.3	197,385	75.9
6460	Plasterers and stucco masons	14,620	14,440	98.8	180	1.2	6,360	43.5	6,690	45.8
6500	Reinforcing iron and rebar workers	4,440	4,435	99.9	4	0.1	1,390	31.3	2,530	57.0
6515	Roofers	79,040	78,045	98.7	995	1.3	26,870	34.0	44,810	56.7
6520	Sheet metal workers	61,795	59,435	96.2	2,360	3.8	7,630	12.3	48,985	79.3
6530	Structural iron and steel workers	30,470	30,115	98.8	355	1.2	3,950	13.0	23,170	76.0
6600	Helpers, construction trades	29,225	28,165	96.4	1,060	3.6	9,425	32.2	15,870	54.3
6660	Construction and building inspectors	27,105	24,210	89.3	2,895	10.7	2,445	9.0	21,920	80.9
6700	Elevator installers and repairers	12,735	12,590	98.9	140	1.1	1,200	9.4	10,670	83.8
6710	Fence erectors	11,585	11,275	97.3	310	2.7	2,595	22.4	8,005	69.1
6720	Hazardous materials removal workers	11,750	9,750	83.0	2,000	17.0	2,695	22.9	6,515	55.4
6730	Highway maintenance workers	53,375	51,775	97.0	1,600	3.0	4,300	8.1	42,655	79.9
6740	Rail-track laying and maintenance equipment operators	6,150	6,085	98.9	65	1.1	675	11.0	4,315	70.2
6765	Miscellaneous construction workers, including solar photovoltaic installers, septic tank servicers, and sewer pipe cleaners	19,905	19,270	96.8	635	3.2	3,480	17.5	14,000	70.3
6800	Derrick, rotary drill, and service unit operators, and roustabouts, oil, gas, and mining	17,080	16,890	98.9	190	1.1	2,960	17.3	12,530	73.4
6820	Earth drillers, except oil and gas	13,845	13,680	98.8	165	1.2	1,250	9.0	11,815	85.3
6830	Explosives workers, ordnance handling experts, and blasters	4,235	4,010	94.7	225	5.3	265	6.3	3,380	79.8
6840	Mining machine operators	30,390	29,775	98.0	615	2.0	2,780	9.1	26,015	85.6
6940	Miscellaneous extraction workers, including roof bolters and helpers	28,850	28,250	97.9	600	2.1	4,320	15.0	22,065	76.5
7000	First-line supervisors of mechanics, installers, and repairers	109,840	104,370	95.0	5,470	5.0	9,380	8.5	90,145	82.1
7010	Computer, automated teller, and office machine repairers	53,810	46,575	86.6	7,240	13.5	6,770	12.6	38,240	71.1
7020	Radio and telecommunications equipment installers and repairers	57,850	51,955	89.8	5,895	10.2	6,335	11.0	44,215	76.4
7030	Avionics technicians	4,510	3,885	86.1	625	13.9	675	15.0	3,265	72.4

A-19 **Workers with High School Diploma or Equivalency: Detailed Occupation, by Sex, Race, and Hispanic Origin, 2006–2010**—Continued

Census occupation code	Detailed Occupation	High school diploma or equivalency									
		Not Hispanic or Latino, one race										Not Hispanic or Latino, two or more races	
		Black or African American alone		American Indian and Alaska Native alone		Asian alone		Native Hawaiian and Other Pacific Islander alone			
		Number	Percent	Number	Percent	Number	Percent	Number	Percent	Number	Percent
6230	Carpenters	28,195	4.8	5,090	0.9	7,010	1.2	1,100	0.2	8,130	1.4
6240	Carpet, floor, and tile installers and finishers	3,845	4.5	395	0.5	975	1.1	40	0.0	1,190	1.4
6250	Cement masons, concrete finishers, and terrazzo workers	4,935	15.1	310	0.9	150	0.5	100	0.3	480	1.5
6260	Construction laborers	51,825	8.2	5,525	0.9	8,240	1.3	1,775	0.3	8,910	1.4
6300	Paving, surfacing, and tamping equipment operators	620	7.7	15	0.2	10	0.1	4	0.0	103	1.3
6320	Construction equipment operators, except paving, surfacing, and tamping equipment operators	11,105	5.9	2,320	1.2	495	0.3	605	0.3	2,560	1.4
6330	Drywall installers, ceiling tile installers, and tapers	3,510	5.2	795	1.2	485	0.7	75	0.1	615	0.9
6355	Electricians	19,185	6.5	1,760	0.6	3,850	1.3	445	0.2	3,215	1.1
6360	Glaziers	935	4.2	215	1.0	340	1.5	20	0.1	270	1.2
6400	Insulation workers	1,510	8.2	180	1.0	115	0.6	10	0.1	410	2.2
6420	Painters, construction and maintenance	16,700	7.5	1,135	0.5	3,450	1.5	360	0.2	3,215	1.4
6430	Paperhangers	115	3.5	20	0.6	80	2.4	0	0.0	14	0.4
6440	Pipelayers, plumbers, pipefitters, and steamfitters	17,560	6.8	2,060	0.8	2,145	0.8	480	0.2	3,095	1.2
6460	Plasterers and stucco masons	1,395	9.5	30	0.2	20	0.1	40	0.3	85	0.6
6500	Reinforcing iron and rebar workers	345	7.8	80	1.8	75	1.7	0	0.0	24	0.5
6515	Roofers	4,935	6.2	725	0.9	460	0.6	240	0.3	995	1.3
6520	Sheet metal workers	3,645	5.9	200	0.3	790	1.3	70	0.1	475	0.8
6530	Structural iron and steel workers	2,155	7.1	550	1.8	205	0.7	115	0.4	320	1.1
6600	Helpers, construction trades	2,675	9.2	365	1.2	250	0.9	25	0.1	605	2.1
6660	Construction and building inspectors	2,175	8.0	155	0.6	140	0.5	50	0.2	220	0.8
6700	Elevator installers and repairers	600	4.7	25	0.2	100	0.8	0	0.0	130	1.0
6710	Fence erectors	630	5.4	45	0.4	75	0.6	90	0.8	144	1.2
6720	Hazardous materials removal workers	2,060	17.5	145	1.2	185	1.6	35	0.3	115	1.0
6730	Highway maintenance workers	5,180	9.7	565	1.1	140	0.3	25	0.0	510	1.0
6740	Rail-track laying and maintenance equipment operators	990	16.1	45	0.7	90	1.5	0	0.0	35	0.6
6765	Miscellaneous construction workers, including solar photovoltaic installers, septic tank servicers, and sewer pipe cleaners	1,620	8.1	115	0.6	165	0.8	70	0.4	450	2.3
6800	Derrick, rotary drill, and service unit operators, and roustabouts, oil, gas, and mining	1,095	6.4	300	1.8	15	0.1	0	0.0	178	1.0
6820	Earth drillers, except oil and gas	405	2.9	120	0.9	70	0.5	30	0.2	149	1.1
6830	Explosives workers, ordnance handling experts, and blasters	450	10.6	70	1.7	10	0.2	20	0.5	39	0.9
6840	Mining machine operators	1,025	3.4	215	0.7	110	0.4	30	0.1	200	0.7
6940	Miscellaneous extraction workers, including roof bolters and helpers	1,615	5.6	425	1.5	120	0.4	50	0.2	260	0.9
7000	First-line supervisors of mechanics, installers, and repairers	7,550	6.9	540	0.5	910	0.8	215	0.2	1,090	1.0
7010	Computer, automated teller, and office machine repairers	5,330	9.9	200	0.4	2,205	4.1	145	0.3	925	1.7
7020	Radio and telecommunications equipment installers and repairers	5,440	9.4	155	0.3	1,270	2.2	50	0.1	385	0.7
7030	Avionics technicians	345	7.6	20	0.4	75	1.7	25	0.6	100	2.2

A-19 Workers with High School Diploma or Equivalency: Detailed Occupation, by Sex, Race, and Hispanic Origin, 2006–2010—*Continued*

Census occupation code	Detailed Occupation	Total	High school diploma or equivalency							
			Male		Female		Hispanic or Latino		Not Hispanic or Latino, one race — White alone	
			Number	Percent	Number	Percent	Number	Percent	Number	Percent
7040	Electric motor, power tool, and related repairers	10,915	10,350	94.8	565	5.2	1,165	10.7	8,810	80.7
7100	Electrical and electronics repairers, transportation equipment, and industrial and utility	5,395	5,235	97.0	160	3.0	340	6.3	4,430	82.1
7110	Electronic equipment installers and repairers, motor vehicles	5,940	5,545	93.4	395	6.6	1,080	18.2	4,230	71.2
7120	Electronic home entertainment equipment installers and repairers	20,325	19,680	96.8	645	3.2	3,920	19.3	13,775	67.8
7130	Security and fire alarm systems installers	21,165	20,830	98.4	335	1.6	3,270	15.5	15,350	72.5
7140	Aircraft mechanics and service technicians	43,250	41,055	94.9	2,200	5.1	5,815	13.4	31,545	72.9
7150	Automotive body and related repairers	77,640	76,540	98.6	1,105	1.4	12,910	16.6	57,765	74.4
7160	Automotive glass installers and repairers	9,505	9,190	96.7	315	3.3	1,495	15.7	7,210	75.9
7200	Automotive service technicians and mechanics	363,790	359,190	98.7	4,600	1.3	56,690	15.6	264,215	72.6
7210	Bus and truck mechanics and diesel engine specialists	140,795	139,525	99.1	1,275	0.9	14,410	10.2	111,985	79.5
7220	Heavy vehicle and mobile equipment service technicians and mechanics	96,155	95,370	99.2	785	0.8	8,670	9.0	80,325	83.5
7240	Small engine mechanics	23,095	22,820	98.8	280	1.2	1,750	7.6	20,205	87.5
7260	Miscellaneous vehicle and mobile equipment mechanics, installers, and repairers	34,815	34,350	98.7	465	1.3	6,565	18.9	24,125	69.3
7300	Control and valve installers and repairers	8,845	8,490	96.0	355	4.0	1,110	12.5	6,580	74.4
7315	Heating, air conditioning, and refrigeration mechanics and installers	147,880	146,415	99.0	1,465	1.0	20,045	13.6	114,895	77.7
7320	Home appliance repairers	18,280	17,850	97.6	430	2.4	2,165	11.8	13,990	76.5
7330	Industrial and refractory machinery mechanics	168,020	161,905	96.4	6,115	3.6	16,765	10.0	134,350	80.0
7340	Maintenance and repair workers, general	196,805	190,680	96.9	6,125	3.1	24,490	12.4	146,605	74.5
7350	Maintenance workers, machinery	15,535	15,050	96.9	480	3.1	1,725	11.1	12,230	78.7
7360	Millwrights	23,300	22,720	97.5	580	2.5	1,015	4.4	20,835	89.4
7410	Electrical power-line installers and repairers	50,960	50,510	99.1	450	0.9	4,265	8.4	41,310	81.1
7420	Telecommunications line installers and repairers	61,360	58,930	96.0	2,435	4.0	9,645	15.7	42,890	69.9
7430	Precision instrument and equipment repairers	13,710	11,835	86.3	1,875	13.7	1,760	12.8	10,255	74.8
7510	Coin, vending, and amusement machine servicers and repairers	19,385	16,270	83.9	3,115	16.1	2,055	10.6	14,785	76.3
7540	Locksmiths and safe repairers	11,475	10,720	93.4	755	6.6	1,090	9.5	9,600	83.7
7550	Manufactured building and mobile home installers	4,135	3,795	91.8	335	8.1	515	12.5	3,295	79.7
7560	Riggers	5,355	5,280	98.6	75	1.4	660	12.3	3,820	71.3
7610	Helpers—installation, maintenance, and repair workers	9,520	8,910	93.6	610	6.4	2,475	26.0	5,650	59.3
7630	Other installation, maintenance, and repair workers, including wind turbine service technicians, and commercial divers, and signal and track switch repairers	87,190	82,770	94.9	4,420	5.1	12,690	14.6	64,055	73.5
7700	First-line supervisors of production and operating workers	373,560	301,000	80.6	72,560	19.4	44,870	12.0	280,985	75.2

A-19 Workers with High School Diploma or Equivalency: Detailed Occupation, by Sex, Race, and Hispanic Origin, 2006–2010—*Continued*

Census occupation code	Detailed Occupation	Black or African American alone Number	Percent	American Indian and Alaska Native alone Number	Percent	Asian alone Number	Percent	Native Hawaiian and Other Pacific Islander alone Number	Percent	Not Hispanic or Latino, two or more races Number	Percent
7040	Electric motor, power tool, and related repairers	505	4.6	60	0.5	265	2.4	0	0.0	104	1.0
7100	Electrical and electronics repairers, transportation equipment, and industrial and utility	420	7.8	55	1.0	75	1.4	0	0.0	74	1.4
7110	Electronic equipment installers and repairers, motor vehicles	375	6.3	55	0.9	160	2.7	0	0.0	40	0.7
7120	Electronic home entertainment equipment installers and repairers	1,700	8.4	65	0.3	625	3.1	30	0.1	219	1.1
7130	Security and fire alarm systems installers	1,910	9.0	60	0.3	205	1.0	35	0.2	340	1.6
7140	Aircraft mechanics and service technicians	3,575	8.3	275	0.6	1,235	2.9	165	0.4	640	1.5
7150	Automotive body and related repairers	4,425	5.7	465	0.6	1,155	1.5	15	0.0	910	1.2
7160	Automotive glass installers and repairers	520	5.5	30	0.3	95	1.0	0	0.0	155	1.6
7200	Automotive service technicians and mechanics	27,175	7.5	2,105	0.6	8,570	2.4	425	0.1	4,615	1.3
7210	Bus and truck mechanics and diesel engine specialists	10,645	7.6	590	0.4	1,335	0.9	290	0.2	1,535	1.1
7220	Heavy vehicle and mobile equipment service technicians and mechanics	4,680	4.9	855	0.9	640	0.7	175	0.2	810	0.8
7240	Small engine mechanics	745	3.2	80	0.3	65	0.3	40	0.2	204	0.9
7260	Miscellaneous vehicle and mobile equipment mechanics, installers, and repairers	3,000	8.6	230	0.7	390	1.1	40	0.1	465	1.3
7300	Control and valve installers and repairers	960	10.9	40	0.5	35	0.4	0	0.0	125	1.4
7315	Heating, air conditioning, and refrigeration mechanics and installers	8,970	6.1	700	0.5	1,745	1.2	60	0.0	1,465	1.0
7320	Home appliance repairers	1,510	8.3	115	0.6	390	2.1	0	0.0	110	0.6
7330	Industrial and refractory machinery mechanics	11,685	7.0	805	0.5	2,560	1.5	255	0.2	1,605	1.0
7340	Maintenance and repair workers, general	18,825	9.6	1,340	0.7	3,010	1.5	465	0.2	2,075	1.1
7350	Maintenance workers, machinery	1,085	7.0	120	0.8	205	1.3	25	0.2	134	0.9
7360	Millwrights	845	3.6	130	0.6	185	0.8	30	0.1	259	1.1
7410	Electrical power-line installers and repairers	4,220	8.3	215	0.4	290	0.6	70	0.1	585	1.1
7420	Telecommunications line installers and repairers	6,790	11.1	205	0.3	890	1.5	150	0.2	790	1.3
7430	Precision instrument and equipment repairers	960	7.0	35	0.3	560	4.1	20	0.1	114	0.8
7510	Coin, vending, and amusement machine servicers and repairers	1,500	7.7	335	1.7	415	2.1	25	0.1	280	1.4
7540	Locksmiths and safe repairers	485	4.2	15	0.1	155	1.4	0	0.0	130	1.1
7550	Manufactured building and mobile home installers	230	5.6	20	0.5	15	0.4	4	0.1	44	1.1
7560	Riggers	755	14.1	0	0.0	20	0.4	20	0.4	84	1.6
7610	Helpers—installation, maintenance, and repair workers	825	8.7	70	0.7	345	3.6	20	0.2	135	1.4
7630	Other installation, maintenance, and repair workers, including wind turbine service technicians, and commercial divers, and signal and track switch repairers	6,665	7.6	775	0.9	1,575	1.8	215	0.2	1,215	1.4
7700	First-line supervisors of production and operating workers	33,800	9.0	1,750	0.5	8,275	2.2	330	0.1	3,545	0.9

A-19 **Workers with High School Diploma or Equivalency: Detailed Occupation, by Sex, Race, and Hispanic Origin, 2006–2010**—*Continued*

| Census occupation code | Detailed Occupation | Total | High school diploma or equivalency |||||||
| | | | Male || Female || Hispanic or Latino || Not Hispanic or Latino, one race — White alone ||
			Number	Percent	Number	Percent	Number	Percent	Number	Percent
7710	Aircraft structure, surfaces, rigging, and systems assemblers	4,350	2,500	57.5	1,850	42.5	1,020	23.4	2,490	57.2
7720	Electrical, electronics, and electromechanical assemblers	77,945	32,205	41.3	45,740	58.7	12,210	15.7	42,850	55.0
7730	Engine and other machine assemblers	8,440	6,700	79.4	1,740	20.6	715	8.5	6,655	78.9
7740	Structural metal fabricators and fitters	13,075	12,705	97.2	365	2.8	930	7.1	11,065	84.6
7750	Miscellaneous assemblers and fabricators	454,580	269,990	59.4	184,590	40.6	64,300	14.1	291,450	64.1
7800	Bakers	66,685	29,230	43.8	37,455	56.2	15,765	23.6	38,075	57.1
7810	Butchers and other meat, poultry, and fish processing workers	104,625	82,910	79.2	21,715	20.8	26,015	24.9	57,795	55.2
7830	Food and tobacco roasting, baking, and drying machine operators and tenders	4,495	3,030	67.4	1,465	32.6	640	14.2	2,750	61.2
7840	Food batchmakers	35,590	15,385	43.2	20,210	56.8	6,865	19.3	21,580	60.6
7850	Food cooking machine operators and tenders	5,110	3,015	59.0	2,095	41.0	1,095	21.4	2,990	58.5
7855	Food processing workers, all other	54,090	34,595	64.0	19,495	36.0	12,265	22.7	28,565	52.8
7900	Computer control programmers and operators	29,985	27,145	90.5	2,845	9.5	2,275	7.6	24,980	83.3
7920	Extruding and drawing machine setters, operators, and tenders, metal and plastic	6,505	5,595	86.0	910	14.0	430	6.6	5,370	82.6
7930	Forging machine setters, operators, and tenders, metal and plastic	5,005	4,800	95.9	205	4.1	390	7.8	4,210	84.1
7940	Rolling machine setters, operators, and tenders, metal and plastic	6,150	4,530	73.7	1,620	26.3	560	9.1	4,705	76.5
7950	Cutting, punching, and press machine setters, operators, and tenders, metal and plastic	51,355	40,855	79.6	10,500	20.4	4,465	8.7	39,880	77.7
7960	Drilling and boring machine tool setters, operators, and tenders, metal and plastic	2,635	2,310	87.7	325	12.3	340	12.9	2,050	77.8
8000	Grinding, lapping, polishing, and buffing machine tool setters, operators, and tenders, metal and plastic	25,400	22,300	87.8	3,100	12.2	3,370	13.3	18,240	71.8
8010	Lathe and turning machine tool setters, operators, and tenders, metal and plastic	6,865	6,085	88.6	780	11.4	655	9.5	5,730	83.5
8030	Machinists	172,820	165,065	95.5	7,755	4.5	14,870	8.6	141,360	81.8
8040	Metal furnace operators, tenders, pourers, and casters	13,425	12,420	92.5	1,005	7.5	1,135	8.5	10,060	74.9
8060	Model makers and patternmakers, metal and plastic	2,380	2,195	92.2	180	7.6	195	8.2	2,035	85.5
8100	Molders and molding machine setters, operators, and tenders, metal and plastic	23,215	18,770	80.9	4,445	19.1	1,970	8.5	17,660	76.1
8130	Tool and die makers	27,710	26,885	97.0	825	3.0	1,125	4.1	25,100	90.6
8140	Welding, soldering, and brazing workers	281,315	265,455	94.4	15,860	5.6	38,925	13.8	209,785	74.6
8150	Heat treating equipment setters, operators, and tenders, metal and plastic	3,970	3,680	92.7	290	7.3	295	7.4	3,085	77.7

PART A—NATIONAL DATA

A-19 Workers with High School Diploma or Equivalency: Detailed Occupation, by Sex, Race, and Hispanic Origin, 2006–2010—*Continued*

Census occupation code	Detailed Occupation	Black or African American alone Number	Percent	American Indian and Alaska Native alone Number	Percent	Asian alone Number	Percent	Native Hawaiian and Other Pacific Islander alone Number	Percent	Not Hispanic or Latino, two or more races Number	Percent
7710	Aircraft structure, surfaces, rigging, and systems assemblers	430	9.9	15	0.3	310	7.1	0	0.0	80	1.8
7720	Electrical, electronics, and electromechanical assemblers	10,685	13.7	415	0.5	10,830	13.9	80	0.1	875	1.1
7730	Engine and other machine assemblers	645	7.6	25	0.3	325	3.9	20	0.2	55	0.7
7740	Structural metal fabricators and fitters	795	6.1	85	0.7	65	0.5	0	0.0	135	1.0
7750	Miscellaneous assemblers and fabricators	68,035	15.0	2,235	0.5	24,010	5.3	540	0.1	4,010	0.9
7800	Bakers	8,910	13.4	365	0.5	2,620	3.9	240	0.4	715	1.1
7810	Butchers and other meat, poultry, and fish processing workers	15,605	14.9	435	0.4	3,290	3.1	235	0.2	1,255	1.2
7830	Food and tobacco roasting, baking, and drying machine operators and tenders	850	18.9	60	1.3	150	3.3	0	0.0	45	1.0
7840	Food batchmakers	5,085	14.3	230	0.6	1,080	3.0	25	0.1	730	2.1
7850	Food cooking machine operators and tenders	730	14.3	0	0.0	215	4.2	25	0.5	54	1.1
7855	Food processing workers, all other	10,510	19.4	345	0.6	1,940	3.6	55	0.1	410	0.8
7900	Computer control programmers and operators	1,550	5.2	55	0.2	800	2.7	4	0.0	315	1.1
7920	Extruding and drawing machine setters, operators, and tenders, metal and plastic	440	6.8	35	0.5	140	2.2	10	0.2	85	1.3
7930	Forging machine setters, operators, and tenders, metal and plastic	285	5.7	30	0.6	40	0.8	0	0.0	50	1.0
7940	Rolling machine setters, operators, and tenders, metal and plastic	715	11.6	65	1.1	35	0.6	0	0.0	75	1.2
7950	Cutting, punching, and press machine setters, operators, and tenders, metal and plastic	5,615	10.9	285	0.6	750	1.5	10	0.0	350	0.7
7960	Drilling and boring machine tool setters, operators, and tenders, metal and plastic	155	5.9	20	0.8	25	0.9	20	0.8	25	0.9
8000	Grinding, lapping, polishing, and buffing machine tool setters, operators, and tenders, metal and plastic	2,940	11.6	125	0.5	475	1.9	60	0.2	190	0.7
8010	Lathe and turning machine tool setters, operators, and tenders, metal and plastic	330	4.8	15	0.2	65	0.9	0	0.0	69	1.0
8030	Machinists	9,135	5.3	775	0.4	4,765	2.8	285	0.2	1,630	0.9
8040	Metal furnace operators, tenders, pourers, and casters	1,880	14.0	115	0.9	125	0.9	0	0.0	115	0.9
8060	Model makers and patternmakers, metal and plastic	95	4.0	0	0.0	15	0.6	4	0.2	40	1.7
8100	Molders and molding machine setters, operators, and tenders, metal and plastic	2,705	11.7	70	0.3	395	1.7	40	0.2	375	1.6
8130	Tool and die makers	865	3.1	30	0.1	435	1.6	20	0.1	134	0.5
8140	Welding, soldering, and brazing workers	22,085	7.9	2,770	1.0	4,685	1.7	350	0.1	2,715	1.0
8150	Heat treating equipment setters, operators, and tenders, metal and plastic	385	9.7	85	2.1	80	2.0	15	0.4	25	0.6

A-19 Workers with High School Diploma or Equivalency: Detailed Occupation, by Sex, Race, and Hispanic Origin, 2006–2010—*Continued*

Census occupation code	Detailed Occupation	Total	High school diploma or equivalency							
			Male		Female		Hispanic or Latino		Not Hispanic or Latino, one race — White alone	
			Number	Percent	Number	Percent	Number	Percent	Number	Percent
8200	Plating and coating machine setters, operators, and tenders, metal and plastic	8,650	7,685	88.8	960	11.1	1,220	14.1	6,100	70.5
8210	Tool grinders, filers, and sharpeners..........	4,005	3,910	97.6	95	2.4	120	3.0	3,575	89.3
8220	Miscellaneous metal workers and plastic workers, including milling and planing machine setters, and multiple machine tool setters, and layout workers...............	204,055	156,210	76.6	47,845	23.4	30,655	15.0	131,880	64.6
8250	Prepress technicians and workers	15,405	7,530	48.9	7,875	51.1	1,730	11.2	10,915	70.9
8255	Printing press operators...........................	107,780	88,265	81.9	19,515	18.1	13,775	12.8	78,880	73.2
8256	Print binding and finishing workers	15,945	8,645	54.2	7,300	45.8	1,680	10.5	12,405	77.8
8300	Laundry and dry-cleaning workers............	79,805	32,645	40.9	47,160	59.1	17,470	21.9	40,640	50.9
8310	Pressers, textile, garment, and related materials..	20,740	6,890	33.2	13,850	66.8	5,950	28.7	8,385	40.4
8320	Sewing machine operators	82,975	16,960	20.4	66,015	79.6	19,690	23.7	40,285	48.6
8330	Shoe and leather workers and repairers	3,845	2,990	77.8	855	22.2	765	19.9	2,490	64.8
8340	Shoe machine operators and tenders	1,920	710	37.0	1,210	63.0	230	12.0	1,260	65.6
8350	Tailors, dressmakers, and sewers...............	29,350	6,185	21.1	23,165	78.9	5,675	19.3	15,520	52.9
8400	Textile bleaching and dyeing, and cutting machine setters, operators, and tenders...	5,655	3,500	61.9	2,155	38.1	1,045	18.5	3,365	59.5
8410	Textile knitting and weaving machine setters, operators, and tenders.................	5,870	2,310	39.4	3,565	60.7	585	10.0	3,655	62.3
8420	Textile winding, twisting, and drawing out machine setters, operators, and tenders..	7,580	2,955	39.0	4,625	61.0	790	10.4	4,295	56.7
8450	Upholsterers	17,980	14,645	81.5	3,335	18.5	3,950	22.0	11,780	65.5
8460	Miscellaneous textile, apparel, and furnishings workers, except upholsterers	11,265	6,370	56.5	4,890	43.4	1,990	17.7	6,085	54.0
8500	Cabinetmakers and bench carpenters.........	29,520	27,625	93.6	1,895	6.4	3,605	12.2	24,025	81.4
8510	Furniture finishers	7,880	6,350	80.6	1,530	19.4	1,680	21.3	5,305	67.3
8530	Sawing machine setters, operators, and tenders, wood..	18,015	15,955	88.6	2,055	11.4	2,245	12.5	13,590	75.4
8540	Woodworking machine setters, operators, and tenders, except sawing.....................	13,175	10,605	80.5	2,575	19.5	1,850	14.0	9,480	72.0
8550	Miscellaneous woodworkers, including model makers and patternmakers............	12,195	11,200	91.8	995	8.2	1,195	9.8	9,725	79.7
8600	Power plant operators, distributors, and dispatchers..	15,490	14,480	93.5	1,015	6.6	825	5.3	13,090	84.5
8610	Stationary engineers and boiler operators .	39,135	37,980	97.0	1,155	3.0	3,920	10.0	28,915	73.9
8620	Water and wastewater treatment plant and system operators.......................................	33,170	32,050	96.6	1,120	3.4	2,940	8.9	26,215	79.0

A-19 Workers with High School Diploma or Equivalency: Detailed Occupation, by Sex, Race, and Hispanic Origin, 2006–2010—*Continued*

Census occupation code	Detailed Occupation	Black or African American alone Number	Percent	American Indian and Alaska Native alone Number	Percent	Asian alone Number	Percent	Native Hawaiian and Other Pacific Islander alone Number	Percent	Not Hispanic or Latino, two or more races Number	Percent
8200	Plating and coating machine setters, operators, and tenders, metal and plastic	1,015	11.7	40	0.5	200	2.3	4	0.0	69	0.8
8210	Tool grinders, filers, and sharpeners..........	185	4.6	4	0.1	60	1.5	0	0.0	55	1.4
8220	Miscellaneous metal workers and plastic workers, including milling and planing machine setters, and multiple machine tool setters, and layout workers...............	27,910	13.7	1,105	0.5	10,730	5.3	180	0.1	1,595	0.8
8250	Prepress technicians and workers	1,900	12.3	25	0.2	610	4.0	25	0.2	205	1.3
8255	Printing press operators.............................	9,905	9.2	480	0.4	3,075	2.9	155	0.1	1,505	1.4
8256	Print binding and finishing workers	1,135	7.1	65	0.4	460	2.9	10	0.1	190	1.2
8300	Laundry and dry-cleaning workers............	15,190	19.0	580	0.7	4,620	5.8	300	0.4	1,010	1.3
8310	Pressers, textile, garment, and related materials	4,670	22.5	135	0.7	1,390	6.7	35	0.2	175	0.8
8320	Sewing machine operators	12,810	15.4	375	0.5	9,085	10.9	170	0.2	550	0.7
8330	Shoe and leather workers and repairers	180	4.7	0	0.0	295	7.7	0	0.0	115	3.0
8340	Shoe machine operators and tenders	260	13.5	0	0.0	140	7.3	4	0.2	20	1.0
8350	Tailors, dressmakers, and sewers...............	2,230	7.6	35	0.1	5,705	19.4	25	0.1	170	0.6
8400	Textile bleaching and dyeing, and cutting machine setters, operators, and tenders...	865	15.3	70	1.2	235	4.2	15	0.3	54	1.0
8410	Textile knitting and weaving machine setters, operators, and tenders.................	1,220	20.8	140	2.4	190	3.2	0	0.0	80	1.4
8420	Textile winding, twisting, and drawing out machine setters, operators, and tenders	2,240	29.6	0	0.0	225	3.0	0	0.0	30	0.4
8450	Upholsterers...	1,450	8.1	175	1.0	420	2.3	0	0.0	210	1.2
8460	Miscellaneous textile, apparel, and furnishings workers, except upholsterers	2,405	21.3	35	0.3	675	6.0	15	0.1	65	0.6
8500	Cabinetmakers and bench carpenters.........	955	3.2	135	0.5	570	1.9	20	0.1	210	0.7
8510	Furniture finishers	570	7.2	4	0.1	105	1.3	0	0.0	210	2.7
8530	Sawing machine setters, operators, and tenders, wood	1,790	9.9	130	0.7	140	0.8	0	0.0	118	0.7
8540	Woodworking machine setters, operators, and tenders, except sawing.....................	1,380	10.5	120	0.9	110	0.8	20	0.2	210	1.6
8550	Miscellaneous woodworkers, including model makers and patternmakers............	540	4.4	280	2.3	180	1.5	35	0.3	245	2.0
8600	Power plant operators, distributors, and dispatchers..	990	6.4	335	2.2	105	0.7	0	0.0	154	1.0
8610	Stationary engineers and boiler operators .	4,970	12.7	265	0.7	680	1.7	50	0.1	339	0.9
8620	Water and wastewater treatment plant and system operators..	2,910	8.8	530	1.6	165	0.5	25	0.1	384	1.2

A-19 **Workers with High School Diploma or Equivalency: Detailed Occupation, by Sex, Race, and Hispanic Origin, 2006–2010**—*Continued*

Census occupation code	Detailed Occupation	Total	Male Number	Male Percent	Female Number	Female Percent	Hispanic or Latino Number	Hispanic or Latino Percent	Not Hispanic or Latino, one race White alone Number	Not Hispanic or Latino, one race White alone Percent
8630	Miscellaneous plant and system operators	16,275	15,480	95.1	795	4.9	1,535	9.4	12,625	77.6
8640	Chemical processing machine setters, operators, and tenders	20,790	18,495	89.0	2,295	11.0	2,050	9.9	14,900	71.7
8650	Crushing, grinding, polishing, mixing, and blending workers	42,975	39,285	91.4	3,690	8.6	6,850	15.9	29,175	67.9
8710	Cutting workers	33,630	25,290	75.2	8,340	24.8	5,400	16.1	22,730	67.6
8720	Extruding, forming, pressing, and compacting machine setters, operators, and tenders	17,135	13,845	80.8	3,290	19.2	1,480	8.6	12,950	75.6
8730	Furnace, kiln, oven, drier, and kettle operators and tenders	5,675	5,000	88.1	675	11.9	315	5.6	4,610	81.2
8740	Inspectors, testers, sorters, samplers, and weighers	281,865	159,045	56.4	122,825	43.6	38,860	13.8	191,930	68.1
8750	Jewelers and precious stone and metal workers	12,275	8,995	73.3	3,285	26.8	3,265	26.6	6,160	50.2
8760	Medical, dental, and ophthalmic laboratory technicians	27,625	13,190	47.7	14,435	52.3	3,975	14.4	19,520	70.7
8800	Packaging and filling machine operators and tenders	108,490	47,545	43.8	60,950	56.2	28,070	25.9	50,780	46.8
8810	Painting workers	72,900	64,365	88.3	8,535	11.7	14,565	20.0	48,095	66.0
8830	Photographic process workers and processing machine operators	20,945	6,970	33.3	13,975	66.7	3,145	15.0	13,390	63.9
8850	Adhesive bonding machine operators and tenders	6,230	3,400	54.6	2,830	45.4	950	15.2	3,920	62.9
8860	Cleaning, washing, and metal pickling equipment operators and tenders	4,285	3,275	76.4	1,010	23.6	865	20.2	2,655	62.0
8910	Etchers and engravers	4,145	2,595	62.6	1,550	37.4	435	10.5	3,315	80.0
8920	Molders, shapers, and casters, except metal and plastic	13,160	11,840	90.0	1,320	10.0	2,295	17.4	9,420	71.6
8930	Paper goods machine setters, operators, and tenders	18,190	13,495	74.2	4,695	25.8	2,565	14.1	11,960	65.8
8940	Tire builders	8,430	7,685	91.2	745	8.8	495	5.9	5,920	70.2
8950	Helpers—production workers	18,950	14,730	77.7	4,220	22.3	4,790	25.3	10,100	53.3
8965	Other production workers, including semiconductor processors and cooling and freezing equipment operators	496,780	346,510	69.8	150,265	30.2	78,085	15.7	318,600	64.1
9000	Supervisors of transportation and material moving workers	83,140	67,655	81.4	15,485	18.6	11,705	14.1	56,750	68.3
9030	Aircraft pilots and flight engineers	6,230	6,085	97.7	145	2.3	280	4.5	5,480	88.0
9040	Air traffic controllers and airfield operations specialists	4,935	3,970	80.4	965	19.6	630	12.8	3,500	70.9
9050	Flight attendants	13,180	2,540	19.3	10,640	80.7	1,395	10.6	9,350	70.9
9110	Ambulance drivers and attendants, except emergency medical technicians	4,900	3,705	75.6	1,195	24.4	660	13.5	2,720	55.5

A-19 Workers with High School Diploma or Equivalency: Detailed Occupation, by Sex, Race, and Hispanic Origin, 2006–2010—*Continued*

Census occupation code	Detailed Occupation	High school diploma or equivalency									
		Not Hispanic or Latino, one race								Not Hispanic or Latino, two or more races	
		Black or African American alone		American Indian and Alaska Native alone		Asian alone		Native Hawaiian and Other Pacific Islander alone			
		Number	Percent	Number	Percent	Number	Percent	Number	Percent	Number	Percent
8630	Miscellaneous plant and system operators	1,605	9.9	130	0.8	85	0.5	70	0.4	220	1.4
8640	Chemical processing machine setters, operators, and tenders	3,310	15.9	30	0.1	265	1.3	50	0.2	185	0.9
8650	Crushing, grinding, polishing, mixing, and blending workers	5,260	12.2	335	0.8	925	2.2	15	0.0	415	1.0
8710	Cutting workers	4,175	12.4	255	0.8	645	1.9	70	0.2	355	1.1
8720	Extruding, forming, pressing, and compacting machine setters, operators, and tenders	2,300	13.4	95	0.6	220	1.3	4	0.0	85	0.5
8730	Furnace, kiln, oven, drier, and kettle operators and tenders	610	10.7	50	0.9	10	0.2	10	0.2	70	1.2
8740	Inspectors, testers, sorters, samplers, and weighers	35,615	12.6	1,420	0.5	10,350	3.7	460	0.2	3,225	1.1
8750	Jewelers and precious stone and metal workers	340	2.8	935	7.6	1,445	11.8	0	0.0	130	1.1
8760	Medical, dental, and ophthalmic laboratory technicians	1,545	5.6	170	0.6	2,065	7.5	60	0.2	295	1.1
8800	Packaging and filling machine operators and tenders	23,245	21.4	560	0.5	4,275	3.9	295	0.3	1,265	1.2
8810	Painting workers	7,120	9.8	400	0.5	1,540	2.1	30	0.0	1,155	1.6
8830	Photographic process workers and processing machine operators	2,950	14.1	120	0.6	790	3.8	35	0.2	515	2.5
8850	Adhesive bonding machine operators and tenders	1,020	16.4	10	0.2	225	3.6	30	0.5	80	1.3
8860	Cleaning, washing, and metal pickling equipment operators and tenders	655	15.3	0	0.0	35	0.8	60	1.4	14	0.3
8910	Etchers and engravers	335	8.1	20	0.5	35	0.8	0	0.0	0	0.0
8920	Molders, shapers, and casters, except metal and plastic	955	7.3	50	0.4	315	2.4	10	0.1	120	0.9
8930	Paper goods machine setters, operators, and tenders	2,865	15.8	200	1.1	390	2.1	35	0.2	170	0.9
8940	Tire builders	1,655	19.6	70	0.8	125	1.5	55	0.7	115	1.4
8950	Helpers—production workers	2,495	13.2	175	0.9	920	4.9	65	0.3	409	2.2
8965	Other production workers, including semiconductor processors and cooling and freezing equipment operators	75,575	15.2	2,860	0.6	16,270	3.3	635	0.1	4,760	1.0
9000	Supervisors of transportation and material moving workers	10,885	13.1	585	0.7	1,580	1.9	435	0.5	1,195	1.4
9030	Aircraft pilots and flight engineers	240	3.9	30	0.5	110	1.8	35	0.6	59	0.9
9040	Air traffic controllers and airfield operations specialists	660	13.4	0	0.0	100	2.0	20	0.4	25	0.5
9050	Flight attendants	1,445	11.0	110	0.8	325	2.5	190	1.4	360	2.7
9110	Ambulance drivers and attendants, except emergency medical technicians	1,270	25.9	160	3.3	70	1.4	0	0.0	19	0.4

A-19 **Workers with High School Diploma or Equivalency: Detailed Occupation, by Sex, Race, and Hispanic Origin, 2006–2010**—*Continued*

Census occupation code	Detailed Occupation	Total	Male Number	Male Percent	Female Number	Female Percent	Hispanic or Latino Number	Hispanic or Latino Percent	Not Hispanic or Latino, one race White alone Number	Not Hispanic or Latino, one race White alone Percent
9120	Bus drivers	255,160	121,915	47.8	133,245	52.2	27,650	10.8	153,755	60.3
9130	Driver/sales workers and truck drivers	1,490,730	1,424,740	95.6	65,990	4.4	205,840	13.8	1,038,695	69.7
9140	Taxi drivers and chauffeurs	117,310	98,205	83.7	19,105	16.3	18,170	15.5	54,650	46.6
9150	Motor vehicle operators, all other	22,080	19,610	88.8	2,470	11.2	2,905	13.2	15,540	70.4
9200	Locomotive engineers and operators	20,770	19,895	95.8	875	4.2	1,450	7.0	16,180	77.9
9230	Railroad brake, signal, and switch operators	3,665	3,500	95.5	170	4.6	565	15.4	2,615	71.4
9240	Railroad conductors and yardmasters	18,615	17,780	95.5	835	4.5	975	5.2	14,915	80.1
9260	Subway, streetcar, and other rail transportation workers	4,180	3,710	88.8	475	11.4	285	6.8	2,860	68.4
9300	Sailors and marine oilers, and ship engineers	10,320	9,965	96.6	355	3.4	970	9.4	7,220	70.0
9310	Ship and boat captains and operators	13,640	13,330	97.7	310	2.3	615	4.5	11,930	87.5
9350	Parking lot attendants	26,200	22,705	86.7	3,495	13.3	6,675	25.5	10,865	41.5
9360	Automotive and watercraft service attendants	49,045	37,685	76.8	11,355	23.2	5,325	10.9	34,855	71.1
9410	Transportation inspectors	16,990	14,325	84.3	2,665	15.7	2,755	16.2	12,135	71.4
9415	Transportation attendants, except flight attendants	14,525	4,240	29.2	10,285	70.8	2,075	14.3	6,460	44.5
9420	Miscellaneous transportation workers, including bridge and lock tenders and traffic technicians	8,050	6,930	86.1	1,120	13.9	995	12.4	5,185	64.4
9510	Crane and tower operators	35,560	34,760	97.8	800	2.2	2,845	8.0	27,680	77.8
9520	Dredge, excavating, and loading machine operators	24,395	24,100	98.8	295	1.2	1,845	7.6	21,235	87.0
9560	Conveyor operators and tenders, and hoist and winch operators	6,375	5,720	89.7	650	10.2	580	9.1	4,865	76.3
9600	Industrial truck and tractor operators	260,695	237,955	91.3	22,740	8.7	47,665	18.3	144,135	55.3
9610	Cleaners of vehicles and equipment	135,065	115,620	85.6	19,445	14.4	34,275	25.4	66,950	49.6
9620	Laborers and freight, stock, and material movers, hand	878,595	718,820	81.8	159,775	18.2	137,985	15.7	562,290	64.0
9630	Machine feeders and offbearers	15,680	8,125	51.8	7,555	48.2	2,070	13.2	10,190	65.0
9640	Packers and packagers, hand	165,115	69,795	42.3	95,320	57.7	50,390	30.5	74,665	45.2
9650	Pumping station operators	10,615	10,365	97.6	250	2.4	905	8.5	9,000	84.8
9720	Refuse and recyclable material collectors	39,670	36,510	92.0	3,160	8.0	5,695	14.4	22,450	56.6
9750	Miscellaneous material moving workers, including mine shuttle car operators, and tank car, truck, and ship loaders	26,860	23,335	86.9	3,525	13.1	3,350	12.5	17,190	64.0

A-19 Workers with High School Diploma or Equivalency: Detailed Occupation, by Sex, Race, and Hispanic Origin, 2006–2010—Continued

Census occupation code	Detailed Occupation	Black or African American alone Number	Percent	American Indian and Alaska Native alone Number	Percent	Asian alone Number	Percent	Native Hawaiian and Other Pacific Islander alone Number	Percent	Not Hispanic or Latino, two or more races Number	Percent
9120	Bus drivers	65,115	25.5	2,360	0.9	2,940	1.2	635	0.2	2,705	1.1
9130	Driver/sales workers and truck drivers	200,980	13.5	8,565	0.6	18,140	1.2	2,635	0.2	15,865	1.1
9140	Taxi drivers and chauffeurs	29,560	25.2	965	0.8	11,865	10.1	200	0.2	1,900	1.6
9150	Motor vehicle operators, all other	3,200	14.5	140	0.6	140	0.6	30	0.1	130	0.6
9200	Locomotive engineers and operators	2,520	12.1	325	1.6	150	0.7	0	0.0	145	0.7
9230	Railroad brake, signal, and switch operators	445	12.1	10	0.3	0	0.0	0	0.0	30	0.8
9240	Railroad conductors and yardmasters	2,225	12.0	150	0.8	100	0.5	40	0.2	205	1.1
9260	Subway, streetcar, and other rail transportation workers	840	20.1	35	0.8	80	1.9	15	0.4	70	1.7
9300	Sailors and marine oilers, and ship engineers	1,715	16.6	60	0.6	70	0.7	20	0.2	260	2.5
9310	Ship and boat captains and operators	620	4.5	215	1.6	130	1.0	20	0.1	110	0.8
9350	Parking lot attendants	6,910	26.4	190	0.7	910	3.5	160	0.6	490	1.9
9360	Automotive and watercraft service attendants	5,180	10.6	770	1.6	2,170	4.4	30	0.1	715	1.5
9410	Transportation inspectors	1,650	9.7	115	0.7	270	1.6	0	0.0	60	0.4
9415	Transportation attendants, except flight attendants	5,295	36.5	85	0.6	370	2.5	40	0.3	205	1.4
9420	Miscellaneous transportation workers, including bridge and lock tenders and traffic technicians	1,145	14.2	115	1.4	225	2.8	200	2.5	185	2.3
9510	Crane and tower operators	4,295	12.1	105	0.3	80	0.2	30	0.1	530	1.5
9520	Dredge, excavating, and loading machine operators	900	3.7	155	0.6	10	0.0	0	0.0	255	1.0
9560	Conveyor operators and tenders, and hoist and winch operators	700	11.0	65	1.0	85	1.3	50	0.8	34	0.5
9600	Industrial truck and tractor operators	60,590	23.2	1,345	0.5	3,355	1.3	835	0.3	2,770	1.1
9610	Cleaners of vehicles and equipment	27,765	20.6	815	0.6	2,740	2.0	555	0.4	1,965	1.5
9620	Laborers and freight, stock, and material movers, hand	141,520	16.1	6,845	0.8	15,745	1.8	2,835	0.3	11,380	1.3
9630	Machine feeders and offbearers	2,825	18.0	70	0.4	295	1.9	70	0.4	165	1.1
9640	Packers and packagers, hand	29,420	17.8	665	0.4	7,580	4.6	475	0.3	1,925	1.2
9650	Pumping station operators	380	3.6	105	1.0	50	0.5	4	0.0	170	1.6
9720	Refuse and recyclable material collectors	10,065	25.4	390	1.0	290	0.7	125	0.3	660	1.7
9750	Miscellaneous material moving workers, including mine shuttle car operators, and tank car, truck, and ship loaders	5,470	20.4	135	0.5	285	1.1	105	0.4	324	1.2

A-20 **Workers with Some College or Associate's Degree: Detailed Occupation, by Sex, Race, and Hispanic Origin, 2006–2010**

Census occupation code	Detailed Occupation	Total	Some college or associate's degree						Not Hispanic or Latino, one race	
			Male		Female		Hispanic or Latino		White alone	
			Number	Percent	Number	Percent	Number	Percent	Number	Percent
	Total, all occupations	43,914,705	21,388,890	48.7	22,525,820	51.3	5,037,390	11.5	30,979,895	70.5
0010	Chief executives and legislators	252,560	188,840	74.8	63,720	25.2	14,305	5.7	219,810	87.0
0020	General and operations managers	303,405	211,875	69.8	91,535	30.2	24,325	8.0	247,525	81.6
0040	Advertising and promotions managers	10,790	4,910	45.5	5,880	54.5	920	8.5	9,030	83.7
0050	Marketing and sales managers	198,840	108,300	54.5	90,540	45.5	16,845	8.5	161,020	81.0
0060	Public relations and fundraising managers	10,440	4,100	39.3	6,340	60.7	810	7.8	8,755	83.9
0100	Administrative services managers	43,375	27,565	63.6	15,805	36.4	4,100	9.5	32,865	75.8
0110	Computer and information systems managers	113,535	79,580	70.1	33,955	29.9	7,355	6.5	93,540	82.4
0120	Financial managers	295,130	91,185	30.9	203,945	69.1	35,190	11.9	216,675	73.4
0135	Compensation and benefits managers	8,025	790	9.8	7,235	90.2	545	6.8	6,595	82.2
0136	Human resources managers	91,480	33,485	36.6	57,990	63.4	12,305	13.5	65,500	71.6
0137	Training and development managers	11,795	5,855	49.6	5,935	50.3	1,000	8.5	8,970	76.0
0140	Industrial production managers	72,380	60,330	83.4	12,050	16.6	6,085	8.4	61,035	84.3
0150	Purchasing managers	55,850	27,650	49.5	28,195	50.5	3,990	7.1	43,990	78.8
0160	Transportation, storage, and distribution managers	79,345	65,000	81.9	14,345	18.1	8,050	10.1	59,825	75.4
0205	Farmers, ranchers, and other agricultural managers	182,855	152,295	83.3	30,560	16.7	4,140	2.3	173,460	94.9
0220	Construction managers	272,575	251,430	92.2	21,145	7.8	21,745	8.0	234,180	85.9
0230	Education administrators	123,855	29,550	23.9	94,305	76.1	12,075	9.7	85,290	68.9
0300	Architectural and engineering managers	17,305	16,560	95.7	745	4.3	950	5.5	15,055	87.0
0310	Food service managers	333,110	183,145	55.0	149,965	45.0	38,660	11.6	235,655	70.7
0330	Gaming managers	7,410	4,660	62.9	2,750	37.1	470	6.3	5,495	74.2
0340	Lodging managers	48,520	22,755	46.9	25,765	53.1	5,255	10.8	33,370	68.8
0350	Medical and health services managers	150,225	33,305	22.2	116,920	77.8	13,955	9.3	110,750	73.7
0360	Natural sciences managers	1,305	755	57.9	550	42.1	125	9.6	985	75.5
0410	Property, real estate, and community association managers	191,020	79,340	41.5	111,680	58.5	21,715	11.4	140,810	73.7
0410	Social and community service managers	68,080	19,970	29.3	48,110	70.7	6,325	9.3	48,055	70.6
0425	Emergency management directors	895	540	60.3	355	39.7	80	8.9	760	84.9
0430	Miscellaneous managers, including funeral service managers and postmasters and mail superintendents	864,065	541,855	62.7	322,210	37.3	72,850	8.4	681,910	78.9
0500	Agents and business managers of artists, performers, and athletes	12,690	6,800	53.6	5,890	46.4	1,725	13.6	8,540	67.3
0510	Buyers and purchasing agents, farm products	3,240	2,380	73.5	860	26.5	290	9.0	2,655	81.9
0520	Wholesale and retail buyers, except farm products	82,005	38,510	47.0	43,495	53.0	8,245	10.1	63,620	77.6
0530	Purchasing agents, except wholesale, retail, and farm products	96,630	41,215	42.7	55,415	57.3	8,530	8.8	75,725	78.4
0540	Claims adjusters, appraisers, examiners, and investigators	101,535	29,720	29.3	71,815	70.7	9,820	9.7	68,570	67.5
0565	Compliance officers	51,705	27,405	53.0	24,300	47.0	6,300	12.2	36,230	70.1
0600	Cost estimators	50,465	43,740	86.7	6,725	13.3	3,555	7.0	44,785	88.7
0630	Human resources workers	187,360	49,110	26.2	138,250	73.8	23,680	12.6	122,870	65.6
0640	Compensation, benefits, and job analysis specialists	35,980	4,335	12.0	31,645	88.0	3,775	10.5	25,465	70.8

PART A—NATIONAL DATA

A-20 Workers with Some College or Associate's Degree: Detailed Occupation, by Sex, Race, and Hispanic Origin, 2006–2010—Continued

Census occupation code	Detailed Occupation	Black or African American alone Number	Black or African American alone Percent	American Indian and Alaska Native alone Number	American Indian and Alaska Native alone Percent	Asian alone Number	Asian alone Percent	Native Hawaiian and Other Pacific Islander alone Number	Native Hawaiian and Other Pacific Islander alone Percent	Not Hispanic or Latino, two or more races Number	Not Hispanic or Latino, two or more races Percent
	Total, all occupations................................	5,321,210	12.1	279,390	0.6	1,502,610	3.4	77,230	0.2	716,980	1.6
0010	Chief executives and legislators	8,280	3.3	1,280	0.5	5,585	2.2	180	0.1	3,120	1.2
0020	General and operations managers	18,165	6.0	1,695	0.6	7,080	2.3	410	0.1	4,205	1.4
0040	Advertising and promotions managers	380	3.5	15	0.1	245	2.3	25	0.2	180	1.7
0050	Marketing and sales managers	11,945	6.0	930	0.5	4,780	2.4	170	0.1	3,150	1.6
0060	Public relations and fundraising managers...	560	5.4	70	0.7	95	0.9	0	0.0	155	1.5
0100	Administrative services managers.................	4,370	10.1	375	0.9	940	2.2	115	0.3	605	1.4
0110	Computer and information systems managers..	7,330	6.5	500	0.4	3,405	3.0	30	0.0	1,370	1.2
0120	Financial managers..	28,440	9.6	1,375	0.5	8,795	3.0	405	0.1	4,240	1.4
0135	Compensation and benefits managers...........	690	8.6	35	0.4	90	1.1	0	0.0	70	0.9
0136	Human resources managers...........................	8,975	9.8	430	0.5	2,985	3.3	135	0.1	1,145	1.3
0137	Training and development managers	1,175	10.0	50	0.4	290	2.5	80	0.7	230	1.9
0140	Industrial production managers....................	2,910	4.0	240	0.3	1,260	1.7	65	0.1	780	1.1
0150	Purchasing managers	4,960	8.9	505	0.9	1,435	2.6	55	0.1	905	1.6
0160	Transportation, storage, and distribution managers...	7,730	9.7	495	0.6	2,190	2.8	190	0.2	860	1.1
0205	Farmers, ranchers, and other agricultural managers...	875	0.5	890	0.5	1,740	1.0	100	0.1	1,654	0.9
0220	Construction managers	8,100	3.0	1,395	0.5	3,480	1.3	285	0.1	3,385	1.2
0230	Education administrators	20,755	16.8	1,335	1.1	2,320	1.9	160	0.1	1,920	1.6
0300	Architectural and engineering managers	730	4.2	40	0.2	340	2.0	10	0.1	185	1.1
0310	Food service managers...................................	29,130	8.7	1,705	0.5	21,910	6.6	505	0.2	5,555	1.7
0330	Gaming managers	560	7.6	470	6.3	200	2.7	20	0.3	190	2.6
0340	Lodging managers	4,280	8.8	440	0.9	4,155	8.6	195	0.4	825	1.7
0350	Medical and health services managers	19,155	12.8	865	0.6	3,165	2.1	245	0.2	2,090	1.4
0360	Natural sciences managers	70	5.4	4	0.3	105	8.0	0	0.0	20	1.5
0410	Property, real estate, and community association managers	19,045	10.0	1,545	0.8	4,185	2.2	295	0.2	3,430	1.8
0410	Social and community service managers	10,380	15.2	895	1.3	1,235	1.8	85	0.1	1,105	1.6
0425	Emergency management directors	45	5.0	10	1.1	0	0.0	0	0.0	0	0.0
0430	Miscellaneous managers, including funeral service managers and postmasters and mail superintendents	70,405	8.1	4,750	0.5	20,420	2.4	1,405	0.2	12,330	1.4
0500	Agents and business managers of artists, performers, and athletes.............................	1,795	14.1	40	0.3	385	3.0	4	0.0	200	1.6
0510	Buyers and purchasing agents, farm products	135	4.2	30	0.9	135	4.2	0	0.0	0	0.0
0520	Wholesale and retail buyers, except farm products	5,470	6.7	220	0.3	2,925	3.6	205	0.2	1,320	1.6
0530	Purchasing agents, except wholesale, retail, and farm products	8,350	8.6	505	0.5	1,985	2.1	190	0.2	1,340	1.4
0540	Claims adjusters, appraisers, examiners, and investigators	18,410	18.1	400	0.4	2,730	2.7	85	0.1	1,525	1.5
0565	Compliance officers..	6,160	11.9	525	1.0	1,575	3.0	160	0.3	755	1.5
0600	Cost estimators	680	1.3	195	0.4	580	1.1	15	0.0	655	1.3
0630	Human resources workers..............................	30,100	16.1	1,790	1.0	5,205	2.8	465	0.2	3,250	1.7
0640	Compensation, benefits, and job analysis specialists...	5,425	15.1	210	0.6	595	1.7	80	0.2	430	1.2

A-20 **Workers with Some College or Associate's Degree: Detailed Occupation, by Sex, Race, and Hispanic Origin, 2006–2010**—*Continued*

Census occupation code	Detailed Occupation	Total	Some college or associate's degree					Not Hispanic or Latino, one race	
			Male		Female		Hispanic or Latino		White alone	
			Number	Percent	Number	Percent	Number	Percent	Number	Percent
0650	Training and development specialists	42,480	19,735	46.5	22,745	53.5	3,750	8.8	29,480	69.4
0700	Logisticians	27,080	17,320	64.0	9,760	36.0	2,575	9.5	17,790	65.7
0710	Management analysts	112,075	57,405	51.2	54,670	48.8	7,920	7.1	88,860	79.3
0725	Meeting, convention, and event planners	15,825	3,790	23.9	12,035	76.1	1,870	11.8	11,075	70.0
0726	Fundraisers	14,625	4,310	29.5	10,315	70.5	1,100	7.5	11,215	76.7
0735	Market research analysts and marketing specialists	30,840	13,120	42.5	17,720	57.5	3,495	11.3	23,100	74.9
0740	Business operations specialists, all other	73,775	24,180	32.8	49,595	67.2	8,365	11.3	49,460	67.0
0800	Accountants and auditors	373,220	71,830	19.2	301,390	80.8	33,285	8.9	274,405	73.5
0810	Appraisers and assessors of real estate	40,045	23,690	59.2	16,350	40.8	2,650	6.6	34,350	85.8
0820	Budget analysts	12,375	2,640	21.3	9,730	78.6	1,055	8.5	8,270	66.8
0830	Credit analysts	7,860	2,100	26.7	5,765	73.3	1,080	13.7	5,150	65.5
0840	Financial analysts	8,950	4,260	47.6	4,690	52.4	670	7.5	6,395	71.5
0850	Personal financial advisors	56,505	29,645	52.5	26,860	47.5	6,205	11.0	41,060	72.7
0860	Insurance underwriters	30,310	5,005	16.5	25,305	83.5	2,610	8.6	21,930	72.4
0900	Financial examiners	1,785	495	27.7	1,290	72.3	240	13.4	1,205	67.5
0910	Credit counselors and loan officers	127,695	45,880	35.9	81,815	64.1	18,320	14.3	86,915	68.1
0930	Tax examiners and collectors, and revenue agents	20,560	5,675	27.6	14,880	72.4	2,790	13.6	12,100	58.9
0940	Tax preparers	30,910	7,910	25.6	23,000	74.4	4,490	14.5	19,425	62.8
0950	Financial specialists, all other	18,625	6,175	33.2	12,450	66.8	2,585	13.9	12,120	65.1
1005	Computer and information research scientists	1,720	975	56.7	750	43.6	170	9.9	1,235	71.8
1006	Computer systems analysts	111,630	68,325	61.2	43,305	38.8	8,520	7.6	82,930	74.3
1007	Information security analysts	13,820	9,945	72.0	3,875	28.0	1,060	7.7	10,385	75.1
1010	Computer programmers	123,650	95,800	77.5	27,850	22.5	7,105	5.7	101,420	82.0
1020	Software developers, applications and systems software	121,230	92,535	76.3	28,700	23.7	7,040	5.8	96,965	80.0
1030	Web developers	45,135	31,320	69.4	13,815	30.6	3,585	7.9	35,525	78.7
1050	Computer support specialists	227,955	164,485	72.2	63,470	27.8	20,605	9.0	166,230	72.9
1060	Database administrators	28,205	16,710	59.2	11,490	40.7	1,955	6.9	22,410	79.5
1105	Network and computer systems administrators	107,265	87,340	81.4	19,920	18.6	8,225	7.7	82,595	77.0
1106	Computer network architects	39,550	36,070	91.2	3,480	8.8	2,515	6.4	30,785	77.8
1107	Computer occupations, all other	103,005	79,420	77.1	23,585	22.9	9,400	9.1	74,455	72.3
1200	Actuaries	695	250	36.0	450	64.7	20	2.9	615	88.5
1220	Operations research analysts	28,775	12,375	43.0	16,405	57.0	2,025	7.0	20,995	73.0
1240	Miscellaneous mathematical science occupations, including mathematicians and statisticians	3,605	1,470	40.8	2,135	59.2	260	7.2	2,795	77.5
1300	Architects, except naval	17,635	13,855	78.6	3,780	21.4	2,025	11.5	14,265	80.9
1310	Surveyors, cartographers, and photogrammetrists	8,830	6,840	77.5	1,990	22.5	640	7.2	7,460	84.5
1320	Aerospace engineers	18,610	16,695	89.7	1,915	10.3	1,350	7.3	14,955	80.4
1340	Biomedical and agricultural engineers	2,970	2,715	91.4	255	8.6	135	4.5	2,525	85.0
1350	Chemical engineers	4,850	4,480	92.4	370	7.6	440	9.1	4,035	83.2
1360	Civil engineers	36,240	32,640	90.1	3,595	9.9	2,695	7.4	29,395	81.1
1400	Computer hardware engineers	13,970	12,080	86.5	1,890	13.5	1,290	9.2	10,510	75.2
1410	Electrical and electronics engineers	41,260	37,765	91.5	3,495	8.5	2,915	7.1	33,350	80.8
1420	Environmental engineers	2,685	2,515	93.7	170	6.3	100	3.7	2,110	78.6
1430	Industrial engineers, including health and safety	39,035	33,295	85.3	5,735	14.7	2,275	5.8	33,560	86.0
1440	Marine engineers and naval architects	2,170	1,995	91.9	175	8.1	70	3.2	1,755	80.9
1450	Materials engineers	6,970	6,430	92.3	540	7.7	345	4.9	5,810	83.4
1460	Mechanical engineers	47,395	45,600	96.2	1,795	3.8	2,715	5.7	40,735	85.9

A-20 Workers with Some College or Associate's Degree: Detailed Occupation, by Sex, Race, and Hispanic Origin, 2006–2010—Continued

Census occupation code	Detailed Occupation	Some college or associate's degree									
		Not Hispanic or Latino, one race								Not Hispanic or Latino, two or more races	
		Black or African American alone		American Indian and Alaska Native alone		Asian alone		Native Hawaiian and Other Pacific Islander alone			
		Number	Percent	Number	Percent	Number	Percent	Number	Percent	Number	Percent
0650	Training and development specialists	6,805	16.0	320	0.8	945	2.2	50	0.1	1,125	2.6
0700	Logisticians	4,810	17.8	200	0.7	1,010	3.7	175	0.6	520	1.9
0710	Management analysts	10,155	9.1	615	0.5	2,905	2.6	165	0.1	1,455	1.3
0725	Meeting, convention, and event planners	1,890	11.9	55	0.3	500	3.2	0	0.0	440	2.8
0726	Fundraisers	1,495	10.2	25	0.2	350	2.4	0	0.0	435	3.0
0735	Market research analysts and marketing specialists	2,240	7.3	60	0.2	1,430	4.6	20	0.1	505	1.6
0740	Business operations specialists, all other	11,160	15.1	335	0.5	3,035	4.1	35	0.0	1,390	1.9
0800	Accountants and auditors	37,175	10.0	2,320	0.6	20,440	5.5	640	0.2	4,950	1.3
0810	Appraisers and assessors of real estate	1,900	4.7	205	0.5	520	1.3	10	0.0	405	1.0
0820	Budget analysts	2,035	16.4	85	0.7	455	3.7	65	0.5	410	3.3
0830	Credit analysts	1,265	16.1	35	0.4	270	3.4	10	0.1	50	0.6
0840	Financial analysts	1,280	14.3	35	0.4	400	4.5	0	0.0	175	2.0
0850	Personal financial advisors	6,235	11.0	275	0.5	1,900	3.4	65	0.1	775	1.4
0860	Insurance underwriters	4,365	14.4	45	0.1	955	3.2	20	0.1	385	1.3
0900	Financial examiners	270	15.1	0	0.0	75	4.2	0	0.0	0	0.0
0910	Credit counselors and loan officers	14,600	11.4	285	0.2	4,880	3.8	405	0.3	2,290	1.8
0930	Tax examiners and collectors, and revenue agents	4,635	22.5	70	0.3	540	2.6	55	0.3	360	1.8
0940	Tax preparers	5,770	18.7	140	0.5	680	2.2	60	0.2	345	1.1
0950	Financial specialists, all other	2,890	15.5	105	0.6	615	3.3	35	0.2	280	1.5
1005	Computer and information research scientists	170	9.9	0	0.0	150	8.7	0	0.0	0	0.0
1006	Computer systems analysts	12,645	11.3	420	0.4	4,895	4.4	55	0.0	2,160	1.9
1007	Information security analysts	1,610	11.6	45	0.3	370	2.7	25	0.2	325	2.4
1010	Computer programmers	7,050	5.7	300	0.2	5,390	4.4	220	0.2	2,165	1.8
1020	Software developers, applications and systems software	8,400	6.9	425	0.4	5,985	4.9	175	0.1	2,240	1.8
1030	Web developers	2,335	5.2	180	0.4	2,160	4.8	80	0.2	1,270	2.8
1050	Computer support specialists	25,440	11.2	850	0.4	10,245	4.5	405	0.2	4,180	1.8
1060	Database administrators	2,180	7.7	60	0.2	1,180	4.2	4	0.0	410	1.5
1105	Network and computer systems administrators	9,410	8.8	610	0.6	4,410	4.1	175	0.2	1,840	1.7
1106	Computer network architects	3,520	8.9	180	0.5	1,645	4.2	95	0.2	810	2.0
1107	Computer occupations, all other	11,335	11.0	645	0.6	5,025	4.9	105	0.1	2,035	2.0
1200	Actuaries	15	2.2	0	0.0	45	6.5	0	0.0	4	0.6
1220	Operations research analysts	4,490	15.6	55	0.2	715	2.5	105	0.4	390	1.4
1240	Miscellaneous mathematical science occupations, including mathematicians and statisticians	330	9.2	75	2.1	105	2.9	0	0.0	40	1.1
1300	Architects, except naval	720	4.1	70	0.4	425	2.4	50	0.3	85	0.5
1310	Surveyors, cartographers, and photogrammetrists	540	6.1	50	0.6	95	1.1	0	0.0	44	0.5
1320	Aerospace engineers	670	3.6	125	0.7	1,285	6.9	0	0.0	230	1.2
1340	Biomedical and agricultural engineers	195	6.6	0	0.0	120	4.0	0	0.0	0	0.0
1350	Chemical engineers	250	5.2	15	0.3	100	2.1	0	0.0	10	0.2
1360	Civil engineers	2,120	5.8	175	0.5	1,310	3.6	60	0.2	475	1.3
1400	Computer hardware engineers	1,125	8.1	155	1.1	630	4.5	20	0.1	245	1.8
1410	Electrical and electronics engineers	2,560	6.2	205	0.5	1,625	3.9	30	0.1	575	1.4
1420	Environmental engineers	330	12.3	30	1.1	60	2.2	0	0.0	55	2.0
1430	Industrial engineers, including health and safety	1,315	3.4	115	0.3	1,080	2.8	170	0.4	520	1.3
1440	Marine engineers and naval architects	190	8.8	30	1.4	115	5.3	0	0.0	10	0.5
1450	Materials engineers	400	5.7	0	0.0	325	4.7	15	0.2	75	1.1
1460	Mechanical engineers	1,950	4.1	125	0.3	1,185	2.5	30	0.1	655	1.4

A-20 **Workers with Some College or Associate's Degree: Detailed Occupation, by Sex, Race, and Hispanic Origin, 2006–2010**—*Continued*

Census occupation code	Detailed Occupation	Total	Male Number	Male Percent	Female Number	Female Percent	Hispanic or Latino Number	Hispanic or Latino Percent	Not Hispanic or Latino, one race White alone Number	Not Hispanic or Latino, one race White alone Percent
1520	Petroleum, mining and geological engineers, including mining safety engineers	3,555	3,200	90.0	360	10.1	300	8.4	2,945	82.8
1530	Miscellaneous engineers, including nuclear engineers	69,310	63,380	91.4	5,930	8.6	4,325	6.2	57,520	83.0
1540	Drafters	118,710	98,050	82.6	20,660	17.4	10,555	8.9	97,010	81.7
1550	Engineering technicians, except drafters	230,200	192,635	83.7	37,565	16.3	20,460	8.9	170,020	73.9
1560	Surveying and mapping technicians	43,995	40,335	91.7	3,660	8.3	2,805	6.4	38,355	87.2
1600	Agricultural and food scientists	5,880	4,665	79.3	1,215	20.7	305	5.2	5,110	86.9
1610	Biological scientists	4,610	2,095	45.4	2,515	54.6	330	7.2	3,920	85.0
1640	Conservation scientists and foresters	3,525	3,020	85.7	505	14.3	75	2.1	3,175	90.1
1650	Medical scientists, and life scientists, all other	1,385	530	38.3	855	61.7	90	6.5	1,040	75.1
1700	Astronomers and physicists	820	650	79.3	175	21.3	65	7.9	730	89.0
1710	Atmospheric and space scientists	1,245	1,050	84.3	195	15.7	105	8.4	960	77.1
1720	Chemists and materials scientists	5,990	4,205	70.2	1,785	29.8	350	5.8	4,640	77.5
1740	Environmental scientists and geoscientists	4,400	3,265	74.2	1,135	25.8	425	9.7	3,065	69.7
1760	Physical scientists, all other	2,970	1,950	65.7	1,020	34.3	220	7.4	2,390	80.5
1800	Economists	50	20	40.0	30	60.0	14	28.0	30	60.0
1820	Psychologists	1,030	315	30.6	715	69.4	205	19.9	705	68.4
1840	Urban and regional planners	1,495	755	50.5	740	49.5	105	7.0	1,235	82.6
1860	Miscellaneous social scientists, including survey researchers and sociologists	5,075	2,590	51.0	2,485	49.0	615	12.1	3,120	61.5
1900	Agricultural and food science technicians	10,260	5,530	53.9	4,730	46.1	1,095	10.7	7,570	73.8
1910	Biological technicians	6,150	3,290	53.5	2,855	46.4	725	11.8	4,225	68.7
1920	Chemical technicians	27,070	17,985	66.4	9,085	33.6	2,505	9.3	19,545	72.2
1930	Geological and petroleum technicians, and nuclear technicians	7,445	5,630	75.6	1,815	24.4	540	7.3	6,145	82.5
1965	Miscellaneous life, physical, and social science technicians, including social science research assistants	70,535	39,185	55.6	31,350	44.4	6,775	9.6	50,455	71.5
2000	Counselors	120,310	45,630	37.9	74,680	62.1	15,185	12.6	61,940	51.5
2010	Social workers	121,055	25,440	21.0	95,620	79.0	19,370	16.0	62,155	51.3
2015	Probation officers and correctional treatment specialists	18,850	9,700	51.5	9,150	48.5	3,555	18.9	9,640	51.1
2016	Social and human service assistants	56,960	11,520	20.2	45,445	79.8	9,470	16.6	29,705	52.2
2025	Miscellaneous community and social service specialists, including health educators and community health workers	24,030	8,005	33.3	16,025	66.7	3,725	15.5	13,360	55.6
2040	Clergy	71,155	57,790	81.2	13,365	18.8	5,205	7.3	53,285	74.9
2050	Directors, religious activities and education	12,745	4,700	36.9	8,045	63.1	780	6.1	10,025	78.7
2060	Religious workers, all other	23,580	7,660	32.5	15,920	67.5	1,410	6.0	18,720	79.4
2100	Lawyers, and judges, magistrates, and other judicial workers	8,700	3,085	35.5	5,615	64.5	960	11.0	6,135	70.5
2105	Judicial law clerks	475	80	16.8	395	83.2	25	5.3	330	69.5
2145	Paralegals and legal assistants	157,945	14,760	9.3	143,185	90.7	19,215	12.2	117,745	74.5
2160	Miscellaneous legal support workers	92,520	16,890	18.3	75,630	81.7	10,655	11.5	67,165	72.6
2200	Postsecondary teachers	89,140	42,235	47.4	46,905	52.6	8,920	10.0	64,075	71.9
2300	Preschool and kindergarten teachers	214,220	4,965	2.3	209,255	97.7	29,020	13.5	132,995	62.1
2310	Elementary and middle school teachers	163,560	27,140	16.6	136,415	83.4	21,540	13.2	104,520	63.9
2320	Secondary school teachers	32,095	14,200	44.2	17,900	55.8	5,000	15.6	20,770	64.7
2330	Special education teachers	19,900	2,455	12.3	17,445	87.7	3,525	17.7	11,985	60.2
2340	Other teachers and instructors	252,120	104,940	41.6	147,185	58.4	28,245	11.2	170,300	67.5

PART A—NATIONAL DATA

A-20 **Workers with Some College or Associate's Degree: Detailed Occupation, by Sex, Race, and Hispanic Origin, 2006–2010**—Continued

Census occupation code	Detailed Occupation	Black or African American alone Number	Black or African American alone Percent	American Indian and Alaska Native alone Number	American Indian and Alaska Native alone Percent	Asian alone Number	Asian alone Percent	Native Hawaiian and Other Pacific Islander alone Number	Native Hawaiian and Other Pacific Islander alone Percent	Not Hispanic or Latino, two or more races Number	Not Hispanic or Latino, two or more races Percent
1520	Petroleum, mining and geological engineers, including mining safety engineers	145	4.1	20	0.6	65	1.8	0	0.0	79	2.2
1530	Miscellaneous engineers, including nuclear engineers	3,605	5.2	455	0.7	2,585	3.7	40	0.1	779	1.1
1540	Drafters	4,770	4.0	540	0.5	4,110	3.5	100	0.1	1,620	1.4
1550	Engineering technicians, except drafters	20,315	8.8	1,160	0.5	14,690	6.4	380	0.2	3,175	1.4
1560	Surveying and mapping technicians	1,215	2.8	470	1.1	490	1.1	120	0.3	545	1.2
1600	Agricultural and food scientists	185	3.1	105	1.8	35	0.6	4	0.1	135	2.3
1610	Biological scientists	65	1.4	45	1.0	195	4.2	0	0.0	60	1.3
1640	Conservation scientists and foresters	75	2.1	80	2.3	35	1.0	0	0.0	85	2.4
1650	Medical scientists, and life scientists, all other	90	6.5	0	0.0	140	10.1	0	0.0	30	2.2
1700	Astronomers and physicists	4	0.5	0	0.0	0	0.0	0	0.0	25	3.0
1710	Atmospheric and space scientists	110	8.8	10	0.8	0	0.0	0	0.0	60	4.8
1720	Chemists and materials scientists	710	11.9	15	0.3	200	3.3	0	0.0	80	1.3
1740	Environmental scientists and geoscientists	510	11.6	155	3.5	105	2.4	0	0.0	145	3.3
1760	Physical scientists, all other	100	3.4	60	2.0	140	4.7	0	0.0	55	1.9
1800	Economists	0	0.0	0	0.0	0	0.0	0	0.0	0	0.0
1820	Psychologists	100	9.7	0	0.0	10	1.0	0	0.0	10	1.0
1840	Urban and regional planners	70	4.7	20	1.3	70	4.7	0	0.0	0	0.0
1860	Miscellaneous social scientists, including survey researchers and sociologists	1,000	19.7	65	1.3	130	2.6	0	0.0	150	3.0
1900	Agricultural and food science technicians	730	7.1	125	1.2	525	5.1	20	0.2	190	1.9
1910	Biological technicians	535	8.7	75	1.2	405	6.6	0	0.0	180	2.9
1920	Chemical technicians	3,495	12.9	170	0.6	1,040	3.8	35	0.1	285	1.1
1930	Geological and petroleum technicians, and nuclear technicians	500	6.7	65	0.9	100	1.3	10	0.1	85	1.1
1965	Miscellaneous life, physical, and social science technicians, including social science research assistants	6,185	8.8	655	0.9	4,795	6.8	115	0.2	1,560	2.2
2000	Counselors	35,335	29.4	1,950	1.6	2,470	2.1	365	0.3	3,060	2.5
2010	Social workers	32,525	26.9	1,785	1.5	2,420	2.0	290	0.2	2,500	2.1
2015	Probation officers and correctional treatment specialists	4,355	23.1	370	2.0	385	2.0	195	1.0	355	1.9
2016	Social and human service assistants	14,370	25.2	935	1.6	1,305	2.3	30	0.1	1,145	2.0
2025	Miscellaneous community and social service specialists, including health educators and community health workers	5,190	21.6	630	2.6	510	2.1	70	0.3	555	2.3
2040	Clergy	9,675	13.6	440	0.6	1,365	1.9	145	0.2	1,030	1.4
2050	Directors, religious activities and education	1,560	12.2	25	0.2	200	1.6	80	0.6	70	0.5
2060	Religious workers, all other	2,285	9.7	95	0.4	685	2.9	35	0.1	359	1.5
2100	Lawyers, and judges, magistrates, and other judicial workers	1,040	12.0	195	2.2	210	2.4	0	0.0	160	1.8
2105	Judicial law clerks	90	18.9	0	0.0	25	5.3	0	0.0	4	0.8
2145	Paralegals and legal assistants	14,655	9.3	710	0.4	2,765	1.8	330	0.2	2,520	1.6
2160	Miscellaneous legal support workers	10,195	11.0	820	0.9	2,080	2.2	95	0.1	1,505	1.6
2200	Postsecondary teachers	8,645	9.7	465	0.5	5,035	5.6	80	0.1	1,910	2.1
2300	Preschool and kindergarten teachers	42,275	19.7	1,965	0.9	4,305	2.0	260	0.1	3,400	1.6
2310	Elementary and middle school teachers	28,690	17.5	1,685	1.0	3,710	2.3	320	0.2	3,090	1.9
2320	Secondary school teachers	4,780	14.9	485	1.5	595	1.9	55	0.2	410	1.3
2330	Special education teachers	3,395	17.1	210	1.1	335	1.7	105	0.5	349	1.8
2340	Other teachers and instructors	32,930	13.1	1,635	0.6	12,910	5.1	490	0.2	5,620	2.2

A-20 **Workers with Some College or Associate's Degree: Detailed Occupation, by Sex, Race, and Hispanic Origin, 2006–2010**—*Continued*

Census occupation code	Detailed Occupation	Total	Male Number	Male Percent	Female Number	Female Percent	Hispanic or Latino Number	Hispanic or Latino Percent	Not Hispanic or Latino, one race White alone Number	Not Hispanic or Latino, one race White alone Percent
2400	Archivists, curators, and museum technicians.	6,390	2,815	44.1	3,570	55.9	435	6.8	4,945	77.4
2430	Librarians	29,110	4,450	15.3	24,665	84.7	2,465	8.5	22,340	76.7
2440	Library technicians	18,975	5,125	27.0	13,850	73.0	1,775	9.4	13,555	71.4
2540	Teacher assistants	418,255	37,660	9.0	380,595	91.0	71,655	17.1	262,400	62.7
2550	Other education, training, and library workers	15,495	4,890	31.6	10,605	68.4	1,875	12.1	10,190	65.8
2600	Artists and related workers	56,115	32,135	57.3	23,980	42.7	4,005	7.1	46,600	83.0
2630	Designers	255,445	132,910	52.0	122,535	48.0	23,620	9.2	204,735	80.1
2700	Actors	8,855	5,080	57.4	3,775	42.6	1,000	11.3	6,085	68.7
2710	Producers and directors	28,855	21,240	73.6	7,615	26.4	3,280	11.4	21,860	75.8
2720	Athletes, coaches, umpires, and related workers	80,305	50,910	63.4	29,395	36.6	6,775	8.4	62,470	77.8
2740	Dancers and choreographers	7,170	1,500	20.9	5,670	79.1	1,290	18.0	4,440	61.9
2750	Musicians, singers, and related workers	50,700	35,755	70.5	14,940	29.5	4,010	7.9	35,870	70.7
2760	Entertainers and performers, sports and related workers, all other	14,025	7,880	56.2	6,140	43.8	1,455	10.4	10,090	71.9
2800	Announcers	19,420	15,640	80.5	3,780	19.5	2,370	12.2	13,625	70.2
2810	News analysts, reporters, and correspondents	13,450	7,400	55.0	6,050	45.0	1,590	11.8	10,675	79.4
2825	Public relations specialists	22,030	7,735	35.1	14,295	64.9	2,340	10.6	16,195	73.5
2830	Editors	28,475	14,205	49.9	14,270	50.1	2,285	8.0	23,025	80.9
2840	Technical writers	12,470	6,150	49.3	6,320	50.7	545	4.4	10,575	84.8
2850	Writers and authors	24,810	11,330	45.7	13,480	54.3	1,335	5.4	20,195	81.4
2860	Miscellaneous media and communication workers	29,275	7,900	27.0	21,375	73.0	12,035	41.1	13,135	44.9
2900	Broadcast and sound engineering technicians and radio operators, and media and communication equipment workers, all other	39,400	35,010	88.9	4,390	11.1	3,610	9.2	29,595	75.1
2910	Photographers	52,835	29,530	55.9	23,300	44.1	5,245	9.9	41,085	77.8
2920	Television, video, and motion picture camera operators and editors	14,670	12,225	83.3	2,445	16.7	1,635	11.1	10,810	73.7
3000	Chiropractors	925	345	37.3	580	62.7	135	14.6	700	75.7
3010	Dentists	95	55	57.9	40	42.1	0	0.0	30	31.6
3030	Dietitians and nutritionists	11,605	1,950	16.8	9,655	83.2	1,190	10.3	6,740	58.1
3040	Optometrists	155	25	16.1	130	83.9	75	48.4	65	41.9
3050	Pharmacists	9,585	3,895	40.6	5,685	59.3	975	10.2	5,950	62.1
3060	Physicians and surgeons	1,555	630	40.5	925	59.5	340	21.9	790	50.8
3110	Physician assistants	24,660	6,220	25.2	18,440	74.8	3,330	13.5	16,935	68.7
3120	Podiatrists	0	0	0	0	0	0	0	0	0
3140	Audiologists	385	135	35.1	250	64.9	0	0.0	360	93.5
3150	Occupational therapists	7,650	820	10.7	6,825	89.2	510	6.7	6,275	82.0
3160	Physical therapists	16,045	4,080	25.4	11,965	74.6	1,560	9.7	12,605	78.6
3200	Radiation therapists	6,740	1,615	24.0	5,125	76.0	455	6.8	5,800	86.1
3210	Recreational therapists	2,730	435	15.9	2,295	84.1	165	6.0	1,690	61.9
3220	Respiratory therapists	66,730	22,320	33.4	44,410	66.6	4,860	7.3	50,470	75.6
3230	Speech-language pathologists	1,060	15	1.4	1,045	98.6	165	15.6	720	67.9
3245	Other therapists, including exercise physiologists	16,555	3,755	22.7	12,800	77.3	1,780	10.8	11,275	68.1
3250	Veterinarians	185	15	8.1	170	91.9	4	2.2	180	97.3
3255	Registered nurses	1,114,155	87,825	7.9	1,026,330	92.1	55,210	5.0	897,185	80.5
3256	Nurse anesthetists	1,705	695	40.8	1,010	59.2	110	6.5	1,435	84.2
3258	Nurse practitioners and nurse midwives	3,050	155	5.1	2,895	94.9	205	6.7	2,435	79.8
3260	Health diagnosing and treating practitioners, all other	1,835	380	20.7	1,455	79.3	120	6.5	1,285	70.0

A-20 Workers with Some College or Associate's Degree: Detailed Occupation, by Sex, Race, and Hispanic Origin, 2006–2010—Continued

Census occupation code	Detailed Occupation	Some college or associate's degree								
		Not Hispanic or Latino, one race								Not Hispanic or Latino, two or more races	
		Black or African American alone		American Indian and Alaska Native alone		Asian alone		Native Hawaiian and Other Pacific Islander alone			
		Number	Percent	Number	Percent	Number	Percent	Number	Percent	Number	Percent
2400	Archivists, curators, and museum technicians	655	10.3	90	1.4	210	3.3	0	0.0	54	0.8
2430	Librarians	2,270	7.8	345	1.2	1,055	3.6	40	0.1	590	2.0
2440	Library technicians	1,820	9.6	100	0.5	1,185	6.2	90	0.5	440	2.3
2540	Teacher assistants	64,255	15.4	3,895	0.9	9,230	2.2	620	0.1	6,210	1.5
2550	Other education, training, and library workers	2,060	13.3	390	2.5	535	3.5	75	0.5	365	2.4
2600	Artists and related workers	2,025	3.6	590	1.1	1,765	3.1	45	0.1	1,090	1.9
2630	Designers	11,145	4.4	700	0.3	11,150	4.4	235	0.1	3,865	1.5
2700	Actors	1,145	12.9	50	0.6	125	1.4	4	0.0	445	5.0
2710	Producers and directors	2,605	9.0	125	0.4	550	1.9	50	0.2	385	1.3
2720	Athletes, coaches, umpires, and related workers	6,370	7.9	320	0.4	2,155	2.7	130	0.2	2,090	2.6
2740	Dancers and choreographers	710	9.9	35	0.5	300	4.2	55	0.8	340	4.7
2750	Musicians, singers, and related workers	7,725	15.2	165	0.3	1,270	2.5	155	0.3	1,505	3.0
2760	Entertainers and performers, sports and related workers, all other	1,545	11.0	125	0.9	230	1.6	70	0.5	510	3.6
2800	Announcers	2,270	11.7	105	0.5	665	3.4	50	0.3	335	1.7
2810	News analysts, reporters, and correspondents	530	3.9	175	1.3	290	2.2	0	0.0	190	1.4
2825	Public relations specialists	2,370	10.8	165	0.7	590	2.7	4	0.0	365	1.7
2830	Editors	1,770	6.2	105	0.4	790	2.8	25	0.1	470	1.7
2840	Technical writers	825	6.6	65	0.5	220	1.8	0	0.0	240	1.9
2850	Writers and authors	1,835	7.4	280	1.1	545	2.2	30	0.1	585	2.4
2860	Miscellaneous media and communication workers	1,520	5.2	275	0.9	1,915	6.5	25	0.1	370	1.3
2900	Broadcast and sound engineering technicians and radio operators, and media and communication equipment workers, all other	4,200	10.7	185	0.5	1,040	2.6	90	0.2	670	1.7
2910	Photographers	3,165	6.0	220	0.4	1,970	3.7	110	0.2	1,030	1.9
2920	Television, video, and motion picture camera operators and editors	1,325	9.0	30	0.2	450	3.1	50	0.3	375	2.6
3000	Chiropractors	75	8.1	0	0.0	10	1.1	0	0.0	10	1.1
3010	Dentists	40	42.1	0	0.0	25	26.3	0	0.0	0	0.0
3030	Dietitians and nutritionists	2,855	24.6	305	2.6	375	3.2	10	0.1	125	1.1
3040	Optometrists	0	0.0	0	0.0	10	6.5	0	0.0	0	0.0
3050	Pharmacists	950	9.9	125	1.3	1,380	14.4	40	0.4	165	1.7
3060	Physicians and surgeons	220	14.1	45	2.9	145	9.3	0	0.0	19	1.2
3110	Physician assistants	2,970	12.0	140	0.6	905	3.7	0	0.0	375	1.5
3120	Podiatrists	0	0	0	0	0	0	0	0	0	0
3140	Audiologists	0	0.0	10	2.6	0	0.0	0	0.0	15	3.9
3150	Occupational therapists	600	7.8	20	0.3	180	2.4	4	0.1	54	0.7
3160	Physical therapists	1,255	7.8	115	0.7	305	1.9	35	0.2	175	1.1
3200	Radiation therapists	175	2.6	20	0.3	205	3.0	0	0.0	84	1.2
3210	Recreational therapists	685	25.1	25	0.9	140	5.1	0	0.0	20	0.7
3220	Respiratory therapists	7,495	11.2	200	0.3	2,700	4.0	40	0.1	975	1.5
3230	Speech-language pathologists	120	11.3	10	0.9	10	0.9	0	0.0	35	3.3
3245	Other therapists, including exercise physiologists	2,395	14.5	115	0.7	565	3.4	0	0.0	420	2.5
3250	Veterinarians	0	0.0	0	0.0	0	0.0	0	0.0	0	0.0
3255	Registered nurses	104,775	9.4	4,605	0.4	38,985	3.5	1,030	0.1	12,380	1.1
3256	Nurse anesthetists	85	5.0	0	0.0	60	3.5	0	0.0	20	1.2
3258	Nurse practitioners and nurse midwives	295	9.7	0	0.0	65	2.1	0	0.0	44	1.4
3260	Health diagnosing and treating practitioners, all other	75	4.1	20	1.1	230	12.5	0	0.0	100	5.4

A-20 **Workers with Some College or Associate's Degree: Detailed Occupation, by Sex, Race, and Hispanic Origin, 2006–2010**—*Continued*

Census occupation code	Detailed Occupation	Total	Male Number	Male Percent	Female Number	Female Percent	Hispanic or Latino Number	Hispanic or Latino Percent	White alone Number	White alone Percent
3300	Clinical laboratory technologists and technicians	118,155	28,160	23.8	89,995	76.2	11,495	9.7	75,825	64.2
3310	Dental hygienists	88,265	2,260	2.6	86,005	97.4	4,945	5.6	78,395	88.8
3320	Diagnostic related technologists and technicians	195,715	51,405	26.3	144,310	73.7	17,435	8.9	154,020	78.7
3400	Emergency medical technicians and paramedics	112,945	77,935	69.0	35,010	31.0	11,430	10.1	91,695	81.2
3420	Health practitioner support technologists and technicians	269,130	54,085	20.1	215,045	79.9	28,135	10.5	184,340	68.5
3500	Licensed practical and licensed vocational nurses	463,630	34,915	7.5	428,720	92.5	31,875	6.9	309,660	66.8
3510	Medical records and health information technicians	52,040	5,340	10.3	46,700	89.7	6,520	12.5	31,365	60.3
3520	Opticians, dispensing	26,875	8,265	30.8	18,615	69.3	3,105	11.6	20,595	76.6
3535	Miscellaneous health technologists and technicians	56,345	16,365	29.0	39,985	71.0	5,670	10.1	33,830	60.0
3540	Other health care practitioners and technical occupations	18,205	11,150	61.2	7,055	38.8	2,410	13.2	12,405	68.1
3600	Nursing, psychiatric, and home health aides	780,115	105,655	13.5	674,455	86.5	79,925	10.2	408,265	52.3
3610	Occupational therapy assistants and aides	10,905	970	8.9	9,935	91.1	785	7.2	8,715	79.9
3620	Physical therapist assistants and aides	41,185	9,370	22.8	31,815	77.2	3,870	9.4	32,060	77.8
3630	Massage therapists	66,235	10,775	16.3	55,460	83.7	5,560	8.4	53,175	80.3
3640	Dental assistants	144,995	3,795	2.6	141,200	97.4	23,150	16.0	104,475	72.1
3645	Medical assistants	224,985	12,130	5.4	212,855	94.6	47,690	21.2	132,610	58.9
3646	Medical transcriptionists	46,465	910	2.0	45,555	98.0	1,940	4.2	41,345	89.0
3647	Pharmacy aides	18,920	4,555	24.1	14,360	75.9	3,080	16.3	11,390	60.2
3648	Veterinary assistants and laboratory animal caretakers	17,650	3,045	17.3	14,605	82.7	1,580	9.0	14,705	83.3
3649	Phlebotomists	51,615	6,380	12.4	45,235	87.6	7,345	14.2	30,915	59.9
3655	Health care support workers, all other, including medical equipment preparers	49,215	13,260	26.9	35,955	73.1	4,915	10.0	28,570	58.1
3700	First-line supervisors of correctional officers	26,960	20,350	75.5	6,605	24.5	2,280	8.5	17,495	64.9
3710	First-line supervisors of police and detectives	54,320	46,405	85.4	7,915	14.6	4,725	8.7	41,755	76.9
3720	First-line supervisors of fire fighting and prevention workers	31,295	30,125	96.3	1,165	3.7	1,770	5.7	26,460	84.6
3730	First-line supervisors of protective service workers, all other	40,550	31,230	77.0	9,320	23.0	4,390	10.8	24,890	61.4
3740	Firefighters	163,835	158,330	96.6	5,505	3.4	14,615	8.9	130,845	79.9
3750	Fire inspectors	9,355	8,440	90.2	915	9.8	790	8.4	7,540	80.6
3800	Bailiffs, correctional officers, and jailers	214,280	152,705	71.3	61,575	28.7	26,890	12.5	130,415	60.9
3820	Detectives and criminal investigators	48,565	38,900	80.1	9,670	19.9	6,145	12.7	35,690	73.5
3840	Miscellaneous law enforcement workers	4,435	3,100	69.9	1,335	30.1	590	13.3	2,705	61.0
3850	Police officers	335,960	291,085	86.6	44,870	13.4	47,540	14.2	235,590	70.1
3900	Animal control workers	4,285	2,325	54.3	1,960	45.7	540	12.6	3,480	81.2
3910	Private detectives and investigators	29,505	17,525	59.4	11,980	40.6	3,890	13.2	20,065	68.0
3930	Security guards and gaming surveillance officers	374,115	294,440	78.7	79,675	21.3	49,030	13.1	198,745	53.1
3940	Crossing guards	14,135	5,470	38.7	8,665	61.3	1,670	11.8	8,960	63.4
3945	Transportation security screeners	12,410	8,255	66.5	4,155	33.5	2,120	17.1	6,045	48.7
3955	Lifeguards and other recreational, and all other protective service workers	58,945	27,135	46.0	31,810	54.0	5,450	9.2	45,550	77.3
4000	Chefs and head cooks	119,645	95,605	79.9	24,045	20.1	14,955	12.5	78,765	65.8
4010	First-line supervisors of food preparation and serving workers	199,045	89,365	44.9	109,675	55.1	27,430	13.8	131,255	65.9

PART A—NATIONAL DATA

A-20 Workers with Some College or Associate's Degree: Detailed Occupation, by Sex, Race, and Hispanic Origin, 2006–2010—Continued

Census occupation code	Detailed Occupation	Black or African American alone Number	Black or African American alone Percent	American Indian and Alaska Native alone Number	American Indian and Alaska Native alone Percent	Asian alone Number	Asian alone Percent	Native Hawaiian and Other Pacific Islander alone Number	Native Hawaiian and Other Pacific Islander alone Percent	Not Hispanic or Latino, two or more races Number	Not Hispanic or Latino, two or more races Percent
3300	Clinical laboratory technologists and technicians	20,305	17.2	800	0.7	7,100	6.0	160	0.1	2,465	2.1
3310	Dental hygienists	1,745	2.0	235	0.3	1,830	2.1	40	0.0	1,070	1.2
3320	Diagnostic related technologists and technicians	14,525	7.4	565	0.3	6,680	3.4	120	0.1	2,370	1.2
3400	Emergency medical technicians and paramedics	6,175	5.5	780	0.7	1,365	1.2	45	0.0	1,450	1.3
3420	Health practitioner support technologists and technicians	35,945	13.4	1,735	0.6	14,160	5.3	345	0.1	4,475	1.7
3500	Licensed practical and licensed vocational nurses	99,335	21.4	2,460	0.5	13,755	3.0	305	0.1	6,255	1.3
3510	Medical records and health information technicians	10,005	19.2	915	1.8	2,465	4.7	30	0.1	745	1.4
3520	Opticians, dispensing	1,745	6.5	150	0.6	705	2.6	0	0.0	580	2.2
3535	Miscellaneous health technologists and technicians	12,635	22.4	570	1.0	2,480	4.4	100	0.2	1,060	1.9
3540	Other health care practitioners and technical occupations	2,480	13.6	155	0.9	290	1.6	40	0.2	425	2.3
3600	Nursing, psychiatric, and home health aides	238,155	30.5	7,180	0.9	29,995	3.8	1,495	0.2	15,100	1.9
3610	Occupational therapy assistants and aides	1,085	9.9	15	0.1	205	1.9	20	0.2	75	0.7
3620	Physical therapist assistants and aides	3,235	7.9	230	0.6	1,150	2.8	130	0.3	510	1.2
3630	Massage therapists	3,010	4.5	330	0.5	2,260	3.4	50	0.1	1,855	2.8
3640	Dental assistants	8,850	6.1	1,095	0.8	5,240	3.6	220	0.2	1,970	1.4
3645	Medical assistants	31,345	13.9	1,210	0.5	7,685	3.4	700	0.3	3,745	1.7
3646	Medical transcriptionists	1,985	4.3	125	0.3	505	1.1	45	0.1	525	1.1
3647	Pharmacy aides	2,525	13.3	25	0.1	1,610	8.5	15	0.1	280	1.5
3648	Veterinary assistants and laboratory animal caretakers	700	4.0	30	0.2	275	1.6	0	0.0	370	2.1
3649	Phlebotomists	10,125	19.6	350	0.7	1,710	3.3	125	0.2	1,045	2.0
3655	Health care support workers, all other, including medical equipment preparers	12,090	24.6	410	0.8	2,105	4.3	90	0.2	1,045	2.1
3700	First-line supervisors of correctional officers	6,320	23.4	220	0.8	185	0.7	35	0.1	425	1.6
3710	First-line supervisors of police and detectives	6,320	11.6	385	0.7	285	0.5	80	0.1	770	1.4
3720	First-line supervisors of fire fighting and prevention workers	2,025	6.5	375	1.2	190	0.6	105	0.3	360	1.2
3730	First-line supervisors of protective service workers, all other	9,060	22.3	380	0.9	940	2.3	240	0.6	650	1.6
3740	Firefighters	12,710	7.8	1,190	0.7	1,690	1.0	170	0.1	2,615	1.6
3750	Fire inspectors	720	7.7	115	1.2	35	0.4	0	0.0	149	1.6
3800	Bailiffs, correctional officers, and jailers	49,010	22.9	2,040	1.0	2,030	0.9	405	0.2	3,485	1.6
3820	Detectives and criminal investigators	5,070	10.4	455	0.9	500	1.0	35	0.1	670	1.4
3840	Miscellaneous law enforcement workers	855	19.3	80	1.8	115	2.6	0	0.0	95	2.1
3850	Police officers	39,780	11.8	1,905	0.6	5,410	1.6	930	0.3	4,815	1.4
3900	Animal control workers	195	4.6	40	0.9	0	0.0	0	0.0	29	0.7
3910	Private detectives and investigators	4,170	14.1	405	1.4	365	1.2	80	0.3	535	1.8
3930	Security guards and gaming surveillance officers	101,775	27.2	3,660	1.0	11,125	3.0	1,620	0.4	8,155	2.2
3940	Crossing guards	2,945	20.8	80	0.6	300	2.1	0	0.0	185	1.3
3945	Transportation security screeners	3,085	24.9	115	0.9	640	5.2	65	0.5	330	2.7
3955	Lifeguards and other recreational, and all other protective service workers	4,625	7.8	425	0.7	975	1.7	205	0.3	1,715	2.9
4000	Chefs and head cooks	12,095	10.1	535	0.4	10,500	8.8	220	0.2	2,585	2.2
4010	First-line supervisors of food preparation and serving workers	27,410	13.8	1,480	0.7	7,125	3.6	255	0.1	4,085	2.1

A-20 Workers with Some College or Associate's Degree: Detailed Occupation, by Sex, Race, and Hispanic Origin, 2006–2010—*Continued*

| Census occupation code | Detailed Occupation | Total | Some college or associate's degree |||||| Not Hispanic or Latino, one race ||
| | | | Male || Female || Hispanic or Latino || White alone ||
			Number	Percent	Number	Percent	Number	Percent	Number	Percent
4020	Cooks	432,510	256,450	59.3	176,060	40.7	69,020	16.0	261,880	60.5
4030	Food preparation workers	202,880	81,125	40.0	121,755	60.0	29,050	14.3	134,450	66.3
4040	Bartenders	175,650	80,570	45.9	95,080	54.1	17,180	9.8	142,235	81.0
4050	Combined food preparation and serving workers, including fast food	81,255	28,815	35.5	52,440	64.5	9,610	11.8	54,925	67.6
4060	Counter attendants, cafeteria, food concession, and coffee shop	52,385	17,730	33.8	34,650	66.1	6,355	12.1	36,185	69.1
4110	Waiters and waitresses	827,015	241,285	29.2	585,730	70.8	102,110	12.3	615,940	74.5
4120	Food servers, nonrestaurant	59,135	21,880	37.0	37,255	63.0	8,590	14.5	32,075	54.2
4130	Miscellaneous food preparation and serving related workers, including dining room and cafeteria attendants and bartender helpers	71,020	39,590	55.7	31,425	44.2	14,945	21.0	41,440	58.3
4140	Dishwashers	37,065	28,695	77.4	8,365	22.6	6,835	18.4	21,820	58.9
4150	Hosts and hostesses, restaurant, lounge, and coffee shop	88,285	11,730	13.3	76,555	86.7	13,125	14.9	60,795	68.9
4200	First-line supervisors of housekeeping and janitorial workers	78,100	53,030	67.9	25,070	32.1	12,950	16.6	49,365	63.2
4210	First-line supervisors of landscaping, lawn service, and groundskeeping workers	58,730	54,085	92.1	4,645	7.9	5,355	9.1	48,715	82.9
4220	Janitors and building cleaners	526,080	388,210	73.8	137,865	26.2	79,185	15.1	330,890	62.9
4230	Maids and housekeeping cleaners	213,335	30,580	14.3	182,755	85.7	56,555	26.5	105,335	49.4
4240	Pest control workers	23,395	22,315	95.4	1,080	4.6	2,635	11.3	17,885	76.4
4250	Grounds maintenance workers	229,745	207,165	90.2	22,580	9.8	36,480	15.9	167,975	73.1
4300	First-line supervisors of gaming workers	29,955	16,775	56.0	13,185	44.0	2,560	8.5	22,145	73.9
4320	First-line supervisors of personal service workers	71,160	25,655	36.1	45,505	63.9	6,955	9.8	51,400	72.2
4340	Animal trainers	13,380	5,670	42.4	7,710	57.6	965	7.2	11,610	86.8
4350	Nonfarm animal caretakers	60,495	15,360	25.4	45,135	74.6	4,275	7.1	51,475	85.1
4400	Gaming services workers	42,165	22,540	53.5	19,625	46.5	4,065	9.6	22,995	54.5
4410	Motion picture projectionists	4,145	3,315	80.0	830	20.0	275	6.6	3,415	82.4
4420	Ushers, lobby attendants, and ticket takers	15,885	8,535	53.7	7,350	46.3	1,855	11.7	10,295	64.8
4430	Miscellaneous entertainment attendants and related workers	64,420	37,470	58.2	26,950	41.8	7,645	11.9	45,620	70.8
4460	Embalmers and funeral attendants	5,855	4,315	73.7	1,535	26.2	410	7.0	4,725	80.7
4465	Morticians, undertakers, and funeral directors	20,625	15,960	77.4	4,665	22.6	1,135	5.5	17,105	82.9
4500	Barbers	31,480	23,700	75.3	7,780	24.7	3,200	10.2	15,720	49.9
4510	Hairdressers, hairstylists, and cosmetologists	293,745	24,530	8.4	269,215	91.6	30,915	10.5	211,350	72.0
4520	Miscellaneous personal appearance workers	70,205	7,255	10.3	62,950	89.7	6,325	9.0	35,210	50.2
4530	Baggage porters, bellhops, and concierges	26,725	21,090	78.9	5,635	21.1	5,670	21.2	12,115	45.3
4540	Tour and travel guides	18,565	9,030	48.6	9,535	51.4	1,405	7.6	14,270	76.9
4600	Childcare workers	489,275	29,100	5.9	460,175	94.1	68,715	14.0	319,535	65.3
4610	Personal care aides	279,260	44,610	16.0	234,650	84.0	34,270	12.3	149,675	53.6
4620	Recreation and fitness workers	140,825	52,135	37.0	88,695	63.0	14,050	10.0	102,000	72.4
4640	Residential advisors	42,855	16,655	38.9	26,195	61.1	2,570	6.0	28,040	65.4
4650	Personal care and service workers, all other	31,070	16,400	52.8	14,670	47.2	4,120	13.3	21,085	67.9
4700	First-line supervisors of retail sales workers	1,146,060	645,990	56.4	500,075	43.6	124,890	10.9	856,290	74.7
4710	First-line supervisors of non-retail sales workers	395,320	270,110	68.3	125,210	31.7	38,290	9.7	308,145	77.9
4720	Cashiers	997,865	272,050	27.3	725,815	72.7	156,050	15.6	582,945	58.4
4740	Counter and rental clerks	42,620	20,835	48.9	21,785	51.1	4,830	11.3	29,285	68.7
4750	Parts salespersons	39,740	35,195	88.6	4,550	11.4	4,155	10.5	31,920	80.3
4760	Retail salespersons	1,353,755	670,155	49.5	683,600	50.5	167,275	12.4	940,105	69.4

PART A—NATIONAL DATA

A-20 Workers with Some College or Associate's Degree: Detailed Occupation, by Sex, Race, and Hispanic Origin, 2006–2010—Continued

Census occupation code	Detailed Occupation	Black or African American alone Number	Black or African American alone Percent	American Indian and Alaska Native alone Number	American Indian and Alaska Native alone Percent	Asian alone Number	Asian alone Percent	Native Hawaiian and Other Pacific Islander alone Number	Native Hawaiian and Other Pacific Islander alone Percent	Not Hispanic or Latino, two or more races Number	Not Hispanic or Latino, two or more races Percent
4020	Cooks	67,800	15.7	3,625	0.8	20,940	4.8	1,250	0.3	7,995	1.8
4030	Food preparation workers	21,620	10.7	1,150	0.6	11,185	5.5	480	0.2	4,950	2.4
4040	Bartenders	7,150	4.1	865	0.5	4,070	2.3	290	0.2	3,865	2.2
4050	Combined food preparation and serving workers, including fast food	11,525	14.2	590	0.7	2,675	3.3	80	0.1	1,845	2.3
4060	Counter attendants, cafeteria, food concession, and coffee shop	5,505	10.5	185	0.4	2,730	5.2	65	0.1	1,355	2.6
4110	Waiters and waitresses	48,390	5.9	3,955	0.5	36,255	4.4	1,025	0.1	19,345	2.3
4120	Food servers, nonrestaurant	12,325	20.8	570	1.0	4,095	6.9	130	0.2	1,355	2.3
4130	Miscellaneous food preparation and serving related workers, including dining room and cafeteria attendants and bartender helpers	7,815	11.0	500	0.7	4,545	6.4	365	0.5	1,395	2.0
4140	Dishwashers	5,715	15.4	310	0.8	1,385	3.7	140	0.4	855	2.3
4150	Hosts and hostesses, restaurant, lounge, and coffee shop	7,535	8.5	375	0.4	3,775	4.3	80	0.1	2,610	3.0
4200	First-line supervisors of housekeeping and janitorial workers	11,990	15.4	465	0.6	1,960	2.5	130	0.2	1,245	1.6
4210	First-line supervisors of landscaping, lawn service, and groundskeeping workers	3,205	5.5	260	0.4	335	0.6	100	0.2	765	1.3
4220	Janitors and building cleaners	85,995	16.3	5,430	1.0	15,565	3.0	790	0.2	8,215	1.6
4230	Maids and housekeeping cleaners	34,795	16.3	2,140	1.0	9,980	4.7	510	0.2	4,025	1.9
4240	Pest control workers	2,075	8.9	90	0.4	335	1.4	30	0.1	345	1.5
4250	Grounds maintenance workers	15,760	6.9	1,930	0.8	3,625	1.6	570	0.2	3,405	1.5
4300	First-line supervisors of gaming workers	1,985	6.6	920	3.1	1,720	5.7	65	0.2	560	1.9
4320	First-line supervisors of personal service workers	6,010	8.4	440	0.6	4,920	6.9	155	0.2	1,285	1.8
4340	Animal trainers	220	1.6	105	0.8	310	2.3	45	0.3	125	0.9
4350	Nonfarm animal caretakers	2,530	4.2	285	0.5	735	1.2	15	0.0	1,170	1.9
4400	Gaming services workers	4,445	10.5	1,390	3.3	8,135	19.3	160	0.4	980	2.3
4410	Motion picture projectionists	275	6.6	15	0.4	140	3.4	0	0.0	24	0.6
4420	Ushers, lobby attendants, and ticket takers	2,640	16.6	45	0.3	725	4.6	25	0.2	305	1.9
4430	Miscellaneous entertainment attendants and related workers	6,575	10.2	550	0.9	2,470	3.8	145	0.2	1,420	2.2
4460	Embalmers and funeral attendants	580	9.9	0	0.0	75	1.3	0	0.0	59	1.0
4465	Morticians, undertakers, and funeral directors	2,130	10.3	55	0.3	70	0.3	0	0.0	130	0.6
4500	Barbers	10,925	34.7	165	0.5	1,035	3.3	30	0.1	410	1.3
4510	Hairdressers, hairstylists, and cosmetologists	33,405	11.4	1,060	0.4	12,530	4.3	145	0.0	4,340	1.5
4520	Miscellaneous personal appearance workers	3,800	5.4	185	0.3	23,535	33.5	40	0.1	1,110	1.6
4530	Baggage porters, bellhops, and concierges	5,770	21.6	205	0.8	1,970	7.4	275	1.0	715	2.7
4540	Tour and travel guides	1,120	6.0	125	0.7	1,105	6.0	115	0.6	430	2.3
4600	Childcare workers	76,630	15.7	3,155	0.6	11,615	2.4	790	0.2	8,840	1.8
4610	Personal care aides	68,700	24.6	3,360	1.2	15,935	5.7	1,420	0.5	5,900	2.1
4620	Recreation and fitness workers	16,485	11.7	1,240	0.9	3,935	2.8	245	0.2	2,875	2.0
4640	Residential advisors	8,870	20.7	545	1.3	1,415	3.3	50	0.1	1,370	3.2
4650	Personal care and service workers, all other	3,230	10.4	270	0.9	1,345	4.3	220	0.7	800	2.6
4700	First-line supervisors of retail sales workers	96,215	8.4	5,075	0.4	43,215	3.8	1,525	0.1	18,845	1.6
4710	First-line supervisors of non-retail sales workers	27,675	7.0	1,510	0.4	14,660	3.7	525	0.1	4,520	1.1
4720	Cashiers	167,510	16.8	7,255	0.7	59,805	6.0	2,400	0.2	21,910	2.2
4740	Counter and rental clerks	5,180	12.2	310	0.7	2,005	4.7	75	0.2	935	2.2
4750	Parts salespersons	1,990	5.0	205	0.5	895	2.3	30	0.1	545	1.4
4760	Retail salespersons	155,830	11.5	6,185	0.5	57,295	4.2	1,820	0.1	25,245	1.9

A-20 **Workers with Some College or Associate's Degree: Detailed Occupation, by Sex, Race, and Hispanic Origin, 2006–2010**—Continued

Census occupation code	Detailed Occupation	Total	Male Number	Male Percent	Female Number	Female Percent	Hispanic or Latino Number	Hispanic or Latino Percent	Not Hispanic or Latino, one race White alone Number	Percent
4800	Advertising sales agents	67,975	32,110	47.2	35,865	52.8	6,725	9.9	52,375	77.1
4810	Insurance sales agents	193,425	89,020	46.0	104,405	54.0	20,790	10.7	149,355	77.2
4820	Securities, commodities, and financial services sales agents	81,325	46,235	56.9	35,090	43.1	9,930	12.2	59,155	72.7
4830	Travel agents	36,170	5,925	16.4	30,245	83.6	3,750	10.4	27,190	75.2
4840	Sales representatives, services, all other	219,530	141,185	64.3	78,350	35.7	23,340	10.6	164,725	75.0
4850	Sales representatives, wholesale and manufacturing	466,635	348,570	74.7	118,065	25.3	41,070	8.8	391,180	83.8
4900	Models, demonstrators, and product promoters	20,110	4,925	24.5	15,185	75.5	2,435	12.1	14,505	72.1
4920	Real estate brokers and sales agents	323,675	126,190	39.0	197,485	61.0	31,340	9.7	258,175	79.8
4930	Sales engineers	7,565	7,210	95.3	355	4.7	505	6.7	6,650	87.9
4940	Telemarketers	55,555	20,110	36.2	35,445	63.8	7,480	13.5	32,465	58.4
4950	Door-to-door sales workers, news and street vendors, and related workers	60,570	23,670	39.1	36,900	60.9	7,460	12.3	44,405	73.3
4965	Sales and related workers, all other	71,465	34,305	48.0	37,160	52.0	6,090	8.5	55,355	77.5
5000	First-line supervisors of office and administrative support workers	645,845	199,040	30.8	446,800	69.2	75,495	11.7	465,040	72.0
5010	Switchboard operators, including answering service	17,495	3,050	17.4	14,440	82.5	1,940	11.1	10,880	62.2
5020	Telephone operators	23,855	5,060	21.2	18,800	78.8	3,525	14.8	12,290	51.5
5030	Communications equipment operators, all other	4,720	2,085	44.2	2,635	55.8	410	8.7	2,960	62.7
5100	Bill and account collectors	104,400	30,240	29.0	74,160	71.0	15,265	14.6	61,345	58.8
5110	Billing and posting clerks	224,580	21,280	9.5	203,300	90.5	27,845	12.4	153,590	68.4
5120	Bookkeeping, accounting, and auditing clerks	721,020	80,365	11.1	640,655	88.9	67,525	9.4	550,095	76.3
5130	Gaming cage workers	5,160	1,355	26.3	3,805	73.7	510	9.9	2,670	51.7
5140	Payroll and timekeeping clerks	87,280	8,060	9.2	79,220	90.8	9,675	11.1	61,610	70.6
5150	Procurement clerks	13,465	4,450	33.0	9,015	67.0	1,065	7.9	9,575	71.1
5160	Tellers	208,310	32,605	15.7	175,705	84.3	35,375	17.0	131,575	63.2
5165	Financial clerks, all other	26,640	6,990	26.2	19,650	73.8	3,115	11.7	17,285	64.9
5200	Brokerage clerks	4,310	1,125	26.1	3,185	73.9	590	13.7	3,145	73.0
5220	Court, municipal, and license clerks	43,715	8,125	18.6	35,590	81.4	5,915	13.5	29,320	67.1
5230	Credit authorizers, checkers, and clerks	23,465	5,510	23.5	17,960	76.5	3,025	12.9	15,035	64.1
5240	Customer service representatives	964,665	301,840	31.3	662,830	68.7	140,520	14.6	584,360	60.6
5250	Eligibility interviewers, government programs	28,520	3,800	13.3	24,715	86.7	7,220	25.3	13,035	45.7
5260	File clerks	167,810	36,675	21.9	131,135	78.1	21,455	12.8	107,620	64.1
5300	Hotel, motel, and resort desk clerks	60,825	20,905	34.4	39,920	65.6	8,985	14.8	36,565	60.1
5310	Interviewers, except eligibility and loan	67,210	13,555	20.2	53,655	79.8	9,950	14.8	39,915	59.4
5320	Library assistants, clerical	56,660	11,370	20.1	45,290	79.9	5,475	9.7	39,690	70.0
5330	Loan interviewers and clerks	65,530	11,250	17.2	54,285	82.8	9,335	14.2	43,585	66.5
5340	New accounts clerks	11,105	1,965	17.7	9,140	82.3	1,910	17.2	7,230	65.1
5350	Correspondence clerks and order clerks	56,365	20,355	36.1	36,015	63.9	7,270	12.9	38,820	68.9
5360	Human resources assistants, except payroll and timekeeping	24,755	4,180	16.9	20,570	83.1	3,515	14.2	15,615	63.1
5400	Receptionists and information clerks	542,365	50,110	9.2	492,255	90.8	83,685	15.4	359,140	66.2
5410	Reservation and transportation ticket agents and travel clerks	61,690	22,755	36.9	38,935	63.1	8,560	13.9	36,630	59.4
5420	Information and record clerks, all other	51,025	6,540	12.8	44,485	87.2	5,700	11.2	34,970	68.5
5500	Cargo and freight agents	7,955	5,320	66.9	2,635	33.1	1,400	17.6	4,715	59.3
5510	Couriers and messengers	119,435	99,115	83.0	20,325	17.0	13,955	11.7	79,950	66.9
5520	Dispatchers	127,430	52,880	41.5	74,555	58.5	13,475	10.6	92,055	72.2
5530	Meter readers, utilities	15,305	13,220	86.4	2,085	13.6	2,045	13.4	10,365	67.7
5540	Postal service clerks	66,710	34,130	51.2	32,580	48.8	5,180	7.8	34,485	51.7

PART A—NATIONAL DATA

A-20 Workers with Some College or Associate's Degree: Detailed Occupation, by Sex, Race, and Hispanic Origin, 2006–2010—Continued

Census occupation code	Detailed Occupation	Black or African American alone Number	Percent	American Indian and Alaska Native alone Number	Percent	Asian alone Number	Percent	Native Hawaiian and Other Pacific Islander alone Number	Percent	Not Hispanic or Latino, two or more races Number	Percent
4800	Advertising sales agents	6,295	9.3	170	0.3	1,285	1.9	85	0.1	1,040	1.5
4810	Insurance sales agents	15,955	8.2	655	0.3	3,940	2.0	130	0.1	2,600	1.3
4820	Securities, commodities, and financial services sales agents	7,565	9.3	180	0.2	3,125	3.8	110	0.1	1,260	1.5
4830	Travel agents	2,630	7.3	150	0.4	2,020	5.6	15	0.0	420	1.2
4840	Sales representatives, services, all other	20,320	9.3	935	0.4	6,695	3.0	210	0.1	3,305	1.5
4850	Sales representatives, wholesale and manufacturing	15,865	3.4	1,485	0.3	11,735	2.5	610	0.1	4,690	1.0
4900	Models, demonstrators, and product promoters	1,965	9.8	90	0.4	655	3.3	100	0.5	365	1.8
4920	Real estate brokers and sales agents	19,310	6.0	1,055	0.3	9,785	3.0	220	0.1	3,795	1.2
4930	Sales engineers	150	2.0	0	0.0	180	2.4	0	0.0	80	1.1
4940	Telemarketers	12,995	23.4	265	0.5	845	1.5	145	0.3	1,355	2.4
4950	Door-to-door sales workers, news and street vendors, and related workers	5,955	9.8	395	0.7	995	1.6	95	0.2	1,260	2.1
4965	Sales and related workers, all other	6,655	9.3	305	0.4	2,110	3.0	125	0.2	825	1.2
5000	First-line supervisors of office and administrative support workers	74,880	11.6	3,640	0.6	16,125	2.5	1,175	0.2	9,480	1.5
5010	Switchboard operators, including answering service	3,915	22.4	105	0.6	290	1.7	55	0.3	310	1.8
5020	Telephone operators	6,505	27.3	160	0.7	635	2.7	55	0.2	695	2.9
5030	Communications equipment operators, all other	1,060	22.5	20	0.4	235	5.0	0	0.0	35	0.7
5100	Bill and account collectors	23,000	22.0	550	0.5	2,165	2.1	205	0.2	1,865	1.8
5110	Billing and posting clerks	29,920	13.3	1,405	0.6	7,855	3.5	525	0.2	3,440	1.5
5120	Bookkeeping, accounting, and auditing clerks	62,120	8.6	4,740	0.7	26,615	3.7	880	0.1	9,035	1.3
5130	Gaming cage workers	855	16.6	310	6.0	465	9.0	15	0.3	335	6.5
5140	Payroll and timekeeping clerks	11,800	13.5	530	0.6	2,340	2.7	90	0.1	1,240	1.4
5150	Procurement clerks	2,010	14.9	155	1.2	340	2.5	10	0.1	304	2.3
5160	Tellers	25,500	12.2	635	0.3	11,450	5.5	350	0.2	3,430	1.6
5165	Financial clerks, all other	4,085	15.3	155	0.6	1,555	5.8	45	0.2	400	1.5
5200	Brokerage clerks	420	9.7	25	0.6	80	1.9	25	0.6	24	0.6
5220	Court, municipal, and license clerks	6,345	14.5	460	1.1	1,055	2.4	105	0.2	520	1.2
5230	Credit authorizers, checkers, and clerks	4,045	17.2	175	0.7	685	2.9	80	0.3	420	1.8
5240	Customer service representatives	182,485	18.9	4,860	0.5	31,575	3.3	1,785	0.2	19,070	2.0
5250	Eligibility interviewers, government programs	6,125	21.5	500	1.8	1,110	3.9	35	0.1	490	1.7
5260	File clerks	26,180	15.6	1,140	0.7	7,910	4.7	390	0.2	3,115	1.9
5300	Hotel, motel, and resort desk clerks	9,335	15.3	730	1.2	3,540	5.8	210	0.3	1,460	2.4
5310	Interviewers, except eligibility and loan	13,230	19.7	970	1.4	1,810	2.7	110	0.2	1,225	1.8
5320	Library assistants, clerical	6,555	11.6	350	0.6	3,310	5.8	25	0.0	1,250	2.2
5330	Loan interviewers and clerks	8,735	13.3	345	0.5	2,165	3.3	135	0.2	1,234	1.9
5340	New accounts clerks	1,130	10.2	20	0.2	630	5.7	10	0.1	170	1.5
5350	Correspondence clerks and order clerks	7,025	12.5	340	0.6	1,855	3.3	85	0.2	970	1.7
5360	Human resources assistants, except payroll and timekeeping	4,265	17.2	365	1.5	550	2.2	0	0.0	435	1.8
5400	Receptionists and information clerks	66,915	12.3	3,475	0.6	17,830	3.3	840	0.2	10,475	1.9
5410	Reservation and transportation ticket agents and travel clerks	11,245	18.2	275	0.4	3,070	5.0	595	1.0	1,320	2.1
5420	Information and record clerks, all other	7,410	14.5	595	1.2	1,520	3.0	35	0.1	790	1.5
5500	Cargo and freight agents	1,095	13.8	35	0.4	530	6.7	95	1.2	85	1.1
5510	Couriers and messengers	19,215	16.1	450	0.4	3,830	3.2	245	0.2	1,790	1.5
5520	Dispatchers	16,945	13.3	880	0.7	1,790	1.4	215	0.2	2,075	1.6
5530	Meter readers, utilities	2,280	14.9	130	0.8	110	0.7	70	0.5	305	2.0
5540	Postal service clerks	19,580	29.4	305	0.5	6,175	9.3	80	0.1	900	1.3

A-20 **Workers with Some College or Associate's Degree: Detailed Occupation, by Sex, Race, and Hispanic Origin, 2006–2010**—*Continued*

| Census occupation code | Detailed Occupation | Total | Some college or associate's degree ||||| Not Hispanic or Latino, one race ||
| | | | Male || Female || Hispanic or Latino || White alone ||
			Number	Percent	Number	Percent	Number	Percent	Number	Percent
5550	Postal service mail carriers	154,905	101,390	65.5	53,515	34.5	14,580	9.4	102,275	66.0
5560	Postal service mail sorters, processors, and processing machine operators	40,265	20,405	50.7	19,865	49.3	3,395	8.4	19,215	47.7
5600	Production, planning, and expediting clerks	114,795	47,660	41.5	67,140	58.5	11,255	9.8	86,190	75.1
5610	Shipping, receiving, and traffic clerks	179,195	124,685	69.6	54,505	30.4	28,040	15.6	111,900	62.4
5620	Stock clerks and order fillers	470,815	305,155	64.8	165,660	35.2	63,270	13.4	294,830	62.6
5630	Weighers, measurers, checkers, and samplers, recordkeeping	24,105	13,260	55.0	10,840	45.0	2,995	12.4	16,495	68.4
5700	Secretaries and administrative assistants	1,812,030	64,765	3.6	1,747,265	96.4	184,705	10.2	1,367,600	75.5
5800	Computer operators	63,615	32,755	51.5	30,860	48.5	6,965	10.9	43,385	68.2
5810	Data entry keyers	209,150	42,300	20.2	166,850	79.8	27,615	13.2	131,295	62.8
5820	Word processors and typists	157,790	16,540	10.5	141,250	89.5	18,140	11.5	104,605	66.3
5840	Insurance claims and policy processing clerks	143,185	21,040	14.7	122,150	85.3	16,845	11.8	93,590	65.4
5850	Mail clerks and mail machine operators, except postal service	44,765	23,230	51.9	21,540	48.1	4,950	11.1	25,335	56.6
5860	Office clerks, general	550,935	94,500	17.2	456,435	82.8	77,625	14.1	354,625	64.4
5900	Office machine operators, except computer	22,350	9,455	42.3	12,895	57.7	2,760	12.3	13,120	58.7
5910	Proofreaders and copy markers	4,410	1,270	28.8	3,140	71.2	335	7.6	3,535	80.2
5920	Statistical assistants	12,025	4,310	35.8	7,715	64.2	1,195	9.9	8,430	70.1
5940	Miscellaneous office and administrative support workers, including desktop publishers	219,890	49,695	22.6	170,195	77.4	25,870	11.8	148,220	67.4
6005	First-line supervisors of farming, fishing, and forestry workers	12,395	10,425	84.1	1,970	15.9	2,185	17.6	9,320	75.2
6010	Agricultural inspectors	5,470	3,515	64.3	1,955	35.7	640	11.7	3,625	66.3
6040	Graders and sorters, agricultural products	5,175	2,840	54.9	2,330	45.0	1,995	38.6	2,245	43.4
6050	Miscellaneous agricultural workers, including animal breeders	100,395	77,540	77.2	22,855	22.8	17,095	17.0	77,715	77.4
6100	Fishing and hunting workers	7,055	6,635	94.0	420	6.0	205	2.9	6,290	89.2
6120	Forest and conservation workers	3,460	2,920	84.4	540	15.6	340	9.8	2,830	81.8
6130	Logging workers	11,400	10,985	96.4	415	3.6	705	6.2	9,615	84.3
6200	First-line supervisors of construction trades and extraction workers	300,490	290,215	96.6	10,275	3.4	28,620	9.5	251,390	83.7
6210	Boilermakers	5,465	5,375	98.4	90	1.6	250	4.6	4,575	83.7
6220	Brickmasons, blockmasons, and stonemasons	30,855	30,480	98.8	370	1.2	5,280	17.1	21,520	69.7
6230	Carpenters	338,430	331,160	97.9	7,270	2.1	45,510	13.4	262,390	77.5
6240	Carpet, floor, and tile installers and finishers	36,510	35,500	97.2	1,010	2.8	7,890	21.6	25,390	69.5
6250	Cement masons, concrete finishers, and terrazzo workers	10,240	10,035	98.0	200	2.0	2,525	24.7	6,150	60.1
6260	Construction laborers	301,090	288,765	95.9	12,320	4.1	54,595	18.1	211,125	70.1
6300	Paving, surfacing, and tamping equipment operators	2,665	2,535	95.1	130	4.9	315	11.8	2,060	77.3
6320	Construction equipment operators, except paving, surfacing, and tamping equipment operators	75,855	73,300	96.6	2,555	3.4	6,495	8.6	61,310	80.8
6330	Drywall installers, ceiling tile installers, and tapers	22,250	21,580	97.0	670	3.0	7,425	33.4	12,510	56.2
6355	Electricians	326,710	319,735	97.9	6,975	2.1	32,775	10.0	258,585	79.1
6360	Glaziers	9,965	9,815	98.5	150	1.5	925	9.3	8,100	81.3
6400	Insulation workers	8,905	8,615	96.7	290	3.3	1,810	20.3	6,135	68.9
6420	Painters, construction and maintenance	110,530	99,465	90.0	11,065	10.0	23,085	20.9	74,810	67.7
6430	Paperhangers	2,500	1,795	71.8	705	28.2	230	9.2	2,135	85.4
6440	Pipelayers, plumbers, pipefitters, and steamfitters	162,965	160,315	98.4	2,650	1.6	19,115	11.7	126,405	77.6
6460	Plasterers and stucco masons	4,230	4,090	96.7	145	3.4	1,685	39.8	2,015	47.6

PART A—NATIONAL DATA

A-20 Workers with Some College or Associate's Degree: Detailed Occupation, by Sex, Race, and Hispanic Origin, 2006–2010—*Continued*

Census occupation code	Detailed Occupation	Some college or associate's degree									Not Hispanic or Latino, two or more races	
		Not Hispanic or Latino, one race										
		Black or African American alone		American Indian and Alaska Native alone		Asian alone		Native Hawaiian and Other Pacific Islander alone			
		Number	Percent	Number	Percent	Number	Percent	Number	Percent	Number	Percent
5550	Postal service mail carriers	25,280	16.3	650	0.4	9,555	6.2	280	0.2	2,280	1.5
5560	Postal service mail sorters, processors, and processing machine operators	12,600	31.3	135	0.3	4,095	10.2	120	0.3	710	1.8
5600	Production, planning, and expediting clerks	11,635	10.1	425	0.4	3,050	2.7	265	0.2	1,970	1.7
5610	Shipping, receiving, and traffic clerks	28,025	15.6	775	0.4	6,490	3.6	775	0.4	3,175	1.8
5620	Stock clerks and order fillers	78,460	16.7	3,625	0.8	19,070	4.1	1,925	0.4	9,640	2.0
5630	Weighers, measurers, checkers, and samplers, recordkeeping	3,145	13.0	200	0.8	875	3.6	0	0.0	394	1.6
5700	Secretaries and administrative assistants	185,500	10.2	11,450	0.6	35,925	2.0	2,325	0.1	24,515	1.4
5800	Computer operators	8,885	14.0	570	0.9	2,785	4.4	80	0.1	945	1.5
5810	Data entry keyers	34,875	16.7	1,250	0.6	9,925	4.7	490	0.2	3,700	1.8
5820	Word processors and typists	24,835	15.7	545	0.3	7,110	4.5	200	0.1	2,365	1.5
5840	Insurance claims and policy processing clerks	26,830	18.7	480	0.3	3,035	2.1	235	0.2	2,175	1.5
5850	Mail clerks and mail machine operators, except postal service	11,115	24.8	230	0.5	2,440	5.5	70	0.2	625	1.4
5860	Office clerks, general	79,370	14.4	3,460	0.6	25,265	4.6	1,250	0.2	9,345	1.7
5900	Office machine operators, except computer	3,480	15.6	135	0.6	1,995	8.9	0	0.0	850	3.8
5910	Proofreaders and copy markers	275	6.2	0	0.0	95	2.2	0	0.0	170	3.9
5920	Statistical assistants	1,415	11.8	70	0.6	500	4.2	25	0.2	385	3.2
5940	Miscellaneous office and administrative support workers, including desktop publishers	32,650	14.8	1,820	0.8	6,590	3.0	500	0.2	4,225	1.9
6005	First-line supervisors of farming, fishing, and forestry workers	455	3.7	55	0.4	210	1.7	0	0.0	174	1.4
6010	Agricultural inspectors	880	16.1	65	1.2	165	3.0	10	0.2	80	1.5
6040	Graders and sorters, agricultural products	675	13.0	0	0.0	175	3.4	40	0.8	45	0.9
6050	Miscellaneous agricultural workers, including animal breeders	2,605	2.6	695	0.7	1,120	1.1	65	0.1	1,100	1.1
6100	Fishing and hunting workers	80	1.1	100	1.4	205	2.9	20	0.3	163	2.3
6120	Forest and conservation workers	100	2.9	55	1.6	65	1.9	15	0.4	60	1.7
6130	Logging workers	620	5.4	295	2.6	4	0.0	0	0.0	160	1.4
6200	First-line supervisors of construction trades and extraction workers	11,445	3.8	1,985	0.7	2,820	0.9	665	0.2	3,565	1.2
6210	Boilermakers	440	8.1	90	1.6	65	1.2	10	0.2	34	0.6
6220	Brickmasons, blockmasons, and stonemasons	2,885	9.4	310	1.0	295	1.0	135	0.4	425	1.4
6230	Carpenters	16,820	5.0	3,470	1.0	4,185	1.2	990	0.3	5,055	1.5
6240	Carpet, floor, and tile installers and finishers	1,875	5.1	250	0.7	440	1.2	90	0.2	575	1.6
6250	Cement masons, concrete finishers, and terrazzo workers	1,245	12.2	145	1.4	45	0.4	10	0.1	120	1.2
6260	Construction laborers	23,450	7.8	2,875	1.0	4,145	1.4	520	0.2	4,375	1.5
6300	Paving, surfacing, and tamping equipment operators	170	6.4	35	1.3	20	0.8	4	0.2	55	2.1
6320	Construction equipment operators, except paving, surfacing, and tamping equipment operators	4,765	6.3	1,470	1.9	405	0.5	95	0.1	1,320	1.7
6330	Drywall installers, ceiling tile installers, and tapers	1,260	5.7	335	1.5	270	1.2	15	0.1	445	2.0
6355	Electricians	22,150	6.8	2,170	0.7	6,085	1.9	535	0.2	4,410	1.3
6360	Glaziers	385	3.9	85	0.9	160	1.6	45	0.5	260	2.6
6400	Insulation workers	770	8.6	45	0.5	65	0.7	0	0.0	80	0.9
6420	Painters, construction and maintenance	7,700	7.0	760	0.7	2,280	2.1	175	0.2	1,715	1.6
6430	Paperhangers	80	3.2	0	0.0	55	2.2	0	0.0	0	0.0
6440	Pipelayers, plumbers, pipefitters, and steamfitters	11,675	7.2	1,070	0.7	2,225	1.4	315	0.2	2,170	1.3
6460	Plasterers and stucco masons	460	10.9	40	0.9	30	0.7	4	0.1	0	0.0

A-20 **Workers with Some College or Associate's Degree: Detailed Occupation, by Sex, Race, and Hispanic Origin, 2006–2010**—*Continued*

| Census occupation code | Detailed Occupation | Total | Some college or associate's degree ||||| Not Hispanic or Latino, one race — White alone ||
| | | | Male || Female || Hispanic or Latino || ||
			Number	Percent	Number	Percent	Number	Percent	Number	Percent
6500	Reinforcing iron and rebar workers...............	1,840	1,765	95.9	75	4.1	295	16.0	1,390	75.5
6515	Roofers..	26,350	25,800	97.9	550	2.1	6,990	26.5	16,690	63.3
6520	Sheet metal workers	41,015	39,530	96.4	1,480	3.6	3,870	9.4	33,120	80.8
6530	Structural iron and steel workers.................	18,370	17,820	97.0	555	3.0	2,380	13.0	13,770	75.0
6600	Helpers, construction trades	13,405	12,480	93.1	920	6.9	3,410	25.4	8,380	62.5
6660	Construction and building inspectors	47,065	42,115	89.5	4,950	10.5	3,770	8.0	37,775	80.3
6700	Elevator installers and repairers.................	11,595	11,320	97.6	275	2.4	1,035	8.9	9,435	81.4
6710	Fence erectors...............................	5,715	5,635	98.6	80	1.4	850	14.9	4,420	77.3
6720	Hazardous materials removal workers..........	9,185	7,810	85.0	1,375	15.0	1,360	14.8	5,670	61.7
6730	Highway maintenance workers	27,405	26,160	95.5	1,245	4.5	2,800	10.2	21,280	77.7
6740	Rail-track laying and maintenance equipment operators.................................	3,460	3,365	97.3	100	2.9	325	9.4	2,170	62.7
6765	Miscellaneous construction workers, including solar photovoltaic installers, septic tank servicers, and sewer pipe cleaners...	11,610	11,175	96.3	440	3.8	1,530	13.2	8,490	73.1
6800	Derrick, rotary drill, and service unit operators, and roustabouts, oil, gas, and mining..	8,010	7,920	98.9	90	1.1	1,345	16.8	5,770	72.0
6820	Earth drillers, except oil and gas	6,175	6,055	98.1	120	1.9	440	7.1	5,385	87.2
6830	Explosives workers, ordnance handling experts, and blasters...........................	3,910	3,725	95.3	185	4.7	415	10.6	3,040	77.7
6840	Mining machine operators............................	14,580	14,050	96.4	530	3.6	1,435	9.8	12,165	83.4
6940	Miscellaneous extraction workers, including roof bolters and helpers	13,830	13,455	97.3	375	2.7	1,730	12.5	10,695	77.3
7000	First-line supervisors of mechanics, installers, and repairers	128,655	119,305	92.7	9,350	7.3	11,330	8.8	103,550	80.5
7010	Computer, automated teller, and office machine repairers	144,990	127,805	88.1	17,185	11.9	13,665	9.4	105,535	72.8
7020	Radio and telecommunications equipment installers and repairers.........................	93,750	82,605	88.1	11,150	11.9	9,175	9.8	67,590	72.1
7030	Avionics technicians	9,820	9,140	93.1	685	7.0	1,145	11.7	7,505	76.4
7040	Electric motor, power tool, and related repairers.......................................	11,990	11,535	96.2	455	3.8	1,535	12.8	8,605	71.8
7100	Electrical and electronics repairers, transportation equipment, and industrial and utility	8,685	8,430	97.1	255	2.9	340	3.9	7,230	83.2
7110	Electronic equipment installers and repairers, motor vehicles............................	8,705	8,310	95.5	395	4.5	705	8.1	6,795	78.1
7120	Electronic home entertainment equipment installers and repairers	26,810	25,945	96.8	865	3.2	3,355	12.5	19,070	71.1
7130	Security and fire alarm systems installers......	24,280	23,355	96.2	925	3.8	3,040	12.5	17,610	72.5
7140	Aircraft mechanics and service technicians ..	83,260	79,930	96.0	3,330	4.0	9,905	11.9	61,175	73.5
7150	Automotive body and related repairers	36,975	36,305	98.2	670	1.8	5,050	13.7	27,955	75.6
7160	Automotive glass installers and repairers......	4,565	4,420	96.8	145	3.2	810	17.7	3,270	71.6
7200	Automotive service technicians and mechanics...................................	267,805	263,210	98.3	4,600	1.7	35,700	13.3	195,775	73.1
7210	Bus and truck mechanics and diesel engine specialists.....................................	96,230	94,905	98.6	1,325	1.4	9,450	9.8	74,910	77.8
7220	Heavy vehicle and mobile equipment service technicians and mechanics...............	69,665	68,575	98.4	1,090	1.6	6,165	8.8	57,625	82.7
7240	Small engine mechanics............................	15,265	14,920	97.7	345	2.3	965	6.3	13,360	87.5
7260	Miscellaneous vehicle and mobile equipment mechanics, installers, and repairers..	19,445	18,915	97.3	530	2.7	3,065	15.8	13,575	69.8

PART A—NATIONAL DATA

A-20 Workers with Some College or Associate's Degree: Detailed Occupation, by Sex, Race, and Hispanic Origin, 2006–2010—Continued

Census occupation code	Detailed Occupation	Black or African American alone Number	Black or African American alone Percent	American Indian and Alaska Native alone Number	American Indian and Alaska Native alone Percent	Asian alone Number	Asian alone Percent	Native Hawaiian and Other Pacific Islander alone Number	Native Hawaiian and Other Pacific Islander alone Percent	Not Hispanic or Latino, two or more races Number	Not Hispanic or Latino, two or more races Percent
6500	Reinforcing iron and rebar workers	110	6.0	35	1.9	0	0.0	0	0.0	10	0.5
6515	Roofers	1,775	6.7	150	0.6	195	0.7	75	0.3	475	1.8
6520	Sheet metal workers	2,280	5.6	245	0.6	810	2.0	40	0.1	650	1.6
6530	Structural iron and steel workers	1,495	8.1	135	0.7	180	1.0	70	0.4	340	1.9
6600	Helpers, construction trades	1,095	8.2	100	0.7	165	1.2	40	0.3	204	1.5
6660	Construction and building inspectors	3,860	8.2	505	1.1	625	1.3	100	0.2	425	0.9
6700	Elevator installers and repairers	705	6.1	20	0.2	185	1.6	65	0.6	155	1.3
6710	Fence erectors	210	3.7	65	1.1	45	0.8	0	0.0	125	2.2
6720	Hazardous materials removal workers	1,795	19.5	130	1.4	135	1.5	0	0.0	90	1.0
6730	Highway maintenance workers	2,550	9.3	275	1.0	130	0.5	40	0.1	330	1.2
6740	Rail-track laying and maintenance equipment operators	780	22.5	65	1.9	55	1.6	0	0.0	64	1.8
6765	Miscellaneous construction workers, including solar photovoltaic installers, septic tank servicers, and sewer pipe cleaners	1,125	9.7	60	0.5	165	1.4	15	0.1	225	1.9
6800	Derrick, rotary drill, and service unit operators, and roustabouts, oil, gas, and mining	530	6.6	170	2.1	0	0.0	0	0.0	195	2.4
6820	Earth drillers, except oil and gas	145	2.3	95	1.5	0	0.0	20	0.3	85	1.4
6830	Explosives workers, ordnance handling experts, and blasters	385	9.8	10	0.3	15	0.4	0	0.0	45	1.2
6840	Mining machine operators	510	3.5	270	1.9	65	0.4	0	0.0	140	1.0
6940	Miscellaneous extraction workers, including roof bolters and helpers	830	6.0	280	2.0	50	0.4	45	0.3	205	1.5
7000	First-line supervisors of mechanics, installers, and repairers	9,115	7.1	675	0.5	2,280	1.8	175	0.1	1,525	1.2
7010	Computer, automated teller, and office machine repairers	14,825	10.2	625	0.4	7,430	5.1	255	0.2	2,655	1.8
7020	Radio and telecommunications equipment installers and repairers	12,465	13.3	530	0.6	2,800	3.0	85	0.1	1,105	1.2
7030	Avionics technicians	625	6.4	55	0.6	320	3.3	10	0.1	165	1.7
7040	Electric motor, power tool, and related repairers	1,130	9.4	130	1.1	455	3.8	45	0.4	100	0.8
7100	Electrical and electronics repairers, transportation equipment, and industrial and utility	680	7.8	70	0.8	270	3.1	15	0.2	80	0.9
7110	Electronic equipment installers and repairers, motor vehicles	745	8.6	55	0.6	230	2.6	20	0.2	159	1.8
7120	Electronic home entertainment equipment installers and repairers	2,695	10.1	190	0.7	980	3.7	15	0.1	500	1.9
7130	Security and fire alarm systems installers	2,075	8.5	160	0.7	770	3.2	130	0.5	490	2.0
7140	Aircraft mechanics and service technicians	6,255	7.5	415	0.5	3,600	4.3	420	0.5	1,495	1.8
7150	Automotive body and related repairers	2,060	5.6	255	0.7	1,205	3.3	40	0.1	410	1.1
7160	Automotive glass installers and repairers	295	6.5	25	0.5	55	1.2	0	0.0	110	2.4
7200	Automotive service technicians and mechanics	17,590	6.6	1,585	0.6	12,265	4.6	685	0.3	4,205	1.6
7210	Bus and truck mechanics and diesel engine specialists	7,520	7.8	660	0.7	2,210	2.3	240	0.2	1,240	1.3
7220	Heavy vehicle and mobile equipment service technicians and mechanics	3,335	4.8	445	0.6	1,065	1.5	130	0.2	900	1.3
7240	Small engine mechanics	415	2.7	100	0.7	235	1.5	4	0.0	190	1.2
7260	Miscellaneous vehicle and mobile equipment mechanics, installers, and repairers	1,740	8.9	205	1.1	505	2.6	0	0.0	365	1.9

A-20 **Workers with Some College or Associate's Degree: Detailed Occupation, by Sex, Race, and Hispanic Origin, 2006–2010**—*Continued*

| Census occupation code | Detailed Occupation | Total | Some college or associate's degree ||||| Not Hispanic or Latino, one race White alone ||
| | | | Male || Female || Hispanic or Latino || |||
			Number	Percent	Number	Percent	Number	Percent	Number	Percent
7300	Control and valve installers and repairers	8,460	7,965	94.1	495	5.9	1,010	11.9	6,375	75.4
7315	Heating, air conditioning, and refrigeration mechanics and installers	137,875	136,225	98.8	1,650	1.2	15,090	10.9	108,130	78.4
7320	Home appliance repairers	14,775	14,275	96.6	500	3.4	1,690	11.4	10,895	73.7
7330	Industrial and refractory machinery mechanics	154,660	149,895	96.9	4,765	3.1	13,090	8.5	123,735	80.0
7340	Maintenance and repair workers, general	168,940	162,995	96.5	5,945	3.5	17,425	10.3	126,600	74.9
7350	Maintenance workers, machinery	13,760	13,290	96.6	470	3.4	1,135	8.2	10,765	78.2
7360	Millwrights	20,690	20,260	97.9	430	2.1	565	2.7	18,695	90.4
7410	Electrical power-line installers and repairers	47,175	46,285	98.1	890	1.9	3,515	7.5	38,970	82.6
7420	Telecommunications line installers and repairers	72,805	68,180	93.6	4,625	6.4	8,505	11.7	49,690	68.3
7430	Precision instrument and equipment repairers	32,410	29,700	91.6	2,705	8.3	2,515	7.8	25,595	79.0
7510	Coin, vending, and amusement machine servicers and repairers	17,000	13,865	81.6	3,135	18.4	1,630	9.6	12,715	74.8
7540	Locksmiths and safe repairers	9,540	8,980	94.1	560	5.9	915	9.6	7,490	78.5
7550	Manufactured building and mobile home installers	1,590	1,420	89.3	170	10.7	180	11.3	1,175	73.9
7560	Riggers	3,185	3,070	96.4	115	3.6	205	6.4	2,200	69.1
7610	Helpers--installation, maintenance, and repair workers	4,795	4,445	92.7	355	7.4	1,140	23.8	2,740	57.1
7630	Other installation, maintenance, and repair workers, including wind turbine service technicians, and commercial divers, and signal and track switch repairers	76,280	71,460	93.7	4,820	6.3	8,030	10.5	58,960	77.3
7700	First-line supervisors of production and operating workers	313,250	262,245	83.7	51,005	16.3	30,525	9.7	238,050	76.0
7710	Aircraft structure, surfaces, rigging, and systems assemblers	3,875	3,065	79.1	805	20.8	570	14.7	2,595	67.0
7720	Electrical, electronics, and electromechanical assemblers	42,460	24,040	56.6	18,425	43.4	4,730	11.1	24,515	57.7
7730	Engine and other machine assemblers	5,425	4,645	85.6	780	14.4	315	5.8	4,215	77.7
7740	Structural metal fabricators and fitters	8,285	7,975	96.3	310	3.7	585	7.1	6,545	79.0
7750	Miscellaneous assemblers and fabricators	238,300	156,155	65.5	82,145	34.5	24,445	10.3	153,610	64.5
7800	Bakers	42,845	17,840	41.6	25,005	58.4	6,830	15.9	28,205	65.8
7810	Butchers and other meat, poultry, and fish processing workers	46,215	38,530	83.4	7,685	16.6	8,005	17.3	29,450	63.7
7830	Food and tobacco roasting, baking, and drying machine operators and tenders	2,405	1,545	64.2	860	35.8	430	17.9	1,435	59.7
7840	Food batchmakers	21,330	7,000	32.8	14,330	67.2	3,445	16.2	13,935	65.3
7850	Food cooking machine operators and tenders	2,430	1,625	66.9	805	33.1	480	19.8	1,220	50.2
7855	Food processing workers, all other	23,290	15,570	66.9	7,720	33.1	3,780	16.2	12,655	54.3
7900	Computer control programmers and operators	26,025	24,160	92.8	1,865	7.2	1,860	7.1	20,920	80.4
7920	Extruding and drawing machine setters, operators, and tenders, metal and plastic	3,215	2,655	82.6	560	17.4	205	6.4	2,610	81.2
7930	Forging machine setters, operators, and tenders, metal and plastic	1,500	1,460	97.3	40	2.7	100	6.7	1,100	73.3
7940	Rolling machine setters, operators, and tenders, metal and plastic	2,260	1,915	84.7	345	15.3	195	8.6	1,720	76.1
7950	Cutting, punching, and press machine setters, operators, and tenders, metal and plastic	20,100	16,495	82.1	3,610	18.0	2,185	10.9	14,260	70.9
7960	Drilling and boring machine tool setters, operators, and tenders, metal and plastic	1,110	835	75.2	275	24.8	40	3.6	875	78.8

PART A—NATIONAL DATA

A-20 Workers with Some College or Associate's Degree: Detailed Occupation, by Sex, Race, and Hispanic Origin, 2006–2010—Continued

Census occupation code	Detailed Occupation	Black or African American alone Number	Percent	American Indian and Alaska Native alone Number	Percent	Asian alone Number	Percent	Native Hawaiian and Other Pacific Islander alone Number	Percent	Not Hispanic or Latino, two or more races Number	Percent
7300	Control and valve installers and repairers....	790	9.3	40	0.5	140	1.7	15	0.2	90	1.1
7315	Heating, air conditioning, and refrigeration mechanics and installers	9,390	6.8	675	0.5	2,535	1.8	80	0.1	1,975	1.4
7320	Home appliance repairers	1,125	7.6	160	1.1	500	3.4	0	0.0	400	2.7
7330	Industrial and refractory machinery mechanics	11,100	7.2	940	0.6	3,955	2.6	115	0.1	1,725	1.1
7340	Maintenance and repair workers, general	15,650	9.3	1,445	0.9	5,135	3.0	510	0.3	2,175	1.3
7350	Maintenance workers, machinery	1,235	9.0	120	0.9	235	1.7	60	0.4	210	1.5
7360	Millwrights	1,005	4.9	80	0.4	180	0.9	4	0.0	160	0.8
7410	Electrical power-line installers and repairers..	3,325	7.0	280	0.6	450	1.0	65	0.1	570	1.2
7420	Telecommunications line installers and repairers	10,715	14.7	365	0.5	2,035	2.8	145	0.2	1,345	1.8
7430	Precision instrument and equipment repairers	2,215	6.8	125	0.4	1,295	4.0	35	0.1	625	1.9
7510	Coin, vending, and amusement machine servicers and repairers	1,685	9.9	205	1.2	470	2.8	0	0.0	290	1.7
7540	Locksmiths and safe repairers	685	7.2	60	0.6	150	1.6	0	0.0	240	2.5
7550	Manufactured building and mobile home installers	120	7.5	50	3.1	25	1.6	0	0.0	35	2.2
7560	Riggers	535	16.8	40	1.3	85	2.7	10	0.3	110	3.5
7610	Helpers--installation, maintenance, and repair workers	590	12.3	45	0.9	170	3.5	45	0.9	74	1.5
7630	Other installation, maintenance, and repair workers, including wind turbine service technicians, and commercial divers, and signal and track switch repairers	5,655	7.4	325	0.4	2,025	2.7	50	0.1	1,230	1.6
7700	First-line supervisors of production and operating workers	31,390	10.0	1,170	0.4	8,215	2.6	335	0.1	3,560	1.1
7710	Aircraft structure, surfaces, rigging, and systems assemblers	505	13.0	55	1.4	120	3.1	0	0.0	35	0.9
7720	Electrical, electronics, and electromechanical assemblers	5,945	14.0	365	0.9	6,255	14.7	90	0.2	565	1.3
7730	Engine and other machine assemblers	630	11.6	65	1.2	135	2.5	0	0.0	75	1.4
7740	Structural metal fabricators and fitters	845	10.2	55	0.7	150	1.8	0	0.0	110	1.3
7750	Miscellaneous assemblers and fabricators....	41,025	17.2	1,410	0.6	14,580	6.1	215	0.1	3,005	1.3
7800	Bakers	4,420	10.3	205	0.5	2,395	5.6	110	0.3	674	1.6
7810	Butchers and other meat, poultry, and fish processing workers	6,330	13.7	360	0.8	1,470	3.2	115	0.2	480	1.0
7830	Food and tobacco roasting, baking, and drying machine operators and tenders	320	13.3	50	2.1	135	5.6	20	0.8	19	0.8
7840	Food batchmakers	2,905	13.6	145	0.7	510	2.4	20	0.1	365	1.7
7850	Food cooking machine operators and tenders.	410	16.9	80	3.3	120	4.9	0	0.0	125	5.1
7855	Food processing workers, all other	4,655	20.0	145	0.6	1,555	6.7	115	0.5	379	1.6
7900	Computer control programmers and operators.	1,535	5.9	115	0.4	1,335	5.1	55	0.2	205	0.8
7920	Extruding and drawing machine setters, operators, and tenders, metal and plastic...	315	9.8	15	0.5	65	2.0	0	0.0	10	0.3
7930	Forging machine setters, operators, and tenders, metal and plastic	230	15.3	0	0.0	65	4.3	4	0.3	4	0.3
7940	Rolling machine setters, operators, and tenders, metal and plastic	150	6.6	0	0.0	155	6.9	0	0.0	44	1.9
7950	Cutting, punching, and press machine setters, operators, and tenders, metal and plastic	2,730	13.6	145	0.7	510	2.5	0	0.0	274	1.4
7960	Drilling and boring machine tool setters, operators, and tenders, metal and plastic...	160	14.4	4	0.4	20	1.8	4	0.4	4	0.4

A-20 **Workers with Some College or Associate's Degree: Detailed Occupation, by Sex, Race, and Hispanic Origin, 2006–2010**—*Continued*

| Census occupation code | Detailed Occupation | Total | Some college or associate's degree |||||| Not Hispanic or Latino, one race ||
|||| Male || Female || Hispanic or Latino || White alone ||
			Number	Percent	Number	Percent	Number	Percent	Number	Percent
8000	Grinding, lapping, polishing, and buffing machine tool setters, operators, and tenders, metal and plastic	9,705	8,735	90.0	965	9.9	1,150	11.8	7,230	74.5
8010	Lathe and turning machine tool setters, operators, and tenders, metal and plastic	2,880	2,520	87.5	360	12.5	290	10.1	2,300	79.9
8030	Machinists	135,155	130,780	96.8	4,375	3.2	9,425	7.0	108,820	80.5
8040	Metal furnace operators, tenders, pourers, and casters	5,710	5,250	91.9	460	8.1	405	7.1	4,400	77.1
8060	Model makers and patternmakers, metal and plastic	2,955	2,505	84.8	450	15.2	115	3.9	2,665	90.2
8100	Molders and molding machine setters, operators, and tenders, metal and plastic	11,545	9,710	84.1	1,835	15.9	675	5.8	9,110	78.9
8130	Tool and die makers	34,700	34,055	98.1	645	1.9	1,460	4.2	31,600	91.1
8140	Welding, soldering, and brazing workers	142,230	134,215	94.4	8,020	5.6	17,455	12.3	105,100	73.9
8150	Heat treating equipment setters, operators, and tenders, metal and plastic	2,415	2,135	88.4	285	11.8	135	5.6	1,885	78.1
8200	Plating and coating machine setters, operators, and tenders, metal and plastic	4,110	3,685	89.7	420	10.2	595	14.5	2,755	67.0
8210	Tool grinders, filers, and sharpeners	2,595	2,440	94.0	155	6.0	170	6.6	2,080	80.2
8220	Miscellaneous metal workers and plastic workers, including milling and planing machine setters, and multiple machine tool setters, and layout workers	94,695	76,330	80.6	18,365	19.4	10,990	11.6	59,695	63.0
8250	Prepress technicians and workers	16,650	8,365	50.2	8,285	49.8	1,490	8.9	12,370	74.3
8255	Printing press operators	67,805	55,930	82.5	11,875	17.5	7,255	10.7	49,410	72.9
8256	Print binding and finishing workers	7,995	4,665	58.3	3,330	41.7	735	9.2	6,170	77.2
8300	Laundry and dry-cleaning workers	32,730	18,240	55.7	14,490	44.3	6,080	18.6	17,785	54.3
8310	Pressers, textile, garment, and related materials	6,745	2,930	43.4	3,810	56.5	1,620	24.0	2,895	42.9
8320	Sewing machine operators	31,160	6,930	22.2	24,230	77.8	5,360	17.2	17,870	57.3
8330	Shoe and leather workers and repairers	2,345	1,845	78.7	500	21.3	395	16.8	1,510	64.4
8340	Shoe machine operators and tenders	640	395	61.7	245	38.3	115	18.0	405	63.3
8350	Tailors, dressmakers, and sewers	19,550	3,770	19.3	15,780	80.7	2,445	12.5	12,160	62.2
8400	Textile bleaching and dyeing, and cutting machine setters, operators, and tenders	2,380	1,265	53.2	1,115	46.8	360	15.1	1,475	62.0
8410	Textile knitting and weaving machine setters, operators, and tenders	1,975	590	29.9	1,380	69.9	285	14.4	1,150	58.2
8420	Textile winding, twisting, and drawing out machine setters, operators, and tenders	1,945	545	28.0	1,405	72.2	290	14.9	1,015	52.2
8450	Upholsterers	7,780	6,350	81.6	1,430	18.4	1,080	13.9	5,695	73.2
8460	Miscellaneous textile, apparel, and furnishings workers, except upholsterers	4,575	2,220	48.5	2,360	51.6	845	18.5	2,315	50.6
8500	Cabinetmakers and bench carpenters	17,295	16,320	94.4	975	5.6	1,585	9.2	14,630	84.6
8510	Furniture finishers	4,485	3,785	84.4	700	15.6	585	13.0	3,595	80.2
8530	Sawing machine setters, operators, and tenders, wood	5,850	4,865	83.2	980	16.8	750	12.8	4,305	73.6
8540	Woodworking machine setters, operators, and tenders, except sawing	4,970	4,105	82.6	865	17.4	460	9.3	3,760	75.7
8550	Miscellaneous woodworkers, including model makers and patternmakers	7,455	6,895	92.5	555	7.4	455	6.1	6,420	86.1
8600	Power plant operators, distributors, and dispatchers	21,850	20,610	94.3	1,240	5.7	1,210	5.5	18,330	83.9
8610	Stationary engineers and boiler operators	38,490	37,200	96.6	1,290	3.4	3,445	9.0	28,060	72.9
8620	Water and wastewater treatment plant and system operators	33,785	32,000	94.7	1,785	5.3	2,555	7.6	26,945	79.8

A-20 Workers with Some College or Associate's Degree: Detailed Occupation, by Sex, Race, and Hispanic Origin, 2006–2010—Continued

Census occupation code	Detailed Occupation	\multicolumn{10}{c}{Some college or associate's degree}
		\multicolumn{8}{c}{Not Hispanic or Latino, one race}	\multicolumn{2}{c}{Not Hispanic or Latino, two or more races}
		Black or African American alone		American Indian and Alaska Native alone		Asian alone		Native Hawaiian and Other Pacific Islander alone			
		Number	Percent	Number	Percent	Number	Percent	Number	Percent	Number	Percent
8000	Grinding, lapping, polishing, and buffing machine tool setters, operators, and tenders, metal and plastic	1,120	11.5	20	0.2	105	1.1	0	0.0	75	0.8
8010	Lathe and turning machine tool setters, operators, and tenders, metal and plastic	200	6.9	30	1.0	30	1.0	0	0.0	29	1.0
8030	Machinists	8,120	6.0	865	0.6	6,085	4.5	130	0.1	1,715	1.3
8040	Metal furnace operators, tenders, pourers, and casters	805	14.1	0	0.0	80	1.4	10	0.2	10	0.2
8060	Model makers and patternmakers, metal and plastic	90	3.0	10	0.3	70	2.4	0	0.0	10	0.3
8100	Molders and molding machine setters, operators, and tenders, metal and plastic	1,405	12.2	4	0.0	315	2.7	0	0.0	30	0.3
8130	Tool and die makers	825	2.4	70	0.2	415	1.2	15	0.0	325	0.9
8140	Welding, soldering, and brazing workers	12,355	8.7	1,985	1.4	3,095	2.2	325	0.2	1,910	1.3
8150	Heat treating equipment setters, operators, and tenders, metal and plastic	360	14.9	0	0.0	10	0.4	0	0.0	30	1.2
8200	Plating and coating machine setters, operators, and tenders, metal and plastic	520	12.7	0	0.0	155	3.8	0	0.0	85	2.1
8210	Tool grinders, filers, and sharpeners	185	7.1	15	0.6	105	4.0	0	0.0	45	1.7
8220	Miscellaneous metal workers and plastic workers, including milling and planing machine setters, and multiple machine tool setters, and layout workers	14,575	15.4	455	0.5	7,375	7.8	95	0.1	1,510	1.6
8250	Prepress technicians and workers	1,965	11.8	70	0.4	515	3.1	0	0.0	235	1.4
8255	Printing press operators	7,185	10.6	215	0.3	2,725	4.0	55	0.1	965	1.4
8256	Print binding and finishing workers	570	7.1	70	0.9	330	4.1	45	0.6	75	0.9
8300	Laundry and dry-cleaning workers	5,405	16.5	165	0.5	2,795	8.5	105	0.3	390	1.2
8310	Pressers, textile, garment, and related materials	1,610	23.9	35	0.5	515	7.6	15	0.2	44	0.7
8320	Sewing machine operators	4,040	13.0	290	0.9	3,135	10.1	40	0.1	425	1.4
8330	Shoe and leather workers and repairers	220	9.4	10	0.4	210	9.0	0	0.0	4	0.2
8340	Shoe machine operators and tenders	75	11.7	0	0.0	45	7.0	0	0.0	0	0.0
8350	Tailors, dressmakers, and sewers	1,585	8.1	65	0.3	3,190	16.3	0	0.0	94	0.5
8400	Textile bleaching and dyeing, and cutting machine setters, operators, and tenders	400	16.8	0	0.0	95	4.0	0	0.0	45	1.9
8410	Textile knitting and weaving machine setters, operators, and tenders	415	21.0	0	0.0	100	5.1	0	0.0	20	1.0
8420	Textile winding, twisting, and drawing out machine setters, operators, and tenders	595	30.6	4	0.2	45	2.3	0	0.0	0	0.0
8450	Upholsterers	725	9.3	10	0.1	220	2.8	0	0.0	55	0.7
8460	Miscellaneous textile, apparel, and furnishings workers, except upholsterers	705	15.4	10	0.2	620	13.6	0	0.0	79	1.7
8500	Cabinetmakers and bench carpenters	595	3.4	25	0.1	320	1.9	10	0.1	130	0.8
8510	Furniture finishers	140	3.1	25	0.6	20	0.4	0	0.0	120	2.7
8530	Sawing machine setters, operators, and tenders, wood	640	10.9	90	1.5	25	0.4	0	0.0	30	0.5
8540	Woodworking machine setters, operators, and tenders, except sawing	450	9.1	65	1.3	95	1.9	0	0.0	135	2.7
8550	Miscellaneous woodworkers, including model makers and patternmakers	225	3.0	95	1.3	115	1.5	0	0.0	149	2.0
8600	Power plant operators, distributors, and dispatchers	1,455	6.7	325	1.5	185	0.8	0	0.0	355	1.6
8610	Stationary engineers and boiler operators	4,970	12.9	355	0.9	1,225	3.2	0	0.0	425	1.1
8620	Water and wastewater treatment plant and system operators	3,010	8.9	375	1.1	305	0.9	30	0.1	570	1.7

A-20 **Workers with Some College or Associate's Degree: Detailed Occupation, by Sex, Race, and Hispanic Origin, 2006–2010**—*Continued*

Census occupation code	Detailed Occupation	Total	Male Number	Male Percent	Female Number	Female Percent	Hispanic or Latino Number	Hispanic or Latino Percent	White alone Number	White alone Percent
8630	Miscellaneous plant and system operators....	16,820	15,785	93.8	1,035	6.2	1,890	11.2	12,810	76.2
8640	Chemical processing machine setters, operators, and tenders..................	19,135	16,925	88.5	2,215	11.6	1,570	8.2	14,010	73.2
8650	Crushing, grinding, polishing, mixing, and blending workers.........................	21,935	19,160	87.3	2,775	12.7	2,865	13.1	13,925	63.5
8710	Cutting workers	13,365	10,535	78.8	2,825	21.1	1,835	13.7	8,870	66.4
8720	Extruding, forming, pressing, and compacting machine setters, operators, and tenders	7,935	6,600	83.2	1,335	16.8	695	8.8	5,735	72.3
8730	Furnace, kiln, oven, drier, and kettle operators and tenders........................	3,975	3,320	83.5	655	16.5	340	8.6	2,635	66.3
8740	Inspectors, testers, sorters, samplers, and weighers...	257,480	179,380	69.7	78,100	30.3	27,525	10.7	180,235	70.0
8750	Jewelers and precious stone and metal workers..	12,240	7,955	65.0	4,280	35.0	1,535	12.5	8,630	70.5
8760	Medical, dental, and ophthalmic laboratory technicians.....................................	39,610	20,050	50.6	19,565	49.4	4,750	12.0	28,265	71.4
8800	Packaging and filling machine operators and tenders	43,200	20,350	47.1	22,850	52.9	8,820	20.4	21,850	50.6
8810	Painting workers..................................	35,550	30,385	85.5	5,165	14.5	5,650	15.9	24,685	69.4
8830	Photographic process workers and processing machine operators.....................	23,405	9,930	42.4	13,475	57.6	2,750	11.7	15,640	66.8
8850	Adhesive bonding machine operators and tenders...	2,945	2,015	68.4	935	31.7	300	10.2	2,030	68.9
8860	Cleaning, washing, and metal pickling equipment operators and tenders............	1,680	1,255	74.7	420	25.0	215	12.8	1,270	75.6
8910	Etchers and engravers	3,825	2,345	61.3	1,475	38.6	260	6.8	2,935	76.7
8920	Molders, shapers, and casters, except metal and plastic	8,195	6,895	84.1	1,305	15.9	845	10.3	6,680	81.5
8930	Paper goods machine setters, operators, and tenders	8,015	6,560	81.8	1,455	18.2	570	7.1	5,540	69.1
8940	Tire builders...	4,400	3,920	89.1	480	10.9	270	6.1	2,980	67.7
8950	Helpers—production workers................	9,525	6,670	70.0	2,855	30.0	2,250	23.6	5,400	56.7
8965	Other production workers, including semiconductor processors and cooling and freezing equipment operators	254,930	189,710	74.4	65,220	25.6	29,505	11.6	166,835	65.4
9000	Supervisors of transportation and material moving workers............................	93,195	71,960	77.2	21,235	22.8	12,195	13.1	61,690	66.2
9030	Aircraft pilots and flight engineers............	27,655	26,540	96.0	1,115	4.0	1,380	5.0	24,990	90.4
9040	Air traffic controllers and airfield operations specialists......................................	16,875	14,065	83.3	2,810	16.7	1,350	8.0	12,995	77.0
9050	Flight attendants	41,540	9,010	21.7	32,535	78.3	4,565	11.0	28,965	69.7
9110	Ambulance drivers and attendants, except emergency medical technicians	4,315	3,350	77.6	970	22.5	780	18.1	2,600	60.3
9120	Bus drivers...	193,070	106,775	55.3	86,295	44.7	18,760	9.7	108,670	56.3
9130	Driver/sales workers and truck drivers.........	824,285	769,330	93.3	54,950	6.7	99,970	12.1	570,520	69.2
9140	Taxi drivers and chauffeurs..................	89,975	76,370	84.9	13,600	15.1	11,345	12.6	45,090	50.1
9150	Motor vehicle operators, all other	15,510	13,920	89.7	1,590	10.3	1,670	10.8	11,175	72.1
9200	Locomotive engineers and operators............	21,965	20,825	94.8	1,135	5.2	1,310	6.0	16,350	74.4

PART A—NATIONAL DATA

A-20 Workers with Some College or Associate's Degree: Detailed Occupation, by Sex, Race, and Hispanic Origin, 2006–2010—*Continued*

Census occupation code	Detailed Occupation	Black or African American alone Number	Black or African American alone Percent	American Indian and Alaska Native alone Number	American Indian and Alaska Native alone Percent	Asian alone Number	Asian alone Percent	Native Hawaiian and Other Pacific Islander alone Number	Native Hawaiian and Other Pacific Islander alone Percent	Not Hispanic or Latino, two or more races Number	Not Hispanic or Latino, two or more races Percent
8630	Miscellaneous plant and system operators...	1,445	8.6	165	1.0	190	1.1	50	0.3	265	1.6
8640	Chemical processing machine setters, operators, and tenders	2,855	14.9	85	0.4	360	1.9	20	0.1	235	1.2
8650	Crushing, grinding, polishing, mixing, and blending workers	4,155	18.9	115	0.5	470	2.1	30	0.1	370	1.7
8710	Cutting workers	1,910	14.3	150	1.1	305	2.3	10	0.1	279	2.1
8720	Extruding, forming, pressing, and compacting machine setters, operators, and tenders	1,235	15.6	45	0.6	140	1.8	0	0.0	85	1.1
8730	Furnace, kiln, oven, drier, and kettle operators and tenders	820	20.6	30	0.8	90	2.3	0	0.0	55	1.4
8740	Inspectors, testers, sorters, samplers, and weighers	29,710	11.5	1,305	0.5	13,945	5.4	640	0.2	4,135	1.6
8750	Jewelers and precious stone and metal workers	370	3.0	555	4.5	920	7.5	10	0.1	215	1.8
8760	Medical, dental, and ophthalmic laboratory technicians	2,465	6.2	70	0.2	3,360	8.5	75	0.2	630	1.6
8800	Packaging and filling machine operators and tenders	9,800	22.7	435	1.0	1,720	4.0	60	0.1	510	1.2
8810	Painting workers	3,575	10.1	110	0.3	715	2.0	0	0.0	810	2.3
8830	Photographic process workers and processing machine operators	3,100	13.2	40	0.2	1,240	5.3	4	0.0	625	2.7
8850	Adhesive bonding machine operators and tenders	400	13.6	30	1.0	115	3.9	10	0.3	59	2.0
8860	Cleaning, washing, and metal pickling equipment operators and tenders	140	8.3	0	0.0	25	1.5	0	0.0	24	1.4
8910	Etchers and engravers	240	6.3	85	2.2	175	4.6	0	0.0	130	3.4
8920	Molders, shapers, and casters, except metal and plastic	230	2.8	100	1.2	135	1.6	0	0.0	210	2.6
8930	Paper goods machine setters, operators, and tenders	1,520	19.0	50	0.6	135	1.7	15	0.2	185	2.3
8940	Tire builders	950	21.6	35	0.8	80	1.8	0	0.0	95	2.2
8950	Helpers—production workers	1,125	11.8	130	1.4	460	4.8	0	0.0	160	1.7
8965	Other production workers, including semiconductor processors and cooling and freezing equipment operators	42,290	16.6	1,460	0.6	10,860	4.3	425	0.2	3,555	1.4
9000	Supervisors of transportation and material moving workers	14,065	15.1	440	0.5	3,060	3.3	350	0.4	1,395	1.5
9030	Aircraft pilots and flight engineers	540	2.0	115	0.4	250	0.9	90	0.3	285	1.0
9040	Air traffic controllers and airfield operations specialists	1,545	9.2	20	0.1	425	2.5	135	0.8	415	2.5
9050	Flight attendants	4,435	10.7	120	0.3	2,135	5.1	290	0.7	1,025	2.5
9110	Ambulance drivers and attendants, except emergency medical technicians	680	15.8	95	2.2	100	2.3	0	0.0	64	1.5
9120	Bus drivers	56,305	29.2	1,505	0.8	3,965	2.1	295	0.2	3,565	1.8
9130	Driver/sales workers and truck drivers	121,840	14.8	4,615	0.6	14,700	1.8	1,750	0.2	10,895	1.3
9140	Taxi drivers and chauffeurs	24,130	26.8	620	0.7	6,840	7.6	150	0.2	1,800	2.0
9150	Motor vehicle operators, all other	2,155	13.9	45	0.3	270	1.7	15	0.1	184	1.2
9200	Locomotive engineers and operators	3,640	16.6	105	0.5	170	0.8	20	0.1	365	1.7

A-20 **Workers with Some College or Associate's Degree: Detailed Occupation, by Sex, Race, and Hispanic Origin, 2006–2010**—*Continued*

Census occupation code	Detailed Occupation	Total	Some college or associate's degree							
			Male		Female		Hispanic or Latino		Not Hispanic or Latino, one race — White alone	
			Number	Percent	Number	Percent	Number	Percent	Number	Percent
9230	Railroad brake, signal, and switch operators	2,615	2,515	96.2	100	3.8	255	9.8	2,105	80.5
9240	Railroad conductors and yardmasters	21,500	19,630	91.3	1,870	8.7	1,365	6.3	16,550	77.0
9260	Subway, streetcar, and other rail transportation workers	4,510	3,925	87.0	590	13.1	380	8.4	2,585	57.3
9300	Sailors and marine oilers, and ship engineers	7,295	6,935	95.1	360	4.9	490	6.7	5,220	71.6
9310	Ship and boat captains and operators	9,690	9,365	96.6	325	3.4	645	6.7	8,145	84.1
9350	Parking lot attendants	25,970	22,805	87.8	3,165	12.2	4,900	18.9	13,625	52.5
9360	Automotive and watercraft service attendants	31,275	22,290	71.3	8,985	28.7	2,900	9.3	22,390	71.6
9410	Transportation inspectors	21,750	18,360	84.4	3,390	15.6	2,790	12.8	15,260	70.2
9415	Transportation attendants, except flight attendants	8,535	3,440	40.3	5,095	59.7	1,470	17.2	3,790	44.4
9420	Miscellaneous transportation workers, including bridge and lock tenders and traffic technicians	9,430	8,355	88.6	1,080	11.5	1,335	14.2	5,685	60.3
9510	Crane and tower operators	15,095	14,560	96.5	535	3.5	1,395	9.2	10,900	72.2
9520	Dredge, excavating, and loading machine operators	8,305	8,115	97.7	195	2.3	645	7.8	7,030	84.6
9560	Conveyor operators and tenders, and hoist and winch operators	3,425	3,035	88.6	390	11.4	295	8.6	2,530	73.9
9600	Industrial truck and tractor operators	106,235	96,965	91.3	9,270	8.7	16,525	15.6	57,230	53.9
9610	Cleaners of vehicles and equipment	65,055	55,240	84.9	9,815	15.1	12,440	19.1	37,945	58.3
9620	Laborers and freight, stock, and material movers, hand	490,455	406,905	83.0	83,555	17.0	63,145	12.9	316,085	64.4
9630	Machine feeders and offbearers	7,565	4,215	55.7	3,350	44.3	1,145	15.1	4,690	62.0
9640	Packers and packagers, hand	67,400	31,460	46.7	35,935	53.3	15,650	23.2	32,880	48.8
9650	Pumping station operators	6,430	6,145	95.6	285	4.4	550	8.6	5,370	83.5
9720	Refuse and recyclable material collectors	16,665	14,975	89.9	1,690	10.1	2,515	15.1	9,370	56.2
9750	Miscellaneous material moving workers, including mine shuttle car operators, and tank car, truck, and ship loaders	13,850	11,420	82.5	2,430	17.5	1,930	13.9	8,905	64.3

A-20 Workers with Some College or Associate's Degree: Detailed Occupation, by Sex, Race, and Hispanic Origin, 2006–2010—Continued

Census occupation code	Detailed Occupation	Black or African American alone Number	Black or African American alone Percent	American Indian and Alaska Native alone Number	American Indian and Alaska Native alone Percent	Asian alone Number	Asian alone Percent	Native Hawaiian and Other Pacific Islander alone Number	Native Hawaiian and Other Pacific Islander alone Percent	Not Hispanic or Latino, two or more races Number	Not Hispanic or Latino, two or more races Percent
9230	Railroad brake, signal, and switch operators	165	6.3	4	0.2	10	0.4	0	0.0	73	2.8
9240	Railroad conductors and yardmasters	3,045	14.2	85	0.4	145	0.7	30	0.1	280	1.3
9260	Subway, streetcar, and other rail transportation workers	1,200	26.6	90	2.0	100	2.2	4	0.1	155	3.4
9300	Sailors and marine oilers, and ship engineers	1,105	15.1	35	0.5	235	3.2	15	0.2	190	2.6
9310	Ship and boat captains and operators	365	3.8	110	1.1	175	1.8	35	0.4	215	2.2
9350	Parking lot attendants	5,305	20.4	95	0.4	1,345	5.2	140	0.5	565	2.2
9360	Automotive and watercraft service attendants	3,120	10.0	240	0.8	1,895	6.1	35	0.1	700	2.2
9410	Transportation inspectors	2,605	12.0	135	0.6	705	3.2	60	0.3	200	0.9
9415	Transportation attendants, except flight attendants	2,735	32.0	50	0.6	365	4.3	20	0.2	104	1.2
9420	Miscellaneous transportation workers, including bridge and lock tenders and traffic technicians	1,835	19.5	0	0.0	300	3.2	80	0.8	195	2.1
9510	Crane and tower operators	2,215	14.7	170	1.1	15	0.1	70	0.5	325	2.2
9520	Dredge, excavating, and loading machine operators	405	4.9	95	1.1	40	0.5	0	0.0	90	1.1
9560	Conveyor operators and tenders, and hoist and winch operators	540	15.8	4	0.1	0	0.0	0	0.0	59	1.7
9600	Industrial truck and tractor operators	27,075	25.5	880	0.8	2,160	2.0	335	0.3	2,025	1.9
9610	Cleaners of vehicles and equipment	11,135	17.1	370	0.6	1,895	2.9	125	0.2	1,145	1.8
9620	Laborers and freight, stock, and material movers, hand	84,325	17.2	3,240	0.7	13,470	2.7	1,200	0.2	8,995	1.8
9630	Machine feeders and offbearers	1,295	17.1	15	0.2	195	2.6	30	0.4	190	2.5
9640	Packers and packagers, hand	13,455	20.0	495	0.7	3,685	5.5	220	0.3	1,005	1.5
9650	Pumping station operators	365	5.7	20	0.3	25	0.4	0	0.0	100	1.6
9720	Refuse and recyclable material collectors	4,020	24.1	145	0.9	235	1.4	25	0.2	354	2.1
9750	Miscellaneous material moving workers, including mine shuttle car operators, and tank car, truck, and ship loaders	2,390	17.3	90	0.6	150	1.1	65	0.5	315	2.3

A-21 **Workers with Bachelor's Degree: Detailed Occupations, by Sex, Race, and Hispanic Origin, 2006–2010**

Census occupation code	Detailed Occupation	Total	Bachelor's degree Male Number	Male Percent	Female Number	Female Percent	Hispanic or Latino Number	Hispanic or Latino Percent	Not Hispanic or Latino, one race White alone Number	White alone Percent
	Total, all occupations	27,140,875	13,908,675	51.2	13,232,200	48.8	1,867,870	6.9	20,594,260	75.9
0010	Chief executives and legislators	429,005	340,745	79.4	88,260	20.6	15,090	3.5	378,740	88.3
0020	General and operations managers	309,815	222,995	72.0	86,820	28.0	17,450	5.6	255,230	82.4
0040	Advertising and promotions managers	35,245	15,820	44.9	19,425	55.1	1,820	5.2	29,625	84.1
0050	Marketing and sales managers	396,940	224,495	56.6	172,445	43.4	20,830	5.2	336,515	84.8
0060	Public relations and fundraising managers	27,265	10,950	40.2	16,315	59.8	1,345	4.9	22,645	83.1
0100	Administrative services managers	28,760	18,495	64.3	10,265	35.7	1,140	4.0	23,400	81.4
0110	Computer and information systems managers	211,945	149,090	70.3	62,855	29.7	9,520	4.5	165,420	78.0
0120	Financial managers	423,055	235,540	55.7	187,510	44.3	26,590	6.3	332,655	78.6
0135	Compensation and benefits managers	10,535	3,080	29.2	7,460	70.8	415	3.9	8,585	81.5
0136	Human resources managers	111,865	46,265	41.4	65,600	58.6	9,055	8.1	84,850	75.9
0137	Training and development managers	14,425	6,850	47.5	7,575	52.5	595	4.1	11,730	81.3
0140	Industrial production managers	70,425	55,565	78.9	14,860	21.1	3,850	5.5	58,965	83.7
0150	Purchasing managers	69,320	41,180	59.4	28,145	40.6	3,780	5.5	55,705	80.4
0160	Transportation, storage, and distribution managers	43,445	33,895	78.0	9,550	22.0	3,225	7.4	33,440	77.0
0205	Farmers, ranchers, and other agricultural managers	111,920	93,650	83.7	18,270	16.3	1,610	1.4	107,570	96.1
0220	Construction managers	200,555	181,345	90.4	19,210	9.6	10,990	5.5	174,360	86.9
0230	Education administrators	181,835	57,590	31.7	124,245	68.3	13,340	7.3	136,065	74.8
0300	Architectural and engineering managers	66,605	61,430	92.2	5,175	7.8	2,695	4.0	57,225	85.9
0310	Food service managers	166,795	103,810	62.2	62,985	37.8	12,980	7.8	118,145	70.8
0330	Gaming managers	3,675	2,515	68.4	1,160	31.6	280	7.6	2,845	77.4
0340	Lodging managers	39,830	21,755	54.6	18,075	45.4	2,115	5.3	28,555	71.7
0350	Medical and health services managers	156,255	48,395	31.0	107,865	69.0	8,080	5.2	119,760	76.6
0360	Natural sciences managers	5,960	3,365	56.5	2,590	43.5	205	3.4	4,980	83.6
0410	Property, real estate, and community association managers	147,050	87,555	59.5	59,495	40.5	8,530	5.8	120,830	82.2
0410	Social and community service managers	115,905	38,340	33.1	77,570	66.9	6,910	6.0	89,065	76.8
0425	Emergency management directors	1,210	785	64.9	425	35.1	50	4.1	935	77.3
0430	Miscellaneous managers, including funeral service managers and postmasters and mail superintendents	1,029,930	673,585	65.4	356,345	34.6	56,325	5.5	830,290	80.6
0500	Agents and business managers of artists, performers, and athletes	17,790	9,650	54.2	8,140	45.8	1,125	6.3	14,445	81.2
0510	Buyers and purchasing agents, farm products	2,710	1,950	72.0	760	28.0	20	0.7	2,485	91.7
0520	Wholesale and retail buyers, except farm products	62,385	28,395	45.5	33,990	54.5	3,460	5.5	50,165	80.4
0530	Purchasing agents, except wholesale, retail, and farm products	82,700	41,935	50.7	40,765	49.3	4,660	5.6	64,965	78.6
0540	Claims adjusters, appraisers, examiners, and investigators	109,225	56,645	51.9	52,585	48.1	7,165	6.6	81,065	74.2
0565	Compliance officers	64,870	34,785	53.6	30,085	46.4	4,665	7.2	48,255	74.4
0600	Cost estimators	34,305	30,035	87.6	4,270	12.4	1,685	4.9	30,055	87.6
0630	Human resources workers	243,010	74,040	30.5	168,975	69.5	19,015	7.8	176,960	72.8

A-21 Workers with Bachelor's Degree: Detailed Occupations, by Sex, Race, and Hispanic Origin, 2006–2010—Continued

Census occupation code	Detailed Occupation	Bachelor's degree									
		Not Hispanic or Latino, one race								Not Hispanic or Latino, two or more races	
		Black or African American alone		American Indian and Alaska Native alone		Asian alone		Native Hawaiian and Other Pacific Islander alone			
		Number	Percent	Number	Percent	Number	Percent	Number	Percent	Number	Percent
	Total, all occupations	2,086,355	7.7	81,485	0.3	2,126,165	7.8	22,855	0.1	361,885	1.3
0010	Chief executives and legislators	11,255	2.6	1,110	0.3	19,190	4.5	100	0.0	3,515	0.8
0020	General and operations managers	16,345	5.3	715	0.2	16,300	5.3	155	0.1	3,620	1.2
0040	Advertising and promotions managers	1,465	4.2	60	0.2	1,740	4.9	55	0.2	485	1.4
0050	Marketing and sales managers	14,235	3.6	795	0.2	19,605	4.9	205	0.1	4,765	1.2
0060	Public relations and fundraising managers	1,825	6.7	100	0.4	940	3.4	0	0.0	405	1.5
0100	Administrative services managers	2,330	8.1	145	0.5	1,330	4.6	55	0.2	370	1.3
0110	Computer and information systems managers	11,310	5.3	275	0.1	22,580	10.7	155	0.1	2,685	1.3
0120	Financial managers	28,190	6.7	695	0.2	29,900	7.1	295	0.1	4,730	1.1
0135	Compensation and benefits managers	890	8.4	50	0.5	405	3.8	0	0.0	194	1.8
0136	Human resources managers	9,860	8.8	440	0.4	6,200	5.5	125	0.1	1,345	1.2
0137	Training and development managers	1,515	10.5	20	0.1	415	2.9	25	0.2	130	0.9
0140	Industrial production managers	2,805	4.0	75	0.1	4,095	5.8	35	0.0	600	0.9
0150	Purchasing managers	5,375	7.8	220	0.3	3,560	5.1	65	0.1	615	0.9
0160	Transportation, storage, and distribution managers	3,940	9.1	75	0.2	2,300	5.3	130	0.3	335	0.8
0205	Farmers, ranchers, and other agricultural managers	420	0.4	270	0.2	1,435	1.3	25	0.0	600	0.5
0220	Construction managers	6,815	3.4	330	0.2	6,390	3.2	105	0.1	1,570	0.8
0230	Education administrators	22,285	12.3	765	0.4	6,735	3.7	160	0.1	2,485	1.4
0300	Architectural and engineering managers	1,480	2.2	185	0.3	4,250	6.4	0	0.0	770	1.2
0310	Food service managers	8,975	5.4	365	0.2	24,040	14.4	205	0.1	2,090	1.3
0330	Gaming managers	150	4.1	140	3.8	225	6.1	0	0.0	40	1.1
0340	Lodging managers	2,255	5.7	125	0.3	5,975	15.0	70	0.2	735	1.8
0350	Medical and health services managers	16,050	10.3	585	0.4	10,160	6.5	90	0.1	1,535	1.0
0360	Natural sciences managers	140	2.3	10	0.2	315	5.3	45	0.8	270	4.5
0410	Property, real estate, and community association managers	8,170	5.6	515	0.4	7,095	4.8	145	0.1	1,765	1.2
0410	Social and community service managers	13,570	11.7	765	0.7	3,635	3.1	90	0.1	1,870	1.6
0425	Emergency management directors	170	14.0	0	0.0	10	0.8	0	0.0	50	4.1
0430	Miscellaneous managers, including funeral service managers and postmasters and mail superintendents	64,175	6.2	2,960	0.3	62,890	6.1	760	0.1	12,535	1.2
0500	Agents and business managers of artists, performers, and athletes	1,180	6.6	110	0.6	555	3.1	25	0.1	345	1.9
0510	Buyers and purchasing agents, farm products	15	0.6	10	0.4	180	6.6	0	0.0	4	0.1
0520	Wholesale and retail buyers, except farm products	2,475	4.0	45	0.1	5,250	8.4	45	0.1	940	1.5
0530	Purchasing agents, except wholesale, retail, and farm products	6,405	7.7	305	0.4	5,415	6.5	115	0.1	835	1.0
0540	Claims adjusters, appraisers, examiners, and investigators	13,835	12.7	180	0.2	5,430	5.0	50	0.0	1,505	1.4
0565	Compliance officers	6,295	9.7	285	0.4	4,330	6.7	55	0.1	985	1.5
0600	Cost estimators	605	1.8	50	0.1	1,720	5.0	0	0.0	190	0.6
0630	Human resources workers	29,500	12.1	800	0.3	12,770	5.3	325	0.1	3,640	1.5

A-21 **Workers with Bachelor's Degree: Detailed Occupations, by Sex, Race, and Hispanic Origin, 2006–2010**—Continued

Census occupation code	Detailed Occupation	Total	Bachelor's degree Male Number	Male Percent	Female Number	Female Percent	Hispanic or Latino Number	Hispanic or Latino Percent	Not Hispanic or Latino, one race White alone Number	White alone Percent
0640	Compensation, benefits, and job analysis specialists	35,675	7,840	22.0	27,835	78.0	2,365	6.6	26,505	74.3
0650	Training and development specialists	40,750	16,415	40.3	24,335	59.7	2,765	6.8	30,465	74.8
0700	Logisticians	22,865	15,350	67.1	7,515	32.9	1,650	7.2	16,725	73.1
0710	Management analysts	272,545	162,590	59.7	109,960	40.3	12,295	4.5	215,835	79.2
0725	Meeting, convention, and event planners	27,885	5,145	18.5	22,740	81.5	1,655	5.9	22,785	81.7
0726	Fundraisers	38,795	9,105	23.5	29,690	76.5	1,115	2.9	34,700	89.4
0735	Market research analysts and marketing specialists	87,275	36,145	41.4	51,130	58.6	4,400	5.0	70,995	81.3
0740	Business operations specialists, all other	73,210	30,340	41.4	42,870	58.6	5,205	7.1	51,820	70.8
0800	Accountants and auditors	1,140,160	505,650	44.3	634,510	55.7	66,980	5.9	845,015	74.1
0810	Appraisers and assessors of real estate	43,255	32,860	76.0	10,395	24.0	1,325	3.1	38,365	88.7
0820	Budget analysts	21,950	9,045	41.2	12,905	58.8	1,375	6.3	14,570	66.4
0830	Credit analysts	12,945	7,145	55.2	5,800	44.8	810	6.3	9,815	75.8
0840	Financial analysts	39,830	26,395	66.3	13,435	33.7	2,335	5.9	28,855	72.4
0850	Personal financial advisors	179,880	133,490	74.2	46,390	25.8	8,635	4.8	148,575	82.6
0860	Insurance underwriters	43,020	21,220	49.3	21,795	50.7	1,620	3.8	34,650	80.5
0900	Financial examiners	7,510	4,615	61.5	2,900	38.6	365	4.9	5,520	73.5
0910	Credit counselors and loan officers	141,470	85,700	60.6	55,770	39.4	9,370	6.6	110,005	77.8
0930	Tax examiners and collectors, and revenue agents	22,440	10,970	48.9	11,470	51.1	2,255	10.0	14,105	62.9
0940	Tax preparers	26,795	12,695	47.4	14,100	52.6	2,075	7.7	20,260	75.6
0950	Financial specialists, all other	22,715	10,700	47.1	12,010	52.9	1,765	7.8	16,170	71.2
1005	Computer and information research scientists	5,625	3,890	69.2	1,735	30.8	290	5.2	3,860	68.6
1006	Computer systems analysts	219,480	145,535	66.3	73,945	33.7	9,595	4.4	151,030	68.8
1007	Information security analysts	15,820	12,255	77.5	3,570	22.6	875	5.5	11,875	75.1
1010	Computer programmers	246,240	187,235	76.0	59,005	24.0	9,605	3.9	178,060	72.3
1020	Software developers, applications and systems software	413,505	330,825	80.0	82,680	20.0	15,750	3.8	269,750	65.2
1030	Web developers	74,340	47,095	63.4	27,245	36.6	3,410	4.6	58,400	78.6
1050	Computer support specialists	154,235	109,690	71.1	44,545	28.9	8,890	5.8	109,125	70.8
1060	Database administrators	47,000	31,260	66.5	15,735	33.5	1,905	4.1	34,280	72.9
1105	Network and computer systems administrators	99,025	78,990	79.8	20,030	20.2	5,975	6.0	71,210	71.9
1106	Computer network architects	42,415	37,555	88.5	4,860	11.5	2,485	5.9	29,490	69.5
1107	Computer occupations, all other	104,710	80,105	76.5	24,610	23.5	6,305	6.0	70,930	67.7
1200	Actuaries	15,155	10,320	68.1	4,835	31.9	300	2.0	13,165	86.9
1220	Operations research analysts	47,200	25,645	54.3	21,555	45.7	3,345	7.1	33,650	71.3
1240	Miscellaneous mathematical science occupations, including mathematicians and statisticians	12,135	6,200	51.1	5,935	48.9	845	7.0	8,720	71.9
1300	Architects, except naval	98,125	75,020	76.5	23,105	23.5	6,790	6.9	78,815	80.3
1310	Surveyors, cartographers, and photogrammetrists	23,020	19,355	84.1	3,660	15.9	1,060	4.6	20,345	88.4
1320	Aerospace engineers	68,170	60,390	88.6	7,780	11.4	4,220	6.2	52,060	76.4
1340	Biomedical and agricultural engineers	6,180	5,055	81.8	1,125	18.2	415	6.7	4,940	79.9
1350	Chemical engineers	34,600	28,890	83.5	5,710	16.5	1,685	4.9	28,250	81.6
1360	Civil engineers	179,245	156,260	87.2	22,985	12.8	9,735	5.4	144,015	80.3
1400	Computer hardware engineers	27,705	23,565	85.1	4,140	14.9	1,475	5.3	17,680	63.8
1410	Electrical and electronics engineers	117,165	106,900	91.2	10,265	8.8	7,185	6.1	86,450	73.8
1420	Environmental engineers	16,055	11,735	73.1	4,325	26.9	580	3.6	13,435	83.7
1430	Industrial engineers, including health and safety	85,290	68,730	80.6	16,560	19.4	4,660	5.5	67,965	79.7
1440	Marine engineers and naval architects	5,825	5,275	90.6	550	9.4	60	1.0	4,950	85.0

PART A—NATIONAL DATA

A-21 Workers with Bachelor's Degree: Detailed Occupations, by Sex, Race, and Hispanic Origin, 2006–2010—Continued

Census occupation code	Detailed Occupation	Bachelor's degree									
		Not Hispanic or Latino, one race								Not Hispanic or Latino, two or more races	
		Black or African American alone		American Indian and Alaska Native alone		Asian alone		Native Hawaiian and Other Pacific Islander alone			
		Number	Percent	Number	Percent	Number	Percent	Number	Percent	Number	Percent
0640	Compensation, benefits, and job analysis specialists	4,155	11.6	165	0.5	2,105	5.9	35	0.1	335	0.9
0650	Training and development specialists	5,045	12.4	170	0.4	1,660	4.1	25	0.1	620	1.5
0700	Logisticians	2,565	11.2	170	0.7	1,400	6.1	70	0.3	280	1.2
0710	Management analysts	16,645	6.1	495	0.2	22,970	8.4	110	0.0	4,190	1.5
0725	Meeting, convention, and event planners	1,730	6.2	75	0.3	1,090	3.9	4	0.0	550	2.0
0726	Fundraisers	1,370	3.5	25	0.1	1,095	2.8	20	0.1	475	1.2
0735	Market research analysts and marketing specialists	3,840	4.4	125	0.1	6,420	7.4	15	0.0	1,485	1.7
0740	Business operations specialists, all other	6,925	9.5	375	0.5	7,555	10.3	70	0.1	1,265	1.7
0800	Accountants and auditors	81,050	7.1	3,115	0.3	129,835	11.4	845	0.1	13,325	1.2
0810	Appraisers and assessors of real estate	1,175	2.7	115	0.3	1,755	4.1	50	0.1	470	1.1
0820	Budget analysts	3,160	14.4	80	0.4	2,200	10.0	45	0.2	515	2.3
0830	Credit analysts	1,035	8.0	45	0.3	1,120	8.7	10	0.1	115	0.9
0840	Financial analysts	2,590	6.5	60	0.2	5,210	13.1	10	0.0	770	1.9
0850	Personal financial advisors	9,510	5.3	295	0.2	10,860	6.0	145	0.1	1,865	1.0
0860	Insurance underwriters	3,610	8.4	60	0.1	2,700	6.3	20	0.0	355	0.8
0900	Financial examiners	850	11.3	25	0.3	625	8.3	0	0.0	130	1.7
0910	Credit counselors and loan officers	11,795	8.3	190	0.1	8,710	6.2	90	0.1	1,310	0.9
0930	Tax examiners and collectors, and revenue agents	3,895	17.4	100	0.4	1,705	7.6	50	0.2	330	1.5
0940	Tax preparers	2,335	8.7	55	0.2	1,855	6.9	10	0.0	205	0.8
0950	Financial specialists, all other	2,565	11.3	85	0.4	1,930	8.5	10	0.0	185	0.8
1005	Computer and information research scientists	515	9.2	0	0.0	910	16.2	0	0.0	55	1.0
1006	Computer systems analysts	16,500	7.5	465	0.2	38,585	17.6	195	0.1	3,105	1.4
1007	Information security analysts	1,445	9.1	20	0.1	1,395	8.8	35	0.2	169	1.1
1010	Computer programmers	11,690	4.7	455	0.2	43,090	17.5	80	0.0	3,255	1.3
1020	Software developers, applications and systems software	17,285	4.2	670	0.2	101,780	24.6	310	0.1	7,965	1.9
1030	Web developers	3,020	4.1	150	0.2	7,685	10.3	50	0.1	1,630	2.2
1050	Computer support specialists	15,100	9.8	385	0.2	17,830	11.6	235	0.2	2,675	1.7
1060	Database administrators	2,980	6.3	100	0.2	7,095	15.1	50	0.1	580	1.2
1105	Network and computer systems administrators	7,470	7.5	115	0.1	12,620	12.7	65	0.1	1,575	1.6
1106	Computer network architects	3,490	8.2	60	0.1	5,990	14.1	65	0.2	830	2.0
1107	Computer occupations, all other	9,760	9.3	260	0.2	15,545	14.8	260	0.2	1,655	1.6
1200	Actuaries	355	2.3	10	0.1	1,100	7.3	0	0.0	225	1.5
1220	Operations research analysts	4,935	10.5	115	0.2	4,425	9.4	25	0.1	695	1.5
1240	Miscellaneous mathematical science occupations, including mathematicians and statisticians	1,250	10.3	10	0.1	1,060	8.7	20	0.2	235	1.9
1300	Architects, except naval	2,460	2.5	185	0.2	8,355	8.5	45	0.0	1,480	1.5
1310	Surveyors, cartographers, and photogrammetrists	630	2.7	110	0.5	565	2.5	0	0.0	310	1.3
1320	Aerospace engineers	2,530	3.7	185	0.3	8,135	11.9	65	0.1	970	1.4
1340	Biomedical and agricultural engineers	275	4.4	4	0.1	475	7.7	0	0.0	75	1.2
1350	Chemical engineers	1,765	5.1	40	0.1	2,515	7.3	0	0.0	350	1.0
1360	Civil engineers	7,210	4.0	365	0.2	15,415	8.6	160	0.1	2,340	1.3
1400	Computer hardware engineers	1,785	6.4	145	0.5	6,030	21.8	0	0.0	590	2.1
1410	Electrical and electronics engineers	6,215	5.3	290	0.2	15,645	13.4	45	0.0	1,330	1.1
1420	Environmental engineers	910	5.7	115	0.7	730	4.5	45	0.3	245	1.5
1430	Industrial engineers, including health and safety	4,000	4.7	150	0.2	7,455	8.7	10	0.0	1,040	1.2
1440	Marine engineers and naval architects	340	5.8	25	0.4	405	7.0	4	0.1	32	0.5

A-21 Workers with Bachelor's Degree: Detailed Occupations, by Sex, Race, and Hispanic Origin, 2006–2010—*Continued*

Census occupation code	Detailed Occupation	Total	Bachelor's degree						
			Male		Female		Hispanic or Latino		Not Hispanic or Latino, one race — White alone	
			Number	Percent	Number	Percent	Number	Percent	Number	Percent
1450	Materials engineers	14,670	12,965	88.4	1,705	11.6	650	4.4	11,535	78.6
1460	Mechanical engineers	117,810	108,795	92.3	9,015	7.7	5,245	4.5	97,445	82.7
1520	Petroleum, mining and geological engineers, including mining safety engineers	16,410	14,635	89.2	1,770	10.8	1,045	6.4	13,495	82.2
1530	Miscellaneous engineers, including nuclear engineers	219,825	193,580	88.1	26,245	11.9	11,500	5.2	170,635	77.6
1540	Drafters	38,535	28,390	73.7	10,140	26.3	3,985	10.3	28,170	73.1
1550	Engineering technicians, except drafters	58,575	44,915	76.7	13,660	23.3	4,470	7.6	39,040	66.6
1560	Surveying and mapping technicians	5,025	4,100	81.6	930	18.5	260	5.2	4,175	83.1
1600	Agricultural and food scientists	12,945	9,400	72.6	3,545	27.4	360	2.8	11,685	90.3
1610	Biological scientists	38,250	18,725	49.0	19,525	51.0	2,245	5.9	30,730	80.3
1640	Conservation scientists and foresters	15,930	13,110	82.3	2,820	17.7	290	1.8	14,815	93.0
1650	Medical scientists, and life scientists, all other	7,280	2,355	32.3	4,925	67.7	325	4.5	4,735	65.0
1700	Astronomers and physicists	2,450	2,035	83.1	415	16.9	120	4.9	2,125	86.7
1710	Atmospheric and space scientists	4,310	3,515	81.6	795	18.4	95	2.2	4,000	92.8
1720	Chemists and materials scientists	47,380	27,410	57.9	19,965	42.1	2,270	4.8	34,105	72.0
1740	Environmental scientists and geoscientists	37,760	27,075	71.7	10,685	28.3	1,470	3.9	33,685	89.2
1760	Physical scientists, all other	43,915	22,190	50.5	21,725	49.5	2,585	5.9	30,980	70.5
1800	Economists	6,375	3,615	56.7	2,760	43.3	595	9.3	4,850	76.1
1820	Psychologists	8,900	3,080	34.6	5,815	65.3	980	11.0	6,415	72.1
1840	Urban and regional planners	9,230	5,555	60.2	3,675	39.8	570	6.2	7,535	81.6
1860	Miscellaneous social scientists, including survey researchers and sociologists	18,655	9,090	48.7	9,565	51.3	1,215	6.5	14,540	77.9
1900	Agricultural and food science technicians	6,605	4,000	60.6	2,605	39.4	480	7.3	5,040	76.3
1910	Biological technicians	7,940	4,245	53.5	3,690	46.5	630	7.9	5,245	66.1
1920	Chemical technicians	18,465	10,570	57.2	7,895	42.8	1,350	7.3	12,730	68.9
1930	Geological and petroleum technicians, and nuclear technicians	4,450	3,190	71.7	1,265	28.4	180	4.0	3,640	81.8
1965	Miscellaneous life, physical, and social science technicians, including social science research assistants	47,315	20,630	43.6	26,685	56.4	2,405	5.1	33,795	71.4
2000	Counselors	166,430	55,830	33.5	110,600	66.5	16,030	9.6	104,680	62.9
2010	Social workers	318,005	65,870	20.7	252,130	79.3	32,175	10.1	197,360	62.1
2015	Probation officers and correctional treatment specialists	53,495	25,555	47.8	27,940	52.2	6,190	11.6	33,320	62.3
2016	Social and human service assistants	37,570	8,760	23.3	28,815	76.7	4,465	11.9	23,210	61.8
2025	Miscellaneous community and social service specialists, including health educators and community health workers	24,865	7,980	32.1	16,885	67.9	2,475	10.0	17,425	70.1
2040	Clergy	106,260	87,685	82.5	18,575	17.5	5,055	4.8	85,865	80.8
2050	Directors, religious activities and education	20,005	6,780	33.9	13,225	66.1	1,180	5.9	17,155	85.8
2060	Religious workers, all other	26,125	9,205	35.2	16,920	64.8	1,500	5.7	21,470	82.2
2100	Lawyers, and judges, magistrates, and other judicial workers	19,210	10,530	54.8	8,680	45.2	1,280	6.7	14,965	77.9
2105	Judicial law clerks	765	425	55.6	340	44.4	65	8.5	605	79.1
2145	Paralegals and legal assistants	136,805	32,090	23.5	104,720	76.5	11,770	8.6	102,720	75.1
2160	Miscellaneous legal support workers	64,835	24,635	38.0	40,200	62.0	4,615	7.1	48,425	74.7
2200	Postsecondary teachers	248,870	117,410	47.2	131,455	52.8	15,605	6.3	177,560	71.3
2300	Preschool and kindergarten teachers	165,280	4,945	3.0	160,330	97.0	14,900	9.0	125,065	75.7
2310	Elementary and middle school teachers	1,496,045	305,615	20.4	1,190,425	79.6	123,435	8.3	1,199,405	80.2

A-21 Workers with Bachelor's Degree: Detailed Occupations, by Sex, Race, and Hispanic Origin, 2006–2010—Continued

Census occupation code	Detailed Occupation	Bachelor's degree								
		Not Hispanic or Latino, one race								Not Hispanic or Latino, two or more races	
		Black or African American alone		American Indian and Alaska Native alone		Asian alone		Native Hawaiian and Other Pacific Islander alone			
		Number	Percent	Number	Percent	Number	Percent	Number	Percent	Number	Percent
1450	Materials engineers	385	2.6	50	0.3	1,890	12.9	0	0.0	160	1.1
1460	Mechanical engineers	4,010	3.4	245	0.2	9,570	8.1	120	0.1	1,175	1.0
1520	Petroleum, mining and geological engineers, including mining safety engineers	710	4.3	35	0.2	795	4.8	0	0.0	330	2.0
1530	Miscellaneous engineers, including nuclear engineers	8,655	3.9	570	0.3	25,450	11.6	195	0.1	2,820	1.3
1540	Drafters	1,210	3.1	120	0.3	4,740	12.3	30	0.1	280	0.7
1550	Engineering technicians, except drafters	5,160	8.8	250	0.4	8,460	14.4	65	0.1	1,130	1.9
1560	Surveying and mapping technicians	135	2.7	50	1.0	360	7.2	4	0.1	45	0.9
1600	Agricultural and food scientists	240	1.9	65	0.5	435	3.4	0	0.0	159	1.2
1610	Biological scientists	1,460	3.8	140	0.4	2,915	7.6	55	0.1	710	1.9
1640	Conservation scientists and foresters	260	1.6	270	1.7	100	0.6	4	0.0	195	1.2
1650	Medical scientists, and life scientists, all other	385	5.3	30	0.4	1,595	21.9	20	0.3	195	2.7
1700	Astronomers and physicists	65	2.7	4	0.2	110	4.5	0	0.0	25	1.0
1710	Atmospheric and space scientists	110	2.6	30	0.7	30	0.7	0	0.0	39	0.9
1720	Chemists and materials scientists	3,580	7.6	125	0.3	6,585	13.9	100	0.2	615	1.3
1740	Environmental scientists and geoscientists	1,205	3.2	175	0.5	925	2.4	45	0.1	260	0.7
1760	Physical scientists, all other	1,935	4.4	180	0.4	7,300	16.6	4	0.0	935	2.1
1800	Economists	370	5.8	35	0.5	470	7.4	10	0.2	49	0.8
1820	Psychologists	1,070	12.0	50	0.6	280	3.1	0	0.0	105	1.2
1840	Urban and regional planners	510	5.5	70	0.8	330	3.6	0	0.0	215	2.3
1860	Miscellaneous social scientists, including survey researchers and sociologists	1,475	7.9	90	0.5	900	4.8	20	0.1	415	2.2
1900	Agricultural and food science technicians	360	5.5	4	0.1	610	9.2	40	0.6	69	1.0
1910	Biological technicians	330	4.2	15	0.2	1,545	19.5	15	0.2	160	2.0
1920	Chemical technicians	1,715	9.3	95	0.5	2,225	12.0	0	0.0	345	1.9
1930	Geological and petroleum technicians, and nuclear technicians	315	7.1	15	0.3	255	5.7	4	0.1	45	1.0
1965	Miscellaneous life, physical, and social science technicians, including social science research assistants	2,655	5.6	200	0.4	7,295	15.4	40	0.1	925	2.0
2000	Counselors	35,415	21.3	1,185	0.7	5,660	3.4	475	0.3	2,990	1.8
2010	Social workers	72,685	22.9	2,015	0.6	8,565	2.7	345	0.1	4,860	1.5
2015	Probation officers and correctional treatment specialists	12,070	22.6	285	0.5	780	1.5	45	0.1	805	1.5
2016	Social and human service assistants	7,445	19.8	220	0.6	1,635	4.4	65	0.2	525	1.4
2025	Miscellaneous community and social service specialists, including health educators and community health workers	3,400	13.7	230	0.9	940	3.8	30	0.1	360	1.4
2040	Clergy	9,145	8.6	520	0.5	4,425	4.2	45	0.0	1,200	1.1
2050	Directors, religious activities and education	740	3.7	75	0.4	535	2.7	15	0.1	315	1.6
2060	Religious workers, all other	1,485	5.7	70	0.3	1,320	5.1	25	0.1	255	1.0
2100	Lawyers, and judges, magistrates, and other judicial workers	2,065	10.7	105	0.5	645	3.4	0	0.0	155	0.8
2105	Judicial law clerks	25	3.3	0	0.0	50	6.5	0	0.0	14	1.8
2145	Paralegals and legal assistants	11,745	8.6	380	0.3	7,895	5.8	50	0.0	2,245	1.6
2160	Miscellaneous legal support workers	6,105	9.4	335	0.5	4,300	6.6	90	0.1	970	1.5
2200	Postsecondary teachers	17,010	6.8	620	0.2	32,855	13.2	135	0.1	5,075	2.0
2300	Preschool and kindergarten teachers	15,560	9.4	890	0.5	6,980	4.2	175	0.1	1,710	1.0
2310	Elementary and middle school teachers	119,290	8.0	6,215	0.4	30,000	2.0	890	0.1	16,805	1.1

A-21 Workers with Bachelor's Degree: Detailed Occupations, by Sex, Race, and Hispanic Origin, 2006–2010—Continued

Census occupation code	Detailed Occupation	Total	Bachelor's degree							
			Male		Female		Hispanic or Latino		Not Hispanic or Latino, one race — White alone	
			Number	Percent	Number	Percent	Number	Percent	Number	Percent
2320	Secondary school teachers	343,045	142,965	41.7	200,085	58.3	29,630	8.6	270,555	78.9
2330	Special education teachers	79,435	12,530	15.8	66,905	84.2	4,815	6.1	63,305	79.7
2340	Other teachers and instructors	240,915	80,670	33.5	160,245	66.5	15,615	6.5	187,735	77.9
2400	Archivists, curators, and museum technicians	14,035	5,545	39.5	8,490	60.5	435	3.1	12,105	86.2
2430	Librarians	39,210	6,095	15.5	33,115	84.5	1,905	4.9	32,560	83.0
2440	Library technicians	8,430	2,005	23.8	6,420	76.2	385	4.6	6,400	75.9
2540	Teacher assistants	148,960	18,885	12.7	130,075	87.3	16,225	10.9	106,340	71.4
2550	Other education, training, and library workers	23,415	6,725	28.7	16,690	71.3	1,910	8.2	17,470	74.6
2600	Artists and related workers	79,300	42,625	53.8	36,675	46.2	4,590	5.8	66,950	84.4
2630	Designers	328,030	141,185	43.0	186,845	57.0	21,630	6.6	262,525	80.0
2700	Actors	12,705	7,155	56.3	5,550	43.7	765	6.0	9,630	75.8
2710	Producers and directors	73,775	43,825	59.4	29,950	40.6	5,185	7.0	59,670	80.9
2720	Athletes, coaches, umpires, and related workers	76,185	52,335	68.7	23,850	31.3	4,015	5.3	60,670	79.6
2740	Dancers and choreographers	2,855	815	28.5	2,040	71.5	510	17.9	1,895	66.4
2750	Musicians, singers, and related workers	50,660	29,425	58.1	21,230	41.9	1,885	3.7	42,520	83.9
2760	Entertainers and performers, sports and related workers, all other	9,635	5,205	54.0	4,425	45.9	715	7.4	7,425	77.1
2800	Announcers	14,785	10,675	72.2	4,115	27.8	850	5.7	12,010	81.2
2810	News analysts, reporters, and correspondents	48,520	26,720	55.1	21,805	44.9	3,225	6.6	39,355	81.1
2825	Public relations specialists	74,325	25,155	33.8	49,170	66.2	3,875	5.2	62,450	84.0
2830	Editors	94,690	42,940	45.3	51,755	54.7	4,215	4.5	81,800	86.4
2840	Technical writers	28,355	12,220	43.1	16,130	56.9	895	3.2	24,065	84.9
2850	Writers and authors	88,535	38,825	43.9	49,710	56.1	3,010	3.4	76,885	86.8
2860	Miscellaneous media and communication workers	22,495	7,230	32.1	15,265	67.9	5,975	26.6	11,595	51.5
2900	Broadcast and sound engineering technicians and radio operators, and media and communication equipment workers, all other	24,290	21,175	87.2	3,115	12.8	2,020	8.3	18,825	77.5
2910	Photographers	48,740	29,255	60.0	19,485	40.0	2,425	5.0	41,570	85.3
2920	Television, video, and motion picture camera operators and editors	19,430	15,520	79.9	3,910	20.1	1,055	5.4	16,060	82.7
3000	Chiropractors	1,500	1,155	77.0	350	23.3	115	7.7	1,310	87.3
3010	Dentists	1,460	1,235	84.6	230	15.8	115	7.9	1,020	69.9
3030	Dietitians and nutritionists	32,645	2,475	7.6	30,170	92.4	2,160	6.6	25,660	78.6
3040	Optometrists	295	200	67.8	95	32.2	20	6.8	240	81.4
3050	Pharmacists	107,300	56,435	52.6	50,865	47.4	3,325	3.1	84,655	78.9
3060	Physicians and surgeons	7,920	5,365	67.7	2,555	32.3	460	5.8	5,165	65.2
3110	Physician assistants	30,165	11,570	38.4	18,600	61.7	2,180	7.2	21,170	70.2
3120	Podiatrists	155	115	74.2	40	25.8	0	0.0	125	80.6
3140	Audiologists	670	165	24.6	505	75.4	0	0.0	575	85.8
3150	Occupational therapists	43,070	4,455	10.3	38,615	89.7	1,645	3.8	36,350	84.4
3160	Physical therapists	71,340	20,270	28.4	51,070	71.6	2,720	3.8	55,165	77.3
3200	Radiation therapists	5,290	1,400	26.5	3,890	73.5	130	2.5	4,530	85.6
3210	Recreational therapists	7,455	1,805	24.2	5,650	75.8	300	4.0	6,020	80.8
3220	Respiratory therapists	22,820	9,505	41.7	13,310	58.3	1,240	5.4	16,370	71.7

PART A—NATIONAL DATA

A-21 Workers with Bachelor's Degree: Detailed Occupations, by Sex, Race, and Hispanic Origin, 2006–2010—Continued

Census occupation code	Detailed Occupation	Bachelor's degree								
		Not Hispanic or Latino, one race								Not Hispanic or Latino, two or more races	
		Black or African American alone		American Indian and Alaska Native alone		Asian alone		Native Hawaiian and Other Pacific Islander alone			
		Number	Percent	Number	Percent	Number	Percent	Number	Percent	Number	Percent
2320	Secondary school teachers	29,560	8.6	1,425	0.4	7,015	2.0	355	0.1	4,510	1.3
2330	Special education teachers	7,585	9.5	440	0.6	2,160	2.7	75	0.1	1,050	1.3
2340	Other teachers and instructors	18,395	7.6	790	0.3	14,160	5.9	130	0.1	4,090	1.7
2400	Archivists, curators, and museum technicians	800	5.7	75	0.5	485	3.5	0	0.0	135	1.0
2430	Librarians	2,390	6.1	150	0.4	1,710	4.4	0	0.0	500	1.3
2440	Library technicians	610	7.2	50	0.6	845	10.0	0	0.0	140	1.7
2540	Teacher assistants	15,475	10.4	575	0.4	8,305	5.6	170	0.1	1,880	1.3
2550	Other education, training, and library workers	2,650	11.3	220	0.9	745	3.2	65	0.3	360	1.5
2600	Artists and related workers	1,780	2.2	135	0.2	4,490	5.7	35	0.0	1,325	1.7
2630	Designers	10,520	3.2	410	0.1	27,910	8.5	245	0.1	4,795	1.5
2700	Actors	1,315	10.4	0	0.0	515	4.1	0	0.0	470	3.7
2710	Producers and directors	4,125	5.6	100	0.1	3,370	4.6	10	0.0	1,310	1.8
2720	Athletes, coaches, umpires, and related workers	7,245	9.5	285	0.4	2,450	3.2	170	0.2	1,350	1.8
2740	Dancers and choreographers	150	5.3	4	0.1	85	3.0	10	0.4	200	7.0
2750	Musicians, singers, and related workers	3,330	6.6	10	0.0	2,020	4.0	20	0.0	865	1.7
2760	Entertainers and performers, sports and related workers, all other	875	9.1	4	0.0	355	3.7	4	0.0	255	2.6
2800	Announcers	1,130	7.6	20	0.1	405	2.7	0	0.0	365	2.5
2810	News analysts, reporters, and correspondents	3,075	6.3	60	0.1	1,665	3.4	0	0.0	1,144	2.4
2825	Public relations specialists	4,390	5.9	155	0.2	2,540	3.4	40	0.1	875	1.2
2830	Editors	3,485	3.7	210	0.2	3,580	3.8	100	0.1	1,300	1.4
2840	Technical writers	1,655	5.8	110	0.4	1,265	4.5	10	0.0	345	1.2
2850	Writers and authors	4,025	4.5	220	0.2	3,195	3.6	0	0.0	1,205	1.4
2860	Miscellaneous media and communication workers	1,040	4.6	15	0.1	3,470	15.4	10	0.0	390	1.7
2900	Broadcast and sound engineering technicians and radio operators, and media and communication equipment workers, all other	1,950	8.0	25	0.1	1,020	4.2	0	0.0	450	1.9
2910	Photographers	1,705	3.5	35	0.1	2,230	4.6	10	0.0	765	1.6
2920	Television, video, and motion picture camera operators and editors	965	5.0	0	0.0	985	5.1	20	0.1	345	1.8
3000	Chiropractors	10	0.7	10	0.7	55	3.7	0	0.0	0	0.0
3010	Dentists	90	6.2	0	0.0	235	16.1	0	0.0	0	0.0
3030	Dietitians and nutritionists	2,280	7.0	100	0.3	1,970	6.0	40	0.1	434	1.3
3040	Optometrists	0	0.0	0	0.0	35	11.9	0	0.0	0	0.0
3050	Pharmacists	5,035	4.7	180	0.2	13,310	12.4	0	0.0	795	0.7
3060	Physicians and surgeons	695	8.8	15	0.2	1,440	18.2	0	0.0	140	1.8
3110	Physician assistants	2,675	8.9	170	0.6	3,475	11.5	20	0.1	470	1.6
3120	Podiatrists	0	0.0	0	0.0	30	19.4	0	0.0	0	0.0
3140	Audiologists	35	5.2	0	0.0	35	5.2	0	0.0	25	3.7
3150	Occupational therapists	2,140	5.0	55	0.1	2,430	5.6	35	0.1	405	0.9
3160	Physical therapists	2,490	3.5	170	0.2	10,115	14.2	45	0.1	640	0.9
3200	Radiation therapists	220	4.2	10	0.2	360	6.8	0	0.0	45	0.9
3210	Recreational therapists	825	11.1	20	0.3	265	3.6	0	0.0	20	0.3
3220	Respiratory therapists	2,845	12.5	65	0.3	2,030	8.9	10	0.0	255	1.1

A-21 **Workers with Bachelor's Degree: Detailed Occupations, by Sex, Race, and Hispanic Origin, 2006–2010**—*Continued*

Census occupation code	Detailed Occupation	Total	Bachelor's degree Male Number	Male Percent	Female Number	Female Percent	Hispanic or Latino Number	Hispanic or Latino Percent	Not Hispanic or Latino, one race White alone Number	White alone Percent
3230	Speech-language pathologists	10,000	430	4.3	9,575	95.8	900	9.0	7,990	79.9
3245	Other therapists, including exercise physiologists	30,645	6,840	22.3	23,805	77.7	2,085	6.8	22,815	74.4
3250	Veterinarians	550	335	60.9	215	39.1	40	7.3	430	78.2
3255	Registered nurses	1,131,400	106,595	9.4	1,024,805	90.6	47,585	4.2	816,385	72.2
3256	Nurse anesthetists	3,550	1,665	46.9	1,885	53.1	175	4.9	3,125	88.0
3258	Nurse practitioners and nurse midwives	4,610	340	7.4	4,265	92.5	210	4.6	3,895	84.5
3260	Health diagnosing and treating practitioners, all other	2,700	845	31.3	1,855	68.7	100	3.7	1,645	60.9
3300	Clinical laboratory technologists and technicians	146,665	38,510	26.3	108,155	73.7	9,120	6.2	97,565	66.5
3310	Dental hygienists	41,870	1,545	3.7	40,325	96.3	2,095	5.0	35,675	85.2
3320	Diagnostic related technologists and technicians	56,940	19,785	34.7	37,155	65.3	3,360	5.9	43,710	76.8
3400	Emergency medical technicians and paramedics	19,180	13,330	69.5	5,850	30.5	1,145	6.0	16,420	85.6
3420	Health practitioner support technologists and technicians	66,665	17,200	25.8	49,470	74.2	4,670	7.0	44,595	66.9
3500	Licensed practical and licensed vocational nurses	25,615	4,475	17.5	21,145	82.5	1,515	5.9	11,785	46.0
3510	Medical records and health information technicians	11,765	2,185	18.6	9,575	81.4	715	6.1	7,605	64.6
3520	Opticians, dispensing	6,855	3,080	44.9	3,770	55.0	345	5.0	5,490	80.1
3535	Miscellaneous health technologists and technicians	20,765	9,385	45.2	11,375	54.8	1,060	5.1	13,565	65.3
3540	Other health care practitioners and technical occupations	27,570	15,475	56.1	12,090	43.9	1,540	5.6	22,125	80.3
3600	Nursing, psychiatric, and home health aides	114,495	25,290	22.1	89,205	77.9	11,015	9.6	57,075	49.8
3610	Occupational therapy assistants and aides	1,500	160	10.7	1,340	89.3	125	8.3	1,055	70.3
3620	Physical therapist assistants and aides	11,380	3,880	34.1	7,500	65.9	750	6.6	8,610	75.7
3630	Massage therapists	24,415	4,300	17.6	20,115	82.4	1,060	4.3	20,715	84.8
3640	Dental assistants	15,440	1,385	9.0	14,055	91.0	2,370	15.3	9,215	59.7
3645	Medical assistants	24,590	2,565	10.4	22,030	89.6	3,375	13.7	14,975	60.9
3646	Medical transcriptionists	9,435	430	4.6	9,005	95.4	330	3.5	8,580	90.9
3647	Pharmacy aides	5,555	2,250	40.5	3,305	59.5	465	8.4	2,815	50.7
3648	Veterinary assistants and laboratory animal caretakers	5,690	900	15.8	4,790	84.2	380	6.7	4,860	85.4
3649	Phlebotomists	6,910	1,545	22.4	5,365	77.6	660	9.6	3,850	55.7
3655	Health care support workers, all other, including medical equipment preparers	10,850	3,540	32.6	7,310	67.4	1,225	11.3	6,580	60.6
3700	First-line supervisors of correctional officers	10,915	7,490	68.6	3,425	31.4	810	7.4	7,030	64.4
3710	First-line supervisors of police and detectives	33,325	28,545	85.7	4,780	14.3	2,255	6.8	26,855	80.6
3720	First-line supervisors of fire fighting and prevention workers	9,315	8,830	94.8	485	5.2	330	3.5	8,085	86.8
3730	First-line supervisors of protective service workers, all other	18,805	14,110	75.0	4,695	25.0	1,285	6.8	13,825	73.5
3740	Firefighters	41,470	39,250	94.6	2,220	5.4	2,920	7.0	33,870	81.7
3750	Fire inspectors	3,900	3,400	87.2	500	12.8	240	6.2	3,300	84.6
3800	Bailiffs, correctional officers, and jailers	46,265	32,490	70.2	13,775	29.8	3,570	7.7	29,240	63.2
3820	Detectives and criminal investigators	51,275	38,540	75.2	12,735	24.8	5,200	10.1	37,640	73.4
3840	Miscellaneous law enforcement workers	2,530	1,965	77.7	565	22.3	345	13.6	1,835	72.5
3850	Police officers	175,280	147,445	84.1	27,835	15.9	17,530	10.0	129,100	73.7
3900	Animal control workers	1,155	725	62.8	430	37.2	35	3.0	995	86.1
3910	Private detectives and investigators	30,120	19,230	63.8	10,890	36.2	2,800	9.3	21,990	73.0

A-21 Workers with Bachelor's Degree: Detailed Occupations, by Sex, Race, and Hispanic Origin, 2006–2010—Continued

Census occupation code	Detailed Occupation	Black or African American alone Number	Percent	American Indian and Alaska Native alone Number	Percent	Asian alone Number	Percent	Native Hawaiian and Other Pacific Islander alone Number	Percent	Not Hispanic or Latino, two or more races Number	Percent
3230	Speech-language pathologists	845	8.5	20	0.2	195	2.0	0	0.0	60	0.6
3245	Other therapists, including exercise physiologists	3,440	11.2	105	0.3	1,690	5.5	0	0.0	510	1.7
3250	Veterinarians	20	3.6	0	0.0	30	5.5	0	0.0	35	6.4
3255	Registered nurses	109,020	9.6	3,850	0.3	140,880	12.5	930	0.1	12,760	1.1
3256	Nurse anesthetists	75	2.1	4	0.1	145	4.1	0	0.0	25	0.7
3258	Nurse practitioners and nurse midwives	265	5.7	4	0.1	140	3.0	0	0.0	95	2.1
3260	Health diagnosing and treating practitioners, all other	15	0.6	4	0.1	885	32.8	10	0.4	45	1.7
3300	Clinical laboratory technologists and technicians	12,470	8.5	320	0.2	24,805	16.9	140	0.1	2,245	1.5
3310	Dental hygienists	1,220	2.9	55	0.1	2,180	5.2	10	0.0	630	1.5
3320	Diagnostic related technologists and technicians	4,140	7.3	150	0.3	4,715	8.3	85	0.1	780	1.4
3400	Emergency medical technicians and paramedics	800	4.2	140	0.7	525	2.7	0	0.0	145	0.8
3420	Health practitioner support technologists and technicians	6,375	9.6	200	0.3	9,690	14.5	95	0.1	1,050	1.6
3500	Licensed practical and licensed vocational nurses	6,095	23.8	135	0.5	5,685	22.2	45	0.2	355	1.4
3510	Medical records and health information technicians	1,550	13.2	115	1.0	1,635	13.9	0	0.0	140	1.2
3520	Opticians, dispensing	300	4.4	25	0.4	570	8.3	0	0.0	120	1.8
3535	Miscellaneous health technologists and technicians	2,585	12.4	90	0.4	3,235	15.6	0	0.0	224	1.1
3540	Other health care practitioners and technical occupations	2,235	8.1	120	0.4	1,260	4.6	10	0.0	279	1.0
3600	Nursing, psychiatric, and home health aides	23,875	20.9	470	0.4	19,995	17.5	130	0.1	1,935	1.7
3610	Occupational therapy assistants and aides	20	1.3	40	2.7	240	16.0	0	0.0	25	1.7
3620	Physical therapist assistants and aides	615	5.4	15	0.1	1,230	10.8	65	0.6	110	1.0
3630	Massage therapists	725	3.0	100	0.4	1,335	5.5	40	0.2	440	1.8
3640	Dental assistants	705	4.6	60	0.4	2,830	18.3	60	0.4	200	1.3
3645	Medical assistants	2,820	11.5	50	0.2	2,975	12.1	15	0.1	384	1.6
3646	Medical transcriptionists	190	2.0	10	0.1	160	1.7	0	0.0	165	1.7
3647	Pharmacy aides	660	11.9	35	0.6	1,470	26.5	4	0.1	100	1.8
3648	Veterinary assistants and laboratory animal caretakers	145	2.5	10	0.2	210	3.7	0	0.0	84	1.5
3649	Phlebotomists	895	13.0	4	0.1	1,395	20.2	20	0.3	79	1.1
3655	Health care support workers, all other, including medical equipment preparers	915	8.4	55	0.5	1,850	17.1	35	0.3	190	1.8
3700	First-line supervisors of correctional officers	2,735	25.1	100	0.9	150	1.4	0	0.0	95	0.9
3710	First-line supervisors of police and detectives	3,080	9.2	180	0.5	505	1.5	15	0.0	440	1.3
3720	First-line supervisors of fire fighting and prevention workers	615	6.6	45	0.5	100	1.1	0	0.0	130	1.4
3730	First-line supervisors of protective service workers, all other	2,730	14.5	75	0.4	575	3.1	0	0.0	315	1.7
3740	Firefighters	3,185	7.7	130	0.3	795	1.9	50	0.1	525	1.3
3750	Fire inspectors	160	4.1	25	0.6	115	2.9	10	0.3	49	1.3
3800	Bailiffs, correctional officers, and jailers	11,480	24.8	210	0.5	1,045	2.3	140	0.3	570	1.2
3820	Detectives and criminal investigators	6,130	12.0	255	0.5	1,330	2.6	30	0.1	695	1.4
3840	Miscellaneous law enforcement workers	110	4.3	15	0.6	140	5.5	0	0.0	90	3.6
3850	Police officers	19,770	11.3	695	0.4	5,160	2.9	230	0.1	2,795	1.6
3900	Animal control workers	75	6.5	0	0.0	20	1.7	0	0.0	29	2.5
3910	Private detectives and investigators	3,810	12.6	165	0.5	905	3.0	45	0.1	420	1.4

A-21 **Workers with Bachelor's Degree: Detailed Occupations, by Sex, Race, and Hispanic Origin, 2006–2010**—*Continued*

Census occupation code	Detailed Occupation	Total	Bachelor's degree Male Number	Male Percent	Female Number	Female Percent	Hispanic or Latino Number	Hispanic or Latino Percent	Not Hispanic or Latino, one race White alone Number	White alone Percent
3930	Security guards and gaming surveillance officers	97,805	80,275	82.1	17,525	17.9	8,220	8.4	61,180	62.6
3940	Crossing guards	1,915	900	47.0	1,010	52.7	150	7.8	1,545	80.7
3945	Transportation security screeners	4,625	3,205	69.3	1,420	30.7	495	10.7	2,820	61.0
3955	Lifeguards and other recreational, and all other protective service workers	13,480	6,970	51.7	6,510	48.3	700	5.2	11,540	85.6
4000	Chefs and head cooks	32,435	24,020	74.1	8,415	25.9	3,740	11.5	20,325	62.7
4010	First-line supervisors of food preparation and serving workers	56,520	31,460	55.7	25,065	44.3	5,230	9.3	39,100	69.2
4020	Cooks	65,290	40,170	61.5	25,125	38.5	14,985	23.0	35,095	53.8
4030	Food preparation workers	34,035	13,775	40.5	20,255	59.5	5,365	15.8	21,490	63.1
4040	Bartenders	56,695	28,915	51.0	27,780	49.0	4,095	7.2	47,560	83.9
4050	Combined food preparation and serving workers, including fast food	10,490	4,330	41.3	6,160	58.7	1,720	16.4	6,760	64.4
4060	Counter attendants, cafeteria, food concession, and coffee shop	6,120	2,580	42.2	3,540	57.8	580	9.5	4,120	67.3
4110	Waiters and waitresses	180,320	60,530	33.6	119,785	66.4	17,765	9.9	135,895	75.4
4120	Food servers, nonrestaurant	9,765	4,400	45.1	5,365	54.9	1,145	11.7	5,745	58.8
4130	Miscellaneous food preparation and serving related workers, including dining room and cafeteria attendants and bartender helpers	10,900	6,430	59.0	4,470	41.0	2,660	24.4	5,410	49.6
4140	Dishwashers	5,210	4,385	84.2	825	15.8	1,950	37.4	2,315	44.4
4150	Hosts and hostesses, restaurant, lounge, and coffee shop	13,580	2,010	14.8	11,570	85.2	1,190	8.8	9,615	70.8
4200	First-line supervisors of housekeeping and janitorial workers	22,965	16,705	72.7	6,260	27.3	3,490	15.2	15,065	65.6
4210	First-line supervisors of landscaping, lawn service, and groundskeeping workers	27,800	25,370	91.3	2,425	8.7	1,425	5.1	25,275	90.9
4220	Janitors and building cleaners	89,620	67,075	74.8	22,545	25.2	18,910	21.1	54,135	60.4
4230	Maids and housekeeping cleaners	48,365	7,665	15.8	40,700	84.2	19,145	39.6	19,085	39.5
4240	Pest control workers	5,065	4,705	92.9	355	7.0	660	13.0	3,635	71.8
4250	Grounds maintenance workers	58,490	50,445	86.2	8,045	13.8	7,680	13.1	46,485	79.5
4300	First-line supervisors of gaming workers	17,735	10,685	60.2	7,050	39.8	905	5.1	14,705	82.9
4320	First-line supervisors of personal service workers	32,970	16,310	49.5	16,660	50.5	2,055	6.2	24,595	74.6
4340	Animal trainers	7,540	2,355	31.2	5,190	68.8	230	3.1	6,935	92.0
4350	Nonfarm animal caretakers	19,375	5,100	26.3	14,275	73.7	1,015	5.2	17,145	88.5
4400	Gaming services workers	11,680	7,220	61.8	4,460	38.2	830	7.1	6,855	58.7
4410	Motion picture projectionists	865	720	83.2	145	16.8	90	10.4	680	78.6
4420	Ushers, lobby attendants, and ticket takers	3,260	1,845	56.6	1,410	43.3	245	7.5	2,510	77.0
4430	Miscellaneous entertainment attendants and related workers	19,105	11,105	58.1	8,000	41.9	1,155	6.0	15,170	79.4
4460	Embalmers and funeral attendants	1,750	1,280	73.1	475	27.1	70	4.0	1,515	86.6
4465	Morticians, undertakers, and funeral directors	11,195	8,895	79.5	2,300	20.5	365	3.3	9,370	83.7
4500	Barbers	3,030	2,255	74.4	780	25.7	430	14.2	1,160	38.3
4510	Hairdressers, hairstylists, and cosmetologists	29,190	3,825	13.1	25,360	86.9	3,840	13.2	17,370	59.5
4520	Miscellaneous personal appearance workers	18,885	2,165	11.5	16,720	88.5	1,660	8.8	8,810	46.7
4530	Baggage porters, bellhops, and concierges	9,830	7,185	73.1	2,645	26.9	1,190	12.1	5,815	59.2
4540	Tour and travel guides	9,295	4,830	52.0	4,465	48.0	240	2.6	7,930	85.3
4600	Childcare workers	129,570	8,900	6.9	120,670	93.1	15,400	11.9	90,115	69.5
4610	Personal care aides	67,470	15,085	22.4	52,380	77.6	6,105	9.0	36,445	54.0
4620	Recreation and fitness workers	101,260	35,370	34.9	65,885	65.1	6,120	6.0	81,890	80.9

A-21 Workers with Bachelor's Degree: Detailed Occupations, by Sex, Race, and Hispanic Origin, 2006–2010—Continued

Census occupation code	Detailed Occupation	Bachelor's degree									
		Not Hispanic or Latino, one race								Not Hispanic or Latino, two or more races	
		Black or African American alone		American Indian and Alaska Native alone		Asian alone		Native Hawaiian and Other Pacific Islander alone			
		Number	Percent	Number	Percent	Number	Percent	Number	Percent	Number	Percent
3930	Security guards and gaming surveillance officers..	19,170	19.6	430	0.4	6,535	6.7	145	0.1	2,125	2.2
3940	Crossing guards	175	9.1	4	0.2	35	1.8	0	0.0	4	0.2
3945	Transportation security screeners	865	18.7	4	0.1	385	8.3	0	0.0	59	1.3
3955	Lifeguards and other recreational, and all other protective service workers	750	5.6	35	0.3	230	1.7	15	0.1	205	1.5
4000	Chefs and head cooks	1,875	5.8	80	0.2	5,955	18.4	40	0.1	420	1.3
4010	First-line supervisors of food preparation and serving workers	4,585	8.1	190	0.3	6,520	11.5	45	0.1	855	1.5
4020	Cooks	4,835	7.4	305	0.5	8,835	13.5	140	0.2	1,095	1.7
4030	Food preparation workers	1,510	4.4	115	0.3	4,865	14.3	30	0.1	665	2.0
4040	Bartenders	1,890	3.3	180	0.3	1,875	3.3	55	0.1	1,040	1.8
4050	Combined food preparation and serving workers, including fast food	585	5.6	0	0.0	1,210	11.5	0	0.0	215	2.0
4060	Counter attendants, cafeteria, food concession, and coffee shop	360	5.9	20	0.3	930	15.2	0	0.0	109	1.8
4110	Waiters and waitresses	7,145	4.0	445	0.2	15,295	8.5	155	0.1	3,625	2.0
4120	Food servers, nonrestaurant	775	7.9	60	0.6	1,900	19.5	20	0.2	120	1.2
4130	Miscellaneous food preparation and serving related workers, including dining room and cafeteria attendants and bartender helpers	590	5.4	55	0.5	1,770	16.2	95	0.9	320	2.9
4140	Dishwashers	325	6.2	15	0.3	410	7.9	75	1.4	124	2.4
4150	Hosts and hostesses, restaurant, lounge, and coffee shop	845	6.2	60	0.4	1,465	10.8	55	0.4	355	2.6
4200	First-line supervisors of housekeeping and janitorial workers	2,175	9.5	175	0.8	1,710	7.4	165	0.7	180	0.8
4210	First-line supervisors of landscaping, lawn service, and groundskeeping workers	370	1.3	50	0.2	425	1.5	50	0.2	200	0.7
4220	Janitors and building cleaners	7,305	8.2	515	0.6	7,570	8.4	25	0.0	1,160	1.3
4230	Maids and housekeeping cleaners	2,980	6.2	195	0.4	5,965	12.3	105	0.2	895	1.9
4240	Pest control workers	385	7.6	20	0.4	250	4.9	0	0.0	110	2.2
4250	Grounds maintenance workers	2,035	3.5	90	0.2	1,490	2.5	55	0.1	660	1.1
4300	First-line supervisors of gaming workers	750	4.2	120	0.7	1,085	6.1	0	0.0	170	1.0
4320	First-line supervisors of personal service workers	2,470	7.5	80	0.2	3,360	10.2	15	0.0	390	1.2
4340	Animal trainers	165	2.2	20	0.3	75	1.0	0	0.0	120	1.6
4350	Nonfarm animal caretakers	340	1.8	65	0.3	435	2.2	0	0.0	369	1.9
4400	Gaming services workers	795	6.8	90	0.8	2,935	25.1	0	0.0	175	1.5
4410	Motion picture projectionists	60	6.9	0	0.0	35	4.0	0	0.0	0	0.0
4420	Ushers, lobby attendants, and ticket takers	300	9.2	15	0.5	105	3.2	0	0.0	85	2.6
4430	Miscellaneous entertainment attendants and related workers	1,020	5.3	65	0.3	1,130	5.9	40	0.2	530	2.8
4460	Embalmers and funeral attendants	155	8.9	0	0.0	4	0.2	0	0.0	4	0.2
4465	Morticians, undertakers, and funeral directors	1,360	12.1	4	0.0	15	0.1	0	0.0	80	0.7
4500	Barbers	1,075	35.5	15	0.5	285	9.4	0	0.0	65	2.1
4510	Hairdressers, hairstylists, and cosmetologists	3,850	13.2	65	0.2	3,505	12.0	0	0.0	554	1.9
4520	Miscellaneous personal appearance workers	685	3.6	10	0.1	7,325	38.8	0	0.0	394	2.1
4530	Baggage porters, bellhops, and concierges	1,065	10.8	40	0.4	1,385	14.1	0	0.0	340	3.5
4540	Tour and travel guides	365	3.9	55	0.6	560	6.0	4	0.0	140	1.5
4600	Childcare workers	13,025	10.1	335	0.3	8,180	6.3	25	0.0	2,500	1.9
4610	Personal care aides	9,280	13.8	270	0.4	13,785	20.4	210	0.3	1,375	2.0
4620	Recreation and fitness workers	7,350	7.3	405	0.4	3,215	3.2	110	0.1	2,170	2.1

A-21 **Workers with Bachelor's Degree: Detailed Occupations, by Sex, Race, and Hispanic Origin, 2006–2010**—*Continued*

Census occupation code	Detailed Occupation	Total	Bachelor's degree				Not Hispanic or Latino, one race	
			Male		Female		Hispanic or Latino		White alone	
			Number	Percent	Number	Percent	Number	Percent	Number	Percent
4640	Residential advisors	9,305	3,665	39.4	5,640	60.6	530	5.7	5,750	61.8
4650	Personal care and service workers, all other	12,225	4,875	39.9	7,350	60.1	1,110	9.1	9,580	78.4
4700	First-line supervisors of retail sales workers	601,590	374,880	62.3	226,710	37.7	36,720	6.1	461,735	76.8
4710	First-line supervisors of non-retail sales workers	354,610	256,545	72.3	98,070	27.7	21,680	6.1	283,220	79.9
4720	Cashiers	172,845	65,970	38.2	106,880	61.8	17,415	10.1	103,815	60.1
4740	Counter and rental clerks	13,030	7,770	59.6	5,260	40.4	840	6.4	9,370	71.9
4750	Parts salespersons	6,135	5,500	89.6	635	10.4	685	11.2	4,715	76.9
4760	Retail salespersons	543,625	299,245	55.0	244,375	45.0	32,120	5.9	431,405	79.4
4800	Advertising sales agents	104,840	51,675	49.3	53,165	50.7	6,045	5.8	88,880	84.8
4810	Insurance sales agents	203,305	142,850	70.3	60,460	29.7	9,050	4.5	172,900	85.0
4820	Securities, commodities, and financial services sales agents	175,975	131,665	74.8	44,315	25.2	9,170	5.2	145,060	82.4
4830	Travel agents	22,115	5,955	26.9	16,160	73.1	1,245	5.6	16,310	73.8
4840	Sales representatives, services, all other	229,310	161,125	70.3	68,185	29.7	11,070	4.8	196,840	85.8
4850	Sales representatives, wholesale and manufacturing	571,575	419,460	73.4	152,115	26.6	24,035	4.2	503,625	88.1
4900	Models, demonstrators, and product promoters	7,530	1,900	25.2	5,630	74.8	530	7.0	5,685	75.5
4920	Real estate brokers and sales agents	295,135	157,400	53.3	137,740	46.7	17,545	5.9	242,420	82.1
4930	Sales engineers	16,805	15,570	92.7	1,235	7.3	935	5.6	14,510	86.3
4940	Telemarketers	13,920	6,975	50.1	6,945	49.9	1,035	7.4	9,875	70.9
4950	Door-to-door sales workers, news and street vendors, and related workers	25,870	8,785	34.0	17,085	66.0	2,440	9.4	20,110	77.7
4965	Sales and related workers, all other	71,545	38,945	54.4	32,600	45.6	3,165	4.4	61,190	85.5
5000	First-line supervisors of office and administrative support workers	349,460	141,635	40.5	207,825	59.5	24,775	7.1	259,445	74.2
5010	Switchboard operators, including answering service	3,020	1,035	34.3	1,990	65.9	225	7.5	1,960	64.9
5020	Telephone operators	4,735	1,430	30.2	3,305	69.8	400	8.4	2,625	55.4
5030	Communications equipment operators, all other	2,275	1,040	45.7	1,230	54.1	280	12.3	1,605	70.5
5100	Bill and account collectors	27,895	11,825	42.4	16,075	57.6	2,520	9.0	18,060	64.7
5110	Billing and posting clerks	60,025	11,730	19.5	48,295	80.5	4,860	8.1	40,290	67.1
5120	Bookkeeping, accounting, and auditing clerks	186,255	36,825	19.8	149,430	80.2	10,960	5.9	141,335	75.9
5130	Gaming cage workers	1,160	610	52.6	550	47.4	75	6.5	560	48.3
5140	Payroll and timekeeping clerks	24,660	4,345	17.6	20,320	82.4	1,660	6.7	17,380	70.5
5150	Procurement clerks	5,630	3,025	53.7	2,605	46.3	265	4.7	4,205	74.7
5160	Tellers	51,290	12,440	24.3	38,845	75.7	4,285	8.4	32,810	64.0
5165	Financial clerks, all other	15,580	7,990	51.3	7,590	48.7	995	6.4	10,620	68.2
5200	Brokerage clerks	2,845	1,145	40.2	1,700	59.8	180	6.3	2,180	76.6
5220	Court, municipal, and license clerks	14,105	4,920	34.9	9,185	65.1	940	6.7	9,820	69.6
5230	Credit authorizers, checkers, and clerks	9,085	4,490	49.4	4,600	50.6	470	5.2	6,465	71.2
5240	Customer service representatives	356,540	144,630	40.6	211,905	59.4	29,130	8.2	247,755	69.5
5250	Eligibility interviewers, government programs	22,530	5,710	25.3	16,820	74.7	3,115	13.8	12,200	54.2
5260	File clerks	49,035	13,725	28.0	35,310	72.0	3,160	6.4	33,675	68.7
5300	Hotel, motel, and resort desk clerks	16,735	6,540	39.1	10,195	60.9	1,565	9.4	10,400	62.1
5310	Interviewers, except eligibility and loan	25,075	8,345	33.3	16,730	66.7	2,440	9.7	16,830	67.1
5320	Library assistants, clerical	28,290	4,975	17.6	23,315	82.4	1,100	3.9	22,215	78.5
5330	Loan interviewers and clerks	26,895	8,510	31.6	18,385	68.4	2,260	8.4	18,790	69.9
5340	New accounts clerks	4,305	1,650	38.3	2,655	61.7	400	9.3	2,655	61.7
5350	Correspondence clerks and order clerks	18,790	7,615	40.5	11,175	59.5	1,455	7.7	13,405	71.3
5360	Human resources assistants, except payroll and timekeeping	10,730	2,230	20.8	8,500	79.2	990	9.2	6,765	63.0

A-21 Workers with Bachelor's Degree: Detailed Occupations, by Sex, Race, and Hispanic Origin, 2006-2010—Continued

Census occupation code	Detailed Occupation	Black or African American alone Number	Black or African American alone Percent	American Indian and Alaska Native alone Number	American Indian and Alaska Native alone Percent	Asian alone Number	Asian alone Percent	Native Hawaiian and Other Pacific Islander alone Number	Native Hawaiian and Other Pacific Islander alone Percent	Not Hispanic or Latino, two or more races Number	Not Hispanic or Latino, two or more races Percent
4640	Residential advisors	2,225	23.9	180	1.9	455	4.9	0	0.0	160	1.7
4650	Personal care and service workers, all other	670	5.5	40	0.3	645	5.3	0	0.0	175	1.4
4700	First-line supervisors of retail sales workers	39,945	6.6	1,180	0.2	54,150	9.0	245	0.0	7,615	1.3
4710	First-line supervisors of non-retail sales workers	18,425	5.2	745	0.2	26,380	7.4	245	0.1	3,910	1.1
4720	Cashiers	15,075	8.7	555	0.3	32,050	18.5	410	0.2	3,530	2.0
4740	Counter and rental clerks	1,010	7.8	45	0.3	1,505	11.6	0	0.0	265	2.0
4750	Parts salespersons	285	4.6	10	0.2	420	6.8	0	0.0	24	0.4
4760	Retail salespersons	35,360	6.5	1,300	0.2	36,030	6.6	190	0.0	7,225	1.3
4800	Advertising sales agents	5,325	5.1	155	0.1	3,300	3.1	130	0.1	1,005	1.0
4810	Insurance sales agents	11,485	5.6	200	0.1	7,835	3.9	85	0.0	1,750	0.9
4820	Securities, commodities, and financial services sales agents	7,880	4.5	115	0.1	11,750	6.7	55	0.0	1,945	1.1
4830	Travel agents	1,360	6.1	15	0.1	2,770	12.5	40	0.2	380	1.7
4840	Sales representatives, services, all other	10,850	4.7	370	0.2	8,050	3.5	160	0.1	1,970	0.9
4850	Sales representatives, wholesale and manufacturing	16,885	3.0	710	0.1	21,035	3.7	165	0.0	5,120	0.9
4900	Models, demonstrators, and product promoters	690	9.2	10	0.1	455	6.0	0	0.0	160	2.1
4920	Real estate brokers and sales agents	14,380	4.9	420	0.1	16,965	5.7	135	0.0	3,270	1.1
4930	Sales engineers	235	1.4	20	0.1	1,010	6.0	0	0.0	89	0.5
4940	Telemarketers	2,000	14.4	15	0.1	650	4.7	0	0.0	345	2.5
4950	Door-to-door sales workers, news and street vendors, and related workers	1,625	6.3	125	0.5	1,165	4.5	30	0.1	379	1.5
4965	Sales and related workers, all other	3,310	4.6	215	0.3	3,020	4.2	65	0.1	585	0.8
5000	First-line supervisors of office and administrative support workers	35,995	10.3	1,005	0.3	23,285	6.7	305	0.1	4,650	1.3
5010	Switchboard operators, including answering service	385	12.7	0	0.0	355	11.8	0	0.0	105	3.5
5020	Telephone operators	1,235	26.1	40	0.8	310	6.5	10	0.2	115	2.4
5030	Communications equipment operators, all other	290	12.7	10	0.4	80	3.5	0	0.0	10	0.4
5100	Bill and account collectors	5,365	19.2	150	0.5	1,450	5.2	0	0.0	345	1.2
5110	Billing and posting clerks	6,505	10.8	150	0.2	7,275	12.1	120	0.2	830	1.4
5120	Bookkeeping, accounting, and auditing clerks	12,025	6.5	635	0.3	18,865	10.1	215	0.1	2,220	1.2
5130	Gaming cage workers	115	9.9	35	3.0	355	30.6	10	0.9	14	1.2
5140	Payroll and timekeeping clerks	2,710	11.0	130	0.5	2,400	9.7	20	0.1	359	1.5
5150	Procurement clerks	600	10.7	4	0.1	490	8.7	0	0.0	70	1.2
5160	Tellers	5,710	11.1	85	0.2	7,400	14.4	85	0.2	915	1.8
5165	Financial clerks, all other	1,450	9.3	35	0.2	2,220	14.2	10	0.1	245	1.6
5200	Brokerage clerks	165	5.8	0	0.0	295	10.4	0	0.0	24	0.8
5220	Court, municipal, and license clerks	2,380	16.9	65	0.5	695	4.9	0	0.0	205	1.5
5230	Credit authorizers, checkers, and clerks	1,230	13.5	30	0.3	690	7.6	15	0.2	185	2.0
5240	Customer service representatives	47,120	13.2	1,120	0.3	25,485	7.1	365	0.1	5,565	1.6
5250	Eligibility interviewers, government programs	5,270	23.4	70	0.3	1,525	6.8	20	0.1	335	1.5
5260	File clerks	5,680	11.6	285	0.6	5,350	10.9	35	0.1	850	1.7
5300	Hotel, motel, and resort desk clerks	1,780	10.6	110	0.7	2,495	14.9	15	0.1	375	2.2
5310	Interviewers, except eligibility and loan	3,565	14.2	140	0.6	1,520	6.1	95	0.4	485	1.9
5320	Library assistants, clerical	2,075	7.3	100	0.4	2,425	8.6	0	0.0	379	1.3
5330	Loan interviewers and clerks	2,705	10.1	110	0.4	2,630	9.8	40	0.1	360	1.3
5340	New accounts clerks	505	11.7	4	0.1	670	15.6	0	0.0	69	1.6
5350	Correspondence clerks and order clerks	1,685	9.0	80	0.4	1,940	10.3	25	0.1	200	1.1
5360	Human resources assistants, except payroll and timekeeping	1,790	16.7	65	0.6	925	8.6	20	0.2	180	1.7

A-21 Workers with Bachelor's Degree: Detailed Occupations, by Sex, Race, and Hispanic Origin, 2006–2010—Continued

Census occupation code	Detailed Occupation	Total	Bachelor's degree							
			Male		Female		Hispanic or Latino		Not Hispanic or Latino, one race — White alone	
			Number	Percent	Number	Percent	Number	Percent	Number	Percent
5400	Receptionists and information clerks	117,480	17,055	14.5	100,425	85.5	9,455	8.0	86,090	73.3
5410	Reservation and transportation ticket agents and travel clerks	29,955	12,225	40.8	17,730	59.2	3,310	11.0	19,820	66.2
5420	Information and record clerks, all other	14,770	3,780	25.6	10,995	74.4	1,200	8.1	10,275	69.6
5500	Cargo and freight agents	3,045	2,160	70.9	890	29.2	345	11.3	1,760	57.8
5510	Couriers and messengers	30,900	25,985	84.1	4,915	15.9	2,740	8.9	21,180	68.5
5520	Dispatchers	26,515	13,940	52.6	12,575	47.4	1,870	7.1	19,870	74.9
5530	Meter readers, utilities	2,630	2,170	82.5	460	17.5	270	10.3	1,840	70.0
5540	Postal service clerks	18,725	10,370	55.4	8,360	44.6	940	5.0	8,915	47.6
5550	Postal service mail carriers	39,085	30,400	77.8	8,680	22.2	2,185	5.6	27,560	70.5
5560	Postal service mail sorters, processors, and processing machine operators	12,475	7,140	57.2	5,335	42.8	750	6.0	5,870	47.1
5600	Production, planning, and expediting clerks	64,990	31,685	48.8	33,305	51.2	3,420	5.3	51,635	79.5
5610	Shipping, receiving, and traffic clerks	33,310	23,750	71.3	9,560	28.7	4,900	14.7	21,540	64.7
5620	Stock clerks and order fillers	84,695	54,460	64.3	30,235	35.7	7,980	9.4	56,720	67.0
5630	Weighers, measurers, checkers, and samplers, recordkeeping	6,215	3,650	58.7	2,560	41.2	565	9.1	4,440	71.4
5700	Secretaries and administrative assistants	548,925	38,855	7.1	510,070	92.9	39,625	7.2	416,890	75.9
5800	Computer operators	27,065	16,600	61.3	10,460	38.6	1,990	7.4	18,930	69.9
5810	Data entry keyers	61,790	19,080	30.9	42,710	69.1	4,535	7.3	41,660	67.4
5820	Word processors and typists	43,810	7,640	17.4	36,170	82.6	3,035	6.9	29,785	68.0
5840	Insurance claims and policy processing clerks	56,135	17,590	31.3	38,545	68.7	3,950	7.0	40,470	72.1
5850	Mail clerks and mail machine operators, except postal service	8,620	5,190	60.2	3,430	39.8	825	9.6	5,605	65.0
5860	Office clerks, general	161,155	38,895	24.1	122,260	75.9	13,645	8.5	108,520	67.3
5900	Office machine operators, except computer	5,095	2,640	51.8	2,460	48.3	300	5.9	3,110	61.0
5910	Proofreaders and copy markers	5,525	1,620	29.3	3,900	70.6	195	3.5	4,720	85.4
5920	Statistical assistants	6,360	2,685	42.2	3,675	57.8	310	4.9	4,700	73.9
5940	Miscellaneous office and administrative support workers, including desktop publishers	121,360	33,770	27.8	87,585	72.2	9,780	8.1	85,975	70.8
6005	First-line supervisors of farming, fishing, and forestry workers	6,930	5,675	81.9	1,250	18.0	410	5.9	5,925	85.5
6010	Agricultural inspectors	4,195	2,635	62.8	1,560	37.2	370	8.8	2,940	70.1
6040	Graders and sorters, agricultural products	1,340	820	61.2	520	38.8	380	28.4	765	57.1
6050	Miscellaneous agricultural workers, including animal breeders	26,345	18,660	70.8	7,685	29.2	3,470	13.2	21,545	81.8
6100	Fishing and hunting workers	2,530	2,365	93.5	165	6.5	120	4.7	2,290	90.5
6120	Forest and conservation workers	1,955	1,410	72.1	550	28.1	54	2.8	1,895	96.9
6130	Logging workers	1,760	1,625	92.3	135	7.7	10	0.6	1,535	87.2
6200	First-line supervisors of construction trades and extraction workers	83,780	79,245	94.6	4,535	5.4	6,300	7.5	70,855	84.6
6210	Boilermakers	580	580	100.0	0	0.0	70	12.1	480	82.8
6220	Brickmasons, blockmasons, and stonemasons	5,525	5,435	98.4	90	1.6	1,115	20.2	3,810	69.0
6230	Carpenters	76,540	74,085	96.8	2,455	3.2	10,320	13.5	61,045	79.8
6240	Carpet, floor, and tile installers and finishers	7,360	7,080	96.2	280	3.8	2,030	27.6	4,850	65.9
6250	Cement masons, concrete finishers, and terrazzo workers	1,355	1,345	99.3	4	0.3	475	35.1	775	57.2
6260	Construction laborers	64,230	61,085	95.1	3,145	4.9	12,615	19.6	45,360	70.6
6300	Paving, surfacing, and tamping equipment operators	235	225	95.7	10	4.3	45	19.1	130	55.3
6320	Construction equipment operators, except paving, surfacing, and tamping equipment operators	9,025	8,720	96.6	305	3.4	860	9.5	7,165	79.4

A-21 Workers with Bachelor's Degree: Detailed Occupations, by Sex, Race, and Hispanic Origin, 2006–2010—Continued

Census occupation code	Detailed Occupation	Bachelor's degree									
		Not Hispanic or Latino, one race								Not Hispanic or Latino, two or more races	
		Black or African American alone		American Indian and Alaska Native alone		Asian alone		Native Hawaiian and Other Pacific Islander alone			
		Number	Percent	Number	Percent	Number	Percent	Number	Percent	Number	Percent
5400	Receptionists and information clerks	11,345	9.7	350	0.3	8,325	7.1	130	0.1	1,780	1.5
5410	Reservation and transportation ticket agents and travel clerks	3,255	10.9	65	0.2	2,975	9.9	75	0.3	450	1.5
5420	Information and record clerks, all other	1,700	11.5	135	0.9	1,195	8.1	25	0.2	240	1.6
5500	Cargo and freight agents	200	6.6	0	0.0	655	21.5	0	0.0	85	2.8
5510	Couriers and messengers	4,325	14.0	140	0.5	2,090	6.8	15	0.0	410	1.3
5520	Dispatchers	3,350	12.6	175	0.7	950	3.6	15	0.1	285	1.1
5530	Meter readers, utilities	280	10.6	0	0.0	215	8.2	0	0.0	34	1.3
5540	Postal service clerks	3,680	19.7	100	0.5	4,765	25.4	45	0.2	285	1.5
5550	Postal service mail carriers	3,920	10.0	110	0.3	4,860	12.4	55	0.1	394	1.0
5560	Postal service mail sorters, processors, and processing machine operators	2,130	17.1	20	0.2	3,620	29.0	10	0.1	75	0.6
5600	Production, planning, and expediting clerks	4,325	6.7	110	0.2	4,180	6.4	70	0.1	1,250	1.9
5610	Shipping, receiving, and traffic clerks	3,295	9.9	45	0.1	2,980	8.9	30	0.1	515	1.5
5620	Stock clerks and order fillers	8,675	10.2	425	0.5	9,565	11.3	130	0.2	1,195	1.4
5630	Weighers, measurers, checkers, and samplers, recordkeeping	500	8.0	15	0.2	575	9.3	0	0.0	115	1.9
5700	Secretaries and administrative assistants	47,010	8.6	1,605	0.3	34,945	6.4	565	0.1	8,290	1.5
5800	Computer operators	2,680	9.9	60	0.2	3,140	11.6	10	0.0	260	1.0
5810	Data entry keyers	7,025	11.4	230	0.4	7,395	12.0	10	0.0	935	1.5
5820	Word processors and typists	5,215	11.9	125	0.3	4,835	11.0	85	0.2	725	1.7
5840	Insurance claims and policy processing clerks	7,895	14.1	115	0.2	2,850	5.1	15	0.0	840	1.5
5850	Mail clerks and mail machine operators, except postal service	820	9.5	30	0.3	1,150	13.3	15	0.2	175	2.0
5860	Office clerks, general	16,245	10.1	600	0.4	19,065	11.8	210	0.1	2,875	1.8
5900	Office machine operators, except computer	845	16.6	25	0.5	735	14.4	0	0.0	85	1.7
5910	Proofreaders and copy markers	280	5.1	4	0.1	215	3.9	25	0.5	80	1.4
5920	Statistical assistants	560	8.8	15	0.2	655	10.3	0	0.0	125	2.0
5940	Miscellaneous office and administrative support workers, including desktop publishers	14,455	11.9	385	0.3	8,685	7.2	80	0.1	1,995	1.6
6005	First-line supervisors of farming, fishing, and forestry workers	160	2.3	50	0.7	220	3.2	4	0.1	160	2.3
6010	Agricultural inspectors	485	11.6	15	0.4	245	5.8	30	0.7	110	2.6
6040	Graders and sorters, agricultural products	40	3.0	4	0.3	145	10.8	0	0.0	10	0.7
6050	Miscellaneous agricultural workers, including animal breeders	280	1.1	65	0.2	760	2.9	4	0.0	219	0.8
6100	Fishing and hunting workers	0	0.0	4	0.2	85	3.4	10	0.4	18	0.7
6120	Forest and conservation workers	0	0.0	0	0.0	10	0.5	0	0.0	0	0.0
6130	Logging workers	210	11.9	0	0.0	0	0.0	0	0.0	4	0.2
6200	First-line supervisors of construction trades and extraction workers	2,910	3.5	355	0.4	2,540	3.0	155	0.2	670	0.8
6210	Boilermakers	4	0.7	4	0.7	0	0.0	15	2.6	0	0.0
6220	Brickmasons, blockmasons, and stonemasons	350	6.3	20	0.4	140	2.5	0	0.0	100	1.8
6230	Carpenters	1,885	2.5	445	0.6	1,745	2.3	105	0.1	995	1.3
6240	Carpet, floor, and tile installers and finishers	180	2.4	15	0.2	155	2.1	0	0.0	130	1.8
6250	Cement masons, concrete finishers, and terrazzo workers	30	2.2	4	0.3	0	0.0	20	1.5	45	3.3
6260	Construction laborers	3,250	5.1	280	0.4	1,930	3.0	40	0.1	755	1.2
6300	Paving, surfacing, and tamping equipment operators	45	19.1	0	0.0	0	0.0	0	0.0	15	6.4
6320	Construction equipment operators, except paving, surfacing, and tamping equipment operators	650	7.2	65	0.7	180	2.0	30	0.3	79	0.9

A-21 Workers with Bachelor's Degree: Detailed Occupations, by Sex, Race, and Hispanic Origin, 2006–2010—*Continued*

Census occupation code	Detailed Occupation	Total	Bachelor's degree Male Number	Male Percent	Female Number	Female Percent	Hispanic or Latino Number	Hispanic or Latino Percent	Not Hispanic or Latino, one race — White alone Number	White alone Percent
6330	Drywall installers, ceiling tile installers, and tapers	3,010	2,915	96.8	95	3.2	1,525	50.7	1,305	43.4
6355	Electricians	41,535	40,030	96.4	1,505	3.6	5,150	12.4	29,805	71.8
6360	Glaziers	1,115	1,100	98.7	10	0.9	215	19.3	805	72.2
6400	Insulation workers	1,365	1,275	93.4	90	6.6	465	34.1	760	55.7
6420	Painters, construction and maintenance	31,825	26,860	84.4	4,965	15.6	6,745	21.2	22,820	71.7
6430	Paperhangers	635	445	70.1	190	29.9	20	3.1	580	91.3
6440	Pipelayers, plumbers, pipefitters, and steamfitters	18,940	18,305	96.6	635	3.4	2,285	12.1	14,595	77.1
6460	Plasterers and stucco masons	1,010	980	97.0	35	3.5	540	53.5	385	38.1
6500	Reinforcing iron and rebar workers	195	190	97.4	4	2.1	25	12.8	165	84.6
6515	Roofers	4,835	4,770	98.7	65	1.3	1,820	37.6	2,660	55.0
6520	Sheet metal workers	3,975	3,675	92.5	295	7.4	370	9.3	3,010	75.7
6530	Structural iron and steel workers	2,080	2,045	98.3	40	1.9	175	8.4	1,620	77.9
6600	Helpers, construction trades	1,620	1,450	89.5	170	10.5	420	25.9	895	55.2
6660	Construction and building inspectors	20,640	18,170	88.0	2,465	11.9	1,425	6.9	15,740	76.3
6700	Elevator installers and repairers	1,690	1,595	94.4	95	5.6	240	14.2	1,305	77.2
6710	Fence erectors	1,070	1,065	99.5	10	0.9	180	16.8	870	81.3
6720	Hazardous materials removal workers	2,170	1,775	81.8	390	18.0	265	12.2	1,440	66.4
6730	Highway maintenance workers	2,770	2,655	95.8	110	4.0	100	3.6	2,390	86.3
6740	Rail-track laying and maintenance equipment operators	265	255	96.2	10	3.8	10	3.8	205	77.4
6765	Miscellaneous construction workers, including solar photovoltaic installers, septic tank servicers, and sewer pipe cleaners	1,725	1,655	95.9	75	4.3	210	12.2	1,305	75.7
6800	Derrick, rotary drill, and service unit operators, and roustabouts, oil, gas, and mining	1,405	1,345	95.7	60	4.3	105	7.5	1,255	89.3
6820	Earth drillers, except oil and gas	1,010	1,010	100.0	4	0.4	25	2.5	910	90.1
6830	Explosives workers, ordnance handling experts, and blasters	600	535	89.2	70	11.7	90	15.0	425	70.8
6840	Mining machine operators	1,715	1,640	95.6	75	4.4	170	9.9	1,500	87.5
6940	Miscellaneous extraction workers, including roof bolters and helpers	1,620	1,580	97.5	40	2.5	120	7.4	1,375	84.9
7000	First-line supervisors of mechanics, installers, and repairers	30,490	26,285	86.2	4,205	13.8	2,345	7.7	23,800	78.1
7010	Computer, automated teller, and office machine repairers	48,015	41,910	87.3	6,105	12.7	3,620	7.5	33,085	68.9
7020	Radio and telecommunications equipment installers and repairers	19,600	16,535	84.4	3,065	15.6	1,800	9.2	13,020	66.4
7030	Avionics technicians	1,880	1,830	97.3	50	2.7	225	12.0	1,275	67.8
7040	Electric motor, power tool, and related repairers	1,690	1,665	98.5	25	1.5	345	20.4	1,150	68.0
7100	Electrical and electronics repairers, transportation equipment, and industrial and utility	1,585	1,515	95.6	70	4.4	120	7.6	1,235	77.9
7110	Electronic equipment installers and repairers, motor vehicles	900	865	96.1	40	4.4	95	10.6	710	78.9
7120	Electronic home entertainment equipment installers and repairers	5,310	5,145	96.9	165	3.1	680	12.8	3,705	69.8
7130	Security and fire alarm systems installers	4,085	3,920	96.0	170	4.2	515	12.6	2,980	72.9
7140	Aircraft mechanics and service technicians	13,335	12,675	95.1	660	4.9	1,630	12.2	8,765	65.7

A-21 Workers with Bachelor's Degree: Detailed Occupations, by Sex, Race, and Hispanic Origin, 2006–2010—Continued

Census occupation code	Detailed Occupation	Black or African American alone Number	Percent	American Indian and Alaska Native alone Number	Percent	Asian alone Number	Percent	Native Hawaiian and Other Pacific Islander alone Number	Percent	Not Hispanic or Latino, two or more races Number	Percent
6330	Drywall installers, ceiling tile installers, and tapers	95	3.2	35	1.2	45	1.5	0	0.0	0	0.0
6355	Electricians	3,270	7.9	270	0.7	2,310	5.6	135	0.3	594	1.4
6360	Glaziers	55	4.9	0	0.0	25	2.2	0	0.0	10	0.9
6400	Insulation workers	125	9.2	0	0.0	0	0.0	4	0.3	4	0.3
6420	Painters, construction and maintenance	845	2.7	20	0.1	1,150	3.6	0	0.0	240	0.8
6430	Paperhangers	0	0.0	0	0.0	15	2.4	0	0.0	25	3.9
6440	Pipelayers, plumbers, pipefitters, and steamfitters	1,410	7.4	85	0.4	390	2.1	0	0.0	175	0.9
6460	Plasterers and stucco masons	85	8.4	0	0.0	0	0.0	0	0.0	0	0.0
6500	Reinforcing iron and rebar workers	0	0.0	0	0.0	0	0.0	0	0.0	0	0.0
6515	Roofers	280	5.8	25	0.5	45	0.9	0	0.0	4	0.1
6520	Sheet metal workers	205	5.2	0	0.0	370	9.3	0	0.0	19	0.5
6530	Structural iron and steel workers	125	6.0	0	0.0	120	5.8	15	0.7	30	1.4
6600	Helpers, construction trades	85	5.2	105	6.5	105	6.5	0	0.0	15	0.9
6660	Construction and building inspectors	1,905	9.2	90	0.4	1,260	6.1	0	0.0	220	1.1
6700	Elevator installers and repairers	100	5.9	0	0.0	50	3.0	0	0.0	0	0.0
6710	Fence erectors	20	1.9	0	0.0	0	0.0	0	0.0	0	0.0
6720	Hazardous materials removal workers	270	12.4	10	0.5	125	5.8	0	0.0	65	3.0
6730	Highway maintenance workers	185	6.7	35	1.3	10	0.4	0	0.0	50	1.8
6740	Rail-track laying and maintenance equipment operators	35	13.2	0	0.0	15	5.7	0	0.0	0	0.0
6765	Miscellaneous construction workers, including solar photovoltaic installers, septic tank servicers, and sewer pipe cleaners	115	6.7	0	0.0	65	3.8	10	0.6	24	1.4
6800	Derrick, rotary drill, and service unit operators, and roustabouts, oil, gas, and mining	0	0.0	0	0.0	35	2.5	0	0.0	15	1.1
6820	Earth drillers, except oil and gas	30	3.0	0	0.0	45	4.5	0	0.0	0	0.0
6830	Explosives workers, ordnance handling experts, and blasters	50	8.3	0	0.0	35	5.8	0	0.0	0	0.0
6840	Mining machine operators	50	2.9	0	0.0	0	0.0	0	0.0	0	0.0
6940	Miscellaneous extraction workers, including roof bolters and helpers	85	5.2	30	1.9	15	0.9	0	0.0	0	0.0
7000	First-line supervisors of mechanics, installers, and repairers	2,470	8.1	115	0.4	1,355	4.4	35	0.1	379	1.2
7010	Computer, automated teller, and office machine repairers	5,285	11.0	125	0.3	5,160	10.7	25	0.1	715	1.5
7020	Radio and telecommunications equipment installers and repairers	2,835	14.5	45	0.2	1,510	7.7	40	0.2	350	1.8
7030	Avionics technicians	205	10.9	0	0.0	155	8.2	0	0.0	15	0.8
7040	Electric motor, power tool, and related repairers	65	3.8	15	0.9	100	5.9	0	0.0	15	0.9
7100	Electrical and electronics repairers, transportation equipment, and industrial and utility	135	8.5	0	0.0	80	5.0	0	0.0	14	0.9
7110	Electronic equipment installers and repairers, motor vehicles	40	4.4	0	0.0	0	0.0	0	0.0	55	6.1
7120	Electronic home entertainment equipment installers and repairers	445	8.4	0	0.0	360	6.8	30	0.6	94	1.8
7130	Security and fire alarm systems installers	295	7.2	10	0.2	270	6.6	0	0.0	20	0.5
7140	Aircraft mechanics and service technicians	1,180	8.8	105	0.8	1,190	8.9	25	0.2	445	3.3

A-21 **Workers with Bachelor's Degree: Detailed Occupations, by Sex, Race, and Hispanic Origin, 2006–2010**—Continued

Census occupation code	Detailed Occupation	Total	Bachelor's degree						
			Male		Female		Hispanic or Latino		Not Hispanic or Latino, one race — White alone	
			Number	Percent	Number	Percent	Number	Percent	Number	Percent
7150	Automotive body and related repairers	3,285	3,175	96.7	110	3.3	875	26.6	1,900	57.8
7160	Automotive glass installers and repairers	800	755	94.4	50	6.3	150	18.8	605	75.6
7200	Automotive service technicians and mechanics	24,480	23,735	97.0	745	3.0	4,825	19.7	15,140	61.8
7210	Bus and truck mechanics and diesel engine specialists	6,490	6,355	97.9	135	2.1	775	11.9	4,275	65.9
7220	Heavy vehicle and mobile equipment service technicians and mechanics	6,005	5,900	98.3	105	1.7	865	14.4	4,550	75.8
7240	Small engine mechanics	1,450	1,375	94.8	80	5.5	55	3.8	1,265	87.2
7260	Miscellaneous vehicle and mobile equipment mechanics, installers, and repairers	2,710	2,570	94.8	135	5.0	440	16.2	1,985	73.2
7300	Control and valve installers and repairers	930	875	94.1	55	5.9	30	3.2	695	74.7
7315	Heating, air conditioning, and refrigeration mechanics and installers	12,920	12,610	97.6	310	2.4	1,675	13.0	9,255	71.6
7320	Home appliance repairers	2,245	2,130	94.9	115	5.1	205	9.1	1,770	78.8
7330	Industrial and refractory machinery mechanics	18,320	17,475	95.4	845	4.6	2,250	12.3	12,505	68.3
7340	Maintenance and repair workers, general	24,845	23,175	93.3	1,670	6.7	2,545	10.2	17,920	72.1
7350	Maintenance workers, machinery	1,530	1,415	92.5	115	7.5	175	11.4	880	57.5
7360	Millwrights	1,340	1,250	93.3	85	6.3	30	2.2	1,175	87.7
7410	Electrical power-line installers and repairers	4,665	4,550	97.5	110	2.4	270	5.8	3,545	76.0
7420	Telecommunications line installers and repairers	12,025	10,780	89.6	1,245	10.4	1,315	10.9	7,750	64.4
7430	Precision instrument and equipment repairers	9,175	7,970	86.9	1,210	13.2	610	6.6	7,300	79.6
7510	Coin, vending, and amusement machine servicers and repairers	3,445	3,030	88.0	415	12.0	220	6.4	2,715	78.8
7540	Locksmiths and safe repairers	2,195	2,030	92.5	160	7.3	75	3.4	1,765	80.4
7550	Manufactured building and mobile home installers	205	205	100.0	0	0.0	15	7.3	170	82.9
7560	Riggers	595	550	92.4	45	7.6	180	30.3	320	53.8
7610	Helpers—installation, maintenance, and repair workers	560	530	94.6	25	4.5	280	50.0	175	31.3
7630	Other installation, maintenance, and repair workers, including wind turbine service technicians, and commercial divers, and signal and track switch repairers	16,050	14,660	91.3	1,395	8.7	1,425	8.9	12,545	78.2
7700	First-line supervisors of production and operating workers	111,905	87,970	78.6	23,930	21.4	7,610	6.8	85,320	76.2
7710	Aircraft structure, surfaces, rigging, and systems assemblers	465	370	79.6	95	20.4	55	11.8	265	57.0
7720	Electrical, electronics, and electromechanical assemblers	7,495	4,470	59.6	3,025	40.4	905	12.1	3,495	46.6
7730	Engine and other machine assemblers	510	445	87.3	65	12.7	50	9.8	350	68.6
7740	Structural metal fabricators and fitters	1,240	1,110	89.5	125	10.1	110	8.9	915	73.8
7750	Miscellaneous assemblers and fabricators	40,555	27,405	67.6	13,150	32.4	4,840	11.9	23,760	58.6
7800	Bakers	11,500	5,060	44.0	6,440	56.0	1,380	12.0	7,960	69.2
7810	Butchers and other meat, poultry, and fish processing workers	6,040	5,160	85.4	875	14.5	1,615	26.7	3,295	54.6
7830	Food and tobacco roasting, baking, and drying machine operators and tenders	645	480	74.4	170	26.4	115	17.8	510	79.1
7840	Food batchmakers	3,790	1,495	39.4	2,295	60.6	600	15.8	2,700	71.2
7850	Food cooking machine operators and tenders	525	240	45.7	285	54.3	135	25.7	240	45.7
7855	Food processing workers, all other	3,415	2,185	64.0	1,230	36.0	710	20.8	1,680	49.2

A-21 Workers with Bachelor's Degree: Detailed Occupations, by Sex, Race, and Hispanic Origin, 2006–2010—Continued

Census occupation code	Detailed Occupation	Bachelor's degree								
		Not Hispanic or Latino, one race								Not Hispanic or Latino, two or more races	
		Black or African American alone		American Indian and Alaska Native alone		Asian alone		Native Hawaiian and Other Pacific Islander alone			
		Number	Percent	Number	Percent	Number	Percent	Number	Percent	Number	Percent
7150	Automotive body and related repairers	200	6.1	10	0.3	250	7.6	0	0.0	49	1.5
7160	Automotive glass installers and repairers	20	2.5	0	0.0	20	2.5	0	0.0	10	1.3
7200	Automotive service technicians and mechanics	1,525	6.2	125	0.5	2,480	10.1	0	0.0	385	1.6
7210	Bus and truck mechanics and diesel engine specialists	755	11.6	100	1.5	580	8.9	0	0.0	4	0.1
7220	Heavy vehicle and mobile equipment service technicians and mechanics	270	4.5	15	0.2	205	3.4	0	0.0	95	1.6
7240	Small engine mechanics	30	2.1	0	0.0	50	3.4	0	0.0	55	3.8
7260	Miscellaneous vehicle and mobile equipment mechanics, installers, and repairers	160	5.9	15	0.6	35	1.3	0	0.0	70	2.6
7300	Control and valve installers and repairers	100	10.8	20	2.2	25	2.7	0	0.0	55	5.9
7315	Heating, air conditioning, and refrigeration mechanics and installers	860	6.7	50	0.4	820	6.3	40	0.3	225	1.7
7320	Home appliance repairers	175	7.8	20	0.9	70	3.1	0	0.0	10	0.4
7330	Industrial and refractory machinery mechanics	1,305	7.1	115	0.6	1,895	10.3	4	0.0	245	1.3
7340	Maintenance and repair workers, general	1,730	7.0	95	0.4	2,185	8.8	30	0.1	335	1.3
7350	Maintenance workers, machinery	170	11.1	15	1.0	295	19.3	0	0.0	0	0.0
7360	Millwrights	50	3.7	15	1.1	70	5.2	0	0.0	0	0.0
7410	Electrical power-line installers and repairers	620	13.3	75	1.6	50	1.1	0	0.0	105	2.3
7420	Telecommunications line installers and repairers	2,010	16.7	10	0.1	790	6.6	20	0.2	125	1.0
7430	Precision instrument and equipment repairers	310	3.4	20	0.2	785	8.6	10	0.1	135	1.5
7510	Coin, vending, and amusement machine servicers and repairers	190	5.5	20	0.6	240	7.0	10	0.3	55	1.6
7540	Locksmiths and safe repairers	140	6.4	25	1.1	100	4.6	0	0.0	85	3.9
7550	Manufactured building and mobile home installers	20	9.8	0	0.0	0	0.0	0	0.0	0	0.0
7560	Riggers	45	7.6	0	0.0	15	2.5	0	0.0	34	5.7
7610	Helpers—installation, maintenance, and repair workers	20	3.6	0	0.0	55	9.8	0	0.0	25	4.5
7630	Other installation, maintenance, and repair workers, including wind turbine service technicians, and commercial divers, and signal and track switch repairers	915	5.7	35	0.2	965	6.0	10	0.1	155	1.0
7700	First-line supervisors of production and operating workers	8,870	7.9	365	0.3	8,650	7.7	230	0.2	870	0.8
7710	Aircraft structure, surfaces, rigging, and systems assemblers	90	19.4	0	0.0	55	11.8	0	0.0	0	0.0
7720	Electrical, electronics, and electromechanical assemblers	615	8.2	50	0.7	2,345	31.3	25	0.3	60	0.8
7730	Engine and other machine assemblers	20	3.9	0	0.0	90	17.6	0	0.0	0	0.0
7740	Structural metal fabricators and fitters	115	9.3	0	0.0	40	3.2	10	0.8	54	4.4
7750	Miscellaneous assemblers and fabricators	4,610	11.4	105	0.3	6,860	16.9	10	0.0	370	0.9
7800	Bakers	615	5.3	30	0.3	1,365	11.9	10	0.1	140	1.2
7810	Butchers and other meat, poultry, and fish processing workers	570	9.4	50	0.8	350	5.8	0	0.0	160	2.6
7830	Food and tobacco roasting, baking, and drying machine operators and tenders	0	0.0	4	0.6	20	3.1	0	0.0	0	0.0
7840	Food batchmakers	185	4.9	0	0.0	300	7.9	0	0.0	0	0.0
7850	Food cooking machine operators and tenders	40	7.6	10	1.9	70	13.3	0	0.0	25	4.8
7855	Food processing workers, all other	520	15.2	0	0.0	440	12.9	4	0.1	65	1.9

A-21. Workers with Bachelor's Degree: Detailed Occupations, by Sex, Race, and Hispanic Origin, 2006–2010—Continued

Census occupation code	Detailed Occupation	Total	Bachelor's degree Male Number	Male Percent	Female Number	Female Percent	Hispanic or Latino Number	Hispanic or Latino Percent	Not Hispanic or Latino, one race White alone Number	White alone Percent
7900	Computer control programmers and operators	3,375	3,025	89.6	350	10.4	305	9.0	2,565	76.0
7920	Extruding and drawing machine setters, operators, and tenders, metal and plastic	445	350	78.7	95	21.3	60	13.5	315	70.8
7930	Forging machine setters, operators, and tenders, metal and plastic	85	85	100.0	0	0.0	10	11.8	50	58.8
7940	Rolling machine setters, operators, and tenders, metal and plastic	275	265	96.4	10	3.6	15	5.5	180	65.5
7950	Cutting, punching, and press machine setters, operators, and tenders, metal and plastic	2,340	1,905	81.4	440	18.8	200	8.5	1,615	69.0
7960	Drilling and boring machine tool setters, operators, and tenders, metal and plastic	55	45	81.8	10	18.2	10	18.2	35	63.6
8000	Grinding, lapping, polishing, and buffing machine tool setters, operators, and tenders, metal and plastic	1,025	875	85.4	145	14.1	210	20.5	670	65.4
8010	Lathe and turning machine tool setters, operators, and tenders, metal and plastic	270	265	98.1	10	3.7	30	11.1	190	70.4
8030	Machinists	10,125	9,700	95.8	425	4.2	810	8.0	7,180	70.9
8040	Metal furnace operators, tenders, pourers, and casters	635	570	89.8	65	10.2	50	7.9	490	77.2
8060	Model makers and patternmakers, metal and plastic	660	505	76.5	155	23.5	30	4.5	575	87.1
8100	Molders and molding machine setters, operators, and tenders, metal and plastic	1,270	1,135	89.4	135	10.6	195	15.4	885	69.7
8130	Tool and die makers	2,425	2,185	90.1	240	9.9	225	9.3	2,050	84.5
8140	Welding, soldering, and brazing workers	10,280	9,520	92.6	765	7.4	1,985	19.3	6,875	66.9
8150	Heat treating equipment setters, operators, and tenders, metal and plastic	235	170	72.3	60	25.5	30	12.8	165	70.2
8200	Plating and coating machine setters, operators, and tenders, metal and plastic	330	240	72.7	90	27.3	45	13.6	280	84.8
8210	Tool grinders, filers, and sharpeners	375	335	89.3	35	9.3	35	9.3	270	72.0
8220	Miscellaneous metal workers and plastic workers, including milling and planing machine setters, and multiple machine tool setters, and layout workers	13,865	10,835	78.1	3,030	21.9	2,700	19.5	6,450	46.5
8250	Prepress technicians and workers	6,215	3,320	53.4	2,895	46.6	290	4.7	4,805	77.3
8255	Printing press operators	13,655	10,260	75.1	3,395	24.9	1,605	11.8	9,400	68.8
8256	Print binding and finishing workers	1,845	1,065	57.7	780	42.3	305	16.5	1,255	68.0
8300	Laundry and dry-cleaning workers	7,875	4,565	58.0	3,310	42.0	1,490	18.9	3,355	42.6
8310	Pressers, textile, garment, and related materials	1,170	485	41.5	690	59.0	495	42.3	310	26.5
8320	Sewing machine operators	8,215	1,240	15.1	6,975	84.9	1,955	23.8	4,725	57.5
8330	Shoe and leather workers and repairers	655	540	82.4	115	17.6	90	13.7	435	66.4
8340	Shoe machine operators and tenders	275	155	56.4	120	43.6	35	12.7	210	76.4
8350	Tailors, dressmakers, and sewers	9,435	2,125	22.5	7,310	77.5	730	7.7	6,275	66.5
8400	Textile bleaching and dyeing, and cutting machine setters, operators, and tenders	375	225	60.0	150	40.0	90	24.0	170	45.3
8410	Textile knitting and weaving machine setters, operators, and tenders	315	60	19.0	250	79.4	20	6.3	240	76.2
8420	Textile winding, twisting, and drawing out machine setters, operators, and tenders	105	85	81.0	20	19.0	20	19.0	65	61.9
8450	Upholsterers	1,445	1,070	74.0	375	26.0	390	27.0	930	64.4
8460	Miscellaneous textile, apparel, and furnishings workers, except upholsterers	2,195	935	42.6	1,260	57.4	245	11.2	1,430	65.1

PART A—NATIONAL DATA

A-21 Workers with Bachelor's Degree: Detailed Occupations, by Sex, Race, and Hispanic Origin, 2006–2010—Continued

Census occupation code	Detailed Occupation	Black or African American alone Number	Black or African American alone Percent	American Indian and Alaska Native alone Number	American Indian and Alaska Native alone Percent	Asian alone Number	Asian alone Percent	Native Hawaiian and Other Pacific Islander alone Number	Native Hawaiian and Other Pacific Islander alone Percent	Not Hispanic or Latino, two or more races Number	Not Hispanic or Latino, two or more races Percent
7900	Computer control programmers and operators	150	4.4	15	0.4	330	9.8	0	0.0	15	0.4
7920	Extruding and drawing machine setters, operators, and tenders, metal and plastic	25	5.6	10	2.2	30	6.7	0	0.0	0	0.0
7930	Forging machine setters, operators, and tenders, metal and plastic	25	29.4	0	0.0	0	0.0	0	0.0	0	0.0
7940	Rolling machine setters, operators, and tenders, metal and plastic	0	0.0	25	9.1	55	20.0	0	0.0	0	0.0
7950	Cutting, punching, and press machine setters, operators, and tenders, metal and plastic	390	16.7	0	0.0	135	5.8	0	0.0	4	0.2
7960	Drilling and boring machine tool setters, operators, and tenders, metal and plastic	0	0.0	0	0.0	4	7.3	0	0.0	0	0.0
8000	Grinding, lapping, polishing, and buffing machine tool setters, operators, and tenders, metal and plastic	60	5.9	0	0.0	65	6.3	0	0.0	15	1.5
8010	Lathe and turning machine tool setters, operators, and tenders, metal and plastic	0	0.0	0	0.0	50	18.5	0	0.0	0	0.0
8030	Machinists	735	7.3	55	0.5	1,220	12.0	30	0.3	100	1.0
8040	Metal furnace operators, tenders, pourers, and casters	70	11.0	0	0.0	20	3.1	0	0.0	0	0.0
8060	Model makers and patternmakers, metal and plastic	30	4.5	0	0.0	0	0.0	0	0.0	19	2.9
8100	Molders and molding machine setters, operators, and tenders, metal and plastic	75	5.9	0	0.0	115	9.1	0	0.0	0	0.0
8130	Tool and die makers	50	2.1	0	0.0	85	3.5	0	0.0	15	0.6
8140	Welding, soldering, and brazing workers	715	7.0	140	1.4	510	5.0	0	0.0	54	0.5
8150	Heat treating equipment setters, operators, and tenders, metal and plastic	40	17.0	0	0.0	0	0.0	0	0.0	0	0.0
8200	Plating and coating machine setters, operators, and tenders, metal and plastic	0	0.0	0	0.0	4	1.2	0	0.0	0	0.0
8210	Tool grinders, filers, and sharpeners	25	6.7	0	0.0	40	10.7	0	0.0	0	0.0
8220	Miscellaneous metal workers and plastic workers, including milling and planing machine setters, and multiple machine tool setters, and layout workers	1,545	11.1	30	0.2	2,920	21.1	15	0.1	204	1.5
8250	Prepress technicians and workers	450	7.2	0	0.0	585	9.4	10	0.2	69	1.1
8255	Printing press operators	1,205	8.8	30	0.2	1,235	9.0	15	0.1	165	1.2
8256	Print binding and finishing workers	115	6.2	0	0.0	155	8.4	0	0.0	10	0.5
8300	Laundry and dry-cleaning workers	640	8.1	15	0.2	2,200	27.9	4	0.1	169	2.1
8310	Pressers, textile, garment, and related materials	90	7.7	0	0.0	215	18.4	0	0.0	60	5.1
8320	Sewing machine operators	345	4.2	4	0.0	1,145	13.9	0	0.0	40	0.5
8330	Shoe and leather workers and repairers	50	7.6	0	0.0	70	10.7	0	0.0	4	0.6
8340	Shoe machine operators and tenders	0	0.0	0	0.0	15	5.5	0	0.0	10	3.6
8350	Tailors, dressmakers, and sewers	330	3.5	20	0.2	2,020	21.4	0	0.0	60	0.6
8400	Textile bleaching and dyeing, and cutting machine setters, operators, and tenders	10	2.7	4	1.1	95	25.3	0	0.0	4	1.1
8410	Textile knitting and weaving machine setters, operators, and tenders	0	0.0	0	0.0	50	15.9	0	0.0	0	0.0
8420	Textile winding, twisting, and drawing out machine setters, operators, and tenders	0	0.0	0	0.0	4	3.8	0	0.0	15	14.3
8450	Upholsterers	60	4.2	15	1.0	45	3.1	0	0.0	0	0.0
8460	Miscellaneous textile, apparel, and furnishings workers, except upholsterers	110	5.0	0	0.0	375	17.1	35	1.6	0	0.0

A-21 Workers with Bachelor's Degree: Detailed Occupations, by Sex, Race, and Hispanic Origin, 2006–2010—Continued

Census occupation code	Detailed Occupation	Total	Bachelor's degree Male Number	Male Percent	Female Number	Female Percent	Hispanic or Latino Number	Hispanic or Latino Percent	Not Hispanic or Latino, one race White alone Number	White alone Percent
8500	Cabinetmakers and bench carpenters	4,535	4,225	93.2	305	6.7	325	7.2	3,895	85.9
8510	Furniture finishers	1,460	1,215	83.2	245	16.8	245	16.8	1,115	76.4
8530	Sawing machine setters, operators, and tenders, wood	700	505	72.1	190	27.1	110	15.7	530	75.7
8540	Woodworking machine setters, operators, and tenders, except sawing	615	395	64.2	220	35.8	99	16.1	380	61.8
8550	Miscellaneous woodworkers, including model makers and patternmakers	3,220	2,885	89.6	340	10.6	150	4.7	2,960	91.9
8600	Power plant operators, distributors, and dispatchers	6,010	5,520	91.8	485	8.1	210	3.5	5,075	84.4
8610	Stationary engineers and boiler operators	8,515	8,290	97.4	225	2.6	815	9.6	5,740	67.4
8620	Water and wastewater treatment plant and system operators	6,525	5,835	89.4	690	10.6	350	5.4	5,120	78.5
8630	Miscellaneous plant and system operators	3,085	2,830	91.7	255	8.3	125	4.1	2,490	80.7
8640	Chemical processing machine setters, operators, and tenders	6,725	5,605	83.3	1,120	16.7	300	4.5	4,895	72.8
8650	Crushing, grinding, polishing, mixing, and blending workers	3,460	2,700	78.0	760	22.0	510	14.7	2,360	68.2
8710	Cutting workers	2,090	1,685	80.6	405	19.4	415	19.9	1,315	62.9
8720	Extruding, forming, pressing, and compacting machine setters, operators, and tenders	855	740	86.5	115	13.5	10	1.2	745	87.1
8730	Furnace, kiln, oven, drier, and kettle operators and tenders	610	470	77.0	140	23.0	90	14.8	390	63.9
8740	Inspectors, testers, sorters, samplers, and weighers	79,645	53,465	67.1	26,180	32.9	6,650	8.3	52,320	65.7
8750	Jewelers and precious stone and metal workers	6,150	3,045	49.5	3,105	50.5	590	9.6	4,520	73.5
8760	Medical, dental, and ophthalmic laboratory technicians	9,070	4,705	51.9	4,365	48.1	960	10.6	5,690	62.7
8800	Packaging and filling machine operators and tenders	7,890	3,965	50.3	3,925	49.7	2,495	31.6	3,065	38.8
8810	Painting workers	3,985	3,050	76.5	935	23.5	855	21.5	2,460	61.7
8830	Photographic process workers and processing machine operators	8,255	4,685	56.8	3,575	43.3	600	7.3	5,960	72.2
8850	Adhesive bonding machine operators and tenders	200	155	77.5	45	22.5	50	25.0	70	35.0
8860	Cleaning, washing, and metal pickling equipment operators and tenders	230	160	69.6	70	30.4	35	15.2	125	54.3
8910	Etchers and engravers	1,025	805	78.5	220	21.5	25	2.4	915	89.3
8920	Molders, shapers, and casters, except metal and plastic	2,985	2,015	67.5	970	32.5	135	4.5	2,650	88.8
8930	Paper goods machine setters, operators, and tenders	1,100	860	78.2	240	21.8	60	5.5	650	59.1
8940	Tire builders	390	320	82.1	70	17.9	15	3.8	160	41.0
8950	Helpers—production workers	1,660	1,010	60.8	650	39.2	435	26.2	760	45.8
8965	Other production workers, including semiconductor processors and cooling and freezing equipment operators	45,680	33,000	72.2	12,680	27.8	6,120	13.4	27,815	60.9
9000	Supervisors of transportation and material moving workers	33,135	26,335	79.5	6,805	20.5	2,875	8.7	22,840	68.9
9030	Aircraft pilots and flight engineers	73,885	70,095	94.9	3,785	5.1	2,655	3.6	67,245	91.0
9040	Air traffic controllers and airfield operations specialists	9,840	7,975	81.0	1,860	18.9	480	4.9	8,160	82.9
9050	Flight attendants	28,020	6,395	22.8	21,625	77.2	2,010	7.2	21,340	76.2
9110	Ambulance drivers and attendants, except emergency medical technicians	1,035	865	83.6	170	16.4	95	9.2	825	79.7

PART A—NATIONAL DATA

A-21 Workers with Bachelor's Degree: Detailed Occupations, by Sex, Race, and Hispanic Origin, 2006–2010—Continued

Census occupation code	Detailed Occupation	Black or African American alone Number	Black or African American alone Percent	American Indian and Alaska Native alone Number	American Indian and Alaska Native alone Percent	Asian alone Number	Asian alone Percent	Native Hawaiian and Other Pacific Islander alone Number	Native Hawaiian and Other Pacific Islander alone Percent	Not Hispanic or Latino, two or more races Number	Not Hispanic or Latino, two or more races Percent
8500	Cabinetmakers and bench carpenters	115	2.5	0	0.0	135	3.0	4	0.1	60	1.3
8510	Furniture finishers	60	4.1	10	0.7	10	0.7	0	0.0	10	0.7
8530	Sawing machine setters, operators, and tenders, wood	0	0.0	15	2.1	25	3.6	0	0.0	15	2.1
8540	Woodworking machine setters, operators, and tenders, except sawing	50	8.1	0	0.0	45	7.3	0	0.0	40	6.5
8550	Miscellaneous woodworkers, including model makers and patternmakers	0	0.0	0	0.0	115	3.6	0	0.0	4	0.1
8600	Power plant operators, distributors, and dispatchers	470	7.8	30	0.5	125	2.1	0	0.0	100	1.7
8610	Stationary engineers and boiler operators	645	7.6	15	0.2	1,210	14.2	0	0.0	90	1.1
8620	Water and wastewater treatment plant and system operators	520	8.0	30	0.5	400	6.1	0	0.0	105	1.6
8630	Miscellaneous plant and system operators	355	11.5	0	0.0	115	3.7	0	0.0	0	0.0
8640	Chemical processing machine setters, operators, and tenders	730	10.9	50	0.7	465	6.9	0	0.0	285	4.2
8650	Crushing, grinding, polishing, mixing, and blending workers	370	10.7	20	0.6	180	5.2	15	0.4	10	0.3
8710	Cutting workers	240	11.5	4	0.2	120	5.7	0	0.0	8	0.4
8720	Extruding, forming, pressing, and compacting machine setters, operators, and tenders	85	9.9	0	0.0	15	1.8	0	0.0	0	0.0
8730	Furnace, kiln, oven, drier, and kettle operators and tenders	90	14.8	0	0.0	25	4.1	0	0.0	15	2.5
8740	Inspectors, testers, sorters, samplers, and weighers	7,195	9.0	265	0.3	11,890	14.9	95	0.1	1,240	1.6
8750	Jewelers and precious stone and metal workers	210	3.4	60	1.0	725	11.8	0	0.0	50	0.8
8760	Medical, dental, and ophthalmic laboratory technicians	300	3.3	4	0.0	2,025	22.3	0	0.0	85	0.9
8800	Packaging and filling machine operators and tenders	1,125	14.3	20	0.3	1,135	14.4	0	0.0	54	0.7
8810	Painting workers	335	8.4	10	0.3	280	7.0	0	0.0	39	1.0
8830	Photographic process workers and processing machine operators	715	8.7	0	0.0	930	11.3	0	0.0	44	0.5
8850	Adhesive bonding machine operators and tenders	60	30.0	0	0.0	20	10.0	0	0.0	0	0.0
8860	Cleaning, washing, and metal pickling equipment operators and tenders	20	8.7	0	0.0	50	21.7	0	0.0	0	0.0
8910	Etchers and engravers	15	1.5	0	0.0	70	6.8	0	0.0	0	0.0
8920	Molders, shapers, and casters, except metal and plastic	4	0.1	15	0.5	160	5.4	0	0.0	14	0.5
8930	Paper goods machine setters, operators, and tenders	220	20.0	0	0.0	160	14.5	0	0.0	10	0.9
8940	Tire builders	200	51.3	0	0.0	15	3.8	0	0.0	0	0.0
8950	Helpers—production workers	275	16.6	10	0.6	160	9.6	10	0.6	10	0.6
8965	Other production workers, including semiconductor processors and cooling and freezing equipment operators	5,050	11.1	160	0.4	5,905	12.9	105	0.2	530	1.2
9000	Supervisors of transportation and material moving workers	4,185	12.6	195	0.6	2,580	7.8	30	0.1	430	1.3
9030	Aircraft pilots and flight engineers	1,690	2.3	305	0.4	1,125	1.5	85	0.1	790	1.1
9040	Air traffic controllers and airfield operations specialists	615	6.3	35	0.4	350	3.6	40	0.4	159	1.6
9050	Flight attendants	2,500	8.9	55	0.2	1,590	5.7	55	0.2	470	1.7
9110	Ambulance drivers and attendants, except emergency medical technicians	115	11.1	0	0.0	0	0.0	0	0.0	0	0.0

A-21 **Workers with Bachelor's Degree: Detailed Occupations, by Sex, Race, and Hispanic Origin, 2006–2010**—*Continued*

Census occupation code	Detailed Occupation	Total	Bachelor's degree						
			Male		Female		Hispanic or Latino		Not Hispanic or Latino, one race — White alone	
			Number	Percent	Number	Percent	Number	Percent	Number	Percent
9120	Bus drivers	32,600	24,535	75.3	8,070	24.8	2,685	8.2	21,425	65.7
9130	Driver/sales workers and truck drivers	125,890	118,175	93.9	7,715	6.1	15,275	12.1	87,510	69.5
9140	Taxi drivers and chauffeurs	36,175	34,170	94.5	2,005	5.5	2,885	8.0	17,695	48.9
9150	Motor vehicle operators, all other	4,150	3,775	91.0	375	9.0	385	9.3	3,380	81.4
9200	Locomotive engineers and operators	4,875	4,620	94.8	250	5.1	260	5.3	3,545	72.7
9230	Railroad brake, signal, and switch operators	350	345	98.6	4	1.1	0	0.0	330	94.3
9240	Railroad conductors and yardmasters	5,040	4,630	91.9	410	8.1	270	5.4	3,630	72.0
9260	Subway, streetcar, and other rail transportation workers	805	620	77.0	185	23.0	90	11.2	475	59.0
9300	Sailors and marine oilers, and ship engineers	2,150	1,940	90.2	210	9.8	140	6.5	1,760	81.9
9310	Ship and boat captains and operators	5,285	5,020	95.0	265	5.0	139	2.6	4,855	91.9
9350	Parking lot attendants	5,960	5,420	90.9	535	9.0	1,445	24.2	3,095	51.9
9360	Automotive and watercraft service attendants	4,950	3,970	80.2	980	19.8	580	11.7	2,890	58.4
9410	Transportation inspectors	5,965	5,180	86.8	785	13.2	480	8.0	4,385	73.5
9415	Transportation attendants, except flight attendants	2,075	970	46.7	1,100	53.0	285	13.7	1,105	53.3
9420	Miscellaneous transportation workers, including bridge and lock tenders and traffic technicians	2,270	1,940	85.5	335	14.8	150	6.6	1,425	62.8
9510	Crane and tower operators	1,070	1,000	93.5	65	6.1	70	6.5	750	70.1
9520	Dredge, excavating, and loading machine operators	1,380	1,360	98.6	20	1.4	160	11.6	1,175	85.1
9560	Conveyor operators and tenders, and hoist and winch operators	455	370	81.3	85	18.7	50	11.0	290	63.7
9600	Industrial truck and tractor operators	10,445	9,570	91.6	875	8.4	2,310	22.1	5,620	53.8
9610	Cleaners of vehicles and equipment	8,975	7,500	83.6	1,475	16.4	2,695	30.0	4,230	47.1
9620	Laborers and freight, stock, and material movers, hand	70,055	57,520	82.1	12,535	17.9	8,020	11.4	47,010	67.1
9630	Machine feeders and offbearers	935	510	54.5	425	45.5	85	9.1	590	63.1
9640	Packers and packagers, hand	12,535	6,235	49.7	6,300	50.3	3,415	27.2	5,410	43.2
9650	Pumping station operators	1,325	1,255	94.7	70	5.3	130	9.8	1,120	84.5
9720	Refuse and recyclable material collectors	2,695	2,140	79.4	555	20.6	365	13.5	1,710	63.5
9750	Miscellaneous material moving workers, including mine shuttle car operators, and tank car, truck, and ship loaders	1,750	1,520	86.9	230	13.1	215	12.3	1,045	59.7

PART A—NATIONAL DATA

A-21 Workers with Bachelor's Degree: Detailed Occupations, by Sex, Race, and Hispanic Origin, 2006–2010—*Continued*

Census occupation code	Detailed Occupation	Bachelor's degree									
		Not Hispanic or Latino, one race									Not Hispanic or Latino, two or more races	
		Black or African American alone		American Indian and Alaska Native alone		Asian alone		Native Hawaiian and Other Pacific Islander alone			
		Number	Percent	Number	Percent	Number	Percent	Number	Percent	Number	Percent
9120	Bus drivers	6,330	19.4	135	0.4	1,515	4.6	35	0.1	475	1.5
9130	Driver/sales workers and truck drivers	14,810	11.8	485	0.4	5,895	4.7	155	0.1	1,750	1.4
9140	Taxi drivers and chauffeurs	7,500	20.7	75	0.2	7,245	20.0	10	0.0	760	2.1
9150	Motor vehicle operators, all other	280	6.7	4	0.1	75	1.8	0	0.0	25	0.6
9200	Locomotive engineers and operators	855	17.5	10	0.2	135	2.8	0	0.0	65	1.3
9230	Railroad brake, signal, and switch operators	20	5.7	0	0.0	0	0.0	0	0.0	0	0.0
9240	Railroad conductors and yardmasters	1,005	19.9	10	0.2	95	1.9	0	0.0	30	0.6
9260	Subway, streetcar, and other rail transportation workers	220	27.3	0	0.0	15	1.9	0	0.0	0	0.0
9300	Sailors and marine oilers, and ship engineers	55	2.6	0	0.0	100	4.7	35	1.6	54	2.5
9310	Ship and boat captains and operators	85	1.6	0	0.0	75	1.4	0	0.0	135	2.6
9350	Parking lot attendants	685	11.5	0	0.0	630	10.6	0	0.0	100	1.7
9360	Automotive and watercraft service attendants	270	5.5	10	0.2	1,075	21.7	0	0.0	124	2.5
9410	Transportation inspectors	725	12.2	0	0.0	365	6.1	0	0.0	8	0.1
9415	Transportation attendants, except flight attendants	405	19.5	0	0.0	265	12.8	0	0.0	14	0.7
9420	Miscellaneous transportation workers, including bridge and lock tenders and traffic technicians	430	18.9	4	0.2	230	10.1	10	0.4	25	1.1
9510	Crane and tower operators	155	14.5	25	2.3	45	4.2	4	0.4	15	1.4
9520	Dredge, excavating, and loading machine operators	30	2.2	15	1.1	0	0.0	0	0.0	0	0.0
9560	Conveyor operators and tenders, and hoist and winch operators	55	12.1	15	3.3	35	7.7	0	0.0	10	2.2
9600	Industrial truck and tractor operators	1,740	16.7	30	0.3	435	4.2	0	0.0	310	3.0
9610	Cleaners of vehicles and equipment	1,235	13.8	10	0.1	500	5.6	45	0.5	265	3.0
9620	Laborers and freight, stock, and material movers, hand	8,575	12.2	185	0.3	5,090	7.3	115	0.2	1,065	1.5
9630	Machine feeders and offbearers	95	10.2	0	0.0	160	17.1	0	0.0	0	0.0
9640	Packers and packagers, hand	1,210	9.7	140	1.1	2,200	17.6	15	0.1	139	1.1
9650	Pumping station operators	60	4.5	10	0.8	10	0.8	0	0.0	0	0.0
9720	Refuse and recyclable material collectors	485	18.0	25	0.9	65	2.4	0	0.0	49	1.8
9750	Miscellaneous material moving workers, including mine shuttle car operators, and tank car, truck, and ship loaders	360	20.6	10	0.6	80	4.6	4	0.2	29	1.7

A-22 Workers with Graduate or Professional Degree: Detailed Occupations, by Sex, Race, and Hispanic Origin, 2006–2010

Census occupation code	Detailed Occupation	Total	Male Number	Male Percent	Female Number	Female Percent	Hispanic or Latino Number	Hispanic or Latino Percent	White alone Number	White alone Percent
	Total, all occupations	15,119,450	7,934,285	52.5	7,185,165	47.5	818,350	5.4	11,537,450	76.3
0010	Chief executives and legislators	284,380	224,805	79.1	59,575	20.9	10,390	3.7	238,890	84.0
0020	General and operations managers	135,400	96,750	71.5	38,650	28.5	7,345	5.4	106,570	78.7
0040	Advertising and promotions managers	6,655	3,425	51.5	3,225	48.5	255	3.8	5,330	80.1
0050	Marketing and sales managers	141,380	86,485	61.2	54,900	38.8	8,215	5.8	111,535	78.9
0060	Public relations and fundraising managers	13,165	5,330	40.5	7,835	59.5	445	3.4	10,980	83.4
0100	Administrative services managers	11,435	7,580	66.3	3,855	33.7	575	5.0	9,005	78.7
0110	Computer and information systems managers	112,080	80,205	71.6	31,875	28.4	4,130	3.7	76,115	67.9
0120	Financial managers	199,705	133,170	66.7	66,535	33.3	9,815	4.9	156,085	78.2
0135	Compensation and benefits managers	4,830	1,710	35.4	3,120	64.6	150	3.1	4,055	84.0
0136	Human resources managers	59,125	26,445	44.7	32,680	55.3	3,880	6.6	43,075	72.9
0137	Training and development managers	10,300	4,720	45.8	5,580	54.2	405	3.9	8,600	83.5
0140	Industrial production managers	27,780	21,750	78.3	6,030	21.7	1,365	4.9	21,510	77.4
0150	Purchasing managers	32,405	19,530	60.3	12,875	39.7	1,715	5.3	24,940	77.0
0160	Transportation, storage, and distribution managers	12,270	9,285	75.7	2,985	24.3	895	7.3	9,025	73.6
0205	Farmers, ranchers, and other agricultural managers	24,800	19,495	78.6	5,305	21.4	775	3.1	22,940	92.5
0220	Construction managers	45,090	39,280	87.1	5,810	12.9	3,050	6.8	36,615	81.2
0230	Education administrators	458,705	197,000	42.9	261,700	57.1	26,915	5.9	359,050	78.3
0300	Architectural and engineering managers	51,515	46,445	90.2	5,065	9.8	1,420	2.8	39,990	77.6
0310	Food service managers	29,345	18,665	63.6	10,685	36.4	3,050	10.4	18,075	61.6
0330	Gaming managers	700	525	75.0	175	25.0	20	2.9	590	84.3
0340	Lodging managers	11,335	6,645	58.6	4,690	41.4	530	4.7	7,850	69.3
0350	Medical and health services managers	151,030	61,450	40.7	89,580	59.3	7,855	5.2	118,100	78.2
0360	Natural sciences managers	11,070	7,315	66.1	3,755	33.9	485	4.4	8,590	77.6
0410	Property, real estate, and community association managers	51,410	34,720	67.5	16,690	32.5	2,325	4.5	42,010	81.7
0410	Social and community service managers	93,135	33,970	36.5	59,165	63.5	5,560	6.0	71,500	76.8
0425	Emergency management directors	715	485	67.8	230	32.2	50	7.0	540	75.5
0430	Miscellaneous managers, including funeral service managers and postmasters and mail superintendents	573,885	386,410	67.3	187,475	32.7	27,510	4.8	440,675	76.8
0500	Agents and business managers of artists, performers, and athletes	5,350	3,125	58.4	2,220	41.5	405	7.6	4,080	76.3
0510	Buyers and purchasing agents, farm products	400	310	77.5	90	22.5	45	11.3	320	80.0
0520	Wholesale and retail buyers, except farm products	8,410	4,550	54.1	3,860	45.9	510	6.1	6,430	76.5
0530	Purchasing agents, except wholesale, retail, and farm products	20,665	11,650	56.4	9,015	43.6	1,180	5.7	14,970	72.4
0540	Claims adjusters, appraisers, examiners, and investigators	18,145	8,835	48.7	9,310	51.3	985	5.4	12,570	69.3
0565	Compliance officers	32,045	17,365	54.2	14,680	45.8	1,675	5.2	23,540	73.5
0600	Cost estimators	4,645	3,890	83.7	760	16.4	290	6.2	3,625	78.0
0630	Human resources workers	91,880	33,080	36.0	58,800	64.0	5,595	6.1	66,130	72.0

A-22 Workers with Graduate or Professional Degree: Detailed Occupations, by Sex, Race, and Hispanic Origin, 2006–2010—Continued

Census occupation code	Detailed Occupation	Black or African American alone Number	Percent	American Indian and Alaska Native alone Number	Percent	Asian alone Number	Percent	Native Hawaiian and Other Pacific Islander alone Number	Percent	Not Hispanic or Latino, two or more races Number	Percent
	Total, all occupations	1,026,135	6.8	40,420	0.3	1,496,970	9.9	8,375	0.1	191,750	1.3
0010	Chief executives and legislators	12,585	4.4	910	0.3	19,260	6.8	65	0.0	2,275	0.8
0020	General and operations managers	9,175	6.8	525	0.4	10,120	7.5	30	0.0	1,630	1.2
0040	Advertising and promotions managers	410	6.2	0	0.0	520	7.8	15	0.2	125	1.9
0050	Marketing and sales managers	6,410	4.5	180	0.1	13,155	9.3	50	0.0	1,835	1.3
0060	Public relations and fundraising managers	1,025	7.8	40	0.3	480	3.6	4	0.0	185	1.4
0100	Administrative services managers	1,035	9.1	15	0.1	605	5.3	4	0.0	195	1.7
0110	Computer and information systems managers	6,775	6.0	210	0.2	23,485	21.0	55	0.0	1,310	1.2
0120	Financial managers	11,565	5.8	540	0.3	19,595	9.8	20	0.0	2,085	1.0
0135	Compensation and benefits managers	295	6.1	15	0.3	240	5.0	0	0.0	75	1.6
0136	Human resources managers	7,655	12.9	130	0.2	3,590	6.1	10	0.0	780	1.3
0137	Training and development managers	950	9.2	20	0.2	310	3.0	0	0.0	14	0.1
0140	Industrial production managers	1,210	4.4	50	0.2	3,310	11.9	0	0.0	340	1.2
0150	Purchasing managers	3,080	9.5	60	0.2	2,285	7.1	0	0.0	330	1.0
0160	Transportation, storage, and distribution managers	1,205	9.8	65	0.5	955	7.8	15	0.1	110	0.9
0205	Farmers, ranchers, and other agricultural managers	360	1.5	110	0.4	420	1.7	0	0.0	195	0.8
0220	Construction managers	2,530	5.6	140	0.3	2,280	5.1	35	0.1	440	1.0
0230	Education administrators	55,070	12.0	1,850	0.4	10,680	2.3	230	0.1	4,915	1.1
0300	Architectural and engineering managers	1,270	2.5	85	0.2	8,205	15.9	10	0.0	535	1.0
0310	Food service managers	1,565	5.3	65	0.2	6,130	20.9	45	0.2	420	1.4
0330	Gaming managers	0	0.0	15	2.1	35	5.0	0	0.0	40	5.7
0340	Lodging managers	545	4.8	70	0.6	2,095	18.5	55	0.5	200	1.8
0350	Medical and health services managers	13,285	8.8	650	0.4	9,610	6.4	65	0.0	1,465	1.0
0360	Natural sciences managers	175	1.6	0	0.0	1,655	15.0	0	0.0	159	1.4
0410	Property, real estate, and community association managers	3,375	6.6	105	0.2	2,940	5.7	45	0.1	605	1.2
0410	Social and community service managers	11,000	11.8	460	0.5	3,310	3.6	40	0.0	1,255	1.3
0425	Emergency management directors	85	11.9	0	0.0	20	2.8	0	0.0	19	2.7
0430	Miscellaneous managers, including funeral service managers and postmasters and mail superintendents	37,615	6.6	1,420	0.2	58,495	10.2	330	0.1	7,840	1.4
0500	Agents and business managers of artists, performers, and athletes	215	4.0	20	0.4	430	8.0	45	0.8	155	2.9
0510	Buyers and purchasing agents, farm products	0	0.0	0	0.0	30	7.5	0	0.0	0	0.0
0520	Wholesale and retail buyers, except farm products	425	5.1	30	0.4	880	10.5	0	0.0	140	1.7
0530	Purchasing agents, except wholesale, retail, and farm products	2,820	13.6	85	0.4	1,445	7.0	0	0.0	165	0.8
0540	Claims adjusters, appraisers, examiners, and investigators	2,670	14.7	50	0.3	1,610	8.9	10	0.1	244	1.3
0565	Compliance officers	3,785	11.8	205	0.6	2,435	7.6	15	0.0	385	1.2
0600	Cost estimators	45	1.0	50	1.1	590	12.7	0	0.0	49	1.1
0630	Human resources workers	13,250	14.4	290	0.3	5,200	5.7	90	0.1	1,315	1.4

A-22 **Workers with Graduate or Professional Degree: Detailed Occupations, by Sex, Race, and Hispanic Origin, 2006–2010**—*Continued*

Census occupation code	Detailed Occupation	Total	Male Number	Male Percent	Female Number	Female Percent	Hispanic or Latino Number	Hispanic or Latino Percent	White alone Number	White alone Percent
0640	Compensation, benefits, and job analysis specialists	9,190	2,900	31.6	6,290	68.4	490	5.3	6,945	75.6
0650	Training and development specialists	18,700	7,425	39.7	11,275	60.3	1,125	6.0	14,340	76.7
0700	Logisticians	6,675	4,775	71.5	1,900	28.5	520	7.8	4,680	70.1
0710	Management analysts	221,935	142,505	64.2	79,430	35.8	8,170	3.7	172,770	77.8
0725	Meeting, convention, and event planners	5,655	1,600	28.3	4,055	71.7	335	5.9	4,360	77.1
0726	Fundraisers	21,430	7,545	35.2	13,880	64.8	670	3.1	19,250	89.8
0735	Market research analysts and marketing specialists	45,535	24,645	54.1	20,890	45.9	2,105	4.6	33,795	74.2
0740	Business operations specialists, all other	32,885	15,500	47.1	17,385	52.9	1,865	5.7	23,460	71.3
0800	Accountants and auditors	392,715	212,510	54.1	180,205	45.9	19,240	4.9	288,200	73.4
0810	Appraisers and assessors of real estate	10,145	7,735	76.2	2,410	23.8	380	3.7	8,785	86.6
0820	Budget analysts	13,015	6,135	47.1	6,880	52.9	825	6.3	9,175	70.5
0830	Credit analysts	4,165	2,360	56.7	1,805	43.3	330	7.9	2,750	66.0
0840	Financial analysts	28,825	21,975	76.2	6,850	23.8	1,145	4.0	21,325	74.0
0850	Personal financial advisors	87,000	67,695	77.8	19,300	22.2	3,055	3.5	72,435	83.3
0860	Insurance underwriters	7,745	4,175	53.9	3,570	46.1	250	3.2	6,015	77.7
0900	Financial examiners	2,440	1,590	65.2	845	34.6	100	4.1	1,770	72.5
0910	Credit counselors and loan officers	29,985	19,705	65.7	10,280	34.3	2,060	6.9	23,205	77.4
0930	Tax examiners and collectors, and revenue agents	6,095	3,650	59.9	2,445	40.1	440	7.2	3,815	62.6
0940	Tax preparers	14,715	8,455	57.5	6,260	42.5	590	4.0	11,640	79.1
0950	Financial specialists, all other	10,610	6,980	65.8	3,630	34.2	530	5.0	7,915	74.6
1005	Computer and information research scientists	7,505	5,680	75.7	1,830	24.4	305	4.1	4,555	60.7
1006	Computer systems analysts	104,365	72,575	69.5	31,790	30.5	3,575	3.4	60,745	58.2
1007	Information security analysts	7,470	5,715	76.5	1,760	23.6	440	5.9	5,260	70.4
1010	Computer programmers	95,830	69,805	72.8	26,030	27.2	2,795	2.9	53,910	56.3
1020	Software developers, applications and systems software	265,320	207,280	78.1	58,040	21.9	6,820	2.6	119,285	45.0
1030	Web developers	20,020	11,310	56.5	8,710	43.5	725	3.6	14,220	71.0
1050	Computer support specialists	37,300	25,000	67.0	12,305	33.0	1,600	4.3	22,960	61.6
1060	Database administrators	21,255	13,810	65.0	7,445	35.0	580	2.7	11,280	53.1
1105	Network and computer systems administrators	27,160	21,225	78.1	5,935	21.9	1,245	4.6	17,110	63.0
1106	Computer network architects	16,060	13,790	85.9	2,265	14.1	745	4.6	8,645	53.8
1107	Computer occupations, all other	37,130	26,705	71.9	10,425	28.1	1,690	4.6	20,615	55.5
1200	Actuaries	7,680	5,120	66.7	2,565	33.4	170	2.2	5,725	74.5
1220	Operations research analysts	31,465	18,765	59.6	12,700	40.4	1,555	4.9	23,095	73.4
1240	Miscellaneous mathematical science occupations, including mathematicians and statisticians	22,585	12,745	56.4	9,840	43.6	770	3.4	15,150	67.1
1300	Architects, except naval	67,160	48,720	72.5	18,440	27.5	3,945	5.9	53,655	79.9
1310	Surveyors, cartographers, and photogrammetrists	5,635	4,390	77.9	1,245	22.1	210	3.7	4,840	85.9
1320	Aerospace engineers	44,765	39,195	87.6	5,565	12.4	1,840	4.1	32,620	72.9
1340	Biomedical and agricultural engineers	3,740	2,985	79.8	750	20.1	140	3.7	2,460	65.8
1350	Chemical engineers	17,215	14,785	85.9	2,430	14.1	700	4.1	11,500	66.8
1360	Civil engineers	84,115	72,660	86.4	11,455	13.6	3,545	4.2	61,695	73.3
1400	Computer hardware engineers	16,960	14,030	82.7	2,930	17.3	540	3.2	7,975	47.0
1410	Electrical and electronics engineers	63,820	57,670	90.4	6,150	9.6	2,610	4.1	38,085	59.7
1420	Environmental engineers	13,055	9,440	72.3	3,615	27.7	500	3.8	9,785	75.0
1430	Industrial engineers, including health and safety	32,300	25,880	80.1	6,420	19.9	1,720	5.3	22,040	68.2

Note: "Not Hispanic or Latino, one race" columns show White alone.

A-22 Workers with Graduate or Professional Degree: Detailed Occupations, by Sex, Race, and Hispanic Origin, 2006–2010—Continued

		Graduate or Professional degree									
		Not Hispanic or Latino, one race								Not Hispanic or Latino, two or more races	
Census occupation code	Detailed Occupation	Black or African American alone		American Indian and Alaska Native alone		Asian alone		Native Hawaiian and Other Pacific Islander alone			
		Number	Percent	Number	Percent	Number	Percent	Number	Percent	Number	Percent
0640	Compensation, benefits, and job analysis specialists	1,065	11.6	25	0.3	505	5.5	0	0.0	155	1.7
0650	Training and development specialists	2,410	12.9	60	0.3	595	3.2	0	0.0	175	0.9
0700	Logisticians	850	12.7	45	0.7	430	6.4	15	0.2	129	1.9
0710	Management analysts	11,330	5.1	580	0.3	26,410	11.9	115	0.1	2,555	1.2
0725	Meeting, convention, and event planners	560	9.9	25	0.4	290	5.1	0	0.0	85	1.5
0726	Fundraisers	820	3.8	15	0.1	485	2.3	35	0.2	155	0.7
0735	Market research analysts and marketing specialists	1,960	4.3	45	0.1	6,900	15.2	0	0.0	730	1.6
0740	Business operations specialists, all other	3,075	9.4	140	0.4	3,640	11.1	10	0.0	700	2.1
0800	Accountants and auditors	28,885	7.4	795	0.2	51,240	13.0	275	0.1	4,080	1.0
0810	Appraisers and assessors of real estate	485	4.8	10	0.1	390	3.8	0	0.0	105	1.0
0820	Budget analysts	1,960	15.1	40	0.3	795	6.1	20	0.2	204	1.6
0830	Credit analysts	435	10.4	4	0.1	620	14.9	0	0.0	20	0.5
0840	Financial analysts	1,445	5.0	25	0.1	4,415	15.3	45	0.2	420	1.5
0850	Personal financial advisors	3,240	3.7	50	0.1	7,215	8.3	0	0.0	1,000	1.1
0860	Insurance underwriters	740	9.6	15	0.2	540	7.0	4	0.1	180	2.3
0900	Financial examiners	255	10.5	10	0.4	240	9.8	0	0.0	65	2.7
0910	Credit counselors and loan officers	2,035	6.8	110	0.4	2,235	7.5	15	0.1	330	1.1
0930	Tax examiners and collectors, and revenue agents	1,135	18.6	35	0.6	525	8.6	0	0.0	150	2.5
0940	Tax preparers	850	5.8	40	0.3	1,465	10.0	0	0.0	125	0.8
0950	Financial specialists, all other	995	9.4	90	0.8	910	8.6	0	0.0	175	1.6
1005	Computer and information research scientists	300	4.0	25	0.3	2,215	29.5	40	0.5	75	1.0
1006	Computer systems analysts	6,525	6.3	150	0.1	31,595	30.3	35	0.0	1,740	1.7
1007	Information security analysts	705	9.4	10	0.1	910	12.2	0	0.0	154	2.1
1010	Computer programmers	3,375	3.5	160	0.2	34,075	35.6	15	0.0	1,495	1.6
1020	Software developers, applications and systems software	8,280	3.1	175	0.1	126,430	47.7	90	0.0	4,235	1.6
1030	Web developers	750	3.7	65	0.3	3,945	19.7	15	0.1	299	1.5
1050	Computer support specialists	3,600	9.7	95	0.3	8,350	22.4	80	0.2	625	1.7
1060	Database administrators	1,545	7.3	4	0.0	7,330	34.5	30	0.1	485	2.3
1105	Network and computer systems administrators	1,785	6.6	90	0.3	6,465	23.8	15	0.1	455	1.7
1106	Computer network architects	1,110	6.9	0	0.0	5,240	32.6	0	0.0	320	2.0
1107	Computer occupations, all other	2,900	7.8	100	0.3	11,020	29.7	0	0.0	805	2.2
1200	Actuaries	215	2.8	0	0.0	1,520	19.8	0	0.0	54	0.7
1220	Operations research analysts	2,665	8.5	80	0.3	3,510	11.2	30	0.1	530	1.7
1240	Miscellaneous mathematical science occupations, including mathematicians and statisticians	750	3.3	70	0.3	5,465	24.2	0	0.0	380	1.7
1300	Architects, except naval	1,360	2.0	45	0.1	7,335	10.9	35	0.1	785	1.2
1310	Surveyors, cartographers, and photogrammetrists	190	3.4	25	0.4	310	5.5	0	0.0	64	1.1
1320	Aerospace engineers	1,640	3.7	20	0.0	7,805	17.4	40	0.1	795	1.8
1340	Biomedical and agricultural engineers	215	5.7	0	0.0	875	23.4	0	0.0	55	1.5
1350	Chemical engineers	815	4.7	10	0.1	3,975	23.1	0	0.0	215	1.2
1360	Civil engineers	3,030	3.6	145	0.2	14,465	17.2	80	0.1	1,160	1.4
1400	Computer hardware engineers	875	5.2	0	0.0	7,380	43.5	4	0.0	185	1.1
1410	Electrical and electronics engineers	2,065	3.2	60	0.1	20,110	31.5	25	0.0	860	1.3
1420	Environmental engineers	400	3.1	0	0.0	2,290	17.5	0	0.0	84	0.6
1430	Industrial engineers, including health and safety	1,690	5.2	25	0.1	6,460	20.0	0	0.0	360	1.1

A-22 **Workers with Graduate or Professional Degree: Detailed Occupations, by Sex, Race, and Hispanic Origin, 2006–2010**—*Continued*

Census occupation code	Detailed Occupation	Total	Male Number	Male Percent	Female Number	Female Percent	Hispanic or Latino Number	Hispanic or Latino Percent	White alone Number	White alone Percent
1440	Marine engineers and naval architects	1,920	1,775	92.4	150	7.8	25	1.3	1,545	80.5
1450	Materials engineers	7,390	6,285	85.0	1,105	15.0	355	4.8	4,425	59.9
1460	Mechanical engineers	48,900	43,895	89.8	5,005	10.2	1,910	3.9	32,890	67.3
1520	Petroleum, mining and geological engineers, including mining safety engineers	6,670	5,975	89.6	695	10.4	495	7.4	4,410	66.1
1530	Miscellaneous engineers, including nuclear engineers	138,495	119,900	86.6	18,600	13.4	5,955	4.3	90,435	65.3
1540	Drafters	7,635	5,460	71.5	2,175	28.5	565	7.4	5,310	69.5
1550	Engineering technicians, except drafters	10,355	7,705	74.4	2,645	25.5	705	6.8	6,930	66.9
1560	Surveying and mapping technicians	625	435	69.6	190	30.4	55	8.8	445	71.2
1600	Agricultural and food scientists	10,555	7,800	73.9	2,755	26.1	655	6.2	7,910	74.9
1610	Biological scientists	39,650	22,305	56.3	17,345	43.7	1,695	4.3	30,265	76.3
1640	Conservation scientists and foresters	5,135	3,690	71.9	1,445	28.1	250	4.9	4,500	87.6
1650	Medical scientists, and life scientists, all other	105,895	53,900	50.9	51,995	49.1	4,525	4.3	61,310	57.9
1700	Astronomers and physicists	9,135	7,745	84.8	1,390	15.2	335	3.7	7,345	80.4
1710	Atmospheric and space scientists	3,310	2,720	82.2	590	17.8	65	2.0	2,810	84.9
1720	Chemists and materials scientists	33,695	22,670	67.3	11,020	32.7	1,220	3.6	21,450	63.7
1740	Environmental scientists and geoscientists	33,600	24,335	72.4	9,265	27.6	1,125	3.3	28,905	86.0
1760	Physical scientists, all other	116,485	78,220	67.2	38,265	32.8	4,385	3.8	74,985	64.4
1800	Economists	17,075	12,085	70.8	4,985	29.2	1,405	8.2	12,395	72.6
1820	Psychologists	165,170	54,540	33.0	110,630	67.0	8,345	5.1	143,775	87.0
1840	Urban and regional planners	12,590	7,570	60.1	5,020	39.9	615	4.9	10,100	80.2
1860	Miscellaneous social scientists, including survey researchers and sociologists	21,370	10,150	47.5	11,225	52.5	1,155	5.4	17,415	81.5
1900	Agricultural and food science technicians	1,065	600	56.3	465	43.7	130	12.2	705	66.2
1910	Biological technicians	3,290	1,975	60.0	1,315	40.0	80	2.4	2,065	62.8
1920	Chemical technicians	4,745	2,850	60.1	1,895	39.9	255	5.4	2,680	56.5
1930	Geological and petroleum technicians, and nuclear technicians	1,130	740	65.5	390	34.5	45	4.0	805	71.2
1965	Miscellaneous life, physical, and social science technicians, including social science research assistants	15,995	7,800	48.8	8,195	51.2	780	4.9	10,135	63.4
2000	Counselors	298,375	76,605	25.7	221,775	74.3	19,890	6.7	228,695	76.6
2010	Social workers	246,215	48,915	19.9	197,300	80.1	19,755	8.0	173,800	70.6
2015	Probation officers and correctional treatment specialists	15,430	7,740	50.2	7,690	49.8	1,280	8.3	10,140	65.7
2016	Social and human service assistants	13,305	4,040	30.4	9,270	69.7	1,130	8.5	8,390	63.1
2025	Miscellaneous community and social service specialists, including health educators and community health workers	14,270	4,135	29.0	10,135	71.0	1,260	8.8	9,390	65.8
2040	Clergy	215,490	179,390	83.2	36,100	16.8	6,575	3.1	179,550	83.3
2050	Directors, religious activities and education	13,845	6,550	47.3	7,290	52.7	500	3.6	11,730	84.7
2060	Religious workers, all other	20,045	11,120	55.5	8,925	44.5	815	4.1	16,950	84.6
2100	Lawyers, and judges, magistrates, and other judicial workers	976,340	661,275	67.7	315,065	32.3	42,190	4.3	843,720	86.4
2105	Judicial law clerks	9,115	4,360	47.8	4,755	52.2	455	5.0	7,680	84.3
2145	Paralegals and legal assistants	26,770	8,500	31.8	18,270	68.2	2,415	9.0	19,030	71.1
2160	Miscellaneous legal support workers	24,610	11,485	46.7	13,130	53.4	1,425	5.8	18,550	75.4
2200	Postsecondary teachers	922,715	501,605	54.4	421,110	45.6	41,755	4.5	707,125	76.6
2300	Preschool and kindergarten teachers	56,355	1,810	3.2	54,545	96.8	4,265	7.6	44,255	78.5
2310	Elementary and middle school teachers	1,484,965	326,800	22.0	1,158,165	78.0	83,305	5.6	1,233,495	83.1
2320	Secondary school teachers	363,160	150,915	41.6	212,245	58.4	20,400	5.6	303,655	83.6
2330	Special education teachers	96,410	14,320	14.9	82,090	85.1	4,645	4.8	81,300	84.3
2340	Other teachers and instructors	147,125	49,835	33.9	97,290	66.1	6,580	4.5	118,360	80.4
2400	Archivists, curators, and museum technicians	18,545	7,235	39.0	11,315	61.0	445	2.4	16,645	89.8

PART A—NATIONAL DATA

A-22 Workers with Graduate or Professional Degree: Detailed Occupations, by Sex, Race, and Hispanic Origin, 2006–2010—Continued

Census occupation code	Detailed Occupation	Black or African American alone Number	Black or African American alone Percent	American Indian and Alaska Native alone Number	American Indian and Alaska Native alone Percent	Asian alone Number	Asian alone Percent	Native Hawaiian and Other Pacific Islander alone Number	Native Hawaiian and Other Pacific Islander alone Percent	Not Hispanic or Latino, two or more races Number	Not Hispanic or Latino, two or more races Percent
1440	Marine engineers and naval architects	40	2.1	0	0.0	265	13.8	0	0.0	49	2.6
1450	Materials engineers	245	3.3	45	0.6	2,250	30.4	0	0.0	75	1.0
1460	Mechanical engineers	1,590	3.3	40	0.1	11,690	23.9	10	0.0	775	1.6
1520	Petroleum, mining and geological engineers, including mining safety engineers	485	7.3	0	0.0	1,180	17.7	0	0.0	100	1.5
1530	Miscellaneous engineers, including nuclear engineers	4,835	3.5	195	0.1	35,380	25.5	0	0.0	1,695	1.2
1540	Drafters	270	3.5	4	0.1	1,350	17.7	0	0.0	130	1.7
1550	Engineering technicians, except drafters	800	7.7	15	0.1	1,700	16.4	10	0.1	195	1.9
1560	Surveying and mapping technicians	70	11.2	15	2.4	40	6.4	0	0.0	0	0.0
1600	Agricultural and food scientists	285	2.7	4	0.0	1,480	14.0	0	0.0	214	2.0
1610	Biological scientists	920	2.3	85	0.2	6,185	15.6	25	0.1	475	1.2
1640	Conservation scientists and foresters	160	3.1	10	0.2	140	2.7	0	0.0	75	1.5
1650	Medical scientists, and life scientists, all other	4,120	3.9	95	0.1	34,355	32.4	90	0.1	1,400	1.3
1700	Astronomers and physicists	135	1.5	15	0.2	1,115	12.2	10	0.1	180	2.0
1710	Atmospheric and space scientists	105	3.2	15	0.5	310	9.4	0	0.0	4	0.1
1720	Chemists and materials scientists	1,265	3.8	100	0.3	9,280	27.5	0	0.0	375	1.1
1740	Environmental scientists and geoscientists	1,150	3.4	55	0.2	1,990	5.9	40	0.1	335	1.0
1760	Physical scientists, all other	3,165	2.7	195	0.2	32,015	27.5	30	0.0	1,705	1.5
1800	Economists	885	5.2	15	0.1	2,260	13.2	4	0.0	110	0.6
1820	Psychologists	6,990	4.2	285	0.2	3,940	2.4	80	0.0	1,760	1.1
1840	Urban and regional planners	940	7.5	15	0.1	750	6.0	0	0.0	175	1.4
1860	Miscellaneous social scientists, including survey researchers and sociologists	1,260	5.9	60	0.3	1,190	5.6	0	0.0	305	1.4
1900	Agricultural and food science technicians	25	2.3	4	0.4	160	15.0	0	0.0	45	4.2
1910	Biological technicians	105	3.2	0	0.0	970	29.5	0	0.0	75	2.3
1920	Chemical technicians	340	7.2	15	0.3	1,385	29.2	0	0.0	70	1.5
1930	Geological and petroleum technicians, and nuclear technicians	70	6.2	0	0.0	215	19.0	0	0.0	0	0.0
1965	Miscellaneous life, physical, and social science technicians, including social science research assistants	830	5.2	25	0.2	3,920	24.5	4	0.0	295	1.8
2000	Counselors	36,800	12.3	1,675	0.6	6,990	2.3	200	0.1	4,130	1.4
2010	Social workers	40,485	16.4	855	0.3	7,640	3.1	110	0.0	3,570	1.4
2015	Probation officers and correctional treatment specialists	3,300	21.4	50	0.3	295	1.9	20	0.1	340	2.2
2016	Social and human service assistants	2,995	22.5	30	0.2	555	4.2	15	0.1	184	1.4
2025	Miscellaneous community and social service specialists, including health educators and community health workers	2,550	17.9	120	0.8	560	3.9	10	0.1	385	2.7
2040	Clergy	15,275	7.1	335	0.2	11,780	5.5	140	0.1	1,830	0.8
2050	Directors, religious activities and education	810	5.9	25	0.2	710	5.1	0	0.0	64	0.5
2060	Religious workers, all other	1,015	5.1	25	0.1	1,085	5.4	0	0.0	159	0.8
2100	Lawyers, and judges, magistrates, and other judicial workers	42,245	4.3	2,215	0.2	34,120	3.5	310	0.0	11,535	1.2
2105	Judicial law clerks	420	4.6	55	0.6	425	4.7	0	0.0	84	0.9
2145	Paralegals and legal assistants	2,845	10.6	110	0.4	1,955	7.3	4	0.0	415	1.6
2160	Miscellaneous legal support workers	2,090	8.5	85	0.3	2,095	8.5	20	0.1	355	1.4
2200	Postsecondary teachers	48,530	5.3	2,415	0.3	108,815	11.8	515	0.1	13,560	1.5
2300	Preschool and kindergarten teachers	4,550	8.1	95	0.2	2,670	4.7	4	0.0	515	0.9
2310	Elementary and middle school teachers	117,630	7.9	4,095	0.3	31,545	2.1	755	0.1	14,140	1.0
2320	Secondary school teachers	24,920	6.9	1,195	0.3	8,445	2.3	320	0.1	4,230	1.2
2330	Special education teachers	7,260	7.5	335	0.3	1,600	1.7	40	0.0	1,240	1.3
2340	Other teachers and instructors	10,595	7.2	480	0.3	8,995	6.1	95	0.1	2,015	1.4
2400	Archivists, curators, and museum technicians	480	2.6	25	0.1	595	3.2	0	0.0	355	1.9

A-22 Workers with Graduate or Professional Degree: Detailed Occupations, by Sex, Race, and Hispanic Origin, 2006–2010—Continued

Census occupation code	Detailed Occupation	Total	Male Number	Male Percent	Female Number	Female Percent	Hispanic or Latino Number	Hispanic or Latino Percent	Not Hispanic or Latino, one race, White alone Number	Not Hispanic or Latino, one race, White alone Percent
2430	Librarians	102,795	17,425	17.0	85,370	83.0	3,070	3.0	90,015	87.6
2440	Library technicians	4,480	975	21.8	3,505	78.2	165	3.7	3,635	81.1
2540	Teacher assistants	31,055	5,800	18.7	25,255	81.3	2,650	8.5	21,495	69.2
2550	Other education, training, and library workers	41,825	10,960	26.2	30,870	73.8	2,500	6.0	32,780	78.4
2600	Artists and related workers	24,200	12,165	50.3	12,035	49.7	1,270	5.2	20,180	83.4
2630	Designers	57,875	29,660	51.2	28,215	48.8	3,675	6.3	43,015	74.3
2700	Actors	3,250	1,940	59.7	1,310	40.3	135	4.2	2,660	81.8
2710	Producers and directors	20,000	10,520	52.6	9,475	47.4	1,425	7.1	15,350	76.8
2720	Athletes, coaches, umpires, and related workers	28,285	19,340	68.4	8,945	31.6	1,310	4.6	23,280	82.3
2740	Dancers and choreographers	425	80	18.8	345	81.2	45	10.6	205	48.2
2750	Musicians, singers, and related workers	34,445	18,845	54.7	15,600	45.3	1,230	3.6	29,255	84.9
2760	Entertainers and performers, sports and related workers, all other	2,770	1,560	56.3	1,210	43.7	225	8.1	2,165	78.2
2800	Announcers	2,610	1,770	67.8	840	32.2	215	8.2	1,970	75.5
2810	News analysts, reporters, and correspondents	15,200	8,235	54.2	6,965	45.8	965	6.3	12,150	79.9
2825	Public relations specialists	26,790	11,360	42.4	15,430	57.6	1,615	6.0	21,940	81.9
2830	Editors	37,990	15,405	40.6	22,585	59.4	1,515	4.0	32,555	85.7
2840	Technical writers	14,970	6,295	42.1	8,675	57.9	435	2.9	12,715	84.9
2850	Writers and authors	57,480	23,965	41.7	33,515	58.3	1,730	3.0	50,425	87.7
2860	Miscellaneous media and communication workers	12,465	4,455	35.7	8,010	64.3	2,635	21.1	7,030	56.4
2900	Broadcast and sound engineering technicians and radio operators, and media and communication equipment workers, all other	3,585	3,090	86.2	495	13.8	285	7.9	2,405	67.1
2910	Photographers	8,155	4,715	57.8	3,435	42.1	435	5.3	6,905	84.7
2920	Television, video, and motion picture camera operators and editors	2,690	2,075	77.1	615	22.9	215	8.0	2,175	80.9
3000	Chiropractors	51,970	39,525	76.1	12,445	23.9	1,660	3.2	46,525	89.5
3010	Dentists	159,455	123,215	77.3	36,240	22.7	8,465	5.3	122,210	76.6
3030	Dietitians and nutritionists	25,275	1,875	7.4	23,400	92.6	845	3.3	20,905	82.7
3040	Optometrists	33,905	22,205	65.5	11,700	34.5	875	2.6	27,905	82.3
3050	Pharmacists	127,030	56,135	44.2	70,895	55.8	4,780	3.8	88,920	70.0
3060	Physicians and surgeons	801,320	544,025	67.9	257,300	32.1	45,290	5.7	556,120	69.4
3110	Physician assistants	37,450	13,945	37.2	23,505	62.8	2,690	7.2	30,115	80.4
3120	Podiatrists	9,535	7,745	81.2	1,790	18.8	470	4.9	7,915	83.0
3140	Audiologists	12,210	2,460	20.1	9,750	79.9	380	3.1	11,080	90.7
3150	Occupational therapists	29,725	3,190	10.7	26,535	89.3	1,380	4.6	24,920	83.8
3160	Physical therapists	88,195	29,200	33.1	58,995	66.9	3,120	3.5	75,730	85.9
3200	Radiation therapists	685	315	46.0	370	54.0	15	2.2	560	81.8
3210	Recreational therapists	1,920	605	31.5	1,320	68.8	95	4.9	1,455	75.8
3220	Respiratory therapists	4,205	2,075	49.3	2,130	50.7	335	8.0	2,615	62.2
3230	Speech-language pathologists	97,795	4,180	4.3	93,615	95.7	4,220	4.3	86,460	88.4
3245	Other therapists, including exercise physiologists	66,795	14,115	21.1	52,680	78.9	4,200	6.3	53,235	79.7
3250	Veterinarians	70,055	35,360	50.5	34,695	49.5	2,250	3.2	64,095	91.5
3255	Registered nurses	247,640	25,950	10.5	221,690	89.5	10,460	4.2	184,100	74.3
3256	Nurse anesthetists	16,940	7,105	41.9	9,835	58.1	435	2.6	15,210	89.8
3258	Nurse practitioners and nurse midwives	71,300	5,345	7.5	65,955	92.5	2,565	3.6	61,500	86.3
3260	Health diagnosing and treating practitioners, all other	12,440	4,490	36.1	7,955	63.9	480	3.9	8,215	66.0
3300	Clinical laboratory technologists and technicians	24,650	9,015	36.6	15,635	63.4	1,520	6.2	14,580	59.1
3310	Dental hygienists	6,520	335	5.1	6,185	94.9	575	8.8	5,145	78.9

PART A—NATIONAL DATA

A-22 Workers with Graduate or Professional Degree: Detailed Occupations, by Sex, Race, and Hispanic Origin, 2006–2010—Continued

Census occupation code	Detailed Occupation	Black or African American alone Number	Percent	American Indian and Alaska Native alone Number	Percent	Asian alone Number	Percent	Native Hawaiian and Other Pacific Islander alone Number	Percent	Not Hispanic or Latino, two or more races Number	Percent
2430	Librarians..	4,740	4.6	215	0.2	3,715	3.6	10	0.0	1,030	1.0
2440	Library technicians.................................	255	5.7	20	0.4	285	6.4	0	0.0	125	2.8
2540	Teacher assistants...................................	3,405	11.0	130	0.4	2,875	9.3	50	0.2	450	1.4
2550	Other education, training, and library workers.......	4,415	10.6	145	0.3	1,410	3.4	4	0.0	570	1.4
2600	Artists and related workers...................	530	2.2	90	0.4	1,730	7.1	0	0.0	405	1.7
2630	Designers...	1,865	3.2	150	0.3	8,290	14.3	35	0.1	850	1.5
2700	Actors...	185	5.7	10	0.3	115	3.5	0	0.0	149	4.6
2710	Producers and directors........................	1,695	8.5	50	0.3	1,110	5.6	4	0.0	360	1.8
2720	Athletes, coaches, umpires, and related workers....	2,550	9.0	110	0.4	590	2.1	15	0.1	430	1.5
2740	Dancers and choreographers................	90	21.2	0	0.0	75	17.6	0	0.0	10	2.4
2750	Musicians, singers, and related workers..............	1,605	4.7	40	0.1	1,860	5.4	4	0.0	445	1.3
2760	Entertainers and performers, sports and related workers, all other..............	125	4.5	15	0.5	120	4.3	0	0.0	125	4.5
2800	Announcers..	145	5.6	15	0.6	250	9.6	0	0.0	10	0.4
2810	News analysts, reporters, and correspondents........	715	4.7	15	0.1	1,130	7.4	0	0.0	235	1.5
2825	Public relations specialists....................	1,855	6.9	105	0.4	870	3.2	35	0.1	365	1.4
2830	Editors..	1,325	3.5	15	0.0	2,020	5.3	0	0.0	560	1.5
2840	Technical writers...................................	735	4.9	50	0.3	805	5.4	0	0.0	235	1.6
2850	Writers and authors...............................	2,435	4.2	195	0.3	1,830	3.2	40	0.1	825	1.4
2860	Miscellaneous media and communication workers	470	3.8	20	0.2	2,155	17.3	0	0.0	165	1.3
2900	Broadcast and sound engineering technicians and radio operators, and media and communication equipment workers, all other..............	330	9.2	35	1.0	415	11.6	0	0.0	120	3.3
2910	Photographers.......................................	340	4.2	70	0.9	305	3.7	0	0.0	100	1.2
2920	Television, video, and motion picture camera operators and editors...................	160	5.9	0	0.0	140	5.2	0	0.0	0	0.0
3000	Chiropractors..	955	1.8	100	0.2	2,095	4.0	10	0.0	625	1.2
3010	Dentists..	5,105	3.2	185	0.1	21,640	13.6	70	0.0	1,790	1.1
3030	Dietitians and nutritionists....................	1,405	5.6	35	0.1	1,930	7.6	0	0.0	150	0.6
3040	Optometrists...	455	1.3	100	0.3	4,290	12.7	45	0.1	240	0.7
3050	Pharmacists...	7,430	5.8	305	0.2	23,995	18.9	135	0.1	1,465	1.2
3060	Physicians and surgeons.......................	37,935	4.7	1,410	0.2	148,615	18.5	290	0.0	11,665	1.5
3110	Physician assistants..............................	1,435	3.8	140	0.4	2,490	6.6	0	0.0	585	1.6
3120	Podiatrists..	450	4.7	0	0.0	650	6.8	15	0.2	34	0.4
3140	Audiologists..	440	3.6	0	0.0	235	1.9	0	0.0	84	0.7
3150	Occupational therapists........................	1,060	3.6	35	0.1	1,940	6.5	0	0.0	390	1.3
3160	Physical therapists................................	2,235	2.5	190	0.2	5,980	6.8	75	0.1	865	1.0
3200	Radiation therapists..............................	55	8.0	0	0.0	55	8.0	0	0.0	0	0.0
3210	Recreational therapists.........................	315	16.4	0	0.0	20	1.0	0	0.0	40	2.1
3220	Respiratory therapists...........................	600	14.3	15	0.4	540	12.8	15	0.4	89	2.1
3230	Speech-language pathologists..............	4,065	4.2	260	0.3	2,025	2.1	25	0.0	740	0.8
3245	Other therapists, including exercise physiologists..	5,815	8.7	240	0.4	2,015	3.0	130	0.2	1,170	1.8
3250	Veterinarians...	1,160	1.7	130	0.2	1,870	2.7	15	0.0	540	0.8
3255	Registered nurses.................................	27,455	11.1	985	0.4	21,380	8.6	40	0.0	3,215	1.3
3256	Nurse anesthetists.................................	485	2.9	25	0.1	530	3.1	0	0.0	250	1.5
3258	Nurse practitioners and nurse midwives..............	3,080	4.3	70	0.1	3,240	4.5	10	0.0	840	1.2
3260	Health diagnosing and treating practitioners, all other..	165	1.3	55	0.4	3,290	26.4	0	0.0	235	1.9
3300	Clinical laboratory technologists and technicians...	2,275	9.2	100	0.4	5,790	23.5	90	0.4	300	1.2
3310	Dental hygienists..................................	320	4.9	20	0.3	380	5.8	0	0.0	80	1.2

A-22 Workers with Graduate or Professional Degree: Detailed Occupations, by Sex, Race, and Hispanic Origin, 2006–2010—*Continued*

| Census occupation code | Detailed Occupation | Total | Graduate or Professional degree |||||| Not Hispanic or Latino, one race ||
| | | | Male || Female || Hispanic or Latino || White alone ||
			Number	Percent	Number	Percent	Number	Percent	Number	Percent
3320	Diagnostic related technologists and technicians....	11,950	4,715	39.5	7,235	60.5	1,030	8.6	8,440	70.6
3400	Emergency medical technicians and paramedics....	3,610	2,605	72.2	1,010	28.0	315	8.7	2,980	82.5
3420	Health practitioner support technologists and technicians..	10,145	3,610	35.6	6,540	64.5	1,000	9.9	6,250	61.6
3500	Licensed practical and licensed vocational nurses.	13,495	1,250	9.3	12,245	90.7	830	6.2	10,245	75.9
3510	Medical records and health information technicians...	2,555	620	24.3	1,935	75.7	69	2.7	1,785	69.9
3520	Opticians, dispensing...................................	1,085	560	51.6	525	48.4	75	6.9	855	78.8
3535	Miscellaneous health technologists and technicians..	10,775	6,005	55.7	4,770	44.3	530	4.9	8,130	75.5
3540	Other health care practitioners and technical occupations...	15,365	8,505	55.4	6,860	44.6	850	5.5	12,540	81.6
3600	Nursing, psychiatric, and home health aides.........	35,695	11,820	33.1	23,875	66.9	3,915	11.0	21,545	60.4
3610	Occupational therapy assistants and aides..............	295	15	5.1	280	94.9	15	5.1	185	62.7
3620	Physical therapist assistants and aides.................	2,095	750	35.8	1,345	64.2	155	7.4	1,405	67.1
3630	Massage therapists.......................................	8,490	1,790	21.1	6,700	78.9	520	6.1	7,290	85.9
3640	Dental assistants..	6,360	1,145	18.0	5,215	82.0	2,185	34.4	2,280	35.8
3645	Medical assistants......................................	8,530	1,930	22.6	6,600	77.4	2,105	24.7	4,850	56.9
3646	Medical transcriptionists...............................	1,945	150	7.7	1,795	92.3	85	4.4	1,695	87.1
3647	Pharmacy aides..	1,490	610	40.9	880	59.1	105	7.0	870	58.4
3648	Veterinary assistants and laboratory animal caretakers..	895	260	29.1	635	70.9	65	7.3	735	82.1
3649	Phlebotomists...	1,205	485	40.2	720	59.8	260	21.6	640	53.1
3655	Health care support workers, all other, including medical equipment preparers..........................	2,160	660	30.6	1,500	69.4	155	7.2	1,340	62.0
3700	First-line supervisors of correctional officers.........	3,425	1,855	54.2	1,570	45.8	220	6.4	2,175	63.5
3710	First-line supervisors of police and detectives........	11,580	9,510	82.1	2,075	17.9	800	6.9	9,155	79.1
3720	First-line supervisors of fire fighting and prevention workers......................................	2,100	1,995	95.0	105	5.0	70	3.3	1,755	83.6
3730	First-line supervisors of protective service workers, all other.......................................	7,450	5,490	73.7	1,960	26.3	270	3.6	5,720	76.8
3740	Firefighters..	4,385	3,990	91.0	395	9.0	555	12.7	3,435	78.3
3750	Fire inspectors..	765	665	86.9	100	13.1	0	0.0	650	85.0
3800	Bailiffs, correctional officers, and jailers..............	5,635	3,530	62.6	2,105	37.4	440	7.8	3,035	53.9
3820	Detectives and criminal investigators.....................	15,075	10,450	69.3	4,625	30.7	1,330	8.8	11,285	74.9
3840	Miscellaneous law enforcement workers...............	410	320	78.0	90	22.0	0	0.0	335	81.7
3850	Police officers..	30,230	23,750	78.6	6,480	21.4	2,625	8.7	22,280	73.7
3900	Animal control workers................................	160	125	78.1	35	21.9	4	2.5	155	96.9
3910	Private detectives and investigators......................	9,960	6,655	66.8	3,305	33.2	940	9.4	7,250	72.8
3930	Security guards and gaming surveillance officers..	20,225	16,870	83.4	3,355	16.6	1,605	7.9	12,855	63.6
3940	Crossing guards...	735	400	54.4	335	45.6	45	6.1	530	72.1
3945	Transportation security screeners......................	775	510	65.8	265	34.2	45	5.8	510	65.8
3955	Lifeguards and other recreational, and all other protective service workers.............................	2,520	1,100	43.7	1,420	56.3	150	6.0	2,130	84.5
4000	Chefs and head cooks..................................	4,965	3,580	72.1	1,380	27.8	565	11.4	2,560	51.6

A-22 Workers with Graduate or Professional Degree: Detailed Occupations, by Sex, Race, and Hispanic Origin, 2006–2010—Continued

Census occupation code	Detailed Occupation	Black or African American alone Number	Percent	American Indian and Alaska Native alone Number	Percent	Asian alone Number	Percent	Native Hawaiian and Other Pacific Islander alone Number	Percent	Not Hispanic or Latino, two or more races Number	Percent
3320	Diagnostic related technologists and technicians....	1,015	8.5	20	0.2	1,245	10.4	25	0.2	170	1.4
3400	Emergency medical technicians and paramedics....	70	1.9	55	1.5	130	3.6	0	0.0	59	1.6
3420	Health practitioner support technologists and technicians.................	940	9.3	15	0.1	1,755	17.3	15	0.1	164	1.6
3500	Licensed practical and licensed vocational nurses.	1,480	11.0	30	0.2	805	6.0	15	0.1	90	0.7
3510	Medical records and health information technicians.................	250	9.8	60	2.3	375	14.7	0	0.0	15	0.6
3520	Opticians, dispensing.................	0	0.0	4	0.4	125	11.5	0	0.0	35	3.2
3535	Miscellaneous health technologists and technicians.................	735	6.8	4	0.0	1,220	11.3	0	0.0	155	1.4
3540	Other health care practitioners and technical occupations.................	800	5.2	55	0.4	805	5.2	0	0.0	320	2.1
3600	Nursing, psychiatric, and home health aides.........	4,890	13.7	225	0.6	4,425	12.4	65	0.2	630	1.8
3610	Occupational therapy assistants and aides.............	95	32.2	0	0.0	0	0.0	0	0.0	0	0.0
3620	Physical therapist assistants and aides..................	115	5.5	4	0.2	350	16.7	10	0.5	60	2.9
3630	Massage therapists.................	115	1.4	50	0.6	315	3.7	0	0.0	195	2.3
3640	Dental assistants.................	235	3.7	10	0.2	1,595	25.1	0	0.0	55	0.9
3645	Medical assistants.................	385	4.5	4	0.0	1,070	12.5	0	0.0	125	1.5
3646	Medical transcriptionists.................	20	1.0	0	0.0	120	6.2	0	0.0	25	1.3
3647	Pharmacy aides.................	100	6.7	0	0.0	410	27.5	0	0.0	0	0.0
3648	Veterinary assistants and laboratory animal caretakers.................	15	1.7	0	0.0	55	6.1	0	0.0	20	2.2
3649	Phlebotomists.................	95	7.9	4	0.3	160	13.3	0	0.0	50	4.1
3655	Health care support workers, all other, including medical equipment preparers.................	275	12.7	20	0.9	250	11.6	0	0.0	120	5.6
3700	First-line supervisors of correctional officers.........	880	25.7	15	0.4	65	1.9	0	0.0	75	2.2
3710	First-line supervisors of police and detectives.......	1,295	11.2	45	0.4	155	1.3	35	0.3	100	0.9
3720	First-line supervisors of fire fighting and prevention workers.................	140	6.7	0	0.0	40	1.9	20	1.0	75	3.6
3730	First-line supervisors of protective service workers, all other.................	1,190	16.0	40	0.5	165	2.2	0	0.0	59	0.8
3740	Firefighters.................	190	4.3	4	0.1	55	1.3	0	0.0	145	3.3
3750	Fire inspectors.................	60	7.8	0	0.0	35	4.6	0	0.0	20	2.6
3800	Bailiffs, correctional officers, and jailers.................	1,760	31.2	35	0.6	230	4.1	20	0.4	120	2.1
3820	Detectives and criminal investigators.................	1,795	11.9	110	0.7	310	2.1	35	0.2	215	1.4
3840	Miscellaneous law enforcement workers.............	50	12.2	20	4.9	4	1.0	0	0.0	0	0.0
3850	Police officers.................	3,490	11.5	150	0.5	1,125	3.7	65	0.2	500	1.7
3900	Animal control workers.................	0	0.0	0	0.0	0	0.0	0	0.0	0	0.0
3910	Private detectives and investigators.................	1,095	11.0	25	0.3	420	4.2	15	0.2	215	2.2
3930	Security guards and gaming surveillance officers..	3,880	19.2	85	0.4	1,295	6.4	10	0.0	490	2.4
3940	Crossing guards.................	130	17.7	0	0.0	30	4.1	0	0.0	0	0.0
3945	Transportation security screeners.................	75	9.7	0	0.0	85	11.0	15	1.9	40	5.2
3955	Lifeguards and other recreational, and all other protective service workers.................	100	4.0	10	0.4	105	4.2	0	0.0	24	1.0
4000	Chefs and head cooks.................	515	10.4	0	0.0	1,215	24.5	0	0.0	110	2.2

A-22 **Workers with Graduate or Professional Degree: Detailed Occupations, by Sex, Race, and Hispanic Origin, 2006–2010**—*Continued*

Census occupation code	Detailed Occupation	Total	Male Number	Male Percent	Female Number	Female Percent	Hispanic or Latino Number	Hispanic or Latino Percent	Not Hispanic or Latino, one race / White alone Number	Percent
4010	First-line supervisors of food preparation and serving workers	8,020	4,465	55.7	3,555	44.3	930	11.6	5,015	62.5
4020	Cooks	9,825	5,190	52.8	4,635	47.2	2,760	28.1	4,750	48.3
4030	Food preparation workers	4,665	1,950	41.8	2,715	58.2	930	19.9	2,620	56.2
4040	Bartenders	5,615	3,145	56.0	2,470	44.0	330	5.9	4,765	84.9
4050	Combined food preparation and serving workers, including fast food	1,375	540	39.3	835	60.7	120	8.7	865	62.9
4060	Counter attendants, cafeteria, food concession, and coffee shop	1,160	470	40.5	690	59.5	90	7.8	790	68.1
4110	Waiters and waitresses	18,795	7,235	38.5	11,565	61.5	2,015	10.7	13,950	74.2
4120	Food servers, nonrestaurant	1,425	690	48.4	735	51.6	195	13.7	820	57.5
4130	Miscellaneous food preparation and serving related workers, including dining room and cafeteria attendants and bartender helpers	1,410	685	48.6	725	51.4	395	28.0	485	34.4
4140	Dishwashers	725	640	88.3	90	12.4	300	41.4	210	29.0
4150	Hosts and hostesses, restaurant, lounge, and coffee shop	1,815	370	20.4	1,440	79.3	240	13.2	1,325	73.0
4200	First-line supervisors of housekeeping and janitorial workers	4,890	3,345	68.4	1,545	31.6	855	17.5	3,020	61.8
4210	First-line supervisors of landscaping, lawn service, and groundskeeping workers	3,395	2,960	87.2	430	12.7	410	12.1	2,815	82.9
4220	Janitors and building cleaners	18,105	13,765	76.0	4,340	24.0	4,515	24.9	10,745	59.3
4230	Maids and housekeeping cleaners	9,105	1,670	18.3	7,440	81.7	3,930	43.2	3,760	41.3
4240	Pest control workers	925	850	91.9	75	8.1	125	13.5	660	71.4
4250	Grounds maintenance workers	10,130	8,480	83.7	1,645	16.2	1,585	15.6	7,840	77.4
4300	First-line supervisors of gaming workers	3,795	2,230	58.8	1,570	41.4	265	7.0	3,000	79.1
4320	First-line supervisors of personal service workers	7,910	4,385	55.4	3,520	44.5	435	5.5	5,875	74.3
4340	Animal trainers	1,365	440	32.2	925	67.8	85	6.2	1,195	87.5
4350	Nonfarm animal caretakers	2,945	870	29.5	2,070	70.3	175	5.9	2,690	91.3
4400	Gaming services workers	1,715	1,225	71.4	490	28.6	155	9.0	925	53.9
4410	Motion picture projectionists	230	155	67.4	75	32.6	0	0.0	155	67.4
4420	Ushers, lobby attendants, and ticket takers	970	585	60.3	385	39.7	4	0.4	890	91.8
4430	Miscellaneous entertainment attendants and related workers	4,630	3,145	67.9	1,485	32.1	345	7.5	3,955	85.4
4460	Embalmers and funeral attendants	835	710	85.0	120	14.4	4	0.5	815	97.6
4465	Morticians, undertakers, and funeral directors	2,995	2,430	81.1	565	18.9	30	1.0	2,500	83.5
4500	Barbers	985	715	72.6	270	27.4	75	7.6	510	51.8
4510	Hairdressers, hairstylists, and cosmetologists	9,620	1,125	11.7	8,495	88.3	695	7.2	7,210	74.9
4520	Miscellaneous personal appearance workers	3,260	300	9.2	2,965	91.0	190	5.8	1,755	53.8
4530	Baggage porters, bellhops, and concierges	1,355	1,015	74.9	340	25.1	150	11.1	980	72.3
4540	Tour and travel guides	3,345	1,730	51.7	1,615	48.3	45	1.3	3,120	93.3
4600	Childcare workers	22,825	1,800	7.9	21,020	92.1	3,020	13.2	15,120	66.2
4610	Personal care aides	16,205	3,705	22.9	12,495	77.1	1,560	9.6	9,655	59.6
4620	Recreation and fitness workers	25,065	7,785	31.1	17,280	68.9	1,185	4.7	21,380	85.3
4640	Residential advisors	2,195	985	44.9	1,210	55.1	65	3.0	1,460	66.5
4650	Personal care and service workers, all other	2,660	1,005	37.8	1,655	62.2	110	4.1	2,210	83.1
4700	First-line supervisors of retail sales workers	107,360	67,665	63.0	39,695	37.0	6,480	6.0	78,875	73.5
4710	First-line supervisors of non-retail sales workers	103,810	73,015	70.3	30,790	29.7	6,010	5.8	79,660	76.7

A-22 Workers with Graduate or Professional Degree: Detailed Occupations, by Sex, Race, and Hispanic Origin, 2006–2010—Continued

		Graduate or Professional degree									
		Not Hispanic or Latino, one race								Not Hispanic or Latino, two or more races	
Census occupation code	Detailed Occupation	Black or African American alone		American Indian and Alaska Native alone		Asian alone		Native Hawaiian and Other Pacific Islander alone			
		Number	Percent	Number	Percent	Number	Percent	Number	Percent	Number	Percent
4010	First-line supervisors of food preparation and serving workers	700	8.7	35	0.4	1,210	15.1	10	0.1	115	1.4
4020	Cooks	805	8.2	55	0.6	1,165	11.9	0	0.0	290	3.0
4030	Food preparation workers	375	8.0	25	0.5	650	13.9	0	0.0	70	1.5
4040	Bartenders	160	2.8	30	0.5	190	3.4	90	1.6	55	1.0
4050	Combined food preparation and serving workers, including fast food	115	8.4	0	0.0	260	18.9	0	0.0	10	0.7
4060	Counter attendants, cafeteria, food concession, and coffee shop	115	9.9	0	0.0	120	10.3	0	0.0	50	4.3
4110	Waiters and waitresses	830	4.4	40	0.2	1,690	9.0	65	0.3	200	1.1
4120	Food servers, nonrestaurant	100	7.0	0	0.0	280	19.6	0	0.0	25	1.8
4130	Miscellaneous food preparation and serving related workers, including dining room and cafeteria attendants and bartender helpers	290	20.6	15	1.1	225	16.0	0	0.0	0	0.0
4140	Dishwashers	85	11.7	4	0.6	130	17.9	0	0.0	0	0.0
4150	Hosts and hostesses, restaurant, lounge, and coffee shop	135	7.4	0	0.0	45	2.5	45	2.5	25	1.4
4200	First-line supervisors of housekeeping and janitorial workers	720	14.7	15	0.3	235	4.8	0	0.0	40	0.8
4210	First-line supervisors of landscaping, lawn service, and groundskeeping workers	140	4.1	0	0.0	15	0.4	10	0.3	4	0.1
4220	Janitors and building cleaners	1,385	7.6	90	0.5	995	5.5	45	0.2	320	1.8
4230	Maids and housekeeping cleaners	715	7.9	10	0.1	530	5.8	0	0.0	155	1.7
4240	Pest control workers	135	14.6	0	0.0	4	0.4	0	0.0	0	0.0
4250	Grounds maintenance workers	315	3.1	65	0.6	190	1.9	15	0.1	114	1.1
4300	First-line supervisors of gaming workers	250	6.6	55	1.4	190	5.0	0	0.0	35	0.9
4320	First-line supervisors of personal service workers	605	7.6	30	0.4	825	10.4	0	0.0	135	1.7
4340	Animal trainers	20	1.5	0	0.0	60	4.4	0	0.0	0	0.0
4350	Nonfarm animal caretakers	4	0.1	0	0.0	55	1.9	0	0.0	15	0.5
4400	Gaming services workers	90	5.2	20	1.2	435	25.4	0	0.0	90	5.2
4410	Motion picture projectionists	30	13.0	0	0.0	45	19.6	0	0.0	0	0.0
4420	Ushers, lobby attendants, and ticket takers	70	7.2	0	0.0	15	1.5	0	0.0	0	0.0
4430	Miscellaneous entertainment attendants and related workers	175	3.8	0	0.0	85	1.8	0	0.0	65	1.4
4460	Embalmers and funeral attendants	15	1.8	0	0.0	0	0.0	0	0.0	0	0.0
4465	Morticians, undertakers, and funeral directors	430	14.4	4	0.1	25	0.8	0	0.0	4	0.1
4500	Barbers	300	30.5	0	0.0	20	2.0	0	0.0	90	9.1
4510	Hairdressers, hairstylists, and cosmetologists	995	10.3	50	0.5	515	5.4	0	0.0	150	1.6
4520	Miscellaneous personal appearance workers	160	4.9	15	0.5	990	30.4	20	0.6	130	4.0
4530	Baggage porters, bellhops, and concierges	110	8.1	0	0.0	75	5.5	0	0.0	40	3.0
4540	Tour and travel guides	30	0.9	0	0.0	80	2.4	0	0.0	70	2.1
4600	Childcare workers	2,515	11.0	115	0.5	1,630	7.1	0	0.0	420	1.8
4610	Personal care aides	2,510	15.5	85	0.5	1,995	12.3	85	0.5	315	1.9
4620	Recreation and fitness workers	1,320	5.3	85	0.3	780	3.1	0	0.0	310	1.2
4640	Residential advisors	475	21.6	0	0.0	125	5.7	0	0.0	70	3.2
4650	Personal care and service workers, all other	110	4.1	0	0.0	140	5.3	0	0.0	85	3.2
4700	First-line supervisors of retail sales workers	6,455	6.0	275	0.3	13,620	12.7	30	0.0	1,630	1.5
4710	First-line supervisors of non-retail sales workers	5,655	5.4	195	0.2	11,145	10.7	4	0.0	1,140	1.1

A-22 **Workers with Graduate or Professional Degree: Detailed Occupations, by Sex, Race, and Hispanic Origin, 2006–2010**—*Continued*

Census occupation code	Detailed Occupation	Total	Graduate or Professional degree						
			Male		Female		Hispanic or Latino		Not Hispanic or Latino, one race – White alone	
			Number	Percent	Number	Percent	Number	Percent	Number	Percent
4720	Cashiers	28,785	12,580	43.7	16,205	56.3	3,340	11.6	16,890	58.7
4740	Counter and rental clerks	1,990	1,285	64.6	700	35.2	195	9.8	1,290	64.8
4750	Parts salespersons	610	545	89.3	70	11.5	100	16.4	440	72.1
4760	Retail salespersons	95,295	51,770	54.3	43,525	45.7	4,890	5.1	75,265	79.0
4800	Advertising sales agents	14,515	7,270	50.1	7,245	49.9	730	5.0	12,005	82.7
4810	Insurance sales agents	40,010	29,025	72.5	10,985	27.5	2,125	5.3	31,685	79.2
4820	Securities, commodities, and financial services sales agents	57,435	47,085	82.0	10,350	18.0	2,830	4.9	45,905	79.9
4830	Travel agents	4,665	1,655	35.5	3,010	64.5	300	6.4	3,370	72.2
4840	Sales representatives, services, all other	44,935	32,205	71.7	12,735	28.3	2,630	5.9	36,620	81.5
4850	Sales representatives, wholesale and manufacturing	100,295	73,005	72.8	27,290	27.2	5,045	5.0	83,040	82.8
4900	Models, demonstrators, and product promoters	1,975	680	34.4	1,295	65.6	90	4.6	1,540	78.0
4920	Real estate brokers and sales agents	82,605	46,020	55.7	36,580	44.3	4,685	5.7	65,470	79.3
4930	Sales engineers	4,965	4,660	93.9	305	6.1	265	5.3	3,640	73.3
4940	Telemarketers	2,795	1,485	53.1	1,315	47.0	340	12.2	2,015	72.1
4950	Door-to-door sales workers, news and street vendors, and related workers	6,335	1,765	27.9	4,570	72.1	485	7.7	4,795	75.7
4965	Sales and related workers, all other	16,895	10,270	60.8	6,620	39.2	710	4.2	14,260	84.4
5000	First-line supervisors of office and administrative support workers	98,175	47,530	48.4	50,645	51.6	6,825	7.0	71,140	72.5
5010	Switchboard operators, including answering service	660	175	26.5	485	73.5	50	7.6	410	62.1
5020	Telephone operators	695	195	28.1	500	71.9	40	5.8	470	67.6
5030	Communications equipment operators, all other	550	275	50.0	275	50.0	15	2.7	460	83.6
5100	Bill and account collectors	4,770	2,175	45.6	2,600	54.5	520	10.9	2,945	61.7
5110	Billing and posting clerks	10,340	2,965	28.7	7,375	71.3	895	8.7	7,025	67.9
5120	Bookkeeping, accounting, and auditing clerks	32,305	9,225	28.6	23,080	71.4	2,140	6.6	24,620	76.2
5130	Gaming cage workers	170	110	64.7	60	35.3	20	11.8	85	50.0
5140	Payroll and timekeeping clerks	3,115	695	22.3	2,420	77.7	265	8.5	2,240	71.9
5150	Procurement clerks	1,660	930	56.0	730	44.0	100	6.0	1,220	73.5
5160	Tellers	5,055	1,205	23.8	3,845	76.1	450	8.9	2,855	56.5
5165	Financial clerks, all other	6,380	3,990	62.5	2,390	37.5	280	4.4	4,590	71.9
5200	Brokerage clerks	430	175	40.7	250	58.1	50	11.6	360	83.7
5220	Court, municipal, and license clerks	3,310	1,325	40.0	1,980	59.8	185	5.6	2,620	79.2
5230	Credit authorizers, checkers, and clerks	2,200	1,250	56.8	955	43.4	74	3.4	1,600	72.7
5240	Customer service representatives	53,480	23,835	44.6	29,645	55.4	3,950	7.4	36,370	68.0
5250	Eligibility interviewers, government programs	3,965	1,440	36.3	2,525	63.7	465	11.7	2,270	57.3
5260	File clerks	10,325	3,365	32.6	6,960	67.4	640	6.2	6,840	66.2
5300	Hotel, motel, and resort desk clerks	2,125	1,200	56.5	920	43.3	100	4.7	1,515	71.3
5310	Interviewers, except eligibility and loan	7,130	2,840	39.8	4,290	60.2	480	6.7	5,570	78.1
5320	Library assistants, clerical	7,635	1,530	20.0	6,105	80.0	290	3.8	6,320	82.8
5330	Loan interviewers and clerks	3,060	1,375	44.9	1,690	55.2	200	6.5	1,935	63.2
5340	New accounts clerks	570	350	61.4	220	38.6	10	1.8	375	65.8
5350	Correspondence clerks and order clerks	2,850	1,235	43.3	1,620	56.8	335	11.8	1,895	66.5
5360	Human resources assistants, except payroll and timekeeping	2,215	845	38.1	1,365	61.6	175	7.9	1,160	52.4
5400	Receptionists and information clerks	19,615	4,005	20.4	15,610	79.6	1,360	6.9	14,755	75.2
5410	Reservation and transportation ticket agents and travel clerks	4,685	2,590	55.3	2,100	44.8	375	8.0	3,445	73.5
5420	Information and record clerks, all other	3,725	1,035	27.8	2,690	72.2	325	8.7	2,375	63.8

A-22 **Workers with Graduate or Professional Degree: Detailed Occupations, by Sex, Race, and Hispanic Origin, 2006–2010**—Continued

Census occupation code	Detailed Occupation	Graduate or Professional degree									
		Not Hispanic or Latino, one race								Not Hispanic or Latino, two or more races	
		Black or African American alone		American Indian and Alaska Native alone		Asian alone		Native Hawaiian and Other Pacific Islander alone			
		Number	Percent	Number	Percent	Number	Percent	Number	Percent	Number	Percent
4720	Cashiers	2,085	7.2	105	0.4	5,810	20.2	10	0.0	535	1.9
4740	Counter and rental clerks	165	8.3	0	0.0	280	14.1	0	0.0	53	2.7
4750	Parts salespersons	25	4.1	0	0.0	0	0.0	0	0.0	55	9.0
4760	Retail salespersons	5,950	6.2	130	0.1	7,520	7.9	65	0.1	1,475	1.5
4800	Advertising sales agents	960	6.6	115	0.8	560	3.9	10	0.1	135	0.9
4810	Insurance sales agents	3,050	7.6	125	0.3	2,710	6.8	10	0.0	305	0.8
4820	Securities, commodities, and financial services sales agents	2,805	4.9	60	0.1	5,125	8.9	0	0.0	715	1.2
4830	Travel agents	270	5.8	30	0.6	655	14.0	0	0.0	35	0.8
4840	Sales representatives, services, all other	2,045	4.6	55	0.1	3,000	6.7	0	0.0	580	1.3
4850	Sales representatives, wholesale and manufacturing	4,175	4.2	115	0.1	6,685	6.7	35	0.0	1,200	1.2
4900	Models, demonstrators, and product promoters	70	3.5	60	3.0	180	9.1	0	0.0	35	1.8
4920	Real estate brokers and sales agents	5,200	6.3	165	0.2	6,155	7.5	110	0.1	815	1.0
4930	Sales engineers	230	4.6	80	1.6	710	14.3	0	0.0	40	0.8
4940	Telemarketers	230	8.2	10	0.4	155	5.5	0	0.0	48	1.7
4950	Door-to-door sales workers, news and street vendors, and related workers	625	9.9	40	0.6	235	3.7	0	0.0	155	2.4
4965	Sales and related workers, all other	670	4.0	15	0.1	1,075	6.4	15	0.1	145	0.9
5000	First-line supervisors of office and administrative support workers	10,720	10.9	565	0.6	7,400	7.5	160	0.2	1,370	1.4
5010	Switchboard operators, including answering service	105	15.9	10	1.5	50	7.6	15	2.3	25	3.8
5020	Telephone operators	105	15.1	35	5.0	45	6.5	0	0.0	0	0.0
5030	Communications equipment operators, all other	40	7.3	0	0.0	20	3.6	0	0.0	15	2.7
5100	Bill and account collectors	935	19.6	45	0.9	290	6.1	0	0.0	34	0.7
5110	Billing and posting clerks	875	8.5	30	0.3	1,365	13.2	0	0.0	145	1.4
5120	Bookkeeping, accounting, and auditing clerks	2,130	6.6	125	0.4	2,940	9.1	0	0.0	355	1.1
5130	Gaming cage workers	0	0.0	40	23.5	30	17.6	0	0.0	0	0.0
5140	Payroll and timekeeping clerks	295	9.5	0	0.0	280	9.0	0	0.0	40	1.3
5150	Procurement clerks	230	13.9	20	1.2	75	4.5	0	0.0	20	1.2
5160	Tellers	480	9.5	4	0.1	1,110	22.0	4	0.1	155	3.1
5165	Financial clerks, all other	380	6.0	15	0.2	1,005	15.8	0	0.0	110	1.7
5200	Brokerage clerks	0	0.0	0	0.0	20	4.7	0	0.0	0	0.0
5220	Court, municipal, and license clerks	305	9.2	4	0.1	160	4.8	0	0.0	39	1.2
5230	Credit authorizers, checkers, and clerks	140	6.4	0	0.0	340	15.5	0	0.0	45	2.0
5240	Customer service representatives	7,125	13.3	90	0.2	5,205	9.7	50	0.1	690	1.3
5250	Eligibility interviewers, government programs	840	21.2	10	0.3	360	9.1	0	0.0	25	0.6
5260	File clerks	1,425	13.8	60	0.6	1,075	10.4	4	0.0	280	2.7
5300	Hotel, motel, and resort desk clerks	125	5.9	20	0.9	360	16.9	0	0.0	0	0.0
5310	Interviewers, except eligibility and loan	480	6.7	55	0.8	370	5.2	0	0.0	175	2.5
5320	Library assistants, clerical	235	3.1	30	0.4	600	7.9	0	0.0	160	2.1
5330	Loan interviewers and clerks	360	11.8	0	0.0	510	16.7	0	0.0	60	2.0
5340	New accounts clerks	80	14.0	0	0.0	40	7.0	20	3.5	45	7.9
5350	Correspondence clerks and order clerks	325	11.4	0	0.0	220	7.7	0	0.0	79	2.8
5360	Human resources assistants, except payroll and timekeeping	640	28.9	0	0.0	205	9.3	0	0.0	30	1.4
5400	Receptionists and information clerks	1,830	9.3	50	0.3	1,245	6.3	0	0.0	375	1.9
5410	Reservation and transportation ticket agents and travel clerks	320	6.8	10	0.2	440	9.4	15	0.3	85	1.8
5420	Information and record clerks, all other	530	14.2	4	0.1	440	11.8	0	0.0	44	1.2

A-22 **Workers with Graduate or Professional Degree: Detailed Occupations, by Sex, Race, and Hispanic Origin, 2006–2010**—*Continued*

Census occupation code	Detailed Occupation	Total	Male Number	Male Percent	Female Number	Female Percent	Hispanic or Latino Number	Hispanic or Latino Percent	Not Hispanic or Latino, one race White alone Number	Percent
5500	Cargo and freight agents	580	405	69.8	170	29.3	65	11.2	405	69.8
5510	Couriers and messengers	5,300	4,770	90.0	535	10.1	490	9.2	3,745	70.7
5520	Dispatchers	3,155	1,720	54.5	1,440	45.6	350	11.1	2,280	72.3
5530	Meter readers, utilities	305	205	67.2	105	34.4	25	8.2	175	57.4
5540	Postal service clerks	2,310	1,385	60.0	925	40.0	155	6.7	950	41.1
5550	Postal service mail carriers	4,110	3,060	74.5	1,050	25.5	160	3.9	2,915	70.9
5560	Postal service mail sorters, processors, and processing machine operators	1,840	1,235	67.1	605	32.9	90	4.9	865	47.0
5600	Production, planning, and expediting clerks	15,885	8,855	55.7	7,030	44.3	1,010	6.4	12,075	76.0
5610	Shipping, receiving, and traffic clerks	4,515	3,195	70.8	1,320	29.2	795	17.6	2,750	60.9
5620	Stock clerks and order fillers	12,945	7,635	59.0	5,310	41.0	1,620	12.5	7,855	60.7
5630	Weighers, measurers, checkers, and samplers, recordkeeping	1,160	735	63.4	425	36.6	95	8.2	795	68.5
5700	Secretaries and administrative assistants	89,860	12,315	13.7	77,545	86.3	6,225	6.9	65,975	73.4
5800	Computer operators	5,260	3,355	63.8	1,905	36.2	340	6.5	3,395	64.5
5810	Data entry keyers	9,885	3,350	33.9	6,535	66.1	690	7.0	6,505	65.8
5820	Word processors and typists	7,620	1,770	23.2	5,850	76.8	575	7.5	4,950	65.0
5840	Insurance claims and policy processing clerks	7,485	3,120	41.7	4,365	58.3	355	4.7	5,295	70.7
5850	Mail clerks and mail machine operators, except postal service	1,495	970	64.9	525	35.1	140	9.4	990	66.2
5860	Office clerks, general	31,170	8,885	28.5	22,285	71.5	2,440	7.8	20,685	66.4
5900	Office machine operators, except computer	635	210	33.1	425	66.9	45	7.1	480	75.6
5910	Proofreaders and copy markers	1,595	640	40.1	955	59.9	74	4.6	1,325	83.1
5920	Statistical assistants	1,425	660	46.3	770	54.0	75	5.3	1,070	75.1
5940	Miscellaneous office and administrative support workers, including desktop publishers	33,095	9,730	29.4	23,365	70.6	2,525	7.6	22,965	69.4
6005	First-line supervisors of farming, fishing, and forestry workers	1,420	1,065	75.0	355	25.0	140	9.9	1,215	85.6
6010	Agricultural inspectors	1,070	810	75.7	260	24.3	80	7.5	675	63.1
6040	Graders and sorters, agricultural products	225	110	48.9	110	48.9	95	42.2	90	40.0
6050	Miscellaneous agricultural workers, including animal breeders	4,835	3,440	71.1	1,400	29.0	775	16.0	3,815	78.9
6100	Fishing and hunting workers	620	570	91.9	50	8.1	10	1.6	500	80.6
6120	Forest and conservation workers	420	290	69.0	130	31.0	10	2.4	400	95.2
6130	Logging workers	335	310	92.5	25	7.5	0	0.0	255	76.1
6200	First-line supervisors of construction trades and extraction workers	15,250	13,920	91.3	1,330	8.7	1,680	11.0	12,080	79.2
6210	Boilermakers	15	15	100.0	0	0.0	15	100.0	0	0.0
6220	Brickmasons, blockmasons, and stonemasons	835	820	98.2	15	1.8	240	28.7	495	59.3
6230	Carpenters	13,420	12,820	95.5	600	4.5	2,250	16.8	10,135	75.5
6240	Carpet, floor, and tile installers and finishers	1,040	1,020	98.1	20	1.9	360	34.6	545	52.4
6250	Cement masons, concrete finishers, and terrazzo workers	225	225	100.0	0	0.0	120	53.3	75	33.3
6260	Construction laborers	11,580	11,070	95.6	505	4.4	2,425	20.9	7,935	68.5
6300	Paving, surfacing, and tamping equipment operators	90	90	100.0	0	0.0	65	72.2	20	22.2
6320	Construction equipment operators, except paving, surfacing, and tamping equipment operators	1,090	1,010	92.7	80	7.3	250	22.9	715	65.6
6330	Drywall installers, ceiling tile installers, and tapers	450	420	93.3	30	6.7	335	74.4	110	24.4

A-22 Workers with Graduate or Professional Degree: Detailed Occupations, by Sex, Race, and Hispanic Origin, 2006–2010—*Continued*

Census occupation code	Detailed Occupation	Graduate or Professional degree									
		Not Hispanic or Latino, one race								Not Hispanic or Latino, two or more races	
		Black or African American alone		American Indian and Alaska Native alone		Asian alone		Native Hawaiian and Other Pacific Islander alone			
		Number	Percent	Number	Percent	Number	Percent	Number	Percent	Number	Percent
5500	Cargo and freight agents	60	10.3	0	0.0	50	8.6	0	0.0	0	0.0
5510	Couriers and messengers	710	13.4	0	0.0	240	4.5	0	0.0	115	2.2
5520	Dispatchers	315	10.0	15	0.5	125	4.0	0	0.0	75	2.4
5530	Meter readers, utilities	10	3.3	0	0.0	100	32.8	0	0.0	0	0.0
5540	Postal service clerks	515	22.3	0	0.0	620	26.8	20	0.9	40	1.7
5550	Postal service mail carriers	370	9.0	30	0.7	590	14.4	0	0.0	44	1.1
5560	Postal service mail sorters, processors, and processing machine operators	445	24.2	0	0.0	430	23.4	4	0.2	4	0.2
5600	Production, planning, and expediting clerks	905	5.7	95	0.6	1,485	9.3	15	0.1	300	1.9
5610	Shipping, receiving, and traffic clerks	425	9.4	25	0.6	430	9.5	15	0.3	75	1.7
5620	Stock clerks and order fillers	1,570	12.1	80	0.6	1,525	11.8	10	0.1	290	2.2
5630	Weighers, measurers, checkers, and samplers, recordkeeping	85	7.3	0	0.0	170	14.7	0	0.0	15	1.3
5700	Secretaries and administrative assistants	9,230	10.3	280	0.3	6,735	7.5	75	0.1	1,345	1.5
5800	Computer operators	570	10.8	4	0.1	920	17.5	0	0.0	25	0.5
5810	Data entry keyers	1,350	13.7	70	0.7	1,060	10.7	25	0.3	190	1.9
5820	Word processors and typists	1,075	14.1	50	0.7	865	11.4	0	0.0	104	1.4
5840	Insurance claims and policy processing clerks	1,105	14.8	0	0.0	560	7.5	45	0.6	120	1.6
5850	Mail clerks and mail machine operators, except postal service	170	11.4	0	0.0	110	7.4	0	0.0	85	5.7
5860	Office clerks, general	3,755	12.0	135	0.4	3,620	11.6	35	0.1	505	1.6
5900	Office machine operators, except computer	60	9.4	0	0.0	50	7.9	0	0.0	0	0.0
5910	Proofreaders and copy markers	85	5.3	0	0.0	115	7.2	0	0.0	0	0.0
5920	Statistical assistants	185	13.0	20	1.4	35	2.5	0	0.0	50	3.5
5940	Miscellaneous office and administrative support workers, including desktop publishers	4,665	14.1	210	0.6	2,260	6.8	60	0.2	425	1.3
6005	First-line supervisors of farming, fishing, and forestry workers	30	2.1	4	0.3	15	1.1	0	0.0	15	1.1
6010	Agricultural inspectors	140	13.1	0	0.0	165	15.4	10	0.9	0	0.0
6040	Graders and sorters, agricultural products	35	15.6	0	0.0	0	0.0	0	0.0	0	0.0
6050	Miscellaneous agricultural workers, including animal breeders	115	2.4	0	0.0	125	2.6	4	0.1	4	0.1
6100	Fishing and hunting workers	20	3.2	30	4.8	35	5.6	0	0.0	20	3.2
6120	Forest and conservation workers	0	0.0	0	0.0	10	2.4	0	0.0	0	0.0
6130	Logging workers	65	19.4	4	1.2	0	0.0	0	0.0	10	3.0
6200	First-line supervisors of construction trades and extraction workers	635	4.2	65	0.4	595	3.9	10	0.1	190	1.2
6210	Boilermakers	0	0.0	0	0.0	0	0.0	0	0.0	0	0.0
6220	Brickmasons, blockmasons, and stonemasons	40	4.8	0	0.0	10	1.2	0	0.0	55	6.6
6230	Carpenters	555	4.1	10	0.1	265	2.0	10	0.1	195	1.5
6240	Carpet, floor, and tile installers and finishers	25	2.4	10	1.0	100	9.6	0	0.0	0	0.0
6250	Cement masons, concrete finishers, and terrazzo workers	30	13.3	0	0.0	0	0.0	0	0.0	0	0.0
6260	Construction laborers	715	6.2	60	0.5	305	2.6	0	0.0	135	1.2
6300	Paving, surfacing, and tamping equipment operators	0	0.0	0	0.0	0	0.0	0	0.0	0	0.0
6320	Construction equipment operators, except paving, surfacing, and tamping equipment operators	95	8.7	15	1.4	0	0.0	0	0.0	15	1.4
6330	Drywall installers, ceiling tile installers, and tapers	0	0.0	0	0.0	4	0.9	0	0.0	0	0.0

A-22 Workers with Graduate or Professional Degree: Detailed Occupations, by Sex, Race, and Hispanic Origin, 2006–2010—Continued

Census occupation code	Detailed Occupation	Total	Male Number	Male Percent	Female Number	Female Percent	Hispanic or Latino Number	Hispanic or Latino Percent	Not Hispanic or Latino, one race / White alone Number	Percent
6355	Electricians	7,665	7,400	96.5	270	3.5	1,145	14.9	5,545	72.3
6360	Glaziers	145	135	93.1	10	6.9	10	6.9	130	89.7
6400	Insulation workers	205	205	100.0	0	0.0	110	53.7	75	36.6
6420	Painters, construction and maintenance	6,055	5,180	85.5	875	14.5	1,135	18.7	4,275	70.6
6430	Paperhangers	80	60	75.0	20	25.0	0	0.0	80	100.0
6440	Pipelayers, plumbers, pipefitters, and steamfitters	3,875	3,765	97.2	110	2.8	515	13.3	2,965	76.5
6460	Plasterers and stucco masons	135	135	100.0	0	0.0	20	14.8	115	85.2
6500	Reinforcing iron and rebar workers	15	15	100.0	0	0.0	0	0.0	15	100.0
6515	Roofers	875	875	100.0	0	0.0	415	47.4	420	48.0
6520	Sheet metal workers	500	485	97.0	15	3.0	45	9.0	385	77.0
6530	Structural iron and steel workers	155	155	100.0	0	0.0	35	22.6	110	71.0
6600	Helpers, construction trades	340	320	94.1	20	5.9	85	25.0	195	57.4
6660	Construction and building inspectors	3,430	3,015	87.9	415	12.1	290	8.5	2,350	68.5
6700	Elevator installers and repairers	300	300	100.0	0	0.0	0	0.0	230	76.7
6710	Fence erectors	125	125	100.0	0	0.0	50	40.0	75	60.0
6720	Hazardous materials removal workers	590	440	74.6	150	25.4	15	2.5	520	88.1
6730	Highway maintenance workers	335	310	92.5	25	7.5	0	0.0	260	77.6
6740	Rail-track laying and maintenance equipment operators	10	10	100.0	0	0.0	0	0.0	0	0.0
6765	Miscellaneous construction workers, including solar photovoltaic installers, septic tank servicers, and sewer pipe cleaners	425	415	97.6	10	2.4	95	22.4	310	72.9
6800	Derrick, rotary drill, and service unit operators, and roustabouts, oil, gas, and mining	190	180	94.7	15	7.9	0	0.0	180	94.7
6820	Earth drillers, except oil and gas	25	25	100.0	0	0.0	0	0.0	20	80.0
6830	Explosives workers, ordnance handling experts, and blasters	140	140	100.0	0	0.0	0	0.0	115	82.1
6840	Mining machine operators	215	195	90.7	20	9.3	4	1.9	190	88.4
6940	Miscellaneous extraction workers, including roof bolters and helpers	175	145	82.9	30	17.1	10	5.7	140	80.0
7000	First-line supervisors of mechanics, installers, and repairers	7,040	5,715	81.2	1,330	18.9	450	6.4	4,800	68.2
7010	Computer, automated teller, and office machine repairers	8,120	6,805	83.8	1,315	16.2	425	5.2	4,745	58.4
7020	Radio and telecommunications equipment installers and repairers	2,850	2,185	76.7	665	23.3	325	11.4	1,715	60.2
7030	Avionics technicians	225	225	100.0	0	0.0	85	37.8	115	51.1
7040	Electric motor, power tool, and related repairers	330	305	92.4	25	7.6	75	22.7	180	54.5
7100	Electrical and electronics repairers, transportation equipment, and industrial and utility	305	260	85.2	40	13.1	4	1.3	285	93.4
7110	Electronic equipment installers and repairers, motor vehicles	200	200	100.0	0	0.0	40	20.0	95	47.5
7120	Electronic home entertainment equipment installers and repairers	680	620	91.2	60	8.8	105	15.4	510	75.0
7130	Security and fire alarm systems installers	605	565	93.4	40	6.6	40	6.6	505	83.5
7140	Aircraft mechanics and service technicians	1,860	1,800	96.8	60	3.2	180	9.7	1,210	65.1
7150	Automotive body and related repairers	590	515	87.3	75	12.7	55	9.3	505	85.6

A-22 Workers with Graduate or Professional Degree: Detailed Occupations, by Sex, Race, and Hispanic Origin, 2006–2010—Continued

Census occupation code	Detailed Occupation	Black or African American alone Number	Black or African American alone Percent	American Indian and Alaska Native alone Number	American Indian and Alaska Native alone Percent	Asian alone Number	Asian alone Percent	Native Hawaiian and Other Pacific Islander alone Number	Native Hawaiian and Other Pacific Islander alone Percent	Not Hispanic or Latino, two or more races Number	Not Hispanic or Latino, two or more races Percent
6355	Electricians	485	6.3	65	0.8	385	5.0	0	0.0	49	0.6
6360	Glaziers	0	0.0	0	0.0	0	0.0	0	0.0	4	2.8
6400	Insulation workers	15	7.3	0	0.0	0	0.0	0	0.0	0	0.0
6420	Painters, construction and maintenance	130	2.1	30	0.5	385	6.4	0	0.0	95	1.6
6430	Paperhangers	0	0.0	0	0.0	0	0.0	0	0.0	0	0.0
6440	Pipelayers, plumbers, pipefitters, and steamfitters	195	5.0	50	1.3	50	1.3	0	0.0	100	2.6
6460	Plasterers and stucco masons	0	0.0	0	0.0	0	0.0	0	0.0	0	0.0
6500	Reinforcing iron and rebar workers	0	0.0	0	0.0	0	0.0	0	0.0	0	0.0
6515	Roofers	20	2.3	4	0.5	15	1.7	0	0.0	0	0.0
6520	Sheet metal workers	25	5.0	0	0.0	45	9.0	0	0.0	4	0.8
6530	Structural iron and steel workers	0	0.0	0	0.0	10	6.5	0	0.0	0	0.0
6600	Helpers, construction trades	30	8.8	0	0.0	30	8.8	0	0.0	0	0.0
6660	Construction and building inspectors	280	8.2	10	0.3	470	13.7	0	0.0	35	1.0
6700	Elevator installers and repairers	25	8.3	0	0.0	35	11.7	0	0.0	10	3.3
6710	Fence erectors	0	0.0	0	0.0	0	0.0	0	0.0	0	0.0
6720	Hazardous materials removal workers	15	2.5	4	0.7	40	6.8	0	0.0	0	0.0
6730	Highway maintenance workers	45	13.4	4	1.2	25	7.5	0	0.0	0	0.0
6740	Rail-track laying and maintenance equipment operators	10	100.0	0	0.0	0	0.0	0	0.0	0	0.0
6765	Miscellaneous construction workers, including solar photovoltaic installers, septic tank servicers, and sewer pipe cleaners	0	0.0	0	0.0	10	2.4	0	0.0	10	2.4
6800	Derrick, rotary drill, and service unit operators, and roustabouts, oil, gas, and mining	0	0.0	0	0.0	0	0.0	0	0.0	10	5.3
6820	Earth drillers, except oil and gas	0	0.0	0	0.0	0	0.0	0	0.0	4	16.0
6830	Explosives workers, ordnance handling experts, and blasters	30	21.4	0	0.0	0	0.0	0	0.0	0	0.0
6840	Mining machine operators	0	0.0	0	0.0	20	9.3	0	0.0	0	0.0
6940	Miscellaneous extraction workers, including roof bolters and helpers	0	0.0	0	0.0	0	0.0	0	0.0	20	11.4
7000	First-line supervisors of mechanics, installers, and repairers	1,050	14.9	10	0.1	680	9.7	4	0.1	55	0.8
7010	Computer, automated teller, and office machine repairers	905	11.1	15	0.2	1,870	23.0	10	0.1	155	1.9
7020	Radio and telecommunications equipment installers and repairers	410	14.4	0	0.0	370	13.0	0	0.0	40	1.4
7030	Avionics technicians	0	0.0	0	0.0	20	8.9	0	0.0	0	0.0
7040	Electric motor, power tool, and related repairers	0	0.0	0	0.0	40	12.1	0	0.0	35	10.6
7100	Electrical and electronics repairers, transportation equipment, and industrial and utility	0	0.0	0	0.0	10	3.3	0	0.0	0	0.0
7110	Electronic equipment installers and repairers, motor vehicles	30	15.0	0	0.0	35	17.5	0	0.0	0	0.0
7120	Electronic home entertainment equipment installers and repairers	10	1.5	4	0.6	55	8.1	0	0.0	0	0.0
7130	Security and fire alarm systems installers	60	9.9	0	0.0	0	0.0	0	0.0	0	0.0
7140	Aircraft mechanics and service technicians	265	14.2	0	0.0	180	9.7	10	0.5	25	1.3
7150	Automotive body and related repairers	0	0.0	0	0.0	10	1.7	0	0.0	20	3.4

A-22 Workers with Graduate or Professional Degree: Detailed Occupations, by Sex, Race, and Hispanic Origin, 2006–2010—*Continued*

Census occupation code	Detailed Occupation	Total	Male Number	Male Percent	Female Number	Female Percent	Hispanic or Latino Number	Hispanic or Latino Percent	Not Hispanic or Latino, one race — White alone Number	White alone Percent
7160	Automotive glass installers and repairers	35	25	71.4	10	28.6	0	0.0	15	42.9
7200	Automotive service technicians and mechanics	4,170	3,950	94.7	220	5.3	930	22.3	2,405	57.7
7210	Bus and truck mechanics and diesel engine specialists	1,075	1,035	96.3	40	3.7	240	22.3	650	60.5
7220	Heavy vehicle and mobile equipment service technicians and mechanics	940	910	96.8	30	3.2	125	13.3	735	78.2
7240	Small engine mechanics	325	310	95.4	15	4.6	30	9.2	270	83.1
7260	Miscellaneous vehicle and mobile equipment mechanics, installers, and repairers	260	260	100.0	0	0.0	40	15.4	185	71.2
7300	Control and valve installers and repairers	90	90	100.0	0	0.0	10	11.1	80	88.9
7315	Heating, air conditioning, and refrigeration mechanics and installers	2,535	2,425	95.7	110	4.3	510	20.1	1,735	68.4
7320	Home appliance repairers	570	535	93.9	35	6.1	110	19.3	400	70.2
7330	Industrial and refractory machinery mechanics	2,200	2,145	97.5	55	2.5	340	15.5	1,445	65.7
7340	Maintenance and repair workers, general	3,990	3,615	90.6	375	9.4	540	13.5	2,865	71.8
7350	Maintenance workers, machinery	210	210	100.0	0	0.0	25	11.9	120	57.1
7360	Millwrights	300	265	88.3	35	11.7	20	6.7	230	76.7
7410	Electrical power-line installers and repairers	575	560	97.4	15	2.6	55	9.6	375	65.2
7420	Telecommunications line installers and repairers	1,485	1,320	88.9	165	11.1	230	15.5	930	62.6
7430	Precision instrument and equipment repairers	2,245	2,025	90.2	220	9.8	195	8.7	1,805	80.4
7510	Coin, vending, and amusement machine servicers and repairers	650	465	71.5	190	29.2	110	16.9	420	64.6
7540	Locksmiths and safe repairers	385	350	90.9	40	10.4	35	9.1	315	81.8
7550	Manufactured building and mobile home installers	40	40	100.0	0	0.0	0	0.0	40	100.0
7560	Riggers	70	70	100.0	0	0.0	0	0.0	70	100.0
7610	Helpers—installation, maintenance, and repair workers	100	100	100.0	0	0.0	95	95.0	10	10.0
7630	Other installation, maintenance, and repair workers, including wind turbine service technicians, and commercial divers, and signal and track switch repairers	2,935	2,620	89.3	320	10.9	320	10.9	2,235	76.1
7700	First-line supervisors of production and operating workers	29,790	23,590	79.2	6,205	20.8	2,430	8.2	20,930	70.3
7710	Aircraft structure, surfaces, rigging, and systems assemblers	65	65	100.0	0	0.0	0	0.0	25	38.5
7720	Electrical, electronics, and electromechanical assemblers	1,135	680	59.9	455	40.1	220	19.4	575	50.7
7730	Engine and other machine assemblers	60	60	100.0	0	0.0	0	0.0	40	66.7
7740	Structural metal fabricators and fitters	180	165	91.7	15	8.3	0	0.0	170	94.4
7750	Miscellaneous assemblers and fabricators	5,640	4,110	72.9	1,530	27.1	790	14.0	3,755	66.6
7800	Bakers	1,950	870	44.6	1,080	55.4	245	12.6	1,400	71.8
7810	Butchers and other meat, poultry, and fish processing workers	895	750	83.8	150	16.8	250	27.9	470	52.5
7830	Food and tobacco roasting, baking, and drying machine operators and tenders	75	30	40.0	40	53.3	0	0.0	55	73.3
7840	Food batchmakers	455	195	42.9	260	57.1	110	24.2	190	41.8
7850	Food cooking machine operators and tenders	4	0	0.0	4	100.0	0	0.0	4	100.0
7855	Food processing workers, all other	670	390	58.2	275	41.0	70	10.4	325	48.5
7900	Computer control programmers and operators	645	605	93.8	40	6.2	165	25.6	395	61.2

A-22 Workers with Graduate or Professional Degree: Detailed Occupations, by Sex, Race, and Hispanic Origin, 2006–2010—*Continued*

Census occupation code	Detailed Occupation	Black or African American alone Number	Black or African American alone Percent	American Indian and Alaska Native alone Number	American Indian and Alaska Native alone Percent	Asian alone Number	Asian alone Percent	Native Hawaiian and Other Pacific Islander alone Number	Native Hawaiian and Other Pacific Islander alone Percent	Not Hispanic or Latino, two or more races Number	Not Hispanic or Latino, two or more races Percent
7160	Automotive glass installers and repairers	0	0.0	20	57.1	0	0.0	0	0.0	0	0.0
7200	Automotive service technicians and mechanics	365	8.8	95	2.3	280	6.7	0	0.0	85	2.0
7210	Bus and truck mechanics and diesel engine specialists	45	4.2	35	3.3	70	6.5	0	0.0	35	3.3
7220	Heavy vehicle and mobile equipment service technicians and mechanics	0	0.0	20	2.1	45	4.8	0	0.0	20	2.1
7240	Small engine mechanics	0	0.0	0	0.0	10	3.1	0	0.0	15	4.6
7260	Miscellaneous vehicle and mobile equipment mechanics, installers, and repairers	30	11.5	0	0.0	4	1.5	0	0.0	0	0.0
7300	Control and valve installers and repairers	0	0.0	0	0.0	0	0.0	0	0.0	0	0.0
7315	Heating, air conditioning, and refrigeration mechanics and installers	55	2.2	4	0.2	185	7.3	0	0.0	45	1.8
7320	Home appliance repairers	15	2.6	0	0.0	45	7.9	0	0.0	0	0.0
7330	Industrial and refractory machinery mechanics	180	8.2	15	0.7	165	7.5	0	0.0	55	2.5
7340	Maintenance and repair workers, general	220	5.5	15	0.4	240	6.0	0	0.0	110	2.8
7350	Maintenance workers, machinery	55	26.2	0	0.0	0	0.0	0	0.0	10	4.8
7360	Millwrights	50	16.7	0	0.0	0	0.0	0	0.0	0	0.0
7410	Electrical power-line installers and repairers	110	19.1	0	0.0	35	6.1	0	0.0	0	0.0
7420	Telecommunications line installers and repairers	185	12.5	10	0.7	110	7.4	0	0.0	20	1.3
7430	Precision instrument and equipment repairers	65	2.9	0	0.0	150	6.7	20	0.9	10	0.4
7510	Coin, vending, and amusement machine servicers and repairers	35	5.4	0	0.0	85	13.1	0	0.0	0	0.0
7540	Locksmiths and safe repairers	10	2.6	0	0.0	25	6.5	0	0.0	0	0.0
7550	Manufactured building and mobile home installers	0	0.0	0	0.0	0	0.0	0	0.0	0	0.0
7560	Riggers	0	0.0	0	0.0	0	0.0	0	0.0	0	0.0
7610	Helpers—installation, maintenance, and repair workers	0	0.0	0	0.0	0	0.0	0	0.0	0	0.0
7630	Other installation, maintenance, and repair workers, including wind turbine service technicians, and commercial divers, and signal and track switch repairers	135	4.6	25	0.9	200	6.8	0	0.0	23	0.8
7700	First-line supervisors of production and operating workers	2,590	8.7	35	0.1	3,600	12.1	25	0.1	175	0.6
7710	Aircraft structure, surfaces, rigging, and systems assemblers	0	0.0	0	0.0	40	61.5	0	0.0	0	0.0
7720	Electrical, electronics, and electromechanical assemblers	25	2.2	0	0.0	285	25.1	20	1.8	15	1.3
7730	Engine and other machine assemblers	20	33.3	0	0.0	0	0.0	0	0.0	0	0.0
7740	Structural metal fabricators and fitters	10	5.6	0	0.0	0	0.0	0	0.0	0	0.0
7750	Miscellaneous assemblers and fabricators	460	8.2	15	0.3	600	10.6	0	0.0	23	0.4
7800	Bakers	45	2.3	0	0.0	195	10.0	0	0.0	70	3.6
7810	Butchers and other meat, poultry, and fish processing workers	125	14.0	0	0.0	35	3.9	0	0.0	14	1.6
7830	Food and tobacco roasting, baking, and drying machine operators and tenders	20	26.7	0	0.0	0	0.0	0	0.0	0	0.0
7840	Food batchmakers	4	0.9	0	0.0	135	29.7	10	2.2	0	0.0
7850	Food cooking machine operators and tenders	0	0.0	0	0.0	0	0.0	0	0.0	0	0.0
7855	Food processing workers, all other	100	14.9	0	0.0	95	14.2	55	8.2	20	3.0
7900	Computer control programmers and operators	30	4.7	0	0.0	60	9.3	0	0.0	0	0.0

A-22 **Workers with Graduate or Professional Degree: Detailed Occupations, by Sex, Race, and Hispanic Origin, 2006–2010**—*Continued*

Census occupation code	Detailed Occupation	Total	Graduate or Professional degree						Not Hispanic or Latino, one race	
			Male		Female		Hispanic or Latino		White alone	
			Number	Percent	Number	Percent	Number	Percent	Number	Percent
7920	Extruding and drawing machine setters, operators, and tenders, metal and plastic..................	35	35	100.0	0	0.0	0	0.0	15	42.9
7930	Forging machine setters, operators, and tenders, metal and plastic................................	10	10	100.0	0	0.0	0	0.0	10	100.0
7940	Rolling machine setters, operators, and tenders, metal and plastic................................	50	50	100.0	0	0.0	35	70.0	15	30.0
7950	Cutting, punching, and press machine setters, operators, and tenders, metal and plastic	335	260	77.6	75	22.4	95	28.4	165	49.3
7960	Drilling and boring machine tool setters, operators, and tenders, metal and plastic	0	0	0	0	0	0	0	0	0
8000	Grinding, lapping, polishing, and buffing machine tool setters, operators, and tenders, metal and plastic...	245	185	75.5	55	22.4	115	46.9	120	49.0
8010	Lathe and turning machine tool setters, operators, and tenders, metal and plastic.................	50	25	50.0	25	50.0	10	20.0	25	50.0
8030	Machinists	1,740	1,685	96.8	50	2.9	150	8.6	1,265	72.7
8040	Metal furnace operators, tenders, pourers, and casters..	95	95	100.0	0	0.0	25	26.3	60	63.2
8060	Model makers and patternmakers, metal and plastic...	210	165	78.6	50	23.8	0	0.0	195	92.9
8100	Molders and molding machine setters, operators, and tenders, metal and plastic.................	120	95	79.2	25	20.8	45	37.5	65	54.2
8130	Tool and die makers	470	470	100.0	0	0.0	34	7.2	430	91.5
8140	Welding, soldering, and brazing workers.............	1,525	1,365	89.5	155	10.2	375	24.6	880	57.7
8150	Heat treating equipment setters, operators, and tenders, metal and plastic.............................	20	20	100.0	0	0.0	0	0.0	0	0.0
8200	Plating and coating machine setters, operators, and tenders, metal and plastic.......................	180	165	91.7	10	5.6	40	22.2	115	63.9
8210	Tool grinders, filers, and sharpeners	50	40	80.0	10	20.0	10	20.0	40	80.0
8220	Miscellaneous metal workers and plastic workers, including milling and planing machine setters, and multiple machine tool setters, and layout workers...	1,980	1,520	76.8	460	23.2	560	28.3	900	45.5
8250	Prepress technicians and workers......................	865	450	52.0	420	48.6	30	3.5	695	80.3
8255	Printing press operators	1,965	1,430	72.8	535	27.2	175	8.9	1,480	75.3
8256	Print binding and finishing workers....................	550	235	42.7	315	57.3	55	10.0	440	80.0
8300	Laundry and dry-cleaning workers.....................	1,440	840	58.3	600	41.7	505	35.1	415	28.8
8310	Pressers, textile, garment, and related materials.....	250	80	32.0	170	68.0	130	52.0	60	24.0
8320	Sewing machine operators................................	1,655	190	11.5	1,460	88.2	510	30.8	1,030	62.2
8330	Shoe and leather workers and repairers	135	125	92.6	10	7.4	0	0.0	100	74.1
8340	Shoe machine operators and tenders..................	35	35	100.0	0	0.0	0	0.0	30	85.7
8350	Tailors, dressmakers, and sewers.......................	2,215	525	23.7	1,690	76.3	215	9.7	1,690	76.3
8400	Textile bleaching and dyeing, and cutting machine setters, operators, and tenders	65	40	61.5	30	46.2	0	0.0	35	53.8
8410	Textile knitting and weaving machine setters, operators, and tenders.................................	90	0	0.0	90	100.0	0	0.0	75	83.3
8420	Textile winding, twisting, and drawing out machine setters, operators, and tenders	25	10	40.0	20	80.0	10	40.0	20	80.0
8450	Upholsterers...	320	255	79.7	65	20.3	55	17.2	235	73.4

PART A—NATIONAL DATA

A-22 **Workers with Graduate or Professional Degree: Detailed Occupations, by Sex, Race, and Hispanic Origin, 2006–2010**—*Continued*

Census occupation code	Detailed Occupation	Graduate or Professional degree									
		Not Hispanic or Latino, one race								Not Hispanic or Latino, two or more races	
		Black or African American alone		American Indian and Alaska Native alone		Asian alone		Native Hawaiian and Other Pacific Islander alone			
		Number	Percent	Number	Percent	Number	Percent	Number	Percent	Number	Percent
7920	Extruding and drawing machine setters, operators, and tenders, metal and plastic	20	57.1	0	0.0	0	0.0	0	0.0	0	0.0
7930	Forging machine setters, operators, and tenders, metal and plastic	0	0.0	0	0.0	0	0.0	0	0.0	0	0.0
7940	Rolling machine setters, operators, and tenders, metal and plastic	0	0.0	0	0.0	0	0.0	0	0.0	0	0.0
7950	Cutting, punching, and press machine setters, operators, and tenders, metal and plastic	20	6.0	0	0.0	60	17.9	0	0.0	0	0.0
7960	Drilling and boring machine tool setters, operators, and tenders, metal and plastic	0	0	0	0	0	0	0	0	0	0
8000	Grinding, lapping, polishing, and buffing machine tool setters, operators, and tenders, metal and plastic	0	0.0	0	0.0	10	4.1	0	0.0	0	0.0
8010	Lathe and turning machine tool setters, operators, and tenders, metal and plastic	0	0.0	0	0.0	15	30.0	0	0.0	0	0.0
8030	Machinists	160	9.2	20	1.1	70	4.0	0	0.0	75	4.3
8040	Metal furnace operators, tenders, pourers, and casters	0	0.0	0	0.0	15	15.8	0	0.0	0	0.0
8060	Model makers and patternmakers, metal and plastic	15	7.1	0	0.0	4	1.9	0	0.0	0	0.0
8100	Molders and molding machine setters, operators, and tenders, metal and plastic	0	0.0	0	0.0	0	0.0	0	0.0	10	8.3
8130	Tool and die makers	4	0.9	0	0.0	0	0.0	0	0.0	4	0.9
8140	Welding, soldering, and brazing workers	125	8.2	0	0.0	130	8.5	0	0.0	20	1.3
8150	Heat treating equipment setters, operators, and tenders, metal and plastic	10	50.0	0	0.0	10	50.0	0	0.0	0	0.0
8200	Plating and coating machine setters, operators, and tenders, metal and plastic	0	0.0	0	0.0	20	11.1	0	0.0	0	0.0
8210	Tool grinders, filers, and sharpeners	0	0.0	0	0.0	0	0.0	0	0.0	0	0.0
8220	Miscellaneous metal workers and plastic workers, including milling and planing machine setters, and multiple machine tool setters, and layout workers	190	9.6	0	0.0	330	16.7	0	0.0	0	0.0
8250	Prepress technicians and workers	20	2.3	20	2.3	105	12.1	0	0.0	0	0.0
8255	Printing press operators	90	4.6	0	0.0	170	8.7	0	0.0	54	2.7
8256	Print binding and finishing workers	35	6.4	0	0.0	20	3.6	0	0.0	0	0.0
8300	Laundry and dry-cleaning workers	60	4.2	0	0.0	415	28.8	4	0.3	30	2.1
8310	Pressers, textile, garment, and related materials	0	0.0	0	0.0	65	26.0	0	0.0	0	0.0
8320	Sewing machine operators	10	0.6	0	0.0	95	5.7	0	0.0	4	0.2
8330	Shoe and leather workers and repairers	0	0.0	0	0.0	30	22.2	0	0.0	10	7.4
8340	Shoe machine operators and tenders	0	0.0	0	0.0	10	28.6	0	0.0	0	0.0
8350	Tailors, dressmakers, and sewers	90	4.1	0	0.0	220	9.9	0	0.0	0	0.0
8400	Textile bleaching and dyeing, and cutting machine setters, operators, and tenders	0	0.0	0	0.0	30	46.2	0	0.0	0	0.0
8410	Textile knitting and weaving machine setters, operators, and tenders	10	11.1	0	0.0	0	0.0	0	0.0	4	4.4
8420	Textile winding, twisting, and drawing out machine setters, operators, and tenders	0	0.0	0	0.0	0	0.0	0	0.0	0	0.0
8450	Upholsterers	25	7.8	0	0.0	0	0.0	0	0.0	0	0.0

A-22 **Workers with Graduate or Professional Degree: Detailed Occupations, by Sex, Race, and Hispanic Origin, 2006–2010**—*Continued*

Census occupation code	Detailed Occupation	Total	Male Number	Male Percent	Female Number	Female Percent	Hispanic or Latino Number	Hispanic or Latino Percent	Not Hispanic or Latino, one race White alone Number	Not Hispanic or Latino, one race White alone Percent
8460	Miscellaneous textile, apparel, and furnishings workers, except upholsterers	430	130	30.2	300	69.8	15	3.5	370	86.0
8500	Cabinetmakers and bench carpenters	885	825	93.2	60	6.8	85	9.6	800	90.4
8510	Furniture finishers	300	190	63.3	110	36.7	35	11.7	260	86.7
8530	Sawing machine setters, operators, and tenders, wood	225	200	88.9	25	11.1	35	15.6	170	75.6
8540	Woodworking machine setters, operators, and tenders, except sawing	320	225	70.3	90	28.1	85	26.6	175	54.7
8550	Miscellaneous woodworkers, including model makers and patternmakers	625	575	92.0	50	8.0	14	2.2	565	90.4
8600	Power plant operators, distributors, and dispatchers	935	835	89.3	95	10.2	70	7.5	765	81.8
8610	Stationary engineers and boiler operators	2,075	1,870	90.1	205	9.9	235	11.3	1,395	67.2
8620	Water and wastewater treatment plant and system operators	960	860	89.6	100	10.4	120	12.5	660	68.8
8630	Miscellaneous plant and system operators	440	420	95.5	15	3.4	55	12.5	275	62.5
8640	Chemical processing machine setters, operators, and tenders	1,510	1,120	74.2	390	25.8	85	5.6	1,045	69.2
8650	Crushing, grinding, polishing, mixing, and blending workers	690	415	60.1	275	39.9	15	2.2	550	79.7
8710	Cutting workers	300	195	65.0	110	36.7	160	53.3	95	31.7
8720	Extruding, forming, pressing, and compacting machine setters, operators, and tenders	65	65	100.0	0	0.0	0	0.0	40	61.5
8730	Furnace, kiln, oven, drier, and kettle operators and tenders	35	10	28.6	25	71.4	0	0.0	30	85.7
8740	Inspectors, testers, sorters, samplers, and weighers	21,170	11,585	54.7	9,585	45.3	1,555	7.3	13,665	64.5
8750	Jewelers and precious stone and metal workers	1,650	760	46.1	895	54.2	145	8.8	1,390	84.2
8760	Medical, dental, and ophthalmic laboratory technicians	2,165	1,205	55.7	960	44.3	315	14.5	1,255	58.0
8800	Packaging and filling machine operators and tenders	1,395	735	52.7	660	47.3	475	34.1	530	38.0
8810	Painting workers	785	645	82.2	140	17.8	195	24.8	440	56.1
8830	Photographic process workers and processing machine operators	1,680	920	54.8	760	45.2	185	11.0	835	49.7
8850	Adhesive bonding machine operators and tenders	55	40	72.7	15	27.3	35	63.6	4	7.3
8860	Cleaning, washing, and metal pickling equipment operators and tenders	10	0	0.0	10	100.0	0	0.0	10	100.0
8910	Etchers and engravers	210	130	61.9	80	38.1	30	14.3	175	83.3
8920	Molders, shapers, and casters, except metal and plastic	1,270	910	71.7	360	28.3	80	6.3	1,090	85.8
8930	Paper goods machine setters, operators, and tenders	110	100	90.9	10	9.1	0	0.0	55	50.0
8940	Tire builders	55	35	63.6	20	36.4	10	18.2	50	90.9
8950	Helpers—production workers	235	160	68.1	80	34.0	20	8.5	180	76.6
8965	Other production workers, including semiconductor processors and cooling and freezing equipment operators	8,435	5,725	67.9	2,710	32.1	1,350	16.0	5,120	60.7
9000	Supervisors of transportation and material moving workers	5,770	4,295	74.4	1,475	25.6	325	5.6	4,045	70.1

A-22 Workers with Graduate or Professional Degree: Detailed Occupations, by Sex, Race, and Hispanic Origin, 2006–2010—*Continued*

			Graduate or Professional degree						
		colspan="8"	Not Hispanic or Latino, one race					Not Hispanic or Latino, two or more races	
Census occupation code	Detailed Occupation	Black or African American alone		American Indian and Alaska Native alone		Asian alone		Native Hawaiian and Other Pacific Islander alone		
		Number	Percent	Number	Percent	Number	Percent	Number	Percent	Number	Percent
---	---	---	---	---	---	---	---	---	---	---	---
8460	Miscellaneous textile, apparel, and furnishings workers, except upholsterers............	35	8.1	0	0.0	10	2.3	0	0.0	0	0.0
8500	Cabinetmakers and bench carpenters........	0	0.0	0	0.0	0	0.0	0	0.0	0	0.0
8510	Furniture finishers............	10	3.3	0	0.0	0	0.0	0	0.0	0	0.0
8530	Sawing machine setters, operators, and tenders, wood............	0	0.0	0	0.0	15	6.7	0	0.0	0	0.0
8540	Woodworking machine setters, operators, and tenders, except sawing............	55	17.2	0	0.0	0	0.0	0	0.0	0	0.0
8550	Miscellaneous woodworkers, including model makers and patternmakers............	4	0.6	10	1.6	10	1.6	0	0.0	14	2.2
8600	Power plant operators, distributors, and dispatchers............	60	6.4	0	0.0	10	1.1	0	0.0	25	2.7
8610	Stationary engineers and boiler operators............	225	10.8	35	1.7	195	9.4	0	0.0	0	0.0
8620	Water and wastewater treatment plant and system operators............	90	9.4	4	0.4	50	5.2	0	0.0	35	3.6
8630	Miscellaneous plant and system operators............	50	11.4	0	0.0	40	9.1	0	0.0	15	3.4
8640	Chemical processing machine setters, operators, and tenders............	160	10.6	10	0.7	215	14.2	0	0.0	0	0.0
8650	Crushing, grinding, polishing, mixing, and blending workers............	65	9.4	10	1.4	25	3.6	0	0.0	20	2.9
8710	Cutting workers............	10	3.3	0	0.0	35	11.7	0	0.0	0	0.0
8720	Extruding, forming, pressing, and compacting machine setters, operators, and tenders............	0	0.0	0	0.0	25	38.5	0	0.0	0	0.0
8730	Furnace, kiln, oven, drier, and kettle operators and tenders............	10	28.6	0	0.0	0	0.0	0	0.0	4	11.4
8740	Inspectors, testers, sorters, samplers, and weighers	1,755	8.3	75	0.4	3,860	18.2	35	0.2	215	1.0
8750	Jewelers and precious stone and metal workers.....	25	1.5	4	0.2	50	3.0	0	0.0	39	2.4
8760	Medical, dental, and ophthalmic laboratory technicians............	225	10.4	0	0.0	360	16.6	0	0.0	10	0.5
8800	Packaging and filling machine operators and tenders............	60	4.3	4	0.3	310	22.2	0	0.0	15	1.1
8810	Painting workers............	20	2.5	0	0.0	35	4.5	0	0.0	95	12.1
8830	Photographic process workers and processing machine operators............	110	6.5	0	0.0	510	30.4	0	0.0	40	2.4
8850	Adhesive bonding machine operators and tenders.	4	7.3	0	0.0	15	27.3	0	0.0	0	0.0
8860	Cleaning, washing, and metal pickling equipment operators and tenders............	0	0.0	0	0.0	0	0.0	0	0.0	0	0.0
8910	Etchers and engravers............	0	0.0	0	0.0	0	0.0	0	0.0	0	0.0
8920	Molders, shapers, and casters, except metal and plastic............	15	1.2	0	0.0	45	3.5	0	0.0	35	2.8
8930	Paper goods machine setters, operators, and tenders............	20	18.2	0	0.0	10	9.1	25	22.7	0	0.0
8940	Tire builders............	0	0.0	0	0.0	0	0.0	0	0.0	0	0.0
8950	Helpers—production workers............	4	1.7	0	0.0	35	14.9	0	0.0	0	0.0
8965	Other production workers, including semiconductor processors and cooling and freezing equipment operators............	865	10.3	15	0.2	910	10.8	45	0.5	130	1.5
9000	Supervisors of transportation and material moving workers............	685	11.9	30	0.5	570	9.9	45	0.8	65	1.1

A-22 **Workers with Graduate or Professional Degree: Detailed Occupations, by Sex, Race, and Hispanic Origin, 2006–2010**—*Continued*

Census occupation code	Detailed Occupation	Total	Male Number	Male Percent	Female Number	Female Percent	Hispanic or Latino Number	Hispanic or Latino Percent	Not Hispanic or Latino, one race White alone Number	Not Hispanic or Latino, one race White alone Percent
9030	Aircraft pilots and flight engineers	15,660	15,060	96.2	600	3.8	465	3.0	14,395	91.9
9040	Air traffic controllers and airfield operations specialists	1,255	900	71.7	360	28.7	70	5.6	1,060	84.5
9050	Flight attendants	3,045	820	26.9	2,230	73.2	265	8.7	2,280	74.9
9110	Ambulance drivers and attendants, except emergency medical technicians	280	270	96.4	10	3.6	20	7.1	240	85.7
9120	Bus drivers	8,340	6,830	81.9	1,510	18.1	575	6.9	5,980	71.7
9130	Driver/sales workers and truck drivers	22,645	21,325	94.2	1,325	5.9	3,885	17.2	15,105	66.7
9140	Taxi drivers and chauffeurs	9,535	8,940	93.8	595	6.2	615	6.4	5,190	54.4
9150	Motor vehicle operators, all other	970	910	93.8	60	6.2	30	3.1	890	91.8
9200	Locomotive engineers and operators	700	685	97.9	20	2.9	30	4.3	465	66.4
9230	Railroad brake, signal, and switch operators	25	25	100.0	0	0.0	0	0.0	15	60.0
9240	Railroad conductors and yardmasters	475	405	85.3	70	14.7	10	2.1	450	94.7
9260	Subway, streetcar, and other rail transportation workers	185	140	75.7	45	24.3	0	0.0	145	78.4
9300	Sailors and marine oilers, and ship engineers	470	450	95.7	20	4.3	24	5.1	430	91.5
9310	Ship and boat captains and operators	1,030	980	95.1	50	4.9	35	3.4	990	96.1
9350	Parking lot attendants	1,090	1,065	97.7	25	2.3	290	26.6	420	38.5
9360	Automotive and watercraft service attendants	770	575	74.7	195	25.3	70	9.1	500	64.9
9410	Transportation inspectors	1,115	990	88.8	125	11.2	140	12.6	855	76.7
9415	Transportation attendants, except flight attendants	500	235	47.0	265	53.0	25	5.0	350	70.0
9420	Miscellaneous transportation workers, including bridge and lock tenders and traffic technicians	545	405	74.3	140	25.7	30	5.5	330	60.6
9510	Crane and tower operators	170	170	100.0	0	0.0	40	23.5	125	73.5
9520	Dredge, excavating, and loading machine operators	245	235	95.9	10	4.1	25	10.2	175	71.4
9560	Conveyor operators and tenders, and hoist and winch operators	115	90	78.3	25	21.7	15	13.0	65	56.5
9600	Industrial truck and tractor operators	1,410	1,315	93.3	95	6.7	490	34.8	560	39.7
9610	Cleaners of vehicles and equipment	1,245	1,055	84.7	190	15.3	335	26.9	650	52.2
9620	Laborers and freight, stock, and material movers, hand	11,505	9,405	81.7	2,100	18.3	2,080	18.1	6,960	60.5
9630	Machine feeders and offbearers	165	50	30.3	120	72.7	90	54.5	55	33.3
9640	Packers and packagers, hand	2,210	1,295	58.6	910	41.2	510	23.1	1,130	51.1
9650	Pumping station operators	115	75	65.2	40	34.8	0	0.0	60	52.2
9720	Refuse and recyclable material collectors	535	320	59.8	210	39.3	65	12.1	415	77.6
9750	Miscellaneous material moving workers, including mine shuttle car operators, and tank car, truck, and ship loaders	275	185	67.3	90	32.7	80	29.1	170	61.8

PART A—NATIONAL DATA

A-22 Workers with Graduate or Professional Degree: Detailed Occupations, by Sex, Race, and Hispanic Origin, 2006–2010—Continued

Census occupation code	Detailed Occupation	Black or African American alone Number	Black or African American alone Percent	American Indian and Alaska Native alone Number	American Indian and Alaska Native alone Percent	Asian alone Number	Asian alone Percent	Native Hawaiian and Other Pacific Islander alone Number	Native Hawaiian and Other Pacific Islander alone Percent	Not Hispanic or Latino, two or more races Number	Not Hispanic or Latino, two or more races Percent
9030	Aircraft pilots and flight engineers	235	1.5	15	0.1	325	2.1	20	0.1	215	1.4
9040	Air traffic controllers and airfield operations specialists	95	7.6	4	0.3	20	1.6	0	0.0	10	0.8
9050	Flight attendants	235	7.7	25	0.8	190	6.2	0	0.0	50	1.6
9110	Ambulance drivers and attendants, except emergency medical technicians	0	0.0	15	5.4	10	3.6	0	0.0	0	0.0
9120	Bus drivers	1,390	16.7	25	0.3	200	2.4	0	0.0	170	2.0
9130	Driver/sales workers and truck drivers	2,205	9.7	50	0.2	1,030	4.5	10	0.0	355	1.6
9140	Taxi drivers and chauffeurs	1,920	20.1	20	0.2	1,650	17.3	0	0.0	140	1.5
9150	Motor vehicle operators, all other	40	4.1	0	0.0	0	0.0	0	0.0	15	1.5
9200	Locomotive engineers and operators	115	16.4	0	0.0	95	13.6	0	0.0	0	0.0
9230	Railroad brake, signal, and switch operators	0	0.0	0	0.0	0	0.0	0	0.0	10	40.0
9240	Railroad conductors and yardmasters	10	2.1	0	0.0	0	0.0	0	0.0	4	0.8
9260	Subway, streetcar, and other rail transportation workers	35	18.9	4	2.2	0	0.0	0	0.0	0	0.0
9300	Sailors and marine oilers, and ship engineers	0	0.0	0	0.0	20	4.3	0	0.0	0	0.0
9310	Ship and boat captains and operators	0	0.0	0	0.0	4	0.4	0	0.0	0	0.0
9350	Parking lot attendants	185	17.0	0	0.0	200	18.3	0	0.0	0	0.0
9360	Automotive and watercraft service attendants	50	6.5	40	5.2	115	14.9	0	0.0	0	0.0
9410	Transportation inspectors	50	4.5	0	0.0	70	6.3	4	0.4	0	0.0
9415	Transportation attendants, except flight attendants	35	7.0	0	0.0	85	17.0	0	0.0	0	0.0
9420	Miscellaneous transportation workers, including bridge and lock tenders and traffic technicians	55	10.1	0	0.0	130	23.9	0	0.0	0	0.0
9510	Crane and tower operators	0	0.0	4	2.4	0	0.0	0	0.0	0	0.0
9520	Dredge, excavating, and loading machine operators	35	14.3	0	0.0	10	4.1	0	0.0	0	0.0
9560	Conveyor operators and tenders, and hoist and winch operators	35	30.4	0	0.0	0	0.0	0	0.0	0	0.0
9600	Industrial truck and tractor operators	235	16.7	0	0.0	110	7.8	0	0.0	15	1.1
9610	Cleaners of vehicles and equipment	195	15.7	10	0.8	45	3.6	0	0.0	14	1.1
9620	Laborers and freight, stock, and material movers, hand	1,490	13.0	100	0.9	740	6.4	4	0.0	124	1.1
9630	Machine feeders and offbearers	10	6.1	0	0.0	15	9.1	0	0.0	0	0.0
9640	Packers and packagers, hand	150	6.8	40	1.8	340	15.4	0	0.0	40	1.8
9650	Pumping station operators	40	34.8	15	13.0	0	0.0	0	0.0	0	0.0
9720	Refuse and recyclable material collectors	10	1.9	0	0.0	0	0.0	10	1.9	30	5.6
9750	Miscellaneous material moving workers, including mine shuttle car operators, and tank car, truck, and ship loaders	4	1.5	0	0.0	20	7.3	0	0.0	0	0.0

PART B

State Data

PART B—STATE TABLES

B-1 All Workers, by State and Occupation Group, 2006–2010

State	Total who worked in the last 5 years Number	Percent	Management, business, and financial workers Number	Percent	Science, engineering, and computer professionals Number	Percent	Health care practitioner professionals Number	Percent	Other professional workers Number	Percent
United States	154,037,475	100.0	18,514,755	12.0	5,907,405	3.8	5,041,270	3.3	16,723,700	10.9
Alabama	2,230,880	100.0	221,485	9.9	69,550	3.1	73,725	3.3	211,625	9.5
Alaska	363,355	100.0	42,405	11.7	15,295	4.2	10,540	2.9	39,215	10.8
Arizona	2,975,165	100.0	366,105	12.3	120,405	4.0	93,815	3.2	299,710	10.1
Arkansas	1,360,940	100.0	137,885	10.1	27,865	2.0	44,670	3.3	125,370	9.2
California	18,274,870	100.0	2,283,685	12.5	827,650	4.5	518,360	2.8	2,062,235	11.3
Colorado	2,636,625	100.0	374,815	14.2	152,625	5.8	83,140	3.2	290,555	11.0
Connecticut	1,910,905	100.0	256,775	13.4	86,220	4.5	69,880	3.7	242,105	12.7
Delaware	451,135	100.0	58,180	12.9	17,750	3.9	16,245	3.6	48,765	10.8
District of Columbia	328,035	100.0	62,195	19.0	19,530	6.0	6,480	2.0	74,200	22.6
Florida	9,128,080	100.0	1,098,395	12.0	264,810	2.9	292,705	3.2	886,050	9.7
Georgia	4,713,920	100.0	590,245	12.5	169,290	3.6	131,950	2.8	497,825	10.6
Hawaii	674,470	100.0	76,650	11.4	20,810	3.1	20,390	3.0	77,255	11.5
Idaho	751,480	100.0	88,250	11.7	27,490	3.7	22,885	3.0	71,320	9.5
Illinois	6,632,590	100.0	819,820	12.4	248,460	3.7	217,910	3.3	729,300	11.0
Indiana	3,274,430	100.0	343,525	10.5	97,980	3.0	107,595	3.3	303,005	9.3
Iowa	1,640,080	100.0	197,025	12.0	46,845	2.9	55,740	3.4	164,995	10.1
Kansas	1,479,515	100.0	183,390	12.4	51,380	3.5	52,930	3.6	162,505	11.0
Kentucky	2,038,920	100.0	209,670	10.3	49,585	2.4	75,080	3.7	197,015	9.7
Louisiana	2,116,795	100.0	206,110	9.7	46,000	2.2	70,630	3.3	207,745	9.8
Maine	703,390	100.0	79,590	11.3	19,940	2.8	26,935	3.8	79,525	11.3
Maryland	3,107,930	100.0	455,235	14.6	208,910	6.7	111,915	3.6	392,040	12.6
Massachusetts	3,531,260	100.0	487,985	13.8	205,130	5.8	143,445	4.1	470,150	13.3
Michigan	4,938,335	100.0	524,445	10.6	197,715	4.0	165,545	3.4	477,030	9.7
Minnesota	2,916,930	100.0	390,150	13.4	126,515	4.3	102,840	3.5	321,010	11.0
Mississippi	1,345,155	100.0	123,375	9.2	25,355	1.9	46,955	3.5	125,310	9.3
Missouri	3,020,900	100.0	347,305	11.5	93,840	3.1	101,875	3.4	309,565	10.2
Montana	504,880	100.0	65,730	13.0	15,125	3.0	17,135	3.4	52,295	10.4
Nebraska	988,060	100.0	129,375	13.1	28,910	2.9	35,425	3.6	99,370	10.1
Nevada	1,377,920	100.0	142,790	10.4	31,380	2.3	33,000	2.4	114,040	8.3
New Hampshire	738,510	100.0	96,500	13.1	39,645	5.4	27,490	3.7	79,485	10.8
New Jersey	4,587,250	100.0	622,305	13.6	214,750	4.7	159,255	3.5	553,275	12.1
New Mexico	957,905	100.0	103,485	10.8	39,125	4.1	28,805	3.0	105,630	11.0
New York	9,781,730	100.0	1,153,145	11.8	305,850	3.1	367,395	3.8	1,339,795	13.7
North Carolina	4,640,230	100.0	531,295	11.4	154,850	3.3	156,105	3.4	490,010	10.6
North Dakota	365,155	100.0	49,700	13.6	10,425	2.9	12,315	3.4	35,665	9.8
Ohio	5,877,985	100.0	645,840	11.0	197,175	3.4	213,100	3.6	580,780	9.9
Oklahoma	1,785,480	100.0	196,195	11.0	48,110	2.7	52,320	2.9	183,020	10.3
Oregon	1,931,995	100.0	236,540	12.2	79,170	4.1	61,555	3.2	201,400	10.4
Pennsylvania	6,408,620	100.0	726,845	11.3	229,190	3.6	252,745	3.9	691,240	10.8
Rhode Island	560,550	100.0	64,475	11.5	20,005	3.6	21,670	3.9	66,305	11.8
South Carolina	2,206,485	100.0	232,560	10.5	60,610	2.7	70,430	3.2	211,710	9.6
South Dakota	430,310	100.0	58,130	13.5	10,795	2.5	16,460	3.8	42,740	9.9
Tennessee	3,081,950	100.0	325,475	10.6	83,505	2.7	106,235	3.4	300,375	9.7
Texas	11,962,845	100.0	1,414,045	11.8	456,760	3.8	323,505	2.7	1,259,015	10.5
Utah	1,313,655	100.0	158,570	12.1	55,330	4.2	35,900	2.7	144,410	11.0
Vermont	350,300	100.0	44,930	12.8	12,530	3.6	13,060	3.7	46,305	13.2
Virginia	4,065,245	100.0	587,575	14.5	252,460	6.2	123,045	3.0	493,250	12.1
Washington	3,380,745	100.0	447,335	13.2	194,965	5.8	107,490	3.2	357,265	10.6
West Virginia	822,340	100.0	70,810	8.6	17,850	2.2	31,240	3.8	79,045	9.6
Wisconsin	3,073,910	100.0	352,235	11.5	103,780	3.4	103,190	3.4	303,410	9.9
Wyoming	297,310	100.0	34,160	11.5	8,175	2.7	8,225	2.8	28,420	9.6

B-1 All Workers, by State and Occupation Group, 2006–2010—Continued

State	Technicians Number	Technicians Percent	Sales workers Number	Sales workers Percent	Administrative support workers Number	Administrative support workers Percent	Construction and extractive craft workers Number	Construction and extractive craft workers Percent	Installation, maintenance, and repair craft workers Number	Installation, maintenance, and repair craft workers Percent
United States	4,244,165	2.8	17,256,510	11.2	23,586,105	15.3	9,205,480	6.0	6,316,335	4.1
Alabama	68,020	3.0	255,510	11.5	326,860	14.7	150,015	6.7	112,255	5.0
Alaska	10,355	2.8	31,815	8.8	60,410	16.6	30,045	8.3	16,805	4.6
Arizona	79,810	2.7	360,160	12.1	479,215	16.1	205,910	6.9	124,800	4.2
Arkansas	40,430	3.0	150,420	11.1	198,390	14.6	87,015	6.4	64,260	4.7
California	441,475	2.4	2,097,545	11.5	2,752,860	15.1	1,036,330	5.7	663,530	3.6
Colorado	67,245	2.6	304,425	11.5	384,820	14.6	185,420	7.0	101,245	3.8
Connecticut	52,650	2.8	216,550	11.3	290,655	15.2	99,100	5.2	73,500	3.8
Delaware	13,485	3.0	49,070	10.9	74,765	16.6	26,620	5.9	17,600	3.9
District of Columbia	6,085	1.9	22,025	6.7	51,620	15.7	7,915	2.4	4,380	1.3
Florida	246,560	2.7	1,208,925	13.2	1,463,445	16.0	601,425	6.6	367,040	4.0
Georgia	123,850	2.6	564,910	12.0	702,460	14.9	293,645	6.2	202,140	4.3
Hawaii	15,020	2.2	77,945	11.6	106,585	15.8	46,365	6.9	25,245	3.7
Idaho	21,075	2.8	80,265	10.7	113,305	15.1	57,480	7.6	32,715	4.4
Illinois	165,930	2.5	739,955	11.2	1,042,310	15.7	343,475	5.2	249,740	3.8
Indiana	93,005	2.8	346,320	10.6	482,465	14.7	186,080	5.7	161,665	4.9
Iowa	44,715	2.7	167,130	10.2	250,295	15.3	89,090	5.4	69,440	4.2
Kansas	40,755	2.8	150,995	10.2	231,000	15.6	86,565	5.9	66,910	4.5
Kentucky	58,740	2.9	216,020	10.6	312,830	15.3	132,925	6.5	92,685	4.5
Louisiana	68,220	3.2	239,715	11.3	319,280	15.1	178,860	8.4	99,400	4.7
Maine	19,005	2.7	76,980	10.9	101,175	14.4	48,700	6.9	32,490	4.6
Maryland	91,490	2.9	306,180	9.9	491,010	15.8	171,810	5.5	111,330	3.6
Massachusetts	104,340	3.0	373,000	10.6	528,180	15.0	175,840	5.0	115,670	3.3
Michigan	135,945	2.8	534,985	10.8	726,595	14.7	238,200	4.8	223,995	4.5
Minnesota	91,645	3.1	320,270	11.0	438,920	15.0	150,445	5.2	118,180	4.1
Mississippi	40,885	3.0	146,530	10.9	189,945	14.1	96,400	7.2	63,840	4.7
Missouri	91,705	3.0	338,585	11.2	468,105	15.5	181,530	6.0	130,680	4.3
Montana	12,020	2.4	53,030	10.5	74,280	14.7	41,770	8.3	22,445	4.4
Nebraska	28,685	2.9	104,185	10.5	155,560	15.7	52,980	5.4	40,490	4.1
Nevada	30,335	2.2	164,670	12.0	207,885	15.1	110,945	8.1	49,415	3.6
New Hampshire	23,430	3.2	87,950	11.9	110,545	15.0	44,180	6.0	31,670	4.3
New Jersey	127,025	2.8	535,245	11.7	758,100	16.5	225,205	4.9	155,945	3.4
New Mexico	28,325	3.0	101,735	10.6	144,400	15.1	75,840	7.9	44,750	4.7
New York	239,175	2.4	1,064,945	10.9	1,581,430	16.2	485,580	5.0	325,710	3.3
North Carolina	134,295	2.9	526,510	11.3	657,415	14.2	300,020	6.5	214,480	4.6
North Dakota	10,910	3.0	38,730	10.6	53,560	14.7	24,700	6.8	15,885	4.4
Ohio	176,110	3.0	623,495	10.6	902,380	15.4	289,700	4.9	261,560	4.4
Oklahoma	55,120	3.1	192,740	10.8	280,550	15.7	126,725	7.1	92,830	5.2
Oregon	48,390	2.5	210,775	10.9	295,295	15.3	111,145	5.8	75,605	3.9
Pennsylvania	201,865	3.1	678,620	10.6	1,015,505	15.8	339,535	5.3	274,820	4.3
Rhode Island	14,765	2.6	60,265	10.8	88,355	15.8	28,690	5.1	20,530	3.7
South Carolina	64,330	2.9	259,915	11.8	321,010	14.5	141,975	6.4	107,900	4.9
South Dakota	12,060	2.8	43,910	10.2	67,085	15.6	24,945	5.8	18,595	4.3
Tennessee	98,240	3.2	351,715	11.4	466,945	15.2	187,580	6.1	137,080	4.4
Texas	331,955	2.8	1,376,480	11.5	1,827,485	15.3	867,480	7.3	522,570	4.4
Utah	37,960	2.9	156,125	11.9	220,930	16.8	89,390	6.8	56,175	4.3
Vermont	10,120	2.9	35,685	10.2	50,115	14.3	23,220	6.6	15,050	4.3
Virginia	111,495	2.7	422,885	10.4	598,125	14.7	243,425	6.0	159,705	3.9
Washington	90,795	2.7	360,730	10.7	491,870	14.5	197,940	5.9	135,340	4.0
West Virginia	28,680	3.5	88,930	10.8	122,970	15.0	73,055	8.9	39,895	4.9
Wisconsin	88,565	2.9	313,095	10.2	463,190	15.1	159,410	5.2	140,710	4.6
Wyoming	7,080	2.4	27,915	9.4	43,600	14.7	32,840	11.0	15,640	5.3

B-1 All Workers, by State and Occupation Group, 2006–2010—Continued

State	Production operative workers Number	Percent	Transportation and material moving operative workers Number	Percent	Laborers and helpers Number	Percent	Protective service workers Number	Percent	Service workers, except protective Number	Percent
United States	7,769,340	5.0	6,984,985	4.5	5,991,240	3.9	3,257,310	2.1	21,572,140	14.0
Alabama	166,840	7.5	119,365	5.4	96,025	4.3	44,730	2.0	287,000	12.9
Alaska	12,430	3.4	15,015	4.1	16,025	4.4	8,595	2.4	52,270	14.4
Arizona	93,825	3.2	110,910	3.7	116,420	3.9	76,990	2.6	417,560	14.0
Arkansas	112,835	8.3	77,260	5.7	67,785	5.0	24,910	1.8	187,995	13.8
California	792,860	4.3	780,745	4.3	870,025	4.8	378,645	2.1	2,510,735	13.7
Colorado	81,590	3.1	93,910	3.6	89,370	3.4	50,955	1.9	359,135	13.6
Connecticut	80,535	4.2	67,830	3.5	55,465	2.9	36,590	1.9	263,435	13.8
Delaware	17,695	3.9	20,140	4.5	14,895	3.3	10,500	2.3	62,015	13.7
District of Columbia	2,175	0.7	8,150	2.5	6,190	1.9	9,060	2.8	43,980	13.4
Florida	263,700	2.9	349,720	3.8	374,780	4.1	225,460	2.5	1,368,995	15.0
Georgia	248,875	5.3	242,680	5.1	182,455	3.9	101,355	2.2	597,190	12.7
Hawaii	15,115	2.2	23,095	3.4	27,440	4.1	20,360	3.0	116,610	17.3
Idaho	36,525	4.9	36,210	4.8	43,535	5.8	14,090	1.9	102,340	13.6
Illinois	385,600	5.8	344,525	5.2	231,570	3.5	139,705	2.1	890,145	13.4
Indiana	292,465	8.9	179,740	5.5	136,830	4.2	57,520	1.8	453,680	13.9
Iowa	126,350	7.7	84,225	5.1	78,660	4.8	21,090	1.3	235,200	14.3
Kansas	91,015	6.2	63,420	4.3	59,790	4.0	25,855	1.7	203,565	13.8
Kentucky	155,430	7.6	112,805	5.5	92,000	4.5	37,915	1.9	275,020	13.5
Louisiana	100,365	4.7	105,905	5.0	82,935	3.9	54,990	2.6	311,605	14.7
Maine	34,160	4.9	29,510	4.2	34,210	4.9	11,035	1.6	105,495	15.0
Maryland	70,025	2.3	116,120	3.7	79,260	2.6	89,120	2.9	385,320	12.4
Massachusetts	131,475	3.7	117,470	3.3	93,120	2.6	72,005	2.0	480,505	13.6
Michigan	371,155	7.5	230,835	4.7	191,180	3.9	87,520	1.8	750,160	15.2
Minnesota	170,005	5.8	122,545	4.2	102,295	3.5	38,000	1.3	404,605	13.9
Mississippi	103,905	7.7	78,935	5.9	57,765	4.3	31,960	2.4	189,955	14.1
Missouri	178,950	5.9	144,630	4.8	117,590	3.9	55,965	1.9	436,045	14.4
Montana	15,805	3.1	20,265	4.0	24,235	4.8	9,690	1.9	78,625	15.6
Nebraska	61,230	6.2	47,780	4.8	44,800	4.5	14,700	1.5	138,735	14.0
Nevada	37,585	2.7	59,035	4.3	48,520	3.5	42,560	3.1	292,675	21.2
New Hampshire	36,235	4.9	28,345	3.8	23,100	3.1	11,220	1.5	93,765	12.7
New Jersey	159,570	3.5	212,385	4.6	129,675	2.8	111,995	2.4	577,155	12.6
New Mexico	29,675	3.1	37,450	3.9	36,300	3.8	25,720	2.7	147,825	15.4
New York	328,590	3.4	414,965	4.2	248,105	2.5	278,350	2.8	1,529,240	15.6
North Carolina	306,930	6.6	221,365	4.8	188,445	4.1	86,400	1.9	620,650	13.4
North Dakota	16,955	4.6	16,975	4.6	16,510	4.5	5,080	1.4	56,560	15.5
Ohio	422,105	7.2	305,720	5.2	237,980	4.0	108,130	1.8	846,015	14.4
Oklahoma	99,390	5.6	85,645	4.8	70,755	4.0	35,575	2.0	253,865	14.2
Oregon	99,380	5.1	81,145	4.2	105,670	5.5	31,995	1.7	277,280	14.4
Pennsylvania	346,925	5.4	317,090	4.9	254,035	4.0	121,595	1.9	894,205	14.0
Rhode Island	31,105	5.5	24,310	4.3	15,130	2.7	12,145	2.2	87,030	15.5
South Carolina	157,800	7.2	111,200	5.0	88,820	4.0	45,055	2.0	307,585	13.9
South Dakota	24,950	5.8	17,915	4.2	21,045	4.9	7,410	1.7	61,815	14.4
Tennessee	222,260	7.2	165,125	5.4	126,940	4.1	61,285	2.0	417,150	13.5
Texas	547,650	4.6	553,600	4.6	466,560	3.9	261,555	2.2	1,636,470	13.7
Utah	65,595	5.0	54,200	4.1	45,455	3.5	22,655	1.7	162,265	12.4
Vermont	16,405	4.7	11,625	3.3	14,390	4.1	5,190	1.5	50,025	14.3
Virginia	156,625	3.9	155,095	3.8	127,975	3.1	98,910	2.4	500,370	12.3
Washington	135,310	4.0	147,770	4.4	158,675	4.7	61,750	1.8	463,750	13.7
West Virginia	38,830	4.7	47,235	5.7	32,865	4.0	18,095	2.2	125,010	15.2
Wisconsin	264,975	8.6	155,130	5.0	134,830	4.4	50,100	1.6	420,710	13.7
Wyoming	11,580	3.9	17,910	6.0	12,805	4.3	5,235	1.8	42,815	14.4

B-2 All Workers, by State, Sex, Race, and Hispanic or Latino Origin, 2006–2010

State	Total who worked in the last 5 years	Male Number	Male Percent	Female Number	Female Percent	Hispanic or Latino Number	Hispanic or Latino Percent	White alone, not Hispanic or Latino Number	White alone, not Hispanic or Latino Percent
United States	154,037,475	81,323,085	52.8	72,714,390	47.2	22,457,110	14.6	103,278,405	67.0
Alabama	2,230,880	1,176,925	52.8	1,053,955	47.2	78,390	3.5	1,550,345	69.5
Alaska	363,355	195,920	53.9	167,435	46.1	18,390	5.1	249,005	68.5
Arizona	2,975,165	1,607,545	54.0	1,367,620	46.0	789,075	26.5	1,851,265	62.2
Arkansas	1,360,940	715,950	52.6	644,990	47.4	74,865	5.5	1,048,135	77.0
California	18,274,870	9,936,510	54.4	8,338,360	45.6	6,270,850	34.3	8,024,060	43.9
Colorado	2,636,625	1,422,345	53.9	1,214,285	46.1	454,585	17.2	1,959,930	74.3
Connecticut	1,910,905	991,235	51.9	919,670	48.1	220,140	11.5	1,415,935	74.1
Delaware	451,135	230,830	51.2	220,305	48.8	30,675	6.8	310,005	68.7
District of Columbia	328,035	159,735	48.7	168,305	51.3	31,080	9.5	133,550	40.7
Florida	9,128,080	4,780,525	52.4	4,347,555	47.6	2,045,300	22.4	5,374,790	58.9
Georgia	4,713,920	2,462,680	52.2	2,251,240	47.8	374,760	8.0	2,757,425	58.5
Hawaii	674,470	350,850	52.0	323,620	48.0	48,535	7.2	161,795	24.0
Idaho	751,480	409,955	54.6	341,525	45.4	71,535	9.5	647,975	86.2
Illinois	6,632,590	3,498,985	52.8	3,133,605	47.2	940,535	14.2	4,479,990	67.5
Indiana	3,274,430	1,728,770	52.8	1,545,660	47.2	165,635	5.1	2,758,755	84.3
Iowa	1,640,080	860,055	52.4	780,025	47.6	62,575	3.8	1,495,320	91.2
Kansas	1,479,515	779,735	52.7	699,780	47.3	126,650	8.6	1,208,755	81.7
Kentucky	2,038,920	1,072,710	52.6	966,210	47.4	53,970	2.6	1,789,090	87.7
Louisiana	2,116,795	1,110,415	52.5	1,006,380	47.5	87,680	4.1	1,352,590	63.9
Maine	703,390	363,625	51.7	339,765	48.3	7,535	1.1	674,020	95.8
Maryland	3,107,930	1,578,080	50.8	1,529,850	49.2	239,705	7.7	1,760,270	56.6
Massachusetts	3,531,260	1,809,580	51.2	1,721,680	48.8	271,100	7.7	2,805,440	79.4
Michigan	4,938,335	2,572,410	52.1	2,365,930	47.9	186,945	3.8	3,941,860	79.8
Minnesota	2,916,930	1,526,435	52.3	1,390,500	47.7	111,040	3.8	2,525,930	86.6
Mississippi	1,345,155	694,550	51.6	650,605	48.4	32,200	2.4	825,655	61.4
Missouri	3,020,900	1,563,955	51.8	1,456,945	48.2	92,480	3.1	2,510,250	83.1
Montana	504,880	267,315	52.9	237,560	47.1	11,520	2.3	456,445	90.4
Nebraska	988,060	519,240	52.6	468,815	47.4	70,500	7.1	846,385	85.7
Nevada	1,377,920	753,075	54.7	624,845	45.3	327,035	23.7	799,975	58.1
New Hampshire	738,510	388,075	52.5	350,435	47.5	16,265	2.2	691,765	93.7
New Jersey	4,587,250	2,416,535	52.7	2,170,715	47.3	764,475	16.7	2,822,720	61.5
New Mexico	957,905	505,980	52.8	451,925	47.2	414,905	43.3	430,415	44.9
New York	9,781,730	5,073,155	51.9	4,708,575	48.1	1,574,075	16.1	5,977,070	61.1
North Carolina	4,640,230	2,409,220	51.9	2,231,010	48.1	340,630	7.3	3,165,610	68.2
North Dakota	365,155	193,220	52.9	171,935	47.1	5,745	1.6	336,220	92.1
Ohio	5,877,985	3,051,365	51.9	2,826,620	48.1	149,175	2.5	4,925,810	83.8
Oklahoma	1,785,480	952,360	53.3	833,120	46.7	133,645	7.5	1,296,480	72.6
Oregon	1,931,995	1,026,790	53.1	905,205	46.9	195,875	10.1	1,566,405	81.1
Pennsylvania	6,408,620	3,351,160	52.3	3,057,460	47.7	278,765	4.3	5,318,095	83.0
Rhode Island	560,550	285,835	51.0	274,715	49.0	58,175	10.4	448,300	80.0
South Carolina	2,206,485	1,139,565	51.6	1,066,920	48.4	101,550	4.6	1,469,010	66.6
South Dakota	430,310	225,015	52.3	205,295	47.7	8,835	2.1	383,735	89.2
Tennessee	3,081,950	1,621,960	52.6	1,459,990	47.4	126,000	4.1	2,382,410	77.3
Texas	11,962,845	6,511,480	54.4	5,451,365	45.6	4,042,355	33.8	5,944,815	49.7
Utah	1,313,655	733,825	55.9	579,830	44.1	153,360	11.7	1,084,610	82.6
Vermont	350,300	180,200	51.4	170,100	48.6	4,670	1.3	334,660	95.5
Virginia	4,065,245	2,103,800	51.8	1,961,445	48.2	305,985	7.5	2,708,285	66.6
Washington	3,380,745	1,806,580	53.4	1,574,165	46.6	314,185	9.3	2,565,235	75.9
West Virginia	822,340	440,505	53.6	381,835	46.4	8,095	1.0	774,540	94.2
Wisconsin	3,073,910	1,603,825	52.2	1,470,085	47.8	142,775	4.6	2,675,355	87.0
Wyoming	297,310	162,695	54.7	134,615	45.3	22,280	7.5	261,910	88.1

B-2 All Workers, by State, Sex, Race, and Hispanic or Latino Origin, 2006–2010—*Continued*

State	Black alone, not Hispanic or Latino Number	Percent	American Indian and Alaska Native alone, not Hispanic or Latino Number	Percent	Asian alone, not Hispanic or Latino Number	Percent	Native Hawaiian and Other Pacific Islander alone, not Hispanic or Latino Number	Percent	Two or more races, not Hispanic or Latino Number	Percent
United States	17,469,155	11.3	894,065	0.6	7,426,010	4.8	234,435	0.2	2,278,295	1.5
Alabama	544,630	24.4	10,730	0.5	25,335	1.1	585	0.0	20,865	0.9
Alaska	11,715	3.2	40,530	11.2	21,530	5.9	3,015	0.8	19,170	5.3
Arizona	106,985	3.6	95,335	3.2	87,105	2.9	5,370	0.2	40,030	1.3
Arkansas	195,305	14.4	8,275	0.6	16,715	1.2	1,640	0.1	15,995	1.2
California	1,012,990	5.5	70,285	0.4	2,452,235	13.4	69,485	0.4	374,960	2.1
Colorado	90,025	3.4	15,360	0.6	71,360	2.7	2,945	0.1	42,420	1.6
Connecticut	172,205	9.0	2,720	0.1	70,390	3.7	835	0.0	28,675	1.5
Delaware	88,815	19.7	1,295	0.3	14,525	3.2	180	0.0	5,645	1.3
District of Columbia	143,010	43.6	765	0.2	13,655	4.2	185	0.1	5,785	1.8
Florida	1,329,950	14.6	19,280	0.2	236,565	2.6	5,205	0.1	116,985	1.3
Georgia	1,366,840	29.0	9,070	0.2	151,665	3.2	2,310	0.0	51,850	1.1
Hawaii	8,490	1.3	985	0.1	278,870	41.3	59,235	8.8	116,560	17.3
Idaho	3,805	0.5	6,885	0.9	8,900	1.2	1,240	0.2	11,140	1.5
Illinois	827,980	12.5	7,250	0.1	310,190	4.7	1,695	0.0	64,945	1.0
Indiana	259,270	7.9	5,965	0.2	46,850	1.4	760	0.0	37,200	1.1
Iowa	36,020	2.2	3,455	0.2	28,000	1.7	585	0.0	14,125	0.9
Kansas	74,630	5.0	9,360	0.6	35,580	2.4	725	0.0	23,820	1.6
Kentucky	151,055	7.4	3,285	0.2	22,925	1.1	1,295	0.1	17,295	0.8
Louisiana	611,295	28.9	10,660	0.5	35,085	1.7	640	0.0	18,840	0.9
Maine	5,270	0.7	3,130	0.4	6,585	0.9	210	0.0	6,645	0.9
Maryland	881,970	28.4	5,970	0.2	169,600	5.5	1,365	0.0	49,045	1.6
Massachusetts	204,215	5.8	4,710	0.1	181,110	5.1	975	0.0	63,705	1.8
Michigan	600,660	12.2	22,635	0.5	120,130	2.4	1,310	0.0	64,805	1.3
Minnesota	119,280	4.1	22,420	0.8	102,315	3.5	1,095	0.0	34,860	1.2
Mississippi	459,805	34.2	5,615	0.4	13,370	1.0	215	0.0	8,290	0.6
Missouri	317,095	10.5	10,240	0.3	48,580	1.6	1,940	0.1	40,305	1.3
Montana	1,670	0.3	24,040	4.8	3,205	0.6	380	0.1	7,620	1.5
Nebraska	38,085	3.9	5,095	0.5	15,665	1.6	510	0.1	11,815	1.2
Nevada	99,320	7.2	11,720	0.9	104,030	7.5	7,915	0.6	27,920	2.0
New Hampshire	7,260	1.0	1,475	0.2	14,710	2.0	175	0.0	6,865	0.9
New Jersey	562,605	12.3	4,845	0.1	373,185	8.1	1,060	0.0	58,355	1.3
New Mexico	16,845	1.8	69,130	7.2	14,205	1.5	485	0.1	11,915	1.2
New York	1,335,260	13.7	21,930	0.2	726,650	7.4	1,950	0.0	144,800	1.5
North Carolina	938,545	20.2	42,115	0.9	97,590	2.1	2,390	0.1	53,350	1.1
North Dakota	3,200	0.9	13,275	3.6	3,300	0.9	245	0.1	3,175	0.9
Ohio	630,925	10.7	9,525	0.2	98,460	1.7	750	0.0	63,340	1.1
Oklahoma	119,160	6.7	110,745	6.2	32,250	1.8	1,860	0.1	91,340	5.1
Oregon	30,045	1.6	17,940	0.9	71,590	3.7	6,255	0.3	43,880	2.3
Pennsylvania	573,645	9.0	6,525	0.1	169,185	2.6	1,440	0.0	60,965	1.0
Rhode Island	26,950	4.8	1,560	0.3	15,075	2.7	100	0.0	10,390	1.9
South Carolina	578,855	26.2	6,315	0.3	29,075	1.3	870	0.0	20,805	0.9
South Dakota	4,020	0.9	25,110	5.8	3,965	0.9	120	0.0	4,535	1.1
Tennessee	490,575	15.9	6,265	0.2	46,055	1.5	1,415	0.0	29,225	0.9
Texas	1,344,670	11.2	34,325	0.3	463,715	3.9	8,350	0.1	124,615	1.0
Utah	11,045	0.8	11,540	0.9	28,015	2.1	10,560	0.8	14,530	1.1
Vermont	2,475	0.7	865	0.2	3,585	1.0	65	0.0	3,980	1.1
Virginia	751,585	18.5	8,375	0.2	228,775	5.6	3,015	0.1	59,220	1.5
Washington	107,595	3.2	37,065	1.1	246,575	7.3	18,370	0.5	91,720	2.7
West Virginia	23,040	2.8	1,170	0.1	6,180	0.8	205	0.0	9,115	1.1
Wisconsin	146,800	4.8	21,875	0.7	59,505	1.9	805	0.0	26,785	0.9
Wyoming	1,670	0.6	5,020	1.7	2,295	0.8	90	0.0	4,040	1.4

B-3 Management, Business, and Financial Workers, by State, Sex, Race, and Hispanic or Latino Origin, 2006–2010

State	Total who worked in the last 5 years	Male Number	Male Percent	Female Number	Female Percent	Hispanic or Latino Number	Hispanic or Latino Percent	White alone, not Hispanic or Latino Number	White alone, not Hispanic or Latino Percent
United States	18,514,755	11,000,315	59.4	7,514,440	40.6	1,466,850	7.9	14,425,760	77.9
Alabama	221,485	133,095	60.1	88,390	39.9	3,125	1.4	180,280	81.4
Alaska	42,405	23,225	54.8	19,180	45.2	1,035	2.4	34,060	80.3
Arizona	366,105	216,650	59.2	149,455	40.8	51,755	14.1	282,310	77.1
Arkansas	137,885	84,330	61.2	53,555	38.8	3,275	2.4	119,955	87.0
California	2,283,685	1,341,595	58.7	942,095	41.3	393,305	17.2	1,396,570	61.2
Colorado	374,815	224,040	59.8	150,775	40.2	32,425	8.7	319,340	85.2
Connecticut	256,775	154,080	60.0	102,690	40.0	12,060	4.7	219,415	85.5
Delaware	58,180	32,895	56.5	25,290	43.5	1,825	3.1	45,065	77.5
District of Columbia	62,195	30,965	49.8	31,230	50.2	4,025	6.5	37,595	60.4
Florida	1,098,395	651,965	59.4	446,430	40.6	184,065	16.8	782,075	71.2
Georgia	590,245	348,550	59.1	241,700	40.9	20,570	3.5	423,465	71.7
Hawaii	76,650	43,375	56.6	33,275	43.4	4,330	5.6	25,295	33.0
Idaho	88,250	56,020	63.5	32,230	36.5	3,605	4.1	82,100	93.0
Illinois	819,820	487,385	59.5	332,430	40.5	54,255	6.6	648,475	79.1
Indiana	343,525	207,580	60.4	135,945	39.6	7,945	2.3	307,870	89.6
Iowa	197,025	124,305	63.1	72,720	36.9	2,770	1.4	188,700	95.8
Kansas	183,390	116,535	63.5	66,855	36.5	5,955	3.2	164,940	89.9
Kentucky	209,670	124,465	59.4	85,205	40.6	2,930	1.4	193,505	92.3
Louisiana	206,110	122,135	59.3	83,975	40.7	5,310	2.6	161,230	78.2
Maine	79,590	44,180	55.5	35,410	44.5	565	0.7	76,955	96.7
Maryland	455,235	250,735	55.1	204,500	44.9	18,155	4.0	304,590	66.9
Massachusetts	487,985	277,590	56.9	210,395	43.1	16,840	3.5	426,495	87.4
Michigan	524,445	311,265	59.4	213,180	40.6	11,105	2.1	450,545	85.9
Minnesota	390,150	233,265	59.8	156,885	40.2	6,625	1.7	359,960	92.3
Mississippi	123,375	73,375	59.5	50,000	40.5	2,145	1.7	96,990	78.6
Missouri	347,305	205,560	59.2	141,745	40.8	5,795	1.7	309,980	89.3
Montana	65,730	41,725	63.5	24,000	36.5	920	1.4	61,495	93.6
Nebraska	129,375	82,905	64.1	46,470	35.9	3,210	2.5	121,130	93.6
Nevada	142,790	84,190	59.0	58,600	41.0	16,095	11.3	106,835	74.8
New Hampshire	96,500	58,395	60.5	38,105	39.5	1,445	1.5	91,980	95.3
New Jersey	622,305	377,935	60.7	244,370	39.3	51,125	8.2	453,575	72.9
New Mexico	103,485	59,550	57.5	43,935	42.5	32,225	31.1	62,875	60.8
New York	1,153,145	671,380	58.2	481,765	41.8	100,265	8.7	849,725	73.7
North Carolina	531,295	312,895	58.9	218,400	41.1	15,240	2.9	430,555	81.0
North Dakota	49,700	33,670	67.7	16,035	32.3	350	0.7	47,740	96.1
Ohio	645,840	387,775	60.0	258,065	40.0	10,615	1.6	573,505	88.8
Oklahoma	196,195	117,660	60.0	78,535	40.0	7,150	3.6	159,195	81.1
Oregon	236,540	137,070	57.9	99,470	42.1	10,225	4.3	209,125	88.4
Pennsylvania	726,845	437,660	60.2	289,185	39.8	17,020	2.3	644,150	88.6
Rhode Island	64,475	36,435	56.5	28,040	43.5	2,305	3.6	57,390	89.0
South Carolina	232,560	136,135	58.5	96,430	41.5	4,885	2.1	191,285	82.3
South Dakota	58,130	38,725	66.6	19,405	33.4	505	0.9	55,030	94.7
Tennessee	325,475	197,615	60.7	127,860	39.3	5,980	1.8	278,000	85.4
Texas	1,414,045	861,705	60.9	552,340	39.1	266,790	18.9	957,675	67.7
Utah	158,570	103,790	65.5	54,785	34.5	9,360	5.9	143,120	90.3
Vermont	44,930	26,045	58.0	18,885	42.0	455	1.0	43,625	97.1
Virginia	587,575	342,295	58.3	245,280	41.7	26,225	4.5	452,015	76.9
Washington	447,335	263,680	58.9	183,655	41.1	19,295	4.3	373,030	83.4
West Virginia	70,810	41,785	59.0	29,025	41.0	600	0.8	67,650	95.5
Wisconsin	352,235	209,100	59.4	143,135	40.6	7,360	2.1	325,810	92.5
Wyoming	34,160	21,035	61.6	13,130	38.4	1,400	4.1	31,500	92.2

PART B—STATE TABLES

B-3 Management, Business, and Financial Workers, by State, Sex, Race, and Hispanic or Latino Origin, 2006–2010—Continued

State	Black alone, not Hispanic or Latino Number	Percent	American Indian and Alaska Native alone, not Hispanic or Latino Number	Percent	Asian alone, not Hispanic or Latino Number	Percent	Native Hawaiian and Other Pacific Islander alone, not Hispanic or Latino Number	Percent	Two or more races, not Hispanic or Latino Number	Percent
United States	1,372,180	7.4	77,300	0.4	920,515	5.0	19,115	0.1	233,045	1.3
Alabama	32,210	14.5	915	0.4	3,130	1.4	125	0.1	1,705	0.8
Alaska	895	2.1	3,310	7.8	1,120	2.6	80	0.2	1,900	4.5
Arizona	11,090	3.0	5,765	1.6	10,220	2.8	655	0.2	4,300	1.2
Arkansas	11,080	8.0	720	0.5	1,605	1.2	40	0.0	1,210	0.9
California	107,850	4.7	8,050	0.4	326,020	14.3	6,855	0.3	45,040	2.0
Colorado	8,875	2.4	1,410	0.4	7,845	2.1	185	0.0	4,730	1.3
Connecticut	11,810	4.6	230	0.1	10,450	4.1	65	0.0	2,745	1.1
Delaware	8,590	14.8	100	0.2	1,930	3.3	15	0.0	655	1.1
District of Columbia	16,005	25.7	165	0.3	2,995	4.8	65	0.1	1,335	2.1
Florida	91,900	8.4	2,220	0.2	25,475	2.3	325	0.0	12,330	1.1
Georgia	118,505	20.1	1,285	0.2	20,455	3.5	200	0.0	5,770	1.0
Hawaii	1,140	1.5	140	0.2	30,475	39.8	4,130	5.4	11,140	14.5
Idaho	260	0.3	490	0.6	580	0.7	40	0.0	1,175	1.3
Illinois	67,310	8.2	915	0.1	41,725	5.1	295	0.0	6,840	0.8
Indiana	19,150	5.6	480	0.1	4,910	1.4	200	0.1	2,975	0.9
Iowa	2,035	1.0	155	0.1	2,235	1.1	20	0.0	1,110	0.6
Kansas	5,900	3.2	985	0.5	3,200	1.7	45	0.0	2,365	1.3
Kentucky	9,255	4.4	250	0.1	2,500	1.2	85	0.0	1,150	0.5
Louisiana	34,215	16.6	740	0.4	2,965	1.4	55	0.0	1,590	0.8
Maine	355	0.4	290	0.4	770	1.0	20	0.0	640	0.8
Maryland	103,235	22.7	905	0.2	21,985	4.8	150	0.0	6,220	1.4
Massachusetts	16,550	3.4	450	0.1	21,900	4.5	55	0.0	5,695	1.2
Michigan	42,315	8.1	1,740	0.3	13,435	2.6	135	0.0	5,175	1.0
Minnesota	8,225	2.1	1,720	0.4	9,745	2.5	130	0.0	3,755	1.0
Mississippi	21,810	17.7	385	0.3	1,360	1.1	15	0.0	675	0.5
Missouri	21,620	6.2	1,030	0.3	4,970	1.4	105	0.0	3,795	1.1
Montana	115	0.2	2,150	3.3	330	0.5	15	0.0	700	1.1
Nebraska	2,340	1.8	360	0.3	1,505	1.2	25	0.0	805	0.6
Nevada	7,445	5.2	1,110	0.8	8,410	5.9	390	0.3	2,510	1.8
New Hampshire	635	0.7	105	0.1	1,595	1.7	0	0.0	755	0.8
New Jersey	51,975	8.4	485	0.1	58,765	9.4	135	0.0	6,245	1.0
New Mexico	1,410	1.4	4,020	3.9	1,690	1.6	55	0.1	1,210	1.2
New York	100,210	8.7	1,750	0.2	86,780	7.5	235	0.0	14,190	1.2
North Carolina	66,720	12.6	3,175	0.6	10,650	2.0	315	0.1	4,640	0.9
North Dakota	165	0.3	890	1.8	215	0.4	100	0.2	244	0.5
Ohio	43,320	6.7	860	0.1	12,350	1.9	90	0.0	5,090	0.8
Oklahoma	8,230	4.2	9,950	5.1	2,605	1.3	110	0.1	8,965	4.6
Oregon	3,050	1.3	1,425	0.6	7,985	3.4	335	0.1	4,395	1.9
Pennsylvania	41,940	5.8	535	0.1	18,010	2.5	45	0.0	5,150	0.7
Rhode Island	2,335	3.6	35	0.1	1,280	2.0	30	0.0	1,095	1.7
South Carolina	31,150	13.4	455	0.2	3,065	1.3	95	0.0	1,630	0.7
South Dakota	250	0.4	1,790	3.1	205	0.4	15	0.0	339	0.6
Tennessee	32,695	10.0	510	0.2	5,425	1.7	195	0.1	2,680	0.8
Texas	114,885	8.1	4,545	0.3	54,765	3.9	670	0.0	14,715	1.0
Utah	1,105	0.7	525	0.3	2,340	1.5	695	0.4	1,430	0.9
Vermont	115	0.3	90	0.2	350	0.8	15	0.0	290	0.6
Virginia	67,525	11.5	1,075	0.2	33,560	5.7	390	0.1	6,790	1.2
Washington	10,510	2.3	4,280	1.0	29,150	6.5	1,015	0.2	10,045	2.2
West Virginia	1,510	2.1	100	0.1	305	0.4	4	0.0	635	0.9
Wisconsin	10,240	2.9	1,750	0.5	4,860	1.4	50	0.0	2,165	0.6
Wyoming	120	0.4	475	1.4	325	1.0	15	0.0	324	0.9

B-4 Science, Engineering, and Computer Professionals, by State, Sex, Race, and Hispanic or Latino Origin, 2006–2010

State	Total who worked in the last 5 years	Male Number	Male Percent	Female Number	Female Percent	Hispanic or Latino Number	Hispanic or Latino Percent	White alone, not Hispanic or Latino Number	White alone, not Hispanic or Latino Percent
United States	5,907,405	4,528,390	76.7	1,379,015	23.3	326,755	5.5	4,246,640	71.9
Alabama	69,550	53,985	77.6	15,560	22.4	1,480	2.1	56,180	80.8
Alaska	15,295	12,080	79.0	3,215	21.0	405	2.6	13,190	86.2
Arizona	120,405	95,070	79.0	25,335	21.0	10,815	9.0	89,695	74.5
Arkansas	27,865	21,130	75.8	6,735	24.2	530	1.9	23,470	84.2
California	827,650	632,475	76.4	195,175	23.6	72,930	8.8	440,870	53.3
Colorado	152,625	118,090	77.4	34,535	22.6	8,545	5.6	126,775	83.1
Connecticut	86,220	66,370	77.0	19,850	23.0	3,195	3.7	66,270	76.9
Delaware	17,750	13,365	75.3	4,385	24.7	230	1.3	12,535	70.6
District of Columbia	19,530	12,070	61.8	7,460	38.2	1,235	6.3	11,925	61.1
Florida	264,810	207,225	78.3	57,585	21.7	37,345	14.1	186,555	70.4
Georgia	169,290	127,470	75.3	41,825	24.7	5,680	3.4	111,525	65.9
Hawaii	20,810	15,915	76.5	4,895	23.5	860	4.1	7,415	35.6
Idaho	27,490	21,975	79.9	5,510	20.0	715	2.6	24,580	89.4
Illinois	248,460	190,095	76.5	58,365	23.5	12,350	5.0	176,975	71.2
Indiana	97,980	76,505	78.1	21,475	21.9	1,935	2.0	83,365	85.1
Iowa	46,845	35,870	76.6	10,980	23.4	975	2.1	41,810	89.3
Kansas	51,380	39,970	77.8	11,410	22.2	1,670	3.3	42,635	83.0
Kentucky	49,585	39,455	79.6	10,125	20.4	870	1.8	43,475	87.7
Louisiana	46,000	35,895	78.0	10,105	22.0	1,565	3.4	37,080	80.6
Maine	19,940	15,415	77.3	4,525	22.7	165	0.8	18,850	94.5
Maryland	208,910	145,390	69.6	63,520	30.4	7,060	3.4	127,140	60.9
Massachusetts	205,130	153,165	74.7	51,965	25.3	6,300	3.1	154,555	75.3
Michigan	197,715	155,815	78.8	41,900	21.2	4,225	2.1	157,335	79.6
Minnesota	126,515	96,700	76.4	29,815	23.6	2,085	1.6	107,110	84.7
Mississippi	25,355	20,060	79.1	5,295	20.9	385	1.5	21,050	83.0
Missouri	93,840	69,970	74.6	23,870	25.4	1,780	1.9	78,240	83.4
Montana	15,125	11,235	74.3	3,890	25.7	200	1.3	14,345	94.8
Nebraska	28,910	22,595	78.2	6,320	21.9	860	3.0	24,430	84.5
Nevada	31,380	24,580	78.3	6,800	21.7	2,170	6.9	23,720	75.6
New Hampshire	39,645	31,405	79.2	8,240	20.8	725	1.8	34,665	87.4
New Jersey	214,750	161,270	75.1	53,480	24.9	13,535	6.3	121,230	56.5
New Mexico	39,125	30,640	78.3	8,485	21.7	8,420	21.5	27,000	69.0
New York	305,850	233,020	76.2	72,825	23.8	20,115	6.6	212,255	69.4
North Carolina	154,850	115,380	74.5	39,475	25.5	4,550	2.9	118,795	76.7
North Dakota	10,425	8,240	79.0	2,185	21.0	140	1.3	9,745	93.5
Ohio	197,175	154,005	78.1	43,175	21.9	3,410	1.7	166,375	84.4
Oklahoma	48,110	37,640	78.2	10,465	21.8	1,620	3.4	38,035	79.1
Oregon	79,170	61,420	77.6	17,750	22.4	2,270	2.9	64,230	81.1
Pennsylvania	229,190	174,150	76.0	55,040	24.0	5,325	2.3	189,125	82.5
Rhode Island	20,005	15,310	76.5	4,695	23.5	725	3.6	17,345	86.7
South Carolina	60,610	48,685	80.3	11,920	19.7	1,030	1.7	48,865	80.6
South Dakota	10,795	8,450	78.3	2,340	21.7	175	1.6	9,575	88.7
Tennessee	83,505	65,580	78.5	17,925	21.5	1,655	2.0	69,325	83.0
Texas	456,760	356,735	78.1	100,030	21.9	53,725	11.8	294,890	64.6
Utah	55,330	45,870	82.9	9,460	17.1	2,295	4.1	49,335	89.2
Vermont	12,530	9,375	74.8	3,155	25.2	155	1.2	11,945	95.3
Virginia	252,460	188,400	74.6	64,055	25.4	9,695	3.8	176,865	70.1
Washington	194,965	153,920	78.9	41,045	21.1	6,310	3.2	147,680	75.7
West Virginia	17,850	14,065	78.8	3,785	21.2	345	1.9	16,210	90.8
Wisconsin	103,780	78,335	75.5	25,445	24.5	1,705	1.6	92,390	89.0
Wyoming	8,175	6,565	80.3	1,610	19.7	260	3.2	7,660	93.7

PART B—STATE TABLES

B-4 Science, Engineering, and Computer Professionals, by State, Sex, Race, and Hispanic or Latino Origin, 2006–2010—Continued

State	Black alone, not Hispanic or Latino		American Indian and Alaska Native alone, not Hispanic or Latino		Asian alone, not Hispanic or Latino		Native Hawaiian and Other Pacific Islander alone, not Hispanic or Latino		Two or more races, not Hispanic or Latino	
	Number	Percent	Number	Percent	Number	Percent	Number	Percent	Number	Percent
United States	351,600	6.0	17,045	0.3	867,955	14.7	6,045	0.1	91,370	1.5
Alabama	7,990	11.5	275	0.4	3,025	4.3	25	0.0	570	0.8
Alaska	155	1.0	515	3.4	475	3.1	10	0.1	550	3.6
Arizona	4,420	3.7	1,335	1.1	12,485	10.4	235	0.2	1,414	1.2
Arkansas	1,840	6.6	185	0.7	1,460	5.2	15	0.1	370	1.3
California	26,000	3.1	1,870	0.2	265,195	32.0	2,040	0.2	18,740	2.3
Colorado	3,815	2.5	495	0.3	9,910	6.5	135	0.1	2,940	1.9
Connecticut	3,890	4.5	80	0.1	11,650	13.5	10	0.0	1,120	1.3
Delaware	1,920	10.8	20	0.1	2,915	16.4	0	0.0	129	0.7
District of Columbia	4,445	22.8	15	0.1	1,435	7.3	0	0.0	470	2.4
Florida	18,345	6.9	470	0.2	18,435	7.0	115	0.0	3,545	1.3
Georgia	31,545	18.6	445	0.3	18,015	10.6	160	0.1	1,920	1.1
Hawaii	450	2.2	20	0.1	9,310	44.7	560	2.7	2,200	10.6
Idaho	105	0.4	105	0.4	1,495	5.4	15	0.1	470	1.7
Illinois	15,435	6.2	200	0.1	40,560	16.3	110	0.0	2,820	1.1
Indiana	4,515	4.6	130	0.1	6,685	6.8	15	0.0	1,330	1.4
Iowa	745	1.6	60	0.1	2,860	6.1	30	0.1	374	0.8
Kansas	1,235	2.4	215	0.4	4,940	9.6	4	0.0	690	1.3
Kentucky	1,810	3.7	35	0.1	2,915	5.9	35	0.1	445	0.9
Louisiana	4,860	10.6	150	0.3	1,890	4.1	4	0.0	450	1.0
Maine	295	1.5	25	0.1	550	2.8	0	0.0	50	0.3
Maryland	38,910	18.6	380	0.2	31,525	15.1	110	0.1	3,790	1.8
Massachusetts	5,965	2.9	145	0.1	35,145	17.1	135	0.1	2,890	1.4
Michigan	11,340	5.7	460	0.2	21,860	11.1	65	0.0	2,435	1.2
Minnesota	3,270	2.6	295	0.2	12,390	9.8	50	0.0	1,310	1.0
Mississippi	2,735	10.8	65	0.3	905	3.6	0	0.0	220	0.9
Missouri	5,345	5.7	250	0.3	6,810	7.3	60	0.1	1,365	1.5
Montana	70	0.5	210	1.4	135	0.9	15	0.1	138	0.9
Nebraska	665	2.3	30	0.1	2,355	8.1	25	0.1	550	1.9
Nevada	1,455	4.6	200	0.6	3,100	9.9	165	0.5	575	1.8
New Hampshire	550	1.4	40	0.1	3,185	8.0	15	0.0	465	1.2
New Jersey	13,750	6.4	160	0.1	63,095	29.4	75	0.0	2,905	1.4
New Mexico	565	1.4	1,170	3.0	1,395	3.6	40	0.1	535	1.4
New York	22,020	7.2	345	0.1	46,340	15.2	65	0.0	4,700	1.5
North Carolina	14,670	9.5	445	0.3	14,275	9.2	185	0.1	1,930	1.2
North Dakota	55	0.5	145	1.4	295	2.8	0	0.0	50	0.5
Ohio	9,755	4.9	210	0.1	15,440	7.8	0	0.0	1,985	1.0
Oklahoma	2,040	4.2	1,605	3.3	2,695	5.6	4	0.0	2,115	4.4
Oregon	705	0.9	375	0.5	9,505	12.0	70	0.1	2,015	2.5
Pennsylvania	9,560	4.2	245	0.1	22,825	10.0	30	0.0	2,080	0.9
Rhode Island	415	2.1	0	0.0	1,300	6.5	0	0.0	215	1.1
South Carolina	6,995	11.5	60	0.1	2,935	4.8	45	0.1	684	1.1
South Dakota	15	0.1	305	2.8	525	4.9	0	0.0	200	1.9
Tennessee	6,465	7.7	85	0.1	5,170	6.2	25	0.0	775	0.9
Texas	30,370	6.6	1,260	0.3	70,335	15.4	230	0.1	5,955	1.3
Utah	360	0.7	220	0.4	2,115	3.8	265	0.5	734	1.3
Vermont	50	0.4	4	0.0	235	1.9	0	0.0	129	1.0
Virginia	23,555	9.3	385	0.2	36,725	14.5	365	0.1	4,870	1.9
Washington	3,345	1.7	920	0.5	32,000	16.4	465	0.2	4,240	2.2
West Virginia	450	2.5	4	0.0	705	3.9	0	0.0	130	0.7
Wisconsin	2,275	2.2	310	0.3	6,355	6.1	20	0.0	715	0.7
Wyoming	65	0.8	75	0.9	65	0.8	0	0.0	54	0.7

B-5 Health Care Practitioner Professionals, by State, Sex, Race, and Hispanic or Latino Origin, 2006–2010

State	Total who worked in the last 5 years	Male Number	Male Percent	Female Number	Female Percent	Hispanic or Latino Number	Hispanic or Latino Percent	White alone, not Hispanic or Latino Number	White alone, not Hispanic or Latino Percent
United States	5,041,270	1,359,170	27.0	3,682,105	73.0	255,010	5.1	3,806,800	75.5
Alabama	73,725	18,620	25.3	55,105	74.7	980	1.3	59,010	80.0
Alaska	10,540	3,230	30.6	7,310	69.4	295	2.8	9,215	87.4
Arizona	93,815	27,240	29.0	66,575	71.0	7,485	8.0	73,090	77.9
Arkansas	44,670	11,950	26.8	32,720	73.2	565	1.3	38,250	85.6
California	518,360	162,370	31.3	355,990	68.7	53,130	10.2	274,875	53.0
Colorado	83,140	22,445	27.0	60,695	73.0	4,675	5.6	72,425	87.1
Connecticut	69,880	18,815	26.9	51,065	73.1	3,000	4.3	56,690	81.1
Delaware	16,245	3,550	21.9	12,695	78.1	315	1.9	12,230	75.3
District of Columbia	6,480	2,350	36.3	4,130	63.7	420	6.5	3,075	47.5
Florida	292,705	83,960	28.7	208,740	71.3	39,100	13.4	192,100	65.6
Georgia	131,950	33,960	25.7	97,990	74.3	3,130	2.4	90,975	68.9
Hawaii	20,390	6,760	33.2	13,635	66.9	885	4.3	7,400	36.3
Idaho	22,885	7,815	34.1	15,065	65.8	850	3.7	21,410	93.6
Illinois	217,910	53,475	24.5	164,440	75.5	8,410	3.9	158,440	72.7
Indiana	107,595	23,995	22.3	83,600	77.7	2,130	2.0	95,475	88.7
Iowa	55,740	12,780	22.9	42,960	77.1	715	1.3	52,780	94.7
Kansas	52,930	13,630	25.8	39,300	74.2	1,705	3.2	46,820	88.5
Kentucky	75,080	18,180	24.2	56,900	75.8	585	0.8	69,325	92.3
Louisiana	70,630	21,125	29.9	49,505	70.1	2,265	3.2	54,310	76.9
Maine	26,935	6,980	25.9	19,955	74.1	125	0.5	26,175	97.2
Maryland	111,915	29,310	26.2	82,605	73.8	3,485	3.1	69,705	62.3
Massachusetts	143,445	33,820	23.6	109,625	76.4	3,365	2.3	121,865	85.0
Michigan	165,545	45,005	27.2	120,535	72.8	2,865	1.7	136,440	82.4
Minnesota	102,840	24,910	24.2	77,930	75.8	1,390	1.4	94,490	91.9
Mississippi	46,955	11,400	24.3	35,555	75.7	410	0.9	37,110	79.0
Missouri	101,875	25,550	25.1	76,320	74.9	1,395	1.4	88,765	87.1
Montana	17,135	4,895	28.6	12,240	71.4	215	1.3	16,180	94.4
Nebraska	35,425	8,690	24.5	26,735	75.5	580	1.6	33,230	93.8
Nevada	33,000	9,985	30.3	23,010	69.7	1,825	5.5	21,320	64.6
New Hampshire	27,490	6,425	23.4	21,065	76.6	370	1.3	25,950	94.4
New Jersey	159,255	42,940	27.0	116,315	73.0	7,875	4.9	103,380	64.9
New Mexico	28,805	8,060	28.0	20,745	72.0	6,475	22.5	19,545	67.9
New York	367,395	103,685	28.2	263,710	71.8	20,640	5.6	242,460	66.0
North Carolina	156,105	38,510	24.7	117,595	75.3	2,620	1.7	126,805	81.2
North Dakota	12,315	2,780	22.6	9,530	77.4	70	0.6	11,780	95.7
Ohio	213,100	51,550	24.2	161,550	75.8	3,200	1.5	185,490	87.0
Oklahoma	52,320	14,715	28.1	37,605	71.9	1,215	2.3	41,745	79.8
Oregon	61,555	17,695	28.7	43,860	71.3	1,670	2.7	54,635	88.8
Pennsylvania	252,745	66,090	26.1	186,655	73.9	4,570	1.8	217,565	86.1
Rhode Island	21,670	5,205	24.0	16,460	76.0	555	2.6	19,105	88.2
South Carolina	70,430	16,260	23.1	54,170	76.9	870	1.2	57,635	81.8
South Dakota	16,460	3,820	23.2	12,645	76.8	75	0.5	15,665	95.2
Tennessee	106,235	29,215	27.5	77,020	72.5	1,870	1.8	90,525	85.2
Texas	323,505	93,515	28.9	229,990	71.1	46,000	14.2	202,140	62.5
Utah	35,900	13,325	37.1	22,575	62.9	990	2.8	33,385	93.0
Vermont	13,060	3,105	23.8	9,955	76.2	235	1.8	12,475	95.5
Virginia	123,045	31,095	25.3	91,955	74.7	3,610	2.9	93,000	75.6
Washington	107,490	30,160	28.1	77,335	71.9	3,790	3.5	88,640	82.5
West Virginia	31,240	8,100	25.9	23,145	74.1	365	1.2	28,955	92.7
Wisconsin	103,190	24,155	23.4	79,035	76.6	1,370	1.3	95,060	92.1
Wyoming	8,225	1,955	23.8	6,270	76.2	280	3.4	7,675	93.3

B-5 Health Care Practitioner Professionals, by State, Sex, Race, and Hispanic or Latino Origin, 2006–2010—*Continued*

State	Black alone, not Hispanic or Latino Number	Percent	American Indian and Alaska Native alone, not Hispanic or Latino Number	Percent	Asian alone, not Hispanic or Latino Number	Percent	Native Hawaiian and Other Pacific Islander alone, not Hispanic or Latino Number	Percent	Two or more races, not Hispanic or Latino Number	Percent
United States	399,915	7.9	16,335	0.3	498,670	9.9	3,360	0.1	61,175	1.2
Alabama	11,415	15.5	310	0.4	1,415	1.9	10	0.0	580	0.8
Alaska	95	0.9	215	2.0	405	3.8	0	0.0	315	3.0
Arizona	3,315	3.5	1,300	1.4	7,095	7.6	215	0.2	1,309	1.4
Arkansas	3,800	8.5	220	0.5	1,280	2.9	4	0.0	550	1.2
California	26,185	5.1	1,220	0.2	150,870	29.1	1,045	0.2	11,035	2.1
Colorado	1,570	1.9	260	0.3	3,165	3.8	155	0.2	895	1.1
Connecticut	4,095	5.9	30	0.0	5,310	7.6	35	0.1	705	1.0
Delaware	2,235	13.8	35	0.2	1,145	7.0	0	0.0	280	1.7
District of Columbia	2,020	31.2	0	0.0	790	12.2	0	0.0	170	2.6
Florida	35,080	12.0	510	0.2	22,480	7.7	255	0.1	3,175	1.1
Georgia	28,450	21.6	105	0.1	7,890	6.0	20	0.0	1,375	1.0
Hawaii	320	1.6	45	0.2	9,400	46.1	595	2.9	1,750	8.6
Idaho	15	0.1	70	0.3	300	1.3	20	0.1	220	1.0
Illinois	18,335	8.4	145	0.1	30,635	14.1	60	0.0	1,880	0.9
Indiana	4,670	4.3	95	0.1	4,205	3.9	10	0.0	1,015	0.9
Iowa	350	0.6	60	0.1	1,570	2.8	4	0.0	265	0.5
Kansas	1,840	3.5	185	0.3	1,840	3.5	4	0.0	540	1.0
Kentucky	2,260	3.0	90	0.1	2,440	3.2	35	0.0	340	0.5
Louisiana	10,490	14.9	175	0.2	2,900	4.1	0	0.0	495	0.7
Maine	80	0.3	90	0.3	325	1.2	0	0.0	135	0.5
Maryland	23,745	21.2	115	0.1	13,085	11.7	15	0.0	1,765	1.6
Massachusetts	6,260	4.4	60	0.0	10,325	7.2	10	0.0	1,560	1.1
Michigan	11,660	7.0	365	0.2	12,295	7.4	15	0.0	1,895	1.1
Minnesota	2,540	2.5	380	0.4	3,375	3.3	0	0.0	670	0.7
Mississippi	8,375	17.8	115	0.2	770	1.6	0	0.0	175	0.4
Missouri	5,500	5.4	430	0.4	4,625	4.5	10	0.0	1,145	1.1
Montana	25	0.1	345	2.0	125	0.7	10	0.1	235	1.4
Nebraska	500	1.4	90	0.3	640	1.8	35	0.1	355	1.0
Nevada	1,760	5.3	170	0.5	7,160	21.7	55	0.2	715	2.2
New Hampshire	200	0.7	70	0.3	680	2.5	0	0.0	220	0.8
New Jersey	15,020	9.4	110	0.1	30,970	19.4	80	0.1	1,815	1.1
New Mexico	315	1.1	775	2.7	1,125	3.9	0	0.0	565	2.0
New York	47,375	12.9	555	0.2	51,890	14.1	60	0.0	4,410	1.2
North Carolina	17,685	11.3	1,045	0.7	6,435	4.1	10	0.0	1,510	1.0
North Dakota	35	0.3	125	1.0	195	1.6	25	0.2	90	0.7
Ohio	13,185	6.2	370	0.2	8,810	4.1	30	0.0	2,015	0.9
Oklahoma	2,495	4.8	2,765	5.3	2,060	3.9	0	0.0	2,035	3.9
Oregon	700	1.1	185	0.3	3,385	5.5	25	0.0	955	1.6
Pennsylvania	13,630	5.4	210	0.1	14,750	5.8	75	0.0	1,945	0.8
Rhode Island	925	4.3	0	0.0	865	4.0	0	0.0	210	1.0
South Carolina	9,465	13.4	200	0.3	1,715	2.4	15	0.0	535	0.8
South Dakota	90	0.5	390	2.4	200	1.2	0	0.0	48	0.3
Tennessee	9,350	8.8	120	0.1	3,470	3.3	20	0.0	885	0.8
Texas	33,815	10.5	990	0.3	36,670	11.3	90	0.0	3,790	1.2
Utah	170	0.5	250	0.7	760	2.1	55	0.2	290	0.8
Vermont	100	0.8	55	0.4	125	1.0	0	0.0	79	0.6
Virginia	13,775	11.2	135	0.1	11,090	9.0	85	0.1	1,350	1.1
Washington	1,715	1.6	365	0.3	10,970	10.2	145	0.1	1,870	1.7
West Virginia	535	1.7	4	0.0	1,150	3.7	0	0.0	235	0.8
Wisconsin	2,360	2.3	290	0.3	3,370	3.3	25	0.0	714	0.7
Wyoming	10	0.1	85	1.0	120	1.5	0	0.0	59	0.7

B-6 Other Professional Workers, by State, Sex, Race, and Hispanic or Latino Origin, 2006–2010

State	Total who worked in the last 5 years	Male Number	Male Percent	Female Number	Female Percent	Hispanic or Latino Number	Hispanic or Latino Percent	White alone, not Hispanic or Latino Number	White alone, not Hispanic or Latino Percent
United States	16,723,700	6,345,860	37.9	10,377,840	62.1	1,299,960	7.8	12,680,020	75.8
Alabama	211,625	73,475	34.7	138,150	65.3	2,975	1.4	160,960	76.1
Alaska	39,215	14,285	36.4	24,930	63.6	1,435	3.7	30,590	78.0
Arizona	299,710	115,480	38.5	184,230	61.5	42,510	14.2	222,705	74.3
Arkansas	125,370	42,375	33.8	82,995	66.2	2,965	2.4	103,380	82.5
California	2,062,235	837,610	40.6	1,224,625	59.4	345,420	16.7	1,264,400	61.3
Colorado	290,555	109,200	37.6	181,355	62.4	23,375	8.0	246,830	85.0
Connecticut	242,105	95,315	39.4	146,790	60.6	12,835	5.3	202,330	83.6
Delaware	48,765	18,550	38.0	30,215	62.0	1,315	2.7	36,665	75.2
District of Columbia	74,200	33,620	45.3	40,580	54.7	4,430	6.0	45,450	61.3
Florida	886,050	334,860	37.8	551,190	62.2	143,760	16.2	597,030	67.4
Georgia	497,825	175,495	35.3	322,330	64.7	15,855	3.2	339,635	68.2
Hawaii	77,255	29,385	38.0	47,870	62.0	4,275	5.5	27,125	35.1
Idaho	71,320	26,910	37.7	44,410	62.3	2,985	4.2	65,425	91.7
Illinois	729,300	280,000	38.4	449,300	61.6	45,000	6.2	562,765	77.2
Indiana	303,005	114,065	37.6	188,940	62.4	7,940	2.6	264,735	87.4
Iowa	164,995	60,025	36.4	104,970	63.6	3,220	2.0	152,980	92.7
Kansas	162,505	59,160	36.4	103,350	63.6	5,535	3.4	144,545	88.9
Kentucky	197,015	72,315	36.7	124,705	63.3	2,930	1.5	175,565	89.1
Louisiana	207,745	70,520	33.9	137,225	66.1	5,385	2.6	150,620	72.5
Maine	79,525	27,880	35.1	51,645	64.9	840	1.1	76,530	96.2
Maryland	392,040	146,110	37.3	245,935	62.7	13,810	3.5	255,120	65.1
Massachusetts	470,150	179,880	38.3	290,270	61.7	19,505	4.1	400,175	85.1
Michigan	477,030	184,490	38.7	292,540	61.3	10,860	2.3	399,080	83.7
Minnesota	321,010	121,110	37.7	199,895	62.3	6,085	1.9	288,880	90.0
Mississippi	125,310	41,995	33.5	83,315	66.5	1,365	1.1	90,115	71.9
Missouri	309,565	110,175	35.6	199,395	64.4	6,325	2.0	269,300	87.0
Montana	52,295	20,450	39.1	31,850	60.9	950	1.8	47,780	91.4
Nebraska	99,370	36,875	37.1	62,495	62.9	2,745	2.8	90,580	91.2
Nevada	114,040	45,410	39.8	68,630	60.2	11,920	10.5	83,705	73.4
New Hampshire	79,485	27,390	34.5	52,095	65.5	1,225	1.5	75,645	95.2
New Jersey	553,275	215,025	38.9	338,245	61.1	44,755	8.1	405,755	73.3
New Mexico	105,630	39,090	37.0	66,540	63.0	30,155	28.5	63,215	59.8
New York	1,339,795	541,825	40.4	797,970	59.6	113,580	8.5	974,050	72.7
North Carolina	490,010	167,300	34.1	322,715	65.9	14,115	2.9	375,370	76.6
North Dakota	35,665	12,235	34.3	23,435	65.7	275	0.8	32,835	92.1
Ohio	580,780	216,935	37.4	363,845	62.6	9,800	1.7	502,210	86.5
Oklahoma	183,020	66,675	36.4	116,345	63.6	5,700	3.1	145,575	79.5
Oregon	201,400	79,870	39.7	121,525	60.3	9,460	4.7	175,735	87.3
Pennsylvania	691,240	272,400	39.4	418,840	60.6	17,130	2.5	596,650	86.3
Rhode Island	66,305	25,460	38.4	40,840	61.6	2,765	4.2	58,325	88.0
South Carolina	211,710	73,080	34.5	138,630	65.5	4,055	1.9	161,360	76.2
South Dakota	42,740	15,770	36.9	26,965	63.1	585	1.4	38,745	90.7
Tennessee	300,375	112,305	37.4	188,070	62.6	5,830	1.9	246,610	82.1
Texas	1,259,015	456,475	36.3	802,540	63.7	242,315	19.2	814,665	64.7
Utah	144,410	61,855	42.8	82,555	57.2	5,800	4.0	130,610	90.4
Vermont	46,305	16,695	36.1	29,610	63.9	560	1.2	44,275	95.6
Virginia	493,250	179,105	36.3	314,145	63.7	18,370	3.7	374,655	76.0
Washington	357,265	138,205	38.7	219,065	61.3	15,480	4.3	296,155	82.9
West Virginia	79,045	29,755	37.6	49,290	62.4	810	1.0	74,335	94.0
Wisconsin	303,410	110,870	36.5	192,540	63.5	7,610	2.5	272,060	89.7
Wyoming	28,420	10,530	37.1	17,895	63.0	1,040	3.7	26,165	92.1

PART B—STATE TABLES

B-6 Other Professional Workers, by State, Sex, Race, and Hispanic or Latino Origin, 2006–2010—Continued

State	Black alone, not Hispanic or Latino Number	Percent	American Indian and Alaska Native alone, not Hispanic or Latino Number	Percent	Asian alone, not Hispanic or Latino Number	Percent	Native Hawaiian and Other Pacific Islander alone, not Hispanic or Latino Number	Percent	Two or more races, not Hispanic or Latino Number	Percent
United States	1,584,760	9.5	74,070	0.4	826,590	4.9	15,995	0.1	242,305	1.4
Alabama	40,895	19.3	815	0.4	4,055	1.9	35	0.0	1,885	0.9
Alaska	1,230	3.1	3,395	8.7	885	2.3	175	0.4	1,505	3.8
Arizona	12,475	4.2	8,005	2.7	9,200	3.1	415	0.1	4,405	1.5
Arkansas	15,785	12.6	630	0.5	1,535	1.2	40	0.0	1,035	0.8
California	119,905	5.8	6,410	0.3	272,890	13.2	4,460	0.2	48,745	2.4
Colorado	7,370	2.5	1,340	0.5	6,765	2.3	190	0.1	4,675	1.6
Connecticut	16,505	6.8	305	0.1	7,430	3.1	25	0.0	2,670	1.1
Delaware	8,140	16.7	40	0.1	1,945	4.0	4	0.0	650	1.3
District of Columbia	18,920	25.5	250	0.3	3,515	4.7	30	0.0	1,600	2.2
Florida	111,620	12.6	1,535	0.2	20,630	2.3	455	0.1	11,025	1.2
Georgia	119,355	24.0	640	0.1	16,145	3.2	165	0.0	6,030	1.2
Hawaii	935	1.2	225	0.3	29,735	38.5	4,350	5.6	10,615	13.7
Idaho	265	0.4	585	0.8	895	1.3	95	0.1	1,065	1.5
Illinois	77,840	10.7	555	0.1	35,345	4.8	155	0.0	7,630	1.0
Indiana	19,675	6.5	305	0.1	7,200	2.4	40	0.0	3,110	1.0
Iowa	3,540	2.1	140	0.1	3,925	2.4	55	0.0	1,135	0.7
Kansas	5,740	3.5	750	0.5	4,115	2.5	55	0.0	1,765	1.1
Kentucky	13,065	6.6	145	0.1	3,670	1.9	65	0.0	1,575	0.8
Louisiana	44,955	21.6	710	0.3	4,160	2.0	50	0.0	1,860	0.9
Maine	530	0.7	270	0.3	845	1.1	40	0.1	465	0.6
Maryland	96,020	24.5	675	0.2	20,665	5.3	115	0.0	5,635	1.4
Massachusetts	20,610	4.4	490	0.1	22,755	4.8	75	0.0	6,530	1.4
Michigan	45,945	9.6	1,435	0.3	13,975	2.9	60	0.0	5,670	1.2
Minnesota	10,440	3.3	1,865	0.6	10,045	3.1	25	0.0	3,665	1.1
Mississippi	30,900	24.7	465	0.4	1,850	1.5	15	0.0	595	0.5
Missouri	24,820	8.0	610	0.2	5,340	1.7	165	0.1	3,010	1.0
Montana	225	0.4	2,120	4.1	325	0.6	25	0.0	870	1.7
Nebraska	2,985	3.0	395	0.4	1,580	1.6	50	0.1	1,040	1.0
Nevada	7,840	6.9	810	0.7	6,795	6.0	480	0.4	2,495	2.2
New Hampshire	490	0.6	185	0.2	1,285	1.6	4	0.0	655	0.8
New Jersey	56,985	10.3	480	0.1	38,520	7.0	50	0.0	6,725	1.2
New Mexico	2,335	2.2	5,925	5.6	2,305	2.2	45	0.0	1,660	1.6
New York	142,420	10.6	1,955	0.1	88,960	6.6	240	0.0	18,595	1.4
North Carolina	81,655	16.7	3,545	0.7	9,645	2.0	35	0.0	5,645	1.2
North Dakota	240	0.7	1,305	3.7	705	2.0	0	0.0	310	0.9
Ohio	48,620	8.4	695	0.1	13,555	2.3	4	0.0	5,895	1.0
Oklahoma	11,140	6.1	9,005	4.9	3,560	1.9	155	0.1	7,875	4.3
Oregon	3,085	1.5	1,000	0.5	7,455	3.7	395	0.2	4,270	2.1
Pennsylvania	52,085	7.5	575	0.1	18,660	2.7	125	0.0	6,020	0.9
Rhode Island	2,455	3.7	165	0.2	1,740	2.6	0	0.0	850	1.3
South Carolina	40,355	19.1	315	0.1	3,775	1.8	35	0.0	1,825	0.9
South Dakota	270	0.6	2,320	5.4	460	1.1	0	0.0	350	0.8
Tennessee	39,895	13.3	480	0.2	4,995	1.7	95	0.0	2,470	0.8
Texas	132,245	10.5	3,665	0.3	51,040	4.1	600	0.0	14,495	1.2
Utah	1,175	0.8	820	0.6	3,755	2.6	645	0.4	1,605	1.1
Vermont	275	0.6	65	0.1	550	1.2	0	0.0	575	1.2
Virginia	65,995	13.4	730	0.1	25,655	5.2	255	0.1	7,590	1.5
Washington	9,385	2.6	2,815	0.8	23,875	6.7	1,265	0.4	8,290	2.3
West Virginia	2,100	2.7	20	0.0	1,020	1.3	45	0.1	710	0.9
Wisconsin	12,960	4.3	1,605	0.5	6,535	2.2	55	0.0	2,585	0.9
Wyoming	75	0.3	490	1.7	310	1.1	15	0.1	330	1.2

B-7 Technicians, by State, Sex, Race, and Hispanic or Latino Origin, 2006–2010

State	Total who worked in the last 5 years	Male Number	Male Percent	Female Number	Female Percent	Hispanic or Latino Number	Hispanic or Latino Percent	White alone, not Hispanic or Latino Number	White alone, not Hispanic or Latino Percent
United States	4,244,165	1,861,185	43.9	2,382,975	56.1	360,235	8.5	3,000,415	70.7
Alabama	68,020	25,825	38.0	42,195	62.0	685	1.0	50,930	74.9
Alaska	10,355	5,115	49.4	5,240	50.6	650	6.3	7,395	71.4
Arizona	79,810	38,975	48.8	40,835	51.2	13,205	16.5	56,160	70.4
Arkansas	40,430	14,985	37.1	25,445	62.9	930	2.3	33,430	82.7
California	441,475	228,815	51.8	212,660	48.2	91,515	20.7	204,695	46.4
Colorado	67,245	34,485	51.3	32,760	48.7	7,635	11.4	53,545	79.6
Connecticut	52,650	22,530	42.8	30,120	57.2	3,410	6.5	40,380	76.7
Delaware	13,485	6,100	45.2	7,385	54.8	420	3.1	9,365	69.4
District of Columbia	6,085	2,630	43.2	3,455	56.8	225	3.7	2,435	40.0
Florida	246,560	105,890	42.9	140,665	57.1	41,810	17.0	152,640	61.9
Georgia	123,850	51,815	41.8	72,035	58.2	3,570	2.9	76,525	61.8
Hawaii	15,020	7,300	48.6	7,720	51.4	980	6.5	3,370	22.4
Idaho	21,075	9,835	46.7	11,240	53.3	955	4.5	18,890	89.6
Illinois	165,930	71,690	43.2	94,240	56.8	11,770	7.1	115,590	69.7
Indiana	93,005	35,235	37.9	57,770	62.1	2,620	2.8	80,210	86.2
Iowa	44,715	17,740	39.7	26,975	60.3	860	1.9	41,510	92.8
Kansas	40,755	17,150	42.1	23,605	57.9	1,970	4.8	34,310	84.2
Kentucky	58,740	21,050	35.8	37,690	64.2	820	1.4	53,000	90.2
Louisiana	68,220	27,975	41.0	40,245	59.0	1,510	2.2	47,640	69.8
Maine	19,005	7,210	37.9	11,795	62.1	190	1.0	18,285	96.2
Maryland	91,490	40,890	44.7	50,605	55.3	3,265	3.6	50,410	55.1
Massachusetts	104,340	45,190	43.3	59,150	56.7	5,810	5.6	82,655	79.2
Michigan	135,945	54,965	40.4	80,975	59.6	3,150	2.3	112,885	83.0
Minnesota	91,645	39,595	43.2	52,050	56.8	1,425	1.6	81,255	88.7
Mississippi	40,885	14,135	34.6	26,750	65.4	545	1.3	27,510	67.3
Missouri	91,705	35,595	38.8	56,115	61.2	1,775	1.9	76,240	83.1
Montana	12,020	4,810	40.0	7,210	60.0	410	3.4	10,760	89.5
Nebraska	28,685	11,425	39.8	17,260	60.2	680	2.4	25,965	90.5
Nevada	30,335	15,270	50.3	15,065	49.7	3,585	11.8	19,405	64.0
New Hampshire	23,430	10,240	43.7	13,190	56.3	345	1.5	21,670	92.5
New Jersey	127,025	60,145	47.3	66,880	52.7	12,140	9.6	74,915	59.0
New Mexico	28,325	14,475	51.1	13,850	48.9	9,800	34.6	15,020	53.0
New York	239,175	107,295	44.9	131,880	55.1	21,370	8.9	156,790	65.6
North Carolina	134,295	52,095	38.8	82,200	61.2	3,475	2.6	97,845	72.9
North Dakota	10,910	3,985	36.5	6,925	63.5	80	0.7	10,305	94.5
Ohio	176,110	68,765	39.0	107,345	61.0	2,905	1.6	149,815	85.1
Oklahoma	55,120	23,055	41.8	32,065	58.2	1,860	3.4	41,840	75.9
Oregon	48,390	23,950	49.5	24,440	50.5	2,155	4.5	41,605	86.0
Pennsylvania	201,865	83,825	41.5	118,040	58.5	4,950	2.5	168,145	83.3
Rhode Island	14,765	6,555	44.4	8,205	55.6	655	4.4	12,700	86.0
South Carolina	64,330	24,955	38.8	39,375	61.2	1,215	1.9	46,485	72.3
South Dakota	12,060	4,325	35.9	7,735	64.1	120	1.0	11,055	91.7
Tennessee	98,240	37,300	38.0	60,940	62.0	1,225	1.2	79,600	81.0
Texas	331,955	159,655	48.1	172,305	51.9	77,540	23.4	183,880	55.4
Utah	37,960	21,480	56.6	16,485	43.4	2,595	6.8	33,025	87.0
Vermont	10,120	4,120	40.7	6,000	59.3	170	1.7	9,750	96.3
Virginia	111,495	46,830	42.0	64,665	58.0	4,185	3.8	74,190	66.5
Washington	90,795	44,150	48.6	46,645	51.4	4,325	4.8	70,635	77.8
West Virginia	28,680	10,955	38.2	17,725	61.8	150	0.5	27,440	95.7
Wisconsin	88,565	35,630	40.2	52,935	59.8	2,335	2.6	79,725	90.0
Wyoming	7,080	3,195	45.1	3,885	54.9	265	3.7	6,575	92.9

B-7 Technicians, by State, Sex, Race, and Hispanic or Latino Origin, 2006–2010—Continued

State	Black alone, not Hispanic or Latino Number	Percent	American Indian and Alaska Native alone, not Hispanic or Latino Number	Percent	Asian alone, not Hispanic or Latino Number	Percent	Native Hawaiian and Other Pacific Islander alone, not Hispanic or Latino Number	Percent	Two or more races, not Hispanic or Latino Number	Percent
United States	484,455	11.4	23,050	0.5	307,115	7.2	4,845	0.1	64,040	1.5
Alabama	14,500	21.3	340	0.5	975	1.4	4	0.0	595	0.9
Alaska	430	4.2	750	7.2	545	5.3	50	0.5	540	5.2
Arizona	3,005	3.8	2,090	2.6	4,045	5.1	160	0.2	1,145	1.4
Arkansas	4,380	10.8	225	0.6	985	2.4	0	0.0	474	1.2
California	27,540	6.2	1,505	0.3	103,155	23.4	1,760	0.4	11,305	2.6
Colorado	1,910	2.8	345	0.5	2,380	3.5	0	0.0	1,440	2.1
Connecticut	4,870	9.2	75	0.1	2,970	5.6	100	0.2	845	1.6
Delaware	2,470	18.3	65	0.5	935	6.9	0	0.0	230	1.7
District of Columbia	2,950	48.5	0	0.0	415	6.8	0	0.0	60	1.0
Florida	38,690	15.7	540	0.2	9,040	3.7	265	0.1	3,575	1.4
Georgia	35,935	29.0	285	0.2	6,125	4.9	30	0.0	1,380	1.1
Hawaii	415	2.8	4	0.0	7,005	46.6	785	5.2	2,454	16.3
Idaho	135	0.6	220	1.0	460	2.2	15	0.1	394	1.9
Illinois	20,225	12.2	230	0.1	16,315	9.8	15	0.0	1,785	1.1
Indiana	7,000	7.5	120	0.1	2,020	2.2	25	0.0	1,005	1.1
Iowa	720	1.6	20	0.0	1,290	2.9	0	0.0	310	0.7
Kansas	2,085	5.1	260	0.6	1,665	4.1	25	0.1	435	1.1
Kentucky	3,540	6.0	115	0.2	950	1.6	0	0.0	325	0.6
Louisiana	16,830	24.7	305	0.4	1,195	1.8	25	0.0	720	1.1
Maine	90	0.5	25	0.1	165	0.9	30	0.2	215	1.1
Maryland	28,515	31.2	205	0.2	7,615	8.3	50	0.1	1,430	1.6
Massachusetts	6,850	6.6	100	0.1	7,410	7.1	30	0.0	1,485	1.4
Michigan	12,140	8.9	495	0.4	5,325	3.9	40	0.0	1,905	1.4
Minnesota	2,845	3.1	440	0.5	4,490	4.9	65	0.1	1,120	1.2
Mississippi	12,120	29.6	110	0.3	415	1.0	35	0.1	154	0.4
Missouri	9,865	10.8	225	0.2	2,385	2.6	30	0.0	1,180	1.3
Montana	15	0.1	520	4.3	125	1.0	0	0.0	185	1.5
Nebraska	920	3.2	100	0.3	810	2.8	0	0.0	215	0.7
Nevada	2,375	7.8	315	1.0	3,700	12.2	165	0.5	780	2.6
New Hampshire	265	1.1	30	0.1	660	2.8	0	0.0	460	2.0
New Jersey	16,975	13.4	210	0.2	20,920	16.5	50	0.0	1,810	1.4
New Mexico	375	1.3	2,050	7.2	600	2.1	0	0.0	475	1.7
New York	36,815	15.4	795	0.3	20,435	8.5	0	0.0	2,970	1.2
North Carolina	26,290	19.6	1,235	0.9	4,115	3.1	20	0.0	1,315	1.0
North Dakota	65	0.6	205	1.9	145	1.3	4	0.0	100	0.9
Ohio	16,445	9.3	315	0.2	4,950	2.8	0	0.0	1,680	1.0
Oklahoma	3,735	6.8	3,560	6.5	1,330	2.4	55	0.1	2,735	5.0
Oregon	555	1.1	525	1.1	2,370	4.9	85	0.2	1,095	2.3
Pennsylvania	18,295	9.1	290	0.1	8,290	4.1	20	0.0	1,875	0.9
Rhode Island	660	4.5	25	0.2	505	3.4	0	0.0	210	1.4
South Carolina	14,465	22.5	135	0.2	1,360	2.1	65	0.1	610	0.9
South Dakota	50	0.4	605	5.0	85	0.7	0	0.0	140	1.2
Tennessee	14,090	14.3	135	0.1	1,945	2.0	0	0.0	1,240	1.3
Texas	42,380	12.8	1,120	0.3	22,990	6.9	330	0.1	3,720	1.1
Utah	225	0.6	230	0.6	1,285	3.4	120	0.3	480	1.3
Vermont	25	0.2	15	0.1	85	0.8	4	0.0	73	0.7
Virginia	22,330	20.0	205	0.2	8,745	7.8	110	0.1	1,725	1.5
Washington	2,995	3.3	715	0.8	9,270	10.2	270	0.3	2,585	2.8
West Virginia	590	2.1	105	0.4	145	0.5	0	0.0	245	0.9
Wisconsin	3,445	3.9	450	0.5	1,930	2.2	4	0.0	675	0.8
Wyoming	15	0.2	60	0.8	35	0.5	0	0.0	125	1.8

B-8 Sales Workers, by State, Sex, Race, and Hispanic or Latino Origin, 2006–2010

State	Total who worked in the last 5 years	Male Number	Male Percent	Female Number	Female Percent	Hispanic or Latino Number	Hispanic or Latino Percent	White alone, not Hispanic or Latino Number	White alone, not Hispanic or Latino Percent
United States	17,256,510	8,552,900	49.6	8,703,610	50.4	2,154,145	12.5	12,163,980	70.5
Alabama	255,510	114,145	44.7	141,360	55.3	3,850	1.5	188,970	74.0
Alaska	31,815	13,925	43.8	17,895	56.2	1,585	5.0	22,115	69.5
Arizona	360,160	186,530	51.8	173,630	48.2	77,185	21.4	249,625	69.3
Arkansas	150,420	70,700	47.0	79,720	53.0	4,525	3.0	123,475	82.1
California	2,097,545	1,081,745	51.6	1,015,800	48.4	634,490	30.2	1,022,925	48.8
Colorado	304,425	157,400	51.7	147,020	48.3	40,980	13.5	239,955	78.8
Connecticut	216,550	111,460	51.5	105,090	48.5	22,800	10.5	165,145	76.3
Delaware	49,070	23,265	47.4	25,810	52.6	1,970	4.0	37,045	75.5
District of Columbia	22,025	9,765	44.3	12,260	55.7	1,430	6.5	7,755	35.2
Florida	1,208,925	595,980	49.3	612,945	50.7	252,895	20.9	757,225	62.6
Georgia	564,910	271,215	48.0	293,690	52.0	25,210	4.5	355,290	62.9
Hawaii	77,945	32,735	42.0	45,210	58.0	5,300	6.8	19,890	25.5
Idaho	80,265	40,550	50.5	39,715	49.5	5,245	6.5	72,290	90.1
Illinois	739,955	371,545	50.2	368,410	49.8	83,800	11.3	530,615	71.7
Indiana	346,320	166,130	48.0	180,190	52.0	11,700	3.4	298,310	86.1
Iowa	167,130	84,220	50.4	82,910	49.6	3,970	2.4	156,185	93.5
Kansas	150,995	77,890	51.6	73,105	48.4	8,685	5.8	129,365	85.7
Kentucky	216,020	100,865	46.7	115,160	53.3	3,410	1.6	194,515	90.0
Louisiana	239,715	103,445	43.2	136,265	56.8	8,120	3.4	157,310	65.6
Maine	76,980	37,485	48.7	39,495	51.3	1,030	1.3	73,910	96.0
Maryland	306,180	150,920	49.3	155,260	50.7	18,575	6.1	185,210	60.5
Massachusetts	373,000	190,535	51.1	182,460	48.9	26,190	7.0	307,865	82.5
Michigan	534,985	255,745	47.8	279,240	52.2	14,145	2.6	444,110	83.0
Minnesota	320,270	169,770	53.0	150,500	47.0	7,975	2.5	285,185	89.0
Mississippi	146,530	61,395	41.9	85,130	58.1	1,860	1.3	96,685	66.0
Missouri	338,585	162,420	48.0	176,165	52.0	7,245	2.1	288,620	85.2
Montana	53,030	26,470	49.9	26,560	50.1	1,315	2.5	49,170	92.7
Nebraska	104,185	53,525	51.4	50,665	48.6	4,320	4.1	92,985	89.2
Nevada	164,670	76,820	46.7	87,850	53.3	29,670	18.0	103,345	62.8
New Hampshire	87,950	45,410	51.6	42,540	48.4	1,610	1.8	84,055	95.6
New Jersey	535,245	287,150	53.6	248,100	46.4	70,190	13.1	358,140	66.9
New Mexico	101,735	46,500	45.7	55,235	54.3	41,480	40.8	49,280	48.4
New York	1,064,945	552,975	51.9	511,970	48.1	152,520	14.3	682,040	64.0
North Carolina	526,510	253,340	48.1	273,170	51.9	21,495	4.1	394,115	74.9
North Dakota	38,730	19,750	51.0	18,985	49.0	605	1.6	35,735	92.3
Ohio	623,495	298,225	47.8	325,270	52.2	12,700	2.0	538,100	86.3
Oklahoma	192,740	92,410	47.9	100,330	52.1	9,440	4.9	147,440	76.5
Oregon	210,775	107,995	51.2	102,780	48.8	14,495	6.9	179,880	85.3
Pennsylvania	678,620	333,300	49.1	345,320	50.9	24,035	3.5	578,275	85.2
Rhode Island	60,265	29,975	49.7	30,290	50.3	4,765	7.9	50,490	83.8
South Carolina	259,915	116,940	45.0	142,975	55.0	5,130	2.0	189,080	72.7
South Dakota	43,910	22,925	52.2	20,980	47.8	625	1.4	41,005	93.4
Tennessee	351,715	170,615	48.5	181,100	51.5	7,560	2.1	288,205	81.9
Texas	1,376,480	692,425	50.3	684,055	49.7	404,160	29.4	758,785	55.1
Utah	156,125	82,880	53.1	73,245	46.9	13,455	8.6	135,615	86.9
Vermont	35,685	17,755	49.8	17,925	50.2	310	0.9	34,290	96.1
Virginia	422,885	196,755	46.5	226,135	53.5	23,555	5.6	289,665	68.5
Washington	360,730	182,235	50.5	178,490	49.5	24,110	6.7	286,790	79.5
West Virginia	88,930	39,540	44.5	49,385	55.5	795	0.9	83,355	93.7
Wisconsin	313,095	152,220	48.6	160,875	51.4	9,930	3.2	279,875	89.4
Wyoming	27,915	12,985	46.5	14,930	53.5	1,700	6.1	24,675	88.4

B-8 Sales Workers, by State, Sex, Race, and Hispanic or Latino Origin, 2006–2010—Continued

State	Black alone, not Hispanic or Latino Number	Percent	American Indian and Alaska Native alone, not Hispanic or Latino Number	Percent	Asian alone, not Hispanic or Latino Number	Percent	Native Hawaiian and Other Pacific Islander alone, not Hispanic or Latino Number	Percent	Two or more races, not Hispanic or Latino Number	Percent
United States	1,746,595	10.1	81,310	0.5	809,545	4.7	23,455	0.1	277,475	1.6
Alabama	55,860	21.9	1,125	0.4	3,055	1.2	45	0.0	2,600	1.0
Alaska	1,115	3.5	2,775	8.7	2,235	7.0	290	0.9	1,700	5.3
Arizona	11,610	3.2	7,015	1.9	9,235	2.6	375	0.1	5,120	1.4
Arkansas	18,210	12.1	970	0.6	1,450	1.0	40	0.0	1,745	1.2
California	104,845	5.0	7,570	0.4	273,085	13.0	6,550	0.3	48,075	2.3
Colorado	9,530	3.1	1,665	0.5	6,840	2.2	260	0.1	5,195	1.7
Connecticut	17,545	8.1	360	0.2	6,830	3.2	110	0.1	3,755	1.7
Delaware	7,760	15.8	65	0.1	1,460	3.0	0	0.0	765	1.6
District of Columbia	11,895	54.0	55	0.2	620	2.8	20	0.1	245	1.1
Florida	146,485	12.1	1,885	0.2	32,325	2.7	825	0.1	17,285	1.4
Georgia	153,645	27.2	1,180	0.2	21,890	3.9	240	0.0	7,450	1.3
Hawaii	740	0.9	40	0.1	33,365	42.8	5,405	6.9	13,209	16.9
Idaho	380	0.5	510	0.6	590	0.7	55	0.1	1,195	1.5
Illinois	84,545	11.4	780	0.1	32,195	4.4	145	0.0	7,870	1.1
Indiana	27,490	7.9	605	0.2	3,595	1.0	25	0.0	4,590	1.3
Iowa	3,250	1.9	440	0.3	1,640	1.0	85	0.1	1,570	0.9
Kansas	7,075	4.7	750	0.5	2,410	1.6	45	0.0	2,675	1.8
Kentucky	13,750	6.4	315	0.1	1,660	0.8	250	0.1	2,125	1.0
Louisiana	66,740	27.8	1,350	0.6	4,435	1.9	70	0.0	1,685	0.7
Maine	445	0.6	260	0.3	575	0.7	4	0.0	759	1.0
Maryland	80,340	26.2	410	0.1	15,665	5.1	185	0.1	5,790	1.9
Massachusetts	17,950	4.8	610	0.2	14,335	3.8	70	0.0	5,975	1.6
Michigan	58,120	10.9	2,300	0.4	8,890	1.7	160	0.0	7,260	1.4
Minnesota	12,235	3.8	1,695	0.5	9,215	2.9	65	0.0	3,900	1.2
Mississippi	44,555	30.4	470	0.3	1,785	1.2	0	0.0	1,170	0.8
Missouri	31,740	9.4	915	0.3	4,525	1.3	170	0.1	5,365	1.6
Montana	250	0.5	1,430	2.7	160	0.3	40	0.1	660	1.2
Nebraska	4,015	3.9	370	0.4	930	0.9	40	0.0	1,530	1.5
Nevada	12,185	7.4	1,320	0.8	13,450	8.2	1,065	0.6	3,640	2.2
New Hampshire	470	0.5	180	0.2	855	1.0	10	0.0	765	0.9
New Jersey	54,785	10.2	645	0.1	44,085	8.2	45	0.0	7,360	1.4
New Mexico	1,765	1.7	6,550	6.4	1,070	1.1	105	0.1	1,490	1.5
New York	119,930	11.3	2,470	0.2	89,925	8.4	230	0.0	17,835	1.7
North Carolina	90,565	17.2	3,415	0.6	9,560	1.8	250	0.0	7,100	1.3
North Dakota	360	0.9	1,335	3.4	290	0.7	0	0.0	410	1.1
Ohio	56,580	9.1	765	0.1	7,525	1.2	60	0.0	7,760	1.2
Oklahoma	12,470	6.5	10,020	5.2	3,215	1.7	275	0.1	9,880	5.1
Oregon	3,010	1.4	1,845	0.9	6,350	3.0	795	0.4	4,400	2.1
Pennsylvania	52,100	7.7	695	0.1	16,425	2.4	135	0.0	6,950	1.0
Rhode Island	2,615	4.3	130	0.2	1,400	2.3	0	0.0	865	1.4
South Carolina	58,355	22.5	890	0.3	3,430	1.3	50	0.0	2,985	1.1
South Dakota	295	0.7	1,460	3.3	195	0.4	0	0.0	335	0.8
Tennessee	46,705	13.3	690	0.2	5,225	1.5	150	0.0	3,185	0.9
Texas	137,565	10.0	3,655	0.3	54,860	4.0	955	0.1	16,490	1.2
Utah	980	0.6	800	0.5	2,510	1.6	1,000	0.6	1,760	1.1
Vermont	205	0.6	75	0.2	300	0.8	10	0.0	500	1.4
Virginia	77,195	18.3	720	0.2	24,175	5.7	485	0.1	7,090	1.7
Washington	9,795	2.7	3,250	0.9	23,725	6.6	2,105	0.6	10,955	3.0
West Virginia	3,145	3.5	120	0.1	425	0.5	65	0.1	1,020	1.1
Wisconsin	13,155	4.2	1,885	0.6	5,195	1.7	90	0.0	2,970	0.9
Wyoming	240	0.9	480	1.7	335	1.2	10	0.0	485	1.7

B-9 Administrative Support Workers, by State, Sex, Race, and Hispanic or Latino Origin, 2006–2010

State	Total who worked in the last 5 years	Male Number	Male Percent	Female Number	Female Percent	Hispanic or Latino Number	Hispanic or Latino Percent	White alone, not Hispanic or Latino Number	White alone, not Hispanic or Latino Percent
United States	23,586,105	5,990,085	25.4	17,596,020	74.6	3,075,280	13.0	15,972,595	67.7
Alabama	326,860	76,070	23.3	250,790	76.7	4,850	1.5	234,655	71.8
Alaska	60,410	15,500	25.7	44,910	74.3	3,200	5.3	38,535	63.8
Arizona	479,215	127,370	26.6	351,845	73.4	119,745	25.0	304,605	63.6
Arkansas	198,390	46,830	23.6	151,560	76.4	5,095	2.6	159,345	80.3
California	2,752,860	794,945	28.9	1,957,920	71.1	905,735	32.9	1,193,460	43.4
Colorado	384,820	97,500	25.3	287,320	74.7	60,980	15.8	288,235	74.9
Connecticut	290,655	69,875	24.0	220,785	76.0	29,440	10.1	218,585	75.2
Delaware	74,765	18,820	25.2	55,945	74.8	3,380	4.5	51,845	69.3
District of Columbia	51,620	17,530	34.0	34,090	66.0	3,030	5.9	16,010	31.0
Florida	1,463,445	368,005	25.1	1,095,440	74.9	320,060	21.9	866,255	59.2
Georgia	702,460	169,210	24.1	533,250	75.9	28,835	4.1	417,795	59.5
Hawaii	106,585	26,020	24.4	80,565	75.6	7,500	7.0	18,800	17.6
Idaho	113,305	25,795	22.8	87,510	77.2	7,530	6.6	101,250	89.4
Illinois	1,042,310	270,620	26.0	771,690	74.0	131,680	12.6	703,840	67.5
Indiana	482,465	113,260	23.5	369,205	76.5	16,400	3.4	411,845	85.4
Iowa	250,295	57,220	22.9	193,075	77.1	5,750	2.3	233,225	93.2
Kansas	231,000	54,605	23.6	176,395	76.4	15,490	6.7	193,645	83.8
Kentucky	312,830	76,250	24.4	236,585	75.6	4,300	1.4	279,440	89.3
Louisiana	319,280	69,890	21.9	249,390	78.1	7,805	2.4	217,600	68.2
Maine	101,175	23,550	23.3	77,630	76.7	1,200	1.2	97,505	96.4
Maryland	491,010	126,045	25.7	364,965	74.3	24,015	4.9	264,365	53.8
Massachusetts	528,180	139,805	26.5	388,380	73.5	36,460	6.9	430,380	81.5
Michigan	726,595	170,185	23.4	556,410	76.6	21,875	3.0	586,905	80.8
Minnesota	438,920	108,550	24.7	330,370	75.3	10,885	2.5	387,170	88.2
Mississippi	189,945	43,005	22.6	146,940	77.4	1,800	0.9	126,510	66.6
Missouri	468,105	110,215	23.5	357,890	76.5	10,035	2.1	386,915	82.7
Montana	74,280	13,985	18.8	60,295	81.2	1,290	1.7	67,505	90.9
Nebraska	155,560	36,895	23.7	118,665	76.3	7,210	4.6	136,345	87.6
Nevada	207,885	56,660	27.3	151,220	72.7	36,165	17.4	129,980	62.5
New Hampshire	110,545	26,230	23.7	84,315	76.3	1,945	1.8	105,145	95.1
New Jersey	758,100	191,470	25.3	566,625	74.7	114,335	15.1	479,455	63.2
New Mexico	144,400	33,225	23.0	111,175	77.0	66,940	46.4	61,440	42.5
New York	1,581,430	435,015	27.5	1,146,415	72.5	239,280	15.1	968,960	61.3
North Carolina	657,415	159,445	24.3	497,970	75.7	24,410	3.7	461,860	70.3
North Dakota	53,560	11,500	21.5	42,060	78.5	865	1.6	49,520	92.5
Ohio	902,380	223,330	24.7	679,050	75.3	16,565	1.8	755,640	83.7
Oklahoma	280,550	65,820	23.5	214,730	76.5	13,615	4.9	209,685	74.7
Oregon	295,295	71,285	24.1	224,010	75.9	21,115	7.2	249,345	84.4
Pennsylvania	1,015,505	249,950	24.6	765,560	75.4	38,170	3.8	840,425	82.8
Rhode Island	88,355	22,935	26.0	65,420	74.0	8,080	9.1	72,515	82.1
South Carolina	321,010	73,845	23.0	247,165	77.0	7,005	2.2	227,160	70.8
South Dakota	67,085	14,360	21.4	52,725	78.6	875	1.3	60,805	90.6
Tennessee	466,945	114,585	24.5	352,360	75.5	9,300	2.0	364,070	78.0
Texas	1,827,485	485,325	26.6	1,342,155	73.4	575,365	31.5	922,460	50.5
Utah	220,930	60,645	27.4	160,290	72.6	19,780	9.0	188,390	85.3
Vermont	50,115	11,545	23.0	38,570	77.0	695	1.4	47,895	95.6
Virginia	598,125	149,065	24.9	449,060	75.1	33,750	5.6	395,455	66.1
Washington	491,870	120,885	24.6	370,985	75.4	31,955	6.5	386,485	78.6
West Virginia	122,970	29,480	24.0	93,495	76.0	915	0.7	115,810	94.2
Wisconsin	463,190	107,890	23.3	355,305	76.7	16,050	3.5	408,160	88.1
Wyoming	43,600	8,055	18.5	35,550	81.5	2,500	5.7	39,355	90.3

B-9 Administrative Support Workers, by State, Sex, Race, and Hispanic or Latino Origin, 2006–2010—*Continued*

State	Black alone, not Hispanic or Latino Number	Percent	American Indian and Alaska Native alone, not Hispanic or Latino Number	Percent	Asian alone, not Hispanic or Latino Number	Percent	Native Hawaiian and Other Pacific Islander alone, not Hispanic or Latino Number	Percent	Two or more races, not Hispanic or Latino Number	Percent
United States	3,079,780	13.1	139,440	0.6	908,890	3.9	44,440	0.2	365,670	1.6
Alabama	81,590	25.0	1,355	0.4	1,495	0.5	30	0.0	2,880	0.9
Alaska	2,345	3.9	8,405	13.9	3,585	5.9	565	0.9	3,770	6.2
Arizona	20,830	4.3	15,865	3.3	9,890	2.1	1,000	0.2	7,275	1.5
Arkansas	28,850	14.5	1,360	0.7	1,355	0.7	260	0.1	2,130	1.1
California	210,755	7.7	12,405	0.5	351,955	12.8	14,800	0.5	63,745	2.3
Colorado	18,110	4.7	2,215	0.6	8,285	2.2	505	0.1	6,490	1.7
Connecticut	31,465	10.8	455	0.2	6,430	2.2	210	0.1	4,065	1.4
Delaware	17,125	22.9	155	0.2	1,305	1.7	85	0.1	870	1.2
District of Columbia	30,165	58.4	125	0.2	1,460	2.8	70	0.1	770	1.5
Florida	227,170	15.5	2,925	0.2	26,545	1.8	585	0.0	19,905	1.4
Georgia	231,715	33.0	1,545	0.2	14,010	2.0	495	0.1	8,055	1.1
Hawaii	1,330	1.2	125	0.1	47,300	44.4	10,420	9.8	21,115	19.8
Idaho	515	0.5	1,175	1.0	855	0.8	485	0.4	1,495	1.3
Illinois	160,065	15.4	1,080	0.1	35,600	3.4	310	0.0	9,730	0.9
Indiana	44,775	9.3	820	0.2	3,995	0.8	60	0.0	4,570	0.9
Iowa	5,915	2.4	590	0.2	2,800	1.1	40	0.0	1,975	0.8
Kansas	13,435	5.8	1,270	0.5	3,065	1.3	130	0.1	3,965	1.7
Kentucky	24,020	7.7	470	0.2	1,985	0.6	210	0.1	2,400	0.8
Louisiana	86,855	27.2	1,445	0.5	2,555	0.8	125	0.0	2,900	0.9
Maine	580	0.6	375	0.4	650	0.6	25	0.0	850	0.8
Maryland	174,755	35.6	1,000	0.2	18,375	3.7	315	0.1	8,190	1.7
Massachusetts	34,130	6.5	595	0.1	18,260	3.5	215	0.0	8,140	1.5
Michigan	95,665	13.2	2,920	0.4	10,295	1.4	115	0.0	8,810	1.2
Minnesota	20,525	4.7	3,585	0.8	10,975	2.5	115	0.0	5,660	1.3
Mississippi	58,805	31.0	690	0.4	910	0.5	45	0.0	1,190	0.6
Missouri	58,980	12.6	1,480	0.3	4,240	0.9	315	0.1	6,130	1.3
Montana	250	0.3	3,660	4.9	420	0.6	40	0.1	1,115	1.5
Nebraska	7,630	4.9	920	0.6	1,600	1.0	125	0.1	1,730	1.1
Nevada	19,220	9.2	1,980	1.0	13,640	6.6	1,640	0.8	5,240	2.5
New Hampshire	1,230	1.1	160	0.1	1,175	1.1	40	0.0	850	0.8
New Jersey	113,485	15.0	525	0.1	41,405	5.5	80	0.0	8,815	1.2
New Mexico	2,560	1.8	10,095	7.0	1,245	0.9	95	0.1	2,020	1.4
New York	250,785	15.9	3,630	0.2	93,345	5.9	385	0.0	25,050	1.6
North Carolina	148,915	22.7	4,635	0.7	8,565	1.3	375	0.1	8,655	1.3
North Dakota	200	0.4	2,205	4.1	280	0.5	0	0.0	495	0.9
Ohio	111,685	12.4	1,110	0.1	7,895	0.9	115	0.0	9,370	1.0
Oklahoma	21,275	7.6	17,330	6.2	3,645	1.3	195	0.1	14,810	5.3
Oregon	4,620	1.6	3,045	1.0	9,010	3.1	955	0.3	7,205	2.4
Pennsylvania	110,580	10.9	905	0.1	15,865	1.6	105	0.0	9,455	0.9
Rhode Island	3,755	4.2	340	0.4	1,550	1.8	35	0.0	2,085	2.4
South Carolina	81,345	25.3	780	0.2	2,160	0.7	55	0.0	2,505	0.8
South Dakota	540	0.8	3,925	5.9	420	0.6	20	0.0	504	0.8
Tennessee	84,615	18.1	795	0.2	3,755	0.8	215	0.0	4,195	0.9
Texas	256,615	14.0	5,350	0.3	45,075	2.5	1,995	0.1	20,620	1.1
Utah	1,975	0.9	1,740	0.8	3,665	1.7	2,290	1.0	3,095	1.4
Vermont	440	0.9	120	0.2	540	1.1	25	0.0	395	0.8
Virginia	130,610	21.8	1,445	0.2	27,410	4.6	550	0.1	8,910	1.5
Washington	17,770	3.6	6,020	1.2	30,605	6.2	3,415	0.7	15,620	3.2
West Virginia	3,905	3.2	155	0.1	675	0.5	25	0.0	1,485	1.2
Wisconsin	25,195	5.4	3,305	0.7	6,445	1.4	120	0.0	3,910	0.8
Wyoming	110	0.3	835	1.9	330	0.8	15	0.0	460	1.1

B-10 **Construction and Extractive Craft Workers, by State, Sex, Race, and Hispanic or Latino Origin, 2006–2010**

State	Total who worked in the last 5 years	Male Number	Male Percent	Female Number	Female Percent	Hispanic or Latino Number	Hispanic or Latino Percent	White alone, not Hispanic or Latino Number	White alone, not Hispanic or Latino Percent
United States	9,205,480	8,951,330	97.2	254,155	2.8	2,481,855	27.0	5,811,335	63.1
Alabama	150,015	144,620	96.4	5,395	3.6	19,125	12.7	104,455	69.6
Alaska	30,045	28,835	96.0	1,210	4.0	1,265	4.2	22,055	73.4
Arizona	205,910	200,205	97.2	5,705	2.8	103,270	50.2	86,675	42.1
Arkansas	87,015	84,650	97.3	2,365	2.7	12,370	14.2	66,755	76.7
California	1,036,330	1,013,790	97.8	22,535	2.2	575,265	55.5	377,420	36.4
Colorado	185,420	179,725	96.9	5,695	3.1	65,835	35.5	111,995	60.4
Connecticut	99,100	97,010	97.9	2,090	2.1	18,635	18.8	72,605	73.3
Delaware	26,620	26,010	97.7	615	2.3	4,595	17.3	19,040	71.5
District of Columbia	7,915	7,640	96.5	275	3.5	3,125	39.5	535	6.8
Florida	601,425	581,150	96.6	20,280	3.4	208,015	34.6	321,595	53.5
Georgia	293,645	284,415	96.9	9,230	3.1	86,150	29.3	157,385	53.6
Hawaii	46,365	45,130	97.3	1,235	2.7	5,280	11.4	11,620	25.1
Idaho	57,480	55,280	96.2	2,200	3.8	7,440	12.9	48,050	83.6
Illinois	343,475	335,320	97.6	8,155	2.4	73,590	21.4	245,140	71.4
Indiana	186,080	180,725	97.1	5,355	2.9	17,540	9.4	158,625	85.2
Iowa	89,090	86,590	97.2	2,500	2.8	6,230	7.0	80,725	90.6
Kansas	86,565	83,770	96.8	2,800	3.2	16,370	18.9	65,110	75.2
Kentucky	132,925	129,055	97.1	3,870	2.9	6,585	5.0	120,485	90.6
Louisiana	178,860	173,090	96.8	5,765	3.2	21,315	11.9	115,725	64.7
Maine	48,700	47,120	96.8	1,575	3.2	345	0.7	47,095	96.7
Maryland	171,810	166,700	97.0	5,110	3.0	45,825	26.7	95,060	55.3
Massachusetts	175,840	171,765	97.7	4,080	2.3	14,165	8.1	148,860	84.7
Michigan	238,200	230,885	96.9	7,315	3.1	13,550	5.7	205,590	86.3
Minnesota	150,445	145,975	97.0	4,470	3.0	8,110	5.4	136,480	90.7
Mississippi	96,400	92,905	96.4	3,490	3.6	7,855	8.1	64,200	66.6
Missouri	181,530	175,990	96.9	5,540	3.1	8,945	4.9	159,730	88.0
Montana	41,770	40,180	96.2	1,585	3.8	1,265	3.0	37,390	89.5
Nebraska	52,980	51,640	97.5	1,340	2.5	7,225	13.6	43,780	82.6
Nevada	110,945	107,515	96.9	3,430	3.1	50,295	45.3	53,560	48.3
New Hampshire	44,180	43,200	97.8	980	2.2	1,305	3.0	42,115	95.3
New Jersey	225,205	220,565	97.9	4,640	2.1	57,520	25.5	145,875	64.8
New Mexico	75,840	73,980	97.5	1,860	2.5	45,610	60.1	22,110	29.2
New York	485,580	474,905	97.8	10,675	2.2	118,080	24.3	294,180	60.6
North Carolina	300,020	291,265	97.1	8,750	2.9	78,165	26.1	181,040	60.3
North Dakota	24,700	24,130	97.7	570	2.3	490	2.0	22,630	91.6
Ohio	289,700	280,605	96.9	9,095	3.1	11,150	3.8	254,910	88.0
Oklahoma	126,725	122,935	97.0	3,790	3.0	23,220	18.3	83,950	66.2
Oregon	111,145	107,940	97.1	3,205	2.9	17,600	15.8	88,180	79.3
Pennsylvania	339,535	331,300	97.6	8,235	2.4	16,485	4.9	300,980	88.6
Rhode Island	28,690	28,045	97.8	645	2.2	2,440	8.5	24,030	83.8
South Carolina	141,975	137,110	96.6	4,865	3.4	26,690	18.8	85,660	60.3
South Dakota	24,945	24,155	96.8	790	3.2	565	2.3	22,085	88.5
Tennessee	187,580	182,190	97.1	5,390	2.9	27,580	14.7	143,360	76.4
Texas	867,480	848,090	97.8	19,390	2.2	526,110	60.6	290,565	33.5
Utah	89,390	87,695	98.1	1,695	1.9	21,825	24.4	64,220	71.8
Vermont	23,220	22,520	97.0	700	3.0	275	1.2	22,615	97.4
Virginia	243,425	235,160	96.6	8,265	3.4	54,485	22.4	149,915	61.6
Washington	197,940	190,340	96.2	7,605	3.8	28,725	14.5	152,855	77.2
West Virginia	73,055	71,690	98.1	1,365	1.9	730	1.0	70,800	96.9
Wisconsin	159,410	154,550	97.0	4,860	3.0	9,060	5.7	144,025	90.3
Wyoming	32,840	31,265	95.2	1,570	4.8	4,160	12.7	27,485	83.7

B-10 Construction and Extractive Craft Workers, by State, Sex, Race, and Hispanic or Latino Origin, 2006-2010—Continued

State	Black alone, not Hispanic or Latino Number	Percent	American Indian and Alaska Native alone, not Hispanic or Latino Number	Percent	Asian alone, not Hispanic or Latino Number	Percent	Native Hawaiian and Other Pacific Islander alone, not Hispanic or Latino Number	Percent	Two or more races, not Hispanic or Latino Number	Percent
United States	593,195	6.4	77,485	0.8	106,950	1.2	15,845	0.2	118,815	1.3
Alabama	23,685	15.8	1,125	0.7	290	0.2	35	0.0	1,305	0.9
Alaska	505	1.7	4,015	13.4	405	1.3	115	0.4	1,695	5.6
Arizona	2,650	1.3	10,545	5.1	690	0.3	505	0.2	1,565	0.8
Arkansas	5,765	6.6	500	0.6	215	0.2	60	0.1	1,350	1.6
California	28,370	2.7	5,310	0.5	32,560	3.1	3,475	0.3	13,925	1.3
Colorado	2,660	1.4	1,585	0.9	905	0.5	170	0.1	2,270	1.2
Connecticut	5,130	5.2	180	0.2	535	0.5	15	0.0	2,000	2.0
Delaware	2,665	10.0	40	0.2	90	0.3	0	0.0	190	0.7
District of Columbia	4,135	52.2	0	0.0	15	0.2	0	0.0	100	1.3
Florida	59,540	9.9	1,670	0.3	2,595	0.4	410	0.1	7,600	1.3
Georgia	44,650	15.2	360	0.1	2,055	0.7	105	0.0	2,945	1.0
Hawaii	355	0.8	50	0.1	12,635	27.3	6,490	14.0	9,940	21.4
Idaho	215	0.4	565	1.0	80	0.1	245	0.4	885	1.5
Illinois	20,170	5.9	440	0.1	1,800	0.5	40	0.0	2,285	0.7
Indiana	7,430	4.0	485	0.3	455	0.2	75	0.0	1,470	0.8
Iowa	1,130	1.3	260	0.3	245	0.3	25	0.0	480	0.5
Kansas	2,475	2.9	695	0.8	770	0.9	125	0.1	1,020	1.2
Kentucky	4,565	3.4	245	0.2	140	0.1	55	0.0	850	0.6
Louisiana	38,190	21.4	910	0.5	1,000	0.6	20	0.0	1,695	0.9
Maine	175	0.4	345	0.7	140	0.3	0	0.0	594	1.2
Maryland	26,350	15.3	275	0.2	2,150	1.3	70	0.0	2,085	1.2
Massachusetts	5,975	3.4	325	0.2	2,025	1.2	40	0.0	4,455	2.5
Michigan	13,775	5.8	1,690	0.7	680	0.3	50	0.0	2,860	1.2
Minnesota	2,215	1.5	1,275	0.8	850	0.6	90	0.1	1,425	0.9
Mississippi	23,280	24.1	430	0.4	280	0.3	15	0.0	349	0.4
Missouri	8,990	5.0	905	0.5	415	0.2	75	0.0	2,470	1.4
Montana	60	0.1	2,420	5.8	105	0.3	0	0.0	525	1.3
Nebraska	840	1.6	365	0.7	130	0.2	20	0.0	625	1.2
Nevada	3,300	3.0	1,080	1.0	885	0.8	370	0.3	1,455	1.3
New Hampshire	130	0.3	105	0.2	115	0.3	15	0.0	400	0.9
New Jersey	14,815	6.6	270	0.1	3,070	1.4	45	0.0	3,600	1.6
New Mexico	700	0.9	6,660	8.8	190	0.3	0	0.0	570	0.8
New York	46,120	9.5	1,825	0.4	18,515	3.8	100	0.0	6,755	1.4
North Carolina	30,820	10.3	6,425	2.1	1,050	0.3	30	0.0	2,490	0.8
North Dakota	140	0.6	1,225	5.0	35	0.1	20	0.1	154	0.6
Ohio	19,390	6.7	655	0.2	880	0.3	15	0.0	2,705	0.9
Oklahoma	3,550	2.8	9,150	7.2	455	0.4	80	0.1	6,330	5.0
Oregon	1,040	0.9	865	0.8	680	0.6	320	0.3	2,465	2.2
Pennsylvania	16,600	4.9	490	0.1	1,920	0.6	75	0.0	2,975	0.9
Rhode Island	990	3.5	170	0.6	500	1.7	0	0.0	555	1.9
South Carolina	26,925	19.0	895	0.6	330	0.2	75	0.1	1,405	1.0
South Dakota	55	0.2	1,840	7.4	50	0.2	0	0.0	355	1.4
Tennessee	13,520	7.2	710	0.4	300	0.2	240	0.1	1,865	1.0
Texas	38,080	4.4	1,885	0.2	4,965	0.6	240	0.0	5,635	0.6
Utah	365	0.4	1,265	1.4	335	0.4	760	0.9	625	0.7
Vermont	25	0.1	60	0.3	40	0.2	4	0.0	205	0.9
Virginia	32,130	13.2	805	0.3	3,580	1.5	80	0.0	2,425	1.0
Washington	4,060	2.1	2,325	1.2	4,250	2.1	1,030	0.5	4,700	2.4
West Virginia	780	1.1	80	0.1	10	0.0	0	0.0	654	0.9
Wisconsin	3,575	2.2	1,230	0.8	485	0.3	25	0.0	1,010	0.6
Wyoming	145	0.4	470	1.4	60	0.2	10	0.0	499	1.5

B-11 **Installation, Maintenance, and Repair Craft Workers, by State, Sex, Race, and Hispanic or Latino Origin, 2006–2010**

State	Total who worked in the last 5 years	Male Number	Male Percent	Female Number	Female Percent	Hispanic or Latino Number	Hispanic or Latino Percent	White alone, not Hispanic or Latino Number	White alone, not Hispanic or Latino Percent
United States	6,316,335	5,871,165	93.0	445,170	7.0	899,470	14.2	4,590,455	72.7
Alabama	112,255	104,065	92.7	8,190	7.3	2,705	2.4	90,235	80.4
Alaska	16,805	15,830	94.2	970	5.8	510	3.0	12,505	74.4
Arizona	124,800	117,050	93.8	7,755	6.2	33,960	27.2	80,225	64.3
Arkansas	64,260	59,980	93.3	4,280	6.7	2,380	3.7	55,025	85.6
California	663,530	615,755	92.8	47,780	7.2	259,565	39.1	285,420	43.0
Colorado	101,245	93,410	92.3	7,830	7.7	16,170	16.0	77,480	76.5
Connecticut	73,500	68,535	93.2	4,960	6.7	8,895	12.1	58,100	79.0
Delaware	17,600	16,400	93.2	1,205	6.8	1,085	6.2	13,745	78.1
District of Columbia	4,380	3,960	90.4	420	9.6	405	9.2	365	8.3
Florida	367,040	342,005	93.2	25,035	6.8	84,005	22.9	232,090	63.2
Georgia	202,140	186,725	92.4	15,415	7.6	13,795	6.8	139,675	69.1
Hawaii	25,245	23,305	92.3	1,940	7.7	1,620	6.4	5,400	21.4
Idaho	32,715	30,585	93.5	2,130	6.5	2,230	6.8	29,295	89.5
Illinois	249,740	231,595	92.7	18,145	7.3	35,685	14.3	185,355	74.2
Indiana	161,665	149,860	92.7	11,805	7.3	6,830	4.2	144,990	89.7
Iowa	69,440	63,880	92.0	5,560	8.0	1,530	2.2	65,740	94.7
Kansas	66,910	61,835	92.4	5,080	7.6	4,670	7.0	57,395	85.8
Kentucky	92,685	86,435	93.3	6,250	6.7	1,715	1.9	86,515	93.3
Louisiana	99,400	93,190	93.8	6,210	6.2	3,630	3.7	73,565	74.0
Maine	32,490	30,235	93.1	2,255	6.9	140	0.4	31,490	96.9
Maryland	111,330	103,625	93.1	7,705	6.9	8,630	7.8	70,035	62.9
Massachusetts	115,670	107,825	93.2	7,845	6.8	8,940	7.7	97,195	84.0
Michigan	223,995	208,070	92.9	15,925	7.1	5,295	2.4	196,600	87.8
Minnesota	118,180	109,455	92.6	8,725	7.4	3,070	2.6	108,425	91.7
Mississippi	63,840	59,800	93.7	4,040	6.3	1,305	2.0	45,635	71.5
Missouri	130,680	121,820	93.2	8,865	6.8	3,505	2.7	117,235	89.7
Montana	22,445	20,940	93.3	1,505	6.7	460	2.0	20,790	92.6
Nebraska	40,490	38,150	94.2	2,340	5.8	2,255	5.6	36,560	90.3
Nevada	49,415	46,090	93.3	3,325	6.7	10,965	22.2	31,800	64.4
New Hampshire	31,670	29,575	93.4	2,095	6.6	480	1.5	30,505	96.3
New Jersey	155,945	145,255	93.1	10,685	6.9	28,910	18.5	104,140	66.8
New Mexico	44,750	40,910	91.4	3,840	8.6	18,830	42.1	19,275	43.1
New York	325,710	302,140	92.8	23,575	7.2	50,660	15.6	218,000	66.9
North Carolina	214,480	199,380	93.0	15,100	7.0	12,905	6.0	164,965	76.9
North Dakota	15,885	14,750	92.9	1,135	7.1	195	1.2	15,090	95.0
Ohio	261,560	243,555	93.1	18,010	6.9	4,910	1.9	236,910	90.6
Oklahoma	92,830	86,520	93.2	6,310	6.8	6,130	6.6	71,895	77.4
Oregon	75,605	69,600	92.1	6,005	7.9	5,595	7.4	64,455	85.3
Pennsylvania	274,820	256,715	93.4	18,105	6.6	8,915	3.2	245,325	89.3
Rhode Island	20,530	18,530	90.3	2,000	9.7	2,210	10.8	16,760	81.6
South Carolina	107,900	100,535	93.2	7,370	6.8	3,505	3.2	82,390	76.4
South Dakota	18,595	17,555	94.4	1,040	5.6	225	1.2	17,340	93.3
Tennessee	137,080	126,850	92.5	10,230	7.5	3,820	2.8	116,540	85.0
Texas	522,570	488,570	93.5	34,000	6.5	191,660	36.7	268,565	51.4
Utah	56,175	52,085	92.7	4,090	7.3	5,785	10.3	47,750	85.0
Vermont	15,050	13,920	92.5	1,130	7.5	150	1.0	14,615	97.1
Virginia	159,705	146,950	92.0	12,755	8.0	12,275	7.7	115,705	72.4
Washington	135,340	124,280	91.8	11,060	8.2	10,445	7.7	108,885	80.5
West Virginia	39,895	37,610	94.3	2,285	5.7	295	0.7	38,665	96.9
Wisconsin	140,710	130,520	92.8	10,190	7.2	4,770	3.4	129,450	92.0
Wyoming	15,640	14,960	95.7	680	4.3	865	5.5	14,340	91.7

PART B—STATE TABLES

B-11 Installation, Maintenance, and Repair Craft Workers, by State, Sex, Race, and Hispanic or Latino Origin, 2006–2010—Continued

State	Black alone, not Hispanic or Latino Number	Percent	American Indian and Alaska Native alone, not Hispanic or Latino Number	Percent	Asian alone, not Hispanic or Latino Number	Percent	Native Hawaiian and Other Pacific Islander alone, not Hispanic or Latino Number	Percent	Two or more races, not Hispanic or Latino Number	Percent
United States	492,785	7.8	40,315	0.6	202,305	3.2	9,395	0.1	81,610	1.3
Alabama	16,675	14.9	625	0.6	885	0.8	45	0.0	1,080	1.0
Alaska	365	2.2	1,980	11.8	405	2.4	145	0.9	899	5.3
Arizona	3,380	2.7	3,430	2.7	1,980	1.6	260	0.2	1,560	1.3
Arkansas	5,310	8.3	500	0.8	350	0.5	65	0.1	635	1.0
California	27,360	4.1	2,605	0.4	73,840	11.1	3,165	0.5	11,570	1.7
Colorado	3,160	3.1	805	0.8	2,090	2.1	200	0.2	1,335	1.3
Connecticut	3,985	5.4	120	0.2	1,485	2.0	20	0.0	895	1.2
Delaware	2,375	13.5	25	0.1	225	1.3	10	0.1	135	0.8
District of Columbia	3,465	79.1	0	0.0	50	1.1	0	0.0	95	2.2
Florida	39,760	10.8	770	0.2	5,965	1.6	135	0.0	4,310	1.2
Georgia	41,820	20.7	550	0.3	4,220	2.1	175	0.1	1,905	0.9
Hawaii	510	2.0	110	0.4	10,810	42.8	1,800	7.1	5,000	19.8
Idaho	355	1.1	255	0.8	185	0.6	20	0.1	375	1.1
Illinois	19,500	7.8	365	0.1	6,740	2.7	40	0.0	2,060	0.8
Indiana	7,175	4.4	205	0.1	810	0.5	20	0.0	1,635	1.0
Iowa	680	1.0	140	0.2	740	1.1	0	0.0	610	0.9
Kansas	2,010	3.0	535	0.8	1,335	2.0	10	0.0	960	1.4
Kentucky	3,375	3.6	150	0.2	355	0.4	60	0.1	525	0.6
Louisiana	19,600	19.7	450	0.5	1,340	1.3	15	0.0	800	0.8
Maine	215	0.7	215	0.7	120	0.4	40	0.1	270	0.8
Maryland	26,210	23.5	260	0.2	4,170	3.7	150	0.1	1,875	1.7
Massachusetts	4,430	3.8	170	0.1	3,275	2.8	10	0.0	1,655	1.4
Michigan	17,090	7.6	965	0.4	2,070	0.9	10	0.0	1,965	0.9
Minnesota	2,195	1.9	795	0.7	2,560	2.2	55	0.0	1,075	0.9
Mississippi	16,045	25.1	190	0.3	285	0.4	25	0.0	360	0.6
Missouri	7,000	5.4	465	0.4	1,040	0.8	125	0.1	1,310	1.0
Montana	60	0.3	665	3.0	95	0.4	4	0.0	365	1.6
Nebraska	625	1.5	250	0.6	505	1.2	10	0.0	290	0.7
Nevada	2,535	5.1	480	1.0	2,585	5.2	360	0.7	690	1.4
New Hampshire	250	0.8	75	0.2	140	0.4	0	0.0	220	0.7
New Jersey	14,450	9.3	235	0.2	6,325	4.1	60	0.0	1,825	1.2
New Mexico	580	1.3	5,090	11.4	545	1.2	10	0.0	430	1.0
New York	35,315	10.8	735	0.2	16,465	5.1	55	0.0	4,485	1.4
North Carolina	29,015	13.5	1,620	0.8	3,380	1.6	180	0.1	2,415	1.1
North Dakota	45	0.3	430	2.7	10	0.1	0	0.0	114	0.7
Ohio	15,475	5.9	470	0.2	1,510	0.6	50	0.0	2,245	0.9
Oklahoma	3,310	3.6	5,660	6.1	1,155	1.2	50	0.1	4,635	5.0
Oregon	675	0.9	885	1.2	2,050	2.7	295	0.4	1,645	2.2
Pennsylvania	14,410	5.2	200	0.1	4,090	1.5	70	0.0	1,810	0.7
Rhode Island	815	4.0	60	0.3	305	1.5	0	0.0	375	1.8
South Carolina	19,785	18.3	295	0.3	805	0.7	65	0.1	1,060	1.0
South Dakota	150	0.8	560	3.0	140	0.8	0	0.0	180	1.0
Tennessee	13,770	10.0	245	0.2	1,680	1.2	25	0.0	1,005	0.7
Texas	37,275	7.1	2,185	0.4	17,115	3.3	320	0.1	5,445	1.0
Utah	230	0.4	830	1.5	735	1.3	325	0.6	520	0.9
Vermont	40	0.3	65	0.4	45	0.3	0	0.0	135	0.9
Virginia	22,850	14.3	245	0.2	6,355	4.0	85	0.1	2,185	1.4
Washington	3,135	2.3	1,420	1.0	7,345	5.4	780	0.6	3,330	2.5
West Virginia	535	1.3	45	0.1	65	0.2	0	0.0	295	0.7
Wisconsin	3,395	2.4	710	0.5	1,535	1.1	30	0.0	815	0.6
Wyoming	25	0.2	200	1.3	0	0.0	15	0.1	194	1.2

B-12 Production Operative Workers, by State, Sex, Race, and Hispanic or Latino Origin, 2006–2010

State	Total who worked in the last 5 years	Male Number	Male Percent	Female Number	Female Percent	Hispanic or Latino Number	Hispanic or Latino Percent	White alone, not Hispanic or Latino Number	White alone, not Hispanic or Latino Percent
United States	7,769,340	5,340,305	68.7	2,429,035	31.3	1,742,115	22.4	4,484,160	57.7
Alabama	166,840	112,190	67.2	54,650	32.8	12,435	7.5	94,130	56.4
Alaska	12,430	9,715	78.2	2,715	21.8	1,550	12.5	5,310	42.7
Arizona	93,825	65,245	69.5	28,580	30.5	43,290	46.1	37,640	40.1
Arkansas	112,835	74,170	65.7	38,660	34.3	14,850	13.2	71,450	63.3
California	792,860	523,175	66.0	269,685	34.0	491,145	61.9	154,245	19.5
Colorado	81,590	57,090	70.0	24,500	30.0	26,620	32.6	44,440	54.5
Connecticut	80,535	53,525	66.5	27,010	33.5	18,820	23.4	47,350	58.8
Delaware	17,695	12,490	70.6	5,205	29.4	3,005	17.0	9,750	55.1
District of Columbia	2,175	1,525	70.1	645	29.7	610	28.0	240	11.0
Florida	263,700	176,250	66.8	87,450	33.2	78,145	29.6	125,435	47.6
Georgia	248,875	161,870	65.0	87,005	35.0	40,140	16.1	109,440	44.0
Hawaii	15,115	10,165	67.3	4,950	32.7	1,130	7.5	1,985	13.1
Idaho	36,525	24,800	67.9	11,725	32.1	7,645	20.9	27,110	74.2
Illinois	385,600	265,035	68.7	120,565	31.3	133,965	34.7	196,245	50.9
Indiana	292,465	201,480	68.9	90,985	31.1	27,560	9.4	236,225	80.8
Iowa	126,350	89,025	70.5	37,325	29.5	13,415	10.6	103,465	81.9
Kansas	91,015	64,265	70.6	26,750	29.4	17,975	19.7	60,370	66.3
Kentucky	155,430	108,880	70.1	46,550	29.9	5,590	3.6	130,000	83.6
Louisiana	100,365	80,705	80.4	19,660	19.6	4,930	4.9	57,715	57.5
Maine	34,160	24,430	71.5	9,730	28.5	805	2.4	31,905	93.4
Maryland	70,025	47,925	68.4	22,100	31.6	7,115	10.2	36,885	52.7
Massachusetts	131,475	87,490	66.5	43,985	33.5	24,165	18.4	84,055	63.9
Michigan	371,155	262,170	70.6	108,980	29.4	25,220	6.8	275,090	74.1
Minnesota	170,005	117,930	69.4	52,075	30.6	16,075	9.5	126,505	74.4
Mississippi	103,905	66,415	63.9	37,490	36.1	4,520	4.4	44,640	43.0
Missouri	178,950	123,565	69.1	55,385	30.9	10,455	5.8	141,975	79.3
Montana	15,805	11,195	70.8	4,610	29.2	320	2.0	14,240	90.1
Nebraska	61,230	42,215	68.9	19,015	31.1	15,680	25.6	39,015	63.7
Nevada	37,585	25,930	69.0	11,660	31.0	17,560	46.7	15,870	42.2
New Hampshire	36,235	23,770	65.6	12,465	34.4	1,895	5.2	30,970	85.5
New Jersey	159,570	105,360	66.0	54,210	34.0	65,010	40.7	62,600	39.2
New Mexico	29,675	21,195	71.4	8,475	28.6	16,220	54.7	9,270	31.2
New York	328,590	219,280	66.7	109,310	33.3	79,400	24.2	183,825	55.9
North Carolina	306,930	191,845	62.5	115,085	37.5	42,935	14.0	163,355	53.2
North Dakota	16,955	12,320	72.7	4,635	27.3	500	2.9	14,950	88.2
Ohio	422,105	294,190	69.7	127,915	30.3	17,070	4.0	343,395	81.4
Oklahoma	99,390	74,855	75.3	24,540	24.7	13,195	13.3	62,860	63.2
Oregon	99,380	72,045	72.5	27,335	27.5	19,655	19.8	68,115	68.5
Pennsylvania	346,925	248,175	71.5	98,745	28.5	28,835	8.3	278,180	80.2
Rhode Island	31,105	19,810	63.7	11,295	36.3	9,640	31.0	16,910	54.4
South Carolina	157,800	103,275	65.4	54,525	34.6	10,595	6.7	76,030	48.2
South Dakota	24,950	17,075	68.4	7,875	31.6	1,425	5.7	20,465	82.0
Tennessee	222,260	146,095	65.7	76,160	34.3	13,770	6.2	159,370	71.7
Texas	547,650	403,025	73.6	144,625	26.4	275,940	50.4	177,810	32.5
Utah	65,595	44,740	68.2	20,855	31.8	18,315	27.9	40,145	61.2
Vermont	16,405	11,630	70.9	4,770	29.1	155	0.9	15,750	96.0
Virginia	156,625	106,495	68.0	50,130	32.0	12,065	7.7	92,220	58.9
Washington	135,310	97,035	71.7	38,270	28.3	24,155	17.9	84,135	62.2
West Virginia	38,830	31,015	79.9	7,810	20.1	435	1.1	37,160	95.7
Wisconsin	264,975	186,735	70.5	78,240	29.5	24,685	9.3	214,485	80.9
Wyoming	11,580	9,470	81.8	2,110	18.2	1,480	12.8	9,435	81.5

B-12 Production Operative Workers, by State, Sex, Race, and Hispanic or Latino Origin, 2006–2010—*Continued*

State	Black alone, not Hispanic or Latino Number	Percent	American Indian and Alaska Native alone, not Hispanic or Latino Number	Percent	Asian alone, not Hispanic or Latino Number	Percent	Native Hawaiian and Other Pacific Islander alone, not Hispanic or Latino Number	Percent	Two or more races, not Hispanic or Latino Number	Percent
United States	1,003,295	12.9	45,105	0.6	397,465	5.1	10,445	0.1	86,760	1.1
Alabama	56,500	33.9	930	0.6	1,595	1.0	40	0.0	1,210	0.7
Alaska	760	6.1	880	7.1	3,390	27.3	205	1.6	329	2.6
Arizona	2,720	2.9	4,620	4.9	4,390	4.7	195	0.2	955	1.0
Arkansas	21,805	19.3	685	0.6	1,950	1.7	500	0.4	1,590	1.4
California	21,190	2.7	1,715	0.2	112,910	14.2	2,730	0.3	8,930	1.1
Colorado	3,425	4.2	570	0.7	5,200	6.4	100	0.1	1,230	1.5
Connecticut	8,445	10.5	135	0.2	4,860	6.0	10	0.0	915	1.1
Delaware	4,405	24.9	90	0.5	310	1.8	0	0.0	140	0.8
District of Columbia	1,260	57.9	0	0.0	30	1.4	0	0.0	34	1.6
Florida	46,410	17.6	675	0.3	10,365	3.9	195	0.1	2,480	0.9
Georgia	87,435	35.1	440	0.2	9,520	3.8	95	0.0	1,805	0.7
Hawaii	125	0.8	4	0.0	7,685	50.8	1,440	9.5	2,740	18.1
Idaho	215	0.6	375	1.0	855	2.3	25	0.1	300	0.8
Illinois	37,555	9.7	635	0.2	14,580	3.8	25	0.0	2,595	0.7
Indiana	21,825	7.5	595	0.2	3,195	1.1	110	0.0	2,950	1.0
Iowa	4,035	3.2	300	0.2	4,100	3.2	35	0.0	1,000	0.8
Kansas	5,605	6.2	565	0.6	5,015	5.5	20	0.0	1,460	1.6
Kentucky	16,935	10.9	235	0.2	1,340	0.9	30	0.0	1,310	0.8
Louisiana	33,930	33.8	705	0.7	2,440	2.4	0	0.0	640	0.6
Maine	355	1.0	160	0.5	600	1.8	4	0.0	334	1.0
Maryland	21,245	30.3	165	0.2	3,825	5.5	45	0.1	740	1.1
Massachusetts	6,805	5.2	160	0.1	12,775	9.7	65	0.0	3,455	2.6
Michigan	55,435	14.9	1,560	0.4	9,550	2.6	75	0.0	4,220	1.1
Minnesota	9,155	5.4	930	0.5	15,500	9.1	115	0.1	1,725	1.0
Mississippi	53,555	51.5	300	0.3	420	0.4	0	0.0	470	0.5
Missouri	20,580	11.5	890	0.5	2,930	1.6	170	0.1	1,950	1.1
Montana	10	0.1	740	4.7	185	1.2	70	0.4	234	1.5
Nebraska	3,620	5.9	285	0.5	2,005	3.3	10	0.0	620	1.0
Nevada	1,525	4.1	335	0.9	1,690	4.5	75	0.2	535	1.4
New Hampshire	685	1.9	45	0.1	2,360	6.5	15	0.0	265	0.7
New Jersey	18,860	11.8	225	0.1	10,965	6.9	20	0.0	1,885	1.2
New Mexico	345	1.2	3,075	10.4	565	1.9	35	0.1	170	0.6
New York	29,685	9.0	880	0.3	29,950	9.1	120	0.0	4,725	1.4
North Carolina	86,320	28.1	3,080	1.0	8,810	2.9	225	0.1	2,210	0.7
North Dakota	400	2.4	700	4.1	260	1.5	45	0.3	95	0.6
Ohio	49,565	11.7	755	0.2	7,410	1.8	90	0.0	3,820	0.9
Oklahoma	6,635	6.7	7,725	7.8	3,295	3.3	295	0.3	5,390	5.4
Oregon	1,440	1.4	1,205	1.2	6,805	6.8	580	0.6	1,580	1.6
Pennsylvania	23,580	6.8	380	0.1	12,815	3.7	165	0.0	2,960	0.9
Rhode Island	1,860	6.0	20	0.1	2,130	6.8	0	0.0	540	1.7
South Carolina	66,955	42.4	625	0.4	2,250	1.4	30	0.0	1,315	0.8
South Dakota	1,135	4.5	985	3.9	505	2.0	15	0.1	424	1.7
Tennessee	42,785	19.2	400	0.2	3,660	1.6	135	0.1	2,140	1.0
Texas	63,815	11.7	1,045	0.2	24,880	4.5	215	0.0	3,945	0.7
Utah	1,145	1.7	915	1.4	3,540	5.4	805	1.2	735	1.1
Vermont	95	0.6	35	0.2	240	1.5	0	0.0	124	0.8
Virginia	43,210	27.6	355	0.2	6,835	4.4	75	0.0	1,860	1.2
Washington	4,495	3.3	1,290	1.0	16,805	12.4	1,150	0.8	3,270	2.4
West Virginia	860	2.2	60	0.2	20	0.1	0	0.0	298	0.8
Wisconsin	12,405	4.7	1,485	0.6	10,050	3.8	40	0.0	1,820	0.7
Wyoming	135	1.2	145	1.3	85	0.7	0	0.0	304	2.6

B-13 Transportation and Material Moving Operative Workers, by State, Sex, Race, and Hispanic or Latino Origin, 2006–2010

State	Total who worked in the last 5 years	Male Number	Male Percent	Female Number	Female Percent	Hispanic or Latino Number	Hispanic or Latino Percent	White alone, not Hispanic or Latino Number	White alone, not Hispanic or Latino Percent
United States	6,984,985	5,695,450	81.5	1,289,535	18.5	1,297,050	18.6	4,211,875	60.3
Alabama	119,365	96,760	81.1	22,605	18.9	2,885	2.4	78,070	65.4
Alaska	15,015	12,650	84.2	2,365	15.8	895	6.0	9,690	64.5
Arizona	110,910	91,480	82.5	19,430	17.5	36,080	32.5	61,205	55.2
Arkansas	77,260	63,195	81.8	14,065	18.2	4,380	5.7	55,890	72.3
California	780,745	629,450	80.6	151,295	19.4	409,600	52.5	226,850	29.1
Colorado	93,910	79,460	84.6	14,450	15.4	21,270	22.6	63,635	67.8
Connecticut	67,830	53,425	78.8	14,405	21.2	10,745	15.8	44,510	65.6
Delaware	20,140	16,250	80.7	3,890	19.3	1,590	7.9	11,700	58.1
District of Columbia	8,150	6,640	81.5	1,510	18.5	590	7.2	215	2.6
Florida	349,720	291,715	83.4	58,005	16.6	97,775	28.0	169,495	48.5
Georgia	242,680	192,560	79.3	50,125	20.7	18,180	7.5	117,335	48.3
Hawaii	23,095	19,705	85.3	3,390	14.7	1,660	7.2	3,440	14.9
Idaho	36,210	29,550	81.6	6,665	18.4	4,325	11.9	30,535	84.3
Illinois	344,525	277,415	80.5	67,110	19.5	72,695	21.1	202,570	58.8
Indiana	179,740	141,450	78.7	38,290	21.3	11,140	6.2	148,890	82.8
Iowa	84,225	71,700	85.1	12,525	14.9	3,780	4.5	77,240	91.7
Kansas	63,420	51,885	81.8	11,530	18.2	6,400	10.1	50,250	79.2
Kentucky	112,805	91,015	80.7	21,790	19.3	2,405	2.1	99,040	87.8
Louisiana	105,905	89,700	84.7	16,205	15.3	3,200	3.0	59,655	56.3
Maine	29,510	25,505	86.4	4,000	13.6	150	0.5	28,495	96.6
Maryland	116,120	96,965	83.5	19,155	16.5	8,445	7.3	52,560	45.3
Massachusetts	117,470	95,295	81.1	22,175	18.9	13,340	11.4	86,200	73.4
Michigan	230,835	182,500	79.1	48,335	20.9	10,750	4.7	179,085	77.6
Minnesota	122,545	102,395	83.6	20,150	16.4	6,150	5.0	103,300	84.3
Mississippi	78,935	65,515	83.0	13,420	17.0	905	1.1	43,260	54.8
Missouri	144,630	118,500	81.9	26,130	18.1	4,165	2.9	118,035	81.6
Montana	20,265	17,650	87.1	2,615	12.9	420	2.1	18,500	91.3
Nebraska	47,780	39,940	83.6	7,840	16.4	3,815	8.0	40,425	84.6
Nevada	59,035	49,870	84.5	9,165	15.5	13,390	22.7	34,175	57.9
New Hampshire	28,345	22,405	79.0	5,940	21.0	610	2.2	26,685	94.1
New Jersey	212,385	169,480	79.8	42,905	20.2	65,020	30.6	97,115	45.7
New Mexico	37,450	31,150	83.2	6,300	16.8	18,130	48.4	15,525	41.5
New York	414,965	350,790	84.5	64,175	15.5	97,970	23.6	205,275	49.5
North Carolina	221,365	173,230	78.3	48,140	21.7	14,815	6.7	129,705	58.6
North Dakota	16,975	14,925	87.9	2,050	12.1	310	1.8	15,800	93.1
Ohio	305,720	242,320	79.3	63,400	20.7	7,700	2.5	252,505	82.6
Oklahoma	85,645	73,260	85.5	12,385	14.5	5,925	6.9	63,185	73.8
Oregon	81,145	65,390	80.6	15,755	19.4	9,750	12.0	64,195	79.1
Pennsylvania	317,090	257,330	81.2	59,760	18.8	21,560	6.8	253,750	80.0
Rhode Island	24,310	19,210	79.0	5,100	21.0	5,100	21.0	16,945	69.7
South Carolina	111,200	84,600	76.1	26,600	23.9	3,845	3.5	57,430	51.6
South Dakota	17,915	15,065	84.1	2,850	15.9	735	4.1	15,985	89.2
Tennessee	165,125	131,880	79.9	33,245	20.1	6,375	3.9	117,285	71.0
Texas	553,600	466,390	84.2	87,210	15.8	222,595	40.2	220,880	39.9
Utah	54,200	44,695	82.5	9,505	17.5	7,170	13.2	43,225	79.8
Vermont	11,625	9,610	82.7	2,015	17.3	110	0.9	11,210	96.4
Virginia	155,095	122,910	79.2	32,185	20.8	9,285	6.0	90,085	58.1
Washington	147,770	118,880	80.4	28,890	19.6	18,615	12.6	107,170	72.5
West Virginia	47,235	41,365	87.6	5,870	12.4	240	0.5	45,350	96.0
Wisconsin	155,130	125,310	80.8	29,820	19.2	9,140	5.9	131,945	85.1
Wyoming	17,910	15,120	84.4	2,795	15.6	910	5.1	16,375	91.4

B-13 Transportation and Material Moving Operative Workers, by State, Sex, Race, and Hispanic or Latino Origin, 2006–2010—Continued

State	Black alone, not Hispanic or Latino Number	Percent	American Indian and Alaska Native alone, not Hispanic or Latino Number	Percent	Asian alone, not Hispanic or Latino Number	Percent	Native Hawaiian and Other Pacific Islander alone, not Hispanic or Latino Number	Percent	Two or more races, not Hispanic or Latino Number	Percent
United States	1,121,360	16.1	42,095	0.6	207,095	3.0	13,920	0.2	91,585	1.3
Alabama	35,875	30.1	650	0.5	490	0.4	4	0.0	1,390	1.2
Alaska	690	4.6	1,525	10.2	1,235	8.2	285	1.9	695	4.6
Arizona	6,480	5.8	4,085	3.7	1,320	1.2	235	0.2	1,510	1.4
Arkansas	14,620	18.9	505	0.7	810	1.0	60	0.1	1,000	1.3
California	56,740	7.3	3,220	0.4	67,475	8.6	4,080	0.5	12,775	1.6
Colorado	5,655	6.0	470	0.5	1,485	1.6	115	0.1	1,290	1.4
Connecticut	10,040	14.8	145	0.2	1,365	2.0	10	0.0	1,010	1.5
Delaware	6,135	30.5	155	0.8	290	1.4	15	0.1	260	1.3
District of Columbia	7,125	87.4	0	0.0	150	1.8	0	0.0	70	0.9
Florida	73,285	21.0	940	0.3	4,465	1.3	200	0.1	3,555	1.0
Georgia	101,050	41.6	300	0.1	3,470	1.4	285	0.1	2,065	0.9
Hawaii	255	1.1	30	0.1	9,295	40.2	3,315	14.4	5,100	22.1
Idaho	185	0.5	450	1.2	130	0.4	25	0.1	560	1.5
Illinois	56,685	16.5	390	0.1	8,940	2.6	35	0.0	3,210	0.9
Indiana	15,845	8.8	430	0.2	1,710	1.0	4	0.0	1,710	1.0
Iowa	1,645	2.0	170	0.2	600	0.7	0	0.0	790	0.9
Kansas	4,130	6.5	540	0.9	855	1.3	10	0.0	1,235	1.9
Kentucky	9,865	8.7	205	0.2	445	0.4	60	0.1	790	0.7
Louisiana	40,450	38.2	1,020	1.0	615	0.6	20	0.0	950	0.9
Maine	305	1.0	125	0.4	165	0.6	0	0.0	265	0.9
Maryland	49,430	42.6	315	0.3	3,740	3.2	0	0.0	1,635	1.4
Massachusetts	11,385	9.7	240	0.2	4,005	3.4	15	0.0	2,280	1.9
Michigan	34,655	15.0	1,275	0.6	2,130	0.9	70	0.0	2,870	1.2
Minnesota	7,905	6.5	760	0.6	3,045	2.5	4	0.0	1,375	1.1
Mississippi	33,675	42.7	305	0.4	175	0.2	0	0.0	620	0.8
Missouri	18,870	13.0	430	0.3	1,005	0.7	135	0.1	1,990	1.4
Montana	65	0.3	955	4.7	30	0.1	10	0.0	280	1.4
Nebraska	2,305	4.8	230	0.5	385	0.8	4	0.0	620	1.3
Nevada	7,100	12.0	560	0.9	2,395	4.1	605	1.0	810	1.4
New Hampshire	305	1.1	95	0.3	390	1.4	0	0.0	265	0.9
New Jersey	36,605	17.2	340	0.2	10,405	4.9	85	0.0	2,820	1.3
New Mexico	750	2.0	2,405	6.4	295	0.8	0	0.0	334	0.9
New York	69,985	16.9	865	0.2	34,435	8.3	50	0.0	6,390	1.5
North Carolina	70,050	31.6	2,380	1.1	2,635	1.2	55	0.0	1,730	0.8
North Dakota	65	0.4	590	3.5	65	0.4	4	0.0	130	0.8
Ohio	39,850	13.0	615	0.2	2,300	0.8	70	0.0	2,675	0.9
Oklahoma	6,050	7.1	5,335	6.2	890	1.0	45	0.1	4,220	4.9
Oregon	2,140	2.6	1,040	1.3	1,690	2.1	365	0.4	1,965	2.4
Pennsylvania	32,980	10.4	415	0.1	5,590	1.8	120	0.0	2,685	0.8
Rhode Island	1,210	5.0	105	0.4	580	2.4	0	0.0	365	1.5
South Carolina	47,920	43.1	440	0.4	790	0.7	85	0.1	695	0.6
South Dakota	115	0.6	815	4.5	65	0.4	0	0.0	189	1.1
Tennessee	38,455	23.3	355	0.2	1,255	0.8	45	0.0	1,350	0.8
Texas	95,010	17.2	1,605	0.3	8,345	1.5	655	0.1	4,500	0.8
Utah	930	1.7	760	1.4	775	1.4	915	1.7	415	0.8
Vermont	70	0.6	60	0.5	75	0.6	0	0.0	105	0.9
Virginia	47,670	30.7	415	0.3	5,665	3.7	40	0.0	1,930	1.2
Washington	8,275	5.6	1,535	1.0	6,410	4.3	1,685	1.1	4,075	2.8
West Virginia	945	2.0	110	0.2	45	0.1	25	0.1	525	1.1
Wisconsin	9,385	6.0	1,180	0.8	2,135	1.4	70	0.0	1,275	0.8
Wyoming	125	0.7	215	1.2	35	0.2	4	0.0	249	1.4

B-14 Laborers and Helpers, by State, Sex, Race, and Hispanic or Latino Origin, 2006–2010

State	Total who worked in the last 5 years	Male Number	Male Percent	Female Number	Female Percent	Hispanic or Latino Number	Hispanic or Latino Percent	White alone, not Hispanic or Latino Number	White alone, not Hispanic or Latino Percent
United States	5,991,240	4,999,790	83.5	991,450	16.5	1,817,710	30.3	3,217,175	53.7
Alabama	96,025	81,920	85.3	14,105	14.7	9,405	9.8	54,770	57.0
Alaska	16,025	13,805	86.1	2,220	13.9	1,095	6.8	9,235	57.6
Arizona	116,420	98,250	84.4	18,170	15.6	66,515	57.1	39,760	34.2
Arkansas	67,785	56,730	83.7	11,055	16.3	7,825	11.5	45,595	67.3
California	870,025	721,675	82.9	148,345	17.1	620,260	71.3	167,320	19.2
Colorado	89,370	73,100	81.8	16,270	18.2	31,205	34.9	51,050	57.1
Connecticut	55,465	47,510	85.7	7,950	14.3	13,695	24.7	34,065	61.4
Delaware	14,895	12,225	82.1	2,670	17.9	3,440	23.1	7,980	53.6
District of Columbia	6,190	4,845	78.3	1,345	21.7	545	8.8	595	9.6
Florida	374,780	316,525	84.5	58,255	15.5	137,510	36.7	162,860	43.5
Georgia	182,455	154,580	84.7	27,875	15.3	38,635	21.2	78,135	42.8
Hawaii	27,440	22,500	82.0	4,940	18.0	2,525	9.2	4,330	15.8
Idaho	43,535	36,445	83.7	7,090	16.3	14,360	33.0	27,750	63.7
Illinois	231,570	191,795	82.8	39,775	17.2	69,265	29.9	127,505	55.1
Indiana	136,830	109,415	80.0	27,415	20.0	15,095	11.0	107,385	78.5
Iowa	78,660	63,540	80.8	15,120	19.2	6,410	8.1	68,440	87.0
Kansas	59,790	49,640	83.0	10,150	17.0	10,245	17.1	43,630	73.0
Kentucky	92,000	75,925	82.5	16,075	17.5	9,325	10.1	74,340	80.8
Louisiana	82,935	72,780	87.8	10,160	12.3	5,525	6.7	42,565	51.3
Maine	34,210	28,890	84.4	5,320	15.6	350	1.0	32,935	96.3
Maryland	79,260	67,955	85.7	11,300	14.3	16,040	20.2	37,425	47.2
Massachusetts	93,120	78,350	84.1	14,770	15.9	14,820	15.9	68,520	73.6
Michigan	191,180	153,105	80.1	38,075	19.9	21,015	11.0	143,060	74.8
Minnesota	102,295	82,500	80.6	19,795	19.4	9,745	9.5	84,410	82.5
Mississippi	57,765	50,385	87.2	7,380	12.8	3,205	5.5	27,145	47.0
Missouri	117,590	97,650	83.0	19,940	17.0	7,410	6.3	94,350	80.2
Montana	24,235	19,605	80.9	4,630	19.1	715	3.0	21,475	88.6
Nebraska	44,800	37,330	83.3	7,475	16.7	6,420	14.3	35,740	79.8
Nevada	48,520	40,235	82.9	8,280	17.1	21,150	43.6	20,330	41.9
New Hampshire	23,100	18,295	79.2	4,805	20.8	850	3.7	21,345	92.4
New Jersey	129,675	111,270	85.8	18,410	14.2	49,150	37.9	58,375	45.0
New Mexico	36,300	30,825	84.9	5,475	15.1	20,990	57.8	10,720	29.5
New York	248,105	211,305	85.2	36,795	14.8	66,880	27.0	140,690	56.7
North Carolina	188,445	160,090	85.0	28,360	15.0	39,050	20.7	99,620	52.9
North Dakota	16,510	14,085	85.3	2,425	14.7	440	2.7	15,180	91.9
Ohio	237,980	192,700	81.0	45,275	19.0	13,485	5.7	193,350	81.2
Oklahoma	70,755	59,640	84.3	11,115	15.7	12,970	18.3	41,810	59.1
Oregon	105,670	87,330	82.6	18,340	17.4	35,390	33.5	63,780	60.4
Pennsylvania	254,035	208,630	82.1	45,405	17.9	24,720	9.7	204,520	80.5
Rhode Island	15,130	12,945	85.6	2,185	14.4	2,895	19.1	11,205	74.1
South Carolina	88,820	75,995	85.6	12,820	14.4	12,030	13.5	45,480	51.2
South Dakota	21,045	17,610	83.7	3,440	16.3	1,155	5.5	17,895	85.0
Tennessee	126,940	104,605	82.4	22,335	17.6	13,860	10.9	83,545	65.8
Texas	466,560	407,360	87.3	59,200	12.7	255,375	54.7	142,935	30.6
Utah	45,455	37,315	82.1	8,140	17.9	11,155	24.5	31,365	69.0
Vermont	14,390	11,465	79.7	2,925	20.3	530	3.7	13,370	92.9
Virginia	127,975	107,015	83.6	20,960	16.4	18,915	14.8	73,455	57.4
Washington	158,675	127,430	80.3	31,245	19.7	56,685	35.7	84,570	53.3
West Virginia	32,865	27,935	85.0	4,930	15.0	485	1.5	30,975	94.2
Wisconsin	134,830	106,450	79.0	28,385	21.1	15,515	11.5	109,555	81.3
Wyoming	12,805	10,280	80.3	2,525	19.7	1,440	11.2	10,735	83.8

PART B—STATE TABLES

B-14 Laborers and Helpers, by State, Sex, Race, and Hispanic or Latino Origin, 2006–2010—*Continued*

State	Black alone, not Hispanic or Latino Number	Percent	American Indian and Alaska Native alone, not Hispanic or Latino Number	Percent	Asian alone, not Hispanic or Latino Number	Percent	Native Hawaiian and Other Pacific Islander alone, not Hispanic or Latino Number	Percent	Two or more races, not Hispanic or Latino Number	Percent
United States	703,955	11.7	45,120	0.8	111,940	1.9	12,490	0.2	82,845	1.4
Alabama	29,865	31.1	495	0.5	465	0.5	25	0.0	1,000	1.0
Alaska	410	2.6	3,280	20.5	815	5.1	280	1.7	915	5.7
Arizona	3,145	2.7	4,670	4.0	785	0.7	215	0.2	1,330	1.1
Arkansas	12,605	18.6	330	0.5	590	0.9	110	0.2	730	1.1
California	29,900	3.4	3,085	0.4	34,505	4.0	3,205	0.4	11,750	1.4
Colorado	3,775	4.2	590	0.7	1,385	1.5	90	0.1	1,275	1.4
Connecticut	5,930	10.7	50	0.1	745	1.3	0	0.0	980	1.8
Delaware	3,165	21.2	30	0.2	155	1.0	0	0.0	134	0.9
District of Columbia	4,985	80.5	30	0.5	25	0.4	0	0.0	10	0.2
Florida	65,150	17.4	1,185	0.3	4,260	1.1	160	0.0	3,665	1.0
Georgia	60,875	33.4	460	0.3	2,525	1.4	100	0.1	1,725	0.9
Hawaii	115	0.4	55	0.2	10,910	39.8	4,435	16.2	5,065	18.5
Idaho	145	0.3	370	0.8	260	0.6	50	0.1	610	1.4
Illinois	29,380	12.7	245	0.1	3,095	1.3	60	0.0	2,015	0.9
Indiana	11,520	8.4	405	0.3	815	0.6	35	0.0	1,575	1.2
Iowa	1,930	2.5	245	0.3	870	1.1	85	0.1	675	0.9
Kansas	3,620	6.1	435	0.7	715	1.2	4	0.0	1,135	1.9
Kentucky	6,930	7.5	265	0.3	305	0.3	10	0.0	830	0.9
Louisiana	31,805	38.3	700	0.8	1,490	1.8	45	0.1	805	1.0
Maine	195	0.6	210	0.6	105	0.3	0	0.0	409	1.2
Maryland	23,280	29.4	250	0.3	1,275	1.6	10	0.0	985	1.2
Massachusetts	4,995	5.4	220	0.2	2,165	2.3	0	0.0	2,395	2.6
Michigan	22,060	11.5	855	0.4	1,555	0.8	25	0.0	2,610	1.4
Minnesota	3,695	3.6	1,000	1.0	1,965	1.9	70	0.1	1,405	1.4
Mississippi	26,375	45.7	145	0.3	455	0.8	25	0.0	415	0.7
Missouri	12,855	10.9	435	0.4	715	0.6	160	0.1	1,665	1.4
Montana	40	0.2	1,575	6.5	45	0.2	20	0.1	365	1.5
Nebraska	1,240	2.8	320	0.7	470	1.0	4	0.0	605	1.4
Nevada	3,850	7.9	565	1.2	1,660	3.4	205	0.4	765	1.6
New Hampshire	265	1.1	130	0.6	160	0.7	15	0.1	329	1.4
New Jersey	16,615	12.8	95	0.1	3,805	2.9	10	0.0	1,630	1.3
New Mexico	905	2.5	3,070	8.5	140	0.4	0	0.0	475	1.3
New York	29,235	11.8	910	0.4	6,785	2.7	4	0.0	3,600	1.5
North Carolina	43,530	23.1	2,120	1.1	1,905	1.0	70	0.0	2,140	1.1
North Dakota	330	2.0	345	2.1	35	0.2	10	0.1	175	1.1
Ohio	26,360	11.1	530	0.2	1,550	0.7	20	0.0	2,690	1.1
Oklahoma	5,685	8.0	5,395	7.6	525	0.7	170	0.2	4,205	5.9
Oregon	1,360	1.3	1,065	1.0	1,460	1.4	485	0.5	2,125	2.0
Pennsylvania	18,975	7.5	265	0.1	3,180	1.3	70	0.0	2,295	0.9
Rhode Island	335	2.2	50	0.3	295	1.9	0	0.0	350	2.3
South Carolina	29,675	33.4	220	0.2	585	0.7	25	0.0	810	0.9
South Dakota	190	0.9	1,360	6.5	205	1.0	0	0.0	240	1.1
Tennessee	26,860	21.2	365	0.3	675	0.5	30	0.0	1,600	1.3
Texas	56,620	12.1	975	0.2	5,910	1.3	345	0.1	4,400	0.9
Utah	550	1.2	555	1.2	515	1.1	760	1.7	555	1.2
Vermont	235	1.6	35	0.2	30	0.2	10	0.1	184	1.3
Virginia	31,230	24.4	440	0.3	2,140	1.7	20	0.0	1,770	1.4
Washington	4,490	2.8	3,100	2.0	5,190	3.3	1,005	0.6	3,630	2.3
West Virginia	870	2.6	20	0.1	110	0.3	0	0.0	400	1.2
Wisconsin	5,755	4.3	1,295	1.0	1,535	1.1	4	0.0	1,170	0.9
Wyoming	60	0.5	290	2.3	60	0.5	0	0.0	225	1.8

B-15 Protective Service Workers, by State, Sex, Race, and Hispanic or Latino Origin, 2006–2010

State	Total who worked in the last 5 years	Male Number	Male Percent	Female Number	Female Percent	Hispanic or Latino Number	Hispanic or Latino Percent	White alone, not Hispanic or Latino Number	White alone, not Hispanic or Latino Percent
United States	3,257,310	2,514,290	77.2	743,020	22.8	388,655	11.9	2,090,840	64.2
Alabama	44,730	35,730	79.9	8,995	20.1	595	1.3	29,610	66.2
Alaska	8,595	6,980	81.2	1,615	18.8	250	2.9	6,145	71.5
Arizona	76,990	60,525	78.6	16,465	21.4	17,215	22.4	50,305	65.3
Arkansas	24,910	19,330	77.6	5,580	22.4	610	2.4	18,235	73.2
California	378,645	302,485	79.9	76,160	20.1	107,605	28.4	179,045	47.3
Colorado	50,955	38,855	76.3	12,100	23.7	7,195	14.1	38,530	75.6
Connecticut	36,590	29,610	80.9	6,980	19.1	3,805	10.4	26,745	73.1
Delaware	10,500	7,520	71.6	2,985	28.4	550	5.2	7,145	68.0
District of Columbia	9,060	5,350	59.1	3,715	41.0	185	2.0	1,130	12.5
Florida	225,460	170,290	75.5	55,175	24.5	38,575	17.1	133,215	59.1
Georgia	101,355	73,615	72.6	27,745	27.4	2,505	2.5	52,630	51.9
Hawaii	20,360	16,585	81.5	3,775	18.5	1,590	7.8	4,405	21.6
Idaho	14,090	11,105	78.8	2,985	21.2	770	5.5	12,520	88.9
Illinois	139,705	107,175	76.7	32,530	23.3	12,900	9.2	88,415	63.3
Indiana	57,520	44,620	77.6	12,900	22.4	1,875	3.3	47,270	82.2
Iowa	21,090	16,500	78.2	4,590	21.8	565	2.7	19,575	92.8
Kansas	25,855	20,280	78.4	5,575	21.6	1,325	5.1	21,975	85.0
Kentucky	37,915	28,890	76.2	9,025	23.8	450	1.2	33,655	88.8
Louisiana	54,990	39,760	72.3	15,225	27.7	970	1.8	30,865	56.1
Maine	11,035	9,385	85.0	1,655	15.0	64	0.6	10,670	96.7
Maryland	89,120	63,365	71.1	25,755	28.9	2,750	3.1	41,605	46.7
Massachusetts	72,005	57,785	80.3	14,220	19.7	4,675	6.5	58,070	80.6
Michigan	87,520	67,115	76.7	20,405	23.3	2,060	2.4	63,000	72.0
Minnesota	38,000	28,370	74.7	9,635	25.4	1,125	3.0	32,460	85.4
Mississippi	31,960	23,190	72.6	8,770	27.4	265	0.8	17,195	53.8
Missouri	55,965	42,925	76.7	13,035	23.3	1,195	2.1	45,405	81.1
Montana	9,690	7,575	78.2	2,115	21.8	145	1.5	8,375	86.4
Nebraska	14,700	10,830	73.7	3,870	26.3	510	3.5	12,935	88.0
Nevada	42,560	33,850	79.5	8,710	20.5	5,235	12.3	28,045	65.9
New Hampshire	11,220	9,550	85.1	1,670	14.9	114	1.0	10,800	96.3
New Jersey	111,995	89,300	79.7	22,695	20.3	13,985	12.5	71,125	63.5
New Mexico	25,720	20,140	78.3	5,585	21.7	11,290	43.9	11,050	43.0
New York	278,350	216,300	77.7	62,050	22.3	44,135	15.9	153,605	55.2
North Carolina	86,400	66,170	76.6	20,230	23.4	2,415	2.8	59,775	69.2
North Dakota	5,080	3,905	76.9	1,175	23.1	150	3.0	4,280	84.3
Ohio	108,130	85,295	78.9	22,835	21.1	2,305	2.1	88,345	81.7
Oklahoma	35,575	28,230	79.4	7,340	20.6	1,300	3.7	26,535	74.6
Oregon	31,995	25,575	79.9	6,420	20.1	1,745	5.5	27,500	86.0
Pennsylvania	121,595	94,935	78.1	26,660	21.9	4,500	3.7	92,305	75.9
Rhode Island	12,145	9,615	79.2	2,530	20.8	730	6.0	10,375	85.4
South Carolina	45,055	34,085	75.7	10,970	24.3	920	2.0	29,750	66.0
South Dakota	7,410	5,470	73.8	1,935	26.1	125	1.7	6,150	83.0
Tennessee	61,285	47,650	77.8	13,635	22.2	715	1.2	44,675	72.9
Texas	261,555	197,855	75.6	63,700	24.4	74,165	28.4	132,245	50.6
Utah	22,655	17,230	76.1	5,420	23.9	1,125	5.0	20,115	88.8
Vermont	5,190	4,090	78.8	1,095	21.1	105	2.0	4,940	95.2
Virginia	98,910	74,655	75.5	24,255	24.5	5,070	5.1	65,260	66.0
Washington	61,750	48,510	78.6	13,240	21.4	3,835	6.2	48,800	79.0
West Virginia	18,095	14,365	79.4	3,730	20.6	210	1.2	17,025	94.1
Wisconsin	50,100	37,915	75.7	12,185	24.3	1,870	3.7	42,400	84.6
Wyoming	5,235	3,870	73.9	1,365	26.1	310	5.9	4,620	88.3

B-15 Protective Service Workers, by State, Sex, Race, and Hispanic or Latino Origin, 2006–2010—Continued

State	Black alone, not Hispanic or Latino Number	Percent	American Indian and Alaska Native alone, not Hispanic or Latino Number	Percent	Asian alone, not Hispanic or Latino Number	Percent	Native Hawaiian and Other Pacific Islander alone, not Hispanic or Latino Number	Percent	Two or more races, not Hispanic or Latino Number	Percent
United States	615,010	18.9	29,220	0.9	67,095	2.1	9,190	0.3	57,295	1.8
Alabama	13,805	30.9	275	0.6	70	0.2	20	0.0	355	0.8
Alaska	445	5.2	1,185	13.8	185	2.2	65	0.8	320	3.7
Arizona	3,790	4.9	3,430	4.5	765	1.0	240	0.3	1,240	1.6
Arkansas	5,375	21.6	200	0.8	30	0.1	30	0.1	435	1.7
California	48,290	12.8	3,055	0.8	27,645	7.3	2,980	0.8	10,030	2.6
Colorado	3,070	6.0	480	0.9	730	1.4	30	0.1	920	1.8
Connecticut	5,090	13.9	105	0.3	220	0.6	30	0.1	600	1.6
Delaware	2,425	23.1	65	0.6	160	1.5	0	0.0	160	1.5
District of Columbia	7,440	82.1	25	0.3	165	1.8	0	0.0	120	1.3
Florida	47,650	21.1	670	0.3	2,430	1.1	175	0.1	2,740	1.2
Georgia	43,840	43.3	335	0.3	640	0.6	75	0.1	1,335	1.3
Hawaii	435	2.1	15	0.1	5,185	25.5	3,465	17.0	5,263	25.8
Idaho	100	0.7	390	2.8	60	0.4	0	0.0	250	1.8
Illinois	34,695	24.8	250	0.2	1,930	1.4	10	0.0	1,500	1.1
Indiana	7,480	13.0	135	0.2	115	0.2	25	0.0	625	1.1
Iowa	475	2.3	80	0.4	145	0.7	4	0.0	245	1.2
Kansas	1,695	6.6	270	1.0	105	0.4	25	0.1	465	1.8
Kentucky	3,245	8.6	65	0.2	30	0.1	90	0.2	385	1.0
Louisiana	21,940	39.9	430	0.8	215	0.4	10	0.0	560	1.0
Maine	65	0.6	130	1.2	25	0.2	0	0.0	89	0.8
Maryland	42,120	47.3	195	0.2	905	1.0	0	0.0	1,540	1.7
Massachusetts	6,615	9.2	135	0.2	1,105	1.5	65	0.1	1,345	1.9
Michigan	19,650	22.5	995	1.1	440	0.5	80	0.1	1,295	1.5
Minnesota	1,945	5.1	885	2.3	945	2.5	0	0.0	640	1.7
Mississippi	14,030	43.9	150	0.5	145	0.5	0	0.0	174	0.5
Missouri	7,985	14.3	225	0.4	140	0.3	35	0.1	980	1.8
Montana	30	0.3	1,010	10.4	20	0.2	20	0.2	94	1.0
Nebraska	780	5.3	140	1.0	55	0.4	35	0.2	240	1.6
Nevada	5,250	12.3	510	1.2	2,025	4.8	295	0.7	1,195	2.8
New Hampshire	105	0.9	60	0.5	10	0.1	0	0.0	125	1.1
New Jersey	23,020	20.6	230	0.2	1,975	1.8	10	0.0	1,650	1.5
New Mexico	685	2.7	2,330	9.1	130	0.5	10	0.0	225	0.9
New York	67,590	24.3	845	0.3	7,960	2.9	35	0.0	4,180	1.5
North Carolina	22,220	25.7	675	0.8	385	0.4	50	0.1	880	1.0
North Dakota	115	2.3	465	9.2	35	0.7	0	0.0	30	0.6
Ohio	15,270	14.1	250	0.2	380	0.4	55	0.1	1,530	1.4
Oklahoma	2,620	7.4	3,105	8.7	90	0.3	35	0.1	1,885	5.3
Oregon	830	2.6	395	1.2	380	1.2	110	0.3	1,035	3.2
Pennsylvania	22,315	18.4	135	0.1	930	0.8	45	0.0	1,370	1.1
Rhode Island	560	4.6	0	0.0	150	1.2	0	0.0	330	2.7
South Carolina	13,630	30.3	185	0.4	145	0.3	0	0.0	425	0.9
South Dakota	30	0.4	980	13.2	0	0.0	0	0.0	125	1.7
Tennessee	14,800	24.1	200	0.3	165	0.3	4	0.0	730	1.2
Texas	48,600	18.6	820	0.3	2,315	0.9	205	0.1	3,210	1.2
Utah	210	0.9	235	1.0	330	1.5	340	1.5	295	1.3
Vermont	35	0.7	35	0.7	30	0.6	0	0.0	45	0.9
Virginia	24,900	25.2	285	0.3	1,935	2.0	45	0.0	1,415	1.4
Washington	3,225	5.2	1,250	2.0	2,555	4.1	405	0.7	1,684	2.7
West Virginia	600	3.3	15	0.1	65	0.4	0	0.0	180	1.0
Wisconsin	3,830	7.6	770	1.5	500	1.0	40	0.1	690	1.4
Wyoming	70	1.3	115	2.2	4	0.1	0	0.0	115	2.2

B-16 Service Workers, except Protective, by State, Sex, Race, and Hispanic or Latino Origin, 2006–2010

State	Total who worked in the last 5 years	Male Number	Male Percent	Female Number	Female Percent	Hispanic or Latino Number	Hispanic or Latino Percent	White alone, not Hispanic or Latino Number	White alone, not Hispanic or Latino Percent
United States	21,572,140	7,477,890	34.7	14,094,250	65.3	4,523,995	21.0	11,868,285	55.0
Alabama	287,000	92,230	32.1	194,770	67.9	12,220	4.3	156,345	54.5
Alaska	52,270	19,660	37.6	32,610	62.4	4,110	7.9	27,945	53.5
Arizona	417,560	152,745	36.6	264,820	63.4	154,770	37.1	205,840	49.3
Arkansas	187,995	58,460	31.1	129,535	68.9	13,535	7.2	126,575	67.3
California	2,510,735	925,885	36.9	1,584,850	63.1	1,188,895	47.4	770,190	30.7
Colorado	359,135	128,715	35.8	230,420	64.2	102,230	28.5	216,720	60.3
Connecticut	263,435	93,330	35.4	170,105	64.6	54,020	20.5	153,920	58.4
Delaware	62,015	21,650	34.9	40,365	65.1	6,605	10.7	34,260	55.2
District of Columbia	43,980	18,725	42.6	25,255	57.4	10,545	24.0	5,975	13.6
Florida	1,368,995	497,750	36.4	871,240	63.6	351,205	25.7	651,415	47.6
Georgia	597,190	198,835	33.3	398,355	66.7	65,730	11.0	266,475	44.6
Hawaii	116,610	48,950	42.0	67,655	58.0	9,800	8.4	20,645	17.7
Idaho	102,340	31,600	30.9	70,740	69.1	12,125	11.8	84,040	82.1
Illinois	890,145	323,700	36.4	566,445	63.6	179,720	20.2	505,145	56.7
Indiana	453,680	148,280	32.7	305,400	67.3	32,070	7.1	352,670	77.7
Iowa	235,200	71,840	30.5	163,365	69.5	11,290	4.8	206,150	87.6
Kansas	203,565	64,275	31.6	139,290	68.4	27,040	13.3	148,470	72.9
Kentucky	275,020	88,995	32.4	186,020	67.6	10,875	4.0	220,885	80.3
Louisiana	311,605	97,330	31.2	214,275	68.8	15,150	4.9	138,725	44.5
Maine	105,495	32,995	31.3	72,505	68.7	1,505	1.4	98,985	93.8
Maryland	385,320	128,380	33.3	256,940	66.7	59,565	15.5	161,740	42.0
Massachusetts	480,505	174,060	36.2	306,445	63.8	70,165	14.6	320,380	66.7
Michigan	750,160	248,540	33.1	501,620	66.9	36,550	4.9	546,510	72.9
Minnesota	404,605	135,760	33.6	268,845	66.4	28,730	7.1	318,775	78.8
Mississippi	189,955	59,120	31.1	130,835	68.9	5,290	2.8	80,665	42.5
Missouri	436,045	150,535	34.5	285,510	65.5	21,185	4.9	320,890	73.6
Montana	78,625	25,415	32.3	53,210	67.7	2,820	3.6	66,845	85.0
Nebraska	138,735	43,230	31.2	95,505	68.8	13,710	9.9	110,165	79.4
Nevada	292,675	130,400	44.6	162,270	55.4	102,435	35.0	122,550	41.9
New Hampshire	93,765	33,300	35.5	60,465	64.5	3,120	3.3	85,970	91.7
New Jersey	577,155	217,495	37.7	359,660	62.3	160,350	27.8	268,540	46.5
New Mexico	147,825	51,645	34.9	96,180	65.1	83,665	56.6	42,025	28.4
New York	1,529,240	592,340	38.7	936,900	61.3	417,655	27.3	654,165	42.8
North Carolina	620,650	202,220	32.6	418,435	67.4	58,730	9.5	339,350	54.7
North Dakota	56,560	16,270	28.8	40,290	71.2	1,210	2.1	49,825	88.1
Ohio	846,015	278,305	32.9	567,710	67.1	30,340	3.6	643,330	76.0
Oklahoma	253,865	81,865	32.2	172,000	67.8	28,715	11.3	155,905	61.4
Oregon	277,280	91,065	32.8	186,215	67.2	41,805	15.1	204,360	73.7
Pennsylvania	894,205	303,785	34.0	590,420	66.0	55,710	6.2	672,705	75.2
Rhode Island	87,030	32,775	37.7	54,255	62.3	13,615	15.6	60,980	70.1
South Carolina	307,585	100,700	32.7	206,885	67.3	18,280	5.9	159,860	52.0
South Dakota	61,815	18,315	29.6	43,500	70.4	1,630	2.6	51,075	82.6
Tennessee	417,150	139,335	33.4	277,815	66.6	25,370	6.1	283,450	67.9
Texas	1,636,470	537,865	32.9	1,098,605	67.1	777,325	47.5	544,175	33.3
Utah	162,265	56,015	34.5	106,255	65.5	31,780	19.6	118,740	73.2
Vermont	50,025	17,515	35.0	32,510	65.0	730	1.5	46,440	92.8
Virginia	500,370	159,335	31.8	341,035	68.2	70,375	14.1	251,370	50.2
Washington	463,750	151,205	32.6	312,540	67.4	63,245	13.6	310,370	66.9
West Virginia	125,010	38,620	30.9	86,390	69.1	1,595	1.3	113,665	90.9
Wisconsin	420,710	133,470	31.7	287,240	68.3	29,370	7.0	337,415	80.2
Wyoming	42,815	13,065	30.5	29,755	69.5	5,510	12.9	34,675	81.0

PART B—STATE TABLES

B-16 Service Workers, except Protective, by State, Sex, Race, and Hispanic or Latino Origin, 2006–2010—Continued

State	Black alone, not Hispanic or Latino Number	Percent	American Indian and Alaska Native alone, not Hispanic or Latino Number	Percent	Asian alone, not Hispanic or Latino Number	Percent	Native Hawaiian and Other Pacific Islander alone, not Hispanic or Latino Number	Percent	Two or more races, not Hispanic or Latino Number	Percent
United States	3,485,605	16.2	168,060	0.8	1,100,785	5.1	41,760	0.2	383,650	1.8
Alabama	109,480	38.1	1,375	0.5	4,130	1.4	140	0.0	3,310	1.2
Alaska	2,190	4.2	7,775	14.9	5,715	10.9	715	1.4	3,820	7.3
Arizona	16,495	4.0	19,615	4.7	14,025	3.4	620	0.1	6,195	1.5
Arkansas	41,290	22.0	1,200	0.6	2,650	1.4	255	0.1	2,485	1.3
California	152,330	6.1	10,920	0.4	325,940	13.0	10,805	0.4	51,650	2.1
Colorado	15,785	4.4	2,845	0.8	13,755	3.8	770	0.2	7,030	2.0
Connecticut	39,625	15.0	380	0.1	9,325	3.5	200	0.1	5,960	2.3
Delaware	18,115	29.2	385	0.6	1,610	2.6	55	0.1	990	1.6
District of Columbia	24,820	56.4	65	0.1	1,900	4.3	0	0.0	670	1.5
Florida	294,120	21.5	2,910	0.2	48,285	3.5	1,030	0.1	20,040	1.5
Georgia	233,720	39.1	1,020	0.2	22,860	3.8	105	0.0	7,285	1.2
Hawaii	1,245	1.1	125	0.1	54,220	46.5	11,225	9.6	19,345	16.6
Idaho	810	0.8	1,245	1.2	2,030	2.0	160	0.2	1,945	1.9
Illinois	156,095	17.5	920	0.1	36,715	4.1	370	0.0	11,180	1.3
Indiana	53,550	11.8	1,120	0.2	6,520	1.4	110	0.0	7,640	1.7
Iowa	8,860	3.8	720	0.3	4,695	2.0	200	0.1	3,280	1.4
Kansas	15,960	7.8	1,855	0.9	5,195	2.6	210	0.1	4,835	2.4
Kentucky	34,820	12.7	625	0.2	3,840	1.4	310	0.1	3,665	1.3
Louisiana	145,215	46.6	1,500	0.5	7,385	2.4	195	0.1	3,440	1.1
Maine	1,435	1.4	560	0.5	1,520	1.4	50	0.0	1,439	1.4
Maryland	133,180	34.6	735	0.2	23,265	6.0	150	0.0	6,685	1.7
Massachusetts	50,825	10.6	905	0.2	23,180	4.8	170	0.0	14,875	3.1
Michigan	132,230	17.6	5,125	0.7	15,685	2.1	395	0.1	13,660	1.8
Minnesota	28,870	7.1	6,225	1.5	15,090	3.7	265	0.1	6,645	1.6
Mississippi	97,250	51.2	1,660	0.9	3,555	1.9	40	0.0	1,495	0.8
Missouri	75,375	17.3	1,870	0.4	9,040	2.1	355	0.1	7,325	1.7
Montana	455	0.6	5,500	7.0	1,100	1.4	115	0.1	1,790	2.3
Nebraska	8,765	6.3	1,165	0.8	2,455	1.8	130	0.1	2,355	1.7
Nevada	21,965	7.5	1,995	0.7	35,610	12.2	1,955	0.7	6,170	2.1
New Hampshire	1,620	1.7	190	0.2	1,780	1.9	45	0.0	1,045	1.1
New Jersey	103,885	18.0	730	0.1	34,895	6.0	310	0.1	8,450	1.5
New Mexico	3,445	2.3	14,175	9.6	2,735	1.9	85	0.1	1,690	1.1
New York	305,695	20.0	3,860	0.3	123,100	8.0	350	0.0	24,420	1.6
North Carolina	189,870	30.6	7,605	1.2	15,010	2.4	595	0.1	9,500	1.5
North Dakota	960	1.7	3,020	5.3	725	1.3	35	0.1	775	1.4
Ohio	145,160	17.2	1,660	0.2	12,880	1.5	125	0.0	12,515	1.5
Oklahoma	28,015	11.0	19,100	7.5	6,540	2.6	395	0.2	15,190	6.0
Oregon	6,220	2.2	3,780	1.4	11,875	4.3	1,330	0.5	7,915	2.9
Pennsylvania	129,010	14.4	1,125	0.1	23,480	2.6	290	0.0	11,885	1.3
Rhode Island	7,600	8.7	445	0.5	2,400	2.8	35	0.0	1,960	2.3
South Carolina	119,000	38.7	690	0.2	5,485	1.8	235	0.1	4,035	1.3
South Dakota	760	1.2	6,360	10.3	830	1.3	70	0.1	1,090	1.8
Tennessee	94,550	22.7	1,105	0.3	7,895	1.9	235	0.1	4,540	1.1
Texas	233,350	14.3	4,895	0.3	59,365	3.6	1,400	0.1	15,970	1.0
Utah	1,380	0.9	2,190	1.3	4,965	3.1	1,320	0.8	1,895	1.2
Vermont	735	1.5	145	0.3	870	1.7	4	0.0	1,100	2.2
Virginia	136,365	27.3	990	0.2	32,740	6.5	345	0.1	8,180	1.6
Washington	21,820	4.7	6,970	1.5	42,185	9.1	3,195	0.7	15,960	3.4
West Virginia	5,925	4.7	315	0.3	1,420	1.1	40	0.0	2,060	1.6
Wisconsin	34,880	8.3	5,355	1.3	7,820	1.9	230	0.1	5,630	1.3
Wyoming	470	1.1	1,020	2.4	510	1.2	10	0.0	620	1.4

PART C

Metropolitan Statistical Area Data

C-1 All Workers, by Metropolitan Statistical Area and Occupation Group, 2006–2010

Metropolitan Statistical Area	Total who worked in the last 5 years Number	Percent	Management, business, and financial workers Number	Percent	Science, engineering, and computer professionals Number	Percent	Health care practitioner professionals Number	Percent	Other professional workers Number	Percent
Abilene, TX	76,065	100.0	7,065	9.3	1,095	1.4	2,385	3.1	8,905	11.7
Akron, OH	375,270	100.0	43,860	11.7	14,105	3.8	13,475	3.6	38,940	10.4
Albany, GA	72,015	100.0	6,600	9.2	1,030	1.4	2,110	2.9	6,830	9.5
Albany–Schenectady–Troy, NY	463,990	100.0	59,095	12.7	22,095	4.8	18,225	3.9	58,025	12.5
Albuquerque, NM	434,835	100.0	52,100	12.0	22,730	5.2	15,470	3.6	48,925	11.3
Alexandria, LA	68,565	100.0	6,595	9.6	840	1.2	3,020	4.4	7,160	10.4
Allentown–Bethlehem–Easton, PA–NJ	420,055	100.0	47,625	11.3	15,775	3.8	16,440	3.9	43,970	10.5
Altoona, PA	62,595	100.0	5,945	9.5	1,165	1.9	2,555	4.1	5,520	8.8
Amarillo, TX	126,675	100.0	12,320	9.7	2,750	2.2	4,345	3.4	13,070	10.3
Ames, IA	52,425	100.0	5,875	11.2	3,240	6.2	1,590	3.0	9,320	17.8
Anchorage, AK	195,975	100.0	25,060	12.8	9,770	5.0	6,865	3.5	21,875	11.2
Anderson, IN	62,785	100.0	5,625	9.0	1,190	1.9	1,945	3.1	5,840	9.3
Anderson, SC	88,610	100.0	8,440	9.5	1,840	2.1	2,905	3.3	7,545	8.5
Ann Arbor, MI	183,005	100.0	24,195	13.2	15,175	8.3	10,915	6.0	31,275	17.1
Anniston–Oxford, AL	54,030	100.0	4,485	8.3	1,260	2.3	1,400	2.6	4,540	8.4
Appleton, WI	125,605	100.0	14,615	11.6	4,430	3.5	3,555	2.8	11,865	9.4
Asheville, NC	208,775	100.0	22,770	10.9	4,530	2.2	9,350	4.5	23,745	11.4
Athens–Clarke County, GA	92,445	100.0	10,425	11.3	2,750	3.0	3,060	3.3	14,050	15.2
Atlanta–Sandy Springs–Marietta, GA	2,730,620	100.0	400,780	14.7	130,170	4.8	72,865	2.7	312,360	11.4
Atlantic City–Hammonton, NJ	142,735	100.0	13,420	9.4	3,030	2.1	4,445	3.1	12,550	8.8
Auburn–Opelika, AL	67,545	100.0	6,940	10.3	1,995	3.0	2,255	3.3	9,140	13.5
Augusta–Richmond County, GA–SC	250,335	100.0	23,320	9.3	9,325	3.7	10,435	4.2	23,925	9.6
Austin–Round Rock–San Marcos, TX	897,255	100.0	134,065	14.9	62,590	7.0	23,290	2.6	116,535	13.0
Bakersfield–Delano, CA	351,110	100.0	28,740	8.2	7,650	2.2	7,670	2.2	28,455	8.1
Baltimore–Towson, MD	1,438,090	100.0	207,880	14.5	91,030	6.3	58,130	4.0	176,570	12.3
Bangor, ME	80,010	100.0	7,565	9.5	1,670	2.1	3,530	4.4	9,395	11.7
Barnstable Town, MA	110,965	100.0	14,520	13.1	3,645	3.3	5,295	4.8	13,060	11.8
Baton Rouge, LA	396,310	100.0	43,080	10.9	12,065	3.0	12,085	3.0	40,850	10.3
Battle Creek, MI	66,535	100.0	6,525	9.8	1,635	2.5	1,830	2.8	5,415	8.1
Bay City, MI	54,050	100.0	4,160	7.7	1,185	2.2	2,085	3.9	4,810	8.9
Beaumont–Port Arthur, TX	175,070	100.0	14,260	8.1	3,925	2.2	5,505	3.1	16,415	9.4
Bellingham, WA	103,245	100.0	12,200	11.8	2,865	2.8	2,855	2.8	11,385	11.0
Bend, OR	79,735	100.0	9,350	11.7	2,745	3.4	2,435	3.1	8,130	10.2
Billings, MT	83,515	100.0	9,145	11.0	2,660	3.2	3,380	4.0	8,625	10.3
Binghamton, NY	126,275	100.0	12,185	9.6	5,565	4.4	4,110	3.3	14,190	11.2
Birmingham–Hoover, AL	555,515	100.0	64,545	11.6	17,350	3.1	22,070	4.0	58,160	10.5
Bismarck, ND	60,895	100.0	7,580	12.4	2,785	4.6	2,625	4.3	6,110	10.0
Blacksburg–Christiansburg–Radford, VA	79,795	100.0	7,890	9.9	4,210	5.3	2,195	2.8	11,285	14.1
Bloomington, IN	94,460	100.0	9,485	10.0	3,715	3.9	2,400	2.5	14,660	15.5
Bloomington–Normal, IL	93,065	100.0	12,575	13.5	6,300	6.8	2,155	2.3	11,160	12.0
Boise City–Nampa, ID	301,285	100.0	38,885	12.9	15,445	5.1	9,955	3.3	30,550	10.1
Boston–Cambridge–Quincy, MA–NH	2,498,630	100.0	371,435	14.9	167,370	6.7	104,450	4.2	350,660	14.0
Boulder, CO	163,620	100.0	26,595	16.3	17,630	10.8	5,895	3.6	26,280	16.1
Bowling Green, KY	63,565	100.0	6,040	9.5	1,735	2.7	1,990	3.1	7,085	11.1
Bremerton–Silverdale, WA	119,380	100.0	14,860	12.4	6,905	5.8	3,440	2.9	11,960	10.0
Bridgeport–Stamford–Norwalk, CT	475,550	100.0	80,200	16.9	18,945	4.0	15,440	3.2	66,925	14.1
Brownsville–Harlingen, TX	150,325	100.0	11,840	7.9	1,555	1.0	3,905	2.6	15,375	10.2
Brunswick, GA	53,415	100.0	5,435	10.2	660	1.2	1,715	3.2	5,495	10.3
Buffalo–Niagara Falls, NY	575,645	100.0	60,745	10.6	18,510	3.2	23,125	4.0	66,505	11.6
Burlington, NC	77,335	100.0	8,085	10.5	1,915	2.5	2,120	2.7	6,895	8.9
Burlington–South Burlington, VT	121,470	100.0	16,060	13.2	6,175	5.1	4,820	4.0	16,380	13.5
Canton–Massillon, OH	206,355	100.0	20,460	9.9	5,220	2.5	7,600	3.7	18,435	8.9
Cape Coral–Fort Myers, FL	285,560	100.0	33,435	11.7	4,905	1.7	9,205	3.2	23,540	8.2
Cape Girardeau–Jackson, MO–IL	48,915	100.0	4,815	9.8	705	1.4	1,785	3.6	5,065	10.4
Carson City, NV	28,715	100.0	2,780	9.7	885	3.1	625	2.2	2,835	9.9

PART C—METROPOLITAN STATISTICAL AREA TABLES

C-1 All Workers, by Metropolitan Statistical Area and Occupation Group, 2006–2010—Continued

Metropolitan Statistical Area	Technicians Number	Technicians Percent	Sales workers Number	Sales workers Percent	Administrative support workers Number	Administrative support workers Percent	Construction and extractive craft workers Number	Construction and extractive craft workers Percent	Installation, maintenance, and repair craft workers Number	Installation, maintenance, and repair craft workers Percent
Abilene, TX	2,775	3.6	8,710	11.5	12,035	15.8	4,755	6.3	3,995	5.3
Akron, OH	10,825	2.9	41,340	11.0	58,910	15.7	17,880	4.8	16,065	4.3
Albany, GA	2,575	3.6	8,345	11.6	10,530	14.6	3,640	5.1	3,420	4.7
Albany–Schenectady–Troy, NY	15,065	3.2	48,930	10.5	84,685	18.3	21,460	4.6	15,790	3.4
Albuquerque, NM	14,590	3.4	47,905	11.0	68,900	15.8	30,185	6.9	17,685	4.1
Alexandria, LA	2,340	3.4	7,410	10.8	10,660	15.5	4,705	6.9	3,340	4.9
Allentown–Bethlehem–Easton, PA–NJ	13,305	3.2	45,170	10.8	68,010	16.2	21,855	5.2	19,240	4.6
Altoona, PA	1,975	3.2	7,220	11.5	9,955	15.9	3,300	5.3	3,410	5.4
Amarillo, TX	3,950	3.1	14,915	11.8	19,765	15.6	7,755	6.1	6,735	5.3
Ames, IA	2,050	3.9	4,810	9.2	7,470	14.2	1,975	3.8	1,520	2.9
Anchorage, AK	5,650	2.9	18,400	9.4	33,440	17.1	14,645	7.5	8,275	4.2
Anderson, IN	1,660	2.6	6,325	10.1	9,690	15.4	4,020	6.4	3,175	5.1
Anderson, SC	3,165	3.6	10,535	11.9	12,425	14.0	4,905	5.5	5,235	5.9
Ann Arbor, MI	5,930	3.2	16,865	9.2	23,155	12.7	4,835	2.6	5,090	2.8
Anniston–Oxford, AL	1,480	2.7	6,190	11.5	7,475	13.8	2,665	4.9	4,015	7.4
Appleton, WI	3,530	2.8	13,795	11.0	19,165	15.3	6,775	5.4	6,010	4.8
Asheville, NC	6,045	2.9	23,490	11.3	29,020	13.9	15,380	7.4	9,965	4.8
Athens–Clarke County, GA	3,175	3.4	10,335	11.2	12,475	13.5	4,845	5.2	3,275	3.5
Atlanta–Sandy Springs–Marietta, GA	65,850	2.4	348,420	12.8	415,475	15.2	161,600	5.9	101,560	3.7
Atlantic City–Hammonton, NJ	3,220	2.3	16,705	11.7	19,695	13.8	7,870	5.5	5,075	3.6
Auburn–Opelika, AL	2,390	3.5	7,160	10.6	9,900	14.7	4,090	6.1	3,355	5.0
Augusta–Richmond County, GA–SC	8,475	3.4	28,105	11.2	36,345	14.5	14,240	5.7	11,840	4.7
Austin–Round Rock–San Marcos, TX	26,595	3.0	104,020	11.6	131,035	14.6	59,685	6.7	29,280	3.3
Bakersfield–Delano, CA	8,220	2.3	35,250	10.0	49,780	14.2	26,445	7.5	16,110	4.6
Baltimore–Towson, MD	44,435	3.1	153,740	10.7	229,065	15.9	69,250	4.8	52,020	3.6
Bangor, ME	2,470	3.1	9,135	11.4	12,425	15.5	4,680	5.8	4,055	5.1
Barnstable Town, MA	3,095	2.8	13,675	12.3	15,220	13.7	8,925	8.0	4,155	3.7
Baton Rouge, LA	13,480	3.4	46,150	11.6	63,585	16.0	30,780	7.8	16,900	4.3
Battle Creek, MI	1,305	2.0	6,710	10.1	9,275	13.9	3,060	4.6	3,250	4.9
Bay City, MI	1,835	3.4	5,940	11.0	8,160	15.1	3,030	5.6	2,935	5.4
Beaumont–Port Arthur, TX	6,140	3.5	17,865	10.2	26,975	15.4	17,545	10.0	8,555	4.9
Bellingham, WA	2,730	2.6	11,890	11.5	15,580	15.1	6,080	5.9	3,965	3.8
Bend, OR	2,110	2.6	10,175	12.8	11,220	14.1	7,180	9.0	3,660	4.6
Billings, MT	2,045	2.4	10,190	12.2	13,115	15.7	5,940	7.1	4,235	5.1
Binghamton, NY	4,350	3.4	14,140	11.2	21,085	16.7	5,890	4.7	4,670	3.7
Birmingham–Hoover, AL	16,660	3.0	70,570	12.7	88,645	16.0	36,275	6.5	24,820	4.5
Bismarck, ND	2,050	3.4	6,865	11.3	9,945	16.3	4,015	6.6	2,415	4.0
Blacksburg–Christiansburg–Radford, VA	3,165	4.0	7,860	9.9	10,275	12.9	3,750	4.7	3,360	4.2
Bloomington, IN	3,040	3.2	8,410	8.9	12,865	13.6	5,360	5.7	3,445	3.6
Bloomington–Normal, IL	2,430	2.6	12,250	13.2	15,865	17.0	3,475	3.7	2,880	3.1
Boise City–Nampa, ID	9,510	3.2	33,400	11.1	47,605	15.8	19,790	6.6	11,415	3.8
Boston–Cambridge–Quincy, MA–NH	73,100	2.9	269,385	10.8	368,240	14.7	114,125	4.6	73,405	2.9
Boulder, CO	4,540	2.8	18,840	11.5	17,840	10.9	6,425	3.9	3,505	2.1
Bowling Green, KY	1,730	2.7	7,525	11.8	9,645	15.2	3,415	5.4	2,545	4.0
Bremerton–Silverdale, WA	4,070	3.4	11,525	9.7	17,215	14.4	8,765	7.3	5,715	4.8
Bridgeport–Stamford–Norwalk, CT	8,875	1.9	60,250	12.7	66,765	14.0	28,530	6.0	13,775	2.9
Brownsville–Harlingen, TX	3,415	2.3	17,620	11.7	23,375	15.5	9,950	6.6	5,855	3.9
Brunswick, GA	1,105	2.1	5,980	11.2	7,585	14.2	4,420	8.3	2,645	5.0
Buffalo–Niagara Falls, NY	16,865	2.9	65,010	11.3	101,235	17.6	23,265	4.0	23,790	4.1
Burlington, NC	2,815	3.6	8,465	10.9	12,250	15.8	4,320	5.6	4,430	5.7
Burlington–South Burlington, VT	3,950	3.3	12,785	10.5	18,095	14.9	5,625	4.6	5,070	4.2
Canton–Massillon, OH	6,170	3.0	21,950	10.6	31,655	15.3	10,125	4.9	9,810	4.8
Cape Coral–Fort Myers, FL	7,235	2.5	41,440	14.5	42,825	15.0	26,210	9.2	13,875	4.9
Cape Girardeau–Jackson, MO–IL	1,100	2.2	5,325	10.9	7,555	15.4	3,350	6.8	2,510	5.1
Carson City, NV	775	2.7	3,085	10.7	4,710	16.4	2,060	7.2	1,230	4.3

C-1 All Workers, by Metropolitan Statistical Area and Occupation Group, 2006–2010—*Continued*

Metropolitan Statistical Area	Production operative workers Number	Percent	Transportation and material moving operative workers Number	Percent	Laborers and helpers Number	Percent	Protective service workers Number	Percent	Service workers, except protective Number	Percent
Abilene, TX	3,120	4.1	2,830	3.7	3,380	4.4	2,190	2.9	12,390	16.3
Akron, OH	26,165	7.0	15,955	4.3	12,675	3.4	5,930	1.6	53,005	14.1
Albany, GA	4,400	6.1	5,020	7.0	3,685	5.1	1,890	2.6	10,710	14.9
Albany–Schenectady–Troy, NY	14,445	3.1	17,365	3.7	12,750	2.7	11,085	2.4	61,995	13.4
Albuquerque, NM	12,725	2.9	15,330	3.5	12,175	2.8	11,880	2.7	60,990	14.0
Alexandria, LA	2,855	4.2	3,535	5.2	2,535	3.7	2,130	3.1	10,885	15.9
Allentown–Bethlehem–Easton, PA–NJ	23,940	5.7	22,895	5.5	15,835	3.8	7,425	1.8	55,065	13.1
Altoona, PA	3,625	5.8	3,870	6.2	2,780	4.4	1,160	1.9	9,505	15.2
Amarillo, TX	6,865	5.4	6,250	4.9	5,380	4.2	3,615	2.9	18,175	14.3
Ames, IA	2,065	3.9	1,855	3.5	2,210	4.2	525	1.0	7,820	14.9
Anchorage, AK	3,935	2.0	7,260	3.7	6,590	3.4	4,115	2.1	29,090	14.8
Anderson, IN	4,960	7.9	3,725	5.9	2,625	4.2	2,010	3.2	9,000	14.3
Anderson, SC	9,165	10.3	5,095	5.7	3,460	3.9	1,140	1.3	11,695	13.2
Ann Arbor, MI	6,045	3.3	5,400	3.0	4,095	2.2	2,460	1.3	25,850	14.1
Anniston–Oxford, AL	5,640	10.4	2,825	5.2	2,750	5.1	945	1.7	7,435	13.8
Appleton, WI	12,945	10.3	6,545	5.2	5,010	4.0	1,780	1.4	14,830	11.8
Asheville, NC	12,230	5.9	8,370	4.0	8,325	4.0	3,135	1.5	31,080	14.9
Athens–Clarke County, GA	4,505	4.9	3,325	3.6	3,805	4.1	1,640	1.8	13,825	15.0
Atlanta–Sandy Springs–Marietta, GA	99,775	3.7	123,030	4.5	87,085	3.2	51,745	1.9	321,715	11.8
Atlantic City–Hammonton, NJ	3,275	2.3	5,470	3.8	4,250	3.0	5,585	3.9	36,935	25.9
Auburn–Opelika, AL	4,190	6.2	3,060	4.5	2,215	3.3	1,390	2.1	9,025	13.4
Augusta–Richmond County, GA–SC	16,065	6.4	12,735	5.1	10,480	4.2	6,030	2.4	35,290	14.1
Austin–Round Rock–San Marcos, TX	23,655	2.6	25,985	2.9	24,345	2.7	14,730	1.6	114,960	12.8
Bakersfield–Delano, CA	15,790	4.5	20,685	5.9	42,700	12.2	11,095	3.2	46,295	13.2
Baltimore–Towson, MD	34,670	2.4	55,185	3.8	35,950	2.5	40,265	2.8	176,165	12.2
Bangor, ME	3,345	4.2	3,575	4.5	3,330	4.2	1,545	1.9	12,805	16.0
Barnstable Town, MA	2,150	1.9	3,055	2.8	4,715	4.2	2,330	2.1	16,590	15.0
Baton Rouge, LA	18,685	4.7	17,725	4.5	12,615	3.2	10,175	2.6	54,450	13.7
Battle Creek, MI	8,300	12.5	3,875	5.8	3,090	4.6	1,140	1.7	10,380	15.6
Bay City, MI	3,795	7.0	2,560	4.7	2,160	4.0	985	1.8	9,560	17.7
Beaumont–Port Arthur, TX	11,870	6.8	8,720	5.0	7,085	4.0	4,885	2.8	23,520	13.4
Bellingham, WA	4,870	4.7	4,030	3.9	5,245	5.1	1,960	1.9	16,595	16.1
Bend, OR	3,170	4.0	2,460	3.1	3,295	4.1	1,085	1.4	12,130	15.2
Billings, MT	3,140	3.8	3,520	4.2	3,190	3.8	1,145	1.4	12,920	15.5
Binghamton, NY	6,870	5.4	6,530	5.2	3,850	3.0	2,440	1.9	19,195	15.2
Birmingham–Hoover, AL	26,335	4.7	25,545	4.6	20,700	3.7	11,220	2.0	66,290	11.9
Bismarck, ND	1,820	3.0	2,590	4.3	1,800	3.0	1,010	1.7	9,195	15.1
Blacksburg–Christiansburg–Radford, VA	5,635	7.1	2,705	3.4	3,020	3.8	1,500	1.9	12,345	15.5
Bloomington, IN	5,810	6.2	4,875	5.2	3,305	3.5	1,280	1.4	15,350	16.3
Bloomington–Normal, IL	2,925	3.1	3,040	3.3	2,785	3.0	1,670	1.8	12,965	13.9
Boise City–Nampa, ID	13,380	4.4	12,965	4.3	12,890	4.3	5,240	1.7	38,230	12.7
Boston–Cambridge–Quincy, MA–NH	76,940	3.1	74,860	3.0	57,890	2.3	48,795	2.0	325,180	13.0
Boulder, CO	5,020	3.1	3,525	2.2	3,935	2.4	1,660	1.0	21,285	13.0
Bowling Green, KY	5,885	9.3	3,310	5.2	2,525	4.0	885	1.4	8,880	14.0
Bremerton–Silverdale, WA	4,195	3.5	4,430	3.7	4,495	3.8	2,830	2.4	17,470	14.6
Bridgeport–Stamford–Norwalk, CT	14,585	3.1	13,365	2.8	14,550	3.1	7,370	1.5	60,975	12.8
Brownsville–Harlingen, TX	6,070	4.0	8,040	5.3	7,685	5.1	4,890	3.3	28,810	19.2
Brunswick, GA	2,065	3.9	2,805	5.3	2,605	4.9	1,295	2.4	8,995	16.8
Buffalo–Niagara Falls, NY	30,040	5.2	23,610	4.1	16,790	2.9	13,515	2.3	87,370	15.2
Burlington, NC	6,680	8.6	4,035	5.2	2,665	3.4	1,460	1.9	10,400	13.4
Burlington–South Burlington, VT	4,780	3.9	3,685	3.0	4,235	3.5	2,250	1.9	16,990	14.0
Canton–Massillon, OH	16,720	8.1	11,060	5.4	9,435	4.6	3,005	1.5	32,770	15.9
Cape Coral–Fort Myers, FL	6,110	2.1	11,160	3.9	11,565	4.0	7,150	2.5	43,680	15.3
Cape Girardeau–Jackson, MO–IL	3,345	6.8	2,415	4.9	1,915	3.9	930	1.9	7,705	15.8
Carson City, NV	1,750	6.1	855	3.0	1,090	3.8	910	3.2	4,660	16.2

PART C—METROPOLITAN STATISTICAL AREA TABLES

C-1 All Workers, by Metropolitan Statistical Area and Occupation Group, 2006–2010—Continued

Metropolitan Statistical Area	Total who worked in the last 5 years Number	Percent	Management, business, and financial workers Number	Percent	Science, engineering, and computer professionals Number	Percent	Health care practitioner professionals Number	Percent	Other professional workers Number	Percent
Casper, WY	39,835	100.0	3,660	9.2	1,185	3.0	1,665	4.2	3,460	8.7
Cedar Rapids, IA	139,835	100.0	17,025	12.2	7,315	5.2	4,695	3.4	13,540	9.7
Champaign–Urbana, IL	122,820	100.0	12,500	10.2	6,020	4.9	3,685	3.0	20,875	17.0
Charleston, WV	140,600	100.0	13,775	9.8	3,790	2.7	6,655	4.7	15,045	10.7
Charleston–North Charleston–Summerville, SC	331,985	100.0	39,365	11.9	11,330	3.4	12,475	3.8	32,705	9.9
Charlotte–Gastonia–Rock Hill, NC–SC	914,240	100.0	128,050	14.0	36,965	4.0	28,125	3.1	101,325	11.1
Charlottesville, VA	101,390	100.0	13,705	13.5	5,515	5.4	5,800	5.7	15,890	15.7
Chattanooga, TN–GA	264,805	100.0	29,155	11.0	7,035	2.7	10,335	3.9	24,805	9.4
Cheyenne, WY	46,530	100.0	5,480	11.8	1,775	3.8	1,540	3.3	4,700	10.1
Chicago–Joliet–Naperville, IL–IN–WI	4,936,190	100.0	643,675	13.0	196,855	4.0	162,720	3.3	564,285	11.4
Chico, CA	102,290	100.0	11,355	11.1	2,425	2.4	3,190	3.1	10,770	10.5
Cincinnati–Middletown, OH–KY–IN	1,100,965	100.0	138,190	12.6	45,680	4.1	39,875	3.6	114,205	10.4
Clarksville, TN–KY	111,840	100.0	10,630	9.5	2,175	1.9	3,175	2.8	10,145	9.1
Cleveland, TN	54,860	100.0	4,210	7.7	1,290	2.4	1,775	3.2	5,450	9.9
Cleveland–Elyria–Mentor, OH	1,081,565	100.0	124,045	11.5	38,695	3.6	44,445	4.1	111,840	10.3
Coeur d'Alene, ID	68,645	100.0	8,370	12.2	1,845	2.7	2,520	3.7	5,620	8.2
College Station–Bryan, TX	109,230	100.0	10,735	9.8	4,450	4.1	2,670	2.4	16,440	15.1
Colorado Springs, CO	309,975	100.0	43,510	14.0	20,615	6.7	9,600	3.1	33,840	10.9
Columbia, MO	94,885	100.0	10,060	10.6	3,510	3.7	4,875	5.1	15,065	15.9
Columbia, SC	382,825	100.0	45,590	11.9	12,895	3.4	13,490	3.5	45,390	11.9
Columbus, GA–AL	127,345	100.0	13,455	10.6	2,405	1.9	4,000	3.1	12,920	10.1
Columbus, IN	39,535	100.0	5,170	13.1	2,735	6.9	1,275	3.2	3,510	8.9
Columbus, OH	962,935	100.0	131,340	13.6	46,015	4.8	34,755	3.6	110,570	11.5
Corpus Christi, TX	200,510	100.0	19,195	9.6	3,845	1.9	5,970	3.0	20,815	10.4
Corvallis, OR	43,835	100.0	5,005	11.4	3,580	8.2	1,595	3.6	7,210	16.4
Crestview–Fort Walton Beach–Destin, FL	89,110	100.0	11,445	12.8	4,200	4.7	2,460	2.8	8,640	9.7
Cumberland, MD–WV	46,650	100.0	4,060	8.7	575	1.2	1,650	3.5	4,145	8.9
Dallas–Fort Worth–Arlington, TX	3,240,180	100.0	440,065	13.6	155,605	4.8	86,040	2.7	351,080	10.8
Dalton, GA	67,210	100.0	5,400	8.0	880	1.3	1,130	1.7	4,170	6.2
Danville, IL	38,480	100.0	3,115	8.1	390	1.0	1,135	2.9	2,870	7.5
Danville, VA	51,165	100.0	3,700	7.2	640	1.3	1,505	2.9	4,290	8.4
Davenport–Moline–Rock Island, IA–IL	195,505	100.0	21,100	10.8	6,200	3.2	6,570	3.4	19,005	9.7
Dayton, OH	426,345	100.0	46,465	10.9	19,065	4.5	15,350	3.6	43,415	10.2
Decatur, AL	73,280	100.0	6,470	8.8	2,125	2.9	1,730	2.4	5,435	7.4
Decatur, IL	53,620	100.0	5,285	9.9	1,735	3.2	1,875	3.5	4,840	9.0
Deltona–Daytona Beach–Ormond Beach, FL	231,415	100.0	25,200	10.9	5,685	2.5	7,300	3.2	21,040	9.1
Denver–Aurora–Broomfield, CO	1,371,265	100.0	202,550	14.8	86,940	6.3	42,775	3.1	152,155	11.1
Des Moines–West Des Moines, IA	313,020	100.0	45,445	14.5	12,520	4.0	10,315	3.3	35,760	11.4
Detroit–Warren–Livonia, MI	2,166,755	100.0	250,470	11.6	110,335	5.1	74,095	3.4	208,150	9.6
Dothan, AL	67,090	100.0	5,890	8.8	1,015	1.5	2,770	4.1	6,065	9.0
Dover, DE	75,070	100.0	7,930	10.6	2,010	2.7	2,480	3.3	7,220	9.6
Dubuque, IA	51,700	100.0	5,805	11.2	1,560	3.0	2,035	3.9	5,415	10.5
Duluth, MN–WI	143,840	100.0	14,925	10.4	3,100	2.2	6,165	4.3	15,150	10.5
Durham–Chapel Hill, NC	261,205	100.0	33,315	12.8	15,890	6.1	15,105	5.8	39,535	15.1
Eau Claire, WI	89,845	100.0	9,545	10.6	2,245	2.5	2,850	3.2	8,335	9.3
El Centro, CA	67,320	100.0	5,565	8.3	595	0.9	1,065	1.6	5,280	7.8
Elizabethtown, KY	50,330	100.0	5,220	10.4	1,110	2.2	1,785	3.5	4,910	9.8
Elkhart–Goshen, IN	102,705	100.0	9,085	8.8	2,090	2.0	2,460	2.4	7,765	7.6
Elmira, NY	42,540	100.0	3,875	9.1	1,405	3.3	1,985	4.7	3,985	9.4
El Paso, TX	328,945	100.0	29,100	8.8	6,420	2.0	8,180	2.5	36,155	11.0
Erie, PA	138,180	100.0	13,100	9.5	3,965	2.9	5,610	4.1	13,925	10.1
Eugene–Springfield, OR	176,945	100.0	19,725	11.1	4,755	2.7	5,250	3.0	20,280	11.5
Evansville, IN–KY	183,595	100.0	18,010	9.8	4,335	2.4	5,845	3.2	15,680	8.5
Fairbanks, AK	47,555	100.0	5,120	10.8	2,025	4.3	1,205	2.5	5,345	11.2
Fargo, ND–MN	121,190	100.0	13,705	11.3	4,780	3.9	4,525	3.7	13,530	11.2

C-1 All Workers, by Metropolitan Statistical Area and Occupation Group, 2006–2010—*Continued*

Metropolitan Statistical Area	Technicians Number	Technicians Percent	Sales workers Number	Sales workers Percent	Administrative support workers Number	Administrative support workers Percent	Construction and extractive craft workers Number	Construction and extractive craft workers Percent	Installation, maintenance, and repair craft workers Number	Installation, maintenance, and repair craft workers Percent
Casper, WY	1,020	2.6	4,585	11.5	6,575	16.5	3,600	9.0	2,620	6.6
Cedar Rapids, IA	4,670	3.3	15,010	10.7	22,095	15.8	7,820	5.6	6,025	4.3
Champaign–Urbana, IL	4,285	3.5	12,100	9.9	18,505	15.1	4,970	4.0	4,115	3.4
Charleston, WV	4,920	3.5	15,505	11.0	24,435	17.4	10,590	7.5	6,000	4.3
Charleston–North Charleston–Summerville, SC	10,385	3.1	40,740	12.3	48,200	14.5	22,845	6.9	16,640	5.0
Charlotte–Gastonia–Rock Hill, NC–SC	22,960	2.5	118,050	12.9	134,725	14.7	53,220	5.8	36,935	4.0
Charlottesville, VA	3,130	3.1	10,105	10.0	13,250	13.1	6,320	6.2	2,770	2.7
Chattanooga, TN–GA	8,665	3.3	29,550	11.2	41,610	15.7	16,240	6.1	10,580	4.0
Cheyenne, WY	1,250	2.7	4,495	9.7	7,815	16.8	3,400	7.3	1,785	3.8
Chicago–Joliet–Naperville, IL–IN–WI	116,845	2.4	573,035	11.6	775,800	15.7	252,265	5.1	177,970	3.6
Chico, CA	3,125	3.1	11,035	10.8	15,560	15.2	6,470	6.3	4,140	4.0
Cincinnati–Middletown, OH–KY–IN	31,715	2.9	123,345	11.2	177,740	16.1	54,445	4.9	46,445	4.2
Clarksville, TN–KY	3,180	2.8	11,910	10.6	16,960	15.2	5,845	5.2	6,560	5.9
Cleveland, TN	1,725	3.1	5,445	9.9	8,315	15.2	3,670	6.7	2,730	5.0
Cleveland–Elyria–Mentor, OH	34,320	3.2	119,215	11.0	174,020	16.1	46,135	4.3	45,300	4.2
Coeur d'Alene, ID	1,720	2.5	7,830	11.4	11,035	16.1	7,075	10.3	3,265	4.8
College Station–Bryan, TX	3,695	3.4	10,455	9.6	17,140	15.7	7,275	6.7	4,890	4.5
Colorado Springs, CO	9,050	2.9	33,490	10.8	47,810	15.4	18,020	5.8	12,935	4.2
Columbia, MO	4,100	4.3	10,475	11.0	14,450	15.2	4,370	4.6	2,875	3.0
Columbia, SC	12,115	3.2	43,905	11.5	62,450	16.3	21,490	5.6	14,965	3.9
Columbus, GA–AL	4,615	3.6	14,245	11.2	21,535	16.9	6,760	5.3	4,660	3.7
Columbus, IN	1,100	2.8	3,815	9.6	5,485	13.9	1,520	3.8	1,715	4.3
Columbus, OH	28,685	3.0	104,050	10.8	162,440	16.9	39,165	4.1	32,590	3.4
Corpus Christi, TX	6,245	3.1	22,445	11.2	30,415	15.2	15,655	7.8	11,560	5.8
Corvallis, OR	1,950	4.4	3,755	8.6	5,965	13.6	1,830	4.2	1,410	3.2
Crestview–Fort Walton Beach–Destin, FL	2,820	3.2	10,655	12.0	12,740	14.3	5,815	6.5	4,665	5.2
Cumberland, MD–WV	1,200	2.6	5,085	10.9	7,355	15.8	3,425	7.3	2,330	5.0
Dallas–Fort Worth–Arlington, TX	81,930	2.5	390,655	12.1	516,285	15.9	204,925	6.3	133,535	4.1
Dalton, GA	1,330	2.0	6,815	10.1	8,850	13.2	3,740	5.6	3,490	5.2
Danville, IL	1,130	2.9	3,890	10.1	5,695	14.8	2,920	7.6	1,555	4.0
Danville, VA	1,360	2.7	4,675	9.1	7,855	15.4	3,600	7.0	2,510	4.9
Davenport–Moline–Rock Island, IA–IL	5,015	2.6	21,665	11.1	29,430	15.1	10,590	5.4	8,925	4.6
Dayton, OH	14,010	3.3	45,490	10.7	65,115	15.3	19,185	4.5	18,745	4.4
Decatur, AL	2,680	3.7	8,175	11.2	10,280	14.0	5,570	7.6	3,955	5.4
Decatur, IL	1,710	3.2	5,195	9.7	8,445	15.7	2,945	5.5	2,500	4.7
Deltona–Daytona Beach–Ormond Beach, FL	6,770	2.9	31,930	13.8	36,365	15.7	16,175	7.0	10,765	4.7
Denver–Aurora–Broomfield, CO	33,490	2.4	166,080	12.1	211,625	15.4	87,320	6.4	50,940	3.7
Des Moines–West Des Moines, IA	8,780	2.8	36,935	11.8	54,855	17.5	16,580	5.3	10,405	3.3
Detroit–Warren–Livonia, MI	57,695	2.7	243,580	11.2	326,860	15.1	92,815	4.3	94,070	4.3
Dothan, AL	2,030	3.0	8,820	13.1	9,505	14.2	4,490	6.7	4,315	6.4
Dover, DE	2,260	3.0	7,645	10.2	12,730	17.0	5,230	7.0	3,705	4.9
Dubuque, IA	1,205	2.3	5,435	10.5	7,935	15.3	2,660	5.1	2,205	4.3
Duluth, MN–WI	4,675	3.3	15,220	10.6	20,830	14.5	9,770	6.8	6,940	4.8
Durham–Chapel Hill, NC	10,245	3.9	23,065	8.8	34,545	13.2	14,510	5.6	8,445	3.2
Eau Claire, WI	2,505	2.8	10,425	11.6	13,265	14.8	4,490	5.0	3,905	4.3
El Centro, CA	1,100	1.6	8,095	12.0	10,290	15.3	3,840	5.7	2,410	3.6
Elizabethtown, KY	1,325	2.6	5,005	9.9	8,240	16.4	3,380	6.7	2,270	4.5
Elkhart–Goshen, IN	2,235	2.2	9,635	9.4	14,270	13.9	4,150	4.0	5,175	5.0
Elmira, NY	1,490	3.5	4,605	10.8	7,210	16.9	1,820	4.3	2,240	5.3
El Paso, TX	7,105	2.2	40,635	12.4	53,065	16.1	18,840	5.7	14,690	4.5
Erie, PA	4,320	3.1	14,740	10.7	20,910	15.1	5,870	4.2	7,430	5.4
Eugene–Springfield, OR	5,145	2.9	20,010	11.3	28,070	15.9	9,615	5.4	7,550	4.3
Evansville, IN–KY	6,285	3.4	20,700	11.3	27,185	14.8	10,420	5.7	9,150	5.0
Fairbanks, AK	1,710	3.6	4,250	8.9	8,000	16.8	4,865	10.2	2,855	6.0
Fargo, ND–MN	4,520	3.7	14,535	12.0	18,205	15.0	6,985	5.8	4,270	3.5

PART C—METROPOLITAN STATISTICAL AREA TABLES

C-1 All Workers, by Metropolitan Statistical Area and Occupation Group, 2006–2010—Continued

Metropolitan Statistical Area	Production operative workers Number	Production operative workers Percent	Transportation and material moving operative workers Number	Transportation and material moving operative workers Percent	Laborers and helpers Number	Laborers and helpers Percent	Protective service workers Number	Protective service workers Percent	Service workers, except protective Number	Service workers, except protective Percent
Casper, WY	1,800	4.5	2,015	5.1	1,400	3.5	410	1.0	5,710	14.3
Cedar Rapids, IA	9,435	6.7	5,855	4.2	5,010	3.6	1,955	1.4	18,635	13.3
Champaign–Urbana, IL	5,085	4.1	4,590	3.7	4,750	3.9	1,925	1.6	18,415	15.0
Charleston, WV	4,615	3.3	7,105	5.1	4,165	3.0	3,020	2.1	20,020	14.2
Charleston–North Charleston–Summerville, SC	13,895	4.2	15,090	4.5	11,120	3.3	6,680	2.0	47,305	14.2
Charlotte–Gastonia–Rock Hill, NC–SC	46,200	5.1	41,920	4.6	30,035	3.3	14,455	1.6	112,015	12.3
Charlottesville, VA	1,880	1.9	3,100	3.1	3,350	3.3	1,825	1.8	13,825	13.6
Chattanooga, TN–GA	18,810	7.1	13,815	5.2	9,300	3.5	4,550	1.7	37,490	14.2
Cheyenne, WY	1,890	4.1	2,505	5.4	2,020	4.3	1,040	2.2	6,660	14.3
Chicago–Joliet–Naperville, IL–IN–WI	265,915	5.4	246,295	5.0	156,110	3.2	105,705	2.1	631,170	12.8
Chico, CA	3,570	3.5	4,105	4.0	5,595	5.5	2,005	2.0	17,750	17.4
Cincinnati–Middletown, OH–KY–IN	60,850	5.5	51,650	4.7	37,120	3.4	19,485	1.8	150,395	13.7
Clarksville, TN–KY	9,155	8.2	6,410	5.7	4,295	3.8	2,940	2.6	17,595	15.7
Cleveland, TN	5,900	10.8	3,640	6.6	2,615	4.8	945	1.7	6,720	12.2
Cleveland–Elyria–Mentor, OH	67,690	6.3	47,215	4.4	35,835	3.3	21,765	2.0	155,760	14.4
Coeur d'Alene, ID	3,005	4.4	2,595	3.8	2,245	3.3	1,100	1.6	10,120	14.7
College Station–Bryan, TX	3,860	3.5	3,920	3.6	4,420	4.0	1,935	1.8	16,460	15.1
Colorado Springs, CO	8,490	2.7	10,090	3.3	8,730	2.8	6,785	2.2	44,300	14.3
Columbia, MO	3,590	3.8	2,875	3.0	2,460	2.6	1,630	1.7	14,145	14.9
Columbia, SC	18,565	4.8	15,635	4.1	13,970	3.6	9,205	2.4	49,915	13.0
Columbus, GA–AL	7,030	5.5	6,510	5.1	4,250	3.3	3,130	2.5	19,760	15.5
Columbus, IN	4,525	11.4	2,020	5.1	1,300	3.3	630	1.6	4,515	11.4
Columbus, OH	41,130	4.3	44,005	4.6	33,070	3.4	19,250	2.0	126,435	13.1
Corpus Christi, TX	8,300	4.1	8,710	4.3	8,220	4.1	5,290	2.6	32,125	16.0
Corvallis, OR	1,540	3.5	1,110	2.5	2,340	5.3	550	1.3	5,715	13.0
Crestview–Fort Walton Beach–Destin, FL	2,370	2.7	2,635	3.0	3,180	3.6	2,075	2.3	14,715	16.5
Cumberland, MD–WV	2,595	5.6	2,530	5.4	1,855	4.0	1,365	2.9	7,975	17.1
Dallas–Fort Worth–Arlington, TX	149,180	4.6	142,450	4.4	106,520	3.3	57,025	1.8	393,180	12.1
Dalton, GA	13,355	19.9	6,745	10.0	2,470	3.7	805	1.2	7,225	10.7
Danville, IL	3,730	9.7	2,810	7.3	2,250	5.8	650	1.7	5,690	14.8
Danville, VA	5,525	10.8	3,400	6.6	2,580	5.0	1,250	2.4	7,395	14.5
Davenport–Moline–Rock Island, IA–IL	14,860	7.6	11,595	5.9	7,370	3.8	3,050	1.6	28,400	14.5
Dayton, OH	29,480	6.9	20,800	4.9	14,690	3.4	7,960	1.9	62,285	14.6
Decatur, AL	8,325	11.4	4,470	6.1	3,400	4.6	1,035	1.4	8,960	12.2
Decatur, IL	3,670	6.8	2,910	5.4	2,410	4.5	925	1.7	8,495	15.8
Deltona–Daytona Beach–Ormond Beach, FL	7,390	3.2	8,505	3.7	10,525	4.5	5,540	2.4	36,065	15.6
Denver–Aurora–Broomfield, CO	38,720	2.8	48,855	3.6	41,540	3.0	25,490	1.9	173,575	12.7
Des Moines–West Des Moines, IA	13,400	4.3	11,725	3.7	10,070	3.2	3,960	1.3	40,405	12.9
Detroit–Warren–Livonia, MI	139,935	6.5	95,000	4.4	68,360	3.2	41,370	1.9	318,055	14.7
Dothan, AL	4,355	6.5	3,860	5.8	3,040	4.5	1,305	1.9	9,135	13.6
Dover, DE	3,415	4.5	3,940	5.2	2,805	3.7	2,275	3.0	10,900	14.5
Dubuque, IA	3,395	6.6	2,380	4.6	2,280	4.4	745	1.4	8,480	16.4
Duluth, MN–WI	5,785	4.0	6,940	4.8	4,455	3.1	2,810	2.0	26,330	18.3
Durham–Chapel Hill, NC	9,515	3.6	8,045	3.1	8,020	3.1	4,020	1.5	34,675	13.3
Eau Claire, WI	7,565	8.4	5,130	5.7	4,065	4.5	1,465	1.6	13,760	15.3
El Centro, CA	2,790	4.1	3,875	5.8	6,645	9.9	3,720	5.5	9,985	14.8
Elizabethtown, KY	3,540	7.0	2,900	5.8	1,780	3.5	1,275	2.5	7,105	14.1
Elkhart–Goshen, IN	20,505	20.0	6,670	6.5	4,650	4.5	950	0.9	11,955	11.6
Elmira, NY	2,315	5.4	1,980	4.7	1,450	3.4	1,645	3.9	6,120	14.4
El Paso, TX	15,565	4.7	21,250	6.5	11,260	3.4	12,060	3.7	50,675	15.4
Erie, PA	11,430	8.3	6,325	4.6	5,135	3.7	2,400	1.7	21,630	15.7
Eugene–Springfield, OR	9,775	5.5	7,185	4.1	8,835	5.0	2,575	1.5	26,830	15.2
Evansville, IN–KY	17,140	9.3	10,685	5.8	7,365	4.0	2,910	1.6	26,320	14.3
Fairbanks, AK	950	2.0	1,865	3.9	1,765	3.7	1,085	2.3	6,200	13.0
Fargo, ND–MN	5,785	4.8	5,450	4.5	4,920	4.1	1,440	1.2	18,075	14.9

C-1 **All Workers, by Metropolitan Statistical Area and Occupation Group, 2006–2010**—*Continued*

Metropolitan Statistical Area	Total who worked in the last 5 years		Management, business, and financial workers		Science, engineering, and computer professionals		Health care practitioner professionals		Other professional workers	
	Number	Percent	Number	Percent	Number	Percent	Number	Percent	Number	Percent
Farmington, NM	55,275	100.0	5,540	10.0	1,360	2.5	1,510	2.7	4,150	7.5
Fayetteville, NC	149,930	100.0	12,990	8.7	2,870	1.9	5,200	3.5	16,490	11.0
Fayetteville–Springdale–Rogers, AR–MO	224,940	100.0	28,295	12.6	6,915	3.1	5,360	2.4	23,065	10.3
Flagstaff, AZ	69,245	100.0	6,500	9.4	1,815	2.6	2,170	3.1	8,545	12.3
Flint, MI	198,305	100.0	16,785	8.5	5,065	2.6	7,130	3.6	17,905	9.0
Florence, SC	97,465	100.0	8,320	8.5	1,950	2.0	3,750	3.8	9,505	9.8
Florence–Muscle Shoals, AL	67,340	100.0	5,450	8.1	1,295	1.9	2,430	3.6	6,355	9.4
Fond du Lac, WI	56,855	100.0	5,650	9.9	1,290	2.3	1,500	2.6	3,950	6.9
Fort Collins–Loveland, CO	163,945	100.0	22,920	14.0	11,405	7.0	6,520	4.0	19,780	12.1
Fort Smith, AR–OK	135,200	100.0	11,685	8.6	2,020	1.5	3,985	2.9	10,825	8.0
Fort Wayne, IN	213,850	100.0	22,750	10.6	7,205	3.4	7,300	3.4	20,695	9.7
Fresno, CA	415,700	100.0	38,710	9.3	7,180	1.7	11,515	2.8	38,860	9.3
Gadsden, AL	45,955	100.0	4,005	8.7	595	1.3	1,895	4.1	3,970	8.6
Gainesville, FL	132,310	100.0	14,835	11.2	6,150	4.6	8,020	6.1	20,175	15.2
Gainesville, GA	84,825	100.0	8,840	10.4	1,970	2.3	2,020	2.4	7,855	9.3
Glens Falls, NY	65,280	100.0	6,420	9.8	1,325	2.0	2,295	3.5	6,370	9.8
Goldsboro, NC	55,700	100.0	5,260	9.4	750	1.3	1,610	2.9	5,010	9.0
Grand Forks, ND–MN	55,125	100.0	6,010	10.9	1,440	2.6	1,995	3.6	5,625	10.2
Grand Junction, CO	73,175	100.0	8,680	11.9	1,950	2.7	3,125	4.3	6,335	8.7
Grand Rapids–Wyoming, MI	400,815	100.0	42,720	10.7	12,785	3.2	12,205	3.0	39,145	9.8
Great Falls, MT	38,710	100.0	4,420	11.4	865	2.2	1,840	4.8	3,580	9.2
Greeley, CO	126,475	100.0	15,460	12.2	5,130	4.1	3,110	2.5	11,165	8.8
Green Bay, WI	165,850	100.0	18,835	11.4	4,610	2.8	5,305	3.2	15,080	9.1
Greensboro–High Point, NC	370,400	100.0	41,310	11.2	9,220	2.5	10,325	2.8	38,745	10.5
Greenville, NC	94,940	100.0	9,015	9.5	2,035	2.1	5,630	5.9	10,630	11.2
Greenville–Mauldin–Easley, SC	311,995	100.0	33,905	10.9	11,850	3.8	10,090	3.2	32,235	10.3
Gulfport–Biloxi, MS	115,200	100.0	11,215	9.7	2,505	2.2	2,825	2.5	10,310	8.9
Hagerstown–Martinsburg, MD–WV	136,740	100.0	14,450	10.6	4,765	3.5	3,780	2.8	11,530	8.4
Hanford–Corcoran, CA	60,000	100.0	4,115	6.9	765	1.3	1,175	2.0	4,975	8.3
Harrisburg–Carlisle, PA	290,055	100.0	36,140	12.5	12,455	4.3	9,715	3.3	32,020	11.0
Harrisonburg, VA	60,145	100.0	5,860	9.7	1,070	1.8	1,440	2.4	6,530	10.9
Hartford–West Hartford–East Hartford, CT	653,940	100.0	88,100	13.5	33,035	5.1	25,440	3.9	80,840	12.4
Hattiesburg, MS	67,460	100.0	7,040	10.4	1,285	1.9	3,145	4.7	7,770	11.5
Hickory–Lenoir–Morganton, NC	179,730	100.0	15,790	8.8	2,690	1.5	5,660	3.1	15,475	8.6
Hinesville–Fort Stewart, GA	31,935	100.0	2,220	7.0	445	1.4	505	1.6	2,695	8.4
Holland–Grand Haven, MI	138,265	100.0	15,785	11.4	4,605	3.3	4,215	3.0	13,830	10.0
Honolulu, HI	462,845	100.0	54,035	11.7	17,110	3.7	15,495	3.3	54,820	11.8
Hot Springs, AR	42,500	100.0	4,605	10.8	525	1.2	1,915	4.5	3,365	7.9
Houma–Bayou Cane–Thibodaux, LA	96,810	100.0	8,240	8.5	1,665	1.7	3,060	3.2	7,440	7.7
Houston–Sugar Land–Baytown, TX	2,915,695	100.0	353,640	12.1	142,680	4.9	79,740	2.7	303,195	10.4
Huntington–Ashland, WV–KY–OH	125,340	100.0	10,550	8.4	2,030	1.6	5,930	4.7	11,715	9.3
Huntsville, AL	205,625	100.0	25,160	12.2	21,000	10.2	6,455	3.1	21,245	10.3
Idaho Falls, ID	60,035	100.0	7,040	11.7	3,005	5.0	1,920	3.2	5,175	8.6
Indianapolis–Carmel, IN	910,210	100.0	117,805	12.9	40,160	4.4	35,625	3.9	93,560	10.3
Iowa City, IA	87,665	100.0	9,695	11.1	3,955	4.5	5,920	6.8	13,090	14.9
Ithaca, NY	53,015	100.0	5,840	11.0	3,280	6.2	1,800	3.4	11,725	22.1
Jackson, MI	76,035	100.0	6,945	9.1	2,395	3.1	2,560	3.4	5,420	7.1
Jackson, MS	263,165	100.0	28,990	11.0	6,675	2.5	12,735	4.8	28,595	10.9
Jackson, TN	57,240	100.0	5,455	9.5	1,015	1.8	2,470	4.3	5,970	10.4
Jacksonville, FL	678,960	100.0	90,180	13.3	22,390	3.3	22,250	3.3	63,010	9.3
Jacksonville, NC	61,645	100.0	5,525	9.0	1,050	1.7	1,495	2.4	6,320	10.3
Janesville, WI	85,060	100.0	7,920	9.3	1,925	2.3	2,485	2.9	7,285	8.6
Jefferson City, MO	75,350	100.0	9,715	12.9	2,675	3.6	2,365	3.1	7,755	10.3
Johnson City, TN	93,205	100.0	9,225	9.9	2,145	2.3	4,245	4.6	8,900	9.5
Johnstown, PA	67,230	100.0	5,550	8.3	1,620	2.4	3,255	4.8	6,015	8.9

C-1 All Workers, by Metropolitan Statistical Area and Occupation Group, 2006–2010—*Continued*

Metropolitan Statistical Area	Technicians Number	Technicians Percent	Sales workers Number	Sales workers Percent	Administrative support workers Number	Administrative support workers Percent	Construction and extractive craft workers Number	Construction and extractive craft workers Percent	Installation, maintenance, and repair craft workers Number	Installation, maintenance, and repair craft workers Percent
Farmington, NM	1,170	2.1	5,405	9.8	8,390	15.2	6,305	11.4	3,825	6.9
Fayetteville, NC	4,500	3.0	17,695	11.8	23,370	15.6	7,080	4.7	7,420	4.9
Fayetteville–Springdale–Rogers, AR–MO	5,880	2.6	27,420	12.2	32,235	14.3	15,685	7.0	9,390	4.2
Flagstaff, AZ	1,895	2.7	7,335	10.6	10,375	15.0	5,120	7.4	2,830	4.1
Flint, MI	5,525	2.8	23,115	11.7	27,430	13.8	10,515	5.3	9,015	4.5
Florence, SC	3,385	3.5	10,990	11.3	15,225	15.6	5,065	5.2	4,835	5.0
Florence–Muscle Shoals, AL	2,000	3.0	8,965	13.3	9,685	14.4	5,380	8.0	3,730	5.5
Fond du Lac, WI	1,620	2.8	5,455	9.6	7,960	14.0	3,315	5.8	3,310	5.8
Fort Collins–Loveland, CO	5,530	3.4	17,790	10.9	20,770	12.7	9,585	5.8	5,675	3.5
Fort Smith, AR–OK	3,710	2.7	14,885	11.0	19,070	14.1	8,585	6.3	6,110	4.5
Fort Wayne, IN	5,815	2.7	23,845	11.2	32,685	15.3	9,785	4.6	10,015	4.7
Fresno, CA	9,210	2.2	45,465	10.9	62,685	15.1	22,060	5.3	15,290	3.7
Gadsden, AL	1,665	3.6	4,525	9.8	6,685	14.5	3,125	6.8	2,340	5.1
Gainesville, FL	4,645	3.5	14,595	11.0	18,885	14.3	4,685	3.5	3,955	3.0
Gainesville, GA	1,450	1.7	9,950	11.7	10,795	12.7	7,615	9.0	4,185	4.9
Glens Falls, NY	1,585	2.4	7,355	11.3	9,990	15.3	4,195	6.4	3,355	5.1
Goldsboro, NC	1,955	3.5	6,415	11.5	6,985	12.5	3,635	6.5	3,080	5.5
Grand Forks, ND–MN	1,895	3.4	6,155	11.2	8,210	14.9	2,990	5.4	2,110	3.8
Grand Junction, CO	1,985	2.7	8,565	11.7	10,745	14.7	7,320	10.0	3,750	5.1
Grand Rapids–Wyoming, MI	10,475	2.6	44,320	11.1	60,650	15.1	19,205	4.8	18,575	4.6
Great Falls, MT	1,100	2.8	4,350	11.2	6,885	17.8	2,795	7.2	1,780	4.6
Greeley, CO	3,480	2.8	13,765	10.9	19,260	15.2	10,785	8.5	5,170	4.1
Green Bay, WI	5,200	3.1	17,435	10.5	26,030	15.7	8,330	5.0	8,675	5.2
Greensboro–High Point, NC	9,280	2.5	43,720	11.8	56,595	15.3	19,865	5.4	17,880	4.8
Greenville, NC	3,035	3.2	10,745	11.3	13,490	14.2	4,955	5.2	3,275	3.4
Greenville–Mauldin–Easley, SC	8,980	2.9	37,800	12.1	44,260	14.2	19,505	6.3	14,845	4.8
Gulfport–Biloxi, MS	3,730	3.2	12,625	11.0	15,705	13.6	11,425	9.9	5,255	4.6
Hagerstown–Martinsburg, MD–WV	4,145	3.0	14,760	10.8	21,570	15.8	10,425	7.6	7,645	5.6
Hanford–Corcoran, CA	1,150	1.9	5,235	8.7	7,350	12.3	2,550	4.3	3,415	5.7
Harrisburg–Carlisle, PA	8,645	3.0	29,490	10.2	53,695	18.5	11,620	4.0	11,085	3.8
Harrisonburg, VA	1,770	2.9	6,710	11.2	7,830	13.0	4,225	7.0	2,790	4.6
Hartford–West Hartford–East Hartford, CT	19,375	3.0	72,520	11.1	104,450	16.0	28,390	4.3	26,085	4.0
Hattiesburg, MS	1,960	2.9	8,745	13.0	9,250	13.7	4,705	7.0	3,180	4.7
Hickory–Lenoir–Morganton, NC	4,520	2.5	17,560	9.8	23,685	13.2	10,295	5.7	11,670	6.5
Hinesville–Fort Stewart, GA	965	3.0	3,485	10.9	5,265	16.5	1,810	5.7	2,965	9.3
Holland–Grand Haven, MI	3,550	2.6	14,925	10.8	19,510	14.1	6,365	4.6	6,330	4.6
Honolulu, HI	11,215	2.4	52,395	11.3	77,000	16.6	28,055	6.1	17,760	3.8
Hot Springs, AR	1,390	3.3	5,870	13.8	5,810	13.7	3,135	7.4	2,065	4.9
Houma–Bayou Cane–Thibodaux, LA	2,860	3.0	10,960	11.3	14,245	14.7	9,825	10.1	5,475	5.7
Houston–Sugar Land–Baytown, TX	82,605	2.8	332,370	11.4	424,230	14.5	231,275	7.9	125,695	4.3
Huntington–Ashland, WV–KY–OH	5,000	4.0	15,100	12.0	20,880	16.7	7,495	6.0	6,285	5.0
Huntsville, AL	6,835	3.3	22,265	10.8	27,950	13.6	9,575	4.7	8,450	4.1
Idaho Falls, ID	2,055	3.4	6,920	11.5	9,360	15.6	4,620	7.7	2,590	4.3
Indianapolis–Carmel, IN	25,585	2.8	106,600	11.7	142,800	15.7	47,640	5.2	37,800	4.2
Iowa City, IA	3,305	3.8	8,690	9.9	12,390	14.1	3,440	3.9	2,690	3.1
Ithaca, NY	2,290	4.3	4,315	8.1	8,145	15.4	2,400	4.5	1,250	2.4
Jackson, MI	2,585	3.4	8,440	11.1	11,200	14.7	3,790	5.0	4,410	5.8
Jackson, MS	8,975	3.4	30,970	11.8	41,300	15.7	16,705	6.3	10,240	3.9
Jackson, TN	1,885	3.3	6,095	10.6	8,175	14.3	3,160	5.5	2,345	4.1
Jacksonville, FL	17,310	2.5	84,220	12.4	121,620	17.9	40,915	6.0	30,240	4.5
Jacksonville, NC	1,960	3.2	7,040	11.4	9,425	15.3	5,125	8.3	3,550	5.8
Janesville, WI	2,300	2.7	8,650	10.2	12,700	14.9	4,605	5.4	4,280	5.0
Jefferson City, MO	2,565	3.4	6,325	8.4	13,915	18.5	5,410	7.2	2,990	4.0
Johnson City, TN	4,080	4.4	11,115	11.9	13,635	14.6	5,400	5.8	4,080	4.4
Johnstown, PA	2,365	3.5	6,710	10.0	10,240	15.2	4,370	6.5	2,890	4.3

C-1 All Workers, by Metropolitan Statistical Area and Occupation Group, 2006–2010—*Continued*

Metropolitan Statistical Area	Production operative workers Number	Percent	Transportation and material moving operative workers Number	Percent	Laborers and helpers Number	Percent	Protective service workers Number	Percent	Service workers, except protective Number	Percent
Farmington, NM	2,390	4.3	3,530	6.4	2,430	4.4	1,070	1.9	7,745	14.0
Fayetteville, NC	8,580	5.7	7,300	4.9	5,745	3.8	3,880	2.6	24,715	16.5
Fayetteville–Springdale–Rogers, AR–MO	16,560	7.4	10,870	4.8	9,275	4.1	3,640	1.6	28,900	12.8
Flagstaff, AZ	2,910	4.2	2,680	3.9	2,410	3.5	1,910	2.8	12,085	17.5
Flint, MI	16,205	8.2	11,035	5.6	7,460	3.8	4,190	2.1	32,435	16.4
Florence, SC	7,995	8.2	5,590	5.7	3,585	3.7	1,825	1.9	14,230	14.6
Florence–Muscle Shoals, AL	5,125	7.6	3,715	5.5	2,675	4.0	1,385	2.1	8,680	12.9
Fond du Lac, WI	6,550	11.5	3,575	6.3	2,945	5.2	1,290	2.3	8,145	14.3
Fort Collins–Loveland, CO	5,910	3.6	4,715	2.9	5,900	3.6	2,755	1.7	23,600	14.4
Fort Smith, AR–OK	16,475	12.2	9,135	6.8	6,870	5.1	2,065	1.5	18,670	13.8
Fort Wayne, IN	19,495	9.1	11,545	5.4	8,165	3.8	3,100	1.4	29,420	13.8
Fresno, CA	19,350	4.7	23,980	5.8	46,120	11.1	9,310	2.2	59,355	14.3
Gadsden, AL	4,160	9.1	2,965	6.5	2,250	4.9	990	2.2	6,295	13.7
Gainesville, FL	3,070	2.3	3,285	2.5	5,120	3.9	2,750	2.1	21,100	15.9
Gainesville, GA	8,990	10.6	5,310	6.3	4,875	5.7	1,065	1.3	9,145	10.8
Glens Falls, NY	4,350	6.7	3,150	4.8	3,070	4.7	1,785	2.7	9,675	14.8
Goldsboro, NC	4,370	7.8	3,290	5.9	3,095	5.6	1,355	2.4	8,080	14.5
Grand Forks, ND–MN	2,785	5.1	2,185	4.0	2,720	4.9	645	1.2	10,200	18.5
Grand Junction, CO	2,260	3.1	3,625	5.0	2,795	3.8	1,295	1.8	10,445	14.3
Grand Rapids–Wyoming, MI	35,335	8.8	20,895	5.2	17,800	4.4	5,325	1.3	56,205	14.0
Great Falls, MT	995	2.6	1,350	3.5	1,700	4.4	895	2.3	5,905	15.3
Greeley, CO	6,590	5.2	6,520	5.2	6,290	5.0	2,305	1.8	16,455	13.0
Green Bay, WI	13,885	8.4	8,390	5.1	8,125	4.9	2,395	1.4	22,465	13.5
Greensboro–High Point, NC	30,485	8.2	20,715	5.6	14,725	4.0	5,950	1.6	47,290	12.8
Greenville, NC	5,425	5.7	4,005	4.2	4,020	4.2	1,870	2.0	15,610	16.4
Greenville–Mauldin–Easley, SC	24,300	7.8	14,005	4.5	11,720	3.8	4,515	1.4	40,530	13.0
Gulfport–Biloxi, MS	4,650	4.0	5,350	4.6	3,935	3.4	3,295	2.9	21,310	18.5
Hagerstown–Martinsburg, MD–WV	6,510	4.8	8,210	6.0	5,875	4.3	4,065	3.0	18,000	13.2
Hanford–Corcoran, CA	3,135	5.2	4,460	7.4	9,520	15.9	2,860	4.8	8,255	13.8
Harrisburg–Carlisle, PA	11,405	3.9	16,910	5.8	13,115	4.5	4,570	1.6	37,595	13.0
Harrisonburg, VA	4,345	7.2	3,460	5.8	4,445	7.4	875	1.5	8,405	14.0
Hartford–West Hartford–East Hartford, CT	28,010	4.3	23,580	3.6	17,820	2.7	12,485	1.9	87,540	13.4
Hattiesburg, MS	3,305	4.9	3,590	5.3	2,350	3.5	1,235	1.8	8,975	13.3
Hickory–Lenoir–Morganton, NC	24,350	13.5	11,790	6.6	7,890	4.4	3,465	1.9	22,555	12.5
Hinesville–Fort Stewart, GA	1,330	4.2	2,265	7.1	1,245	3.9	1,300	4.1	4,755	14.9
Holland–Grand Haven, MI	15,110	10.9	6,660	4.8	6,715	4.9	1,230	0.9	18,285	13.2
Honolulu, HI	9,590	2.1	16,510	3.6	15,165	3.3	13,925	3.0	76,265	16.5
Hot Springs, AR	1,865	4.4	2,005	4.7	1,735	4.1	775	1.8	7,145	16.8
Houma–Bayou Cane–Thibodaux, LA	7,345	7.6	7,065	7.3	4,295	4.4	2,035	2.1	11,530	11.9
Houston–Sugar Land–Baytown, TX	134,760	4.6	133,645	4.6	106,235	3.6	56,415	1.9	378,195	13.0
Huntington–Ashland, WV–KY–OH	6,100	4.9	6,375	5.1	4,010	3.2	2,370	1.9	20,425	16.3
Huntsville, AL	12,200	5.9	8,515	4.1	6,375	3.1	3,555	1.7	24,130	11.7
Idaho Falls, ID	2,480	4.1	2,890	4.8	2,990	5.0	1,160	1.9	7,630	12.7
Indianapolis–Carmel, IN	45,985	5.1	42,155	4.6	31,075	3.4	16,905	1.9	117,370	12.9
Iowa City, IA	2,985	3.4	3,365	3.8	2,370	2.7	1,025	1.2	14,340	16.4
Ithaca, NY	1,305	2.5	1,460	2.8	1,590	3.0	735	1.4	6,605	12.5
Jackson, MI	6,780	8.9	4,075	5.4	2,915	3.8	1,815	2.4	11,565	15.2
Jackson, MS	11,555	4.4	12,435	4.7	9,330	3.5	6,265	2.4	35,250	13.4
Jackson, TN	5,300	9.3	2,970	5.2	1,940	3.4	1,070	1.9	8,670	15.1
Jacksonville, FL	20,310	3.0	29,185	4.3	23,600	3.5	15,710	2.3	90,525	13.3
Jacksonville, NC	2,045	3.3	2,740	4.4	2,445	4.0	1,335	2.2	11,145	18.1
Janesville, WI	9,775	11.5	5,425	6.4	3,640	4.3	1,005	1.2	12,445	14.6
Jefferson City, MO	4,135	5.5	2,940	3.9	2,820	3.7	2,130	2.8	9,290	12.3
Johnson City, TN	6,760	7.3	4,135	4.4	3,275	3.5	1,660	1.8	14,110	15.1
Johnstown, PA	4,045	6.0	3,820	5.7	2,730	4.1	1,835	2.7	11,130	16.6

PART C—METROPOLITAN STATISTICAL AREA TABLES

C-1 All Workers, by Metropolitan Statistical Area and Occupation Group, 2006–2010—Continued

Metropolitan Statistical Area	Total who worked in the last 5 years Number	Percent	Management, business, and financial workers Number	Percent	Science, engineering, and computer professionals Number	Percent	Health care practitioner professionals Number	Percent	Other professional workers Number	Percent
Jonesboro, AR	58,115	100.0	5,410	9.3	940	1.6	2,065	3.6	5,795	10.0
Joplin, MO	86,305	100.0	7,870	9.1	1,505	1.7	2,755	3.2	7,095	8.2
Kalamazoo–Portage, MI	170,005	100.0	18,070	10.6	6,130	3.6	6,175	3.6	18,420	10.8
Kankakee–Bradley, IL	56,315	100.0	4,655	8.3	895	1.6	1,975	3.5	5,035	8.9
Kansas City, MO–KS	1,074,060	100.0	145,175	13.5	46,855	4.4	38,275	3.6	116,180	10.8
Kennewick–Pasco–Richland, WA	116,110	100.0	13,550	11.7	7,010	6.0	3,075	2.6	9,420	8.1
Killeen–Temple–Fort Hood, TX	161,360	100.0	15,095	9.4	3,465	2.1	5,070	3.1	16,805	10.4
Kingsport–Bristol–Bristol, TN–VA	143,115	100.0	13,270	9.3	3,430	2.4	5,345	3.7	12,020	8.4
Kingston, NY	95,990	100.0	10,775	11.2	2,690	2.8	3,805	4.0	13,725	14.3
Knoxville, TN	347,520	100.0	40,065	11.5	14,165	4.1	13,975	4.0	37,480	10.8
Kokomo, IN	46,070	100.0	3,735	8.1	1,655	3.6	1,265	2.7	3,985	8.6
La Crosse, WI–MN	74,895	100.0	7,095	9.5	2,020	2.7	3,115	4.2	8,355	11.2
Lafayette, IN	103,435	100.0	10,110	9.8	4,125	4.0	3,125	3.0	14,845	14.4
Lafayette, LA	138,620	100.0	13,960	10.1	4,135	3.0	4,725	3.4	14,480	10.4
Lake Charles, LA	95,640	100.0	8,830	9.2	1,610	1.7	2,735	2.9	8,515	8.9
Lake Havasu City–Kingman, AZ	84,485	100.0	7,650	9.1	1,035	1.2	1,985	2.3	5,615	6.6
Lakeland–Winter Haven, FL	272,540	100.0	27,950	10.3	4,870	1.8	8,020	2.9	24,250	8.9
Lancaster, PA	266,220	100.0	29,930	11.2	6,540	2.5	8,425	3.2	24,825	9.3
Lansing–East Lansing, MI	243,125	100.0	26,390	10.9	10,410	4.3	6,905	2.8	31,020	12.8
Laredo, TX	104,070	100.0	9,445	9.1	775	0.7	1,810	1.7	9,890	9.5
Las Cruces, NM	92,900	100.0	7,865	8.5	3,330	3.6	2,280	2.5	11,610	12.5
Las Vegas–Paradise, NV	997,625	100.0	100,430	10.1	20,660	2.1	23,050	2.3	79,810	8.0
Lawrence, KS	63,700	100.0	7,245	11.4	2,700	4.2	1,990	3.1	11,425	17.9
Lawton, OK	50,730	100.0	4,200	8.3	970	1.9	1,765	3.5	5,175	10.2
Lebanon, PA	68,330	100.0	6,865	10.0	1,435	2.1	2,315	3.4	5,305	7.8
Lewiston, ID–WA	29,785	100.0	2,945	9.9	570	1.9	980	3.3	2,465	8.3
Lewiston–Auburn, ME	57,170	100.0	5,900	10.3	1,075	1.9	1,900	3.3	5,925	10.4
Lexington–Fayette, KY	251,860	100.0	29,445	11.7	9,995	4.0	12,560	5.0	31,450	12.5
Lima, OH	53,195	100.0	4,525	8.5	705	1.3	1,555	2.9	4,485	8.4
Lincoln, NE	171,905	100.0	21,535	12.5	6,820	4.0	5,845	3.4	21,655	12.6
Little Rock–North Little Rock–Conway, AR	349,855	100.0	39,015	11.2	11,260	3.2	16,430	4.7	37,670	10.8
Logan, UT–ID	60,630	100.0	6,120	10.1	2,485	4.1	1,240	2.0	7,605	12.5
Longview, TX	100,375	100.0	9,580	9.5	1,845	1.8	2,675	2.7	8,800	8.8
Longview, WA	46,705	100.0	4,200	9.0	1,010	2.2	1,820	3.9	3,530	7.6
Los Angeles–Long Beach–Santa Ana, CA	6,510,485	100.0	805,460	12.4	233,510	3.6	176,820	2.7	804,480	12.4
Louisville/Jefferson County, KY–IN	653,945	100.0	72,530	11.1	18,420	2.8	24,440	3.7	65,700	10.0
Lubbock, TX	142,160	100.0	14,115	9.9	2,915	2.1	5,530	3.9	16,265	11.4
Lynchburg, VA	125,640	100.0	13,155	10.5	3,765	3.0	3,865	3.1	12,230	9.7
Macon, GA	104,525	100.0	10,325	9.9	2,925	2.8	3,800	3.6	10,440	10.0
Madera–Chowchilla, CA	59,670	100.0	5,655	9.5	810	1.4	1,120	1.9	3,690	6.2
Madison, WI	330,970	100.0	45,120	13.6	21,525	6.5	13,475	4.1	47,210	14.3
Manchester–Nashua, NH	227,720	100.0	32,730	14.4	16,325	7.2	7,690	3.4	22,950	10.1
Manhattan, KS	57,660	100.0	6,075	10.5	1,530	2.7	1,795	3.1	8,645	15.0
Mankato–North Mankato, MN	57,325	100.0	6,225	10.9	1,505	2.6	1,380	2.4	6,225	10.9
Mansfield, OH	59,780	100.0	5,190	8.7	1,205	2.0	1,930	3.2	4,985	8.3
McAllen–Edinburg–Mission, TX	297,890	100.0	22,330	7.5	3,000	1.0	6,905	2.3	29,440	9.9
Medford, OR	98,875	100.0	10,510	10.6	1,955	2.0	3,800	3.8	8,690	8.8
Memphis, TN–MS–AR	655,310	100.0	72,340	11.0	18,530	2.8	20,065	3.1	65,680	10.0
Merced, CA	109,910	100.0	8,100	7.4	970	0.9	1,970	1.8	8,220	7.5
Miami–Fort Lauderdale–Pompano Beach, FL	2,809,665	100.0	346,420	12.3	68,020	2.4	87,775	3.1	281,810	10.0
Michigan City–La Porte, IN	54,160	100.0	5,120	9.5	845	1.6	1,385	2.6	4,085	7.5
Midland, TX	68,290	100.0	7,445	10.9	2,445	3.6	1,780	2.6	6,335	9.3
Milwaukee–Waukesha–West Allis, WI	826,530	100.0	102,235	12.4	34,080	4.1	32,655	4.0	91,250	11.0
Minneapolis–St. Paul–Bloomington, MN–WI	1,840,260	100.0	271,575	14.8	102,585	5.6	62,530	3.4	222,270	12.1
Missoula, MT	59,355	100.0	6,640	11.2	2,110	3.6	2,460	4.1	7,415	12.5

C-1 **All Workers, by Metropolitan Statistical Area and Occupation Group, 2006–2010**—*Continued*

Metropolitan Statistical Area	Technicians Number	Technicians Percent	Sales workers Number	Sales workers Percent	Administrative support workers Number	Administrative support workers Percent	Construction and extractive craft workers Number	Construction and extractive craft workers Percent	Installation, maintenance, and repair craft workers Number	Installation, maintenance, and repair craft workers Percent
Jonesboro, AR	2,010	3.5	7,285	12.5	8,330	14.3	3,425	5.9	2,535	4.4
Joplin, MO	2,620	3.0	10,245	11.9	12,270	14.2	4,755	5.5	4,815	5.6
Kalamazoo–Portage, MI	4,700	2.8	18,915	11.1	24,670	14.5	7,420	4.4	6,845	4.0
Kankakee–Bradley, IL	1,590	2.8	5,585	9.9	8,735	15.5	3,555	6.3	2,370	4.2
Kansas City, MO–KS	32,850	3.1	122,815	11.4	177,850	16.6	57,080	5.3	42,410	3.9
Kennewick–Pasco–Richland, WA	3,845	3.3	10,975	9.5	15,615	13.4	7,455	6.4	4,715	4.1
Killeen–Temple–Fort Hood, TX	5,385	3.3	17,025	10.6	26,715	16.6	10,000	6.2	8,500	5.3
Kingsport–Bristol–Bristol, TN–VA	5,755	4.0	16,045	11.2	20,710	14.5	9,585	6.7	7,825	5.5
Kingston, NY	2,430	2.5	11,055	11.5	14,860	15.5	6,235	6.5	3,705	3.9
Knoxville, TN	11,565	3.3	43,790	12.6	55,975	16.1	20,645	5.9	13,025	3.7
Kokomo, IN	1,285	2.8	4,225	9.2	6,605	14.3	2,570	5.6	2,490	5.4
La Crosse, WI–MN	2,690	3.6	8,200	10.9	11,545	15.4	3,610	4.8	2,970	4.0
Lafayette, IN	3,670	3.5	10,235	9.9	13,485	13.0	4,445	4.3	4,405	4.3
Lafayette, LA	4,795	3.5	17,405	12.6	22,150	16.0	9,515	6.9	7,890	5.7
Lake Charles, LA	3,200	3.3	10,810	11.3	14,350	15.0	9,755	10.2	4,920	5.1
Lake Havasu City–Kingman, AZ	2,125	2.5	11,175	13.2	13,940	16.5	6,480	7.7	4,520	5.4
Lakeland–Winter Haven, FL	6,460	2.4	30,895	11.3	43,015	15.8	21,065	7.7	11,645	4.3
Lancaster, PA	7,665	2.9	27,285	10.2	41,145	15.5	17,570	6.6	13,780	5.2
Lansing–East Lansing, MI	8,085	3.3	24,225	10.0	40,090	16.5	9,560	3.9	8,605	3.5
Laredo, TX	1,495	1.4	13,350	12.8	19,815	19.0	6,745	6.5	3,530	3.4
Las Cruces, NM	2,495	2.7	9,515	10.2	13,605	14.6	6,930	7.5	3,900	4.2
Las Vegas–Paradise, NV	21,210	2.1	122,470	12.3	148,995	14.9	78,715	7.9	33,280	3.3
Lawrence, KS	2,405	3.8	6,340	10.0	10,310	16.2	2,590	4.1	1,920	3.0
Lawton, OK	2,145	4.2	5,580	11.0	7,960	15.7	3,195	6.3	2,595	5.1
Lebanon, PA	2,410	3.5	7,050	10.3	10,655	15.6	3,415	5.0	3,890	5.7
Lewiston, ID–WA	785	2.6	3,025	10.2	4,720	15.8	1,700	5.7	1,415	4.8
Lewiston–Auburn, ME	1,565	2.7	6,780	11.9	9,985	17.5	3,900	6.8	2,850	5.0
Lexington–Fayette, KY	8,055	3.2	29,305	11.6	36,420	14.5	10,990	4.4	8,415	3.3
Lima, OH	1,355	2.5	5,815	10.9	7,710	14.5	2,730	5.1	2,455	4.6
Lincoln, NE	5,745	3.3	17,525	10.2	28,820	16.8	8,520	5.0	6,575	3.8
Little Rock–North Little Rock–Conway, AR	11,845	3.4	39,895	11.4	57,450	16.4	21,410	6.1	15,140	4.3
Logan, UT–ID	1,900	3.1	6,485	10.7	9,360	15.4	3,370	5.6	2,720	4.5
Longview, TX	2,910	2.9	11,840	11.8	14,190	14.1	8,420	8.4	5,825	5.8
Longview, WA	1,085	2.3	4,720	10.1	6,100	13.1	3,210	6.9	2,875	6.2
Los Angeles–Long Beach–Santa Ana, CA	148,070	2.3	771,455	11.8	1,024,100	15.7	336,655	5.2	230,535	3.5
Louisville/Jefferson County, KY–IN	17,770	2.7	70,455	10.8	105,825	16.2	36,610	5.6	28,105	4.3
Lubbock, TX	4,110	2.9	17,525	12.3	23,875	16.8	7,690	5.4	6,070	4.3
Lynchburg, VA	3,520	2.8	13,205	10.5	19,580	15.6	7,500	6.0	6,470	5.1
Macon, GA	3,180	3.0	11,935	11.4	16,010	15.3	5,940	5.7	4,630	4.4
Madera–Chowchilla, CA	1,295	2.2	6,395	10.7	7,900	13.2	3,345	5.6	2,560	4.3
Madison, WI	12,225	3.7	32,755	9.9	50,815	15.4	13,995	4.2	10,570	3.2
Manchester–Nashua, NH	7,375	3.2	26,335	11.6	35,200	15.5	12,495	5.5	8,805	3.9
Manhattan, KS	1,725	3.0	5,355	9.3	9,555	16.6	3,500	6.1	2,455	4.3
Mankato–North Mankato, MN	1,430	2.5	6,810	11.9	9,060	15.8	2,565	4.5	2,070	3.6
Mansfield, OH	1,720	2.9	5,930	9.9	8,880	14.9	2,770	4.6	3,055	5.1
McAllen–Edinburg–Mission, TX	5,920	2.0	38,060	12.8	42,960	14.4	24,965	8.4	11,820	4.0
Medford, OR	2,450	2.5	13,200	13.4	15,780	16.0	6,490	6.6	3,995	4.0
Memphis, TN–MS–AR	18,010	2.7	74,845	11.4	106,460	16.2	32,775	5.0	26,650	4.1
Merced, CA	2,355	2.1	10,690	9.7	14,960	13.6	7,970	7.3	3,970	3.6
Miami–Fort Lauderdale–Pompano Beach, FL	67,780	2.4	387,305	13.8	454,165	16.2	177,385	6.3	103,310	3.7
Michigan City–La Porte, IN	1,440	2.7	5,585	10.3	7,935	14.7	3,940	7.3	3,275	6.0
Midland, TX	2,370	3.5	8,240	12.1	10,860	15.9	6,765	9.9	3,260	4.8
Milwaukee–Waukesha–West Allis, WI	22,965	2.8	90,435	10.9	132,530	16.0	34,435	4.2	33,675	4.1
Minneapolis–St. Paul–Bloomington, MN–WI	55,740	3.0	215,710	11.7	284,220	15.4	80,820	4.4	68,285	3.7
Missoula, MT	1,470	2.5	7,730	13.0	8,925	15.0	3,540	6.0	1,990	3.4

PART C—METROPOLITAN STATISTICAL AREA TABLES

C-1 All Workers, by Metropolitan Statistical Area and Occupation Group, 2006–2010—Continued

Metropolitan Statistical Area	Production operative workers Number	Percent	Transportation and material moving operative workers Number	Percent	Laborers and helpers Number	Percent	Protective service workers Number	Percent	Service workers, except protective Number	Percent
Jonesboro, AR	4,650	8.0	2,910	5.0	3,585	6.2	685	1.2	7,970	13.7
Joplin, MO	7,615	8.8	5,340	6.2	3,795	4.4	1,140	1.3	13,755	15.9
Kalamazoo–Portage, MI	12,455	7.3	7,650	4.5	7,425	4.4	2,570	1.5	26,695	15.7
Kankakee–Bradley, IL	3,915	7.0	4,350	7.7	2,935	5.2	1,075	1.9	8,565	15.2
Kansas City, MO–KS	49,350	4.6	46,840	4.4	35,295	3.3	20,735	1.9	134,205	12.5
Kennewick–Pasco–Richland, WA	5,205	4.5	6,175	5.3	10,025	8.6	2,170	1.9	15,760	13.6
Killeen–Temple–Fort Hood, TX	5,470	3.4	7,540	4.7	6,170	3.8	6,560	4.1	25,530	15.8
Kingsport–Bristol–Bristol, TN–VA	12,880	9.0	6,910	4.8	5,430	3.8	2,585	1.8	20,020	14.0
Kingston, NY	2,845	3.0	4,250	4.4	3,175	3.3	2,510	2.6	13,310	13.9
Knoxville, TN	17,285	5.0	13,625	3.9	12,210	3.5	5,420	1.6	46,030	13.2
Kokomo, IN	5,485	11.9	2,325	5.0	1,885	4.1	725	1.6	7,365	16.0
La Crosse, WI–MN	5,240	7.0	3,920	5.2	3,270	4.4	840	1.1	11,685	15.6
Lafayette, IN	7,830	7.6	4,320	4.2	4,090	4.0	1,445	1.4	16,465	15.9
Lafayette, LA	4,780	3.4	6,100	4.4	5,000	3.6	2,800	2.0	19,590	14.1
Lake Charles, LA	4,685	4.9	5,105	5.3	3,155	3.3	2,750	2.9	14,330	15.0
Lake Havasu City–Kingman, AZ	3,240	3.8	4,025	4.8	3,210	3.8	2,365	2.8	16,175	19.1
Lakeland–Winter Haven, FL	11,925	4.4	14,735	5.4	17,480	6.4	6,275	2.3	40,505	14.9
Lancaster, PA	21,040	7.9	15,555	5.8	13,175	4.9	2,805	1.1	33,835	12.7
Lansing–East Lansing, MI	14,075	5.8	9,815	4.0	9,165	3.8	4,425	1.8	37,860	15.6
Laredo, TX	2,325	2.2	7,895	7.6	4,455	4.3	4,590	4.4	16,450	15.8
Las Cruces, NM	3,560	3.8	3,450	3.7	4,545	4.9	2,620	2.8	16,035	17.3
Las Vegas–Paradise, NV	23,060	2.3	40,285	4.0	33,635	3.4	31,420	3.1	230,695	23.1
Lawrence, KS	2,320	3.6	1,420	2.2	2,170	3.4	615	1.0	9,845	15.5
Lawton, OK	2,420	4.8	2,275	4.5	1,910	3.8	1,740	3.4	8,185	16.1
Lebanon, PA	5,245	7.7	4,680	6.8	3,190	4.7	1,150	1.7	10,390	15.2
Lewiston, ID–WA	2,320	7.8	1,545	5.2	1,380	4.6	615	2.1	5,135	17.2
Lewiston–Auburn, ME	3,200	5.6	2,535	4.4	2,180	3.8	745	1.3	8,150	14.3
Lexington–Fayette, KY	13,665	5.4	9,770	3.9	11,600	4.6	4,045	1.6	34,320	13.6
Lima, OH	5,085	9.6	3,320	6.2	2,555	4.8	1,235	2.3	9,060	17.0
Lincoln, NE	9,170	5.3	6,530	3.8	5,535	3.2	2,515	1.5	24,290	14.1
Little Rock–North Little Rock–Conway, AR	16,035	4.6	14,985	4.3	12,120	3.5	6,110	1.7	47,220	13.5
Logan, UT–ID	5,040	8.3	2,355	3.9	2,600	4.3	810	1.3	8,275	13.6
Longview, TX	7,230	7.2	5,540	5.5	4,770	4.8	2,010	2.0	13,975	13.9
Longview, WA	3,275	7.0	2,565	5.5	3,435	7.4	870	1.9	7,340	15.7
Los Angeles–Long Beach–Santa Ana, CA	345,850	5.3	283,090	4.3	231,940	3.6	118,625	1.8	906,025	13.9
Louisville/Jefferson County, KY–IN	43,815	6.7	34,460	5.3	29,360	4.5	11,520	1.8	87,525	13.4
Lubbock, TX	5,220	3.7	5,360	3.8	6,090	4.3	2,820	2.0	23,580	16.6
Lynchburg, VA	8,875	7.1	6,420	5.1	5,125	4.1	2,305	1.8	18,505	14.7
Macon, GA	4,895	4.7	5,810	5.6	4,120	3.9	2,815	2.7	16,250	15.5
Madera–Chowchilla, CA	2,995	5.0	3,065	5.1	10,145	17.0	1,620	2.7	8,130	13.6
Madison, WI	14,030	4.2	11,195	3.4	10,175	3.1	4,690	1.4	41,820	12.6
Manchester–Nashua, NH	11,825	5.2	8,630	3.8	6,615	2.9	3,095	1.4	26,000	11.4
Manhattan, KS	2,210	3.8	2,135	3.7	2,095	3.6	1,160	2.0	9,025	15.7
Mankato–North Mankato, MN	4,510	7.9	2,665	4.6	2,405	4.2	995	1.7	9,120	15.9
Mansfield, OH	7,310	12.2	3,625	6.1	3,170	5.3	1,535	2.6	8,060	13.5
McAllen–Edinburg–Mission, TX	10,665	3.6	15,235	5.1	19,670	6.6	7,125	2.4	54,440	18.3
Medford, OR	4,555	4.6	4,315	4.4	5,510	5.6	1,400	1.4	15,320	15.5
Memphis, TN–MS–AR	31,710	4.8	40,710	6.2	29,230	4.5	17,560	2.7	89,425	13.6
Merced, CA	8,210	7.5	8,835	8.0	13,835	12.6	1,930	1.8	15,365	14.0
Miami–Fort Lauderdale–Pompano Beach, FL	72,800	2.6	106,110	3.8	102,130	3.6	76,850	2.7	436,730	15.5
Michigan City–La Porte, IN	5,095	9.4	3,335	6.2	2,495	4.6	1,410	2.6	7,620	14.1
Midland, TX	2,355	3.4	3,185	4.7	2,695	3.9	1,000	1.5	9,205	13.5
Milwaukee–Waukesha–West Allis, WI	58,095	7.0	34,995	4.2	27,520	3.3	15,125	1.8	108,825	13.2
Minneapolis–St. Paul–Bloomington, MN–WI	92,340	5.0	64,975	3.5	48,615	2.6	22,385	1.2	234,435	12.7
Missoula, MT	1,310	2.2	1,920	3.2	2,445	4.1	885	1.5	10,285	17.3

C-1 All Workers, by Metropolitan Statistical Area and Occupation Group, 2006–2010—*Continued*

Metropolitan Statistical Area	Total who worked in the last 5 years Number	Percent	Management, business, and financial workers Number	Percent	Science, engineering, and computer professionals Number	Percent	Health care practitioner professionals Number	Percent	Other professional workers Number	Percent
Mobile, AL	193,015	100.0	17,145	8.9	4,520	2.3	6,725	3.5	17,865	9.3
Modesto, CA	237,095	100.0	20,970	8.8	3,520	1.5	5,790	2.4	20,080	8.5
Monroe, LA	81,880	100.0	7,355	9.0	1,145	1.4	3,260	4.0	8,440	10.3
Monroe, MI	77,790	100.0	6,610	8.5	2,175	2.8	2,225	2.9	5,560	7.1
Montgomery, AL	177,485	100.0	19,405	10.9	5,760	3.2	5,230	2.9	19,875	11.2
Morgantown, WV	61,165	100.0	5,440	8.9	2,085	3.4	2,770	4.5	7,875	12.9
Morristown, TN	64,795	100.0	5,695	8.8	890	1.4	1,635	2.5	4,220	6.5
Mount Vernon–Anacortes, WA	55,410	100.0	6,190	11.2	1,390	2.5	1,710	3.1	5,010	9.0
Muncie, IN	58,470	100.0	4,975	8.5	1,195	2.0	2,100	3.6	6,410	11.0
Muskegon–Norton Shores, MI	82,545	100.0	6,350	7.7	1,830	2.2	2,260	2.7	6,705	8.1
Myrtle Beach–North Myrtle Beach–Conway, SC	132,990	100.0	14,210	10.7	1,480	1.1	3,890	2.9	11,180	8.4
Napa, CA	68,980	100.0	9,720	14.1	1,830	2.7	3,120	4.5	6,805	9.9
Naples–Marco Island, FL	144,445	100.0	17,600	12.2	2,230	1.5	4,355	3.0	11,860	8.2
Nashville-Davidson–Murfreesboro–Franklin, TN	819,770	100.0	101,815	12.4	26,445	3.2	31,850	3.9	93,315	11.4
New Haven–Milford, CT	465,055	100.0	53,020	11.4	20,090	4.3	19,120	4.1	59,105	12.7
New Orleans–Metairie–Kenner, LA	558,690	100.0	61,940	11.1	15,470	2.8	21,960	3.9	62,420	11.2
New York–Northern New Jersey–Long Island, NY–NJ–PA	9,654,290	100.0	1,247,080	12.9	349,960	3.6	348,655	3.6	1,344,275	13.9
Niles–Benton Harbor, MI	78,070	100.0	8,010	10.3	2,180	2.8	2,535	3.2	7,850	10.1
North Port–Bradenton–Sarasota, FL	318,635	100.0	39,735	12.5	7,130	2.2	12,415	3.9	29,845	9.4
Norwich–New London, CT	143,095	100.0	15,530	10.9	8,610	6.0	4,405	3.1	16,280	11.4
Ocala, FL	137,090	100.0	13,230	9.7	1,820	1.3	5,180	3.8	10,525	7.7
Ocean City, NJ	48,330	100.0	5,570	11.5	825	1.7	2,055	4.3	5,590	11.6
Odessa, TX	65,035	100.0	5,080	7.8	590	0.9	1,560	2.4	4,795	7.4
Ogden–Clearfield, UT	255,640	100.0	33,595	13.1	11,735	4.6	7,085	2.8	26,820	10.5
Oklahoma City, OK	624,140	100.0	72,965	11.7	22,120	3.5	20,940	3.4	67,790	10.9
Olympia, WA	122,585	100.0	17,555	14.3	6,360	5.2	4,185	3.4	14,730	12.0
Omaha–Council Bluffs, NE–IA	465,810	100.0	59,430	12.8	18,760	4.0	19,800	4.3	49,090	10.5
Orlando–Kissimmee–Sanford, FL	1,109,310	100.0	139,240	12.6	41,070	3.7	31,710	2.9	110,775	10.0
Oshkosh–Neenah, WI	90,270	100.0	9,275	10.3	2,705	3.0	2,760	3.1	7,900	8.8
Owensboro, KY	53,730	100.0	5,080	9.5	920	1.7	1,915	3.6	4,755	8.8
Oxnard–Thousand Oaks–Ventura, CA	415,150	100.0	58,860	14.2	19,825	4.8	11,255	2.7	45,930	11.1
Palm Bay–Melbourne–Titusville, FL	261,135	100.0	30,805	11.8	18,760	7.2	8,095	3.1	23,455	9.0
Palm Coast, FL	38,585	100.0	5,365	13.9	855	2.2	1,340	3.5	3,925	10.2
Panama City–Lynn Haven–Panama City Beach, FL	82,595	100.0	8,995	10.9	2,680	3.2	2,500	3.0	7,230	8.8
Parkersburg–Marietta–Vienna, WV–OH	76,200	100.0	6,410	8.4	1,850	2.4	2,495	3.3	6,905	9.1
Pascagoula, MS	74,930	100.0	7,415	9.9	2,270	3.0	2,135	2.8	6,120	8.2
Pensacola–Ferry Pass–Brent, FL	210,670	100.0	20,985	10.0	6,640	3.2	7,010	3.3	20,180	9.6
Peoria, IL	191,510	100.0	21,680	11.3	8,955	4.7	7,985	4.2	18,520	9.7
Philadelphia–Camden–Wilmington, PA–NJ–DE–MD	3,073,915	100.0	404,785	13.2	139,810	4.5	129,505	4.2	374,295	12.2
Phoenix–Mesa–Glendale, AZ	2,009,550	100.0	268,725	13.4	88,685	4.4	64,435	3.2	201,575	10.0
Pine Bluff, AR	44,845	100.0	3,820	8.5	630	1.4	1,420	3.2	3,480	7.8
Pittsburgh, PA	1,200,920	100.0	139,095	11.6	47,215	3.9	55,250	4.6	132,650	11.0
Pittsfield, MA	68,570	100.0	7,415	10.8	1,915	2.8	2,840	4.1	8,375	12.2
Pocatello, ID	44,250	100.0	4,150	9.4	1,365	3.1	1,575	3.6	4,810	10.9
Portland–South Portland–Biddeford, ME	285,140	100.0	37,835	13.3	11,630	4.1	11,600	4.1	34,340	12.0
Portland–Vancouver–Hillsboro, OR–WA	1,169,465	100.0	156,580	13.4	63,810	5.5	39,415	3.4	129,735	11.1
Port St. Lucie, FL	192,585	100.0	20,715	10.8	4,440	2.3	6,945	3.6	16,385	8.5
Poughkeepsie–Newburgh–Middletown, NY	335,485	100.0	41,475	12.4	12,555	3.7	13,430	4.0	38,680	11.5
Prescott, AZ	93,800	100.0	10,440	11.1	1,930	2.1	3,105	3.3	8,995	9.6
Providence–New Bedford–Fall River, RI–MA	856,225	100.0	96,280	11.2	29,475	3.4	31,200	3.6	96,220	11.2
Provo–Orem, UT	228,880	100.0	27,130	11.9	11,650	5.1	6,025	2.6	29,650	13.0
Pueblo, CO	72,410	100.0	6,985	9.6	1,590	2.2	3,175	4.4	6,540	9.0
Punta Gorda, FL	64,655	100.0	6,165	9.5	1,415	2.2	2,465	3.8	4,910	7.6
Racine, WI	100,730	100.0	10,395	10.3	3,105	3.1	3,035	3.0	9,680	9.6
Raleigh–Cary, NC	580,680	100.0	90,455	15.6	46,780	8.1	19,815	3.4	72,455	12.5

PART C—METROPOLITAN STATISTICAL AREA TABLES

C-1 All Workers, by Metropolitan Statistical Area and Occupation Group, 2006–2010—Continued

Metropolitan Statistical Area	Technicians Number	Technicians Percent	Sales workers Number	Sales workers Percent	Administrative support workers Number	Administrative support workers Percent	Construction and extractive craft workers Number	Construction and extractive craft workers Percent	Installation, maintenance, and repair craft workers Number	Installation, maintenance, and repair craft workers Percent
Mobile, AL	5,575	2.9	22,655	11.7	30,745	15.9	15,060	7.8	9,105	4.7
Modesto, CA	5,625	2.4	25,980	11.0	35,715	15.1	16,935	7.1	10,785	4.5
Monroe, LA	3,070	3.7	9,855	12.0	13,875	16.9	5,375	6.6	3,240	4.0
Monroe, MI	2,290	2.9	7,640	9.8	11,850	15.2	4,900	6.3	4,890	6.3
Montgomery, AL	5,110	2.9	19,640	11.1	28,815	16.2	9,080	5.1	7,605	4.3
Morgantown, WV	2,640	4.3	5,720	9.4	8,655	14.2	5,635	9.2	2,290	3.7
Morristown, TN	1,790	2.8	7,030	10.8	8,980	13.9	4,735	7.3	3,425	5.3
Mount Vernon–Anacortes, WA	1,225	2.2	6,260	11.3	7,690	13.9	3,805	6.9	2,540	4.6
Muncie, IN	1,480	2.5	6,140	10.5	9,160	15.7	2,840	4.9	2,530	4.3
Muskegon–Norton Shores, MI	2,250	2.7	8,330	10.1	11,495	13.9	3,845	4.7	4,425	5.4
Myrtle Beach–North Myrtle Beach–Conway, SC	3,190	2.4	21,625	16.3	20,045	15.1	11,145	8.4	5,590	4.2
Napa, CA	1,485	2.2	6,710	9.7	9,145	13.3	3,755	5.4	2,400	3.5
Naples–Marco Island, FL	3,540	2.5	20,130	13.9	18,195	12.6	13,695	9.5	5,265	3.6
Nashville-Davidson–Murfreesboro–Franklin, TN	24,220	3.0	99,660	12.2	129,325	15.8	46,730	5.7	33,275	4.1
New Haven–Milford, CT	14,280	3.1	51,065	11.0	72,165	15.5	23,030	5.0	18,445	4.0
New Orleans–Metairie–Kenner, LA	15,345	2.7	65,755	11.8	82,205	14.7	45,925	8.2	22,925	4.1
New York–Northern New Jersey–Long Island, NY–NJ–PA	225,205	2.3	1,096,315	11.4	1,556,335	16.1	469,150	4.9	286,935	3.0
Niles–Benton Harbor, MI	2,230	2.9	7,735	9.9	11,605	14.9	3,770	4.8	3,620	4.6
North Port–Bradenton–Sarasota, FL	9,035	2.8	44,770	14.1	47,755	15.0	23,305	7.3	12,830	4.0
Norwich–New London, CT	4,590	3.2	14,330	10.0	20,225	14.1	8,045	5.6	6,260	4.4
Ocala, FL	3,895	2.8	17,610	12.8	21,630	15.8	10,155	7.4	6,785	4.9
Ocean City, NJ	975	2.0	5,550	11.5	7,145	14.8	3,875	8.0	2,265	4.7
Odessa, TX	1,490	2.3	7,890	12.1	10,045	15.4	6,800	10.5	4,615	7.1
Ogden–Clearfield, UT	7,745	3.0	29,815	11.7	42,325	16.6	14,645	5.7	12,435	4.9
Oklahoma City, OK	20,935	3.4	71,000	11.4	103,920	16.7	40,790	6.5	28,355	4.5
Olympia, WA	3,565	2.9	11,325	9.2	21,415	17.5	6,700	5.5	4,790	3.9
Omaha–Council Bluffs, NE–IA	14,310	3.1	52,690	11.3	79,300	17.0	24,645	5.3	17,055	3.7
Orlando–Kissimmee–Sanford, FL	28,345	2.6	152,640	13.8	178,910	16.1	69,800	6.3	39,225	3.5
Oshkosh–Neenah, WI	2,705	3.0	10,185	11.3	13,355	14.8	3,590	4.0	4,160	4.6
Owensboro, KY	1,105	2.1	5,210	9.7	8,100	15.1	3,745	7.0	2,860	5.3
Oxnard–Thousand Oaks–Ventura, CA	10,505	2.5	49,570	11.9	62,350	15.0	20,905	5.0	15,495	3.7
Palm Bay–Melbourne–Titusville, FL	9,400	3.6	31,025	11.9	38,140	14.6	16,085	6.2	11,750	4.5
Palm Coast, FL	1,345	3.5	4,650	12.1	6,045	15.7	2,140	5.5	1,340	3.5
Panama City–Lynn Haven–Panama City Beach, FL	2,800	3.4	10,400	12.6	13,195	16.0	6,585	8.0	4,210	5.1
Parkersburg–Marietta–Vienna, WV–OH	2,630	3.5	8,280	10.9	12,230	16.0	5,755	7.6	3,465	4.5
Pascagoula, MS	1,945	2.6	7,490	10.0	10,050	13.4	8,510	11.4	3,640	4.9
Pensacola–Ferry Pass–Brent, FL	7,345	3.5	26,505	12.6	34,055	16.2	15,010	7.1	9,795	4.6
Peoria, IL	5,905	3.1	19,655	10.3	29,185	15.2	9,795	5.1	8,880	4.6
Philadelphia–Camden–Wilmington, PA–NJ–DE–MD	93,035	3.0	340,700	11.1	515,530	16.8	140,715	4.6	107,465	3.5
Phoenix–Mesa–Glendale, AZ	52,810	2.6	252,270	12.6	325,520	16.2	134,405	6.7	80,920	4.0
Pine Bluff, AR	1,425	3.2	3,990	8.9	7,220	16.1	2,100	4.7	2,195	4.9
Pittsburgh, PA	40,515	3.4	132,005	11.0	189,970	15.8	63,895	5.3	49,395	4.1
Pittsfield, MA	1,905	2.8	7,125	10.4	10,220	14.9	4,520	6.6	2,440	3.6
Pocatello, ID	1,245	2.8	5,175	11.7	7,140	16.1	2,520	5.7	1,745	3.9
Portland–South Portland–Biddeford, ME	8,165	2.9	32,690	11.5	40,295	14.1	17,120	6.0	11,730	4.1
Portland–Vancouver–Hillsboro, OR–WA	30,540	2.6	129,920	11.1	179,280	15.3	60,260	5.2	43,715	3.7
Port St. Lucie, FL	5,010	2.6	26,095	13.5	28,395	14.7	16,125	8.4	8,920	4.6
Poughkeepsie–Newburgh–Middletown, NY	9,780	2.9	35,800	10.7	54,440	16.2	20,390	6.1	14,705	4.4
Prescott, AZ	2,725	2.9	12,395	13.2	14,035	15.0	7,990	8.5	4,155	4.4
Providence–New Bedford–Fall River, RI–MA	24,660	2.9	92,630	10.8	134,805	15.7	49,370	5.8	32,585	3.8
Provo–Orem, UT	7,130	3.1	28,310	12.4	38,455	16.8	14,165	6.2	8,485	3.7
Pueblo, CO	1,785	2.5	8,595	11.9	11,790	16.3	5,455	7.5	3,250	4.5
Punta Gorda, FL	2,240	3.5	9,655	14.9	10,730	16.6	5,055	7.8	3,000	4.6
Racine, WI	3,050	3.0	10,235	10.2	15,310	15.2	5,690	5.6	5,720	5.7
Raleigh–Cary, NC	18,890	3.3	70,025	12.1	83,275	14.3	34,355	5.9	19,460	3.4

C-1 **All Workers, by Metropolitan Statistical Area and Occupation Group, 2006–2010**—*Continued*

Metropolitan Statistical Area	Production operative workers Number	Percent	Transportation and material moving operative workers Number	Percent	Laborers and helpers Number	Percent	Protective service workers Number	Percent	Service workers, except protective Number	Percent
Mobile, AL	10,880	5.6	10,005	5.2	7,965	4.1	3,950	2.0	27,225	14.1
Modesto, CA	16,995	7.2	16,055	6.8	16,835	7.1	4,595	1.9	32,345	13.6
Monroe, LA	4,315	5.3	3,895	4.8	3,630	4.4	1,735	2.1	11,875	14.5
Monroe, MI	7,015	9.0	4,930	6.3	3,745	4.8	1,425	1.8	11,505	14.8
Montgomery, AL	11,180	6.3	8,240	4.6	7,190	4.1	4,660	2.6	23,280	13.1
Morgantown, WV	2,415	3.9	2,375	3.9	1,985	3.2	1,450	2.4	9,440	15.4
Morristown, TN	7,925	12.2	4,605	7.1	3,190	4.9	1,140	1.8	8,915	13.8
Mount Vernon–Anacortes, WA	3,585	6.5	3,005	5.4	3,730	6.7	1,060	1.9	7,910	14.3
Muncie, IN	3,775	6.5	2,320	4.0	2,580	4.4	1,160	2.0	11,110	19.0
Muskegon–Norton Shores, MI	10,425	12.6	4,225	5.1	4,125	5.0	1,545	1.9	12,910	15.6
Myrtle Beach–North Myrtle Beach–Conway, SC	3,180	2.4	4,355	3.3	4,435	3.3	3,805	2.9	24,130	18.1
Napa, CA	3,110	4.5	2,435	3.5	6,405	9.3	985	1.4	10,055	14.6
Naples–Marco Island, FL	2,960	2.0	4,810	3.3	10,165	7.0	3,155	2.2	25,170	17.4
Nashville-Davidson–Murfreesboro–Franklin, TN	42,475	5.2	37,205	4.5	28,315	3.5	14,760	1.8	104,125	12.7
New Haven–Milford, CT	24,295	5.2	18,720	4.0	12,175	2.6	9,635	2.1	64,500	13.9
New Orleans–Metairie–Kenner, LA	19,670	3.5	24,600	4.4	18,890	3.4	14,415	2.6	80,545	14.4
New York–Northern New Jersey–Long Island, NY–NJ–PA	273,910	2.8	418,325	4.3	220,125	2.3	264,370	2.7	1,430,770	14.8
Niles–Benton Harbor, MI	6,350	8.1	3,840	4.9	3,885	5.0	1,160	1.5	12,355	15.8
North Port–Bradenton–Sarasota, FL	10,360	3.3	10,430	3.3	13,705	4.3	5,595	1.8	48,155	15.1
Norwich–New London, CT	4,830	3.4	4,910	3.4	3,975	2.8	4,040	2.8	25,935	18.1
Ocala, FL	5,945	4.3	6,695	4.9	7,430	5.4	3,785	2.8	20,575	15.0
Ocean City, NJ	915	1.9	1,650	3.4	1,820	3.8	1,435	3.0	8,430	17.4
Odessa, TX	4,185	6.4	4,170	6.4	2,770	4.3	1,005	1.5	9,645	14.8
Ogden–Clearfield, UT	14,885	5.8	11,150	4.4	7,995	3.1	4,525	1.8	29,510	11.5
Oklahoma City, OK	25,605	4.1	25,975	4.2	21,115	3.4	12,135	1.9	86,285	13.8
Olympia, WA	3,180	2.6	4,115	3.4	4,135	3.4	3,100	2.5	16,465	13.4
Omaha–Council Bluffs, NE–IA	20,905	4.5	19,060	4.1	15,750	3.4	7,610	1.6	64,115	13.8
Orlando–Kissimmee–Sanford, FL	26,035	2.3	41,815	3.8	40,500	3.7	23,400	2.1	173,275	15.6
Oshkosh–Neenah, WI	9,210	10.2	4,575	5.1	3,990	4.4	1,805	2.0	13,470	14.9
Owensboro, KY	5,395	10.0	3,095	5.8	2,440	4.5	890	1.7	7,805	14.5
Oxnard–Thousand Oaks–Ventura, CA	17,215	4.1	15,465	3.7	26,510	6.4	7,910	1.9	49,710	12.0
Palm Bay–Melbourne–Titusville, FL	9,610	3.7	9,530	3.6	7,970	3.1	6,395	2.4	37,290	14.3
Palm Coast, FL	1,880	4.9	1,125	2.9	1,605	4.2	990	2.6	5,465	14.2
Panama City–Lynn Haven–Panama City Beach, FL	2,800	3.4	2,850	3.5	2,710	3.3	2,270	2.7	12,720	15.4
Parkersburg–Marietta–Vienna, WV–OH	5,590	7.3	4,475	5.9	2,830	3.7	1,245	1.6	11,320	14.9
Pascagoula, MS	5,345	7.1	3,135	4.2	2,480	3.3	2,070	2.8	11,305	15.1
Pensacola–Ferry Pass–Brent, FL	5,695	2.7	8,190	3.9	7,700	3.7	4,875	2.3	32,355	15.4
Peoria, IL	12,310	6.4	9,735	5.1	6,695	3.5	3,095	1.6	27,815	14.5
Philadelphia–Camden–Wilmington, PA–NJ–DE–MD	109,400	3.6	127,885	4.2	88,105	2.9	68,915	2.2	395,150	12.9
Phoenix–Mesa–Glendale, AZ	63,445	3.2	74,055	3.7	75,240	3.7	45,250	2.3	263,775	13.1
Pine Bluff, AR	3,890	8.7	2,875	6.4	2,715	6.1	2,155	4.8	5,895	13.1
Pittsburgh, PA	48,815	4.1	52,460	4.4	39,215	3.3	21,775	1.8	180,095	15.0
Pittsfield, MA	3,000	4.4	2,355	3.4	2,450	3.6	1,255	1.8	12,330	18.0
Pocatello, ID	2,260	5.1	2,515	5.7	2,290	5.2	780	1.8	6,540	14.8
Portland–South Portland–Biddeford, ME	12,025	4.2	9,765	3.4	10,265	3.6	4,140	1.5	42,235	14.8
Portland–Vancouver–Hillsboro, OR–WA	57,325	4.9	48,095	4.1	47,330	4.0	17,575	1.5	154,390	13.2
Port St. Lucie, FL	5,520	2.9	6,725	3.5	10,010	5.2	5,890	3.1	28,325	14.7
Poughkeepsie–Newburgh–Middletown, NY	10,585	3.2	13,520	4.0	10,050	3.0	13,535	4.0	43,860	13.1
Prescott, AZ	2,830	3.0	3,260	3.5	3,545	3.8	2,730	2.9	15,250	16.3
Providence–New Bedford–Fall River, RI–MA	49,125	5.7	37,845	4.4	24,260	2.8	18,620	2.2	130,165	15.2
Provo–Orem, UT	10,545	4.6	6,880	3.0	6,740	2.9	3,385	1.5	29,055	12.7
Pueblo, CO	2,830	3.9	2,415	3.3	3,015	4.2	2,600	3.6	11,585	16.0
Punta Gorda, FL	1,990	3.1	2,635	4.1	2,470	3.8	1,905	2.9	9,250	14.3
Racine, WI	9,775	9.7	5,675	5.6	3,765	3.7	2,015	2.0	12,430	12.3
Raleigh–Cary, NC	17,455	3.0	18,285	3.1	15,275	2.6	9,435	1.6	60,370	10.4

PART C—METROPOLITAN STATISTICAL AREA TABLES

C-1 All Workers, by Metropolitan Statistical Area and Occupation Group, 2006–2010—Continued

Metropolitan Statistical Area	Total who worked in the last 5 years Number	Percent	Management, business, and financial workers Number	Percent	Science, engineering, and computer professionals Number	Percent	Health care practitioner professionals Number	Percent	Other professional workers Number	Percent
Rapid City, SD	65,140	100.0	7,155	11.0	1,975	3.0	2,475	3.8	6,820	10.5
Reading, PA	212,665	100.0	21,750	10.2	6,045	2.8	6,560	3.1	19,955	9.4
Redding, CA	79,430	100.0	8,605	10.8	1,965	2.5	2,825	3.6	7,670	9.7
Reno–Sparks, NV	227,115	100.0	26,845	11.8	7,145	3.1	6,950	3.1	21,835	9.6
Richmond, VA	647,365	100.0	88,995	13.7	27,775	4.3	21,750	3.4	72,080	11.1
Riverside–San Bernardino–Ontario, CA	1,901,430	100.0	188,570	9.9	41,575	2.2	50,245	2.6	166,495	8.8
Roanoke, VA	157,385	100.0	17,550	11.2	4,630	2.9	6,390	4.1	16,065	10.2
Rochester, MN	102,730	100.0	10,355	10.1	5,820	5.7	10,295	10.0	9,550	9.3
Rochester, NY	536,310	100.0	59,885	11.2	26,790	5.0	21,605	4.0	68,115	12.7
Rockford, IL	175,105	100.0	16,485	9.4	5,345	3.1	5,375	3.1	14,665	8.4
Rocky Mount, NC	72,975	100.0	6,695	9.2	1,245	1.7	2,090	2.9	5,935	8.1
Rome, GA	45,080	100.0	4,325	9.6	655	1.5	1,665	3.7	4,390	9.7
Sacramento–Arden-Arcade–Roseville, CA	1,056,940	100.0	144,215	13.6	54,575	5.2	31,790	3.0	115,275	10.9
Saginaw–Saginaw Township North, MI	92,670	100.0	8,110	8.8	2,370	2.6	3,125	3.4	7,810	8.4
St. Cloud, MN	106,535	100.0	11,420	10.7	2,055	1.9	2,935	2.8	10,295	9.7
St. George, UT	57,495	100.0	6,320	11.0	1,240	2.2	1,960	3.4	5,555	9.7
St. Joseph, MO–KS	62,580	100.0	6,465	10.3	925	1.5	1,970	3.1	5,485	8.8
St. Louis, MO–IL	1,464,850	100.0	177,485	12.1	62,320	4.3	55,350	3.8	157,350	10.7
Salem, OR	185,690	100.0	21,170	11.4	4,600	2.5	4,690	2.5	17,370	9.4
Salinas, CA	196,235	100.0	18,430	9.4	5,035	2.6	4,710	2.4	17,720	9.0
Salisbury, MD	62,185	100.0	6,460	10.4	1,400	2.3	2,580	4.1	6,850	11.0
Salt Lake City, UT	577,550	100.0	70,425	12.2	24,855	4.3	16,765	2.9	61,700	10.7
San Angelo, TX	52,760	100.0	4,955	9.4	840	1.6	1,765	3.3	5,165	9.8
San Antonio–New Braunfels, TX	993,330	100.0	120,265	12.1	31,185	3.1	30,700	3.1	104,845	10.6
San Diego–Carlsbad–San Marcos, CA	1,497,805	100.0	204,260	13.6	93,155	6.2	45,995	3.1	171,525	11.5
Sandusky, OH	39,430	100.0	3,610	9.2	820	2.1	1,405	3.6	3,565	9.0
San Francisco–Oakland–Fremont, CA	2,306,445	100.0	365,475	15.8	168,525	7.3	79,625	3.5	311,130	13.5
San Jose–Sunnyvale–Santa Clara, CA	942,880	100.0	145,760	15.5	126,615	13.4	26,785	2.8	105,885	11.2
San Luis Obispo–Paso Robles, CA	131,210	100.0	15,675	11.9	5,410	4.1	4,685	3.6	14,775	11.3
Santa Barbara–Santa Maria–Goleta, CA	209,665	100.0	23,920	11.4	9,070	4.3	5,165	2.5	25,360	12.1
Santa Cruz–Watsonville, CA	137,890	100.0	18,470	13.4	7,475	5.4	4,600	3.3	18,775	13.6
Santa Fe, NM	76,445	100.0	10,400	13.6	3,990	5.2	2,350	3.1	11,250	14.7
Santa Rosa–Petaluma, CA	253,110	100.0	32,685	12.9	8,590	3.4	7,685	3.0	27,285	10.8
Savannah, GA	163,670	100.0	18,495	11.3	4,505	2.8	6,290	3.8	16,935	10.3
Scranton–Wilkes-Barre, PA	280,610	100.0	26,115	9.3	5,575	2.0	11,450	4.1	26,290	9.4
Seattle–Tacoma–Bellevue, WA	1,833,705	100.0	271,410	14.8	140,235	7.6	58,550	3.2	206,185	11.2
Sebastian–Vero Beach, FL	61,560	100.0	7,375	12.0	1,320	2.1	2,125	3.5	5,625	9.1
Sheboygan, WI	63,255	100.0	6,230	9.8	1,775	2.8	1,825	2.9	4,870	7.7
Sherman–Denison, TX	58,850	100.0	5,565	9.5	1,345	2.3	1,825	3.1	5,665	9.6
Shreveport–Bossier City, LA	189,435	100.0	16,305	8.6	3,600	1.9	7,955	4.2	18,085	9.5
Sioux City, IA–NE–SD	76,160	100.0	7,375	9.7	1,150	1.5	2,580	3.4	6,670	8.8
Sioux Falls, SD	128,290	100.0	15,585	12.1	4,320	3.4	6,210	4.8	12,010	9.4
South Bend–Mishawaka, IN–MI	161,550	100.0	16,945	10.5	3,880	2.4	4,290	2.7	17,025	10.5
Spartanburg, SC	135,060	100.0	13,915	10.3	3,305	2.4	4,005	3.0	11,750	8.7
Spokane, WA	231,110	100.0	25,645	11.1	6,825	3.0	10,025	4.3	25,225	10.9
Springfield, IL	112,285	100.0	13,585	12.1	4,355	3.9	5,370	4.8	12,660	11.3
Springfield, MA	355,390	100.0	37,540	10.6	10,920	3.1	12,920	3.6	46,445	13.1
Springfield, MO	218,960	100.0	23,460	10.7	4,125	1.9	8,330	3.8	22,475	10.3
Springfield, OH	68,370	100.0	6,295	9.2	1,565	2.3	2,290	3.3	5,490	8.0
State College, PA	76,610	100.0	7,895	10.3	4,265	5.6	2,215	2.9	13,555	17.7
Steubenville–Weirton, OH–WV	58,010	100.0	4,380	7.6	655	1.1	2,585	4.5	4,255	7.3
Stockton, CA	309,845	100.0	31,145	10.1	7,200	2.3	7,465	2.4	25,205	8.1
Sumter, SC	46,225	100.0	3,390	7.3	595	1.3	1,170	2.5	4,265	9.2
Syracuse, NY	333,980	100.0	34,405	10.3	11,540	3.5	12,945	3.9	41,405	12.4
Tallahassee, FL	187,465	100.0	23,915	12.8	8,025	4.3	4,775	2.5	28,140	15.0

C-1 All Workers, by Metropolitan Statistical Area and Occupation Group, 2006–2010—Continued

Metropolitan Statistical Area	Technicians Number	Technicians Percent	Sales workers Number	Sales workers Percent	Administrative support workers Number	Administrative support workers Percent	Construction and extractive craft workers Number	Construction and extractive craft workers Percent	Installation, maintenance, and repair craft workers Number	Installation, maintenance, and repair craft workers Percent
Rapid City, SD	2,080	3.2	7,530	11.6	10,505	16.1	4,720	7.2	3,105	4.8
Reading, PA	6,540	3.1	22,235	10.5	33,020	15.5	10,775	5.1	10,180	4.8
Redding, CA	1,825	2.3	10,330	13.0	12,775	16.1	5,565	7.0	3,510	4.4
Reno–Sparks, NV	5,415	2.4	26,935	11.9	36,885	16.2	16,350	7.2	8,030	3.5
Richmond, VA	18,720	2.9	76,070	11.8	103,210	15.9	38,320	5.9	26,295	4.1
Riverside–San Bernardino–Ontario, CA	43,335	2.3	227,880	12.0	300,970	15.8	142,175	7.5	87,765	4.6
Roanoke, VA	4,765	3.0	18,600	11.8	26,210	16.7	9,205	5.8	6,620	4.2
Rochester, MN	6,370	6.2	8,795	8.6	14,440	14.1	5,170	5.0	3,450	3.4
Rochester, NY	17,555	3.3	55,350	10.3	84,960	15.8	22,640	4.2	23,115	4.3
Rockford, IL	4,720	2.7	18,620	10.6	28,300	16.2	9,415	5.4	8,330	4.8
Rocky Mount, NC	2,025	2.8	8,080	11.1	11,385	15.6	4,065	5.6	3,205	4.4
Rome, GA	1,470	3.3	4,610	10.2	6,425	14.3	3,600	8.0	2,085	4.6
Sacramento–Arden-Arcade–Roseville, CA	27,545	2.6	123,625	11.7	175,530	16.6	62,220	5.9	37,475	3.5
Saginaw–Saginaw Township North, MI	2,935	3.2	11,080	12.0	14,465	15.6	3,960	4.3	3,950	4.3
St. Cloud, MN	3,485	3.3	11,015	10.3	16,615	15.6	6,860	6.4	5,155	4.8
St. George, UT	1,520	2.6	7,615	13.2	8,315	14.5	5,685	9.9	2,495	4.3
St. Joseph, MO–KS	2,265	3.6	6,630	10.6	9,055	14.5	4,005	6.4	3,090	4.9
St. Louis, MO–IL	43,255	3.0	167,430	11.4	230,390	15.7	80,410	5.5	58,460	4.0
Salem, OR	4,230	2.3	17,825	9.6	30,070	16.2	12,485	6.7	6,395	3.4
Salinas, CA	3,280	1.7	20,290	10.3	24,695	12.6	10,525	5.4	5,975	3.0
Salisbury, MD	1,745	2.8	7,245	11.7	8,970	14.4	4,465	7.2	2,540	4.1
Salt Lake City, UT	16,530	2.9	70,485	12.2	103,175	17.9	38,585	6.7	22,825	4.0
San Angelo, TX	1,775	3.4	5,810	11.0	8,825	16.7	4,230	8.0	2,140	4.1
San Antonio–New Braunfels, TX	30,755	3.1	114,930	11.6	167,775	16.9	67,830	6.8	41,570	4.2
San Diego–Carlsbad–San Marcos, CA	42,650	2.8	178,695	11.9	218,465	14.6	85,685	5.7	50,780	3.4
Sandusky, OH	1,395	3.5	4,735	12.0	5,440	13.8	2,105	5.3	1,860	4.7
San Francisco–Oakland–Fremont, CA	57,995	2.5	256,365	11.1	327,660	14.2	109,045	4.7	65,775	2.9
San Jose–Sunnyvale–Santa Clara, CA	27,645	2.9	95,880	10.2	118,625	12.6	43,310	4.6	28,520	3.0
San Luis Obispo–Paso Robles, CA	3,755	2.9	16,275	12.4	19,230	14.7	8,295	6.3	5,135	3.9
Santa Barbara–Santa Maria–Goleta, CA	4,775	2.3	20,945	10.0	28,365	13.5	11,565	5.5	6,245	3.0
Santa Cruz–Watsonville, CA	3,620	2.6	14,890	10.8	16,245	11.8	8,200	5.9	4,375	3.2
Santa Fe, NM	1,740	2.3	8,660	11.3	10,165	13.3	5,530	7.2	2,960	3.9
Santa Rosa–Petaluma, CA	5,660	2.2	32,730	12.9	36,100	14.3	18,520	7.3	9,150	3.6
Savannah, GA	3,990	2.4	20,695	12.6	23,380	14.3	9,965	6.1	8,235	5.0
Scranton–Wilkes-Barre, PA	9,415	3.4	30,470	10.9	47,860	17.1	14,375	5.1	12,580	4.5
Seattle–Tacoma–Bellevue, WA	50,010	2.7	199,590	10.9	264,425	14.4	101,950	5.6	69,210	3.8
Sebastian–Vero Beach, FL	1,265	2.1	7,735	12.6	7,985	13.0	5,945	9.7	2,570	4.2
Sheboygan, WI	1,745	2.8	5,945	9.4	8,570	13.5	3,290	5.2	3,080	4.9
Sherman–Denison, TX	2,195	3.7	6,705	11.4	8,535	14.5	3,790	6.4	2,965	5.0
Shreveport–Bossier City, LA	5,760	3.0	21,840	11.5	28,750	15.2	12,835	6.8	8,970	4.7
Sioux City, IA–NE–SD	1,615	2.1	8,795	11.5	12,280	16.1	3,780	5.0	3,115	4.1
Sioux Falls, SD	4,110	3.2	14,470	11.3	22,845	17.8	6,705	5.2	5,020	3.9
South Bend–Mishawaka, IN–MI	4,625	2.9	18,005	11.1	25,805	16.0	7,815	4.8	7,230	4.5
Spartanburg, SC	4,035	3.0	15,170	11.2	18,745	13.9	7,850	5.8	7,090	5.2
Spokane, WA	6,170	2.7	27,560	11.9	38,170	16.5	11,910	5.2	8,715	3.8
Springfield, IL	4,010	3.6	12,285	10.9	21,885	19.5	4,635	4.1	3,855	3.4
Springfield, MA	10,515	3.0	35,575	10.0	55,455	15.6	15,895	4.5	15,955	4.5
Springfield, MO	6,350	2.9	27,665	12.6	35,065	16.0	13,455	6.1	9,280	4.2
Springfield, OH	1,835	2.7	6,905	10.1	11,125	16.3	3,415	5.0	3,640	5.3
State College, PA	2,925	3.8	7,355	9.6	10,150	13.2	3,460	4.5	2,685	3.5
Steubenville–Weirton, OH–WV	2,075	3.6	6,190	10.7	8,775	15.1	3,965	6.8	3,500	6.0
Stockton, CA	7,185	2.3	33,785	10.9	49,330	15.9	19,915	6.4	13,790	4.5
Sumter, SC	1,625	3.5	4,440	9.6	6,255	13.5	3,000	6.5	2,695	5.8
Syracuse, NY	10,150	3.0	37,700	11.3	56,190	16.8	15,970	4.8	14,850	4.4
Tallahassee, FL	5,560	3.0	19,535	10.4	32,595	17.4	9,185	4.9	6,290	3.4

PART C—METROPOLITAN STATISTICAL AREA TABLES

C-1 All Workers, by Metropolitan Statistical Area and Occupation Group, 2006-2010—Continued

Metropolitan Statistical Area	Production operative workers Number	Percent	Transportation and material moving operative workers Number	Percent	Laborers and helpers Number	Percent	Protective service workers Number	Percent	Service workers, except protective Number	Percent
Rapid City, SD	2,400	3.7	2,580	4.0	2,395	3.7	1,335	2.0	9,775	15.0
Reading, PA	19,040	9.0	11,560	5.4	9,965	4.7	3,405	1.6	29,170	13.7
Redding, CA	2,265	2.9	3,140	4.0	3,510	4.4	1,930	2.4	12,110	15.2
Reno-Sparks, NV	7,740	3.4	10,685	4.7	8,530	3.8	5,515	2.4	36,750	16.2
Richmond, VA	25,055	3.9	26,060	4.0	20,115	3.1	15,865	2.5	80,025	12.4
Riverside-San Bernardino-Ontario, CA	92,335	4.9	114,505	6.0	95,355	5.0	50,450	2.7	262,680	13.8
Roanoke, VA	10,285	6.5	8,220	5.2	5,630	3.6	2,785	1.8	19,600	12.5
Rochester, MN	5,255	5.1	3,825	3.7	2,940	2.9	1,235	1.2	14,785	14.4
Rochester, NY	29,345	5.5	22,220	4.1	15,850	3.0	10,300	1.9	73,035	13.6
Rockford, IL	18,050	10.3	10,665	6.1	6,670	3.8	2,970	1.7	23,085	13.2
Rocky Mount, NC	6,910	9.5	5,935	8.1	3,655	5.0	1,330	1.8	9,520	13.0
Rome, GA	3,630	8.1	2,030	4.5	1,820	4.0	975	2.2	6,755	15.0
Sacramento-Arden-Arcade-Roseville, CA	28,175	2.7	37,040	3.5	36,935	3.5	24,555	2.3	144,360	13.7
Saginaw-Saginaw Township North, MI	6,730	7.3	4,165	4.5	3,340	3.6	1,570	1.7	16,795	18.1
St. Cloud, MN	7,840	7.4	5,690	5.3	4,950	4.6	1,725	1.6	15,785	14.8
St. George, UT	1,845	3.2	2,680	4.7	2,475	4.3	620	1.1	8,535	14.8
St. Joseph, MO-KS	5,060	8.1	3,490	5.6	2,985	4.8	1,640	2.6	9,135	14.6
St. Louis, MO-IL	69,095	4.7	61,510	4.2	48,040	3.3	25,850	1.8	213,305	14.6
Salem, OR	10,475	5.6	9,110	4.9	14,660	7.9	4,125	2.2	26,685	14.4
Salinas, CA	8,095	4.1	10,260	5.2	30,715	15.7	4,570	2.3	29,145	14.9
Salisbury, MD	2,990	4.8	3,335	5.4	1,950	3.1	1,835	3.0	9,375	15.1
Salt Lake City, UT	27,015	4.7	23,435	4.1	19,195	3.3	10,165	1.8	68,155	11.8
San Angelo, TX	2,495	4.7	2,040	3.9	2,080	3.9	1,275	2.4	9,025	17.1
San Antonio-New Braunfels, TX	34,600	3.5	40,065	4.0	34,075	3.4	21,080	2.1	144,095	14.5
San Diego-Carlsbad-San Marcos, CA	48,165	3.2	44,830	3.0	49,390	3.3	32,855	2.2	212,950	14.2
Sandusky, OH	3,490	8.9	2,000	5.1	1,595	4.0	730	1.9	6,380	16.2
San Francisco-Oakland-Fremont, CA	60,985	2.6	72,425	3.1	64,845	2.8	36,800	1.6	304,585	13.2
San Jose-Sunnyvale-Santa Clara, CA	37,315	4.0	28,290	3.0	26,760	2.8	13,350	1.4	106,670	11.3
San Luis Obispo-Paso Robles, CA	3,535	2.7	2,985	2.3	6,285	4.8	4,240	3.2	19,890	15.2
Santa Barbara-Santa Maria-Goleta, CA	6,200	3.0	7,475	3.6	20,860	9.9	4,155	2.0	33,315	15.9
Santa Cruz-Watsonville, CA	4,190	3.0	4,090	3.0	10,005	7.3	2,255	1.6	19,445	14.1
Santa Fe, NM	1,450	1.9	1,660	2.2	2,695	3.5	1,380	1.8	11,805	15.4
Santa Rosa-Petaluma, CA	9,875	3.9	8,360	3.3	13,705	5.4	4,450	1.8	36,385	14.4
Savannah, GA	6,570	4.0	8,920	5.4	6,140	3.8	3,870	2.4	24,055	14.7
Scranton-Wilkes-Barre, PA	18,805	6.7	17,010	6.1	11,195	4.0	6,445	2.3	41,200	14.7
Seattle-Tacoma-Bellevue, WA	62,980	3.4	72,090	3.9	57,880	3.2	29,570	1.6	234,925	12.8
Sebastian-Vero Beach, FL	1,960	3.2	2,045	3.3	4,300	7.0	935	1.5	9,750	15.8
Sheboygan, WI	8,600	13.6	3,650	5.8	3,595	5.7	860	1.4	8,920	14.1
Sherman-Denison, TX	4,360	7.4	3,090	5.3	2,455	4.2	915	1.6	8,995	15.3
Shreveport-Bossier City, LA	8,060	4.3	9,310	4.9	7,945	4.2	5,200	2.7	31,860	16.8
Sioux City, IA-NE-SD	8,395	11.0	4,135	5.4	4,150	5.4	1,020	1.3	10,595	13.9
Sioux Falls, SD	7,855	6.1	5,595	4.4	5,110	4.0	2,135	1.7	15,785	12.3
South Bend-Mishawaka, IN-MI	14,195	8.8	8,585	5.3	6,395	4.0	2,230	1.4	22,610	14.0
Spartanburg, SC	13,310	9.9	8,910	6.6	5,540	4.1	1,830	1.4	17,900	13.3
Spokane, WA	9,460	4.1	9,155	4.0	8,145	3.5	4,435	1.9	37,565	16.3
Springfield, IL	3,215	2.9	3,535	3.1	3,015	2.7	2,370	2.1	16,600	14.8
Springfield, MA	20,470	5.8	14,985	4.2	12,265	3.5	7,535	2.1	54,925	15.5
Springfield, MO	11,340	5.2	11,135	5.1	8,680	4.0	3,475	1.6	32,700	14.9
Springfield, OH	6,120	9.0	4,095	6.0	3,085	4.5	1,430	2.1	10,125	14.8
State College, PA	3,115	4.1	2,380	3.1	2,815	3.7	1,325	1.7	11,925	15.6
Steubenville-Weirton, OH-WV	3,660	6.3	3,390	5.8	2,530	4.4	1,220	2.1	10,225	17.6
Stockton, CA	18,275	5.9	20,300	6.6	22,330	7.2	7,405	2.4	40,355	13.0
Sumter, SC	4,725	10.2	3,095	6.7	1,590	3.4	1,380	3.0	7,080	15.3
Syracuse, NY	15,985	4.8	13,770	4.1	10,730	3.2	6,890	2.1	48,675	14.6
Tallahassee, FL	3,335	1.8	5,025	2.7	6,115	3.3	5,190	2.8	26,935	14.4

C-1 All Workers, by Metropolitan Statistical Area and Occupation Group, 2006–2010—*Continued*

Metropolitan Statistical Area	Total who worked in the last 5 years Number	Percent	Management, business, and financial workers Number	Percent	Science, engineering, and computer professionals Number	Percent	Health care practitioner professionals Number	Percent	Other professional workers Number	Percent
Tampa–St. Petersburg–Clearwater, FL	1,372,115	100.0	174,760	12.7	46,060	3.4	48,275	3.5	137,105	10.0
Terre Haute, IN	82,160	100.0	6,520	7.9	1,630	2.0	2,950	3.6	7,690	9.4
Texarkana, TX–Texarkana, AR	62,730	100.0	5,580	8.9	855	1.4	2,065	3.3	5,605	8.9
Toledo, OH	341,835	100.0	32,470	9.5	8,745	2.6	13,460	3.9	33,515	9.8
Topeka, KS	121,930	100.0	14,105	11.6	3,165	2.6	4,290	3.5	13,985	11.5
Trenton–Ewing, NJ	192,230	100.0	26,655	13.9	12,310	6.4	5,645	2.9	26,020	13.5
Tucson, AZ	460,140	100.0	50,410	11.0	21,155	4.6	16,685	3.6	50,770	11.0
Tulsa, OK	467,790	100.0	54,005	11.5	15,700	3.4	13,825	3.0	48,130	10.3
Tuscaloosa, AL	102,505	100.0	8,830	8.6	2,285	2.2	3,840	3.7	11,285	11.0
Tyler, TX	100,970	100.0	9,655	9.6	2,160	2.1	4,685	4.6	9,830	9.7
Utica–Rome, NY	144,850	100.0	14,860	10.3	3,520	2.4	5,835	4.0	15,350	10.6
Valdosta, GA	64,870	100.0	5,565	8.6	895	1.4	1,780	2.7	5,700	8.8
Vallejo–Fairfield, CA	204,570	100.0	23,485	11.5	7,025	3.4	6,555	3.2	18,905	9.2
Victoria, TX	56,975	100.0	5,390	9.5	980	1.7	1,875	3.3	4,965	8.7
Vineland–Millville–Bridgeton, NJ	73,170	100.0	5,280	7.2	1,170	1.6	1,535	2.1	6,455	8.8
Virginia Beach–Norfolk–Newport News, VA–NC	824,655	100.0	98,550	12.0	38,480	4.7	24,785	3.0	90,095	10.9
Visalia–Porterville, CA	189,285	100.0	14,865	7.9	1,925	1.0	3,975	2.1	14,760	7.8
Waco, TX	112,195	100.0	10,585	9.4	2,220	2.0	3,020	2.7	12,810	11.4
Warner Robins, GA	65,710	100.0	9,035	13.7	3,290	5.0	1,935	2.9	6,850	10.4
Washington–Arlington–Alexandria, DC–VA–MD–WV	3,067,930	100.0	550,405	17.9	277,420	9.0	87,360	2.8	469,555	15.3
Waterloo–Cedar Falls, IA	89,345	100.0	8,820	9.9	2,470	2.8	2,445	2.7	9,625	10.8
Wausau, WI	74,835	100.0	8,065	10.8	2,030	2.7	2,825	3.8	6,205	8.3
Wenatchee–East Wenatchee, WA	53,045	100.0	5,165	9.7	1,285	2.4	1,750	3.3	4,430	8.4
Wheeling, WV–OH	69,265	100.0	5,420	7.8	930	1.3	3,580	5.2	6,295	9.1
Wichita, KS	317,885	100.0	33,590	10.6	13,550	4.3	10,665	3.4	32,545	10.2
Wichita Falls, TX	69,795	100.0	5,960	8.5	1,165	1.7	2,250	3.2	6,980	10.0
Williamsport, PA	59,280	100.0	4,975	8.4	1,140	1.9	1,900	3.2	5,170	8.7
Wilmington, NC	179,945	100.0	20,605	11.5	4,600	2.6	6,745	3.7	18,230	10.1
Winchester, VA–WV	64,905	100.0	7,105	10.9	2,310	3.6	2,185	3.4	5,650	8.7
Winston-Salem, NC	235,660	100.0	27,005	11.5	6,910	2.9	9,835	4.2	25,245	10.7
Worcester, MA	425,625	100.0	56,375	13.2	25,160	5.9	16,770	3.9	47,400	11.1
Yakima, WA	109,320	100.0	8,975	8.2	1,565	1.4	2,940	2.7	8,450	7.7
York–Hanover, PA	231,710	100.0	25,860	11.2	8,020	3.5	6,820	2.9	20,825	9.0
Youngstown–Warren–Boardman, OH–PA	270,585	100.0	22,685	8.4	5,155	1.9	10,435	3.9	23,330	8.6
Yuba City, CA	74,740	100.0	7,175	9.6	1,660	2.2	1,565	2.1	5,900	7.9
Yuma, AZ	76,590	100.0	6,380	8.3	1,200	1.6	1,420	1.9	5,755	7.5

C-1 All Workers, by Metropolitan Statistical Area and Occupation Group, 2006–2010—Continued

Metropolitan Statistical Area	Technicians Number	Technicians Percent	Sales workers Number	Sales workers Percent	Administrative support workers Number	Administrative support workers Percent	Construction and extractive craft workers Number	Construction and extractive craft workers Percent	Installation, maintenance, and repair craft workers Number	Installation, maintenance, and repair craft workers Percent
Tampa–St. Petersburg–Clearwater, FL	41,580	3.0	187,225	13.6	233,725	17.0	76,330	5.6	54,930	4.0
Terre Haute, IN	2,895	3.5	9,195	11.2	11,690	14.2	5,045	6.1	3,745	4.6
Texarkana, TX–Texarkana, AR	2,100	3.3	7,900	12.6	9,045	14.4	3,950	6.3	4,180	6.7
Toledo, OH	8,930	2.6	36,030	10.5	50,940	14.9	16,800	4.9	15,105	4.4
Topeka, KS	3,325	2.7	11,425	9.4	22,005	18.0	6,820	5.6	5,750	4.7
Trenton–Ewing, NJ	5,530	2.9	19,210	10.0	33,040	17.2	7,750	4.0	4,915	2.6
Tucson, AZ	13,745	3.0	51,060	11.1	75,675	16.4	29,670	6.4	19,055	4.1
Tulsa, OK	14,165	3.0	53,290	11.4	76,180	16.3	29,490	6.3	26,675	5.7
Tuscaloosa, AL	3,695	3.6	10,680	10.4	14,425	14.1	7,650	7.5	4,540	4.4
Tyler, TX	3,480	3.4	12,130	12.0	15,490	15.3	6,365	6.3	3,480	3.4
Utica–Rome, NY	4,840	3.3	14,265	9.8	25,390	17.5	7,210	5.0	5,955	4.1
Valdosta, GA	1,840	2.8	8,030	12.4	10,640	16.4	3,960	6.1	3,255	5.0
Vallejo–Fairfield, CA	5,980	2.9	22,510	11.0	35,190	17.2	13,455	6.6	9,220	4.5
Victoria, TX	2,400	4.2	6,345	11.1	7,970	14.0	4,895	8.6	3,370	5.9
Vineland–Millville–Bridgeton, NJ	1,995	2.7	6,910	9.4	11,470	15.7	3,860	5.3	3,055	4.2
Virginia Beach–Norfolk–Newport News, VA–NC	25,805	3.1	94,900	11.5	130,720	15.9	53,630	6.5	38,955	4.7
Visalia–Porterville, CA	3,500	1.8	17,620	9.3	24,560	13.0	9,990	5.3	7,340	3.9
Waco, TX	3,505	3.1	12,215	10.9	18,300	16.3	6,365	5.7	5,430	4.8
Warner Robins, GA	2,375	3.6	6,835	10.4	9,880	15.0	3,740	5.7	3,575	5.4
Washington–Arlington–Alexandria, DC–VA–MD–WV	74,485	2.4	268,005	8.7	451,390	14.7	154,815	5.0	83,350	2.7
Waterloo–Cedar Falls, IA	2,300	2.6	9,140	10.2	13,790	15.4	4,060	4.5	3,750	4.2
Wausau, WI	2,230	3.0	7,045	9.4	11,840	15.8	3,995	5.3	3,730	5.0
Wenatchee–East Wenatchee, WA	1,130	2.1	5,690	10.7	7,285	13.7	3,490	6.6	2,110	4.0
Wheeling, WV–OH	2,215	3.2	7,560	10.9	10,600	15.3	5,865	8.5	3,175	4.6
Wichita, KS	8,755	2.8	32,285	10.2	49,975	15.7	20,855	6.6	17,625	5.5
Wichita Falls, TX	2,550	3.7	8,300	11.9	10,365	14.9	4,175	6.0	3,820	5.5
Williamsport, PA	2,120	3.6	6,245	10.5	9,430	15.9	3,650	6.2	3,050	5.1
Wilmington, NC	5,415	3.0	23,490	13.1	24,005	13.3	15,260	8.5	7,150	4.0
Winchester, VA–WV	1,875	2.9	6,855	10.6	8,995	13.9	5,215	8.0	3,155	4.9
Winston–Salem, NC	7,030	3.0	26,365	11.2	35,335	15.0	14,010	5.9	10,485	4.4
Worcester, MA	12,670	3.0	44,735	10.5	65,580	15.4	21,670	5.1	17,045	4.0
Yakima, WA	2,295	2.1	10,840	9.9	14,190	13.0	4,555	4.2	4,115	3.8
York–Hanover, PA	7,165	3.1	23,575	10.2	36,625	15.8	13,650	5.9	12,630	5.5
Youngstown–Warren–Boardman, OH–PA	8,685	3.2	30,420	11.2	39,020	14.4	15,005	5.5	13,315	4.9
Yuba City, CA	2,090	2.8	7,965	10.7	11,420	15.3	5,920	7.9	3,170	4.2
Yuma, AZ	1,815	2.4	7,640	10.0	11,685	15.3	5,185	6.8	4,185	5.5

C-1 All Workers, by Metropolitan Statistical Area and Occupation Group, 2006–2010—*Continued*

Metropolitan Statistical Area	Production operative workers Number	Percent	Transportation and material moving operative workers Number	Percent	Laborers and helpers Number	Percent	Protective service workers Number	Percent	Service workers, except protective Number	Percent
Tampa–St. Petersburg–Clearwater, FL	43,255	3.2	48,485	3.5	48,725	3.6	26,100	1.9	190,030	13.8
Terre Haute, IN	7,185	8.7	4,660	5.7	3,410	4.2	2,495	3.0	12,370	15.1
Texarkana, TX–Texarkana, AR	4,175	6.7	3,205	5.1	2,965	4.7	1,555	2.5	8,795	14.0
Toledo, OH	25,255	7.4	20,480	6.0	15,195	4.4	6,200	1.8	53,245	15.6
Topeka, KS	6,095	5.0	5,175	4.2	4,450	3.6	2,915	2.4	17,445	14.3
Trenton–Ewing, NJ	6,270	3.3	7,665	4.0	6,885	3.6	4,690	2.4	23,890	12.4
Tucson, AZ	12,895	2.8	14,770	3.2	15,970	3.5	13,250	2.9	70,440	15.3
Tulsa, OK	27,325	5.8	19,790	4.2	15,100	3.2	7,385	1.6	63,835	13.6
Tuscaloosa, AL	7,585	7.4	5,245	5.1	4,685	4.6	1,950	1.9	14,595	14.2
Tyler, TX	6,490	6.4	4,930	4.9	4,330	4.3	1,800	1.8	15,285	15.1
Utica–Rome, NY	8,535	5.9	6,440	4.4	5,080	3.5	4,675	3.2	21,675	15.0
Valdosta, GA	3,120	4.8	3,915	6.0	3,090	4.8	2,130	3.3	9,920	15.3
Vallejo–Fairfield, CA	7,810	3.8	9,250	4.5	7,815	3.8	6,380	3.1	28,555	14.0
Victoria, TX	4,075	7.2	2,895	5.1	2,370	4.2	1,005	1.8	8,035	14.1
Vineland–Millville–Bridgeton, NJ	5,555	7.6	5,375	7.3	4,135	5.7	3,215	4.4	11,670	15.9
Virginia Beach–Norfolk–Newport News, VA–NC	30,755	3.7	31,935	3.9	25,465	3.1	21,860	2.7	111,185	13.5
Visalia–Porterville, CA	11,320	6.0	12,115	6.4	33,275	17.6	5,880	3.1	24,995	13.2
Waco, TX	6,940	6.2	5,855	5.2	4,455	4.0	1,915	1.7	17,365	15.5
Warner Robins, GA	2,815	4.3	2,390	3.6	2,145	3.3	1,590	2.4	8,380	12.8
Washington–Arlington–Alexandria, DC–VA–MD–WV	42,855	1.4	84,890	2.8	62,455	2.0	83,110	2.7	352,010	11.5
Waterloo–Cedar Falls, IA	7,640	8.6	4,650	5.2	4,210	4.7	1,200	1.3	14,430	16.2
Wausau, WI	8,530	11.4	3,720	5.0	3,970	5.3	675	0.9	9,620	12.9
Wenatchee–East Wenatchee, WA	2,520	4.8	2,990	5.6	5,880	11.1	1,005	1.9	8,070	15.2
Wheeling, WV–OH	3,045	4.4	3,565	5.1	3,295	4.8	1,375	2.0	11,765	17.0
Wichita, KS	24,370	7.7	12,375	3.9	10,000	3.1	5,515	1.7	43,395	13.7
Wichita Falls, TX	4,450	6.4	3,585	5.1	2,545	3.6	2,200	3.2	10,990	15.7
Williamsport, PA	5,115	8.6	3,075	5.2	3,690	6.2	1,240	2.1	7,770	13.1
Wilmington, NC	6,610	3.7	7,150	4.0	7,390	4.1	3,505	1.9	28,275	15.7
Winchester, VA–WV	3,625	5.6	3,585	5.5	4,145	6.4	1,235	1.9	8,455	13.0
Winston–Salem, NC	15,170	6.4	12,020	5.1	8,205	3.5	4,025	1.7	30,830	13.1
Worcester, MA	21,145	5.0	16,975	4.0	12,400	2.9	9,375	2.2	54,865	12.9
Yakima, WA	7,935	7.3	8,460	7.7	16,565	15.2	1,620	1.5	15,870	14.5
York–Hanover, PA	18,820	8.1	12,625	5.4	10,710	4.6	3,905	1.7	28,880	12.5
Youngstown–Warren–Boardman, OH–PA	21,910	8.1	15,535	5.7	12,330	4.6	5,275	1.9	43,280	16.0
Yuba City, CA	3,370	4.5	4,315	5.8	6,565	8.8	1,525	2.0	10,315	13.8
Yuma, AZ	3,085	4.0	4,535	5.9	8,110	10.6	3,360	4.4	11,430	14.9

PART C—METROPOLITAN STATISTICAL AREA TABLES

C-2 All Workers, by Metropolitan Statistical Area, Sex, Race, and Hispanic or Latino Origin, 2006–2010

Metropolitan Statistical Area	Total who worked in the last 5 years	Male Number	Male Percent	Female Number	Female Percent	Hispanic or Latino Number	Hispanic or Latino Percent	White alone, not Hispanic or Latino Number	White alone, not Hispanic or Latino Percent
Abilene, TX	76,065	38,995	51.3	37,070	48.7	14,210	18.7	55,145	72.5
Akron, OH	375,270	194,810	51.9	180,460	48.1	4,850	1.3	319,030	85.0
Albany, GA	72,015	35,590	49.4	36,425	50.6	1,305	1.8	34,505	47.9
Albany-Schenectady-Troy, NY	463,990	237,810	51.3	226,175	48.7	15,220	3.3	398,385	85.9
Albuquerque, NM	434,835	228,170	52.5	206,665	47.5	185,290	42.6	203,145	46.7
Alexandria, LA	68,565	34,620	50.5	33,945	49.5	1,655	2.4	46,615	68.0
Allentown-Bethlehem-Easton, PA-NJ	420,055	221,040	52.6	199,015	47.4	41,605	9.9	347,975	82.8
Altoona, PA	62,595	32,995	52.7	29,600	47.3	570	0.9	60,795	97.1
Amarillo, TX	126,675	69,020	54.5	57,655	45.5	27,665	21.8	87,310	68.9
Ames, IA	52,425	28,115	53.6	24,310	46.4	1,375	2.6	46,520	88.7
Anchorage, AK	195,975	103,930	53.0	92,050	47.0	10,935	5.6	142,365	72.6
Anderson, IN	62,785	32,960	52.5	29,825	47.5	1,480	2.4	56,005	89.2
Anderson, SC	88,610	46,250	52.2	42,360	47.8	2,280	2.6	70,300	79.3
Ann Arbor, MI	183,005	93,930	51.3	89,075	48.7	6,385	3.5	138,110	75.5
Anniston-Oxford, AL	54,030	28,915	53.5	25,115	46.5	1,740	3.2	40,255	74.5
Appleton, WI	125,605	66,390	52.9	59,210	47.1	3,310	2.6	116,615	92.8
Asheville, NC	208,775	108,615	52.0	100,155	48.0	11,980	5.7	183,145	87.7
Athens-Clarke County, GA	92,445	48,175	52.1	44,270	47.9	6,050	6.5	65,860	71.2
Atlanta-Sandy Springs-Marietta, GA	2,730,620	1,433,060	52.5	1,297,560	47.5	252,345	9.2	1,459,145	53.4
Atlantic City-Hammonton, NJ	142,735	73,440	51.5	69,295	48.5	21,835	15.3	87,040	61.0
Auburn-Opelika, AL	67,545	35,730	52.9	31,820	47.1	2,220	3.3	48,095	71.2
Augusta-Richmond County, GA-SC	250,335	127,810	51.1	122,520	48.9	9,795	3.9	147,425	58.9
Austin-Round Rock-San Marcos, TX	897,255	491,955	54.8	405,300	45.2	255,270	28.5	525,250	58.5
Bakersfield-Delano, CA	351,110	195,870	55.8	155,240	44.2	160,415	45.7	151,525	43.2
Baltimore-Towson, MD	1,438,090	726,565	50.5	711,525	49.5	59,155	4.1	913,890	63.5
Bangor, ME	80,010	41,510	51.9	38,500	48.1	635	0.8	76,725	95.9
Barnstable Town, MA	110,965	56,875	51.3	54,090	48.7	2,215	2.0	102,940	92.8
Baton Rouge, LA	396,310	206,000	52.0	190,305	48.0	12,490	3.2	241,900	61.0
Battle Creek, MI	66,535	34,290	51.5	32,245	48.5	2,460	3.7	55,610	83.6
Bay City, MI	54,050	27,745	51.3	26,305	48.7	2,235	4.1	50,110	92.7
Beaumont-Port Arthur, TX	175,070	95,010	54.3	80,060	45.7	18,240	10.4	110,550	63.1
Bellingham, WA	103,245	54,530	52.8	48,715	47.2	6,850	6.6	87,095	84.4
Bend, OR	79,735	42,390	53.2	37,340	46.8	5,360	6.7	71,445	89.6
Billings, MT	83,515	43,515	52.1	40,005	47.9	2,940	3.5	75,965	91.0
Binghamton, NY	126,275	66,500	52.7	59,775	47.3	2,995	2.4	114,670	90.8
Birmingham-Hoover, AL	555,515	291,630	52.5	263,890	47.5	21,985	4.0	373,375	67.2
Bismarck, ND	60,895	30,920	50.8	29,975	49.2	585	1.0	57,830	95.0
Blacksburg-Christiansburg-Radford, VA	79,795	42,000	52.6	37,795	47.4	1,745	2.2	70,965	88.9
Bloomington, IN	94,460	49,770	52.7	44,690	47.3	2,370	2.5	85,415	90.4
Bloomington-Normal, IL	93,065	47,590	51.1	45,475	48.9	3,335	3.6	79,250	85.2
Boise City-Nampa, ID	301,285	163,435	54.2	137,850	45.8	31,775	10.5	254,785	84.6
Boston-Cambridge-Quincy, MA-NH	2,498,630	1,283,405	51.4	1,215,230	48.6	190,335	7.6	1,945,880	77.9
Boulder, CO	163,620	89,430	54.7	74,190	45.3	17,790	10.9	135,305	82.7
Bowling Green, KY	63,565	33,200	52.2	30,365	47.8	2,070	3.3	54,005	85.0
Bremerton-Silverdale, WA	119,380	63,790	53.4	55,590	46.6	6,245	5.2	97,315	81.5
Bridgeport-Stamford-Norwalk, CT	475,550	255,060	53.6	220,485	46.4	76,845	16.2	319,915	67.3
Brownsville-Harlingen, TX	150,325	80,695	53.7	69,630	46.3	131,430	87.4	16,535	11.0
Brunswick, GA	53,415	28,265	52.9	25,145	47.1	2,440	4.6	37,760	70.7
Buffalo-Niagara Falls, NY	575,645	294,005	51.1	281,640	48.9	16,495	2.9	483,465	84.0
Burlington, NC	77,335	39,820	51.5	37,515	48.5	7,600	9.8	53,365	69.0
Burlington-South Burlington, VT	121,470	62,625	51.6	58,845	48.4	1,920	1.6	113,855	93.7
Canton-Massillon, OH	206,355	107,070	51.9	99,290	48.1	2,785	1.3	186,930	90.6
Cape Coral-Fort Myers, FL	285,560	153,450	53.7	132,110	46.3	52,615	18.4	202,950	71.1
Cape Girardeau-Jackson, MO-IL	48,915	25,470	52.1	23,445	47.9	745	1.5	43,555	89.0
Carson City, NV	28,715	15,775	54.9	12,935	45.0	5,365	18.7	21,225	73.9

C-2 **All Workers, by Metropolitan Statistical Area, Sex, Race, and Hispanic or Latino Origin, 2006–2010**—*Continued*

Metropolitan Statistical Area	Black alone, not Hispanic or Latino Number	Percent	American Indian and Alaska Native alone, not Hispanic or Latino Number	Percent	Asian alone, not Hispanic or Latino Number	Percent	Native Hawaiian and Other Pacific Islander alone, not Hispanic or Latino Number	Percent	Two or more races, not Hispanic or Latino Number	Percent
Abilene, TX	3,970	5.2	295	0.4	945	1.2	100	0.1	1,400	1.8
Akron, OH	39,860	10.6	505	0.1	7,045	1.9	60	0.0	3,920	1.0
Albany, GA	34,985	48.6	175	0.2	580	0.8	0	0.0	465	0.6
Albany–Schenectady–Troy, NY	27,430	5.9	1,245	0.3	13,480	2.9	125	0.0	8,105	1.7
Albuquerque, NM	10,115	2.3	20,165	4.6	9,310	2.1	345	0.1	6,460	1.5
Alexandria, LA	18,160	26.5	485	0.7	895	1.3	10	0.0	745	1.1
Allentown–Bethlehem–Easton, PA–NJ	16,120	3.8	290	0.1	9,985	2.4	4	0.0	4,065	1.0
Altoona, PA	645	1.0	30	0.0	300	0.5	0	0.0	260	0.4
Amarillo, TX	6,820	5.4	560	0.4	2,745	2.2	105	0.1	1,475	1.2
Ames, IA	1,105	2.1	60	0.1	2,860	5.5	0	0.0	504	1.0
Anchorage, AK	8,140	4.2	9,480	4.8	11,660	5.9	2,365	1.2	11,020	5.6
Anderson, IN	3,460	5.5	35	0.1	260	0.4	20	0.0	1,525	2.4
Anderson, SC	14,520	16.4	90	0.1	655	0.7	15	0.0	750	0.8
Ann Arbor, MI	20,335	11.1	420	0.2	13,440	7.3	25	0.0	4,300	2.3
Anniston–Oxford, AL	10,910	20.2	225	0.4	445	0.8	20	0.0	429	0.8
Appleton, WI	755	0.6	1,405	1.1	2,665	2.1	15	0.0	845	0.7
Asheville, NC	9,260	4.4	735	0.4	1,710	0.8	75	0.0	1,870	0.9
Athens–Clarke County, GA	16,530	17.9	110	0.1	2,605	2.8	4	0.0	1,285	1.4
Atlanta–Sandy Springs–Marietta, GA	854,050	31.3	5,285	0.2	125,010	4.6	1,250	0.0	33,535	1.2
Atlantic City–Hammonton, NJ	20,380	14.3	175	0.1	11,060	7.7	150	0.1	2,095	1.5
Auburn–Opelika, AL	14,600	21.6	155	0.2	1,850	2.7	45	0.1	580	0.9
Augusta–Richmond County, GA–SC	84,605	33.8	495	0.2	4,580	1.8	355	0.1	3,085	1.2
Austin–Round Rock–San Marcos, TX	61,560	6.9	2,425	0.3	40,105	4.5	565	0.1	12,075	1.3
Bakersfield–Delano, CA	15,440	4.4	2,390	0.7	14,905	4.2	285	0.1	6,150	1.8
Baltimore–Towson, MD	377,950	26.3	2,880	0.2	61,960	4.3	480	0.0	21,770	1.5
Bangor, ME	415	0.5	710	0.9	785	1.0	0	0.0	740	0.9
Barnstable Town, MA	2,130	1.9	580	0.5	1,025	0.9	15	0.0	2,055	1.9
Baton Rouge, LA	130,370	32.9	610	0.2	7,750	2.0	25	0.0	3,170	0.8
Battle Creek, MI	6,000	9.0	295	0.4	1,165	1.8	10	0.0	1,000	1.5
Bay City, MI	580	1.1	135	0.2	330	0.6	30	0.1	620	1.1
Beaumont–Port Arthur, TX	39,785	22.7	605	0.3	4,275	2.4	65	0.0	1,550	0.9
Bellingham, WA	980	0.9	2,400	2.3	3,635	3.5	230	0.2	2,055	2.0
Bend, OR	235	0.3	640	0.8	805	1.0	115	0.1	1,135	1.4
Billings, MT	530	0.6	2,320	2.8	680	0.8	115	0.1	965	1.2
Binghamton, NY	3,725	2.9	345	0.3	3,045	2.4	30	0.0	1,465	1.2
Birmingham–Hoover, AL	148,170	26.7	1,100	0.2	7,245	1.3	110	0.0	3,525	0.6
Bismarck, ND	220	0.4	1,580	2.6	160	0.3	15	0.0	510	0.8
Blacksburg–Christiansburg–Radford, VA	3,225	4.0	45	0.1	2,885	3.6	15	0.0	920	1.2
Bloomington, IN	2,450	2.6	195	0.2	2,600	2.8	25	0.0	1,410	1.5
Bloomington–Normal, IL	6,140	6.6	95	0.1	3,305	3.6	15	0.0	920	1.0
Boise City–Nampa, ID	2,250	0.7	1,530	0.5	5,585	1.9	675	0.2	4,685	1.6
Boston–Cambridge–Quincy, MA–NH	159,575	6.4	2,820	0.1	154,180	6.2	750	0.0	45,095	1.8
Boulder, CO	1,090	0.7	535	0.3	6,280	3.8	30	0.0	2,590	1.6
Bowling Green, KY	5,390	8.5	60	0.1	1,360	2.1	90	0.1	585	0.9
Bremerton–Silverdale, WA	3,300	2.8	1,530	1.3	6,070	5.1	1,100	0.9	3,820	3.2
Bridgeport–Stamford–Norwalk, CT	49,015	10.3	605	0.1	21,425	4.5	125	0.0	7,615	1.6
Brownsville–Harlingen, TX	665	0.4	220	0.1	1,085	0.7	25	0.0	370	0.2
Brunswick, GA	12,115	22.7	0	0.0	645	1.2	0	0.0	455	0.9
Buffalo–Niagara Falls, NY	55,740	9.7	2,720	0.5	11,535	2.0	95	0.0	5,595	1.0
Burlington, NC	14,360	18.6	205	0.3	895	1.2	100	0.1	805	1.0
Burlington–South Burlington, VT	1,490	1.2	475	0.4	2,245	1.8	4	0.0	1,479	1.2
Canton–Massillon, OH	12,595	6.1	450	0.2	1,515	0.7	0	0.0	2,085	1.0
Cape Coral–Fort Myers, FL	22,085	7.7	475	0.2	4,285	1.5	15	0.0	3,140	1.1
Cape Girardeau–Jackson, MO–IL	3,485	7.1	45	0.1	595	1.2	25	0.1	460	0.9
Carson City, NV	450	1.6	415	1.4	625	2.2	85	0.3	560	2.0

C-2 All Workers, by Metropolitan Statistical Area, Sex, Race, and Hispanic or Latino Origin, 2006–2010—Continued

Metropolitan Statistical Area	Total who worked in the last 5 years	Male Number	Male Percent	Female Number	Female Percent	Hispanic or Latino Number	Hispanic or Latino Percent	White alone, not Hispanic or Latino Number	White alone, not Hispanic or Latino Percent
Casper, WY	39,835	21,515	54.0	18,320	46.0	2,415	6.1	36,130	90.7
Cedar Rapids, IA	139,835	73,165	52.3	66,670	47.7	2,785	2.0	129,700	92.8
Champaign–Urbana, IL	122,820	64,190	52.3	58,625	47.7	5,295	4.3	96,135	78.3
Charleston, WV	140,600	74,460	53.0	66,140	47.0	1,100	0.8	129,990	92.5
Charleston–North Charleston–Summerville, SC	331,985	171,575	51.7	160,410	48.3	15,435	4.6	220,125	66.3
Charlotte–Gastonia–Rock Hill, NC–SC	914,240	479,120	52.4	435,120	47.6	77,825	8.5	586,325	64.1
Charlottesville, VA	101,390	51,605	50.9	49,785	49.1	4,510	4.4	79,655	78.6
Chattanooga, TN–GA	264,805	138,640	52.4	126,165	47.6	7,960	3.0	214,705	81.1
Cheyenne, WY	46,530	24,260	52.1	22,265	47.9	5,040	10.8	39,455	84.8
Chicago–Joliet–Naperville, IL–IN–WI	4,936,190	2,614,675	53.0	2,321,515	47.0	910,725	18.4	2,941,695	59.6
Chico, CA	102,290	54,325	53.1	47,970	46.9	13,215	12.9	79,600	77.8
Cincinnati–Middletown, OH–KY–IN	1,100,965	572,635	52.0	528,330	48.0	23,300	2.1	926,485	84.2
Clarksville, TN–KY	111,840	56,355	50.4	55,480	49.6	6,040	5.4	79,785	71.3
Cleveland, TN	54,860	29,810	54.3	25,050	45.7	1,985	3.6	49,670	90.5
Cleveland–Elyria–Mentor, OH	1,081,565	551,230	51.0	530,335	49.0	41,460	3.8	816,825	75.5
Coeur d'Alene, ID	68,645	36,065	52.5	32,585	47.5	2,225	3.2	64,075	93.3
College Station–Bryan, TX	109,230	59,890	54.8	49,345	45.2	21,425	19.6	70,805	64.8
Colorado Springs, CO	309,975	163,590	52.8	146,385	47.2	39,355	12.7	235,265	75.9
Columbia, MO	94,885	47,405	50.0	47,480	50.0	2,570	2.7	79,855	84.2
Columbia, SC	382,825	194,210	50.7	188,615	49.3	15,960	4.2	233,895	61.1
Columbus, GA–AL	127,345	59,865	47.0	67,480	53.0	6,015	4.7	65,555	51.5
Columbus, IN	39,535	21,565	54.5	17,970	45.5	2,130	5.4	34,910	88.3
Columbus, OH	962,935	501,435	52.1	461,500	47.9	29,100	3.0	763,480	79.3
Corpus Christi, TX	200,510	106,785	53.3	93,720	46.7	110,220	55.0	78,680	39.2
Corvallis, OR	43,835	23,145	52.8	20,690	47.2	2,570	5.9	37,430	85.4
Crestview–Fort Walton Beach–Destin, FL	89,110	46,735	52.4	42,375	47.6	5,675	6.4	70,205	78.8
Cumberland, MD–WV	46,650	24,375	52.3	22,275	47.7	430	0.9	43,985	94.3
Dallas–Fort Worth–Arlington, TX	3,240,180	1,760,155	54.3	1,480,025	45.7	783,825	24.2	1,779,100	54.9
Dalton, GA	67,210	38,320	57.0	28,890	43.0	16,385	24.4	47,510	70.7
Danville, IL	38,480	20,405	53.0	18,075	47.0	1,480	3.8	32,090	83.4
Danville, VA	51,165	26,070	51.0	25,095	49.0	1,175	2.3	32,725	64.0
Davenport–Moline–Rock Island, IA–IL	195,505	101,730	52.0	93,770	48.0	12,570	6.4	167,565	85.7
Dayton, OH	426,345	218,800	51.3	207,545	48.7	7,710	1.8	347,680	81.5
Decatur, AL	73,280	40,295	55.0	32,985	45.0	4,025	5.5	57,875	79.0
Decatur, IL	53,620	27,675	51.6	25,945	48.4	960	1.8	44,185	82.4
Deltona–Daytona Beach–Ormond Beach, FL	231,415	119,785	51.8	111,630	48.2	22,960	9.9	179,550	77.6
Denver–Aurora–Broomfield, CO	1,371,265	737,920	53.8	633,340	46.2	257,635	18.8	968,740	70.6
Des Moines–West Des Moines, IA	313,020	161,950	51.7	151,070	48.3	16,265	5.2	273,000	87.2
Detroit–Warren–Livonia, MI	2,166,755	1,127,370	52.0	1,039,385	48.0	72,825	3.4	1,552,140	71.6
Dothan, AL	67,090	35,505	52.9	31,590	47.1	1,695	2.5	50,505	75.3
Dover, DE	75,070	37,650	50.2	37,425	49.9	3,625	4.8	51,805	69.0
Dubuque, IA	51,700	26,650	51.5	25,050	48.5	910	1.8	48,950	94.7
Duluth, MN–WI	143,840	75,005	52.1	68,835	47.9	1,605	1.1	135,005	93.9
Durham–Chapel Hill, NC	261,205	130,600	50.0	130,605	50.0	26,510	10.1	150,905	57.8
Eau Claire, WI	89,845	46,705	52.0	43,140	48.0	1,170	1.3	85,245	94.9
El Centro, CA	67,320	36,390	54.1	30,930	45.9	53,135	78.9	10,975	16.3
Elizabethtown, KY	50,330	25,745	51.2	24,580	48.8	1,620	3.2	41,530	82.5
Elkhart–Goshen, IN	102,705	56,270	54.8	46,430	45.2	12,340	12.0	82,985	80.8
Elmira, NY	42,540	21,705	51.0	20,835	49.0	630	1.5	38,775	91.1
El Paso, TX	328,945	177,930	54.1	151,020	45.9	267,450	81.3	47,685	14.5
Erie, PA	138,180	71,800	52.0	66,380	48.0	3,400	2.5	125,095	90.5
Eugene–Springfield, OR	176,945	93,205	52.7	83,735	47.3	10,920	6.2	153,885	87.0
Evansville, IN–KY	183,595	96,750	52.7	86,845	47.3	2,965	1.6	167,570	91.3
Fairbanks, AK	47,555	24,910	52.4	22,645	47.6	2,335	4.9	36,985	77.8
Fargo, ND–MN	121,190	63,570	52.5	57,620	47.5	2,460	2.0	112,115	92.5

C-2 All Workers, by Metropolitan Statistical Area, Sex, Race, and Hispanic or Latino Origin, 2006–2010—*Continued*

Metropolitan Statistical Area	Black alone, not Hispanic or Latino Number	Percent	American Indian and Alaska Native alone, not Hispanic or Latino Number	Percent	Asian alone, not Hispanic or Latino Number	Percent	Native Hawaiian and Other Pacific Islander alone, not Hispanic or Latino Number	Percent	Two or more races, not Hispanic or Latino Number	Percent
Casper, WY	175	0.4	225	0.6	285	0.7	0	0.0	605	1.5
Cedar Rapids, IA	3,505	2.5	260	0.2	2,055	1.5	105	0.1	1,420	1.0
Champaign–Urbana, IL	11,805	9.6	245	0.2	7,955	6.5	0	0.0	1,385	1.1
Charleston, WV	4,955	3.5	135	0.1	1,270	0.9	25	0.0	3,130	2.2
Charleston–North Charleston–Summerville, SC	84,890	25.6	1,320	0.4	5,720	1.7	245	0.1	4,250	1.3
Charlotte–Gastonia–Rock Hill, NC–SC	208,680	22.8	3,045	0.3	27,305	3.0	550	0.1	10,510	1.1
Charlottesville, VA	12,440	12.3	70	0.1	3,290	3.2	20	0.0	1,405	1.4
Chattanooga, TN–GA	35,205	13.3	485	0.2	3,665	1.4	130	0.0	2,655	1.0
Cheyenne, WY	725	1.6	340	0.7	465	1.0	10	0.0	500	1.1
Chicago–Joliet–Naperville, IL–IN–WI	743,655	15.1	4,925	0.1	284,490	5.8	1,155	0.0	49,550	1.0
Chico, CA	1,375	1.3	845	0.8	3,835	3.7	215	0.2	3,200	3.1
Cincinnati–Middletown, OH–KY–IN	118,180	10.7	1,485	0.1	20,105	1.8	370	0.0	11,035	1.0
Clarksville, TN–KY	21,820	19.5	495	0.4	1,960	1.8	205	0.2	1,535	1.4
Cleveland, TN	2,015	3.7	155	0.3	445	0.8	70	0.1	515	0.9
Cleveland–Elyria–Mentor, OH	189,530	17.5	1,785	0.2	22,215	2.1	30	0.0	9,720	0.9
Coeur d'Alene, ID	195	0.3	465	0.7	270	0.4	85	0.1	1,340	2.0
College Station–Bryan, TX	10,990	10.1	165	0.2	4,655	4.3	25	0.0	1,160	1.1
Colorado Springs, CO	16,990	5.5	1,810	0.6	7,965	2.6	735	0.2	7,855	2.5
Columbia, MO	7,465	7.9	255	0.3	3,055	3.2	80	0.1	1,600	1.7
Columbia, SC	121,970	31.9	785	0.2	6,125	1.6	45	0.0	4,040	1.1
Columbus, GA–AL	51,290	40.3	240	0.2	2,110	1.7	265	0.2	1,875	1.5
Columbus, IN	665	1.7	90	0.2	1,290	3.3	0	0.0	455	1.2
Columbus, OH	125,655	13.0	1,455	0.2	29,275	3.0	120	0.0	13,855	1.4
Corpus Christi, TX	6,380	3.2	325	0.2	3,145	1.6	10	0.0	1,745	0.9
Corvallis, OR	365	0.8	345	0.8	2,140	4.9	55	0.1	925	2.1
Crestview–Fort Walton Beach–Destin, FL	7,785	8.7	600	0.7	2,885	3.2	35	0.0	1,920	2.2
Cumberland, MD–WV	1,530	3.3	60	0.1	245	0.5	15	0.0	390	0.8
Dallas–Fort Worth–Arlington, TX	455,530	14.1	10,745	0.3	166,375	5.1	3,020	0.1	41,590	1.3
Dalton, GA	2,155	3.2	245	0.4	540	0.8	15	0.0	365	0.5
Danville, IL	4,015	10.4	15	0.0	220	0.6	0	0.0	665	1.7
Danville, VA	16,730	32.7	10	0.0	270	0.5	15	0.0	234	0.5
Davenport–Moline–Rock Island, IA–IL	10,040	5.1	350	0.2	2,625	1.3	30	0.0	2,325	1.2
Dayton, OH	56,750	13.3	570	0.1	7,430	1.7	30	0.0	6,170	1.4
Decatur, AL	8,295	11.3	1,420	1.9	335	0.5	35	0.0	1,290	1.8
Decatur, IL	7,065	13.2	105	0.2	555	1.0	0	0.0	750	1.4
Deltona–Daytona Beach–Ormond Beach, FL	21,630	9.3	460	0.2	3,505	1.5	60	0.0	3,255	1.4
Denver–Aurora–Broomfield, CO	66,965	4.9	6,715	0.5	48,215	3.5	1,215	0.1	21,775	1.6
Des Moines–West Des Moines, IA	11,275	3.6	375	0.1	9,290	3.0	80	0.0	2,740	0.9
Detroit–Warren–Livonia, MI	435,160	20.1	5,710	0.3	73,625	3.4	425	0.0	26,875	1.2
Dothan, AL	13,585	20.2	225	0.3	520	0.8	20	0.0	545	0.8
Dover, DE	16,205	21.6	395	0.5	1,670	2.2	75	0.1	1,300	1.7
Dubuque, IA	575	1.1	75	0.1	355	0.7	55	0.1	780	1.5
Duluth, MN–WI	1,135	0.8	3,135	2.2	1,370	1.0	15	0.0	1,574	1.1
Durham–Chapel Hill, NC	67,980	26.0	670	0.3	10,720	4.1	50	0.0	4,365	1.7
Eau Claire, WI	720	0.8	385	0.4	1,785	2.0	60	0.1	470	0.5
El Centro, CA	1,440	2.1	445	0.7	990	1.5	15	0.0	325	0.5
Elizabethtown, KY	5,030	10.0	175	0.3	820	1.6	145	0.3	1,005	2.0
Elkhart–Goshen, IN	4,930	4.8	285	0.3	1,255	1.2	60	0.1	860	0.8
Elmira, NY	1,950	4.6	50	0.1	465	1.1	25	0.1	645	1.5
El Paso, TX	7,595	2.3	665	0.2	3,555	1.1	85	0.0	1,915	0.6
Erie, PA	6,420	4.6	195	0.1	1,495	1.1	35	0.0	1,540	1.1
Eugene–Springfield, OR	1,685	1.0	1,775	1.0	3,735	2.1	405	0.2	4,540	2.6
Evansville, IN–KY	9,395	5.1	240	0.1	1,505	0.8	10	0.0	1,915	1.0
Fairbanks, AK	1,855	3.9	2,770	5.8	1,510	3.2	145	0.3	1,950	4.1
Fargo, ND–MN	1,865	1.5	1,440	1.2	2,185	1.8	160	0.1	960	0.8

PART C—METROPOLITAN STATISTICAL AREA TABLES

C-2 All Workers, by Metropolitan Statistical Area, Sex, Race, and Hispanic or Latino Origin, 2006–2010—Continued

Metropolitan Statistical Area	Total who worked in the last 5 years	Male Number	Male Percent	Female Number	Female Percent	Hispanic or Latino Number	Hispanic or Latino Percent	White alone, not Hispanic or Latino Number	White alone, not Hispanic or Latino Percent
Farmington, NM	55,275	30,575	55.3	24,705	44.7	9,375	17.0	27,420	49.6
Fayetteville, NC	149,930	69,865	46.6	80,065	53.4	11,655	7.8	71,765	47.9
Fayetteville–Springdale–Rogers, AR–MO	224,940	121,990	54.2	102,945	45.8	28,700	12.8	178,175	79.2
Flagstaff, AZ	69,245	35,730	51.6	33,515	48.4	8,765	12.7	43,170	62.3
Flint, MI	198,305	100,775	50.8	97,530	49.2	5,115	2.6	153,735	77.5
Florence, SC	97,465	48,745	50.0	48,720	50.0	1,855	1.9	57,420	58.9
Florence–Muscle Shoals, AL	67,340	35,535	52.8	31,805	47.2	1,215	1.8	57,640	85.6
Fond du Lac, WI	56,855	29,855	52.5	27,000	47.5	2,055	3.6	53,245	93.7
Fort Collins–Loveland, CO	163,945	87,935	53.6	76,005	46.4	14,810	9.0	142,260	86.8
Fort Smith, AR–OK	135,200	72,435	53.6	62,765	46.4	9,420	7.0	106,975	79.1
Fort Wayne, IN	213,850	113,015	52.8	100,835	47.2	10,120	4.7	178,750	83.6
Fresno, CA	415,700	226,940	54.6	188,760	45.4	194,830	46.9	157,705	37.9
Gadsden, AL	45,955	24,780	53.9	21,170	46.1	1,355	2.9	37,360	81.3
Gainesville, FL	132,310	67,640	51.1	64,670	48.9	10,280	7.8	91,705	69.3
Gainesville, GA	84,825	47,010	55.4	37,815	44.6	19,700	23.2	57,660	68.0
Glens Falls, NY	65,280	33,995	52.1	31,285	47.9	880	1.3	63,260	96.9
Goldsboro, NC	55,700	28,160	50.6	27,540	49.4	5,015	9.0	32,480	58.3
Grand Forks, ND–MN	55,125	28,930	52.5	26,195	47.5	1,550	2.8	50,885	92.3
Grand Junction, CO	73,175	39,645	54.2	33,525	45.8	8,290	11.3	62,380	85.2
Grand Rapids–Wyoming, MI	400,815	211,795	52.8	189,025	47.2	27,940	7.0	333,000	83.1
Great Falls, MT	38,710	19,475	50.3	19,235	49.7	1,035	2.7	34,930	90.2
Greeley, CO	126,475	69,150	54.7	57,325	45.3	29,420	23.3	92,185	72.9
Green Bay, WI	165,850	87,530	52.8	78,315	47.2	7,245	4.4	149,130	89.9
Greensboro–High Point, NC	370,400	192,310	51.9	178,090	48.1	23,495	6.3	240,470	64.9
Greenville, NC	94,940	47,240	49.8	47,700	50.2	5,145	5.4	57,520	60.6
Greenville–Mauldin–Easley, SC	311,995	165,785	53.1	146,210	46.9	20,075	6.4	232,535	74.5
Gulfport–Biloxi, MS	115,200	61,295	53.2	53,900	46.8	5,220	4.5	84,370	73.2
Hagerstown–Martinsburg, MD–WV	136,740	72,570	53.1	64,170	46.9	3,515	2.6	120,530	88.1
Hanford–Corcoran, CA	60,000	35,980	60.0	24,020	40.0	28,205	47.0	24,845	41.4
Harrisburg–Carlisle, PA	290,055	150,295	51.8	139,765	48.2	10,315	3.6	242,885	83.7
Harrisonburg, VA	60,145	31,525	52.4	28,620	47.6	5,095	8.5	51,260	85.2
Hartford–West Hartford–East Hartford, CT	653,940	335,505	51.3	318,435	48.7	67,020	10.2	490,435	75.0
Hattiesburg, MS	67,460	35,240	52.2	32,220	47.8	1,560	2.3	46,775	69.3
Hickory–Lenoir–Morganton, NC	179,730	96,330	53.6	83,400	46.4	10,125	5.6	152,700	85.0
Hinesville–Fort Stewart, GA	31,935	15,625	48.9	16,305	51.1	2,390	7.5	14,650	45.9
Holland–Grand Haven, MI	138,265	73,525	53.2	64,740	46.8	10,350	7.5	121,370	87.8
Honolulu, HI	462,845	239,510	51.7	223,330	48.3	29,595	6.4	88,095	19.0
Hot Springs, AR	42,500	22,440	52.8	20,060	47.2	1,580	3.7	36,650	86.2
Houma–Bayou Cane–Thibodaux, LA	96,810	54,180	56.0	42,630	44.0	3,615	3.7	74,170	76.6
Houston–Sugar Land–Baytown, TX	2,915,695	1,618,265	55.5	1,297,435	44.5	928,900	31.9	1,279,095	43.9
Huntington–Ashland, WV–KY–OH	125,340	65,995	52.7	59,345	47.3	840	0.7	119,270	95.2
Huntsville, AL	205,625	110,010	53.5	95,615	46.5	8,565	4.2	141,895	69.0
Idaho Falls, ID	60,035	33,305	55.5	26,730	44.5	5,685	9.5	52,635	87.7
Indianapolis–Carmel, IN	910,210	473,180	52.0	437,030	48.0	47,190	5.2	705,940	77.6
Iowa City, IA	87,665	45,245	51.6	42,425	48.4	3,350	3.8	76,680	87.5
Ithaca, NY	53,015	27,565	52.0	25,450	48.0	2,165	4.1	44,330	83.6
Jackson, MI	76,035	39,825	52.4	36,210	47.6	1,885	2.5	68,650	90.3
Jackson, MS	263,165	131,715	50.1	131,450	49.9	5,720	2.2	136,870	52.0
Jackson, TN	57,240	29,125	50.9	28,115	49.1	1,675	2.9	37,075	64.8
Jacksonville, FL	678,960	351,725	51.8	327,235	48.2	42,350	6.2	465,415	68.5
Jacksonville, NC	61,645	29,460	47.8	32,185	52.2	5,225	8.5	42,545	69.0
Janesville, WI	85,060	44,175	51.9	40,885	48.1	5,160	6.1	74,895	88.0
Jefferson City, MO	75,350	38,415	51.0	36,935	49.0	1,460	1.9	68,930	91.5
Johnson City, TN	93,205	49,215	52.8	43,990	47.2	2,255	2.4	86,745	93.1
Johnstown, PA	67,230	35,255	52.4	31,975	47.6	645	1.0	64,385	95.8

C-2 **All Workers, by Metropolitan Statistical Area, Sex, Race, and Hispanic or Latino Origin, 2006–2010**—*Continued*

Metropolitan Statistical Area	Black alone, not Hispanic or Latino Number	Percent	American Indian and Alaska Native alone, not Hispanic or Latino Number	Percent	Asian alone, not Hispanic or Latino Number	Percent	Native Hawaiian and Other Pacific Islander alone, not Hispanic or Latino Number	Percent	Two or more races, not Hispanic or Latino Number	Percent
Farmington, NM	345	0.6	17,335	31.4	335	0.6	4	0.0	465	0.8
Fayetteville, NC	55,000	36.7	2,675	1.8	3,425	2.3	470	0.3	4,940	3.3
Fayetteville–Springdale–Rogers, AR–MO	4,200	1.9	3,380	1.5	4,810	2.1	1,515	0.7	4,150	1.8
Flagstaff, AZ	710	1.0	14,400	20.8	960	1.4	70	0.1	1,160	1.7
Flint, MI	33,245	16.8	905	0.5	1,880	0.9	65	0.0	3,355	1.7
Florence, SC	36,350	37.3	130	0.1	920	0.9	0	0.0	795	0.8
Florence–Muscle Shoals, AL	7,430	11.0	295	0.4	400	0.6	0	0.0	364	0.5
Fond du Lac, WI	585	1.0	175	0.3	440	0.8	4	0.0	349	0.6
Fort Collins–Loveland, CO	1,115	0.7	575	0.4	2,975	1.8	175	0.1	2,030	1.2
Fort Smith, AR–OK	4,445	3.3	4,220	3.1	3,440	2.5	15	0.0	6,680	4.9
Fort Wayne, IN	18,075	8.5	445	0.2	3,925	1.8	65	0.0	2,470	1.2
Fresno, CA	17,185	4.1	1,805	0.4	35,945	8.6	590	0.1	7,645	1.8
Gadsden, AL	6,490	14.1	135	0.3	245	0.5	15	0.0	355	0.8
Gainesville, FL	21,950	16.6	265	0.2	6,125	4.6	110	0.1	1,880	1.4
Gainesville, GA	5,265	6.2	135	0.2	1,605	1.9	15	0.0	440	0.5
Glens Falls, NY	310	0.5	145	0.2	295	0.5	20	0.0	370	0.6
Goldsboro, NC	16,935	30.4	75	0.1	570	1.0	25	0.0	600	1.1
Grand Forks, ND–MN	660	1.2	930	1.7	605	1.1	4	0.0	495	0.9
Grand Junction, CO	445	0.6	365	0.5	470	0.6	120	0.2	1,100	1.5
Grand Rapids–Wyoming, MI	25,755	6.4	1,305	0.3	7,590	1.9	130	0.0	5,090	1.3
Great Falls, MT	335	0.9	1,270	3.3	295	0.8	0	0.0	840	2.2
Greeley, CO	1,100	0.9	745	0.6	1,530	1.2	65	0.1	1,430	1.1
Green Bay, WI	1,865	1.1	3,205	1.9	2,990	1.8	90	0.1	1,330	0.8
Greensboro–High Point, NC	91,700	24.8	1,475	0.4	9,360	2.5	45	0.0	3,855	1.0
Greenville, NC	29,725	31.3	210	0.2	1,250	1.3	0	0.0	1,090	1.1
Greenville–Mauldin–Easley, SC	50,425	16.2	595	0.2	5,470	1.8	235	0.1	2,660	0.9
Gulfport–Biloxi, MS	20,475	17.8	385	0.3	3,315	2.9	60	0.1	1,380	1.2
Hagerstown–Martinsburg, MD–WV	9,600	7.0	210	0.2	1,505	1.1	15	0.0	1,370	1.0
Hanford–Corcoran, CA	3,435	5.7	295	0.5	2,460	4.1	35	0.1	724	1.2
Harrisburg–Carlisle, PA	24,585	8.5	355	0.1	7,940	2.7	140	0.0	3,835	1.3
Harrisonburg, VA	2,335	3.9	90	0.1	990	1.6	95	0.2	280	0.5
Hartford–West Hartford–East Hartford, CT	62,505	9.6	725	0.1	24,050	3.7	265	0.0	8,940	1.4
Hattiesburg, MS	17,850	26.5	125	0.2	770	1.1	0	0.0	375	0.6
Hickory–Lenoir–Morganton, NC	11,125	6.2	370	0.2	4,095	2.3	20	0.0	1,290	0.7
Hinesville–Fort Stewart, GA	13,680	42.8	140	0.4	455	1.4	120	0.4	490	1.5
Holland–Grand Haven, MI	1,645	1.2	315	0.2	3,170	2.3	55	0.0	1,365	1.0
Honolulu, HI	7,030	1.5	535	0.1	222,480	48.1	38,610	8.3	76,490	16.5
Hot Springs, AR	3,330	7.8	225	0.5	325	0.8	0	0.0	389	0.9
Houma–Bayou Cane–Thibodaux, LA	14,005	14.5	3,060	3.2	1,000	1.0	4	0.0	955	1.0
Houston–Sugar Land–Baytown, TX	483,850	16.6	5,650	0.2	189,210	6.5	1,485	0.1	27,500	0.9
Huntington–Ashland, WV–KY–OH	3,240	2.6	115	0.1	730	0.6	15	0.0	1,125	0.9
Huntsville, AL	45,875	22.3	1,345	0.7	4,330	2.1	180	0.1	3,435	1.7
Idaho Falls, ID	145	0.2	410	0.7	440	0.7	40	0.1	675	1.1
Indianapolis–Carmel, IN	124,770	13.7	1,465	0.2	18,805	2.1	180	0.0	11,865	1.3
Iowa City, IA	2,620	3.0	155	0.2	3,940	4.5	35	0.0	890	1.0
Ithaca, NY	1,540	2.9	150	0.3	3,895	7.3	25	0.0	910	1.7
Jackson, MI	4,245	5.6	100	0.1	515	0.7	10	0.0	635	0.8
Jackson, MS	116,310	44.2	220	0.1	2,835	1.1	40	0.0	1,180	0.4
Jackson, TN	17,415	30.4	100	0.2	530	0.9	40	0.1	415	0.7
Jacksonville, FL	135,580	20.0	1,855	0.3	23,550	3.5	440	0.1	9,770	1.4
Jacksonville, NC	10,780	17.5	330	0.5	1,130	1.8	160	0.3	1,475	2.4
Janesville, WI	3,005	3.5	105	0.1	790	0.9	30	0.0	1,075	1.3
Jefferson City, MO	3,465	4.6	170	0.2	630	0.8	25	0.0	665	0.9
Johnson City, TN	2,625	2.8	240	0.3	760	0.8	4	0.0	585	0.6
Johnstown, PA	1,435	2.1	55	0.1	405	0.6	35	0.1	264	0.4

PART C—METROPOLITAN STATISTICAL AREA TABLES

C-2 All Workers, by Metropolitan Statistical Area, Sex, Race, and Hispanic or Latino Origin, 2006–2010—Continued

Metropolitan Statistical Area	Total who worked in the last 5 years	Male Number	Male Percent	Female Number	Female Percent	Hispanic or Latino Number	Hispanic or Latino Percent	White alone, not Hispanic or Latino Number	White alone, not Hispanic or Latino Percent
Jonesboro, AR	58,115	30,555	52.6	27,560	47.4	2,100	3.6	49,440	85.1
Joplin, MO	86,305	46,085	53.4	40,220	46.6	4,205	4.9	76,665	88.8
Kalamazoo–Portage, MI	170,005	88,545	52.1	81,460	47.9	7,780	4.6	142,455	83.8
Kankakee–Bradley, IL	56,315	28,860	51.2	27,455	48.8	4,560	8.1	43,535	77.3
Kansas City, MO–KS	1,074,060	559,170	52.1	514,890	47.9	73,800	6.9	836,910	77.9
Kennewick–Pasco–Richland, WA	116,110	64,465	55.5	51,640	44.5	27,710	23.9	81,580	70.3
Killeen–Temple–Fort Hood, TX	161,360	79,840	49.5	81,520	50.5	27,995	17.3	94,255	58.4
Kingsport–Bristol–Bristol, TN–VA	143,115	76,700	53.6	66,415	46.4	1,635	1.1	137,020	95.7
Kingston, NY	95,990	49,885	52.0	46,105	48.0	6,700	7.0	82,740	86.2
Knoxville, TN	347,520	185,350	53.3	162,170	46.7	10,560	3.0	307,265	88.4
Kokomo, IN	46,070	23,905	51.9	22,165	48.1	965	2.1	42,260	91.7
La Crosse, WI–MN	74,895	38,145	50.9	36,750	49.1	950	1.3	70,305	93.9
Lafayette, IN	103,435	55,695	53.8	47,740	46.2	6,305	6.1	88,360	85.4
Lafayette, LA	138,620	73,225	52.8	65,395	47.2	4,385	3.2	97,755	70.5
Lake Charles, LA	95,640	50,965	53.3	44,675	46.7	2,170	2.3	69,930	73.1
Lake Havasu City–Kingman, AZ	84,485	44,740	53.0	39,745	47.0	12,120	14.3	67,855	80.3
Lakeland–Winter Haven, FL	272,540	143,945	52.8	128,590	47.2	43,820	16.1	183,080	67.2
Lancaster, PA	266,220	144,645	54.3	121,575	45.7	18,060	6.8	232,945	87.5
Lansing–East Lansing, MI	243,125	123,240	50.7	119,885	49.3	12,545	5.2	197,980	81.4
Laredo, TX	104,070	57,000	54.8	47,070	45.2	98,665	94.8	4,255	4.1
Las Cruces, NM	92,900	48,895	52.6	44,005	47.4	58,605	63.1	29,975	32.3
Las Vegas–Paradise, NV	997,625	546,120	54.7	451,505	45.3	261,430	26.2	520,300	52.2
Lawrence, KS	63,700	32,555	51.1	31,145	48.9	3,095	4.9	53,945	84.7
Lawton, OK	50,730	24,920	49.1	25,810	50.9	4,805	9.5	31,085	61.3
Lebanon, PA	68,330	36,410	53.3	31,920	46.7	4,475	6.5	61,680	90.3
Lewiston, ID–WA	29,785	15,445	51.9	14,340	48.1	845	2.8	27,105	91.0
Lewiston–Auburn, ME	57,170	29,205	51.1	27,965	48.9	705	1.2	54,420	95.2
Lexington–Fayette, KY	251,860	132,280	52.5	119,575	47.5	12,745	5.1	205,630	81.6
Lima, OH	53,195	28,250	53.1	24,945	46.9	925	1.7	45,815	86.1
Lincoln, NE	171,905	89,385	52.0	82,525	48.0	7,745	4.5	151,880	88.4
Little Rock–North Little Rock–Conway, AR	349,855	179,480	51.3	170,370	48.7	14,635	4.2	251,680	71.9
Logan, UT–ID	60,630	33,990	56.1	26,645	43.9	5,095	8.4	53,290	87.9
Longview, TX	100,375	54,400	54.2	45,975	45.8	11,550	11.5	69,690	69.4
Longview, WA	46,705	25,480	54.6	21,225	45.4	3,120	6.7	41,010	87.8
Los Angeles–Long Beach–Santa Ana, CA	6,510,485	3,560,030	54.7	2,950,455	45.3	2,686,765	41.3	2,289,425	35.2
Louisville/Jefferson County, KY–IN	653,945	340,170	52.0	313,780	48.0	22,570	3.5	532,545	81.4
Lubbock, TX	142,160	74,745	52.6	67,415	47.4	41,960	29.5	86,675	61.0
Lynchburg, VA	125,640	65,230	51.9	60,410	48.1	2,550	2.0	98,975	78.8
Macon, GA	104,525	53,505	51.2	51,020	48.8	2,645	2.5	58,385	55.9
Madera–Chowchilla, CA	59,670	34,540	57.9	25,130	42.1	29,265	49.0	25,995	43.6
Madison, WI	330,970	171,335	51.8	159,635	48.2	15,200	4.6	288,865	87.3
Manchester–Nashua, NH	227,720	121,180	53.2	106,545	46.8	9,445	4.1	204,755	89.9
Manhattan, KS	57,660	29,240	50.7	28,420	49.3	3,335	5.8	46,350	80.4
Mankato–North Mankato, MN	57,325	30,170	52.6	27,155	47.4	1,430	2.5	53,210	92.8
Mansfield, OH	59,780	30,545	51.1	29,235	48.9	555	0.9	54,075	90.5
McAllen–Edinburg–Mission, TX	297,890	164,565	55.2	133,325	44.8	271,030	91.0	21,480	7.2
Medford, OR	98,875	51,195	51.8	47,680	48.2	9,910	10.0	84,155	85.1
Memphis, TN–MS–AR	655,310	332,495	50.7	322,815	49.3	28,920	4.4	329,985	50.4
Merced, CA	109,910	62,140	56.5	47,770	43.5	56,770	51.7	39,740	36.2
Miami–Fort Lauderdale–Pompano Beach, FL	2,809,665	1,468,715	52.3	1,340,950	47.7	1,177,275	41.9	995,920	35.4
Michigan City–La Porte, IN	54,160	28,470	52.6	25,690	47.4	2,230	4.1	47,205	87.2
Midland, TX	68,290	37,795	55.3	30,500	44.7	23,140	33.9	39,325	57.6
Milwaukee–Waukesha–West Allis, WI	826,530	424,610	51.4	401,920	48.6	62,970	7.6	619,985	75.0
Minneapolis–St. Paul–Bloomington, MN–WI	1,840,260	959,110	52.1	881,155	47.9	80,680	4.4	1,527,900	83.0
Missoula, MT	59,355	31,145	52.5	28,215	47.5	1,165	2.0	55,245	93.1

C-2 All Workers, by Metropolitan Statistical Area, Sex, Race, and Hispanic or Latino Origin, 2006-2010—Continued

Metropolitan Statistical Area	Black alone, not Hispanic or Latino Number	Percent	American Indian and Alaska Native alone, not Hispanic or Latino Number	Percent	Asian alone, not Hispanic or Latino Number	Percent	Native Hawaiian and Other Pacific Islander alone, not Hispanic or Latino Number	Percent	Two or more races, not Hispanic or Latino Number	Percent
Jonesboro, AR	5,480	9.4	170	0.3	575	1.0	0	0.0	345	0.6
Joplin, MO	1,210	1.4	1,635	1.9	815	0.9	280	0.3	1,485	1.7
Kalamazoo–Portage, MI	13,825	8.1	635	0.4	2,640	1.6	100	0.1	2,575	1.5
Kankakee–Bradley, IL	7,280	12.9	155	0.3	480	0.9	20	0.0	280	0.5
Kansas City, MO–KS	118,385	11.0	3,905	0.4	23,720	2.2	1,050	0.1	16,295	1.5
Kennewick–Pasco–Richland, WA	1,455	1.3	905	0.8	2,990	2.6	150	0.1	1,320	1.1
Killeen–Temple–Fort Hood, TX	29,775	18.5	705	0.4	4,040	2.5	895	0.6	3,695	2.3
Kingsport–Bristol–Bristol, TN–VA	2,505	1.8	250	0.2	785	0.5	35	0.0	880	0.6
Kingston, NY	3,630	3.8	230	0.2	1,415	1.5	0	0.0	1,275	1.3
Knoxville, TN	20,355	5.9	865	0.2	5,050	1.5	150	0.0	3,280	0.9
Kokomo, IN	2,150	4.7	45	0.1	320	0.7	10	0.0	315	0.7
La Crosse, WI–MN	760	1.0	255	0.3	2,130	2.8	4	0.0	489	0.7
Lafayette, IN	2,940	2.8	105	0.1	4,630	4.5	40	0.0	1,050	1.0
Lafayette, LA	33,580	24.2	415	0.3	1,690	1.2	95	0.1	695	0.5
Lake Charles, LA	20,930	21.9	390	0.4	1,085	1.1	25	0.0	1,105	1.2
Lake Havasu City–Kingman, AZ	765	0.9	1,145	1.4	1,005	1.2	140	0.2	1,465	1.7
Lakeland–Winter Haven, FL	36,925	13.5	650	0.2	4,880	1.8	150	0.1	3,030	1.1
Lancaster, PA	7,615	2.9	275	0.1	4,640	1.7	100	0.0	2,590	1.0
Lansing–East Lansing, MI	19,120	7.9	665	0.3	7,645	3.1	120	0.0	5,060	2.1
Laredo, TX	400	0.4	60	0.1	535	0.5	10	0.0	150	0.1
Las Cruces, NM	1,435	1.5	765	0.8	1,110	1.2	15	0.0	990	1.1
Las Vegas–Paradise, NV	93,330	9.4	4,820	0.5	89,355	9.0	6,510	0.7	21,880	2.2
Lawrence, KS	2,250	3.5	1,070	1.7	2,155	3.4	45	0.1	1,145	1.8
Lawton, OK	8,660	17.1	2,550	5.0	1,020	2.0	355	0.7	2,260	4.5
Lebanon, PA	935	1.4	55	0.1	670	1.0	0	0.0	520	0.8
Lewiston, ID–WA	120	0.4	780	2.6	290	1.0	45	0.2	595	2.0
Lewiston–Auburn, ME	405	0.7	90	0.2	350	0.6	0	0.0	1,200	2.1
Lexington–Fayette, KY	24,935	9.9	535	0.2	5,640	2.2	135	0.1	2,235	0.9
Lima, OH	5,430	10.2	45	0.1	415	0.8	0	0.0	565	1.1
Lincoln, NE	4,645	2.7	705	0.4	4,975	2.9	110	0.1	1,845	1.1
Little Rock–North Little Rock–Conway, AR	73,325	21.0	1,245	0.4	5,180	1.5	65	0.0	3,725	1.1
Logan, UT–ID	335	0.6	355	0.6	1,025	1.7	90	0.1	435	0.7
Longview, TX	16,870	16.8	390	0.4	830	0.8	110	0.1	930	0.9
Longview, WA	220	0.5	400	0.9	750	1.6	95	0.2	1,115	2.4
Los Angeles–Long Beach–Santa Ana, CA	423,265	6.5	13,510	0.2	970,035	14.9	17,155	0.3	110,340	1.7
Louisville/Jefferson County, KY–IN	80,720	12.3	1,090	0.2	9,670	1.5	365	0.1	6,995	1.1
Lubbock, TX	8,510	6.0	570	0.4	3,010	2.1	85	0.1	1,350	0.9
Lynchburg, VA	21,190	16.9	300	0.2	1,355	1.1	10	0.0	1,255	1.0
Macon, GA	40,915	39.1	210	0.2	1,445	1.4	4	0.0	920	0.9
Madera–Chowchilla, CA	1,640	2.7	585	1.0	1,315	2.2	55	0.1	815	1.4
Madison, WI	10,890	3.3	695	0.2	11,195	3.4	20	0.0	4,105	1.2
Manchester–Nashua, NH	3,865	1.7	330	0.1	6,990	3.1	85	0.0	2,255	1.0
Manhattan, KS	4,280	7.4	295	0.5	2,070	3.6	90	0.2	1,245	2.2
Mankato–North Mankato, MN	895	1.6	80	0.1	1,070	1.9	0	0.0	640	1.1
Mansfield, OH	4,000	6.7	235	0.4	375	0.6	0	0.0	535	0.9
McAllen–Edinburg–Mission, TX	1,075	0.4	150	0.1	3,390	1.1	0	0.0	760	0.3
Medford, OR	365	0.4	630	0.6	1,310	1.3	160	0.2	2,350	2.4
Memphis, TN–MS–AR	275,220	42.0	1,150	0.2	12,945	2.0	195	0.0	6,890	1.1
Merced, CA	3,320	3.0	575	0.5	7,650	7.0	365	0.3	1,495	1.4
Miami–Fort Lauderdale–Pompano Beach, FL	532,585	19.0	3,240	0.1	68,100	2.4	970	0.0	31,580	1.1
Michigan City–La Porte, IN	3,940	7.3	50	0.1	280	0.5	4	0.0	439	0.8
Midland, TX	4,175	6.1	265	0.4	965	1.4	0	0.0	420	0.6
Milwaukee–Waukesha–West Allis, WI	109,835	13.3	3,150	0.4	21,735	2.6	240	0.0	8,615	1.0
Minneapolis–St. Paul–Bloomington, MN–WI	108,525	5.9	8,525	0.5	88,190	4.8	750	0.0	25,685	1.4
Missoula, MT	130	0.2	1,215	2.0	585	1.0	85	0.1	930	1.6

PART C—METROPOLITAN STATISTICAL AREA TABLES

C-2 All Workers, by Metropolitan Statistical Area, Sex, Race, and Hispanic or Latino Origin, 2006–2010—Continued

Metropolitan Statistical Area	Total who worked in the last 5 years	Male Number	Male Percent	Female Number	Female Percent	Hispanic or Latino Number	Hispanic or Latino Percent	White alone, not Hispanic or Latino Number	White alone, not Hispanic or Latino Percent
Mobile, AL	193,015	100,355	52.0	92,660	48.0	4,465	2.3	121,075	62.7
Modesto, CA	237,095	130,485	55.0	106,615	45.0	90,315	38.1	121,490	51.2
Monroe, LA	81,880	41,770	51.0	40,115	49.0	1,555	1.9	53,725	65.6
Monroe, MI	77,790	41,175	52.9	36,615	47.1	2,070	2.7	73,055	93.9
Montgomery, AL	177,485	89,605	50.5	87,885	49.5	5,090	2.9	97,690	55.0
Morgantown, WV	61,165	33,050	54.0	28,115	46.0	770	1.3	56,915	93.1
Morristown, TN	64,795	35,455	54.7	29,345	45.3	3,785	5.8	58,285	90.0
Mount Vernon–Anacortes, WA	55,410	29,715	53.6	25,695	46.4	7,650	13.8	45,035	81.3
Muncie, IN	58,470	29,465	50.4	29,010	49.6	925	1.6	52,655	90.1
Muskegon–Norton Shores, MI	82,545	41,915	50.8	40,635	49.2	3,220	3.9	68,350	82.8
Myrtle Beach–North Myrtle Beach–Conway, SC	132,990	69,335	52.1	63,655	47.9	7,970	6.0	105,420	79.3
Napa, CA	68,980	37,700	54.7	31,285	45.4	20,795	30.1	40,930	59.3
Naples–Marco Island, FL	144,445	80,060	55.4	64,385	44.6	40,975	28.4	91,270	63.2
Nashville-Davidson–Murfreesboro–Franklin, TN	819,770	434,795	53.0	384,980	47.0	47,225	5.8	627,135	76.5
New Haven–Milford, CT	465,055	236,300	50.8	228,755	49.2	57,990	12.5	331,340	71.2
New Orleans–Metairie–Kenner, LA	558,690	293,065	52.5	265,625	47.5	44,675	8.0	324,410	58.1
New York–Northern New Jersey–Long Island, NY–NJ–PA	9,654,290	5,050,260	52.3	4,604,030	47.7	2,069,115	21.4	4,933,525	51.1
Niles–Benton Harbor, MI	78,070	40,560	52.0	37,505	48.0	3,130	4.0	62,825	80.5
North Port–Bradenton–Sarasota, FL	318,635	167,315	52.5	151,320	47.5	35,215	11.1	254,975	80.0
Norwich–New London, CT	143,095	74,565	52.1	68,530	47.9	9,320	6.5	116,855	81.7
Ocala, FL	137,090	69,665	50.8	67,425	49.2	14,335	10.5	101,485	74.0
Ocean City, NJ	48,330	25,520	52.8	22,810	47.2	2,615	5.4	42,355	87.6
Odessa, TX	65,035	36,635	56.3	28,400	43.7	31,180	47.9	30,230	46.5
Ogden–Clearfield, UT	255,640	142,865	55.9	112,775	44.1	27,055	10.6	216,940	84.9
Oklahoma City, OK	624,140	332,050	53.2	292,090	46.8	58,245	9.3	444,300	71.2
Olympia, WA	122,585	62,220	50.8	60,365	49.2	6,970	5.7	99,460	81.1
Omaha–Council Bluffs, NE–IA	465,810	241,990	52.0	223,820	48.0	33,130	7.1	383,890	82.4
Orlando–Kissimmee–Sanford, FL	1,109,310	583,025	52.6	526,285	47.4	256,520	23.1	624,810	56.3
Oshkosh–Neenah, WI	90,270	46,370	51.4	43,900	48.6	2,245	2.5	84,705	93.8
Owensboro, KY	53,730	28,440	52.9	25,295	47.1	1,090	2.0	50,010	93.1
Oxnard–Thousand Oaks–Ventura, CA	415,150	228,165	55.0	186,985	45.0	152,145	36.6	217,580	52.4
Palm Bay–Melbourne–Titusville, FL	261,135	139,470	53.4	121,665	46.6	19,960	7.6	207,085	79.3
Palm Coast, FL	38,585	19,535	50.6	19,050	49.4	2,920	7.6	30,575	79.2
Panama City–Lynn Haven–Panama City Beach, FL	82,595	42,755	51.8	39,840	48.2	3,705	4.5	67,955	82.3
Parkersburg–Marietta–Vienna, WV–OH	76,200	40,535	53.2	35,665	46.8	650	0.9	73,685	96.7
Pascagoula, MS	74,930	40,705	54.3	34,225	45.7	2,860	3.8	55,410	73.9
Pensacola–Ferry Pass–Brent, FL	210,670	109,085	51.8	101,585	48.2	8,470	4.0	161,010	76.4
Peoria, IL	191,510	101,235	52.9	90,270	47.1	4,460	2.3	167,530	87.5
Philadelphia–Camden–Wilmington, PA–NJ–DE–MD	3,073,915	1,577,090	51.3	1,496,825	48.7	193,155	6.3	2,144,185	69.8
Phoenix–Mesa–Glendale, AZ	2,009,550	1,098,335	54.7	911,220	45.3	512,570	25.5	1,278,295	63.6
Pine Bluff, AR	44,845	22,365	49.9	22,480	50.1	425	0.9	23,200	51.7
Pittsburgh, PA	1,200,920	626,845	52.2	574,080	47.8	13,000	1.1	1,072,640	89.3
Pittsfield, MA	68,570	34,625	50.5	33,945	49.5	2,215	3.2	63,045	91.9
Pocatello, ID	44,250	23,795	53.8	20,455	46.2	3,030	6.8	38,715	87.5
Portland–South Portland–Biddeford, ME	285,140	146,305	51.3	138,840	48.7	3,715	1.3	271,045	95.1
Portland–Vancouver–Hillsboro, OR–WA	1,169,465	624,985	53.4	544,480	46.6	107,100	9.2	929,010	79.4
Port St. Lucie, FL	192,585	102,450	53.2	90,135	46.8	27,570	14.3	133,525	69.3
Poughkeepsie–Newburgh–Middletown, NY	335,485	177,895	53.0	157,590	47.0	43,325	12.9	248,025	73.9
Prescott, AZ	93,800	48,765	52.0	45,035	48.0	11,865	12.6	77,970	83.1
Providence–New Bedford–Fall River, RI–MA	856,225	436,970	51.0	419,255	49.0	70,885	8.3	710,410	83.0

C-2 All Workers, by Metropolitan Statistical Area, Sex, Race, and Hispanic or Latino Origin, 2006–2010—Continued

Metropolitan Statistical Area	Black alone, not Hispanic or Latino Number	Percent	American Indian and Alaska Native alone, not Hispanic or Latino Number	Percent	Asian alone, not Hispanic or Latino Number	Percent	Native Hawaiian and Other Pacific Islander alone, not Hispanic or Latino Number	Percent	Two or more races, not Hispanic or Latino Number	Percent
Mobile, AL	61,100	31.7	1,055	0.5	3,485	1.8	60	0.0	1,775	0.9
Modesto, CA	5,615	2.4	1,480	0.6	12,595	5.3	1,325	0.6	4,285	1.8
Monroe, LA	25,140	30.7	195	0.2	685	0.8	25	0.0	565	0.7
Monroe, MI	1,375	1.8	145	0.2	305	0.4	30	0.0	805	1.0
Montgomery, AL	70,110	39.5	480	0.3	2,530	1.4	10	0.0	1,580	0.9
Morgantown, WV	1,270	2.1	110	0.2	1,475	2.4	20	0.0	610	1.0
Morristown, TN	1,820	2.8	95	0.1	210	0.3	40	0.1	560	0.9
Mount Vernon–Anacortes, WA	255	0.5	785	1.4	730	1.3	85	0.2	870	1.6
Muncie, IN	2,985	5.1	220	0.4	520	0.9	0	0.0	1,160	2.0
Muskegon–Norton Shores, MI	8,950	10.8	490	0.6	410	0.5	45	0.1	1,085	1.3
Myrtle Beach–North Myrtle Beach–Conway, SC	16,380	12.3	605	0.5	1,490	1.1	75	0.1	1,045	0.8
Napa, CA	1,040	1.5	275	0.4	4,610	6.7	200	0.3	1,130	1.6
Naples–Marco Island, FL	9,195	6.4	340	0.2	1,850	1.3	55	0.0	755	0.5
Nashville-Davidson–Murfreesboro–Franklin, TN	117,090	14.3	1,775	0.2	18,505	2.3	485	0.1	7,560	0.9
New Haven–Milford, CT	51,580	11.1	485	0.1	16,470	3.5	235	0.1	6,955	1.5
New Orleans–Metairie–Kenner, LA	166,205	29.7	2,180	0.4	15,540	2.8	165	0.0	5,515	1.0
New York–Northern New Jersey–Long Island, NY–NJ–PA	1,521,415	15.8	12,070	0.1	970,475	10.1	1,750	0.0	145,935	1.5
Niles–Benton Harbor, MI	9,805	12.6	310	0.4	1,250	1.6	25	0.0	725	0.9
North Port–Bradenton–Sarasota, FL	19,235	6.0	660	0.2	5,230	1.6	120	0.0	3,190	1.0
Norwich–New London, CT	6,790	4.7	610	0.4	6,230	4.4	170	0.1	3,115	2.2
Ocala, FL	16,960	12.4	530	0.4	2,070	1.5	140	0.1	1,575	1.1
Ocean City, NJ	2,290	4.7	175	0.4	455	0.9	0	0.0	445	0.9
Odessa, TX	2,155	3.3	90	0.1	480	0.7	35	0.1	870	1.3
Ogden–Clearfield, UT	2,600	1.0	1,090	0.4	4,150	1.6	810	0.3	2,995	1.2
Oklahoma City, OK	59,105	9.5	20,115	3.2	18,090	2.9	420	0.1	23,860	3.8
Olympia, WA	3,425	2.8	1,620	1.3	6,665	5.4	1,030	0.8	3,420	2.8
Omaha–Council Bluffs, NE–IA	31,355	6.7	930	0.2	8,670	1.9	345	0.1	7,485	1.6
Orlando–Kissimmee–Sanford, FL	160,920	14.5	2,310	0.2	44,640	4.0	1,070	0.1	19,035	1.7
Oshkosh–Neenah, WI	515	0.6	300	0.3	1,975	2.2	0	0.0	535	0.6
Owensboro, KY	1,980	3.7	90	0.2	265	0.5	10	0.0	280	0.5
Oxnard–Thousand Oaks–Ventura, CA	7,135	1.7	1,020	0.2	29,460	7.1	710	0.2	7,100	1.7
Palm Bay–Melbourne–Titusville, FL	22,860	8.8	1,100	0.4	5,915	2.3	195	0.1	4,025	1.5
Palm Coast, FL	3,695	9.6	150	0.4	795	2.1	20	0.1	440	1.1
Panama City–Lynn Haven–Panama City Beach, FL	7,300	8.8	375	0.5	1,765	2.1	45	0.1	1,450	1.8
Parkersburg–Marietta–Vienna, WV–OH	580	0.8	50	0.1	410	0.5	0	0.0	830	1.1
Pascagoula, MS	14,260	19.0	140	0.2	1,440	1.9	30	0.0	790	1.1
Pensacola–Ferry Pass–Brent, FL	29,880	14.2	1,145	0.5	5,355	2.5	340	0.2	4,465	2.1
Peoria, IL	14,200	7.4	120	0.1	3,295	1.7	25	0.0	1,885	1.0
Philadelphia–Camden–Wilmington, PA–NJ–DE–MD	549,650	17.9	3,495	0.1	145,400	4.7	640	0.0	37,395	1.2
Phoenix–Mesa–Glendale, AZ	86,895	4.3	33,545	1.7	68,145	3.4	3,915	0.2	26,180	1.3
Pine Bluff, AR	20,570	45.9	65	0.1	250	0.6	0	0.0	330	0.7
Pittsburgh, PA	82,470	6.9	1,050	0.1	19,980	1.7	370	0.0	11,410	1.0
Pittsfield, MA	1,570	2.3	145	0.2	750	1.1	30	0.0	815	1.2
Pocatello, ID	285	0.6	970	2.2	480	1.1	155	0.4	615	1.4
Portland–South Portland–Biddeford, ME	3,435	1.2	605	0.2	3,870	1.4	95	0.0	2,370	0.8
Portland–Vancouver–Hillsboro, OR–WA	28,420	2.4	5,985	0.5	65,730	5.6	4,890	0.4	28,325	2.4
Port St. Lucie, FL	25,775	13.4	385	0.2	3,060	1.6	50	0.0	2,220	1.2
Poughkeepsie–Newburgh–Middletown, NY	29,180	8.7	545	0.2	9,535	2.8	120	0.0	4,755	1.4
Prescott, AZ	545	0.6	1,395	1.5	760	0.8	55	0.1	1,210	1.3
Providence–New Bedford–Fall River, RI–MA	35,230	4.1	1,895	0.2	20,260	2.4	130	0.0	17,420	2.0

PART C—METROPOLITAN STATISTICAL AREA TABLES

C-2. All Workers, by Metropolitan Statistical Area, Sex, Race, and Hispanic or Latino Origin, 2006–2010—Continued

Metropolitan Statistical Area	Total who worked in the last 5 years	Male Number	Male Percent	Female Number	Female Percent	Hispanic or Latino Number	Hispanic or Latino Percent	White alone, not Hispanic or Latino Number	White alone, not Hispanic or Latino Percent
Provo–Orem, UT	228,880	130,845	57.2	98,035	42.8	22,405	9.8	196,810	86.0
Pueblo, CO	72,410	37,470	51.7	34,940	48.3	27,435	37.9	42,035	58.1
Punta Gorda, FL	64,655	33,665	52.1	30,990	47.9	3,725	5.8	55,175	85.3
Racine, WI	100,730	52,890	52.5	47,835	47.5	8,995	8.9	80,805	80.2
Raleigh–Cary, NC	580,680	308,055	53.1	272,625	46.9	49,830	8.6	388,130	66.8
Rapid City, SD	65,140	33,775	51.8	31,365	48.2	1,710	2.6	56,990	87.5
Reading, PA	212,665	111,385	52.4	101,285	47.6	25,165	11.8	175,270	82.4
Redding, CA	79,430	41,860	52.7	37,570	47.3	6,235	7.8	66,975	84.3
Reno–Sparks, NV	227,115	122,160	53.8	104,955	46.2	42,735	18.8	159,640	70.3
Richmond, VA	647,365	328,950	50.8	318,420	49.2	29,020	4.5	404,765	62.5
Riverside–San Bernardino–Ontario, CA	1,901,430	1,044,545	54.9	856,885	45.1	829,870	43.6	763,985	40.2
Roanoke, VA	157,385	80,760	51.3	76,625	48.7	4,540	2.9	130,075	82.6
Rochester, MN	102,730	52,520	51.1	50,215	48.9	3,190	3.1	92,090	89.6
Rochester, NY	536,310	274,710	51.2	261,600	48.8	24,895	4.6	444,225	82.8
Rockford, IL	175,105	92,415	52.8	82,690	47.2	17,535	10.0	137,435	78.5
Rocky Mount, NC	72,975	36,825	50.5	36,150	49.5	3,640	5.0	37,185	51.0
Rome, GA	45,080	23,675	52.5	21,405	47.5	3,420	7.6	34,875	77.4
Sacramento–Arden-Arcade–Roseville, CA	1,056,940	552,425	52.3	504,515	47.7	188,215	17.8	634,575	60.0
Saginaw–Saginaw Township North, MI	92,670	46,200	49.9	46,470	50.1	6,080	6.6	71,175	76.8
St. Cloud, MN	106,535	55,960	52.5	50,575	47.5	2,045	1.9	99,750	93.6
St. George, UT	57,495	32,405	56.4	25,090	43.6	5,495	9.6	49,850	86.7
St. Joseph, MO–KS	62,580	32,680	52.2	29,900	47.8	2,060	3.3	57,360	91.7
St. Louis, MO–IL	1,464,850	749,765	51.2	715,085	48.8	33,345	2.3	1,144,100	78.1
Salem, OR	185,690	98,580	53.1	87,105	46.9	36,215	19.5	137,655	74.1
Salinas, CA	196,235	108,220	55.1	88,015	44.9	103,325	52.7	69,970	35.7
Salisbury, MD	62,185	31,015	49.9	31,170	50.1	2,200	3.5	42,870	68.9
Salt Lake City, UT	577,550	318,395	55.1	259,155	44.9	83,775	14.5	451,225	78.1
San Angelo, TX	52,760	27,485	52.1	25,275	47.9	18,000	34.1	31,830	60.3
San Antonio–New Braunfels, TX	993,330	528,340	53.2	464,990	46.8	510,890	51.4	388,115	39.1
San Diego–Carlsbad–San Marcos, CA	1,497,805	809,920	54.1	687,890	45.9	427,055	28.5	791,435	52.8
Sandusky, OH	39,430	20,155	51.1	19,270	48.9	1,145	2.9	34,670	87.9
San Francisco–Oakland–Fremont, CA	2,306,445	1,227,900	53.2	1,078,540	46.8	457,155	19.8	1,067,110	46.3
San Jose–Sunnyvale–Santa Clara, CA	942,880	526,460	55.8	416,420	44.2	240,305	25.5	364,195	38.6
San Luis Obispo–Paso Robles, CA	131,210	69,945	53.3	61,270	46.7	24,480	18.7	97,650	74.4
Santa Barbara–Santa Maria–Goleta, CA	209,665	113,545	54.2	96,120	45.8	82,365	39.3	108,395	51.7
Santa Cruz–Watsonville, CA	137,890	73,660	53.4	64,225	46.6	38,890	28.2	88,385	64.1
Santa Fe, NM	76,445	39,490	51.7	36,955	48.3	36,050	47.2	36,490	47.7
Santa Rosa–Petaluma, CA	253,110	135,110	53.4	118,000	46.6	55,820	22.1	176,380	69.7
Savannah, GA	163,670	84,265	51.5	79,405	48.5	7,105	4.3	99,620	60.9
Scranton–Wilkes-Barre, PA	280,610	146,415	52.2	134,195	47.8	10,625	3.8	259,595	92.5
Seattle–Tacoma–Bellevue, WA	1,833,705	980,855	53.5	852,850	46.5	135,775	7.4	1,321,260	72.1
Sebastian–Vero Beach, FL	61,560	32,375	52.6	29,185	47.4	7,350	11.9	46,985	76.3
Sheboygan, WI	63,255	33,645	53.2	29,610	46.8	2,595	4.1	57,200	90.4
Sherman–Denison, TX	58,850	30,965	52.6	27,885	47.4	5,815	9.9	47,535	80.8
Shreveport–Bossier City, LA	189,435	94,760	50.0	94,670	50.0	6,205	3.3	108,750	57.4
Sioux City, IA–NE–SD	76,160	39,980	52.5	36,180	47.5	9,285	12.2	61,675	81.0
Sioux Falls, SD	128,290	65,960	51.4	62,330	48.6	3,310	2.6	118,370	92.3
South Bend–Mishawaka, IN–MI	161,550	83,740	51.8	77,810	48.2	8,960	5.5	131,430	81.4
Spartanburg, SC	135,060	70,025	51.8	65,035	48.2	6,845	5.1	97,695	72.3
Spokane, WA	231,110	120,250	52.0	110,860	48.0	8,310	3.6	206,820	89.5
Springfield, IL	112,285	55,975	49.9	56,310	50.1	1,750	1.6	97,160	86.5
Springfield, MA	355,390	177,815	50.0	177,575	50.0	37,100	10.4	285,450	80.3
Springfield, MO	218,960	115,160	52.6	103,795	47.4	5,120	2.3	202,695	92.6
Springfield, OH	68,370	34,670	50.7	33,700	49.3	1,495	2.2	60,005	87.8
State College, PA	76,610	41,900	54.7	34,710	45.3	1,655	2.2	68,565	89.5

C-2 All Workers, by Metropolitan Statistical Area, Sex, Race, and Hispanic or Latino Origin, 2006–2010—*Continued*

Metropolitan Statistical Area	Black alone, not Hispanic or Latino Number	Percent	American Indian and Alaska Native alone, not Hispanic or Latino Number	Percent	Asian alone, not Hispanic or Latino Number	Percent	Native Hawaiian and Other Pacific Islander alone, not Hispanic or Latino Number	Percent	Two or more races, not Hispanic or Latino Number	Percent
Provo–Orem, UT	1,065	0.5	1,065	0.5	2,905	1.3	1,510	0.7	3,125	1.4
Pueblo, CO	835	1.2	425	0.6	525	0.7	125	0.2	1,025	1.4
Punta Gorda, FL	3,700	5.7	160	0.2	975	1.5	0	0.0	920	1.4
Racine, WI	8,315	8.3	200	0.2	1,225	1.2	15	0.0	1,170	1.2
Raleigh–Cary, NC	111,245	19.2	1,430	0.2	23,625	4.1	155	0.0	6,265	1.1
Rapid City, SD	555	0.9	3,720	5.7	725	1.1	0	0.0	1,440	2.2
Reading, PA	7,500	3.5	95	0.0	2,650	1.2	110	0.1	1,870	0.9
Redding, CA	575	0.7	1,335	1.7	2,100	2.6	170	0.2	2,035	2.6
Reno–Sparks, NV	4,550	2.0	3,015	1.3	12,275	5.4	1,080	0.5	3,825	1.7
Richmond, VA	183,205	28.3	1,930	0.3	19,695	3.0	325	0.1	8,430	1.3
Riverside–San Bernardino–Ontario, CA	135,240	7.1	7,260	0.4	121,525	6.4	5,500	0.3	38,040	2.0
Roanoke, VA	18,505	11.8	215	0.1	2,500	1.6	4	0.0	1,545	1.0
Rochester, MN	2,350	2.3	90	0.1	4,255	4.1	25	0.0	730	0.7
Rochester, NY	47,610	8.9	1,110	0.2	12,545	2.3	125	0.0	5,795	1.1
Rockford, IL	14,320	8.2	290	0.2	3,930	2.2	25	0.0	1,570	0.9
Rocky Mount, NC	30,810	42.2	185	0.3	425	0.6	0	0.0	735	1.0
Rome, GA	5,560	12.3	60	0.1	730	1.6	0	0.0	440	1.0
Sacramento–Arden-Arcade–Roseville, CA	67,955	6.4	6,530	0.6	121,650	11.5	8,545	0.8	29,465	2.8
Saginaw–Saginaw Township North, MI	13,110	14.1	255	0.3	970	1.0	10	0.0	1,080	1.2
St. Cloud, MN	2,120	2.0	235	0.2	1,710	1.6	4	0.0	670	0.6
St. George, UT	200	0.3	560	1.0	540	0.9	375	0.7	470	0.8
St. Joseph, MO–KS	1,880	3.0	180	0.3	395	0.6	60	0.1	644	1.0
St. Louis, MO–IL	238,390	16.3	2,165	0.1	30,460	2.1	420	0.0	15,975	1.1
Salem, OR	1,335	0.7	2,055	1.1	3,655	2.0	880	0.5	3,895	2.1
Salinas, CA	4,715	2.4	580	0.3	12,545	6.4	1,130	0.6	3,970	2.0
Salisbury, MD	15,000	24.1	90	0.1	1,520	2.4	10	0.0	490	0.8
Salt Lake City, UT	6,675	1.2	3,825	0.7	18,480	3.2	7,295	1.3	6,275	1.1
San Angelo, TX	1,805	3.4	200	0.4	455	0.9	0	0.0	475	0.9
San Antonio–New Braunfels, TX	59,220	6.0	2,455	0.2	20,640	2.1	850	0.1	11,165	1.1
San Diego–Carlsbad–San Marcos, CA	67,915	4.5	5,240	0.3	165,075	11.0	7,360	0.5	33,735	2.3
Sandusky, OH	2,735	6.9	100	0.3	230	0.6	0	0.0	550	1.4
San Francisco–Oakland–Fremont, CA	168,980	7.3	5,440	0.2	530,645	23.0	15,995	0.7	61,120	2.6
San Jose–Sunnyvale–Santa Clara, CA	23,615	2.5	2,730	0.3	289,040	30.7	3,195	0.3	19,795	2.1
San Luis Obispo–Paso Robles, CA	1,380	1.1	820	0.6	4,125	3.1	135	0.1	2,629	2.0
Santa Barbara–Santa Maria–Goleta, CA	3,595	1.7	790	0.4	10,495	5.0	510	0.2	3,515	1.7
Santa Cruz–Watsonville, CA	1,345	1.0	425	0.3	5,755	4.2	265	0.2	2,835	2.1
Santa Fe, NM	405	0.5	1,940	2.5	890	1.2	15	0.0	650	0.9
Santa Rosa–Petaluma, CA	3,490	1.4	1,970	0.8	9,955	3.9	855	0.3	4,645	1.8
Savannah, GA	51,475	31.5	300	0.2	3,525	2.2	120	0.1	1,515	0.9
Scranton–Wilkes-Barre, PA	5,025	1.8	280	0.1	3,250	1.2	75	0.0	1,760	0.6
Seattle–Tacoma–Bellevue, WA	88,105	4.8	13,665	0.7	203,735	11.1	13,250	0.7	57,915	3.2
Sebastian–Vero Beach, FL	5,855	9.5	110	0.2	710	1.2	15	0.0	540	0.9
Sheboygan, WI	600	0.9	275	0.4	2,220	3.5	0	0.0	359	0.6
Sherman–Denison, TX	3,235	5.5	790	1.3	550	0.9	45	0.1	875	1.5
Shreveport–Bossier City, LA	69,785	36.8	650	0.3	2,380	1.3	75	0.0	1,595	0.8
Sioux City, IA–NE–SD	1,625	2.1	855	1.1	2,000	2.6	50	0.1	670	0.9
Sioux Falls, SD	2,480	1.9	1,565	1.2	1,670	1.3	20	0.0	880	0.7
South Bend–Mishawaka, IN–MI	15,810	9.8	520	0.3	2,625	1.6	75	0.0	2,125	1.3
Spartanburg, SC	26,225	19.4	245	0.2	2,910	2.2	65	0.0	1,075	0.8
Spokane, WA	2,755	1.2	2,260	1.0	5,045	2.2	675	0.3	5,240	2.3
Springfield, IL	10,275	9.2	140	0.1	1,760	1.6	55	0.0	1,140	1.0
Springfield, MA	19,720	5.5	530	0.1	8,245	2.3	65	0.0	4,275	1.2
Springfield, MO	4,060	1.9	945	0.4	2,310	1.1	35	0.0	3,795	1.7
Springfield, OH	5,350	7.8	150	0.2	495	0.7	0	0.0	875	1.3
State College, PA	1,800	2.3	140	0.2	3,620	4.7	45	0.1	785	1.0

C-2 All Workers, by Metropolitan Statistical Area, Sex, Race, and Hispanic or Latino Origin, 2006–2010—Continued

Metropolitan Statistical Area	Total who worked in the last 5 years	Male Number	Male Percent	Female Number	Female Percent	Hispanic or Latino Number	Hispanic or Latino Percent	White alone, not Hispanic or Latino Number	White alone, not Hispanic or Latino Percent
Steubenville–Weirton, OH–WV	58,010	30,315	52.3	27,695	47.7	470	0.8	54,970	94.8
Stockton, CA	309,845	168,100	54.3	141,745	45.7	110,395	35.6	125,270	40.4
Sumter, SC	46,225	23,070	49.9	23,150	50.1	1,440	3.1	22,690	49.1
Syracuse, NY	333,980	170,975	51.2	163,005	48.8	8,755	2.6	291,575	87.3
Tallahassee, FL	187,465	93,750	50.0	93,715	50.0	9,035	4.8	116,500	62.1
Tampa–St. Petersburg–Clearwater, FL	1,372,115	711,110	51.8	661,005	48.2	204,845	14.9	957,235	69.8
Terre Haute, IN	82,160	43,930	53.5	38,235	46.5	1,125	1.4	76,615	93.3
Texarkana, TX–Texarkana, AR	62,730	33,160	52.9	29,570	47.1	3,220	5.1	44,145	70.4
Toledo, OH	341,835	175,935	51.5	165,900	48.5	15,785	4.6	278,150	81.4
Topeka, KS	121,930	62,050	50.9	59,880	49.1	8,590	7.0	101,290	83.1
Trenton–Ewing, NJ	192,230	100,700	52.4	91,530	47.6	27,325	14.2	111,150	57.8
Tucson, AZ	460,140	242,530	52.7	217,610	47.3	148,270	32.2	267,950	58.2
Tulsa, OK	467,790	250,630	53.6	217,155	46.4	33,325	7.1	336,325	71.9
Tuscaloosa, AL	102,505	53,595	52.3	48,905	47.7	2,980	2.9	66,385	64.8
Tyler, TX	100,970	53,240	52.7	47,730	47.3	15,400	15.3	65,190	64.6
Utica–Rome, NY	144,850	74,445	51.4	70,405	48.6	3,805	2.6	132,545	91.5
Valdosta, GA	64,870	32,750	50.5	32,120	49.5	3,390	5.2	39,140	60.3
Vallejo–Fairfield, CA	204,570	105,935	51.8	98,635	48.2	44,085	21.6	91,040	44.5
Victoria, TX	56,975	30,805	54.1	26,170	45.9	22,565	39.6	30,075	52.8
Vineland–Millville–Bridgeton, NJ	73,170	38,455	52.6	34,715	47.4	17,255	23.6	41,790	57.1
Virginia Beach–Norfolk–Newport News, VA–NC	824,655	410,895	49.8	413,760	50.2	36,645	4.4	492,340	59.7
Visalia–Porterville, CA	189,285	107,825	57.0	81,460	43.0	106,680	56.4	69,965	37.0
Waco, TX	112,195	58,250	51.9	53,945	48.1	23,715	21.1	70,585	62.9
Warner Robins, GA	65,710	33,340	50.7	32,370	49.3	3,460	5.3	41,350	62.9
Washington–Arlington–Alexandria, DC–VA–MD–WV	3,067,930	1,581,335	51.5	1,486,595	48.5	404,025	13.2	1,551,175	50.6
Waterloo–Cedar Falls, IA	89,345	46,290	51.8	43,060	48.2	2,165	2.4	80,060	89.6
Wausau, WI	74,835	39,885	53.3	34,950	46.7	1,265	1.7	69,485	92.9
Wenatchee–East Wenatchee, WA	53,045	28,730	54.2	24,320	45.8	13,215	24.9	38,210	72.0
Wheeling, WV–OH	69,265	36,505	52.7	32,760	47.3	460	0.7	66,575	96.1
Wichita, KS	317,885	169,095	53.2	148,790	46.8	29,905	9.4	246,990	77.7
Wichita Falls, TX	69,795	36,390	52.1	33,410	47.9	8,795	12.6	52,980	75.9
Williamsport, PA	59,280	31,150	52.5	28,130	47.5	660	1.1	55,730	94.0
Wilmington, NC	179,945	92,820	51.6	87,130	48.4	8,400	4.7	143,910	80.0
Winchester, VA–WV	64,905	34,785	53.6	30,120	46.4	4,265	6.6	55,680	85.8
Winston-Salem, NC	235,660	121,130	51.4	114,530	48.6	20,575	8.7	163,400	69.3
Worcester, MA	425,625	223,160	52.4	202,465	47.6	29,840	7.0	359,510	84.5
Yakima, WA	109,320	59,875	54.8	49,445	45.2	44,670	40.9	57,720	52.8
York–Hanover, PA	231,710	122,700	53.0	109,005	47.0	8,630	3.7	208,205	89.9
Youngstown–Warren–Boardman, OH–PA	270,585	141,450	52.3	129,130	47.7	5,955	2.2	236,145	87.3
Yuba City, CA	74,740	40,670	54.4	34,070	45.6	18,630	24.9	42,795	57.3
Yuma, AZ	76,590	41,395	54.0	35,195	46.0	47,630	62.2	24,980	32.6

C-2 **All Workers, by Metropolitan Statistical Area, Sex, Race, and Hispanic or Latino Origin, 2006–2010**—*Continued*

Metropolitan Statistical Area	Black alone, not Hispanic or Latino Number	Black alone, not Hispanic or Latino Percent	American Indian and Alaska Native alone, not Hispanic or Latino Number	American Indian and Alaska Native alone, not Hispanic or Latino Percent	Asian alone, not Hispanic or Latino Number	Asian alone, not Hispanic or Latino Percent	Native Hawaiian and Other Pacific Islander alone, not Hispanic or Latino Number	Native Hawaiian and Other Pacific Islander alone, not Hispanic or Latino Percent	Two or more races, not Hispanic or Latino Number	Two or more races, not Hispanic or Latino Percent
Steubenville–Weirton, OH–WV	1,690	2.9	45	0.1	190	0.3	25	0.0	615	1.1
Stockton, CA	19,915	6.4	1,445	0.5	43,465	14.0	1,455	0.5	7,900	2.5
Sumter, SC	20,935	45.3	175	0.4	660	1.4	10	0.0	320	0.7
Syracuse, NY	20,230	6.1	2,220	0.7	7,570	2.3	135	0.0	3,485	1.0
Tallahassee, FL	54,760	29.2	620	0.3	4,555	2.4	100	0.1	1,890	1.0
Tampa–St. Petersburg–Clearwater, FL	146,715	10.7	2,445	0.2	42,060	3.1	1,020	0.1	17,795	1.3
Terre Haute, IN	2,535	3.1	170	0.2	950	1.2	35	0.0	730	0.9
Texarkana, TX–Texarkana, AR	13,785	22.0	345	0.5	390	0.6	30	0.0	825	1.3
Toledo, OH	39,030	11.4	495	0.1	4,985	1.5	85	0.0	3,305	1.0
Topeka, KS	7,395	6.1	1,495	1.2	1,140	0.9	40	0.0	1,990	1.6
Trenton–Ewing, NJ	34,915	18.2	395	0.2	16,155	8.4	4	0.0	2,275	1.2
Tucson, AZ	13,855	3.0	9,095	2.0	13,370	2.9	660	0.1	6,940	1.5
Tulsa, OK	34,705	7.4	29,695	6.3	8,090	1.7	285	0.1	25,370	5.4
Tuscaloosa, AL	31,175	30.4	205	0.2	935	0.9	0	0.0	825	0.8
Tyler, TX	18,195	18.0	255	0.3	1,005	1.0	25	0.0	905	0.9
Utica–Rome, NY	4,205	2.9	170	0.1	2,745	1.9	40	0.0	1,345	0.9
Valdosta, GA	20,560	31.7	105	0.2	905	1.4	0	0.0	770	1.2
Vallejo–Fairfield, CA	26,650	13.0	795	0.4	31,895	15.6	1,905	0.9	8,200	4.0
Victoria, TX	2,865	5.0	4	0.0	865	1.5	0	0.0	600	1.1
Vineland–Millville–Bridgeton, NJ	11,695	16.0	420	0.6	950	1.3	40	0.1	1,020	1.4
Virginia Beach–Norfolk–Newport News, VA–NC	247,530	30.0	2,130	0.3	30,010	3.6	975	0.1	15,030	1.8
Visalia–Porterville, CA	2,125	1.1	1,285	0.7	6,415	3.4	180	0.1	2,635	1.4
Waco, TX	15,245	13.6	310	0.3	1,490	1.3	15	0.0	835	0.7
Warner Robins, GA	18,220	27.7	155	0.2	1,490	2.3	0	0.0	1,035	1.6
Washington–Arlington–Alexandria, DC–VA–MD–WV	768,640	25.1	5,765	0.2	280,830	9.2	2,070	0.1	55,430	1.8
Waterloo–Cedar Falls, IA	4,990	5.6	115	0.1	1,015	1.1	75	0.1	935	1.0
Wausau, WI	390	0.5	260	0.3	2,880	3.8	4	0.0	555	0.7
Wenatchee–East Wenatchee, WA	105	0.2	320	0.6	315	0.6	75	0.1	805	1.5
Wheeling, WV–OH	1,125	1.6	45	0.1	450	0.6	0	0.0	610	0.9
Wichita, KS	21,215	6.7	2,075	0.7	11,140	3.5	215	0.1	6,345	2.0
Wichita Falls, TX	5,345	7.7	495	0.7	1,380	2.0	60	0.1	735	1.1
Williamsport, PA	1,855	3.1	140	0.2	320	0.5	4	0.0	575	1.0
Wilmington, NC	23,195	12.9	660	0.4	1,525	0.8	80	0.0	2,185	1.2
Winchester, VA–WV	3,295	5.1	130	0.2	775	1.2	80	0.1	680	1.0
Winston-Salem, NC	45,765	19.4	425	0.2	3,200	1.4	200	0.1	2,100	0.9
Worcester, MA	13,870	3.3	505	0.1	16,010	3.8	165	0.0	5,725	1.3
Yakima, WA	675	0.6	3,090	2.8	1,040	1.0	85	0.1	2,045	1.9
York–Hanover, PA	9,785	4.2	350	0.2	2,595	1.1	10	0.0	2,135	0.9
Youngstown–Warren–Boardman, OH–PA	24,410	9.0	420	0.2	1,595	0.6	25	0.0	2,030	0.8
Yuba City, CA	1,445	1.9	740	1.0	8,060	10.8	220	0.3	2,850	3.8
Yuma, AZ	1,410	1.8	785	1.0	950	1.2	100	0.1	730	1.0

C-3 Management, Business, and Financial Workers, by Metropolitan Statistical Area, Sex, Race, and Hispanic or Latino Origin, 2006–2010

Metropolitan Statistical Area	Total who worked in the last 5 years	Male Number	Male Percent	Female Number	Female Percent	Hispanic or Latino Number	Hispanic or Latino Percent	White alone, not Hispanic or Latino Number	White alone, not Hispanic or Latino Percent
Abilene, TX	7,065	4,195	59.4	2,865	40.6	655	9.3	5,815	82.3
Akron, OH	43,860	26,870	61.3	16,990	38.7	445	1.0	39,460	90.0
Albany, GA	6,600	3,685	55.8	2,910	44.1	125	1.9	4,360	66.1
Albany–Schenectady–Troy, NY	59,095	33,570	56.8	25,525	43.2	1,045	1.8	53,590	90.7
Albuquerque, NM	52,100	29,860	57.3	22,240	42.7	16,750	32.1	31,215	59.9
Alexandria, LA	6,595	3,870	58.7	2,725	41.3	130	2.0	5,275	80.0
Allentown–Bethlehem–Easton, PA–NJ	47,625	29,435	61.8	18,195	38.2	2,115	4.4	42,215	88.6
Altoona, PA	5,945	3,675	61.8	2,270	38.2	45	0.8	5,790	97.4
Amarillo, TX	12,320	7,470	60.6	4,850	39.4	1,670	13.6	10,010	81.3
Ames, IA	5,875	3,660	62.3	2,215	37.7	75	1.3	5,540	94.3
Anchorage, AK	25,060	13,895	55.4	11,165	44.6	620	2.5	20,910	83.4
Anderson, IN	5,625	3,130	55.6	2,495	44.4	65	1.2	5,200	92.4
Anderson, SC	8,440	5,395	63.9	3,045	36.1	115	1.4	7,525	89.2
Ann Arbor, MI	24,195	14,085	58.2	10,110	41.8	505	2.1	19,605	81.0
Anniston–Oxford, AL	4,485	2,805	62.5	1,680	37.5	140	3.1	3,880	86.5
Appleton, WI	14,615	8,825	60.4	5,795	39.7	295	2.0	13,870	94.9
Asheville, NC	22,770	13,540	59.5	9,230	40.5	435	1.9	21,325	93.7
Athens–Clarke County, GA	10,425	6,385	61.2	4,040	38.8	405	3.9	8,360	80.2
Atlanta–Sandy Springs–Marietta, GA	400,780	236,085	58.9	164,695	41.1	16,020	4.0	271,255	67.7
Atlantic City–Hammonton, NJ	13,420	7,770	57.9	5,650	42.1	790	5.9	10,455	77.9
Auburn–Opelika, AL	6,940	3,965	57.1	2,975	42.9	80	1.2	5,735	82.6
Augusta–Richmond County, GA–SC	23,320	13,300	57.0	10,020	43.0	600	2.6	17,385	74.5
Austin–Round Rock–San Marcos, TX	134,065	78,260	58.4	55,810	41.6	21,545	16.1	98,040	73.1
Bakersfield–Delano, CA	28,740	16,345	56.9	12,390	43.1	6,540	22.8	19,070	66.4
Baltimore–Towson, MD	207,880	117,245	56.4	90,635	43.6	4,950	2.4	156,070	75.1
Bangor, ME	7,565	4,375	57.8	3,190	42.2	104	1.4	7,310	96.6
Barnstable Town, MA	14,520	8,220	56.6	6,300	43.4	305	2.1	13,550	93.3
Baton Rouge, LA	43,080	24,365	56.6	18,710	43.4	690	1.6	32,760	76.0
Battle Creek, MI	6,525	3,655	56.0	2,870	44.0	130	2.0	5,830	89.3
Bay City, MI	4,160	2,275	54.7	1,880	45.2	95	2.3	3,930	94.5
Beaumont–Port Arthur, TX	14,260	8,680	60.9	5,585	39.2	825	5.8	10,950	76.8
Bellingham, WA	12,200	7,675	62.9	4,525	37.1	695	5.7	10,690	87.6
Bend, OR	9,350	6,000	64.2	3,350	35.8	340	3.6	8,660	92.6
Billings, MT	9,145	5,675	62.1	3,470	37.9	175	1.9	8,605	94.1
Binghamton, NY	12,185	7,820	64.2	4,360	35.8	230	1.9	11,585	95.1
Birmingham–Hoover, AL	64,545	38,055	59.0	26,490	41.0	780	1.2	51,645	80.0
Bismarck, ND	7,580	4,465	58.9	3,110	41.0	35	0.5	7,380	97.4
Blacksburg–Christiansburg–Radford, VA	7,890	4,885	61.9	3,005	38.1	245	3.1	7,215	91.4
Bloomington, IN	9,485	5,575	58.8	3,910	41.2	155	1.6	8,700	91.7
Bloomington–Normal, IL	12,575	6,835	54.4	5,740	45.6	365	2.9	11,125	88.5
Boise City–Nampa, ID	38,885	23,800	61.2	15,090	38.8	1,985	5.1	35,870	92.2
Boston–Cambridge–Quincy, MA–NH	371,435	213,000	57.3	158,435	42.7	12,795	3.4	321,840	86.6
Boulder, CO	26,595	16,310	61.3	10,285	38.7	1,525	5.7	23,740	89.3
Bowling Green, KY	6,040	3,875	64.2	2,160	35.8	60	1.0	5,645	93.5
Bremerton–Silverdale, WA	14,860	8,640	58.1	6,220	41.9	405	2.7	13,100	88.2
Bridgeport–Stamford–Norwalk, CT	80,200	51,845	64.6	28,355	35.4	4,840	6.0	67,375	84.0
Brownsville–Harlingen, TX	11,840	7,590	64.1	4,250	35.9	8,575	72.4	3,040	25.7
Brunswick, GA	5,435	3,160	58.1	2,275	41.9	65	1.2	4,660	85.7
Buffalo–Niagara Falls, NY	60,745	36,050	59.3	24,695	40.7	1,105	1.8	54,440	89.6
Burlington, NC	8,085	5,060	62.6	3,025	37.4	295	3.6	6,585	81.4
Burlington–South Burlington, VT	16,060	9,420	58.7	6,640	41.3	120	0.7	15,520	96.6
Canton–Massillon, OH	20,460	12,740	62.3	7,715	37.7	200	1.0	19,300	94.3
Cape Coral–Fort Myers, FL	33,435	21,380	63.9	12,055	36.1	3,065	9.2	28,605	85.6
Cape Girardeau–Jackson, MO–IL	4,815	2,850	59.2	1,960	40.7	45	0.9	4,410	91.6
Carson City, NV	2,780	1,445	52.0	1,330	47.8	255	9.2	2,445	87.9

C-3 **Management, Business, and Financial Workers, by Metropolitan Statistical Area, Sex, Race, and Hispanic or Latino Origin, 2006–2010**—*Continued*

Metropolitan Statistical Area	Black alone, not Hispanic or Latino Number	Black alone, not Hispanic or Latino Percent	American Indian and Alaska Native alone, not Hispanic or Latino Number	American Indian and Alaska Native alone, not Hispanic or Latino Percent	Asian alone, not Hispanic or Latino Number	Asian alone, not Hispanic or Latino Percent	Native Hawaiian and Other Pacific Islander alone, not Hispanic or Latino Number	Native Hawaiian and Other Pacific Islander alone, not Hispanic or Latino Percent	Two or more races, not Hispanic or Latino Number	Two or more races, not Hispanic or Latino Percent
Abilene, TX	240	3.4	45	0.6	190	2.7	4	0.1	115	1.6
Akron, OH	2,725	6.2	25	0.1	945	2.2	0	0.0	255	0.6
Albany, GA	2,015	30.5	25	0.4	50	0.8	0	0.0	24	0.4
Albany–Schenectady–Troy, NY	2,075	3.5	110	0.2	1,695	2.9	25	0.0	555	0.9
Albuquerque, NM	805	1.5	1,655	3.2	1,095	2.1	35	0.1	555	1.1
Alexandria, LA	1,020	15.5	55	0.8	50	0.8	0	0.0	65	1.0
Allentown–Bethlehem–Easton, PA–NJ	1,600	3.4	30	0.1	1,305	2.7	0	0.0	365	0.8
Altoona, PA	60	1.0	0	0.0	50	0.8	0	0.0	0	0.0
Amarillo, TX	430	3.5	45	0.4	80	0.6	4	0.0	75	0.6
Ames, IA	80	1.4	0	0.0	175	3.0	0	0.0	8	0.1
Anchorage, AK	680	2.7	885	3.5	710	2.8	55	0.2	1,195	4.8
Anderson, IN	225	4.0	0	0.0	30	0.5	0	0.0	100	1.8
Anderson, SC	565	6.7	45	0.5	85	1.0	0	0.0	105	1.2
Ann Arbor, MI	1,955	8.1	25	0.1	1,665	6.9	0	0.0	430	1.8
Anniston–Oxford, AL	410	9.1	0	0.0	40	0.9	15	0.3	10	0.2
Appleton, WI	0	0.0	100	0.7	275	1.9	0	0.0	75	0.5
Asheville, NC	450	2.0	125	0.5	225	1.0	15	0.1	195	0.9
Athens–Clarke County, GA	1,250	12.0	4	0.0	310	3.0	0	0.0	95	0.9
Atlanta–Sandy Springs–Marietta, GA	89,965	22.4	905	0.2	18,215	4.5	95	0.0	4,325	1.1
Atlantic City–Hammonton, NJ	1,310	9.8	15	0.1	580	4.3	0	0.0	275	2.0
Auburn–Opelika, AL	855	12.3	30	0.4	150	2.2	45	0.6	45	0.6
Augusta–Richmond County, GA–SC	4,745	20.3	25	0.1	325	1.4	45	0.2	195	0.8
Austin–Round Rock–San Marcos, TX	6,720	5.0	375	0.3	5,365	4.0	55	0.0	1,970	1.5
Bakersfield–Delano, CA	1,320	4.6	280	1.0	1,150	4.0	15	0.1	365	1.3
Baltimore–Towson, MD	37,140	17.9	355	0.2	7,145	3.4	25	0.0	2,195	1.1
Bangor, ME	20	0.3	25	0.3	50	0.7	0	0.0	55	0.7
Barnstable Town, MA	190	1.3	20	0.1	105	0.7	0	0.0	350	2.4
Baton Rouge, LA	8,685	20.2	65	0.2	615	1.4	10	0.0	250	0.6
Battle Creek, MI	320	4.9	40	0.6	175	2.7	0	0.0	30	0.5
Bay City, MI	30	0.7	20	0.5	40	1.0	0	0.0	35	0.8
Beaumont–Port Arthur, TX	2,060	14.4	55	0.4	245	1.7	10	0.1	115	0.8
Bellingham, WA	155	1.3	245	2.0	305	2.5	20	0.2	90	0.7
Bend, OR	25	0.3	30	0.3	125	1.3	0	0.0	170	1.8
Billings, MT	25	0.3	160	1.7	105	1.1	0	0.0	75	0.8
Binghamton, NY	130	1.1	35	0.3	175	1.4	0	0.0	24	0.2
Birmingham–Hoover, AL	10,965	17.0	95	0.1	740	1.1	0	0.0	325	0.5
Bismarck, ND	45	0.6	100	1.3	0	0.0	0	0.0	20	0.3
Blacksburg–Christiansburg–Radford, VA	225	2.9	0	0.0	180	2.3	0	0.0	25	0.3
Bloomington, IN	215	2.3	20	0.2	200	2.1	25	0.3	170	1.8
Bloomington–Normal, IL	735	5.8	4	0.0	315	2.5	15	0.1	14	0.1
Boise City–Nampa, ID	180	0.5	100	0.3	355	0.9	0	0.0	400	1.0
Boston–Cambridge–Quincy, MA–NH	13,270	3.6	295	0.1	18,840	5.1	55	0.0	4,330	1.2
Boulder, CO	170	0.6	15	0.1	810	3.0	15	0.1	325	1.2
Bowling Green, KY	225	3.7	0	0.0	65	1.1	0	0.0	50	0.8
Bremerton–Silverdale, WA	215	1.4	140	0.9	525	3.5	90	0.6	400	2.7
Bridgeport–Stamford–Norwalk, CT	3,200	4.0	10	0.0	3,945	4.9	15	0.0	825	1.0
Brownsville–Harlingen, TX	45	0.4	25	0.2	145	1.2	0	0.0	10	0.1
Brunswick, GA	675	12.4	0	0.0	15	0.3	0	0.0	19	0.3
Buffalo–Niagara Falls, NY	3,140	5.2	290	0.5	1,185	2.0	0	0.0	580	1.0
Burlington, NC	1,020	12.6	20	0.2	105	1.3	20	0.2	40	0.5
Burlington–South Burlington, VT	80	0.5	30	0.2	225	1.4	4	0.0	74	0.5
Canton–Massillon, OH	685	3.3	30	0.1	160	0.8	0	0.0	85	0.4
Cape Coral–Fort Myers, FL	1,090	3.3	70	0.2	270	0.8	0	0.0	335	1.0
Cape Girardeau–Jackson, MO–IL	265	5.5	0	0.0	90	1.9	0	0.0	4	0.1
Carson City, NV	25	0.9	30	1.1	25	0.9	0	0.0	0	0.0

PART C—METROPOLITAN STATISTICAL AREA TABLES

C-3 Management, Business, and Financial Workers, by Metropolitan Statistical Area, Sex, Race, and Hispanic or Latino Origin, 2006–2010—Continued

Metropolitan Statistical Area	Total who worked in the last 5 years	Male Number	Male Percent	Female Number	Female Percent	Hispanic or Latino Number	Hispanic or Latino Percent	White alone, not Hispanic or Latino Number	White alone, not Hispanic or Latino Percent
Casper, WY	3,660	2,295	62.7	1,365	37.3	130	3.6	3,440	94.0
Cedar Rapids, IA	17,025	10,355	60.8	6,670	39.2	230	1.4	16,260	95.5
Champaign–Urbana, IL	12,500	7,055	56.4	5,445	43.6	260	2.1	10,975	87.8
Charleston, WV	13,775	8,245	59.9	5,530	40.1	45	0.3	13,105	95.1
Charleston–North Charleston–Summerville, SC	39,365	22,530	57.2	16,840	42.8	750	1.9	33,055	84.0
Charlotte–Gastonia–Rock Hill, NC–SC	128,050	75,360	58.9	52,695	41.2	4,750	3.7	99,040	77.3
Charlottesville, VA	13,705	7,735	56.4	5,970	43.6	355	2.6	11,875	86.6
Chattanooga, TN–GA	29,155	18,225	62.5	10,930	37.5	415	1.4	25,235	86.6
Cheyenne, WY	5,480	3,060	55.8	2,420	44.2	325	5.9	5,010	91.4
Chicago–Joliet–Naperville, IL–IN–WI	643,675	379,495	59.0	264,180	41.0	53,060	8.2	481,805	74.9
Chico, CA	11,355	6,700	59.0	4,650	41.0	995	8.8	9,590	84.5
Cincinnati–Middletown, OH–KY–IN	138,190	82,045	59.4	56,145	40.6	1,950	1.4	124,120	89.8
Clarksville, TN–KY	10,630	6,495	61.1	4,135	38.9	615	5.8	8,355	78.6
Cleveland, TN	4,210	2,705	64.3	1,505	35.7	105	2.5	3,910	92.9
Cleveland–Elyria–Mentor, OH	124,045	73,405	59.2	50,640	40.8	3,195	2.6	105,890	85.4
Coeur d'Alene, ID	8,370	5,150	61.5	3,220	38.5	205	2.4	7,810	93.3
College Station–Bryan, TX	10,735	6,550	61.0	4,185	39.0	1,175	10.9	8,575	79.9
Colorado Springs, CO	43,510	25,995	59.7	17,520	40.3	3,390	7.8	36,110	83.0
Columbia, MO	10,060	5,675	56.4	4,385	43.6	205	2.0	9,135	90.8
Columbia, SC	45,590	25,915	56.8	19,675	43.2	820	1.8	35,125	77.0
Columbus, GA–AL	13,455	7,650	56.9	5,805	43.1	445	3.3	8,970	66.7
Columbus, IN	5,170	3,430	66.3	1,740	33.7	115	2.2	4,705	91.0
Columbus, OH	131,340	77,160	58.7	54,185	41.3	2,140	1.6	112,045	85.3
Corpus Christi, TX	19,195	11,390	59.3	7,805	40.7	7,415	38.6	10,850	56.5
Corvallis, OR	5,005	3,045	60.8	1,960	39.2	190	3.8	4,400	87.9
Crestview–Fort Walton Beach–Destin, FL	11,445	7,045	61.6	4,405	38.5	450	3.9	9,815	85.8
Cumberland, MD–WV	4,060	2,435	60.0	1,625	40.0	19	0.5	3,870	95.3
Dallas–Fort Worth–Arlington, TX	440,065	265,105	60.2	174,960	39.8	48,200	11.0	318,015	72.3
Dalton, GA	5,400	3,515	65.1	1,885	34.9	485	9.0	4,715	87.3
Danville, IL	3,115	1,920	61.6	1,200	38.5	70	2.2	2,765	88.8
Danville, VA	3,700	2,400	64.9	1,300	35.1	0	0.0	3,050	82.4
Davenport–Moline–Rock Island, IA–IL	21,100	12,585	59.6	8,515	40.4	710	3.4	19,405	92.0
Dayton, OH	46,465	27,515	59.2	18,955	40.8	565	1.2	40,005	86.1
Decatur, AL	6,470	4,040	62.4	2,430	37.6	35	0.5	5,565	86.0
Decatur, IL	5,285	3,165	59.9	2,120	40.1	75	1.4	4,760	90.1
Deltona–Daytona Beach–Ormond Beach, FL	25,200	14,845	58.9	10,350	41.1	1,560	6.2	21,970	87.2
Denver–Aurora–Broomfield, CO	202,550	118,415	58.5	84,130	41.5	18,420	9.1	169,785	83.8
Des Moines–West Des Moines, IA	45,445	25,735	56.6	19,705	43.4	725	1.6	42,645	93.8
Detroit–Warren–Livonia, MI	250,470	148,770	59.4	101,700	40.6	4,980	2.0	201,890	80.6
Dothan, AL	5,890	3,955	67.1	1,935	32.9	65	1.1	5,115	86.8
Dover, DE	7,930	4,565	57.6	3,365	42.4	210	2.6	5,875	74.1
Dubuque, IA	5,805	3,400	58.6	2,400	41.3	105	1.8	5,575	96.0
Duluth, MN–WI	14,925	8,640	57.9	6,285	42.1	75	0.5	14,235	95.4
Durham–Chapel Hill, NC	33,315	17,830	53.5	15,480	46.5	1,040	3.1	24,440	73.4
Eau Claire, WI	9,545	5,770	60.5	3,775	39.5	90	0.9	9,255	97.0
El Centro, CA	5,565	3,505	63.0	2,060	37.0	3,170	57.0	2,085	37.5
Elizabethtown, KY	5,220	3,080	59.0	2,140	41.0	155	3.0	4,425	84.8
Elkhart–Goshen, IN	9,085	6,230	68.6	2,855	31.4	420	4.6	8,265	91.0
Elmira, NY	3,875	2,205	56.9	1,670	43.1	65	1.7	3,580	92.4
El Paso, TX	29,100	17,650	60.7	11,450	39.3	20,085	69.0	7,660	26.3
Erie, PA	13,100	8,000	61.1	5,100	38.9	285	2.2	12,235	93.4
Eugene–Springfield, OR	19,725	11,025	55.9	8,705	44.1	875	4.4	17,890	90.7
Evansville, IN–KY	18,010	11,030	61.2	6,980	38.8	45	0.2	17,070	94.8
Fairbanks, AK	5,120	2,570	50.2	2,550	49.8	165	3.2	4,405	86.0
Fargo, ND–MN	13,705	8,470	61.8	5,235	38.2	205	1.5	13,035	95.1

C-3 **Management, Business, and Financial Workers, by Metropolitan Statistical Area, Sex, Race, and Hispanic or Latino Origin, 2006–2010**—*Continued*

Metropolitan Statistical Area	Black alone, not Hispanic or Latino Number	Percent	American Indian and Alaska Native alone, not Hispanic or Latino Number	Percent	Asian alone, not Hispanic or Latino Number	Percent	Native Hawaiian and Other Pacific Islander alone, not Hispanic or Latino Number	Percent	Two or more races, not Hispanic or Latino Number	Percent
Casper, WY	25	0.7	35	1.0	25	0.7	0	0.0	4	0.1
Cedar Rapids, IA	160	0.9	30	0.2	195	1.1	0	0.0	150	0.9
Champaign–Urbana, IL	605	4.8	40	0.3	590	4.7	0	0.0	25	0.2
Charleston, WV	225	1.6	0	0.0	90	0.7	0	0.0	305	2.2
Charleston–North Charleston–Summerville, SC	4,490	11.4	135	0.3	555	1.4	35	0.1	350	0.9
Charlotte–Gastonia–Rock Hill, NC–SC	19,290	15.1	395	0.3	3,490	2.7	40	0.0	1,055	0.8
Charlottesville, VA	1,120	8.2	15	0.1	230	1.7	0	0.0	110	0.8
Chattanooga, TN–GA	2,610	9.0	10	0.0	530	1.8	30	0.1	320	1.1
Cheyenne, WY	0	0.0	35	0.6	15	0.3	0	0.0	90	1.6
Chicago–Joliet–Naperville, IL–IN–WI	62,780	9.8	620	0.1	39,265	6.1	200	0.0	5,945	0.9
Chico, CA	110	1.0	90	0.8	320	2.8	20	0.2	230	2.0
Cincinnati–Middletown, OH–KY–IN	8,010	5.8	185	0.1	2,925	2.1	40	0.0	960	0.7
Clarksville, TN–KY	1,360	12.8	25	0.2	170	1.6	0	0.0	105	1.0
Cleveland, TN	65	1.5	0	0.0	55	1.3	0	0.0	80	1.9
Cleveland–Elyria–Mentor, OH	11,480	9.3	210	0.2	2,550	2.1	0	0.0	720	0.6
Coeur d'Alene, ID	4	0.0	65	0.8	35	0.4	20	0.2	230	2.7
College Station–Bryan, TX	675	6.3	25	0.2	125	1.2	0	0.0	159	1.5
Colorado Springs, CO	1,935	4.4	240	0.6	795	1.8	75	0.2	970	2.2
Columbia, MO	355	3.5	35	0.3	205	2.0	25	0.2	105	1.0
Columbia, SC	8,480	18.6	130	0.3	570	1.3	10	0.0	450	1.0
Columbus, GA–AL	3,480	25.9	30	0.2	255	1.9	0	0.0	275	2.0
Columbus, IN	115	2.2	10	0.2	195	3.8	0	0.0	30	0.6
Columbus, OH	11,525	8.8	210	0.2	4,095	3.1	30	0.0	1,295	1.0
Corpus Christi, TX	610	3.2	20	0.1	145	0.8	0	0.0	160	0.8
Corvallis, OR	20	0.4	95	1.9	240	4.8	0	0.0	65	1.3
Crestview–Fort Walton Beach–Destin, FL	765	6.7	45	0.4	190	1.7	0	0.0	175	1.5
Cumberland, MD–WV	105	2.6	0	0.0	35	0.9	0	0.0	29	0.7
Dallas–Fort Worth–Arlington, TX	45,130	10.3	1,520	0.3	21,720	4.9	230	0.1	5,255	1.2
Dalton, GA	115	2.1	0	0.0	65	1.2	0	0.0	19	0.4
Danville, IL	165	5.3	0	0.0	55	1.8	0	0.0	60	1.9
Danville, VA	625	16.9	0	0.0	20	0.5	0	0.0	0	0.0
Davenport–Moline–Rock Island, IA–IL	435	2.1	25	0.1	375	1.8	15	0.1	140	0.7
Dayton, OH	4,470	9.6	65	0.1	720	1.5	10	0.0	635	1.4
Decatur, AL	595	9.2	130	2.0	25	0.4	0	0.0	124	1.9
Decatur, IL	360	6.8	15	0.3	20	0.4	0	0.0	60	1.1
Deltona–Daytona Beach–Ormond Beach, FL	1,090	4.3	95	0.4	365	1.4	0	0.0	120	0.5
Denver–Aurora–Broomfield, CO	6,270	3.1	560	0.3	5,105	2.5	70	0.0	2,340	1.2
Des Moines–West Des Moines, IA	800	1.8	50	0.1	970	2.1	0	0.0	250	0.6
Detroit–Warren–Livonia, MI	31,650	12.6	460	0.2	9,170	3.7	40	0.0	2,280	0.9
Dothan, AL	535	9.1	40	0.7	95	1.6	0	0.0	38	0.6
Dover, DE	1,515	19.1	15	0.2	180	2.3	0	0.0	135	1.7
Dubuque, IA	75	1.3	0	0.0	30	0.5	0	0.0	19	0.3
Duluth, MN–WI	90	0.6	215	1.4	165	1.1	0	0.0	140	0.9
Durham–Chapel Hill, NC	6,245	18.7	65	0.2	1,100	3.3	15	0.0	410	1.2
Eau Claire, WI	0	0.0	25	0.3	165	1.7	0	0.0	4	0.0
El Centro, CA	45	0.8	70	1.3	150	2.7	0	0.0	40	0.7
Elizabethtown, KY	550	10.5	4	0.1	45	0.9	0	0.0	40	0.8
Elkhart–Goshen, IN	265	2.9	20	0.2	65	0.7	0	0.0	50	0.6
Elmira, NY	115	3.0	0	0.0	65	1.7	0	0.0	50	1.3
El Paso, TX	545	1.9	60	0.2	495	1.7	0	0.0	265	0.9
Erie, PA	375	2.9	40	0.3	110	0.8	0	0.0	54	0.4
Eugene–Springfield, OR	170	0.9	140	0.7	245	1.2	4	0.0	400	2.0
Evansville, IN–KY	590	3.3	35	0.2	80	0.4	0	0.0	189	1.0
Fairbanks, AK	140	2.7	110	2.1	160	3.1	0	0.0	140	2.7
Fargo, ND–MN	90	0.7	100	0.7	155	1.1	80	0.6	39	0.3

C-3 Management, Business, and Financial Workers, by Metropolitan Statistical Area, Sex, Race, and Hispanic or Latino Origin, 2006–2010—Continued

Metropolitan Statistical Area	Total who worked in the last 5 years	Male Number	Male Percent	Female Number	Female Percent	Hispanic or Latino Number	Hispanic or Latino Percent	White alone, not Hispanic or Latino Number	White alone, not Hispanic or Latino Percent
Farmington, NM	5,540	3,300	59.6	2,240	40.4	685	12.4	3,800	68.6
Fayetteville, NC	12,990	7,265	55.9	5,725	44.1	715	5.5	7,720	59.4
Fayetteville–Springdale–Rogers, AR–MO	28,295	17,980	63.5	10,315	36.5	1,215	4.3	25,250	89.2
Flagstaff, AZ	6,500	3,900	60.0	2,600	40.0	370	5.7	5,035	77.5
Flint, MI	16,785	8,685	51.7	8,100	48.3	225	1.3	14,320	85.3
Florence, SC	8,320	4,865	58.5	3,455	41.5	35	0.4	6,440	77.4
Florence–Muscle Shoals, AL	5,450	3,205	58.8	2,245	41.2	24	0.4	4,745	87.1
Fond du Lac, WI	5,650	3,575	63.3	2,075	36.7	65	1.2	5,480	97.0
Fort Collins–Loveland, CO	22,920	13,880	60.6	9,035	39.4	1,305	5.7	20,965	91.5
Fort Smith, AR–OK	11,685	7,520	64.4	4,165	35.6	385	3.3	10,275	87.9
Fort Wayne, IN	22,750	14,095	62.0	8,655	38.0	300	1.3	20,510	90.2
Fresno, CA	38,710	22,935	59.2	15,780	40.8	10,445	27.0	22,835	59.0
Gadsden, AL	4,005	2,385	59.6	1,620	40.4	45	1.1	3,470	86.6
Gainesville, FL	14,835	8,490	57.2	6,345	42.8	540	3.6	11,495	77.5
Gainesville, GA	8,840	5,295	59.9	3,545	40.1	285	3.2	8,095	91.6
Glens Falls, NY	6,420	3,905	60.8	2,515	39.2	29	0.5	6,330	98.6
Goldsboro, NC	5,260	2,945	56.0	2,315	44.0	100	1.9	4,105	78.0
Grand Forks, ND–MN	6,010	3,850	64.1	2,160	35.9	40	0.7	5,865	97.6
Grand Junction, CO	8,680	5,105	58.8	3,575	41.2	685	7.9	7,610	87.7
Grand Rapids–Wyoming, MI	42,720	25,540	59.8	17,180	40.2	1,105	2.6	39,195	91.7
Great Falls, MT	4,420	2,510	56.8	1,910	43.2	85	1.9	4,020	91.0
Greeley, CO	15,460	9,715	62.8	5,745	37.2	1,815	11.7	13,055	84.4
Green Bay, WI	18,835	10,990	58.3	7,845	41.7	245	1.3	17,940	95.2
Greensboro–High Point, NC	41,310	23,830	57.7	17,475	42.3	1,150	2.8	32,375	78.4
Greenville, NC	9,015	5,515	61.2	3,500	38.8	175	1.9	7,195	79.8
Greenville–Mauldin–Easley, SC	33,905	21,145	62.4	12,760	37.6	630	1.9	29,310	86.4
Gulfport–Biloxi, MS	11,215	6,655	59.3	4,560	40.7	190	1.7	9,235	82.3
Hagerstown–Martinsburg, MD–WV	14,450	8,240	57.0	6,210	43.0	305	2.1	12,885	89.2
Hanford–Corcoran, CA	4,115	2,595	63.1	1,520	36.9	1,070	26.0	2,735	66.5
Harrisburg–Carlisle, PA	36,140	20,730	57.4	15,410	42.6	530	1.5	32,090	88.8
Harrisonburg, VA	5,860	3,550	60.6	2,310	39.4	140	2.4	5,565	95.0
Hartford–West Hartford–East Hartford, CT	88,100	50,865	57.7	37,235	42.3	3,910	4.4	74,875	85.0
Hattiesburg, MS	7,040	4,290	60.9	2,750	39.1	125	1.8	5,755	81.7
Hickory–Lenoir–Morganton, NC	15,790	9,660	61.2	6,130	38.8	405	2.6	14,680	93.0
Hinesville–Fort Stewart, GA	2,220	1,180	53.2	1,035	46.6	135	6.1	1,175	52.9
Holland–Grand Haven, MI	15,785	10,315	65.3	5,470	34.7	580	3.7	14,700	93.1
Honolulu, HI	54,035	30,165	55.8	23,870	44.2	2,945	5.5	14,840	27.5
Hot Springs, AR	4,605	2,930	63.6	1,675	36.4	84	1.8	4,175	90.7
Houma–Bayou Cane–Thibodaux, LA	8,240	5,250	63.7	2,990	36.3	70	0.8	7,270	88.2
Houston–Sugar Land–Baytown, TX	353,640	219,525	62.1	134,115	37.9	55,540	15.7	231,495	65.5
Huntington–Ashland, WV–KY–OH	10,550	6,435	61.0	4,110	39.0	10	0.1	10,140	96.1
Huntsville, AL	25,160	15,320	60.9	9,840	39.1	595	2.4	19,890	79.1
Idaho Falls, ID	7,040	4,795	68.1	2,245	31.9	300	4.3	6,530	92.8
Indianapolis–Carmel, IN	117,805	70,405	59.8	47,405	40.2	2,390	2.0	101,205	85.9
Iowa City, IA	9,695	6,160	63.5	3,540	36.5	75	0.8	9,215	95.0
Ithaca, NY	5,840	3,080	52.7	2,760	47.3	130	2.2	5,225	89.5
Jackson, MI	6,945	3,885	55.9	3,060	44.1	135	1.9	6,370	91.7
Jackson, MS	28,990	16,375	56.5	12,615	43.5	460	1.6	20,930	72.2
Jackson, TN	5,455	3,250	59.6	2,205	40.4	125	2.3	4,210	77.2
Jacksonville, FL	90,180	51,530	57.1	38,650	42.9	3,655	4.1	71,390	79.2
Jacksonville, NC	5,525	2,975	53.8	2,550	46.2	275	5.0	4,120	74.6
Janesville, WI	7,920	4,855	61.3	3,070	38.8	295	3.7	7,385	93.2
Jefferson City, MO	9,715	5,775	59.4	3,945	40.6	55	0.6	9,270	95.4
Johnson City, TN	9,225	5,735	62.2	3,490	37.8	95	1.0	8,835	95.8
Johnstown, PA	5,550	3,300	59.5	2,250	40.5	79	1.4	5,285	95.2

C-3 **Management, Business, and Financial Workers, by Metropolitan Statistical Area, Sex, Race, and Hispanic or Latino Origin, 2006–2010**—*Continued*

Metropolitan Statistical Area	Black alone, not Hispanic or Latino Number	Percent	American Indian and Alaska Native alone, not Hispanic or Latino Number	Percent	Asian alone, not Hispanic or Latino Number	Percent	Native Hawaiian and Other Pacific Islander alone, not Hispanic or Latino Number	Percent	Two or more races, not Hispanic or Latino Number	Percent
Farmington, NM	15	0.3	960	17.3	40	0.7	0	0.0	40	0.7
Fayetteville, NC	3,825	29.4	170	1.3	190	1.5	65	0.5	305	2.3
Fayetteville–Springdale–Rogers, AR–MO	515	1.8	220	0.8	695	2.5	40	0.1	370	1.3
Flagstaff, AZ	55	0.8	665	10.2	285	4.4	4	0.1	85	1.3
Flint, MI	1,820	10.8	55	0.3	115	0.7	4	0.0	240	1.4
Florence, SC	1,655	19.9	0	0.0	185	2.2	0	0.0	0	0.0
Florence–Muscle Shoals, AL	575	10.6	15	0.3	55	1.0	0	0.0	45	0.8
Fond du Lac, WI	4	0.1	4	0.1	70	1.2	0	0.0	19	0.3
Fort Collins–Loveland, CO	110	0.5	65	0.3	360	1.6	0	0.0	109	0.5
Fort Smith, AR–OK	145	1.2	325	2.8	115	1.0	0	0.0	443	3.8
Fort Wayne, IN	1,260	5.5	55	0.2	415	1.8	15	0.1	200	0.9
Fresno, CA	1,525	3.9	105	0.3	3,050	7.9	20	0.1	735	1.9
Gadsden, AL	410	10.2	10	0.2	30	0.7	15	0.4	20	0.5
Gainesville, FL	1,970	13.3	60	0.4	500	3.4	0	0.0	275	1.9
Gainesville, GA	335	3.8	35	0.4	80	0.9	0	0.0	8	0.1
Glens Falls, NY	30	0.5	0	0.0	20	0.3	0	0.0	15	0.2
Goldsboro, NC	915	17.4	20	0.4	30	0.6	0	0.0	90	1.7
Grand Forks, ND–MN	10	0.2	40	0.7	45	0.7	4	0.1	18	0.3
Grand Junction, CO	90	1.0	20	0.2	145	1.7	20	0.2	110	1.3
Grand Rapids–Wyoming, MI	1,480	3.5	90	0.2	460	1.1	20	0.0	370	0.9
Great Falls, MT	70	1.6	145	3.3	0	0.0	0	0.0	100	2.3
Greeley, CO	130	0.8	50	0.3	170	1.1	0	0.0	240	1.6
Green Bay, WI	150	0.8	205	1.1	205	1.1	0	0.0	94	0.5
Greensboro–High Point, NC	6,505	15.7	170	0.4	755	1.8	0	0.0	355	0.9
Greenville, NC	1,355	15.0	55	0.6	195	2.2	0	0.0	35	0.4
Greenville–Mauldin–Easley, SC	3,000	8.8	20	0.1	785	2.3	4	0.0	154	0.5
Gulfport–Biloxi, MS	1,345	12.0	0	0.0	320	2.9	0	0.0	125	1.1
Hagerstown–Martinsburg, MD–WV	825	5.7	60	0.4	205	1.4	0	0.0	174	1.2
Hanford–Corcoran, CA	145	3.5	20	0.5	110	2.7	0	0.0	33	0.8
Harrisburg–Carlisle, PA	2,170	6.0	45	0.1	870	2.4	0	0.0	435	1.2
Harrisonburg, VA	95	1.6	0	0.0	60	1.0	0	0.0	0	0.0
Hartford–West Hartford–East Hartford, CT	4,520	5.1	90	0.1	3,745	4.3	35	0.0	915	1.0
Hattiesburg, MS	945	13.4	10	0.1	160	2.3	0	0.0	45	0.6
Hickory–Lenoir–Morganton, NC	595	3.8	15	0.1	55	0.3	4	0.0	40	0.3
Hinesville–Fort Stewart, GA	775	34.9	30	1.4	80	3.6	0	0.0	25	1.1
Holland–Grand Haven, MI	125	0.8	55	0.3	215	1.4	15	0.1	100	0.6
Honolulu, HI	1,035	1.9	35	0.1	25,025	46.3	2,940	5.4	7,225	13.4
Hot Springs, AR	250	5.4	10	0.2	15	0.3	0	0.0	70	1.5
Houma–Bayou Cane–Thibodaux, LA	620	7.5	110	1.3	120	1.5	0	0.0	49	0.6
Houston–Sugar Land–Baytown, TX	40,850	11.6	840	0.2	21,255	6.0	200	0.1	3,455	1.0
Huntington–Ashland, WV–KY–OH	275	2.6	10	0.1	35	0.3	0	0.0	79	0.7
Huntsville, AL	3,460	13.8	180	0.7	640	2.5	55	0.2	335	1.3
Idaho Falls, ID	0	0.0	40	0.6	75	1.1	10	0.1	80	1.1
Indianapolis–Carmel, IN	10,535	8.9	85	0.1	2,360	2.0	85	0.1	1,155	1.0
Iowa City, IA	90	0.9	0	0.0	255	2.6	10	0.1	45	0.5
Ithaca, NY	190	3.3	35	0.6	115	2.0	0	0.0	140	2.4
Jackson, MI	270	3.9	0	0.0	115	1.7	0	0.0	50	0.7
Jackson, MS	7,190	24.8	10	0.0	265	0.9	0	0.0	135	0.5
Jackson, TN	1,040	19.1	0	0.0	55	1.0	15	0.3	4	0.1
Jacksonville, FL	11,390	12.6	280	0.3	2,255	2.5	65	0.1	1,140	1.3
Jacksonville, NC	800	14.5	20	0.4	140	2.5	20	0.4	149	2.7
Janesville, WI	130	1.6	10	0.1	25	0.3	0	0.0	70	0.9
Jefferson City, MO	295	3.0	15	0.2	40	0.4	0	0.0	40	0.4
Johnson City, TN	145	1.6	45	0.5	55	0.6	0	0.0	49	0.5
Johnstown, PA	120	2.2	0	0.0	45	0.8	0	0.0	20	0.4

PART C—METROPOLITAN STATISTICAL AREA TABLES

C-3 Management, Business, and Financial Workers, by Metropolitan Statistical Area, Sex, Race, and Hispanic or Latino Origin, 2006–2010—Continued

Metropolitan Statistical Area	Total who worked in the last 5 years	Male Number	Male Percent	Female Number	Female Percent	Hispanic or Latino Number	Hispanic or Latino Percent	White alone, not Hispanic or Latino Number	White alone, not Hispanic or Latino Percent
Jonesboro, AR	5,410	3,550	65.6	1,865	34.5	65	1.2	5,015	92.7
Joplin, MO	7,870	4,690	59.6	3,185	40.5	60	0.8	7,290	92.6
Kalamazoo–Portage, MI	18,070	10,940	60.5	7,125	39.4	490	2.7	16,020	88.7
Kankakee–Bradley, IL	4,655	2,690	57.8	1,965	42.2	165	3.5	4,000	85.9
Kansas City, MO–KS	145,175	85,410	58.8	59,765	41.2	4,515	3.1	126,305	87.0
Kennewick–Pasco–Richland, WA	13,550	8,815	65.1	4,735	34.9	1,330	9.8	11,735	86.6
Killeen–Temple–Fort Hood, TX	15,095	8,010	53.1	7,085	46.9	1,575	10.4	10,785	71.4
Kingsport–Bristol–Bristol, TN–VA	13,270	7,920	59.7	5,350	40.3	15	0.1	12,885	97.1
Kingston, NY	10,775	6,060	56.2	4,715	43.8	415	3.9	10,020	93.0
Knoxville, TN	40,065	25,205	62.9	14,865	37.1	585	1.5	36,885	92.1
Kokomo, IN	3,735	2,310	61.8	1,425	38.2	4	0.1	3,670	98.3
La Crosse, WI–MN	7,095	4,395	61.9	2,700	38.1	90	1.3	6,780	95.6
Lafayette, IN	10,110	6,310	62.4	3,800	37.6	195	1.9	9,400	93.0
Lafayette, LA	13,960	8,875	63.6	5,085	36.4	155	1.1	12,050	86.3
Lake Charles, LA	8,830	5,290	59.9	3,540	40.1	170	1.9	7,395	83.7
Lake Havasu City–Kingman, AZ	7,650	4,205	55.0	3,445	45.0	470	6.1	6,840	89.4
Lakeland–Winter Haven, FL	27,950	16,410	58.7	11,540	41.3	2,385	8.5	22,405	80.2
Lancaster, PA	29,930	19,855	66.3	10,075	33.7	845	2.8	28,210	94.3
Lansing–East Lansing, MI	26,390	14,715	55.8	11,675	44.2	1,145	4.3	22,670	85.9
Laredo, TX	9,445	6,190	65.5	3,255	34.5	8,780	93.0	460	4.9
Las Cruces, NM	7,865	4,620	58.7	3,245	41.3	3,310	42.1	4,010	51.0
Las Vegas–Paradise, NV	100,430	59,185	58.9	41,245	41.1	12,455	12.4	71,480	71.2
Lawrence, KS	7,245	4,570	63.1	2,675	36.9	295	4.1	6,385	88.1
Lawton, OK	4,200	2,390	56.9	1,810	43.1	215	5.1	3,115	74.2
Lebanon, PA	6,865	4,445	64.7	2,420	35.3	180	2.6	6,500	94.7
Lewiston, ID–WA	2,945	1,675	56.9	1,270	43.1	45	1.5	2,790	94.7
Lewiston–Auburn, ME	5,900	3,535	59.9	2,370	40.2	80	1.4	5,705	96.7
Lexington–Fayette, KY	29,445	18,000	61.1	11,445	38.9	440	1.5	26,840	91.2
Lima, OH	4,525	2,860	63.2	1,670	36.9	34	0.8	4,170	92.2
Lincoln, NE	21,535	12,335	57.3	9,200	42.7	555	2.6	20,220	93.9
Little Rock–North Little Rock–Conway, AR	39,015	22,695	58.2	16,320	41.8	735	1.9	31,805	81.5
Logan, UT–ID	6,120	4,305	70.3	1,815	29.7	215	3.5	5,775	94.4
Longview, TX	9,580	5,770	60.2	3,810	39.8	410	4.3	7,870	82.2
Longview, WA	4,200	2,295	54.6	1,905	45.4	175	4.2	3,765	89.6
Los Angeles–Long Beach–Santa Ana, CA	805,460	475,885	59.1	329,575	40.9	167,640	20.8	437,550	54.3
Louisville/Jefferson County, KY–IN	72,530	41,740	57.5	30,795	42.5	1,005	1.4	64,270	88.6
Lubbock, TX	14,115	8,625	61.1	5,490	38.9	2,455	17.4	10,750	76.2
Lynchburg, VA	13,155	7,805	59.3	5,350	40.7	65	0.5	11,595	88.1
Macon, GA	10,325	5,980	57.9	4,340	42.0	125	1.2	7,450	72.2
Madera–Chowchilla, CA	5,655	3,660	64.7	1,995	35.3	1,420	25.1	3,645	64.5
Madison, WI	45,120	25,295	56.1	19,825	43.9	900	2.0	41,610	92.2
Manchester–Nashua, NH	32,730	20,460	62.5	12,270	37.5	605	1.8	30,610	93.5
Manhattan, KS	6,075	3,570	58.8	2,505	41.2	225	3.7	5,270	86.7
Mankato–North Mankato, MN	6,225	4,100	65.9	2,125	34.1	19	0.3	6,085	97.8
Mansfield, OH	5,190	2,995	57.7	2,195	42.3	60	1.2	4,665	89.9
McAllen–Edinburg–Mission, TX	22,330	14,180	63.5	8,155	36.5	17,905	80.2	3,820	17.1
Medford, OR	10,510	5,660	53.9	4,845	46.1	525	5.0	9,505	90.4
Memphis, TN–MS–AR	72,340	42,020	58.1	30,320	41.9	1,575	2.2	49,925	69.0
Merced, CA	8,100	4,930	60.9	3,170	39.1	2,830	34.9	4,410	54.4
Miami–Fort Lauderdale–Pompano Beach, FL	346,420	208,345	60.1	138,075	39.9	123,615	35.7	173,910	50.2
Michigan City–La Porte, IN	5,120	2,990	58.4	2,130	41.6	135	2.6	4,690	91.6
Midland, TX	7,445	5,425	72.9	2,020	27.1	1,150	15.4	5,840	78.4
Milwaukee–Waukesha–West Allis, WI	102,235	58,570	57.3	43,665	42.7	3,140	3.1	88,660	86.7
Minneapolis–St. Paul–Bloomington, MN–WI	271,575	154,890	57.0	116,685	43.0	5,545	2.0	245,065	90.2
Missoula, MT	6,640	3,770	56.8	2,865	43.1	120	1.8	6,365	95.9

C-3 **Management, Business, and Financial Workers, by Metropolitan Statistical Area, Sex, Race, and Hispanic or Latino Origin, 2006–2010**—*Continued*

Metropolitan Statistical Area	Black alone, not Hispanic or Latino Number	Percent	American Indian and Alaska Native alone, not Hispanic or Latino Number	Percent	Asian alone, not Hispanic or Latino Number	Percent	Native Hawaiian and Other Pacific Islander alone, not Hispanic or Latino Number	Percent	Two or more races, not Hispanic or Latino Number	Percent
Jonesboro, AR	195	3.6	25	0.5	70	1.3	0	0.0	45	0.8
Joplin, MO	40	0.5	135	1.7	160	2.0	0	0.0	179	2.3
Kalamazoo–Portage, MI	1,055	5.8	20	0.1	290	1.6	40	0.2	160	0.9
Kankakee–Bradley, IL	395	8.5	40	0.9	35	0.8	0	0.0	20	0.4
Kansas City, MO–KS	9,655	6.7	565	0.4	2,410	1.7	50	0.0	1,680	1.2
Kennewick–Pasco–Richland, WA	120	0.9	30	0.2	245	1.8	10	0.1	85	0.6
Killeen–Temple–Fort Hood, TX	1,965	13.0	30	0.2	470	3.1	20	0.1	245	1.6
Kingsport–Bristol–Bristol, TN–VA	165	1.2	30	0.2	135	1.0	15	0.1	30	0.2
Kingston, NY	240	2.2	10	0.1	65	0.6	0	0.0	24	0.2
Knoxville, TN	1,635	4.1	80	0.2	535	1.3	75	0.2	275	0.7
Kokomo, IN	30	0.8	0	0.0	15	0.4	0	0.0	15	0.4
La Crosse, WI–MN	90	1.3	50	0.7	70	1.0	0	0.0	18	0.3
Lafayette, IN	165	1.6	10	0.1	310	3.1	0	0.0	23	0.2
Lafayette, LA	1,575	11.3	10	0.1	100	0.7	0	0.0	75	0.5
Lake Charles, LA	1,100	12.5	15	0.2	130	1.5	0	0.0	20	0.2
Lake Havasu City–Kingman, AZ	40	0.5	125	1.6	105	1.4	0	0.0	70	0.9
Lakeland–Winter Haven, FL	2,030	7.3	90	0.3	725	2.6	0	0.0	320	1.1
Lancaster, PA	265	0.9	35	0.1	340	1.1	25	0.1	210	0.7
Lansing–East Lansing, MI	1,740	6.6	35	0.1	360	1.4	20	0.1	415	1.6
Laredo, TX	120	1.3	0	0.0	65	0.7	0	0.0	19	0.2
Las Cruces, NM	155	2.0	35	0.4	160	2.0	0	0.0	190	2.4
Las Vegas–Paradise, NV	6,970	6.9	525	0.5	6,760	6.7	345	0.3	1,900	1.9
Lawrence, KS	130	1.8	100	1.4	180	2.5	0	0.0	150	2.1
Lawton, OK	470	11.2	215	5.1	90	2.1	0	0.0	95	2.3
Lebanon, PA	70	1.0	0	0.0	85	1.2	0	0.0	30	0.4
Lewiston, ID–WA	0	0.0	40	1.4	15	0.5	0	0.0	59	2.0
Lewiston–Auburn, ME	4	0.1	4	0.1	15	0.3	0	0.0	100	1.7
Lexington–Fayette, KY	1,360	4.6	25	0.1	530	1.8	0	0.0	245	0.8
Lima, OH	245	5.4	0	0.0	35	0.8	0	0.0	34	0.8
Lincoln, NE	240	1.1	25	0.1	370	1.7	0	0.0	130	0.6
Little Rock–North Little Rock–Conway, AR	5,490	14.1	185	0.5	470	1.2	0	0.0	325	0.8
Logan, UT–ID	65	1.1	15	0.2	45	0.7	0	0.0	4	0.1
Longview, TX	1,085	11.3	40	0.4	65	0.7	0	0.0	110	1.1
Longview, WA	55	1.3	25	0.6	135	3.2	0	0.0	45	1.1
Los Angeles–Long Beach–Santa Ana, CA	46,005	5.7	1,435	0.2	137,305	17.0	1,925	0.2	13,595	1.7
Louisville/Jefferson County, KY–IN	5,450	7.5	95	0.1	1,125	1.6	85	0.1	510	0.7
Lubbock, TX	485	3.4	45	0.3	295	2.1	10	0.1	79	0.6
Lynchburg, VA	1,290	9.8	20	0.2	70	0.5	0	0.0	110	0.8
Macon, GA	2,605	25.2	4	0.0	40	0.4	4	0.0	90	0.9
Madera–Chowchilla, CA	205	3.6	115	2.0	95	1.7	10	0.2	165	2.9
Madison, WI	1,025	2.3	95	0.2	1,070	2.4	0	0.0	420	0.9
Manchester–Nashua, NH	385	1.2	20	0.1	850	2.6	0	0.0	260	0.8
Manhattan, KS	370	6.1	50	0.8	90	1.5	0	0.0	74	1.2
Mankato–North Mankato, MN	30	0.5	15	0.2	40	0.6	0	0.0	35	0.6
Mansfield, OH	240	4.6	40	0.8	95	1.8	0	0.0	90	1.7
McAllen–Edinburg–Mission, TX	155	0.7	45	0.2	315	1.4	0	0.0	89	0.4
Medford, OR	60	0.6	0	0.0	190	1.8	4	0.0	220	2.1
Memphis, TN–MS–AR	18,445	25.5	135	0.2	1,635	2.3	15	0.0	615	0.9
Merced, CA	270	3.3	10	0.1	465	5.7	0	0.0	114	1.4
Miami–Fort Lauderdale–Pompano Beach, FL	35,750	10.3	405	0.1	8,925	2.6	20	0.0	3,795	1.1
Michigan City–La Porte, IN	280	5.5	0	0.0	0	0.0	0	0.0	19	0.4
Midland, TX	205	2.8	10	0.1	185	2.5	0	0.0	50	0.7
Milwaukee–Waukesha–West Allis, WI	7,405	7.2	215	0.2	2,075	2.0	40	0.0	700	0.7
Minneapolis–St. Paul–Bloomington, MN–WI	8,015	3.0	870	0.3	8,880	3.3	110	0.0	3,095	1.1
Missoula, MT	0	0.0	65	1.0	30	0.5	0	0.0	65	1.0

C-3 Management, Business, and Financial Workers, by Metropolitan Statistical Area, Sex, Race, and Hispanic or Latino Origin, 2006–2010—Continued

Metropolitan Statistical Area	Total who worked in the last 5 years	Male Number	Male Percent	Female Number	Female Percent	Hispanic or Latino Number	Hispanic or Latino Percent	White alone, not Hispanic or Latino Number	White alone, not Hispanic or Latino Percent
Mobile, AL	17,145	10,010	58.4	7,135	41.6	275	1.6	13,630	79.5
Modesto, CA	20,970	12,920	61.6	8,045	38.4	4,280	20.4	15,105	72.0
Monroe, LA	7,355	4,435	60.3	2,915	39.6	95	1.3	5,830	79.3
Monroe, MI	6,610	4,130	62.5	2,480	37.5	150	2.3	6,290	95.2
Montgomery, AL	19,405	11,105	57.2	8,300	42.8	165	0.9	13,730	70.8
Morgantown, WV	5,440	3,145	57.8	2,300	42.3	100	1.8	5,050	92.8
Morristown, TN	5,695	3,405	59.8	2,295	40.3	150	2.6	5,380	94.5
Mount Vernon–Anacortes, WA	6,190	3,715	60.0	2,475	40.0	430	6.9	5,480	88.5
Muncie, IN	4,975	3,000	60.3	1,975	39.7	55	1.1	4,630	93.1
Muskegon–Norton Shores, MI	6,350	3,815	60.1	2,535	39.9	29	0.5	5,730	90.2
Myrtle Beach–North Myrtle Beach–Conway, SC	14,210	8,635	60.8	5,575	39.2	340	2.4	12,860	90.5
Napa, CA	9,720	5,585	57.5	4,140	42.6	1,065	11.0	7,765	79.9
Naples–Marco Island, FL	17,600	11,405	64.8	6,195	35.2	1,775	10.1	15,275	86.8
Nashville-Davidson–Murfreesboro–Franklin, TN	101,815	61,470	60.4	40,340	39.6	2,090	2.1	88,300	86.7
New Haven–Milford, CT	53,020	30,835	58.2	22,185	41.8	2,575	4.9	44,535	84.0
New Orleans–Metairie–Kenner, LA	61,940	36,665	59.2	25,275	40.8	3,080	5.0	45,800	73.9
New York–Northern New Jersey–Long Island, NY–NJ–PA	1,247,080	736,550	59.1	510,530	40.9	135,520	10.9	838,165	67.2
Niles–Benton Harbor, MI	8,010	4,970	62.0	3,040	38.0	160	2.0	7,290	91.0
North Port–Bradenton–Sarasota, FL	39,735	23,555	59.3	16,180	40.7	1,920	4.8	35,495	89.3
Norwich–New London, CT	15,530	9,180	59.1	6,345	40.9	410	2.6	13,960	89.9
Ocala, FL	13,230	8,005	60.5	5,225	39.5	980	7.4	11,075	83.7
Ocean City, NJ	5,570	3,515	63.1	2,055	36.9	30	0.5	5,350	96.1
Odessa, TX	5,080	3,180	62.6	1,905	37.5	1,620	31.9	3,175	62.5
Ogden–Clearfield, UT	33,595	21,975	65.4	11,620	34.6	1,880	5.6	30,525	90.9
Oklahoma City, OK	72,965	42,585	58.4	30,380	41.6	3,365	4.6	58,970	80.8
Olympia, WA	17,555	9,555	54.4	8,000	45.6	820	4.7	14,945	85.1
Omaha–Council Bluffs, NE–IA	59,430	34,685	58.4	24,745	41.6	1,705	2.9	54,205	91.2
Orlando–Kissimmee–Sanford, FL	139,240	80,565	57.9	58,675	42.1	19,000	13.6	101,670	73.0
Oshkosh–Neenah, WI	9,275	5,200	56.1	4,080	44.0	90	1.0	9,050	97.6
Owensboro, KY	5,080	3,105	61.1	1,975	38.9	40	0.8	4,875	96.0
Oxnard–Thousand Oaks–Ventura, CA	58,860	35,670	60.6	23,190	39.4	10,605	18.0	41,660	70.8
Palm Bay–Melbourne–Titusville, FL	30,805	18,975	61.6	11,835	38.4	1,675	5.4	26,485	86.0
Palm Coast, FL	5,365	3,245	60.5	2,120	39.5	170	3.2	4,670	87.0
Panama City–Lynn Haven–Panama City Beach, FL	8,995	5,385	59.9	3,610	40.1	270	3.0	8,045	89.4
Parkersburg–Marietta–Vienna, WV–OH	6,410	3,655	57.0	2,755	43.0	60	0.9	6,250	97.5
Pascagoula, MS	7,415	4,150	56.0	3,265	44.0	315	4.2	6,375	86.0
Pensacola–Ferry Pass–Brent, FL	20,985	12,180	58.0	8,805	42.0	575	2.7	17,965	85.6
Peoria, IL	21,680	13,200	60.9	8,475	39.1	390	1.8	20,065	92.6
Philadelphia–Camden–Wilmington, PA–NJ–DE–MD	404,785	237,590	58.7	167,195	41.3	12,720	3.1	327,215	80.8
Phoenix–Mesa–Glendale, AZ	268,725	160,380	59.7	108,345	40.3	35,545	13.2	209,975	78.1
Pine Bluff, AR	3,820	2,230	58.4	1,590	41.6	60	1.6	2,665	69.8
Pittsburgh, PA	139,095	82,120	59.0	56,975	41.0	1,470	1.1	128,295	92.2
Pittsfield, MA	7,415	4,095	55.2	3,325	44.8	109	1.5	7,125	96.1
Pocatello, ID	4,150	2,515	60.6	1,635	39.4	65	1.6	3,940	94.9
Portland–South Portland–Biddeford, ME	37,835	20,835	55.1	17,000	44.9	230	0.6	36,575	96.7
Portland–Vancouver–Hillsboro, OR–WA	156,580	91,180	58.2	65,400	41.8	5,850	3.7	136,560	87.2
Port St. Lucie, FL	20,715	12,805	61.8	7,910	38.2	1,620	7.8	16,925	81.7
Poughkeepsie–Newburgh–Middletown, NY	41,475	25,760	62.1	15,715	37.9	3,090	7.5	33,935	81.8
Prescott, AZ	10,440	6,015	57.6	4,425	42.4	520	5.0	9,655	92.5
Providence–New Bedford–Fall River, RI–MA	96,280	55,315	57.5	40,965	42.5	2,965	3.1	86,635	90.0

C-3 Management, Business, and Financial Workers, by Metropolitan Statistical Area, Sex, Race, and Hispanic or Latino Origin, 2006–2010—Continued

Metropolitan Statistical Area	Black alone, not Hispanic or Latino Number	Percent	American Indian and Alaska Native alone, not Hispanic or Latino Number	Percent	Asian alone, not Hispanic or Latino Number	Percent	Native Hawaiian and Other Pacific Islander alone, not Hispanic or Latino Number	Percent	Two or more races, not Hispanic or Latino Number	Percent
Mobile, AL	2,845	16.6	80	0.5	200	1.2	0	0.0	109	0.6
Modesto, CA	205	1.0	115	0.5	755	3.6	160	0.8	355	1.7
Monroe, LA	1,280	17.4	30	0.4	105	1.4	0	0.0	15	0.2
Monroe, MI	65	1.0	0	0.0	35	0.5	0	0.0	70	1.1
Montgomery, AL	4,830	24.9	110	0.6	485	2.5	0	0.0	90	0.5
Morgantown, WV	170	3.1	10	0.2	75	1.4	0	0.0	35	0.6
Morristown, TN	45	0.8	20	0.4	75	1.3	0	0.0	29	0.5
Mount Vernon–Anacortes, WA	15	0.2	85	1.4	85	1.4	20	0.3	74	1.2
Muncie, IN	160	3.2	4	0.1	10	0.2	0	0.0	115	2.3
Muskegon–Norton Shores, MI	450	7.1	15	0.2	35	0.6	0	0.0	95	1.5
Myrtle Beach–North Myrtle Beach–Conway, SC	840	5.9	0	0.0	135	1.0	15	0.1	25	0.2
Napa, CA	155	1.6	45	0.5	545	5.6	20	0.2	130	1.3
Naples–Marco Island, FL	340	1.9	0	0.0	175	1.0	0	0.0	30	0.2
Nashville–Davidson–Murfreesboro–Franklin, TN	8,355	8.2	200	0.2	1,980	1.9	25	0.0	860	0.8
New Haven–Milford, CT	3,585	6.8	30	0.1	1,855	3.5	0	0.0	435	0.8
New Orleans–Metairie–Kenner, LA	10,840	17.5	120	0.2	1,440	2.3	30	0.0	630	1.0
New York–Northern New Jersey–Long Island, NY–NJ–PA	124,465	10.0	1,095	0.1	132,090	10.6	265	0.0	15,485	1.2
Niles–Benton Harbor, MI	300	3.7	75	0.9	85	1.1	0	0.0	95	1.2
North Port–Bradenton–Sarasota, FL	1,205	3.0	15	0.0	620	1.6	0	0.0	485	1.2
Norwich–New London, CT	220	1.4	60	0.4	535	3.4	15	0.1	325	2.1
Ocala, FL	895	6.8	4	0.0	110	0.8	15	0.1	139	1.1
Ocean City, NJ	165	3.0	15	0.3	0	0.0	0	0.0	10	0.2
Odessa, TX	165	3.2	0	0.0	35	0.7	4	0.1	85	1.7
Ogden–Clearfield, UT	260	0.8	55	0.2	485	1.4	40	0.1	355	1.1
Oklahoma City, OK	4,485	6.1	2,275	3.1	1,455	2.0	70	0.1	2,345	3.2
Olympia, WA	280	1.6	415	2.4	635	3.6	105	0.6	350	2.0
Omaha–Council Bluffs, NE–IA	1,975	3.3	20	0.0	975	1.6	25	0.0	520	0.9
Orlando–Kissimmee–Sanford, FL	11,490	8.3	175	0.1	4,765	3.4	55	0.0	2,085	1.5
Oshkosh–Neenah, WI	10	0.1	20	0.2	100	1.1	0	0.0	14	0.2
Owensboro, KY	130	2.6	4	0.1	25	0.5	0	0.0	4	0.1
Oxnard–Thousand Oaks–Ventura, CA	880	1.5	170	0.3	4,560	7.7	135	0.2	840	1.4
Palm Bay–Melbourne–Titusville, FL	1,510	4.9	190	0.6	540	1.8	25	0.1	385	1.2
Palm Coast, FL	390	7.3	20	0.4	60	1.1	10	0.2	45	0.8
Panama City–Lynn Haven–Panama City Beach, FL	380	4.2	20	0.2	140	1.6	0	0.0	140	1.6
Parkersburg–Marietta–Vienna, WV–OH	55	0.9	0	0.0	0	0.0	0	0.0	44	0.7
Pascagoula, MS	500	6.7	40	0.5	130	1.8	0	0.0	50	0.7
Pensacola–Ferry Pass–Brent, FL	1,725	8.2	70	0.3	340	1.6	50	0.2	260	1.2
Peoria, IL	770	3.6	15	0.1	370	1.7	0	0.0	70	0.3
Philadelphia–Camden–Wilmington, PA–NJ–DE–MD	44,390	11.0	260	0.1	15,795	3.9	50	0.0	4,345	1.1
Phoenix–Mesa–Glendale, AZ	9,295	3.5	2,320	0.9	8,115	3.0	405	0.2	3,070	1.1
Pine Bluff, AR	1,045	27.4	0	0.0	25	0.7	0	0.0	29	0.8
Pittsburgh, PA	5,665	4.1	140	0.1	2,615	1.9	0	0.0	920	0.7
Pittsfield, MA	80	1.1	15	0.2	75	1.0	0	0.0	10	0.1
Pocatello, ID	0	0.0	60	1.4	20	0.5	0	0.0	65	1.6
Portland–South Portland–Biddeford, ME	265	0.7	85	0.2	445	1.2	20	0.1	210	0.6
Portland–Vancouver–Hillsboro, OR–WA	2,850	1.8	670	0.4	7,230	4.6	280	0.2	3,140	2.0
Port St. Lucie, FL	1,615	7.8	15	0.1	285	1.4	10	0.0	250	1.2
Poughkeepsie–Newburgh–Middletown, NY	2,925	7.1	35	0.1	1,145	2.8	30	0.1	315	0.8
Prescott, AZ	30	0.3	65	0.6	70	0.7	40	0.4	60	0.6
Providence–New Bedford–Fall River, RI–MA	3,275	3.4	65	0.1	1,695	1.8	30	0.0	1,610	1.7

PART C—METROPOLITAN STATISTICAL AREA TABLES

C-3 Management, Business, and Financial Workers, by Metropolitan Statistical Area, Sex, Race, and Hispanic or Latino Origin, 2006–2010—Continued

Metropolitan Statistical Area	Total who worked in the last 5 years	Male Number	Male Percent	Female Number	Female Percent	Hispanic or Latino Number	Hispanic or Latino Percent	White alone, not Hispanic or Latino Number	White alone, not Hispanic or Latino Percent
Provo–Orem, UT	27,130	20,020	73.8	7,110	26.2	1,255	4.6	24,975	92.1
Pueblo, CO	6,985	4,230	60.6	2,755	39.4	1,840	26.3	4,785	68.5
Punta Gorda, FL	6,165	3,685	59.8	2,480	40.2	145	2.4	5,705	92.5
Racine, WI	10,395	6,325	60.8	4,070	39.2	540	5.2	9,190	88.4
Raleigh–Cary, NC	90,455	54,280	60.0	36,175	40.0	2,405	2.7	72,525	80.2
Rapid City, SD	7,155	4,195	58.6	2,960	41.4	120	1.7	6,565	91.8
Reading, PA	21,750	13,120	60.3	8,630	39.7	860	4.0	20,045	92.2
Redding, CA	8,605	5,260	61.1	3,345	38.9	240	2.8	7,655	89.0
Reno–Sparks, NV	26,845	15,655	58.3	11,190	41.7	2,555	9.5	22,015	82.0
Richmond, VA	88,995	50,220	56.4	38,775	43.6	1,725	1.9	68,350	76.8
Riverside–San Bernardino–Ontario, CA	188,570	113,955	60.4	74,620	39.6	49,325	26.2	107,805	57.2
Roanoke, VA	17,550	10,160	57.9	7,390	42.1	230	1.3	15,595	88.9
Rochester, MN	10,355	6,640	64.1	3,715	35.9	150	1.4	9,860	95.2
Rochester, NY	59,885	36,315	60.6	23,570	39.4	1,550	2.6	54,640	91.2
Rockford, IL	16,485	10,295	62.5	6,190	37.5	780	4.7	14,465	87.7
Rocky Mount, NC	6,695	3,655	54.6	3,035	45.3	275	4.1	4,525	67.6
Rome, GA	4,325	2,620	60.6	1,705	39.4	34	0.8	3,890	89.9
Sacramento–Arden-Arcade–Roseville, CA	144,215	80,075	55.5	64,140	44.5	15,240	10.6	103,555	71.8
Saginaw–Saginaw Township North, MI	8,110	4,720	58.2	3,395	41.9	335	4.1	6,950	85.7
St. Cloud, MN	11,420	7,080	62.0	4,340	38.0	70	0.6	11,190	98.0
St. George, UT	6,320	4,195	66.4	2,125	33.6	225	3.6	6,010	95.1
St. Joseph, MO–KS	6,465	4,055	62.7	2,410	37.3	70	1.1	6,160	95.3
St. Louis, MO–IL	177,485	103,305	58.2	74,180	41.8	2,590	1.5	153,680	86.6
Salem, OR	21,170	12,255	57.9	8,915	42.1	1,370	6.5	18,875	89.2
Salinas, CA	18,430	10,865	59.0	7,565	41.0	4,230	23.0	11,920	64.7
Salisbury, MD	6,460	3,725	57.7	2,740	42.4	105	1.6	5,360	83.0
Salt Lake City, UT	70,425	43,435	61.7	26,990	38.3	5,410	7.7	61,685	87.6
San Angelo, TX	4,955	3,135	63.3	1,820	36.7	885	17.9	3,810	76.9
San Antonio–New Braunfels, TX	120,265	70,435	58.6	49,830	41.4	43,510	36.2	65,905	54.8
San Diego–Carlsbad–San Marcos, CA	204,260	121,280	59.4	82,980	40.6	32,210	15.8	140,640	68.9
Sandusky, OH	3,610	2,200	60.9	1,410	39.1	80	2.2	3,375	93.5
San Francisco–Oakland–Fremont, CA	365,475	206,835	56.6	158,640	43.4	34,330	9.4	223,855	61.3
San Jose–Sunnyvale–Santa Clara, CA	145,760	89,160	61.2	56,600	38.8	18,105	12.4	77,810	53.4
San Luis Obispo–Paso Robles, CA	15,675	9,655	61.6	6,020	38.4	1,595	10.2	13,090	83.5
Santa Barbara–Santa Maria–Goleta, CA	23,920	14,355	60.0	9,565	40.0	4,550	19.0	17,305	72.3
Santa Cruz–Watsonville, CA	18,470	11,245	60.9	7,225	39.1	1,855	10.0	15,035	81.4
Santa Fe, NM	10,400	5,630	54.1	4,770	45.9	3,390	32.6	6,490	62.4
Santa Rosa–Petaluma, CA	32,685	19,130	58.5	13,555	41.5	3,245	9.9	27,120	83.0
Savannah, GA	18,495	10,845	58.6	7,650	41.4	475	2.6	14,185	76.7
Scranton–Wilkes-Barre, PA	26,115	15,810	60.5	10,305	39.5	465	1.8	24,855	95.2
Seattle–Tacoma–Bellevue, WA	271,410	157,390	58.0	114,020	42.0	10,190	3.8	217,605	80.2
Sebastian–Vero Beach, FL	7,375	4,695	63.7	2,680	36.3	315	4.3	6,620	89.8
Sheboygan, WI	6,230	3,745	60.1	2,490	40.0	75	1.2	6,010	96.5
Sherman–Denison, TX	5,565	3,180	57.1	2,380	42.8	300	5.4	4,960	89.1
Shreveport–Bossier City, LA	16,305	9,015	55.3	7,290	44.7	345	2.1	12,225	75.0
Sioux City, IA–NE–SD	7,375	4,815	65.3	2,560	34.7	240	3.3	6,880	93.3
Sioux Falls, SD	15,585	9,340	59.9	6,250	40.1	215	1.4	15,090	96.8
South Bend–Mishawaka, IN–MI	16,945	10,195	60.2	6,750	39.8	615	3.6	14,915	88.0
Spartanburg, SC	13,915	8,425	60.5	5,485	39.4	370	2.7	12,035	86.5
Spokane, WA	25,645	15,485	60.4	10,160	39.6	590	2.3	23,630	92.1
Springfield, IL	13,585	7,590	55.9	5,995	44.1	275	2.0	12,530	92.2
Springfield, MA	37,540	19,650	52.3	17,890	47.7	2,085	5.6	33,365	88.9
Springfield, MO	23,460	13,810	58.9	9,650	41.1	320	1.4	22,200	94.6
Springfield, OH	6,295	3,615	57.4	2,680	42.6	55	0.9	5,635	89.5
State College, PA	7,895	4,585	58.1	3,305	41.9	65	0.8	7,370	93.4

C-3. Management, Business, and Financial Workers, by Metropolitan Statistical Area, Sex, Race, and Hispanic or Latino Origin, 2006–2010—*Continued*

Metropolitan Statistical Area	Black alone, not Hispanic or Latino Number	Percent	American Indian and Alaska Native alone, not Hispanic or Latino Number	Percent	Asian alone, not Hispanic or Latino Number	Percent	Native Hawaiian and Other Pacific Islander alone, not Hispanic or Latino Number	Percent	Two or more races, not Hispanic or Latino Number	Percent
Provo–Orem, UT	125	0.5	80	0.3	250	0.9	105	0.4	340	1.3
Pueblo, CO	70	1.0	55	0.8	135	1.9	0	0.0	104	1.5
Punta Gorda, FL	260	4.2	0	0.0	40	0.6	0	0.0	15	0.2
Racine, WI	380	3.7	25	0.2	150	1.4	0	0.0	104	1.0
Raleigh–Cary, NC	11,495	12.7	150	0.2	3,020	3.3	55	0.1	810	0.9
Rapid City, SD	95	1.3	205	2.9	45	0.6	0	0.0	125	1.7
Reading, PA	540	2.5	0	0.0	180	0.8	20	0.1	105	0.5
Redding, CA	50	0.6	260	3.0	145	1.7	4	0.0	260	3.0
Reno–Sparks, NV	415	1.5	280	1.0	1,250	4.7	40	0.1	300	1.1
Richmond, VA	14,875	16.7	315	0.4	2,620	2.9	25	0.0	1,085	1.2
Riverside–San Bernardino–Ontario, CA	13,095	6.9	760	0.4	13,325	7.1	550	0.3	3,710	2.0
Roanoke, VA	1,380	7.9	0	0.0	250	1.4	0	0.0	100	0.6
Rochester, MN	30	0.3	20	0.2	255	2.5	0	0.0	40	0.4
Rochester, NY	2,145	3.6	50	0.1	970	1.6	0	0.0	530	0.9
Rockford, IL	605	3.7	10	0.1	420	2.5	0	0.0	210	1.3
Rocky Mount, NC	1,730	25.8	15	0.2	95	1.4	0	0.0	53	0.8
Rome, GA	265	6.1	10	0.2	50	1.2	0	0.0	75	1.7
Sacramento–Arden-Arcade–Roseville, CA	7,360	5.1	790	0.5	13,245	9.2	480	0.3	3,540	2.5
Saginaw–Saginaw Township North, MI	660	8.1	10	0.1	55	0.7	0	0.0	100	1.2
St. Cloud, MN	40	0.4	0	0.0	95	0.8	0	0.0	18	0.2
St. George, UT	0	0.0	55	0.9	30	0.5	0	0.0	0	0.0
St. Joseph, MO–KS	55	0.9	10	0.2	125	1.9	0	0.0	54	0.8
St. Louis, MO–IL	16,155	9.1	300	0.2	3,055	1.7	130	0.1	1,570	0.9
Salem, OR	120	0.6	160	0.8	380	1.8	4	0.0	260	1.2
Salinas, CA	520	2.8	105	0.6	1,105	6.0	165	0.9	385	2.1
Salisbury, MD	755	11.7	0	0.0	220	3.4	0	0.0	19	0.3
Salt Lake City, UT	645	0.9	115	0.2	1,470	2.1	465	0.7	640	0.9
San Angelo, TX	165	3.3	20	0.4	50	1.0	0	0.0	23	0.5
San Antonio–New Braunfels, TX	6,960	5.8	350	0.3	2,125	1.8	80	0.1	1,340	1.1
San Diego–Carlsbad–San Marcos, CA	7,505	3.7	690	0.3	18,645	9.1	725	0.4	3,845	1.9
Sandusky, OH	155	4.3	0	0.0	0	0.0	0	0.0	0	0.0
San Francisco–Oakland–Fremont, CA	20,245	5.5	855	0.2	74,835	20.5	1,895	0.5	9,460	2.6
San Jose–Sunnyvale–Santa Clara, CA	2,670	1.8	275	0.2	43,535	29.9	325	0.2	3,040	2.1
San Luis Obispo–Paso Robles, CA	145	0.9	75	0.5	610	3.9	0	0.0	160	1.0
Santa Barbara–Santa Maria–Goleta, CA	515	2.2	105	0.4	1,155	4.8	15	0.1	280	1.2
Santa Cruz–Watsonville, CA	130	0.7	50	0.3	1,025	5.5	60	0.3	315	1.7
Santa Fe, NM	40	0.4	235	2.3	135	1.3	4	0.0	95	0.9
Santa Rosa–Petaluma, CA	305	0.9	215	0.7	1,290	3.9	0	0.0	509	1.6
Savannah, GA	3,435	18.6	55	0.3	205	1.1	0	0.0	140	0.8
Scranton–Wilkes-Barre, PA	225	0.9	45	0.2	450	1.7	0	0.0	79	0.3
Seattle–Tacoma–Bellevue, WA	8,980	3.3	1,780	0.7	25,135	9.3	560	0.2	7,160	2.6
Sebastian–Vero Beach, FL	300	4.1	0	0.0	90	1.2	0	0.0	45	0.6
Sheboygan, WI	35	0.6	0	0.0	75	1.2	0	0.0	39	0.6
Sherman–Denison, TX	105	1.9	110	2.0	30	0.5	0	0.0	60	1.1
Shreveport–Bossier City, LA	3,400	20.9	30	0.2	170	1.0	0	0.0	135	0.8
Sioux City, IA–NE–SD	115	1.6	20	0.3	65	0.9	0	0.0	55	0.7
Sioux Falls, SD	120	0.8	45	0.3	90	0.6	0	0.0	29	0.2
South Bend–Mishawaka, IN–MI	1,005	5.9	4	0.0	300	1.8	0	0.0	115	0.7
Spartanburg, SC	1,320	9.5	10	0.1	115	0.8	0	0.0	60	0.4
Spokane, WA	115	0.4	265	1.0	570	2.2	35	0.1	445	1.7
Springfield, IL	485	3.6	15	0.1	230	1.7	0	0.0	40	0.3
Springfield, MA	1,130	3.0	10	0.0	590	1.6	0	0.0	365	1.0
Springfield, MO	305	1.3	30	0.1	250	1.1	0	0.0	360	1.5
Springfield, OH	470	7.5	0	0.0	70	1.1	0	0.0	65	1.0
State College, PA	140	1.8	4	0.1	245	3.1	0	0.0	69	0.9

PART C—METROPOLITAN STATISTICAL AREA TABLES

C-3 Management, Business, and Financial Workers, by Metropolitan Statistical Area, Sex, Race, and Hispanic or Latino Origin, 2006–2010—Continued

Metropolitan Statistical Area	Total who worked in the last 5 years	Male Number	Male Percent	Female Number	Female Percent	Hispanic or Latino Number	Hispanic or Latino Percent	White alone, not Hispanic or Latino Number	White alone, not Hispanic or Latino Percent
Steubenville–Weirton, OH–WV	4,380	2,485	56.7	1,895	43.3	4	0.1	4,175	95.3
Stockton, CA	31,145	17,925	57.6	13,220	42.4	6,275	20.1	18,615	59.8
Sumter, SC	3,390	1,905	56.2	1,490	44.0	40	1.2	2,430	71.7
Syracuse, NY	34,405	19,955	58.0	14,450	42.0	550	1.6	31,685	92.1
Tallahassee, FL	23,915	12,690	53.1	11,225	46.9	820	3.4	17,565	73.4
Tampa–St. Petersburg–Clearwater, FL	174,760	102,690	58.8	72,065	41.2	16,905	9.7	140,150	80.2
Terre Haute, IN	6,520	3,855	59.1	2,665	40.9	45	0.7	6,175	94.7
Texarkana, TX–Texarkana, AR	5,580	3,325	59.6	2,255	40.4	90	1.6	4,785	85.8
Toledo, OH	32,470	20,130	62.0	12,340	38.0	895	2.8	28,650	88.2
Topeka, KS	14,105	8,195	58.1	5,910	41.9	430	3.0	12,620	89.5
Trenton–Ewing, NJ	26,655	15,860	59.5	10,795	40.5	1,465	5.5	19,145	71.8
Tucson, AZ	50,410	28,860	57.3	21,550	42.7	9,625	19.1	36,650	72.7
Tulsa, OK	54,005	32,555	60.3	21,450	39.7	1,770	3.3	44,195	81.8
Tuscaloosa, AL	8,830	4,990	56.5	3,840	43.5	90	1.0	6,810	77.1
Tyler, TX	9,655	6,100	63.2	3,560	36.9	395	4.1	8,320	86.2
Utica–Rome, NY	14,860	8,500	57.2	6,360	42.8	95	0.6	14,295	96.2
Valdosta, GA	5,565	3,125	56.2	2,435	43.8	150	2.7	4,465	80.2
Vallejo–Fairfield, CA	23,485	11,815	50.3	11,675	49.7	3,730	15.9	13,115	55.8
Victoria, TX	5,390	3,265	60.6	2,125	39.4	1,460	27.1	3,420	63.5
Vineland–Millville–Bridgeton, NJ	5,280	3,155	59.8	2,125	40.2	655	12.4	3,975	75.3
Virginia Beach–Norfolk–Newport News, VA–NC	98,550	56,070	56.9	42,480	43.1	2,705	2.7	72,300	73.4
Visalia–Porterville, CA	14,865	9,605	64.6	5,260	35.4	4,610	31.0	9,375	63.1
Waco, TX	10,585	6,255	59.1	4,330	40.9	1,035	9.8	8,580	81.1
Warner Robins, GA	9,035	5,245	58.1	3,790	41.9	350	3.9	6,330	70.1
Washington–Arlington–Alexandria, DC–VA–MD–WV	550,405	305,605	55.5	244,800	44.5	36,320	6.6	355,825	64.6
Waterloo–Cedar Falls, IA	8,820	5,445	61.7	3,375	38.3	115	1.3	8,310	94.2
Wausau, WI	8,065	5,030	62.4	3,035	37.6	75	0.9	7,750	96.1
Wenatchee–East Wenatchee, WA	5,165	3,070	59.4	2,095	40.6	485	9.4	4,580	88.7
Wheeling, WV–OH	5,420	3,175	58.6	2,245	41.4	50	0.9	5,315	98.1
Wichita, KS	33,590	20,680	61.6	12,910	38.4	1,305	3.9	29,425	87.6
Wichita Falls, TX	5,960	3,450	57.9	2,510	42.1	325	5.5	5,120	85.9
Williamsport, PA	4,975	3,270	65.7	1,705	34.3	110	2.2	4,730	95.1
Wilmington, NC	20,605	12,715	61.7	7,890	38.3	530	2.6	18,885	91.7
Winchester, VA–WV	7,105	4,205	59.2	2,900	40.8	100	1.4	6,655	93.7
Winston-Salem, NC	27,005	15,540	57.5	11,460	42.4	770	2.9	22,360	82.8
Worcester, MA	56,375	33,000	58.5	23,375	41.5	1,435	2.5	51,245	90.9
Yakima, WA	8,975	5,965	66.5	3,010	33.5	1,400	15.6	7,070	78.8
York–Hanover, PA	25,860	16,105	62.3	9,755	37.7	440	1.7	24,150	93.4
Youngstown–Warren–Boardman, OH–PA	22,685	14,270	62.9	8,415	37.1	420	1.9	20,980	92.5
Yuba City, CA	7,175	4,300	59.9	2,875	40.1	845	11.8	5,380	75.0
Yuma, AZ	6,380	3,975	62.3	2,405	37.7	2,475	38.8	3,600	56.4

C-3. Management, Business, and Financial Workers, by Metropolitan Statistical Area, Sex, Race, and Hispanic or Latino Origin, 2006–2010—*Continued*

Metropolitan Statistical Area	Black alone, not Hispanic or Latino Number	Percent	American Indian and Alaska Native alone, not Hispanic or Latino Number	Percent	Asian alone, not Hispanic or Latino Number	Percent	Native Hawaiian and Other Pacific Islander alone, not Hispanic or Latino Number	Percent	Two or more races, not Hispanic or Latino Number	Percent
Steubenville–Weirton, OH–WV	195	4.5	0	0.0	0	0.0	4	0.1	0	0.0
Stockton, CA	1,830	5.9	205	0.7	3,325	10.7	75	0.2	820	2.6
Sumter, SC	860	25.4	0	0.0	65	1.9	0	0.0	0	0.0
Syracuse, NY	1,250	3.6	195	0.6	530	1.5	20	0.1	170	0.5
Tallahassee, FL	4,855	20.3	120	0.5	320	1.3	20	0.1	210	0.9
Tampa–St. Petersburg–Clearwater, FL	11,010	6.3	405	0.2	4,410	2.5	40	0.0	1,845	1.1
Terre Haute, IN	180	2.8	15	0.2	90	1.4	0	0.0	15	0.2
Texarkana, TX–Texarkana, AR	640	11.5	4	0.1	60	1.1	0	0.0	0	0.0
Toledo, OH	1,900	5.9	35	0.1	605	1.9	0	0.0	380	1.2
Topeka, KS	535	3.8	215	1.5	110	0.8	0	0.0	195	1.4
Trenton–Ewing, NJ	2,940	11.0	30	0.1	2,810	10.5	0	0.0	269	1.0
Tucson, AZ	1,415	2.8	535	1.1	1,260	2.5	130	0.3	790	1.6
Tulsa, OK	2,275	4.2	2,675	5.0	610	1.1	25	0.0	2,460	4.6
Tuscaloosa, AL	1,615	18.3	10	0.1	230	2.6	0	0.0	75	0.8
Tyler, TX	745	7.7	35	0.4	85	0.9	0	0.0	70	0.7
Utica–Rome, NY	265	1.8	15	0.1	140	0.9	4	0.0	38	0.3
Valdosta, GA	705	12.7	10	0.2	115	2.1	0	0.0	120	2.2
Vallejo–Fairfield, CA	2,190	9.3	60	0.3	3,415	14.5	135	0.6	850	3.6
Victoria, TX	140	2.6	0	0.0	305	5.7	0	0.0	65	1.2
Vineland–Millville–Bridgeton, NJ	510	9.7	35	0.7	60	1.1	0	0.0	48	0.9
Virginia Beach–Norfolk–Newport News, VA–NC	18,845	19.1	200	0.2	3,070	3.1	105	0.1	1,325	1.3
Visalia–Porterville, CA	200	1.3	80	0.5	415	2.8	20	0.1	164	1.1
Waco, TX	815	7.7	25	0.2	50	0.5	4	0.0	80	0.8
Warner Robins, GA	2,080	23.0	15	0.2	165	1.8	0	0.0	94	1.0
Washington–Arlington–Alexandria, DC–VA–MD–WV	104,485	19.0	1,050	0.2	43,630	7.9	385	0.1	8,710	1.6
Waterloo–Cedar Falls, IA	210	2.4	0	0.0	40	0.5	4	0.0	145	1.6
Wausau, WI	35	0.4	4	0.0	140	1.7	0	0.0	65	0.8
Wenatchee–East Wenatchee, WA	0	0.0	4	0.1	10	0.2	40	0.8	45	0.9
Wheeling, WV–OH	35	0.6	0	0.0	25	0.5	0	0.0	0	0.0
Wichita, KS	1,330	4.0	130	0.4	805	2.4	0	0.0	600	1.8
Wichita Falls, TX	315	5.3	85	1.4	55	0.9	0	0.0	55	0.9
Williamsport, PA	40	0.8	0	0.0	40	0.8	0	0.0	55	1.1
Wilmington, NC	975	4.7	20	0.1	80	0.4	0	0.0	115	0.6
Winchester, VA–WV	60	0.8	105	1.5	165	2.3	0	0.0	19	0.3
Winston–Salem, NC	3,425	12.7	30	0.1	240	0.9	0	0.0	180	0.7
Worcester, MA	1,005	1.8	55	0.1	2,255	4.0	0	0.0	380	0.7
Yakima, WA	20	0.2	255	2.8	60	0.7	0	0.0	170	1.9
York–Hanover, PA	785	3.0	50	0.2	345	1.3	0	0.0	90	0.3
Youngstown–Warren–Boardman, OH–PA	980	4.3	15	0.1	140	0.6	10	0.0	140	0.6
Yuba City, CA	100	1.4	65	0.9	560	7.8	35	0.5	195	2.7
Yuma, AZ	75	1.2	20	0.3	175	2.7	25	0.4	10	0.2

PART C—METROPOLITAN STATISTICAL AREA TABLES

C-4 Science, Engineering, and Computer Professionals, by Metropolitan Statistical Area, Sex, Race, and Hispanic or Latino Origin, 2006–2010

Metropolitan Statistical Area	Total who worked in the last 5 years	Male Number	Male Percent	Female Number	Female Percent	Hispanic or Latino Number	Hispanic or Latino Percent	White alone, not Hispanic or Latino Number	White alone, not Hispanic or Latino Percent
Abilene, TX	1,095	915	83.6	180	16.4	75	6.8	975	89.0
Akron, OH	14,105	11,020	78.1	3,085	21.9	225	1.6	12,245	86.8
Albany, GA	1,030	725	70.4	305	29.6	15	1.5	665	64.6
Albany–Schenectady–Troy, NY	22,095	16,385	74.2	5,710	25.8	365	1.7	18,515	83.8
Albuquerque, NM	22,730	17,720	78.0	5,010	22.0	5,075	22.3	15,550	68.4
Alexandria, LA	840	755	89.9	85	10.1	20	2.4	775	92.3
Allentown–Bethlehem–Easton, PA–NJ	15,775	12,510	79.3	3,265	20.7	980	6.2	12,465	79.0
Altoona, PA	1,165	945	81.1	220	18.9	55	4.7	1,075	92.3
Amarillo, TX	2,750	2,105	76.5	650	23.6	385	14.0	2,130	77.5
Ames, IA	3,240	2,470	76.2	770	23.8	30	0.9	2,780	85.8
Anchorage, AK	9,770	7,940	81.3	1,835	18.8	285	2.9	8,600	88.0
Anderson, IN	1,190	845	71.0	345	29.0	10	0.8	1,130	95.0
Anderson, SC	1,840	1,460	79.3	380	20.7	10	0.5	1,570	85.3
Ann Arbor, MI	15,175	11,785	77.7	3,385	22.3	300	2.0	11,090	73.1
Anniston–Oxford, AL	1,260	1,020	81.0	235	18.7	45	3.6	1,035	82.1
Appleton, WI	4,430	3,515	79.3	915	20.7	25	0.6	4,185	94.5
Asheville, NC	4,530	3,490	77.0	1,040	23.0	80	1.8	4,245	93.7
Athens–Clarke County, GA	2,750	1,955	71.1	795	28.9	105	3.8	2,375	86.4
Atlanta–Sandy Springs–Marietta, GA	130,170	96,775	74.3	33,400	25.7	4,330	3.3	80,490	61.8
Atlantic City–Hammonton, NJ	3,030	2,230	73.6	800	26.4	190	6.3	2,145	70.8
Auburn–Opelika, AL	1,995	1,485	74.4	510	25.6	24	1.2	1,580	79.2
Augusta–Richmond County, GA–SC	9,325	7,630	81.8	1,695	18.2	205	2.2	7,300	78.3
Austin–Round Rock–San Marcos, TX	62,590	48,805	78.0	13,785	22.0	6,625	10.6	43,030	68.7
Bakersfield–Delano, CA	7,650	6,170	80.7	1,485	19.4	870	11.4	5,795	75.8
Baltimore–Towson, MD	91,030	64,485	70.8	26,545	29.2	2,490	2.7	65,110	71.5
Bangor, ME	1,670	1,335	79.9	335	20.1	15	0.9	1,530	91.6
Barnstable Town, MA	3,645	2,690	73.8	955	26.2	190	5.2	3,290	90.3
Baton Rouge, LA	12,065	9,435	78.2	2,630	21.8	295	2.4	9,410	78.0
Battle Creek, MI	1,635	1,100	67.3	535	32.7	19	1.2	1,475	90.2
Bay City, MI	1,185	895	75.5	290	24.5	0	0.0	1,160	97.9
Beaumont–Port Arthur, TX	3,925	3,075	78.3	850	21.7	120	3.1	3,070	78.2
Bellingham, WA	2,865	2,435	85.0	435	15.2	54	1.9	2,625	91.6
Bend, OR	2,745	1,925	70.1	825	30.1	30	1.1	2,580	94.0
Billings, MT	2,660	1,995	75.0	665	25.0	90	3.4	2,385	89.7
Binghamton, NY	5,565	4,600	82.7	965	17.3	105	1.9	5,015	90.1
Birmingham–Hoover, AL	17,350	12,850	74.1	4,500	25.9	325	1.9	13,355	77.0
Bismarck, ND	2,785	2,055	73.8	730	26.2	0	0.0	2,730	98.0
Blacksburg–Christiansburg–Radford, VA	4,210	3,385	80.4	830	19.7	35	0.8	3,540	84.1
Bloomington, IN	3,715	2,755	74.2	960	25.8	45	1.2	3,300	88.8
Bloomington–Normal, IL	6,300	4,620	73.3	1,680	26.7	110	1.7	4,360	69.2
Boise City–Nampa, ID	15,445	12,625	81.7	2,820	18.3	555	3.6	13,240	85.7
Boston–Cambridge–Quincy, MA–NH	167,370	124,395	74.3	42,975	25.7	4,935	2.9	125,245	74.8
Boulder, CO	17,630	13,940	79.1	3,690	20.9	560	3.2	15,050	85.4
Bowling Green, KY	1,735	1,320	76.1	420	24.2	15	0.9	1,550	89.3
Bremerton–Silverdale, WA	6,905	5,730	83.0	1,175	17.0	280	4.1	6,165	89.3
Bridgeport–Stamford–Norwalk, CT	18,945	14,415	76.1	4,530	23.9	1,025	5.4	13,340	70.4
Brownsville–Harlingen, TX	1,555	1,220	78.5	335	21.5	1,105	71.1	425	27.3
Brunswick, GA	660	580	87.9	80	12.1	30	4.5	570	86.4
Buffalo–Niagara Falls, NY	18,510	14,645	79.1	3,860	20.9	260	1.4	16,020	86.5
Burlington, NC	1,915	1,345	70.2	570	29.8	25	1.3	1,610	84.1
Burlington–South Burlington, VT	6,175	4,615	74.7	1,560	25.3	110	1.8	5,805	94.0
Canton–Massillon, OH	5,220	4,320	82.8	895	17.1	80	1.5	4,805	92.0
Cape Coral–Fort Myers, FL	4,905	3,670	74.8	1,235	25.2	335	6.8	4,145	84.5
Cape Girardeau–Jackson, MO–IL	705	585	83.0	120	17.0	0	0.0	630	89.4
Carson City, NV	885	730	82.5	155	17.5	50	5.6	785	88.7

C-4 **Science, Engineering, and Computer Professionals, by Metropolitan Statistical Area, Sex, Race, and Hispanic or Latino Origin, 2006–2010**—*Continued*

Metropolitan Statistical Area	Black alone, not Hispanic or Latino Number	Percent	American Indian and Alaska Native alone, not Hispanic or Latino Number	Percent	Asian alone, not Hispanic or Latino Number	Percent	Native Hawaiian and Other Pacific Islander alone, not Hispanic or Latino Number	Percent	Two or more races, not Hispanic or Latino Number	Percent
Abilene, TX	25	2.3	0	0.0	25	2.3	0	0.0	0	0.0
Akron, OH	695	4.9	0	0.0	690	4.9	0	0.0	250	1.8
Albany, GA	290	28.2	50	4.9	0	0.0	0	0.0	15	1.5
Albany–Schenectady–Troy, NY	565	2.6	15	0.1	2,465	11.2	0	0.0	175	0.8
Albuquerque, NM	450	2.0	540	2.4	685	3.0	40	0.2	385	1.7
Alexandria, LA	20	2.4	10	1.2	15	1.8	0	0.0	4	0.5
Allentown–Bethlehem–Easton, PA–NJ	605	3.8	20	0.1	1,580	10.0	0	0.0	120	0.8
Altoona, PA	0	0.0	0	0.0	20	1.7	0	0.0	15	1.3
Amarillo, TX	115	4.2	10	0.4	100	3.6	0	0.0	10	0.4
Ames, IA	30	0.9	0	0.0	370	11.4	0	0.0	34	1.0
Anchorage, AK	95	1.0	145	1.5	285	2.9	0	0.0	360	3.7
Anderson, IN	20	1.7	0	0.0	0	0.0	0	0.0	30	2.5
Anderson, SC	205	11.1	0	0.0	0	0.0	0	0.0	54	2.9
Ann Arbor, MI	575	3.8	20	0.1	2,970	19.6	10	0.1	205	1.4
Anniston–Oxford, AL	130	10.3	20	1.6	30	2.4	0	0.0	0	0.0
Appleton, WI	20	0.5	4	0.1	150	3.4	0	0.0	44	1.0
Asheville, NC	80	1.8	0	0.0	85	1.9	25	0.6	20	0.4
Athens–Clarke County, GA	70	2.5	10	0.4	175	6.4	0	0.0	10	0.4
Atlanta–Sandy Springs–Marietta, GA	27,265	20.9	260	0.2	16,225	12.5	60	0.0	1,545	1.2
Atlantic City–Hammonton, NJ	210	6.9	0	0.0	460	15.2	0	0.0	19	0.6
Auburn–Opelika, AL	165	8.3	20	1.0	195	9.8	0	0.0	8	0.4
Augusta–Richmond County, GA–SC	1,055	11.3	30	0.3	600	6.4	95	1.0	39	0.4
Austin–Round Rock–San Marcos, TX	2,180	3.5	140	0.2	9,620	15.4	0	0.0	995	1.6
Bakersfield–Delano, CA	240	3.1	40	0.5	605	7.9	0	0.0	105	1.4
Baltimore–Towson, MD	11,205	12.3	145	0.2	10,355	11.4	45	0.0	1,685	1.9
Bangor, ME	100	6.0	15	0.9	4	0.2	0	0.0	4	0.2
Barnstable Town, MA	0	0.0	0	0.0	145	4.0	0	0.0	23	0.6
Baton Rouge, LA	1,615	13.4	4	0.0	605	5.0	0	0.0	130	1.1
Battle Creek, MI	45	2.8	35	2.1	65	4.0	0	0.0	4	0.2
Bay City, MI	0	0.0	10	0.8	0	0.0	0	0.0	15	1.3
Beaumont–Port Arthur, TX	430	11.0	15	0.4	295	7.5	0	0.0	0	0.0
Bellingham, WA	10	0.3	35	1.2	135	4.7	0	0.0	4	0.1
Bend, OR	0	0.0	15	0.5	85	3.1	0	0.0	35	1.3
Billings, MT	65	2.4	80	3.0	0	0.0	10	0.4	30	1.1
Binghamton, NY	85	1.5	15	0.3	295	5.3	0	0.0	45	0.8
Birmingham–Hoover, AL	2,515	14.5	4	0.0	1,115	6.4	0	0.0	28	0.2
Bismarck, ND	0	0.0	0	0.0	20	0.7	0	0.0	35	1.3
Blacksburg–Christiansburg–Radford, VA	225	5.3	0	0.0	355	8.4	0	0.0	60	1.4
Bloomington, IN	65	1.7	4	0.1	255	6.9	0	0.0	35	0.9
Bloomington–Normal, IL	295	4.7	25	0.4	1,355	21.5	0	0.0	159	2.5
Boise City–Nampa, ID	45	0.3	85	0.6	1,140	7.4	15	0.1	370	2.4
Boston–Cambridge–Quincy, MA–NH	4,925	2.9	65	0.0	29,870	17.8	110	0.1	2,225	1.3
Boulder, CO	65	0.4	15	0.1	1,620	9.2	0	0.0	320	1.8
Bowling Green, KY	15	0.9	4	0.2	150	8.6	0	0.0	0	0.0
Bremerton–Silverdale, WA	0	0.0	10	0.1	285	4.1	10	0.1	155	2.2
Bridgeport–Stamford–Norwalk, CT	815	4.3	25	0.1	3,470	18.3	10	0.1	250	1.3
Brownsville–Harlingen, TX	0	0.0	0	0.0	25	1.6	0	0.0	0	0.0
Brunswick, GA	60	9.1	0	0.0	0	0.0	0	0.0	0	0.0
Buffalo–Niagara Falls, NY	715	3.9	55	0.3	1,370	7.4	0	0.0	90	0.5
Burlington, NC	235	12.3	0	0.0	45	2.3	0	0.0	0	0.0
Burlington–South Burlington, VT	20	0.3	0	0.0	170	2.8	0	0.0	65	1.1
Canton–Massillon, OH	20	0.4	95	1.8	210	4.0	0	0.0	10	0.2
Cape Coral–Fort Myers, FL	120	2.4	15	0.3	205	4.2	0	0.0	80	1.6
Cape Girardeau–Jackson, MO–IL	15	2.1	0	0.0	10	1.4	0	0.0	50	7.1
Carson City, NV	0	0.0	4	0.5	35	4.0	0	0.0	10	1.1

PART C—METROPOLITAN STATISTICAL AREA TABLES

C-4 **Science, Engineering, and Computer Professionals, by Metropolitan Statistical Area, Sex, Race, and Hispanic or Latino Origin, 2006–2010**—Continued

Metropolitan Statistical Area	Total who worked in the last 5 years	Male Number	Male Percent	Female Number	Female Percent	Hispanic or Latino Number	Hispanic or Latino Percent	White alone, not Hispanic or Latino Number	White alone, not Hispanic or Latino Percent
Casper, WY	1,185	950	80.2	235	19.8	10	0.8	1,145	96.6
Cedar Rapids, IA	7,315	5,630	77.0	1,690	23.1	85	1.2	6,595	90.2
Champaign–Urbana, IL	6,020	4,750	78.9	1,270	21.1	135	2.2	4,575	76.0
Charleston, WV	3,790	2,985	78.8	805	21.2	120	3.2	3,425	90.4
Charleston–North Charleston–Summerville, SC	11,330	9,150	80.8	2,180	19.2	225	2.0	9,325	82.3
Charlotte–Gastonia–Rock Hill, NC–SC	36,965	28,235	76.4	8,730	23.6	1,105	3.0	26,470	71.6
Charlottesville, VA	5,515	3,770	68.4	1,745	31.6	95	1.7	4,705	85.3
Chattanooga, TN–GA	7,035	5,565	79.1	1,470	20.9	85	1.2	6,265	89.1
Cheyenne, WY	1,775	1,400	78.9	375	21.1	85	4.8	1,655	93.2
Chicago–Joliet–Naperville, IL–IN–WI	196,855	149,610	76.0	47,245	24.0	11,580	5.9	132,430	67.3
Chico, CA	2,425	1,835	75.7	590	24.3	115	4.7	2,155	88.9
Cincinnati–Middletown, OH–KY–IN	45,680	35,570	77.9	10,110	22.1	830	1.8	38,510	84.3
Clarksville, TN–KY	2,175	1,630	74.9	550	25.3	84	3.9	1,745	80.2
Cleveland, TN	1,290	950	73.6	340	26.4	40	3.1	1,145	88.8
Cleveland–Elyria–Mentor, OH	38,695	30,090	77.8	8,605	22.2	890	2.3	31,725	82.0
Coeur d'Alene, ID	1,845	1,610	87.3	240	13.0	15	0.8	1,805	97.8
College Station–Bryan, TX	4,450	3,725	83.7	725	16.3	450	10.1	3,245	72.9
Colorado Springs, CO	20,615	16,695	81.0	3,920	19.0	1,270	6.2	17,190	83.4
Columbia, MO	3,510	2,605	74.2	905	25.8	85	2.4	2,705	77.1
Columbia, SC	12,895	9,845	76.3	3,050	23.7	255	2.0	9,110	70.6
Columbus, GA–AL	2,405	1,745	72.6	665	27.7	205	8.5	1,560	64.9
Columbus, IN	2,735	2,240	81.9	495	18.1	75	2.7	1,870	68.4
Columbus, OH	46,015	35,105	76.3	10,910	23.7	715	1.6	36,420	79.1
Corpus Christi, TX	3,845	3,255	84.7	590	15.3	1,125	29.3	2,485	64.6
Corvallis, OR	3,580	2,750	76.8	835	23.3	145	4.1	2,895	80.9
Crestview–Fort Walton Beach–Destin, FL	4,200	3,185	75.8	1,010	24.0	180	4.3	3,445	82.0
Cumberland, MD–WV	575	505	87.8	70	12.2	0	0.0	530	92.2
Dallas–Fort Worth–Arlington, TX	155,605	120,895	77.7	34,710	22.3	11,270	7.2	102,275	65.7
Dalton, GA	880	640	72.7	245	27.8	90	10.2	795	90.3
Danville, IL	390	325	83.3	65	16.7	20	5.1	335	85.9
Danville, VA	640	475	74.2	165	25.8	0	0.0	485	75.8
Davenport–Moline–Rock Island, IA–IL	6,200	4,895	79.0	1,305	21.0	235	3.8	5,390	86.9
Dayton, OH	19,065	15,120	79.3	3,945	20.7	405	2.1	16,130	84.6
Decatur, AL	2,125	1,720	80.9	405	19.1	25	1.2	2,005	94.4
Decatur, IL	1,735	1,310	75.5	425	24.5	60	3.5	1,340	77.2
Deltona–Daytona Beach–Ormond Beach, FL	5,685	4,595	80.8	1,090	19.2	310	5.5	4,985	87.7
Denver–Aurora–Broomfield, CO	86,940	65,655	75.5	21,285	24.5	4,900	5.6	70,605	81.2
Des Moines–West Des Moines, IA	12,520	9,135	73.0	3,385	27.0	240	1.9	10,915	87.2
Detroit–Warren–Livonia, MI	110,335	87,530	79.3	22,800	20.7	2,330	2.1	81,535	73.9
Dothan, AL	1,015	845	83.3	175	17.2	25	2.5	890	87.7
Dover, DE	2,010	1,660	82.6	350	17.4	40	2.0	1,410	70.1
Dubuque, IA	1,560	1,360	87.2	195	12.5	70	4.5	1,445	92.6
Duluth, MN–WI	3,100	2,480	80.0	620	20.0	14	0.5	2,965	95.6
Durham–Chapel Hill, NC	15,890	11,075	69.7	4,815	30.3	680	4.3	11,330	71.3
Eau Claire, WI	2,245	1,740	77.5	505	22.5	15	0.7	2,160	96.2
El Centro, CA	595	515	86.6	80	13.4	310	52.1	195	32.8
Elizabethtown, KY	1,110	825	74.3	280	25.2	40	3.6	880	79.3
Elkhart–Goshen, IN	2,090	1,720	82.3	365	17.5	10	0.5	1,940	92.8
Elmira, NY	1,405	1,020	72.6	390	27.8	0	0.0	1,255	89.3
El Paso, TX	6,420	5,110	79.6	1,315	20.5	4,045	63.0	1,870	29.1
Erie, PA	3,965	3,260	82.2	700	17.7	60	1.5	3,615	91.2
Eugene–Springfield, OR	4,755	3,680	77.4	1,075	22.6	100	2.1	4,060	85.4
Evansville, IN–KY	4,335	3,365	77.6	975	22.5	60	1.4	4,040	93.2
Fairbanks, AK	2,025	1,565	77.3	460	22.7	35	1.7	1,840	90.9
Fargo, ND–MN	4,780	3,995	83.6	785	16.4	90	1.9	4,285	89.6

C-4 **Science, Engineering, and Computer Professionals, by Metropolitan Statistical Area, Sex, Race, and Hispanic or Latino Origin, 2006–2010**—*Continued*

Metropolitan Statistical Area	Black alone, not Hispanic or Latino		American Indian and Alaska Native alone, not Hispanic or Latino		Asian alone, not Hispanic or Latino		Native Hawaiian and Other Pacific Islander alone, not Hispanic or Latino		Two or more races, not Hispanic or Latino	
	Number	Percent	Number	Percent	Number	Percent	Number	Percent	Number	Percent
Casper, WY	0	0.0	0	0.0	30	2.5	0	0.0	0	0.0
Cedar Rapids, IA	175	2.4	10	0.1	310	4.2	30	0.4	115	1.6
Champaign–Urbana, IL	145	2.4	20	0.3	1,120	18.6	0	0.0	20	0.3
Charleston, WV	45	1.2	4	0.1	145	3.8	0	0.0	50	1.3
Charleston–North Charleston–Summerville, SC	1,200	10.6	20	0.2	430	3.8	0	0.0	130	1.1
Charlotte–Gastonia–Rock Hill, NC–SC	4,420	12.0	70	0.2	4,330	11.7	145	0.4	425	1.1
Charlottesville, VA	225	4.1	25	0.5	410	7.4	0	0.0	55	1.0
Chattanooga, TN–GA	265	3.8	15	0.2	350	5.0	0	0.0	60	0.9
Cheyenne, WY	35	2.0	0	0.0	0	0.0	0	0.0	0	0.0
Chicago–Joliet–Naperville, IL–IN–WI	14,365	7.3	170	0.1	35,875	18.2	40	0.0	2,390	1.2
Chico, CA	0	0.0	0	0.0	90	3.7	4	0.2	59	2.4
Cincinnati–Middletown, OH–KY–IN	2,205	4.8	45	0.1	3,620	7.9	0	0.0	470	1.0
Clarksville, TN–KY	165	7.6	4	0.2	135	6.2	0	0.0	40	1.8
Cleveland, TN	4	0.3	0	0.0	50	3.9	0	0.0	45	3.5
Cleveland–Elyria–Mentor, OH	2,400	6.2	30	0.1	3,420	8.8	0	0.0	235	0.6
Coeur d'Alene, ID	0	0.0	4	0.2	15	0.8	0	0.0	10	0.5
College Station–Bryan, TX	110	2.5	4	0.1	580	13.0	0	0.0	65	1.5
Colorado Springs, CO	720	3.5	80	0.4	760	3.7	25	0.1	570	2.8
Columbia, MO	135	3.8	0	0.0	530	15.1	0	0.0	58	1.7
Columbia, SC	2,510	19.5	4	0.0	835	6.5	0	0.0	180	1.4
Columbus, GA–AL	420	17.5	0	0.0	210	8.7	0	0.0	15	0.6
Columbus, IN	40	1.5	0	0.0	640	23.4	0	0.0	110	4.0
Columbus, OH	2,920	6.3	20	0.0	5,550	12.1	0	0.0	390	0.8
Corpus Christi, TX	75	2.0	0	0.0	80	2.1	0	0.0	80	2.1
Corvallis, OR	35	1.0	0	0.0	335	9.4	0	0.0	175	4.9
Crestview–Fort Walton Beach–Destin, FL	280	6.7	10	0.2	140	3.3	0	0.0	150	3.6
Cumberland, MD–WV	20	3.5	0	0.0	25	4.3	0	0.0	0	0.0
Dallas–Fort Worth–Arlington, TX	11,270	7.2	530	0.3	28,145	18.1	135	0.1	1,980	1.3
Dalton, GA	0	0.0	0	0.0	0	0.0	0	0.0	0	0.0
Danville, IL	0	0.0	0	0.0	35	9.0	0	0.0	0	0.0
Danville, VA	155	24.2	0	0.0	0	0.0	0	0.0	0	0.0
Davenport–Moline–Rock Island, IA–IL	230	3.7	10	0.2	285	4.6	0	0.0	50	0.8
Dayton, OH	970	5.1	10	0.1	1,205	6.3	0	0.0	340	1.8
Decatur, AL	20	0.9	35	1.6	10	0.5	0	0.0	25	1.2
Decatur, IL	90	5.2	0	0.0	225	13.0	0	0.0	25	1.4
Deltona–Daytona Beach–Ormond Beach, FL	165	2.9	4	0.1	180	3.2	0	0.0	45	0.8
Denver–Aurora–Broomfield, CO	2,855	3.3	225	0.3	6,630	7.6	90	0.1	1,630	1.9
Des Moines–West Des Moines, IA	185	1.5	4	0.0	1,035	8.3	0	0.0	140	1.1
Detroit–Warren–Livonia, MI	8,650	7.8	140	0.1	15,990	14.5	45	0.0	1,640	1.5
Dothan, AL	95	9.4	0	0.0	4	0.4	0	0.0	4	0.4
Dover, DE	440	21.9	0	0.0	115	5.7	0	0.0	0	0.0
Dubuque, IA	0	0.0	0	0.0	40	2.6	0	0.0	0	0.0
Duluth, MN–WI	0	0.0	35	1.1	65	2.1	0	0.0	15	0.5
Durham–Chapel Hill, NC	1,625	10.2	15	0.1	1,970	12.4	0	0.0	275	1.7
Eau Claire, WI	25	1.1	0	0.0	35	1.6	0	0.0	10	0.4
El Centro, CA	65	10.9	0	0.0	20	3.4	0	0.0	10	1.7
Elizabethtown, KY	140	12.6	0	0.0	35	3.2	0	0.0	20	1.8
Elkhart–Goshen, IN	60	2.9	4	0.2	60	2.9	0	0.0	10	0.5
Elmira, NY	55	3.9	0	0.0	50	3.6	0	0.0	45	3.2
El Paso, TX	170	2.6	20	0.3	305	4.8	0	0.0	10	0.2
Erie, PA	40	1.0	0	0.0	225	5.7	0	0.0	28	0.7
Eugene–Springfield, OR	80	1.7	25	0.5	305	6.4	0	0.0	175	3.7
Evansville, IN–KY	45	1.0	0	0.0	110	2.5	0	0.0	79	1.8
Fairbanks, AK	45	2.2	0	0.0	95	4.7	0	0.0	19	0.9
Fargo, ND–MN	45	0.9	75	1.6	245	5.1	0	0.0	40	0.8

PART C—METROPOLITAN STATISTICAL AREA TABLES

C-4 Science, Engineering, and Computer Professionals, by Metropolitan Statistical Area, Sex, Race, and Hispanic or Latino Origin, 2006–2010—*Continued*

Metropolitan Statistical Area	Total who worked in the last 5 years	Male Number	Male Percent	Female Number	Female Percent	Hispanic or Latino Number	Hispanic or Latino Percent	White alone, not Hispanic or Latino Number	White alone, not Hispanic or Latino Percent
Farmington, NM	1,360	1,190	87.5	170	12.5	105	7.7	1,010	74.3
Fayetteville, NC	2,870	2,000	69.7	870	30.3	250	8.7	1,675	58.4
Fayetteville–Springdale–Rogers, AR–MO	6,915	5,305	76.7	1,610	23.3	145	2.1	5,750	83.2
Flagstaff, AZ	1,815	1,485	81.8	330	18.2	130	7.2	1,520	83.7
Flint, MI	5,065	4,095	80.8	970	19.2	110	2.2	4,415	87.2
Florence, SC	1,950	1,530	78.5	420	21.5	85	4.4	1,470	75.4
Florence–Muscle Shoals, AL	1,295	960	74.1	335	25.9	0	0.0	1,265	97.7
Fond du Lac, WI	1,290	940	72.9	350	27.1	25	1.9	1,160	89.9
Fort Collins–Loveland, CO	11,405	9,145	80.2	2,260	19.8	480	4.2	10,060	88.2
Fort Smith, AR–OK	2,020	1,650	81.7	370	18.3	55	2.7	1,705	84.4
Fort Wayne, IN	7,205	6,095	84.6	1,110	15.4	185	2.6	6,210	86.2
Fresno, CA	7,180	5,510	76.7	1,675	23.3	985	13.7	4,685	65.3
Gadsden, AL	595	525	88.2	70	11.8	20	3.4	545	91.6
Gainesville, FL	6,150	4,560	74.1	1,590	25.9	345	5.6	4,515	73.4
Gainesville, GA	1,970	1,695	86.0	270	13.7	115	5.8	1,555	78.9
Glens Falls, NY	1,325	985	74.3	340	25.7	40	3.0	1,240	93.6
Goldsboro, NC	750	545	72.7	205	27.3	0	0.0	645	86.0
Grand Forks, ND–MN	1,440	1,080	75.0	360	25.0	4	0.3	1,405	97.6
Grand Junction, CO	1,950	1,730	88.7	220	11.3	29	1.5	1,885	96.7
Grand Rapids–Wyoming, MI	12,785	10,325	80.8	2,460	19.2	295	2.3	11,600	90.7
Great Falls, MT	865	655	75.7	210	24.3	0	0.0	855	98.8
Greeley, CO	5,130	3,855	75.1	1,275	24.9	515	10.0	4,295	83.7
Green Bay, WI	4,610	3,530	76.6	1,080	23.4	20	0.4	4,370	94.8
Greensboro–High Point, NC	9,220	6,820	74.0	2,400	26.0	190	2.1	7,095	77.0
Greenville, NC	2,035	1,520	74.7	515	25.3	60	2.9	1,635	80.3
Greenville–Mauldin–Easley, SC	11,850	9,775	82.5	2,080	17.6	175	1.5	9,815	82.8
Gulfport–Biloxi, MS	2,505	1,825	72.9	685	27.3	110	4.4	2,195	87.6
Hagerstown–Martinsburg, MD–WV	4,765	3,700	77.6	1,060	22.2	120	2.5	4,020	84.4
Hanford–Corcoran, CA	765	560	73.2	205	26.8	95	12.4	565	73.9
Harrisburg–Carlisle, PA	12,455	9,125	73.3	3,335	26.8	200	1.6	10,260	82.4
Harrisonburg, VA	1,070	845	79.0	230	21.5	40	3.7	885	82.7
Hartford–West Hartford–East Hartford, CT	33,035	25,595	77.5	7,440	22.5	1,100	3.3	25,720	77.9
Hattiesburg, MS	1,285	1,155	89.9	130	10.1	15	1.2	1,160	90.3
Hickory–Lenoir–Morganton, NC	2,690	2,085	77.5	605	22.5	75	2.8	2,325	86.4
Hinesville–Fort Stewart, GA	445	350	78.7	95	21.3	0	0.0	250	56.2
Holland–Grand Haven, MI	4,605	3,985	86.5	620	13.5	55	1.2	4,285	93.1
Honolulu, HI	17,110	12,905	75.4	4,205	24.6	760	4.4	5,420	31.7
Hot Springs, AR	525	380	72.4	145	27.6	0	0.0	435	82.9
Houma–Bayou Cane–Thibodaux, LA	1,665	1,355	81.4	310	18.6	30	1.8	1,405	84.4
Houston–Sugar Land–Baytown, TX	142,680	111,140	77.9	31,540	22.1	14,345	10.1	86,185	60.4
Huntington–Ashland, WV–KY–OH	2,030	1,700	83.7	330	16.3	45	2.2	1,960	96.6
Huntsville, AL	21,000	16,665	79.4	4,340	20.7	495	2.4	17,195	81.9
Idaho Falls, ID	3,005	2,350	78.2	650	21.6	50	1.7	2,815	93.7
Indianapolis–Carmel, IN	40,160	30,175	75.1	9,980	24.9	665	1.7	32,610	81.2
Iowa City, IA	3,955	2,900	73.3	1,055	26.7	155	3.9	3,160	79.9
Ithaca, NY	3,280	2,405	73.3	875	26.7	135	4.1	2,615	79.7
Jackson, MI	2,395	1,920	80.2	470	19.6	115	4.8	2,085	87.1
Jackson, MS	6,675	5,420	81.2	1,260	18.9	120	1.8	4,825	72.3
Jackson, TN	1,015	800	78.8	215	21.2	0	0.0	830	81.8
Jacksonville, FL	22,390	16,540	73.9	5,850	26.1	1,010	4.5	16,535	73.8
Jacksonville, NC	1,050	730	69.5	320	30.5	40	3.8	815	77.6
Janesville, WI	1,925	1,545	80.3	375	19.5	25	1.3	1,850	96.1
Jefferson City, MO	2,675	1,890	70.7	785	29.3	0	0.0	2,265	84.7
Johnson City, TN	2,145	1,750	81.6	390	18.2	15	0.7	2,025	94.4
Johnstown, PA	1,620	1,400	86.4	220	13.6	30	1.9	1,555	96.0

C-4 Science, Engineering, and Computer Professionals, by Metropolitan Statistical Area, Sex, Race, and Hispanic or Latino Origin, 2006–2010—*Continued*

Metropolitan Statistical Area	Black alone, not Hispanic or Latino Number	Percent	American Indian and Alaska Native alone, not Hispanic or Latino Number	Percent	Asian alone, not Hispanic or Latino Number	Percent	Native Hawaiian and Other Pacific Islander alone, not Hispanic or Latino Number	Percent	Two or more races, not Hispanic or Latino Number	Percent
Farmington, NM	35	2.6	165	12.1	35	2.6	0	0.0	8	0.6
Fayetteville, NC	795	27.7	4	0.1	110	3.8	0	0.0	39	1.4
Fayetteville–Springdale–Rogers, AR–MO	125	1.8	35	0.5	620	9.0	15	0.2	225	3.3
Flagstaff, AZ	25	1.4	60	3.3	60	3.3	0	0.0	25	1.4
Flint, MI	370	7.3	10	0.2	125	2.5	0	0.0	34	0.7
Florence, SC	245	12.6	0	0.0	80	4.1	0	0.0	70	3.6
Florence–Muscle Shoals, AL	25	1.9	0	0.0	0	0.0	0	0.0	4	0.3
Fond du Lac, WI	0	0.0	0	0.0	105	8.1	0	0.0	0	0.0
Fort Collins–Loveland, CO	15	0.1	0	0.0	645	5.7	0	0.0	210	1.8
Fort Smith, AR–OK	25	1.2	45	2.2	130	6.4	0	0.0	60	3.0
Fort Wayne, IN	265	3.7	0	0.0	450	6.2	0	0.0	89	1.2
Fresno, CA	220	3.1	40	0.6	1,140	15.9	0	0.0	110	1.5
Gadsden, AL	15	2.5	0	0.0	10	1.7	0	0.0	10	1.7
Gainesville, FL	155	2.5	10	0.2	1,025	16.7	10	0.2	90	1.5
Gainesville, GA	95	4.8	0	0.0	205	10.4	0	0.0	4	0.2
Glens Falls, NY	4	0.3	0	0.0	25	1.9	0	0.0	15	1.1
Goldsboro, NC	75	10.0	0	0.0	30	4.0	0	0.0	0	0.0
Grand Forks, ND–MN	0	0.0	0	0.0	20	1.4	0	0.0	15	1.0
Grand Junction, CO	0	0.0	20	1.0	15	0.8	0	0.0	0	0.0
Grand Rapids–Wyoming, MI	260	2.0	70	0.5	445	3.5	0	0.0	100	0.8
Great Falls, MT	0	0.0	0	0.0	0	0.0	0	0.0	10	1.2
Greeley, CO	115	2.2	70	1.4	90	1.8	0	0.0	49	1.0
Green Bay, WI	0	0.0	15	0.3	190	4.1	0	0.0	15	0.3
Greensboro–High Point, NC	1,250	13.6	50	0.5	480	5.2	0	0.0	160	1.7
Greenville, NC	245	12.0	0	0.0	70	3.4	0	0.0	25	1.2
Greenville–Mauldin–Easley, SC	880	7.4	4	0.0	815	6.9	0	0.0	165	1.4
Gulfport–Biloxi, MS	125	5.0	15	0.6	25	1.0	0	0.0	30	1.2
Hagerstown–Martinsburg, MD–WV	435	9.1	0	0.0	160	3.4	0	0.0	23	0.5
Hanford–Corcoran, CA	0	0.0	10	1.3	90	11.8	0	0.0	0	0.0
Harrisburg–Carlisle, PA	630	5.1	20	0.2	1,245	10.0	0	0.0	105	0.8
Harrisonburg, VA	50	4.7	25	2.3	25	2.3	15	1.4	30	2.8
Hartford–West Hartford–East Hartford, CT	1,240	3.8	20	0.1	4,475	13.5	0	0.0	480	1.5
Hattiesburg, MS	70	5.4	0	0.0	40	3.1	0	0.0	0	0.0
Hickory–Lenoir–Morganton, NC	270	10.0	0	0.0	4	0.1	0	0.0	14	0.5
Hinesville–Fort Stewart, GA	160	36.0	0	0.0	0	0.0	35	7.9	0	0.0
Holland–Grand Haven, MI	25	0.5	0	0.0	210	4.6	0	0.0	25	0.5
Honolulu, HI	435	2.5	10	0.1	8,250	48.2	480	2.8	1,760	10.3
Hot Springs, AR	90	17.1	0	0.0	0	0.0	0	0.0	0	0.0
Houma–Bayou Cane–Thibodaux, LA	70	4.2	40	2.4	75	4.5	0	0.0	45	2.7
Houston–Sugar Land–Baytown, TX	12,730	8.9	160	0.1	27,260	19.1	20	0.0	1,980	1.4
Huntington–Ashland, WV–KY–OH	10	0.5	0	0.0	15	0.7	0	0.0	0	0.0
Huntsville, AL	2,135	10.2	90	0.4	885	4.2	15	0.1	190	0.9
Idaho Falls, ID	25	0.8	0	0.0	85	2.8	0	0.0	30	1.0
Indianapolis–Carmel, IN	2,730	6.8	55	0.1	3,610	9.0	0	0.0	490	1.2
Iowa City, IA	85	2.1	0	0.0	550	13.9	0	0.0	8	0.2
Ithaca, NY	0	0.0	0	0.0	520	15.9	0	0.0	10	0.3
Jackson, MI	120	5.0	0	0.0	75	3.1	0	0.0	0	0.0
Jackson, MS	1,270	19.0	0	0.0	365	5.5	0	0.0	90	1.3
Jackson, TN	150	14.8	0	0.0	35	3.4	0	0.0	0	0.0
Jacksonville, FL	2,420	10.8	60	0.3	2,170	9.7	0	0.0	195	0.9
Jacksonville, NC	95	9.0	10	1.0	55	5.2	0	0.0	35	3.3
Janesville, WI	0	0.0	10	0.5	40	2.1	0	0.0	0	0.0
Jefferson City, MO	165	6.2	0	0.0	195	7.3	0	0.0	55	2.1
Johnson City, TN	55	2.6	0	0.0	15	0.7	0	0.0	30	1.4
Johnstown, PA	20	1.2	0	0.0	15	0.9	0	0.0	4	0.2

C-4 Science, Engineering, and Computer Professionals, by Metropolitan Statistical Area, Sex, Race, and Hispanic or Latino Origin, 2006–2010—Continued

Metropolitan Statistical Area	Total who worked in the last 5 years	Male Number	Male Percent	Female Number	Female Percent	Hispanic or Latino Number	Hispanic or Latino Percent	White alone, not Hispanic or Latino Number	White alone, not Hispanic or Latino Percent
Jonesboro, AR	940	695	73.9	245	26.1	20	2.1	790	84.0
Joplin, MO	1,505	1,145	76.1	360	23.9	30	2.0	1,305	86.7
Kalamazoo–Portage, MI	6,130	4,840	79.0	1,290	21.0	85	1.4	5,310	86.6
Kankakee–Bradley, IL	895	705	78.8	190	21.2	15	1.7	855	95.5
Kansas City, MO–KS	46,855	34,780	74.2	12,075	25.8	1,310	2.8	38,575	82.3
Kennewick–Pasco–Richland, WA	7,010	5,735	81.8	1,275	18.2	230	3.3	6,165	87.9
Killeen–Temple–Fort Hood, TX	3,465	2,435	70.3	1,025	29.6	430	12.4	2,415	69.7
Kingsport–Bristol–Bristol, TN–VA	3,430	2,720	79.3	710	20.7	0	0.0	3,295	96.1
Kingston, NY	2,690	2,095	77.9	590	21.9	59	2.2	2,390	88.8
Knoxville, TN	14,165	11,560	81.6	2,605	18.4	305	2.2	12,610	89.0
Kokomo, IN	1,655	1,450	87.6	205	12.4	40	2.4	1,515	91.5
La Crosse, WI–MN	2,020	1,565	77.5	455	22.5	35	1.7	1,890	93.6
Lafayette, IN	4,125	3,360	81.5	765	18.5	80	1.9	3,285	79.6
Lafayette, LA	4,135	3,385	81.9	745	18.0	89	2.2	3,705	89.6
Lake Charles, LA	1,610	1,340	83.2	270	16.8	10	0.6	1,440	89.4
Lake Havasu City–Kingman, AZ	1,035	870	84.1	165	15.9	75	7.2	835	80.7
Lakeland–Winter Haven, FL	4,870	3,885	79.8	985	20.2	455	9.3	3,770	77.4
Lancaster, PA	6,540	5,260	80.4	1,280	19.6	150	2.3	5,980	91.4
Lansing–East Lansing, MI	10,410	7,060	67.8	3,350	32.2	285	2.7	8,680	83.4
Laredo, TX	775	635	81.9	145	18.7	665	85.8	90	11.6
Las Cruces, NM	3,330	2,570	77.2	760	22.8	920	27.6	2,240	67.3
Las Vegas–Paradise, NV	20,660	16,365	79.2	4,295	20.8	1,645	8.0	14,565	70.5
Lawrence, KS	2,700	1,950	72.2	750	27.8	60	2.2	2,325	86.1
Lawton, OK	970	795	82.0	180	18.6	60	6.2	565	58.2
Lebanon, PA	1,435	1,090	76.0	345	24.0	120	8.4	1,290	89.9
Lewiston, ID–WA	570	420	73.7	150	26.3	0	0.0	480	84.2
Lewiston–Auburn, ME	1,075	820	76.3	255	23.7	0	0.0	1,065	99.1
Lexington–Fayette, KY	9,995	7,910	79.1	2,080	20.8	140	1.4	8,190	81.9
Lima, OH	705	605	85.8	95	13.5	30	4.3	560	79.4
Lincoln, NE	6,820	5,160	75.7	1,655	24.3	140	2.1	5,695	83.5
Little Rock–North Little Rock–Conway, AR	11,260	8,195	72.8	3,065	27.2	230	2.0	9,190	81.6
Logan, UT–ID	2,485	2,240	90.1	250	10.1	130	5.2	2,265	91.1
Longview, TX	1,845	1,575	85.4	270	14.6	45	2.4	1,580	85.6
Longview, WA	1,010	680	67.3	330	32.7	30	3.0	940	93.1
Los Angeles–Long Beach–Santa Ana, CA	233,510	181,765	77.8	51,745	22.2	27,510	11.8	113,570	48.6
Louisville/Jefferson County, KY–IN	18,420	14,145	76.8	4,275	23.2	430	2.3	15,660	85.0
Lubbock, TX	2,915	2,195	75.3	720	24.7	375	12.9	2,060	70.7
Lynchburg, VA	3,765	3,365	89.4	400	10.6	55	1.5	3,335	88.6
Macon, GA	2,925	2,210	75.6	720	24.6	135	4.6	2,165	74.0
Madera–Chowchilla, CA	810	595	73.5	215	26.5	95	11.7	660	81.5
Madison, WI	21,525	15,795	73.4	5,730	26.6	415	1.9	18,295	85.0
Manchester–Nashua, NH	16,325	13,050	79.9	3,280	20.1	405	2.5	13,510	82.8
Manhattan, KS	1,530	1,150	75.2	380	24.8	34	2.2	1,140	74.5
Mankato–North Mankato, MN	1,505	1,110	73.8	390	25.9	0	0.0	1,400	93.0
Mansfield, OH	1,205	905	75.1	300	24.9	0	0.0	1,030	85.5
McAllen–Edinburg–Mission, TX	3,000	2,505	83.5	495	16.5	2,170	72.3	620	20.7
Medford, OR	1,955	1,585	81.1	375	19.2	35	1.8	1,820	93.1
Memphis, TN–MS–AR	18,530	14,230	76.8	4,300	23.2	395	2.1	12,860	69.4
Merced, CA	970	710	73.2	255	26.3	265	27.3	425	43.8
Miami–Fort Lauderdale–Pompano Beach, FL	68,020	54,480	80.1	13,545	19.9	22,860	33.6	32,900	48.4
Michigan City–La Porte, IN	845	725	85.8	120	14.2	20	2.4	745	88.2
Midland, TX	2,445	1,975	80.8	470	19.2	220	9.0	2,045	83.6
Milwaukee–Waukesha–West Allis, WI	34,080	26,090	76.6	7,995	23.5	815	2.4	28,665	84.1
Minneapolis–St. Paul–Bloomington, MN–WI	102,585	78,210	76.2	24,375	23.8	1,730	1.7	85,170	83.0
Missoula, MT	2,110	1,545	73.2	565	26.8	40	1.9	2,005	95.0

C-4 **Science, Engineering, and Computer Professionals, by Metropolitan Statistical Area, Sex, Race, and Hispanic or Latino Origin, 2006–2010**—*Continued*

Metropolitan Statistical Area	Black alone, not Hispanic or Latino		American Indian and Alaska Native alone, not Hispanic or Latino		Asian alone, not Hispanic or Latino		Native Hawaiian and Other Pacific Islander alone, not Hispanic or Latino		Two or more races, not Hispanic or Latino	
	Number	Percent	Number	Percent	Number	Percent	Number	Percent	Number	Percent
Jonesboro, AR	40	4.3	15	1.6	75	8.0	0	0.0	0	0.0
Joplin, MO	0	0.0	20	1.3	115	7.6	20	1.3	10	0.7
Kalamazoo–Portage, MI	235	3.8	10	0.2	430	7.0	0	0.0	60	1.0
Kankakee–Bradley, IL	10	1.1	0	0.0	15	1.7	0	0.0	0	0.0
Kansas City, MO–KS	2,430	5.2	110	0.2	3,755	8.0	0	0.0	680	1.5
Kennewick–Pasco–Richland, WA	25	0.4	4	0.1	535	7.6	0	0.0	50	0.7
Killeen–Temple–Fort Hood, TX	365	10.5	25	0.7	205	5.9	0	0.0	24	0.7
Kingsport–Bristol–Bristol, TN–VA	85	2.5	0	0.0	30	0.9	0	0.0	25	0.7
Kingston, NY	30	1.1	0	0.0	165	6.1	0	0.0	45	1.7
Knoxville, TN	485	3.4	0	0.0	650	4.6	0	0.0	110	0.8
Kokomo, IN	40	2.4	0	0.0	10	0.6	0	0.0	50	3.0
La Crosse, WI–MN	50	2.5	4	0.2	40	2.0	4	0.2	0	0.0
Lafayette, IN	65	1.6	0	0.0	630	15.3	0	0.0	70	1.7
Lafayette, LA	170	4.1	0	0.0	135	3.3	0	0.0	30	0.7
Lake Charles, LA	115	7.1	20	1.2	15	0.9	0	0.0	15	0.9
Lake Havasu City–Kingman, AZ	85	8.2	4	0.4	25	2.4	10	1.0	0	0.0
Lakeland–Winter Haven, FL	320	6.6	0	0.0	200	4.1	4	0.1	125	2.6
Lancaster, PA	55	0.8	25	0.4	295	4.5	0	0.0	29	0.4
Lansing–East Lansing, MI	470	4.5	4	0.0	845	8.1	0	0.0	120	1.2
Laredo, TX	0	0.0	20	2.6	0	0.0	0	0.0	0	0.0
Las Cruces, NM	10	0.3	20	0.6	85	2.6	0	0.0	60	1.8
Las Vegas–Paradise, NV	1,395	6.8	55	0.3	2,450	11.9	110	0.5	445	2.2
Lawrence, KS	50	1.9	65	2.4	150	5.6	0	0.0	50	1.9
Lawton, OK	270	27.8	30	3.1	40	4.1	0	0.0	4	0.4
Lebanon, PA	20	1.4	0	0.0	4	0.3	0	0.0	0	0.0
Lewiston, ID–WA	35	6.1	4	0.7	45	7.9	4	0.7	4	0.7
Lewiston–Auburn, ME	4	0.4	4	0.4	0	0.0	0	0.0	0	0.0
Lexington–Fayette, KY	395	4.0	0	0.0	1,160	11.6	0	0.0	105	1.1
Lima, OH	15	2.1	0	0.0	65	9.2	0	0.0	35	5.0
Lincoln, NE	95	1.4	0	0.0	800	11.7	0	0.0	85	1.2
Little Rock–North Little Rock–Conway, AR	1,130	10.0	80	0.7	535	4.8	0	0.0	95	0.8
Logan, UT–ID	4	0.2	15	0.6	45	1.8	0	0.0	25	1.0
Longview, TX	150	8.1	20	1.1	45	2.4	0	0.0	10	0.5
Longview, WA	0	0.0	10	1.0	0	0.0	0	0.0	30	3.0
Los Angeles–Long Beach–Santa Ana, CA	9,590	4.1	375	0.2	76,270	32.7	620	0.3	5,570	2.4
Louisville/Jefferson County, KY–IN	865	4.7	25	0.1	1,150	6.2	35	0.2	260	1.4
Lubbock, TX	135	4.6	40	1.4	290	9.9	0	0.0	15	0.5
Lynchburg, VA	195	5.2	0	0.0	155	4.1	0	0.0	30	0.8
Macon, GA	475	16.2	15	0.5	100	3.4	0	0.0	40	1.4
Madera–Chowchilla, CA	40	4.9	0	0.0	10	1.2	0	0.0	0	0.0
Madison, WI	245	1.1	15	0.1	2,390	11.1	0	0.0	164	0.8
Manchester–Nashua, NH	300	1.8	20	0.1	1,845	11.3	15	0.1	225	1.4
Manhattan, KS	65	4.2	0	0.0	295	19.3	0	0.0	0	0.0
Mankato–North Mankato, MN	20	1.3	0	0.0	65	4.3	0	0.0	19	1.3
Mansfield, OH	125	10.4	0	0.0	40	3.3	0	0.0	15	1.2
McAllen–Edinburg–Mission, TX	0	0.0	10	0.3	190	6.3	0	0.0	10	0.3
Medford, OR	0	0.0	25	1.3	50	2.6	15	0.8	15	0.8
Memphis, TN–MS–AR	3,085	16.6	10	0.1	1,985	10.7	4	0.0	195	1.1
Merced, CA	25	2.6	20	2.1	195	20.1	30	3.1	4	0.4
Miami–Fort Lauderdale–Pompano Beach, FL	6,410	9.4	65	0.1	4,890	7.2	15	0.0	885	1.3
Michigan City–La Porte, IN	55	6.5	4	0.5	10	1.2	0	0.0	15	1.8
Midland, TX	45	1.8	25	1.0	100	4.1	0	0.0	0	0.0
Milwaukee–Waukesha–West Allis, WI	1,480	4.3	105	0.3	2,735	8.0	0	0.0	280	0.8
Minneapolis–St. Paul–Bloomington, MN–WI	2,965	2.9	100	0.1	11,460	11.2	45	0.0	1,110	1.1
Missoula, MT	0	0.0	10	0.5	35	1.7	0	0.0	14	0.7

C-4 Science, Engineering, and Computer Professionals, by Metropolitan Statistical Area, Sex, Race, and Hispanic or Latino Origin, 2006–2010—Continued

Metropolitan Statistical Area	Total who worked in the last 5 years	Male Number	Male Percent	Female Number	Female Percent	Hispanic or Latino Number	Hispanic or Latino Percent	White alone, not Hispanic or Latino Number	White alone, not Hispanic or Latino Percent
Mobile, AL	4,520	3,775	83.5	745	16.5	54	1.2	3,570	79.0
Modesto, CA	3,520	2,825	80.3	695	19.7	640	18.2	2,485	70.6
Monroe, LA	1,145	1,045	91.3	100	8.7	19	1.7	1,050	91.7
Monroe, MI	2,175	1,645	75.6	525	24.1	35	1.6	2,010	92.4
Montgomery, AL	5,760	4,500	78.1	1,255	21.8	115	2.0	3,905	67.8
Morgantown, WV	2,085	1,660	79.6	430	20.6	4	0.2	1,680	80.6
Morristown, TN	890	685	77.0	200	22.5	4	0.4	870	97.8
Mount Vernon–Anacortes, WA	1,390	1,085	78.1	305	21.9	4	0.3	1,315	94.6
Muncie, IN	1,195	980	82.0	215	18.0	15	1.3	1,135	95.0
Muskegon–Norton Shores, MI	1,830	1,545	84.4	285	15.6	80	4.4	1,565	85.5
Myrtle Beach–North Myrtle Beach–Conway, SC	1,480	1,200	81.1	285	19.3	4	0.3	1,365	92.2
Napa, CA	1,830	1,450	79.2	380	20.8	175	9.6	1,000	54.6
Naples–Marco Island, FL	2,230	2,005	89.9	225	10.1	235	10.5	1,765	79.1
Nashville-Davidson–Murfreesboro–Franklin, TN	26,445	20,350	77.0	6,095	23.0	585	2.2	21,500	81.3
New Haven–Milford, CT	20,090	15,145	75.4	4,950	24.6	855	4.3	14,855	73.9
New Orleans–Metairie–Kenner, LA	15,470	11,625	75.1	3,840	24.8	825	5.3	11,495	74.3
New York–Northern New Jersey–Long Island, NY–NJ–PA	349,960	262,320	75.0	87,640	25.0	29,595	8.5	193,890	55.4
Niles–Benton Harbor, MI	2,180	1,820	83.5	355	16.3	25	1.1	1,860	85.3
North Port–Bradenton–Sarasota, FL	7,130	5,550	77.8	1,585	22.2	210	2.9	6,310	88.5
Norwich–New London, CT	8,610	6,655	77.3	1,950	22.6	185	2.1	7,130	82.8
Ocala, FL	1,820	1,465	80.5	355	19.5	105	5.8	1,545	84.9
Ocean City, NJ	825	540	65.5	285	34.5	55	6.7	765	92.7
Odessa, TX	590	490	83.1	100	16.9	180	30.5	340	57.6
Ogden–Clearfield, UT	11,735	9,665	82.4	2,070	17.6	425	3.6	10,905	92.9
Oklahoma City, OK	22,120	17,125	77.4	4,995	22.6	665	3.0	17,405	78.7
Olympia, WA	6,360	4,500	70.8	1,860	29.2	195	3.1	5,515	86.7
Omaha–Council Bluffs, NE–IA	18,760	14,640	78.0	4,120	22.0	545	2.9	15,700	83.7
Orlando–Kissimmee–Sanford, FL	41,070	33,175	80.8	7,895	19.2	4,990	12.1	28,250	68.8
Oshkosh–Neenah, WI	2,705	2,015	74.5	685	25.3	55	2.0	2,525	93.3
Owensboro, KY	920	770	83.7	150	16.3	0	0.0	875	95.1
Oxnard–Thousand Oaks–Ventura, CA	19,825	15,660	79.0	4,165	21.0	2,030	10.2	12,785	64.5
Palm Bay–Melbourne–Titusville, FL	18,760	14,965	79.8	3,795	20.2	965	5.1	16,005	85.3
Palm Coast, FL	855	620	72.5	235	27.5	55	6.4	635	74.3
Panama City–Lynn Haven–Panama City Beach, FL	2,680	2,100	78.4	580	21.6	25	0.9	2,495	93.1
Parkersburg–Marietta–Vienna, WV–OH	1,850	1,315	71.1	540	29.2	0	0.0	1,780	96.2
Pascagoula, MS	2,270	1,735	76.4	535	23.6	50	2.2	2,050	90.3
Pensacola–Ferry Pass–Brent, FL	6,640	5,335	80.3	1,305	19.7	209	3.1	5,760	86.7
Peoria, IL	8,955	7,175	80.1	1,780	19.9	145	1.6	7,570	84.5
Philadelphia–Camden–Wilmington, PA–NJ–DE–MD	139,810	102,815	73.5	36,990	26.5	3,575	2.6	103,800	74.2
Phoenix–Mesa–Glendale, AZ	88,685	70,165	79.1	18,515	20.9	7,365	8.3	65,185	73.5
Pine Bluff, AR	630	350	55.6	280	44.4	0	0.0	425	67.5
Pittsburgh, PA	47,215	36,680	77.7	10,540	22.3	600	1.3	41,155	87.2
Pittsfield, MA	1,915	1,470	76.8	445	23.2	24	1.3	1,775	92.7
Pocatello, ID	1,365	1,095	80.2	270	19.8	4	0.3	1,265	92.7
Portland–South Portland–Biddeford, ME	11,630	9,160	78.8	2,470	21.2	130	1.1	10,930	94.0
Portland–Vancouver–Hillsboro, OR–WA	63,810	50,445	79.1	13,365	20.9	1,935	3.0	50,475	79.1
Port St. Lucie, FL	4,440	3,475	78.3	965	21.7	180	4.1	3,920	88.3
Poughkeepsie–Newburgh–Middletown, NY	12,555	10,215	81.4	2,340	18.6	710	5.7	9,625	76.7
Prescott, AZ	1,930	1,375	71.2	555	28.8	110	5.7	1,750	90.7
Providence–New Bedford–Fall River, RI–MA	29,475	22,780	77.3	6,695	22.7	1,015	3.4	25,475	86.4

C-4 **Science, Engineering, and Computer Professionals, by Metropolitan Statistical Area, Sex, Race, and Hispanic or Latino Origin, 2006–2010**—*Continued*

Metropolitan Statistical Area	Black alone, not Hispanic or Latino Number	Black alone, not Hispanic or Latino Percent	American Indian and Alaska Native alone, not Hispanic or Latino Number	American Indian and Alaska Native alone, not Hispanic or Latino Percent	Asian alone, not Hispanic or Latino Number	Asian alone, not Hispanic or Latino Percent	Native Hawaiian and Other Pacific Islander alone, not Hispanic or Latino Number	Native Hawaiian and Other Pacific Islander alone, not Hispanic or Latino Percent	Two or more races, not Hispanic or Latino Number	Two or more races, not Hispanic or Latino Percent
Mobile, AL	650	14.4	0	0.0	180	4.0	0	0.0	65	1.4
Modesto, CA	70	2.0	10	0.3	255	7.2	45	1.3	20	0.6
Monroe, LA	55	4.8	0	0.0	4	0.3	0	0.0	14	1.2
Monroe, MI	15	0.7	0	0.0	60	2.8	0	0.0	50	2.3
Montgomery, AL	1,240	21.5	25	0.4	415	7.2	10	0.2	54	0.9
Morgantown, WV	25	1.2	0	0.0	360	17.3	0	0.0	14	0.7
Morristown, TN	0	0.0	0	0.0	10	1.1	0	0.0	0	0.0
Mount Vernon–Anacortes, WA	0	0.0	4	0.3	55	4.0	0	0.0	14	1.0
Muncie, IN	30	2.5	0	0.0	15	1.3	0	0.0	0	0.0
Muskegon–Norton Shores, MI	160	8.7	0	0.0	20	1.1	0	0.0	4	0.2
Myrtle Beach–North Myrtle Beach–Conway, SC	40	2.7	0	0.0	70	4.7	0	0.0	0	0.0
Napa, CA	0	0.0	0	0.0	630	34.4	0	0.0	24	1.3
Naples–Marco Island, FL	115	5.2	0	0.0	105	4.7	0	0.0	10	0.4
Nashville-Davidson–Murfreesboro–Franklin, TN	2,195	8.3	30	0.1	1,895	7.2	25	0.1	215	0.8
New Haven–Milford, CT	1,465	7.3	25	0.1	2,645	13.2	0	0.0	250	1.2
New Orleans–Metairie–Kenner, LA	2,040	13.2	45	0.3	915	5.9	0	0.0	145	0.9
New York–Northern New Jersey–Long Island, NY–NJ–PA	28,705	8.2	280	0.1	92,165	26.3	120	0.0	5,205	1.5
Niles–Benton Harbor, MI	175	8.0	0	0.0	120	5.5	0	0.0	0	0.0
North Port–Bradenton–Sarasota, FL	185	2.6	25	0.4	320	4.5	0	0.0	80	1.1
Norwich–New London, CT	230	2.7	0	0.0	955	11.1	0	0.0	110	1.3
Ocala, FL	100	5.5	10	0.5	35	1.9	0	0.0	25	1.4
Ocean City, NJ	4	0.5	0	0.0	0	0.0	0	0.0	0	0.0
Odessa, TX	0	0.0	0	0.0	35	5.9	0	0.0	34	5.8
Ogden–Clearfield, UT	100	0.9	0	0.0	210	1.8	15	0.1	73	0.6
Oklahoma City, OK	930	4.2	550	2.5	1,585	7.2	0	0.0	980	4.4
Olympia, WA	35	0.6	85	1.3	440	6.9	0	0.0	84	1.3
Omaha–Council Bluffs, NE–IA	535	2.9	20	0.1	1,520	8.1	0	0.0	435	2.3
Orlando–Kissimmee–Sanford, FL	3,260	7.9	120	0.3	3,750	9.1	50	0.1	655	1.6
Oshkosh–Neenah, WI	20	0.7	0	0.0	90	3.3	0	0.0	20	0.7
Owensboro, KY	30	3.3	0	0.0	10	1.1	0	0.0	0	0.0
Oxnard–Thousand Oaks–Ventura, CA	320	1.6	50	0.3	4,305	21.7	95	0.5	245	1.2
Palm Bay–Melbourne–Titusville, FL	525	2.8	40	0.2	835	4.5	25	0.1	365	1.9
Palm Coast, FL	55	6.4	0	0.0	70	8.2	10	1.2	30	3.5
Panama City–Lynn Haven–Panama City Beach, FL	70	2.6	0	0.0	60	2.2	0	0.0	29	1.1
Parkersburg–Marietta–Vienna, WV–OH	25	1.4	0	0.0	45	2.4	0	0.0	0	0.0
Pascagoula, MS	115	5.1	0	0.0	50	2.2	0	0.0	4	0.2
Pensacola–Ferry Pass–Brent, FL	365	5.5	30	0.5	150	2.3	0	0.0	120	1.8
Peoria, IL	240	2.7	0	0.0	935	10.4	10	0.1	60	0.7
Philadelphia–Camden–Wilmington, PA–NJ–DE–MD	10,015	7.2	40	0.0	20,480	14.6	15	0.0	1,880	1.3
Phoenix–Mesa–Glendale, AZ	3,285	3.7	840	0.9	10,755	12.1	110	0.1	1,134	1.3
Pine Bluff, AR	200	31.7	0	0.0	4	0.6	0	0.0	0	0.0
Pittsburgh, PA	1,170	2.5	55	0.1	3,840	8.1	10	0.0	385	0.8
Pittsfield, MA	55	2.9	4	0.2	50	2.6	4	0.2	0	0.0
Pocatello, ID	0	0.0	4	0.3	55	4.0	0	0.0	35	2.6
Portland–South Portland–Biddeford, ME	145	1.2	0	0.0	390	3.4	0	0.0	35	0.3
Portland–Vancouver–Hillsboro, OR–WA	585	0.9	90	0.1	9,105	14.3	60	0.1	1,560	2.4
Port St. Lucie, FL	170	3.8	0	0.0	105	2.4	0	0.0	64	1.4
Poughkeepsie–Newburgh–Middletown, NY	700	5.6	20	0.2	1,340	10.7	0	0.0	164	1.3
Prescott, AZ	0	0.0	25	1.3	35	1.8	0	0.0	4	0.2
Providence–New Bedford–Fall River, RI–MA	645	2.2	0	0.0	1,925	6.5	0	0.0	415	1.4

C-4 Science, Engineering, and Computer Professionals, by Metropolitan Statistical Area, Sex, Race, and Hispanic or Latino Origin, 2006–2010—Continued

Metropolitan Statistical Area	Total who worked in the last 5 years	Male Number	Male Percent	Female Number	Female Percent	Hispanic or Latino Number	Hispanic or Latino Percent	White alone, not Hispanic or Latino Number	White alone, not Hispanic or Latino Percent
Provo–Orem, UT	11,650	10,285	88.3	1,365	11.7	590	5.1	10,520	90.3
Pueblo, CO	1,590	1,205	75.8	385	24.2	390	24.5	1,070	67.3
Punta Gorda, FL	1,415	1,230	86.9	185	13.1	50	3.5	1,280	90.5
Racine, WI	3,105	2,200	70.9	905	29.1	65	2.1	2,745	88.4
Raleigh–Cary, NC	46,780	34,850	74.5	11,935	25.5	1,250	2.7	34,815	74.4
Rapid City, SD	1,975	1,455	73.7	520	26.3	65	3.3	1,705	86.3
Reading, PA	6,045	4,555	75.4	1,490	24.6	80	1.3	5,595	92.6
Redding, CA	1,965	1,425	72.5	540	27.5	145	7.4	1,610	81.9
Reno–Sparks, NV	7,145	5,390	75.4	1,760	24.6	380	5.3	6,025	84.3
Richmond, VA	27,775	20,370	73.3	7,400	26.6	670	2.4	20,345	73.2
Riverside–San Bernardino–Ontario, CA	41,575	32,685	78.6	8,890	21.4	6,685	16.1	22,750	54.7
Roanoke, VA	4,630	3,470	74.9	1,160	25.1	35	0.8	4,185	90.4
Rochester, MN	5,820	4,495	77.2	1,325	22.8	125	2.1	4,815	82.7
Rochester, NY	26,790	21,285	79.5	5,505	20.5	575	2.1	23,235	86.7
Rockford, IL	5,345	4,475	83.7	870	16.3	175	3.3	4,660	87.2
Rocky Mount, NC	1,245	870	69.9	375	30.1	4	0.3	950	76.3
Rome, GA	655	520	79.4	135	20.6	25	3.8	550	84.0
Sacramento–Arden-Arcade–Roseville, CA	54,575	37,625	68.9	16,950	31.1	4,395	8.1	35,930	65.8
Saginaw–Saginaw Township North, MI	2,370	1,920	81.0	445	18.8	140	5.9	1,940	81.9
St. Cloud, MN	2,055	1,415	68.9	640	31.1	55	2.7	1,905	92.7
St. George, UT	1,240	1,055	85.1	185	14.9	25	2.0	1,180	95.2
St. Joseph, MO–KS	925	655	70.8	270	29.2	10	1.1	885	95.7
St. Louis, MO–IL	62,320	46,705	74.9	15,615	25.1	1,200	1.9	50,985	81.8
Salem, OR	4,600	3,325	72.3	1,275	27.7	160	3.5	3,880	84.3
Salinas, CA	5,035	3,765	74.8	1,270	25.2	750	14.9	3,480	69.1
Salisbury, MD	1,400	1,095	78.2	305	21.8	65	4.6	1,035	73.9
Salt Lake City, UT	24,855	19,770	79.5	5,085	20.5	1,060	4.3	21,295	85.7
San Angelo, TX	840	685	81.5	155	18.5	125	14.9	685	81.5
San Antonio–New Braunfels, TX	31,185	24,440	78.4	6,745	21.6	8,380	26.9	18,405	59.0
San Diego–Carlsbad–San Marcos, CA	93,155	71,775	77.0	21,380	23.0	9,135	9.8	58,045	62.3
Sandusky, OH	820	775	94.5	45	5.5	0	0.0	760	92.7
San Francisco–Oakland–Fremont, CA	168,525	124,980	74.2	43,545	25.8	9,285	5.5	85,310	50.6
San Jose–Sunnyvale–Santa Clara, CA	126,615	98,620	77.9	27,990	22.1	4,965	3.9	46,190	36.5
San Luis Obispo–Paso Robles, CA	5,410	4,250	78.6	1,160	21.4	425	7.9	4,500	83.2
Santa Barbara–Santa Maria–Goleta, CA	9,070	7,050	77.7	2,025	22.3	690	7.6	7,130	78.6
Santa Cruz–Watsonville, CA	7,475	6,090	81.5	1,385	18.5	415	5.6	6,515	87.2
Santa Fe, NM	3,990	2,945	73.8	1,040	26.1	950	23.8	2,855	71.6
Santa Rosa–Petaluma, CA	8,590	6,570	76.5	2,020	23.5	555	6.5	7,145	83.2
Savannah, GA	4,505	3,760	83.5	740	16.4	130	2.9	3,750	83.2
Scranton–Wilkes-Barre, PA	5,575	4,215	75.6	1,360	24.4	65	1.2	5,065	90.9
Seattle–Tacoma–Bellevue, WA	140,235	109,930	78.4	30,310	21.6	4,410	3.1	99,605	71.0
Sebastian–Vero Beach, FL	1,320	1,075	81.4	245	18.6	20	1.5	1,185	89.8
Sheboygan, WI	1,775	1,470	82.8	300	16.9	0	0.0	1,625	91.5
Sherman–Denison, TX	1,345	1,095	81.4	250	18.6	4	0.3	1,275	94.8
Shreveport–Bossier City, LA	3,600	2,620	72.8	980	27.2	150	4.2	3,060	85.0
Sioux City, IA–NE–SD	1,150	960	83.5	195	17.0	75	6.5	1,020	88.7
Sioux Falls, SD	4,320	3,555	82.3	770	17.8	45	1.0	3,815	88.3
South Bend–Mishawaka, IN–MI	3,880	2,970	76.5	910	23.5	95	2.4	3,390	87.4
Spartanburg, SC	3,305	2,790	84.4	520	15.7	105	3.2	2,845	86.1
Spokane, WA	6,825	5,545	81.2	1,285	18.8	85	1.2	6,265	91.8
Springfield, IL	4,355	3,430	78.8	925	21.2	15	0.3	3,905	89.7
Springfield, MA	10,920	8,345	76.4	2,575	23.6	555	5.1	9,020	82.6
Springfield, MO	4,125	3,275	79.4	850	20.6	100	2.4	3,895	94.4
Springfield, OH	1,565	1,220	78.0	345	22.0	8	0.5	1,390	88.8
State College, PA	4,265	3,425	80.3	835	19.6	65	1.5	3,635	85.2

C-4 **Science, Engineering, and Computer Professionals, by Metropolitan Statistical Area, Sex, Race, and Hispanic or Latino Origin, 2006–2010**—*Continued*

Metropolitan Statistical Area	Black alone, not Hispanic or Latino Number	Percent	American Indian and Alaska Native alone, not Hispanic or Latino Number	Percent	Asian alone, not Hispanic or Latino Number	Percent	Native Hawaiian and Other Pacific Islander alone, not Hispanic or Latino Number	Percent	Two or more races, not Hispanic or Latino Number	Percent
Provo–Orem, UT	40	0.3	30	0.3	190	1.6	105	0.9	175	1.5
Pueblo, CO	50	3.1	0	0.0	40	2.5	20	1.3	25	1.6
Punta Gorda, FL	70	4.9	0	0.0	20	1.4	0	0.0	0	0.0
Racine, WI	120	3.9	0	0.0	160	5.2	0	0.0	14	0.5
Raleigh–Cary, NC	3,960	8.5	55	0.1	6,040	12.9	0	0.0	660	1.4
Rapid City, SD	0	0.0	110	5.6	35	1.8	0	0.0	60	3.0
Reading, PA	110	1.8	0	0.0	200	3.3	0	0.0	60	1.0
Redding, CA	20	1.0	40	2.0	105	5.3	0	0.0	35	1.8
Reno–Sparks, NV	45	0.6	50	0.7	560	7.8	10	0.1	80	1.1
Richmond, VA	3,500	12.6	25	0.1	2,825	10.2	20	0.1	380	1.4
Riverside–San Bernardino–Ontario, CA	2,605	6.3	265	0.6	8,050	19.4	275	0.7	945	2.3
Roanoke, VA	90	1.9	0	0.0	260	5.6	4	0.1	59	1.3
Rochester, MN	185	3.2	0	0.0	680	11.7	0	0.0	10	0.2
Rochester, NY	710	2.7	35	0.1	1,600	6.0	0	0.0	635	2.4
Rockford, IL	145	2.7	4	0.1	335	6.3	0	0.0	35	0.7
Rocky Mount, NC	175	14.1	0	0.0	100	8.0	0	0.0	15	1.2
Rome, GA	50	7.6	0	0.0	30	4.6	0	0.0	0	0.0
Sacramento–Arden-Arcade–Roseville, CA	2,200	4.0	195	0.4	10,300	18.9	250	0.5	1,300	2.4
Saginaw–Saginaw Township North, MI	185	7.8	0	0.0	65	2.7	10	0.4	30	1.3
St. Cloud, MN	40	1.9	15	0.7	15	0.7	0	0.0	25	1.2
St. George, UT	0	0.0	0	0.0	30	2.4	0	0.0	4	0.3
St. Joseph, MO–KS	0	0.0	0	0.0	0	0.0	20	2.2	10	1.1
St. Louis, MO–IL	3,855	6.2	130	0.2	5,305	8.5	20	0.0	825	1.3
Salem, OR	30	0.7	90	2.0	310	6.7	25	0.5	104	2.3
Salinas, CA	80	1.6	15	0.3	490	9.7	40	0.8	185	3.7
Salisbury, MD	240	17.1	10	0.7	50	3.6	0	0.0	0	0.0
Salt Lake City, UT	215	0.9	100	0.4	1,630	6.6	140	0.6	415	1.7
San Angelo, TX	0	0.0	0	0.0	10	1.2	0	0.0	20	2.4
San Antonio–New Braunfels, TX	1,610	5.2	75	0.2	2,200	7.1	35	0.1	485	1.6
San Diego–Carlsbad–San Marcos, CA	2,305	2.5	215	0.2	21,415	23.0	100	0.1	1,940	2.1
Sandusky, OH	20	2.4	0	0.0	15	1.8	0	0.0	25	3.0
San Francisco–Oakland–Fremont, CA	5,315	3.2	180	0.1	63,720	37.8	340	0.2	4,375	2.6
San Jose–Sunnyvale–Santa Clara, CA	1,375	1.1	65	0.1	71,355	56.4	150	0.1	2,520	2.0
San Luis Obispo–Paso Robles, CA	20	0.4	50	0.9	295	5.5	30	0.6	90	1.7
Santa Barbara–Santa Maria–Goleta, CA	165	1.8	0	0.0	960	10.6	0	0.0	130	1.4
Santa Cruz–Watsonville, CA	45	0.6	40	0.5	300	4.0	0	0.0	165	2.2
Santa Fe, NM	0	0.0	35	0.9	105	2.6	0	0.0	50	1.3
Santa Rosa–Petaluma, CA	20	0.2	60	0.7	620	7.2	0	0.0	190	2.2
Savannah, GA	360	8.0	10	0.2	150	3.3	0	0.0	100	2.2
Scranton–Wilkes-Barre, PA	150	2.7	20	0.4	255	4.6	0	0.0	20	0.4
Seattle–Tacoma–Bellevue, WA	2,990	2.1	450	0.3	29,015	20.7	410	0.3	3,355	2.4
Sebastian–Vero Beach, FL	50	3.8	0	0.0	30	2.3	0	0.0	35	2.7
Sheboygan, WI	0	0.0	15	0.8	130	7.3	0	0.0	4	0.2
Sherman–Denison, TX	0	0.0	20	1.5	10	0.7	30	2.2	10	0.7
Shreveport–Bossier City, LA	325	9.0	10	0.3	45	1.3	0	0.0	15	0.4
Sioux City, IA–NE–SD	35	3.0	0	0.0	10	0.9	0	0.0	10	0.9
Sioux Falls, SD	0	0.0	10	0.2	370	8.6	0	0.0	80	1.9
South Bend–Mishawaka, IN–MI	105	2.7	25	0.6	175	4.5	15	0.4	74	1.9
Spartanburg, SC	150	4.5	25	0.8	165	5.0	20	0.6	0	0.0
Spokane, WA	0	0.0	70	1.0	275	4.0	0	0.0	125	1.8
Springfield, IL	165	3.8	0	0.0	260	6.0	0	0.0	10	0.2
Springfield, MA	395	3.6	20	0.2	800	7.3	0	0.0	124	1.1
Springfield, MO	30	0.7	0	0.0	65	1.6	0	0.0	35	0.8
Springfield, OH	115	7.3	0	0.0	45	2.9	0	0.0	0	0.0
State College, PA	45	1.1	35	0.8	470	11.0	0	0.0	10	0.2

PART C—METROPOLITAN STATISTICAL AREA TABLES

C-4 Science, Engineering, and Computer Professionals, by Metropolitan Statistical Area, Sex, Race, and Hispanic or Latino Origin, 2006–2010—Continued

Metropolitan Statistical Area	Total who worked in the last 5 years	Male Number	Male Percent	Female Number	Female Percent	Hispanic or Latino Number	Hispanic or Latino Percent	White alone, not Hispanic or Latino Number	White alone, not Hispanic or Latino Percent
Steubenville–Weirton, OH–WV	655	510	77.9	145	22.1	0	0.0	615	93.9
Stockton, CA	7,200	5,405	75.1	1,795	24.9	940	13.1	3,610	50.1
Sumter, SC	595	480	80.7	115	19.3	0	0.0	455	76.5
Syracuse, NY	11,540	9,450	81.9	2,085	18.1	195	1.7	10,165	88.1
Tallahassee, FL	8,025	5,755	71.7	2,275	28.3	250	3.1	6,130	76.4
Tampa–St. Petersburg–Clearwater, FL	46,060	34,995	76.0	11,065	24.0	4,020	8.7	35,710	77.5
Terre Haute, IN	1,630	1,350	82.8	280	17.2	15	0.9	1,565	96.0
Texarkana, TX–Texarkana, AR	855	665	77.8	195	22.8	10	1.2	825	96.5
Toledo, OH	8,745	7,160	81.9	1,580	18.1	185	2.1	7,765	88.8
Topeka, KS	3,165	2,330	73.6	840	26.5	65	2.1	2,645	83.6
Trenton–Ewing, NJ	12,310	8,590	69.8	3,720	30.2	275	2.2	7,355	59.7
Tucson, AZ	21,155	16,620	78.6	4,535	21.4	2,425	11.5	16,180	76.5
Tulsa, OK	15,700	12,280	78.2	3,420	21.8	460	2.9	12,695	80.9
Tuscaloosa, AL	2,285	1,635	71.6	650	28.4	45	2.0	1,945	85.1
Tyler, TX	2,160	1,670	77.3	490	22.7	44	2.0	1,815	84.0
Utica–Rome, NY	3,520	2,705	76.8	815	23.2	10	0.3	3,175	90.2
Valdosta, GA	895	660	73.7	230	25.7	40	4.5	685	76.5
Vallejo–Fairfield, CA	7,025	5,130	73.0	1,900	27.0	655	9.3	3,850	54.8
Victoria, TX	980	820	83.7	160	16.3	120	12.2	575	58.7
Vineland–Millville–Bridgeton, NJ	1,170	945	80.8	225	19.2	15	1.3	860	73.5
Virginia Beach–Norfolk–Newport News, VA–NC	38,480	29,610	76.9	8,870	23.1	1,335	3.5	27,985	72.7
Visalia–Porterville, CA	1,925	1,510	78.4	420	21.8	420	21.8	1,225	63.6
Waco, TX	2,220	1,755	79.1	465	20.9	150	6.8	1,785	80.4
Warner Robins, GA	3,290	2,675	81.3	620	18.8	155	4.7	2,460	74.8
Washington–Arlington–Alexandria, DC–VA–MD–WV	277,420	196,070	70.7	81,350	29.3	12,620	4.5	162,730	58.7
Waterloo–Cedar Falls, IA	2,470	2,090	84.6	380	15.4	75	3.0	2,265	91.7
Wausau, WI	2,030	1,560	76.8	470	23.2	0	0.0	1,910	94.1
Wenatchee–East Wenatchee, WA	1,285	1,115	86.8	175	13.6	95	7.4	1,170	91.1
Wheeling, WV–OH	930	745	80.1	185	19.9	0	0.0	880	94.6
Wichita, KS	13,550	11,345	83.7	2,205	16.3	480	3.5	11,700	86.3
Wichita Falls, TX	1,165	970	83.3	200	17.2	20	1.7	1,070	91.8
Williamsport, PA	1,140	985	86.4	155	13.6	0	0.0	1,120	98.2
Wilmington, NC	4,600	3,485	75.8	1,110	24.1	120	2.6	4,140	90.0
Winchester, VA–WV	2,310	1,805	78.1	505	21.9	0	0.0	2,255	97.6
Winston–Salem, NC	6,910	5,245	75.9	1,670	24.2	109	1.6	5,670	82.1
Worcester, MA	25,160	19,710	78.3	5,450	21.7	520	2.1	19,340	76.9
Yakima, WA	1,565	1,315	84.0	245	15.7	320	20.4	1,145	73.2
York–Hanover, PA	8,020	6,690	83.4	1,330	16.6	80	1.0	7,425	92.6
Youngstown–Warren–Boardman, OH–PA	5,155	4,260	82.6	895	17.4	39	0.8	4,815	93.4
Yuba City, CA	1,660	1,210	72.9	455	27.4	100	6.0	1,290	77.7
Yuma, AZ	1,200	855	71.3	345	28.8	165	13.8	915	76.3

C-4 **Science, Engineering, and Computer Professionals, by Metropolitan Statistical Area, Sex, Race, and Hispanic or Latino Origin, 2006–2010**—*Continued*

Metropolitan Statistical Area	Black alone, not Hispanic or Latino Number	Black alone, not Hispanic or Latino Percent	American Indian and Alaska Native alone, not Hispanic or Latino Number	American Indian and Alaska Native alone, not Hispanic or Latino Percent	Asian alone, not Hispanic or Latino Number	Asian alone, not Hispanic or Latino Percent	Native Hawaiian and Other Pacific Islander alone, not Hispanic or Latino Number	Native Hawaiian and Other Pacific Islander alone, not Hispanic or Latino Percent	Two or more races, not Hispanic or Latino Number	Two or more races, not Hispanic or Latino Percent
Steubenville–Weirton, OH–WV	25	3.8	0	0.0	0	0.0	0	0.0	14	2.1
Stockton, CA	380	5.3	30	0.4	1,860	25.8	25	0.3	360	5.0
Sumter, SC	140	23.5	0	0.0	0	0.0	0	0.0	0	0.0
Syracuse, NY	205	1.8	10	0.1	815	7.1	0	0.0	144	1.2
Tallahassee, FL	895	11.2	50	0.6	655	8.2	0	0.0	50	0.6
Tampa–St. Petersburg–Clearwater, FL	2,500	5.4	30	0.1	3,370	7.3	0	0.0	425	0.9
Terre Haute, IN	0	0.0	0	0.0	50	3.1	0	0.0	0	0.0
Texarkana, TX–Texarkana, AR	0	0.0	10	1.2	10	1.2	0	0.0	0	0.0
Toledo, OH	285	3.3	0	0.0	405	4.6	0	0.0	109	1.2
Topeka, KS	70	2.2	30	0.9	240	7.6	0	0.0	110	3.5
Trenton–Ewing, NJ	765	6.2	10	0.1	3,770	30.6	0	0.0	140	1.1
Tucson, AZ	850	4.0	155	0.7	1,330	6.3	60	0.3	155	0.7
Tulsa, OK	665	4.2	545	3.5	785	5.0	0	0.0	555	3.5
Tuscaloosa, AL	250	10.9	0	0.0	15	0.7	0	0.0	30	1.3
Tyler, TX	205	9.5	45	2.1	40	1.9	0	0.0	15	0.7
Utica–Rome, NY	15	0.4	4	0.1	315	8.9	0	0.0	0	0.0
Valdosta, GA	135	15.1	4	0.4	25	2.8	0	0.0	4	0.4
Vallejo–Fairfield, CA	860	12.2	0	0.0	1,475	21.0	25	0.4	170	2.4
Victoria, TX	65	6.6	0	0.0	200	20.4	0	0.0	25	2.6
Vineland–Millville–Bridgeton, NJ	275	23.5	0	0.0	4	0.3	15	1.3	0	0.0
Virginia Beach–Norfolk–Newport News, VA–NC	6,305	16.4	80	0.2	2,010	5.2	30	0.1	735	1.9
Visalia–Porterville, CA	15	0.8	30	1.6	205	10.6	0	0.0	29	1.5
Waco, TX	140	6.3	25	1.1	85	3.8	0	0.0	40	1.8
Warner Robins, GA	500	15.2	0	0.0	160	4.9	0	0.0	20	0.6
Washington–Arlington–Alexandria, DC–VA–MD–WV	42,885	15.5	420	0.2	52,765	19.0	270	0.1	5,740	2.1
Waterloo–Cedar Falls, IA	40	1.6	0	0.0	75	3.0	0	0.0	20	0.8
Wausau, WI	0	0.0	20	1.0	55	2.7	0	0.0	39	1.9
Wenatchee–East Wenatchee, WA	0	0.0	0	0.0	0	0.0	0	0.0	25	1.9
Wheeling, WV–OH	15	1.6	0	0.0	10	1.1	0	0.0	24	2.6
Wichita, KS	235	1.7	55	0.4	970	7.2	4	0.0	105	0.8
Wichita Falls, TX	65	5.6	10	0.9	0	0.0	0	0.0	0	0.0
Williamsport, PA	10	0.9	0	0.0	0	0.0	0	0.0	10	0.9
Wilmington, NC	145	3.2	4	0.1	160	3.5	0	0.0	30	0.7
Winchester, VA–WV	30	1.3	0	0.0	4	0.2	0	0.0	20	0.9
Winston–Salem, NC	570	8.2	20	0.3	460	6.7	0	0.0	78	1.1
Worcester, MA	485	1.9	55	0.2	4,300	17.1	15	0.1	445	1.8
Yakima, WA	0	0.0	25	1.6	10	0.6	0	0.0	65	4.2
York–Hanover, PA	290	3.6	10	0.1	165	2.1	0	0.0	50	0.6
Youngstown–Warren–Boardman, OH–PA	145	2.8	15	0.3	85	1.6	0	0.0	60	1.2
Yuba City, CA	4	0.2	20	1.2	190	11.4	0	0.0	55	3.3
Yuma, AZ	40	3.3	65	5.4	10	0.8	0	0.0	4	0.3

PART C—METROPOLITAN STATISTICAL AREA TABLES

C-5 Health Care Practitioner Professionals, by Metropolitan Statistical Area, Sex, Race, and Hispanic or Latino Origin, 2006–2010

Metropolitan Statistical Area	Total who worked in the last 5 years	Male Number	Male Percent	Female Number	Female Percent	Hispanic or Latino Number	Hispanic or Latino Percent	White alone, not Hispanic or Latino Number	White alone, not Hispanic or Latino Percent
Abilene, TX	2,385	775	32.5	1,610	67.5	135	5.7	1,970	82.6
Akron, OH	13,475	3,375	25.0	10,100	75.0	195	1.4	11,785	87.5
Albany, GA	2,110	675	32.0	1,440	68.2	0	0.0	1,500	71.1
Albany–Schenectady–Troy, NY	18,225	4,870	26.7	13,355	73.3	280	1.5	15,945	87.5
Albuquerque, NM	15,470	4,385	28.3	11,085	71.7	3,445	22.3	10,665	68.9
Alexandria, LA	3,020	920	30.5	2,095	69.4	105	3.5	2,400	79.5
Allentown–Bethlehem–Easton, PA–NJ	16,440	4,260	25.9	12,180	74.1	480	2.9	14,480	88.1
Altoona, PA	2,555	745	29.2	1,815	71.0	0	0.0	2,475	96.9
Amarillo, TX	4,345	1,260	29.0	3,085	71.0	270	6.2	3,800	87.5
Ames, IA	1,590	305	19.2	1,280	80.5	35	2.2	1,370	86.2
Anchorage, AK	6,865	2,185	31.8	4,680	68.2	240	3.5	5,935	86.5
Anderson, IN	1,945	305	15.7	1,640	84.3	25	1.3	1,780	91.5
Anderson, SC	2,905	480	16.5	2,425	83.5	0	0.0	2,710	93.3
Ann Arbor, MI	10,915	3,485	31.9	7,430	68.1	345	3.2	8,355	76.5
Anniston–Oxford, AL	1,400	345	24.6	1,055	75.4	45	3.2	1,075	76.8
Appleton, WI	3,555	615	17.3	2,940	82.7	30	0.8	3,460	97.3
Asheville, NC	9,350	3,020	32.3	6,330	67.7	130	1.4	8,725	93.3
Athens–Clarke County, GA	3,060	1,115	36.4	1,950	63.7	90	2.9	2,530	82.7
Atlanta–Sandy Springs–Marietta, GA	72,865	18,475	25.4	54,390	74.6	2,050	2.8	44,520	61.1
Atlantic City–Hammonton, NJ	4,445	1,035	23.3	3,410	76.7	170	3.8	2,980	67.0
Auburn–Opelika, AL	2,255	620	27.5	1,635	72.5	29	1.3	1,945	86.3
Augusta–Richmond County, GA–SC	10,435	2,575	24.7	7,860	75.3	170	1.6	7,290	69.9
Austin–Round Rock–San Marcos, TX	23,290	6,245	26.8	17,050	73.2	2,280	9.8	17,260	74.1
Bakersfield–Delano, CA	7,670	2,340	30.5	5,330	69.5	1,040	13.6	4,070	53.1
Baltimore–Towson, MD	58,130	15,020	25.8	43,110	74.2	1,400	2.4	39,180	67.4
Bangor, ME	3,530	940	26.6	2,590	73.4	24	0.7	3,355	95.0
Barnstable Town, MA	5,295	1,300	24.6	3,990	75.4	4	0.1	5,125	96.8
Baton Rouge, LA	12,085	3,315	27.4	8,765	72.5	325	2.7	8,980	74.3
Battle Creek, MI	1,830	480	26.2	1,350	73.8	65	3.6	1,495	81.7
Bay City, MI	2,085	495	23.7	1,585	76.0	85	4.1	1,965	94.2
Beaumont–Port Arthur, TX	5,505	1,435	26.1	4,070	73.9	225	4.1	4,040	73.4
Bellingham, WA	2,855	675	23.6	2,180	76.4	89	3.1	2,545	89.1
Bend, OR	2,435	725	29.8	1,715	70.4	15	0.6	2,310	94.9
Billings, MT	3,380	1,105	32.7	2,275	67.3	34	1.0	3,235	95.7
Binghamton, NY	4,110	1,090	26.5	3,020	73.5	50	1.2	3,580	87.1
Birmingham–Hoover, AL	22,070	5,915	26.8	16,160	73.2	295	1.3	17,430	79.0
Bismarck, ND	2,625	415	15.8	2,205	84.0	0	0.0	2,555	97.3
Blacksburg–Christiansburg–Radford, VA	2,195	430	19.6	1,760	80.2	10	0.5	2,110	96.1
Bloomington, IN	2,400	600	25.0	1,800	75.0	35	1.5	2,235	93.1
Bloomington–Normal, IL	2,155	585	27.1	1,570	72.9	10	0.5	2,000	92.8
Boise City–Nampa, ID	9,955	3,180	31.9	6,775	68.1	550	5.5	9,005	90.5
Boston–Cambridge–Quincy, MA–NH	104,450	25,560	24.5	78,890	75.5	2,425	2.3	86,875	83.2
Boulder, CO	5,895	1,740	29.5	4,155	70.5	170	2.9	5,535	93.9
Bowling Green, KY	1,990	575	28.9	1,415	71.1	40	2.0	1,825	91.7
Bremerton–Silverdale, WA	3,440	785	22.8	2,660	77.3	75	2.2	3,045	88.5
Bridgeport–Stamford–Norwalk, CT	15,440	4,610	29.9	10,830	70.1	835	5.4	11,895	77.0
Brownsville–Harlingen, TX	3,905	1,250	32.0	2,655	68.0	2,530	64.8	910	23.3
Brunswick, GA	1,715	520	30.3	1,195	69.7	35	2.0	1,355	79.0
Buffalo–Niagara Falls, NY	23,125	5,440	23.5	17,685	76.5	270	1.2	19,840	85.8
Burlington, NC	2,120	615	29.0	1,500	70.8	15	0.7	1,920	90.6
Burlington–South Burlington, VT	4,820	1,195	24.8	3,625	75.2	125	2.6	4,540	94.2
Canton–Massillon, OH	7,600	1,780	23.4	5,820	76.6	45	0.6	7,065	93.0
Cape Coral–Fort Myers, FL	9,205	2,605	28.3	6,600	71.7	630	6.8	7,430	80.7
Cape Girardeau–Jackson, MO–IL	1,785	290	16.2	1,495	83.8	25	1.4	1,705	95.5
Carson City, NV	625	320	51.2	305	48.8	15	2.4	535	85.6

C-5 Health Care Practitioner Professionals, by Metropolitan Statistical Area, Sex, Race, and Hispanic or Latino Origin, 2006–2010—*Continued*

Metropolitan Statistical Area	Black alone, not Hispanic or Latino Number	Black alone, not Hispanic or Latino Percent	American Indian and Alaska Native alone, not Hispanic or Latino Number	American Indian and Alaska Native alone, not Hispanic or Latino Percent	Asian alone, not Hispanic or Latino Number	Asian alone, not Hispanic or Latino Percent	Native Hawaiian and Other Pacific Islander alone, not Hispanic or Latino Number	Native Hawaiian and Other Pacific Islander alone, not Hispanic or Latino Percent	Two or more races, not Hispanic or Latino Number	Two or more races, not Hispanic or Latino Percent
Abilene, TX	80	3.4	30	1.3	95	4.0	0	0.0	69	2.9
Akron, OH	985	7.3	0	0.0	405	3.0	0	0.0	110	0.8
Albany, GA	495	23.5	4	0.2	75	3.6	0	0.0	35	1.7
Albany–Schenectady–Troy, NY	355	1.9	20	0.1	1,480	8.1	0	0.0	145	0.8
Albuquerque, NM	160	1.0	220	1.4	685	4.4	0	0.0	300	1.9
Alexandria, LA	390	12.9	10	0.3	100	3.3	0	0.0	14	0.5
Allentown–Bethlehem–Easton, PA–NJ	360	2.2	30	0.2	900	5.5	0	0.0	190	1.2
Altoona, PA	45	1.8	0	0.0	35	1.4	0	0.0	4	0.2
Amarillo, TX	90	2.1	10	0.2	95	2.2	4	0.1	80	1.8
Ames, IA	30	1.9	0	0.0	135	8.5	0	0.0	14	0.9
Anchorage, AK	70	1.0	115	1.7	295	4.3	0	0.0	210	3.1
Anderson, IN	120	6.2	0	0.0	30	1.5	0	0.0	0	0.0
Anderson, SC	130	4.5	0	0.0	25	0.9	0	0.0	45	1.5
Ann Arbor, MI	670	6.1	35	0.3	1,380	12.6	0	0.0	130	1.2
Anniston–Oxford, AL	200	14.3	4	0.3	70	5.0	0	0.0	10	0.7
Appleton, WI	4	0.1	20	0.6	35	1.0	0	0.0	0	0.0
Asheville, NC	140	1.5	15	0.2	255	2.7	0	0.0	90	1.0
Athens–Clarke County, GA	165	5.4	0	0.0	280	9.2	0	0.0	0	0.0
Atlanta–Sandy Springs–Marietta, GA	19,690	27.0	45	0.1	5,585	7.7	20	0.0	955	1.3
Atlantic City–Hammonton, NJ	450	10.1	0	0.0	735	16.5	0	0.0	110	2.5
Auburn–Opelika, AL	195	8.6	0	0.0	55	2.4	0	0.0	30	1.3
Augusta–Richmond County, GA–SC	2,350	22.5	0	0.0	535	5.1	0	0.0	84	0.8
Austin–Round Rock–San Marcos, TX	1,170	5.0	70	0.3	2,300	9.9	0	0.0	210	0.9
Bakersfield–Delano, CA	365	4.8	50	0.7	1,770	23.1	35	0.5	335	4.4
Baltimore–Towson, MD	9,570	16.5	85	0.1	7,060	12.1	15	0.0	810	1.4
Bangor, ME	0	0.0	70	2.0	75	2.1	0	0.0	4	0.1
Barnstable Town, MA	120	2.3	0	0.0	25	0.5	0	0.0	14	0.3
Baton Rouge, LA	2,300	19.0	30	0.2	415	3.4	0	0.0	35	0.3
Battle Creek, MI	105	5.7	0	0.0	150	8.2	0	0.0	15	0.8
Bay City, MI	0	0.0	4	0.2	30	1.4	0	0.0	0	0.0
Beaumont–Port Arthur, TX	780	14.2	15	0.3	370	6.7	0	0.0	75	1.4
Bellingham, WA	25	0.9	4	0.1	85	3.0	0	0.0	105	3.7
Bend, OR	15	0.6	0	0.0	65	2.7	0	0.0	29	1.2
Billings, MT	15	0.4	10	0.3	65	1.9	0	0.0	20	0.6
Binghamton, NY	95	2.3	0	0.0	295	7.2	0	0.0	90	2.2
Birmingham–Hoover, AL	3,690	16.7	25	0.1	555	2.5	0	0.0	85	0.4
Bismarck, ND	0	0.0	0	0.0	25	1.0	15	0.6	30	1.1
Blacksburg–Christiansburg–Radford, VA	45	2.1	0	0.0	20	0.9	0	0.0	10	0.5
Bloomington, IN	75	3.1	0	0.0	35	1.5	0	0.0	20	0.8
Bloomington–Normal, IL	65	3.0	0	0.0	70	3.2	0	0.0	14	0.6
Boise City–Nampa, ID	15	0.2	30	0.3	240	2.4	0	0.0	109	1.1
Boston–Cambridge–Quincy, MA–NH	4,875	4.7	65	0.1	8,940	8.6	0	0.0	1,270	1.2
Boulder, CO	0	0.0	10	0.2	120	2.0	0	0.0	55	0.9
Bowling Green, KY	35	1.8	0	0.0	70	3.5	0	0.0	15	0.8
Bremerton–Silverdale, WA	10	0.3	20	0.6	230	6.7	4	0.1	55	1.6
Bridgeport–Stamford–Norwalk, CT	1,220	7.9	30	0.2	1,315	8.5	0	0.0	135	0.9
Brownsville–Harlingen, TX	70	1.8	0	0.0	365	9.3	0	0.0	35	0.9
Brunswick, GA	275	16.0	0	0.0	55	3.2	0	0.0	0	0.0
Buffalo–Niagara Falls, NY	1,535	6.6	70	0.3	1,225	5.3	0	0.0	185	0.8
Burlington, NC	140	6.6	0	0.0	45	2.1	0	0.0	0	0.0
Burlington–South Burlington, VT	15	0.3	25	0.5	95	2.0	0	0.0	20	0.4
Canton–Massillon, OH	220	2.9	0	0.0	235	3.1	0	0.0	39	0.5
Cape Coral–Fort Myers, FL	495	5.4	0	0.0	585	6.4	0	0.0	65	0.7
Cape Girardeau–Jackson, MO–IL	55	3.1	0	0.0	0	0.0	0	0.0	0	0.0
Carson City, NV	0	0.0	4	0.6	55	8.8	0	0.0	10	1.6

PART C—METROPOLITAN STATISTICAL AREA TABLES

C-5 **Health Care Practitioner Professionals, by Metropolitan Statistical Area, Sex, Race, and Hispanic or Latino Origin, 2006–2010**—Continued

Metropolitan Statistical Area	Total who worked in the last 5 years	Male Number	Male Percent	Female Number	Female Percent	Hispanic or Latino Number	Hispanic or Latino Percent	White alone, not Hispanic or Latino Number	White alone, not Hispanic or Latino Percent
Casper, WY	1,665	430	25.8	1,240	74.5	30	1.8	1,570	94.3
Cedar Rapids, IA	4,695	810	17.3	3,890	82.9	74	1.6	4,505	96.0
Champaign–Urbana, IL	3,685	835	22.7	2,850	77.3	115	3.1	3,030	82.2
Charleston, WV	6,655	2,015	30.3	4,640	69.7	90	1.4	6,050	90.9
Charleston–North Charleston–Summerville, SC	12,475	2,975	23.8	9,500	76.2	170	1.4	10,475	84.0
Charlotte–Gastonia–Rock Hill, NC–SC	28,125	6,755	24.0	21,375	76.0	460	1.6	21,595	76.8
Charlottesville, VA	5,800	1,995	34.4	3,805	65.6	90	1.6	5,035	86.8
Chattanooga, TN–GA	10,335	2,780	26.9	7,555	73.1	115	1.1	9,030	87.4
Cheyenne, WY	1,540	390	25.3	1,150	74.7	125	8.1	1,410	91.6
Chicago–Joliet–Naperville, IL–IN–WI	162,720	41,115	25.3	121,600	74.7	8,205	5.0	106,520	65.5
Chico, CA	3,190	1,040	32.6	2,150	67.4	250	7.8	2,720	85.3
Cincinnati–Middletown, OH–KY–IN	39,875	9,645	24.2	30,230	75.8	395	1.0	34,850	87.4
Clarksville, TN–KY	3,175	775	24.4	2,400	75.6	140	4.4	2,550	80.3
Cleveland, TN	1,775	435	24.5	1,345	75.8	15	0.8	1,630	91.8
Cleveland–Elyria–Mentor, OH	44,445	11,250	25.3	33,195	74.7	1,045	2.4	35,985	81.0
Coeur d'Alene, ID	2,520	760	30.2	1,755	69.6	75	3.0	2,365	93.8
College Station–Bryan, TX	2,670	855	32.0	1,815	68.0	160	6.0	2,125	79.6
Colorado Springs, CO	9,600	2,910	30.3	6,690	69.7	435	4.5	8,260	86.0
Columbia, MO	4,875	1,555	31.9	3,320	68.1	90	1.8	4,365	89.5
Columbia, SC	13,490	3,310	24.5	10,180	75.5	210	1.6	9,740	72.2
Columbus, GA–AL	4,000	1,255	31.4	2,740	68.5	145	3.6	2,460	61.5
Columbus, IN	1,275	355	27.8	920	72.2	10	0.8	1,235	96.9
Columbus, OH	34,755	9,060	26.1	25,695	73.9	470	1.4	29,310	84.3
Corpus Christi, TX	5,970	1,865	31.2	4,110	68.8	1,935	32.4	3,325	55.7
Corvallis, OR	1,595	375	23.5	1,220	76.5	15	0.9	1,495	93.7
Crestview–Fort Walton Beach–Destin, FL	2,460	760	30.9	1,705	69.3	130	5.3	2,025	82.3
Cumberland, MD–WV	1,650	475	28.8	1,175	71.2	4	0.2	1,610	97.6
Dallas–Fort Worth–Arlington, TX	86,040	23,235	27.0	62,805	73.0	5,490	6.4	57,125	66.4
Dalton, GA	1,130	380	33.6	750	66.4	45	4.0	960	85.0
Danville, IL	1,135	260	22.9	875	77.1	0	0.0	1,005	88.5
Danville, VA	1,505	415	27.6	1,090	72.4	0	0.0	1,225	81.4
Davenport–Moline–Rock Island, IA–IL	6,570	1,595	24.3	4,970	75.6	75	1.1	6,155	93.7
Dayton, OH	15,350	3,925	25.6	11,425	74.4	260	1.7	13,135	85.6
Decatur, AL	1,730	370	21.4	1,360	78.6	15	0.9	1,545	89.3
Decatur, IL	1,875	640	34.1	1,235	65.9	60	3.2	1,610	85.9
Deltona–Daytona Beach–Ormond Beach, FL	7,300	1,845	25.3	5,455	74.7	455	6.2	6,025	82.5
Denver–Aurora–Broomfield, CO	42,775	11,285	26.4	31,490	73.6	2,350	5.5	36,240	84.7
Des Moines–West Des Moines, IA	10,315	2,530	24.5	7,785	75.5	150	1.5	9,640	93.5
Detroit–Warren–Livonia, MI	74,095	20,660	27.9	53,435	72.1	1,120	1.5	54,975	74.2
Dothan, AL	2,770	695	25.1	2,080	75.1	10	0.4	2,430	87.7
Dover, DE	2,480	440	17.7	2,040	82.3	44	1.8	1,880	75.8
Dubuque, IA	2,035	515	25.3	1,520	74.7	15	0.7	1,985	97.5
Duluth, MN–WI	6,165	1,645	26.7	4,520	73.3	29	0.5	5,970	96.8
Durham–Chapel Hill, NC	15,105	4,290	28.4	10,815	71.6	465	3.1	10,960	72.6
Eau Claire, WI	2,850	630	22.1	2,215	77.7	10	0.4	2,800	98.2
El Centro, CA	1,065	445	41.8	625	58.7	695	65.3	310	29.1
Elizabethtown, KY	1,785	545	30.5	1,240	69.5	40	2.2	1,550	86.8
Elkhart–Goshen, IN	2,460	685	27.8	1,775	72.2	55	2.2	2,275	92.5
Elmira, NY	1,985	625	31.5	1,360	68.5	0	0.0	1,800	90.7
El Paso, TX	8,180	3,360	41.1	4,820	58.9	4,760	58.2	2,400	29.3
Erie, PA	5,610	1,210	21.6	4,400	78.4	35	0.6	5,310	94.7
Eugene–Springfield, OR	5,250	1,545	29.4	3,710	70.7	105	2.0	4,835	92.1
Evansville, IN–KY	5,845	1,195	20.4	4,650	79.6	0	0.0	5,365	91.8
Fairbanks, AK	1,205	355	29.5	850	70.5	0	0.0	1,095	90.9
Fargo, ND–MN	4,525	1,275	28.2	3,255	71.9	50	1.1	4,265	94.3

C-5 Health Care Practitioner Professionals, by Metropolitan Statistical Area, Sex, Race, and Hispanic or Latino Origin, 2006–2010—*Continued*

Metropolitan Statistical Area	Black alone, not Hispanic or Latino Number	Black alone, not Hispanic or Latino Percent	American Indian and Alaska Native alone, not Hispanic or Latino Number	American Indian and Alaska Native alone, not Hispanic or Latino Percent	Asian alone, not Hispanic or Latino Number	Asian alone, not Hispanic or Latino Percent	Native Hawaiian and Other Pacific Islander alone, not Hispanic or Latino Number	Native Hawaiian and Other Pacific Islander alone, not Hispanic or Latino Percent	Two or more races, not Hispanic or Latino Number	Two or more races, not Hispanic or Latino Percent
Casper, WY	0	0.0	4	0.2	30	1.8	0	0.0	30	1.8
Cedar Rapids, IA	30	0.6	0	0.0	90	1.9	0	0.0	0	0.0
Champaign–Urbana, IL	80	2.2	0	0.0	440	11.9	0	0.0	19	0.5
Charleston, WV	115	1.7	0	0.0	360	5.4	0	0.0	40	0.6
Charleston–North Charleston–Summerville, SC	1,425	11.4	40	0.3	220	1.8	15	0.1	130	1.0
Charlotte–Gastonia–Rock Hill, NC–SC	4,790	17.0	70	0.2	1,040	3.7	0	0.0	170	0.6
Charlottesville, VA	160	2.8	0	0.0	465	8.0	10	0.2	40	0.7
Chattanooga, TN–GA	560	5.4	10	0.1	550	5.3	0	0.0	65	0.6
Cheyenne, WY	10	0.6	0	0.0	0	0.0	0	0.0	0	0.0
Chicago–Joliet–Naperville, IL–IN–WI	17,520	10.8	60	0.0	28,805	17.7	65	0.0	1,550	1.0
Chico, CA	25	0.8	25	0.8	135	4.2	0	0.0	34	1.1
Cincinnati–Middletown, OH–KY–IN	2,635	6.6	30	0.1	1,595	4.0	25	0.1	345	0.9
Clarksville, TN–KY	380	12.0	4	0.1	85	2.7	0	0.0	15	0.5
Cleveland, TN	25	1.4	20	1.1	70	3.9	0	0.0	10	0.6
Cleveland–Elyria–Mentor, OH	3,940	8.9	125	0.3	2,890	6.5	0	0.0	455	1.0
Coeur d'Alene, ID	0	0.0	0	0.0	10	0.4	0	0.0	70	2.8
College Station–Bryan, TX	95	3.6	10	0.4	265	9.9	0	0.0	20	0.7
Colorado Springs, CO	305	3.2	25	0.3	340	3.5	95	1.0	145	1.5
Columbia, MO	145	3.0	30	0.6	225	4.6	0	0.0	19	0.4
Columbia, SC	2,910	21.6	60	0.4	465	3.4	0	0.0	100	0.7
Columbus, GA–AL	1,220	30.5	4	0.1	135	3.4	0	0.0	35	0.9
Columbus, IN	0	0.0	30	2.4	0	0.0	0	0.0	0	0.0
Columbus, OH	2,910	8.4	110	0.3	1,570	4.5	0	0.0	380	1.1
Corpus Christi, TX	240	4.0	25	0.4	310	5.2	0	0.0	140	2.3
Corvallis, OR	0	0.0	0	0.0	65	4.1	0	0.0	20	1.3
Crestview–Fort Walton Beach–Destin, FL	55	2.2	20	0.8	170	6.9	0	0.0	60	2.4
Cumberland, MD–WV	15	0.9	0	0.0	10	0.6	0	0.0	10	0.6
Dallas–Fort Worth–Arlington, TX	11,490	13.4	260	0.3	10,570	12.3	45	0.1	1,050	1.2
Dalton, GA	35	3.1	0	0.0	90	8.0	0	0.0	0	0.0
Danville, IL	80	7.0	0	0.0	50	4.4	0	0.0	0	0.0
Danville, VA	230	15.3	0	0.0	30	2.0	0	0.0	15	1.0
Davenport–Moline–Rock Island, IA–IL	130	2.0	10	0.2	145	2.2	10	0.2	44	0.7
Dayton, OH	1,080	7.0	15	0.1	705	4.6	0	0.0	150	1.0
Decatur, AL	60	3.5	70	4.0	4	0.2	0	0.0	30	1.7
Decatur, IL	120	6.4	15	0.8	70	3.7	0	0.0	0	0.0
Deltona–Daytona Beach–Ormond Beach, FL	335	4.6	10	0.1	345	4.7	0	0.0	130	1.8
Denver–Aurora–Broomfield, CO	1,235	2.9	120	0.3	2,220	5.2	25	0.1	585	1.4
Des Moines–West Des Moines, IA	90	0.9	25	0.2	400	3.9	0	0.0	4	0.0
Detroit–Warren–Livonia, MI	8,850	11.9	135	0.2	8,150	11.0	15	0.0	855	1.2
Dothan, AL	285	10.3	20	0.7	15	0.5	0	0.0	12	0.4
Dover, DE	375	15.1	0	0.0	105	4.2	0	0.0	75	3.0
Dubuque, IA	10	0.5	0	0.0	25	1.2	0	0.0	0	0.0
Duluth, MN–WI	25	0.4	70	1.1	20	0.3	0	0.0	49	0.8
Durham–Chapel Hill, NC	2,000	13.2	70	0.5	1,365	9.0	0	0.0	240	1.6
Eau Claire, WI	0	0.0	4	0.1	30	1.1	0	0.0	4	0.1
El Centro, CA	15	1.4	0	0.0	40	3.8	0	0.0	10	0.9
Elizabethtown, KY	60	3.4	0	0.0	115	6.4	0	0.0	14	0.8
Elkhart–Goshen, IN	40	1.6	0	0.0	65	2.6	0	0.0	25	1.0
Elmira, NY	40	2.0	0	0.0	145	7.3	0	0.0	4	0.2
El Paso, TX	370	4.5	0	0.0	555	6.8	0	0.0	100	1.2
Erie, PA	120	2.1	10	0.2	95	1.7	0	0.0	40	0.7
Eugene–Springfield, OR	10	0.2	15	0.3	215	4.1	0	0.0	75	1.4
Evansville, IN–KY	180	3.1	30	0.5	145	2.5	0	0.0	120	2.1
Fairbanks, AK	4	0.3	50	4.1	25	2.1	0	0.0	35	2.9
Fargo, ND–MN	25	0.6	25	0.6	140	3.1	0	0.0	24	0.5

PART C—METROPOLITAN STATISTICAL AREA TABLES

C-5 Health Care Practitioner Professionals, by Metropolitan Statistical Area, Sex, Race, and Hispanic or Latino Origin, 2006–2010—Continued

Metropolitan Statistical Area	Total who worked in the last 5 years	Male Number	Male Percent	Female Number	Female Percent	Hispanic or Latino Number	Hispanic or Latino Percent	White alone, not Hispanic or Latino Number	White alone, not Hispanic or Latino Percent
Farmington, NM	1,510	455	30.1	1,060	70.2	120	7.9	1,060	70.2
Fayetteville, NC	5,200	1,250	24.0	3,950	76.0	210	4.0	3,120	60.0
Fayetteville–Springdale–Rogers, AR–MO	5,360	1,285	24.0	4,075	76.0	40	0.7	4,895	91.3
Flagstaff, AZ	2,170	715	32.9	1,455	67.1	65	3.0	1,810	83.4
Flint, MI	7,130	1,895	26.6	5,235	73.4	145	2.0	5,735	80.4
Florence, SC	3,750	875	23.3	2,870	76.5	70	1.9	3,025	80.7
Florence–Muscle Shoals, AL	2,430	615	25.3	1,815	74.7	10	0.4	2,145	88.3
Fond du Lac, WI	1,500	235	15.7	1,260	84.0	25	1.7	1,365	91.0
Fort Collins–Loveland, CO	6,520	1,800	27.6	4,725	72.5	205	3.1	6,165	94.6
Fort Smith, AR–OK	3,985	1,070	26.9	2,915	73.1	80	2.0	3,480	87.3
Fort Wayne, IN	7,300	1,435	19.7	5,860	80.3	110	1.5	6,670	91.4
Fresno, CA	11,515	3,935	34.2	7,580	65.8	1,630	14.2	5,935	51.5
Gadsden, AL	1,895	555	29.3	1,340	70.7	20	1.1	1,650	87.1
Gainesville, FL	8,020	2,625	32.7	5,395	67.3	330	4.1	6,285	78.4
Gainesville, GA	2,020	660	32.7	1,360	67.3	100	5.0	1,785	88.4
Glens Falls, NY	2,295	550	24.0	1,740	75.8	60	2.6	2,150	93.7
Goldsboro, NC	1,610	315	19.6	1,290	80.1	10	0.6	1,165	72.4
Grand Forks, ND–MN	1,995	510	25.6	1,480	74.2	15	0.8	1,930	96.7
Grand Junction, CO	3,125	745	23.8	2,380	76.2	70	2.2	3,020	96.6
Grand Rapids–Wyoming, MI	12,205	3,300	27.0	8,905	73.0	175	1.4	11,325	92.8
Great Falls, MT	1,840	455	24.7	1,385	75.3	25	1.4	1,750	95.1
Greeley, CO	3,110	840	27.0	2,270	73.0	95	3.1	2,785	89.5
Green Bay, WI	5,305	1,300	24.5	4,005	75.5	10	0.2	5,060	95.4
Greensboro–High Point, NC	10,325	2,470	23.9	7,855	76.1	140	1.4	8,205	79.5
Greenville, NC	5,630	1,415	25.1	4,215	74.9	160	2.8	4,205	74.7
Greenville–Mauldin–Easley, SC	10,090	2,540	25.2	7,550	74.8	125	1.2	8,765	86.9
Gulfport–Biloxi, MS	2,825	740	26.2	2,085	73.8	85	3.0	2,580	91.3
Hagerstown–Martinsburg, MD–WV	3,780	615	16.3	3,165	83.7	95	2.5	3,360	88.9
Hanford–Corcoran, CA	1,175	385	32.8	790	67.2	185	15.7	660	56.2
Harrisburg–Carlisle, PA	9,715	3,145	32.4	6,570	67.6	140	1.4	8,545	88.0
Harrisonburg, VA	1,440	335	23.3	1,105	76.7	15	1.0	1,330	92.4
Hartford–West Hartford–East Hartford, CT	25,440	6,535	25.7	18,905	74.3	820	3.2	20,980	82.5
Hattiesburg, MS	3,145	940	29.9	2,205	70.1	0	0.0	2,480	78.9
Hickory–Lenoir–Morganton, NC	5,660	1,335	23.6	4,325	76.4	80	1.4	5,200	91.9
Hinesville–Fort Stewart, GA	505	25	5.0	480	95.0	14	2.8	185	36.6
Holland–Grand Haven, MI	4,215	985	23.4	3,230	76.6	60	1.4	3,940	93.5
Honolulu, HI	15,495	5,165	33.3	10,330	66.7	590	3.8	4,870	31.4
Hot Springs, AR	1,915	490	25.6	1,430	74.7	25	1.3	1,785	93.2
Houma–Bayou Cane–Thibodaux, LA	3,060	885	28.9	2,170	70.9	65	2.1	2,460	80.4
Houston–Sugar Land–Baytown, TX	79,740	23,170	29.1	56,570	70.9	8,225	10.3	40,860	51.2
Huntington–Ashland, WV–KY–OH	5,930	1,565	26.4	4,365	73.6	80	1.3	5,420	91.4
Huntsville, AL	6,455	1,840	28.5	4,610	71.4	84	1.3	5,250	81.3
Idaho Falls, ID	1,920	790	41.1	1,130	58.9	35	1.8	1,890	98.4
Indianapolis–Carmel, IN	35,625	8,730	24.5	26,895	75.5	715	2.0	30,625	86.0
Iowa City, IA	5,920	2,040	34.5	3,880	65.5	55	0.9	5,240	88.5
Ithaca, NY	1,800	695	38.6	1,100	61.1	100	5.6	1,565	86.9
Jackson, MI	2,560	465	18.2	2,095	81.8	24	0.9	2,400	93.8
Jackson, MS	12,735	3,375	26.5	9,360	73.5	115	0.9	8,895	69.8
Jackson, TN	2,470	885	35.8	1,580	64.0	65	2.6	2,025	82.0
Jacksonville, FL	22,250	6,055	27.2	16,195	72.8	1,230	5.5	15,820	71.1
Jacksonville, NC	1,495	240	16.1	1,255	83.9	34	2.3	1,230	82.3
Janesville, WI	2,485	550	22.1	1,935	77.9	19	0.8	2,340	94.2
Jefferson City, MO	2,365	485	20.5	1,880	79.5	0	0.0	2,245	94.9
Johnson City, TN	4,245	1,535	36.2	2,710	63.8	70	1.6	3,970	93.5
Johnstown, PA	3,255	800	24.6	2,455	75.4	10	0.3	3,095	95.1

C-5 **Health Care Practitioner Professionals, by Metropolitan Statistical Area, Sex, Race, and Hispanic or Latino Origin, 2006–2010**—*Continued*

Metropolitan Statistical Area	Black alone, not Hispanic or Latino Number	Percent	American Indian and Alaska Native alone, not Hispanic or Latino Number	Percent	Asian alone, not Hispanic or Latino Number	Percent	Native Hawaiian and Other Pacific Islander alone, not Hispanic or Latino Number	Percent	Two or more races, not Hispanic or Latino Number	Percent
Farmington, NM	0	0.0	220	14.6	55	3.6	0	0.0	59	3.9
Fayetteville, NC	1,355	26.1	60	1.2	355	6.8	10	0.2	85	1.6
Fayetteville–Springdale–Rogers, AR–MO	50	0.9	135	2.5	105	2.0	0	0.0	140	2.6
Flagstaff, AZ	50	2.3	165	7.6	55	2.5	10	0.5	15	0.7
Flint, MI	695	9.7	0	0.0	485	6.8	0	0.0	70	1.0
Florence, SC	610	16.3	0	0.0	35	0.9	0	0.0	4	0.1
Florence–Muscle Shoals, AL	225	9.3	4	0.2	45	1.9	0	0.0	4	0.2
Fond du Lac, WI	0	0.0	0	0.0	90	6.0	0	0.0	20	1.3
Fort Collins–Loveland, CO	0	0.0	10	0.2	75	1.2	0	0.0	75	1.2
Fort Smith, AR–OK	50	1.3	115	2.9	65	1.6	0	0.0	195	4.9
Fort Wayne, IN	215	2.9	0	0.0	300	4.1	0	0.0	4	0.1
Fresno, CA	340	3.0	65	0.6	3,170	27.5	65	0.6	310	2.7
Gadsden, AL	185	9.8	0	0.0	25	1.3	0	0.0	20	1.1
Gainesville, FL	710	8.9	0	0.0	645	8.0	0	0.0	44	0.5
Gainesville, GA	45	2.2	30	1.5	60	3.0	0	0.0	0	0.0
Glens Falls, NY	0	0.0	15	0.7	25	1.1	4	0.2	34	1.5
Goldsboro, NC	350	21.7	4	0.2	75	4.7	0	0.0	4	0.2
Grand Forks, ND–MN	15	0.8	0	0.0	30	1.5	0	0.0	0	0.0
Grand Junction, CO	0	0.0	0	0.0	10	0.3	30	1.0	0	0.0
Grand Rapids–Wyoming, MI	200	1.6	40	0.3	370	3.0	0	0.0	95	0.8
Great Falls, MT	0	0.0	15	0.8	30	1.6	0	0.0	25	1.4
Greeley, CO	0	0.0	0	0.0	210	6.8	0	0.0	20	0.6
Green Bay, WI	20	0.4	50	0.9	115	2.2	15	0.3	30	0.6
Greensboro–High Point, NC	1,560	15.1	4	0.0	315	3.1	0	0.0	94	0.9
Greenville, NC	780	13.9	15	0.3	345	6.1	0	0.0	129	2.3
Greenville–Mauldin–Easley, SC	785	7.8	15	0.1	325	3.2	0	0.0	69	0.7
Gulfport–Biloxi, MS	95	3.4	0	0.0	65	2.3	0	0.0	0	0.0
Hagerstown–Martinsburg, MD–WV	180	4.8	10	0.3	110	2.9	0	0.0	25	0.7
Hanford–Corcoran, CA	100	8.5	0	0.0	220	18.7	0	0.0	15	1.3
Harrisburg–Carlisle, PA	345	3.6	4	0.0	635	6.5	0	0.0	44	0.5
Harrisonburg, VA	35	2.4	0	0.0	60	4.2	0	0.0	0	0.0
Hartford–West Hartford–East Hartford, CT	1,600	6.3	0	0.0	1,690	6.6	0	0.0	350	1.4
Hattiesburg, MS	620	19.7	0	0.0	10	0.3	0	0.0	40	1.3
Hickory–Lenoir–Morganton, NC	185	3.3	15	0.3	130	2.3	0	0.0	50	0.9
Hinesville–Fort Stewart, GA	290	57.4	0	0.0	4	0.8	0	0.0	10	2.0
Holland–Grand Haven, MI	45	1.1	0	0.0	135	3.2	0	0.0	35	0.8
Honolulu, HI	295	1.9	30	0.2	8,025	51.8	310	2.0	1,370	8.8
Hot Springs, AR	70	3.7	0	0.0	35	1.8	0	0.0	0	0.0
Houma–Bayou Cane–Thibodaux, LA	395	12.9	35	1.1	100	3.3	0	0.0	0	0.0
Houston–Sugar Land–Baytown, TX	13,350	16.7	155	0.2	16,110	20.2	25	0.0	1,020	1.3
Huntington–Ashland, WV–KY–OH	110	1.9	4	0.1	240	4.0	0	0.0	75	1.3
Huntsville, AL	780	12.1	55	0.9	210	3.3	10	0.2	55	0.9
Idaho Falls, ID	0	0.0	0	0.0	0	0.0	0	0.0	0	0.0
Indianapolis–Carmel, IN	2,220	6.2	25	0.1	1,750	4.9	0	0.0	295	0.8
Iowa City, IA	45	0.8	0	0.0	545	9.2	0	0.0	35	0.6
Ithaca, NY	25	1.4	0	0.0	110	6.1	0	0.0	0	0.0
Jackson, MI	40	1.6	0	0.0	85	3.3	0	0.0	14	0.5
Jackson, MS	3,315	26.0	0	0.0	365	2.9	0	0.0	35	0.3
Jackson, TN	280	11.3	20	0.8	70	2.8	0	0.0	10	0.4
Jacksonville, FL	2,575	11.6	60	0.3	2,220	10.0	50	0.2	300	1.3
Jacksonville, NC	85	5.7	0	0.0	120	8.0	0	0.0	20	1.3
Janesville, WI	75	3.0	4	0.2	30	1.2	0	0.0	8	0.3
Jefferson City, MO	55	2.3	4	0.2	20	0.8	0	0.0	49	2.1
Johnson City, TN	50	1.2	0	0.0	125	2.9	0	0.0	35	0.8
Johnstown, PA	0	0.0	0	0.0	140	4.3	0	0.0	8	0.2

PART C—METROPOLITAN STATISTICAL AREA TABLES

C-5 Health Care Practitioner Professionals, by Metropolitan Statistical Area, Sex, Race, and Hispanic or Latino Origin, 2006-2010—Continued

Metropolitan Statistical Area	Total who worked in the last 5 years	Male Number	Male Percent	Female Number	Female Percent	Hispanic or Latino Number	Hispanic or Latino Percent	White alone, not Hispanic or Latino Number	White alone, not Hispanic or Latino Percent
Jonesboro, AR	2,065	465	22.5	1,600	77.5	25	1.2	1,860	90.1
Joplin, MO	2,755	830	30.1	1,925	69.9	110	4.0	2,465	89.5
Kalamazoo-Portage, MI	6,175	1,750	28.3	4,430	71.7	205	3.3	5,400	87.4
Kankakee-Bradley, IL	1,975	405	20.5	1,570	79.5	0	0.0	1,705	86.3
Kansas City, MO-KS	38,275	9,490	24.8	28,780	75.2	815	2.1	33,020	86.3
Kennewick-Pasco-Richland, WA	3,075	860	28.0	2,215	72.0	170	5.5	2,595	84.4
Killeen-Temple-Fort Hood, TX	5,070	1,625	32.1	3,445	67.9	440	8.7	3,750	74.0
Kingsport-Bristol-Bristol, TN-VA	5,345	1,605	30.0	3,740	70.0	45	0.8	5,235	97.9
Kingston, NY	3,805	1,100	28.9	2,705	71.1	130	3.4	3,460	90.9
Knoxville, TN	13,975	3,945	28.2	10,030	71.8	245	1.8	12,625	90.3
Kokomo, IN	1,265	290	22.9	975	77.1	0	0.0	1,220	96.4
La Crosse, WI-MN	3,115	840	27.0	2,275	73.0	14	0.4	3,000	96.3
Lafayette, IN	3,125	630	20.2	2,495	79.8	40	1.3	2,795	89.4
Lafayette, LA	4,725	1,550	32.8	3,175	67.2	160	3.4	3,935	83.3
Lake Charles, LA	2,735	910	33.3	1,830	66.9	110	4.0	1,960	71.7
Lake Havasu City-Kingman, AZ	1,985	480	24.2	1,505	75.8	165	8.3	1,645	82.9
Lakeland-Winter Haven, FL	8,020	1,915	23.9	6,100	76.1	530	6.6	5,900	73.6
Lancaster, PA	8,425	2,170	25.8	6,255	74.2	255	3.0	7,535	89.4
Lansing-East Lansing, MI	6,905	1,740	25.2	5,170	74.9	150	2.2	6,040	87.5
Laredo, TX	1,810	695	38.4	1,115	61.6	1,445	79.8	185	10.2
Las Cruces, NM	2,280	620	27.2	1,660	72.8	865	37.9	1,250	54.8
Las Vegas-Paradise, NV	23,050	6,630	28.8	16,420	71.2	1,505	6.5	12,985	56.3
Lawrence, KS	1,990	695	34.9	1,295	65.1	50	2.5	1,805	90.7
Lawton, OK	1,765	550	31.2	1,220	69.1	180	10.2	1,230	69.7
Lebanon, PA	2,315	725	31.3	1,590	68.7	45	1.9	2,160	93.3
Lewiston, ID-WA	980	335	34.2	645	65.8	15	1.5	950	96.9
Lewiston-Auburn, ME	1,900	400	21.1	1,500	78.9	10	0.5	1,835	96.6
Lexington-Fayette, KY	12,560	3,620	28.8	8,940	71.2	35	0.3	11,515	91.7
Lima, OH	1,555	350	22.5	1,210	77.8	14	0.9	1,435	92.3
Lincoln, NE	5,845	1,570	26.9	4,275	73.1	50	0.9	5,520	94.4
Little Rock-North Little Rock-Conway, AR	16,430	4,940	30.1	11,490	69.9	200	1.2	13,290	80.9
Logan, UT-ID	1,240	485	39.1	755	60.9	10	0.8	1,220	98.4
Longview, TX	2,675	745	27.9	1,930	72.1	39	1.5	2,335	87.3
Longview, WA	1,820	435	23.9	1,385	76.1	45	2.5	1,750	96.2
Los Angeles-Long Beach-Santa Ana, CA	176,820	57,650	32.6	119,170	67.4	21,040	11.9	76,575	43.3
Louisville/Jefferson County, KY-IN	24,440	6,075	24.9	18,365	75.1	290	1.2	21,590	88.3
Lubbock, TX	5,530	1,730	31.3	3,800	68.7	520	9.4	4,480	81.0
Lynchburg, VA	3,865	985	25.5	2,880	74.5	40	1.0	3,495	90.4
Macon, GA	3,800	1,110	29.2	2,690	70.8	25	0.7	2,530	66.6
Madera-Chowchilla, CA	1,120	305	27.2	820	73.2	205	18.3	795	71.0
Madison, WI	13,475	3,560	26.4	9,915	73.6	210	1.6	12,395	92.0
Manchester-Nashua, NH	7,690	1,675	21.8	6,015	78.2	140	1.8	7,080	92.1
Manhattan, KS	1,795	720	40.1	1,075	59.9	60	3.3	1,550	86.4
Mankato-North Mankato, MN	1,380	295	21.4	1,085	78.6	15	1.1	1,335	96.7
Mansfield, OH	1,930	390	20.2	1,540	79.8	10	0.5	1,720	89.1
McAllen-Edinburg-Mission, TX	6,905	2,215	32.1	4,690	67.9	4,425	64.1	1,100	15.9
Medford, OR	3,800	1,190	31.3	2,605	68.6	130	3.4	3,535	93.0
Memphis, TN-MS-AR	20,065	4,810	24.0	15,255	76.0	355	1.8	13,610	67.8
Merced, CA	1,970	720	36.5	1,255	63.7	230	11.7	1,200	60.9
Miami-Fort Lauderdale-Pompano Beach, FL	87,775	27,935	31.8	59,840	68.2	23,805	27.1	40,060	45.6
Michigan City-La Porte, IN	1,385	225	16.2	1,160	83.8	55	4.0	1,230	88.8
Midland, TX	1,780	590	33.1	1,190	66.9	235	13.2	1,210	68.0
Milwaukee-Waukesha-West Allis, WI	32,655	8,195	25.1	24,460	74.9	645	2.0	28,185	86.3
Minneapolis-St. Paul-Bloomington, MN-WI	62,530	14,720	23.5	47,810	76.5	935	1.5	56,530	90.4
Missoula, MT	2,460	740	30.1	1,720	69.9	30	1.2	2,305	93.7

C-5 **Health Care Practitioner Professionals, by Metropolitan Statistical Area, Sex, Race, and Hispanic or Latino Origin, 2006–2010**—*Continued*

Metropolitan Statistical Area	Black alone, not Hispanic or Latino Number	Percent	American Indian and Alaska Native alone, not Hispanic or Latino Number	Percent	Asian alone, not Hispanic or Latino Number	Percent	Native Hawaiian and Other Pacific Islander alone, not Hispanic or Latino Number	Percent	Two or more races, not Hispanic or Latino Number	Percent
Jonesboro, AR	115	5.6	0	0.0	65	3.1	0	0.0	0	0.0
Joplin, MO	0	0.0	60	2.2	80	2.9	0	0.0	44	1.6
Kalamazoo–Portage, MI	145	2.3	4	0.1	330	5.3	0	0.0	85	1.4
Kankakee–Bradley, IL	165	8.4	0	0.0	105	5.3	0	0.0	0	0.0
Kansas City, MO–KS	2,130	5.6	90	0.2	1,825	4.8	4	0.0	390	1.0
Kennewick–Pasco–Richland, WA	0	0.0	40	1.3	195	6.3	0	0.0	75	2.4
Killeen–Temple–Fort Hood, TX	495	9.8	40	0.8	250	4.9	4	0.1	85	1.7
Kingsport–Bristol–Bristol, TN–VA	4	0.1	0	0.0	60	1.1	0	0.0	0	0.0
Kingston, NY	40	1.1	0	0.0	160	4.2	0	0.0	15	0.4
Knoxville, TN	430	3.1	4	0.0	535	3.8	0	0.0	130	0.9
Kokomo, IN	25	2.0	0	0.0	0	0.0	0	0.0	20	1.6
La Crosse, WI–MN	0	0.0	0	0.0	35	1.1	0	0.0	65	2.1
Lafayette, IN	50	1.6	0	0.0	215	6.9	0	0.0	29	0.9
Lafayette, LA	445	9.4	10	0.2	165	3.5	0	0.0	10	0.2
Lake Charles, LA	520	19.0	10	0.4	110	4.0	0	0.0	25	0.9
Lake Havasu City–Kingman, AZ	25	1.3	25	1.3	60	3.0	0	0.0	60	3.0
Lakeland–Winter Haven, FL	960	12.0	0	0.0	535	6.7	15	0.2	75	0.9
Lancaster, PA	365	4.3	4	0.0	225	2.7	0	0.0	35	0.4
Lansing–East Lansing, MI	340	4.9	0	0.0	275	4.0	0	0.0	99	1.4
Laredo, TX	80	4.4	0	0.0	105	5.8	0	0.0	0	0.0
Las Cruces, NM	25	1.1	0	0.0	90	3.9	0	0.0	50	2.2
Las Vegas–Paradise, NV	1,610	7.0	95	0.4	6,300	27.3	4	0.0	550	2.4
Lawrence, KS	40	2.0	10	0.5	65	3.3	0	0.0	24	1.2
Lawton, OK	240	13.6	60	3.4	10	0.6	0	0.0	50	2.8
Lebanon, PA	20	0.9	0	0.0	65	2.8	0	0.0	20	0.9
Lewiston, ID–WA	0	0.0	15	1.5	0	0.0	0	0.0	0	0.0
Lewiston–Auburn, ME	10	0.5	0	0.0	25	1.3	0	0.0	20	1.1
Lexington–Fayette, KY	350	2.8	35	0.3	510	4.1	4	0.0	110	0.9
Lima, OH	85	5.5	0	0.0	10	0.6	0	0.0	10	0.6
Lincoln, NE	75	1.3	45	0.8	120	2.1	0	0.0	40	0.7
Little Rock–North Little Rock–Conway, AR	1,915	11.7	25	0.2	725	4.4	0	0.0	270	1.6
Logan, UT–ID	0	0.0	0	0.0	10	0.8	0	0.0	0	0.0
Longview, TX	215	8.0	0	0.0	85	3.2	0	0.0	0	0.0
Longview, WA	0	0.0	0	0.0	10	0.5	0	0.0	14	0.8
Los Angeles–Long Beach–Santa Ana, CA	12,070	6.8	250	0.1	63,490	35.9	205	0.1	3,190	1.8
Louisville/Jefferson County, KY–IN	1,355	5.5	20	0.1	1,020	4.2	0	0.0	165	0.7
Lubbock, TX	165	3.0	60	1.1	275	5.0	0	0.0	30	0.5
Lynchburg, VA	295	7.6	0	0.0	20	0.5	0	0.0	15	0.4
Macon, GA	910	23.9	0	0.0	255	6.7	0	0.0	80	2.1
Madera–Chowchilla, CA	65	5.8	0	0.0	35	3.1	0	0.0	20	1.8
Madison, WI	260	1.9	10	0.1	495	3.7	0	0.0	114	0.8
Manchester–Nashua, NH	65	0.8	50	0.7	305	4.0	0	0.0	57	0.7
Manhattan, KS	105	5.8	4	0.2	70	3.9	0	0.0	4	0.2
Mankato–North Mankato, MN	0	0.0	0	0.0	30	2.2	0	0.0	4	0.3
Mansfield, OH	115	6.0	0	0.0	85	4.4	0	0.0	0	0.0
McAllen–Edinburg–Mission, TX	65	0.9	0	0.0	1,265	18.3	0	0.0	45	0.7
Medford, OR	0	0.0	0	0.0	95	2.5	0	0.0	34	0.9
Memphis, TN–MS–AR	4,990	24.9	35	0.2	895	4.5	20	0.1	150	0.7
Merced, CA	60	3.0	30	1.5	420	21.3	0	0.0	39	2.0
Miami–Fort Lauderdale–Pompano Beach, FL	16,575	18.9	90	0.1	6,265	7.1	105	0.1	875	1.0
Michigan City–La Porte, IN	55	4.0	0	0.0	45	3.2	0	0.0	4	0.3
Midland, TX	75	4.2	0	0.0	260	14.6	0	0.0	4	0.2
Milwaukee–Waukesha–West Allis, WI	1,685	5.2	115	0.4	1,785	5.5	0	0.0	239	0.7
Minneapolis–St. Paul–Bloomington, MN–WI	2,295	3.7	175	0.3	2,145	3.4	0	0.0	450	0.7
Missoula, MT	0	0.0	75	3.0	10	0.4	0	0.0	40	1.6

PART C—METROPOLITAN STATISTICAL AREA TABLES

C-5 **Health Care Practitioner Professionals, by Metropolitan Statistical Area, Sex, Race, and Hispanic or Latino Origin, 2006–2010**—*Continued*

Metropolitan Statistical Area	Total who worked in the last 5 years	Male Number	Male Percent	Female Number	Female Percent	Hispanic or Latino Number	Hispanic or Latino Percent	White alone, not Hispanic or Latino Number	White alone, not Hispanic or Latino Percent
Mobile, AL	6,725	1,660	24.7	5,065	75.3	120	1.8	4,785	71.2
Modesto, CA	5,790	1,985	34.3	3,805	65.7	510	8.8	3,925	67.8
Monroe, LA	3,260	985	30.2	2,275	69.8	4	0.1	2,680	82.2
Monroe, MI	2,225	400	18.0	1,825	82.0	44	2.0	2,065	92.8
Montgomery, AL	5,230	1,545	29.5	3,685	70.5	65	1.2	3,640	69.6
Morgantown, WV	2,770	985	35.6	1,785	64.4	0	0.0	2,565	92.6
Morristown, TN	1,635	435	26.6	1,200	73.4	25	1.5	1,575	96.3
Mount Vernon–Anacortes, WA	1,710	580	33.9	1,135	66.4	65	3.8	1,585	92.7
Muncie, IN	2,100	515	24.5	1,585	75.5	25	1.2	1,920	91.4
Muskegon–Norton Shores, MI	2,260	575	25.4	1,685	74.6	40	1.8	2,060	91.2
Myrtle Beach–North Myrtle Beach–Conway, SC	3,890	1,135	29.2	2,755	70.8	14	0.4	3,515	90.4
Napa, CA	3,120	1,325	42.5	1,795	57.5	155	5.0	2,345	75.2
Naples–Marco Island, FL	4,355	1,480	34.0	2,875	66.0	345	7.9	3,610	82.9
Nashville-Davidson–Murfreesboro–Franklin, TN	31,850	8,720	27.4	23,130	72.6	565	1.8	26,895	84.4
New Haven–Milford, CT	19,120	5,385	28.2	13,735	71.8	1,110	5.8	14,905	78.0
New Orleans–Metairie–Kenner, LA	21,960	6,520	29.7	15,440	70.3	1,165	5.3	16,020	73.0
New York–Northern New Jersey–Long Island, NY–NJ–PA	348,655	102,910	29.5	245,745	70.5	24,430	7.0	196,380	56.3
Niles–Benton Harbor, MI	2,535	740	29.2	1,795	70.8	14	0.6	2,235	88.2
North Port–Bradenton–Sarasota, FL	12,415	3,690	29.7	8,725	70.3	605	4.9	10,695	86.1
Norwich–New London, CT	4,405	1,045	23.7	3,360	76.3	90	2.0	3,820	86.7
Ocala, FL	5,180	1,375	26.5	3,805	73.5	185	3.6	3,950	76.3
Ocean City, NJ	2,055	555	27.0	1,500	73.0	184	9.0	1,780	86.6
Odessa, TX	1,560	540	34.6	1,020	65.4	260	16.7	1,055	67.6
Ogden–Clearfield, UT	7,085	2,655	37.5	4,430	62.5	185	2.6	6,540	92.3
Oklahoma City, OK	20,940	6,315	30.2	14,625	69.8	375	1.8	16,565	79.1
Olympia, WA	4,185	1,275	30.5	2,915	69.7	155	3.7	3,545	84.7
Omaha–Council Bluffs, NE–IA	19,800	4,915	24.8	14,885	75.2	425	2.1	18,200	91.9
Orlando–Kissimmee–Sanford, FL	31,710	8,595	27.1	23,120	72.9	4,040	12.7	18,760	59.2
Oshkosh–Neenah, WI	2,760	570	20.7	2,190	79.3	15	0.5	2,625	95.1
Owensboro, KY	1,915	385	20.1	1,530	79.9	10	0.5	1,890	98.7
Oxnard–Thousand Oaks–Ventura, CA	11,255	3,375	30.0	7,880	70.0	1,150	10.2	7,410	65.8
Palm Bay–Melbourne–Titusville, FL	8,095	2,145	26.5	5,950	73.5	555	6.9	6,230	77.0
Palm Coast, FL	1,340	215	16.0	1,125	84.0	10	0.7	1,095	81.7
Panama City–Lynn Haven–Panama City Beach, FL	2,500	650	26.0	1,850	74.0	50	2.0	2,255	90.2
Parkersburg–Marietta–Vienna, WV–OH	2,495	755	30.3	1,740	69.7	50	2.0	2,405	96.4
Pascagoula, MS	2,135	545	25.5	1,595	74.7	60	2.8	1,730	81.0
Pensacola–Ferry Pass–Brent, FL	7,010	1,820	26.0	5,190	74.0	255	3.6	6,080	86.7
Peoria, IL	7,985	1,975	24.7	6,005	75.2	225	2.8	7,115	89.1
Philadelphia–Camden–Wilmington, PA–NJ–DE–MD	129,505	33,230	25.7	96,275	74.3	3,290	2.5	97,505	75.3
Phoenix–Mesa–Glendale, AZ	64,435	18,710	29.0	45,725	71.0	4,465	6.9	50,555	78.5
Pine Bluff, AR	1,420	285	20.1	1,135	79.9	4	0.3	860	60.6
Pittsburgh, PA	55,250	14,825	26.8	40,430	73.2	675	1.2	50,065	90.6
Pittsfield, MA	2,840	865	30.5	1,980	69.7	25	0.9	2,700	95.1
Pocatello, ID	1,575	630	40.0	945	60.0	4	0.3	1,545	98.1
Portland–South Portland–Biddeford, ME	11,600	3,050	26.3	8,555	73.8	54	0.5	11,295	97.4
Portland–Vancouver–Hillsboro, OR–WA	39,415	10,705	27.2	28,715	72.9	1,170	3.0	33,685	85.5
Port St. Lucie, FL	6,945	1,630	23.5	5,315	76.5	420	6.0	4,860	70.0
Poughkeepsie–Newburgh–Middletown, NY	13,430	3,310	24.6	10,120	75.4	600	4.5	10,175	75.8
Prescott, AZ	3,105	815	26.2	2,285	73.6	165	5.3	2,815	90.7
Providence–New Bedford–Fall River, RI–MA	31,200	6,745	21.6	24,455	78.4	675	2.2	28,055	89.9

C-5 **Health Care Practitioner Professionals, by Metropolitan Statistical Area, Sex, Race, and Hispanic or Latino Origin, 2006–2010**—*Continued*

Metropolitan Statistical Area	Black alone, not Hispanic or Latino Number	Percent	American Indian and Alaska Native alone, not Hispanic or Latino Number	Percent	Asian alone, not Hispanic or Latino Number	Percent	Native Hawaiian and Other Pacific Islander alone, not Hispanic or Latino Number	Percent	Two or more races, not Hispanic or Latino Number	Percent
Mobile, AL	1,680	25.0	0	0.0	55	0.8	0	0.0	80	1.2
Modesto, CA	170	2.9	25	0.4	1,025	17.7	4	0.1	135	2.3
Monroe, LA	485	14.9	0	0.0	95	2.9	0	0.0	0	0.0
Monroe, MI	10	0.4	0	0.0	50	2.2	0	0.0	60	2.7
Montgomery, AL	1,300	24.9	15	0.3	100	1.9	0	0.0	105	2.0
Morgantown, WV	4	0.1	0	0.0	165	6.0	0	0.0	40	1.4
Morristown, TN	10	0.6	0	0.0	25	1.5	0	0.0	0	0.0
Mount Vernon–Anacortes, WA	0	0.0	4	0.2	50	2.9	0	0.0	4	0.2
Muncie, IN	30	1.4	0	0.0	115	5.5	0	0.0	10	0.5
Muskegon–Norton Shores, MI	95	4.2	20	0.9	4	0.2	0	0.0	50	2.2
Myrtle Beach–North Myrtle Beach–Conway, SC	220	5.7	0	0.0	85	2.2	0	0.0	55	1.4
Napa, CA	20	0.6	10	0.3	500	16.0	0	0.0	80	2.6
Naples–Marco Island, FL	210	4.8	35	0.8	155	3.6	0	0.0	4	0.1
Nashville-Davidson–Murfreesboro–Franklin, TN	3,015	9.5	25	0.1	980	3.1	0	0.0	370	1.2
New Haven–Milford, CT	1,105	5.8	0	0.0	1,810	9.5	35	0.2	145	0.8
New Orleans–Metairie–Kenner, LA	3,375	15.4	40	0.2	1,140	5.2	0	0.0	210	1.0
New York–Northern New Jersey–Long Island, NY–NJ–PA	52,545	15.1	325	0.1	70,150	20.1	80	0.0	4,745	1.4
Niles–Benton Harbor, MI	150	5.9	0	0.0	100	3.9	0	0.0	34	1.3
North Port–Bradenton–Sarasota, FL	570	4.6	15	0.1	420	3.4	10	0.1	95	0.8
Norwich–New London, CT	120	2.7	0	0.0	330	7.5	0	0.0	45	1.0
Ocala, FL	615	11.9	0	0.0	380	7.3	0	0.0	50	1.0
Ocean City, NJ	4	0.2	0	0.0	85	4.1	0	0.0	0	0.0
Odessa, TX	75	4.8	10	0.6	150	9.6	0	0.0	15	1.0
Ogden–Clearfield, UT	110	1.6	25	0.4	115	1.6	25	0.4	80	1.1
Oklahoma City, OK	1,360	6.5	505	2.4	1,410	6.7	0	0.0	725	3.5
Olympia, WA	25	0.6	0	0.0	370	8.8	0	0.0	90	2.2
Omaha–Council Bluffs, NE–IA	410	2.1	15	0.1	450	2.3	20	0.1	280	1.4
Orlando–Kissimmee–Sanford, FL	4,505	14.2	35	0.1	3,845	12.1	30	0.1	495	1.6
Oshkosh–Neenah, WI	4	0.1	0	0.0	110	4.0	0	0.0	4	0.1
Owensboro, KY	0	0.0	0	0.0	15	0.8	0	0.0	0	0.0
Oxnard–Thousand Oaks–Ventura, CA	140	1.2	30	0.3	2,120	18.8	15	0.1	385	3.4
Palm Bay–Melbourne–Titusville, FL	505	6.2	0	0.0	680	8.4	0	0.0	124	1.5
Palm Coast, FL	125	9.3	0	0.0	110	8.2	0	0.0	0	0.0
Panama City–Lynn Haven–Panama City Beach, FL	110	4.4	10	0.4	75	3.0	0	0.0	0	0.0
Parkersburg–Marietta–Vienna, WV–OH	0	0.0	0	0.0	40	1.6	0	0.0	0	0.0
Pascagoula, MS	285	13.3	10	0.5	40	1.9	0	0.0	15	0.7
Pensacola–Ferry Pass–Brent, FL	410	5.8	20	0.3	190	2.7	0	0.0	50	0.7
Peoria, IL	215	2.7	0	0.0	355	4.4	0	0.0	80	1.0
Philadelphia–Camden–Wilmington, PA–NJ–DE–MD	14,520	11.2	180	0.1	12,620	9.7	25	0.0	1,365	1.1
Phoenix–Mesa–Glendale, AZ	2,625	4.1	385	0.6	5,410	8.4	155	0.2	839	1.3
Pine Bluff, AR	515	36.3	0	0.0	25	1.8	0	0.0	15	1.1
Pittsburgh, PA	1,710	3.1	25	0.0	2,430	4.4	0	0.0	350	0.6
Pittsfield, MA	20	0.7	0	0.0	60	2.1	0	0.0	35	1.2
Pocatello, ID	0	0.0	4	0.3	0	0.0	20	1.3	0	0.0
Portland–South Portland–Biddeford, ME	40	0.3	4	0.0	150	1.3	0	0.0	59	0.5
Portland–Vancouver–Hillsboro, OR–WA	685	1.7	100	0.3	2,990	7.6	25	0.1	765	1.9
Port St. Lucie, FL	1,145	16.5	60	0.9	440	6.3	0	0.0	25	0.4
Poughkeepsie–Newburgh–Middletown, NY	1,240	9.2	20	0.1	1,310	9.8	10	0.1	74	0.6
Prescott, AZ	0	0.0	0	0.0	95	3.1	0	0.0	30	1.0
Providence–New Bedford–Fall River, RI–MA	1,035	3.3	0	0.0	1,140	3.7	0	0.0	290	0.9

PART C—METROPOLITAN STATISTICAL AREA TABLES

C-5 Health Care Practitioner Professionals, by Metropolitan Statistical Area, Sex, Race, and Hispanic or Latino Origin, 2006–2010—Continued

Metropolitan Statistical Area	Total who worked in the last 5 years	Male Number	Male Percent	Female Number	Female Percent	Hispanic or Latino Number	Hispanic or Latino Percent	White alone, not Hispanic or Latino Number	White alone, not Hispanic or Latino Percent
Provo–Orem, UT	6,025	2,290	38.0	3,735	62.0	155	2.6	5,685	94.4
Pueblo, CO	3,175	900	28.3	2,275	71.7	785	24.7	2,260	71.2
Punta Gorda, FL	2,465	780	31.6	1,685	68.4	205	8.3	1,935	78.5
Racine, WI	3,035	670	22.1	2,365	77.9	65	2.1	2,725	89.8
Raleigh–Cary, NC	19,815	5,005	25.3	14,810	74.7	270	1.4	15,640	78.9
Rapid City, SD	2,475	600	24.2	1,875	75.8	10	0.4	2,355	95.2
Reading, PA	6,560	1,400	21.3	5,160	78.7	225	3.4	5,855	89.3
Redding, CA	2,825	955	33.8	1,870	66.2	80	2.8	2,575	91.2
Reno–Sparks, NV	6,950	2,450	35.3	4,500	64.7	240	3.5	5,750	82.7
Richmond, VA	21,750	5,475	25.2	16,275	74.8	280	1.3	16,155	74.3
Riverside–San Bernardino–Ontario, CA	50,245	15,320	30.5	34,925	69.5	7,555	15.0	23,545	46.9
Roanoke, VA	6,390	1,830	28.6	4,555	71.3	30	0.5	5,770	90.3
Rochester, MN	10,295	3,145	30.5	7,155	69.5	185	1.8	9,215	89.5
Rochester, NY	21,605	5,110	23.7	16,495	76.3	640	3.0	18,625	86.2
Rockford, IL	5,375	1,220	22.7	4,155	77.3	130	2.4	4,555	84.7
Rocky Mount, NC	2,090	365	17.5	1,730	82.8	30	1.4	1,720	82.3
Rome, GA	1,665	445	26.7	1,215	73.0	10	0.6	1,545	92.8
Sacramento–Arden-Arcade–Roseville, CA	31,790	9,860	31.0	21,930	69.0	1,975	6.2	20,595	64.8
Saginaw–Saginaw Township North, MI	3,125	1,020	32.6	2,105	67.4	70	2.2	2,550	81.6
St. Cloud, MN	2,935	910	31.0	2,020	68.8	50	1.7	2,805	95.6
St. George, UT	1,960	750	38.3	1,205	61.5	55	2.8	1,790	91.3
St. Joseph, MO–KS	1,970	385	19.5	1,580	80.2	0	0.0	1,870	94.9
St. Louis, MO–IL	55,350	13,965	25.2	41,385	74.8	800	1.4	45,835	82.8
Salem, OR	4,690	1,380	29.4	3,310	70.6	165	3.5	4,200	89.6
Salinas, CA	4,710	1,580	33.5	3,130	66.5	655	13.9	2,910	61.8
Salisbury, MD	2,580	745	28.9	1,835	71.1	60	2.3	2,080	80.6
Salt Lake City, UT	16,765	6,030	36.0	10,735	64.0	480	2.9	15,505	92.5
San Angelo, TX	1,765	515	29.2	1,250	70.8	175	9.9	1,530	86.7
San Antonio–New Braunfels, TX	30,700	9,330	30.4	21,370	69.6	8,465	27.6	17,370	56.6
San Diego–Carlsbad–San Marcos, CA	45,995	14,480	31.5	31,510	68.5	4,660	10.1	28,295	61.5
Sandusky, OH	1,405	420	29.9	985	70.1	10	0.7	1,275	90.7
San Francisco–Oakland–Fremont, CA	79,625	23,905	30.0	55,720	70.0	5,175	6.5	42,505	53.4
San Jose–Sunnyvale–Santa Clara, CA	26,785	7,750	28.9	19,040	71.1	1,915	7.1	11,770	43.9
San Luis Obispo–Paso Robles, CA	4,685	1,700	36.3	2,985	63.7	300	6.4	3,825	81.6
Santa Barbara–Santa Maria–Goleta, CA	5,165	1,530	29.6	3,635	70.4	585	11.3	3,755	72.7
Santa Cruz–Watsonville, CA	4,600	1,145	24.9	3,455	75.1	325	7.1	3,585	77.9
Santa Fe, NM	2,350	665	28.3	1,685	71.7	375	16.0	1,750	74.5
Santa Rosa–Petaluma, CA	7,685	2,355	30.6	5,335	69.4	390	5.1	6,575	85.6
Savannah, GA	6,290	1,595	25.4	4,690	74.6	165	2.6	5,155	82.0
Scranton–Wilkes-Barre, PA	11,450	2,980	26.0	8,470	74.0	99	0.9	10,790	94.2
Seattle–Tacoma–Bellevue, WA	58,550	16,450	28.1	42,100	71.9	1,765	3.0	45,095	77.0
Sebastian–Vero Beach, FL	2,125	610	28.7	1,515	71.3	95	4.5	1,890	88.9
Sheboygan, WI	1,825	315	17.3	1,510	82.7	4	0.2	1,780	97.5
Sherman–Denison, TX	1,825	270	14.8	1,555	85.2	30	1.6	1,620	88.8
Shreveport–Bossier City, LA	7,955	2,725	34.3	5,230	65.7	175	2.2	6,065	76.2
Sioux City, IA–NE–SD	2,580	635	24.6	1,940	75.2	74	2.9	2,430	94.2
Sioux Falls, SD	6,210	1,560	25.1	4,650	74.9	20	0.3	6,060	97.6
South Bend–Mishawaka, IN–MI	4,290	1,235	28.8	3,050	71.1	70	1.6	3,800	88.6
Spartanburg, SC	4,005	1,090	27.2	2,915	72.8	65	1.6	3,435	85.8
Spokane, WA	10,025	3,185	31.8	6,835	68.2	245	2.4	9,225	92.0
Springfield, IL	5,370	1,520	28.3	3,850	71.7	0	0.0	4,700	87.5
Springfield, MA	12,920	2,820	21.8	10,100	78.2	500	3.9	11,515	89.1
Springfield, MO	8,330	2,380	28.6	5,950	71.4	114	1.4	7,840	94.1
Springfield, OH	2,290	445	19.4	1,845	80.6	0	0.0	2,115	92.4
State College, PA	2,215	795	35.9	1,415	63.9	4	0.2	1,920	86.7

C-5 **Health Care Practitioner Professionals, by Metropolitan Statistical Area, Sex, Race, and Hispanic or Latino Origin, 2006–2010**—*Continued*

Metropolitan Statistical Area	Black alone, not Hispanic or Latino		American Indian and Alaska Native alone, not Hispanic or Latino		Asian alone, not Hispanic or Latino		Native Hawaiian and Other Pacific Islander alone, not Hispanic or Latino		Two or more races, not Hispanic or Latino	
	Number	Percent	Number	Percent	Number	Percent	Number	Percent	Number	Percent
Provo–Orem, UT	0	0.0	40	0.7	85	1.4	4	0.1	60	1.0
Pueblo, CO	20	0.6	40	1.3	55	1.7	0	0.0	8	0.3
Punta Gorda, FL	150	6.1	0	0.0	165	6.7	0	0.0	10	0.4
Racine, WI	160	5.3	0	0.0	60	2.0	10	0.3	10	0.3
Raleigh–Cary, NC	2,095	10.6	160	0.8	1,430	7.2	0	0.0	225	1.1
Rapid City, SD	0	0.0	90	3.6	4	0.2	0	0.0	10	0.4
Reading, PA	95	1.4	20	0.3	245	3.7	50	0.8	65	1.0
Redding, CA	4	0.1	4	0.1	135	4.8	0	0.0	33	1.2
Reno–Sparks, NV	75	1.1	30	0.4	670	9.6	30	0.4	150	2.2
Richmond, VA	3,775	17.4	60	0.3	1,290	5.9	0	0.0	200	0.9
Riverside–San Bernardino–Ontario, CA	4,220	8.4	130	0.3	13,395	26.7	120	0.2	1,285	2.6
Roanoke, VA	295	4.6	0	0.0	200	3.1	0	0.0	95	1.5
Rochester, MN	160	1.6	0	0.0	680	6.6	0	0.0	60	0.6
Rochester, NY	1,130	5.2	55	0.3	1,000	4.6	15	0.1	139	0.6
Rockford, IL	220	4.1	0	0.0	440	8.2	0	0.0	30	0.6
Rocky Mount, NC	320	15.3	10	0.5	0	0.0	0	0.0	15	0.7
Rome, GA	55	3.3	0	0.0	55	3.3	0	0.0	0	0.0
Sacramento–Arden-Arcade–Roseville, CA	1,245	3.9	130	0.4	7,035	22.1	100	0.3	710	2.2
Saginaw–Saginaw Township North, MI	205	6.6	0	0.0	245	7.8	0	0.0	60	1.9
St. Cloud, MN	30	1.0	0	0.0	45	1.5	0	0.0	4	0.1
St. George, UT	0	0.0	0	0.0	110	5.6	0	0.0	10	0.5
St. Joseph, MO–KS	40	2.0	0	0.0	55	2.8	0	0.0	0	0.0
St. Louis, MO–IL	4,745	8.6	105	0.2	3,095	5.6	10	0.0	755	1.4
Salem, OR	40	0.9	35	0.7	205	4.4	0	0.0	40	0.9
Salinas, CA	30	0.6	0	0.0	910	19.3	20	0.4	175	3.7
Salisbury, MD	265	10.3	0	0.0	160	6.2	0	0.0	19	0.7
Salt Lake City, UT	60	0.4	140	0.8	425	2.5	25	0.1	130	0.8
San Angelo, TX	40	2.3	0	0.0	4	0.2	0	0.0	10	0.6
San Antonio–New Braunfels, TX	2,285	7.4	90	0.3	2,095	6.8	15	0.0	385	1.3
San Diego–Carlsbad–San Marcos, CA	1,425	3.1	110	0.2	10,575	23.0	105	0.2	825	1.8
Sandusky, OH	75	5.3	0	0.0	25	1.8	0	0.0	19	1.4
San Francisco–Oakland–Fremont, CA	3,915	4.9	60	0.1	25,870	32.5	230	0.3	1,860	2.3
San Jose–Sunnyvale–Santa Clara, CA	590	2.2	15	0.1	12,035	44.9	80	0.3	385	1.4
San Luis Obispo–Paso Robles, CA	20	0.4	30	0.6	320	6.8	0	0.0	190	4.1
Santa Barbara–Santa Maria–Goleta, CA	90	1.7	55	1.1	555	10.7	15	0.3	104	2.0
Santa Cruz–Watsonville, CA	65	1.4	10	0.2	545	11.8	0	0.0	75	1.6
Santa Fe, NM	15	0.6	50	2.1	130	5.5	0	0.0	35	1.5
Santa Rosa–Petaluma, CA	0	0.0	0	0.0	670	8.7	0	0.0	55	0.7
Savannah, GA	720	11.4	0	0.0	195	3.1	0	0.0	55	0.9
Scranton–Wilkes-Barre, PA	85	0.7	0	0.0	390	3.4	10	0.1	84	0.7
Seattle–Tacoma–Bellevue, WA	1,440	2.5	200	0.3	8,890	15.2	140	0.2	1,025	1.8
Sebastian–Vero Beach, FL	65	3.1	30	1.4	30	1.4	0	0.0	15	0.7
Sheboygan, WI	0	0.0	0	0.0	40	2.2	0	0.0	4	0.2
Sherman–Denison, TX	20	1.1	85	4.7	45	2.5	0	0.0	25	1.4
Shreveport–Bossier City, LA	1,100	13.8	10	0.1	535	6.7	0	0.0	70	0.9
Sioux City, IA–NE–SD	70	2.7	0	0.0	0	0.0	0	0.0	0	0.0
Sioux Falls, SD	25	0.4	20	0.3	85	1.4	0	0.0	0	0.0
South Bend–Mishawaka, IN–MI	180	4.2	0	0.0	220	5.1	0	0.0	18	0.4
Spartanburg, SC	325	8.1	0	0.0	160	4.0	0	0.0	25	0.6
Spokane, WA	105	1.0	4	0.0	330	3.3	0	0.0	110	1.1
Springfield, IL	180	3.4	4	0.1	450	8.4	0	0.0	39	0.7
Springfield, MA	440	3.4	4	0.0	370	2.9	10	0.1	74	0.6
Springfield, MO	40	0.5	70	0.8	195	2.3	0	0.0	75	0.9
Springfield, OH	75	3.3	10	0.4	90	3.9	0	0.0	0	0.0
State College, PA	20	0.9	4	0.2	205	9.3	20	0.9	40	1.8

C-5 Health Care Practitioner Professionals, by Metropolitan Statistical Area, Sex, Race, and Hispanic or Latino Origin, 2006–2010—*Continued*

Metropolitan Statistical Area	Total who worked in the last 5 years	Male Number	Male Percent	Female Number	Female Percent	Hispanic or Latino Number	Hispanic or Latino Percent	White alone, not Hispanic or Latino Number	White alone, not Hispanic or Latino Percent
Steubenville–Weirton, OH–WV	2,585	485	18.8	2,100	81.2	0	0.0	2,445	94.6
Stockton, CA	7,465	2,335	31.3	5,130	68.7	740	9.9	3,640	48.8
Sumter, SC	1,170	235	20.1	935	79.9	0	0.0	885	75.6
Syracuse, NY	12,945	3,400	26.3	9,545	73.7	165	1.3	11,545	89.2
Tallahassee, FL	4,775	1,180	24.7	3,595	75.3	145	3.0	3,455	72.4
Tampa–St. Petersburg–Clearwater, FL	48,275	13,510	28.0	34,765	72.0	4,535	9.4	35,145	72.8
Terre Haute, IN	2,950	770	26.1	2,180	73.9	35	1.2	2,705	91.7
Texarkana, TX–Texarkana, AR	2,065	600	29.1	1,465	70.9	40	1.9	1,710	82.8
Toledo, OH	13,460	2,775	20.6	10,680	79.3	365	2.7	11,675	86.7
Topeka, KS	4,290	1,070	24.9	3,220	75.1	105	2.4	3,900	90.9
Trenton–Ewing, NJ	5,645	1,385	24.5	4,260	75.5	120	2.1	3,395	60.1
Tucson, AZ	16,685	5,030	30.1	11,660	69.9	2,050	12.3	12,415	74.4
Tulsa, OK	13,825	3,915	28.3	9,910	71.7	415	3.0	11,100	80.3
Tuscaloosa, AL	3,840	985	25.7	2,855	74.3	85	2.2	2,490	64.8
Tyler, TX	4,685	1,685	36.0	3,000	64.0	285	6.1	3,715	79.3
Utica–Rome, NY	5,835	1,410	24.2	4,425	75.8	35	0.6	5,550	95.1
Valdosta, GA	1,780	425	23.9	1,355	76.1	55	3.1	1,420	79.8
Vallejo–Fairfield, CA	6,555	1,430	21.8	5,125	78.2	420	6.4	2,845	43.4
Victoria, TX	1,875	625	33.3	1,250	66.7	560	29.9	1,180	62.9
Vineland–Millville–Bridgeton, NJ	1,535	230	15.0	1,300	84.7	80	5.2	1,170	76.2
Virginia Beach–Norfolk–Newport News, VA–NC	24,785	6,095	24.6	18,690	75.4	590	2.4	16,920	68.3
Visalia–Porterville, CA	3,975	1,110	27.9	2,865	72.1	785	19.7	2,380	59.9
Waco, TX	3,020	755	25.0	2,265	75.0	270	8.9	2,340	77.5
Warner Robins, GA	1,935	565	29.2	1,370	70.8	60	3.1	1,500	77.5
Washington–Arlington–Alexandria, DC–VA–MD–WV	87,360	24,270	27.8	63,085	72.2	4,585	5.2	49,365	56.5
Waterloo–Cedar Falls, IA	2,445	445	18.2	2,000	81.8	25	1.0	2,305	94.3
Wausau, WI	2,825	755	26.7	2,070	73.3	55	1.9	2,665	94.3
Wenatchee–East Wenatchee, WA	1,750	505	28.9	1,245	71.1	45	2.6	1,665	95.1
Wheeling, WV–OH	3,580	905	25.3	2,670	74.6	65	1.8	3,385	94.6
Wichita, KS	10,665	2,880	27.0	7,785	73.0	485	4.5	9,085	85.2
Wichita Falls, TX	2,250	675	30.0	1,575	70.0	60	2.7	2,015	89.6
Williamsport, PA	1,900	295	15.5	1,605	84.5	0	0.0	1,840	96.8
Wilmington, NC	6,745	1,930	28.6	4,815	71.4	45	0.7	6,100	90.4
Winchester, VA–WV	2,185	615	28.1	1,570	71.9	115	5.3	1,945	89.0
Winston-Salem, NC	9,835	2,785	28.3	7,050	71.7	120	1.2	8,180	83.2
Worcester, MA	16,770	3,445	20.5	13,325	79.5	400	2.4	14,620	87.2
Yakima, WA	2,940	1,080	36.7	1,855	63.1	355	12.1	2,440	83.0
York–Hanover, PA	6,820	1,435	21.0	5,385	79.0	60	0.9	6,300	92.4
Youngstown–Warren–Boardman, OH–PA	10,435	2,850	27.3	7,585	72.7	210	2.0	9,505	91.1
Yuba City, CA	1,565	405	25.9	1,165	74.4	150	9.6	1,125	71.9
Yuma, AZ	1,420	335	23.6	1,085	76.4	245	17.3	1,000	70.4

C-5 Health Care Practitioner Professionals, by Metropolitan Statistical Area, Sex, Race, and Hispanic or Latino Origin, 2006–2010—*Continued*

Metropolitan Statistical Area	Black alone, not Hispanic or Latino Number	Percent	American Indian and Alaska Native alone, not Hispanic or Latino Number	Percent	Asian alone, not Hispanic or Latino Number	Percent	Native Hawaiian and Other Pacific Islander alone, not Hispanic or Latino Number	Percent	Two or more races, not Hispanic or Latino Number	Percent
Steubenville–Weirton, OH–WV	30	1.2	0	0.0	100	3.9	0	0.0	4	0.2
Stockton, CA	220	2.9	40	0.5	2,610	35.0	10	0.1	210	2.8
Sumter, SC	240	20.5	0	0.0	25	2.1	0	0.0	15	1.3
Syracuse, NY	390	3.0	50	0.4	710	5.5	0	0.0	80	0.6
Tallahassee, FL	800	16.8	0	0.0	290	6.1	0	0.0	90	1.9
Tampa–St. Petersburg–Clearwater, FL	3,535	7.3	65	0.1	4,340	9.0	50	0.1	604	1.3
Terre Haute, IN	50	1.7	10	0.3	115	3.9	0	0.0	30	1.0
Texarkana, TX–Texarkana, AR	190	9.2	0	0.0	55	2.7	0	0.0	70	3.4
Toledo, OH	690	5.1	4	0.0	585	4.3	0	0.0	130	1.0
Topeka, KS	120	2.8	10	0.2	110	2.6	0	0.0	39	0.9
Trenton–Ewing, NJ	665	11.8	0	0.0	1,420	25.2	0	0.0	49	0.9
Tucson, AZ	485	2.9	205	1.2	1,265	7.6	0	0.0	265	1.6
Tulsa, OK	685	5.0	765	5.5	375	2.7	0	0.0	485	3.5
Tuscaloosa, AL	1,105	28.8	0	0.0	120	3.1	0	0.0	40	1.0
Tyler, TX	445	9.5	0	0.0	230	4.9	0	0.0	15	0.3
Utica–Rome, NY	65	1.1	4	0.1	155	2.7	0	0.0	28	0.5
Valdosta, GA	300	16.9	0	0.0	4	0.2	0	0.0	0	0.0
Vallejo–Fairfield, CA	850	13.0	25	0.4	2,190	33.4	25	0.4	195	3.0
Victoria, TX	70	3.7	0	0.0	55	2.9	0	0.0	4	0.2
Vineland–Millville–Bridgeton, NJ	185	12.1	10	0.7	60	3.9	0	0.0	30	2.0
Virginia Beach–Norfolk–Newport News, VA–NC	4,615	18.6	15	0.1	2,150	8.7	0	0.0	500	2.0
Visalia–Porterville, CA	85	2.1	15	0.4	645	16.2	0	0.0	70	1.8
Waco, TX	315	10.4	0	0.0	85	2.8	0	0.0	4	0.1
Warner Robins, GA	245	12.7	0	0.0	135	7.0	0	0.0	0	0.0
Washington–Arlington–Alexandria, DC–VA–MD–WV	18,725	21.4	75	0.1	13,100	15.0	75	0.1	1,430	1.6
Waterloo–Cedar Falls, IA	0	0.0	10	0.4	70	2.9	0	0.0	30	1.2
Wausau, WI	10	0.4	0	0.0	50	1.8	0	0.0	39	1.4
Wenatchee–East Wenatchee, WA	0	0.0	0	0.0	20	1.1	0	0.0	25	1.4
Wheeling, WV–OH	4	0.1	0	0.0	95	2.7	0	0.0	35	1.0
Wichita, KS	485	4.5	65	0.6	390	3.7	0	0.0	160	1.5
Wichita Falls, TX	75	3.3	35	1.6	45	2.0	0	0.0	20	0.9
Williamsport, PA	40	2.1	15	0.8	4	0.2	0	0.0	0	0.0
Wilmington, NC	450	6.7	0	0.0	120	1.8	0	0.0	34	0.5
Winchester, VA–WV	60	2.7	0	0.0	50	2.3	0	0.0	10	0.5
Winston–Salem, NC	1,200	12.2	25	0.3	215	2.2	0	0.0	95	1.0
Worcester, MA	725	4.3	4	0.0	865	5.2	0	0.0	155	0.9
Yakima, WA	10	0.3	0	0.0	90	3.1	0	0.0	39	1.3
York–Hanover, PA	260	3.8	0	0.0	110	1.6	0	0.0	95	1.4
Youngstown–Warren–Boardman, OH–PA	340	3.3	15	0.1	320	3.1	0	0.0	45	0.4
Yuba City, CA	20	1.3	20	1.3	175	11.2	0	0.0	70	4.5
Yuma, AZ	40	2.8	4	0.3	90	6.3	0	0.0	40	2.8

PART C—METROPOLITAN STATISTICAL AREA TABLES

C-6 Other Professional Workers, by Metropolitan Statistical Area, Sex, Race, and Hispanic or Latino Origin, 2006–2010

Metropolitan Statistical Area	Total who worked in the last 5 years	Male Number	Male Percent	Female Number	Female Percent	Hispanic or Latino Number	Hispanic or Latino Percent	White alone, not Hispanic or Latino Number	White alone, not Hispanic or Latino Percent
Abilene, TX	8,905	3,620	40.7	5,285	59.3	630	7.1	7,790	87.5
Akron, OH	38,940	14,685	37.7	24,255	62.3	510	1.3	33,660	86.4
Albany, GA	6,830	2,205	32.3	4,625	67.7	85	1.2	4,215	61.7
Albany–Schenectady–Troy, NY	58,025	22,530	38.8	35,495	61.2	1,375	2.4	52,335	90.2
Albuquerque, NM	48,925	18,045	36.9	30,880	63.1	13,335	27.3	29,895	61.1
Alexandria, LA	7,160	2,210	30.9	4,950	69.1	200	2.8	5,040	70.4
Allentown–Bethlehem–Easton, PA–NJ	43,970	16,245	36.9	27,725	63.1	2,150	4.9	39,185	89.1
Altoona, PA	5,520	2,030	36.8	3,490	63.2	0	0.0	5,410	98.0
Amarillo, TX	13,070	4,735	36.2	8,335	63.8	1,110	8.5	11,030	84.4
Ames, IA	9,320	4,365	46.8	4,950	53.1	295	3.2	7,415	79.6
Anchorage, AK	21,875	8,275	37.8	13,600	62.2	880	4.0	17,520	80.1
Anderson, IN	5,840	2,335	40.0	3,505	60.0	85	1.5	5,325	91.2
Anderson, SC	7,545	2,910	38.6	4,635	61.4	50	0.7	6,730	89.2
Ann Arbor, MI	31,275	13,435	43.0	17,840	57.0	770	2.5	24,765	79.2
Anniston–Oxford, AL	4,540	1,560	34.4	2,980	65.6	105	2.3	3,715	81.8
Appleton, WI	11,865	4,425	37.3	7,440	62.7	140	1.2	11,215	94.5
Asheville, NC	23,745	8,880	37.4	14,870	62.6	500	2.1	22,185	93.2
Athens–Clarke County, GA	14,050	6,025	42.9	8,030	57.2	400	2.8	11,435	81.4
Atlanta–Sandy Springs–Marietta, GA	312,360	112,790	36.1	199,570	63.9	11,430	3.7	198,240	63.5
Atlantic City–Hammonton, NJ	12,550	4,610	36.7	7,940	63.3	670	5.3	9,535	76.0
Auburn–Opelika, AL	9,140	4,075	44.6	5,065	55.4	220	2.4	6,700	73.3
Augusta–Richmond County, GA–SC	23,925	8,125	34.0	15,800	66.0	535	2.2	15,790	66.0
Austin–Round Rock–San Marcos, TX	116,535	46,240	39.7	70,295	60.3	16,745	14.4	86,215	74.0
Bakersfield–Delano, CA	28,455	10,040	35.3	18,415	64.7	6,595	23.2	18,520	65.1
Baltimore–Towson, MD	176,570	64,155	36.3	112,415	63.7	3,850	2.2	124,655	70.6
Bangor, ME	9,395	3,600	38.3	5,795	61.7	140	1.5	8,730	92.9
Barnstable Town, MA	13,060	4,535	34.7	8,525	65.3	130	1.0	12,520	95.9
Baton Rouge, LA	40,850	14,365	35.2	26,485	64.8	810	2.0	28,765	70.4
Battle Creek, MI	5,415	1,905	35.2	3,505	64.7	139	2.6	4,620	85.3
Bay City, MI	4,810	1,735	36.1	3,070	63.8	70	1.5	4,675	97.2
Beaumont–Port Arthur, TX	16,415	5,665	34.5	10,750	65.5	755	4.6	12,035	73.3
Bellingham, WA	11,385	4,370	38.4	7,010	61.6	220	1.9	10,275	90.3
Bend, OR	8,130	3,295	40.5	4,835	59.5	180	2.2	7,710	94.8
Billings, MT	8,625	3,395	39.4	5,230	60.6	185	2.1	7,990	92.6
Binghamton, NY	14,190	5,580	39.3	8,610	60.7	395	2.8	12,830	90.4
Birmingham–Hoover, AL	58,160	21,205	36.5	36,950	63.5	795	1.4	43,480	74.8
Bismarck, ND	6,110	2,245	36.7	3,865	63.3	30	0.5	5,765	94.4
Blacksburg–Christiansburg–Radford, VA	11,285	4,930	43.7	6,350	56.3	190	1.7	9,490	84.1
Bloomington, IN	14,660	6,640	45.3	8,020	54.7	395	2.7	12,370	84.4
Bloomington–Normal, IL	11,160	4,325	38.8	6,835	61.2	245	2.2	9,810	87.9
Boise City–Nampa, ID	30,550	11,585	37.9	18,970	62.1	1,635	5.4	27,750	90.8
Boston–Cambridge–Quincy, MA–NH	350,660	136,305	38.9	214,350	61.1	13,690	3.9	296,225	84.5
Boulder, CO	26,280	11,105	42.3	15,175	57.7	1,300	4.9	23,155	88.1
Bowling Green, KY	7,085	2,705	38.2	4,380	61.8	220	3.1	6,130	86.5
Bremerton–Silverdale, WA	11,960	4,465	37.3	7,495	62.7	225	1.9	10,915	91.3
Bridgeport–Stamford–Norwalk, CT	66,925	28,800	43.0	38,130	57.0	4,325	6.5	55,535	83.0
Brownsville–Harlingen, TX	15,375	5,960	38.8	9,415	61.2	11,505	74.8	3,450	22.4
Brunswick, GA	5,495	2,475	45.0	3,015	54.9	270	4.9	4,380	79.7
Buffalo–Niagara Falls, NY	66,505	26,210	39.4	40,295	60.6	1,425	2.1	57,470	86.4
Burlington, NC	6,895	2,525	36.6	4,370	63.4	85	1.2	5,780	83.8
Burlington–South Burlington, VT	16,380	5,965	36.4	10,415	63.6	260	1.6	15,310	93.5
Canton–Massillon, OH	18,435	6,880	37.3	11,560	62.7	90	0.5	17,210	93.4
Cape Coral–Fort Myers, FL	23,540	8,620	36.6	14,920	63.4	2,355	10.0	19,185	81.5
Cape Girardeau–Jackson, MO–IL	5,065	1,920	37.9	3,145	62.1	15	0.3	4,725	93.3
Carson City, NV	2,835	1,305	46.0	1,530	54.0	285	10.1	2,450	86.4

C-6 Other Professional Workers, by Metropolitan Statistical Area, Sex, Race, and Hispanic or Latino Origin, 2006–2010—*Continued*

Metropolitan Statistical Area	Black alone, not Hispanic or Latino Number	Percent	American Indian and Alaska Native alone, not Hispanic or Latino Number	Percent	Asian alone, not Hispanic or Latino Number	Percent	Native Hawaiian and Other Pacific Islander alone, not Hispanic or Latino Number	Percent	Two or more races, not Hispanic or Latino Number	Percent
Abilene, TX	300	3.4	15	0.2	30	0.3	0	0.0	139	1.6
Akron, OH	3,385	8.7	10	0.0	945	2.4	0	0.0	425	1.1
Albany, GA	2,450	35.9	0	0.0	50	0.7	0	0.0	29	0.4
Albany–Schenectady–Troy, NY	2,305	4.0	25	0.0	1,590	2.7	15	0.0	375	0.6
Albuquerque, NM	1,305	2.7	1,805	3.7	1,555	3.2	20	0.0	1,015	2.1
Alexandria, LA	1,780	24.9	10	0.1	55	0.8	0	0.0	70	1.0
Allentown–Bethlehem–Easton, PA–NJ	1,260	2.9	30	0.1	1,055	2.4	4	0.0	280	0.6
Altoona, PA	55	1.0	4	0.1	15	0.3	0	0.0	40	0.7
Amarillo, TX	575	4.4	45	0.3	165	1.3	0	0.0	144	1.1
Ames, IA	305	3.3	0	0.0	1,195	12.8	0	0.0	105	1.1
Anchorage, AK	1,000	4.6	895	4.1	605	2.8	115	0.5	860	3.9
Anderson, IN	210	3.6	4	0.1	4	0.1	4	0.1	209	3.6
Anderson, SC	640	8.5	0	0.0	85	1.1	0	0.0	40	0.5
Ann Arbor, MI	2,125	6.8	45	0.1	2,955	9.4	0	0.0	610	2.0
Anniston–Oxford, AL	625	13.8	25	0.6	40	0.9	0	0.0	30	0.7
Appleton, WI	130	1.1	100	0.8	230	1.9	0	0.0	50	0.4
Asheville, NC	795	3.3	50	0.2	90	0.4	0	0.0	190	0.8
Athens–Clarke County, GA	1,265	9.0	4	0.0	725	5.2	4	0.0	220	1.6
Atlanta–Sandy Springs–Marietta, GA	84,520	27.1	435	0.1	13,370	4.3	140	0.0	4,220	1.4
Atlantic City–Hammonton, NJ	1,730	13.8	4	0.0	445	3.5	0	0.0	165	1.3
Auburn–Opelika, AL	1,370	15.0	0	0.0	790	8.6	0	0.0	54	0.6
Augusta–Richmond County, GA–SC	6,685	27.9	65	0.3	580	2.4	0	0.0	265	1.1
Austin–Round Rock–San Marcos, TX	6,220	5.3	300	0.3	5,395	4.6	65	0.1	1,605	1.4
Bakersfield–Delano, CA	1,415	5.0	195	0.7	1,065	3.7	45	0.2	615	2.2
Baltimore–Towson, MD	38,265	21.7	330	0.2	7,020	4.0	45	0.0	2,400	1.4
Bangor, ME	30	0.3	70	0.7	365	3.9	0	0.0	59	0.6
Barnstable Town, MA	175	1.3	70	0.5	45	0.3	0	0.0	120	0.9
Baton Rouge, LA	9,590	23.5	60	0.1	1,260	3.1	15	0.0	350	0.9
Battle Creek, MI	495	9.1	4	0.1	105	1.9	0	0.0	45	0.8
Bay City, MI	10	0.2	4	0.1	35	0.7	0	0.0	20	0.4
Beaumont–Port Arthur, TX	2,955	18.0	35	0.2	550	3.4	0	0.0	80	0.5
Bellingham, WA	65	0.6	210	1.8	380	3.3	20	0.2	210	1.8
Bend, OR	0	0.0	50	0.6	25	0.3	0	0.0	160	2.0
Billings, MT	75	0.9	200	2.3	70	0.8	0	0.0	100	1.2
Binghamton, NY	370	2.6	25	0.2	370	2.6	0	0.0	200	1.4
Birmingham–Hoover, AL	11,995	20.6	120	0.2	1,450	2.5	0	0.0	320	0.6
Bismarck, ND	15	0.2	230	3.8	30	0.5	0	0.0	39	0.6
Blacksburg–Christiansburg–Radford, VA	430	3.8	0	0.0	975	8.6	0	0.0	190	1.7
Bloomington, IN	510	3.5	10	0.1	1,105	7.5	0	0.0	265	1.8
Bloomington–Normal, IL	515	4.6	0	0.0	425	3.8	0	0.0	165	1.5
Boise City–Nampa, ID	135	0.4	85	0.3	445	1.5	35	0.1	470	1.5
Boston–Cambridge–Quincy, MA–NH	15,930	4.5	330	0.1	19,475	5.6	55	0.0	4,950	1.4
Boulder, CO	220	0.8	85	0.3	975	3.7	0	0.0	545	2.1
Bowling Green, KY	580	8.2	0	0.0	120	1.7	0	0.0	35	0.5
Bremerton–Silverdale, WA	140	1.2	165	1.4	275	2.3	45	0.4	200	1.7
Bridgeport–Stamford–Norwalk, CT	3,855	5.8	120	0.2	2,515	3.8	20	0.0	560	0.8
Brownsville–Harlingen, TX	60	0.4	75	0.5	210	1.4	25	0.2	55	0.4
Brunswick, GA	710	12.9	0	0.0	90	1.6	0	0.0	50	0.9
Buffalo–Niagara Falls, NY	4,885	7.3	205	0.3	1,910	2.9	35	0.1	580	0.9
Burlington, NC	795	11.5	0	0.0	145	2.1	0	0.0	90	1.3
Burlington–South Burlington, VT	135	0.8	15	0.1	365	2.2	0	0.0	300	1.8
Canton–Massillon, OH	725	3.9	15	0.1	255	1.4	0	0.0	140	0.8
Cape Coral–Fort Myers, FL	1,440	6.1	45	0.2	220	0.9	0	0.0	295	1.3
Cape Girardeau–Jackson, MO–IL	185	3.7	15	0.3	55	1.1	0	0.0	65	1.3
Carson City, NV	15	0.5	20	0.7	45	1.6	0	0.0	19	0.7

PART C—METROPOLITAN STATISTICAL AREA TABLES

C-6 Other Professional Workers, by Metropolitan Statistical Area, Sex, Race, and Hispanic or Latino Origin, 2006–2010—Continued

Metropolitan Statistical Area	Total who worked in the last 5 years	Male Number	Male Percent	Female Number	Female Percent	Hispanic or Latino Number	Hispanic or Latino Percent	White alone, not Hispanic or Latino Number	White alone, not Hispanic or Latino Percent
Casper, WY	3,460	1,285	37.1	2,175	62.9	40	1.2	3,330	96.2
Cedar Rapids, IA	13,540	4,585	33.9	8,955	66.1	345	2.5	12,540	92.6
Champaign–Urbana, IL	20,875	9,835	47.1	11,045	52.9	1,090	5.2	15,640	74.9
Charleston, WV	15,045	6,080	40.4	8,970	59.6	75	0.5	14,020	93.2
Charleston–North Charleston–Summerville, SC	32,705	10,915	33.4	21,790	66.6	730	2.2	25,165	76.9
Charlotte–Gastonia–Rock Hill, NC–SC	101,325	34,635	34.2	66,690	65.8	3,305	3.3	74,745	73.8
Charlottesville, VA	15,890	6,730	42.4	9,160	57.6	290	1.8	13,920	87.6
Chattanooga, TN–GA	24,805	9,190	37.0	15,615	63.0	495	2.0	21,465	86.5
Cheyenne, WY	4,700	1,655	35.2	3,045	64.8	330	7.0	4,240	90.2
Chicago–Joliet–Naperville, IL–IN–WI	564,285	218,870	38.8	345,415	61.2	42,745	7.6	412,495	73.1
Chico, CA	10,770	4,190	38.9	6,580	61.1	795	7.4	9,105	84.5
Cincinnati–Middletown, OH–KY–IN	114,205	42,605	37.3	71,595	62.7	1,545	1.4	99,840	87.4
Clarksville, TN–KY	10,145	3,340	32.9	6,805	67.1	370	3.6	8,040	79.3
Cleveland, TN	5,450	2,270	41.7	3,180	58.3	90	1.7	4,955	90.9
Cleveland–Elyria–Mentor, OH	111,840	42,850	38.3	68,990	61.7	2,265	2.0	91,265	81.6
Coeur d'Alene, ID	5,620	1,785	31.8	3,830	68.1	30	0.5	5,305	94.4
College Station–Bryan, TX	16,440	7,550	45.9	8,890	54.1	1,420	8.6	11,955	72.7
Colorado Springs, CO	33,840	12,295	36.3	21,545	63.7	1,695	5.0	29,275	86.5
Columbia, MO	15,065	6,385	42.4	8,680	57.6	300	2.0	13,160	87.4
Columbia, SC	45,390	16,670	36.7	28,720	63.3	935	2.1	32,060	70.6
Columbus, GA–AL	12,920	4,015	31.1	8,905	68.9	435	3.4	8,130	62.9
Columbus, IN	3,510	1,190	33.9	2,320	66.1	19	0.5	3,255	92.7
Columbus, OH	110,570	43,010	38.9	67,555	61.1	2,010	1.8	92,620	83.8
Corpus Christi, TX	20,815	7,020	33.7	13,795	66.3	8,240	39.6	11,115	53.4
Corvallis, OR	7,210	3,165	43.9	4,050	56.2	290	4.0	6,135	85.1
Crestview–Fort Walton Beach–Destin, FL	8,640	3,180	36.8	5,460	63.2	240	2.8	7,385	85.5
Cumberland, MD–WV	4,145	1,635	39.4	2,515	60.7	70	1.7	3,855	93.0
Dallas–Fort Worth–Arlington, TX	351,080	129,290	36.8	221,790	63.2	34,355	9.8	247,375	70.5
Dalton, GA	4,170	1,380	33.1	2,790	66.9	190	4.6	3,825	91.7
Danville, IL	2,870	945	32.9	1,930	67.2	105	3.7	2,480	86.4
Danville, VA	4,290	1,275	29.7	3,010	70.2	4	0.1	3,190	74.4
Davenport–Moline–Rock Island, IA–IL	19,005	6,580	34.6	12,425	65.4	745	3.9	17,220	90.6
Dayton, OH	43,415	15,830	36.5	27,580	63.5	645	1.5	36,240	83.5
Decatur, AL	5,435	2,045	37.6	3,390	62.4	55	1.0	4,790	88.1
Decatur, IL	4,840	1,920	39.7	2,920	60.3	65	1.3	4,265	88.1
Deltona–Daytona Beach–Ormond Beach, FL	21,040	8,290	39.4	12,750	60.6	1,350	6.4	16,675	79.3
Denver–Aurora–Broomfield, CO	152,155	57,795	38.0	94,360	62.0	13,175	8.7	126,265	83.0
Des Moines–West Des Moines, IA	35,760	13,430	37.6	22,330	62.4	620	1.7	33,405	93.4
Detroit–Warren–Livonia, MI	208,150	79,095	38.0	129,055	62.0	4,475	2.1	161,935	77.8
Dothan, AL	6,065	2,035	33.6	4,030	66.4	80	1.3	5,185	85.5
Dover, DE	7,220	2,385	33.0	4,835	67.0	195	2.7	5,230	72.4
Dubuque, IA	5,415	1,975	36.5	3,440	63.5	50	0.9	5,120	94.6
Duluth, MN–WI	15,150	5,650	37.3	9,500	62.7	60	0.4	14,400	95.0
Durham–Chapel Hill, NC	39,535	15,265	38.6	24,270	61.4	1,315	3.3	27,845	70.4
Eau Claire, WI	8,335	2,995	35.9	5,340	64.1	50	0.6	8,025	96.3
El Centro, CA	5,280	1,760	33.3	3,520	66.7	3,410	64.6	1,425	27.0
Elizabethtown, KY	4,910	1,770	36.0	3,140	64.0	145	3.0	4,075	83.0
Elkhart–Goshen, IN	7,765	2,870	37.0	4,895	63.0	435	5.6	7,085	91.2
Elmira, NY	3,985	1,690	42.4	2,295	57.6	45	1.1	3,750	94.1
El Paso, TX	36,155	13,780	38.1	22,370	61.9	24,955	69.0	9,205	25.5
Erie, PA	13,925	5,240	37.6	8,685	62.4	195	1.4	13,070	93.9
Eugene–Springfield, OR	20,280	7,985	39.4	12,295	60.6	765	3.8	18,090	89.2
Evansville, IN–KY	15,680	5,795	37.0	9,885	63.0	140	0.9	14,660	93.5
Fairbanks, AK	5,345	2,115	39.6	3,235	60.5	215	4.0	4,270	79.9
Fargo, ND–MN	13,530	4,715	34.8	8,815	65.2	95	0.7	12,645	93.5

C-6 Other Professional Workers, by Metropolitan Statistical Area, Sex, Race, and Hispanic or Latino Origin, 2006–2010—Continued

Metropolitan Statistical Area	Black alone, not Hispanic or Latino Number	Percent	American Indian and Alaska Native alone, not Hispanic or Latino Number	Percent	Asian alone, not Hispanic or Latino Number	Percent	Native Hawaiian and Other Pacific Islander alone, not Hispanic or Latino Number	Percent	Two or more races, not Hispanic or Latino Number	Percent
Casper, WY	0	0.0	15	0.4	0	0.0	0	0.0	70	2.0
Cedar Rapids, IA	205	1.5	4	0.0	305	2.3	10	0.1	135	1.0
Champaign–Urbana, IL	1,100	5.3	0	0.0	2,795	13.4	0	0.0	250	1.2
Charleston, WV	490	3.3	4	0.0	125	0.8	25	0.2	310	2.1
Charleston–North Charleston–Summerville, SC	5,840	17.9	50	0.2	590	1.8	20	0.1	305	0.9
Charlotte–Gastonia–Rock Hill, NC–SC	19,615	19.4	305	0.3	2,100	2.1	0	0.0	1,250	1.2
Charlottesville, VA	570	3.6	0	0.0	915	5.8	0	0.0	195	1.2
Chattanooga, TN–GA	2,230	9.0	80	0.3	330	1.3	10	0.0	190	0.8
Cheyenne, WY	75	1.6	10	0.2	0	0.0	0	0.0	45	1.0
Chicago–Joliet–Naperville, IL–IN–WI	72,180	12.8	345	0.1	30,340	5.4	90	0.0	6,095	1.1
Chico, CA	85	0.8	100	0.9	335	3.1	15	0.1	335	3.1
Cincinnati–Middletown, OH–KY–IN	9,075	7.9	95	0.1	2,590	2.3	0	0.0	1,055	0.9
Clarksville, TN–KY	1,460	14.4	50	0.5	145	1.4	0	0.0	90	0.9
Cleveland, TN	215	3.9	10	0.2	135	2.5	0	0.0	45	0.8
Cleveland–Elyria–Mentor, OH	14,420	12.9	205	0.2	2,815	2.5	4	0.0	865	0.8
Coeur d'Alene, ID	20	0.4	15	0.3	20	0.4	0	0.0	225	4.0
College Station–Bryan, TX	1,050	6.4	10	0.1	1,855	11.3	0	0.0	155	0.9
Colorado Springs, CO	1,285	3.8	170	0.5	560	1.7	20	0.1	840	2.5
Columbia, MO	445	3.0	15	0.1	985	6.5	10	0.1	150	1.0
Columbia, SC	10,875	24.0	45	0.1	975	2.1	0	0.0	500	1.1
Columbus, GA–AL	4,085	31.6	15	0.1	135	1.0	0	0.0	125	1.0
Columbus, IN	125	3.6	0	0.0	70	2.0	0	0.0	40	1.1
Columbus, OH	10,230	9.3	180	0.2	4,150	3.8	0	0.0	1,380	1.2
Corpus Christi, TX	670	3.2	110	0.5	415	2.0	0	0.0	260	1.2
Corvallis, OR	85	1.2	0	0.0	495	6.9	4	0.1	205	2.8
Crestview–Fort Walton Beach–Destin, FL	545	6.3	90	1.0	240	2.8	0	0.0	139	1.6
Cumberland, MD–WV	170	4.1	0	0.0	4	0.1	0	0.0	55	1.3
Dallas–Fort Worth–Arlington, TX	46,125	13.1	1,365	0.4	16,670	4.7	150	0.0	5,040	1.4
Dalton, GA	85	2.0	15	0.4	40	1.0	0	0.0	24	0.6
Danville, IL	185	6.4	0	0.0	4	0.1	0	0.0	100	3.5
Danville, VA	1,010	23.5	0	0.0	15	0.3	15	0.3	55	1.3
Davenport–Moline–Rock Island, IA–IL	730	3.8	0	0.0	115	0.6	0	0.0	195	1.0
Dayton, OH	4,935	11.4	30	0.1	885	2.0	0	0.0	675	1.6
Decatur, AL	200	3.7	290	5.3	40	0.7	0	0.0	55	1.0
Decatur, IL	405	8.4	20	0.4	20	0.4	0	0.0	70	1.4
Deltona–Daytona Beach–Ormond Beach, FL	2,240	10.6	80	0.4	350	1.7	0	0.0	355	1.7
Denver–Aurora–Broomfield, CO	5,485	3.6	640	0.4	4,180	2.7	65	0.0	2,350	1.5
Des Moines–West Des Moines, IA	885	2.5	15	0.0	595	1.7	0	0.0	240	0.7
Detroit–Warren–Livonia, MI	32,810	15.8	350	0.2	6,230	3.0	30	0.0	2,320	1.1
Dothan, AL	675	11.1	4	0.1	45	0.7	10	0.2	59	1.0
Dover, DE	1,365	18.9	0	0.0	240	3.3	4	0.1	185	2.6
Dubuque, IA	65	1.2	0	0.0	40	0.7	0	0.0	140	2.6
Duluth, MN–WI	95	0.6	240	1.6	215	1.4	0	0.0	144	1.0
Durham–Chapel Hill, NC	7,705	19.5	65	0.2	1,950	4.9	0	0.0	660	1.7
Eau Claire, WI	100	1.2	50	0.6	90	1.1	0	0.0	29	0.3
El Centro, CA	210	4.0	35	0.7	170	3.2	0	0.0	24	0.5
Elizabethtown, KY	510	10.4	15	0.3	70	1.4	0	0.0	99	2.0
Elkhart–Goshen, IN	175	2.3	4	0.1	50	0.6	0	0.0	20	0.3
Elmira, NY	145	3.6	10	0.3	25	0.6	0	0.0	10	0.3
El Paso, TX	1,145	3.2	25	0.1	580	1.6	0	0.0	245	0.7
Erie, PA	410	2.9	4	0.0	165	1.2	0	0.0	80	0.6
Eugene–Springfield, OR	195	1.0	30	0.1	695	3.4	45	0.2	465	2.3
Evansville, IN–KY	515	3.3	0	0.0	225	1.4	0	0.0	140	0.9
Fairbanks, AK	175	3.3	350	6.5	130	2.4	15	0.3	195	3.6
Fargo, ND–MN	140	1.0	80	0.6	450	3.3	0	0.0	115	0.8

PART C—METROPOLITAN STATISTICAL AREA TABLES

C-6 Other Professional Workers, by Metropolitan Statistical Area, Sex, Race, and Hispanic or Latino Origin, 2006–2010—*Continued*

Metropolitan Statistical Area	Total who worked in the last 5 years	Male Number	Male Percent	Female Number	Female Percent	Hispanic or Latino Number	Hispanic or Latino Percent	White alone, not Hispanic or Latino Number	White alone, not Hispanic or Latino Percent
Farmington, NM	4,150	1,590	38.3	2,560	61.7	495	11.9	2,400	57.8
Fayetteville, NC	16,490	4,525	27.4	11,965	72.6	910	5.5	8,980	54.5
Fayetteville-Springdale-Rogers, AR-MO	23,065	8,270	35.9	14,795	64.1	1,090	4.7	20,340	88.2
Flagstaff, AZ	8,545	3,190	37.3	5,355	62.7	645	7.5	6,450	75.5
Flint, MI	17,905	6,590	36.8	11,315	63.2	325	1.8	14,355	80.2
Florence, SC	9,505	3,000	31.6	6,510	68.5	150	1.6	6,385	67.2
Florence-Muscle Shoals, AL	6,355	2,505	39.4	3,850	60.6	105	1.7	5,525	86.9
Fond du Lac, WI	3,950	1,390	35.2	2,560	64.8	60	1.5	3,775	95.6
Fort Collins-Loveland, CO	19,780	7,480	37.8	12,305	62.2	975	4.9	17,825	90.1
Fort Smith, AR-OK	10,825	3,935	36.4	6,885	63.6	215	2.0	9,510	87.9
Fort Wayne, IN	20,695	7,445	36.0	13,250	64.0	395	1.9	18,100	87.5
Fresno, CA	38,860	14,585	37.5	24,280	62.5	10,520	27.1	22,135	57.0
Gadsden, AL	3,970	1,380	34.8	2,585	65.1	65	1.6	3,590	90.4
Gainesville, FL	20,175	9,185	45.5	10,990	54.5	1,465	7.3	15,240	75.5
Gainesville, GA	7,855	2,340	29.8	5,515	70.2	345	4.4	7,085	90.2
Glens Falls, NY	6,370	2,550	40.0	3,820	60.0	95	1.5	6,175	96.9
Goldsboro, NC	5,010	1,400	27.9	3,610	72.1	220	4.4	3,230	64.5
Grand Forks, ND-MN	5,625	2,365	42.0	3,255	57.9	55	1.0	5,130	91.2
Grand Junction, CO	6,335	2,340	36.9	3,995	63.1	375	5.9	5,735	90.5
Grand Rapids-Wyoming, MI	39,145	15,650	40.0	23,495	60.0	1,300	3.3	34,630	88.5
Great Falls, MT	3,580	1,340	37.4	2,240	62.6	40	1.1	3,305	92.3
Greeley, CO	11,165	3,790	33.9	7,375	66.1	1,595	14.3	9,185	82.3
Green Bay, WI	15,080	5,340	35.4	9,740	64.6	335	2.2	13,975	92.7
Greensboro-High Point, NC	38,745	13,875	35.8	24,870	64.2	970	2.5	28,260	72.9
Greenville, NC	10,630	3,890	36.6	6,740	63.4	280	2.6	7,985	75.1
Greenville-Mauldin-Easley, SC	32,235	12,490	38.7	19,745	61.3	970	3.0	26,930	83.5
Gulfport-Biloxi, MS	10,310	3,545	34.4	6,760	65.6	285	2.8	8,095	78.5
Hagerstown-Martinsburg, MD-WV	11,530	3,915	34.0	7,615	66.0	270	2.3	10,470	90.8
Hanford-Corcoran, CA	4,975	2,115	42.5	2,855	57.4	1,165	23.4	3,050	61.3
Harrisburg-Carlisle, PA	32,020	12,700	39.7	19,320	60.3	670	2.1	28,700	89.6
Harrisonburg, VA	6,530	2,420	37.1	4,110	62.9	75	1.1	6,080	93.1
Hartford-West Hartford-East Hartford, CT	80,840	30,975	38.3	49,865	61.7	3,635	4.5	67,395	83.4
Hattiesburg, MS	7,770	2,705	34.8	5,065	65.2	90	1.2	5,825	75.0
Hickory-Lenoir-Morganton, NC	15,475	5,160	33.3	10,310	66.6	330	2.1	14,175	91.6
Hinesville-Fort Stewart, GA	2,695	830	30.8	1,870	69.4	85	3.2	1,545	57.3
Holland-Grand Haven, MI	13,830	4,935	35.7	8,895	64.3	455	3.3	12,965	93.7
Honolulu, HI	54,820	21,275	38.8	33,545	61.2	2,890	5.3	15,995	29.2
Hot Springs, AR	3,365	1,205	35.8	2,155	64.0	75	2.2	3,025	89.9
Houma-Bayou Cane-Thibodaux, LA	7,440	2,215	29.8	5,225	70.2	320	4.3	6,040	81.2
Houston-Sugar Land-Baytown, TX	303,195	108,010	35.6	195,190	64.4	42,550	14.0	184,345	60.8
Huntington-Ashland, WV-KY-OH	11,715	4,610	39.4	7,105	60.6	60	0.5	11,230	95.9
Huntsville, AL	21,245	7,165	33.7	14,080	66.3	335	1.6	15,160	71.4
Idaho Falls, ID	5,175	1,910	36.9	3,265	63.1	160	3.1	4,855	93.8
Indianapolis-Carmel, IN	93,560	34,795	37.2	58,765	62.8	2,100	2.2	79,755	85.2
Iowa City, IA	13,090	5,545	42.4	7,545	57.6	420	3.2	11,320	86.5
Ithaca, NY	11,725	5,745	49.0	5,980	51.0	445	3.8	9,650	82.3
Jackson, MI	5,420	2,035	37.5	3,385	62.5	100	1.8	5,060	93.4
Jackson, MS	28,595	10,370	36.3	18,225	63.7	235	0.8	18,540	64.8
Jackson, TN	5,970	2,035	34.1	3,935	65.9	95	1.6	4,415	74.0
Jacksonville, FL	63,010	21,985	34.9	41,020	65.1	3,070	4.9	47,165	74.9
Jacksonville, NC	6,320	1,820	28.8	4,500	71.2	290	4.6	5,020	79.4
Janesville, WI	7,285	2,095	28.8	5,190	71.2	290	4.0	6,665	91.5
Jefferson City, MO	7,755	2,415	31.1	5,340	68.9	89	1.1	7,040	90.8
Johnson City, TN	8,900	3,645	41.0	5,255	59.0	145	1.6	8,360	93.9
Johnstown, PA	6,015	2,160	35.9	3,855	64.1	55	0.9	5,820	96.8

C-6 Other Professional Workers, by Metropolitan Statistical Area, Sex, Race, and Hispanic or Latino Origin, 2006–2010—*Continued*

Metropolitan Statistical Area	Black alone, not Hispanic or Latino Number	Percent	American Indian and Alaska Native alone, not Hispanic or Latino Number	Percent	Asian alone, not Hispanic or Latino Number	Percent	Native Hawaiian and Other Pacific Islander alone, not Hispanic or Latino Number	Percent	Two or more races, not Hispanic or Latino Number	Percent
Farmington, NM	0	0.0	1,185	28.6	20	0.5	0	0.0	50	1.2
Fayetteville, NC	5,725	34.7	110	0.7	295	1.8	0	0.0	470	2.9
Fayetteville-Springdale-Rogers, AR-MO	495	2.1	280	1.2	635	2.8	35	0.2	189	0.8
Flagstaff, AZ	60	0.7	1,070	12.5	145	1.7	4	0.0	175	2.0
Flint, MI	2,660	14.9	120	0.7	120	0.7	15	0.1	315	1.8
Florence, SC	2,705	28.5	0	0.0	190	2.0	0	0.0	65	0.7
Florence-Muscle Shoals, AL	655	10.3	25	0.4	25	0.4	0	0.0	15	0.2
Fond du Lac, WI	65	1.6	4	0.1	30	0.8	0	0.0	20	0.5
Fort Collins-Loveland, CO	130	0.7	15	0.1	620	3.1	45	0.2	175	0.9
Fort Smith, AR-OK	230	2.1	275	2.5	190	1.8	4	0.0	394	3.6
Fort Wayne, IN	1,665	8.0	15	0.1	315	1.5	0	0.0	205	1.0
Fresno, CA	1,640	4.2	150	0.4	3,485	9.0	15	0.0	910	2.3
Gadsden, AL	295	7.4	0	0.0	0	0.0	0	0.0	18	0.5
Gainesville, FL	1,725	8.6	25	0.1	1,425	7.1	10	0.0	290	1.4
Gainesville, GA	290	3.7	0	0.0	80	1.0	0	0.0	54	0.7
Glens Falls, NY	4	0.1	0	0.0	45	0.7	0	0.0	55	0.9
Goldsboro, NC	1,415	28.2	4	0.1	35	0.7	0	0.0	93	1.9
Grand Forks, ND-MN	125	2.2	70	1.2	220	3.9	0	0.0	24	0.4
Grand Junction, CO	85	1.3	10	0.2	55	0.9	10	0.2	65	1.0
Grand Rapids-Wyoming, MI	1,890	4.8	60	0.2	800	2.0	0	0.0	465	1.2
Great Falls, MT	40	1.1	90	2.5	0	0.0	0	0.0	105	2.9
Greeley, CO	65	0.6	120	1.1	65	0.6	0	0.0	135	1.2
Green Bay, WI	150	1.0	285	1.9	180	1.2	0	0.0	150	1.0
Greensboro-High Point, NC	7,975	20.6	65	0.2	945	2.4	0	0.0	530	1.4
Greenville, NC	2,170	20.4	0	0.0	125	1.2	0	0.0	70	0.7
Greenville-Mauldin-Easley, SC	3,240	10.1	35	0.1	850	2.6	10	0.0	200	0.6
Gulfport-Biloxi, MS	1,510	14.6	10	0.1	315	3.1	15	0.1	75	0.7
Hagerstown-Martinsburg, MD-WV	530	4.6	30	0.3	130	1.1	0	0.0	105	0.9
Hanford-Corcoran, CA	515	10.4	4	0.1	175	3.5	0	0.0	64	1.3
Harrisburg-Carlisle, PA	1,600	5.0	65	0.2	750	2.3	0	0.0	235	0.7
Harrisonburg, VA	175	2.7	0	0.0	185	2.8	0	0.0	20	0.3
Hartford-West Hartford-East Hartford, CT	6,505	8.0	85	0.1	2,150	2.7	0	0.0	1,065	1.3
Hattiesburg, MS	1,545	19.9	25	0.3	285	3.7	0	0.0	0	0.0
Hickory-Lenoir-Morganton, NC	685	4.4	55	0.4	85	0.5	0	0.0	145	0.9
Hinesville-Fort Stewart, GA	975	36.2	15	0.6	75	2.8	0	0.0	0	0.0
Holland-Grand Haven, MI	40	0.3	15	0.1	250	1.8	0	0.0	110	0.8
Honolulu, HI	880	1.6	75	0.1	24,610	44.9	2,870	5.2	7,490	13.7
Hot Springs, AR	200	5.9	15	0.4	40	1.2	0	0.0	15	0.4
Houma-Bayou Cane-Thibodaux, LA	845	11.4	110	1.5	110	1.5	0	0.0	20	0.3
Houston-Sugar Land-Baytown, TX	52,210	17.2	560	0.2	20,210	6.7	85	0.0	3,235	1.1
Huntington-Ashland, WV-KY-OH	195	1.7	4	0.0	155	1.3	0	0.0	75	0.6
Huntsville, AL	4,560	21.5	90	0.4	605	2.8	30	0.1	470	2.2
Idaho Falls, ID	0	0.0	55	1.1	90	1.7	0	0.0	8	0.2
Indianapolis-Carmel, IN	8,525	9.1	55	0.1	1,975	2.1	15	0.0	1,135	1.2
Iowa City, IA	210	1.6	4	0.0	1,035	7.9	25	0.2	70	0.5
Ithaca, NY	230	2.0	80	0.7	1,105	9.4	0	0.0	215	1.8
Jackson, MI	210	3.9	0	0.0	30	0.6	0	0.0	20	0.4
Jackson, MS	9,330	32.6	20	0.1	395	1.4	0	0.0	69	0.2
Jackson, TN	1,380	23.1	4	0.1	25	0.4	10	0.2	40	0.7
Jacksonville, FL	10,420	16.5	150	0.2	1,470	2.3	75	0.1	655	1.0
Jacksonville, NC	875	13.8	0	0.0	40	0.6	0	0.0	100	1.6
Janesville, WI	240	3.3	0	0.0	55	0.8	0	0.0	34	0.5
Jefferson City, MO	525	6.8	30	0.4	25	0.3	0	0.0	53	0.7
Johnson City, TN	190	2.1	30	0.3	85	1.0	0	0.0	95	1.1
Johnstown, PA	125	2.1	0	0.0	10	0.2	0	0.0	4	0.1

C-6 Other Professional Workers, by Metropolitan Statistical Area, Sex, Race, and Hispanic or Latino Origin, 2006–2010—Continued

Metropolitan Statistical Area	Total who worked in the last 5 years	Male Number	Male Percent	Female Number	Female Percent	Hispanic or Latino Number	Hispanic or Latino Percent	White alone, not Hispanic or Latino Number	White alone, not Hispanic or Latino Percent
Jonesboro, AR	5,795	2,005	34.6	3,790	65.4	55	0.9	4,985	86.0
Joplin, MO	7,095	2,690	37.9	4,405	62.1	115	1.6	6,730	94.9
Kalamazoo–Portage, MI	18,420	6,955	37.8	11,465	62.2	460	2.5	16,160	87.7
Kankakee–Bradley, IL	5,035	1,720	34.2	3,315	65.8	239	4.7	4,175	82.9
Kansas City, MO–KS	116,180	41,830	36.0	74,350	64.0	3,625	3.1	100,550	86.5
Kennewick–Pasco–Richland, WA	9,420	3,445	36.6	5,975	63.4	1,130	12.0	7,750	82.3
Killeen–Temple–Fort Hood, TX	16,805	5,195	30.9	11,610	69.1	1,735	10.3	11,620	69.1
Kingsport–Bristol–Bristol, TN–VA	12,020	4,240	35.3	7,780	64.7	200	1.7	11,540	96.0
Kingston, NY	13,725	5,495	40.0	8,230	60.0	440	3.2	12,435	90.6
Knoxville, TN	37,480	14,660	39.1	22,820	60.9	745	2.0	33,555	89.5
Kokomo, IN	3,985	1,445	36.3	2,540	63.7	25	0.6	3,830	96.1
La Crosse, WI–MN	8,355	3,160	37.8	5,195	62.2	125	1.5	7,975	95.5
Lafayette, IN	14,845	7,150	48.2	7,695	51.8	615	4.1	11,600	78.1
Lafayette, LA	14,480	4,890	33.8	9,590	66.2	205	1.4	11,795	81.5
Lake Charles, LA	8,515	2,550	29.9	5,960	70.0	85	1.0	6,920	81.3
Lake Havasu City–Kingman, AZ	5,615	2,055	36.6	3,555	63.3	320	5.7	5,010	89.2
Lakeland–Winter Haven, FL	24,250	8,320	34.3	15,930	65.7	1,850	7.6	18,555	76.5
Lancaster, PA	24,825	9,285	37.4	15,540	62.6	840	3.4	22,660	91.3
Lansing–East Lansing, MI	31,020	13,545	43.7	17,475	56.3	830	2.7	25,745	83.0
Laredo, TX	9,890	3,225	32.6	6,665	67.4	8,905	90.0	820	8.3
Las Cruces, NM	11,610	4,670	40.2	6,940	59.8	4,975	42.9	5,785	49.8
Las Vegas–Paradise, NV	79,810	32,370	40.6	47,440	59.4	9,235	11.6	54,800	68.7
Lawrence, KS	11,425	4,445	38.9	6,980	61.1	370	3.2	9,770	85.5
Lawton, OK	5,175	2,080	40.2	3,095	59.8	205	4.0	3,575	69.1
Lebanon, PA	5,305	2,040	38.5	3,260	61.5	250	4.7	4,885	92.1
Lewiston, ID–WA	2,465	950	38.5	1,515	61.5	50	2.0	2,255	91.5
Lewiston–Auburn, ME	5,925	1,885	31.8	4,040	68.2	45	0.8	5,670	95.7
Lexington–Fayette, KY	31,450	13,105	41.7	18,345	58.3	770	2.4	26,600	84.6
Lima, OH	4,485	1,580	35.2	2,905	64.8	30	0.7	3,920	87.4
Lincoln, NE	21,655	8,785	40.6	12,865	59.4	685	3.2	19,485	90.0
Little Rock–North Little Rock–Conway, AR	37,670	13,765	36.5	23,905	63.5	780	2.1	29,090	77.2
Logan, UT–ID	7,605	3,340	43.9	4,265	56.1	255	3.4	6,790	89.3
Longview, TX	8,800	2,925	33.2	5,875	66.8	315	3.6	7,225	82.1
Longview, WA	3,530	1,050	29.7	2,480	70.3	85	2.4	3,225	91.4
Los Angeles–Long Beach–Santa Ana, CA	804,480	356,645	44.3	447,835	55.7	151,820	18.9	451,410	56.1
Louisville/Jefferson County, KY–IN	65,700	24,050	36.6	41,650	63.4	1,180	1.8	55,140	83.9
Lubbock, TX	16,265	5,830	35.8	10,435	64.2	2,185	13.4	12,400	76.2
Lynchburg, VA	12,230	4,345	35.5	7,885	64.5	185	1.5	10,650	87.1
Macon, GA	10,440	3,615	34.6	6,825	65.4	90	0.9	7,180	68.8
Madera–Chowchilla, CA	3,690	1,295	35.1	2,395	64.9	1,065	28.9	2,295	62.2
Madison, WI	47,210	18,635	39.5	28,575	60.5	1,560	3.3	41,805	88.6
Manchester–Nashua, NH	22,950	7,475	32.6	15,475	67.4	510	2.2	21,435	93.4
Manhattan, KS	8,645	3,390	39.2	5,255	60.8	345	4.0	6,755	78.1
Mankato–North Mankato, MN	6,225	2,595	41.7	3,630	58.3	70	1.1	5,825	93.6
Mansfield, OH	4,985	1,705	34.2	3,280	65.8	20	0.4	4,730	94.9
McAllen–Edinburg–Mission, TX	29,440	11,140	37.8	18,295	62.1	23,885	81.1	4,620	15.7
Medford, OR	8,690	3,335	38.4	5,355	61.6	615	7.1	7,735	89.0
Memphis, TN–MS–AR	65,680	22,465	34.2	43,215	65.8	1,170	1.8	40,810	62.1
Merced, CA	8,220	3,165	38.5	5,060	61.6	2,170	26.4	4,845	58.9
Miami–Fort Lauderdale–Pompano Beach, FL	281,810	110,510	39.2	171,300	60.8	90,870	32.2	136,680	48.5
Michigan City–La Porte, IN	4,085	1,260	30.8	2,825	69.2	50	1.2	3,665	89.7
Midland, TX	6,335	2,205	34.8	4,130	65.2	1,050	16.6	4,665	73.6
Milwaukee–Waukesha–West Allis, WI	91,250	34,480	37.8	56,770	62.2	3,110	3.4	75,155	82.4
Minneapolis–St. Paul–Bloomington, MN–WI	222,270	85,425	38.4	136,845	61.6	4,980	2.2	195,655	88.0
Missoula, MT	7,415	2,845	38.4	4,565	61.6	155	2.1	7,020	94.7

C-6 Other Professional Workers, by Metropolitan Statistical Area, Sex, Race, and Hispanic or Latino Origin, 2006–2010—*Continued*

Metropolitan Statistical Area	Black alone, not Hispanic or Latino Number	Percent	American Indian and Alaska Native alone, not Hispanic or Latino Number	Percent	Asian alone, not Hispanic or Latino Number	Percent	Native Hawaiian and Other Pacific Islander alone, not Hispanic or Latino Number	Percent	Two or more races, not Hispanic or Latino Number	Percent
Jonesboro, AR	630	10.9	15	0.3	115	2.0	0	0.0	0	0.0
Joplin, MO	30	0.4	55	0.8	55	0.8	20	0.3	93	1.3
Kalamazoo–Portage, MI	1,210	6.6	25	0.1	360	2.0	0	0.0	205	1.1
Kankakee–Bradley, IL	495	9.8	4	0.1	75	1.5	4	0.1	30	0.6
Kansas City, MO–KS	8,360	7.2	295	0.3	2,060	1.8	80	0.1	1,210	1.0
Kennewick–Pasco–Richland, WA	200	2.1	35	0.4	190	2.0	0	0.0	115	1.2
Killeen–Temple–Fort Hood, TX	2,835	16.9	40	0.2	125	0.7	70	0.4	375	2.2
Kingsport–Bristol–Bristol, TN–VA	150	1.2	20	0.2	50	0.4	0	0.0	60	0.5
Kingston, NY	465	3.4	40	0.3	105	0.8	0	0.0	240	1.7
Knoxville, TN	1,820	4.9	85	0.2	1,020	2.7	0	0.0	255	0.7
Kokomo, IN	85	2.1	0	0.0	45	1.1	0	0.0	0	0.0
La Crosse, WI–MN	45	0.5	4	0.0	130	1.6	0	0.0	80	1.0
Lafayette, IN	450	3.0	10	0.1	1,975	13.3	20	0.1	175	1.2
Lafayette, LA	2,175	15.0	20	0.1	240	1.7	0	0.0	49	0.3
Lake Charles, LA	1,305	15.3	35	0.4	105	1.2	0	0.0	58	0.7
Lake Havasu City–Kingman, AZ	55	1.0	35	0.6	85	1.5	45	0.8	70	1.2
Lakeland–Winter Haven, FL	3,205	13.2	45	0.2	240	1.0	20	0.1	340	1.4
Lancaster, PA	710	2.9	15	0.1	395	1.6	0	0.0	204	0.8
Lansing–East Lansing, MI	1,900	6.1	80	0.3	1,850	6.0	10	0.0	605	2.0
Laredo, TX	30	0.3	0	0.0	120	1.2	0	0.0	15	0.2
Las Cruces, NM	385	3.3	30	0.3	240	2.1	0	0.0	195	1.7
Las Vegas–Paradise, NV	7,330	9.2	275	0.3	5,625	7.0	375	0.5	2,175	2.7
Lawrence, KS	320	2.8	145	1.3	635	5.6	0	0.0	180	1.6
Lawton, OK	855	16.5	225	4.3	115	2.2	0	0.0	205	4.0
Lebanon, PA	75	1.4	4	0.1	65	1.2	0	0.0	20	0.4
Lewiston, ID–WA	35	1.4	90	3.7	20	0.8	0	0.0	14	0.6
Lewiston–Auburn, ME	30	0.5	4	0.1	90	1.5	0	0.0	89	1.5
Lexington–Fayette, KY	2,245	7.1	35	0.1	1,555	4.9	15	0.0	219	0.7
Lima, OH	485	10.8	4	0.1	30	0.7	0	0.0	20	0.4
Lincoln, NE	575	2.7	60	0.3	590	2.7	0	0.0	255	1.2
Little Rock–North Little Rock–Conway, AR	6,945	18.4	125	0.3	345	0.9	0	0.0	385	1.0
Logan, UT–ID	65	0.9	30	0.4	375	4.9	15	0.2	80	1.1
Longview, TX	1,095	12.4	30	0.3	30	0.3	25	0.3	78	0.9
Longview, WA	0	0.0	0	0.0	65	1.8	30	0.8	125	3.5
Los Angeles–Long Beach–Santa Ana, CA	55,700	6.9	1,475	0.2	125,945	15.7	1,085	0.1	17,045	2.1
Louisville/Jefferson County, KY–IN	7,270	11.1	20	0.0	1,375	2.1	55	0.1	665	1.0
Lubbock, TX	665	4.1	135	0.8	780	4.8	0	0.0	95	0.6
Lynchburg, VA	1,115	9.1	10	0.1	180	1.5	0	0.0	85	0.7
Macon, GA	3,015	28.9	0	0.0	80	0.8	0	0.0	75	0.7
Madera–Chowchilla, CA	180	4.9	30	0.8	45	1.2	0	0.0	74	2.0
Madison, WI	1,105	2.3	125	0.3	2,050	4.3	0	0.0	565	1.2
Manchester–Nashua, NH	180	0.8	0	0.0	580	2.5	4	0.0	240	1.0
Manhattan, KS	675	7.8	25	0.3	705	8.2	4	0.0	130	1.5
Mankato–North Mankato, MN	75	1.2	20	0.3	200	3.2	0	0.0	39	0.6
Mansfield, OH	205	4.1	0	0.0	0	0.0	0	0.0	25	0.5
McAllen–Edinburg–Mission, TX	255	0.9	10	0.0	545	1.9	0	0.0	130	0.4
Medford, OR	0	0.0	20	0.2	185	2.1	0	0.0	140	1.6
Memphis, TN–MS–AR	21,400	32.6	60	0.1	1,365	2.1	10	0.0	865	1.3
Merced, CA	305	3.7	75	0.9	680	8.3	0	0.0	145	1.8
Miami–Fort Lauderdale–Pompano Beach, FL	44,245	15.7	250	0.1	6,140	2.2	55	0.0	3,565	1.3
Michigan City–La Porte, IN	345	8.4	0	0.0	4	0.1	0	0.0	18	0.4
Midland, TX	450	7.1	30	0.5	35	0.6	0	0.0	105	1.7
Milwaukee–Waukesha–West Allis, WI	9,625	10.5	150	0.2	2,395	2.6	40	0.0	780	0.9
Minneapolis–St. Paul–Bloomington, MN–WI	9,455	4.3	740	0.3	8,645	3.9	20	0.0	2,775	1.2
Missoula, MT	0	0.0	130	1.8	45	0.6	0	0.0	65	0.9

PART C—METROPOLITAN STATISTICAL AREA TABLES

C-6 Other Professional Workers, by Metropolitan Statistical Area, Sex, Race, and Hispanic or Latino Origin, 2006–2010—Continued

Metropolitan Statistical Area	Total who worked in the last 5 years	Male Number	Male Percent	Female Number	Female Percent	Hispanic or Latino Number	Hispanic or Latino Percent	White alone, not Hispanic or Latino Number	White alone, not Hispanic or Latino Percent
Mobile, AL	17,865	5,605	31.4	12,260	68.6	200	1.1	12,600	70.5
Modesto, CA	20,080	7,665	38.2	12,410	61.8	3,995	19.9	14,260	71.0
Monroe, LA	8,440	2,690	31.9	5,750	68.1	80	0.9	6,300	74.6
Monroe, MI	5,560	2,090	37.6	3,475	62.5	90	1.6	5,290	95.1
Montgomery, AL	19,875	6,610	33.3	13,260	66.7	235	1.2	12,935	65.1
Morgantown, WV	7,875	3,255	41.3	4,620	58.7	175	2.2	7,040	89.4
Morristown, TN	4,220	1,390	32.9	2,830	67.1	145	3.4	3,980	94.3
Mount Vernon–Anacortes, WA	5,010	1,770	35.3	3,240	64.7	270	5.4	4,500	89.8
Muncie, IN	6,410	2,640	41.2	3,765	58.7	40	0.6	5,945	92.7
Muskegon–Norton Shores, MI	6,705	2,470	36.8	4,235	63.2	210	3.1	5,830	87.0
Myrtle Beach–North Myrtle Beach–Conway, SC	11,180	3,890	34.8	7,295	65.3	195	1.7	9,765	87.3
Napa, CA	6,805	2,690	39.5	4,115	60.5	655	9.6	5,315	78.1
Naples–Marco Island, FL	11,860	4,525	38.2	7,340	61.9	1,625	13.7	9,555	80.6
Nashville-Davidson–Murfreesboro–Franklin, TN	93,315	37,210	39.9	56,105	60.1	2,130	2.3	77,260	82.8
New Haven–Milford, CT	59,105	22,925	38.8	36,185	61.2	3,750	6.3	47,155	79.8
New Orleans–Metairie–Kenner, LA	62,420	23,415	37.5	39,010	62.5	2,740	4.4	43,130	69.1
New York–Northern New Jersey–Long Island, NY–NJ–PA	1,344,275	548,490	40.8	795,785	59.2	139,655	10.4	906,630	67.4
Niles–Benton Harbor, MI	7,850	3,165	40.3	4,685	59.7	275	3.5	6,675	85.0
North Port–Bradenton–Sarasota, FL	29,845	10,955	36.7	18,885	63.3	1,530	5.1	25,930	86.9
Norwich–New London, CT	16,280	5,790	35.6	10,490	64.4	520	3.2	14,485	89.0
Ocala, FL	10,525	3,785	36.0	6,740	64.0	710	6.7	8,200	77.9
Ocean City, NJ	5,590	1,950	34.9	3,645	65.2	190	3.4	5,105	91.3
Odessa, TX	4,795	1,490	31.1	3,305	68.9	1,305	27.2	3,060	63.8
Ogden–Clearfield, UT	26,820	10,880	40.6	15,940	59.4	1,120	4.2	24,735	92.2
Oklahoma City, OK	67,790	26,165	38.6	41,625	61.4	2,555	3.8	54,040	79.7
Olympia, WA	14,730	5,420	36.8	9,315	63.2	620	4.2	12,620	85.7
Omaha–Council Bluffs, NE–IA	49,090	18,175	37.0	30,920	63.0	1,380	2.8	43,730	89.1
Orlando–Kissimmee–Sanford, FL	110,775	42,945	38.8	67,830	61.2	16,800	15.2	74,050	66.8
Oshkosh–Neenah, WI	7,900	3,070	38.9	4,830	61.1	120	1.5	7,500	94.9
Owensboro, KY	4,755	1,755	36.9	3,000	63.1	90	1.9	4,555	95.8
Oxnard–Thousand Oaks–Ventura, CA	45,930	18,950	41.3	26,985	58.8	8,150	17.7	32,610	71.0
Palm Bay–Melbourne–Titusville, FL	23,455	8,765	37.4	14,690	62.6	1,605	6.8	19,780	84.3
Palm Coast, FL	3,925	1,400	35.7	2,525	64.3	250	6.4	3,025	77.1
Panama City–Lynn Haven–Panama City Beach, FL	7,230	2,230	30.8	5,005	69.2	305	4.2	6,145	85.0
Parkersburg–Marietta–Vienna, WV–OH	6,905	2,660	38.5	4,250	61.5	85	1.2	6,665	96.5
Pascagoula, MS	6,120	1,935	31.6	4,185	68.4	100	1.6	5,185	84.7
Pensacola–Ferry Pass–Brent, FL	20,180	7,555	37.4	12,625	62.6	600	3.0	16,240	80.5
Peoria, IL	18,520	6,855	37.0	11,665	63.0	245	1.3	16,900	91.3
Philadelphia–Camden–Wilmington, PA–NJ–DE–MD	374,295	146,350	39.1	227,945	60.9	12,415	3.3	289,070	77.2
Phoenix–Mesa–Glendale, AZ	201,575	77,945	38.7	123,630	61.3	25,300	12.6	153,675	76.2
Pine Bluff, AR	3,480	1,060	30.5	2,415	69.4	35	1.0	1,760	50.6
Pittsburgh, PA	132,650	54,360	41.0	78,295	59.0	1,435	1.1	119,785	90.3
Pittsfield, MA	8,375	3,445	41.1	4,930	58.9	330	3.9	7,800	93.1
Pocatello, ID	4,810	1,895	39.4	2,915	60.6	135	2.8	4,335	90.1
Portland–South Portland–Biddeford, ME	34,340	12,570	36.6	21,770	63.4	535	1.6	33,050	96.2
Portland–Vancouver–Hillsboro, OR–WA	129,735	51,175	39.4	78,560	60.6	5,405	4.2	111,665	86.1
Port St. Lucie, FL	16,385	6,040	36.9	10,345	63.1	1,480	9.0	13,115	80.0
Poughkeepsie–Newburgh–Middletown, NY	38,680	14,110	36.5	24,570	63.5	3,080	8.0	31,550	81.6
Prescott, AZ	8,995	3,680	40.9	5,315	59.1	460	5.1	8,040	89.4
Providence–New Bedford–Fall River, RI–MA	96,220	36,335	37.8	59,885	62.2	3,545	3.7	85,355	88.7

C-6 Other Professional Workers, by Metropolitan Statistical Area, Sex, Race, and Hispanic or Latino Origin, 2006–2010—Continued

Metropolitan Statistical Area	Black alone, not Hispanic or Latino Number	Percent	American Indian and Alaska Native alone, not Hispanic or Latino Number	Percent	Asian alone, not Hispanic or Latino Number	Percent	Native Hawaiian and Other Pacific Islander alone, not Hispanic or Latino Number	Percent	Two or more races, not Hispanic or Latino Number	Percent
Mobile, AL	4,610	25.8	60	0.3	290	1.6	0	0.0	100	0.6
Modesto, CA	580	2.9	115	0.6	770	3.8	20	0.1	340	1.7
Monroe, LA	1,885	22.3	4	0.0	55	0.7	0	0.0	120	1.4
Monroe, MI	80	1.4	4	0.1	60	1.1	0	0.0	35	0.6
Montgomery, AL	6,300	31.7	75	0.4	210	1.1	0	0.0	120	0.6
Morgantown, WV	230	2.9	10	0.1	390	5.0	0	0.0	34	0.4
Morristown, TN	50	1.2	15	0.4	0	0.0	0	0.0	24	0.6
Mount Vernon–Anacortes, WA	20	0.4	135	2.7	20	0.4	4	0.1	59	1.2
Muncie, IN	190	3.0	40	0.6	95	1.5	0	0.0	105	1.6
Muskegon–Norton Shores, MI	505	7.5	25	0.4	60	0.9	0	0.0	80	1.2
Myrtle Beach–North Myrtle Beach–Conway, SC	970	8.7	55	0.5	115	1.0	0	0.0	85	0.8
Napa, CA	150	2.2	45	0.7	330	4.8	45	0.7	270	4.0
Naples–Marco Island, FL	525	4.4	10	0.1	85	0.7	0	0.0	60	0.5
Nashville-Davidson–Murfreesboro–Franklin, TN	11,445	12.3	120	0.1	1,670	1.8	50	0.1	650	0.7
New Haven–Milford, CT	5,095	8.6	55	0.1	2,275	3.8	10	0.0	775	1.3
New Orleans–Metairie–Kenner, LA	13,990	22.4	135	0.2	1,755	2.8	0	0.0	670	1.1
New York–Northern New Jersey–Long Island, NY–NJ–PA	164,380	12.2	1,080	0.1	112,560	8.4	165	0.0	19,805	1.5
Niles–Benton Harbor, MI	600	7.6	15	0.2	215	2.7	0	0.0	70	0.9
North Port–Bradenton–Sarasota, FL	1,615	5.4	100	0.3	380	1.3	0	0.0	290	1.0
Norwich–New London, CT	690	4.2	40	0.2	350	2.1	0	0.0	190	1.2
Ocala, FL	1,250	11.9	20	0.2	165	1.6	0	0.0	185	1.8
Ocean City, NJ	265	4.7	0	0.0	25	0.4	0	0.0	0	0.0
Odessa, TX	285	5.9	20	0.4	35	0.7	0	0.0	90	1.9
Ogden–Clearfield, UT	315	1.2	105	0.4	295	1.1	70	0.3	180	0.7
Oklahoma City, OK	5,525	8.2	1,520	2.2	1,910	2.8	40	0.1	2,200	3.2
Olympia, WA	445	3.0	105	0.7	620	4.2	55	0.4	270	1.8
Omaha–Council Bluffs, NE–IA	2,440	5.0	50	0.1	800	1.6	35	0.1	655	1.3
Orlando–Kissimmee–Sanford, FL	14,305	12.9	160	0.1	3,755	3.4	170	0.2	1,540	1.4
Oshkosh–Neenah, WI	70	0.9	0	0.0	130	1.6	0	0.0	80	1.0
Owensboro, KY	90	1.9	0	0.0	10	0.2	0	0.0	10	0.2
Oxnard–Thousand Oaks–Ventura, CA	890	1.9	125	0.3	3,120	6.8	65	0.1	970	2.1
Palm Bay–Melbourne–Titusville, FL	1,365	5.8	45	0.2	285	1.2	25	0.1	345	1.5
Palm Coast, FL	575	14.6	10	0.3	30	0.8	0	0.0	35	0.9
Panama City–Lynn Haven–Panama City Beach, FL	525	7.3	25	0.3	90	1.2	0	0.0	155	2.1
Parkersburg–Marietta–Vienna, WV–OH	0	0.0	0	0.0	105	1.5	0	0.0	55	0.8
Pascagoula, MS	700	11.4	4	0.1	30	0.5	0	0.0	105	1.7
Pensacola–Ferry Pass–Brent, FL	2,405	11.9	95	0.5	565	2.8	20	0.1	250	1.2
Peoria, IL	890	4.8	15	0.1	340	1.8	4	0.0	124	0.7
Philadelphia–Camden–Wilmington, PA–NJ–DE–MD	53,045	14.2	330	0.1	14,780	3.9	30	0.0	4,625	1.2
Phoenix–Mesa–Glendale, AZ	10,160	5.0	2,540	1.3	6,820	3.4	255	0.1	2,830	1.4
Pine Bluff, AR	1,645	47.3	10	0.3	4	0.1	0	0.0	20	0.6
Pittsburgh, PA	7,580	5.7	100	0.1	2,585	1.9	55	0.0	1,110	0.8
Pittsfield, MA	95	1.1	20	0.2	90	1.1	0	0.0	40	0.5
Pocatello, ID	30	0.6	80	1.7	70	1.5	45	0.9	110	2.3
Portland–South Portland–Biddeford, ME	275	0.8	50	0.1	240	0.7	0	0.0	195	0.6
Portland–Vancouver–Hillsboro, OR–WA	2,820	2.2	400	0.3	6,270	4.8	295	0.2	2,880	2.2
Port St. Lucie, FL	1,455	8.9	0	0.0	180	1.1	0	0.0	155	0.9
Poughkeepsie–Newburgh–Middletown, NY	2,580	6.7	30	0.1	1,015	2.6	0	0.0	415	1.1
Prescott, AZ	130	1.4	155	1.7	100	1.1	0	0.0	115	1.3
Providence–New Bedford–Fall River, RI–MA	3,380	3.5	180	0.2	2,305	2.4	0	0.0	1,460	1.5

C-6 Other Professional Workers, by Metropolitan Statistical Area, Sex, Race, and Hispanic or Latino Origin, 2006–2010—Continued

Metropolitan Statistical Area	Total who worked in the last 5 years	Male Number	Male Percent	Female Number	Female Percent	Hispanic or Latino Number	Hispanic or Latino Percent	White alone, not Hispanic or Latino Number	White alone, not Hispanic or Latino Percent
Provo–Orem, UT	29,650	13,770	46.4	15,880	53.6	1,195	4.0	27,260	91.9
Pueblo, CO	6,540	2,245	34.3	4,295	65.7	1,620	24.8	4,725	72.2
Punta Gorda, FL	4,910	1,435	29.2	3,475	70.8	200	4.1	4,165	84.8
Racine, WI	9,680	3,200	33.1	6,480	66.9	425	4.4	8,325	86.0
Raleigh–Cary, NC	72,455	25,255	34.9	47,200	65.1	2,235	3.1	55,050	76.0
Rapid City, SD	6,820	2,715	39.8	4,105	60.2	85	1.2	6,175	90.5
Reading, PA	19,955	7,190	36.0	12,765	64.0	1,005	5.0	17,825	89.3
Redding, CA	7,670	2,475	32.3	5,195	67.7	265	3.5	6,785	88.5
Reno–Sparks, NV	21,835	8,575	39.3	13,265	60.8	1,640	7.5	18,180	83.3
Richmond, VA	72,080	24,975	34.6	47,105	65.4	1,495	2.1	51,965	72.1
Riverside–San Bernardino–Ontario, CA	166,495	63,000	37.8	103,495	62.2	40,145	24.1	93,930	56.4
Roanoke, VA	16,065	5,525	34.4	10,540	65.6	165	1.0	14,225	88.5
Rochester, MN	9,550	3,740	39.2	5,810	60.8	135	1.4	8,825	92.4
Rochester, NY	68,115	24,955	36.6	43,160	63.4	2,045	3.0	59,295	87.1
Rockford, IL	14,665	5,140	35.0	9,525	65.0	560	3.8	12,625	86.1
Rocky Mount, NC	5,935	1,850	31.2	4,085	68.8	140	2.4	4,005	67.5
Rome, GA	4,390	1,520	34.6	2,870	65.4	115	2.6	3,785	86.2
Sacramento–Arden-Arcade–Roseville, CA	115,275	43,100	37.4	72,175	62.6	11,925	10.3	78,815	68.4
Saginaw–Saginaw Township North, MI	7,810	2,990	38.3	4,815	61.7	345	4.4	6,265	80.2
St. Cloud, MN	10,295	3,715	36.1	6,580	63.9	65	0.6	9,615	93.4
St. George, UT	5,555	2,400	43.2	3,155	56.8	85	1.5	5,195	93.5
St. Joseph, MO–KS	5,485	1,950	35.6	3,530	64.4	105	1.9	5,085	92.7
St. Louis, MO–IL	157,350	56,665	36.0	100,680	64.0	3,015	1.9	130,110	82.7
Salem, OR	17,370	6,955	40.0	10,415	60.0	1,525	8.8	14,860	85.5
Salinas, CA	17,720	6,950	39.2	10,770	60.8	4,090	23.1	11,145	62.9
Salisbury, MD	6,850	2,305	33.6	4,545	66.4	160	2.3	5,060	73.9
Salt Lake City, UT	61,700	25,910	42.0	35,795	58.0	2,710	4.4	54,630	88.5
San Angelo, TX	5,165	2,005	38.8	3,160	61.2	1,045	20.2	3,950	76.5
San Antonio–New Braunfels, TX	104,845	38,025	36.3	66,820	63.7	37,905	36.2	57,425	54.8
San Diego–Carlsbad–San Marcos, CA	171,525	66,825	39.0	104,700	61.0	28,650	16.7	115,650	67.4
Sandusky, OH	3,565	1,325	37.2	2,235	62.7	295	8.3	3,115	87.4
San Francisco–Oakland–Fremont, CA	311,130	125,215	40.2	185,915	59.8	30,805	9.9	194,355	62.5
San Jose–Sunnyvale–Santa Clara, CA	105,885	38,085	36.0	67,800	64.0	14,215	13.4	57,450	54.3
San Luis Obispo–Paso Robles, CA	14,775	5,560	37.6	9,215	62.4	1,170	7.9	12,605	85.3
Santa Barbara–Santa Maria–Goleta, CA	25,360	10,465	41.3	14,895	58.7	3,920	15.5	18,515	73.0
Santa Cruz–Watsonville, CA	18,775	7,045	37.5	11,730	62.5	2,265	12.1	15,260	81.3
Santa Fe, NM	11,250	4,345	38.6	6,905	61.4	2,890	25.7	7,800	69.3
Santa Rosa–Petaluma, CA	27,285	9,550	35.0	17,730	65.0	2,360	8.6	23,450	85.9
Savannah, GA	16,935	6,005	35.5	10,935	64.6	340	2.0	11,840	69.9
Scranton–Wilkes-Barre, PA	26,290	11,095	42.2	15,195	57.8	415	1.6	24,920	94.8
Seattle–Tacoma–Bellevue, WA	206,185	80,040	38.8	126,140	61.2	7,405	3.6	163,705	79.4
Sebastian–Vero Beach, FL	5,625	1,875	33.3	3,745	66.6	240	4.3	4,830	85.9
Sheboygan, WI	4,870	1,800	37.0	3,070	63.0	85	1.7	4,480	92.0
Sherman–Denison, TX	5,665	2,160	38.1	3,505	61.9	175	3.1	4,940	87.2
Shreveport–Bossier City, LA	18,085	6,195	34.3	11,890	65.7	365	2.0	12,050	66.6
Sioux City, IA–NE–SD	6,670	2,170	32.5	4,500	67.5	215	3.2	6,170	92.5
Sioux Falls, SD	12,010	4,285	35.7	7,725	64.3	160	1.3	11,505	95.8
South Bend–Mishawaka, IN–MI	17,025	6,970	40.9	10,055	59.1	625	3.7	14,545	85.4
Spartanburg, SC	11,750	3,570	30.4	8,185	69.7	135	1.1	9,725	82.8
Spokane, WA	25,225	10,445	41.4	14,780	58.6	725	2.9	23,005	91.2
Springfield, IL	12,660	4,800	37.9	7,860	62.1	165	1.3	11,395	90.0
Springfield, MA	46,445	16,715	36.0	29,730	64.0	3,050	6.6	39,215	84.4
Springfield, MO	22,475	8,205	36.5	14,270	63.5	350	1.6	21,275	94.7
Springfield, OH	5,490	1,765	32.1	3,725	67.9	29	0.5	4,920	89.6
State College, PA	13,555	6,655	49.1	6,900	50.9	230	1.7	11,535	85.1

C-6 Other Professional Workers, by Metropolitan Statistical Area, Sex, Race, and Hispanic or Latino Origin, 2006–2010—*Continued*

Metropolitan Statistical Area	Black alone, not Hispanic or Latino Number	Percent	American Indian and Alaska Native alone, not Hispanic or Latino Number	Percent	Asian alone, not Hispanic or Latino Number	Percent	Native Hawaiian and Other Pacific Islander alone, not Hispanic or Latino Number	Percent	Two or more races, not Hispanic or Latino Number	Percent
Provo–Orem, UT	45	0.2	110	0.4	445	1.5	105	0.4	490	1.7
Pueblo, CO	30	0.5	0	0.0	60	0.9	25	0.4	85	1.3
Punta Gorda, FL	345	7.0	25	0.5	115	2.3	0	0.0	60	1.2
Racine, WI	595	6.1	65	0.7	165	1.7	0	0.0	110	1.1
Raleigh–Cary, NC	11,445	15.8	230	0.3	2,735	3.8	10	0.0	745	1.0
Rapid City, SD	45	0.7	315	4.6	35	0.5	0	0.0	160	2.3
Reading, PA	855	4.3	0	0.0	110	0.6	0	0.0	150	0.8
Redding, CA	70	0.9	170	2.2	185	2.4	20	0.3	173	2.3
Reno–Sparks, NV	440	2.0	190	0.9	1,050	4.8	80	0.4	255	1.2
Richmond, VA	15,685	21.8	210	0.3	1,760	2.4	45	0.1	925	1.3
Riverside–San Bernardino–Ontario, CA	14,905	9.0	715	0.4	12,970	7.8	440	0.3	3,390	2.0
Roanoke, VA	1,255	7.8	25	0.2	110	0.7	0	0.0	285	1.8
Rochester, MN	250	2.6	15	0.2	260	2.7	0	0.0	69	0.7
Rochester, NY	4,580	6.7	85	0.1	1,590	2.3	15	0.0	505	0.7
Rockford, IL	975	6.6	85	0.6	325	2.2	0	0.0	90	0.6
Rocky Mount, NC	1,725	29.1	30	0.5	20	0.3	0	0.0	19	0.3
Rome, GA	380	8.7	0	0.0	90	2.1	0	0.0	18	0.4
Sacramento–Arden-Arcade–Roseville, CA	6,755	5.9	545	0.5	13,355	11.6	510	0.4	3,370	2.9
Saginaw–Saginaw Township North, MI	890	11.4	15	0.2	165	2.1	0	0.0	130	1.7
St. Cloud, MN	305	3.0	15	0.1	215	2.1	0	0.0	70	0.7
St. George, UT	40	0.7	85	1.5	75	1.4	60	1.1	15	0.3
St. Joseph, MO–KS	235	4.3	0	0.0	40	0.7	0	0.0	19	0.3
St. Louis, MO–IL	19,735	12.5	195	0.1	2,975	1.9	40	0.0	1,280	0.8
Salem, OR	80	0.5	155	0.9	375	2.2	65	0.4	310	1.8
Salinas, CA	590	3.3	80	0.5	1,310	7.4	75	0.4	425	2.4
Salisbury, MD	1,350	19.7	75	1.1	165	2.4	0	0.0	34	0.5
Salt Lake City, UT	695	1.1	175	0.3	2,425	3.9	365	0.6	695	1.1
San Angelo, TX	140	2.7	0	0.0	0	0.0	0	0.0	35	0.7
San Antonio–New Braunfels, TX	5,995	5.7	240	0.2	1,895	1.8	60	0.1	1,335	1.3
San Diego–Carlsbad–San Marcos, CA	6,485	3.8	475	0.3	15,410	9.0	540	0.3	4,315	2.5
Sandusky, OH	130	3.6	0	0.0	20	0.6	0	0.0	0	0.0
San Francisco–Oakland–Fremont, CA	19,525	6.3	470	0.2	55,655	17.9	890	0.3	9,430	3.0
San Jose–Sunnyvale–Santa Clara, CA	3,020	2.9	365	0.3	28,120	26.6	195	0.2	2,520	2.4
San Luis Obispo–Paso Robles, CA	195	1.3	45	0.3	415	2.8	70	0.5	285	1.9
Santa Barbara–Santa Maria–Goleta, CA	410	1.6	40	0.2	1,685	6.6	80	0.3	705	2.8
Santa Cruz–Watsonville, CA	165	0.9	30	0.2	750	4.0	0	0.0	310	1.7
Santa Fe, NM	50	0.4	230	2.0	155	1.4	4	0.0	119	1.1
Santa Rosa–Petaluma, CA	295	1.1	115	0.4	605	2.2	25	0.1	435	1.6
Savannah, GA	4,095	24.2	20	0.1	370	2.2	0	0.0	275	1.6
Scranton–Wilkes-Barre, PA	300	1.1	20	0.1	440	1.7	30	0.1	165	0.6
Seattle–Tacoma–Bellevue, WA	7,705	3.7	1,000	0.5	19,885	9.6	970	0.5	5,505	2.7
Sebastian–Vero Beach, FL	490	8.7	0	0.0	40	0.7	0	0.0	20	0.4
Sheboygan, WI	105	2.2	15	0.3	105	2.2	0	0.0	69	1.4
Sherman–Denison, TX	370	6.5	50	0.9	85	1.5	0	0.0	39	0.7
Shreveport–Bossier City, LA	5,195	28.7	75	0.4	220	1.2	15	0.1	170	0.9
Sioux City, IA–NE–SD	150	2.2	10	0.1	85	1.3	0	0.0	40	0.6
Sioux Falls, SD	120	1.0	80	0.7	65	0.5	0	0.0	89	0.7
South Bend–Mishawaka, IN–MI	1,275	7.5	45	0.3	355	2.1	0	0.0	175	1.0
Spartanburg, SC	1,505	12.8	20	0.2	235	2.0	4	0.0	140	1.2
Spokane, WA	280	1.1	190	0.8	580	2.3	50	0.2	395	1.6
Springfield, IL	860	6.8	10	0.1	175	1.4	0	0.0	53	0.4
Springfield, MA	2,335	5.0	20	0.0	1,260	2.7	20	0.0	550	1.2
Springfield, MO	325	1.4	0	0.0	245	1.1	0	0.0	280	1.2
Springfield, OH	435	7.9	10	0.2	40	0.7	0	0.0	60	1.1
State College, PA	240	1.8	35	0.3	1,460	10.8	0	0.0	60	0.4

C-6 Other Professional Workers, by Metropolitan Statistical Area, Sex, Race, and Hispanic or Latino Origin, 2006–2010—Continued

Metropolitan Statistical Area	Total who worked in the last 5 years	Male Number	Male Percent	Female Number	Female Percent	Hispanic or Latino Number	Hispanic or Latino Percent	White alone, not Hispanic or Latino Number	White alone, not Hispanic or Latino Percent
Steubenville–Weirton, OH–WV	4,255	1,485	34.9	2,765	65.0	115	2.7	3,965	93.2
Stockton, CA	25,205	8,580	34.0	16,625	66.0	4,580	18.2	14,055	55.8
Sumter, SC	4,265	1,395	32.7	2,870	67.3	95	2.2	2,640	61.9
Syracuse, NY	41,405	15,710	37.9	25,695	62.1	825	2.0	37,140	89.7
Tallahassee, FL	28,140	11,520	40.9	16,620	59.1	1,140	4.1	19,305	68.6
Tampa–St. Petersburg–Clearwater, FL	137,105	50,595	36.9	86,515	63.1	13,730	10.0	104,435	76.2
Terre Haute, IN	7,690	2,665	34.7	5,025	65.3	85	1.1	7,185	93.4
Texarkana, TX–Texarkana, AR	5,605	1,915	34.2	3,690	65.8	70	1.2	4,330	77.3
Toledo, OH	33,515	12,575	37.5	20,940	62.5	910	2.7	28,720	85.7
Topeka, KS	13,985	5,135	36.7	8,850	63.3	425	3.0	12,555	89.8
Trenton–Ewing, NJ	26,020	10,700	41.1	15,320	58.9	1,440	5.5	19,280	74.1
Tucson, AZ	50,770	19,920	39.2	30,850	60.8	9,980	19.7	35,895	70.7
Tulsa, OK	48,130	17,320	36.0	30,810	64.0	1,475	3.1	38,285	79.5
Tuscaloosa, AL	11,285	3,730	33.1	7,555	66.9	140	1.2	8,550	75.8
Tyler, TX	9,830	3,520	35.8	6,310	64.2	465	4.7	8,240	83.8
Utica–Rome, NY	15,350	5,270	34.3	10,080	65.7	315	2.1	14,015	91.3
Valdosta, GA	5,700	2,110	37.0	3,595	63.1	160	2.8	4,255	74.6
Vallejo–Fairfield, CA	18,905	7,000	37.0	11,905	63.0	2,340	12.4	10,950	57.9
Victoria, TX	4,965	1,325	26.7	3,640	73.3	915	18.4	3,660	73.7
Vineland–Millville–Bridgeton, NJ	6,455	1,915	29.7	4,540	70.3	885	13.7	4,440	68.8
Virginia Beach–Norfolk–Newport News, VA–NC	90,095	28,370	31.5	61,725	68.5	2,740	3.0	60,545	67.2
Visalia–Porterville, CA	14,760	5,205	35.3	9,550	64.7	4,805	32.6	9,035	61.2
Waco, TX	12,810	5,015	39.1	7,795	60.9	920	7.2	10,130	79.1
Warner Robins, GA	6,850	2,125	31.0	4,725	69.0	135	2.0	4,615	67.4
Washington–Arlington–Alexandria, DC–VA–MD–WV	469,555	187,015	39.8	282,540	60.2	26,280	5.6	305,755	65.1
Waterloo–Cedar Falls, IA	9,625	3,380	35.1	6,250	64.9	150	1.6	8,745	90.9
Wausau, WI	6,205	2,205	35.5	4,000	64.5	50	0.8	5,795	93.4
Wenatchee–East Wenatchee, WA	4,430	1,655	37.4	2,775	62.6	440	9.9	3,895	87.9
Wheeling, WV–OH	6,295	2,700	42.9	3,600	57.2	35	0.6	6,130	97.4
Wichita, KS	32,545	11,990	36.8	20,555	63.2	1,355	4.2	28,070	86.2
Wichita Falls, TX	6,980	2,735	39.2	4,245	60.8	600	8.6	5,760	82.5
Williamsport, PA	5,170	2,055	39.7	3,115	60.3	95	1.8	4,910	95.0
Wilmington, NC	18,230	6,435	35.3	11,795	64.7	385	2.1	16,000	87.8
Winchester, VA–WV	5,650	1,955	34.6	3,695	65.4	120	2.1	5,080	89.9
Winston–Salem, NC	25,245	8,765	34.7	16,480	65.3	840	3.3	19,790	78.4
Worcester, MA	47,400	16,720	35.3	30,680	64.7	1,985	4.2	42,000	88.6
Yakima, WA	8,450	3,395	40.2	5,055	59.8	1,890	22.4	5,990	70.9
York–Hanover, PA	20,825	7,710	37.0	13,115	63.0	480	2.3	19,250	92.4
Youngstown–Warren–Boardman, OH–PA	23,330	8,660	37.1	14,665	62.9	270	1.2	21,150	90.7
Yuba City, CA	5,900	1,990	33.7	3,910	66.3	740	12.5	4,340	73.6
Yuma, AZ	5,755	1,870	32.5	3,885	67.5	2,375	41.3	2,975	51.7

C-6 Other Professional Workers, by Metropolitan Statistical Area, Sex, Race, and Hispanic or Latino Origin, 2006–2010—*Continued*

Metropolitan Statistical Area	Black alone, not Hispanic or Latino Number	Percent	American Indian and Alaska Native alone, not Hispanic or Latino Number	Percent	Asian alone, not Hispanic or Latino Number	Percent	Native Hawaiian and Other Pacific Islander alone, not Hispanic or Latino Number	Percent	Two or more races, not Hispanic or Latino Number	Percent
Steubenville–Weirton, OH–WV	120	2.8	0	0.0	20	0.5	15	0.4	18	0.4
Stockton, CA	2,220	8.8	110	0.4	3,355	13.3	125	0.5	755	3.0
Sumter, SC	1,485	34.8	0	0.0	15	0.4	0	0.0	35	0.8
Syracuse, NY	1,765	4.3	160	0.4	1,280	3.1	0	0.0	240	0.6
Tallahassee, FL	6,275	22.3	0	0.0	1,035	3.7	15	0.1	370	1.3
Tampa–St. Petersburg–Clearwater, FL	13,540	9.9	170	0.1	3,505	2.6	30	0.0	1,695	1.2
Terre Haute, IN	130	1.7	20	0.3	200	2.6	0	0.0	69	0.9
Texarkana, TX–Texarkana, AR	1,045	18.6	40	0.7	35	0.6	0	0.0	85	1.5
Toledo, OH	2,685	8.0	4	0.0	1,010	3.0	0	0.0	190	0.6
Topeka, KS	725	5.2	100	0.7	75	0.5	0	0.0	104	0.7
Trenton–Ewing, NJ	2,725	10.5	80	0.3	2,090	8.0	0	0.0	405	1.6
Tucson, AZ	1,385	2.7	700	1.4	1,790	3.5	65	0.1	955	1.9
Tulsa, OK	3,165	6.6	2,505	5.2	495	1.0	55	0.1	2,145	4.5
Tuscaloosa, AL	2,125	18.8	4	0.0	325	2.9	0	0.0	145	1.3
Tyler, TX	915	9.3	50	0.5	110	1.1	25	0.3	30	0.3
Utica–Rome, NY	490	3.2	25	0.2	340	2.2	0	0.0	160	1.0
Valdosta, GA	1,170	20.5	0	0.0	35	0.6	0	0.0	79	1.4
Vallejo–Fairfield, CA	3,025	16.0	90	0.5	1,880	9.9	90	0.5	535	2.8
Victoria, TX	230	4.6	0	0.0	65	1.3	0	0.0	94	1.9
Vineland–Millville–Bridgeton, NJ	820	12.7	20	0.3	70	1.1	0	0.0	219	3.4
Virginia Beach–Norfolk–Newport News, VA–NC	22,620	25.1	210	0.2	2,385	2.6	75	0.1	1,510	1.7
Visalia–Porterville, CA	220	1.5	135	0.9	320	2.2	4	0.0	230	1.6
Waco, TX	1,460	11.4	35	0.3	150	1.2	0	0.0	110	0.9
Warner Robins, GA	1,900	27.7	0	0.0	65	0.9	0	0.0	139	2.0
Washington–Arlington–Alexandria, DC–VA–MD–WV	92,675	19.7	720	0.2	35,555	7.6	200	0.0	8,370	1.8
Waterloo–Cedar Falls, IA	545	5.7	4	0.0	110	1.1	4	0.0	70	0.7
Wausau, WI	90	1.5	20	0.3	220	3.5	0	0.0	30	0.5
Wenatchee–East Wenatchee, WA	30	0.7	0	0.0	15	0.3	0	0.0	40	0.9
Wheeling, WV–OH	40	0.6	0	0.0	50	0.8	0	0.0	44	0.7
Wichita, KS	1,505	4.6	195	0.6	985	3.0	15	0.0	415	1.3
Wichita Falls, TX	450	6.4	15	0.2	130	1.9	0	0.0	25	0.4
Williamsport, PA	150	2.9	0	0.0	10	0.2	0	0.0	4	0.1
Wilmington, NC	1,500	8.2	30	0.2	105	0.6	0	0.0	215	1.2
Winchester, VA–WV	215	3.8	0	0.0	95	1.7	0	0.0	140	2.5
Winston-Salem, NC	4,050	16.0	4	0.0	410	1.6	0	0.0	150	0.6
Worcester, MA	1,250	2.6	85	0.2	1,670	3.5	0	0.0	415	0.9
Yakima, WA	55	0.7	170	2.0	75	0.9	0	0.0	270	3.2
York–Hanover, PA	765	3.7	0	0.0	175	0.8	10	0.0	140	0.7
Youngstown–Warren–Boardman, OH–PA	1,525	6.5	15	0.1	105	0.5	0	0.0	265	1.1
Yuba City, CA	95	1.6	95	1.6	315	5.3	20	0.3	295	5.0
Yuma, AZ	155	2.7	125	2.2	90	1.6	0	0.0	40	0.7

PART C—METROPOLITAN STATISTICAL AREA TABLES

C-7 **Technicians, by Metropolitan Statistical Area, Sex, Race, and Hispanic or Latino Origin, 2006–2010**

Metropolitan Statistical Area	Total who worked in the last 5 years	Male Number	Male Percent	Female Number	Female Percent	Hispanic or Latino Number	Hispanic or Latino Percent	White alone, not Hispanic or Latino Number	White alone, not Hispanic or Latino Percent
Abilene, TX	2,775	1,045	37.7	1,735	62.5	520	18.7	1,970	71.0
Akron, OH	10,825	4,970	45.9	5,855	54.1	65	0.6	9,620	88.9
Albany, GA	2,575	730	28.3	1,850	71.8	0	0.0	1,390	54.0
Albany–Schenectady–Troy, NY	15,065	6,880	45.7	8,190	54.4	385	2.6	12,920	85.8
Albuquerque, NM	14,590	7,455	51.1	7,135	48.9	5,125	35.1	7,920	54.3
Alexandria, LA	2,340	880	37.6	1,460	62.4	15	0.6	1,575	67.3
Allentown–Bethlehem–Easton, PA–NJ	13,305	5,965	44.8	7,340	55.2	760	5.7	11,195	84.1
Altoona, PA	1,975	710	35.9	1,265	64.1	0	0.0	1,935	98.0
Amarillo, TX	3,950	1,435	36.3	2,515	63.7	625	15.8	2,925	74.1
Ames, IA	2,050	1,010	49.3	1,040	50.7	60	2.9	1,800	87.8
Anchorage, AK	5,650	2,670	47.3	2,975	52.7	420	7.4	4,160	73.6
Anderson, IN	1,660	565	34.0	1,095	66.0	50	3.0	1,535	92.5
Anderson, SC	3,165	1,180	37.3	1,990	62.9	0	0.0	2,730	86.3
Ann Arbor, MI	5,930	2,860	48.2	3,075	51.9	170	2.9	4,210	71.0
Anniston–Oxford, AL	1,480	670	45.3	810	54.7	0	0.0	1,305	88.2
Appleton, WI	3,530	1,525	43.2	2,005	56.8	14	0.4	3,365	95.3
Asheville, NC	6,045	2,160	35.7	3,880	64.2	115	1.9	5,530	91.5
Athens–Clarke County, GA	3,175	1,350	42.5	1,825	57.5	145	4.6	2,430	76.5
Atlanta–Sandy Springs–Marietta, GA	65,850	31,210	47.4	34,640	52.6	2,025	3.1	36,140	54.9
Atlantic City–Hammonton, NJ	3,220	1,290	40.1	1,930	59.9	205	6.4	2,210	68.6
Auburn–Opelika, AL	2,390	945	39.5	1,445	60.5	35	1.5	1,870	78.2
Augusta–Richmond County, GA–SC	8,475	3,285	38.8	5,190	61.2	215	2.5	5,125	60.5
Austin–Round Rock–San Marcos, TX	26,595	15,090	56.7	11,505	43.3	5,090	19.1	16,615	62.5
Bakersfield–Delano, CA	8,220	4,195	51.0	4,025	49.0	2,410	29.3	4,325	52.6
Baltimore–Towson, MD	44,435	19,505	43.9	24,925	56.1	1,165	2.6	27,140	61.1
Bangor, ME	2,470	865	35.0	1,600	64.8	20	0.8	2,355	95.3
Barnstable Town, MA	3,095	1,230	39.7	1,865	60.3	95	3.1	2,890	93.4
Baton Rouge, LA	13,480	6,545	48.6	6,935	51.4	195	1.4	8,975	66.6
Battle Creek, MI	1,305	425	32.6	880	67.4	4	0.3	1,225	93.9
Bay City, MI	1,835	805	43.9	1,030	56.1	4	0.2	1,745	95.1
Beaumont–Port Arthur, TX	6,140	2,680	43.6	3,460	56.4	370	6.0	4,400	71.7
Bellingham, WA	2,730	1,085	39.7	1,645	60.3	200	7.3	2,355	86.3
Bend, OR	2,110	720	34.1	1,390	65.9	90	4.3	1,985	94.1
Billings, MT	2,045	880	43.0	1,165	57.0	40	2.0	1,990	97.3
Binghamton, NY	4,350	1,835	42.2	2,515	57.8	100	2.3	4,065	93.4
Birmingham–Hoover, AL	16,660	6,295	37.8	10,365	62.2	190	1.1	11,365	68.2
Bismarck, ND	2,050	905	44.1	1,145	55.9	30	1.5	2,015	98.3
Blacksburg–Christiansburg–Radford, VA	3,165	1,350	42.7	1,810	57.2	80	2.5	2,725	86.1
Bloomington, IN	3,040	1,365	44.9	1,675	55.1	35	1.2	2,895	95.2
Bloomington–Normal, IL	2,430	1,075	44.2	1,355	55.8	30	1.2	2,050	84.4
Boise City–Nampa, ID	9,510	5,005	52.6	4,505	47.4	515	5.4	8,395	88.3
Boston–Cambridge–Quincy, MA–NH	73,100	33,695	46.1	39,405	53.9	3,755	5.1	56,210	76.9
Boulder, CO	4,540	2,895	63.8	1,645	36.2	250	5.5	3,980	87.7
Bowling Green, KY	1,730	800	46.2	930	53.8	0	0.0	1,585	91.6
Bremerton–Silverdale, WA	4,070	1,920	47.2	2,150	52.8	225	5.5	3,250	79.9
Bridgeport–Stamford–Norwalk, CT	8,875	4,190	47.2	4,685	52.8	905	10.2	5,475	61.7
Brownsville–Harlingen, TX	3,415	1,670	48.9	1,745	51.1	2,990	87.6	330	9.7
Brunswick, GA	1,105	345	31.2	760	68.8	0	0.0	850	76.9
Buffalo–Niagara Falls, NY	16,865	6,550	38.8	10,315	61.2	290	1.7	14,100	83.6
Burlington, NC	2,815	1,365	48.5	1,450	51.5	45	1.6	2,230	79.2
Burlington–South Burlington, VT	3,950	1,760	44.6	2,195	55.6	70	1.8	3,805	96.3
Canton–Massillon, OH	6,170	2,505	40.6	3,665	59.4	14	0.2	5,780	93.7
Cape Coral–Fort Myers, FL	7,235	2,850	39.4	4,385	60.6	915	12.6	5,200	71.9
Cape Girardeau–Jackson, MO–IL	1,100	310	28.2	790	71.8	30	2.7	1,045	95.0
Carson City, NV	775	315	40.6	465	60.0	54	7.0	545	70.3

C-7 Technicians, by Metropolitan Statistical Area, Sex, Race, and Hispanic or Latino Origin, 2006–2010—*Continued*

Metropolitan Statistical Area	Black alone, not Hispanic or Latino Number	Percent	American Indian and Alaska Native alone, not Hispanic or Latino Number	Percent	Asian alone, not Hispanic or Latino Number	Percent	Native Hawaiian and Other Pacific Islander alone, not Hispanic or Latino Number	Percent	Two or more races, not Hispanic or Latino Number	Percent
Abilene, TX	245	8.8	0	0.0	30	1.1	0	0.0	10	0.4
Akron, OH	590	5.5	10	0.1	375	3.5	0	0.0	170	1.6
Albany, GA	1,165	45.2	4	0.2	0	0.0	0	0.0	15	0.6
Albany–Schenectady–Troy, NY	845	5.6	60	0.4	630	4.2	0	0.0	230	1.5
Albuquerque, NM	290	2.0	730	5.0	310	2.1	0	0.0	220	1.5
Alexandria, LA	580	24.8	40	1.7	40	1.7	0	0.0	84	3.6
Allentown–Bethlehem–Easton, PA–NJ	470	3.5	0	0.0	725	5.4	0	0.0	150	1.1
Altoona, PA	0	0.0	0	0.0	0	0.0	0	0.0	40	2.0
Amarillo, TX	200	5.1	30	0.8	100	2.5	0	0.0	65	1.6
Ames, IA	0	0.0	0	0.0	170	8.3	0	0.0	15	0.7
Anchorage, AK	250	4.4	180	3.2	325	5.8	35	0.6	285	5.0
Anderson, IN	40	2.4	0	0.0	4	0.2	0	0.0	39	2.3
Anderson, SC	435	13.7	0	0.0	0	0.0	0	0.0	0	0.0
Ann Arbor, MI	495	8.3	20	0.3	855	14.4	0	0.0	179	3.0
Anniston–Oxford, AL	125	8.4	0	0.0	0	0.0	0	0.0	50	3.4
Appleton, WI	4	0.1	60	1.7	85	2.4	0	0.0	0	0.0
Asheville, NC	280	4.6	10	0.2	95	1.6	0	0.0	15	0.2
Athens–Clarke County, GA	430	13.5	0	0.0	170	5.4	0	0.0	0	0.0
Atlanta–Sandy Springs–Marietta, GA	21,410	32.5	120	0.2	5,090	7.7	30	0.0	1,030	1.6
Atlantic City–Hammonton, NJ	500	15.5	10	0.3	185	5.7	50	1.6	60	1.9
Auburn–Opelika, AL	385	16.1	0	0.0	95	4.0	0	0.0	10	0.4
Augusta–Richmond County, GA–SC	2,730	32.2	4	0.0	255	3.0	0	0.0	150	1.8
Austin–Round Rock–San Marcos, TX	1,885	7.1	45	0.2	2,545	9.6	15	0.1	400	1.5
Bakersfield–Delano, CA	575	7.0	20	0.2	700	8.5	15	0.2	175	2.1
Baltimore–Towson, MD	12,395	27.9	60	0.1	3,010	6.8	20	0.0	640	1.4
Bangor, ME	25	1.0	10	0.4	10	0.4	0	0.0	49	2.0
Barnstable Town, MA	60	1.9	0	0.0	15	0.5	0	0.0	40	1.3
Baton Rouge, LA	3,860	28.6	0	0.0	340	2.5	0	0.0	110	0.8
Battle Creek, MI	50	3.8	0	0.0	15	1.1	0	0.0	10	0.8
Bay City, MI	50	2.7	0	0.0	0	0.0	0	0.0	35	1.9
Beaumont–Port Arthur, TX	1,120	18.2	4	0.1	170	2.8	0	0.0	75	1.2
Bellingham, WA	20	0.7	25	0.9	105	3.8	0	0.0	25	0.9
Bend, OR	0	0.0	0	0.0	0	0.0	10	0.5	25	1.2
Billings, MT	0	0.0	10	0.5	10	0.5	0	0.0	0	0.0
Binghamton, NY	110	2.5	15	0.3	40	0.9	0	0.0	25	0.6
Birmingham–Hoover, AL	4,620	27.7	30	0.2	365	2.2	0	0.0	90	0.5
Bismarck, ND	0	0.0	0	0.0	0	0.0	0	0.0	4	0.2
Blacksburg–Christiansburg–Radford, VA	65	2.1	0	0.0	290	9.2	0	0.0	0	0.0
Bloomington, IN	40	1.3	10	0.3	35	1.2	0	0.0	24	0.8
Bloomington–Normal, IL	40	1.6	0	0.0	310	12.8	0	0.0	0	0.0
Boise City–Nampa, ID	25	0.3	55	0.6	340	3.6	15	0.2	164	1.7
Boston–Cambridge–Quincy, MA–NH	5,535	7.6	60	0.1	6,360	8.7	0	0.00	1,180	1.6
Boulder, CO	45	1.0	4	0.1	155	3.4	0	0.0	100	2.2
Bowling Green, KY	65	3.8	10	0.6	60	3.5	0	0.0	4	0.2
Bremerton–Silverdale, WA	80	2.0	4	0.1	285	7.0	30	0.7	195	4.8
Bridgeport–Stamford–Norwalk, CT	1,415	15.9	0	0.0	820	9.2	10	0.1	250	2.8
Brownsville–Harlingen, TX	40	1.2	4	0.1	35	1.0	0	0.0	15	0.4
Brunswick, GA	255	23.1	0	0.0	0	0.0	0	0.0	0	0.0
Buffalo–Niagara Falls, NY	1,830	10.9	75	0.4	480	2.8	0	0.0	94	0.6
Burlington, NC	390	13.9	15	0.5	40	1.4	0	0.0	100	3.6
Burlington–South Burlington, VT	0	0.0	0	0.0	50	1.3	0	0.0	32	0.8
Canton–Massillon, OH	200	3.2	10	0.2	45	0.7	0	0.0	120	1.9
Cape Coral–Fort Myers, FL	910	12.6	0	0.0	90	1.2	0	0.0	120	1.7
Cape Girardeau–Jackson, MO–IL	15	1.4	0	0.0	10	0.9	0	0.0	0	0.0
Carson City, NV	35	4.5	15	1.9	10	1.3	0	0.0	115	14.8

PART C—METROPOLITAN STATISTICAL AREA TABLES

C-7 **Technicians, by Metropolitan Statistical Area, Sex, Race, and Hispanic or Latino Origin, 2006–2010**—*Continued*

Metropolitan Statistical Area	Total who worked in the last 5 years	Male Number	Male Percent	Female Number	Female Percent	Hispanic or Latino Number	Hispanic or Latino Percent	White alone, not Hispanic or Latino Number	White alone, not Hispanic or Latino Percent
Casper, WY	1,020	525	51.5	495	48.5	15	1.5	960	94.1
Cedar Rapids, IA	4,670	2,150	46.0	2,520	54.0	75	1.6	4,405	94.3
Champaign–Urbana, IL	4,285	1,975	46.1	2,315	54.0	60	1.4	3,345	78.1
Charleston, WV	4,920	2,110	42.9	2,810	57.1	4	0.1	4,535	92.2
Charleston–North Charleston–Summerville, SC	10,385	4,540	43.7	5,845	56.3	305	2.9	7,135	68.7
Charlotte–Gastonia–Rock Hill, NC–SC	22,960	10,425	45.4	12,535	54.6	785	3.4	15,525	67.6
Charlottesville, VA	3,130	1,400	44.7	1,730	55.3	25	0.8	2,415	77.2
Chattanooga, TN–GA	8,665	3,535	40.8	5,130	59.2	85	1.0	7,115	82.1
Cheyenne, WY	1,250	375	30.0	870	69.6	120	9.6	1,105	88.4
Chicago–Joliet–Naperville, IL–IN–WI	116,845	52,930	45.3	63,915	54.7	11,895	10.2	69,820	59.8
Chico, CA	3,125	1,335	42.7	1,790	57.3	100	3.2	2,885	92.3
Cincinnati–Middletown, OH–KY–IN	31,715	11,820	37.3	19,895	62.7	455	1.4	27,230	85.9
Clarksville, TN–KY	3,180	1,210	38.1	1,970	61.9	140	4.4	2,395	75.3
Cleveland, TN	1,725	650	37.7	1,070	62.0	30	1.7	1,550	89.9
Cleveland–Elyria–Mentor, OH	34,320	13,835	40.3	20,485	59.7	975	2.8	25,810	75.2
Coeur d'Alene, ID	1,720	805	46.8	910	52.9	40	2.3	1,600	93.0
College Station–Bryan, TX	3,695	1,785	48.3	1,915	51.8	380	10.3	2,785	75.4
Colorado Springs, CO	9,050	4,675	51.7	4,380	48.4	1,005	11.1	6,860	75.8
Columbia, MO	4,100	1,765	43.0	2,335	57.0	50	1.2	3,595	87.7
Columbia, SC	12,115	5,185	42.8	6,935	57.2	215	1.8	8,135	67.1
Columbus, GA–AL	4,615	1,585	34.3	3,030	65.7	150	3.3	2,535	54.9
Columbus, IN	1,100	375	34.1	730	66.4	0	0.0	1,010	91.8
Columbus, OH	28,685	13,555	47.3	15,130	52.7	380	1.3	23,115	80.6
Corpus Christi, TX	6,245	2,850	45.6	3,400	54.4	3,515	56.3	2,460	39.4
Corvallis, OR	1,950	1,010	51.8	935	47.9	75	3.8	1,575	80.8
Crestview–Fort Walton Beach–Destin, FL	2,820	1,285	45.6	1,535	54.4	150	5.3	2,305	81.7
Cumberland, MD–WV	1,200	375	31.3	820	68.3	10	0.8	1,130	94.2
Dallas–Fort Worth–Arlington, TX	81,930	41,745	51.0	40,185	49.0	9,880	12.1	49,205	60.1
Dalton, GA	1,330	480	36.1	845	63.5	105	7.9	1,055	79.3
Danville, IL	1,130	320	28.3	810	71.7	15	1.3	935	82.7
Danville, VA	1,360	385	28.3	970	71.3	15	1.1	1,050	77.2
Davenport–Moline–Rock Island, IA–IL	5,015	2,065	41.2	2,950	58.8	280	5.6	4,310	85.9
Dayton, OH	14,010	5,710	40.8	8,300	59.2	270	1.9	11,155	79.6
Decatur, AL	2,680	1,270	47.4	1,410	52.6	54	2.0	2,205	82.3
Decatur, IL	1,710	470	27.5	1,240	72.5	10	0.6	1,475	86.3
Deltona–Daytona Beach–Ormond Beach, FL	6,770	2,615	38.6	4,155	61.4	455	6.7	5,515	81.5
Denver–Aurora–Broomfield, CO	33,490	18,225	54.4	15,265	45.6	3,665	10.9	26,195	78.2
Des Moines–West Des Moines, IA	8,780	4,065	46.3	4,715	53.7	195	2.2	7,925	90.3
Detroit–Warren–Livonia, MI	57,695	23,145	40.1	34,550	59.9	1,310	2.3	43,240	74.9
Dothan, AL	2,030	705	34.7	1,325	65.3	24	1.2	1,580	77.8
Dover, DE	2,260	855	37.8	1,410	62.4	39	1.7	1,610	71.2
Dubuque, IA	1,205	495	41.1	710	58.9	20	1.7	1,080	89.6
Duluth, MN–WI	4,675	1,455	31.1	3,220	68.9	45	1.0	4,545	97.2
Durham–Chapel Hill, NC	10,245	4,055	39.6	6,190	60.4	295	2.9	6,360	62.1
Eau Claire, WI	2,505	995	39.7	1,510	60.3	4	0.2	2,460	98.2
El Centro, CA	1,100	430	39.1	670	60.9	800	72.7	210	19.1
Elizabethtown, KY	1,325	495	37.4	830	62.6	35	2.6	1,110	83.8
Elkhart–Goshen, IN	2,235	915	40.9	1,320	59.1	145	6.5	1,900	85.0
Elmira, NY	1,490	650	43.6	840	56.4	15	1.0	1,385	93.0
El Paso, TX	7,105	3,690	51.9	3,415	48.1	5,565	78.3	1,105	15.6
Erie, PA	4,320	1,485	34.4	2,835	65.6	45	1.0	4,085	94.6
Eugene–Springfield, OR	5,145	2,435	47.3	2,710	52.7	230	4.5	4,740	92.1
Evansville, IN–KY	6,285	2,310	36.8	3,970	63.2	45	0.7	5,765	91.7
Fairbanks, AK	1,710	890	52.0	820	48.0	55	3.2	1,260	73.7
Fargo, ND–MN	4,520	1,905	42.1	2,615	57.9	85	1.9	4,315	95.5

C-7 **Technicians, by Metropolitan Statistical Area, Sex, Race, and Hispanic or Latino Origin, 2006–2010**—*Continued*

Metropolitan Statistical Area	Black alone, not Hispanic or Latino Number	Black alone, not Hispanic or Latino Percent	American Indian and Alaska Native alone, not Hispanic or Latino Number	American Indian and Alaska Native alone, not Hispanic or Latino Percent	Asian alone, not Hispanic or Latino Number	Asian alone, not Hispanic or Latino Percent	Native Hawaiian and Other Pacific Islander alone, not Hispanic or Latino Number	Native Hawaiian and Other Pacific Islander alone, not Hispanic or Latino Percent	Two or more races, not Hispanic or Latino Number	Two or more races, not Hispanic or Latino Percent
Casper, WY	0	0.0	0	0.0	0	0.0	0	0.0	50	4.9
Cedar Rapids, IA	45	1.0	0	0.0	135	2.9	0	0.0	15	0.3
Champaign–Urbana, IL	240	5.6	0	0.0	570	13.3	0	0.0	74	1.7
Charleston, WV	215	4.4	0	0.0	40	0.8	0	0.0	120	2.4
Charleston–North Charleston–Summerville, SC	2,345	22.6	0	0.0	380	3.7	65	0.6	155	1.5
Charlotte–Gastonia–Rock Hill, NC–SC	5,390	23.5	20	0.1	990	4.3	0	0.0	260	1.1
Charlottesville, VA	440	14.1	0	0.0	195	6.2	0	0.0	50	1.6
Chattanooga, TN–GA	1,120	12.9	10	0.1	205	2.4	0	0.0	130	1.5
Cheyenne, WY	4	0.3	0	0.0	0	0.0	0	0.0	15	1.2
Chicago–Joliet–Naperville, IL–IN–WI	18,900	16.2	150	0.1	14,785	12.7	15	0.0	1,280	1.1
Chico, CA	30	1.0	20	0.6	65	2.1	0	0.0	29	0.9
Cincinnati–Middletown, OH–KY–IN	2,705	8.5	20	0.1	1,035	3.3	0	0.0	270	0.9
Clarksville, TN–KY	600	18.9	0	0.0	15	0.5	0	0.0	35	1.1
Cleveland, TN	145	8.4	0	0.0	0	0.0	0	0.0	0	0.0
Cleveland–Elyria–Mentor, OH	6,025	17.6	75	0.2	1,265	3.7	0	0.0	160	0.5
Coeur d'Alene, ID	0	0.0	0	0.0	10	0.6	0	0.0	70	4.1
College Station–Bryan, TX	260	7.0	10	0.3	175	4.7	0	0.0	80	2.2
Colorado Springs, CO	455	5.0	65	0.7	335	3.7	0	0.0	330	3.6
Columbia, MO	195	4.8	4	0.1	150	3.7	0	0.0	104	2.5
Columbia, SC	3,345	27.6	4	0.0	345	2.8	0	0.0	80	0.7
Columbus, GA–AL	1,690	36.6	15	0.3	205	4.4	0	0.0	19	0.4
Columbus, IN	65	5.9	0	0.0	25	2.3	0	0.0	0	0.0
Columbus, OH	3,105	10.8	20	0.1	1,760	6.1	0	0.0	305	1.1
Corpus Christi, TX	60	1.0	10	0.2	110	1.8	0	0.0	90	1.4
Corvallis, OR	10	0.5	50	2.6	120	6.2	0	0.0	114	5.8
Crestview–Fort Walton Beach–Destin, FL	175	6.2	20	0.7	110	3.9	15	0.5	50	1.8
Cumberland, MD–WV	20	1.7	0	0.0	30	2.5	0	0.0	10	0.8
Dallas–Fort Worth–Arlington, TX	12,840	15.7	330	0.4	8,445	10.3	110	0.1	1,120	1.4
Dalton, GA	120	9.0	25	1.9	0	0.0	0	0.0	20	1.5
Danville, IL	165	14.6	0	0.0	0	0.0	0	0.0	15	1.3
Danville, VA	295	21.7	0	0.0	0	0.0	0	0.0	0	0.0
Davenport–Moline–Rock Island, IA–IL	290	5.8	20	0.4	95	1.9	0	0.0	23	0.5
Dayton, OH	1,970	14.1	90	0.6	320	2.3	0	0.0	205	1.5
Decatur, AL	295	11.0	20	0.7	45	1.7	0	0.0	65	2.4
Decatur, IL	95	5.6	20	1.2	105	6.1	0	0.0	4	0.2
Deltona–Daytona Beach–Ormond Beach, FL	530	7.8	15	0.2	140	2.1	0	0.0	115	1.7
Denver–Aurora–Broomfield, CO	1,250	3.7	110	0.3	1,610	4.8	0	0.0	660	2.0
Des Moines–West Des Moines, IA	225	2.6	4	0.0	345	3.9	0	0.0	85	1.0
Detroit–Warren–Livonia, MI	9,035	15.7	115	0.2	3,235	5.6	35	0.1	720	1.2
Dothan, AL	390	19.2	4	0.2	20	1.0	0	0.0	10	0.5
Dover, DE	410	18.1	0	0.0	110	4.9	0	0.0	85	3.8
Dubuque, IA	0	0.0	0	0.0	65	5.4	0	0.0	39	3.2
Duluth, MN–WI	30	0.6	30	0.6	4	0.1	0	0.0	25	0.5
Durham–Chapel Hill, NC	2,500	24.4	20	0.2	930	9.1	0	0.0	145	1.4
Eau Claire, WI	0	0.0	15	0.6	15	0.6	0	0.0	10	0.4
El Centro, CA	60	5.5	10	0.9	20	1.8	0	0.0	0	0.0
Elizabethtown, KY	135	10.2	0	0.0	0	0.0	0	0.0	45	3.4
Elkhart–Goshen, IN	90	4.0	15	0.7	45	2.0	0	0.0	40	1.8
Elmira, NY	75	5.0	0	0.0	10	0.7	0	0.0	4	0.3
El Paso, TX	235	3.3	40	0.6	135	1.9	0	0.0	30	0.4
Erie, PA	150	3.5	0	0.0	15	0.3	0	0.0	25	0.6
Eugene–Springfield, OR	15	0.3	65	1.3	25	0.5	0	0.0	70	1.4
Evansville, IN–KY	295	4.7	0	0.0	100	1.6	0	0.0	80	1.3
Fairbanks, AK	120	7.0	100	5.8	75	4.4	4	0.2	95	5.6
Fargo, ND–MN	10	0.2	10	0.2	85	1.9	0	0.0	15	0.3

PART C—METROPOLITAN STATISTICAL AREA TABLES

C-7 **Technicians, by Metropolitan Statistical Area, Sex, Race, and Hispanic or Latino Origin, 2006–2010**—*Continued*

Metropolitan Statistical Area	Total who worked in the last 5 years	Male Number	Male Percent	Female Number	Female Percent	Hispanic or Latino Number	Hispanic or Latino Percent	White alone, not Hispanic or Latino Number	White alone, not Hispanic or Latino Percent
Farmington, NM	1,170	445	38.0	725	62.0	115	9.8	610	52.1
Fayetteville, NC	4,500	1,300	28.9	3,195	71.0	290	6.4	2,530	56.2
Fayetteville–Springdale–Rogers, AR–MO	5,880	2,515	42.8	3,365	57.2	330	5.6	4,835	82.2
Flagstaff, AZ	1,895	800	42.2	1,095	57.8	80	4.2	1,470	77.6
Flint, MI	5,525	2,180	39.5	3,345	60.5	120	2.2	4,495	81.4
Florence, SC	3,385	1,125	33.2	2,260	66.8	50	1.5	2,155	63.7
Florence–Muscle Shoals, AL	2,000	590	29.5	1,410	70.5	0	0.0	1,860	93.0
Fond du Lac, WI	1,620	505	31.2	1,115	68.8	55	3.4	1,560	96.3
Fort Collins–Loveland, CO	5,530	2,690	48.6	2,840	51.4	560	10.1	4,655	84.2
Fort Smith, AR–OK	3,710	1,450	39.1	2,260	60.9	130	3.5	3,075	82.9
Fort Wayne, IN	5,815	2,200	37.8	3,610	62.1	125	2.1	5,215	89.7
Fresno, CA	9,210	3,765	40.9	5,440	59.1	2,835	30.8	4,195	45.5
Gadsden, AL	1,665	605	36.3	1,060	63.7	0	0.0	1,460	87.7
Gainesville, FL	4,645	2,210	47.6	2,435	52.4	355	7.6	3,595	77.4
Gainesville, GA	1,450	500	34.5	950	65.5	140	9.7	1,220	84.1
Glens Falls, NY	1,585	645	40.7	940	59.3	0	0.0	1,580	99.7
Goldsboro, NC	1,955	595	30.4	1,360	69.6	105	5.4	1,015	51.9
Grand Forks, ND–MN	1,895	575	30.3	1,320	69.7	15	0.8	1,780	93.9
Grand Junction, CO	1,985	770	38.8	1,215	61.2	130	6.5	1,835	92.4
Grand Rapids–Wyoming, MI	10,475	4,440	42.4	6,035	57.6	355	3.4	9,370	89.5
Great Falls, MT	1,100	495	45.0	605	55.0	30	2.7	1,035	94.1
Greeley, CO	3,480	1,530	44.0	1,950	56.0	555	15.9	2,810	80.7
Green Bay, WI	5,200	2,040	39.2	3,165	60.9	55	1.1	4,960	95.4
Greensboro–High Point, NC	9,280	3,330	35.9	5,955	64.2	100	1.1	6,735	72.6
Greenville, NC	3,035	1,125	37.1	1,910	62.9	44	1.4	1,845	60.8
Greenville–Mauldin–Easley, SC	8,980	3,700	41.2	5,280	58.8	185	2.1	7,265	80.9
Gulfport–Biloxi, MS	3,730	1,670	44.8	2,060	55.2	150	4.0	2,780	74.5
Hagerstown–Martinsburg, MD–WV	4,145	1,635	39.4	2,510	60.6	80	1.9	3,805	91.8
Hanford–Corcoran, CA	1,150	350	30.4	800	69.6	245	21.3	630	54.8
Harrisburg–Carlisle, PA	8,645	4,325	50.0	4,325	50.0	155	1.8	7,345	85.0
Harrisonburg, VA	1,770	755	42.7	1,010	57.1	15	0.8	1,725	97.5
Hartford–West Hartford–East Hartford, CT	19,375	8,650	44.6	10,725	55.4	1,315	6.8	15,110	78.0
Hattiesburg, MS	1,960	735	37.5	1,220	62.2	110	5.6	1,550	79.1
Hickory–Lenoir–Morganton, NC	4,520	1,675	37.1	2,845	62.9	110	2.4	4,015	88.8
Hinesville–Fort Stewart, GA	965	330	34.2	640	66.3	35	3.6	440	45.6
Holland–Grand Haven, MI	3,550	1,550	43.7	2,000	56.3	130	3.7	3,350	94.4
Honolulu, HI	11,215	5,610	50.0	5,605	50.0	695	6.2	2,180	19.4
Hot Springs, AR	1,390	520	37.4	870	62.6	15	1.1	1,305	93.9
Houma–Bayou Cane–Thibodaux, LA	2,860	1,280	44.8	1,580	55.2	15	0.5	2,250	78.7
Houston–Sugar Land–Baytown, TX	82,605	42,670	51.7	39,935	48.3	15,840	19.2	40,420	48.9
Huntington–Ashland, WV–KY–OH	5,000	1,900	38.0	3,100	62.0	40	0.8	4,795	95.9
Huntsville, AL	6,835	3,180	46.5	3,660	53.5	115	1.7	5,060	74.0
Idaho Falls, ID	2,055	985	47.9	1,070	52.1	55	2.7	1,950	94.9
Indianapolis–Carmel, IN	25,585	10,110	39.5	15,480	60.5	540	2.1	20,580	80.4
Iowa City, IA	3,305	1,380	41.8	1,920	58.1	65	2.0	2,810	85.0
Ithaca, NY	2,290	1,175	51.3	1,115	48.7	85	3.7	1,975	86.2
Jackson, MI	2,585	1,170	45.3	1,415	54.7	85	3.3	2,405	93.0
Jackson, MS	8,975	3,365	37.5	5,610	62.5	30	0.3	4,705	52.4
Jackson, TN	1,885	535	28.4	1,350	71.6	35	1.9	1,345	71.4
Jacksonville, FL	17,310	7,850	45.3	9,465	54.7	895	5.2	11,745	67.9
Jacksonville, NC	1,960	545	27.8	1,415	72.2	160	8.2	1,385	70.7
Janesville, WI	2,300	840	36.5	1,465	63.7	20	0.9	2,135	92.8
Jefferson City, MO	2,565	1,070	41.7	1,495	58.3	4	0.2	2,315	90.3
Johnson City, TN	4,080	1,165	28.6	2,915	71.4	0	0.0	3,910	95.8
Johnstown, PA	2,365	915	38.7	1,450	61.3	4	0.2	2,310	97.7

C-7 Technicians, by Metropolitan Statistical Area, Sex, Race, and Hispanic or Latino Origin, 2006–2010—Continued

Metropolitan Statistical Area	Black alone, not Hispanic or Latino Number	Percent	American Indian and Alaska Native alone, not Hispanic or Latino Number	Percent	Asian alone, not Hispanic or Latino Number	Percent	Native Hawaiian and Other Pacific Islander alone, not Hispanic or Latino Number	Percent	Two or more races, not Hispanic or Latino Number	Percent
Farmington, NM	0	0.0	425	36.3	25	2.1	0	0.0	0	0.0
Fayetteville, NC	1,290	28.7	100	2.2	110	2.4	0	0.0	180	4.0
Fayetteville–Springdale–Rogers, AR–MO	225	3.8	50	0.9	280	4.8	0	0.0	155	2.6
Flagstaff, AZ	15	0.8	305	16.1	20	1.1	0	0.0	0	0.0
Flint, MI	745	13.5	10	0.2	50	0.9	0	0.0	110	2.0
Florence, SC	1,170	34.6	0	0.0	4	0.1	0	0.0	4	0.1
Florence–Muscle Shoals, AL	110	5.5	15	0.8	4	0.2	0	0.0	15	0.8
Fond du Lac, WI	0	0.0	0	0.0	4	0.2	0	0.0	0	0.0
Fort Collins–Loveland, CO	65	1.2	45	0.8	145	2.6	0	0.0	60	1.1
Fort Smith, AR–OK	80	2.2	165	4.4	135	3.6	0	0.0	125	3.4
Fort Wayne, IN	295	5.1	10	0.2	70	1.2	25	0.4	70	1.2
Fresno, CA	480	5.2	30	0.3	1,385	15.0	25	0.3	260	2.8
Gadsden, AL	190	11.4	0	0.0	0	0.0	0	0.0	19	1.1
Gainesville, FL	450	9.7	0	0.0	150	3.2	0	0.0	95	2.0
Gainesville, GA	45	3.1	0	0.0	40	2.8	0	0.0	4	0.3
Glens Falls, NY	0	0.0	0	0.0	4	0.3	0	0.0	0	0.0
Goldsboro, NC	830	42.5	0	0.0	0	0.0	0	0.0	4	0.2
Grand Forks, ND–MN	25	1.3	20	1.1	0	0.0	0	0.0	55	2.9
Grand Junction, CO	0	0.0	4	0.2	0	0.0	0	0.0	15	0.8
Grand Rapids–Wyoming, MI	365	3.5	10	0.1	160	1.5	0	0.0	220	2.1
Great Falls, MT	0	0.0	0	0.0	0	0.0	0	0.0	30	2.7
Greeley, CO	40	1.1	30	0.9	35	1.0	0	0.0	14	0.4
Green Bay, WI	0	0.0	110	2.1	75	1.4	0	0.0	0	0.0
Greensboro–High Point, NC	2,230	24.0	20	0.2	150	1.6	0	0.0	50	0.5
Greenville, NC	1,065	35.1	50	1.6	30	1.0	0	0.0	4	0.1
Greenville–Mauldin–Easley, SC	1,305	14.5	0	0.0	165	1.8	0	0.0	60	0.7
Gulfport–Biloxi, MS	575	15.4	0	0.0	160	4.3	35	0.9	25	0.7
Hagerstown–Martinsburg, MD–WV	185	4.5	15	0.4	65	1.6	0	0.0	4	0.1
Hanford–Corcoran, CA	90	7.8	10	0.9	125	10.9	0	0.0	50	4.3
Harrisburg–Carlisle, PA	605	7.0	25	0.3	400	4.6	0	0.0	115	1.3
Harrisonburg, VA	20	1.1	0	0.0	0	0.0	0	0.0	10	0.6
Hartford–West Hartford–East Hartford, CT	1,370	7.1	70	0.4	1,200	6.2	80	0.4	240	1.2
Hattiesburg, MS	300	15.3	0	0.0	0	0.0	0	0.0	0	0.0
Hickory–Lenoir–Morganton, NC	330	7.3	0	0.0	55	1.2	4	0.1	4	0.1
Hinesville–Fort Stewart, GA	430	44.6	40	4.1	20	2.1	0	0.0	4	0.4
Holland–Grand Haven, MI	0	0.0	0	0.0	55	1.5	0	0.0	10	0.3
Honolulu, HI	345	3.1	4	0.0	5,775	51.5	545	4.9	1,664	14.8
Hot Springs, AR	4	0.3	35	2.5	15	1.1	0	0.0	10	0.7
Houma–Bayou Cane–Thibodaux, LA	515	18.0	35	1.2	0	0.0	0	0.0	40	1.4
Houston–Sugar Land–Baytown, TX	16,505	20.0	175	0.2	8,990	10.9	25	0.0	650	0.8
Huntington–Ashland, WV–KY–OH	80	1.6	0	0.0	0	0.0	0	0.0	80	1.6
Huntsville, AL	1,310	19.2	60	0.9	220	3.2	0	0.0	74	1.1
Idaho Falls, ID	35	1.7	15	0.7	0	0.0	0	0.0	4	0.2
Indianapolis–Carmel, IN	3,205	12.5	55	0.2	830	3.2	0	0.0	380	1.5
Iowa City, IA	100	3.0	0	0.0	300	9.1	0	0.0	30	0.9
Ithaca, NY	35	1.5	0	0.0	175	7.6	0	0.0	19	0.8
Jackson, MI	55	2.1	0	0.0	15	0.6	0	0.0	25	1.0
Jackson, MS	4,140	46.1	0	0.0	70	0.8	0	0.0	29	0.3
Jackson, TN	355	18.8	0	0.0	70	3.7	0	0.0	80	4.2
Jacksonville, FL	3,165	18.3	55	0.3	1,010	5.8	30	0.2	415	2.4
Jacksonville, NC	340	17.3	0	0.0	30	1.5	0	0.0	40	2.0
Janesville, WI	70	3.0	0	0.0	15	0.7	0	0.0	55	2.4
Jefferson City, MO	165	6.4	4	0.2	30	1.2	0	0.0	44	1.7
Johnson City, TN	75	1.8	10	0.2	60	1.5	0	0.0	25	0.6
Johnstown, PA	15	0.6	0	0.0	30	1.3	0	0.0	4	0.2

PART C—METROPOLITAN STATISTICAL AREA TABLES

C-7 Technicians, by Metropolitan Statistical Area, Sex, Race, and Hispanic or Latino Origin, 2006–2010—Continued

Metropolitan Statistical Area	Total who worked in the last 5 years	Male Number	Male Percent	Female Number	Female Percent	Hispanic or Latino Number	Hispanic or Latino Percent	White alone, not Hispanic or Latino Number	White alone, not Hispanic or Latino Percent
Jonesboro, AR	2,010	590	29.4	1,420	70.6	4	0.2	1,930	96.0
Joplin, MO	2,620	1,105	42.2	1,515	57.8	24	0.9	2,425	92.6
Kalamazoo–Portage, MI	4,700	2,170	46.2	2,535	53.9	125	2.7	4,150	88.3
Kankakee–Bradley, IL	1,590	480	30.2	1,110	69.8	4	0.3	1,315	82.7
Kansas City, MO–KS	32,850	13,695	41.7	19,155	58.3	1,190	3.6	26,490	80.6
Kennewick–Pasco–Richland, WA	3,845	1,850	48.1	2,000	52.0	470	12.2	3,165	82.3
Killeen–Temple–Fort Hood, TX	5,385	2,275	42.2	3,110	57.8	805	14.9	3,135	58.2
Kingsport–Bristol–Bristol, TN–VA	5,755	2,140	37.2	3,615	62.8	35	0.6	5,480	95.2
Kingston, NY	2,430	1,100	45.3	1,330	54.7	105	4.3	2,130	87.7
Knoxville, TN	11,565	5,175	44.7	6,390	55.3	80	0.7	10,435	90.2
Kokomo, IN	1,285	420	32.7	865	67.3	10	0.8	1,200	93.4
La Crosse, WI–MN	2,690	1,170	43.5	1,520	56.5	4	0.1	2,625	97.6
Lafayette, IN	3,670	1,495	40.7	2,175	59.3	130	3.5	3,085	84.1
Lafayette, LA	4,795	2,295	47.9	2,505	52.2	35	0.7	3,500	73.0
Lake Charles, LA	3,200	1,130	35.3	2,070	64.7	79	2.5	2,490	77.8
Lake Havasu City–Kingman, AZ	2,125	1,055	49.6	1,070	50.4	405	19.1	1,615	76.0
Lakeland–Winter Haven, FL	6,460	2,215	34.3	4,245	65.7	555	8.6	4,785	74.1
Lancaster, PA	7,665	2,975	38.8	4,690	61.2	355	4.6	6,915	90.2
Lansing–East Lansing, MI	8,085	3,860	47.7	4,230	52.3	120	1.5	6,735	83.3
Laredo, TX	1,495	800	53.5	700	46.8	1,305	87.3	80	5.4
Las Cruces, NM	2,495	1,430	57.3	1,065	42.7	1,225	49.1	980	39.3
Las Vegas–Paradise, NV	21,210	10,900	51.4	10,310	48.6	2,790	13.2	12,435	58.6
Lawrence, KS	2,405	1,430	59.5	970	40.3	65	2.7	2,070	86.1
Lawton, OK	2,145	795	37.1	1,350	62.9	240	11.2	1,350	62.9
Lebanon, PA	2,410	830	34.4	1,580	65.6	10	0.4	2,245	93.2
Lewiston, ID–WA	785	235	29.9	550	70.1	10	1.3	745	94.9
Lewiston–Auburn, ME	1,565	550	35.1	1,015	64.9	0	0.0	1,525	97.4
Lexington–Fayette, KY	8,055	3,225	40.0	4,830	60.0	135	1.7	6,965	86.5
Lima, OH	1,355	520	38.4	835	61.6	10	0.7	1,295	95.6
Lincoln, NE	5,745	2,575	44.8	3,170	55.2	144	2.5	5,190	90.3
Little Rock–North Little Rock–Conway, AR	11,845	4,515	38.1	7,330	61.9	270	2.3	8,965	75.7
Logan, UT–ID	1,900	1,195	62.9	705	37.1	19	1.0	1,855	97.6
Longview, TX	2,910	1,170	40.2	1,740	59.8	50	1.7	2,320	79.7
Longview, WA	1,085	485	44.7	595	54.8	10	0.9	1,025	94.5
Los Angeles–Long Beach–Santa Ana, CA	148,070	79,760	53.9	68,310	46.1	38,300	25.9	54,375	36.7
Louisville/Jefferson County, KY–IN	17,770	7,020	39.5	10,750	60.5	320	1.8	14,845	83.5
Lubbock, TX	4,110	1,900	46.2	2,210	53.8	960	23.4	2,755	67.0
Lynchburg, VA	3,520	1,300	36.9	2,220	63.1	30	0.9	2,905	82.5
Macon, GA	3,180	1,235	38.8	1,945	61.2	95	3.0	2,045	64.3
Madera–Chowchilla, CA	1,295	635	49.0	655	50.6	570	44.0	600	46.3
Madison, WI	12,225	6,025	49.3	6,205	50.8	395	3.2	10,645	87.1
Manchester–Nashua, NH	7,375	3,380	45.8	3,995	54.2	215	2.9	6,595	89.4
Manhattan, KS	1,725	865	50.1	865	50.1	70	4.1	1,455	84.3
Mankato–North Mankato, MN	1,430	585	40.9	845	59.1	19	1.3	1,385	96.9
Mansfield, OH	1,720	585	34.0	1,135	66.0	10	0.6	1,590	92.4
McAllen–Edinburg–Mission, TX	5,920	2,925	49.4	2,995	50.6	5,520	93.2	250	4.2
Medford, OR	2,450	1,175	48.0	1,275	52.0	105	4.3	2,185	89.2
Memphis, TN–MS–AR	18,010	6,255	34.7	11,755	65.3	210	1.2	10,515	58.4
Merced, CA	2,355	840	35.7	1,515	64.3	890	37.8	895	38.0
Miami–Fort Lauderdale–Pompano Beach, FL	67,780	29,725	43.9	38,050	56.1	23,765	35.1	24,155	35.6
Michigan City–La Porte, IN	1,440	375	26.0	1,070	74.3	35	2.4	1,230	85.4
Midland, TX	2,370	1,085	45.8	1,285	54.2	530	22.4	1,660	70.0
Milwaukee–Waukesha–West Allis, WI	22,965	9,740	42.4	13,225	57.6	1,140	5.0	18,190	79.2
Minneapolis–St. Paul–Bloomington, MN–WI	55,740	27,280	48.9	28,460	51.1	910	1.6	47,335	84.9
Missoula, MT	1,470	705	48.0	765	52.0	170	11.6	1,165	79.3

C-7 **Technicians, by Metropolitan Statistical Area, Sex, Race, and Hispanic or Latino Origin, 2006–2010**—*Continued*

Metropolitan Statistical Area	Black alone, not Hispanic or Latino Number	Percent	American Indian and Alaska Native alone, not Hispanic or Latino Number	Percent	Asian alone, not Hispanic or Latino Number	Percent	Native Hawaiian and Other Pacific Islander alone, not Hispanic or Latino Number	Percent	Two or more races, not Hispanic or Latino Number	Percent
Jonesboro, AR	75	3.7	0	0.0	0	0.0	0	0.0	0	0.0
Joplin, MO	30	1.1	50	1.9	55	2.1	0	0.0	40	1.5
Kalamazoo–Portage, MI	235	5.0	30	0.6	50	1.1	0	0.0	114	2.4
Kankakee–Bradley, IL	270	17.0	0	0.0	0	0.0	0	0.0	0	0.0
Kansas City, MO–KS	3,665	11.2	50	0.2	975	3.0	15	0.0	475	1.4
Kennewick–Pasco–Richland, WA	25	0.7	15	0.4	130	3.4	0	0.0	39	1.0
Killeen–Temple–Fort Hood, TX	1,075	20.0	60	1.1	60	1.1	90	1.7	160	3.0
Kingsport–Bristol–Bristol, TN–VA	110	1.9	25	0.4	0	0.0	0	0.0	105	1.8
Kingston, NY	125	5.1	15	0.6	40	1.6	0	0.0	18	0.7
Knoxville, TN	660	5.7	10	0.1	140	1.2	0	0.0	240	2.1
Kokomo, IN	65	5.1	0	0.0	15	1.2	0	0.0	0	0.0
La Crosse, WI–MN	10	0.4	0	0.0	40	1.5	0	0.0	14	0.5
Lafayette, IN	140	3.8	0	0.0	290	7.9	0	0.0	18	0.5
Lafayette, LA	1,100	22.9	30	0.6	115	2.4	0	0.0	15	0.3
Lake Charles, LA	515	16.1	15	0.5	10	0.3	10	0.3	75	2.3
Lake Havasu City–Kingman, AZ	0	0.0	15	0.7	55	2.6	15	0.7	20	0.9
Lakeland–Winter Haven, FL	855	13.2	50	0.8	70	1.1	25	0.4	120	1.9
Lancaster, PA	210	2.7	0	0.0	100	1.3	20	0.3	63	0.8
Lansing–East Lansing, MI	500	6.2	30	0.4	565	7.0	0	0.0	145	1.8
Laredo, TX	75	5.0	0	0.0	20	1.3	0	0.0	20	1.3
Las Cruces, NM	15	0.6	25	1.0	190	7.6	0	0.0	50	2.0
Las Vegas–Paradise, NV	2,140	10.1	50	0.2	3,185	15.0	120	0.6	480	2.3
Lawrence, KS	70	2.9	35	1.5	150	6.2	0	0.0	14	0.6
Lawton, OK	180	8.4	175	8.2	45	2.1	35	1.6	120	5.6
Lebanon, PA	55	2.3	20	0.8	40	1.7	0	0.0	39	1.6
Lewiston, ID–WA	0	0.0	35	4.5	0	0.0	0	0.0	0	0.0
Lewiston–Auburn, ME	4	0.3	4	0.3	10	0.6	0	0.0	20	1.3
Lexington–Fayette, KY	655	8.1	4	0.0	210	2.6	0	0.0	80	1.0
Lima, OH	25	1.8	0	0.0	0	0.0	0	0.0	30	2.2
Lincoln, NE	110	1.9	0	0.0	275	4.8	0	0.0	29	0.5
Little Rock–North Little Rock–Conway, AR	2,055	17.3	4	0.0	440	3.7	0	0.0	110	0.9
Logan, UT–ID	0	0.0	0	0.0	25	1.3	0	0.0	0	0.0
Longview, TX	515	17.7	0	0.0	10	0.3	0	0.0	10	0.3
Longview, WA	0	0.0	15	1.4	25	2.3	0	0.0	10	0.9
Los Angeles–Long Beach–Santa Ana, CA	11,980	8.1	220	0.1	39,975	27.0	325	0.2	2,890	2.0
Louisville/Jefferson County, KY–IN	1,905	10.7	20	0.1	460	2.6	0	0.0	220	1.2
Lubbock, TX	205	5.0	25	0.6	135	3.3	0	0.0	23	0.6
Lynchburg, VA	465	13.2	0	0.0	90	2.6	0	0.0	25	0.7
Macon, GA	1,000	31.4	0	0.0	40	1.3	0	0.0	4	0.1
Madera–Chowchilla, CA	50	3.9	20	1.5	15	1.2	0	0.0	40	3.1
Madison, WI	350	2.9	0	0.0	565	4.6	0	0.0	280	2.3
Manchester–Nashua, NH	115	1.6	0	0.0	330	4.5	0	0.0	125	1.7
Manhattan, KS	115	6.7	15	0.9	50	2.9	25	1.4	0	0.0
Mankato–North Mankato, MN	20	1.4	0	0.0	4	0.3	0	0.0	0	0.0
Mansfield, OH	125	7.3	0	0.0	0	0.0	0	0.0	0	0.0
McAllen–Edinburg–Mission, TX	35	0.6	10	0.2	100	1.7	0	0.0	10	0.2
Medford, OR	0	0.0	45	1.8	40	1.6	0	0.0	75	3.1
Memphis, TN–MS–AR	6,535	36.3	10	0.1	585	3.2	0	0.0	155	0.9
Merced, CA	135	5.7	20	0.8	385	16.3	0	0.0	25	1.1
Miami–Fort Lauderdale–Pompano Beach, FL	16,470	24.3	80	0.1	2,460	3.6	130	0.2	725	1.1
Michigan City–La Porte, IN	180	12.5	0	0.0	0	0.0	0	0.0	0	0.0
Midland, TX	145	6.1	0	0.0	35	1.5	0	0.0	0	0.0
Milwaukee–Waukesha–West Allis, WI	2,620	11.4	40	0.2	835	3.6	0	0.0	134	0.6
Minneapolis–St. Paul–Bloomington, MN–WI	2,610	4.7	185	0.3	3,830	6.9	65	0.1	805	1.4
Missoula, MT	15	1.0	10	0.7	70	4.8	0	0.0	45	3.1

PART C—METROPOLITAN STATISTICAL AREA TABLES

C-7 Technicians, by Metropolitan Statistical Area, Sex, Race, and Hispanic or Latino Origin, 2006–2010—Continued

Metropolitan Statistical Area	Total who worked in the last 5 years	Male Number	Male Percent	Female Number	Female Percent	Hispanic or Latino Number	Hispanic or Latino Percent	White alone, not Hispanic or Latino Number	White alone, not Hispanic or Latino Percent
Mobile, AL	5,575	2,045	36.7	3,525	63.2	24	0.4	3,490	62.6
Modesto, CA	5,625	2,580	45.9	3,050	54.2	1,430	25.4	3,120	55.5
Monroe, LA	3,070	1,285	41.9	1,785	58.1	10	0.3	2,245	73.1
Monroe, MI	2,290	825	36.0	1,470	64.2	55	2.4	2,180	95.2
Montgomery, AL	5,110	1,960	38.4	3,150	61.6	29	0.6	3,575	70.0
Morgantown, WV	2,640	1,100	41.7	1,540	58.3	45	1.7	2,520	95.5
Morristown, TN	1,790	500	27.9	1,290	72.1	0	0.0	1,690	94.4
Mount Vernon–Anacortes, WA	1,225	650	53.1	575	46.9	65	5.3	1,095	89.4
Muncie, IN	1,480	560	37.8	920	62.2	15	1.0	1,345	90.9
Muskegon–Norton Shores, MI	2,250	790	35.1	1,460	64.9	75	3.3	2,050	91.1
Myrtle Beach–North Myrtle Beach–Conway, SC	3,190	1,250	39.2	1,940	60.8	65	2.0	2,610	81.8
Napa, CA	1,485	560	37.7	925	62.3	385	25.9	835	56.2
Naples–Marco Island, FL	3,540	1,340	37.9	2,195	62.0	840	23.7	2,415	68.2
Nashville-Davidson–Murfreesboro–Franklin, TN	24,220	10,605	43.8	13,615	56.2	345	1.4	18,350	75.8
New Haven–Milford, CT	14,280	5,275	36.9	9,005	63.1	900	6.3	10,460	73.2
New Orleans–Metairie–Kenner, LA	15,345	6,215	40.5	9,125	59.5	690	4.5	9,930	64.7
New York–Northern New Jersey–Long Island, NY–NJ–PA	225,205	109,930	48.8	115,270	51.2	28,865	12.8	114,460	50.8
Niles–Benton Harbor, MI	2,230	950	42.6	1,275	57.2	35	1.6	1,875	84.1
North Port–Bradenton–Sarasota, FL	9,035	3,450	38.2	5,585	61.8	655	7.2	7,345	81.3
Norwich–New London, CT	4,590	2,095	45.6	2,495	54.4	190	4.1	4,105	89.4
Ocala, FL	3,895	1,285	33.0	2,610	67.0	275	7.1	2,960	76.0
Ocean City, NJ	975	230	23.6	745	76.4	30	3.1	850	87.2
Odessa, TX	1,490	850	57.0	640	43.0	425	28.5	985	66.1
Ogden–Clearfield, UT	7,745	4,125	53.3	3,620	46.7	715	9.2	6,640	85.7
Oklahoma City, OK	20,935	9,315	44.5	11,620	55.5	655	3.1	16,005	76.5
Olympia, WA	3,565	1,605	45.0	1,960	55.0	225	6.3	2,650	74.3
Omaha–Council Bluffs, NE–IA	14,310	6,320	44.2	7,995	55.9	280	2.0	12,655	88.4
Orlando–Kissimmee–Sanford, FL	28,345	13,450	47.5	14,895	52.5	5,250	18.5	16,415	57.9
Oshkosh–Neenah, WI	2,705	920	34.0	1,790	66.2	25	0.9	2,600	96.1
Owensboro, KY	1,105	380	34.4	725	65.6	10	0.9	1,080	97.7
Oxnard–Thousand Oaks–Ventura, CA	10,505	5,960	56.7	4,545	43.3	2,845	27.1	5,420	51.6
Palm Bay–Melbourne–Titusville, FL	9,400	4,770	50.7	4,630	49.3	670	7.1	7,170	76.3
Palm Coast, FL	1,345	440	32.7	905	67.3	130	9.7	1,075	79.9
Panama City–Lynn Haven–Panama City Beach, FL	2,800	1,175	42.0	1,625	58.0	75	2.7	2,335	83.4
Parkersburg–Marietta–Vienna, WV–OH	2,630	1,020	38.8	1,610	61.2	0	0.0	2,545	96.8
Pascagoula, MS	1,945	915	47.0	1,030	53.0	55	2.8	1,450	74.6
Pensacola–Ferry Pass–Brent, FL	7,345	3,160	43.0	4,180	56.9	185	2.5	5,845	79.6
Peoria, IL	5,905	2,275	38.5	3,630	61.5	35	0.6	5,375	91.0
Philadelphia–Camden–Wilmington, PA–NJ–DE–MD	93,035	40,305	43.3	52,730	56.7	3,265	3.5	62,960	67.7
Phoenix–Mesa–Glendale, AZ	52,810	27,095	51.3	25,715	48.7	7,585	14.4	37,955	71.9
Pine Bluff, AR	1,425	320	22.5	1,105	77.5	10	0.7	860	60.4
Pittsburgh, PA	40,515	18,370	45.3	22,145	54.7	300	0.7	36,195	89.3
Pittsfield, MA	1,905	745	39.1	1,160	60.9	45	2.4	1,820	95.5
Pocatello, ID	1,245	575	46.2	665	53.4	20	1.6	1,045	83.9
Portland–South Portland–Biddeford, ME	8,165	3,320	40.7	4,845	59.3	140	1.7	7,785	95.3
Portland–Vancouver–Hillsboro, OR–WA	30,540	16,070	52.6	14,470	47.4	1,320	4.3	25,420	83.2
Port St. Lucie, FL	5,010	2,095	41.8	2,915	58.2	390	7.8	3,825	76.3
Poughkeepsie–Newburgh–Middletown, NY	9,780	4,230	43.3	5,550	56.7	835	8.5	7,395	75.6
Prescott, AZ	2,725	1,185	43.5	1,540	56.5	110	4.0	2,555	93.8
Providence–New Bedford–Fall River, RI–MA	24,660	9,525	38.6	15,135	61.4	875	3.5	21,565	87.4

C-7 Technicians, by Metropolitan Statistical Area, Sex, Race, and Hispanic or Latino Origin, 2006–2010—*Continued*

Metropolitan Statistical Area	Black alone, not Hispanic or Latino Number	Percent	American Indian and Alaska Native alone, not Hispanic or Latino Number	Percent	Asian alone, not Hispanic or Latino Number	Percent	Native Hawaiian and Other Pacific Islander alone, not Hispanic or Latino Number	Percent	Two or more races, not Hispanic or Latino Number	Percent
Mobile, AL	1,890	33.9	15	0.3	115	2.1	0	0.0	35	0.6
Modesto, CA	345	6.1	40	0.7	585	10.4	10	0.2	105	1.9
Monroe, LA	765	24.9	10	0.3	4	0.1	0	0.0	40	1.3
Monroe, MI	0	0.0	0	0.0	20	0.9	0	0.0	40	1.7
Montgomery, AL	1,340	26.2	15	0.3	70	1.4	0	0.0	79	1.5
Morgantown, WV	15	0.6	15	0.6	45	1.7	0	0.0	4	0.2
Morristown, TN	100	5.6	0	0.0	0	0.0	0	0.0	4	0.2
Mount Vernon–Anacortes, WA	15	1.2	4	0.3	10	0.8	0	0.0	34	2.8
Muncie, IN	45	3.0	0	0.0	55	3.7	0	0.0	20	1.4
Muskegon–Norton Shores, MI	105	4.7	0	0.0	15	0.7	0	0.0	0	0.0
Myrtle Beach–North Myrtle Beach–Conway, SC	390	12.2	20	0.6	95	3.0	0	0.0	15	0.5
Napa, CA	30	2.0	15	1.0	185	12.5	0	0.0	30	2.0
Naples–Marco Island, FL	190	5.4	0	0.0	30	0.8	45	1.3	25	0.7
Nashville-Davidson–Murfreesboro–Franklin, TN	4,390	18.1	50	0.2	785	3.2	0	0.0	300	1.2
New Haven–Milford, CT	1,890	13.2	0	0.0	815	5.7	0	0.0	215	1.5
New Orleans–Metairie–Kenner, LA	3,975	25.9	25	0.2	585	3.8	0	0.0	140	0.9
New York–Northern New Jersey–Long Island, NY–NJ–PA	42,020	18.7	435	0.2	36,055	16.0	0	0.0	3,365	1.5
Niles–Benton Harbor, MI	210	9.4	10	0.4	85	3.8	0	0.0	8	0.4
North Port–Bradenton–Sarasota, FL	770	8.5	15	0.2	170	1.9	0	0.0	80	0.9
Norwich–New London, CT	135	2.9	0	0.0	55	1.2	15	0.3	90	2.0
Ocala, FL	470	12.1	15	0.4	130	3.3	15	0.4	40	1.0
Ocean City, NJ	95	9.7	4	0.4	4	0.4	0	0.0	0	0.0
Odessa, TX	65	4.4	0	0.0	4	0.3	0	0.0	4	0.3
Ogden–Clearfield, UT	55	0.7	30	0.4	230	3.0	0	0.0	75	1.0
Oklahoma City, OK	1,930	9.2	820	3.9	880	4.2	15	0.1	625	3.0
Olympia, WA	240	6.7	75	2.1	250	7.0	10	0.3	115	3.2
Omaha–Council Bluffs, NE–IA	805	5.6	0	0.0	390	2.7	0	0.0	180	1.3
Orlando–Kissimmee–Sanford, FL	4,845	17.1	75	0.3	1,225	4.3	10	0.0	520	1.8
Oshkosh–Neenah, WI	0	0.0	15	0.6	35	1.3	0	0.0	40	1.5
Owensboro, KY	15	1.4	0	0.0	0	0.0	0	0.0	0	0.0
Oxnard–Thousand Oaks–Ventura, CA	415	4.0	0	0.0	1,485	14.1	15	0.1	325	3.1
Palm Bay–Melbourne–Titusville, FL	1,010	10.7	0	0.0	320	3.4	0	0.0	230	2.4
Palm Coast, FL	110	8.2	0	0.0	25	1.9	0	0.0	14	1.0
Panama City–Lynn Haven–Panama City Beach, FL	245	8.8	40	1.4	40	1.4	0	0.0	60	2.1
Parkersburg–Marietta–Vienna, WV–OH	45	1.7	10	0.4	0	0.0	0	0.0	30	1.1
Pascagoula, MS	430	22.1	0	0.0	15	0.8	0	0.0	0	0.0
Pensacola–Ferry Pass–Brent, FL	910	12.4	40	0.5	255	3.5	0	0.0	105	1.4
Peoria, IL	215	3.6	0	0.0	170	2.9	0	0.0	115	1.9
Philadelphia–Camden–Wilmington, PA–NJ–DE–MD	18,120	19.5	185	0.2	7,330	7.9	0	0.0	1,170	1.3
Phoenix–Mesa–Glendale, AZ	2,355	4.5	865	1.6	3,215	6.1	100	0.2	740	1.4
Pine Bluff, AR	545	38.2	0	0.0	4	0.3	0	0.0	0	0.0
Pittsburgh, PA	2,465	6.1	25	0.1	1,150	2.8	0	0.0	385	1.0
Pittsfield, MA	15	0.8	0	0.0	10	0.5	0	0.0	10	0.5
Pocatello, ID	75	6.0	55	4.4	35	2.8	0	0.0	10	0.8
Portland–South Portland–Biddeford, ME	40	0.5	0	0.0	120	1.5	20	0.2	60	0.7
Portland–Vancouver–Hillsboro, OR–WA	530	1.7	195	0.6	2,330	7.6	75	0.2	675	2.2
Port St. Lucie, FL	625	12.5	10	0.2	65	1.3	0	0.0	94	1.9
Poughkeepsie–Newburgh–Middletown, NY	1,115	11.4	0	0.0	380	3.9	0	0.0	65	0.7
Prescott, AZ	0	0.0	30	1.1	0	0.0	0	0.0	35	1.3
Providence–New Bedford–Fall River, RI–MA	950	3.9	35	0.1	710	2.9	30	0.1	495	2.0

PART C—METROPOLITAN STATISTICAL AREA TABLES

C-7 **Technicians, by Metropolitan Statistical Area, Sex, Race, and Hispanic or Latino Origin, 2006–2010**—*Continued*

Metropolitan Statistical Area	Total who worked in the last 5 years	Male Number	Male Percent	Female Number	Female Percent	Hispanic or Latino Number	Hispanic or Latino Percent	White alone, not Hispanic or Latino Number	White alone, not Hispanic or Latino Percent
Provo–Orem, UT	7,130	4,490	63.0	2,640	37.0	385	5.4	6,195	86.9
Pueblo, CO	1,785	555	31.1	1,230	68.9	670	37.5	1,040	58.3
Punta Gorda, FL	2,240	720	32.1	1,520	67.9	75	3.3	1,905	85.0
Racine, WI	3,050	1,305	42.8	1,750	57.4	140	4.6	2,695	88.4
Raleigh–Cary, NC	18,890	9,190	48.7	9,695	51.3	520	2.8	13,165	69.7
Rapid City, SD	2,080	900	43.3	1,180	56.7	30	1.4	1,965	94.5
Reading, PA	6,540	2,645	40.4	3,890	59.5	240	3.7	5,945	90.9
Redding, CA	1,825	910	49.9	915	50.1	145	7.9	1,575	86.3
Reno–Sparks, NV	5,415	2,610	48.2	2,800	51.7	435	8.0	4,080	75.3
Richmond, VA	18,720	7,495	40.0	11,220	59.9	530	2.8	10,945	58.5
Riverside–San Bernardino–Ontario, CA	43,335	21,685	50.0	21,650	50.0	11,755	27.1	20,065	46.3
Roanoke, VA	4,765	1,750	36.7	3,020	63.4	25	0.5	4,160	87.3
Rochester, MN	6,370	2,740	43.0	3,630	57.0	70	1.1	5,815	91.3
Rochester, NY	17,555	7,540	43.0	10,015	57.0	605	3.4	14,680	83.6
Rockford, IL	4,720	1,800	38.1	2,920	61.9	80	1.7	4,195	88.9
Rocky Mount, NC	2,025	645	31.9	1,375	67.9	30	1.5	1,275	63.0
Rome, GA	1,470	435	29.6	1,035	70.4	30	2.0	1,220	83.0
Sacramento–Arden-Arcade–Roseville, CA	27,545	14,025	50.9	13,520	49.1	2,600	9.4	17,005	61.7
Saginaw–Saginaw Township North, MI	2,935	855	29.1	2,085	71.0	155	5.3	2,550	86.9
St. Cloud, MN	3,485	1,175	33.7	2,310	66.3	30	0.9	3,365	96.6
St. George, UT	1,520	730	48.0	790	52.0	110	7.2	1,405	92.4
St. Joseph, MO–KS	2,265	675	29.8	1,590	70.2	10	0.4	2,035	89.8
St. Louis, MO–IL	43,255	18,215	42.1	25,040	57.9	765	1.8	32,835	75.9
Salem, OR	4,230	2,110	49.9	2,120	50.1	170	4.0	3,815	90.2
Salinas, CA	3,280	1,310	39.9	1,970	60.1	1,305	39.8	1,360	41.5
Salisbury, MD	1,745	640	36.7	1,105	63.3	10	0.6	1,255	71.9
Salt Lake City, UT	16,530	9,295	56.2	7,240	43.8	1,285	7.8	14,105	85.3
San Angelo, TX	1,775	675	38.0	1,100	62.0	470	26.5	1,230	69.3
San Antonio–New Braunfels, TX	30,755	15,015	48.8	15,740	51.2	13,455	43.7	12,930	42.0
San Diego–Carlsbad–San Marcos, CA	42,650	22,565	52.9	20,090	47.1	7,460	17.5	22,330	52.4
Sandusky, OH	1,395	385	27.6	1,005	72.0	20	1.4	1,270	91.0
San Francisco–Oakland–Fremont, CA	57,995	31,360	54.1	26,640	45.9	6,435	11.1	26,510	45.7
San Jose–Sunnyvale–Santa Clara, CA	27,645	15,485	56.0	12,160	44.0	3,795	13.7	9,480	34.3
San Luis Obispo–Paso Robles, CA	3,755	1,895	50.5	1,860	49.5	445	11.9	3,030	80.7
Santa Barbara–Santa Maria–Goleta, CA	4,775	2,620	54.9	2,160	45.2	795	16.6	3,345	70.1
Santa Cruz–Watsonville, CA	3,620	1,960	54.1	1,660	45.9	575	15.9	2,840	78.5
Santa Fe, NM	1,740	880	50.6	860	49.4	730	42.0	920	52.9
Santa Rosa–Petaluma, CA	5,660	2,735	48.3	2,925	51.7	650	11.5	4,190	74.0
Savannah, GA	3,990	1,495	37.5	2,490	62.4	135	3.4	2,655	66.5
Scranton–Wilkes-Barre, PA	9,415	3,770	40.0	5,645	60.0	110	1.2	9,080	96.4
Seattle–Tacoma–Bellevue, WA	50,010	25,325	50.6	24,690	49.4	1,850	3.7	35,890	71.8
Sebastian–Vero Beach, FL	1,265	445	35.2	820	64.8	65	5.1	1,065	84.2
Sheboygan, WI	1,745	655	37.5	1,090	62.5	50	2.9	1,625	93.1
Sherman–Denison, TX	2,195	970	44.2	1,225	55.8	75	3.4	1,945	88.6
Shreveport–Bossier City, LA	5,760	2,005	34.8	3,755	65.2	185	3.2	3,595	62.4
Sioux City, IA–NE–SD	1,615	540	33.4	1,080	66.9	50	3.1	1,475	91.3
Sioux Falls, SD	4,110	1,390	33.8	2,720	66.2	20	0.5	3,985	97.0
South Bend–Mishawaka, IN–MI	4,625	1,980	42.8	2,645	57.2	100	2.2	3,715	80.3
Spartanburg, SC	4,035	1,375	34.1	2,660	65.9	70	1.7	2,940	72.9
Spokane, WA	6,170	2,885	46.8	3,285	53.2	185	3.0	5,615	91.0
Springfield, IL	4,010	1,620	40.4	2,390	59.6	20	0.5	3,585	89.4
Springfield, MA	10,515	4,015	38.2	6,495	61.8	735	7.0	8,920	84.8
Springfield, MO	6,350	2,330	36.7	4,015	63.2	175	2.8	6,015	94.7
Springfield, OH	1,835	610	33.2	1,225	66.8	25	1.4	1,670	91.0
State College, PA	2,925	1,580	54.0	1,345	46.0	40	1.4	2,680	91.6

C-7 Technicians, by Metropolitan Statistical Area, Sex, Race, and Hispanic or Latino Origin, 2006–2010—Continued

Metropolitan Statistical Area	Black alone, not Hispanic or Latino Number	Black alone, not Hispanic or Latino Percent	American Indian and Alaska Native alone, not Hispanic or Latino Number	American Indian and Alaska Native alone, not Hispanic or Latino Percent	Asian alone, not Hispanic or Latino Number	Asian alone, not Hispanic or Latino Percent	Native Hawaiian and Other Pacific Islander alone, not Hispanic or Latino Number	Native Hawaiian and Other Pacific Islander alone, not Hispanic or Latino Percent	Two or more races, not Hispanic or Latino Number	Two or more races, not Hispanic or Latino Percent
Provo–Orem, UT	75	1.1	15	0.2	215	3.0	25	0.4	220	3.1
Pueblo, CO	45	2.5	25	1.4	0	0.0	0	0.0	10	0.6
Punta Gorda, FL	170	7.6	0	0.0	20	0.9	0	0.0	70	3.1
Racine, WI	100	3.3	50	1.6	45	1.5	0	0.0	25	0.8
Raleigh–Cary, NC	3,570	18.9	45	0.2	1,300	6.9	0	0.0	290	1.5
Rapid City, SD	4	0.2	45	2.2	20	1.0	0	0.0	10	0.5
Reading, PA	190	2.9	0	0.0	120	1.8	0	0.0	39	0.6
Redding, CA	10	0.5	0	0.0	4	0.2	4	0.2	84	4.6
Reno–Sparks, NV	180	3.3	120	2.2	445	8.2	45	0.8	110	2.0
Richmond, VA	6,100	32.6	15	0.1	850	4.5	0	0.0	280	1.5
Riverside–San Bernardino–Ontario, CA	4,100	9.5	180	0.4	6,185	14.3	135	0.3	920	2.1
Roanoke, VA	500	10.5	0	0.0	80	1.7	0	0.0	4	0.1
Rochester, MN	70	1.1	0	0.0	335	5.3	0	0.0	80	1.3
Rochester, NY	1,415	8.1	90	0.5	695	4.0	0	0.0	74	0.4
Rockford, IL	230	4.9	0	0.0	195	4.1	0	0.0	25	0.5
Rocky Mount, NC	650	32.1	4	0.2	10	0.5	0	0.0	50	2.5
Rome, GA	195	13.3	10	0.7	15	1.0	0	0.0	0	0.0
Sacramento–Arden-Arcade–Roseville, CA	1,615	5.9	145	0.5	5,080	18.4	195	0.7	905	3.3
Saginaw–Saginaw Township North, MI	175	6.0	0	0.0	40	1.4	0	0.0	20	0.7
St. Cloud, MN	25	0.7	0	0.0	45	1.3	0	0.0	20	0.6
St. George, UT	0	0.0	0	0.0	0	0.0	0	0.0	4	0.3
St. Joseph, MO–KS	185	8.2	15	0.7	0	0.0	0	0.0	15	0.7
St. Louis, MO–IL	7,315	16.9	45	0.1	1,785	4.1	0	0.0	520	1.2
Salem, OR	30	0.7	30	0.7	110	2.6	0	0.0	75	1.8
Salinas, CA	55	1.7	10	0.3	460	14.0	0	0.0	90	2.7
Salisbury, MD	435	24.9	0	0.0	35	2.0	0	0.0	14	0.8
Salt Lake City, UT	90	0.5	115	0.7	685	4.1	75	0.5	175	1.1
San Angelo, TX	45	2.5	0	0.0	15	0.8	0	0.0	15	0.8
San Antonio–New Braunfels, TX	2,425	7.9	120	0.4	1,360	4.4	30	0.1	435	1.4
San Diego–Carlsbad–San Marcos, CA	2,095	4.9	95	0.2	9,190	21.5	280	0.7	1,200	2.8
Sandusky, OH	60	4.3	0	0.0	0	0.0	0	0.0	34	2.4
San Francisco–Oakland–Fremont, CA	3,330	5.7	135	0.2	18,710	32.3	550	0.9	2,330	4.0
San Jose–Sunnyvale–Santa Clara, CA	635	2.3	50	0.2	12,945	46.8	20	0.1	720	2.6
San Luis Obispo–Paso Robles, CA	60	1.6	35	0.9	165	4.4	0	0.0	25	0.7
Santa Barbara–Santa Maria–Goleta, CA	80	1.7	10	0.2	425	8.9	0	0.0	135	2.8
Santa Cruz–Watsonville, CA	25	0.7	0	0.0	145	4.0	0	0.0	40	1.1
Santa Fe, NM	0	0.0	55	3.2	20	1.1	0	0.0	15	0.9
Santa Rosa–Petaluma, CA	95	1.7	50	0.9	465	8.2	65	1.1	144	2.5
Savannah, GA	1,040	26.1	0	0.0	145	3.6	0	0.0	15	0.4
Scranton–Wilkes-Barre, PA	125	1.3	45	0.5	35	0.4	0	0.0	15	0.2
Seattle–Tacoma–Bellevue, WA	2,420	4.8	220	0.4	7,765	15.5	160	0.3	1,700	3.4
Sebastian–Vero Beach, FL	70	5.5	0	0.0	65	5.1	0	0.0	0	0.0
Sheboygan, WI	25	1.4	0	0.0	40	2.3	0	0.0	0	0.0
Sherman–Denison, TX	95	4.3	50	2.3	0	0.0	0	0.0	29	1.3
Shreveport–Bossier City, LA	1,805	31.3	35	0.6	70	1.2	4	0.1	55	1.0
Sioux City, IA–NE–SD	40	2.5	4	0.2	40	2.5	0	0.0	15	0.9
Sioux Falls, SD	35	0.9	20	0.5	30	0.7	0	0.0	14	0.3
South Bend–Mishawaka, IN–MI	525	11.4	0	0.0	170	3.7	0	0.0	120	2.6
Spartanburg, SC	830	20.6	20	0.5	135	3.3	0	0.0	35	0.9
Spokane, WA	40	0.6	40	0.6	170	2.8	55	0.9	70	1.1
Springfield, IL	260	6.5	0	0.0	90	2.2	0	0.0	60	1.5
Springfield, MA	405	3.9	4	0.0	400	3.8	0	0.0	45	0.4
Springfield, MO	80	1.3	0	0.0	45	0.7	0	0.0	30	0.5
Springfield, OH	115	6.3	0	0.0	15	0.8	0	0.0	10	0.5
State College, PA	90	3.1	0	0.0	50	1.7	0	0.0	70	2.4

PART C—METROPOLITAN STATISTICAL AREA TABLES

C-7 Technicians, by Metropolitan Statistical Area, Sex, Race, and Hispanic or Latino Origin, 2006–2010—Continued

Metropolitan Statistical Area	Total who worked in the last 5 years	Male Number	Male Percent	Female Number	Female Percent	Hispanic or Latino Number	Hispanic or Latino Percent	White alone, not Hispanic or Latino Number	White alone, not Hispanic or Latino Percent
Steubenville–Weirton, OH–WV	2,075	645	31.1	1,430	68.9	14	0.7	2,055	99.0
Stockton, CA	7,185	3,160	44.0	4,025	56.0	1,495	20.8	2,905	40.4
Sumter, SC	1,625	380	23.4	1,245	76.6	95	5.8	835	51.4
Syracuse, NY	10,150	3,505	34.5	6,645	65.5	200	2.0	8,750	86.2
Tallahassee, FL	5,560	2,825	50.8	2,735	49.2	330	5.9	3,735	67.2
Tampa–St. Petersburg–Clearwater, FL	41,580	17,725	42.6	23,855	57.4	4,995	12.0	29,205	70.2
Terre Haute, IN	2,895	1,055	36.4	1,845	63.7	65	2.2	2,700	93.3
Texarkana, TX–Texarkana, AR	2,100	565	26.9	1,535	73.1	85	4.0	1,515	72.1
Toledo, OH	8,930	3,100	34.7	5,830	65.3	255	2.9	7,685	86.1
Topeka, KS	3,325	1,450	43.6	1,870	56.2	44	1.3	3,050	91.7
Trenton–Ewing, NJ	5,530	2,705	48.9	2,825	51.1	245	4.4	3,415	61.8
Tucson, AZ	13,745	6,005	43.7	7,740	56.3	3,365	24.5	8,850	64.4
Tulsa, OK	14,165	6,640	46.9	7,525	53.1	400	2.8	10,370	73.2
Tuscaloosa, AL	3,695	1,295	35.0	2,400	65.0	65	1.8	2,515	68.1
Tyler, TX	3,480	1,600	46.0	1,885	54.2	220	6.3	2,595	74.6
Utica–Rome, NY	4,840	1,725	35.6	3,115	64.4	75	1.5	4,520	93.4
Valdosta, GA	1,840	625	34.0	1,215	66.0	14	0.8	1,330	72.3
Vallejo–Fairfield, CA	5,980	2,810	47.0	3,170	53.0	960	16.1	2,560	42.8
Victoria, TX	2,400	915	38.1	1,485	61.9	750	31.3	1,395	58.1
Vineland–Millville–Bridgeton, NJ	1,995	565	28.3	1,430	71.7	270	13.5	1,215	60.9
Virginia Beach–Norfolk–Newport News, VA–NC	25,805	10,700	41.5	15,105	58.5	935	3.6	15,035	58.3
Visalia–Porterville, CA	3,500	1,460	41.7	2,040	58.3	1,275	36.4	1,725	49.3
Waco, TX	3,505	1,160	33.1	2,345	66.9	420	12.0	2,455	70.0
Warner Robins, GA	2,375	1,000	42.1	1,375	57.9	40	1.7	1,735	73.1
Washington–Arlington–Alexandria, DC–VA–MD–WV	74,485	35,710	47.9	38,775	52.1	4,490	6.0	35,755	48.0
Waterloo–Cedar Falls, IA	2,300	785	34.1	1,515	65.9	10	0.4	2,170	94.3
Wausau, WI	2,230	850	38.1	1,380	61.9	80	3.6	2,130	95.5
Wenatchee–East Wenatchee, WA	1,130	510	45.1	615	54.4	30	2.7	1,055	93.4
Wheeling, WV–OH	2,215	755	34.1	1,465	66.1	0	0.0	2,185	98.6
Wichita, KS	8,755	3,480	39.7	5,275	60.3	545	6.2	7,030	80.3
Wichita Falls, TX	2,550	815	32.0	1,730	67.8	255	10.0	2,035	79.8
Williamsport, PA	2,120	650	30.7	1,470	69.3	40	1.9	1,995	94.1
Wilmington, NC	5,415	2,025	37.4	3,385	62.5	105	1.9	4,665	86.1
Winchester, VA–WV	1,875	740	39.5	1,135	60.5	90	4.8	1,645	87.7
Winston–Salem, NC	7,030	2,430	34.6	4,600	65.4	280	4.0	5,180	73.7
Worcester, MA	12,670	5,390	42.5	7,280	57.5	1,010	8.0	10,365	81.8
Yakima, WA	2,295	845	36.8	1,450	63.2	520	22.7	1,540	67.1
York–Hanover, PA	7,165	2,910	40.6	4,250	59.3	130	1.8	6,545	91.3
Youngstown–Warren–Boardman, OH–PA	8,685	2,870	33.0	5,815	67.0	110	1.3	7,845	90.3
Yuba City, CA	2,090	835	40.0	1,255	60.0	330	15.8	1,390	66.5
Yuma, AZ	1,815	850	46.8	960	52.9	765	42.1	755	41.6

C-7 Technicians, by Metropolitan Statistical Area, Sex, Race, and Hispanic or Latino Origin, 2006–2010—Continued

Metropolitan Statistical Area	Black alone, not Hispanic or Latino Number	Percent	American Indian and Alaska Native alone, not Hispanic or Latino Number	Percent	Asian alone, not Hispanic or Latino Number	Percent	Native Hawaiian and Other Pacific Islander alone, not Hispanic or Latino Number	Percent	Two or more races, not Hispanic or Latino Number	Percent
Steubenville–Weirton, OH–WV	4	0.2	0	0.0	0	0.0	0	0.0	0	0.0
Stockton, CA	430	6.0	40	0.6	2,145	29.9	45	0.6	135	1.9
Sumter, SC	630	38.8	0	0.0	30	1.8	0	0.0	35	2.2
Syracuse, NY	725	7.1	80	0.8	275	2.7	0	0.0	120	1.2
Tallahassee, FL	1,095	19.7	15	0.3	365	6.6	0	0.0	20	0.4
Tampa–St. Petersburg–Clearwater, FL	4,805	11.6	85	0.2	2,020	4.9	0	0.0	470	1.1
Terre Haute, IN	105	3.6	0	0.0	30	1.0	0	0.0	0	0.0
Texarkana, TX–Texarkana, AR	405	19.3	0	0.0	15	0.7	0	0.0	80	3.8
Toledo, OH	770	8.6	15	0.2	180	2.0	0	0.0	24	0.3
Topeka, KS	115	3.5	35	1.1	70	2.1	0	0.0	10	0.3
Trenton–Ewing, NJ	975	17.6	0	0.0	815	14.7	0	0.0	80	1.4
Tucson, AZ	500	3.6	115	0.8	635	4.6	0	0.0	275	2.0
Tulsa, OK	1,150	8.1	955	6.7	200	1.4	4	0.0	1,090	7.7
Tuscaloosa, AL	1,045	28.3	15	0.4	20	0.5	0	0.0	29	0.8
Tyler, TX	615	17.7	0	0.0	55	1.6	0	0.0	0	0.0
Utica–Rome, NY	165	3.4	10	0.2	65	1.3	0	0.0	4	0.1
Valdosta, GA	475	25.8	0	0.0	10	0.5	0	0.0	10	0.5
Vallejo–Fairfield, CA	480	8.0	0	0.0	1,620	27.1	65	1.1	294	4.9
Victoria, TX	185	7.7	0	0.0	40	1.7	0	0.0	35	1.5
Vineland–Millville–Bridgeton, NJ	270	13.5	60	3.0	120	6.0	0	0.0	65	3.3
Virginia Beach–Norfolk–Newport News, VA–NC	7,435	28.8	165	0.6	1,560	6.0	55	0.2	615	2.4
Visalia–Porterville, CA	35	1.0	60	1.7	335	9.6	0	0.0	70	2.0
Waco, TX	580	16.5	0	0.0	25	0.7	0	0.0	30	0.9
Warner Robins, GA	515	21.7	0	0.0	40	1.7	0	0.0	45	1.9
Washington–Arlington–Alexandria, DC–VA–MD–WV	22,410	30.1	140	0.2	10,310	13.8	85	0.1	1,295	1.7
Waterloo–Cedar Falls, IA	75	3.3	0	0.0	45	2.0	0	0.0	0	0.0
Wausau, WI	0	0.0	0	0.0	10	0.4	0	0.0	15	0.7
Wenatchee–East Wenatchee, WA	0	0.0	15	1.3	20	1.8	0	0.0	10	0.9
Wheeling, WV–OH	20	0.9	0	0.0	0	0.0	0	0.0	8	0.4
Wichita, KS	530	6.1	60	0.7	455	5.2	0	0.0	135	1.5
Wichita Falls, TX	80	3.1	0	0.0	45	1.8	60	2.4	80	3.1
Williamsport, PA	35	1.7	15	0.7	30	1.4	0	0.0	10	0.5
Wilmington, NC	585	10.8	0	0.0	0	0.0	0	0.0	60	1.1
Winchester, VA–WV	100	5.3	0	0.0	40	2.1	0	0.0	0	0.0
Winston–Salem, NC	1,330	18.9	10	0.1	220	3.1	0	0.0	10	0.1
Worcester, MA	590	4.7	25	0.2	585	4.6	0	0.0	95	0.7
Yakima, WA	10	0.4	95	4.1	20	0.9	0	0.0	110	4.8
York–Hanover, PA	355	5.0	30	0.4	85	1.2	0	0.0	20	0.3
Youngstown–Warren–Boardman, OH–PA	625	7.2	15	0.2	10	0.1	0	0.0	75	0.9
Yuba City, CA	110	5.3	15	0.7	125	6.0	0	0.0	120	5.7
Yuma, AZ	115	6.3	55	3.0	85	4.7	15	0.8	19	1.0

PART C—METROPOLITAN STATISTICAL AREA TABLES

C-8 Sales Workers, by Metropolitan Statistical Area, Sex, Race, and Hispanic or Latino Origin, 2006–2010

Metropolitan Statistical Area	Total who worked in the last 5 years	Male Number	Male Percent	Female Number	Female Percent	Hispanic or Latino Number	Hispanic or Latino Percent	White alone, not Hispanic or Latino Number	White alone, not Hispanic or Latino Percent
Abilene, TX	8,710	3,935	45.2	4,780	54.9	1,665	19.1	5,935	68.1
Akron, OH	41,340	19,285	46.6	22,050	53.3	415	1.0	36,160	87.5
Albany, GA	8,345	3,245	38.9	5,105	61.2	160	1.9	4,405	52.8
Albany–Schenectady–Troy, NY	48,930	25,310	51.7	23,620	48.3	1,440	2.9	42,735	87.3
Albuquerque, NM	47,905	23,415	48.9	24,485	51.1	19,285	40.3	24,105	50.3
Alexandria, LA	7,410	3,115	42.0	4,295	58.0	165	2.2	4,995	67.4
Allentown–Bethlehem–Easton, PA–NJ	45,170	22,980	50.9	22,190	49.1	3,505	7.8	38,545	85.3
Altoona, PA	7,220	2,970	41.1	4,255	58.9	45	0.6	7,005	97.0
Amarillo, TX	14,915	7,650	51.3	7,265	48.7	3,070	20.6	10,655	71.4
Ames, IA	4,810	2,460	51.1	2,350	48.9	90	1.9	4,465	92.8
Anchorage, AK	18,400	8,750	47.6	9,650	52.4	1,095	6.0	13,025	70.8
Anderson, IN	6,325	2,875	45.5	3,450	54.5	130	2.1	5,815	91.9
Anderson, SC	10,535	4,850	46.0	5,685	54.0	115	1.1	8,500	80.7
Ann Arbor, MI	16,865	8,530	50.6	8,335	49.4	495	2.9	12,970	76.9
Anniston–Oxford, AL	6,190	2,530	40.9	3,660	59.1	59	1.0	4,715	76.2
Appleton, WI	13,795	6,675	48.4	7,120	51.6	135	1.0	13,105	95.0
Asheville, NC	23,490	10,880	46.3	12,610	53.7	685	2.9	21,480	91.4
Athens–Clarke County, GA	10,335	4,725	45.7	5,610	54.3	370	3.6	7,295	70.6
Atlanta–Sandy Springs–Marietta, GA	348,420	176,300	50.6	172,120	49.4	18,065	5.2	204,580	58.7
Atlantic City–Hammonton, NJ	16,705	7,630	45.7	9,075	54.3	2,170	13.0	10,645	63.7
Auburn–Opelika, AL	7,160	3,225	45.0	3,940	55.0	75	1.0	5,475	76.5
Augusta–Richmond County, GA–SC	28,105	11,975	42.6	16,130	57.4	700	2.5	17,150	61.0
Austin–Round Rock–San Marcos, TX	104,020	55,430	53.3	48,590	46.7	24,355	23.4	68,185	65.5
Bakersfield–Delano, CA	35,250	16,095	45.7	19,155	54.3	13,900	39.4	17,260	49.0
Baltimore–Towson, MD	153,740	76,940	50.0	76,795	50.0	5,140	3.3	103,720	67.5
Bangor, ME	9,135	4,520	49.5	4,615	50.5	15	0.2	8,740	95.7
Barnstable Town, MA	13,675	7,015	51.3	6,660	48.7	135	1.0	12,935	94.6
Baton Rouge, LA	46,150	19,945	43.2	26,200	56.8	1,110	2.4	29,120	63.1
Battle Creek, MI	6,710	3,045	45.4	3,665	54.6	190	2.8	5,625	83.8
Bay City, MI	5,940	2,610	43.9	3,330	56.1	245	4.1	5,620	94.6
Beaumont–Port Arthur, TX	17,865	7,740	43.3	10,130	56.7	1,320	7.4	11,640	65.2
Bellingham, WA	11,890	6,080	51.1	5,810	48.9	530	4.5	10,355	87.1
Bend, OR	10,175	5,255	51.6	4,920	48.4	385	3.8	9,390	92.3
Billings, MT	10,190	5,005	49.1	5,185	50.9	475	4.7	9,270	91.0
Binghamton, NY	14,140	7,335	51.9	6,805	48.1	270	1.9	12,985	91.8
Birmingham–Hoover, AL	70,570	34,775	49.3	35,800	50.7	1,010	1.4	51,670	73.2
Bismarck, ND	6,865	3,625	52.8	3,235	47.1	70	1.0	6,445	93.9
Blacksburg–Christiansburg–Radford, VA	7,860	3,085	39.2	4,775	60.8	205	2.6	7,040	89.6
Bloomington, IN	8,410	4,020	47.8	4,390	52.2	100	1.2	7,845	93.3
Bloomington–Normal, IL	12,250	6,245	51.0	6,000	49.0	455	3.7	10,665	87.1
Boise City–Nampa, ID	33,400	17,750	53.1	15,650	46.9	2,210	6.6	29,820	89.3
Boston–Cambridge–Quincy, MA–NH	269,385	139,880	51.9	129,505	48.1	19,095	7.1	219,220	81.4
Boulder, CO	18,840	10,355	55.0	8,485	45.0	1,670	8.9	16,390	87.0
Bowling Green, KY	7,525	3,525	46.8	4,000	53.2	130	1.7	6,450	85.7
Bremerton–Silverdale, WA	11,525	5,100	44.3	6,425	55.7	595	5.2	9,300	80.7
Bridgeport–Stamford–Norwalk, CT	60,250	33,035	54.8	27,215	45.2	7,945	13.2	43,035	71.4
Brownsville–Harlingen, TX	17,620	8,705	49.4	8,915	50.6	15,345	87.1	1,985	11.3
Brunswick, GA	5,980	2,590	43.3	3,390	56.7	160	2.7	4,070	68.1
Buffalo–Niagara Falls, NY	65,010	31,925	49.1	33,085	50.9	1,650	2.5	56,905	87.5
Burlington, NC	8,465	3,895	46.0	4,575	54.0	375	4.4	6,460	76.3
Burlington–South Burlington, VT	12,785	6,690	52.3	6,095	47.7	110	0.9	12,060	94.3
Canton–Massillon, OH	21,950	10,375	47.3	11,575	52.7	270	1.2	20,150	91.8
Cape Coral–Fort Myers, FL	41,440	20,565	49.6	20,880	50.4	5,465	13.2	32,160	77.6
Cape Girardeau–Jackson, MO–IL	5,325	2,790	52.4	2,535	47.6	105	2.0	4,705	88.4
Carson City, NV	3,085	1,465	47.5	1,620	52.5	695	22.5	2,290	74.2

C-8 Sales Workers, by Metropolitan Statistical Area, Sex, Race, and Hispanic or Latino Origin, 2006–2010—*Continued*

Metropolitan Statistical Area	Black alone, not Hispanic or Latino Number	Percent	American Indian and Alaska Native alone, not Hispanic or Latino Number	Percent	Asian alone, not Hispanic or Latino Number	Percent	Native Hawaiian and Other Pacific Islander alone, not Hispanic or Latino Number	Percent	Two or more races, not Hispanic or Latino Number	Percent
Abilene, TX	650	7.5	30	0.3	140	1.6	4	0.0	285	3.3
Akron, OH	3,700	9.0	10	0.0	505	1.2	0	0.0	550	1.3
Albany, GA	3,490	41.8	30	0.4	235	2.8	0	0.0	25	0.3
Albany–Schenectady–Troy, NY	2,385	4.9	100	0.2	1,200	2.5	25	0.1	1,045	2.1
Albuquerque, NM	810	1.7	1,925	4.0	800	1.7	105	0.2	880	1.8
Alexandria, LA	2,045	27.6	35	0.5	100	1.3	0	0.0	65	0.9
Allentown–Bethlehem–Easton, PA–NJ	1,545	3.4	10	0.0	1,060	2.3	0	0.0	505	1.1
Altoona, PA	90	1.2	0	0.0	40	0.6	0	0.0	40	0.6
Amarillo, TX	535	3.6	75	0.5	470	3.2	15	0.1	95	0.6
Ames, IA	80	1.7	15	0.3	125	2.6	0	0.0	24	0.5
Anchorage, AK	840	4.6	620	3.4	1,620	8.8	240	1.3	965	5.2
Anderson, IN	260	4.1	10	0.2	15	0.2	0	0.0	100	1.6
Anderson, SC	1,630	15.5	10	0.1	135	1.3	0	0.0	145	1.4
Ann Arbor, MI	2,070	12.3	35	0.2	765	4.5	10	0.1	520	3.1
Anniston–Oxford, AL	1,315	21.2	10	0.2	90	1.5	0	0.0	0	0.0
Appleton, WI	70	0.5	140	1.0	220	1.6	0	0.0	130	0.9
Asheville, NC	880	3.7	95	0.4	150	0.6	4	0.0	200	0.9
Athens–Clarke County, GA	2,075	20.1	10	0.1	265	2.6	0	0.0	325	3.1
Atlanta–Sandy Springs–Marietta, GA	103,080	29.6	775	0.2	17,425	5.0	70	0.0	4,430	1.3
Atlantic City–Hammonton, NJ	2,030	12.2	40	0.2	1,460	8.7	0	0.0	355	2.1
Auburn–Opelika, AL	1,400	19.6	4	0.1	75	1.0	0	0.0	129	1.8
Augusta–Richmond County, GA–SC	9,125	32.5	65	0.2	580	2.1	60	0.2	425	1.5
Austin–Round Rock–San Marcos, TX	6,145	5.9	120	0.1	3,655	3.5	40	0.0	1,520	1.5
Bakersfield–Delano, CA	1,600	4.5	100	0.3	1,545	4.4	15	0.0	825	2.3
Baltimore–Towson, MD	35,270	22.9	265	0.2	6,575	4.3	60	0.0	2,710	1.8
Bangor, ME	110	1.2	115	1.3	45	0.5	0	0.0	105	1.1
Barnstable Town, MA	70	0.5	45	0.3	290	2.1	0	0.0	195	1.4
Baton Rouge, LA	14,585	31.6	140	0.3	1,015	2.2	0	0.0	185	0.4
Battle Creek, MI	620	9.2	40	0.6	95	1.4	0	0.0	135	2.0
Bay City, MI	20	0.3	4	0.1	45	0.8	0	0.0	10	0.2
Beaumont–Port Arthur, TX	3,970	22.2	120	0.7	630	3.5	4	0.0	185	1.0
Bellingham, WA	35	0.3	225	1.9	410	3.4	65	0.5	265	2.2
Bend, OR	45	0.4	110	1.1	130	1.3	15	0.1	98	1.0
Billings, MT	75	0.7	215	2.1	80	0.8	30	0.3	45	0.4
Binghamton, NY	490	3.5	70	0.5	200	1.4	0	0.0	135	1.0
Birmingham–Hoover, AL	16,140	22.9	165	0.2	1,120	1.6	20	0.0	440	0.6
Bismarck, ND	0	0.0	320	4.7	4	0.1	0	0.0	20	0.3
Blacksburg–Christiansburg–Radford, VA	365	4.6	15	0.2	165	2.1	0	0.0	69	0.9
Bloomington, IN	150	1.8	30	0.4	140	1.7	0	0.0	140	1.7
Bloomington–Normal, IL	800	6.5	15	0.1	195	1.6	0	0.0	110	0.9
Boise City–Nampa, ID	270	0.8	180	0.5	385	1.2	25	0.1	515	1.5
Boston–Cambridge–Quincy, MA–NH	14,580	5.4	415	0.2	12,120	4.5	35	0.0	3,910	1.5
Boulder, CO	45	0.2	45	0.2	460	2.4	0	0.0	235	1.2
Bowling Green, KY	770	10.2	10	0.1	80	1.1	0	0.0	89	1.2
Bremerton–Silverdale, WA	320	2.8	110	1.0	675	5.9	40	0.3	490	4.3
Bridgeport–Stamford–Norwalk, CT	5,915	9.8	115	0.2	2,385	4.0	10	0.0	850	1.4
Brownsville–Harlingen, TX	70	0.4	10	0.1	75	0.4	0	0.0	139	0.8
Brunswick, GA	1,380	23.1	0	0.0	235	3.9	0	0.0	135	2.3
Buffalo–Niagara Falls, NY	4,540	7.0	375	0.6	975	1.5	10	0.0	555	0.9
Burlington, NC	1,490	17.6	0	0.0	115	1.4	0	0.0	30	0.4
Burlington–South Burlington, VT	145	1.1	65	0.5	245	1.9	0	0.0	155	1.2
Canton–Massillon, OH	1,040	4.7	55	0.3	140	0.6	0	0.0	295	1.3
Cape Coral–Fort Myers, FL	2,815	6.8	45	0.1	565	1.4	0	0.0	395	1.0
Cape Girardeau–Jackson, MO–IL	355	6.7	0	0.0	95	1.8	20	0.4	50	0.9
Carson City, NV	15	0.5	4	0.1	45	1.5	0	0.0	35	1.1

C-8 Sales Workers, by Metropolitan Statistical Area, Sex, Race, and Hispanic or Latino Origin, 2006–2010—Continued

Metropolitan Statistical Area	Total who worked in the last 5 years	Male Number	Male Percent	Female Number	Female Percent	Hispanic or Latino Number	Hispanic or Latino Percent	White alone, not Hispanic or Latino Number	White alone, not Hispanic or Latino Percent
Casper, WY	4,585	2,495	54.4	2,090	45.6	245	5.3	4,220	92.0
Cedar Rapids, IA	15,010	8,010	53.4	7,000	46.6	215	1.4	14,085	93.8
Champaign–Urbana, IL	12,100	5,760	47.6	6,340	52.4	425	3.5	9,865	81.5
Charleston, WV	15,505	7,520	48.5	7,985	51.5	150	1.0	14,265	92.0
Charleston–North Charleston–Summerville, SC	40,740	19,060	46.8	21,675	53.2	690	1.7	29,705	72.9
Charlotte–Gastonia–Rock Hill, NC–SC	118,050	60,410	51.2	57,645	48.8	5,520	4.7	86,615	73.4
Charlottesville, VA	10,105	4,920	48.7	5,185	51.3	180	1.8	8,270	81.8
Chattanooga, TN–GA	29,550	14,280	48.3	15,275	51.7	295	1.0	25,100	84.9
Cheyenne, WY	4,495	2,005	44.6	2,490	55.4	330	7.3	3,910	87.0
Chicago–Joliet–Naperville, IL–IN–WI	573,035	292,795	51.1	280,240	48.9	81,865	14.3	375,850	65.6
Chico, CA	11,035	5,670	51.4	5,370	48.7	1,140	10.3	8,795	79.7
Cincinnati–Middletown, OH–KY–IN	123,345	62,680	50.8	60,665	49.2	1,550	1.3	107,065	86.8
Clarksville, TN–KY	11,910	4,720	39.6	7,190	60.4	775	6.5	8,705	73.1
Cleveland, TN	5,445	2,380	43.7	3,065	56.3	90	1.7	5,075	93.2
Cleveland–Elyria–Mentor, OH	119,215	58,420	49.0	60,800	51.0	3,970	3.3	95,265	79.9
Coeur d'Alene, ID	7,830	3,625	46.3	4,205	53.7	285	3.6	7,325	93.6
College Station–Bryan, TX	10,455	4,965	47.5	5,490	52.5	1,695	16.2	7,150	68.4
Colorado Springs, CO	33,490	16,155	48.2	17,335	51.8	4,185	12.5	25,985	77.6
Columbia, MO	10,475	5,140	49.1	5,335	50.9	220	2.1	8,780	83.8
Columbia, SC	43,905	20,820	47.4	23,080	52.6	870	2.0	29,695	67.6
Columbus, GA–AL	14,245	5,520	38.8	8,730	61.3	535	3.8	8,065	56.6
Columbus, IN	3,815	1,720	45.1	2,095	54.9	70	1.8	3,570	93.6
Columbus, OH	104,050	53,905	51.8	50,145	48.2	1,995	1.9	86,915	83.5
Corpus Christi, TX	22,445	9,975	44.4	12,475	55.6	11,825	52.7	9,560	42.6
Corvallis, OR	3,755	1,780	47.4	1,975	52.6	195	5.2	3,265	87.0
Crestview–Fort Walton Beach–Destin, FL	10,655	4,685	44.0	5,965	56.0	675	6.3	8,720	81.8
Cumberland, MD–WV	5,085	2,165	42.6	2,915	57.3	35	0.7	4,755	93.5
Dallas–Fort Worth–Arlington, TX	390,655	204,500	52.3	186,155	47.7	68,115	17.4	248,250	63.5
Dalton, GA	6,815	3,435	50.4	3,385	49.7	900	13.2	5,675	83.3
Danville, IL	3,890	1,730	44.5	2,160	55.5	85	2.2	3,250	83.5
Danville, VA	4,675	1,765	37.8	2,910	62.2	55	1.2	3,380	72.3
Davenport–Moline–Rock Island, IA–IL	21,665	10,115	46.7	11,550	53.3	1,120	5.2	19,115	88.2
Dayton, OH	45,490	20,805	45.7	24,685	54.3	780	1.7	38,385	84.4
Decatur, AL	8,175	3,535	43.2	4,640	56.8	185	2.3	6,765	82.8
Decatur, IL	5,195	2,210	42.5	2,985	57.5	85	1.6	4,480	86.2
Deltona–Daytona Beach–Ormond Beach, FL	31,930	15,340	48.0	16,590	52.0	3,165	9.9	25,230	79.0
Denver–Aurora–Broomfield, CO	166,080	87,720	52.8	78,360	47.2	22,815	13.7	126,580	76.2
Des Moines–West Des Moines, IA	36,935	20,085	54.4	16,845	45.6	1,225	3.3	33,500	90.7
Detroit–Warren–Livonia, MI	243,580	119,330	49.0	124,250	51.0	6,110	2.5	185,890	76.3
Dothan, AL	8,820	4,115	46.7	4,705	53.3	130	1.5	6,840	77.6
Dover, DE	7,645	3,275	42.8	4,370	57.2	280	3.7	5,840	76.4
Dubuque, IA	5,435	2,440	44.9	2,995	55.1	25	0.5	5,200	95.7
Duluth, MN–WI	15,220	7,765	51.0	7,455	49.0	155	1.0	14,220	93.4
Durham–Chapel Hill, NC	23,065	10,675	46.3	12,385	53.7	1,535	6.7	13,890	60.2
Eau Claire, WI	10,425	5,585	53.6	4,840	46.4	170	1.6	9,915	95.1
El Centro, CA	8,095	4,005	49.5	4,090	50.5	6,635	82.0	1,135	14.0
Elizabethtown, KY	5,005	2,040	40.8	2,970	59.3	105	2.1	4,195	83.8
Elkhart–Goshen, IN	9,635	4,830	50.1	4,805	49.9	620	6.4	8,340	86.6
Elmira, NY	4,605	2,055	44.6	2,555	55.5	80	1.7	4,265	92.6
El Paso, TX	40,635	19,235	47.3	21,395	52.7	33,310	82.0	5,685	14.0
Erie, PA	14,740	6,710	45.5	8,025	54.4	230	1.6	13,490	91.5
Eugene–Springfield, OR	20,010	10,495	52.4	9,510	47.5	925	4.6	18,010	90.0
Evansville, IN–KY	20,700	10,050	48.6	10,650	51.4	285	1.4	18,810	90.9
Fairbanks, AK	4,250	1,485	34.9	2,765	65.1	210	4.9	3,235	76.1
Fargo, ND–MN	14,535	7,885	54.2	6,650	45.8	260	1.8	13,745	94.6

C-8 Sales Workers, by Metropolitan Statistical Area, Sex, Race, and Hispanic or Latino Origin, 2006–2010—*Continued*

Metropolitan Statistical Area	Black alone, not Hispanic or Latino Number	Percent	American Indian and Alaska Native alone, not Hispanic or Latino Number	Percent	Asian alone, not Hispanic or Latino Number	Percent	Native Hawaiian and Other Pacific Islander alone, not Hispanic or Latino Number	Percent	Two or more races, not Hispanic or Latino Number	Percent
Casper, WY	35	0.8	0	0.0	70	1.5	0	0.0	15	0.3
Cedar Rapids, IA	320	2.1	60	0.4	140	0.9	15	0.1	180	1.2
Champaign–Urbana, IL	1,330	11.0	25	0.2	335	2.8	0	0.0	114	0.9
Charleston, WV	790	5.1	25	0.2	75	0.5	0	0.0	190	1.2
Charleston–North Charleston–Summerville, SC	9,110	22.4	165	0.4	535	1.3	20	0.0	520	1.3
Charlotte–Gastonia–Rock Hill, NC–SC	21,230	18.0	290	0.2	2,915	2.5	4	0.0	1,470	1.2
Charlottesville, VA	1,275	12.6	10	0.1	225	2.2	0	0.0	145	1.4
Chattanooga, TN–GA	3,365	11.4	40	0.1	485	1.6	0	0.0	275	0.9
Cheyenne, WY	100	2.2	50	1.1	85	1.9	0	0.0	20	0.4
Chicago–Joliet–Naperville, IL–IN–WI	77,590	13.5	540	0.1	30,690	5.4	105	0.0	6,395	1.1
Chico, CA	145	1.3	80	0.7	535	4.8	30	0.3	315	2.9
Cincinnati–Middletown, OH–KY–IN	11,580	9.4	140	0.1	1,555	1.3	40	0.0	1,420	1.2
Clarksville, TN–KY	1,880	15.8	35	0.3	325	2.7	0	0.0	190	1.6
Cleveland, TN	150	2.8	60	1.1	30	0.6	15	0.3	30	0.6
Cleveland–Elyria–Mentor, OH	16,950	14.2	140	0.1	1,760	1.5	0	0.0	1,125	0.9
Coeur d'Alene, ID	0	0.0	55	0.7	20	0.3	0	0.0	145	1.9
College Station–Bryan, TX	965	9.2	45	0.4	560	5.4	0	0.0	50	0.5
Colorado Springs, CO	1,485	4.4	135	0.4	725	2.2	60	0.2	920	2.7
Columbia, MO	1,015	9.7	40	0.4	170	1.6	20	0.2	235	2.2
Columbia, SC	12,125	27.6	75	0.2	705	1.6	0	0.0	440	1.0
Columbus, GA–AL	4,960	34.8	55	0.4	365	2.6	20	0.1	245	1.7
Columbus, IN	50	1.3	0	0.0	65	1.7	0	0.0	55	1.4
Columbus, OH	11,090	10.7	155	0.1	2,285	2.2	0	0.0	1,610	1.5
Corpus Christi, TX	290	1.3	10	0.0	460	2.0	0	0.0	299	1.3
Corvallis, OR	10	0.3	45	1.2	170	4.5	40	1.1	30	0.8
Crestview–Fort Walton Beach–Destin, FL	695	6.5	90	0.8	230	2.2	0	0.0	239	2.2
Cumberland, MD–WV	235	4.6	25	0.5	4	0.1	0	0.0	34	0.7
Dallas–Fort Worth–Arlington, TX	48,265	12.4	1,300	0.3	18,765	4.8	405	0.1	5,555	1.4
Dalton, GA	135	2.0	10	0.1	35	0.5	0	0.0	60	0.9
Danville, IL	495	12.7	0	0.0	4	0.1	0	0.0	54	1.4
Danville, VA	1,220	26.1	0	0.0	10	0.2	0	0.0	4	0.1
Davenport–Moline–Rock Island, IA–IL	975	4.5	40	0.2	235	1.1	4	0.0	175	0.8
Dayton, OH	5,170	11.4	40	0.1	520	1.1	0	0.0	600	1.3
Decatur, AL	880	10.8	125	1.5	95	1.2	0	0.0	119	1.5
Decatur, IL	510	9.8	0	0.0	30	0.6	0	0.0	94	1.8
Deltona–Daytona Beach–Ormond Beach, FL	2,395	7.5	40	0.1	675	2.1	0	0.0	425	1.3
Denver–Aurora–Broomfield, CO	7,790	4.7	875	0.5	5,100	3.1	80	0.0	2,845	1.7
Des Moines–West Des Moines, IA	1,125	3.0	70	0.2	615	1.7	20	0.1	375	1.0
Detroit–Warren–Livonia, MI	42,350	17.4	585	0.2	5,570	2.3	55	0.0	3,015	1.2
Dothan, AL	1,610	18.3	20	0.2	140	1.6	0	0.0	79	0.9
Dover, DE	1,190	15.6	25	0.3	155	2.0	0	0.0	160	2.1
Dubuque, IA	60	1.1	0	0.0	35	0.6	0	0.0	110	2.0
Duluth, MN–WI	200	1.3	250	1.6	225	1.5	4	0.0	175	1.1
Durham–Chapel Hill, NC	6,535	28.3	110	0.5	450	2.0	10	0.0	535	2.3
Eau Claire, WI	20	0.2	30	0.3	205	2.0	40	0.4	49	0.5
El Centro, CA	115	1.4	20	0.2	175	2.2	0	0.0	20	0.2
Elizabethtown, KY	335	6.7	35	0.7	100	2.0	10	0.2	225	4.5
Elkhart–Goshen, IN	370	3.8	15	0.2	80	0.8	0	0.0	205	2.1
Elmira, NY	130	2.8	10	0.2	20	0.4	0	0.0	110	2.4
El Paso, TX	875	2.2	30	0.1	455	1.1	40	0.1	235	0.6
Erie, PA	660	4.5	15	0.1	115	0.8	0	0.0	230	1.6
Eugene–Springfield, OR	195	1.0	110	0.5	400	2.0	10	0.0	355	1.8
Evansville, IN–KY	1,045	5.0	4	0.0	210	1.0	0	0.0	345	1.7
Fairbanks, AK	185	4.4	230	5.4	170	4.0	45	1.1	175	4.1
Fargo, ND–MN	175	1.2	135	0.9	145	1.0	0	0.0	75	0.5

PART C—METROPOLITAN STATISTICAL AREA TABLES

C-8 Sales Workers, by Metropolitan Statistical Area, Sex, Race, and Hispanic or Latino Origin, 2006–2010—Continued

Metropolitan Statistical Area	Total who worked in the last 5 years	Male Number	Male Percent	Female Number	Female Percent	Hispanic or Latino Number	Hispanic or Latino Percent	White alone, not Hispanic or Latino Number	White alone, not Hispanic or Latino Percent
Farmington, NM	5,405	2,265	41.9	3,140	58.1	605	11.2	2,990	55.3
Fayetteville, NC	17,695	6,770	38.3	10,925	61.7	1,400	7.9	9,030	51.0
Fayetteville–Springdale–Rogers, AR–MO	27,420	14,590	53.2	12,830	46.8	1,955	7.1	23,510	85.7
Flagstaff, AZ	7,335	3,650	49.8	3,685	50.2	795	10.8	4,920	67.1
Flint, MI	23,115	10,055	43.5	13,060	56.5	655	2.8	18,440	79.8
Florence, SC	10,990	4,885	44.4	6,100	55.5	49	0.4	6,715	61.1
Florence–Muscle Shoals, AL	8,965	4,055	45.2	4,910	54.8	90	1.0	7,855	87.6
Fond du Lac, WI	5,455	2,555	46.8	2,900	53.2	280	5.1	5,095	93.4
Fort Collins–Loveland, CO	17,790	9,575	53.8	8,215	46.2	1,140	6.4	16,090	90.4
Fort Smith, AR–OK	14,885	7,335	49.3	7,555	50.8	590	4.0	12,695	85.3
Fort Wayne, IN	23,845	12,040	50.5	11,810	49.5	710	3.0	21,070	88.4
Fresno, CA	45,465	24,160	53.1	21,305	46.9	16,880	37.1	21,175	46.6
Gadsden, AL	4,525	2,020	44.6	2,505	55.4	65	1.4	3,885	85.9
Gainesville, FL	14,595	6,975	47.8	7,620	52.2	1,370	9.4	9,725	66.6
Gainesville, GA	9,950	5,065	50.9	4,885	49.1	890	8.9	8,070	81.1
Glens Falls, NY	7,355	3,380	46.0	3,975	54.0	69	0.9	7,180	97.6
Goldsboro, NC	6,415	2,665	41.5	3,755	58.5	200	3.1	4,315	67.3
Grand Forks, ND–MN	6,155	3,000	48.7	3,155	51.3	105	1.7	5,690	92.4
Grand Junction, CO	8,565	4,545	53.1	4,020	46.9	875	10.2	7,605	88.8
Grand Rapids–Wyoming, MI	44,320	22,305	50.3	22,010	49.7	1,510	3.4	39,075	88.2
Great Falls, MT	4,350	2,305	53.0	2,045	47.0	75	1.7	4,110	94.5
Greeley, CO	13,765	7,015	51.0	6,750	49.0	2,685	19.5	10,700	77.7
Green Bay, WI	17,435	9,130	52.4	8,305	47.6	520	3.0	15,940	91.4
Greensboro–High Point, NC	43,720	21,530	49.2	22,190	50.8	1,180	2.7	31,170	71.3
Greenville, NC	10,745	4,680	43.6	6,065	56.4	355	3.3	7,115	66.2
Greenville–Mauldin–Easley, SC	37,800	18,005	47.6	19,795	52.4	1,235	3.3	29,945	79.2
Gulfport–Biloxi, MS	12,625	5,415	42.9	7,215	57.1	220	1.7	9,675	76.6
Hagerstown–Martinsburg, MD–WV	14,760	6,975	47.3	7,785	52.7	270	1.8	12,670	85.8
Hanford–Corcoran, CA	5,235	2,410	46.0	2,820	53.9	2,145	41.0	2,390	45.7
Harrisburg–Carlisle, PA	29,490	14,985	50.8	14,505	49.2	845	2.9	25,330	85.9
Harrisonburg, VA	6,710	3,130	46.6	3,580	53.4	135	2.0	5,990	89.3
Hartford–West Hartford–East Hartford, CT	72,520	37,070	51.1	35,450	48.9	6,645	9.2	55,910	77.1
Hattiesburg, MS	8,745	3,670	42.0	5,075	58.0	35	0.4	6,395	73.1
Hickory–Lenoir–Morganton, NC	17,560	8,730	49.7	8,830	50.3	460	2.6	15,975	91.0
Hinesville–Fort Stewart, GA	3,485	920	26.4	2,570	73.7	325	9.3	1,875	53.8
Holland–Grand Haven, MI	14,925	8,065	54.0	6,860	46.0	570	3.8	13,640	91.4
Honolulu, HI	52,395	22,650	43.2	29,745	56.8	3,220	6.1	9,995	19.1
Hot Springs, AR	5,870	2,640	45.0	3,225	54.9	55	0.9	5,360	91.3
Houma–Bayou Cane–Thibodaux, LA	10,960	4,750	43.3	6,210	56.7	380	3.5	8,040	73.4
Houston–Sugar Land–Baytown, TX	332,370	170,975	51.4	161,390	48.6	87,310	26.3	165,590	49.8
Huntington–Ashland, WV–KY–OH	15,100	6,865	45.5	8,235	54.5	105	0.7	14,345	95.0
Huntsville, AL	22,265	10,005	44.9	12,260	55.1	480	2.2	15,330	68.9
Idaho Falls, ID	6,920	3,475	50.2	3,450	49.9	570	8.2	6,210	89.7
Indianapolis–Carmel, IN	106,600	54,555	51.2	52,050	48.8	3,135	2.9	87,325	81.9
Iowa City, IA	8,690	4,675	53.8	4,015	46.2	235	2.7	7,745	89.1
Ithaca, NY	4,315	2,260	52.4	2,055	47.6	195	4.5	3,615	83.8
Jackson, MI	8,440	3,940	46.7	4,500	53.3	255	3.0	7,805	92.5
Jackson, MS	30,970	14,200	45.9	16,770	54.1	590	1.9	17,690	57.1
Jackson, TN	6,095	2,840	46.6	3,255	53.4	70	1.1	4,270	70.1
Jacksonville, FL	84,220	40,540	48.1	43,680	51.9	4,745	5.6	61,370	72.9
Jacksonville, NC	7,040	2,895	41.1	4,145	58.9	495	7.0	5,460	77.6
Janesville, WI	8,650	3,835	44.3	4,810	55.6	275	3.2	7,710	89.1
Jefferson City, MO	6,325	3,165	50.0	3,160	50.0	100	1.6	5,765	91.1
Johnson City, TN	11,115	5,720	51.5	5,395	48.5	205	1.8	10,505	94.5
Johnstown, PA	6,710	3,160	47.1	3,550	52.9	95	1.4	6,375	95.0

C-8 Sales Workers, by Metropolitan Statistical Area, Sex, Race, and Hispanic or Latino Origin, 2006–2010—Continued

Metropolitan Statistical Area	Black alone, not Hispanic or Latino Number	Percent	American Indian and Alaska Native alone, not Hispanic or Latino Number	Percent	Asian alone, not Hispanic or Latino Number	Percent	Native Hawaiian and Other Pacific Islander alone, not Hispanic or Latino Number	Percent	Two or more races, not Hispanic or Latino Number	Percent
Farmington, NM	80	1.5	1,675	31.0	15	0.3	0	0.0	40	0.7
Fayetteville, NC	5,820	32.9	280	1.6	340	1.9	30	0.2	795	4.5
Fayetteville–Springdale–Rogers, AR–MO	565	2.1	470	1.7	270	1.0	25	0.1	620	2.3
Flagstaff, AZ	60	0.8	1,405	19.2	70	1.0	25	0.3	59	0.8
Flint, MI	3,325	14.4	105	0.5	220	1.0	4	0.0	365	1.6
Florence, SC	4,035	36.7	20	0.2	55	0.5	0	0.0	115	1.0
Florence–Muscle Shoals, AL	835	9.3	100	1.1	30	0.3	0	0.0	54	0.6
Fond du Lac, WI	0	0.0	70	1.3	0	0.0	0	0.0	8	0.1
Fort Collins–Loveland, CO	35	0.2	35	0.2	170	1.0	25	0.1	294	1.7
Fort Smith, AR–OK	510	3.4	390	2.6	180	1.2	0	0.0	520	3.5
Fort Wayne, IN	1,480	6.2	40	0.2	280	1.2	0	0.0	270	1.1
Fresno, CA	1,565	3.4	250	0.5	4,620	10.2	60	0.1	910	2.0
Gadsden, AL	515	11.4	25	0.6	15	0.3	0	0.0	14	0.3
Gainesville, FL	2,715	18.6	35	0.2	520	3.6	10	0.1	215	1.5
Gainesville, GA	630	6.3	4	0.0	300	3.0	0	0.0	50	0.5
Glens Falls, NY	30	0.4	25	0.3	15	0.2	0	0.0	28	0.4
Goldsboro, NC	1,605	25.0	20	0.3	135	2.1	10	0.2	130	2.0
Grand Forks, ND–MN	50	0.8	140	2.3	75	1.2	0	0.0	90	1.5
Grand Junction, CO	0	0.0	0	0.0	10	0.1	0	0.0	80	0.9
Grand Rapids–Wyoming, MI	2,445	5.5	110	0.2	610	1.4	0	0.0	570	1.3
Great Falls, MT	40	0.9	15	0.3	0	0.0	0	0.0	105	2.4
Greeley, CO	55	0.4	15	0.1	115	0.8	20	0.1	180	1.3
Green Bay, WI	165	0.9	460	2.6	265	1.5	0	0.0	89	0.5
Greensboro–High Point, NC	9,665	22.1	175	0.4	1,150	2.6	0	0.0	380	0.9
Greenville, NC	2,810	26.2	0	0.0	230	2.1	0	0.0	235	2.2
Greenville–Mauldin–Easley, SC	5,420	14.3	90	0.2	605	1.6	0	0.0	505	1.3
Gulfport–Biloxi, MS	1,780	14.1	4	0.0	670	5.3	0	0.0	275	2.2
Hagerstown–Martinsburg, MD–WV	1,360	9.2	20	0.1	140	0.9	0	0.0	300	2.0
Hanford–Corcoran, CA	185	3.5	50	1.0	350	6.7	0	0.0	118	2.3
Harrisburg–Carlisle, PA	2,125	7.2	25	0.1	735	2.5	0	0.0	430	1.5
Harrisonburg, VA	380	5.7	25	0.4	85	1.3	80	1.2	19	0.3
Hartford–West Hartford–East Hartford, CT	6,485	8.9	115	0.2	2,130	2.9	10	0.0	1,225	1.7
Hattiesburg, MS	2,230	25.5	20	0.2	10	0.1	0	0.0	59	0.7
Hickory–Lenoir–Morganton, NC	470	2.7	55	0.3	390	2.2	10	0.1	200	1.1
Hinesville–Fort Stewart, GA	1,190	34.1	0	0.0	50	1.4	4	0.1	40	1.1
Holland–Grand Haven, MI	165	1.1	50	0.3	315	2.1	10	0.1	170	1.1
Honolulu, HI	405	0.8	10	0.0	26,630	50.8	3,460	6.6	8,659	16.5
Hot Springs, AR	305	5.2	45	0.8	65	1.1	0	0.0	44	0.7
Houma–Bayou Cane–Thibodaux, LA	1,815	16.6	545	5.0	20	0.2	0	0.0	160	1.5
Houston–Sugar Land–Baytown, TX	51,780	15.6	590	0.2	23,545	7.1	155	0.0	3,395	1.0
Huntington–Ashland, WV–KY–OH	365	2.4	0	0.0	100	0.7	0	0.0	185	1.2
Huntsville, AL	5,375	24.1	170	0.8	460	2.1	20	0.1	425	1.9
Idaho Falls, ID	0	0.0	35	0.5	30	0.4	10	0.1	69	1.0
Indianapolis–Carmel, IN	13,155	12.3	240	0.2	1,300	1.2	15	0.0	1,435	1.3
Iowa City, IA	325	3.7	50	0.6	240	2.8	0	0.0	89	1.0
Ithaca, NY	100	2.3	0	0.0	285	6.6	0	0.0	120	2.8
Jackson, MI	305	3.6	0	0.0	45	0.5	0	0.0	34	0.4
Jackson, MS	11,975	38.7	50	0.2	465	1.5	0	0.0	195	0.6
Jackson, TN	1,575	25.8	20	0.3	60	1.0	4	0.1	95	1.6
Jacksonville, FL	13,970	16.6	220	0.3	2,845	3.4	4	0.0	1,065	1.3
Jacksonville, NC	745	10.6	35	0.5	40	0.6	0	0.0	265	3.8
Janesville, WI	345	4.0	4	0.0	120	1.4	0	0.0	190	2.2
Jefferson City, MO	310	4.9	45	0.7	35	0.6	0	0.0	74	1.2
Johnson City, TN	185	1.7	40	0.4	90	0.8	0	0.0	95	0.9
Johnstown, PA	160	2.4	0	0.0	15	0.2	0	0.0	53	0.8

PART C—METROPOLITAN STATISTICAL AREA TABLES

C-8 Sales Workers, by Metropolitan Statistical Area, Sex, Race, and Hispanic or Latino Origin, 2006–2010—Continued

Metropolitan Statistical Area	Total who worked in the last 5 years	Male Number	Male Percent	Female Number	Female Percent	Hispanic or Latino Number	Hispanic or Latino Percent	White alone, not Hispanic or Latino Number	White alone, not Hispanic or Latino Percent
Jonesboro, AR	7,285	3,505	48.1	3,785	52.0	140	1.9	6,440	88.4
Joplin, MO	10,245	4,955	48.4	5,290	51.6	300	2.9	9,295	90.7
Kalamazoo–Portage, MI	18,915	9,695	51.3	9,220	48.7	500	2.6	16,400	86.7
Kankakee–Bradley, IL	5,585	2,235	40.0	3,350	60.0	300	5.4	4,505	80.7
Kansas City, MO–KS	122,815	64,110	52.2	58,710	47.8	5,295	4.3	101,255	82.4
Kennewick–Pasco–Richland, WA	10,975	5,450	49.7	5,525	50.3	2,180	19.9	8,200	74.7
Killeen–Temple–Fort Hood, TX	17,025	7,090	41.6	9,935	58.4	2,610	15.3	10,140	59.6
Kingsport–Bristol–Bristol, TN–VA	16,045	7,575	47.2	8,465	52.8	145	0.9	15,485	96.5
Kingston, NY	11,055	5,445	49.3	5,610	50.7	545	4.9	9,790	88.6
Knoxville, TN	43,790	23,070	52.7	20,725	47.3	685	1.6	39,935	91.2
Kokomo, IN	4,225	1,870	44.3	2,355	55.7	54	1.3	4,060	96.1
La Crosse, WI–MN	8,200	3,780	46.1	4,425	54.0	55	0.7	7,790	95.0
Lafayette, IN	10,235	4,810	47.0	5,430	53.1	370	3.6	9,095	88.9
Lafayette, LA	17,405	8,335	47.9	9,070	52.1	315	1.8	12,610	72.5
Lake Charles, LA	10,810	4,655	43.1	6,155	56.9	170	1.6	7,850	72.6
Lake Havasu City–Kingman, AZ	11,175	5,220	46.7	5,960	53.3	975	8.7	9,635	86.2
Lakeland–Winter Haven, FL	30,895	14,595	47.2	16,300	52.8	3,850	12.5	22,310	72.2
Lancaster, PA	27,285	13,960	51.2	13,325	48.8	1,410	5.2	24,215	88.7
Lansing–East Lansing, MI	24,225	12,265	50.6	11,965	49.4	725	3.0	20,580	85.0
Laredo, TX	13,350	6,150	46.1	7,200	53.9	12,725	95.3	450	3.4
Las Cruces, NM	9,515	4,345	45.7	5,170	54.3	5,995	63.0	3,190	33.5
Las Vegas–Paradise, NV	122,470	56,320	46.0	66,150	54.0	24,500	20.0	69,710	56.9
Lawrence, KS	6,340	3,110	49.1	3,230	50.9	225	3.5	5,420	85.5
Lawton, OK	5,580	1,755	31.5	3,825	68.5	495	8.9	3,615	64.8
Lebanon, PA	7,050	3,545	50.3	3,505	49.7	535	7.6	6,345	90.0
Lewiston, ID–WA	3,025	1,455	48.1	1,565	51.7	130	4.3	2,765	91.4
Lewiston–Auburn, ME	6,780	3,520	51.9	3,260	48.1	90	1.3	6,525	96.2
Lexington–Fayette, KY	29,305	14,445	49.3	14,855	50.7	745	2.5	25,355	86.5
Lima, OH	5,815	2,690	46.3	3,125	53.7	210	3.6	4,940	85.0
Lincoln, NE	17,525	9,590	54.7	7,935	45.3	450	2.6	15,865	90.5
Little Rock–North Little Rock–Conway, AR	39,895	19,610	49.2	20,280	50.8	810	2.0	30,550	76.6
Logan, UT–ID	6,485	3,070	47.3	3,420	52.7	250	3.9	6,050	93.3
Longview, TX	11,840	5,405	45.7	6,435	54.3	745	6.3	9,090	76.8
Longview, WA	4,720	2,500	53.0	2,220	47.0	160	3.4	4,240	89.8
Los Angeles–Long Beach–Santa Ana, CA	771,455	406,435	52.7	365,025	47.3	279,220	36.2	309,910	40.2
Louisville/Jefferson County, KY–IN	70,455	34,970	49.6	35,485	50.4	1,595	2.3	60,030	85.2
Lubbock, TX	17,525	9,250	52.8	8,275	47.2	4,325	24.7	12,070	68.9
Lynchburg, VA	13,205	6,135	46.5	7,070	53.5	245	1.9	10,715	81.1
Macon, GA	11,935	5,525	46.3	6,405	53.7	134	1.1	7,350	61.6
Madera–Chowchilla, CA	6,395	3,200	50.0	3,190	49.9	2,230	34.9	3,500	54.7
Madison, WI	32,755	17,335	52.9	15,420	47.1	705	2.2	29,330	89.5
Manchester–Nashua, NH	26,335	13,745	52.2	12,590	47.8	775	2.9	24,605	93.4
Manhattan, KS	5,355	2,390	44.6	2,960	55.3	165	3.1	4,660	87.0
Mankato–North Mankato, MN	6,810	3,395	49.9	3,415	50.1	95	1.4	6,370	93.5
Mansfield, OH	5,930	2,615	44.1	3,315	55.9	45	0.8	5,530	93.3
McAllen–Edinburg–Mission, TX	38,060	19,650	51.6	18,410	48.4	35,130	92.3	2,440	6.4
Medford, OR	13,200	6,620	50.2	6,585	49.9	905	6.9	11,775	89.2
Memphis, TN–MS–AR	74,845	34,715	46.4	40,130	53.6	1,420	1.9	44,285	59.2
Merced, CA	10,690	5,205	48.7	5,485	51.3	5,060	47.3	3,865	36.2
Miami–Fort Lauderdale–Pompano Beach, FL	387,305	196,380	50.7	190,925	49.3	155,335	40.1	155,720	40.2
Michigan City–La Porte, IN	5,585	2,275	40.7	3,315	59.4	145	2.6	4,875	87.3
Midland, TX	8,240	3,930	47.7	4,310	52.3	2,535	30.8	5,035	61.1
Milwaukee–Waukesha–West Allis, WI	90,435	45,130	49.9	45,310	50.1	4,780	5.3	72,665	80.4
Minneapolis–St. Paul–Bloomington, MN–WI	215,710	116,765	54.1	98,950	45.9	6,370	3.0	186,375	86.4
Missoula, MT	7,730	4,535	58.7	3,190	41.3	190	2.5	7,300	94.4

C-8 Sales Workers, by Metropolitan Statistical Area, Sex, Race, and Hispanic or Latino Origin, 2006–2010—*Continued*

Metropolitan Statistical Area	Black alone, not Hispanic or Latino Number	Percent	American Indian and Alaska Native alone, not Hispanic or Latino Number	Percent	Asian alone, not Hispanic or Latino Number	Percent	Native Hawaiian and Other Pacific Islander alone, not Hispanic or Latino Number	Percent	Two or more races, not Hispanic or Latino Number	Percent
Jonesboro, AR	685	9.4	4	0.1	4	0.1	0	0.0	15	0.2
Joplin, MO	110	1.1	305	3.0	25	0.2	0	0.0	214	2.1
Kalamazoo–Portage, MI	1,460	7.7	55	0.3	235	1.2	0	0.0	270	1.4
Kankakee–Bradley, IL	635	11.4	30	0.5	95	1.7	0	0.0	29	0.5
Kansas City, MO–KS	11,720	9.5	335	0.3	2,170	1.8	85	0.1	1,965	1.6
Kennewick–Pasco–Richland, WA	100	0.9	125	1.1	190	1.7	0	0.0	180	1.6
Killeen–Temple–Fort Hood, TX	2,975	17.5	75	0.4	515	3.0	70	0.4	640	3.8
Kingsport–Bristol–Bristol, TN–VA	205	1.3	0	0.0	120	0.7	0	0.0	90	0.6
Kingston, NY	290	2.6	25	0.2	255	2.3	0	0.0	150	1.4
Knoxville, TN	2,270	5.2	40	0.1	370	0.8	40	0.1	450	1.0
Kokomo, IN	95	2.2	0	0.0	15	0.4	0	0.0	0	0.0
La Crosse, WI–MN	15	0.2	25	0.3	285	3.5	0	0.0	24	0.3
Lafayette, IN	330	3.2	20	0.2	280	2.7	0	0.0	145	1.4
Lafayette, LA	4,085	23.5	105	0.6	220	1.3	0	0.0	65	0.4
Lake Charles, LA	2,435	22.5	35	0.3	240	2.2	0	0.0	79	0.7
Lake Havasu City–Kingman, AZ	140	1.3	65	0.6	95	0.9	25	0.2	250	2.2
Lakeland–Winter Haven, FL	3,240	10.5	85	0.3	970	3.1	0	0.0	440	1.4
Lancaster, PA	880	3.2	45	0.2	410	1.5	0	0.0	325	1.2
Lansing–East Lansing, MI	1,905	7.9	110	0.5	430	1.8	35	0.1	450	1.9
Laredo, TX	0	0.0	10	0.1	135	1.0	0	0.0	24	0.2
Las Cruces, NM	80	0.8	145	1.5	35	0.4	0	0.0	75	0.8
Las Vegas–Paradise, NV	11,580	9.5	685	0.6	12,130	9.9	925	0.8	2,935	2.4
Lawrence, KS	340	5.4	110	1.7	85	1.3	0	0.0	160	2.5
Lawton, OK	1,030	18.5	135	2.4	105	1.9	30	0.5	165	3.0
Lebanon, PA	25	0.4	15	0.2	65	0.9	0	0.0	60	0.9
Lewiston, ID–WA	0	0.0	10	0.3	0	0.0	0	0.0	120	4.0
Lewiston–Auburn, ME	45	0.7	4	0.1	4	0.1	0	0.0	114	1.7
Lexington–Fayette, KY	2,475	8.4	50	0.2	345	1.2	65	0.2	265	0.9
Lima, OH	600	10.3	4	0.1	25	0.4	0	0.0	50	0.9
Lincoln, NE	550	3.1	65	0.4	195	1.1	10	0.1	390	2.2
Little Rock–North Little Rock–Conway, AR	7,350	18.4	90	0.2	710	1.8	4	0.0	380	1.0
Logan, UT–ID	0	0.0	0	0.0	85	1.3	20	0.3	84	1.3
Longview, TX	1,620	13.7	65	0.5	180	1.5	0	0.0	139	1.2
Longview, WA	15	0.3	75	1.6	60	1.3	0	0.0	169	3.6
Los Angeles–Long Beach–Santa Ana, CA	43,975	5.7	1,510	0.2	120,285	15.6	1,770	0.2	14,790	1.9
Louisville/Jefferson County, KY–IN	7,360	10.4	75	0.1	585	0.8	95	0.1	720	1.0
Lubbock, TX	690	3.9	15	0.1	140	0.8	35	0.2	260	1.5
Lynchburg, VA	1,870	14.2	75	0.6	115	0.9	0	0.0	190	1.4
Macon, GA	3,965	33.2	0	0.0	355	3.0	0	0.0	125	1.0
Madera–Chowchilla, CA	165	2.6	0	0.0	435	6.8	15	0.2	49	0.8
Madison, WI	1,320	4.0	110	0.3	730	2.2	4	0.0	550	1.7
Manchester–Nashua, NH	220	0.8	35	0.1	450	1.7	0	0.0	255	1.0
Manhattan, KS	270	5.0	0	0.0	155	2.9	0	0.0	115	2.1
Mankato–North Mankato, MN	205	3.0	4	0.1	85	1.2	0	0.0	45	0.7
Mansfield, OH	245	4.1	0	0.0	55	0.9	0	0.0	50	0.8
McAllen–Edinburg–Mission, TX	105	0.3	0	0.0	290	0.8	0	0.0	100	0.3
Medford, OR	80	0.6	15	0.1	75	0.6	30	0.2	320	2.4
Memphis, TN–MS–AR	26,760	35.8	135	0.2	1,560	2.1	0	0.0	680	0.9
Merced, CA	450	4.2	45	0.4	1,035	9.7	85	0.8	140	1.3
Miami–Fort Lauderdale–Pompano Beach, FL	60,495	15.6	300	0.1	10,245	2.6	190	0.0	5,015	1.3
Michigan City–La Porte, IN	475	8.5	4	0.1	15	0.3	4	0.1	69	1.2
Midland, TX	505	6.1	45	0.5	60	0.7	0	0.0	59	0.7
Milwaukee–Waukesha–West Allis, WI	9,725	10.8	240	0.3	1,950	2.2	20	0.0	1,060	1.2
Minneapolis–St. Paul–Bloomington, MN–WI	11,215	5.2	750	0.3	7,815	3.6	65	0.0	3,125	1.4
Missoula, MT	30	0.4	50	0.6	10	0.1	10	0.1	134	1.7

PART C—METROPOLITAN STATISTICAL AREA TABLES

C-8 Sales Workers, by Metropolitan Statistical Area, Sex, Race, and Hispanic or Latino Origin, 2006–2010—Continued

Metropolitan Statistical Area	Total who worked in the last 5 years	Male Number	Male Percent	Female Number	Female Percent	Hispanic or Latino Number	Hispanic or Latino Percent	White alone, not Hispanic or Latino Number	White alone, not Hispanic or Latino Percent
Mobile, AL	22,655	9,770	43.1	12,885	56.9	225	1.0	15,745	69.5
Modesto, CA	25,980	13,315	51.3	12,665	48.7	8,195	31.5	14,725	56.7
Monroe, LA	9,855	4,445	45.1	5,410	54.9	220	2.2	6,670	67.7
Monroe, MI	7,640	3,480	45.5	4,160	54.5	145	1.9	7,250	94.9
Montgomery, AL	19,640	8,580	43.7	11,060	56.3	435	2.2	11,605	59.1
Morgantown, WV	5,720	2,650	46.3	3,070	53.7	20	0.3	5,335	93.3
Morristown, TN	7,030	3,295	46.9	3,735	53.1	280	4.0	6,620	94.2
Mount Vernon–Anacortes, WA	6,260	2,910	46.5	3,355	53.6	475	7.6	5,400	86.3
Muncie, IN	6,140	2,665	43.4	3,480	56.7	95	1.5	5,515	89.8
Muskegon–Norton Shores, MI	8,330	3,585	43.0	4,745	57.0	260	3.1	6,675	80.1
Myrtle Beach–North Myrtle Beach–Conway, SC	21,625	10,205	47.2	11,420	52.8	340	1.6	18,255	84.4
Napa, CA	6,710	3,135	46.7	3,570	53.2	1,390	20.7	4,465	66.5
Naples–Marco Island, FL	20,130	9,695	48.2	10,435	51.8	3,825	19.0	14,865	73.8
Nashville-Davidson–Murfreesboro–Franklin, TN	99,660	52,450	52.6	47,215	47.4	3,015	3.0	81,960	82.2
New Haven–Milford, CT	51,065	25,230	49.4	25,835	50.6	6,325	12.4	37,645	73.7
New Orleans–Metairie–Kenner, LA	65,755	29,305	44.6	36,450	55.4	4,665	7.1	40,425	61.5
New York–Northern New Jersey–Long Island, NY–NJ–PA	1,096,315	588,980	53.7	507,335	46.3	198,525	18.1	616,220	56.2
Niles–Benton Harbor, MI	7,735	3,115	40.3	4,620	59.7	205	2.7	6,465	83.6
North Port–Bradenton–Sarasota, FL	44,770	22,040	49.2	22,730	50.8	3,630	8.1	38,545	86.1
Norwich–New London, CT	14,330	6,500	45.4	7,830	54.6	830	5.8	12,015	83.8
Ocala, FL	17,610	7,950	45.1	9,660	54.9	1,685	9.6	13,940	79.2
Ocean City, NJ	5,550	2,970	53.5	2,585	46.6	175	3.2	5,030	90.6
Odessa, TX	7,890	3,600	45.6	4,295	54.4	3,555	45.1	3,930	49.8
Ogden–Clearfield, UT	29,815	15,980	53.6	13,830	46.4	2,630	8.8	26,135	87.7
Oklahoma City, OK	71,000	36,665	51.6	34,335	48.4	4,630	6.5	52,725	74.3
Olympia, WA	11,325	5,820	51.4	5,500	48.6	265	2.3	9,545	84.3
Omaha–Council Bluffs, NE–IA	52,690	27,940	53.0	24,745	47.0	2,305	4.4	45,480	86.3
Orlando–Kissimmee–Sanford, FL	152,640	74,775	49.0	77,865	51.0	32,635	21.4	89,875	58.9
Oshkosh–Neenah, WI	10,185	4,985	48.9	5,200	51.1	160	1.6	9,735	95.6
Owensboro, KY	5,210	2,300	44.1	2,905	55.8	74	1.4	4,770	91.6
Oxnard–Thousand Oaks–Ventura, CA	49,570	26,640	53.7	22,930	46.3	15,550	31.4	29,730	60.0
Palm Bay–Melbourne–Titusville, FL	31,025	14,545	46.9	16,480	53.1	2,210	7.1	25,315	81.6
Palm Coast, FL	4,650	2,190	47.1	2,460	52.9	330	7.1	4,040	86.9
Panama City–Lynn Haven–Panama City Beach, FL	10,400	5,060	48.7	5,340	51.3	535	5.1	8,565	82.4
Parkersburg–Marietta–Vienna, WV–OH	8,280	3,645	44.0	4,635	56.0	30	0.4	8,080	97.6
Pascagoula, MS	7,490	2,635	35.2	4,855	64.8	210	2.8	5,470	73.0
Pensacola–Ferry Pass–Brent, FL	26,505	12,400	46.8	14,105	53.2	1,135	4.3	20,560	77.6
Peoria, IL	19,655	9,760	49.7	9,895	50.3	465	2.4	17,565	89.4
Philadelphia–Camden–Wilmington, PA–NJ–DE–MD	340,700	175,555	51.5	165,145	48.5	16,540	4.9	253,510	74.4
Phoenix–Mesa–Glendale, AZ	252,270	135,785	53.8	116,485	46.2	49,115	19.5	179,815	71.3
Pine Bluff, AR	3,990	1,465	36.7	2,525	63.3	15	0.4	2,030	50.9
Pittsburgh, PA	132,005	64,885	49.2	67,120	50.8	1,415	1.1	119,700	90.7
Pittsfield, MA	7,125	3,190	44.8	3,935	55.2	170	2.4	6,600	92.6
Pocatello, ID	5,175	2,585	50.0	2,595	50.1	405	7.8	4,610	89.1
Portland–South Portland–Biddeford, ME	32,690	16,330	50.0	16,360	50.0	410	1.3	31,370	96.0
Portland–Vancouver–Hillsboro, OR–WA	129,920	69,230	53.3	60,690	46.7	8,235	6.3	108,770	83.7
Port St. Lucie, FL	26,095	12,710	48.7	13,385	51.3	3,035	11.6	18,580	71.2
Poughkeepsie–Newburgh–Middletown, NY	35,800	17,155	47.9	18,645	52.1	4,385	12.2	27,215	76.0
Prescott, AZ	12,395	6,000	48.4	6,390	51.6	1,170	9.4	10,725	86.5
Providence–New Bedford–Fall River, RI–MA	92,630	45,680	49.3	46,950	50.7	5,985	6.5	79,895	86.3

C-8 Sales Workers, by Metropolitan Statistical Area, Sex, Race, and Hispanic or Latino Origin, 2006–2010—*Continued*

Metropolitan Statistical Area	Black alone, not Hispanic or Latino Number	Percent	American Indian and Alaska Native alone, not Hispanic or Latino Number	Percent	Asian alone, not Hispanic or Latino Number	Percent	Native Hawaiian and Other Pacific Islander alone, not Hispanic or Latino Number	Percent	Two or more races, not Hispanic or Latino Number	Percent
Mobile, AL	6,110	27.0	90	0.4	280	1.2	0	0.0	200	0.9
Modesto, CA	515	2.0	215	0.8	1,595	6.1	205	0.8	525	2.0
Monroe, LA	2,770	28.1	0	0.0	170	1.7	0	0.0	20	0.2
Monroe, MI	70	0.9	90	1.2	0	0.0	0	0.0	95	1.2
Montgomery, AL	7,160	36.5	40	0.2	185	0.9	0	0.0	210	1.1
Morgantown, WV	195	3.4	4	0.1	80	1.4	0	0.0	80	1.4
Morristown, TN	45	0.6	20	0.3	25	0.4	0	0.0	39	0.6
Mount Vernon–Anacortes, WA	65	1.0	50	0.8	115	1.8	4	0.1	140	2.2
Muncie, IN	360	5.9	20	0.3	10	0.2	0	0.0	140	2.3
Muskegon–Norton Shores, MI	945	11.3	60	0.7	85	1.0	40	0.5	265	3.2
Myrtle Beach–North Myrtle Beach–Conway, SC	2,400	11.1	225	1.0	190	0.9	30	0.1	185	0.9
Napa, CA	205	3.1	85	1.3	475	7.1	25	0.4	65	1.0
Naples–Marco Island, FL	1,015	5.0	15	0.1	260	1.3	10	0.0	140	0.7
Nashville-Davidson–Murfreesboro–Franklin, TN	11,720	11.8	195	0.2	1,835	1.8	90	0.1	850	0.9
New Haven–Milford, CT	4,495	8.8	4	0.0	1,495	2.9	60	0.1	1,045	2.0
New Orleans–Metairie–Kenner, LA	17,825	27.1	205	0.3	1,995	3.0	0	0.0	644	1.0
New York–Northern New Jersey–Long Island, NY–NJ–PA	141,100	12.9	1,390	0.1	121,175	11.1	145	0.0	17,765	1.6
Niles–Benton Harbor, MI	970	12.5	0	0.0	40	0.5	0	0.0	55	0.7
North Port–Bradenton–Sarasota, FL	1,350	3.0	85	0.2	785	1.8	25	0.1	355	0.8
Norwich–New London, CT	480	3.3	35	0.2	675	4.7	0	0.0	300	2.1
Ocala, FL	1,465	8.3	35	0.2	240	1.4	0	0.0	240	1.4
Ocean City, NJ	250	4.5	55	1.0	0	0.0	0	0.0	43	0.8
Odessa, TX	220	2.8	15	0.2	50	0.6	0	0.0	125	1.6
Ogden–Clearfield, UT	240	0.8	50	0.2	360	1.2	70	0.2	330	1.1
Oklahoma City, OK	6,540	9.2	2,125	3.0	1,800	2.5	40	0.1	3,140	4.4
Olympia, WA	350	3.1	50	0.4	700	6.2	85	0.8	330	2.9
Omaha–Council Bluffs, NE–IA	3,315	6.3	65	0.1	670	1.3	60	0.1	795	1.5
Orlando–Kissimmee–Sanford, FL	20,220	13.2	230	0.2	6,765	4.4	270	0.2	2,640	1.7
Oshkosh–Neenah, WI	65	0.6	20	0.2	130	1.3	0	0.0	70	0.7
Owensboro, KY	230	4.4	30	0.6	35	0.7	0	0.0	64	1.2
Oxnard–Thousand Oaks–Ventura, CA	775	1.6	160	0.3	2,630	5.3	50	0.1	680	1.4
Palm Bay–Melbourne–Titusville, FL	2,165	7.0	65	0.2	630	2.0	20	0.1	615	2.0
Palm Coast, FL	170	3.7	0	0.0	75	1.6	0	0.0	29	0.6
Panama City–Lynn Haven–Panama City Beach, FL	745	7.2	10	0.1	165	1.6	20	0.2	365	3.5
Parkersburg–Marietta–Vienna, WV–OH	50	0.6	4	0.0	35	0.4	0	0.0	80	1.0
Pascagoula, MS	1,580	21.1	4	0.1	130	1.7	0	0.0	90	1.2
Pensacola–Ferry Pass–Brent, FL	3,165	11.9	185	0.7	815	3.1	35	0.1	605	2.3
Peoria, IL	1,415	7.2	15	0.1	80	0.4	0	0.0	105	0.5
Philadelphia–Camden–Wilmington, PA–NJ–DE–MD	50,245	14.7	335	0.1	15,810	4.6	95	0.0	4,165	1.2
Phoenix–Mesa–Glendale, AZ	9,590	3.8	2,740	1.1	7,160	2.8	235	0.1	3,615	1.4
Pine Bluff, AR	1,815	45.5	0	0.0	85	2.1	0	0.0	45	1.1
Pittsburgh, PA	7,645	5.8	125	0.1	1,580	1.2	65	0.0	1,475	1.1
Pittsfield, MA	195	2.7	15	0.2	55	0.8	0	0.0	95	1.3
Pocatello, ID	55	1.1	75	1.4	10	0.2	15	0.3	10	0.2
Portland–South Portland–Biddeford, ME	225	0.7	20	0.1	345	1.1	0	0.0	320	1.0
Portland–Vancouver–Hillsboro, OR–WA	2,925	2.3	730	0.6	5,720	4.4	595	0.5	2,945	2.3
Port St. Lucie, FL	3,465	13.3	20	0.1	590	2.3	0	0.0	410	1.6
Poughkeepsie–Newburgh–Middletown, NY	2,620	7.3	35	0.1	865	2.4	0	0.0	675	1.9
Prescott, AZ	100	0.8	125	1.0	120	1.0	0	0.0	150	1.2
Providence–New Bedford–Fall River, RI–MA	3,220	3.5	200	0.2	1,855	2.0	0	0.0	1,470	1.6

PART C—METROPOLITAN STATISTICAL AREA TABLES

C-8 Sales Workers, by Metropolitan Statistical Area, Sex, Race, and Hispanic or Latino Origin, 2006–2010—Continued

Metropolitan Statistical Area	Total who worked in the last 5 years	Male Number	Male Percent	Female Number	Female Percent	Hispanic or Latino Number	Hispanic or Latino Percent	White alone, not Hispanic or Latino Number	White alone, not Hispanic or Latino Percent
Provo–Orem, UT	28,310	16,165	57.1	12,145	42.9	1,875	6.6	25,395	89.7
Pueblo, CO	8,595	4,485	52.2	4,110	47.8	3,035	35.3	5,340	62.1
Punta Gorda, FL	9,655	4,755	49.2	4,900	50.8	435	4.5	8,485	87.9
Racine, WI	10,235	4,640	45.3	5,595	54.7	785	7.7	8,545	83.5
Raleigh–Cary, NC	70,025	38,010	54.3	32,015	45.7	3,685	5.3	50,630	72.3
Rapid City, SD	7,530	3,815	50.7	3,715	49.3	115	1.5	6,890	91.5
Reading, PA	22,235	10,935	49.2	11,300	50.8	2,010	9.0	19,270	86.7
Redding, CA	10,330	4,890	47.3	5,440	52.7	970	9.4	8,485	82.1
Reno–Sparks, NV	26,935	13,560	50.3	13,375	49.7	3,155	11.7	21,290	79.0
Richmond, VA	76,070	37,355	49.1	38,720	50.9	1,940	2.6	51,355	67.5
Riverside–San Bernardino–Ontario, CA	227,880	111,220	48.8	116,660	51.2	89,025	39.1	103,335	45.3
Roanoke, VA	18,600	9,905	53.3	8,695	46.7	360	1.9	15,940	85.7
Rochester, MN	8,795	4,825	54.9	3,970	45.1	195	2.2	8,155	92.7
Rochester, NY	55,350	27,420	49.5	27,930	50.5	1,915	3.5	47,370	85.6
Rockford, IL	18,620	9,030	48.5	9,590	51.5	1,235	6.6	15,445	82.9
Rocky Mount, NC	8,080	3,730	46.2	4,350	53.8	189	2.3	4,875	60.3
Rome, GA	4,610	2,300	49.9	2,310	50.1	200	4.3	3,905	84.7
Sacramento–Arden-Arcade–Roseville, CA	123,625	65,360	52.9	58,265	47.1	18,745	15.2	79,575	64.4
Saginaw–Saginaw Township North, MI	11,080	4,985	45.0	6,095	55.0	485	4.4	9,455	85.3
St. Cloud, MN	11,015	5,860	53.2	5,155	46.8	99	0.9	10,560	95.9
St. George, UT	7,615	3,795	49.8	3,820	50.2	490	6.4	6,860	90.1
St. Joseph, MO–KS	6,630	2,995	45.2	3,630	54.8	180	2.7	6,085	91.8
St. Louis, MO–IL	167,430	79,885	47.7	87,550	52.3	2,885	1.7	135,780	81.1
Salem, OR	17,825	8,650	48.5	9,175	51.5	2,535	14.2	14,040	78.8
Salinas, CA	20,290	9,945	49.0	10,350	51.0	9,255	45.6	8,325	41.0
Salisbury, MD	7,245	3,385	46.7	3,860	53.3	75	1.0	5,310	73.3
Salt Lake City, UT	70,485	38,125	54.1	32,365	45.9	7,565	10.7	59,070	83.8
San Angelo, TX	5,810	2,955	50.9	2,855	49.1	1,640	28.2	3,930	67.6
San Antonio–New Braunfels, TX	114,930	56,260	49.0	58,670	51.0	55,400	48.2	49,505	43.1
San Diego–Carlsbad–San Marcos, CA	178,695	92,090	51.5	86,605	48.5	47,905	26.8	103,140	57.7
Sandusky, OH	4,735	2,020	42.7	2,720	57.4	90	1.9	4,205	88.8
San Francisco–Oakland–Fremont, CA	256,365	135,125	52.7	121,240	47.3	43,740	17.1	130,290	50.8
San Jose–Sunnyvale–Santa Clara, CA	95,880	50,025	52.2	45,860	47.8	25,565	26.7	40,540	42.3
San Luis Obispo–Paso Robles, CA	16,275	8,140	50.0	8,135	50.0	2,605	16.0	12,780	78.5
Santa Barbara–Santa Maria–Goleta, CA	20,945	9,545	45.6	11,400	54.4	7,065	33.7	11,905	56.8
Santa Cruz–Watsonville, CA	14,890	7,375	49.5	7,520	50.5	3,190	21.4	10,365	69.6
Santa Fe, NM	8,660	3,690	42.6	4,970	57.4	3,605	41.6	4,655	53.8
Santa Rosa–Petaluma, CA	32,730	16,520	50.5	16,210	49.5	5,580	17.0	24,495	74.8
Savannah, GA	20,695	9,170	44.3	11,525	55.7	430	2.1	12,700	61.4
Scranton–Wilkes-Barre, PA	30,470	14,275	46.8	16,195	53.2	845	2.8	28,665	94.1
Seattle–Tacoma–Bellevue, WA	199,590	101,830	51.0	97,755	49.0	11,230	5.6	150,960	75.6
Sebastian–Vero Beach, FL	7,735	3,600	46.5	4,135	53.5	515	6.7	6,700	86.6
Sheboygan, WI	5,945	2,740	46.1	3,210	54.0	135	2.3	5,630	94.7
Sherman–Denison, TX	6,705	2,930	43.7	3,775	56.3	385	5.7	5,620	83.8
Shreveport–Bossier City, LA	21,840	9,725	44.5	12,115	55.5	440	2.0	13,240	60.6
Sioux City, IA–NE–SD	8,795	4,380	49.8	4,415	50.2	520	5.9	7,920	90.1
Sioux Falls, SD	14,470	7,995	55.3	6,480	44.8	335	2.3	13,735	94.9
South Bend–Mishawaka, IN–MI	18,005	8,475	47.1	9,530	52.9	570	3.2	15,155	84.2
Spartanburg, SC	15,170	6,705	44.2	8,465	55.8	260	1.7	11,730	77.3
Spokane, WA	27,560	14,310	51.9	13,250	48.1	945	3.4	25,225	91.5
Springfield, IL	12,285	6,385	52.0	5,895	48.0	160	1.3	10,730	87.3
Springfield, MA	35,575	17,630	49.6	17,945	50.4	3,230	9.1	29,710	83.5
Springfield, MO	27,665	14,435	52.2	13,230	47.8	540	2.0	25,715	93.0
Springfield, OH	6,905	2,735	39.6	4,170	60.4	155	2.2	6,165	89.3
State College, PA	7,355	3,405	46.3	3,945	53.6	225	3.1	6,635	90.2

C-8 Sales Workers, by Metropolitan Statistical Area, Sex, Race, and Hispanic or Latino Origin, 2006–2010—Continued

Metropolitan Statistical Area	Black alone, not Hispanic or Latino Number	Percent	American Indian and Alaska Native alone, not Hispanic or Latino Number	Percent	Asian alone, not Hispanic or Latino Number	Percent	Native Hawaiian and Other Pacific Islander alone, not Hispanic or Latino Number	Percent	Two or more races, not Hispanic or Latino Number	Percent
Provo–Orem, UT	90	0.3	165	0.6	230	0.8	180	0.6	375	1.3
Pueblo, CO	50	0.6	25	0.3	10	0.1	10	0.1	120	1.4
Punta Gorda, FL	390	4.0	20	0.2	95	1.0	0	0.0	230	2.4
Racine, WI	685	6.7	4	0.0	175	1.7	0	0.0	35	0.3
Raleigh–Cary, NC	12,600	18.0	205	0.3	2,065	2.9	55	0.1	785	1.1
Rapid City, SD	50	0.7	330	4.4	20	0.3	0	0.0	120	1.6
Reading, PA	500	2.2	60	0.3	230	1.0	0	0.0	160	0.7
Redding, CA	65	0.6	215	2.1	230	2.2	4	0.0	360	3.5
Reno–Sparks, NV	460	1.7	395	1.5	1,035	3.8	110	0.4	490	1.8
Richmond, VA	19,270	25.3	90	0.1	2,245	3.0	0	0.0	1,170	1.5
Riverside–San Bernardino–Ontario, CA	13,750	6.0	795	0.3	15,685	6.9	330	0.1	4,955	2.2
Roanoke, VA	1,720	9.2	65	0.3	305	1.6	0	0.0	205	1.1
Rochester, MN	105	1.2	4	0.0	305	3.5	0	0.0	29	0.3
Rochester, NY	4,275	7.7	90	0.2	860	1.6	30	0.1	815	1.5
Rockford, IL	1,250	6.7	4	0.0	345	1.9	15	0.1	335	1.8
Rocky Mount, NC	2,865	35.5	4	0.0	65	0.8	0	0.0	85	1.1
Rome, GA	410	8.9	10	0.2	50	1.1	0	0.0	30	0.7
Sacramento–Arden-Arcade–Roseville, CA	7,410	6.0	785	0.6	12,790	10.3	705	0.6	3,615	2.9
Saginaw–Saginaw Township North, MI	930	8.4	25	0.2	40	0.4	0	0.0	144	1.3
St. Cloud, MN	65	0.6	0	0.0	210	1.9	0	0.0	80	0.7
St. George, UT	15	0.2	55	0.7	50	0.7	100	1.3	50	0.7
St. Joseph, MO–KS	155	2.3	0	0.0	55	0.8	0	0.0	160	2.4
St. Louis, MO–IL	23,335	13.9	155	0.1	3,135	1.9	50	0.0	2,085	1.2
Salem, OR	110	0.6	240	1.3	235	1.3	70	0.4	595	3.3
Salinas, CA	445	2.2	65	0.3	1,610	7.9	55	0.3	540	2.7
Salisbury, MD	1,570	21.7	0	0.0	210	2.9	0	0.0	74	1.0
Salt Lake City, UT	610	0.9	185	0.3	1,740	2.5	555	0.8	770	1.1
San Angelo, TX	80	1.4	20	0.3	65	1.1	0	0.0	75	1.3
San Antonio–New Braunfels, TX	5,590	4.9	205	0.2	2,675	2.3	40	0.0	1,510	1.3
San Diego–Carlsbad–San Marcos, CA	7,095	4.0	620	0.3	14,300	8.0	655	0.4	4,975	2.8
Sandusky, OH	300	6.3	10	0.2	20	0.4	0	0.0	110	2.3
San Francisco–Oakland–Fremont, CA	16,770	6.5	565	0.2	56,635	22.1	1,460	0.6	6,905	2.7
San Jose–Sunnyvale–Santa Clara, CA	2,510	2.6	275	0.3	24,095	25.1	360	0.4	2,525	2.6
San Luis Obispo–Paso Robles, CA	125	0.8	105	0.6	405	2.5	20	0.1	240	1.5
Santa Barbara–Santa Maria–Goleta, CA	445	2.1	55	0.3	950	4.5	85	0.4	450	2.1
Santa Cruz–Watsonville, CA	185	1.2	65	0.4	590	4.0	50	0.3	450	3.0
Santa Fe, NM	60	0.7	155	1.8	35	0.4	0	0.0	140	1.6
Santa Rosa–Petaluma, CA	520	1.6	100	0.3	1,250	3.8	25	0.1	755	2.3
Savannah, GA	6,580	31.8	70	0.3	615	3.0	70	0.3	225	1.1
Scranton–Wilkes-Barre, PA	395	1.3	25	0.1	235	0.8	0	0.0	300	1.0
Seattle–Tacoma–Bellevue, WA	7,730	3.9	1,415	0.7	19,315	9.7	1,760	0.9	7,180	3.6
Sebastian–Vero Beach, FL	335	4.3	0	0.0	135	1.7	0	0.0	50	0.6
Sheboygan, WI	45	0.8	15	0.3	105	1.8	0	0.0	20	0.3
Sherman–Denison, TX	385	5.7	30	0.4	205	3.1	0	0.0	75	1.1
Shreveport–Bossier City, LA	7,690	35.2	130	0.6	265	1.2	0	0.0	75	0.3
Sioux City, IA–NE–SD	95	1.1	120	1.4	115	1.3	0	0.0	30	0.3
Sioux Falls, SD	195	1.3	90	0.6	55	0.4	0	0.0	55	0.4
South Bend–Mishawaka, IN–MI	1,720	9.6	15	0.1	280	1.6	0	0.0	264	1.5
Spartanburg, SC	2,535	16.7	20	0.1	430	2.8	0	0.0	195	1.3
Spokane, WA	265	1.0	135	0.5	385	1.4	80	0.3	535	1.9
Springfield, IL	1,155	9.4	45	0.4	55	0.4	0	0.0	140	1.1
Springfield, MA	1,440	4.0	110	0.3	690	1.9	20	0.1	375	1.1
Springfield, MO	465	1.7	105	0.4	305	1.1	4	0.0	530	1.9
Springfield, OH	370	5.4	0	0.0	40	0.6	0	0.0	175	2.5
State College, PA	165	2.2	0	0.0	210	2.9	0	0.0	115	1.6

PART C—METROPOLITAN STATISTICAL AREA TABLES

C-8 Sales Workers, by Metropolitan Statistical Area, Sex, Race, and Hispanic or Latino Origin, 2006–2010—Continued

Metropolitan Statistical Area	Total who worked in the last 5 years	Male Number	Male Percent	Female Number	Female Percent	Hispanic or Latino Number	Hispanic or Latino Percent	White alone, not Hispanic or Latino Number	White alone, not Hispanic or Latino Percent
Steubenville–Weirton, OH–WV	6,190	2,405	38.9	3,790	61.2	124	2.0	5,830	94.2
Stockton, CA	33,785	17,000	50.3	16,785	49.7	10,755	31.8	14,995	44.4
Sumter, SC	4,440	1,500	33.8	2,940	66.2	120	2.7	2,445	55.1
Syracuse, NY	37,700	18,785	49.8	18,915	50.2	975	2.6	33,495	88.8
Tallahassee, FL	19,535	9,115	46.7	10,420	53.3	1,100	5.6	11,870	60.8
Tampa–St. Petersburg–Clearwater, FL	187,225	96,050	51.3	91,170	48.7	22,890	12.2	139,935	74.7
Terre Haute, IN	9,195	4,330	47.1	4,865	52.9	85	0.9	8,575	93.3
Texarkana, TX–Texarkana, AR	7,900	3,605	45.6	4,295	54.4	380	4.8	5,450	69.0
Toledo, OH	36,030	17,200	47.7	18,830	52.3	1,395	3.9	30,910	85.8
Topeka, KS	11,425	5,445	47.7	5,980	52.3	530	4.6	9,605	84.1
Trenton–Ewing, NJ	19,210	10,040	52.3	9,170	47.7	2,290	11.9	12,135	63.2
Tucson, AZ	51,060	25,125	49.2	25,935	50.8	14,960	29.3	31,710	62.1
Tulsa, OK	53,290	26,960	50.6	26,330	49.4	1,745	3.3	41,505	77.9
Tuscaloosa, AL	10,680	4,765	44.6	5,915	55.4	25	0.2	7,550	70.7
Tyler, TX	12,130	6,355	52.4	5,775	47.6	1,290	10.6	8,950	73.8
Utica–Rome, NY	14,265	7,275	51.0	6,995	49.0	255	1.8	13,300	93.2
Valdosta, GA	8,030	3,250	40.5	4,775	59.5	195	2.4	4,960	61.8
Vallejo–Fairfield, CA	22,510	10,740	47.7	11,770	52.3	4,005	17.8	10,325	45.9
Victoria, TX	6,345	2,615	41.2	3,730	58.8	2,265	35.7	3,790	59.7
Vineland–Millville–Bridgeton, NJ	6,910	3,395	49.1	3,515	50.9	1,240	17.9	4,450	64.4
Virginia Beach–Norfolk–Newport News, VA–NC	94,900	38,765	40.8	56,135	59.2	4,040	4.3	56,940	60.0
Visalia–Porterville, CA	17,620	8,735	49.6	8,880	50.4	7,915	44.9	8,325	47.2
Waco, TX	12,215	6,110	50.0	6,105	50.0	1,980	16.2	8,395	68.7
Warner Robins, GA	6,835	2,825	41.3	4,015	58.7	245	3.6	4,335	63.4
Washington–Arlington–Alexandria, DC–VA–MD–WV	268,005	131,020	48.9	136,985	51.1	29,505	11.0	136,965	51.1
Waterloo–Cedar Falls, IA	9,140	4,440	48.6	4,700	51.4	160	1.8	8,380	91.7
Wausau, WI	7,045	3,345	47.5	3,695	52.4	40	0.6	6,490	92.1
Wenatchee–East Wenatchee, WA	5,690	3,155	55.4	2,535	44.6	960	16.9	4,595	80.8
Wheeling, WV–OH	7,560	3,535	46.8	4,025	53.2	50	0.7	7,250	95.9
Wichita, KS	32,285	16,405	50.8	15,880	49.2	2,640	8.2	25,925	80.3
Wichita Falls, TX	8,300	3,725	44.9	4,575	55.1	805	9.7	6,605	79.6
Williamsport, PA	6,245	2,670	42.8	3,575	57.2	24	0.4	5,895	94.4
Wilmington, NC	23,490	10,750	45.8	12,740	54.2	490	2.1	20,065	85.4
Winchester, VA–WV	6,855	3,485	50.8	3,370	49.2	155	2.3	6,420	93.7
Winston–Salem, NC	26,365	13,210	50.1	13,160	49.9	1,430	5.4	19,435	73.7
Worcester, MA	44,735	23,085	51.6	21,650	48.4	2,810	6.3	38,780	86.7
Yakima, WA	10,840	5,925	54.7	4,915	45.3	3,190	29.4	7,025	64.8
York–Hanover, PA	23,575	11,295	47.9	12,285	52.1	670	2.8	21,545	91.4
Youngstown–Warren–Boardman, OH–PA	30,420	13,575	44.6	16,845	55.4	450	1.5	27,230	89.5
Yuba City, CA	7,965	4,155	52.2	3,810	47.8	1,345	16.9	4,880	61.3
Yuma, AZ	7,640	3,265	42.7	4,375	57.3	4,375	57.3	2,940	38.5

C-8 Sales Workers, by Metropolitan Statistical Area, Sex, Race, and Hispanic or Latino Origin, 2006–2010—*Continued*

Metropolitan Statistical Area	Black alone, not Hispanic or Latino Number	Percent	American Indian and Alaska Native alone, not Hispanic or Latino Number	Percent	Asian alone, not Hispanic or Latino Number	Percent	Native Hawaiian and Other Pacific Islander alone, not Hispanic or Latino Number	Percent	Two or more races, not Hispanic or Latino Number	Percent
Steubenville–Weirton, OH–WV	155	2.5	0	0.0	10	0.2	0	0.0	73	1.2
Stockton, CA	2,210	6.5	215	0.6	4,420	13.1	160	0.5	1,030	3.0
Sumter, SC	1,715	38.6	0	0.0	95	2.1	0	0.0	65	1.5
Syracuse, NY	1,770	4.7	290	0.8	660	1.8	0	0.0	515	1.4
Tallahassee, FL	5,990	30.7	25	0.1	215	1.1	20	0.1	310	1.6
Tampa–St. Petersburg–Clearwater, FL	15,900	8.5	335	0.2	4,935	2.6	205	0.1	3,025	1.6
Terre Haute, IN	315	3.4	4	0.0	35	0.4	0	0.0	180	2.0
Texarkana, TX–Texarkana, AR	1,920	24.3	10	0.1	55	0.7	0	0.0	85	1.1
Toledo, OH	2,945	8.2	90	0.2	160	0.4	0	0.0	535	1.5
Topeka, KS	980	8.6	60	0.5	45	0.4	0	0.0	209	1.8
Trenton–Ewing, NJ	2,920	15.2	85	0.4	1,450	7.5	0	0.0	330	1.7
Tucson, AZ	1,275	2.5	765	1.5	1,475	2.9	60	0.1	815	1.6
Tulsa, OK	3,125	5.9	3,075	5.8	920	1.7	55	0.1	2,875	5.4
Tuscaloosa, AL	2,860	26.8	4	0.0	100	0.9	0	0.0	145	1.4
Tyler, TX	1,620	13.4	20	0.2	95	0.8	0	0.0	159	1.3
Utica–Rome, NY	320	2.2	35	0.2	180	1.3	35	0.2	145	1.0
Valdosta, GA	2,420	30.1	25	0.3	310	3.9	0	0.0	115	1.4
Vallejo–Fairfield, CA	2,770	12.3	110	0.5	3,870	17.2	275	1.2	1,155	5.1
Victoria, TX	175	2.8	0	0.0	55	0.9	0	0.0	65	1.0
Vineland–Millville–Bridgeton, NJ	965	14.0	20	0.3	165	2.4	0	0.0	74	1.1
Virginia Beach–Norfolk–Newport News, VA–NC	28,015	29.5	200	0.2	3,610	3.8	295	0.3	1,795	1.9
Visalia–Porterville, CA	230	1.3	85	0.5	735	4.2	10	0.1	320	1.8
Waco, TX	1,345	11.0	25	0.2	360	2.9	0	0.0	115	0.9
Warner Robins, GA	1,900	27.8	20	0.3	170	2.5	0	0.0	170	2.5
Washington–Arlington–Alexandria, DC–VA–MD–WV	69,085	25.8	345	0.1	26,015	9.7	215	0.1	5,870	2.2
Waterloo–Cedar Falls, IA	440	4.8	10	0.1	45	0.5	4	0.0	105	1.1
Wausau, WI	65	0.9	10	0.1	405	5.7	0	0.0	39	0.6
Wenatchee–East Wenatchee, WA	0	0.0	20	0.4	50	0.9	0	0.0	63	1.1
Wheeling, WV–OH	120	1.6	0	0.0	25	0.3	0	0.0	110	1.5
Wichita, KS	2,215	6.9	185	0.6	625	1.9	45	0.1	650	2.0
Wichita Falls, TX	595	7.2	40	0.5	195	2.3	0	0.0	64	0.8
Williamsport, PA	140	2.2	45	0.7	70	1.1	0	0.0	69	1.1
Wilmington, NC	2,185	9.3	125	0.5	280	1.2	0	0.0	345	1.5
Winchester, VA–WV	90	1.3	0	0.0	115	1.7	30	0.4	35	0.5
Winston–Salem, NC	4,740	18.0	0	0.0	320	1.2	55	0.2	385	1.5
Worcester, MA	1,235	2.8	4	0.0	1,000	2.2	25	0.1	875	2.0
Yakima, WA	100	0.9	265	2.4	75	0.7	10	0.1	175	1.6
York–Hanover, PA	960	4.1	0	0.0	215	0.9	0	0.0	195	0.8
Youngstown–Warren–Boardman, OH–PA	2,305	7.6	25	0.1	175	0.6	0	0.0	235	0.8
Yuba City, CA	180	2.3	35	0.4	1,150	14.4	4	0.1	370	4.6
Yuma, AZ	145	1.9	35	0.5	100	1.3	0	0.0	54	0.7

C-9 Administrative Support Workers, by Metropolitan Statistical Area, Sex, Race, and Hispanic or Latino Origin, 2006–2010

Metropolitan Statistical Area	Total who worked in the last 5 years	Male Number	Male Percent	Female Number	Female Percent	Hispanic or Latino Number	Hispanic or Latino Percent	White alone, not Hispanic or Latino Number	White alone, not Hispanic or Latino Percent
Abilene, TX	12,035	2,925	24.3	9,110	75.7	1,745	14.5	9,235	76.7
Akron, OH	58,910	14,665	24.9	44,245	75.1	575	1.0	50,165	85.2
Albany, GA	10,530	2,455	23.3	8,075	76.7	85	0.8	5,995	56.9
Albany–Schenectady–Troy, NY	84,685	21,470	25.4	63,220	74.7	2,480	2.9	73,415	86.7
Albuquerque, NM	68,900	16,850	24.5	52,055	75.6	31,605	45.9	30,105	43.7
Alexandria, LA	10,660	2,075	19.5	8,585	80.5	110	1.0	8,050	75.5
Allentown–Bethlehem–Easton, PA–NJ	68,010	16,255	23.9	51,755	76.1	6,525	9.6	56,905	83.7
Altoona, PA	9,955	2,855	28.7	7,105	71.4	65	0.7	9,785	98.3
Amarillo, TX	19,765	5,145	26.0	14,620	74.0	4,005	20.3	14,320	72.5
Ames, IA	7,470	2,135	28.6	5,335	71.4	140	1.9	7,050	94.4
Anchorage, AK	33,440	9,025	27.0	24,415	73.0	2,075	6.2	22,675	67.8
Anderson, IN	9,690	2,215	22.9	7,470	77.1	85	0.9	8,965	92.5
Anderson, SC	12,425	2,680	21.6	9,745	78.4	165	1.3	9,940	80.0
Ann Arbor, MI	23,155	6,310	27.3	16,845	72.7	985	4.3	17,570	75.9
Anniston–Oxford, AL	7,475	1,940	26.0	5,540	74.1	200	2.7	5,755	77.0
Appleton, WI	19,165	3,795	19.8	15,370	80.2	265	1.4	18,275	95.4
Asheville, NC	29,020	6,630	22.8	22,390	77.2	785	2.7	26,375	90.9
Athens–Clarke County, GA	12,475	3,200	25.7	9,270	74.3	300	2.4	9,675	77.6
Atlanta–Sandy Springs–Marietta, GA	415,475	106,330	25.6	309,145	74.4	20,020	4.8	214,330	51.6
Atlantic City–Hammonton, NJ	19,695	4,630	23.5	15,065	76.5	2,145	10.9	13,565	68.9
Auburn–Opelika, AL	9,900	2,480	25.1	7,415	74.9	195	2.0	7,055	71.3
Augusta–Richmond County, GA–SC	36,345	8,290	22.8	28,050	77.2	1,410	3.9	21,420	58.9
Austin–Round Rock–San Marcos, TX	131,035	39,065	29.8	91,970	70.2	37,725	28.8	74,340	56.7
Bakersfield–Delano, CA	49,780	11,305	22.7	38,470	77.3	19,400	39.0	24,680	49.6
Baltimore–Towson, MD	229,065	57,075	24.9	171,990	75.1	5,895	2.6	140,295	61.2
Bangor, ME	12,425	2,940	23.7	9,480	76.3	115	0.9	12,045	96.9
Barnstable Town, MA	15,220	3,115	20.5	12,105	79.5	210	1.4	14,295	93.9
Baton Rouge, LA	63,585	14,475	22.8	49,105	77.2	1,300	2.0	39,785	62.6
Battle Creek, MI	9,275	2,465	26.6	6,815	73.5	370	4.0	7,970	85.9
Bay City, MI	8,160	1,860	22.8	6,305	77.3	305	3.7	7,730	94.7
Beaumont–Port Arthur, TX	26,975	5,550	20.6	21,425	79.4	2,090	7.7	18,195	67.5
Bellingham, WA	15,580	3,985	25.6	11,595	74.4	645	4.1	13,620	87.4
Bend, OR	11,220	2,355	21.0	8,870	79.1	505	4.5	10,145	90.4
Billings, MT	13,115	2,650	20.2	10,470	79.8	325	2.5	12,290	93.7
Binghamton, NY	21,085	5,010	23.8	16,075	76.2	475	2.3	19,180	91.0
Birmingham–Hoover, AL	88,645	20,675	23.3	67,970	76.7	1,095	1.2	58,695	66.2
Bismarck, ND	9,945	2,130	21.4	7,815	78.6	105	1.1	9,530	95.8
Blacksburg–Christiansburg–Radford, VA	10,275	2,755	26.8	7,520	73.2	120	1.2	9,475	92.2
Bloomington, IN	12,865	3,495	27.2	9,370	72.8	355	2.8	11,675	90.8
Bloomington–Normal, IL	15,865	3,840	24.2	12,025	75.8	430	2.7	13,810	87.0
Boise City–Nampa, ID	47,605	11,720	24.6	35,880	75.4	4,120	8.7	41,355	86.9
Boston–Cambridge–Quincy, MA–NH	368,240	99,940	27.1	268,305	72.9	25,235	6.9	293,555	79.7
Boulder, CO	17,840	4,885	27.4	12,955	72.6	1,485	8.3	15,515	87.0
Bowling Green, KY	9,645	2,080	21.6	7,565	78.4	200	2.1	8,410	87.2
Bremerton–Silverdale, WA	17,215	4,450	25.8	12,765	74.2	840	4.9	13,955	81.1
Bridgeport–Stamford–Norwalk, CT	66,765	16,375	24.5	50,385	75.5	8,915	13.4	45,695	68.4
Brownsville–Harlingen, TX	23,375	6,845	29.3	16,530	70.7	20,825	89.1	2,285	9.8
Brunswick, GA	7,585	1,350	17.8	6,235	82.2	125	1.6	5,800	76.5
Buffalo–Niagara Falls, NY	101,235	26,295	26.0	74,945	74.0	2,705	2.7	85,765	84.7
Burlington, NC	12,250	2,725	22.2	9,525	77.8	495	4.0	9,075	74.1
Burlington–South Burlington, VT	18,095	4,735	26.2	13,360	73.8	310	1.7	17,080	94.4
Canton–Massillon, OH	31,655	7,255	22.9	24,400	77.1	320	1.0	28,985	91.6
Cape Coral–Fort Myers, FL	42,825	9,895	23.1	32,930	76.9	6,340	14.8	33,135	77.4
Cape Girardeau–Jackson, MO–IL	7,555	1,675	22.2	5,880	77.8	35	0.5	6,530	86.4
Carson City, NV	4,710	1,365	29.0	3,345	71.0	400	8.5	3,785	80.4

C-9 Administrative Support Workers, by Metropolitan Statistical Area, Sex, Race, and Hispanic or Latino Origin, 2006–2010—Continued

Metropolitan Statistical Area	Black alone, not Hispanic or Latino Number	Percent	American Indian and Alaska Native alone, not Hispanic or Latino Number	Percent	Asian alone, not Hispanic or Latino Number	Percent	Native Hawaiian and Other Pacific Islander alone, not Hispanic or Latino Number	Percent	Two or more races, not Hispanic or Latino Number	Percent
Abilene, TX	720	6.0	35	0.3	55	0.5	4	0.0	235	2.0
Akron, OH	6,925	11.8	90	0.2	585	1.0	0	0.0	575	1.0
Albany, GA	4,370	41.5	30	0.3	25	0.2	0	0.0	25	0.2
Albany–Schenectady–Troy, NY	5,895	7.0	200	0.2	1,315	1.6	10	0.0	1,375	1.6
Albuquerque, NM	1,890	2.7	3,355	4.9	885	1.3	55	0.1	1,009	1.5
Alexandria, LA	2,280	21.4	80	0.8	35	0.3	0	0.0	99	0.9
Allentown–Bethlehem–Easton, PA–NJ	2,970	4.4	40	0.1	895	1.3	0	0.0	664	1.0
Altoona, PA	25	0.3	25	0.3	40	0.4	0	0.0	19	0.2
Amarillo, TX	760	3.8	100	0.5	335	1.7	65	0.3	185	0.9
Ames, IA	140	1.9	15	0.2	75	1.0	0	0.0	48	0.6
Anchorage, AK	1,765	5.3	2,070	6.2	2,075	6.2	475	1.4	2,300	6.9
Anderson, IN	495	5.1	0	0.0	30	0.3	0	0.0	110	1.1
Anderson, SC	2,180	17.5	0	0.0	70	0.6	0	0.0	70	0.6
Ann Arbor, MI	3,090	13.3	15	0.1	930	4.0	0	0.0	570	2.5
Anniston–Oxford, AL	1,395	18.7	25	0.3	0	0.0	0	0.0	105	1.4
Appleton, WI	90	0.5	180	0.9	255	1.3	0	0.0	105	0.5
Asheville, NC	1,400	4.8	90	0.3	155	0.5	0	0.0	215	0.7
Athens–Clarke County, GA	2,150	17.2	4	0.0	220	1.8	0	0.0	114	0.9
Atlanta–Sandy Springs–Marietta, GA	163,655	39.4	835	0.2	11,160	2.7	280	0.1	5,200	1.3
Atlantic City–Hammonton, NJ	2,715	13.8	40	0.2	905	4.6	0	0.0	315	1.6
Auburn–Opelika, AL	2,435	24.6	25	0.3	65	0.7	0	0.0	120	1.2
Augusta–Richmond County, GA–SC	12,255	33.7	95	0.3	495	1.4	0	0.0	675	1.9
Austin–Round Rock–San Marcos, TX	13,030	9.9	480	0.4	3,510	2.7	200	0.2	1,750	1.3
Bakersfield–Delano, CA	2,725	5.5	315	0.6	1,640	3.3	70	0.1	945	1.9
Baltimore–Towson, MD	73,035	31.9	440	0.2	5,815	2.5	100	0.0	3,485	1.5
Bangor, ME	50	0.4	85	0.7	55	0.4	0	0.0	75	0.6
Barnstable Town, MA	240	1.6	90	0.6	70	0.5	15	0.1	305	2.0
Baton Rouge, LA	21,145	33.3	75	0.1	750	1.2	0	0.0	530	0.8
Battle Creek, MI	720	7.8	15	0.2	105	1.1	0	0.0	95	1.0
Bay City, MI	50	0.6	4	0.0	20	0.2	0	0.0	50	0.6
Beaumont–Port Arthur, TX	5,910	21.9	50	0.2	345	1.3	50	0.2	345	1.3
Bellingham, WA	200	1.3	420	2.7	350	2.2	4	0.0	340	2.2
Bend, OR	20	0.2	150	1.3	150	1.3	0	0.0	245	2.2
Billings, MT	60	0.5	205	1.6	50	0.4	10	0.1	179	1.4
Binghamton, NY	660	3.1	70	0.3	385	1.8	30	0.1	290	1.4
Birmingham–Hoover, AL	27,920	31.5	175	0.2	275	0.3	20	0.0	470	0.5
Bismarck, ND	10	0.1	215	2.2	20	0.2	0	0.0	60	0.6
Blacksburg–Christiansburg–Radford, VA	435	4.2	15	0.1	90	0.9	0	0.0	140	1.4
Bloomington, IN	420	3.3	10	0.1	210	1.6	0	0.0	190	1.5
Bloomington–Normal, IL	1,145	7.2	50	0.3	290	1.8	0	0.0	145	0.9
Boise City–Nampa, ID	300	0.6	185	0.4	570	1.2	360	0.8	710	1.5
Boston–Cambridge–Quincy, MA–NH	27,340	7.4	275	0.1	16,070	4.4	100	0.0	5,670	1.5
Boulder, CO	125	0.7	35	0.2	345	1.9	15	0.1	320	1.8
Bowling Green, KY	800	8.3	10	0.1	155	1.6	4	0.0	63	0.7
Bremerton–Silverdale, WA	400	2.3	305	1.8	845	4.9	300	1.7	565	3.3
Bridgeport–Stamford–Norwalk, CT	9,015	13.5	95	0.1	2,250	3.4	0	0.0	795	1.2
Brownsville–Harlingen, TX	160	0.7	20	0.1	35	0.1	0	0.0	50	0.2
Brunswick, GA	1,565	20.6	0	0.0	50	0.7	0	0.0	45	0.6
Buffalo–Niagara Falls, NY	10,010	9.9	435	0.4	1,350	1.3	10	0.0	955	0.9
Burlington, NC	2,360	19.3	35	0.3	75	0.6	30	0.2	179	1.5
Burlington–South Burlington, VT	260	1.4	75	0.4	260	1.4	0	0.0	110	0.6
Canton–Massillon, OH	1,815	5.7	90	0.3	80	0.3	0	0.0	350	1.1
Cape Coral–Fort Myers, FL	2,495	5.8	135	0.3	390	0.9	0	0.0	340	0.8
Cape Girardeau–Jackson, MO–IL	885	11.7	0	0.0	65	0.9	0	0.0	35	0.5
Carson City, NV	145	3.1	135	2.9	80	1.7	40	0.8	130	2.8

PART C—METROPOLITAN STATISTICAL AREA TABLES

C-9 Administrative Support Workers, by Metropolitan Statistical Area, Sex, Race, and Hispanic or Latino Origin, 2006–2010—*Continued*

Metropolitan Statistical Area	Total who worked in the last 5 years	Male Number	Male Percent	Female Number	Female Percent	Hispanic or Latino Number	Hispanic or Latino Percent	White alone, not Hispanic or Latino Number	White alone, not Hispanic or Latino Percent
Casper, WY	6,575	1,225	18.6	5,350	81.4	285	4.3	6,040	91.9
Cedar Rapids, IA	22,095	5,405	24.5	16,690	75.5	390	1.8	20,725	93.8
Champaign–Urbana, IL	18,505	4,630	25.0	13,875	75.0	585	3.2	14,945	80.8
Charleston, WV	24,435	5,460	22.3	18,975	77.7	155	0.6	22,690	92.9
Charleston–North Charleston–Summerville, SC.	48,200	11,080	23.0	37,120	77.0	1,035	2.1	32,765	68.0
Charlotte–Gastonia–Rock Hill, NC–SC	134,725	34,780	25.8	99,945	74.2	6,535	4.9	84,700	62.9
Charlottesville, VA	13,250	3,045	23.0	10,200	77.0	340	2.6	10,275	77.5
Chattanooga, TN–GA	41,610	9,395	22.6	32,215	77.4	515	1.2	35,255	84.7
Cheyenne, WY	7,815	1,755	22.5	6,060	77.5	835	10.7	6,665	85.3
Chicago–Joliet–Naperville, IL–IN–WI	775,800	210,690	27.2	565,105	72.8	128,520	16.6	459,540	59.2
Chico, CA	15,560	4,020	25.8	11,540	74.2	1,455	9.4	12,845	82.6
Cincinnati–Middletown, OH–KY–IN	177,740	44,610	25.1	133,130	74.9	2,710	1.5	149,815	84.3
Clarksville, TN–KY	16,960	4,060	23.9	12,900	76.1	580	3.4	12,175	71.8
Cleveland, TN	8,315	2,080	25.0	6,240	75.0	200	2.4	7,890	94.9
Cleveland–Elyria–Mentor, OH	174,020	42,235	24.3	131,785	75.7	4,875	2.8	131,970	75.8
Coeur d'Alene, ID	11,035	2,385	21.6	8,645	78.3	430	3.9	10,285	93.2
College Station–Bryan, TX	17,140	4,355	25.4	12,785	74.6	3,130	18.3	11,610	67.7
Colorado Springs, CO	47,810	12,505	26.2	35,310	73.9	5,925	12.4	36,150	75.6
Columbia, MO	14,450	4,160	28.8	10,285	71.2	170	1.2	12,590	87.1
Columbia, SC	62,450	15,155	24.3	47,300	75.7	975	1.6	39,370	63.0
Columbus, GA–AL	21,535	4,955	23.0	16,580	77.0	995	4.6	10,845	50.4
Columbus, IN	5,485	1,130	20.6	4,360	79.5	110	2.0	5,195	94.7
Columbus, OH	162,440	45,615	28.1	116,825	71.9	3,140	1.9	127,880	78.7
Corpus Christi, TX	30,415	7,160	23.5	23,255	76.5	17,305	56.9	11,565	38.0
Corvallis, OR	5,965	1,550	26.0	4,415	74.0	365	6.1	5,135	86.1
Crestview–Fort Walton Beach–Destin, FL	12,740	2,660	20.9	10,080	79.1	660	5.2	10,080	79.1
Cumberland, MD–WV	7,355	1,860	25.3	5,495	74.7	50	0.7	7,040	95.7
Dallas–Fort Worth–Arlington, TX	516,285	140,260	27.2	376,020	72.8	100,580	19.5	288,555	55.9
Dalton, GA	8,850	2,330	26.3	6,520	73.7	1,045	11.8	7,290	82.4
Danville, IL	5,695	1,100	19.3	4,595	80.7	115	2.0	5,230	91.8
Danville, VA	7,855	1,685	21.5	6,170	78.5	40	0.5	5,250	66.8
Davenport–Moline–Rock Island, IA–IL	29,430	6,805	23.1	22,625	76.9	1,760	6.0	25,565	86.9
Dayton, OH	65,115	16,995	26.1	48,120	73.9	950	1.5	53,250	81.8
Decatur, AL	10,280	2,315	22.5	7,970	77.5	300	2.9	8,665	84.3
Decatur, IL	8,445	1,840	21.8	6,600	78.2	200	2.4	7,095	84.0
Deltona–Daytona Beach–Ormond Beach, FL	36,365	7,600	20.9	28,765	79.1	3,265	9.0	28,820	79.3
Denver–Aurora–Broomfield, CO	211,625	57,060	27.0	154,565	73.0	36,930	17.5	149,625	70.7
Des Moines–West Des Moines, IA	54,855	14,135	25.8	40,720	74.2	1,585	2.9	48,740	88.9
Detroit–Warren–Livonia, MI	326,860	77,655	23.8	249,200	76.2	8,430	2.6	235,870	72.2
Dothan, AL	9,505	2,035	21.4	7,475	78.6	155	1.6	7,765	81.7
Dover, DE	12,730	2,955	23.2	9,775	76.8	500	3.9	8,920	70.1
Dubuque, IA	7,935	1,985	25.0	5,950	75.0	190	2.4	7,610	95.9
Duluth, MN–WI	20,830	5,305	25.5	15,525	74.5	155	0.7	19,510	93.7
Durham–Chapel Hill, NC	34,545	9,205	26.6	25,340	73.4	1,355	3.9	19,250	55.7
Eau Claire, WI	13,265	2,885	21.7	10,380	78.3	180	1.4	12,620	95.1
El Centro, CA	10,290	2,590	25.2	7,705	74.9	8,185	79.5	1,410	13.7
Elizabethtown, KY	8,240	2,250	27.3	5,990	72.7	215	2.6	6,855	83.2
Elkhart–Goshen, IN	14,270	3,340	23.4	10,935	76.6	860	6.0	12,515	87.7
Elmira, NY	7,210	1,455	20.2	5,755	79.8	225	3.1	6,555	90.9
El Paso, TX	53,065	17,250	32.5	35,815	67.5	45,170	85.1	6,055	11.4
Erie, PA	20,910	5,155	24.7	15,750	75.3	440	2.1	19,085	91.3
Eugene–Springfield, OR	28,070	6,655	23.7	21,415	76.3	1,155	4.1	24,875	88.6
Evansville, IN–KY	27,185	5,540	20.4	21,645	79.6	345	1.3	25,300	93.1
Fairbanks, AK	8,000	2,135	26.7	5,865	73.3	485	6.1	5,770	72.1
Fargo, ND–MN	18,205	4,275	23.5	13,930	76.5	235	1.3	17,410	95.6

C-9 Administrative Support Workers, by Metropolitan Statistical Area, Sex, Race, and Hispanic or Latino Origin, 2006–2010—*Continued*

Metropolitan Statistical Area	Black alone, not Hispanic or Latino Number	Percent	American Indian and Alaska Native alone, not Hispanic or Latino Number	Percent	Asian alone, not Hispanic or Latino Number	Percent	Native Hawaiian and Other Pacific Islander alone, not Hispanic or Latino Number	Percent	Two or more races, not Hispanic or Latino Number	Percent
Casper, WY	0	0.0	55	0.8	75	1.1	0	0.0	120	1.8
Cedar Rapids, IA	540	2.4	75	0.3	160	0.7	0	0.0	210	1.0
Champaign–Urbana, IL	2,065	11.2	30	0.2	660	3.6	0	0.0	230	1.2
Charleston, WV	850	3.5	25	0.1	140	0.6	0	0.0	580	2.4
Charleston–North Charleston–Summerville, SC	13,210	27.4	100	0.2	515	1.1	15	0.0	555	1.2
Charlotte–Gastonia–Rock Hill, NC–SC	38,295	28.4	455	0.3	2,725	2.0	85	0.1	1,930	1.4
Charlottesville, VA	2,010	15.2	10	0.1	445	3.4	0	0.0	165	1.2
Chattanooga, TN–GA	5,300	12.7	90	0.2	210	0.5	4	0.0	240	0.6
Cheyenne, WY	45	0.6	45	0.6	135	1.7	0	0.0	95	1.2
Chicago–Joliet–Naperville, IL–IN–WI	146,160	18.8	665	0.1	33,270	4.3	215	0.0	7,430	1.0
Chico, CA	150	1.0	130	0.8	400	2.6	15	0.1	565	3.6
Cincinnati–Middletown, OH–KY–IN	21,885	12.3	180	0.1	1,445	0.8	60	0.0	1,640	0.9
Clarksville, TN–KY	3,550	20.9	75	0.4	220	1.3	45	0.3	310	1.8
Cleveland, TN	170	2.0	0	0.0	0	0.0	0	0.0	60	0.7
Cleveland–Elyria–Mentor, OH	33,690	19.4	270	0.2	1,660	1.0	0	0.0	1,545	0.9
Coeur d'Alene, ID	45	0.4	85	0.8	10	0.1	20	0.2	160	1.4
College Station–Bryan, TX	1,895	11.1	15	0.1	300	1.8	15	0.1	180	1.1
Colorado Springs, CO	3,330	7.0	245	0.5	960	2.0	155	0.3	1,050	2.2
Columbia, MO	1,060	7.3	35	0.2	245	1.7	10	0.1	335	2.3
Columbia, SC	20,865	33.4	125	0.2	495	0.8	0	0.0	615	1.0
Columbus, GA–AL	9,040	42.0	25	0.1	205	1.0	145	0.7	280	1.3
Columbus, IN	55	1.0	20	0.4	85	1.5	0	0.0	20	0.4
Columbus, OH	25,835	15.9	235	0.1	2,580	1.6	30	0.0	2,735	1.7
Corpus Christi, TX	990	3.3	55	0.2	235	0.8	10	0.0	245	0.8
Corvallis, OR	110	1.8	40	0.7	195	3.3	0	0.0	120	2.0
Crestview–Fort Walton Beach–Destin, FL	1,335	10.5	30	0.2	295	2.3	0	0.0	340	2.7
Cumberland, MD–WV	140	1.9	0	0.0	25	0.3	15	0.2	90	1.2
Dallas–Fort Worth–Arlington, TX	100,300	19.4	1,775	0.3	16,665	3.2	630	0.1	7,775	1.5
Dalton, GA	295	3.3	30	0.3	110	1.2	0	0.0	80	0.9
Danville, IL	315	5.5	0	0.0	0	0.0	0	0.0	34	0.6
Danville, VA	2,460	31.3	0	0.0	85	1.1	0	0.0	15	0.2
Davenport–Moline–Rock Island, IA–IL	1,510	5.1	45	0.2	160	0.5	0	0.0	395	1.3
Dayton, OH	9,515	14.6	20	0.0	565	0.9	0	0.0	810	1.2
Decatur, AL	900	8.8	195	1.9	30	0.3	0	0.0	185	1.8
Decatur, IL	1,045	12.4	0	0.0	10	0.1	0	0.0	100	1.2
Deltona–Daytona Beach–Ormond Beach, FL	3,345	9.2	65	0.2	420	1.2	15	0.0	440	1.2
Denver–Aurora–Broomfield, CO	14,020	6.6	1,170	0.6	6,165	2.9	175	0.1	3,540	1.7
Des Moines–West Des Moines, IA	2,685	4.9	25	0.0	1,390	2.5	20	0.0	400	0.7
Detroit–Warren–Livonia, MI	71,945	22.0	730	0.2	6,090	1.9	15	0.0	3,785	1.2
Dothan, AL	1,480	15.6	20	0.2	30	0.3	0	0.0	60	0.6
Dover, DE	2,865	22.5	65	0.5	160	1.3	15	0.1	200	1.6
Dubuque, IA	55	0.7	0	0.0	35	0.4	0	0.0	50	0.6
Duluth, MN–WI	215	1.0	555	2.7	100	0.5	10	0.0	274	1.3
Durham–Chapel Hill, NC	12,495	36.2	60	0.2	655	1.9	0	0.0	725	2.1
Eau Claire, WI	50	0.4	90	0.7	295	2.2	0	0.0	35	0.3
El Centro, CA	335	3.3	80	0.8	230	2.2	15	0.1	35	0.3
Elizabethtown, KY	915	11.1	0	0.0	105	1.3	35	0.4	115	1.4
Elkhart–Goshen, IN	745	5.2	65	0.5	60	0.4	10	0.1	20	0.1
Elmira, NY	280	3.9	0	0.0	45	0.6	0	0.0	105	1.5
El Paso, TX	1,150	2.2	175	0.3	155	0.3	0	0.0	360	0.7
Erie, PA	985	4.7	20	0.1	160	0.8	0	0.0	220	1.1
Eugene–Springfield, OR	200	0.7	280	1.0	560	2.0	45	0.2	960	3.4
Evansville, IN–KY	1,270	4.7	40	0.1	50	0.2	10	0.0	175	0.6
Fairbanks, AK	495	6.2	465	5.8	330	4.1	15	0.2	435	5.4
Fargo, ND–MN	80	0.4	200	1.1	160	0.9	10	0.1	110	0.6

C-9 Administrative Support Workers, by Metropolitan Statistical Area, Sex, Race, and Hispanic or Latino Origin, 2006–2010—Continued

Metropolitan Statistical Area	Total who worked in the last 5 years	Male Number	Male Percent	Female Number	Female Percent	Hispanic or Latino Number	Hispanic or Latino Percent	White alone, not Hispanic or Latino Number	White alone, not Hispanic or Latino Percent
Farmington, NM	8,390	1,545	18.4	6,845	81.6	1,445	17.2	4,480	53.4
Fayetteville, NC	23,370	5,960	25.5	17,415	74.5	2,040	8.7	11,265	48.2
Fayetteville–Springdale–Rogers, AR–MO	32,235	9,130	28.3	23,105	71.7	2,305	7.2	28,050	87.0
Flagstaff, AZ	10,375	2,450	23.6	7,925	76.4	1,225	11.8	6,745	65.0
Flint, MI	27,430	6,410	23.4	21,020	76.6	620	2.3	21,655	78.9
Florence, SC	15,225	3,215	21.1	12,010	78.9	95	0.6	9,910	65.1
Florence–Muscle Shoals, AL	9,685	2,110	21.8	7,570	78.2	115	1.2	8,330	86.0
Fond du Lac, WI	7,960	1,655	20.8	6,305	79.2	140	1.8	7,735	97.2
Fort Collins–Loveland, CO	20,770	5,210	25.1	15,560	74.9	1,600	7.7	18,430	88.7
Fort Smith, AR–OK	19,070	3,930	20.6	15,140	79.4	725	3.8	15,860	83.2
Fort Wayne, IN	32,685	7,985	24.4	24,700	75.6	1,070	3.3	28,290	86.6
Fresno, CA	62,685	16,375	26.1	46,310	73.9	25,550	40.8	27,600	44.0
Gadsden, AL	6,685	1,630	24.4	5,050	75.5	90	1.3	5,545	82.9
Gainesville, FL	18,885	4,965	26.3	13,920	73.7	1,685	8.9	13,220	70.0
Gainesville, GA	10,795	2,625	24.3	8,170	75.7	1,115	10.3	9,020	83.6
Glens Falls, NY	9,990	2,015	20.2	7,975	79.8	250	2.5	9,550	95.6
Goldsboro, NC	6,985	1,495	21.4	5,490	78.6	180	2.6	4,755	68.1
Grand Forks, ND–MN	8,210	2,160	26.3	6,050	73.7	125	1.5	7,685	93.6
Grand Junction, CO	10,745	2,095	19.5	8,645	80.5	1,075	10.0	9,220	85.8
Grand Rapids–Wyoming, MI	60,650	14,650	24.2	46,000	75.8	3,240	5.3	52,290	86.2
Great Falls, MT	6,885	1,300	18.9	5,580	81.0	225	3.3	6,275	91.1
Greeley, CO	19,260	4,490	23.3	14,770	76.7	3,745	19.4	14,920	77.5
Green Bay, WI	26,030	5,630	21.6	20,400	78.4	560	2.2	24,040	92.4
Greensboro–High Point, NC	56,595	14,565	25.7	42,030	74.3	1,375	2.4	37,350	66.0
Greenville, NC	13,490	3,225	23.9	10,265	76.1	325	2.4	8,125	60.2
Greenville–Mauldin–Easley, SC	44,260	10,740	24.3	33,520	75.7	1,370	3.1	34,560	78.1
Gulfport–Biloxi, MS	15,705	3,005	19.1	12,700	80.9	300	1.9	11,920	75.9
Hagerstown–Martinsburg, MD–WV	21,570	5,310	24.6	16,260	75.4	395	1.8	19,330	89.6
Hanford–Corcoran, CA	7,350	1,945	26.5	5,405	73.5	2,695	36.7	3,555	48.4
Harrisburg–Carlisle, PA	53,695	13,600	25.3	40,095	74.7	1,645	3.1	44,595	83.1
Harrisonburg, VA	7,830	1,820	23.2	6,010	76.8	465	5.9	6,845	87.4
Hartford–West Hartford–East Hartford, CT	104,450	25,800	24.7	78,650	75.3	10,955	10.5	77,475	74.2
Hattiesburg, MS	9,250	2,405	26.0	6,845	74.0	120	1.3	6,745	72.9
Hickory–Lenoir–Morganton, NC	23,685	5,635	23.8	18,050	76.2	570	2.4	21,040	88.8
Hinesville–Fort Stewart, GA	5,265	1,625	30.9	3,640	69.1	345	6.6	2,195	41.7
Holland–Grand Haven, MI	19,510	4,600	23.6	14,905	76.4	975	5.0	17,685	90.6
Honolulu, HI	77,000	19,715	25.6	57,285	74.4	5,155	6.7	10,450	13.6
Hot Springs, AR	5,810	1,225	21.1	4,585	78.9	230	4.0	4,955	85.3
Houma–Bayou Cane–Thibodaux, LA	14,245	2,895	20.3	11,350	79.7	200	1.4	12,385	86.9
Houston–Sugar Land–Baytown, TX	424,230	108,850	25.7	315,380	74.3	115,965	27.3	191,885	45.2
Huntington–Ashland, WV–KY–OH	20,880	5,905	28.3	14,975	71.7	130	0.6	19,745	94.6
Huntsville, AL	27,950	7,535	27.0	20,415	73.0	630	2.3	19,565	70.0
Idaho Falls, ID	9,360	2,050	21.9	7,315	78.2	550	5.9	8,655	92.5
Indianapolis–Carmel, IN	142,800	37,235	26.1	105,565	73.9	4,245	3.0	110,310	77.2
Iowa City, IA	12,390	3,455	27.9	8,930	72.1	310	2.5	11,240	90.7
Ithaca, NY	8,145	1,980	24.3	6,165	75.7	355	4.4	6,430	78.9
Jackson, MI	11,200	2,435	21.7	8,765	78.3	250	2.2	10,115	90.3
Jackson, MS	41,300	8,765	21.2	32,535	78.8	345	0.8	22,665	54.9
Jackson, TN	8,175	1,925	23.5	6,250	76.5	75	0.9	5,780	70.7
Jacksonville, FL	121,620	31,985	26.3	89,635	73.7	7,015	5.8	80,000	65.8
Jacksonville, NC	9,425	2,435	25.8	6,995	74.2	575	6.1	6,615	70.2
Janesville, WI	12,700	2,755	21.7	9,945	78.3	340	2.7	11,825	93.1
Jefferson City, MO	13,915	2,795	20.1	11,115	79.9	210	1.5	13,055	93.8
Johnson City, TN	13,635	3,150	23.1	10,485	76.9	170	1.2	12,775	93.7
Johnstown, PA	10,240	2,440	23.8	7,800	76.2	55	0.5	9,875	96.4

C-9 Administrative Support Workers, by Metropolitan Statistical Area, Sex, Race, and Hispanic or Latino Origin, 2006–2010—*Continued*

Metropolitan Statistical Area	Black alone, not Hispanic or Latino Number	Percent	American Indian and Alaska Native alone, not Hispanic or Latino Number	Percent	Asian alone, not Hispanic or Latino Number	Percent	Native Hawaiian and Other Pacific Islander alone, not Hispanic or Latino Number	Percent	Two or more races, not Hispanic or Latino Number	Percent
Farmington, NM	55	0.7	2,270	27.1	30	0.4	4	0.0	95	1.1
Fayetteville, NC	8,630	36.9	250	1.1	460	2.0	70	0.3	650	2.8
Fayetteville–Springdale–Rogers, AR–MO	325	1.0	470	1.5	365	1.1	225	0.7	495	1.5
Flagstaff, AZ	165	1.6	2,015	19.4	60	0.6	20	0.2	140	1.3
Flint, MI	4,505	16.4	120	0.4	130	0.5	30	0.1	370	1.3
Florence, SC	5,005	32.9	35	0.2	55	0.4	0	0.0	125	0.8
Florence–Muscle Shoals, AL	1,095	11.3	30	0.3	40	0.4	0	0.0	75	0.8
Fond du Lac, WI	0	0.0	4	0.1	55	0.7	0	0.0	30	0.4
Fort Collins–Loveland, CO	100	0.5	100	0.5	230	1.1	55	0.3	250	1.2
Fort Smith, AR–OK	705	3.7	605	3.2	255	1.3	0	0.0	914	4.8
Fort Wayne, IN	2,535	7.8	65	0.2	430	1.3	20	0.1	280	0.9
Fresno, CA	3,080	4.9	320	0.5	4,990	8.0	130	0.2	1,020	1.6
Gadsden, AL	1,000	15.0	20	0.3	15	0.2	0	0.0	12	0.2
Gainesville, FL	3,135	16.6	40	0.2	550	2.9	4	0.0	254	1.3
Gainesville, GA	520	4.8	25	0.2	35	0.3	0	0.0	85	0.8
Glens Falls, NY	55	0.6	15	0.2	50	0.5	0	0.0	69	0.7
Goldsboro, NC	1,905	27.3	4	0.1	30	0.4	15	0.2	88	1.3
Grand Forks, ND–MN	70	0.9	230	2.8	30	0.4	0	0.0	65	0.8
Grand Junction, CO	50	0.5	35	0.3	65	0.6	10	0.1	290	2.7
Grand Rapids–Wyoming, MI	3,385	5.6	140	0.2	860	1.4	15	0.0	725	1.2
Great Falls, MT	40	0.6	165	2.4	65	0.9	0	0.0	115	1.7
Greeley, CO	155	0.8	60	0.3	190	1.0	10	0.1	185	1.0
Green Bay, WI	160	0.6	585	2.2	530	2.0	25	0.1	130	0.5
Greensboro–High Point, NC	16,435	29.0	160	0.3	665	1.2	10	0.0	595	1.1
Greenville, NC	4,720	35.0	45	0.3	115	0.9	0	0.0	160	1.2
Greenville–Mauldin–Easley, SC	7,655	17.3	105	0.2	285	0.6	15	0.0	270	0.6
Gulfport–Biloxi, MS	3,070	19.5	160	1.0	160	1.0	4	0.0	85	0.5
Hagerstown–Martinsburg, MD–WV	1,570	7.3	15	0.1	70	0.3	0	0.0	180	0.8
Hanford–Corcoran, CA	465	6.3	70	1.0	350	4.8	0	0.0	215	2.9
Harrisburg–Carlisle, PA	5,830	10.9	35	0.1	810	1.5	0	0.0	784	1.5
Harrisonburg, VA	290	3.7	0	0.0	150	1.9	0	0.0	85	1.1
Hartford–West Hartford–East Hartford, CT	12,215	11.7	135	0.1	2,365	2.3	20	0.0	1,285	1.2
Hattiesburg, MS	2,205	23.8	0	0.0	95	1.0	0	0.0	90	1.0
Hickory–Lenoir–Morganton, NC	1,325	5.6	30	0.1	530	2.2	0	0.0	190	0.8
Hinesville–Fort Stewart, GA	2,455	46.6	0	0.0	90	1.7	40	0.8	140	2.7
Holland–Grand Haven, MI	255	1.3	50	0.3	345	1.8	0	0.0	200	1.0
Honolulu, HI	1,155	1.5	110	0.1	38,885	50.5	7,065	9.2	14,180	18.4
Hot Springs, AR	540	9.3	25	0.4	15	0.3	0	0.0	44	0.8
Houma–Bayou Cane–Thibodaux, LA	1,220	8.6	315	2.2	45	0.3	4	0.0	75	0.5
Houston–Sugar Land–Baytown, TX	91,675	21.6	900	0.2	18,745	4.4	465	0.1	4,600	1.1
Huntington–Ashland, WV–KY–OH	720	3.4	20	0.1	45	0.2	0	0.0	214	1.0
Huntsville, AL	6,840	24.5	125	0.4	355	1.3	10	0.0	425	1.5
Idaho Falls, ID	0	0.0	0	0.0	45	0.5	0	0.0	110	1.2
Indianapolis–Carmel, IN	24,335	17.0	230	0.2	1,755	1.2	0	0.0	1,920	1.3
Iowa City, IA	380	3.1	10	0.1	315	2.5	0	0.0	134	1.1
Ithaca, NY	360	4.4	20	0.2	785	9.6	25	0.3	170	2.1
Jackson, MI	680	6.1	15	0.1	25	0.2	0	0.0	114	1.0
Jackson, MS	17,960	43.5	4	0.0	160	0.4	0	0.0	155	0.4
Jackson, TN	2,235	27.3	10	0.1	10	0.1	4	0.0	65	0.8
Jacksonville, FL	28,740	23.6	225	0.2	3,210	2.6	10	0.0	2,425	2.0
Jacksonville, NC	1,630	17.3	45	0.5	165	1.8	70	0.7	330	3.5
Janesville, WI	360	2.8	4	0.0	50	0.4	4	0.0	120	0.9
Jefferson City, MO	435	3.1	15	0.1	80	0.6	15	0.1	94	0.7
Johnson City, TN	525	3.9	40	0.3	10	0.1	0	0.0	115	0.8
Johnstown, PA	180	1.8	35	0.3	35	0.3	25	0.2	29	0.3

C-9 Administrative Support Workers, by Metropolitan Statistical Area, Sex, Race, and Hispanic or Latino Origin, 2006–2010—*Continued*

Metropolitan Statistical Area	Total who worked in the last 5 years	Male Number	Male Percent	Female Number	Female Percent	Hispanic or Latino Number	Hispanic or Latino Percent	White alone, not Hispanic or Latino Number	White alone, not Hispanic or Latino Percent
Jonesboro, AR	8,330	1,885	22.6	6,445	77.4	100	1.2	7,410	89.0
Joplin, MO	12,270	2,950	24.0	9,320	76.0	345	2.8	11,420	93.1
Kalamazoo–Portage, MI	24,670	6,110	24.8	18,560	75.2	785	3.2	21,080	85.4
Kankakee–Bradley, IL	8,735	1,830	21.0	6,900	79.0	410	4.7	7,525	86.1
Kansas City, MO–KS	177,850	45,640	25.7	132,210	74.3	9,790	5.5	136,840	76.9
Kennewick–Pasco–Richland, WA	15,615	3,240	20.7	12,375	79.3	2,530	16.2	12,255	78.5
Killeen–Temple–Fort Hood, TX	26,715	7,360	27.6	19,350	72.4	4,375	16.4	15,305	57.3
Kingsport–Bristol–Bristol, TN–VA	20,710	5,080	24.5	15,625	75.4	120	0.6	19,970	96.4
Kingston, NY	14,860	3,265	22.0	11,590	78.0	960	6.5	12,875	86.6
Knoxville, TN	55,975	14,085	25.2	41,890	74.8	770	1.4	50,750	90.7
Kokomo, IN	6,605	1,355	20.5	5,250	79.5	55	0.8	6,220	94.2
La Crosse, WI–MN	11,545	2,795	24.2	8,750	75.8	85	0.7	11,140	96.5
Lafayette, IN	13,485	3,420	25.4	10,065	74.6	525	3.9	12,120	89.9
Lafayette, LA	22,150	4,725	21.3	17,430	78.7	505	2.3	16,270	73.5
Lake Charles, LA	14,350	3,005	20.9	11,345	79.1	300	2.1	10,535	73.4
Lake Havasu City–Kingman, AZ	13,940	3,490	25.0	10,450	75.0	1,950	14.0	11,040	79.2
Lakeland–Winter Haven, FL	43,015	9,935	23.1	33,080	76.9	5,120	11.9	30,740	71.5
Lancaster, PA	41,145	10,290	25.0	30,855	75.0	2,485	6.0	36,445	88.6
Lansing–East Lansing, MI	40,090	9,360	23.3	30,735	76.7	1,900	4.7	33,355	83.2
Laredo, TX	19,815	7,190	36.3	12,625	63.7	18,820	95.0	840	4.2
Las Cruces, NM	13,605	3,770	27.7	9,835	72.3	9,075	66.7	4,105	30.2
Las Vegas–Paradise, NV	148,995	42,290	28.4	106,705	71.6	28,730	19.3	84,230	56.5
Lawrence, KS	10,310	3,285	31.9	7,030	68.2	560	5.4	8,755	84.9
Lawton, OK	7,960	1,760	22.1	6,200	77.9	835	10.5	4,925	61.9
Lebanon, PA	10,655	2,510	23.6	8,145	76.4	770	7.2	9,675	90.8
Lewiston, ID–WA	4,720	880	18.6	3,845	81.5	100	2.1	4,275	90.6
Lewiston–Auburn, ME	9,985	2,385	23.9	7,600	76.1	175	1.8	9,595	96.1
Lexington–Fayette, KY	36,420	9,665	26.5	26,755	73.5	595	1.6	30,785	84.5
Lima, OH	7,710	1,875	24.3	5,835	75.7	70	0.9	6,845	88.8
Lincoln, NE	28,820	7,405	25.7	21,420	74.3	700	2.4	26,590	92.3
Little Rock–North Little Rock–Conway, AR	57,450	13,990	24.4	43,460	75.6	800	1.4	41,735	72.6
Logan, UT–ID	9,360	2,740	29.3	6,620	70.7	425	4.5	8,715	93.1
Longview, TX	14,190	2,905	20.5	11,285	79.5	830	5.8	10,910	76.9
Longview, WA	6,100	1,165	19.1	4,935	80.9	215	3.5	5,640	92.5
Los Angeles–Long Beach–Santa Ana, CA	1,024,100	323,315	31.6	700,790	68.4	414,860	40.5	340,750	33.3
Louisville/Jefferson County, KY–IN	105,825	25,915	24.5	79,915	75.5	1,830	1.7	87,950	83.1
Lubbock, TX	23,875	6,940	29.1	16,940	71.0	6,895	28.9	14,635	61.3
Lynchburg, VA	19,580	4,415	22.5	15,165	77.5	240	1.2	16,245	83.0
Macon, GA	16,010	3,915	24.5	12,095	75.5	120	0.7	9,875	61.7
Madera–Chowchilla, CA	7,900	1,705	21.6	6,200	78.5	3,290	41.6	4,105	52.0
Madison, WI	50,815	14,445	28.4	36,370	71.6	1,625	3.2	45,815	90.2
Manchester–Nashua, NH	35,200	9,225	26.2	25,975	73.8	1,160	3.3	32,495	92.3
Manhattan, KS	9,555	2,200	23.0	7,350	76.9	575	6.0	7,850	82.2
Mankato–North Mankato, MN	9,060	2,205	24.3	6,855	75.7	200	2.2	8,530	94.2
Mansfield, OH	8,880	1,875	21.1	7,005	78.9	150	1.7	8,150	91.8
McAllen–Edinburg–Mission, TX	42,960	13,375	31.1	29,585	68.9	39,600	92.2	2,930	6.8
Medford, OR	15,780	3,340	21.2	12,435	78.8	1,050	6.7	14,110	89.4
Memphis, TN–MS–AR	106,460	27,165	25.5	79,290	74.5	2,020	1.9	52,445	49.3
Merced, CA	14,960	3,495	23.4	11,470	76.7	6,555	43.8	6,650	44.5
Miami–Fort Lauderdale–Pompano Beach, FL	454,165	120,130	26.5	334,035	73.5	195,675	43.1	154,050	33.9
Michigan City–La Porte, IN	7,935	1,725	21.7	6,210	78.3	165	2.1	7,205	90.8
Midland, TX	10,860	2,395	22.1	8,465	77.9	3,350	30.8	6,535	60.2
Milwaukee–Waukesha–West Allis, WI	132,530	33,820	25.5	98,710	74.5	8,295	6.3	99,795	75.3
Minneapolis–St. Paul–Bloomington, MN–WI	284,220	75,575	26.6	208,640	73.4	8,530	3.0	240,590	84.6
Missoula, MT	8,925	2,000	22.4	6,925	77.6	75	0.8	8,440	94.6

C-9 Administrative Support Workers, by Metropolitan Statistical Area, Sex, Race, and Hispanic or Latino Origin, 2006–2010—*Continued*

Metropolitan Statistical Area	Black alone, not Hispanic or Latino Number	Percent	American Indian and Alaska Native alone, not Hispanic or Latino Number	Percent	Asian alone, not Hispanic or Latino Number	Percent	Native Hawaiian and Other Pacific Islander alone, not Hispanic or Latino Number	Percent	Two or more races, not Hispanic or Latino Number	Percent
Jonesboro, AR	685	8.2	0	0.0	50	0.6	0	0.0	80	1.0
Joplin, MO	50	0.4	230	1.9	10	0.1	0	0.0	215	1.8
Kalamazoo–Portage, MI	2,100	8.5	60	0.2	265	1.1	0	0.0	385	1.6
Kankakee–Bradley, IL	690	7.9	10	0.1	40	0.5	0	0.0	50	0.6
Kansas City, MO–KS	24,880	14.0	735	0.4	2,330	1.3	240	0.1	3,035	1.7
Kennewick–Pasco–Richland, WA	215	1.4	135	0.9	275	1.8	40	0.3	165	1.1
Killeen–Temple–Fort Hood, TX	5,770	21.6	85	0.3	500	1.9	125	0.5	560	2.1
Kingsport–Bristol–Bristol, TN–VA	380	1.8	25	0.1	120	0.6	0	0.0	100	0.5
Kingston, NY	580	3.9	10	0.1	125	0.8	0	0.0	315	2.1
Knoxville, TN	3,525	6.3	120	0.2	290	0.5	30	0.1	490	0.9
Kokomo, IN	265	4.0	0	0.0	0	0.0	0	0.0	65	1.0
La Crosse, WI–MN	130	1.1	20	0.2	135	1.2	0	0.0	30	0.3
Lafayette, IN	385	2.9	10	0.1	300	2.2	0	0.0	140	1.0
Lafayette, LA	5,125	23.1	60	0.3	50	0.2	0	0.0	140	0.6
Lake Charles, LA	3,245	22.6	65	0.5	90	0.6	0	0.0	110	0.8
Lake Havasu City–Kingman, AZ	70	0.5	355	2.5	235	1.7	15	0.1	275	2.0
Lakeland–Winter Haven, FL	6,315	14.7	60	0.1	410	1.0	0	0.0	380	0.9
Lancaster, PA	1,300	3.2	20	0.0	395	1.0	0	0.0	505	1.2
Lansing–East Lansing, MI	3,195	8.0	105	0.3	680	1.7	0	0.0	850	2.1
Laredo, TX	80	0.4	25	0.1	35	0.2	10	0.1	0	0.0
Las Cruces, NM	50	0.4	150	1.1	50	0.4	0	0.0	180	1.3
Las Vegas–Paradise, NV	17,995	12.1	820	0.6	11,510	7.7	1,425	1.0	4,280	2.9
Lawrence, KS	410	4.0	190	1.8	180	1.7	45	0.4	164	1.6
Lawton, OK	1,250	15.7	400	5.0	75	0.9	90	1.1	380	4.8
Lebanon, PA	70	0.7	0	0.0	20	0.2	0	0.0	115	1.1
Lewiston, ID–WA	0	0.0	185	3.9	50	1.1	0	0.0	105	2.2
Lewiston–Auburn, ME	45	0.5	10	0.1	35	0.4	0	0.0	134	1.3
Lexington–Fayette, KY	4,255	11.7	155	0.4	280	0.8	15	0.0	335	0.9
Lima, OH	775	10.1	0	0.0	25	0.3	0	0.0	0	0.0
Lincoln, NE	815	2.8	95	0.3	380	1.3	25	0.1	220	0.8
Little Rock–North Little Rock–Conway, AR	13,625	23.7	255	0.4	485	0.8	15	0.0	530	0.9
Logan, UT–ID	10	0.1	90	1.0	55	0.6	0	0.0	60	0.6
Longview, TX	2,090	14.7	125	0.9	85	0.6	20	0.1	135	1.0
Longview, WA	30	0.5	4	0.1	55	0.9	35	0.6	125	2.0
Los Angeles–Long Beach–Santa Ana, CA	92,970	9.1	2,995	0.3	148,325	14.5	4,465	0.4	19,735	1.9
Louisville/Jefferson County, KY–IN	13,760	13.0	135	0.1	860	0.8	55	0.1	1,235	1.2
Lubbock, TX	1,605	6.7	70	0.3	440	1.8	10	0.0	225	0.9
Lynchburg, VA	2,670	13.6	40	0.2	220	1.1	0	0.0	170	0.9
Macon, GA	5,705	35.6	10	0.1	140	0.9	0	0.0	160	1.0
Madera–Chowchilla, CA	175	2.2	75	0.9	180	2.3	0	0.0	80	1.0
Madison, WI	1,540	3.0	50	0.1	1,135	2.2	4	0.0	645	1.3
Manchester–Nashua, NH	645	1.8	70	0.2	525	1.5	30	0.1	275	0.8
Manhattan, KS	760	8.0	20	0.2	155	1.6	4	0.0	190	2.0
Mankato–North Mankato, MN	105	1.2	30	0.3	105	1.2	0	0.0	84	0.9
Mansfield, OH	360	4.1	4	0.0	60	0.7	0	0.0	150	1.7
McAllen–Edinburg–Mission, TX	135	0.3	0	0.0	230	0.5	0	0.0	60	0.1
Medford, OR	75	0.5	45	0.3	60	0.4	10	0.1	440	2.8
Memphis, TN–MS–AR	49,425	46.4	195	0.2	1,030	1.0	45	0.0	1,305	1.2
Merced, CA	370	2.5	150	1.0	955	6.4	50	0.3	230	1.5
Miami–Fort Lauderdale–Pompano Beach, FL	90,165	19.9	535	0.1	7,665	1.7	135	0.0	5,945	1.3
Michigan City–La Porte, IN	460	5.8	4	0.1	30	0.4	0	0.0	74	0.9
Midland, TX	805	7.4	40	0.4	65	0.6	0	0.0	70	0.6
Milwaukee–Waukesha–West Allis, WI	20,310	15.3	345	0.3	2,425	1.8	10	0.0	1,340	1.0
Minneapolis–St. Paul–Bloomington, MN–WI	19,255	6.8	1,500	0.5	9,720	3.4	90	0.0	4,535	1.6
Missoula, MT	30	0.3	150	1.7	135	1.5	4	0.0	100	1.1

C-9 Administrative Support Workers, by Metropolitan Statistical Area, Sex, Race, and Hispanic or Latino Origin, 2006–2010—Continued

Metropolitan Statistical Area	Total who worked in the last 5 years	Male Number	Male Percent	Female Number	Female Percent	Hispanic or Latino Number	Hispanic or Latino Percent	White alone, not Hispanic or Latino Number	White alone, not Hispanic or Latino Percent
Mobile, AL	30,745	6,530	21.2	24,215	78.8	390	1.3	20,225	65.8
Modesto, CA	35,715	8,835	24.7	26,880	75.3	11,385	31.9	20,365	57.0
Monroe, LA	13,875	3,080	22.2	10,795	77.8	220	1.6	9,230	66.5
Monroe, MI	11,850	2,595	21.9	9,255	78.1	200	1.7	11,380	96.0
Montgomery, AL	28,815	6,615	23.0	22,205	77.1	255	0.9	17,295	60.0
Morgantown, WV	8,655	2,100	24.3	6,555	75.7	100	1.2	8,150	94.2
Morristown, TN	8,980	2,365	26.3	6,615	73.7	270	3.0	8,315	92.6
Mount Vernon–Anacortes, WA	7,690	1,410	18.3	6,280	81.7	675	8.8	6,650	86.5
Muncie, IN	9,160	2,300	25.1	6,860	74.9	215	2.3	8,340	91.0
Muskegon–Norton Shores, MI	11,495	2,420	21.1	9,075	78.9	235	2.0	10,090	87.8
Myrtle Beach–North Myrtle Beach–Conway, SC	20,045	4,535	22.6	15,510	77.4	495	2.5	17,170	85.7
Napa, CA	9,145	2,040	22.3	7,105	77.7	2,140	23.4	5,940	65.0
Naples–Marco Island, FL	18,195	3,950	21.7	14,245	78.3	3,275	18.0	13,410	73.7
Nashville-Davidson–Murfreesboro–Franklin, TN	129,325	33,695	26.1	95,635	73.9	3,470	2.7	100,510	77.7
New Haven–Milford, CT	72,165	17,555	24.3	54,615	75.7	7,870	10.9	53,255	73.8
New Orleans–Metairie–Kenner, LA	82,205	18,905	23.0	63,300	77.0	3,865	4.7	51,305	62.4
New York–Northern New Jersey–Long Island, NY–NJ–PA	1,556,335	436,220	28.0	1,120,115	72.0	313,765	20.2	800,680	51.4
Niles–Benton Harbor, MI	11,605	2,660	22.9	8,940	77.0	270	2.3	9,565	82.4
North Port–Bradenton–Sarasota, FL	47,755	11,430	23.9	36,325	76.1	2,885	6.0	41,370	86.6
Norwich–New London, CT	20,225	4,410	21.8	15,820	78.2	860	4.3	16,935	83.7
Ocala, FL	21,630	4,215	19.5	17,415	80.5	1,825	8.4	17,050	78.8
Ocean City, NJ	7,145	1,460	20.4	5,685	79.6	190	2.7	6,590	92.2
Odessa, TX	10,045	2,165	21.6	7,880	78.4	4,430	44.1	5,145	51.2
Ogden–Clearfield, UT	42,325	11,610	27.4	30,715	72.6	3,535	8.4	36,730	86.8
Oklahoma City, OK	103,920	26,960	25.9	76,960	74.1	6,090	5.9	76,575	73.7
Olympia, WA	21,415	5,415	25.3	16,000	74.7	1,080	5.0	17,460	81.5
Omaha–Council Bluffs, NE–IA	79,300	21,170	26.7	58,130	73.3	3,810	4.8	66,180	83.5
Orlando–Kissimmee–Sanford, FL	178,910	47,055	26.3	131,850	73.7	42,630	23.8	100,500	56.2
Oshkosh–Neenah, WI	13,355	3,170	23.7	10,180	76.2	120	0.9	12,870	96.4
Owensboro, KY	8,100	1,555	19.2	6,545	80.8	115	1.4	7,755	95.7
Oxnard–Thousand Oaks–Ventura, CA	62,350	17,015	27.3	45,335	72.7	22,390	35.9	33,620	53.9
Palm Bay–Melbourne–Titusville, FL	38,140	9,180	24.1	28,955	75.9	2,925	7.7	30,325	79.5
Palm Coast, FL	6,045	1,435	23.7	4,605	76.2	410	6.8	4,795	79.3
Panama City–Lynn Haven–Panama City Beach, FL	13,195	2,865	21.7	10,330	78.3	475	3.6	10,890	82.5
Parkersburg–Marietta–Vienna, WV–OH	12,230	2,725	22.3	9,500	77.7	100	0.8	11,855	96.9
Pascagoula, MS	10,050	2,420	24.1	7,630	75.9	160	1.6	7,895	78.6
Pensacola–Ferry Pass–Brent, FL	34,055	8,375	24.6	25,680	75.4	1,255	3.7	26,585	78.1
Peoria, IL	29,185	6,520	22.3	22,665	77.7	835	2.9	25,330	86.8
Philadelphia–Camden–Wilmington, PA–NJ–DE–MD	515,530	130,365	25.3	385,165	74.7	27,135	5.3	357,595	69.4
Phoenix–Mesa–Glendale, AZ	325,520	88,435	27.2	237,090	72.8	74,540	22.9	214,075	65.8
Pine Bluff, AR	7,220	1,660	23.0	5,560	77.0	60	0.8	4,130	57.2
Pittsburgh, PA	189,970	48,135	25.3	141,835	74.7	1,580	0.8	169,485	89.2
Pittsfield, MA	10,220	2,210	21.6	8,015	78.4	165	1.6	9,620	94.1
Pocatello, ID	7,140	1,900	26.6	5,240	73.4	300	4.2	6,450	90.3
Portland–South Portland–Biddeford, ME	40,295	9,760	24.2	30,535	75.8	550	1.4	38,525	95.6
Portland–Vancouver–Hillsboro, OR–WA	179,280	46,975	26.2	132,305	73.8	11,965	6.7	148,480	82.8
Port St. Lucie, FL	28,395	5,890	20.7	22,510	79.3	3,485	12.3	21,045	74.1
Poughkeepsie–Newburgh–Middletown, NY	54,440	13,235	24.3	41,205	75.7	6,430	11.8	41,425	76.1
Prescott, AZ	14,035	2,980	21.2	11,055	78.8	1,355	9.7	12,165	86.7
Providence–New Bedford–Fall River, RI–MA	134,805	33,995	25.2	100,810	74.8	9,675	7.2	114,535	85.0

C-9 Administrative Support Workers, by Metropolitan Statistical Area, Sex, Race, and Hispanic or Latino Origin, 2006–2010—Continued

Metropolitan Statistical Area	Black alone, not Hispanic or Latino Number	Percent	American Indian and Alaska Native alone, not Hispanic or Latino Number	Percent	Asian alone, not Hispanic or Latino Number	Percent	Native Hawaiian and Other Pacific Islander alone, not Hispanic or Latino Number	Percent	Two or more races, not Hispanic or Latino Number	Percent
Mobile, AL	9,535	31.0	115	0.4	215	0.7	0	0.0	270	0.9
Modesto, CA	995	2.8	235	0.7	1,905	5.3	220	0.6	615	1.7
Monroe, LA	4,250	30.6	4	0.0	90	0.6	15	0.1	69	0.5
Monroe, MI	140	1.2	0	0.0	30	0.3	0	0.0	100	0.8
Montgomery, AL	10,640	36.9	45	0.2	230	0.8	0	0.0	345	1.2
Morgantown, WV	190	2.2	0	0.0	145	1.7	0	0.0	80	0.9
Morristown, TN	330	3.7	0	0.0	50	0.6	0	0.0	14	0.2
Mount Vernon–Anacortes, WA	40	0.5	90	1.2	65	0.8	4	0.1	168	2.2
Muncie, IN	315	3.4	65	0.7	60	0.7	0	0.0	170	1.9
Muskegon–Norton Shores, MI	980	8.5	35	0.3	30	0.3	0	0.0	120	1.0
Myrtle Beach–North Myrtle Beach–Conway, SC	2,100	10.5	35	0.2	115	0.6	0	0.0	130	0.6
Napa, CA	180	2.0	15	0.2	665	7.3	35	0.4	175	1.9
Naples–Marco Island, FL	1,000	5.5	80	0.4	165	0.9	0	0.0	260	1.4
Nashville-Davidson–Murfreesboro–Franklin, TN	22,040	17.0	215	0.2	1,755	1.4	55	0.0	1,280	1.0
New Haven–Milford, CT	8,940	12.4	65	0.1	1,160	1.6	40	0.1	835	1.2
New Orleans–Metairie–Kenner, LA	24,740	30.1	425	0.5	880	1.1	55	0.1	935	1.1
New York–Northern New Jersey–Long Island, NY–NJ–PA	294,720	18.9	1,980	0.1	120,765	7.8	300	0.0	24,120	1.5
Niles–Benton Harbor, MI	1,445	12.5	40	0.3	135	1.2	10	0.1	140	1.2
North Port–Bradenton–Sarasota, FL	2,625	5.5	10	0.0	410	0.9	10	0.0	445	0.9
Norwich–New London, CT	995	4.9	110	0.5	400	2.0	140	0.7	785	3.9
Ocala, FL	2,220	10.3	130	0.6	220	1.0	20	0.1	169	0.8
Ocean City, NJ	250	3.5	25	0.3	55	0.8	0	0.0	35	0.5
Odessa, TX	275	2.7	4	0.0	20	0.2	25	0.2	150	1.5
Ogden–Clearfield, UT	420	1.0	195	0.5	605	1.4	125	0.3	715	1.7
Oklahoma City, OK	11,340	10.9	3,385	3.3	1,940	1.9	30	0.0	4,555	4.4
Olympia, WA	690	3.2	235	1.1	1,130	5.3	260	1.2	560	2.6
Omaha–Council Bluffs, NE–IA	6,720	8.5	235	0.3	1,055	1.3	100	0.1	1,205	1.5
Orlando–Kissimmee–Sanford, FL	26,130	14.6	395	0.2	6,200	3.5	105	0.1	2,960	1.7
Oshkosh–Neenah, WI	45	0.3	55	0.4	235	1.8	0	0.0	25	0.2
Owensboro, KY	175	2.2	0	0.0	20	0.2	0	0.0	34	0.4
Oxnard–Thousand Oaks–Ventura, CA	1,410	2.3	130	0.2	3,245	5.2	190	0.3	1,360	2.2
Palm Bay–Melbourne–Titusville, FL	3,545	9.3	95	0.2	535	1.4	40	0.1	670	1.8
Palm Coast, FL	650	10.8	55	0.9	15	0.2	0	0.0	115	1.9
Panama City–Lynn Haven–Panama City Beach, FL	1,280	9.7	45	0.3	270	2.0	15	0.1	215	1.6
Parkersburg–Marietta–Vienna, WV–OH	140	1.1	15	0.1	30	0.2	0	0.0	90	0.7
Pascagoula, MS	1,740	17.3	0	0.0	110	1.1	30	0.3	115	1.1
Pensacola–Ferry Pass–Brent, FL	4,980	14.6	220	0.6	455	1.3	15	0.0	545	1.6
Peoria, IL	2,290	7.8	20	0.1	365	1.3	0	0.0	350	1.2
Philadelphia–Camden–Wilmington, PA–NJ–DE–MD	109,205	21.2	485	0.1	14,895	2.9	70	0.0	6,150	1.2
Phoenix–Mesa–Glendale, AZ	17,690	5.4	6,165	1.9	7,370	2.3	690	0.2	4,990	1.5
Pine Bluff, AR	3,000	41.6	0	0.0	15	0.2	0	0.0	15	0.2
Pittsburgh, PA	15,500	8.2	130	0.1	1,415	0.7	65	0.0	1,800	0.9
Pittsfield, MA	170	1.7	4	0.0	60	0.6	10	0.1	190	1.9
Pocatello, ID	30	0.4	195	2.7	55	0.8	50	0.7	60	0.8
Portland–South Portland–Biddeford, ME	330	0.8	80	0.2	405	1.0	10	0.0	390	1.0
Portland–Vancouver–Hillsboro, OR–WA	4,285	2.4	1,030	0.6	8,310	4.6	830	0.5	4,380	2.4
Port St. Lucie, FL	3,300	11.6	30	0.1	215	0.8	0	0.0	329	1.2
Poughkeepsie–Newburgh–Middletown, NY	4,600	8.4	120	0.2	865	1.6	0	0.0	1,005	1.8
Prescott, AZ	70	0.5	285	2.0	90	0.6	0	0.0	75	0.5
Providence–New Bedford–Fall River, RI–MA	5,050	3.7	435	0.3	2,125	1.6	35	0.0	2,950	2.2

PART C—METROPOLITAN STATISTICAL AREA TABLES

C-9 Administrative Support Workers, by Metropolitan Statistical Area, Sex, Race, and Hispanic or Latino Origin, 2006–2010—Continued

Metropolitan Statistical Area	Total who worked in the last 5 years	Male Number	Male Percent	Female Number	Female Percent	Hispanic or Latino Number	Hispanic or Latino Percent	White alone, not Hispanic or Latino Number	White alone, not Hispanic or Latino Percent
Provo–Orem, UT	38,455	11,320	29.4	27,140	70.6	3,310	8.6	33,345	86.7
Pueblo, CO	11,790	2,805	23.8	8,985	76.2	4,525	38.4	6,880	58.4
Punta Gorda, FL	10,730	2,510	23.4	8,220	76.6	695	6.5	9,275	86.4
Racine, WI	15,310	3,705	24.2	11,605	75.8	1,405	9.2	12,375	80.8
Raleigh–Cary, NC	83,275	21,035	25.3	62,240	74.7	3,740	4.5	56,800	68.2
Rapid City, SD	10,505	2,190	20.8	8,315	79.2	350	3.3	9,370	89.2
Reading, PA	33,020	8,205	24.8	24,815	75.2	3,470	10.5	27,955	84.7
Redding, CA	12,775	3,130	24.5	9,645	75.5	940	7.4	10,960	85.8
Reno–Sparks, NV	36,885	9,585	26.0	27,300	74.0	5,555	15.1	27,330	74.1
Richmond, VA	103,210	23,990	23.2	79,220	76.8	2,450	2.4	62,255	60.3
Riverside–San Bernardino–Ontario, CA	300,970	81,890	27.2	219,080	72.8	123,955	41.2	124,385	41.3
Roanoke, VA	26,210	5,885	22.5	20,325	77.5	420	1.6	22,425	85.6
Rochester, MN	14,440	3,030	21.0	11,410	79.0	80	0.6	13,765	95.3
Rochester, NY	84,960	21,210	25.0	63,750	75.0	3,815	4.5	70,870	83.4
Rockford, IL	28,300	6,490	22.9	21,810	77.1	1,675	5.9	23,890	84.4
Rocky Mount, NC	11,385	2,960	26.0	8,430	74.0	260	2.3	6,355	55.8
Rome, GA	6,425	1,380	21.5	5,045	78.5	165	2.6	5,375	83.7
Sacramento–Arden-Arcade–Roseville, CA	175,530	47,775	27.2	127,755	72.8	28,305	16.1	104,440	59.5
Saginaw–Saginaw Township North, MI	14,465	3,585	24.8	10,885	75.3	1,030	7.1	11,195	77.4
St. Cloud, MN	16,615	4,155	25.0	12,455	75.0	160	1.0	15,690	94.4
St. George, UT	8,315	1,750	21.0	6,565	79.0	355	4.3	7,685	92.4
St. Joseph, MO–KS	9,055	2,020	22.3	7,035	77.7	180	2.0	8,630	95.3
St. Louis, MO–IL	230,390	54,985	23.9	175,405	76.1	3,795	1.6	178,400	77.4
Salem, OR	30,070	7,140	23.7	22,925	76.2	3,860	12.8	24,085	80.1
Salinas, CA	24,695	5,910	23.9	18,785	76.1	10,990	44.5	10,400	42.1
Salisbury, MD	8,970	1,905	21.2	7,065	78.8	75	0.8	6,520	72.7
Salt Lake City, UT	103,175	29,455	28.5	73,725	71.5	11,275	10.9	84,475	81.9
San Angelo, TX	8,825	2,100	23.8	6,725	76.2	3,150	35.7	5,170	58.6
San Antonio–New Braunfels, TX	167,775	48,430	28.9	119,345	71.1	92,100	54.9	60,160	35.9
San Diego–Carlsbad–San Marcos, CA	218,465	63,960	29.3	154,505	70.7	60,590	27.7	111,970	51.3
Sandusky, OH	5,440	1,070	19.7	4,370	80.3	75	1.4	5,075	93.3
San Francisco–Oakland–Fremont, CA	327,660	98,455	30.0	229,205	70.0	60,925	18.6	137,140	41.9
San Jose–Sunnyvale–Santa Clara, CA	118,625	33,915	28.6	84,710	71.4	35,325	29.8	46,690	39.4
San Luis Obispo–Paso Robles, CA	19,230	4,565	23.7	14,660	76.2	3,565	18.5	14,155	73.6
Santa Barbara–Santa Maria–Goleta, CA	28,365	7,540	26.6	20,825	73.4	10,025	35.3	16,135	56.9
Santa Cruz–Watsonville, CA	16,245	3,915	24.1	12,330	75.9	4,365	26.9	10,280	63.3
Santa Fe, NM	10,165	2,425	23.9	7,740	76.1	5,710	56.2	3,820	37.6
Santa Rosa–Petaluma, CA	36,100	8,890	24.6	27,210	75.4	5,905	16.4	27,000	74.8
Savannah, GA	23,380	4,560	19.5	18,820	80.5	790	3.4	14,070	60.2
Scranton–Wilkes-Barre, PA	47,860	12,205	25.5	35,655	74.5	1,415	3.0	44,900	93.8
Seattle–Tacoma–Bellevue, WA	264,425	69,730	26.4	194,695	73.6	14,735	5.6	194,380	73.5
Sebastian–Vero Beach, FL	7,985	1,645	20.6	6,345	79.5	625	7.8	6,625	83.0
Sheboygan, WI	8,570	1,960	22.9	6,610	77.1	145	1.7	8,225	96.0
Sherman–Denison, TX	8,535	2,140	25.1	6,395	74.9	605	7.1	7,410	86.8
Shreveport–Bossier City, LA	28,750	6,660	23.2	22,090	76.8	485	1.7	17,395	60.5
Sioux City, IA–NE–SD	12,280	3,080	25.1	9,200	74.9	635	5.2	10,955	89.2
Sioux Falls, SD	22,845	5,650	24.7	17,190	75.2	265	1.2	21,705	95.0
South Bend–Mishawaka, IN–MI	25,805	5,695	22.1	20,115	78.0	1,175	4.6	21,290	82.5
Spartanburg, SC	18,745	4,220	22.5	14,525	77.5	400	2.1	14,685	78.3
Spokane, WA	38,170	9,670	25.3	28,500	74.7	1,305	3.4	34,530	90.5
Springfield, IL	21,885	5,350	24.4	16,535	75.6	245	1.1	19,035	87.0
Springfield, MA	55,455	14,725	26.6	40,730	73.4	5,090	9.2	45,130	81.4
Springfield, MO	35,065	8,645	24.7	26,420	75.3	540	1.5	33,110	94.4
Springfield, OH	11,125	2,545	22.9	8,585	77.2	145	1.3	9,840	88.4
State College, PA	10,150	2,590	25.5	7,560	74.5	390	3.8	9,175	90.4

C-9 Administrative Support Workers, by Metropolitan Statistical Area, Sex, Race, and Hispanic or Latino Origin, 2006–2010—*Continued*

Metropolitan Statistical Area	Black alone, not Hispanic or Latino Number	Percent	American Indian and Alaska Native alone, not Hispanic or Latino Number	Percent	Asian alone, not Hispanic or Latino Number	Percent	Native Hawaiian and Other Pacific Islander alone, not Hispanic or Latino Number	Percent	Two or more races, not Hispanic or Latino Number	Percent
Provo–Orem, UT	275	0.7	140	0.4	460	1.2	345	0.9	575	1.5
Pueblo, CO	85	0.7	25	0.2	55	0.5	10	0.1	198	1.7
Punta Gorda, FL	525	4.9	0	0.0	115	1.1	0	0.0	125	1.2
Racine, WI	1,185	7.7	15	0.1	110	0.7	0	0.0	220	1.4
Raleigh–Cary, NC	19,885	23.9	170	0.2	1,640	2.0	30	0.0	1,005	1.2
Rapid City, SD	90	0.9	490	4.7	90	0.9	0	0.0	114	1.1
Reading, PA	1,045	3.2	4	0.0	295	0.9	0	0.0	250	0.8
Redding, CA	95	0.7	105	0.8	320	2.5	30	0.2	330	2.6
Reno–Sparks, NV	860	2.3	540	1.5	1,820	4.9	130	0.4	655	1.8
Richmond, VA	35,390	34.3	375	0.4	1,565	1.5	115	0.1	1,055	1.0
Riverside–San Bernardino–Ontario, CA	27,515	9.1	1,185	0.4	15,760	5.2	1,035	0.3	7,140	2.4
Roanoke, VA	2,995	11.4	15	0.1	200	0.8	0	0.0	155	0.6
Rochester, MN	230	1.6	0	0.0	300	2.1	0	0.0	70	0.5
Rochester, NY	8,205	9.7	165	0.2	1,235	1.5	20	0.0	650	0.8
Rockford, IL	2,330	8.2	35	0.1	210	0.7	0	0.0	165	0.6
Rocky Mount, NC	4,535	39.8	55	0.5	50	0.4	0	0.0	130	1.1
Rome, GA	770	12.0	20	0.3	55	0.9	0	0.0	40	0.6
Sacramento–Arden-Arcade–Roseville, CA	15,240	8.7	1,255	0.7	18,425	10.5	1,740	1.0	6,125	3.5
Saginaw–Saginaw Township North, MI	2,000	13.8	75	0.5	90	0.6	0	0.0	74	0.5
St. Cloud, MN	405	2.4	15	0.1	250	1.5	0	0.0	95	0.6
St. George, UT	55	0.7	55	0.7	0	0.0	60	0.7	105	1.3
St. Joseph, MO–KS	120	1.3	50	0.6	15	0.2	0	0.0	67	0.7
St. Louis, MO–IL	42,750	18.6	370	0.2	2,400	1.0	50	0.0	2,625	1.1
Salem, OR	235	0.8	375	1.2	645	2.1	120	0.4	745	2.5
Salinas, CA	680	2.8	70	0.3	1,870	7.6	150	0.6	535	2.2
Salisbury, MD	2,230	24.9	0	0.0	115	1.3	0	0.0	35	0.4
Salt Lake City, UT	1,190	1.2	655	0.6	2,435	2.4	1,745	1.7	1,400	1.4
San Angelo, TX	295	3.3	0	0.0	125	1.4	0	0.0	84	1.0
San Antonio–New Braunfels, TX	11,135	6.6	435	0.3	1,915	1.1	205	0.1	1,815	1.1
San Diego–Carlsbad–San Marcos, CA	13,355	6.1	665	0.3	24,345	11.1	1,575	0.7	5,970	2.7
Sandusky, OH	245	4.5	0	0.0	15	0.3	0	0.0	25	0.5
San Francisco–Oakland–Fremont, CA	34,625	10.6	970	0.3	81,300	24.8	3,355	1.0	9,350	2.9
San Jose–Sunnyvale–Santa Clara, CA	4,400	3.7	585	0.5	28,105	23.7	600	0.5	2,925	2.5
San Luis Obispo–Paso Robles, CA	330	1.7	120	0.6	640	3.3	0	0.0	420	2.2
Santa Barbara–Santa Maria–Goleta, CA	590	2.1	170	0.6	1,060	3.7	25	0.1	360	1.3
Santa Cruz–Watsonville, CA	185	1.1	85	0.5	890	5.5	50	0.3	385	2.4
Santa Fe, NM	95	0.9	385	3.8	90	0.9	0	0.0	65	0.6
Santa Rosa–Petaluma, CA	580	1.6	520	1.4	1,230	3.4	135	0.4	735	2.0
Savannah, GA	7,850	33.6	90	0.4	360	1.5	0	0.0	210	0.9
Scranton–Wilkes-Barre, PA	935	2.0	50	0.1	265	0.6	0	0.0	300	0.6
Seattle–Tacoma–Bellevue, WA	15,095	5.7	2,420	0.9	25,020	9.5	2,350	0.9	10,425	3.9
Sebastian–Vero Beach, FL	615	7.7	25	0.3	75	0.9	0	0.0	20	0.3
Sheboygan, WI	55	0.6	0	0.0	145	1.7	0	0.0	4	0.0
Sherman–Denison, TX	260	3.0	165	1.9	4	0.0	0	0.0	85	1.0
Shreveport–Bossier City, LA	10,405	36.2	70	0.2	190	0.7	25	0.1	184	0.6
Sioux City, IA–NE–SD	210	1.7	190	1.5	110	0.9	0	0.0	190	1.5
Sioux Falls, SD	340	1.5	215	0.9	185	0.8	20	0.1	120	0.5
South Bend–Mishawaka, IN–MI	2,765	10.7	80	0.3	265	1.0	10	0.0	219	0.8
Spartanburg, SC	3,395	18.1	35	0.2	110	0.6	4	0.0	115	0.6
Spokane, WA	365	1.0	220	0.6	575	1.5	100	0.3	1,070	2.8
Springfield, IL	2,170	9.9	4	0.0	160	0.7	10	0.0	265	1.2
Springfield, MA	3,370	6.1	75	0.1	995	1.8	0	0.0	790	1.4
Springfield, MO	570	1.6	155	0.4	225	0.6	0	0.0	470	1.3
Springfield, OH	1,020	9.2	25	0.2	50	0.4	0	0.0	44	0.4
State College, PA	340	3.3	10	0.1	205	2.0	0	0.0	30	0.3

C-9 Administrative Support Workers, by Metropolitan Statistical Area, Sex, Race, and Hispanic or Latino Origin, 2006–2010—Continued

Metropolitan Statistical Area	Total who worked in the last 5 years	Male Number	Male Percent	Female Number	Female Percent	Hispanic or Latino Number	Hispanic or Latino Percent	White alone, not Hispanic or Latino Number	White alone, not Hispanic or Latino Percent
Steubenville–Weirton, OH–WV	8,775	2,315	26.4	6,465	73.7	125	1.4	8,410	95.8
Stockton, CA	49,330	12,400	25.1	36,930	74.9	15,920	32.3	21,390	43.4
Sumter, SC	6,255	1,740	27.8	4,515	72.2	50	0.8	3,740	59.8
Syracuse, NY	56,190	14,000	24.9	42,190	75.1	1,225	2.2	49,755	88.5
Tallahassee, FL	32,595	8,765	26.9	23,830	73.1	1,365	4.2	19,815	60.8
Tampa–St. Petersburg–Clearwater, FL	233,725	61,145	26.2	172,580	73.8	33,090	14.2	164,005	70.2
Terre Haute, IN	11,690	3,205	27.4	8,480	72.5	80	0.7	11,055	94.6
Texarkana, TX–Texarkana, AR	9,045	1,925	21.3	7,125	78.8	125	1.4	6,695	74.0
Toledo, OH	50,940	12,345	24.2	38,595	75.8	1,720	3.4	42,840	84.1
Topeka, KS	22,005	5,045	22.9	16,960	77.1	1,280	5.8	18,730	85.1
Trenton–Ewing, NJ	33,040	8,760	26.5	24,280	73.5	3,875	11.7	19,750	59.8
Tucson, AZ	75,675	21,075	27.8	54,600	72.2	25,930	34.3	42,670	56.4
Tulsa, OK	76,180	17,970	23.6	58,210	76.4	3,355	4.4	55,860	73.3
Tuscaloosa, AL	14,425	3,665	25.4	10,760	74.6	205	1.4	10,635	73.7
Tyler, TX	15,490	3,955	25.5	11,535	74.5	1,550	10.0	10,605	68.5
Utica–Rome, NY	25,390	6,315	24.9	19,075	75.1	670	2.6	22,985	90.5
Valdosta, GA	10,640	2,185	20.5	8,450	79.4	315	3.0	6,660	62.6
Vallejo–Fairfield, CA	35,190	9,660	27.5	25,530	72.5	6,855	19.5	15,010	42.7
Victoria, TX	7,970	1,940	24.3	6,035	75.7	2,905	36.4	4,695	58.9
Vineland–Millville–Bridgeton, NJ	11,470	2,535	22.1	8,940	77.9	2,200	19.2	7,260	63.3
Virginia Beach–Norfolk–Newport News, VA–NC	130,720	30,650	23.4	100,070	76.6	5,675	4.3	75,210	57.5
Visalia–Porterville, CA	24,560	6,235	25.4	18,325	74.6	12,355	50.3	10,445	42.5
Waco, TX	18,300	5,005	27.3	13,295	72.7	3,250	17.8	12,245	66.9
Warner Robins, GA	9,880	2,440	24.7	7,445	75.4	440	4.5	6,175	62.5
Washington–Arlington–Alexandria, DC–VA–MD–WV	451,390	130,915	29.0	320,475	71.0	42,745	9.5	208,580	46.2
Waterloo–Cedar Falls, IA	13,790	3,215	23.3	10,575	76.7	124	0.9	12,605	91.4
Wausau, WI	11,840	2,485	21.0	9,355	79.0	95	0.8	11,180	94.4
Wenatchee–East Wenatchee, WA	7,285	1,705	23.4	5,580	76.6	1,165	16.0	5,830	80.0
Wheeling, WV–OH	10,600	2,420	22.8	8,180	77.2	80	0.8	10,275	96.9
Wichita, KS	49,975	11,820	23.7	38,155	76.3	3,640	7.3	40,390	80.8
Wichita Falls, TX	10,365	2,530	24.4	7,835	75.6	1,160	11.2	8,030	77.5
Williamsport, PA	9,430	2,385	25.3	7,045	74.7	75	0.8	8,980	95.2
Wilmington, NC	24,005	4,870	20.3	19,135	79.7	465	1.9	19,990	83.3
Winchester, VA–WV	8,995	1,810	20.1	7,185	79.9	380	4.2	7,855	87.3
Winston–Salem, NC	35,335	8,500	24.1	26,840	76.0	1,585	4.5	25,240	71.4
Worcester, MA	65,580	16,505	25.2	49,080	74.8	4,535	6.9	57,640	87.9
Yakima, WA	14,190	2,855	20.1	11,330	79.8	4,195	29.6	9,165	64.6
York–Hanover, PA	36,625	7,780	21.2	28,845	78.8	960	2.6	33,820	92.3
Youngstown–Warren–Boardman, OH–PA	39,020	8,900	22.8	30,120	77.2	995	2.5	34,415	88.2
Yuba City, CA	11,420	2,660	23.3	8,760	76.7	2,145	18.8	7,065	61.9
Yuma, AZ	11,685	2,990	25.6	8,695	74.4	6,940	59.4	4,230	36.2

C-9. Administrative Support Workers, by Metropolitan Statistical Area, Sex, Race, and Hispanic or Latino Origin, 2006–2010—*Continued*

Metropolitan Statistical Area	Black alone, not Hispanic or Latino		American Indian and Alaska Native alone, not Hispanic or Latino		Asian alone, not Hispanic or Latino		Native Hawaiian and Other Pacific Islander alone, not Hispanic or Latino		Two or more races, not Hispanic or Latino	
	Number	Percent	Number	Percent	Number	Percent	Number	Percent	Number	Percent
Steubenville–Weirton, OH–WV	190	2.2	0	0.0	0	0.0	0	0.0	55	0.6
Stockton, CA	3,680	7.5	235	0.5	6,610	13.4	185	0.4	1,310	2.7
Sumter, SC	2,335	37.3	0	0.0	65	1.0	10	0.2	49	0.8
Syracuse, NY	3,365	6.0	430	0.8	695	1.2	35	0.1	685	1.2
Tallahassee, FL	10,585	32.5	125	0.4	430	1.3	0	0.0	275	0.8
Tampa–St. Petersburg–Clearwater, FL	29,035	12.4	415	0.2	4,185	1.8	175	0.1	2,815	1.2
Terre Haute, IN	340	2.9	20	0.2	85	0.7	0	0.0	109	0.9
Texarkana, TX–Texarkana, AR	2,015	22.3	25	0.3	20	0.2	30	0.3	140	1.5
Toledo, OH	5,400	10.6	0	0.0	490	1.0	35	0.1	455	0.9
Topeka, KS	1,195	5.4	220	1.0	175	0.8	0	0.0	405	1.8
Trenton–Ewing, NJ	7,565	22.9	0	0.0	1,465	4.4	0	0.0	390	1.2
Tucson, AZ	2,260	3.0	1,645	2.2	1,855	2.5	170	0.2	1,145	1.5
Tulsa, OK	6,980	9.2	4,915	6.5	1,010	1.3	30	0.0	4,030	5.3
Tuscaloosa, AL	3,435	23.8	4	0.0	35	0.2	0	0.0	105	0.7
Tyler, TX	3,095	20.0	0	0.0	50	0.3	0	0.0	185	1.2
Utica–Rome, NY	1,015	4.0	10	0.0	450	1.8	0	0.0	270	1.1
Valdosta, GA	3,405	32.0	10	0.1	115	1.1	0	0.0	135	1.3
Vallejo–Fairfield, CA	5,475	15.6	230	0.7	5,995	17.0	365	1.0	1,265	3.6
Victoria, TX	250	3.1	0	0.0	50	0.6	0	0.0	75	0.9
Vineland–Millville–Bridgeton, NJ	1,640	14.3	85	0.7	90	0.8	25	0.2	180	1.6
Virginia Beach–Norfolk–Newport News, VA–NC	43,025	32.9	260	0.2	3,955	3.0	165	0.1	2,430	1.9
Visalia–Porterville, CA	410	1.7	215	0.9	550	2.2	20	0.1	560	2.3
Waco, TX	2,580	14.1	40	0.2	125	0.7	0	0.0	60	0.3
Warner Robins, GA	2,740	27.7	30	0.3	270	2.7	0	0.0	230	2.3
Washington–Arlington–Alexandria, DC–VA–MD–WV	155,395	34.4	1,105	0.2	34,030	7.5	355	0.1	9,185	2.0
Waterloo–Cedar Falls, IA	765	5.5	45	0.3	135	1.0	4	0.0	115	0.8
Wausau, WI	65	0.5	75	0.6	330	2.8	4	0.0	90	0.8
Wenatchee–East Wenatchee, WA	0	0.0	100	1.4	90	1.2	0	0.0	100	1.4
Wheeling, WV–OH	135	1.3	15	0.1	95	0.9	0	0.0	0	0.0
Wichita, KS	3,645	7.3	225	0.5	820	1.6	45	0.1	1,210	2.4
Wichita Falls, TX	840	8.1	45	0.4	145	1.4	0	0.0	145	1.4
Williamsport, PA	265	2.8	10	0.1	50	0.5	0	0.0	50	0.5
Wilmington, NC	2,960	12.3	100	0.4	135	0.6	40	0.2	310	1.3
Winchester, VA–WV	545	6.1	25	0.3	150	1.7	20	0.2	14	0.2
Winston–Salem, NC	7,905	22.4	55	0.2	255	0.7	0	0.0	290	0.8
Worcester, MA	1,760	2.7	75	0.1	905	1.4	100	0.2	570	0.9
Yakima, WA	25	0.2	385	2.7	135	1.0	35	0.2	250	1.8
York–Hanover, PA	1,185	3.2	95	0.3	230	0.6	0	0.0	340	0.9
Youngstown–Warren–Boardman, OH–PA	3,200	8.2	30	0.1	155	0.4	0	0.0	225	0.6
Yuba City, CA	315	2.8	130	1.1	1,335	11.7	85	0.7	345	3.0
Yuma, AZ	135	1.2	125	1.1	45	0.4	45	0.4	169	1.4

C-10 Construction and Extractive Craft Workers, by Metropolitan Statistical Area, Sex, Race, and Hispanic or Latino Origin, 2006–2010

Metropolitan Statistical Area	Total who worked in the last 5 years	Male Number	Male Percent	Female Number	Female Percent	Hispanic or Latino Number	Hispanic or Latino Percent	White alone, not Hispanic or Latino Number	White alone, not Hispanic or Latino Percent
Abilene, TX	4,755	4,670	98.2	90	1.9	1,515	31.9	3,010	63.3
Akron, OH	17,880	17,340	97.0	545	3.0	325	1.8	15,855	88.7
Albany, GA	3,640	3,590	98.6	50	1.4	115	3.2	2,220	61.0
Albany–Schenectady–Troy, NY	21,460	20,975	97.7	485	2.3	750	3.5	19,420	90.5
Albuquerque, NM	30,185	29,560	97.9	630	2.1	20,390	67.6	7,150	23.7
Alexandria, LA	4,705	4,545	96.6	160	3.4	169	3.6	3,810	81.0
Allentown–Bethlehem–Easton, PA–NJ	21,855	21,295	97.4	560	2.6	2,245	10.3	18,875	86.4
Altoona, PA	3,300	3,255	98.6	45	1.4	10	0.3	3,270	99.1
Amarillo, TX	7,755	7,560	97.5	195	2.5	3,015	38.9	4,540	58.5
Ames, IA	1,975	1,850	93.7	130	6.6	20	1.0	1,870	94.7
Anchorage, AK	14,645	14,145	96.6	500	3.4	560	3.8	11,500	78.5
Anderson, IN	4,020	3,890	96.8	135	3.4	175	4.4	3,615	89.9
Anderson, SC	4,905	4,785	97.6	115	2.3	520	10.6	4,085	83.3
Ann Arbor, MI	4,835	4,680	96.8	155	3.2	230	4.8	4,125	85.3
Anniston–Oxford, AL	2,665	2,485	93.2	180	6.8	320	12.0	1,860	69.8
Appleton, WI	6,775	6,540	96.5	235	3.5	245	3.6	6,290	92.8
Asheville, NC	15,380	14,945	97.2	435	2.8	2,965	19.3	11,885	77.3
Athens–Clarke County, GA	4,845	4,775	98.6	70	1.4	1,120	23.1	3,175	65.5
Atlanta–Sandy Springs–Marietta, GA	161,600	156,995	97.2	4,605	2.8	66,580	41.2	68,300	42.3
Atlantic City–Hammonton, NJ	7,870	7,570	96.2	300	3.8	1,245	15.8	5,840	74.2
Auburn–Opelika, AL	4,090	3,915	95.7	175	4.3	695	17.0	2,915	71.3
Augusta–Richmond County, GA–SC	14,240	13,430	94.3	810	5.7	1,300	9.1	9,115	64.0
Austin–Round Rock–San Marcos, TX	59,685	58,220	97.5	1,465	2.5	40,025	67.1	17,740	29.7
Bakersfield–Delano, CA	26,445	26,045	98.5	400	1.5	13,785	52.1	11,080	41.9
Baltimore–Towson, MD	69,250	67,190	97.0	2,060	3.0	8,905	12.9	47,180	68.1
Bangor, ME	4,680	4,495	96.0	185	4.0	10	0.2	4,555	97.3
Barnstable Town, MA	8,925	8,715	97.6	210	2.4	220	2.5	8,330	93.3
Baton Rouge, LA	30,780	29,695	96.5	1,085	3.5	3,840	12.5	17,950	58.3
Battle Creek, MI	3,060	2,925	95.6	135	4.4	180	5.9	2,660	86.9
Bay City, MI	3,030	2,875	94.9	155	5.1	40	1.3	2,810	92.7
Beaumont–Port Arthur, TX	17,545	17,200	98.0	345	2.0	3,635	20.7	10,940	62.4
Bellingham, WA	6,080	5,845	96.1	235	3.9	425	7.0	5,115	84.1
Bend, OR	7,180	6,905	96.2	270	3.8	605	8.4	6,445	89.8
Billings, MT	5,940	5,820	98.0	120	2.0	280	4.7	5,255	88.5
Binghamton, NY	5,890	5,765	97.9	125	2.1	15	0.3	5,600	95.1
Birmingham–Hoover, AL	36,275	35,190	97.0	1,085	3.0	6,480	17.9	23,840	65.7
Bismarck, ND	4,015	3,945	98.3	70	1.7	119	3.0	3,680	91.7
Blacksburg–Christiansburg–Radford, VA	3,750	3,685	98.3	65	1.7	90	2.4	3,565	95.1
Bloomington, IN	5,360	5,175	96.5	180	3.4	160	3.0	5,090	95.0
Bloomington–Normal, IL	3,475	3,435	98.8	40	1.2	250	7.2	3,185	91.7
Boise City–Nampa, ID	19,790	19,115	96.6	670	3.4	4,140	20.9	15,000	75.8
Boston–Cambridge–Quincy, MA–NH	114,125	111,365	97.6	2,760	2.4	10,200	8.9	94,035	82.4
Boulder, CO	6,425	6,215	96.7	210	3.3	1,395	21.7	4,800	74.7
Bowling Green, KY	3,415	3,360	98.4	55	1.6	245	7.2	2,810	82.3
Bremerton–Silverdale, WA	8,765	8,325	95.0	440	5.0	585	6.7	7,370	84.1
Bridgeport–Stamford–Norwalk, CT	28,530	28,020	98.2	510	1.8	9,490	33.3	16,235	56.9
Brownsville–Harlingen, TX	9,950	9,900	99.5	45	0.5	9,350	94.0	535	5.4
Brunswick, GA	4,420	4,310	97.5	110	2.5	390	8.8	3,365	76.1
Buffalo–Niagara Falls, NY	23,265	22,645	97.3	620	2.7	785	3.4	20,485	88.1
Burlington, NC	4,320	4,290	99.3	30	0.7	1,385	32.1	2,400	55.6
Burlington–South Burlington, VT	5,625	5,535	98.4	90	1.6	105	1.9	5,445	96.8
Canton–Massillon, OH	10,125	9,750	96.3	370	3.7	280	2.8	9,470	93.5
Cape Coral–Fort Myers, FL	26,210	25,165	96.0	1,045	4.0	9,825	37.5	14,275	54.5
Cape Girardeau–Jackson, MO–IL	3,350	3,235	96.6	115	3.4	24	0.7	3,155	94.2
Carson City, NV	2,060	2,030	98.5	30	1.5	540	26.2	1,435	69.7

C-10 **Construction and Extractive Craft Workers, by Metropolitan Statistical Area, Sex, Race, and Hispanic or Latino Origin, 2006–2010**—*Continued*

Metropolitan Statistical Area	Black alone, not Hispanic or Latino Number	Percent	American Indian and Alaska Native alone, not Hispanic or Latino Number	Percent	Asian alone, not Hispanic or Latino Number	Percent	Native Hawaiian and Other Pacific Islander alone, not Hispanic or Latino Number	Percent	Two or more races, not Hispanic or Latino Number	Percent
Abilene, TX	130	2.7	10	0.2	0	0.0	0	0.0	95	2.0
Akron, OH	1,400	7.8	60	0.3	125	0.7	0	0.0	110	0.6
Albany, GA	1,240	34.1	0	0.0	0	0.0	0	0.0	65	1.8
Albany–Schenectady–Troy, NY	785	3.7	85	0.4	0	0.0	0	0.0	415	1.9
Albuquerque, NM	435	1.4	1,760	5.8	155	0.5	0	0.0	293	1.0
Alexandria, LA	595	12.6	15	0.3	35	0.7	10	0.2	75	1.6
Allentown–Bethlehem–Easton, PA–NJ	420	1.9	20	0.1	80	0.4	0	0.0	210	1.0
Altoona, PA	20	0.6	0	0.0	4	0.1	0	0.0	4	0.1
Amarillo, TX	125	1.6	10	0.1	25	0.3	0	0.0	44	0.6
Ames, IA	0	0.0	0	0.0	80	4.1	0	0.0	8	0.4
Anchorage, AK	430	2.9	950	6.5	195	1.3	95	0.6	920	6.3
Anderson, IN	110	2.7	10	0.2	0	0.0	0	0.0	105	2.6
Anderson, SC	300	6.1	0	0.0	0	0.0	0	0.0	0	0.0
Ann Arbor, MI	265	5.5	40	0.8	35	0.7	0	0.0	140	2.9
Anniston–Oxford, AL	375	14.1	20	0.8	40	1.5	4	0.2	40	1.5
Appleton, WI	15	0.2	160	2.4	10	0.1	0	0.0	54	0.8
Asheville, NC	380	2.5	95	0.6	10	0.1	0	0.0	49	0.3
Athens–Clarke County, GA	470	9.7	0	0.0	40	0.8	0	0.0	35	0.7
Atlanta–Sandy Springs–Marietta, GA	22,875	14.2	225	0.1	1,795	1.1	40	0.0	1,775	1.1
Atlantic City–Hammonton, NJ	555	7.1	10	0.1	215	2.7	0	0.0	8	0.1
Auburn–Opelika, AL	450	11.0	20	0.5	4	0.1	0	0.0	10	0.2
Augusta–Richmond County, GA–SC	3,540	24.9	50	0.4	20	0.1	65	0.5	145	1.0
Austin–Round Rock–San Marcos, TX	1,250	2.1	120	0.2	170	0.3	0	0.0	375	0.6
Bakersfield–Delano, CA	805	3.0	150	0.6	235	0.9	15	0.1	369	1.4
Baltimore–Towson, MD	11,615	16.8	200	0.3	505	0.7	30	0.0	820	1.2
Bangor, ME	15	0.3	35	0.7	4	0.1	0	0.0	60	1.3
Barnstable Town, MA	110	1.2	40	0.4	10	0.1	0	0.0	215	2.4
Baton Rouge, LA	8,630	28.0	35	0.1	55	0.2	0	0.0	270	0.9
Battle Creek, MI	115	3.8	70	2.3	0	0.0	0	0.0	34	1.1
Bay City, MI	80	2.6	20	0.7	15	0.5	0	0.0	65	2.1
Beaumont–Port Arthur, TX	2,645	15.1	50	0.3	50	0.3	0	0.0	230	1.3
Bellingham, WA	25	0.4	190	3.1	155	2.5	10	0.2	160	2.6
Bend, OR	0	0.0	35	0.5	10	0.1	0	0.0	79	1.1
Billings, MT	0	0.0	190	3.2	85	1.4	0	0.0	130	2.2
Binghamton, NY	130	2.2	75	1.3	30	0.5	0	0.0	45	0.8
Birmingham–Hoover, AL	5,590	15.4	70	0.2	55	0.2	25	0.1	215	0.6
Bismarck, ND	4	0.1	175	4.4	0	0.0	0	0.0	35	0.9
Blacksburg–Christiansburg–Radford, VA	70	1.9	0	0.0	0	0.0	0	0.0	30	0.8
Bloomington, IN	60	1.1	4	0.1	40	0.7	0	0.0	0	0.0
Bloomington–Normal, IL	35	1.0	4	0.1	0	0.0	0	0.0	0	0.0
Boise City–Nampa, ID	80	0.4	120	0.6	20	0.1	175	0.9	254	1.3
Boston–Cambridge–Quincy, MA–NH	4,680	4.1	215	0.2	1,800	1.6	40	0.0	3,160	2.8
Boulder, CO	30	0.5	60	0.9	85	1.3	0	0.0	55	0.9
Bowling Green, KY	260	7.6	0	0.0	55	1.6	0	0.0	45	1.3
Bremerton–Silverdale, WA	145	1.7	95	1.1	170	1.9	75	0.9	320	3.7
Bridgeport–Stamford–Norwalk, CT	1,515	5.3	0	0.0	170	0.6	0	0.0	1,120	3.9
Brownsville–Harlingen, TX	40	0.4	0	0.0	4	0.0	0	0.0	10	0.1
Brunswick, GA	615	13.9	0	0.0	40	0.9	0	0.0	4	0.1
Buffalo–Niagara Falls, NY	1,580	6.8	170	0.7	35	0.2	0	0.0	215	0.9
Burlington, NC	505	11.7	25	0.6	0	0.0	0	0.0	4	0.1
Burlington–South Burlington, VT	0	0.0	15	0.3	25	0.4	0	0.0	34	0.6
Canton–Massillon, OH	255	2.5	10	0.1	0	0.0	0	0.0	115	1.1
Cape Coral–Fort Myers, FL	1,600	6.1	30	0.1	80	0.3	0	0.0	395	1.5
Cape Girardeau–Jackson, MO–IL	130	3.9	0	0.0	0	0.0	0	0.0	45	1.3
Carson City, NV	40	1.9	30	1.5	15	0.7	0	0.0	4	0.2

C-10 Construction and Extractive Craft Workers, by Metropolitan Statistical Area, Sex, Race, and Hispanic or Latino Origin, 2006–2010—Continued

Metropolitan Statistical Area	Total who worked in the last 5 years	Male Number	Male Percent	Female Number	Female Percent	Hispanic or Latino Number	Hispanic or Latino Percent	White alone, not Hispanic or Latino Number	White alone, not Hispanic or Latino Percent
Casper, WY	3,600	3,350	93.1	250	6.9	460	12.8	3,105	86.3
Cedar Rapids, IA	7,820	7,685	98.3	135	1.7	185	2.4	7,360	94.1
Champaign–Urbana, IL	4,970	4,780	96.2	190	3.8	145	2.9	4,500	90.5
Charleston, WV	10,590	10,455	98.7	135	1.3	80	0.8	10,165	96.0
Charleston–North Charleston–Summerville, SC	22,845	21,820	95.5	1,025	4.5	4,805	21.0	12,340	54.0
Charlotte–Gastonia–Rock Hill, NC–SC	53,220	51,620	97.0	1,600	3.0	19,270	36.2	26,645	50.1
Charlottesville, VA	6,320	6,165	97.5	160	2.5	950	15.0	4,875	77.1
Chattanooga, TN–GA	16,240	15,720	96.8	520	3.2	1,300	8.0	13,615	83.8
Cheyenne, WY	3,400	3,275	96.3	125	3.7	570	16.8	2,745	80.7
Chicago–Joliet–Naperville, IL–IN–WI	252,265	246,255	97.6	6,005	2.4	72,940	28.9	157,025	62.2
Chico, CA	6,470	6,320	97.7	150	2.3	930	14.4	5,020	77.6
Cincinnati–Middletown, OH–KY–IN	54,445	52,905	97.2	1,540	2.8	2,650	4.9	47,410	87.1
Clarksville, TN–KY	5,845	5,650	96.7	195	3.3	130	2.2	4,885	83.6
Cleveland, TN	3,670	3,625	98.8	50	1.4	220	6.0	3,330	90.7
Cleveland–Elyria–Mentor, OH	46,135	44,845	97.2	1,290	2.8	1,740	3.8	38,125	82.6
Coeur d'Alene, ID	7,075	6,990	98.8	85	1.2	265	3.7	6,625	93.6
College Station–Bryan, TX	7,275	7,190	98.8	85	1.2	3,015	41.4	3,475	47.8
Colorado Springs, CO	18,020	17,665	98.0	355	2.0	5,305	29.4	11,495	63.8
Columbia, MO	4,370	4,230	96.8	140	3.2	210	4.8	3,920	89.7
Columbia, SC	21,490	20,765	96.6	725	3.4	4,530	21.1	11,545	53.7
Columbus, GA–AL	6,760	6,545	96.8	215	3.2	690	10.2	3,935	58.2
Columbus, IN	1,520	1,505	99.0	15	1.0	150	9.9	1,340	88.2
Columbus, OH	39,165	37,985	97.0	1,180	3.0	3,940	10.1	31,230	79.7
Corpus Christi, TX	15,655	15,285	97.6	370	2.4	10,605	67.7	4,550	29.1
Corvallis, OR	1,830	1,710	93.4	120	6.6	135	7.4	1,515	82.8
Crestview–Fort Walton Beach–Destin, FL	5,815	5,525	95.0	290	5.0	1,060	18.2	4,380	75.3
Cumberland, MD–WV	3,425	3,370	98.4	55	1.6	39	1.1	3,310	96.6
Dallas–Fort Worth–Arlington, TX	204,925	200,545	97.9	4,380	2.1	129,715	63.3	63,590	31.0
Dalton, GA	3,740	3,580	95.7	160	4.3	1,245	33.3	2,445	65.4
Danville, IL	2,920	2,755	94.3	165	5.7	310	10.6	2,390	81.8
Danville, VA	3,600	3,360	93.3	240	6.7	235	6.5	2,655	73.8
Davenport–Moline–Rock Island, IA–IL	10,590	10,180	96.1	410	3.9	435	4.1	9,740	92.0
Dayton, OH	19,185	18,595	96.9	590	3.1	565	2.9	16,535	86.2
Decatur, AL	5,570	5,400	96.9	170	3.1	1,220	21.9	3,880	69.7
Decatur, IL	2,945	2,890	98.1	55	1.9	50	1.7	2,590	87.9
Deltona–Daytona Beach–Ormond Beach, FL	16,175	15,715	97.2	460	2.8	1,855	11.5	13,125	81.1
Denver–Aurora–Broomfield, CO	87,320	84,700	97.0	2,620	3.0	39,845	45.6	43,605	49.9
Des Moines–West Des Moines, IA	16,580	16,275	98.2	305	1.8	2,010	12.1	14,100	85.0
Detroit–Warren–Livonia, MI	92,815	90,080	97.1	2,735	2.9	7,465	8.0	73,235	78.9
Dothan, AL	4,490	4,390	97.8	100	2.2	200	4.5	3,525	78.5
Dover, DE	5,230	5,115	97.8	115	2.2	505	9.7	4,130	79.0
Dubuque, IA	2,660	2,605	97.9	50	1.9	45	1.7	2,590	97.4
Duluth, MN–WI	9,770	9,495	97.2	275	2.8	90	0.9	9,390	96.1
Durham–Chapel Hill, NC	14,510	14,260	98.3	250	1.7	6,870	47.3	5,565	38.4
Eau Claire, WI	4,490	4,330	96.4	160	3.6	80	1.8	4,365	97.2
El Centro, CA	3,840	3,790	98.7	50	1.3	3,000	78.1	725	18.9
Elizabethtown, KY	3,380	3,285	97.2	95	2.8	90	2.7	3,080	91.1
Elkhart–Goshen, IN	4,150	3,990	96.1	160	3.9	585	14.1	3,305	79.6
Elmira, NY	1,820	1,725	94.8	95	5.2	0	0.0	1,755	96.4
El Paso, TX	18,840	18,565	98.5	275	1.5	17,185	91.2	1,395	7.4
Erie, PA	5,870	5,830	99.3	40	0.7	185	3.2	5,400	92.0
Eugene–Springfield, OR	9,615	9,405	97.8	210	2.2	795	8.3	8,225	85.5
Evansville, IN–KY	10,420	10,100	96.9	320	3.1	260	2.5	9,755	93.6
Fairbanks, AK	4,865	4,505	92.6	365	7.5	420	8.6	3,990	82.0
Fargo, ND–MN	6,985	6,795	97.3	190	2.7	170	2.4	6,410	91.8

C-10 **Construction and Extractive Craft Workers, by Metropolitan Statistical Area, Sex, Race, and Hispanic or Latino Origin, 2006–2010**—*Continued*

Metropolitan Statistical Area	Black alone, not Hispanic or Latino Number	Black alone, not Hispanic or Latino Percent	American Indian and Alaska Native alone, not Hispanic or Latino Number	American Indian and Alaska Native alone, not Hispanic or Latino Percent	Asian alone, not Hispanic or Latino Number	Asian alone, not Hispanic or Latino Percent	Native Hawaiian and Other Pacific Islander alone, not Hispanic or Latino Number	Native Hawaiian and Other Pacific Islander alone, not Hispanic or Latino Percent	Two or more races, not Hispanic or Latino Number	Two or more races, not Hispanic or Latino Percent
Casper, WY	15	0.4	15	0.4	0	0.0	0	0.0	4	0.1
Cedar Rapids, IA	175	2.2	0	0.0	10	0.1	0	0.0	84	1.1
Champaign–Urbana, IL	270	5.4	0	0.0	25	0.5	0	0.0	35	0.7
Charleston, WV	115	1.1	20	0.2	0	0.0	0	0.0	219	2.1
Charleston–North Charleston–Summerville, SC	4,970	21.8	285	1.2	50	0.2	0	0.0	389	1.7
Charlotte–Gastonia–Rock Hill, NC–SC	6,070	11.4	275	0.5	475	0.9	0	0.0	490	0.9
Charlottesville, VA	425	6.7	0	0.0	20	0.3	0	0.0	55	0.9
Chattanooga, TN–GA	965	5.9	35	0.2	30	0.2	85	0.5	210	1.3
Cheyenne, WY	0	0.0	50	1.5	35	1.0	0	0.0	0	0.0
Chicago–Joliet–Naperville, IL–IN–WI	18,835	7.5	325	0.1	1,575	0.6	15	0.0	1,555	0.6
Chico, CA	65	1.0	75	1.2	40	0.6	25	0.4	315	4.9
Cincinnati–Middletown, OH–KY–IN	3,510	6.4	145	0.3	215	0.4	0	0.0	520	1.0
Clarksville, TN–KY	625	10.7	80	1.4	15	0.3	65	1.1	50	0.9
Cleveland, TN	45	1.2	0	0.0	0	0.0	40	1.1	35	1.0
Cleveland–Elyria–Mentor, OH	5,725	12.4	65	0.1	85	0.2	0	0.0	390	0.8
Coeur d'Alene, ID	20	0.3	35	0.5	0	0.0	0	0.0	135	1.9
College Station–Bryan, TX	630	8.7	0	0.0	30	0.4	0	0.0	120	1.6
Colorado Springs, CO	520	2.9	165	0.9	150	0.8	80	0.4	305	1.7
Columbia, MO	155	3.5	4	0.1	25	0.6	0	0.0	60	1.4
Columbia, SC	5,110	23.8	65	0.3	50	0.2	0	0.0	185	0.9
Columbus, GA–AL	2,060	30.5	10	0.1	20	0.3	0	0.0	40	0.6
Columbus, IN	0	0.0	20	1.3	0	0.0	0	0.0	10	0.7
Columbus, OH	3,130	8.0	105	0.3	215	0.5	0	0.0	540	1.4
Corpus Christi, TX	350	2.2	0	0.0	80	0.5	0	0.0	70	0.4
Corvallis, OR	20	1.1	30	1.6	60	3.3	0	0.0	65	3.6
Crestview–Fort Walton Beach–Destin, FL	280	4.8	45	0.8	15	0.3	20	0.3	20	0.3
Cumberland, MD–WV	30	0.9	0	0.0	0	0.0	0	0.0	44	1.3
Dallas–Fort Worth–Arlington, TX	8,295	4.0	500	0.2	1,395	0.7	65	0.0	1,360	0.7
Dalton, GA	50	1.3	0	0.0	0	0.0	0	0.0	4	0.1
Danville, IL	170	5.8	0	0.0	0	0.0	0	0.0	48	1.6
Danville, VA	695	19.3	0	0.0	0	0.0	0	0.0	10	0.3
Davenport–Moline–Rock Island, IA–IL	285	2.7	25	0.2	50	0.5	0	0.0	60	0.6
Dayton, OH	1,800	9.4	0	0.0	75	0.4	0	0.0	210	1.1
Decatur, AL	300	5.4	95	1.7	0	0.0	0	0.0	74	1.3
Decatur, IL	195	6.6	35	1.2	0	0.0	0	0.0	75	2.5
Deltona–Daytona Beach–Ormond Beach, FL	740	4.6	40	0.2	0	0.0	0	0.0	415	2.6
Denver–Aurora–Broomfield, CO	1,760	2.0	575	0.7	510	0.6	30	0.0	990	1.1
Des Moines–West Des Moines, IA	280	1.7	0	0.0	65	0.4	25	0.2	105	0.6
Detroit–Warren–Livonia, MI	10,040	10.8	490	0.5	325	0.4	0	0.0	1,260	1.4
Dothan, AL	665	14.8	15	0.3	25	0.6	0	0.0	64	1.4
Dover, DE	520	9.9	20	0.4	40	0.8	0	0.0	20	0.4
Dubuque, IA	15	0.6	0	0.0	0	0.0	0	0.0	4	0.2
Duluth, MN–WI	10	0.1	175	1.8	0	0.0	0	0.0	99	1.0
Durham–Chapel Hill, NC	1,905	13.1	30	0.2	100	0.7	0	0.0	40	0.3
Eau Claire, WI	0	0.0	25	0.6	10	0.2	0	0.0	4	0.1
El Centro, CA	85	2.2	20	0.5	0	0.0	0	0.0	10	0.3
Elizabethtown, KY	180	5.3	0	0.0	10	0.3	0	0.0	20	0.6
Elkhart–Goshen, IN	180	4.3	10	0.2	0	0.0	10	0.2	60	1.4
Elmira, NY	25	1.4	4	0.2	0	0.0	0	0.0	35	1.9
El Paso, TX	155	0.8	25	0.1	0	0.0	0	0.0	80	0.4
Erie, PA	175	3.0	15	0.3	25	0.4	0	0.0	70	1.2
Eugene–Springfield, OR	65	0.7	100	1.0	15	0.2	65	0.7	350	3.6
Evansville, IN–KY	340	3.3	0	0.0	45	0.4	0	0.0	20	0.2
Fairbanks, AK	0	0.0	225	4.6	55	1.1	0	0.0	175	3.6
Fargo, ND–MN	50	0.7	215	3.1	30	0.4	0	0.0	105	1.5

PART C—METROPOLITAN STATISTICAL AREA TABLES

C-10 Construction and Extractive Craft Workers, by Metropolitan Statistical Area, Sex, Race, and Hispanic or Latino Origin, 2006–2010—Continued

Metropolitan Statistical Area	Total who worked in the last 5 years	Male Number	Male Percent	Female Number	Female Percent	Hispanic or Latino Number	Hispanic or Latino Percent	White alone, not Hispanic or Latino Number	White alone, not Hispanic or Latino Percent
Farmington, NM	6,305	6,025	95.6	280	4.4	1,360	21.6	2,390	37.9
Fayetteville, NC	7,080	6,725	95.0	355	5.0	685	9.7	4,135	58.4
Fayetteville–Springdale–Rogers, AR–MO	15,685	15,320	97.7	365	2.3	4,445	28.3	10,425	66.5
Flagstaff, AZ	5,120	4,860	94.9	265	5.2	1,255	24.5	1,900	37.1
Flint, MI	10,515	10,145	96.5	365	3.5	280	2.7	8,955	85.2
Florence, SC	5,065	4,885	96.4	180	3.6	265	5.2	3,025	59.7
Florence–Muscle Shoals, AL	5,380	5,245	97.5	130	2.4	355	6.6	4,680	87.0
Fond du Lac, WI	3,315	3,205	96.7	110	3.3	130	3.9	3,130	94.4
Fort Collins–Loveland, CO	9,585	9,095	94.9	490	5.1	1,580	16.5	7,720	80.5
Fort Smith, AR–OK	8,585	8,330	97.0	255	3.0	1,155	13.5	6,165	71.8
Fort Wayne, IN	9,785	9,500	97.1	285	2.9	695	7.1	8,500	86.9
Fresno, CA	22,060	21,730	98.5	330	1.5	12,630	57.3	8,195	37.1
Gadsden, AL	3,125	3,080	98.6	45	1.4	370	11.8	2,515	80.5
Gainesville, FL	4,685	4,540	96.9	145	3.1	350	7.5	3,395	72.5
Gainesville, GA	7,615	7,230	94.9	385	5.1	3,890	51.1	3,565	46.8
Glens Falls, NY	4,195	3,995	95.2	195	4.6	10	0.2	4,145	98.8
Goldsboro, NC	3,635	3,510	96.6	125	3.4	740	20.4	2,430	66.9
Grand Forks, ND–MN	2,990	2,915	97.5	75	2.5	165	5.5	2,675	89.5
Grand Junction, CO	7,320	7,090	96.9	230	3.1	1,360	18.6	5,780	79.0
Grand Rapids–Wyoming, MI	19,205	18,550	96.6	650	3.4	1,905	9.9	16,415	85.5
Great Falls, MT	2,795	2,675	95.7	125	4.5	130	4.7	2,495	89.3
Greeley, CO	10,785	10,545	97.8	240	2.2	3,835	35.6	6,580	61.0
Green Bay, WI	8,330	8,085	97.1	245	2.9	215	2.6	7,930	95.2
Greensboro–High Point, NC	19,865	19,185	96.6	680	3.4	5,315	26.8	11,560	58.2
Greenville, NC	4,955	4,905	99.0	50	1.0	1,240	25.0	2,855	57.6
Greenville–Mauldin–Easley, SC	19,505	18,995	97.4	510	2.6	5,275	27.0	12,565	64.4
Gulfport–Biloxi, MS	11,425	10,695	93.6	730	6.4	1,340	11.7	8,715	76.3
Hagerstown–Martinsburg, MD–WV	10,425	10,175	97.6	250	2.4	475	4.6	9,380	90.0
Hanford–Corcoran, CA	2,550	2,425	95.1	125	4.9	1,145	44.9	1,230	48.2
Harrisburg–Carlisle, PA	11,620	11,265	96.9	355	3.1	460	4.0	10,365	89.2
Harrisonburg, VA	4,225	4,085	96.7	140	3.3	540	12.8	3,600	85.2
Hartford–West Hartford–East Hartford, CT	28,390	27,725	97.7	665	2.3	3,160	11.1	22,965	80.9
Hattiesburg, MS	4,705	4,570	97.1	135	2.9	325	6.9	3,530	75.0
Hickory–Lenoir–Morganton, NC	10,295	10,115	98.3	180	1.7	1,515	14.7	8,550	83.1
Hinesville–Fort Stewart, GA	1,810	1,725	95.3	90	5.0	250	13.8	1,120	61.9
Holland–Grand Haven, MI	6,365	6,215	97.6	150	2.4	465	7.3	5,800	91.1
Honolulu, HI	28,055	27,275	97.2	780	2.8	2,570	9.2	4,700	16.8
Hot Springs, AR	3,135	3,035	96.8	100	3.2	275	8.8	2,710	86.4
Houma–Bayou Cane–Thibodaux, LA	9,825	9,590	97.6	235	2.4	550	5.6	7,685	78.2
Houston–Sugar Land–Baytown, TX	231,275	225,675	97.6	5,605	2.4	155,110	67.1	56,815	24.6
Huntington–Ashland, WV–KY–OH	7,495	7,325	97.7	170	2.3	0	0.0	7,340	97.9
Huntsville, AL	9,575	9,155	95.6	425	4.4	1,640	17.1	6,535	68.3
Idaho Falls, ID	4,620	4,505	97.5	115	2.5	685	14.8	3,790	82.0
Indianapolis–Carmel, IN	47,640	46,335	97.3	1,305	2.7	8,040	16.9	35,550	74.6
Iowa City, IA	3,440	3,350	97.4	90	2.6	260	7.6	3,140	91.3
Ithaca, NY	2,400	2,285	95.2	120	5.0	60	2.5	2,190	91.3
Jackson, MI	3,790	3,675	97.0	110	2.9	50	1.3	3,675	97.0
Jackson, MS	16,705	16,260	97.3	445	2.7	1,745	10.4	8,615	51.6
Jackson, TN	3,160	3,110	98.4	50	1.6	410	13.0	2,105	66.6
Jacksonville, FL	40,915	39,485	96.5	1,435	3.5	5,080	12.4	29,600	72.3
Jacksonville, NC	5,125	4,815	94.0	310	6.0	1,050	20.5	3,385	66.0
Janesville, WI	4,605	4,505	97.8	100	2.2	275	6.0	4,230	91.9
Jefferson City, MO	5,410	5,340	98.7	65	1.2	125	2.3	5,220	96.5
Johnson City, TN	5,400	5,210	96.5	190	3.5	350	6.5	4,960	91.9
Johnstown, PA	4,370	4,335	99.2	35	0.8	10	0.2	4,270	97.7

C-10 **Construction and Extractive Craft Workers, by Metropolitan Statistical Area, Sex, Race, and Hispanic or Latino Origin, 2006–2010**—*Continued*

Metropolitan Statistical Area	Black alone, not Hispanic or Latino Number	Percent	American Indian and Alaska Native alone, not Hispanic or Latino Number	Percent	Asian alone, not Hispanic or Latino Number	Percent	Native Hawaiian and Other Pacific Islander alone, not Hispanic or Latino Number	Percent	Two or more races, not Hispanic or Latino Number	Percent
Farmington, NM	0	0.0	2,545	40.4	0	0.0	0	0.0	10	0.2
Fayetteville, NC	1,545	21.8	465	6.6	0	0.0	10	0.1	249	3.5
Fayetteville–Springdale–Rogers, AR–MO	165	1.1	220	1.4	90	0.6	50	0.3	285	1.8
Flagstaff, AZ	4	0.1	1,955	38.2	0	0.0	4	0.1	0	0.0
Flint, MI	1,090	10.4	45	0.4	4	0.0	0	0.0	145	1.4
Florence, SC	1,720	34.0	10	0.2	0	0.0	0	0.0	49	1.0
Florence–Muscle Shoals, AL	300	5.6	4	0.1	35	0.7	0	0.0	0	0.0
Fond du Lac, WI	10	0.3	15	0.5	4	0.1	4	0.1	20	0.6
Fort Collins–Loveland, CO	70	0.7	55	0.6	4	0.0	0	0.0	155	1.6
Fort Smith, AR–OK	90	1.0	365	4.3	0	0.0	4	0.0	805	9.4
Fort Wayne, IN	385	3.9	50	0.5	85	0.9	0	0.0	70	0.7
Fresno, CA	435	2.0	120	0.5	395	1.8	15	0.1	270	1.2
Gadsden, AL	205	6.6	10	0.3	0	0.0	0	0.0	25	0.8
Gainesville, FL	785	16.8	30	0.6	0	0.0	65	1.4	65	1.4
Gainesville, GA	130	1.7	10	0.1	20	0.3	0	0.0	0	0.0
Glens Falls, NY	25	0.6	0	0.0	10	0.2	0	0.0	4	0.1
Goldsboro, NC	460	12.7	0	0.0	10	0.3	0	0.0	4	0.1
Grand Forks, ND–MN	35	1.2	55	1.8	0	0.0	0	0.0	64	2.1
Grand Junction, CO	30	0.4	55	0.8	15	0.2	10	0.1	65	0.9
Grand Rapids–Wyoming, MI	570	3.0	75	0.4	55	0.3	0	0.0	194	1.0
Great Falls, MT	0	0.0	105	3.8	0	0.0	0	0.0	70	2.5
Greeley, CO	45	0.4	90	0.8	55	0.5	0	0.0	184	1.7
Green Bay, WI	0	0.0	125	1.5	25	0.3	0	0.0	30	0.4
Greensboro–High Point, NC	2,540	12.8	145	0.7	100	0.5	0	0.0	210	1.1
Greenville, NC	775	15.6	40	0.8	0	0.0	0	0.0	50	1.0
Greenville–Mauldin–Easley, SC	1,455	7.5	55	0.3	55	0.3	15	0.1	74	0.4
Gulfport–Biloxi, MS	1,180	10.3	45	0.4	30	0.3	0	0.0	115	1.0
Hagerstown–Martinsburg, MD–WV	480	4.6	15	0.1	10	0.1	0	0.0	60	0.6
Hanford–Corcoran, CA	45	1.8	4	0.2	80	3.1	0	0.0	55	2.2
Harrisburg–Carlisle, PA	620	5.3	10	0.1	50	0.4	0	0.0	115	1.0
Harrisonburg, VA	30	0.7	0	0.0	0	0.0	0	0.0	55	1.3
Hartford–West Hartford–East Hartford, CT	1,625	5.7	20	0.1	155	0.5	15	0.1	450	1.6
Hattiesburg, MS	825	17.5	15	0.3	0	0.0	0	0.0	10	0.2
Hickory–Lenoir–Morganton, NC	150	1.5	25	0.2	30	0.3	0	0.0	25	0.2
Hinesville–Fort Stewart, GA	440	24.3	0	0.0	0	0.0	0	0.0	0	0.0
Holland–Grand Haven, MI	4	0.1	30	0.5	40	0.6	0	0.0	20	0.3
Honolulu, HI	330	1.2	20	0.1	9,855	35.1	4,360	15.5	6,215	22.2
Hot Springs, AR	90	2.9	40	1.3	0	0.0	0	0.0	25	0.8
Houma–Bayou Cane–Thibodaux, LA	1,125	11.5	285	2.9	50	0.5	0	0.0	125	1.3
Houston–Sugar Land–Baytown, TX	14,780	6.4	260	0.1	2,775	1.2	45	0.0	1,495	0.6
Huntington–Ashland, WV–KY–OH	135	1.8	0	0.0	0	0.0	0	0.0	20	0.3
Huntsville, AL	1,185	12.4	20	0.2	30	0.3	0	0.0	170	1.8
Idaho Falls, ID	4	0.1	10	0.2	10	0.2	4	0.1	115	2.5
Indianapolis–Carmel, IN	3,480	7.3	95	0.2	115	0.2	0	0.0	355	0.7
Iowa City, IA	25	0.7	0	0.0	0	0.0	0	0.0	15	0.4
Ithaca, NY	90	3.8	0	0.0	50	2.1	0	0.0	10	0.4
Jackson, MI	0	0.0	25	0.7	4	0.1	0	0.0	30	0.8
Jackson, MS	6,225	37.3	25	0.1	45	0.3	15	0.1	34	0.2
Jackson, TN	625	19.8	0	0.0	0	0.0	0	0.0	23	0.7
Jacksonville, FL	5,310	13.0	85	0.2	300	0.7	65	0.2	470	1.1
Jacksonville, NC	620	12.1	50	1.0	0	0.0	0	0.0	14	0.3
Janesville, WI	50	1.1	0	0.0	20	0.4	0	0.0	29	0.6
Jefferson City, MO	40	0.7	0	0.0	0	0.0	4	0.1	24	0.4
Johnson City, TN	65	1.2	0	0.0	20	0.4	0	0.0	0	0.0
Johnstown, PA	65	1.5	4	0.1	0	0.0	0	0.0	24	0.5

C-10 Construction and Extractive Craft Workers, by Metropolitan Statistical Area, Sex, Race, and Hispanic or Latino Origin, 2006–2010—Continued

Metropolitan Statistical Area	Total who worked in the last 5 years	Male Number	Male Percent	Female Number	Female Percent	Hispanic or Latino Number	Hispanic or Latino Percent	White alone, not Hispanic or Latino Number	White alone, not Hispanic or Latino Percent
Jonesboro, AR	3,425	3,280	95.8	145	4.2	420	12.3	2,795	81.6
Joplin, MO	4,755	4,560	95.9	190	4.0	525	11.0	4,085	85.9
Kalamazoo–Portage, MI	7,420	7,190	96.9	225	3.0	485	6.5	6,455	87.0
Kankakee–Bradley, IL	3,555	3,520	99.0	35	1.0	300	8.4	3,100	87.2
Kansas City, MO–KS	57,080	55,270	96.8	1,810	3.2	10,200	17.9	42,165	73.9
Kennewick–Pasco–Richland, WA	7,455	7,090	95.1	365	4.9	1,440	19.3	5,815	78.0
Killeen–Temple–Fort Hood, TX	10,000	9,405	94.1	600	6.0	3,445	34.5	5,160	51.6
Kingsport–Bristol–Bristol, TN–VA	9,585	9,275	96.8	305	3.2	290	3.0	9,000	93.9
Kingston, NY	6,235	6,065	97.3	165	2.6	355	5.7	5,730	91.9
Knoxville, TN	20,645	19,855	96.2	790	3.8	2,095	10.1	17,435	84.5
Kokomo, IN	2,570	2,460	95.7	105	4.1	170	6.6	2,335	90.9
La Crosse, WI–MN	3,610	3,555	98.5	50	1.4	30	0.8	3,565	98.8
Lafayette, IN	4,445	4,245	95.5	205	4.6	430	9.7	3,950	88.9
Lafayette, LA	9,515	9,330	98.1	180	1.9	1,085	11.4	6,310	66.3
Lake Charles, LA	9,755	9,135	93.6	620	6.4	465	4.8	7,710	79.0
Lake Havasu City–Kingman, AZ	6,480	6,355	98.1	130	2.0	1,280	19.8	5,040	77.8
Lakeland–Winter Haven, FL	21,065	20,470	97.2	595	2.8	6,470	30.7	12,545	59.6
Lancaster, PA	17,570	17,240	98.1	330	1.9	1,205	6.9	15,930	90.7
Lansing–East Lansing, MI	9,560	9,175	96.0	385	4.0	855	8.9	8,105	84.8
Laredo, TX	6,745	6,685	99.1	60	0.9	6,600	97.9	110	1.6
Las Cruces, NM	6,930	6,805	98.2	125	1.8	5,590	80.7	1,305	18.8
Las Vegas–Paradise, NV	78,715	76,140	96.7	2,575	3.3	40,485	51.4	32,400	41.2
Lawrence, KS	2,590	2,445	94.4	145	5.6	55	2.1	2,380	91.9
Lawton, OK	3,195	3,060	95.8	135	4.2	470	14.7	2,385	74.6
Lebanon, PA	3,415	3,345	98.0	70	2.0	260	7.6	3,070	89.9
Lewiston, ID–WA	1,700	1,575	92.6	125	7.4	65	3.8	1,590	93.5
Lewiston–Auburn, ME	3,900	3,785	97.1	115	2.9	0	0.0	3,730	95.6
Lexington–Fayette, KY	10,990	10,720	97.5	275	2.5	1,660	15.1	8,530	77.6
Lima, OH	2,730	2,640	96.7	90	3.3	70	2.6	2,500	91.6
Lincoln, NE	8,520	8,335	97.8	185	2.2	1,025	12.0	7,125	83.6
Little Rock–North Little Rock–Conway, AR	21,410	20,935	97.8	475	2.2	3,900	18.2	15,065	70.4
Logan, UT–ID	3,370	3,325	98.7	50	1.5	305	9.1	2,900	86.1
Longview, TX	8,420	8,110	96.3	310	3.7	2,755	32.7	4,765	56.6
Longview, WA	3,210	3,055	95.2	155	4.8	235	7.3	2,715	84.6
Los Angeles–Long Beach–Santa Ana, CA	336,655	330,095	98.1	6,560	1.9	234,855	69.8	75,005	22.3
Louisville/Jefferson County, KY–IN	36,610	35,530	97.0	1,080	3.0	3,245	8.9	30,870	84.3
Lubbock, TX	7,690	7,595	98.8	100	1.3	3,160	41.1	4,150	54.0
Lynchburg, VA	7,500	7,160	95.5	340	4.5	405	5.4	6,155	82.1
Macon, GA	5,940	5,780	97.3	155	2.6	425	7.2	3,690	62.1
Madera–Chowchilla, CA	3,345	3,290	98.4	55	1.6	1,595	47.7	1,665	49.8
Madison, WI	13,995	13,535	96.7	460	3.3	890	6.4	12,670	90.5
Manchester–Nashua, NH	12,495	12,280	98.3	210	1.7	905	7.2	11,325	90.6
Manhattan, KS	3,500	3,425	97.9	70	2.0	260	7.4	2,785	79.6
Mankato–North Mankato, MN	2,565	2,495	97.3	70	2.7	65	2.5	2,425	94.5
Mansfield, OH	2,770	2,705	97.7	65	2.3	29	1.0	2,605	94.0
McAllen–Edinburg–Mission, TX	24,965	24,635	98.7	325	1.3	24,345	97.5	485	1.9
Medford, OR	6,490	6,360	98.0	130	2.0	935	14.4	5,350	82.4
Memphis, TN–MS–AR	32,775	31,995	97.6	775	2.4	8,315	25.4	16,210	49.5
Merced, CA	7,970	7,770	97.5	195	2.4	4,975	62.4	2,590	32.5
Miami–Fort Lauderdale–Pompano Beach, FL	177,385	172,600	97.3	4,785	2.7	105,640	59.6	45,705	25.8
Michigan City–La Porte, IN	3,940	3,860	98.0	80	2.0	295	7.5	3,530	89.6
Midland, TX	6,765	6,645	98.2	120	1.8	3,630	53.7	2,895	42.8
Milwaukee–Waukesha–West Allis, WI	34,435	33,380	96.9	1,055	3.1	4,495	13.1	26,380	76.6
Minneapolis–St. Paul–Bloomington, MN–WI	80,820	78,310	96.9	2,510	3.1	6,360	7.9	70,545	87.3
Missoula, MT	3,540	3,405	96.2	135	3.8	35	1.0	3,345	94.5

C-10 **Construction and Extractive Craft Workers, by Metropolitan Statistical Area, Sex, Race, and Hispanic or Latino Origin, 2006–2010**—*Continued*

Metropolitan Statistical Area	Black alone, not Hispanic or Latino Number	Percent	American Indian and Alaska Native alone, not Hispanic or Latino Number	Percent	Asian alone, not Hispanic or Latino Number	Percent	Native Hawaiian and Other Pacific Islander alone, not Hispanic or Latino Number	Percent	Two or more races, not Hispanic or Latino Number	Percent
Jonesboro, AR	185	5.4	0	0.0	0	0.0	0	0.0	25	0.7
Joplin, MO	15	0.3	80	1.7	10	0.2	0	0.0	35	0.7
Kalamazoo–Portage, MI	280	3.8	70	0.9	0	0.0	35	0.5	95	1.3
Kankakee–Bradley, IL	110	3.1	20	0.6	20	0.6	0	0.0	0	0.0
Kansas City, MO–KS	3,180	5.6	395	0.7	180	0.3	115	0.2	845	1.5
Kennewick–Pasco–Richland, WA	50	0.7	70	0.9	30	0.4	0	0.0	55	0.7
Killeen–Temple–Fort Hood, TX	1,110	11.1	45	0.5	80	0.8	0	0.0	160	1.6
Kingsport–Bristol–Bristol, TN–VA	165	1.7	70	0.7	0	0.0	20	0.2	45	0.5
Kingston, NY	75	1.2	20	0.3	4	0.1	0	0.0	45	0.7
Knoxville, TN	845	4.1	100	0.5	0	0.0	0	0.0	175	0.8
Kokomo, IN	15	0.6	20	0.8	0	0.0	0	0.0	30	1.2
La Crosse, WI–MN	0	0.0	4	0.1	0	0.0	0	0.0	4	0.1
Lafayette, IN	15	0.3	0	0.0	0	0.0	0	0.0	45	1.0
Lafayette, LA	1,985	20.9	10	0.1	80	0.8	0	0.0	40	0.4
Lake Charles, LA	1,450	14.9	0	0.0	30	0.3	0	0.0	105	1.1
Lake Havasu City–Kingman, AZ	15	0.2	90	1.4	4	0.1	0	0.0	55	0.8
Lakeland–Winter Haven, FL	1,790	8.5	45	0.2	85	0.4	0	0.0	135	0.6
Lancaster, PA	215	1.2	35	0.2	50	0.3	0	0.0	130	0.7
Lansing–East Lansing, MI	380	4.0	40	0.4	95	1.0	0	0.0	85	0.9
Laredo, TX	0	0.0	0	0.0	20	0.3	0	0.0	15	0.2
Las Cruces, NM	15	0.2	4	0.1	0	0.0	0	0.0	10	0.1
Las Vegas–Paradise, NV	3,130	4.0	540	0.7	750	1.0	350	0.4	1,055	1.3
Lawrence, KS	60	2.3	60	2.3	10	0.4	0	0.0	29	1.1
Lawton, OK	120	3.8	170	5.3	0	0.0	0	0.0	50	1.6
Lebanon, PA	60	1.8	0	0.0	10	0.3	0	0.0	19	0.6
Lewiston, ID–WA	0	0.0	30	1.8	0	0.0	0	0.0	10	0.6
Lewiston–Auburn, ME	20	0.5	4	0.1	20	0.5	0	0.0	125	3.2
Lexington–Fayette, KY	625	5.7	110	1.0	15	0.1	15	0.1	35	0.3
Lima, OH	160	5.9	4	0.1	0	0.0	0	0.0	0	0.0
Lincoln, NE	70	0.8	100	1.2	90	1.1	0	0.0	100	1.2
Little Rock–North Little Rock–Conway, AR	2,195	10.3	0	0.0	65	0.3	4	0.0	175	0.8
Logan, UT–ID	20	0.6	65	1.9	40	1.2	25	0.7	15	0.4
Longview, TX	720	8.6	65	0.8	0	0.0	0	0.0	105	1.2
Longview, WA	60	1.9	135	4.2	15	0.5	0	0.0	54	1.7
Los Angeles–Long Beach–Santa Ana, CA	9,785	2.9	710	0.2	12,305	3.7	625	0.2	3,370	1.0
Louisville/Jefferson County, KY–IN	2,205	6.0	65	0.2	55	0.2	0	0.0	170	0.5
Lubbock, TX	265	3.4	45	0.6	25	0.3	0	0.0	45	0.6
Lynchburg, VA	895	11.9	30	0.4	0	0.0	0	0.0	14	0.2
Macon, GA	1,785	30.1	0	0.0	15	0.3	0	0.0	30	0.5
Madera–Chowchilla, CA	40	1.2	15	0.4	0	0.0	15	0.4	15	0.4
Madison, WI	260	1.9	20	0.1	110	0.8	0	0.0	50	0.4
Manchester–Nashua, NH	15	0.1	10	0.1	35	0.3	15	0.1	185	1.5
Manhattan, KS	250	7.1	35	1.0	0	0.0	30	0.9	135	3.9
Mankato–North Mankato, MN	60	2.3	0	0.0	0	0.0	0	0.0	15	0.6
Mansfield, OH	80	2.9	50	1.8	0	0.0	0	0.0	10	0.4
McAllen–Edinburg–Mission, TX	0	0.0	0	0.0	20	0.1	0	0.0	115	0.5
Medford, OR	0	0.0	25	0.4	30	0.5	0	0.0	159	2.4
Memphis, TN–MS–AR	7,740	23.6	115	0.4	110	0.3	0	0.0	285	0.9
Merced, CA	130	1.6	0	0.0	55	0.7	125	1.6	95	1.2
Miami–Fort Lauderdale–Pompano Beach, FL	23,460	13.2	245	0.1	655	0.4	25	0.0	1,655	0.9
Michigan City–La Porte, IN	100	2.5	4	0.1	0	0.0	0	0.0	10	0.3
Midland, TX	185	2.7	15	0.2	0	0.0	0	0.0	45	0.7
Milwaukee–Waukesha–West Allis, WI	2,790	8.1	135	0.4	145	0.4	0	0.0	490	1.4
Minneapolis–St. Paul–Bloomington, MN–WI	1,990	2.5	380	0.5	665	0.8	85	0.1	795	1.0
Missoula, MT	20	0.6	85	2.4	15	0.4	0	0.0	35	1.0

PART C—METROPOLITAN STATISTICAL AREA TABLES

C-10 Construction and Extractive Craft Workers, by Metropolitan Statistical Area, Sex, Race, and Hispanic or Latino Origin, 2006–2010—Continued

Metropolitan Statistical Area	Total who worked in the last 5 years	Male Number	Male Percent	Female Number	Female Percent	Hispanic or Latino Number	Hispanic or Latino Percent	White alone, not Hispanic or Latino Number	White alone, not Hispanic or Latino Percent
Mobile, AL	15,060	14,300	95.0	760	5.0	780	5.2	10,225	67.9
Modesto, CA	16,935	16,610	98.1	330	1.9	9,160	54.1	7,320	43.2
Monroe, LA	5,375	5,235	97.4	140	2.6	270	5.0	4,210	78.3
Monroe, MI	4,900	4,645	94.8	255	5.2	145	3.0	4,590	93.7
Montgomery, AL	9,080	8,715	96.0	365	4.0	1,215	13.4	5,265	58.0
Morgantown, WV	5,635	5,515	97.9	120	2.1	14	0.2	5,460	96.9
Morristown, TN	4,735	4,645	98.1	95	2.0	810	17.1	3,715	78.5
Mount Vernon–Anacortes, WA	3,805	3,560	93.6	245	6.4	335	8.8	3,385	89.0
Muncie, IN	2,840	2,715	95.6	125	4.4	19	0.7	2,630	92.6
Muskegon–Norton Shores, MI	3,845	3,740	97.3	105	2.7	35	0.9	3,510	91.3
Myrtle Beach–North Myrtle Beach–Conway, SC	11,145	10,800	96.9	345	3.1	3,055	27.4	6,945	62.3
Napa, CA	3,755	3,660	97.5	90	2.4	1,515	40.3	2,145	57.1
Naples–Marco Island, FL	13,695	13,195	96.3	500	3.7	7,650	55.9	5,565	40.6
Nashville-Davidson–Murfreesboro–Franklin, TN	46,730	45,710	97.8	1,020	2.2	12,035	25.8	31,320	67.0
New Haven–Milford, CT	23,030	22,560	98.0	470	2.0	4,935	21.4	15,995	69.5
New Orleans–Metairie–Kenner, LA	45,925	44,100	96.0	1,825	4.0	11,685	25.4	21,545	46.9
New York–Northern New Jersey–Long Island, NY–NJ–PA	469,150	459,750	98.0	9,400	2.0	160,335	34.2	228,425	48.7
Niles–Benton Harbor, MI	3,770	3,705	98.3	65	1.7	150	4.0	3,350	88.9
North Port–Bradenton–Sarasota, FL	23,305	22,455	96.4	850	3.6	5,555	23.8	16,460	70.6
Norwich–New London, CT	8,045	7,800	97.0	245	3.0	685	8.5	6,990	86.9
Ocala, FL	10,155	9,885	97.3	270	2.7	1,340	13.2	7,770	76.5
Ocean City, NJ	3,875	3,845	99.2	25	0.6	95	2.5	3,615	93.3
Odessa, TX	6,800	6,730	99.0	70	1.0	4,245	62.4	2,435	35.8
Ogden–Clearfield, UT	14,645	14,270	97.4	375	2.6	2,675	18.3	11,595	79.2
Oklahoma City, OK	40,790	39,390	96.6	1,400	3.4	11,045	27.1	25,205	61.8
Olympia, WA	6,700	6,380	95.2	325	4.9	680	10.1	5,530	82.5
Omaha–Council Bluffs, NE–IA	24,645	24,130	97.9	515	2.1	4,080	16.6	19,490	79.1
Orlando–Kissimmee–Sanford, FL	69,800	67,010	96.0	2,785	4.0	26,270	37.6	33,305	47.7
Oshkosh–Neenah, WI	3,590	3,530	98.3	60	1.7	100	2.8	3,480	96.9
Owensboro, KY	3,745	3,630	96.9	115	3.1	170	4.5	3,525	94.1
Oxnard–Thousand Oaks–Ventura, CA	20,905	20,325	97.2	585	2.8	10,480	50.1	9,545	45.7
Palm Bay–Melbourne–Titusville, FL	16,085	15,475	96.2	610	3.8	1,330	8.3	12,900	80.2
Palm Coast, FL	2,140	2,075	97.0	65	3.0	245	11.4	1,760	82.2
Panama City–Lynn Haven–Panama City Beach, FL	6,585	6,195	94.1	390	5.9	770	11.7	5,065	76.9
Parkersburg–Marietta–Vienna, WV–OH	5,755	5,595	97.2	160	2.8	0	0.0	5,645	98.1
Pascagoula, MS	8,510	7,965	93.6	545	6.4	905	10.6	6,185	72.7
Pensacola–Ferry Pass–Brent, FL	15,010	14,410	96.0	600	4.0	1,025	6.8	11,795	78.6
Peoria, IL	9,795	9,530	97.3	265	2.7	325	3.3	8,975	91.6
Philadelphia–Camden–Wilmington, PA–NJ–DE–MD	140,715	137,280	97.6	3,435	2.4	14,165	10.1	108,165	76.9
Phoenix–Mesa–Glendale, AZ	134,405	131,290	97.7	3,115	2.3	73,750	54.9	53,365	39.7
Pine Bluff, AR	2,100	1,995	95.0	110	5.2	94	4.5	1,355	64.5
Pittsburgh, PA	63,895	62,405	97.7	1,490	2.3	430	0.7	60,525	94.7
Pittsfield, MA	4,520	4,445	98.3	70	1.5	255	5.6	4,140	91.6
Pocatello, ID	2,520	2,440	96.8	80	3.2	200	7.9	2,265	89.9
Portland–South Portland–Biddeford, ME	17,120	16,670	97.4	455	2.7	155	0.9	16,540	96.6
Portland–Vancouver–Hillsboro, OR–WA	60,260	58,635	97.3	1,625	2.7	10,790	17.9	45,925	76.2
Port St. Lucie, FL	16,125	15,565	96.5	555	3.4	4,670	29.0	10,100	62.6
Poughkeepsie–Newburgh–Middletown, NY	20,390	20,040	98.3	350	1.7	3,215	15.8	16,030	78.6
Prescott, AZ	7,990	7,575	94.8	410	5.1	2,110	26.4	5,635	70.5
Providence–New Bedford–Fall River, RI–MA	49,370	48,305	97.8	1,060	2.1	3,545	7.2	42,725	86.5

C-10 **Construction and Extractive Craft Workers, by Metropolitan Statistical Area, Sex, Race, and Hispanic or Latino Origin, 2006–2010**—*Continued*

Metropolitan Statistical Area	Black alone, not Hispanic or Latino Number	Percent	American Indian and Alaska Native alone, not Hispanic or Latino Number	Percent	Asian alone, not Hispanic or Latino Number	Percent	Native Hawaiian and Other Pacific Islander alone, not Hispanic or Latino Number	Percent	Two or more races, not Hispanic or Latino Number	Percent
Mobile, AL	3,555	23.6	330	2.2	15	0.1	0	0.0	150	1.0
Modesto, CA	135	0.8	25	0.1	120	0.7	10	0.1	170	1.0
Monroe, LA	790	14.7	70	1.3	20	0.4	0	0.0	10	0.2
Monroe, MI	110	2.2	4	0.1	0	0.0	0	0.0	45	0.9
Montgomery, AL	2,520	27.8	35	0.4	0	0.0	0	0.0	39	0.4
Morgantown, WV	15	0.3	20	0.4	0	0.0	0	0.0	129	2.3
Morristown, TN	95	2.0	35	0.7	0	0.0	0	0.0	75	1.6
Mount Vernon–Anacortes, WA	10	0.3	20	0.5	10	0.3	0	0.0	52	1.4
Muncie, IN	70	2.5	15	0.5	15	0.5	0	0.0	84	3.0
Muskegon–Norton Shores, MI	215	5.6	60	1.6	0	0.0	0	0.0	30	0.8
Myrtle Beach–North Myrtle Beach–Conway, SC	840	7.5	125	1.1	0	0.0	0	0.0	180	1.6
Napa, CA	20	0.5	10	0.3	35	0.9	0	0.0	30	0.8
Naples–Marco Island, FL	430	3.1	30	0.2	4	0.0	0	0.0	10	0.1
Nashville-Davidson–Murfreesboro–Franklin, TN	2,665	5.7	155	0.3	200	0.4	25	0.1	325	0.7
New Haven–Milford, CT	1,675	7.3	25	0.1	120	0.5	0	0.0	280	1.2
New Orleans–Metairie–Kenner, LA	11,355	24.7	70	0.2	600	1.3	0	0.0	665	1.4
New York–Northern New Jersey–Long Island, NY-NJ-PA	50,915	10.9	800	0.2	20,570	4.4	90	0.0	8,005	1.7
Niles–Benton Harbor, MI	200	5.3	15	0.4	25	0.7	15	0.4	10	0.3
North Port–Bradenton–Sarasota, FL	920	3.9	80	0.3	70	0.3	0	0.0	225	1.0
Norwich–New London, CT	215	2.7	65	0.8	40	0.5	0	0.0	45	0.6
Ocala, FL	855	8.4	4	0.0	55	0.5	25	0.2	110	1.1
Ocean City, NJ	105	2.7	25	0.6	4	0.1	0	0.0	30	0.8
Odessa, TX	40	0.6	4	0.1	0	0.0	0	0.0	64	0.9
Ogden–Clearfield, UT	80	0.5	90	0.6	100	0.7	4	0.0	90	0.6
Oklahoma City, OK	1,715	4.2	1,625	4.0	175	0.4	20	0.0	1,010	2.5
Olympia, WA	120	1.8	65	1.0	130	1.9	25	0.4	150	2.2
Omaha–Council Bluffs, NE-IA	665	2.7	40	0.2	30	0.1	10	0.0	325	1.3
Orlando–Kissimmee–Sanford, FL	7,380	10.6	285	0.4	470	0.7	75	0.1	2,005	2.9
Oshkosh–Neenah, WI	0	0.0	0	0.0	10	0.3	0	0.0	0	0.0
Owensboro, KY	40	1.1	0	0.0	15	0.4	0	0.0	0	0.0
Oxnard–Thousand Oaks–Ventura, CA	315	1.5	20	0.1	195	0.9	0	0.0	350	1.7
Palm Bay–Melbourne–Titusville, FL	1,480	9.2	210	1.3	40	0.2	15	0.1	115	0.7
Palm Coast, FL	115	5.4	15	0.7	4	0.2	0	0.0	0	0.0
Panama City–Lynn Haven–Panama City Beach, FL	535	8.1	65	1.0	30	0.5	0	0.0	115	1.7
Parkersburg–Marietta–Vienna, WV-OH	30	0.5	0	0.0	0	0.0	0	0.0	75	1.3
Pascagoula, MS	1,255	14.7	15	0.2	60	0.7	0	0.0	90	1.1
Pensacola–Ferry Pass–Brent, FL	1,575	10.5	135	0.9	155	1.0	30	0.2	295	2.0
Peoria, IL	400	4.1	4	0.0	4	0.0	15	0.2	69	0.7
Philadelphia–Camden–Wilmington, PA-NJ-DE-MD	14,880	10.6	180	0.1	1,595	1.1	55	0.0	1,680	1.2
Phoenix–Mesa–Glendale, AZ	2,225	1.7	3,050	2.3	545	0.4	455	0.3	1,030	0.8
Pine Bluff, AR	540	25.7	15	0.7	0	0.0	0	0.0	100	4.8
Pittsburgh, PA	2,210	3.5	80	0.1	70	0.1	0	0.0	580	0.9
Pittsfield, MA	75	1.7	35	0.8	4	0.1	0	0.0	8	0.2
Pocatello, ID	15	0.6	25	1.0	0	0.0	0	0.0	14	0.6
Portland–South Portland–Biddeford, ME	80	0.5	65	0.4	75	0.4	0	0.0	204	1.2
Portland–Vancouver–Hillsboro, OR-WA	1,090	1.8	275	0.5	620	1.0	285	0.5	1,275	2.1
Port St. Lucie, FL	1,130	7.0	10	0.1	65	0.4	0	0.0	155	1.0
Poughkeepsie–Newburgh–Middletown, NY	695	3.4	115	0.6	75	0.4	10	0.0	255	1.3
Prescott, AZ	0	0.0	190	2.4	0	0.0	0	0.0	55	0.7
Providence–New Bedford–Fall River, RI-MA	1,325	2.7	190	0.4	600	1.2	0	0.0	985	2.0

PART C—METROPOLITAN STATISTICAL AREA TABLES

C-10 Construction and Extractive Craft Workers, by Metropolitan Statistical Area, Sex, Race, and Hispanic or Latino Origin, 2006–2010—Continued

Metropolitan Statistical Area	Total who worked in the last 5 years	Male Number	Male Percent	Female Number	Female Percent	Hispanic or Latino Number	Hispanic or Latino Percent	White alone, not Hispanic or Latino Number	White alone, not Hispanic or Latino Percent
Provo–Orem, UT	14,165	13,830	97.6	335	2.4	2,750	19.4	11,095	78.3
Pueblo, CO	5,455	5,315	97.4	140	2.6	2,600	47.7	2,675	49.0
Punta Gorda, FL	5,055	4,815	95.3	240	4.7	495	9.8	4,335	85.8
Racine, WI	5,690	5,530	97.2	160	2.8	365	6.4	5,050	88.8
Raleigh–Cary, NC	34,355	33,495	97.5	860	2.5	15,275	44.5	14,910	43.4
Rapid City, SD	4,720	4,555	96.5	165	3.5	160	3.4	4,060	86.0
Reading, PA	10,775	10,600	98.4	175	1.6	995	9.2	9,415	87.4
Redding, CA	5,565	5,335	95.9	230	4.1	740	13.3	4,525	81.3
Reno–Sparks, NV	16,350	15,870	97.1	480	2.9	6,615	40.5	9,000	55.0
Richmond, VA	38,320	36,995	96.5	1,330	3.5	6,835	17.8	23,765	62.0
Riverside–San Bernardino–Ontario, CA	142,175	139,300	98.0	2,875	2.0	86,845	61.1	47,050	33.1
Roanoke, VA	9,205	8,940	97.1	265	2.9	1,020	11.1	7,370	80.1
Rochester, MN	5,170	5,060	97.9	110	2.1	235	4.5	4,825	93.3
Rochester, NY	22,640	22,030	97.3	610	2.7	1,225	5.4	19,740	87.2
Rockford, IL	9,415	9,150	97.2	265	2.8	1,335	14.2	7,700	81.8
Rocky Mount, NC	4,065	3,875	95.3	185	4.6	530	13.0	2,440	60.0
Rome, GA	3,600	3,420	95.0	180	5.0	825	22.9	2,445	67.9
Sacramento–Arden-Arcade–Roseville, CA	62,220	60,725	97.6	1,495	2.4	21,305	34.2	35,110	56.4
Saginaw–Saginaw Township North, MI	3,960	3,825	96.6	140	3.5	220	5.6	3,495	88.3
St. Cloud, MN	6,860	6,630	96.6	230	3.4	165	2.4	6,525	95.1
St. George, UT	5,685	5,650	99.4	35	0.6	1,355	23.8	4,160	73.2
St. Joseph, MO–KS	4,005	3,860	96.4	145	3.6	75	1.9	3,765	94.0
St. Louis, MO–IL	80,410	78,390	97.5	2,020	2.5	2,310	2.9	70,625	87.8
Salem, OR	12,485	12,130	97.2	355	2.8	3,610	28.9	8,340	66.8
Salinas, CA	10,525	10,205	97.0	320	3.0	5,955	56.6	3,850	36.6
Salisbury, MD	4,465	4,240	95.0	225	5.0	505	11.3	3,320	74.4
Salt Lake City, UT	38,585	37,915	98.3	665	1.7	13,165	34.1	23,800	61.7
San Angelo, TX	4,230	4,110	97.2	120	2.8	1,920	45.4	2,210	52.2
San Antonio–New Braunfels, TX	67,830	66,110	97.5	1,720	2.5	48,345	71.3	17,580	25.9
San Diego–Carlsbad–San Marcos, CA	85,685	83,505	97.5	2,185	2.6	41,580	48.5	37,905	44.2
Sandusky, OH	2,105	2,060	97.9	40	1.9	50	2.4	1,850	87.9
San Francisco–Oakland–Fremont, CA	109,045	106,400	97.6	2,645	2.4	52,020	47.7	39,490	36.2
San Jose–Sunnyvale–Santa Clara, CA	43,310	42,505	98.1	805	1.9	26,675	61.6	12,825	29.6
San Luis Obispo–Paso Robles, CA	8,295	7,995	96.4	300	3.6	1,905	23.0	6,065	73.1
Santa Barbara–Santa Maria–Goleta, CA	11,565	11,310	97.8	250	2.2	6,235	53.9	4,965	42.9
Santa Cruz–Watsonville, CA	8,200	7,840	95.6	365	4.5	3,375	41.2	4,525	55.2
Santa Fe, NM	5,530	5,375	97.2	155	2.8	4,145	75.0	1,305	23.6
Santa Rosa–Petaluma, CA	18,520	18,040	97.4	475	2.6	5,910	31.9	11,820	63.8
Savannah, GA	9,965	9,655	96.9	310	3.1	1,345	13.5	6,115	61.4
Scranton–Wilkes-Barre, PA	14,375	14,115	98.2	260	1.8	490	3.4	13,625	94.8
Seattle–Tacoma–Bellevue, WA	101,950	98,275	96.4	3,675	3.6	19,480	19.1	71,675	70.3
Sebastian–Vero Beach, FL	5,945	5,810	97.7	135	2.3	1,595	26.8	3,965	66.7
Sheboygan, WI	3,290	3,175	96.5	115	3.5	215	6.5	3,020	91.8
Sherman–Denison, TX	3,790	3,740	98.7	55	1.5	850	22.4	2,815	74.3
Shreveport–Bossier City, LA	12,835	12,330	96.1	505	3.9	1,435	11.2	8,435	65.7
Sioux City, IA–NE–SD	3,780	3,675	97.2	105	2.8	635	16.8	2,835	75.0
Sioux Falls, SD	6,705	6,580	98.1	125	1.9	185	2.8	6,305	94.0
South Bend–Mishawaka, IN–MI	7,815	7,615	97.4	200	2.6	530	6.8	6,730	86.1
Spartanburg, SC	7,850	7,655	97.5	195	2.5	1,665	21.2	5,245	66.8
Spokane, WA	11,910	11,405	95.8	505	4.2	445	3.7	10,935	91.8
Springfield, IL	4,635	4,630	99.9	4	0.1	70	1.5	4,200	90.6
Springfield, MA	15,895	15,360	96.6	535	3.4	1,125	7.1	13,935	87.7
Springfield, MO	13,455	12,985	96.5	465	3.5	465	3.5	12,325	91.6
Springfield, OH	3,415	3,320	97.2	95	2.8	170	5.0	3,115	91.2
State College, PA	3,460	3,375	97.5	85	2.5	10	0.3	3,270	94.5

C-10 Construction and Extractive Craft Workers, by Metropolitan Statistical Area, Sex, Race, and Hispanic or Latino Origin, 2006–2010—*Continued*

Metropolitan Statistical Area	Black alone, not Hispanic or Latino		American Indian and Alaska Native alone, not Hispanic or Latino		Asian alone, not Hispanic or Latino		Native Hawaiian and Other Pacific Islander alone, not Hispanic or Latino		Two or more races, not Hispanic or Latino	
	Number	Percent	Number	Percent	Number	Percent	Number	Percent	Number	Percent
Provo–Orem, UT	80	0.6	125	0.9	10	0.1	45	0.3	55	0.4
Pueblo, CO	80	1.5	65	1.2	0	0.0	0	0.0	44	0.8
Punta Gorda, FL	125	2.5	4	0.1	30	0.6	0	0.0	60	1.2
Racine, WI	240	4.2	0	0.0	0	0.0	0	0.0	35	0.6
Raleigh–Cary, NC	3,635	10.6	120	0.3	190	0.6	0	0.0	235	0.7
Rapid City, SD	10	0.2	385	8.2	0	0.0	0	0.0	100	2.1
Reading, PA	260	2.4	0	0.0	25	0.2	0	0.0	89	0.8
Redding, CA	40	0.7	150	2.7	35	0.6	4	0.1	70	1.3
Reno–Sparks, NV	90	0.6	230	1.4	100	0.6	20	0.1	295	1.8
Richmond, VA	6,495	16.9	180	0.5	450	1.2	0	0.0	595	1.6
Riverside–San Bernardino–Ontario, CA	3,550	2.5	395	0.3	1,790	1.3	515	0.4	2,020	1.4
Roanoke, VA	725	7.9	70	0.8	0	0.0	0	0.0	20	0.2
Rochester, MN	20	0.4	0	0.0	70	1.4	0	0.0	20	0.4
Rochester, NY	1,260	5.6	100	0.4	125	0.6	0	0.0	200	0.9
Rockford, IL	290	3.1	15	0.2	30	0.3	0	0.0	49	0.5
Rocky Mount, NC	1,035	25.5	30	0.7	0	0.0	0	0.0	29	0.7
Rome, GA	305	8.5	0	0.0	0	0.0	0	0.0	20	0.6
Sacramento–Arden-Arcade–Roseville, CA	2,215	3.6	585	0.9	1,585	2.5	340	0.5	1,075	1.7
Saginaw–Saginaw Township North, MI	205	5.2	10	0.3	0	0.0	0	0.0	30	0.8
St. Cloud, MN	0	0.0	10	0.1	100	1.5	0	0.0	64	0.9
St. George, UT	0	0.0	75	1.3	25	0.4	0	0.0	70	1.2
St. Joseph, MO–KS	105	2.6	4	0.1	4	0.1	0	0.0	49	1.2
St. Louis, MO–IL	6,315	7.9	105	0.1	400	0.5	25	0.0	630	0.8
Salem, OR	75	0.6	125	1.0	10	0.1	30	0.2	290	2.3
Salinas, CA	110	1.0	80	0.8	205	1.9	60	0.6	265	2.5
Salisbury, MD	475	10.6	0	0.0	30	0.7	0	0.0	124	2.8
Salt Lake City, UT	165	0.4	320	0.8	160	0.4	640	1.7	330	0.9
San Angelo, TX	85	2.0	15	0.4	0	0.0	0	0.0	4	0.1
San Antonio–New Braunfels, TX	1,295	1.9	200	0.3	130	0.2	60	0.1	220	0.3
San Diego–Carlsbad–San Marcos, CA	2,265	2.6	455	0.5	2,050	2.4	300	0.4	1,130	1.3
Sandusky, OH	95	4.5	10	0.5	55	2.6	0	0.0	45	2.1
San Francisco–Oakland–Fremont, CA	5,050	4.6	395	0.4	9,635	8.8	845	0.8	1,605	1.5
San Jose–Sunnyvale–Santa Clara, CA	635	1.5	230	0.5	2,375	5.5	60	0.1	510	1.2
San Luis Obispo–Paso Robles, CA	4	0.0	125	1.5	100	1.2	0	0.0	104	1.3
Santa Barbara–Santa Maria–Goleta, CA	120	1.0	80	0.7	85	0.7	40	0.3	35	0.3
Santa Cruz–Watsonville, CA	60	0.7	50	0.6	25	0.3	40	0.5	140	1.7
Santa Fe, NM	0	0.0	75	1.4	0	0.0	0	0.0	10	0.2
Santa Rosa–Petaluma, CA	315	1.7	200	1.1	80	0.4	25	0.1	170	0.9
Savannah, GA	2,380	23.9	0	0.0	105	1.1	0	0.0	24	0.2
Scranton–Wilkes-Barre, PA	140	1.0	4	0.0	30	0.2	15	0.1	69	0.5
Seattle–Tacoma–Bellevue, WA	3,190	3.1	795	0.8	3,485	3.4	730	0.7	2,595	2.5
Sebastian–Vero Beach, FL	290	4.9	0	0.0	0	0.0	15	0.3	80	1.3
Sheboygan, WI	0	0.0	15	0.5	30	0.9	0	0.0	4	0.1
Sherman–Denison, TX	95	2.5	10	0.3	0	0.0	0	0.0	20	0.5
Shreveport–Bossier City, LA	2,770	21.6	80	0.6	20	0.2	0	0.0	95	0.7
Sioux City, IA–NE–SD	165	4.4	95	2.5	15	0.4	0	0.0	30	0.8
Sioux Falls, SD	30	0.4	115	1.7	0	0.0	0	0.0	70	1.0
South Bend–Mishawaka, IN–MI	370	4.7	45	0.6	30	0.4	0	0.0	110	1.4
Spartanburg, SC	880	11.2	10	0.1	10	0.1	20	0.3	19	0.2
Spokane, WA	200	1.7	95	0.8	10	0.1	30	0.3	195	1.6
Springfield, IL	340	7.3	25	0.5	0	0.0	0	0.0	0	0.0
Springfield, MA	535	3.4	45	0.3	60	0.4	0	0.0	195	1.2
Springfield, MO	205	1.5	115	0.9	0	0.0	0	0.0	344	2.6
Springfield, OH	65	1.9	45	1.3	15	0.4	0	0.0	4	0.1
State College, PA	100	2.9	4	0.1	0	0.0	0	0.0	75	2.2

PART C—METROPOLITAN STATISTICAL AREA TABLES

C-10 **Construction and Extractive Craft Workers, by Metropolitan Statistical Area, Sex, Race, and Hispanic or Latino Origin, 2006–2010**—*Continued*

Metropolitan Statistical Area	Total who worked in the last 5 years	Male Number	Male Percent	Female Number	Female Percent	Hispanic or Latino Number	Hispanic or Latino Percent	White alone, not Hispanic or Latino Number	White alone, not Hispanic or Latino Percent
Steubenville–Weirton, OH–WV	3,965	3,750	94.6	215	5.4	20	0.5	3,885	98.0
Stockton, CA	19,915	19,480	97.8	430	2.2	10,640	53.4	7,245	36.4
Sumter, SC	3,000	2,865	95.5	135	4.5	235	7.8	1,350	45.0
Syracuse, NY	15,970	15,500	97.1	475	3.0	325	2.0	14,705	92.1
Tallahassee, FL	9,185	8,840	96.2	345	3.8	810	8.8	6,145	66.9
Tampa–St. Petersburg–Clearwater, FL	76,330	73,550	96.4	2,775	3.6	19,900	26.1	49,630	65.0
Terre Haute, IN	5,045	4,900	97.1	145	2.9	45	0.9	4,855	96.2
Texarkana, TX–Texarkana, AR	3,950	3,730	94.4	220	5.6	265	6.7	3,135	79.4
Toledo, OH	16,800	16,080	95.7	720	4.3	710	4.2	14,095	83.9
Topeka, KS	6,820	6,685	98.0	135	2.0	780	11.4	5,445	79.8
Trenton–Ewing, NJ	7,750	7,590	97.9	160	2.1	2,140	27.6	4,585	59.2
Tucson, AZ	29,670	28,720	96.8	950	3.2	16,080	54.2	11,965	40.3
Tulsa, OK	29,490	28,685	97.3	805	2.7	6,625	22.5	17,815	60.4
Tuscaloosa, AL	7,650	7,505	98.1	145	1.9	1,020	13.3	4,800	62.7
Tyler, TX	6,365	6,205	97.5	160	2.5	2,465	38.7	3,180	50.0
Utica–Rome, NY	7,210	7,095	98.4	115	1.6	160	2.2	6,920	96.0
Valdosta, GA	3,960	3,835	96.8	125	3.2	885	22.3	2,135	53.9
Vallejo–Fairfield, CA	13,455	13,295	98.8	165	1.2	5,650	42.0	5,920	44.0
Victoria, TX	4,895	4,870	99.5	25	0.5	2,955	60.4	1,825	37.3
Vineland–Millville–Bridgeton, NJ	3,860	3,825	99.1	35	0.9	895	23.2	2,675	69.3
Virginia Beach–Norfolk–Newport News, VA–NC	53,630	51,020	95.1	2,610	4.9	5,200	9.7	33,325	62.1
Visalia–Porterville, CA	9,990	9,795	98.0	200	2.0	5,745	57.5	3,805	38.1
Waco, TX	6,365	6,155	96.7	215	3.4	2,995	47.1	2,965	46.6
Warner Robins, GA	3,740	3,585	95.9	155	4.1	730	19.5	2,190	58.6
Washington–Arlington–Alexandria, DC–VA–MD–WV	154,815	150,275	97.1	4,535	2.9	74,680	48.2	52,015	33.6
Waterloo–Cedar Falls, IA	4,060	3,970	97.8	90	2.2	110	2.7	3,760	92.6
Wausau, WI	3,995	3,870	96.9	125	3.1	10	0.3	3,945	98.7
Wenatchee–East Wenatchee, WA	3,490	3,360	96.3	130	3.7	800	22.9	2,475	70.9
Wheeling, WV–OH	5,865	5,835	99.5	30	0.5	10	0.2	5,710	97.4
Wichita, KS	20,855	19,805	95.0	1,050	5.0	5,060	24.3	13,690	65.6
Wichita Falls, TX	4,175	4,055	97.1	125	3.0	930	22.3	2,945	70.5
Williamsport, PA	3,650	3,475	95.2	175	4.8	0	0.0	3,620	99.2
Wilmington, NC	15,260	14,645	96.0	615	4.0	2,510	16.4	10,570	69.3
Winchester, VA–WV	5,215	5,145	98.7	70	1.3	905	17.4	4,180	80.2
Winston–Salem, NC	14,010	13,580	96.9	435	3.1	4,570	32.6	8,260	59.0
Worcester, MA	21,670	21,370	98.6	300	1.4	1,070	4.9	19,860	91.6
Yakima, WA	4,555	4,390	96.4	165	3.6	1,110	24.4	3,165	69.5
York–Hanover, PA	13,650	13,330	97.7	320	2.3	465	3.4	12,600	92.3
Youngstown–Warren–Boardman, OH–PA	15,005	14,575	97.1	435	2.9	335	2.2	13,705	91.3
Yuba City, CA	5,920	5,865	99.1	55	0.9	2,455	41.5	2,935	49.6
Yuma, AZ	5,185	5,080	98.0	110	2.1	3,885	74.9	1,190	23.0

C-10 **Construction and Extractive Craft Workers, by Metropolitan Statistical Area, Sex, Race, and Hispanic or Latino Origin, 2006–2010**—*Continued*

Metropolitan Statistical Area	Black alone, not Hispanic or Latino Number	Percent	American Indian and Alaska Native alone, not Hispanic or Latino Number	Percent	Asian alone, not Hispanic or Latino Number	Percent	Native Hawaiian and Other Pacific Islander alone, not Hispanic or Latino Number	Percent	Two or more races, not Hispanic or Latino Number	Percent
Steubenville–Weirton, OH–WV	30	0.8	4	0.1	0	0.0	0	0.0	20	0.5
Stockton, CA	760	3.8	180	0.9	500	2.5	90	0.5	495	2.5
Sumter, SC	1,325	44.2	10	0.3	80	2.7	0	0.0	0	0.0
Syracuse, NY	630	3.9	100	0.6	65	0.4	0	0.0	144	0.9
Tallahassee, FL	2,045	22.3	40	0.4	40	0.4	0	0.0	105	1.1
Tampa–St. Petersburg–Clearwater, FL	5,470	7.2	145	0.2	425	0.6	30	0.0	725	0.9
Terre Haute, IN	50	1.0	4	0.1	50	1.0	25	0.5	4	0.1
Texarkana, TX–Texarkana, AR	485	12.3	60	1.5	0	0.0	0	0.0	0	0.0
Toledo, OH	1,735	10.3	30	0.2	30	0.2	15	0.1	185	1.1
Topeka, KS	365	5.4	140	2.1	0	0.0	0	0.0	90	1.3
Trenton–Ewing, NJ	840	10.8	30	0.4	110	1.4	0	0.0	45	0.6
Tucson, AZ	305	1.0	905	3.1	110	0.4	25	0.1	270	0.9
Tulsa, OK	935	3.2	2,175	7.4	225	0.8	30	0.1	1,685	5.7
Tuscaloosa, AL	1,750	22.9	20	0.3	0	0.0	0	0.0	50	0.7
Tyler, TX	660	10.4	25	0.4	10	0.2	0	0.0	35	0.5
Utica–Rome, NY	65	0.9	10	0.1	4	0.1	0	0.0	54	0.7
Valdosta, GA	850	21.5	0	0.0	0	0.0	0	0.0	88	2.2
Vallejo–Fairfield, CA	860	6.4	85	0.6	325	2.4	120	0.9	495	3.7
Victoria, TX	100	2.0	0	0.0	0	0.0	0	0.0	20	0.4
Vineland–Millville–Bridgeton, NJ	275	7.1	10	0.3	0	0.0	0	0.0	4	0.1
Virginia Beach–Norfolk–Newport News, VA–NC	13,720	25.6	220	0.4	530	1.0	20	0.0	610	1.1
Visalia–Porterville, CA	120	1.2	95	1.0	105	1.1	40	0.4	80	0.8
Waco, TX	365	5.7	0	0.0	15	0.2	0	0.0	29	0.5
Warner Robins, GA	750	20.1	10	0.3	4	0.1	0	0.0	55	1.5
Washington–Arlington–Alexandria, DC–VA–MD–WV	21,665	14.0	305	0.2	4,205	2.7	100	0.1	1,845	1.2
Waterloo–Cedar Falls, IA	160	3.9	4	0.1	0	0.0	0	0.0	20	0.5
Wausau, WI	20	0.5	4	0.1	10	0.3	0	0.0	8	0.2
Wenatchee–East Wenatchee, WA	0	0.0	80	2.3	15	0.4	0	0.0	125	3.6
Wheeling, WV–OH	115	2.0	0	0.0	0	0.0	0	0.0	30	0.5
Wichita, KS	945	4.5	185	0.9	615	2.9	0	0.0	370	1.8
Wichita Falls, TX	140	3.4	60	1.4	70	1.7	0	0.0	35	0.8
Williamsport, PA	10	0.3	0	0.0	10	0.3	4	0.1	4	0.1
Wilmington, NC	1,815	11.9	190	1.2	0	0.0	0	0.0	175	1.1
Winchester, VA–WV	105	2.0	0	0.0	0	0.0	0	0.0	30	0.6
Winston–Salem, NC	1,030	7.4	20	0.1	35	0.2	0	0.0	99	0.7
Worcester, MA	300	1.4	30	0.1	130	0.6	0	0.0	290	1.3
Yakima, WA	0	0.0	150	3.3	25	0.5	0	0.0	115	2.5
York–Hanover, PA	455	3.3	40	0.3	50	0.4	0	0.0	40	0.3
Youngstown–Warren–Boardman, OH–PA	810	5.4	20	0.1	30	0.2	0	0.0	105	0.7
Yuba City, CA	165	2.8	85	1.4	95	1.6	20	0.3	165	2.8
Yuma, AZ	20	0.4	10	0.2	15	0.3	20	0.4	45	0.9

PART C—METROPOLITAN STATISTICAL AREA TABLES 393

C-11 Installation, Maintenance, and Repair Craft Workers, by Metropolitan Statistical Area, Sex, Race, and Hispanic or Latino Origin, 2006–2010

Metropolitan Statistical Area	Total who worked in the last 5 years	Male Number	Male Percent	Female Number	Female Percent	Hispanic or Latino Number	Hispanic or Latino Percent	White alone, not Hispanic or Latino Number	White alone, not Hispanic or Latino Percent
Abilene, TX	3,995	3,740	93.6	255	6.4	780	19.5	2,950	73.8
Akron, OH	16,065	14,830	92.3	1,235	7.7	95	0.6	14,845	92.4
Albany, GA	3,420	3,245	94.9	175	5.1	0	0.0	2,350	68.7
Albany–Schenectady–Troy, NY	15,790	14,695	93.1	1,100	7.0	505	3.2	14,125	89.5
Albuquerque, NM	17,685	15,745	89.0	1,940	11.0	7,585	42.9	7,960	45.0
Alexandria, LA	3,340	3,135	93.9	210	6.3	24	0.7	2,835	84.9
Allentown–Bethlehem–Easton, PA–NJ	19,240	18,130	94.2	1,110	5.8	1,400	7.3	16,985	88.3
Altoona, PA	3,410	3,150	92.4	260	7.6	0	0.0	3,380	99.1
Amarillo, TX	6,735	6,500	96.5	235	3.5	1,575	23.4	4,775	70.9
Ames, IA	1,520	1,370	90.1	145	9.5	10	0.7	1,455	95.7
Anchorage, AK	8,275	7,680	92.8	595	7.2	275	3.3	6,600	79.8
Anderson, IN	3,175	3,055	96.2	120	3.8	85	2.7	2,895	91.2
Anderson, SC	5,235	4,890	93.4	345	6.6	140	2.7	4,610	88.1
Ann Arbor, MI	5,090	4,505	88.5	585	11.5	100	2.0	4,415	86.7
Anniston–Oxford, AL	4,015	3,650	90.9	360	9.0	125	3.1	3,255	81.1
Appleton, WI	6,010	5,500	91.5	515	8.6	60	1.0	5,875	97.8
Asheville, NC	9,965	9,175	92.1	790	7.9	530	5.3	8,800	88.3
Athens–Clarke County, GA	3,275	3,120	95.3	160	4.9	115	3.5	2,725	83.2
Atlanta–Sandy Springs–Marietta, GA	101,560	92,770	91.3	8,790	8.7	8,750	8.6	61,935	61.0
Atlantic City–Hammonton, NJ	5,075	4,860	95.8	220	4.3	685	13.5	3,390	66.8
Auburn–Opelika, AL	3,355	3,210	95.7	150	4.5	105	3.1	2,655	79.1
Augusta–Richmond County, GA–SC	11,840	10,855	91.7	985	8.3	410	3.5	8,840	74.7
Austin–Round Rock–San Marcos, TX	29,280	27,135	92.7	2,145	7.3	9,100	31.1	16,730	57.1
Bakersfield–Delano, CA	16,110	15,500	96.2	610	3.8	6,745	41.9	8,175	50.7
Baltimore–Towson, MD	52,020	48,345	92.9	3,680	7.1	1,900	3.7	36,525	70.2
Bangor, ME	4,055	3,850	94.9	205	5.1	4	0.1	3,950	97.4
Barnstable Town, MA	4,155	3,820	91.9	335	8.1	55	1.3	3,955	95.2
Baton Rouge, LA	16,900	15,635	92.5	1,270	7.5	560	3.3	11,425	67.6
Battle Creek, MI	3,250	3,020	92.9	230	7.1	125	3.8	2,935	90.3
Bay City, MI	2,935	2,695	91.8	240	8.2	40	1.4	2,880	98.1
Beaumont–Port Arthur, TX	8,555	8,055	94.2	505	5.9	765	8.9	6,345	74.2
Bellingham, WA	3,965	3,745	94.5	220	5.5	150	3.8	3,555	89.7
Bend, OR	3,660	3,380	92.3	285	7.8	165	4.5	3,410	93.2
Billings, MT	4,235	3,830	90.4	410	9.7	150	3.5	4,010	94.7
Binghamton, NY	4,670	4,265	91.3	410	8.8	90	1.9	4,360	93.4
Birmingham–Hoover, AL	24,820	23,195	93.5	1,620	6.5	590	2.4	19,195	77.3
Bismarck, ND	2,415	2,240	92.8	175	7.2	25	1.0	2,340	96.9
Blacksburg–Christiansburg–Radford, VA	3,360	3,080	91.7	280	8.3	35	1.0	3,185	94.8
Bloomington, IN	3,445	3,000	87.1	445	12.9	65	1.9	3,355	97.4
Bloomington–Normal, IL	2,880	2,515	87.3	365	12.7	110	3.8	2,575	89.4
Boise City–Nampa, ID	11,415	10,560	92.5	855	7.5	805	7.1	10,040	88.0
Boston–Cambridge–Quincy, MA–NH	73,405	68,295	93.0	5,115	7.0	6,375	8.7	59,505	81.1
Boulder, CO	3,505	3,175	90.6	330	9.4	530	15.1	2,680	76.5
Bowling Green, KY	2,545	2,380	93.5	165	6.5	60	2.4	2,335	91.7
Bremerton–Silverdale, WA	5,715	5,300	92.7	415	7.3	170	3.0	4,700	82.2
Bridgeport–Stamford–Norwalk, CT	13,775	12,680	92.1	1,090	7.9	3,050	22.1	9,040	65.6
Brownsville–Harlingen, TX	5,855	5,495	93.9	360	6.1	5,400	92.2	390	6.7
Brunswick, GA	2,645	2,550	96.4	100	3.8	95	3.6	2,095	79.2
Buffalo–Niagara Falls, NY	23,790	22,395	94.1	1,395	5.9	375	1.6	21,855	91.9
Burlington, NC	4,430	3,975	89.7	455	10.3	605	13.7	3,365	76.0
Burlington–South Burlington, VT	5,070	4,690	92.5	380	7.5	35	0.7	4,895	96.5
Canton–Massillon, OH	9,810	9,120	93.0	690	7.0	95	1.0	9,125	93.0
Cape Coral–Fort Myers, FL	13,875	12,925	93.2	950	6.8	2,665	19.2	10,150	73.2
Cape Girardeau–Jackson, MO–IL	2,510	2,365	94.2	145	5.8	0	0.0	2,420	96.4
Carson City, NV	1,230	1,180	95.9	50	4.1	280	22.8	900	73.2

C-11 Installation, Maintenance, and Repair Craft Workers, by Metropolitan Statistical Area, Sex, Race, and Hispanic or Latino Origin, 2006–2010—*Continued*

Metropolitan Statistical Area	Black alone, not Hispanic or Latino Number	Percent	American Indian and Alaska Native alone, not Hispanic or Latino Number	Percent	Asian alone, not Hispanic or Latino Number	Percent	Native Hawaiian and Other Pacific Islander alone, not Hispanic or Latino Number	Percent	Two or more races, not Hispanic or Latino Number	Percent
Abilene, TX	145	3.6	4	0.1	55	1.4	0	0.0	60	1.5
Akron, OH	990	6.2	10	0.1	25	0.2	0	0.0	110	0.7
Albany, GA	1,025	30.0	0	0.0	0	0.0	0	0.0	44	1.3
Albany–Schenectady–Troy, NY	670	4.2	45	0.3	65	0.4	0	0.0	385	2.4
Albuquerque, NM	320	1.8	1,195	6.8	430	2.4	10	0.1	190	1.1
Alexandria, LA	375	11.2	45	1.3	15	0.4	0	0.0	44	1.3
Allentown–Bethlehem–Easton, PA–NJ	535	2.8	15	0.1	175	0.9	0	0.0	120	0.6
Altoona, PA	15	0.4	0	0.0	0	0.0	0	0.0	14	0.4
Amarillo, TX	150	2.2	65	1.0	70	1.0	0	0.0	105	1.6
Ames, IA	35	2.3	4	0.3	0	0.0	0	0.0	12	0.8
Anchorage, AK	220	2.7	365	4.4	245	3.0	145	1.8	420	5.1
Anderson, IN	90	2.8	0	0.0	0	0.0	0	0.0	100	3.1
Anderson, SC	375	7.2	0	0.0	35	0.7	15	0.3	65	1.2
Ann Arbor, MI	380	7.5	25	0.5	130	2.6	0	0.0	34	0.7
Anniston–Oxford, AL	615	15.3	0	0.0	20	0.5	0	0.0	0	0.0
Appleton, WI	0	0.0	35	0.6	30	0.5	0	0.0	15	0.2
Asheville, NC	260	2.6	25	0.3	145	1.5	4	0.0	195	2.0
Athens–Clarke County, GA	415	12.7	0	0.0	20	0.6	0	0.0	4	0.1
Atlanta–Sandy Springs–Marietta, GA	25,920	25.5	345	0.3	3,570	3.5	20	0.0	1,020	1.0
Atlantic City–Hammonton, NJ	720	14.2	4	0.1	175	3.4	60	1.2	45	0.9
Auburn–Opelika, AL	510	15.2	10	0.3	60	1.8	0	0.0	20	0.6
Augusta–Richmond County, GA–SC	2,230	18.8	4	0.0	100	0.8	45	0.4	210	1.8
Austin–Round Rock–San Marcos, TX	1,810	6.2	180	0.6	955	3.3	25	0.1	480	1.6
Bakersfield–Delano, CA	425	2.6	95	0.6	465	2.9	0	0.0	205	1.3
Baltimore–Towson, MD	10,870	20.9	160	0.3	1,440	2.8	90	0.2	1,035	2.0
Bangor, ME	0	0.0	70	1.7	4	0.1	0	0.0	25	0.6
Barnstable Town, MA	50	1.2	0	0.0	70	1.7	0	0.0	19	0.5
Baton Rouge, LA	4,280	25.3	30	0.2	525	3.1	0	0.0	80	0.5
Battle Creek, MI	105	3.2	10	0.3	55	1.7	0	0.0	25	0.8
Bay City, MI	15	0.5	4	0.1	0	0.0	0	0.0	0	0.0
Beaumont–Port Arthur, TX	1,270	14.8	70	0.8	70	0.8	0	0.0	35	0.4
Bellingham, WA	0	0.0	65	1.6	150	3.8	4	0.1	45	1.1
Bend, OR	10	0.3	40	1.1	0	0.0	0	0.0	35	1.0
Billings, MT	25	0.6	30	0.7	0	0.0	0	0.0	20	0.5
Binghamton, NY	100	2.1	10	0.2	80	1.7	0	0.0	29	0.6
Birmingham–Hoover, AL	4,400	17.7	60	0.2	175	0.7	20	0.1	380	1.5
Bismarck, ND	0	0.0	30	1.2	0	0.0	0	0.0	20	0.8
Blacksburg–Christiansburg–Radford, VA	60	1.8	0	0.0	20	0.6	0	0.0	60	1.8
Bloomington, IN	0	0.0	10	0.3	0	0.0	0	0.0	20	0.6
Bloomington–Normal, IL	150	5.2	0	0.0	25	0.9	0	0.0	24	0.8
Boise City–Nampa, ID	260	2.3	40	0.4	100	0.9	0	0.0	170	1.5
Boston–Cambridge–Quincy, MA–NH	3,490	4.8	110	0.1	2,760	3.8	0	0.0	1,160	1.6
Boulder, CO	20	0.6	0	0.0	235	6.7	0	0.0	40	1.1
Bowling Green, KY	120	4.7	0	0.0	30	1.2	0	0.0	0	0.0
Bremerton–Silverdale, WA	270	4.7	90	1.6	285	5.0	40	0.7	155	2.7
Bridgeport–Stamford–Norwalk, CT	1,155	8.4	0	0.0	375	2.7	0	0.0	155	1.1
Brownsville–Harlingen, TX	25	0.4	30	0.5	0	0.0	0	0.0	10	0.2
Brunswick, GA	405	15.3	0	0.0	0	0.0	0	0.0	50	1.9
Buffalo–Niagara Falls, NY	1,125	4.7	115	0.5	60	0.3	0	0.0	265	1.1
Burlington, NC	390	8.8	0	0.0	45	1.0	0	0.0	15	0.3
Burlington–South Burlington, VT	20	0.4	30	0.6	45	0.9	0	0.0	40	0.8
Canton–Massillon, OH	545	5.6	0	0.0	15	0.2	0	0.0	30	0.3
Cape Coral–Fort Myers, FL	845	6.1	25	0.2	95	0.7	0	0.0	90	0.6
Cape Girardeau–Jackson, MO–IL	80	3.2	0	0.0	0	0.0	0	0.0	10	0.4
Carson City, NV	0	0.0	10	0.8	35	2.8	0	0.0	4	0.3

PART C—METROPOLITAN STATISTICAL AREA TABLES

C-11 Installation, Maintenance, and Repair Craft Workers, by Metropolitan Statistical Area, Sex, Race, and Hispanic or Latino Origin, 2006–2010—*Continued*

Metropolitan Statistical Area	Total who worked in the last 5 years	Male Number	Male Percent	Female Number	Female Percent	Hispanic or Latino Number	Hispanic or Latino Percent	White alone, not Hispanic or Latino Number	White alone, not Hispanic or Latino Percent
Casper, WY	2,620	2,465	94.1	150	5.7	165	6.3	2,415	92.2
Cedar Rapids, IA	6,025	5,610	93.1	415	6.9	75	1.2	5,715	94.9
Champaign–Urbana, IL	4,115	3,785	92.0	325	7.9	60	1.5	3,555	86.4
Charleston, WV	6,000	5,550	92.5	450	7.5	50	0.8	5,830	97.2
Charleston–North Charleston–Summerville, SC.	16,640	15,335	92.2	1,305	7.8	785	4.7	11,230	67.5
Charlotte–Gastonia–Rock Hill, NC–SC	36,935	34,530	93.5	2,405	6.5	2,875	7.8	26,945	73.0
Charlottesville, VA	2,770	2,605	94.0	165	6.0	190	6.9	2,045	73.8
Chattanooga, TN–GA	10,580	9,915	93.7	670	6.3	120	1.1	9,590	90.6
Cheyenne, WY	1,785	1,715	96.1	70	3.9	170	9.5	1,510	84.6
Chicago–Joliet–Naperville, IL–IN–WI	177,970	164,780	92.6	13,185	7.4	36,165	20.3	116,410	65.4
Chico, CA	4,140	3,945	95.3	195	4.7	720	17.4	3,110	75.1
Cincinnati–Middletown, OH–KY–IN	46,445	43,120	92.8	3,325	7.2	620	1.3	42,495	91.5
Clarksville, TN–KY	6,560	6,060	92.4	500	7.6	380	5.8	5,135	78.3
Cleveland, TN	2,730	2,580	94.5	150	5.5	45	1.6	2,620	96.0
Cleveland–Elyria–Mentor, OH	45,300	42,285	93.3	3,015	6.7	1,715	3.8	37,680	83.2
Coeur d'Alene, ID	3,265	3,120	95.6	145	4.4	60	1.8	3,110	95.3
College Station–Bryan, TX	4,890	4,610	94.3	280	5.7	540	11.0	3,905	79.9
Colorado Springs, CO	12,935	11,715	90.6	1,220	9.4	1,575	12.2	10,300	79.6
Columbia, MO	2,875	2,690	93.6	185	6.4	25	0.9	2,640	91.8
Columbia, SC	14,965	14,020	93.7	945	6.3	295	2.0	11,020	73.6
Columbus, GA–AL	4,660	4,290	92.1	370	7.9	155	3.3	3,070	65.9
Columbus, IN	1,715	1,635	95.3	80	4.7	30	1.7	1,600	93.3
Columbus, OH	32,590	29,975	92.0	2,615	8.0	910	2.8	28,030	86.0
Corpus Christi, TX	11,560	10,750	93.0	810	7.0	6,205	53.7	4,845	41.9
Corvallis, OR	1,410	1,215	86.2	200	14.2	45	3.2	1,305	92.6
Crestview–Fort Walton Beach–Destin, FL	4,665	4,395	94.2	270	5.8	200	4.3	3,560	76.3
Cumberland, MD–WV	2,330	2,125	91.2	205	8.8	4	0.2	2,315	99.4
Dallas–Fort Worth–Arlington, TX	133,535	123,100	92.2	10,435	7.8	39,345	29.5	72,950	54.6
Dalton, GA	3,490	3,320	95.1	170	4.9	830	23.8	2,490	71.3
Danville, IL	1,555	1,470	94.5	85	5.5	30	1.9	1,475	94.9
Danville, VA	2,510	2,275	90.6	235	9.4	0	0.0	1,905	75.9
Davenport–Moline–Rock Island, IA–IL	8,925	8,125	91.0	795	8.9	325	3.6	8,145	91.3
Dayton, OH	18,745	17,390	92.8	1,355	7.2	280	1.5	16,775	89.5
Decatur, AL	3,955	3,670	92.8	285	7.2	125	3.2	3,355	84.8
Decatur, IL	2,500	2,315	92.6	190	7.6	80	3.2	2,265	90.6
Deltona–Daytona Beach–Ormond Beach, FL	10,765	10,065	93.5	700	6.5	1,220	11.3	8,810	81.8
Denver–Aurora–Broomfield, CO	50,940	46,640	91.6	4,300	8.4	9,280	18.2	36,310	71.3
Des Moines–West Des Moines, IA	10,405	9,590	92.2	820	7.9	385	3.7	9,370	90.1
Detroit–Warren–Livonia, MI	94,070	87,025	92.5	7,045	7.5	2,190	2.3	75,865	80.6
Dothan, AL	4,315	4,050	93.9	265	6.1	85	2.0	3,615	83.8
Dover, DE	3,705	3,460	93.4	245	6.6	215	5.8	2,940	79.4
Dubuque, IA	2,205	1,975	89.6	235	10.7	20	0.9	2,105	95.5
Duluth, MN–WI	6,940	6,620	95.4	320	4.6	10	0.1	6,760	97.4
Durham–Chapel Hill, NC	8,445	7,905	93.6	540	6.4	685	8.1	5,600	66.3
Eau Claire, WI	3,905	3,715	95.1	190	4.9	34	0.9	3,805	97.4
El Centro, CA	2,410	2,245	93.2	165	6.8	1,855	77.0	520	21.6
Elizabethtown, KY	2,270	2,120	93.4	155	6.8	15	0.7	2,065	91.0
Elkhart–Goshen, IN	5,175	4,595	88.8	585	11.3	630	12.2	4,320	83.5
Elmira, NY	2,240	2,165	96.7	75	3.3	55	2.5	2,050	91.5
El Paso, TX	14,690	13,585	92.5	1,110	7.6	11,730	79.9	2,360	16.1
Erie, PA	7,430	7,010	94.3	420	5.7	95	1.3	6,765	91.0
Eugene–Springfield, OR	7,550	7,065	93.6	485	6.4	400	5.3	6,805	90.1
Evansville, IN–KY	9,150	8,685	94.9	465	5.1	35	0.4	8,835	96.6
Fairbanks, AK	2,855	2,645	92.6	210	7.4	50	1.8	2,400	84.1
Fargo, ND–MN	4,270	3,940	92.3	325	7.6	19	0.4	4,170	97.7

C-11. Installation, Maintenance, and Repair Craft Workers, by Metropolitan Statistical Area, Sex, Race, and Hispanic or Latino Origin, 2006–2010—Continued

Metropolitan Statistical Area	Black alone, not Hispanic or Latino Number	Black alone, not Hispanic or Latino Percent	American Indian and Alaska Native alone, not Hispanic or Latino Number	American Indian and Alaska Native alone, not Hispanic or Latino Percent	Asian alone, not Hispanic or Latino Number	Asian alone, not Hispanic or Latino Percent	Native Hawaiian and Other Pacific Islander alone, not Hispanic or Latino Number	Native Hawaiian and Other Pacific Islander alone, not Hispanic or Latino Percent	Two or more races, not Hispanic or Latino Number	Two or more races, not Hispanic or Latino Percent
Casper, WY	0	0.0	25	1.0	0	0.0	0	0.0	10	0.4
Cedar Rapids, IA	110	1.8	25	0.4	30	0.5	0	0.0	65	1.1
Champaign–Urbana, IL	290	7.0	0	0.0	160	3.9	0	0.0	50	1.2
Charleston, WV	50	0.8	0	0.0	20	0.3	0	0.0	45	0.8
Charleston–North Charleston–Summerville, SC	4,075	24.5	30	0.2	190	1.1	0	0.0	325	2.0
Charlotte–Gastonia–Rock Hill, NC–SC	5,555	15.0	205	0.6	1,040	2.8	0	0.0	305	0.8
Charlottesville, VA	425	15.3	0	0.0	15	0.5	0	0.0	95	3.4
Chattanooga, TN–GA	700	6.6	10	0.1	90	0.9	0	0.0	75	0.7
Cheyenne, WY	25	1.4	50	2.8	0	0.0	0	0.0	30	1.7
Chicago–Joliet–Naperville, IL–IN–WI	17,615	9.9	190	0.1	6,185	3.5	45	0.0	1,360	0.8
Chico, CA	35	0.8	25	0.6	125	3.0	0	0.0	120	2.9
Cincinnati–Middletown, OH–KY–IN	2,570	5.5	85	0.2	315	0.7	0	0.0	355	0.8
Clarksville, TN–KY	865	13.2	0	0.0	100	1.5	15	0.2	65	1.0
Cleveland, TN	45	1.6	0	0.0	0	0.0	0	0.0	20	0.7
Cleveland–Elyria–Mentor, OH	5,010	11.1	50	0.1	345	0.8	10	0.0	490	1.1
Coeur d'Alene, ID	0	0.0	55	1.7	0	0.0	20	0.6	20	0.6
College Station–Bryan, TX	365	7.5	0	0.0	75	1.5	0	0.0	10	0.2
Colorado Springs, CO	450	3.5	115	0.9	90	0.7	75	0.6	320	2.5
Columbia, MO	180	6.3	0	0.0	0	0.0	0	0.0	35	1.2
Columbia, SC	3,245	21.7	80	0.5	155	1.0	20	0.1	155	1.0
Columbus, GA–AL	1,250	26.8	25	0.5	25	0.5	75	1.6	60	1.3
Columbus, IN	30	1.7	4	0.2	20	1.2	0	0.0	30	1.7
Columbus, OH	2,650	8.1	85	0.3	425	1.3	0	0.0	490	1.5
Corpus Christi, TX	385	3.3	30	0.3	45	0.4	0	0.0	55	0.5
Corvallis, OR	4	0.3	30	2.1	25	1.8	0	0.0	0	0.0
Crestview–Fort Walton Beach–Destin, FL	560	12.0	10	0.2	160	3.4	0	0.0	170	3.6
Cumberland, MD–WV	10	0.4	0	0.0	0	0.0	0	0.0	4	0.2
Dallas–Fort Worth–Arlington, TX	12,340	9.2	525	0.4	6,545	4.9	120	0.1	1,705	1.3
Dalton, GA	40	1.1	70	2.0	60	1.7	0	0.0	0	0.0
Danville, IL	25	1.6	15	1.0	0	0.0	0	0.0	10	0.6
Danville, VA	560	22.3	0	0.0	45	1.8	0	0.0	0	0.0
Davenport–Moline–Rock Island, IA–IL	305	3.4	10	0.1	65	0.7	0	0.0	80	0.9
Dayton, OH	1,360	7.3	10	0.1	150	0.8	0	0.0	175	0.9
Decatur, AL	270	6.8	115	2.9	0	0.0	0	0.0	90	2.3
Decatur, IL	95	3.8	0	0.0	25	1.0	0	0.0	39	1.6
Deltona–Daytona Beach–Ormond Beach, FL	530	4.9	30	0.3	85	0.8	0	0.0	90	0.8
Denver–Aurora–Broomfield, CO	2,520	4.9	510	1.0	1,645	3.2	85	0.2	580	1.1
Des Moines–West Des Moines, IA	190	1.8	0	0.0	340	3.3	0	0.0	120	1.2
Detroit–Warren–Livonia, MI	13,715	14.6	230	0.2	1,185	1.3	10	0.0	865	0.9
Dothan, AL	550	12.7	15	0.3	10	0.2	10	0.2	34	0.8
Dover, DE	435	11.7	0	0.0	45	1.2	0	0.0	70	1.9
Dubuque, IA	15	0.7	35	1.6	0	0.0	0	0.0	35	1.6
Duluth, MN–WI	0	0.0	85	1.2	30	0.4	0	0.0	55	0.8
Durham–Chapel Hill, NC	1,780	21.1	20	0.2	230	2.7	15	0.2	114	1.3
Eau Claire, WI	10	0.3	15	0.4	20	0.5	0	0.0	25	0.6
El Centro, CA	25	1.0	4	0.2	0	0.0	0	0.0	0	0.0
Elizabethtown, KY	140	6.2	0	0.0	35	1.5	0	0.0	20	0.9
Elkhart–Goshen, IN	195	3.8	0	0.0	30	0.6	0	0.0	4	0.1
Elmira, NY	95	4.2	0	0.0	25	1.1	0	0.0	14	0.6
El Paso, TX	395	2.7	10	0.1	110	0.7	0	0.0	85	0.6
Erie, PA	415	5.6	4	0.1	35	0.5	0	0.0	120	1.6
Eugene–Springfield, OR	45	0.6	35	0.5	60	0.8	4	0.1	195	2.6
Evansville, IN–KY	195	2.1	0	0.0	30	0.3	0	0.0	55	0.6
Fairbanks, AK	115	4.0	165	5.8	4	0.1	0	0.0	120	4.2
Fargo, ND–MN	30	0.7	10	0.2	0	0.0	0	0.0	40	0.9

PART C—METROPOLITAN STATISTICAL AREA TABLES

C-11 Installation, Maintenance, and Repair Craft Workers, by Metropolitan Statistical Area, Sex, Race, and Hispanic or Latino Origin, 2006–2010—Continued

Metropolitan Statistical Area	Total who worked in the last 5 years	Male Number	Male Percent	Female Number	Female Percent	Hispanic or Latino Number	Hispanic or Latino Percent	White alone, not Hispanic or Latino Number	White alone, not Hispanic or Latino Percent
Farmington, NM	3,825	3,675	96.1	150	3.9	760	19.9	1,925	50.3
Fayetteville, NC	7,420	6,895	92.9	525	7.1	560	7.5	4,380	59.0
Fayetteville–Springdale–Rogers, AR–MO	9,390	8,395	89.4	995	10.6	860	9.2	7,970	84.9
Flagstaff, AZ	2,830	2,670	94.3	160	5.7	220	7.8	1,820	64.3
Flint, MI	9,015	8,395	93.1	625	6.9	150	1.7	8,085	89.7
Florence, SC	4,835	4,650	96.2	185	3.8	50	1.0	3,450	71.4
Florence–Muscle Shoals, AL	3,730	3,585	96.1	150	4.0	55	1.5	3,295	88.3
Fond du Lac, WI	3,310	3,010	90.9	300	9.1	30	0.9	3,260	98.5
Fort Collins–Loveland, CO	5,675	5,350	94.3	325	5.7	500	8.8	5,025	88.5
Fort Smith, AR–OK	6,110	5,855	95.8	250	4.1	240	3.9	5,175	84.7
Fort Wayne, IN	10,015	9,115	91.0	900	9.0	370	3.7	8,975	89.6
Fresno, CA	15,290	14,425	94.3	865	5.7	6,655	43.5	6,815	44.6
Gadsden, AL	2,340	2,225	95.1	120	5.1	10	0.4	2,200	94.0
Gainesville, FL	3,955	3,705	93.7	255	6.4	320	8.1	3,190	80.7
Gainesville, GA	4,185	3,885	92.8	300	7.2	880	21.0	3,100	74.1
Glens Falls, NY	3,355	3,140	93.6	215	6.4	10	0.3	3,300	98.4
Goldsboro, NC	3,080	2,940	95.5	140	4.5	225	7.3	2,295	74.5
Grand Forks, ND–MN	2,110	2,010	95.3	95	4.5	44	2.1	2,015	95.5
Grand Junction, CO	3,750	3,485	92.9	265	7.1	320	8.5	3,310	88.3
Grand Rapids–Wyoming, MI	18,575	17,550	94.5	1,025	5.5	665	3.6	16,715	90.0
Great Falls, MT	1,780	1,695	95.2	85	4.8	90	5.1	1,520	85.4
Greeley, CO	5,170	4,905	94.9	265	5.1	975	18.9	4,070	78.7
Green Bay, WI	8,675	8,095	93.3	580	6.7	140	1.6	8,225	94.8
Greensboro–High Point, NC	17,880	16,465	92.1	1,415	7.9	1,240	6.9	13,220	73.9
Greenville, NC	3,275	2,985	91.1	290	8.9	85	2.6	2,270	69.3
Greenville–Mauldin–Easley, SC	14,845	13,505	91.0	1,340	9.0	775	5.2	11,990	80.8
Gulfport–Biloxi, MS	5,255	5,055	96.2	200	3.8	180	3.4	4,445	84.6
Hagerstown–Martinsburg, MD–WV	7,645	7,110	93.0	530	6.9	54	0.7	7,120	93.1
Hanford–Corcoran, CA	3,415	3,235	94.7	180	5.3	1,240	36.3	1,755	51.4
Harrisburg–Carlisle, PA	11,085	10,305	93.0	785	7.1	410	3.7	10,310	93.0
Harrisonburg, VA	2,790	2,505	89.8	285	10.2	105	3.8	2,545	91.2
Hartford–West Hartford–East Hartford, CT	26,085	24,165	92.6	1,920	7.4	2,380	9.1	21,195	81.3
Hattiesburg, MS	3,180	3,040	95.6	140	4.4	65	2.0	2,390	75.2
Hickory–Lenoir–Morganton, NC	11,670	10,595	90.8	1,080	9.3	540	4.6	10,550	90.4
Hinesville–Fort Stewart, GA	2,965	2,805	94.6	160	5.4	220	7.4	1,765	59.5
Holland–Grand Haven, MI	6,330	5,840	92.3	490	7.7	215	3.4	5,940	93.8
Honolulu, HI	17,760	16,360	92.1	1,400	7.9	980	5.5	2,910	16.4
Hot Springs, AR	2,065	1,960	94.9	110	5.3	0	0.0	1,925	93.2
Houma–Bayou Cane–Thibodaux, LA	5,475	5,225	95.4	255	4.7	145	2.6	4,735	86.5
Houston–Sugar Land–Baytown, TX	125,695	118,705	94.4	6,990	5.6	48,735	38.8	54,340	43.2
Huntington–Ashland, WV–KY–OH	6,285	6,030	95.9	255	4.1	79	1.3	6,075	96.7
Huntsville, AL	8,450	7,640	90.4	810	9.6	280	3.3	6,525	77.2
Idaho Falls, ID	2,590	2,450	94.6	140	5.4	180	6.9	2,385	92.1
Indianapolis–Carmel, IN	37,800	34,975	92.5	2,825	7.5	1,640	4.3	31,785	84.1
Iowa City, IA	2,690	2,480	92.2	205	7.6	60	2.2	2,540	94.4
Ithaca, NY	1,250	1,095	87.6	155	12.4	4	0.3	1,180	94.4
Jackson, MI	4,410	4,055	92.0	355	8.0	80	1.8	4,185	94.9
Jackson, MS	10,240	9,465	92.4	775	7.6	165	1.6	6,030	58.9
Jackson, TN	2,345	2,150	91.7	195	8.3	60	2.6	1,875	80.0
Jacksonville, FL	30,240	28,425	94.0	1,815	6.0	2,130	7.0	22,675	75.0
Jacksonville, NC	3,550	3,265	92.0	285	8.0	275	7.7	2,875	81.0
Janesville, WI	4,280	3,990	93.2	290	6.8	220	5.1	3,965	92.6
Jefferson City, MO	2,990	2,830	94.6	160	5.4	55	1.8	2,815	94.1
Johnson City, TN	4,080	3,525	86.4	555	13.6	45	1.1	3,920	96.1
Johnstown, PA	2,890	2,825	97.8	65	2.2	24	0.8	2,865	99.1

C-11 **Installation, Maintenance, and Repair Craft Workers, by Metropolitan Statistical Area, Sex, Race, and Hispanic or Latino Origin, 2006–2010**—*Continued*

Metropolitan Statistical Area	Black alone, not Hispanic or Latino Number	Percent	American Indian and Alaska Native alone, not Hispanic or Latino Number	Percent	Asian alone, not Hispanic or Latino Number	Percent	Native Hawaiian and Other Pacific Islander alone, not Hispanic or Latino Number	Percent	Two or more races, not Hispanic or Latino Number	Percent
Farmington, NM	15	0.4	1,085	28.4	4	0.1	0	0.0	30	0.8
Fayetteville, NC	1,955	26.3	155	2.1	85	1.1	50	0.7	230	3.1
Fayetteville–Springdale–Rogers, AR–MO	75	0.8	205	2.2	50	0.5	65	0.7	170	1.8
Flagstaff, AZ	25	0.9	710	25.1	4	0.1	0	0.0	50	1.8
Flint, MI	565	6.3	10	0.1	60	0.7	0	0.0	145	1.6
Florence, SC	1,230	25.4	15	0.3	25	0.5	0	0.0	70	1.4
Florence–Muscle Shoals, AL	365	9.8	0	0.0	0	0.0	0	0.0	14	0.4
Fond du Lac, WI	10	0.3	4	0.1	0	0.0	0	0.0	4	0.1
Fort Collins–Loveland, CO	50	0.9	4	0.1	35	0.6	15	0.3	54	1.0
Fort Smith, AR–OK	140	2.3	175	2.9	180	2.9	0	0.0	200	3.3
Fort Wayne, IN	315	3.1	20	0.2	110	1.1	0	0.0	224	2.2
Fresno, CA	340	2.2	50	0.3	1,200	7.8	10	0.1	235	1.5
Gadsden, AL	100	4.3	0	0.0	30	1.3	0	0.0	4	0.2
Gainesville, FL	350	8.8	25	0.6	15	0.4	0	0.0	55	1.4
Gainesville, GA	155	3.7	0	0.0	35	0.8	0	0.0	20	0.5
Glens Falls, NY	25	0.7	0	0.0	0	0.0	0	0.0	20	0.6
Goldsboro, NC	525	17.0	15	0.5	15	0.5	0	0.0	4	0.1
Grand Forks, ND–MN	15	0.7	0	0.0	15	0.7	0	0.0	25	1.2
Grand Junction, CO	15	0.4	30	0.8	0	0.0	0	0.0	74	2.0
Grand Rapids–Wyoming, MI	660	3.6	90	0.5	235	1.3	0	0.0	205	1.1
Great Falls, MT	35	2.0	30	1.7	30	1.7	0	0.0	79	4.4
Greeley, CO	65	1.3	0	0.0	15	0.3	15	0.3	30	0.6
Green Bay, WI	90	1.0	155	1.8	40	0.5	0	0.0	19	0.2
Greensboro–High Point, NC	2,710	15.2	85	0.5	425	2.4	0	0.0	199	1.1
Greenville, NC	850	26.0	0	0.0	0	0.0	0	0.0	70	2.1
Greenville–Mauldin–Easley, SC	1,800	12.1	20	0.1	105	0.7	20	0.1	140	0.9
Gulfport–Biloxi, MS	435	8.3	0	0.0	120	2.3	0	0.0	65	1.2
Hagerstown–Martinsburg, MD–WV	390	5.1	0	0.0	30	0.4	0	0.0	44	0.6
Hanford–Corcoran, CA	260	7.6	15	0.4	120	3.5	0	0.0	29	0.8
Harrisburg–Carlisle, PA	270	2.4	0	0.0	50	0.5	0	0.0	49	0.4
Harrisonburg, VA	75	2.7	0	0.0	30	1.1	0	0.0	34	1.2
Hartford–West Hartford–East Hartford, CT	1,600	6.1	15	0.1	610	2.3	0	0.0	285	1.1
Hattiesburg, MS	670	21.1	25	0.8	25	0.8	0	0.0	0	0.0
Hickory–Lenoir–Morganton, NC	215	1.8	0	0.0	235	2.0	0	0.0	125	1.1
Hinesville–Fort Stewart, GA	980	33.1	0	0.0	0	0.0	0	0.0	0	0.0
Holland–Grand Haven, MI	80	1.3	10	0.2	50	0.8	0	0.0	30	0.5
Honolulu, HI	470	2.6	80	0.5	8,660	48.8	1,240	7.0	3,415	19.2
Hot Springs, AR	140	6.8	0	0.0	0	0.0	0	0.0	0	0.0
Houma–Bayou Cane–Thibodaux, LA	425	7.8	135	2.5	0	0.0	0	0.0	40	0.7
Houston–Sugar Land–Baytown, TX	13,185	10.5	565	0.4	7,595	6.0	90	0.1	1,190	0.9
Huntington–Ashland, WV–KY–OH	40	0.6	15	0.2	35	0.6	0	0.0	40	0.6
Huntsville, AL	1,320	15.6	80	0.9	85	1.0	10	0.1	150	1.8
Idaho Falls, ID	15	0.6	0	0.0	0	0.0	0	0.0	10	0.4
Indianapolis–Carmel, IN	3,635	9.6	55	0.1	425	1.1	0	0.0	260	0.7
Iowa City, IA	0	0.0	0	0.0	35	1.3	0	0.0	55	2.0
Ithaca, NY	0	0.0	0	0.0	40	3.2	0	0.0	20	1.6
Jackson, MI	125	2.8	0	0.0	10	0.2	0	0.0	4	0.1
Jackson, MS	3,895	38.0	40	0.4	20	0.2	25	0.2	70	0.7
Jackson, TN	390	16.6	10	0.4	0	0.0	4	0.2	4	0.2
Jacksonville, FL	4,400	14.6	75	0.2	625	2.1	10	0.0	320	1.1
Jacksonville, NC	315	8.9	4	0.1	50	1.4	0	0.0	35	1.0
Janesville, WI	15	0.4	4	0.1	30	0.7	4	0.1	34	0.8
Jefferson City, MO	35	1.2	15	0.5	35	1.2	0	0.0	40	1.3
Johnson City, TN	100	2.5	0	0.0	0	0.0	0	0.0	15	0.4
Johnstown, PA	0	0.0	0	0.0	0	0.0	0	0.0	8	0.3

PART C—METROPOLITAN STATISTICAL AREA TABLES

C-11 **Installation, Maintenance, and Repair Craft Workers, by Metropolitan Statistical Area, Sex, Race, and Hispanic or Latino Origin, 2006–2010**—Continued

Metropolitan Statistical Area	Total who worked in the last 5 years	Male Number	Male Percent	Female Number	Female Percent	Hispanic or Latino Number	Hispanic or Latino Percent	White alone, not Hispanic or Latino Number	White alone, not Hispanic or Latino Percent
Jonesboro, AR	2,535	2,320	91.5	215	8.5	55	2.2	2,310	91.1
Joplin, MO	4,815	4,595	95.4	220	4.6	290	6.0	4,215	87.5
Kalamazoo–Portage, MI	6,845	6,215	90.8	630	9.2	185	2.7	6,165	90.1
Kankakee–Bradley, IL	2,370	2,275	96.0	95	4.0	70	3.0	2,215	93.5
Kansas City, MO–KS	42,410	39,260	92.6	3,150	7.4	2,535	6.0	35,925	84.7
Kennewick–Pasco–Richland, WA	4,715	4,385	93.0	335	7.1	1,010	21.4	3,500	74.2
Killeen–Temple–Fort Hood, TX	8,500	8,040	94.6	460	5.4	1,345	15.8	5,705	67.1
Kingsport–Bristol–Bristol, TN–VA	7,825	7,290	93.2	535	6.8	70	0.9	7,620	97.4
Kingston, NY	3,705	3,475	93.8	230	6.2	345	9.3	3,205	86.5
Knoxville, TN	13,025	12,275	94.2	750	5.8	225	1.7	12,040	92.4
Kokomo, IN	2,490	2,385	95.8	105	4.2	60	2.4	2,365	95.0
La Crosse, WI–MN	2,970	2,795	94.1	175	5.9	50	1.7	2,725	91.8
Lafayette, IN	4,405	4,075	92.5	330	7.5	95	2.2	4,135	93.9
Lafayette, LA	7,890	7,370	93.4	520	6.6	405	5.1	6,315	80.0
Lake Charles, LA	4,920	4,645	94.4	275	5.6	8	0.2	3,945	80.2
Lake Havasu City–Kingman, AZ	4,520	4,285	94.8	230	5.1	620	13.7	3,740	82.7
Lakeland–Winter Haven, FL	11,645	11,095	95.3	545	4.7	1,735	14.9	8,985	77.2
Lancaster, PA	13,780	12,515	90.8	1,265	9.2	645	4.7	12,765	92.6
Lansing–East Lansing, MI	8,605	8,040	93.4	565	6.6	265	3.1	7,805	90.7
Laredo, TX	3,530	3,395	96.2	135	3.8	3,380	95.8	150	4.2
Las Cruces, NM	3,900	3,745	96.0	155	4.0	2,570	65.9	1,140	29.2
Las Vegas–Paradise, NV	33,280	30,835	92.7	2,445	7.3	8,480	25.5	19,045	57.2
Lawrence, KS	1,920	1,770	92.2	155	8.1	65	3.4	1,725	89.8
Lawton, OK	2,595	2,450	94.4	145	5.6	105	4.0	1,750	67.4
Lebanon, PA	3,890	3,665	94.2	225	5.8	100	2.6	3,765	96.8
Lewiston, ID–WA	1,415	1,295	91.5	120	8.5	20	1.4	1,315	92.9
Lewiston–Auburn, ME	2,850	2,595	91.1	255	8.9	4	0.1	2,765	97.0
Lexington–Fayette, KY	8,415	7,745	92.0	670	8.0	310	3.7	7,230	85.9
Lima, OH	2,455	2,390	97.4	65	2.6	0	0.0	2,360	96.1
Lincoln, NE	6,575	6,270	95.4	305	4.6	300	4.6	5,905	89.8
Little Rock–North Little Rock–Conway, AR	15,140	14,085	93.0	1,050	6.9	390	2.6	12,535	82.8
Logan, UT–ID	2,720	2,605	95.8	115	4.2	140	5.1	2,540	93.4
Longview, TX	5,825	5,520	94.8	300	5.2	510	8.8	4,460	76.6
Longview, WA	2,875	2,710	94.3	165	5.7	100	3.5	2,685	93.4
Los Angeles–Long Beach–Santa Ana, CA	230,535	212,055	92.0	18,475	8.0	118,805	51.5	66,620	28.9
Louisville/Jefferson County, KY–IN	28,105	25,545	90.9	2,560	9.1	680	2.4	25,125	89.4
Lubbock, TX	6,070	5,515	90.9	555	9.1	2,270	37.4	3,395	55.9
Lynchburg, VA	6,470	5,865	90.6	605	9.4	150	2.3	5,545	85.7
Macon, GA	4,630	4,260	92.0	370	8.0	80	1.7	3,020	65.2
Madera–Chowchilla, CA	2,560	2,460	96.1	100	3.9	880	34.4	1,530	59.8
Madison, WI	10,570	9,690	91.7	875	8.3	320	3.0	9,760	92.3
Manchester–Nashua, NH	8,805	8,230	93.5	580	6.6	245	2.8	8,345	94.8
Manhattan, KS	2,455	2,245	91.4	210	8.6	70	2.9	2,110	85.9
Mankato–North Mankato, MN	2,070	1,910	92.3	160	7.7	30	1.4	2,025	97.8
Mansfield, OH	3,055	2,650	86.7	405	13.3	19	0.6	2,835	92.8
McAllen–Edinburg–Mission, TX	11,820	11,210	94.8	610	5.2	10,940	92.6	780	6.6
Medford, OR	3,995	3,690	92.4	310	7.8	235	5.9	3,520	88.1
Memphis, TN–MS–AR	26,650	24,110	90.5	2,540	9.5	1,130	4.2	15,740	59.1
Merced, CA	3,970	3,835	96.6	140	3.5	2,000	50.4	1,690	42.6
Miami–Fort Lauderdale–Pompano Beach, FL	103,310	95,660	92.6	7,650	7.4	47,695	46.2	35,855	34.7
Michigan City–La Porte, IN	3,275	3,125	95.4	150	4.6	165	5.0	3,025	92.4
Midland, TX	3,260	3,095	94.9	165	5.1	1,525	46.8	1,485	45.6
Milwaukee–Waukesha–West Allis, WI	33,675	30,895	91.7	2,780	8.3	2,300	6.8	27,585	81.9
Minneapolis–St. Paul–Bloomington, MN–WI	68,285	62,625	91.7	5,660	8.3	2,505	3.7	60,305	88.3
Missoula, MT	1,990	1,860	93.5	135	6.8	0	0.0	1,850	93.0

C-11 **Installation, Maintenance, and Repair Craft Workers, by Metropolitan Statistical Area, Sex, Race, and Hispanic or Latino Origin, 2006–2010**—*Continued*

Metropolitan Statistical Area	Black alone, not Hispanic or Latino Number	Percent	American Indian and Alaska Native alone, not Hispanic or Latino Number	Percent	Asian alone, not Hispanic or Latino Number	Percent	Native Hawaiian and Other Pacific Islander alone, not Hispanic or Latino Number	Percent	Two or more races, not Hispanic or Latino Number	Percent
Jonesboro, AR	135	5.3	10	0.4	0	0.0	0	0.0	30	1.2
Joplin, MO	115	2.4	90	1.9	25	0.5	20	0.4	60	1.2
Kalamazoo–Portage, MI	345	5.0	40	0.6	4	0.1	0	0.0	110	1.6
Kankakee–Bradley, IL	65	2.7	0	0.0	4	0.2	0	0.0	15	0.6
Kansas City, MO–KS	2,575	6.1	95	0.2	670	1.6	100	0.2	505	1.2
Kennewick–Pasco–Richland, WA	75	1.6	0	0.0	40	0.8	0	0.0	95	2.0
Killeen–Temple–Fort Hood, TX	1,015	11.9	95	1.1	115	1.4	30	0.4	195	2.3
Kingsport–Bristol–Bristol, TN–VA	95	1.2	0	0.0	4	0.1	0	0.0	30	0.4
Kingston, NY	90	2.4	0	0.0	50	1.3	0	0.0	14	0.4
Knoxville, TN	505	3.9	40	0.3	125	1.0	0	0.0	95	0.7
Kokomo, IN	50	2.0	15	0.6	0	0.0	0	0.0	0	0.0
La Crosse, WI–MN	50	1.7	0	0.0	90	3.0	0	0.0	59	2.0
Lafayette, IN	80	1.8	0	0.0	45	1.0	0	0.0	50	1.1
Lafayette, LA	1,050	13.3	0	0.0	75	1.0	0	0.0	40	0.5
Lake Charles, LA	845	17.2	0	0.0	0	0.0	0	0.0	120	2.4
Lake Havasu City–Kingman, AZ	35	0.8	25	0.6	35	0.8	0	0.0	65	1.4
Lakeland–Winter Haven, FL	755	6.5	10	0.1	100	0.9	0	0.0	55	0.5
Lancaster, PA	130	0.9	0	0.0	130	0.9	0	0.0	115	0.8
Lansing–East Lansing, MI	245	2.8	35	0.4	160	1.9	0	0.0	94	1.1
Laredo, TX	0	0.0	0	0.0	0	0.0	0	0.0	0	0.0
Las Cruces, NM	70	1.8	90	2.3	0	0.0	0	0.0	25	0.6
Las Vegas–Paradise, NV	2,450	7.4	125	0.4	2,275	6.8	325	1.0	575	1.7
Lawrence, KS	0	0.0	75	3.9	15	0.8	0	0.0	44	2.3
Lawton, OK	420	16.2	150	5.8	40	1.5	4	0.2	125	4.8
Lebanon, PA	0	0.0	0	0.0	20	0.5	0	0.0	4	0.1
Lewiston, ID–WA	0	0.0	45	3.2	0	0.0	0	0.0	29	2.0
Lewiston–Auburn, ME	0	0.0	0	0.0	0	0.0	0	0.0	79	2.8
Lexington–Fayette, KY	695	8.3	20	0.2	100	1.2	25	0.3	34	0.4
Lima, OH	70	2.9	0	0.0	15	0.6	0	0.0	10	0.4
Lincoln, NE	110	1.7	70	1.1	165	2.5	0	0.0	20	0.3
Little Rock–North Little Rock–Conway, AR	1,880	12.4	100	0.7	95	0.6	0	0.0	135	0.9
Logan, UT–ID	0	0.0	0	0.0	30	1.1	0	0.0	4	0.1
Longview, TX	720	12.4	20	0.3	60	1.0	0	0.0	55	0.9
Longview, WA	0	0.0	0	0.0	10	0.3	0	0.0	80	2.8
Los Angeles–Long Beach–Santa Ana, CA	10,825	4.7	670	0.3	30,100	13.1	605	0.3	2,905	1.3
Louisville/Jefferson County, KY–IN	1,750	6.2	55	0.2	140	0.5	0	0.0	360	1.3
Lubbock, TX	275	4.5	15	0.2	70	1.2	10	0.2	30	0.5
Lynchburg, VA	685	10.6	0	0.0	55	0.9	0	0.0	35	0.5
Macon, GA	1,430	30.9	0	0.0	15	0.3	0	0.0	85	1.8
Madera–Chowchilla, CA	80	3.1	35	1.4	30	1.2	0	0.0	0	0.0
Madison, WI	160	1.5	20	0.2	215	2.0	0	0.0	94	0.9
Manchester–Nashua, NH	125	1.4	0	0.0	90	1.0	0	0.0	0	0.0
Manhattan, KS	175	7.1	0	0.0	45	1.8	10	0.4	40	1.6
Mankato–North Mankato, MN	0	0.0	0	0.0	4	0.2	0	0.0	10	0.5
Mansfield, OH	195	6.4	0	0.0	0	0.0	0	0.0	0	0.0
McAllen–Edinburg–Mission, TX	55	0.5	4	0.0	15	0.1	0	0.0	20	0.2
Medford, OR	25	0.6	45	1.1	25	0.6	40	1.0	110	2.8
Memphis, TN–MS–AR	8,990	33.7	35	0.1	580	2.2	20	0.1	160	0.6
Merced, CA	55	1.4	20	0.5	110	2.8	40	1.0	65	1.6
Miami–Fort Lauderdale–Pompano Beach, FL	16,530	16.0	115	0.1	1,780	1.7	20	0.0	1,315	1.3
Michigan City–La Porte, IN	60	1.8	4	0.1	0	0.0	0	0.0	25	0.8
Midland, TX	125	3.8	65	2.0	45	1.4	0	0.0	10	0.3
Milwaukee–Waukesha–West Allis, WI	2,770	8.2	150	0.4	610	1.8	0	0.0	265	0.8
Minneapolis–St. Paul–Bloomington, MN–WI	2,070	3.0	340	0.5	2,270	3.3	50	0.1	745	1.1
Missoula, MT	0	0.0	100	5.0	20	1.0	0	0.0	20	1.0

PART C—METROPOLITAN STATISTICAL AREA TABLES

C-11 Installation, Maintenance, and Repair Craft Workers, by Metropolitan Statistical Area, Sex, Race, and Hispanic or Latino Origin, 2006–2010—Continued

Metropolitan Statistical Area	Total who worked in the last 5 years	Male Number	Male Percent	Female Number	Female Percent	Hispanic or Latino Number	Hispanic or Latino Percent	White alone, not Hispanic or Latino Number	White alone, not Hispanic or Latino Percent
Mobile, AL	9,105	8,680	95.3	420	4.6	260	2.9	6,680	73.4
Modesto, CA	10,785	10,140	94.0	645	6.0	4,090	37.9	5,655	52.4
Monroe, LA	3,240	3,000	92.6	240	7.4	30	0.9	2,535	78.2
Monroe, MI	4,890	4,765	97.4	125	2.6	90	1.8	4,670	95.5
Montgomery, AL	7,605	6,825	89.7	775	10.2	380	5.0	5,045	66.3
Morgantown, WV	2,290	2,075	90.6	215	9.4	10	0.4	2,195	95.9
Morristown, TN	3,425	3,110	90.8	320	9.3	4	0.1	3,330	97.2
Mount Vernon–Anacortes, WA	2,540	2,405	94.7	135	5.3	315	12.4	2,050	80.7
Muncie, IN	2,530	2,355	93.1	170	6.7	90	3.6	2,340	92.5
Muskegon–Norton Shores, MI	4,425	4,120	93.1	305	6.9	95	2.1	4,020	90.8
Myrtle Beach–North Myrtle Beach–Conway, SC	5,590	5,455	97.6	135	2.4	230	4.1	4,765	85.2
Napa, CA	2,400	2,220	92.5	180	7.5	555	23.1	1,585	66.0
Naples–Marco Island, FL	5,265	4,715	89.6	555	10.5	1,390	26.4	3,665	69.6
Nashville-Davidson–Murfreesboro–Franklin, TN	33,275	30,680	92.2	2,595	7.8	1,525	4.6	28,100	84.4
New Haven–Milford, CT	18,445	17,260	93.6	1,185	6.4	2,640	14.3	14,180	76.9
New Orleans–Metairie–Kenner, LA	22,925	21,380	93.3	1,545	6.7	1,815	7.9	14,745	64.3
New York–Northern New Jersey–Long Island, NY–NJ–PA	286,935	264,365	92.1	22,570	7.9	70,555	24.6	150,455	52.4
Niles–Benton Harbor, MI	3,620	3,395	93.8	225	6.2	30	0.8	3,445	95.2
North Port–Bradenton–Sarasota, FL	12,830	11,775	91.8	1,055	8.2	1,410	11.0	10,935	85.2
Norwich–New London, CT	6,260	5,900	94.2	360	5.8	370	5.9	5,435	86.8
Ocala, FL	6,785	6,385	94.1	400	5.9	725	10.7	5,410	79.7
Ocean City, NJ	2,265	2,170	95.8	95	4.2	145	6.4	2,085	92.1
Odessa, TX	4,615	4,385	95.0	230	5.0	2,190	47.5	2,230	48.3
Ogden–Clearfield, UT	12,435	11,485	92.4	950	7.6	1,005	8.1	10,805	86.9
Oklahoma City, OK	28,355	26,060	91.9	2,295	8.1	2,500	8.8	21,605	76.2
Olympia, WA	4,790	4,495	93.8	300	6.3	285	5.9	4,065	84.9
Omaha–Council Bluffs, NE–IA	17,055	15,885	93.1	1,170	6.9	935	5.5	15,100	88.5
Orlando–Kissimmee–Sanford, FL	39,225	36,400	92.8	2,825	7.2	10,970	28.0	22,055	56.2
Oshkosh–Neenah, WI	4,160	3,755	90.3	405	9.7	35	0.8	3,900	93.8
Owensboro, KY	2,860	2,635	92.1	225	7.9	0	0.0	2,825	98.8
Oxnard–Thousand Oaks–Ventura, CA	15,495	14,600	94.2	895	5.8	6,670	43.0	7,535	48.6
Palm Bay–Melbourne–Titusville, FL	11,750	10,805	92.0	950	8.1	755	6.4	9,655	82.2
Palm Coast, FL	1,340	1,275	95.1	60	4.5	90	6.7	1,120	83.6
Panama City–Lynn Haven–Panama City Beach, FL	4,210	3,925	93.2	285	6.8	170	4.0	3,730	88.6
Parkersburg–Marietta–Vienna, WV–OH	3,465	3,195	92.2	270	7.8	0	0.0	3,430	99.0
Pascagoula, MS	3,640	3,400	93.4	240	6.6	50	1.4	3,055	83.9
Pensacola–Ferry Pass–Brent, FL	9,795	9,245	94.4	550	5.6	515	5.3	8,125	83.0
Peoria, IL	8,880	8,390	94.5	490	5.5	170	1.9	8,155	91.8
Philadelphia–Camden–Wilmington, PA–NJ–DE–MD	107,465	100,395	93.4	7,065	6.6	6,190	5.8	82,465	76.7
Phoenix–Mesa–Glendale, AZ	80,920	75,650	93.5	5,270	6.5	21,890	27.1	52,755	65.2
Pine Bluff, AR	2,195	2,100	95.7	95	4.3	40	1.8	1,585	72.2
Pittsburgh, PA	49,395	46,420	94.0	2,975	6.0	400	0.8	46,520	94.2
Pittsfield, MA	2,440	2,225	91.2	215	8.8	25	1.0	2,285	93.6
Pocatello, ID	1,745	1,610	92.3	140	8.0	100	5.7	1,565	89.7
Portland–South Portland–Biddeford, ME	11,730	10,965	93.5	765	6.5	75	0.6	11,255	96.0
Portland–Vancouver–Hillsboro, OR–WA	43,715	39,990	91.5	3,725	8.5	3,195	7.3	36,410	83.3
Port St. Lucie, FL	8,920	8,350	93.6	570	6.4	975	10.9	6,740	75.6
Poughkeepsie–Newburgh–Middletown, NY	14,705	13,900	94.5	805	5.5	1,650	11.2	11,865	80.7
Prescott, AZ	4,155	3,830	92.2	325	7.8	505	12.2	3,490	84.0
Providence–New Bedford–Fall River, RI–MA	32,585	29,895	91.7	2,690	8.3	2,515	7.7	28,110	86.3

C-11 Installation, Maintenance, and Repair Craft Workers, by Metropolitan Statistical Area, Sex, Race, and Hispanic or Latino Origin, 2006–2010—Continued

Metropolitan Statistical Area	Black alone, not Hispanic or Latino Number	Percent	American Indian and Alaska Native alone, not Hispanic or Latino Number	Percent	Asian alone, not Hispanic or Latino Number	Percent	Native Hawaiian and Other Pacific Islander alone, not Hispanic or Latino Number	Percent	Two or more races, not Hispanic or Latino Number	Percent
Mobile, AL	1,775	19.5	50	0.5	280	3.1	0	0.0	55	0.6
Modesto, CA	215	2.0	45	0.4	555	5.1	75	0.7	144	1.3
Monroe, LA	640	19.8	4	0.1	15	0.5	0	0.0	20	0.6
Monroe, MI	75	1.5	0	0.0	0	0.0	0	0.0	55	1.1
Montgomery, AL	2,065	27.2	0	0.0	75	1.0	0	0.0	40	0.5
Morgantown, WV	0	0.0	20	0.9	4	0.2	0	0.0	60	2.6
Morristown, TN	70	2.0	0	0.0	0	0.0	0	0.0	20	0.6
Mount Vernon–Anacortes, WA	10	0.4	35	1.4	10	0.4	10	0.4	115	4.5
Muncie, IN	40	1.6	0	0.0	35	1.4	0	0.0	25	1.0
Muskegon–Norton Shores, MI	250	5.6	25	0.6	30	0.7	0	0.0	4	0.1
Myrtle Beach–North Myrtle Beach–Conway, SC	535	9.6	0	0.0	60	1.1	0	0.0	0	0.0
Napa, CA	15	0.6	0	0.0	195	8.1	4	0.2	45	1.9
Naples–Marco Island, FL	185	3.5	10	0.2	4	0.1	0	0.0	10	0.2
Nashville-Davidson–Murfreesboro–Franklin, TN	2,605	7.8	65	0.2	740	2.2	0	0.0	240	0.7
New Haven–Milford, CT	1,140	6.2	40	0.2	215	1.2	20	0.1	215	1.2
New Orleans–Metairie–Kenner, LA	5,520	24.1	120	0.5	550	2.4	15	0.1	170	0.7
New York–Northern New Jersey–Long Island, NY–NJ–PA	40,805	14.2	400	0.1	20,460	7.1	70	0.0	4,195	1.5
Niles–Benton Harbor, MI	105	2.9	0	0.0	20	0.6	0	0.0	19	0.5
North Port–Bradenton–Sarasota, FL	225	1.8	20	0.2	120	0.9	0	0.0	125	1.0
Norwich–New London, CT	60	1.0	65	1.0	215	3.4	0	0.0	109	1.7
Ocala, FL	520	7.7	50	0.7	20	0.3	0	0.0	55	0.8
Ocean City, NJ	20	0.9	0	0.0	15	0.7	0	0.0	0	0.0
Odessa, TX	80	1.7	0	0.0	15	0.3	0	0.0	99	2.1
Ogden–Clearfield, UT	125	1.0	145	1.2	105	0.8	45	0.4	205	1.6
Oklahoma City, OK	1,575	5.6	840	3.0	665	2.3	0	0.0	1,175	4.1
Olympia, WA	135	2.8	35	0.7	215	4.5	0	0.0	60	1.3
Omaha–Council Bluffs, NE–IA	485	2.8	95	0.6	275	1.6	10	0.1	145	0.9
Orlando–Kissimmee–Sanford, FL	4,570	11.7	35	0.1	985	2.5	40	0.1	570	1.5
Oshkosh–Neenah, WI	0	0.0	10	0.2	195	4.7	0	0.0	20	0.5
Owensboro, KY	25	0.9	0	0.0	0	0.0	0	0.0	10	0.3
Oxnard–Thousand Oaks–Ventura, CA	300	1.9	0	0.0	705	4.5	20	0.1	265	1.7
Palm Bay–Melbourne–Titusville, FL	900	7.7	90	0.8	185	1.6	10	0.1	155	1.3
Palm Coast, FL	95	7.1	0	0.0	35	2.6	0	0.0	0	0.0
Panama City–Lynn Haven–Panama City Beach, FL	190	4.5	40	1.0	35	0.8	15	0.4	30	0.7
Parkersburg–Marietta–Vienna, WV–OH	15	0.4	10	0.3	4	0.1	0	0.0	0	0.0
Pascagoula, MS	505	13.9	0	0.0	0	0.0	0	0.0	30	0.8
Pensacola–Ferry Pass–Brent, FL	890	9.1	55	0.6	90	0.9	0	0.0	130	1.3
Peoria, IL	350	3.9	4	0.0	100	1.1	0	0.0	94	1.1
Philadelphia–Camden–Wilmington, PA–NJ–DE–MD	13,750	12.8	90	0.1	3,930	3.7	25	0.0	1,020	0.9
Phoenix–Mesa–Glendale, AZ	2,550	3.2	1,035	1.3	1,505	1.9	215	0.3	975	1.2
Pine Bluff, AR	550	25.1	15	0.7	0	0.0	0	0.0	4	0.2
Pittsburgh, PA	1,825	3.7	45	0.1	275	0.6	20	0.0	315	0.6
Pittsfield, MA	45	1.8	15	0.6	20	0.8	0	0.0	44	1.8
Pocatello, ID	0	0.0	75	4.3	0	0.0	0	0.0	10	0.6
Portland–South Portland–Biddeford, ME	205	1.7	50	0.4	65	0.6	40	0.3	35	0.3
Portland–Vancouver–Hillsboro, OR–WA	580	1.3	385	0.9	2,060	4.7	200	0.5	880	2.0
Port St. Lucie, FL	870	9.8	15	0.2	145	1.6	25	0.3	150	1.7
Poughkeepsie–Newburgh–Middletown, NY	785	5.3	45	0.3	150	1.0	0	0.0	210	1.4
Prescott, AZ	15	0.4	35	0.8	35	0.8	0	0.0	80	1.9
Providence–New Bedford–Fall River, RI–MA	975	3.0	70	0.2	340	1.0	0	0.0	575	1.8

PART C—METROPOLITAN STATISTICAL AREA TABLES

C-11 Installation, Maintenance, and Repair Craft Workers, by Metropolitan Statistical Area, Sex, Race, and Hispanic or Latino Origin, 2006–2010—Continued

Metropolitan Statistical Area	Total who worked in the last 5 years	Male Number	Male Percent	Female Number	Female Percent	Hispanic or Latino Number	Hispanic or Latino Percent	White alone, not Hispanic or Latino Number	White alone, not Hispanic or Latino Percent
Provo–Orem, UT	8,485	7,725	91.0	760	9.0	845	10.0	7,500	88.4
Pueblo, CO	3,250	2,950	90.8	300	9.2	1,050	32.3	2,125	65.4
Punta Gorda, FL	3,000	2,800	93.3	200	6.7	50	1.7	2,795	93.2
Racine, WI	5,720	5,360	93.7	360	6.3	440	7.7	5,090	89.0
Raleigh–Cary, NC	19,460	18,060	92.8	1,400	7.2	1,790	9.2	13,180	67.7
Rapid City, SD	3,105	2,905	93.6	200	6.4	50	1.6	2,820	90.8
Reading, PA	10,180	9,450	92.8	730	7.2	670	6.6	9,145	89.8
Redding, CA	3,510	3,395	96.7	115	3.3	210	6.0	3,045	86.8
Reno–Sparks, NV	8,030	7,485	93.2	545	6.8	1,405	17.5	6,005	74.8
Richmond, VA	26,295	24,045	91.4	2,255	8.6	985	3.7	18,755	71.3
Riverside–San Bernardino–Ontario, CA	87,765	83,030	94.6	4,735	5.4	41,710	47.5	36,490	41.6
Roanoke, VA	6,620	5,960	90.0	660	10.0	100	1.5	5,915	89.4
Rochester, MN	3,450	3,230	93.6	220	6.4	110	3.2	3,195	92.6
Rochester, NY	23,115	21,405	92.6	1,710	7.4	745	3.2	20,495	88.7
Rockford, IL	8,330	7,730	92.8	600	7.2	590	7.1	7,050	84.6
Rocky Mount, NC	3,205	3,015	94.1	190	5.9	150	4.7	2,000	62.4
Rome, GA	2,085	2,025	97.1	60	2.9	55	2.6	1,865	89.4
Sacramento–Arden-Arcade–Roseville, CA	37,475	34,475	92.0	3,000	8.0	6,060	16.2	24,470	65.3
Saginaw–Saginaw Township North, MI	3,950	3,590	90.9	355	9.0	115	2.9	3,565	90.3
St. Cloud, MN	5,155	4,480	86.9	675	13.1	45	0.9	5,000	97.0
St. George, UT	2,495	2,435	97.6	60	2.4	80	3.2	2,370	95.0
St. Joseph, MO–KS	3,090	2,970	96.1	115	3.7	130	4.2	2,885	93.4
St. Louis, MO–IL	58,460	54,015	92.4	4,440	7.6	1,100	1.9	50,675	86.7
Salem, OR	6,395	6,000	93.8	395	6.2	1,005	15.7	5,100	79.7
Salinas, CA	5,975	5,580	93.4	395	6.6	3,025	50.6	2,400	40.2
Salisbury, MD	2,540	2,150	84.6	390	15.4	340	13.4	1,700	66.9
Salt Lake City, UT	22,825	21,010	92.0	1,810	7.9	3,325	14.6	18,205	79.8
San Angelo, TX	2,140	1,925	90.0	215	10.0	735	34.3	1,280	59.8
San Antonio–New Braunfels, TX	41,570	38,845	93.4	2,725	6.6	23,190	55.8	15,385	37.0
San Diego–Carlsbad–San Marcos, CA	50,780	47,120	92.8	3,660	7.2	14,940	29.4	26,015	51.2
Sandusky, OH	1,860	1,695	91.1	165	8.9	40	2.2	1,730	93.0
San Francisco–Oakland–Fremont, CA	65,775	60,015	91.2	5,760	8.8	15,990	24.3	28,600	43.5
San Jose–Sunnyvale–Santa Clara, CA	28,520	25,885	90.8	2,640	9.3	9,010	31.6	10,365	36.3
San Luis Obispo–Paso Robles, CA	5,135	4,990	97.2	145	2.8	885	17.2	3,920	76.3
Santa Barbara–Santa Maria–Goleta, CA	6,245	5,735	91.8	510	8.2	2,200	35.2	3,395	54.4
Santa Cruz–Watsonville, CA	4,375	4,125	94.3	250	5.7	1,305	29.8	2,890	66.1
Santa Fe, NM	2,960	2,665	90.0	295	10.0	1,700	57.4	1,175	39.7
Santa Rosa–Petaluma, CA	9,150	8,275	90.4	875	9.6	1,960	21.4	6,585	72.0
Savannah, GA	8,235	7,795	94.7	440	5.3	585	7.1	5,590	67.9
Scranton–Wilkes-Barre, PA	12,580	11,590	92.1	990	7.9	375	3.0	11,935	94.9
Seattle–Tacoma–Bellevue, WA	69,210	62,710	90.6	6,500	9.4	4,320	6.2	53,215	76.9
Sebastian–Vero Beach, FL	2,570	2,220	86.4	350	13.6	195	7.6	2,195	85.4
Sheboygan, WI	3,080	2,895	94.0	190	6.2	24	0.8	2,955	95.9
Sherman–Denison, TX	2,965	2,810	94.8	155	5.2	270	9.1	2,525	85.2
Shreveport–Bossier City, LA	8,970	8,265	92.1	705	7.9	215	2.4	6,215	69.3
Sioux City, IA–NE–SD	3,115	2,975	95.5	140	4.5	190	6.1	2,805	90.0
Sioux Falls, SD	5,020	4,770	95.0	250	5.0	40	0.8	4,830	96.2
South Bend–Mishawaka, IN–MI	7,230	6,665	92.2	565	7.8	225	3.1	6,440	89.1
Spartanburg, SC	7,090	6,425	90.6	665	9.4	115	1.6	5,975	84.3
Spokane, WA	8,715	7,885	90.5	835	9.6	260	3.0	8,000	91.8
Springfield, IL	3,855	3,670	95.2	185	4.8	69	1.8	3,485	90.4
Springfield, MA	15,955	14,865	93.2	1,090	6.8	1,290	8.1	13,945	87.4
Springfield, MO	9,280	8,900	95.9	380	4.1	310	3.3	8,600	92.7
Springfield, OH	3,640	3,505	96.3	140	3.8	25	0.7	3,395	93.3
State College, PA	2,685	2,450	91.2	235	8.8	80	3.0	2,515	93.7

C-11 **Installation, Maintenance, and Repair Craft Workers, by Metropolitan Statistical Area, Sex, Race, and Hispanic or Latino Origin, 2006–2010**—Continued

Metropolitan Statistical Area	Black alone, not Hispanic or Latino Number	Percent	American Indian and Alaska Native alone, not Hispanic or Latino Number	Percent	Asian alone, not Hispanic or Latino Number	Percent	Native Hawaiian and Other Pacific Islander alone, not Hispanic or Latino Number	Percent	Two or more races, not Hispanic or Latino Number	Percent
Provo–Orem, UT	0	0.0	10	0.1	65	0.8	25	0.3	34	0.4
Pueblo, CO	30	0.9	4	0.1	0	0.0	0	0.0	44	1.4
Punta Gorda, FL	85	2.8	0	0.0	55	1.8	0	0.0	10	0.3
Racine, WI	150	2.6	0	0.0	0	0.0	0	0.0	35	0.6
Raleigh–Cary, NC	3,655	18.8	35	0.2	560	2.9	0	0.0	234	1.2
Rapid City, SD	75	2.4	130	4.2	4	0.1	0	0.0	25	0.8
Reading, PA	185	1.8	0	0.0	35	0.3	0	0.0	140	1.4
Redding, CA	0	0.0	80	2.3	70	2.0	25	0.7	84	2.4
Reno–Sparks, NV	85	1.1	195	2.4	240	3.0	25	0.3	70	0.9
Richmond, VA	5,420	20.6	75	0.3	735	2.8	0	0.0	325	1.2
Riverside–San Bernardino–Ontario, CA	4,035	4.6	195	0.2	3,620	4.1	160	0.2	1,570	1.8
Roanoke, VA	425	6.4	4	0.1	40	0.6	0	0.0	130	2.0
Rochester, MN	65	1.9	0	0.0	20	0.6	15	0.4	40	1.2
Rochester, NY	1,220	5.3	50	0.2	415	1.8	0	0.0	190	0.8
Rockford, IL	410	4.9	50	0.6	160	1.9	0	0.0	65	0.8
Rocky Mount, NC	1,005	31.4	4	0.1	20	0.6	0	0.0	24	0.7
Rome, GA	120	5.8	0	0.0	25	1.2	0	0.0	25	1.2
Sacramento–Arden-Arcade–Roseville, CA	1,775	4.7	210	0.6	3,525	9.4	460	1.2	970	2.6
Saginaw–Saginaw Township North, MI	210	5.3	15	0.4	10	0.3	0	0.0	29	0.7
St. Cloud, MN	25	0.5	0	0.0	55	1.1	0	0.0	35	0.7
St. George, UT	4	0.2	30	1.2	4	0.2	0	0.0	0	0.0
St. Joseph, MO–KS	65	2.1	0	0.0	0	0.0	4	0.1	4	0.1
St. Louis, MO–IL	5,435	9.3	115	0.2	655	1.1	0	0.0	475	0.8
Salem, OR	65	1.0	55	0.9	60	0.9	30	0.5	75	1.2
Salinas, CA	130	2.2	20	0.3	360	6.0	0	0.0	44	0.7
Salisbury, MD	475	18.7	0	0.0	25	1.0	0	0.0	0	0.0
Salt Lake City, UT	95	0.4	285	1.2	495	2.2	245	1.1	175	0.8
San Angelo, TX	15	0.7	50	2.3	4	0.2	0	0.0	55	2.6
San Antonio–New Braunfels, TX	1,425	3.4	90	0.2	890	2.1	40	0.1	545	1.3
San Diego–Carlsbad–San Marcos, CA	2,490	4.9	270	0.5	5,680	11.2	345	0.7	1,040	2.0
Sandusky, OH	65	3.5	0	0.0	4	0.2	0	0.0	25	1.3
San Francisco–Oakland–Fremont, CA	3,650	5.5	150	0.2	15,035	22.9	810	1.2	1,530	2.3
San Jose–Sunnyvale–Santa Clara, CA	600	2.1	135	0.5	7,780	27.3	145	0.5	485	1.7
San Luis Obispo–Paso Robles, CA	150	2.9	25	0.5	80	1.6	0	0.0	85	1.7
Santa Barbara–Santa Maria–Goleta, CA	150	2.4	10	0.2	270	4.3	40	0.6	185	3.0
Santa Cruz–Watsonville, CA	25	0.6	25	0.6	65	1.5	10	0.2	50	1.1
Santa Fe, NM	4	0.1	75	2.5	0	0.0	4	0.1	0	0.0
Santa Rosa–Petaluma, CA	80	0.9	75	0.8	205	2.2	50	0.5	195	2.1
Savannah, GA	1,845	22.4	0	0.0	150	1.8	15	0.2	49	0.6
Scranton–Wilkes-Barre, PA	110	0.9	0	0.0	40	0.3	10	0.1	109	0.9
Seattle–Tacoma–Bellevue, WA	2,390	3.5	525	0.8	6,065	8.8	690	1.0	2,005	2.9
Sebastian–Vero Beach, FL	100	3.9	0	0.0	40	1.6	0	0.0	40	1.6
Sheboygan, WI	0	0.0	4	0.1	75	2.4	0	0.0	30	1.0
Sherman–Denison, TX	75	2.5	20	0.7	10	0.3	0	0.0	64	2.2
Shreveport–Bossier City, LA	2,485	27.7	35	0.4	0	0.0	0	0.0	15	0.2
Sioux City, IA–NE–SD	30	1.0	15	0.5	70	2.2	0	0.0	4	0.1
Sioux Falls, SD	75	1.5	20	0.4	35	0.7	0	0.0	15	0.3
South Bend–Mishawaka, IN–MI	415	5.7	35	0.5	15	0.2	0	0.0	105	1.5
Spartanburg, SC	815	11.5	0	0.0	135	1.9	0	0.0	55	0.8
Spokane, WA	110	1.3	15	0.2	160	1.8	0	0.0	169	1.9
Springfield, IL	240	6.2	15	0.4	25	0.6	0	0.0	25	0.6
Springfield, MA	430	2.7	4	0.0	140	0.9	0	0.0	145	0.9
Springfield, MO	65	0.7	70	0.8	55	0.6	0	0.0	175	1.9
Springfield, OH	185	5.1	0	0.0	0	0.0	0	0.0	40	1.1
State College, PA	30	1.1	10	0.4	40	1.5	0	0.0	4	0.1

C-11 Installation, Maintenance, and Repair Craft Workers, by Metropolitan Statistical Area, Sex, Race, and Hispanic or Latino Origin, 2006–2010—Continued

Metropolitan Statistical Area	Total who worked in the last 5 years	Male Number	Male Percent	Female Number	Female Percent	Hispanic or Latino Number	Hispanic or Latino Percent	White alone, not Hispanic or Latino Number	White alone, not Hispanic or Latino Percent
Steubenville–Weirton, OH–WV	3,500	3,385	96.7	110	3.1	4	0.1	3,385	96.7
Stockton, CA	13,790	12,895	93.5	895	6.5	4,660	33.8	6,305	45.7
Sumter, SC	2,695	2,440	90.5	255	9.5	165	6.1	1,750	64.9
Syracuse, NY	14,850	14,115	95.1	735	4.9	265	1.8	13,605	91.6
Tallahassee, FL	6,290	5,845	92.9	445	7.1	310	4.9	4,125	65.6
Tampa–St. Petersburg–Clearwater, FL	54,930	51,285	93.4	3,645	6.6	9,090	16.5	39,790	72.4
Terre Haute, IN	3,745	3,385	90.4	355	9.5	50	1.3	3,560	95.1
Texarkana, TX–Texarkana, AR	4,180	3,890	93.1	295	7.1	165	3.9	3,360	80.4
Toledo, OH	15,105	14,065	93.1	1,040	6.9	500	3.3	13,555	89.7
Topeka, KS	5,750	5,450	94.8	300	5.2	310	5.4	5,035	87.6
Trenton–Ewing, NJ	4,915	4,415	89.8	500	10.2	915	18.6	2,930	59.6
Tucson, AZ	19,055	17,930	94.1	1,120	5.9	6,155	32.3	11,495	60.3
Tulsa, OK	26,675	24,905	93.4	1,770	6.6	1,760	6.6	20,380	76.4
Tuscaloosa, AL	4,540	4,095	90.2	440	9.7	40	0.9	3,635	80.1
Tyler, TX	3,480	3,285	94.4	200	5.7	615	17.7	2,490	71.6
Utica–Rome, NY	5,955	5,560	93.4	390	6.5	44	0.7	5,735	96.3
Valdosta, GA	3,255	3,020	92.8	235	7.2	110	3.4	2,595	79.7
Vallejo–Fairfield, CA	9,220	8,860	96.1	360	3.9	1,910	20.7	4,490	48.7
Victoria, TX	3,370	3,260	96.7	105	3.1	945	28.0	2,190	65.0
Vineland–Millville–Bridgeton, NJ	3,055	2,925	95.7	130	4.3	600	19.6	2,090	68.4
Virginia Beach–Norfolk–Newport News, VA–NC	38,955	35,795	91.9	3,160	8.1	2,540	6.5	25,890	66.5
Visalia–Porterville, CA	7,340	7,090	96.6	250	3.4	3,430	46.7	3,565	48.6
Waco, TX	5,430	4,925	90.7	500	9.2	1,170	21.5	3,885	71.5
Warner Robins, GA	3,575	3,350	93.7	225	6.3	110	3.1	2,910	81.4
Washington–Arlington–Alexandria, DC–VA–MD–WV	83,350	77,375	92.8	5,975	7.2	14,075	16.9	39,315	47.2
Waterloo–Cedar Falls, IA	3,750	3,415	91.1	335	8.9	115	3.1	3,480	92.8
Wausau, WI	3,730	3,430	92.0	295	7.9	40	1.1	3,650	97.9
Wenatchee–East Wenatchee, WA	2,110	2,005	95.0	105	5.0	305	14.5	1,785	84.6
Wheeling, WV–OH	3,175	3,055	96.2	120	3.8	0	0.0	3,090	97.3
Wichita, KS	17,625	15,950	90.5	1,675	9.5	1,355	7.7	14,350	81.4
Wichita Falls, TX	3,820	3,640	95.3	180	4.7	380	9.9	3,290	86.1
Williamsport, PA	3,050	2,850	93.4	200	6.6	15	0.5	3,000	98.4
Wilmington, NC	7,150	6,655	93.1	495	6.9	60	0.8	5,990	83.8
Winchester, VA–WV	3,155	2,865	90.8	290	9.2	70	2.2	2,905	92.1
Winston-Salem, NC	10,485	9,915	94.6	570	5.4	605	5.8	8,335	79.5
Worcester, MA	17,045	15,945	93.5	1,100	6.5	975	5.7	15,305	89.8
Yakima, WA	4,115	3,885	94.4	235	5.7	1,415	34.4	2,355	57.2
York–Hanover, PA	12,630	11,630	92.1	1,000	7.9	300	2.4	11,845	93.8
Youngstown–Warren–Boardman, OH–PA	13,315	12,385	93.0	930	7.0	195	1.5	12,470	93.7
Yuba City, CA	3,170	2,895	91.3	275	8.7	535	16.9	2,125	67.0
Yuma, AZ	4,185	4,040	96.5	150	3.6	2,195	52.4	1,840	44.0

C-11 Installation, Maintenance, and Repair Craft Workers, by Metropolitan Statistical Area, Sex, Race, and Hispanic or Latino Origin, 2006–2010—*Continued*

Metropolitan Statistical Area	Black alone, not Hispanic or Latino Number	Percent	American Indian and Alaska Native alone, not Hispanic or Latino Number	Percent	Asian alone, not Hispanic or Latino Number	Percent	Native Hawaiian and Other Pacific Islander alone, not Hispanic or Latino Number	Percent	Two or more races, not Hispanic or Latino Number	Percent
Steubenville–Weirton, OH–WV	80	2.3	0	0.0	0	0.0	10	0.3	25	0.7
Stockton, CA	675	4.9	40	0.3	1,770	12.8	55	0.4	284	2.1
Sumter, SC	700	26.0	55	2.0	10	0.4	0	0.0	20	0.7
Syracuse, NY	600	4.0	90	0.6	165	1.1	0	0.0	120	0.8
Tallahassee, FL	1,610	25.6	30	0.5	145	2.3	0	0.0	74	1.2
Tampa–St. Petersburg–Clearwater, FL	4,135	7.5	75	0.1	1,065	1.9	10	0.0	765	1.4
Terre Haute, IN	65	1.7	0	0.0	30	0.8	0	0.0	30	0.8
Texarkana, TX–Texarkana, AR	580	13.9	15	0.4	40	1.0	0	0.0	14	0.3
Toledo, OH	820	5.4	60	0.4	75	0.5	0	0.0	95	0.6
Topeka, KS	265	4.6	75	1.3	20	0.3	4	0.1	34	0.6
Trenton–Ewing, NJ	760	15.5	0	0.0	170	3.5	0	0.0	140	2.8
Tucson, AZ	520	2.7	350	1.8	295	1.5	40	0.2	200	1.0
Tulsa, OK	1,070	4.0	1,790	6.7	375	1.4	0	0.0	1,300	4.9
Tuscaloosa, AL	800	17.6	25	0.6	15	0.3	0	0.0	23	0.5
Tyler, TX	315	9.1	0	0.0	20	0.6	0	0.0	40	1.1
Utica–Rome, NY	95	1.6	20	0.3	25	0.4	0	0.0	30	0.5
Valdosta, GA	510	15.7	10	0.3	4	0.1	0	0.0	25	0.8
Vallejo–Fairfield, CA	950	10.3	40	0.4	1,170	12.7	240	2.6	420	4.6
Victoria, TX	140	4.2	0	0.0	25	0.7	0	0.0	65	1.9
Vineland–Millville–Bridgeton, NJ	275	9.0	25	0.8	0	0.0	0	0.0	60	2.0
Virginia Beach–Norfolk–Newport News, VA–NC	8,685	22.3	110	0.3	1,090	2.8	0	0.0	640	1.6
Visalia–Porterville, CA	0	0.0	20	0.3	105	1.4	0	0.0	215	2.9
Waco, TX	235	4.3	20	0.4	100	1.8	0	0.0	20	0.4
Warner Robins, GA	480	13.4	20	0.6	4	0.1	0	0.0	55	1.5
Washington–Arlington–Alexandria, DC–VA–MD–WV	21,475	25.8	135	0.2	6,845	8.2	100	0.1	1,400	1.7
Waterloo–Cedar Falls, IA	100	2.7	4	0.1	0	0.0	0	0.0	50	1.3
Wausau, WI	0	0.0	4	0.1	4	0.1	0	0.0	25	0.7
Wenatchee–East Wenatchee, WA	0	0.0	4	0.2	10	0.5	0	0.0	0	0.0
Wheeling, WV–OH	60	1.9	0	0.0	4	0.1	0	0.0	20	0.6
Wichita, KS	750	4.3	120	0.7	745	4.2	0	0.0	315	1.8
Wichita Falls, TX	90	2.4	0	0.0	10	0.3	0	0.0	54	1.4
Williamsport, PA	10	0.3	0	0.0	10	0.3	0	0.0	14	0.5
Wilmington, NC	985	13.8	10	0.1	10	0.1	15	0.2	85	1.2
Winchester, VA–WV	85	2.7	0	0.0	25	0.8	0	0.0	65	2.1
Winston–Salem, NC	1,260	12.0	30	0.3	95	0.9	35	0.3	135	1.3
Worcester, MA	280	1.6	45	0.3	245	1.4	10	0.1	185	1.1
Yakima, WA	0	0.0	245	6.0	0	0.0	0	0.0	104	2.5
York–Hanover, PA	305	2.4	55	0.4	70	0.6	0	0.0	43	0.3
Youngstown–Warren–Boardman, OH–PA	555	4.2	35	0.3	4	0.0	0	0.0	64	0.5
Yuba City, CA	50	1.6	30	0.9	285	9.0	0	0.0	150	4.7
Yuma, AZ	60	1.4	15	0.4	45	1.1	0	0.0	30	0.7

PART C—METROPOLITAN STATISTICAL AREA TABLES

C-12 **Production Operative Workers, by Metropolitan Statistical Area, Sex, Race, and Hispanic or Latino Origin, 2006–2010**

Metropolitan Statistical Area	Total who worked in the last 5 years	Male Number	Male Percent	Female Number	Female Percent	Hispanic or Latino Number	Hispanic or Latino Percent	White alone, not Hispanic or Latino Number	White alone, not Hispanic or Latino Percent
Abilene, TX	3,120	2,225	71.3	900	28.8	955	30.6	1,910	61.2
Akron, OH	26,165	18,810	71.9	7,355	28.1	560	2.1	20,490	78.3
Albany, GA	4,400	2,805	63.8	1,595	36.3	190	4.3	1,245	28.3
Albany–Schenectady–Troy, NY	14,445	11,105	76.9	3,345	23.2	720	5.0	11,990	83.0
Albuquerque, NM	12,725	9,010	70.8	3,715	29.2	7,095	55.8	4,055	31.9
Alexandria, LA	2,855	2,340	82.0	515	18.0	60	2.1	1,930	67.6
Allentown–Bethlehem–Easton, PA–NJ	23,940	16,890	70.6	7,050	29.4	4,825	20.2	17,540	73.3
Altoona, PA	3,625	2,720	75.0	905	25.0	49	1.4	3,400	93.8
Amarillo, TX	6,865	5,345	77.9	1,520	22.1	2,470	36.0	3,125	45.5
Ames, IA	2,065	1,475	71.4	590	28.6	75	3.6	1,855	89.8
Anchorage, AK	3,935	3,050	77.5	885	22.5	300	7.6	2,645	67.2
Anderson, IN	4,960	3,375	68.0	1,585	32.0	140	2.8	4,240	85.5
Anderson, SC	9,165	5,980	65.2	3,185	34.8	345	3.8	5,835	63.7
Ann Arbor, MI	6,045	4,035	66.7	2,010	33.3	245	4.1	4,220	69.8
Anniston–Oxford, AL	5,640	3,840	68.1	1,800	31.9	295	5.2	3,995	70.8
Appleton, WI	12,945	9,490	73.3	3,455	26.7	555	4.3	11,465	88.6
Asheville, NC	12,230	7,940	64.9	4,290	35.1	1,660	13.6	9,745	79.7
Athens–Clarke County, GA	4,505	2,580	57.3	1,925	42.7	660	14.7	2,145	47.6
Atlanta–Sandy Springs–Marietta, GA	99,775	65,785	65.9	33,990	34.1	17,375	17.4	37,945	38.0
Atlantic City–Hammonton, NJ	3,275	2,250	68.7	1,025	31.3	1,190	36.3	1,305	39.8
Auburn–Opelika, AL	4,190	2,935	70.0	1,255	30.0	190	4.5	1,880	44.9
Augusta–Richmond County, GA–SC	16,065	11,345	70.6	4,720	29.4	945	5.9	6,835	42.5
Austin–Round Rock–San Marcos, TX	23,655	15,810	66.8	7,840	33.1	11,815	49.9	8,125	34.3
Bakersfield–Delano, CA	15,790	11,180	70.8	4,610	29.2	9,865	62.5	4,335	27.5
Baltimore–Towson, MD	34,670	24,450	70.5	10,220	29.5	1,935	5.6	19,105	55.1
Bangor, ME	3,345	2,550	76.2	795	23.8	50	1.5	3,175	94.9
Barnstable Town, MA	2,150	1,565	72.8	585	27.2	100	4.7	1,865	86.7
Baton Rouge, LA	18,685	15,775	84.4	2,910	15.6	385	2.1	11,430	61.2
Battle Creek, MI	8,300	5,575	67.2	2,725	32.8	390	4.7	6,315	76.1
Bay City, MI	3,795	2,955	77.9	845	22.3	275	7.2	3,305	87.1
Beaumont–Port Arthur, TX	11,870	10,355	87.2	1,515	12.8	2,125	17.9	6,845	57.7
Bellingham, WA	4,870	3,505	72.0	1,365	28.0	650	13.3	3,475	71.4
Bend, OR	3,170	2,450	77.3	720	22.7	415	13.1	2,640	83.3
Billings, MT	3,140	2,180	69.4	960	30.6	150	4.8	2,785	88.7
Binghamton, NY	6,870	4,745	69.1	2,125	30.9	140	2.0	5,995	87.3
Birmingham–Hoover, AL	26,335	19,605	74.4	6,730	25.6	1,965	7.5	14,140	53.7
Bismarck, ND	1,820	1,400	76.9	420	23.1	65	3.6	1,670	91.8
Blacksburg–Christiansburg–Radford, VA	5,635	3,520	62.5	2,115	37.5	15	0.3	5,290	93.9
Bloomington, IN	5,810	3,335	57.4	2,475	42.6	175	3.0	5,455	93.9
Bloomington–Normal, IL	2,925	2,230	76.2	695	23.8	190	6.5	2,370	81.0
Boise City–Nampa, ID	13,380	9,210	68.8	4,170	31.2	3,350	25.0	9,025	67.5
Boston–Cambridge–Quincy, MA–NH	76,940	49,860	64.8	27,080	35.2	14,470	18.8	44,750	58.2
Boulder, CO	5,020	3,330	66.3	1,690	33.7	1,765	35.2	2,800	55.8
Bowling Green, KY	5,885	4,005	68.1	1,880	31.9	370	6.3	4,455	75.7
Bremerton–Silverdale, WA	4,195	3,300	78.7	895	21.3	210	5.0	3,060	72.9
Bridgeport–Stamford–Norwalk, CT	14,585	8,950	61.4	5,635	38.6	4,760	32.6	5,840	40.0
Brownsville–Harlingen, TX	6,070	4,630	76.3	1,440	23.7	5,725	94.3	300	4.9
Brunswick, GA	2,065	1,450	70.2	610	29.5	280	13.6	1,130	54.7
Buffalo–Niagara Falls, NY	30,040	22,320	74.3	7,720	25.7	1,580	5.3	23,970	79.8
Burlington, NC	6,680	3,505	52.5	3,175	47.5	1,640	24.6	2,860	42.8
Burlington–South Burlington, VT	4,780	3,405	71.2	1,375	28.8	14	0.3	4,490	93.9
Canton–Massillon, OH	16,720	11,900	71.2	4,820	28.8	485	2.9	14,115	84.4
Cape Coral–Fort Myers, FL	6,110	4,260	69.7	1,850	30.3	2,045	33.5	3,280	53.7
Cape Girardeau–Jackson, MO–IL	3,345	2,285	68.3	1,060	31.7	230	6.9	2,930	87.6
Carson City, NV	1,750	1,265	72.3	485	27.7	895	51.1	740	42.3

C-12 Production Operative Workers, by Metropolitan Statistical Area, Sex, Race, and Hispanic or Latino Origin, 2006–2010—*Continued*

Metropolitan Statistical Area	Black alone, not Hispanic or Latino Number	Black alone, not Hispanic or Latino Percent	American Indian and Alaska Native alone, not Hispanic or Latino Number	American Indian and Alaska Native alone, not Hispanic or Latino Percent	Asian alone, not Hispanic or Latino Number	Asian alone, not Hispanic or Latino Percent	Native Hawaiian and Other Pacific Islander alone, not Hispanic or Latino Number	Native Hawaiian and Other Pacific Islander alone, not Hispanic or Latino Percent	Two or more races, not Hispanic or Latino Number	Two or more races, not Hispanic or Latino Percent
Abilene, TX	125	4.0	0	0.0	35	1.1	15	0.5	80	2.6
Akron, OH	3,560	13.6	35	0.1	1,250	4.8	50	0.2	215	0.8
Albany, GA	2,880	65.5	30	0.7	10	0.2	0	0.0	45	1.0
Albany–Schenectady–Troy, NY	715	4.9	30	0.2	560	3.9	25	0.2	405	2.8
Albuquerque, NM	185	1.5	775	6.1	545	4.3	0	0.0	79	0.6
Alexandria, LA	770	27.0	30	1.1	50	1.8	0	0.0	19	0.7
Allentown–Bethlehem–Easton, PA–NJ	665	2.8	0	0.0	650	2.7	0	0.0	250	1.0
Altoona, PA	100	2.8	0	0.0	30	0.8	0	0.0	49	1.4
Amarillo, TX	895	13.0	4	0.1	325	4.7	0	0.0	50	0.7
Ames, IA	0	0.0	15	0.7	55	2.7	0	0.0	60	2.9
Anchorage, AK	135	3.4	160	4.1	395	10.0	105	2.7	194	4.9
Anderson, IN	455	9.2	0	0.0	10	0.2	0	0.0	125	2.5
Anderson, SC	2,885	31.5	15	0.2	50	0.5	0	0.0	39	0.4
Ann Arbor, MI	1,285	21.3	0	0.0	195	3.2	0	0.0	95	1.6
Anniston–Oxford, AL	1,235	21.9	25	0.4	20	0.4	0	0.0	70	1.2
Appleton, WI	115	0.9	95	0.7	625	4.8	0	0.0	85	0.7
Asheville, NC	705	5.8	35	0.3	65	0.5	0	0.0	15	0.1
Athens–Clarke County, GA	1,575	35.0	0	0.0	75	1.7	0	0.0	50	1.1
Atlanta–Sandy Springs–Marietta, GA	35,695	35.8	215	0.2	7,615	7.6	70	0.1	860	0.9
Atlantic City–Hammonton, NJ	570	17.4	10	0.3	170	5.2	0	0.0	24	0.7
Auburn–Opelika, AL	1,985	47.4	0	0.0	110	2.6	0	0.0	24	0.6
Augusta–Richmond County, GA–SC	8,010	49.9	10	0.1	135	0.8	0	0.0	135	0.8
Austin–Round Rock–San Marcos, TX	2,075	8.8	25	0.1	1,465	6.2	0	0.0	160	0.7
Bakersfield–Delano, CA	475	3.0	245	1.6	780	4.9	4	0.0	83	0.5
Baltimore–Towson, MD	11,815	34.1	115	0.3	1,355	3.9	0	0.0	340	1.0
Bangor, ME	10	0.3	20	0.6	4	0.1	0	0.0	90	2.7
Barnstable Town, MA	35	1.6	45	2.1	35	1.6	0	0.0	75	3.5
Baton Rouge, LA	6,280	33.6	25	0.1	505	2.7	0	0.0	60	0.3
Battle Creek, MI	1,135	13.7	10	0.1	290	3.5	0	0.0	155	1.9
Bay City, MI	70	1.8	0	0.0	70	1.8	0	0.0	70	1.8
Beaumont–Port Arthur, TX	2,255	19.0	15	0.1	575	4.8	0	0.0	55	0.5
Bellingham, WA	120	2.5	65	1.3	415	8.5	0	0.0	145	3.0
Bend, OR	0	0.0	0	0.0	25	0.8	15	0.5	70	2.2
Billings, MT	4	0.1	85	2.7	35	1.1	60	1.9	20	0.6
Binghamton, NY	245	3.6	0	0.0	420	6.1	0	0.0	70	1.0
Birmingham–Hoover, AL	9,840	37.4	105	0.4	100	0.4	0	0.0	184	0.7
Bismarck, ND	45	2.5	30	1.6	0	0.0	0	0.0	10	0.5
Blacksburg–Christiansburg–Radford, VA	240	4.3	0	0.0	50	0.9	0	0.0	45	0.8
Bloomington, IN	85	1.5	4	0.1	50	0.9	0	0.0	40	0.7
Bloomington–Normal, IL	275	9.4	0	0.0	60	2.1	0	0.0	30	1.0
Boise City–Nampa, ID	140	1.0	125	0.9	550	4.1	0	0.0	185	1.4
Boston–Cambridge–Quincy, MA–NH	4,590	6.0	85	0.1	10,905	14.2	80	0.1	2,055	2.7
Boulder, CO	0	0.0	30	0.6	385	7.7	0	0.0	40	0.8
Bowling Green, KY	850	14.4	0	0.0	125	2.1	0	0.0	80	1.4
Bremerton–Silverdale, WA	355	8.5	135	3.2	255	6.1	55	1.3	125	3.0
Bridgeport–Stamford–Norwalk, CT	2,335	16.0	75	0.5	1,305	8.9	10	0.1	255	1.7
Brownsville–Harlingen, TX	20	0.3	0	0.0	20	0.3	0	0.0	0	0.0
Brunswick, GA	615	29.8	0	0.0	15	0.7	0	0.0	20	1.0
Buffalo–Niagara Falls, NY	3,485	11.6	115	0.4	540	1.8	0	0.0	355	1.2
Burlington, NC	1,975	29.6	20	0.3	100	1.5	0	0.0	85	1.3
Burlington–South Burlington, VT	60	1.3	35	0.7	140	2.9	0	0.0	38	0.8
Canton–Massillon, OH	1,870	11.2	75	0.4	65	0.4	0	0.0	110	0.7
Cape Coral–Fort Myers, FL	615	10.1	0	0.0	150	2.5	0	0.0	19	0.3
Cape Girardeau–Jackson, MO–IL	175	5.2	0	0.0	0	0.0	0	0.0	4	0.1
Carson City, NV	0	0.0	10	0.6	70	4.0	0	0.0	35	2.0

PART C—METROPOLITAN STATISTICAL AREA TABLES

C-12 Production Operative Workers, by Metropolitan Statistical Area, Sex, Race, and Hispanic or Latino Origin, 2006–2010—Continued

Metropolitan Statistical Area	Total who worked in the last 5 years	Male Number	Male Percent	Female Number	Female Percent	Hispanic or Latino Number	Hispanic or Latino Percent	White alone, not Hispanic or Latino Number	White alone, not Hispanic or Latino Percent
Casper, WY	1,800	1,495	83.1	305	16.9	175	9.7	1,490	82.8
Cedar Rapids, IA	9,435	6,710	71.1	2,720	28.8	285	3.0	8,390	88.9
Champaign–Urbana, IL	5,085	3,570	70.2	1,515	29.8	360	7.1	3,610	71.0
Charleston, WV	4,615	3,825	82.9	790	17.1	110	2.4	4,370	94.7
Charleston–North Charleston–Summerville, SC	13,895	9,810	70.6	4,085	29.4	1,025	7.4	6,335	45.6
Charlotte–Gastonia–Rock Hill, NC–SC	46,200	29,405	63.6	16,795	36.4	6,560	14.2	22,210	48.1
Charlottesville, VA	1,880	1,455	77.4	420	22.3	280	14.9	1,270	67.6
Chattanooga, TN–GA	18,810	12,655	67.3	6,160	32.7	1,020	5.4	13,685	72.8
Cheyenne, WY	1,890	1,510	79.9	380	20.1	375	19.8	1,415	74.9
Chicago–Joliet–Naperville, IL–IN–WI	265,915	178,970	67.3	86,945	32.7	127,190	47.8	92,075	34.6
Chico, CA	3,570	2,830	79.3	740	20.7	730	20.4	2,485	69.6
Cincinnati–Middletown, OH–KY–IN	60,850	44,190	72.6	16,660	27.4	1,820	3.0	48,760	80.1
Clarksville, TN–KY	9,155	5,815	63.5	3,340	36.5	470	5.1	5,480	59.9
Cleveland, TN	5,900	3,645	61.8	2,255	38.2	435	7.4	4,990	84.6
Cleveland–Elyria–Mentor, OH	67,690	46,705	69.0	20,985	31.0	4,780	7.1	46,010	68.0
Coeur d'Alene, ID	3,005	2,030	67.6	975	32.4	135	4.5	2,820	93.8
College Station–Bryan, TX	3,860	2,785	72.2	1,075	27.8	1,310	33.9	1,770	45.9
Colorado Springs, CO	8,490	5,650	66.5	2,840	33.5	1,460	17.2	5,460	64.3
Columbia, MO	3,590	2,365	65.9	1,225	34.1	235	6.5	2,655	74.0
Columbia, SC	18,565	12,635	68.1	5,930	31.9	1,305	7.0	7,395	39.8
Columbus, GA–AL	7,030	4,535	64.5	2,495	35.5	260	3.7	2,445	34.8
Columbus, IN	4,525	3,235	71.5	1,285	28.4	850	18.8	3,525	77.9
Columbus, OH	41,130	29,280	71.2	11,855	28.8	2,265	5.5	30,680	74.6
Corpus Christi, TX	8,300	6,840	82.4	1,460	17.6	5,400	65.1	2,420	29.2
Corvallis, OR	1,540	1,255	81.5	285	18.5	120	7.8	1,275	82.8
Crestview–Fort Walton Beach–Destin, FL	2,370	1,545	65.2	830	35.0	165	7.0	1,530	64.6
Cumberland, MD–WV	2,595	1,840	70.9	755	29.1	50	1.9	2,450	94.4
Dallas–Fort Worth–Arlington, TX	149,180	102,705	68.8	46,475	31.2	72,545	48.6	44,805	30.0
Dalton, GA	13,355	8,325	62.3	5,030	37.7	6,865	51.4	5,970	44.7
Danville, IL	3,730	2,605	69.8	1,125	30.2	235	6.3	2,860	76.7
Danville, VA	5,525	3,665	66.3	1,860	33.7	100	1.8	2,940	53.2
Davenport–Moline–Rock Island, IA–IL	14,860	10,625	71.5	4,235	28.5	2,160	14.5	11,160	75.1
Dayton, OH	29,480	19,035	64.6	10,445	35.4	585	2.0	22,805	77.4
Decatur, AL	8,325	5,630	67.6	2,695	32.4	895	10.8	5,600	67.3
Decatur, IL	3,670	2,795	76.2	875	23.8	25	0.7	2,965	80.8
Deltona–Daytona Beach–Ormond Beach, FL	7,390	4,750	64.3	2,640	35.7	1,130	15.3	5,335	72.2
Denver–Aurora–Broomfield, CO	38,720	26,785	69.2	11,935	30.8	13,985	36.1	18,285	47.2
Des Moines–West Des Moines, IA	13,400	10,070	75.1	3,330	24.9	2,320	17.3	8,515	63.5
Detroit–Warren–Livonia, MI	139,935	99,265	70.9	40,670	29.1	7,550	5.4	88,760	63.4
Dothan, AL	4,355	2,995	68.8	1,360	31.2	215	4.9	2,540	58.3
Dover, DE	3,415	2,325	68.1	1,095	32.1	355	10.4	1,790	52.4
Dubuque, IA	3,395	2,560	75.4	835	24.6	70	2.1	3,240	95.4
Duluth, MN–WI	5,785	4,555	78.7	1,230	21.3	65	1.1	5,440	94.0
Durham–Chapel Hill, NC	9,515	5,905	62.1	3,610	37.9	2,455	25.8	3,595	37.8
Eau Claire, WI	7,565	5,250	69.4	2,315	30.6	8	0.1	6,890	91.1
El Centro, CA	2,790	2,070	74.2	725	26.0	2,410	86.4	275	9.9
Elizabethtown, KY	3,540	2,225	62.9	1,320	37.3	150	4.2	2,750	77.7
Elkhart–Goshen, IN	20,505	13,710	66.9	6,795	33.1	4,720	23.0	14,145	69.0
Elmira, NY	2,315	1,760	76.0	555	24.0	0	0.0	2,140	92.4
El Paso, TX	15,565	9,415	60.5	6,150	39.5	14,350	92.2	685	4.4
Erie, PA	11,430	8,465	74.1	2,965	25.9	370	3.2	10,180	89.1
Eugene–Springfield, OR	9,775	7,675	78.5	2,100	21.5	925	9.5	8,180	83.7
Evansville, IN–KY	17,140	12,285	71.7	4,850	28.3	520	3.0	15,195	88.7
Fairbanks, AK	950	660	69.5	290	30.5	8	0.8	830	87.4
Fargo, ND–MN	5,785	4,255	73.6	1,530	26.4	305	5.3	4,710	81.4

C-12 **Production Operative Workers, by Metropolitan Statistical Area, Sex, Race, and Hispanic or Latino Origin, 2006–2010**—*Continued*

Metropolitan Statistical Area	Black alone, not Hispanic or Latino Number	Percent	American Indian and Alaska Native alone, not Hispanic or Latino Number	Percent	Asian alone, not Hispanic or Latino Number	Percent	Native Hawaiian and Other Pacific Islander alone, not Hispanic or Latino Number	Percent	Two or more races, not Hispanic or Latino Number	Percent
Casper, WY	40	2.2	50	2.8	0	0.0	0	0.0	45	2.5
Cedar Rapids, IA	470	5.0	25	0.3	165	1.7	0	0.0	95	1.0
Champaign–Urbana, IL	660	13.0	35	0.7	330	6.5	0	0.0	95	1.9
Charleston, WV	105	2.3	0	0.0	10	0.2	0	0.0	29	0.6
Charleston–North Charleston–Summerville, SC	5,845	42.1	75	0.5	380	2.7	10	0.1	224	1.6
Charlotte–Gastonia–Rock Hill, NC–SC	14,330	31.0	325	0.7	2,375	5.1	70	0.2	325	0.7
Charlottesville, VA	270	14.4	0	0.0	15	0.8	0	0.0	45	2.4
Chattanooga, TN–GA	3,640	19.4	70	0.4	270	1.4	0	0.0	130	0.7
Cheyenne, WY	55	2.9	0	0.0	0	0.0	0	0.0	45	2.4
Chicago–Joliet–Naperville, IL–IN–WI	31,050	11.7	505	0.2	13,430	5.1	10	0.0	1,655	0.6
Chico, CA	45	1.3	30	0.8	200	5.6	0	0.0	79	2.2
Cincinnati–Middletown, OH–KY–IN	8,360	13.7	90	0.1	1,200	2.0	15	0.0	605	1.0
Clarksville, TN–KY	2,920	31.9	4	0.0	130	1.4	25	0.3	125	1.4
Cleveland, TN	350	5.9	35	0.6	10	0.2	0	0.0	84	1.4
Cleveland–Elyria–Mentor, OH	14,315	21.1	150	0.2	1,795	2.7	0	0.0	645	1.0
Coeur d'Alene, ID	0	0.0	4	0.1	25	0.8	0	0.0	25	0.8
College Station–Bryan, TX	675	17.5	0	0.0	70	1.8	0	0.0	35	0.9
Colorado Springs, CO	685	8.1	15	0.2	600	7.1	10	0.1	255	3.0
Columbia, MO	485	13.5	4	0.1	180	5.0	0	0.0	34	0.9
Columbia, SC	9,525	51.3	55	0.3	170	0.9	0	0.0	115	0.6
Columbus, GA–AL	4,170	59.3	10	0.1	35	0.5	20	0.3	85	1.2
Columbus, IN	95	2.1	4	0.1	4	0.1	0	0.0	43	1.0
Columbus, OH	6,340	15.4	4	0.0	1,290	3.1	0	0.0	555	1.3
Corpus Christi, TX	300	3.6	0	0.0	135	1.6	0	0.0	50	0.6
Corvallis, OR	20	1.3	4	0.3	95	6.2	0	0.0	30	1.9
Crestview–Fort Walton Beach–Destin, FL	290	12.2	15	0.6	300	12.7	0	0.0	75	3.2
Cumberland, MD–WV	90	3.5	4	0.2	0	0.0	0	0.0	0	0.0
Dallas–Fort Worth–Arlington, TX	19,840	13.3	305	0.2	10,255	6.9	90	0.1	1,340	0.9
Dalton, GA	370	2.8	20	0.1	90	0.7	0	0.0	39	0.3
Danville, IL	550	14.7	0	0.0	0	0.0	0	0.0	85	2.3
Danville, VA	2,425	43.9	0	0.0	0	0.0	0	0.0	60	1.1
Davenport–Moline–Rock Island, IA–IL	1,195	8.0	4	0.0	225	1.5	4	0.0	110	0.7
Dayton, OH	5,185	17.6	35	0.1	615	2.1	0	0.0	259	0.9
Decatur, AL	1,635	19.6	70	0.8	0	0.0	35	0.4	79	0.9
Decatur, IL	640	17.4	0	0.0	35	1.0	0	0.0	4	0.1
Deltona–Daytona Beach–Ormond Beach, FL	660	8.9	0	0.0	200	2.7	0	0.0	70	0.9
Denver–Aurora–Broomfield, CO	1,820	4.7	180	0.5	3,725	9.6	40	0.1	685	1.8
Des Moines–West Des Moines, IA	985	7.4	15	0.1	1,445	10.8	0	0.0	115	0.9
Detroit–Warren–Livonia, MI	36,835	26.3	305	0.2	5,050	3.6	4	0.0	1,435	1.0
Dothan, AL	1,560	35.8	4	0.1	0	0.0	0	0.0	34	0.8
Dover, DE	1,170	34.3	10	0.3	75	2.2	0	0.0	15	0.4
Dubuque, IA	25	0.7	25	0.7	0	0.0	0	0.0	29	0.9
Duluth, MN–WI	30	0.5	95	1.6	100	1.7	0	0.0	59	1.0
Durham–Chapel Hill, NC	3,175	33.4	25	0.3	170	1.8	0	0.0	90	0.9
Eau Claire, WI	245	3.2	40	0.5	360	4.8	10	0.1	14	0.2
El Centro, CA	10	0.4	15	0.5	80	2.9	0	0.0	0	0.0
Elizabethtown, KY	445	12.6	30	0.8	110	3.1	15	0.4	40	1.1
Elkhart–Goshen, IN	1,140	5.6	50	0.2	315	1.5	10	0.0	125	0.6
Elmira, NY	125	5.4	10	0.4	0	0.0	0	0.0	39	1.7
El Paso, TX	385	2.5	30	0.2	100	0.6	0	0.0	20	0.1
Erie, PA	530	4.6	0	0.0	85	0.7	0	0.0	265	2.3
Eugene–Springfield, OR	140	1.4	180	1.8	130	1.3	30	0.3	179	1.8
Evansville, IN–KY	1,200	7.0	0	0.0	60	0.4	0	0.0	160	0.9
Fairbanks, AK	20	2.1	35	3.7	30	3.2	0	0.0	20	2.1
Fargo, ND–MN	290	5.0	135	2.3	260	4.5	45	0.8	40	0.7

PART C—METROPOLITAN STATISTICAL AREA TABLES

C-12 Production Operative Workers, by Metropolitan Statistical Area, Sex, Race, and Hispanic or Latino Origin, 2006–2010—Continued

Metropolitan Statistical Area	Total who worked in the last 5 years	Male Number	Male Percent	Female Number	Female Percent	Hispanic or Latino Number	Hispanic or Latino Percent	White alone, not Hispanic or Latino Number	White alone, not Hispanic or Latino Percent
Farmington, NM	2,390	1,830	76.6	560	23.4	360	15.1	720	30.1
Fayetteville, NC	8,580	5,000	58.3	3,580	41.7	745	8.7	2,730	31.8
Fayetteville–Springdale–Rogers, AR–MO	16,560	10,420	62.9	6,140	37.1	6,705	40.5	7,850	47.4
Flagstaff, AZ	2,910	1,835	63.1	1,080	37.1	415	14.3	1,325	45.5
Flint, MI	16,205	11,420	70.5	4,785	29.5	890	5.5	11,335	69.9
Florence, SC	7,995	5,765	72.1	2,230	27.9	295	3.7	3,580	44.8
Florence–Muscle Shoals, AL	5,125	3,610	70.4	1,515	29.6	160	3.1	4,055	79.1
Fond du Lac, WI	6,550	4,490	68.5	2,060	31.5	490	7.5	5,855	89.4
Fort Collins–Loveland, CO	5,910	4,055	68.6	1,855	31.4	900	15.2	4,610	78.0
Fort Smith, AR–OK	16,475	10,490	63.7	5,985	36.3	2,280	13.8	10,865	65.9
Fort Wayne, IN	19,495	13,700	70.3	5,795	29.7	2,170	11.1	13,740	70.5
Fresno, CA	19,350	12,140	62.7	7,210	37.3	13,140	67.9	2,985	15.4
Gadsden, AL	4,160	2,900	69.7	1,260	30.3	275	6.6	2,610	62.7
Gainesville, FL	3,070	2,255	73.5	810	26.4	235	7.7	1,890	61.6
Gainesville, GA	8,990	5,660	63.0	3,335	37.1	5,165	57.5	2,710	30.1
Glens Falls, NY	4,350	2,925	67.2	1,420	32.6	85	2.0	4,175	96.0
Goldsboro, NC	4,370	2,970	68.0	1,400	32.0	1,000	22.9	1,560	35.7
Grand Forks, ND–MN	2,785	2,100	75.4	685	24.6	155	5.6	2,480	89.0
Grand Junction, CO	2,260	1,795	79.4	465	20.6	450	19.9	1,670	73.9
Grand Rapids–Wyoming, MI	35,335	24,145	68.3	11,190	31.7	5,345	15.1	24,240	68.6
Great Falls, MT	995	625	62.8	370	37.2	15	1.5	900	90.5
Greeley, CO	6,590	4,545	69.0	2,045	31.0	2,895	43.9	3,150	47.8
Green Bay, WI	13,885	10,035	72.3	3,850	27.7	1,875	13.5	10,870	78.3
Greensboro–High Point, NC	30,485	18,305	60.0	12,180	40.0	4,390	14.4	15,555	51.0
Greenville, NC	5,425	3,715	68.5	1,710	31.5	695	12.8	1,855	34.2
Greenville–Mauldin–Easley, SC	24,300	15,700	64.6	8,600	35.4	2,655	10.9	14,445	59.4
Gulfport–Biloxi, MS	4,650	3,455	74.3	1,195	25.7	405	8.7	2,700	58.1
Hagerstown–Martinsburg, MD–WV	6,510	4,730	72.7	1,780	27.3	355	5.5	5,560	85.4
Hanford–Corcoran, CA	3,135	2,125	67.8	1,010	32.2	2,130	67.9	870	27.8
Harrisburg–Carlisle, PA	11,405	8,035	70.5	3,370	29.5	675	5.9	9,185	80.5
Harrisonburg, VA	4,345	2,615	60.2	1,730	39.8	1,055	24.3	2,890	66.5
Hartford–West Hartford–East Hartford, CT	28,010	19,425	69.4	8,585	30.6	5,660	20.2	17,615	62.9
Hattiesburg, MS	3,305	2,410	72.9	900	27.2	310	9.4	1,505	45.5
Hickory–Lenoir–Morganton, NC	24,350	14,280	58.6	10,070	41.4	2,465	10.1	18,345	75.3
Hinesville–Fort Stewart, GA	1,330	950	71.4	375	28.2	115	8.6	485	36.5
Holland–Grand Haven, MI	15,110	10,000	66.2	5,110	33.8	2,745	18.2	10,645	70.5
Honolulu, HI	9,590	6,660	69.4	2,930	30.6	580	6.0	795	8.3
Hot Springs, AR	1,865	1,245	66.8	620	33.2	120	6.4	1,630	87.4
Houma–Bayou Cane–Thibodaux, LA	7,345	6,315	86.0	1,030	14.0	1,100	15.0	4,720	64.3
Houston–Sugar Land–Baytown, TX	134,760	105,645	78.4	29,115	21.6	69,665	51.7	35,665	26.5
Huntington–Ashland, WV–KY–OH	6,100	4,735	77.6	1,365	22.4	0	0.0	5,810	95.2
Huntsville, AL	12,200	7,695	63.1	4,505	36.9	1,020	8.4	6,615	54.2
Idaho Falls, ID	2,480	1,645	66.3	835	33.7	690	27.8	1,740	70.2
Indianapolis–Carmel, IN	45,985	30,730	66.8	15,255	33.2	4,720	10.3	31,360	68.2
Iowa City, IA	2,985	2,255	75.5	730	24.5	235	7.9	2,395	80.2
Ithaca, NY	1,305	880	67.4	420	32.2	75	5.7	1,115	85.4
Jackson, MI	6,780	4,995	73.7	1,785	26.3	205	3.0	6,025	88.9
Jackson, MS	11,555	7,370	63.8	4,185	36.2	380	3.3	3,340	28.9
Jackson, TN	5,300	3,395	64.1	1,905	35.9	140	2.6	2,275	42.9
Jacksonville, FL	20,310	14,780	72.8	5,530	27.2	1,495	7.4	11,790	58.1
Jacksonville, NC	2,045	1,270	62.1	775	37.9	60	2.9	1,220	59.7
Janesville, WI	9,775	6,690	68.4	3,085	31.6	1,230	12.6	7,955	81.4
Jefferson City, MO	4,135	2,830	68.4	1,305	31.6	265	6.4	3,535	85.5
Johnson City, TN	6,760	4,860	71.9	1,900	28.1	200	3.0	6,180	91.4
Johnstown, PA	4,045	3,170	78.4	875	21.6	0	0.0	3,925	97.0

C-12 Production Operative Workers, by Metropolitan Statistical Area, Sex, Race, and Hispanic or Latino Origin, 2006–2010—*Continued*

Metropolitan Statistical Area	Black alone, not Hispanic or Latino Number	Percent	American Indian and Alaska Native alone, not Hispanic or Latino Number	Percent	Asian alone, not Hispanic or Latino Number	Percent	Native Hawaiian and Other Pacific Islander alone, not Hispanic or Latino Number	Percent	Two or more races, not Hispanic or Latino Number	Percent
Farmington, NM	0	0.0	1,290	54.0	0	0.0	0	0.0	20	0.8
Fayetteville, NC	4,400	51.3	200	2.3	210	2.4	60	0.7	240	2.8
Fayetteville–Springdale–Rogers, AR–MO	480	2.9	255	1.5	400	2.4	480	2.9	384	2.3
Flagstaff, AZ	35	1.2	1,060	36.4	45	1.5	0	0.0	30	1.0
Flint, MI	3,660	22.6	80	0.5	35	0.2	4	0.0	205	1.3
Florence, SC	3,935	49.2	0	0.0	85	1.1	0	0.0	105	1.3
Florence–Muscle Shoals, AL	830	16.2	4	0.1	45	0.9	0	0.0	39	0.8
Fond du Lac, WI	95	1.5	10	0.2	45	0.7	0	0.0	60	0.9
Fort Collins–Loveland, CO	100	1.7	105	1.8	125	2.1	25	0.4	40	0.7
Fort Smith, AR–OK	660	4.0	580	3.5	1,070	6.5	0	0.0	1,029	6.2
Fort Wayne, IN	2,555	13.1	35	0.2	715	3.7	0	0.0	275	1.4
Fresno, CA	500	2.6	20	0.1	2,520	13.0	15	0.1	160	0.8
Gadsden, AL	1,220	29.3	10	0.2	30	0.7	0	0.0	24	0.6
Gainesville, FL	710	23.1	20	0.7	165	5.4	0	0.0	50	1.6
Gainesville, GA	825	9.2	0	0.0	240	2.7	0	0.0	55	0.6
Glens Falls, NY	20	0.5	10	0.2	35	0.8	4	0.1	14	0.3
Goldsboro, NC	1,775	40.6	0	0.0	15	0.3	0	0.0	19	0.4
Grand Forks, ND–MN	40	1.4	80	2.9	15	0.5	0	0.0	19	0.7
Grand Junction, CO	70	3.1	0	0.0	30	1.3	0	0.0	35	1.5
Grand Rapids–Wyoming, MI	3,335	9.4	155	0.4	1,825	5.2	0	0.0	435	1.2
Great Falls, MT	0	0.0	80	8.0	0	0.0	0	0.0	0	0.0
Greeley, CO	185	2.8	75	1.1	215	3.3	0	0.0	70	1.1
Green Bay, WI	140	1.0	255	1.8	610	4.4	0	0.0	140	1.0
Greensboro–High Point, NC	8,630	28.3	4	0.0	1,710	5.6	0	0.0	200	0.7
Greenville, NC	2,830	52.2	10	0.2	15	0.3	0	0.0	23	0.4
Greenville–Mauldin–Easley, SC	6,435	26.5	115	0.5	470	1.9	10	0.0	175	0.7
Gulfport–Biloxi, MS	1,365	29.4	10	0.2	105	2.3	0	0.0	65	1.4
Hagerstown–Martinsburg, MD–WV	495	7.6	4	0.1	70	1.1	0	0.0	30	0.5
Hanford–Corcoran, CA	30	1.0	0	0.0	70	2.2	0	0.0	35	1.1
Harrisburg–Carlisle, PA	1,095	9.6	4	0.0	295	2.6	90	0.8	70	0.6
Harrisonburg, VA	270	6.2	4	0.1	125	2.9	0	0.0	0	0.0
Hartford–West Hartford–East Hartford, CT	3,020	10.8	40	0.1	1,575	5.6	0	0.0	100	0.4
Hattiesburg, MS	1,465	44.3	15	0.5	0	0.0	0	0.0	15	0.5
Hickory–Lenoir–Morganton, NC	2,100	8.6	20	0.1	1,315	5.4	0	0.0	100	0.4
Hinesville–Fort Stewart, GA	675	50.8	0	0.0	45	3.4	0	0.0	10	0.8
Holland–Grand Haven, MI	390	2.6	45	0.3	1,065	7.0	0	0.0	225	1.5
Honolulu, HI	75	0.8	0	0.0	5,675	59.2	785	8.2	1,680	17.5
Hot Springs, AR	100	5.4	15	0.8	0	0.0	0	0.0	0	0.0
Houma–Bayou Cane–Thibodaux, LA	1,040	14.2	190	2.6	175	2.4	0	0.0	120	1.6
Houston–Sugar Land–Baytown, TX	18,450	13.7	150	0.1	9,945	7.4	45	0.0	845	0.6
Huntington–Ashland, WV–KY–OH	255	4.2	0	0.0	15	0.2	0	0.0	20	0.3
Huntsville, AL	4,125	33.8	65	0.5	170	1.4	0	0.0	200	1.6
Idaho Falls, ID	10	0.4	0	0.0	30	1.2	0	0.0	8	0.3
Indianapolis–Carmel, IN	8,235	17.9	45	0.1	1,015	2.2	30	0.1	585	1.3
Iowa City, IA	210	7.0	4	0.1	100	3.4	0	0.0	40	1.3
Ithaca, NY	25	1.9	0	0.0	50	3.8	0	0.0	40	3.1
Jackson, MI	475	7.0	0	0.0	35	0.5	0	0.0	35	0.5
Jackson, MS	7,785	67.4	0	0.0	10	0.1	0	0.0	43	0.4
Jackson, TN	2,780	52.5	0	0.0	45	0.8	0	0.0	60	1.1
Jacksonville, FL	5,495	27.1	80	0.4	1,350	6.6	0	0.0	105	0.5
Jacksonville, NC	630	30.8	0	0.0	130	6.4	0	0.0	4	0.2
Janesville, WI	345	3.5	4	0.0	155	1.6	10	0.1	75	0.8
Jefferson City, MO	265	6.4	15	0.4	0	0.0	0	0.0	59	1.4
Johnson City, TN	325	4.8	10	0.1	45	0.7	0	0.0	0	0.0
Johnstown, PA	90	2.2	0	0.0	25	0.6	0	0.0	4	0.1

C-12 Production Operative Workers, by Metropolitan Statistical Area, Sex, Race, and Hispanic or Latino Origin, 2006–2010—Continued

Metropolitan Statistical Area	Total who worked in the last 5 years	Male Number	Male Percent	Female Number	Female Percent	Hispanic or Latino Number	Hispanic or Latino Percent	White alone, not Hispanic or Latino Number	White alone, not Hispanic or Latino Percent
Jonesboro, AR	4,650	3,185	68.5	1,465	31.5	320	6.9	3,445	74.1
Joplin, MO	7,615	5,025	66.0	2,595	34.1	800	10.5	6,115	80.3
Kalamazoo–Portage, MI	12,455	8,875	71.3	3,580	28.7	1,010	8.1	9,775	78.5
Kankakee–Bradley, IL	3,915	2,840	72.5	1,075	27.5	755	19.3	2,410	61.6
Kansas City, MO–KS	49,350	34,530	70.0	14,820	30.0	7,065	14.3	31,345	63.5
Kennewick–Pasco–Richland, WA	5,205	3,545	68.1	1,665	32.0	2,380	45.7	2,470	47.5
Killeen–Temple–Fort Hood, TX	5,470	4,110	75.1	1,360	24.9	1,390	25.4	2,525	46.2
Kingsport–Bristol–Bristol, TN–VA	12,880	9,525	74.0	3,350	26.0	185	1.4	12,290	95.4
Kingston, NY	2,845	2,190	77.0	655	23.0	395	13.9	2,235	78.6
Knoxville, TN	17,285	12,295	71.1	4,990	28.9	965	5.6	14,515	84.0
Kokomo, IN	5,485	3,700	67.5	1,785	32.5	170	3.1	4,660	85.0
La Crosse, WI–MN	5,240	3,750	71.6	1,490	28.4	120	2.3	4,350	83.0
Lafayette, IN	7,830	5,720	73.1	2,110	26.9	810	10.3	6,555	83.7
Lafayette, LA	4,780	3,665	76.7	1,115	23.3	150	3.1	2,975	62.2
Lake Charles, LA	4,685	3,985	85.1	700	14.9	65	1.4	3,665	78.2
Lake Havasu City–Kingman, AZ	3,240	2,190	67.6	1,050	32.4	670	20.7	2,390	73.8
Lakeland–Winter Haven, FL	11,925	8,555	71.7	3,370	28.3	2,730	22.9	6,485	54.4
Lancaster, PA	21,040	14,985	71.2	6,055	28.8	3,010	14.3	15,970	75.9
Lansing–East Lansing, MI	14,075	10,100	71.8	3,975	28.2	1,485	10.6	10,080	71.6
Laredo, TX	2,325	1,610	69.2	715	30.8	2,135	91.8	165	7.1
Las Cruces, NM	3,560	2,285	64.2	1,275	35.8	3,115	87.5	415	11.7
Las Vegas–Paradise, NV	23,060	15,420	66.9	7,640	33.1	12,475	54.1	7,655	33.2
Lawrence, KS	2,320	1,560	67.2	760	32.8	65	2.8	1,930	83.2
Lawton, OK	2,420	1,610	66.5	815	33.7	185	7.6	1,400	57.9
Lebanon, PA	5,245	3,385	64.5	1,865	35.6	500	9.5	4,410	84.1
Lewiston, ID–WA	2,320	1,820	78.4	500	21.6	20	0.9	2,245	96.8
Lewiston–Auburn, ME	3,200	2,235	69.8	965	30.2	65	2.0	2,965	92.7
Lexington–Fayette, KY	13,665	9,400	68.8	4,265	31.2	940	6.9	9,850	72.1
Lima, OH	5,085	3,720	73.2	1,365	26.8	125	2.5	4,050	79.6
Lincoln, NE	9,170	6,510	71.0	2,660	29.0	930	10.1	6,530	71.2
Little Rock–North Little Rock–Conway, AR	16,035	10,925	68.1	5,115	31.9	1,265	7.9	9,965	62.1
Logan, UT–ID	5,040	3,270	64.9	1,770	35.1	1,360	27.0	3,365	66.8
Longview, TX	7,230	5,910	81.7	1,320	18.3	1,580	21.9	3,650	50.5
Longview, WA	3,275	2,610	79.7	665	20.3	415	12.7	2,530	77.3
Los Angeles–Long Beach–Santa Ana, CA	345,850	224,180	64.8	121,670	35.2	256,625	74.2	36,920	10.7
Louisville/Jefferson County, KY–IN	43,815	30,725	70.1	13,090	29.9	2,470	5.6	33,405	76.2
Lubbock, TX	5,220	3,620	69.3	1,600	30.7	2,635	50.5	2,015	38.6
Lynchburg, VA	8,875	6,480	73.0	2,400	27.0	220	2.5	5,710	64.3
Macon, GA	4,895	2,860	58.4	2,040	41.7	135	2.8	1,820	37.2
Madera–Chowchilla, CA	2,995	2,270	75.8	725	24.2	2,120	70.8	685	22.9
Madison, WI	14,030	10,035	71.5	3,995	28.5	1,800	12.8	10,700	76.3
Manchester–Nashua, NH	11,825	6,980	59.0	4,845	41.0	1,355	11.5	8,890	75.2
Manhattan, KS	2,210	1,585	71.7	625	28.3	120	5.4	1,705	77.1
Mankato–North Mankato, MN	4,510	3,190	70.7	1,320	29.3	255	5.7	3,855	85.5
Mansfield, OH	7,310	5,095	69.7	2,215	30.3	74	1.0	6,715	91.9
McAllen–Edinburg–Mission, TX	10,665	8,140	76.3	2,530	23.7	10,255	96.2	335	3.1
Medford, OR	4,555	3,395	74.5	1,160	25.5	970	21.3	3,475	76.3
Memphis, TN–MS–AR	31,710	20,285	64.0	11,425	36.0	2,400	7.6	9,930	31.3
Merced, CA	8,210	5,005	61.0	3,205	39.0	5,595	68.1	1,745	21.3
Miami–Fort Lauderdale–Pompano Beach, FL	72,800	45,245	62.1	27,560	37.9	42,580	58.5	13,810	19.0
Michigan City–La Porte, IN	5,095	3,455	67.8	1,640	32.2	360	7.1	4,190	82.2
Midland, TX	2,355	1,880	79.8	475	20.2	1,365	58.0	885	37.6
Milwaukee–Waukesha–West Allis, WI	58,095	42,125	72.5	15,965	27.5	10,665	18.4	35,425	61.0
Minneapolis–St. Paul–Bloomington, MN–WI	92,340	63,925	69.2	28,420	30.8	9,045	9.8	60,805	65.8
Missoula, MT	1,310	1,035	79.0	275	21.0	15	1.1	1,260	96.2

C-12 **Production Operative Workers, by Metropolitan Statistical Area, Sex, Race, and Hispanic or Latino Origin, 2006–2010**—*Continued*

Metropolitan Statistical Area	Black alone, not Hispanic or Latino Number	Percent	American Indian and Alaska Native alone, not Hispanic or Latino Number	Percent	Asian alone, not Hispanic or Latino Number	Percent	Native Hawaiian and Other Pacific Islander alone, not Hispanic or Latino Number	Percent	Two or more races, not Hispanic or Latino Number	Percent
Jonesboro, AR	815	17.5	40	0.9	10	0.2	0	0.0	15	0.3
Joplin, MO	180	2.4	240	3.2	80	1.1	115	1.5	90	1.2
Kalamazoo–Portage, MI	1,370	11.0	115	0.9	80	0.6	0	0.0	110	0.9
Kankakee–Bradley, IL	675	17.2	0	0.0	30	0.8	0	0.0	49	1.3
Kansas City, MO–KS	7,980	16.2	210	0.4	1,990	4.0	0	0.0	755	1.5
Kennewick–Pasco–Richland, WA	0	0.0	25	0.5	300	5.8	0	0.0	35	0.7
Killeen–Temple–Fort Hood, TX	1,335	24.4	20	0.4	130	2.4	0	0.0	75	1.4
Kingsport–Bristol–Bristol, TN–VA	250	1.9	40	0.3	30	0.2	0	0.0	85	0.7
Kingston, NY	120	4.2	0	0.0	50	1.8	0	0.0	50	1.8
Knoxville, TN	1,350	7.8	40	0.2	170	1.0	0	0.0	240	1.4
Kokomo, IN	580	10.6	4	0.1	50	0.9	0	0.0	19	0.3
La Crosse, WI–MN	65	1.2	15	0.3	675	12.9	0	0.0	14	0.3
Lafayette, IN	320	4.1	4	0.1	65	0.8	0	0.0	69	0.9
Lafayette, LA	1,590	33.3	10	0.2	40	0.8	0	0.0	10	0.2
Lake Charles, LA	930	19.9	0	0.0	0	0.0	0	0.0	25	0.5
Lake Havasu City–Kingman, AZ	65	2.0	30	0.9	15	0.5	10	0.3	55	1.7
Lakeland–Winter Haven, FL	2,260	19.0	90	0.8	240	2.0	25	0.2	105	0.9
Lancaster, PA	885	4.2	10	0.0	1,040	4.9	15	0.1	115	0.5
Lansing–East Lansing, MI	1,570	11.2	55	0.4	550	3.9	45	0.3	290	2.1
Laredo, TX	0	0.0	0	0.0	0	0.0	0	0.0	25	1.1
Las Cruces, NM	15	0.4	0	0.0	0	0.0	15	0.4	0	0.0
Las Vegas–Paradise, NV	1,320	5.7	120	0.5	1,165	5.1	60	0.3	270	1.2
Lawrence, KS	90	3.9	40	1.7	165	7.1	0	0.0	30	1.3
Lawton, OK	460	19.0	65	2.7	165	6.8	55	2.3	90	3.7
Lebanon, PA	65	1.2	0	0.0	215	4.1	0	0.0	55	1.0
Lewiston, ID–WA	0	0.0	35	1.5	20	0.9	0	0.0	4	0.2
Lewiston–Auburn, ME	30	0.9	10	0.3	30	0.9	0	0.0	100	3.1
Lexington–Fayette, KY	2,585	18.9	60	0.4	145	1.1	0	0.0	85	0.6
Lima, OH	775	15.2	25	0.5	30	0.6	0	0.0	80	1.6
Lincoln, NE	580	6.3	75	0.8	960	10.5	0	0.0	94	1.0
Little Rock–North Little Rock–Conway, AR	4,270	26.6	40	0.2	190	1.2	20	0.1	285	1.8
Logan, UT–ID	20	0.4	95	1.9	110	2.2	0	0.0	95	1.9
Longview, TX	1,895	26.2	0	0.0	45	0.6	0	0.0	50	0.7
Longview, WA	50	1.5	50	1.5	125	3.8	10	0.3	95	2.9
Los Angeles–Long Beach–Santa Ana, CA	7,570	2.2	310	0.1	41,305	11.9	570	0.2	2,545	0.7
Louisville/Jefferson County, KY–IN	6,810	15.5	4	0.0	820	1.9	0	0.0	300	0.7
Lubbock, TX	335	6.4	30	0.6	75	1.4	10	0.2	120	2.3
Lynchburg, VA	2,865	32.3	4	0.0	25	0.3	0	0.0	50	0.6
Macon, GA	2,735	55.9	35	0.7	80	1.6	0	0.0	95	1.9
Madera–Chowchilla, CA	90	3.0	4	0.1	95	3.2	0	0.0	0	0.0
Madison, WI	630	4.5	30	0.2	745	5.3	0	0.0	119	0.8
Manchester–Nashua, NH	505	4.3	0	0.0	990	8.4	0	0.0	85	0.7
Manhattan, KS	200	9.0	20	0.9	120	5.4	0	0.0	45	2.0
Mankato–North Mankato, MN	80	1.8	4	0.1	175	3.9	0	0.0	140	3.1
Mansfield, OH	455	6.2	35	0.5	10	0.1	0	0.0	10	0.1
McAllen–Edinburg–Mission, TX	35	0.3	0	0.0	40	0.4	0	0.0	4	0.0
Medford, OR	0	0.0	55	1.2	4	0.1	10	0.2	45	1.0
Memphis, TN–MS–AR	18,455	58.2	10	0.0	660	2.1	15	0.0	240	0.8
Merced, CA	200	2.4	0	0.0	670	8.2	0	0.0	0	0.0
Miami–Fort Lauderdale–Pompano Beach, FL	14,240	19.6	200	0.3	1,485	2.0	10	0.0	475	0.7
Michigan City–La Porte, IN	490	9.6	15	0.3	30	0.6	0	0.0	18	0.4
Midland, TX	65	2.8	0	0.0	30	1.3	0	0.0	15	0.6
Milwaukee–Waukesha–West Allis, WI	8,460	14.6	255	0.4	2,890	5.0	10	0.0	385	0.7
Minneapolis–St. Paul–Bloomington, MN–WI	7,535	8.2	370	0.4	13,415	14.5	75	0.1	1,100	1.2
Missoula, MT	10	0.8	0	0.0	30	2.3	0	0.0	4	0.3

PART C—METROPOLITAN STATISTICAL AREA TABLES

C-12 **Production Operative Workers, by Metropolitan Statistical Area, Sex, Race, and Hispanic or Latino Origin, 2006–2010**—*Continued*

Metropolitan Statistical Area	Total who worked in the last 5 years	Male Number	Male Percent	Female Number	Female Percent	Hispanic or Latino Number	Hispanic or Latino Percent	White alone, not Hispanic or Latino Number	White alone, not Hispanic or Latino Percent
Mobile, AL	10,880	8,490	78.0	2,390	22.0	480	4.4	5,295	48.7
Modesto, CA	16,995	10,570	62.2	6,425	37.8	10,365	61.0	4,660	27.4
Monroe, LA	4,315	3,640	84.4	680	15.8	100	2.3	2,535	58.7
Monroe, MI	7,015	5,180	73.8	1,830	26.1	180	2.6	6,585	93.9
Montgomery, AL	11,180	6,920	61.9	4,260	38.1	685	6.1	3,440	30.8
Morgantown, WV	2,415	1,885	78.1	530	21.9	0	0.0	2,345	97.1
Morristown, TN	7,925	5,285	66.7	2,640	33.3	835	10.5	6,600	83.3
Mount Vernon–Anacortes, WA	3,585	2,900	80.9	685	19.1	1,270	35.4	2,155	60.1
Muncie, IN	3,775	2,830	75.0	940	24.9	10	0.3	3,410	90.3
Muskegon–Norton Shores, MI	10,425	7,290	69.9	3,135	30.1	505	4.8	8,235	79.0
Myrtle Beach–North Myrtle Beach–Conway, SC	3,180	1,920	60.4	1,260	39.6	110	3.5	2,230	70.1
Napa, CA	3,110	2,165	69.6	945	30.4	1,685	54.2	1,250	40.2
Naples–Marco Island, FL	2,960	1,890	63.9	1,070	36.1	1,300	43.9	1,330	44.9
Nashville-Davidson–Murfreesboro–Franklin, TN	42,475	28,790	67.8	13,685	32.2	4,420	10.4	27,090	63.8
New Haven–Milford, CT	24,295	15,815	65.1	8,480	34.9	6,925	28.5	12,765	52.5
New Orleans–Metairie–Kenner, LA	19,670	15,475	78.7	4,190	21.3	1,675	8.5	8,885	45.2
New York–Northern New Jersey–Long Island, NY-NJ-PA	273,910	172,235	62.9	101,675	37.1	123,265	45.0	79,810	29.1
Niles–Benton Harbor, MI	6,350	4,485	70.6	1,865	29.4	435	6.9	4,465	70.3
North Port–Bradenton–Sarasota, FL	10,360	7,005	67.6	3,360	32.4	2,230	21.5	6,650	64.2
Norwich–New London, CT	4,830	3,440	71.2	1,390	28.8	555	11.5	3,855	79.8
Ocala, FL	5,945	4,105	69.0	1,840	31.0	975	16.4	3,525	59.3
Ocean City, NJ	915	640	69.9	275	30.1	145	15.8	685	74.9
Odessa, TX	4,185	3,665	87.6	520	12.4	2,850	68.1	1,195	28.6
Ogden–Clearfield, UT	14,885	10,455	70.2	4,430	29.8	4,250	28.6	9,655	64.9
Oklahoma City, OK	25,605	18,560	72.5	7,045	27.5	4,860	19.0	14,605	57.0
Olympia, WA	3,180	2,455	77.2	725	22.8	305	9.6	2,480	78.0
Omaha–Council Bluffs, NE-IA	20,905	14,825	70.9	6,080	29.1	5,545	26.5	12,130	58.0
Orlando–Kissimmee–Sanford, FL	26,035	17,055	65.5	8,980	34.5	8,690	33.4	10,220	39.3
Oshkosh–Neenah, WI	9,210	6,750	73.3	2,460	26.7	380	4.1	8,220	89.3
Owensboro, KY	5,395	4,215	78.1	1,180	21.9	210	3.9	4,790	88.8
Oxnard–Thousand Oaks–Ventura, CA	17,215	10,260	59.6	6,955	40.4	11,360	66.0	3,585	20.8
Palm Bay–Melbourne–Titusville, FL	9,610	6,350	66.1	3,260	33.9	1,235	12.9	6,815	70.9
Palm Coast, FL	1,880	1,355	72.1	525	27.9	295	15.7	1,320	70.2
Panama City–Lynn Haven–Panama City Beach, FL	2,800	2,275	81.3	525	18.8	165	5.9	2,170	77.5
Parkersburg–Marietta–Vienna, WV-OH	5,590	4,845	86.7	745	13.3	0	0.0	5,440	97.3
Pascagoula, MS	5,345	4,195	78.5	1,155	21.6	285	5.3	3,605	67.4
Pensacola–Ferry Pass–Brent, FL	5,695	4,275	75.1	1,420	24.9	84	1.5	4,060	71.3
Peoria, IL	12,310	9,600	78.0	2,710	22.0	400	3.2	10,330	83.9
Philadelphia–Camden–Wilmington, PA-NJ-DE-MD	109,400	77,225	70.6	32,170	29.4	14,460	13.2	64,225	58.7
Phoenix–Mesa–Glendale, AZ	63,445	44,590	70.3	18,855	29.7	30,540	48.1	24,655	38.9
Pine Bluff, AR	3,890	2,395	61.6	1,490	38.3	50	1.3	1,640	42.2
Pittsburgh, PA	48,815	37,095	76.0	11,720	24.0	360	0.7	43,790	89.7
Pittsfield, MA	3,000	2,215	73.8	785	26.2	280	9.3	2,540	84.7
Pocatello, ID	2,260	1,345	59.5	920	40.7	285	12.6	1,765	78.1
Portland–South Portland–Biddeford, ME	12,025	8,695	72.3	3,325	27.7	450	3.7	10,750	89.4
Portland–Vancouver–Hillsboro, OR-WA	57,325	41,390	72.2	15,935	27.8	9,990	17.4	36,800	64.2
Port St. Lucie, FL	5,520	3,805	68.9	1,710	31.0	955	17.3	3,275	59.3
Poughkeepsie–Newburgh–Middletown, NY	10,585	7,460	70.5	3,125	29.5	3,025	28.6	5,780	54.6
Prescott, AZ	2,830	1,930	68.2	900	31.8	585	20.7	2,150	76.0
Providence–New Bedford–Fall River, RI-MA	49,125	31,495	64.1	17,630	35.9	11,705	23.8	31,030	63.2

C-12 Production Operative Workers, by Metropolitan Statistical Area, Sex, Race, and Hispanic or Latino Origin, 2006–2010—*Continued*

Metropolitan Statistical Area	Black alone, not Hispanic or Latino Number	Percent	American Indian and Alaska Native alone, not Hispanic or Latino Number	Percent	Asian alone, not Hispanic or Latino Number	Percent	Native Hawaiian and Other Pacific Islander alone, not Hispanic or Latino Number	Percent	Two or more races, not Hispanic or Latino Number	Percent
Mobile, AL	4,110	37.8	135	1.2	775	7.1	0	0.0	80	0.7
Modesto, CA	230	1.4	85	0.5	1,145	6.7	125	0.7	380	2.2
Monroe, LA	1,670	38.7	10	0.2	0	0.0	0	0.0	4	0.1
Monroe, MI	200	2.9	10	0.1	0	0.0	0	0.0	35	0.5
Montgomery, AL	6,880	61.5	4	0.0	120	1.1	0	0.0	55	0.5
Morgantown, WV	30	1.2	0	0.0	0	0.0	0	0.0	40	1.7
Morristown, TN	385	4.9	0	0.0	0	0.0	0	0.0	95	1.2
Mount Vernon–Anacortes, WA	4	0.1	30	0.8	80	2.2	4	0.1	34	0.9
Muncie, IN	265	7.0	30	0.8	0	0.0	0	0.0	65	1.7
Muskegon–Norton Shores, MI	1,475	14.1	60	0.6	4	0.0	0	0.0	140	1.3
Myrtle Beach–North Myrtle Beach–Conway, SC	770	24.2	20	0.6	45	1.4	0	0.0	10	0.3
Napa, CA	30	1.0	0	0.0	120	3.9	0	0.0	30	1.0
Naples–Marco Island, FL	290	9.8	0	0.0	10	0.3	0	0.0	30	1.0
Nashville-Davidson–Murfreesboro–Franklin, TN	8,495	20.0	60	0.1	2,070	4.9	40	0.1	310	0.7
New Haven–Milford, CT	2,750	11.3	15	0.1	1,405	5.8	0	0.0	440	1.8
New Orleans–Metairie–Kenner, LA	7,735	39.3	170	0.9	1,080	5.5	0	0.0	125	0.6
New York–Northern New Jersey–Long Island, NY-NJ-PA	31,840	11.6	505	0.2	34,300	12.5	40	0.0	4,150	1.5
Niles–Benton Harbor, MI	1,340	21.1	25	0.4	30	0.5	0	0.0	59	0.9
North Port–Bradenton–Sarasota, FL	950	9.2	0	0.0	425	4.1	0	0.0	110	1.1
Norwich–New London, CT	215	4.5	4	0.1	165	3.4	0	0.0	35	0.7
Ocala, FL	1,185	19.9	50	0.8	130	2.2	0	0.0	80	1.3
Ocean City, NJ	80	8.7	0	0.0	0	0.0	0	0.0	0	0.0
Odessa, TX	75	1.8	4	0.1	15	0.4	0	0.0	48	1.1
Ogden–Clearfield, UT	220	1.5	70	0.5	500	3.4	15	0.1	175	1.2
Oklahoma City, OK	2,520	9.8	1,080	4.2	1,780	7.0	50	0.2	705	2.8
Olympia, WA	25	0.8	45	1.4	250	7.9	15	0.5	60	1.9
Omaha–Council Bluffs, NE–IA	2,255	10.8	90	0.4	565	2.7	10	0.0	320	1.5
Orlando–Kissimmee–Sanford, FL	5,190	19.9	20	0.1	1,465	5.6	25	0.1	420	1.6
Oshkosh–Neenah, WI	50	0.5	40	0.4	490	5.3	0	0.0	29	0.3
Owensboro, KY	330	6.1	0	0.0	15	0.3	0	0.0	55	1.0
Oxnard–Thousand Oaks–Ventura, CA	165	1.0	35	0.2	1,960	11.4	25	0.1	85	0.5
Palm Bay–Melbourne–Titusville, FL	1,085	11.3	0	0.0	305	3.2	40	0.4	135	1.4
Palm Coast, FL	135	7.2	0	0.0	80	4.3	0	0.0	60	3.2
Panama City–Lynn Haven–Panama City Beach, FL	315	11.3	0	0.0	65	2.3	0	0.0	85	3.0
Parkersburg–Marietta–Vienna, WV–OH	45	0.8	4	0.1	30	0.5	0	0.0	65	1.2
Pascagoula, MS	1,350	25.3	25	0.5	35	0.7	0	0.0	45	0.8
Pensacola–Ferry Pass–Brent, FL	1,110	19.5	50	0.9	225	4.0	20	0.4	145	2.5
Peoria, IL	1,255	10.2	0	0.0	140	1.1	0	0.0	185	1.5
Philadelphia–Camden–Wilmington, PA-NJ-DE-MD	19,055	17.4	205	0.2	10,010	9.1	20	0.0	1,420	1.3
Phoenix–Mesa–Glendale, AZ	2,185	3.4	1,380	2.2	3,810	6.0	145	0.2	730	1.2
Pine Bluff, AR	2,190	56.3	0	0.0	10	0.3	0	0.0	0	0.0
Pittsburgh, PA	3,730	7.6	50	0.1	580	1.2	10	0.0	290	0.6
Pittsfield, MA	75	2.5	15	0.5	15	0.5	0	0.0	74	2.5
Pocatello, ID	0	0.0	95	4.2	95	4.2	25	1.1	0	0.0
Portland–South Portland–Biddeford, ME	255	2.1	10	0.1	510	4.2	4	0.0	50	0.4
Portland–Vancouver–Hillsboro, OR–WA	1,375	2.4	330	0.6	7,190	12.5	500	0.9	1,140	2.0
Port St. Lucie, FL	1,170	21.2	0	0.0	115	2.1	0	0.0	0	0.0
Poughkeepsie–Newburgh–Middletown, NY	1,110	10.5	4	0.0	475	4.5	0	0.0	185	1.7
Prescott, AZ	4	0.1	55	1.9	0	0.0	0	0.0	34	1.2
Providence–New Bedford–Fall River, RI–MA	2,335	4.8	20	0.0	2,830	5.8	0	0.0	1,200	2.4

PART C—METROPOLITAN STATISTICAL AREA TABLES

C-12 Production Operative Workers, by Metropolitan Statistical Area, Sex, Race, and Hispanic or Latino Origin, 2006–2010—Continued

Metropolitan Statistical Area	Total who worked in the last 5 years	Male Number	Male Percent	Female Number	Female Percent	Hispanic or Latino Number	Hispanic or Latino Percent	White alone, not Hispanic or Latino Number	White alone, not Hispanic or Latino Percent
Provo–Orem, UT	10,545	7,150	67.8	3,395	32.2	3,265	31.0	6,830	64.8
Pueblo, CO	2,830	2,250	79.5	580	20.5	1,500	53.0	1,165	41.2
Punta Gorda, FL	1,990	1,420	71.4	570	28.6	195	9.8	1,620	81.4
Racine, WI	9,775	6,515	66.6	3,260	33.4	1,590	16.3	6,805	69.6
Raleigh–Cary, NC	17,455	11,285	64.7	6,170	35.3	2,910	16.7	7,150	41.0
Rapid City, SD	2,400	1,435	59.8	965	40.2	45	1.9	1,880	78.3
Reading, PA	19,040	12,755	67.0	6,285	33.0	5,185	27.2	12,785	67.1
Redding, CA	2,265	1,620	71.5	645	28.5	235	10.4	1,840	81.2
Reno–Sparks, NV	7,740	5,560	71.8	2,180	28.2	3,070	39.7	3,830	49.5
Richmond, VA	25,055	18,245	72.8	6,810	27.2	1,570	6.3	11,175	44.6
Riverside–San Bernardino–Ontario, CA	92,335	62,600	67.8	29,730	32.2	62,770	68.0	19,350	21.0
Roanoke, VA	10,285	6,910	67.2	3,375	32.8	545	5.3	7,125	69.3
Rochester, MN	5,255	3,710	70.6	1,540	29.3	435	8.3	3,920	74.6
Rochester, NY	29,345	19,500	66.5	9,850	33.6	2,055	7.0	22,620	77.1
Rockford, IL	18,050	12,925	71.6	5,125	28.4	4,450	24.7	10,915	60.5
Rocky Mount, NC	6,910	3,555	51.4	3,360	48.6	645	9.3	1,895	27.4
Rome, GA	3,630	2,405	66.3	1,225	33.7	765	21.1	2,215	61.0
Sacramento–Arden-Arcade–Roseville, CA	28,175	20,320	72.1	7,860	27.9	8,615	30.6	11,615	41.2
Saginaw–Saginaw Township North, MI	6,730	5,040	74.9	1,690	25.1	675	10.0	4,775	71.0
St. Cloud, MN	7,840	5,480	69.9	2,360	30.1	340	4.3	6,910	88.1
St. George, UT	1,845	1,265	68.6	580	31.4	365	19.8	1,485	80.5
St. Joseph, MO–KS	5,060	3,940	77.9	1,120	22.1	545	10.8	4,145	81.9
St. Louis, MO–IL	69,095	48,360	70.0	20,735	30.0	2,360	3.4	50,925	73.7
Salem, OR	10,475	6,990	66.7	3,485	33.3	4,470	42.7	5,305	50.6
Salinas, CA	8,095	5,300	65.5	2,795	34.5	5,890	72.8	1,055	13.0
Salisbury, MD	2,990	1,700	56.9	1,290	43.1	150	5.0	1,110	37.1
Salt Lake City, UT	27,015	17,665	65.4	9,350	34.6	8,065	29.9	13,955	51.7
San Angelo, TX	2,495	1,725	69.1	765	30.7	1,385	55.5	985	39.5
San Antonio–New Braunfels, TX	34,600	24,505	70.8	10,095	29.2	24,735	71.5	7,740	22.4
San Diego–Carlsbad–San Marcos, CA	48,165	32,845	68.2	15,320	31.8	23,005	47.8	13,225	27.5
Sandusky, OH	3,490	2,360	67.6	1,125	32.2	155	4.4	2,850	81.7
San Francisco–Oakland–Fremont, CA	60,985	40,180	65.9	20,805	34.1	22,405	36.7	14,595	23.9
San Jose–Sunnyvale–Santa Clara, CA	37,315	23,470	62.9	13,845	37.1	14,910	40.0	5,375	14.4
San Luis Obispo–Paso Robles, CA	3,535	2,475	70.0	1,065	30.1	1,300	36.8	2,005	56.7
Santa Barbara–Santa Maria–Goleta, CA	6,200	4,150	66.9	2,050	33.1	3,690	59.5	1,740	28.1
Santa Cruz–Watsonville, CA	4,190	2,590	61.8	1,600	38.2	2,550	60.9	1,445	34.5
Santa Fe, NM	1,450	1,005	69.3	445	30.7	955	65.9	470	32.4
Santa Rosa–Petaluma, CA	9,875	6,645	67.3	3,230	32.7	4,550	46.1	4,510	45.7
Savannah, GA	6,570	5,040	76.7	1,530	23.3	345	5.3	3,280	49.9
Scranton–Wilkes-Barre, PA	18,805	13,280	70.6	5,530	29.4	1,895	10.1	16,365	87.0
Seattle–Tacoma–Bellevue, WA	62,980	44,000	69.9	18,980	30.1	7,145	11.3	36,390	57.8
Sebastian–Vero Beach, FL	1,960	1,030	52.6	930	47.4	395	20.2	1,140	58.2
Sheboygan, WI	8,600	5,740	66.7	2,860	33.3	610	7.1	6,925	80.5
Sherman–Denison, TX	4,360	3,105	71.2	1,255	28.8	755	17.3	2,925	67.1
Shreveport–Bossier City, LA	8,060	5,455	67.7	2,605	32.3	225	2.8	3,700	45.9
Sioux City, IA–NE–SD	8,395	5,435	64.7	2,960	35.3	3,345	39.8	3,730	44.4
Sioux Falls, SD	7,855	5,370	68.4	2,485	31.6	910	11.6	5,515	70.2
South Bend–Mishawaka, IN–MI	14,195	9,635	67.9	4,560	32.1	1,550	10.9	10,555	74.4
Spartanburg, SC	13,310	8,990	67.5	4,320	32.5	1,090	8.2	7,185	54.0
Spokane, WA	9,460	7,370	77.9	2,085	22.0	490	5.2	7,870	83.2
Springfield, IL	3,215	2,250	70.0	965	30.0	155	4.8	2,540	79.0
Springfield, MA	20,470	14,315	69.9	6,155	30.1	3,725	18.2	14,680	71.7
Springfield, MO	11,340	8,145	71.8	3,200	28.2	415	3.7	10,205	90.0
Springfield, OH	6,120	4,295	70.2	1,825	29.8	190	3.1	5,305	86.7
State College, PA	3,115	2,370	76.1	745	23.9	45	1.4	2,830	90.9

C-12 **Production Operative Workers, by Metropolitan Statistical Area, Sex, Race, and Hispanic or Latino Origin, 2006–2010**—*Continued*

Metropolitan Statistical Area	Black alone, not Hispanic or Latino Number	Percent	American Indian and Alaska Native alone, not Hispanic or Latino Number	Percent	Asian alone, not Hispanic or Latino Number	Percent	Native Hawaiian and Other Pacific Islander alone, not Hispanic or Latino Number	Percent	Two or more races, not Hispanic or Latino Number	Percent
Provo–Orem, UT	110	1.0	100	0.9	145	1.4	25	0.2	65	0.6
Pueblo, CO	65	2.3	30	1.1	60	2.1	0	0.0	10	0.4
Punta Gorda, FL	160	8.0	0	0.0	10	0.5	0	0.0	0	0.0
Racine, WI	1,100	11.3	25	0.3	170	1.7	10	0.1	80	0.8
Raleigh–Cary, NC	6,235	35.7	45	0.3	935	5.4	0	0.0	180	1.0
Rapid City, SD	65	2.7	280	11.7	65	2.7	0	0.0	65	2.7
Reading, PA	555	2.9	0	0.0	400	2.1	25	0.1	94	0.5
Redding, CA	0	0.0	40	1.8	110	4.9	4	0.2	30	1.3
Reno–Sparks, NV	165	2.1	115	1.5	365	4.7	15	0.2	180	2.3
Richmond, VA	10,605	42.3	110	0.4	1,145	4.6	50	0.2	400	1.6
Riverside–San Bernardino–Ontario, CA	3,635	3.9	260	0.3	4,810	5.2	385	0.4	1,120	1.2
Roanoke, VA	2,230	21.7	4	0.0	265	2.6	0	0.0	120	1.2
Rochester, MN	470	8.9	0	0.0	405	7.7	10	0.2	15	0.3
Rochester, NY	2,910	9.9	90	0.3	1,360	4.6	4	0.0	310	1.1
Rockford, IL	2,130	11.8	15	0.1	480	2.7	0	0.0	65	0.4
Rocky Mount, NC	4,295	62.2	0	0.0	10	0.1	0	0.0	60	0.9
Rome, GA	530	14.6	0	0.0	120	3.3	0	0.0	0	0.0
Sacramento–Arden-Arcade–Roseville, CA	1,270	4.5	75	0.3	5,670	20.1	265	0.9	669	2.4
Saginaw–Saginaw Township North, MI	1,120	16.6	10	0.1	35	0.5	0	0.0	114	1.7
St. Cloud, MN	330	4.2	0	0.0	245	3.1	0	0.0	18	0.2
St. George, UT	0	0.0	0	0.0	0	0.0	0	0.0	0	0.0
St. Joseph, MO–KS	270	5.3	15	0.3	45	0.9	0	0.0	35	0.7
St. Louis, MO–IL	13,700	19.8	135	0.2	1,360	2.0	15	0.0	610	0.9
Salem, OR	95	0.9	135	1.3	215	2.1	115	1.1	140	1.3
Salinas, CA	220	2.7	15	0.2	810	10.0	15	0.2	90	1.1
Salisbury, MD	1,570	52.5	0	0.0	135	4.5	0	0.0	29	1.0
Salt Lake City, UT	790	2.9	330	1.2	2,765	10.2	740	2.7	365	1.4
San Angelo, TX	65	2.6	0	0.0	55	2.2	0	0.0	4	0.2
San Antonio–New Braunfels, TX	1,255	3.6	60	0.2	635	1.8	25	0.1	144	0.4
San Diego–Carlsbad–San Marcos, CA	1,485	3.1	105	0.2	9,350	19.4	390	0.8	605	1.3
Sandusky, OH	455	13.0	0	0.0	15	0.4	0	0.0	14	0.4
San Francisco–Oakland–Fremont, CA	2,785	4.6	85	0.1	19,415	31.8	630	1.0	1,075	1.8
San Jose–Sunnyvale–Santa Clara, CA	685	1.8	45	0.1	15,885	42.6	35	0.1	375	1.0
San Luis Obispo–Paso Robles, CA	75	2.1	0	0.0	70	2.0	0	0.0	80	2.3
Santa Barbara–Santa Maria–Goleta, CA	30	0.5	0	0.0	595	9.6	0	0.0	140	2.3
Santa Cruz–Watsonville, CA	0	0.0	20	0.5	160	3.8	4	0.1	10	0.2
Santa Fe, NM	0	0.0	30	2.1	0	0.0	0	0.0	0	0.0
Santa Rosa–Petaluma, CA	75	0.8	70	0.7	590	6.0	15	0.2	65	0.7
Savannah, GA	2,560	39.0	15	0.2	350	5.3	0	0.0	20	0.3
Scranton–Wilkes-Barre, PA	285	1.5	10	0.1	230	1.2	10	0.1	24	0.1
Seattle–Tacoma–Bellevue, WA	3,425	5.4	285	0.5	13,270	21.1	835	1.3	1,635	2.6
Sebastian–Vero Beach, FL	415	21.2	0	0.0	15	0.8	0	0.0	0	0.0
Sheboygan, WI	165	1.9	65	0.8	795	9.2	0	0.0	39	0.5
Sherman–Denison, TX	445	10.2	70	1.6	45	1.0	0	0.0	120	2.8
Shreveport–Bossier City, LA	3,910	48.5	90	1.1	40	0.5	0	0.0	95	1.2
Sioux City, IA–NE–SD	310	3.7	50	0.6	910	10.8	0	0.0	50	0.6
Sioux Falls, SD	715	9.1	185	2.4	370	4.7	0	0.0	155	2.0
South Bend–Mishawaka, IN–MI	1,435	10.1	65	0.5	295	2.1	35	0.2	264	1.9
Spartanburg, SC	4,195	31.5	35	0.3	640	4.8	10	0.1	160	1.2
Spokane, WA	125	1.3	100	1.1	530	5.6	70	0.7	275	2.9
Springfield, IL	500	15.6	0	0.0	20	0.6	0	0.0	0	0.0
Springfield, MA	1,025	5.0	0	0.0	780	3.8	0	0.0	260	1.3
Springfield, MO	275	2.4	100	0.9	170	1.5	25	0.2	165	1.5
Springfield, OH	490	8.0	10	0.2	45	0.7	0	0.0	85	1.4
State College, PA	25	0.8	0	0.0	200	6.4	0	0.0	20	0.6

C-12 Production Operative Workers, by Metropolitan Statistical Area, Sex, Race, and Hispanic or Latino Origin, 2006–2010—Continued

Metropolitan Statistical Area	Total who worked in the last 5 years	Male Number	Male Percent	Female Number	Female Percent	Hispanic or Latino Number	Hispanic or Latino Percent	White alone, not Hispanic or Latino Number	White alone, not Hispanic or Latino Percent
Steubenville–Weirton, OH–WV	3,660	3,070	83.9	590	16.1	20	0.5	3,545	96.9
Stockton, CA	18,275	12,370	67.7	5,910	32.3	9,605	52.6	3,755	20.5
Sumter, SC	4,725	2,560	54.2	2,165	45.8	65	1.4	1,570	33.2
Syracuse, NY	15,985	11,235	70.3	4,750	29.7	660	4.1	13,460	84.2
Tallahassee, FL	3,335	2,385	71.5	945	28.3	245	7.3	1,600	48.0
Tampa–St. Petersburg–Clearwater, FL	43,255	28,660	66.3	14,595	33.7	9,175	21.2	24,510	56.7
Terre Haute, IN	7,185	5,485	76.3	1,700	23.7	125	1.7	6,700	93.2
Texarkana, TX–Texarkana, AR	4,175	3,310	79.3	860	20.6	310	7.4	2,580	61.8
Toledo, OH	25,255	16,995	67.3	8,260	32.7	2,540	10.1	18,330	72.6
Topeka, KS	6,095	4,830	79.2	1,265	20.8	690	11.3	4,750	77.9
Trenton–Ewing, NJ	6,270	4,235	67.5	2,035	32.5	2,260	36.0	2,000	31.9
Tucson, AZ	12,895	8,815	68.4	4,075	31.6	6,630	51.4	4,960	38.5
Tulsa, OK	27,325	21,695	79.4	5,630	20.6	3,355	12.3	16,790	61.4
Tuscaloosa, AL	7,585	5,315	70.1	2,270	29.9	290	3.8	3,980	52.5
Tyler, TX	6,490	4,375	67.4	2,115	32.6	2,025	31.2	2,395	36.9
Utica–Rome, NY	8,535	6,240	73.1	2,290	26.8	310	3.6	7,635	89.5
Valdosta, GA	3,120	2,095	67.1	1,025	32.9	110	3.5	1,330	42.6
Vallejo–Fairfield, CA	7,810	5,545	71.0	2,265	29.0	2,930	37.5	2,360	30.2
Victoria, TX	4,075	3,465	85.0	605	14.8	2,305	56.6	1,460	35.8
Vineland–Millville–Bridgeton, NJ	5,555	3,905	70.3	1,650	29.7	2,560	46.1	2,020	36.4
Virginia Beach–Norfolk–Newport News, VA–NC	30,755	21,250	69.1	9,505	30.9	1,170	3.8	14,165	46.1
Visalia–Porterville, CA	11,320	7,005	61.9	4,315	38.1	8,190	72.3	2,300	20.3
Waco, TX	6,940	4,985	71.8	1,955	28.2	2,785	40.1	2,865	41.3
Warner Robins, GA	2,815	1,905	67.7	910	32.3	250	8.9	1,400	49.7
Washington–Arlington–Alexandria, DC–VA–MD–WV	42,855	28,055	65.5	14,795	34.5	10,065	23.5	16,430	38.3
Waterloo–Cedar Falls, IA	7,640	5,395	70.6	2,245	29.4	560	7.3	6,110	80.0
Wausau, WI	8,530	6,275	73.6	2,255	26.4	320	3.8	7,175	84.1
Wenatchee–East Wenatchee, WA	2,520	1,480	58.7	1,040	41.3	1,140	45.2	1,325	52.6
Wheeling, WV–OH	3,045	2,500	82.1	545	17.9	10	0.3	2,900	95.2
Wichita, KS	24,370	17,120	70.3	7,245	29.7	3,760	15.4	15,645	64.2
Wichita Falls, TX	4,450	3,135	70.4	1,310	29.4	860	19.3	2,800	62.9
Williamsport, PA	5,115	3,555	69.5	1,560	30.5	70	1.4	4,800	93.8
Wilmington, NC	6,610	4,380	66.3	2,230	33.7	300	4.5	4,095	62.0
Winchester, VA–WV	3,625	2,445	67.4	1,180	32.6	580	16.0	2,815	77.7
Winston–Salem, NC	15,170	9,640	63.5	5,530	36.5	2,735	18.0	8,615	56.8
Worcester, MA	21,145	15,165	71.7	5,980	28.3	3,875	18.3	14,840	70.2
Yakima, WA	7,935	4,715	59.4	3,220	40.6	5,085	64.1	2,185	27.5
York–Hanover, PA	18,820	12,910	68.6	5,910	31.4	1,555	8.3	15,995	85.0
Youngstown–Warren–Boardman, OH–PA	21,910	16,155	73.7	5,755	26.3	480	2.2	18,605	84.9
Yuba City, CA	3,370	2,355	69.9	1,015	30.1	1,135	33.7	1,560	46.3
Yuma, AZ	3,085	1,945	63.0	1,140	37.0	2,635	85.4	380	12.3

C-12 **Production Operative Workers, by Metropolitan Statistical Area, Sex, Race, and Hispanic or Latino Origin, 2006–2010**—*Continued*

Metropolitan Statistical Area	Black alone, not Hispanic or Latino Number	Percent	American Indian and Alaska Native alone, not Hispanic or Latino Number	Percent	Asian alone, not Hispanic or Latino Number	Percent	Native Hawaiian and Other Pacific Islander alone, not Hispanic or Latino Number	Percent	Two or more races, not Hispanic or Latino Number	Percent
Steubenville–Weirton, OH–WV	55	1.5	0	0.0	15	0.4	0	0.0	20	0.5
Stockton, CA	795	4.4	4	0.0	3,720	20.4	30	0.2	365	2.0
Sumter, SC	2,975	63.0	25	0.5	80	1.7	0	0.0	15	0.3
Syracuse, NY	1,060	6.6	65	0.4	565	3.5	55	0.3	120	0.8
Tallahassee, FL	1,365	40.9	0	0.0	125	3.7	0	0.0	0	0.0
Tampa–St. Petersburg–Clearwater, FL	5,680	13.1	50	0.1	3,360	7.8	80	0.2	410	0.9
Terre Haute, IN	270	3.8	15	0.2	0	0.0	10	0.1	70	1.0
Texarkana, TX–Texarkana, AR	1,165	27.9	60	1.4	0	0.0	0	0.0	55	1.3
Toledo, OH	3,720	14.7	90	0.4	400	1.6	0	0.0	174	0.7
Topeka, KS	510	8.4	45	0.7	25	0.4	0	0.0	80	1.3
Trenton–Ewing, NJ	1,550	24.7	65	1.0	365	5.8	0	0.0	35	0.6
Tucson, AZ	340	2.6	425	3.3	465	3.6	15	0.1	60	0.5
Tulsa, OK	2,445	8.9	1,925	7.0	1,115	4.1	0	0.0	1,695	6.2
Tuscaloosa, AL	3,245	42.8	40	0.5	35	0.5	0	0.0	0	0.0
Tyler, TX	2,000	30.8	0	0.0	25	0.4	0	0.0	45	0.7
Utica–Rome, NY	180	2.1	4	0.0	260	3.0	0	0.0	150	1.8
Valdosta, GA	1,640	52.6	0	0.0	20	0.6	0	0.0	15	0.5
Vallejo–Fairfield, CA	690	8.8	20	0.3	1,315	16.8	150	1.9	350	4.5
Victoria, TX	290	7.1	0	0.0	15	0.4	0	0.0	4	0.1
Vineland–Millville–Bridgeton, NJ	825	14.9	45	0.8	45	0.8	0	0.0	64	1.2
Virginia Beach–Norfolk–Newport News, VA–NC	12,620	41.0	80	0.3	2,140	7.0	0	0.0	575	1.9
Visalia–Porterville, CA	50	0.4	0	0.0	655	5.8	20	0.2	105	0.9
Waco, TX	1,170	16.9	25	0.4	70	1.0	0	0.0	30	0.4
Warner Robins, GA	1,045	37.1	30	1.1	30	1.1	0	0.0	59	2.1
Washington–Arlington–Alexandria, DC–VA–MD–WV	10,350	24.2	145	0.3	5,180	12.1	50	0.1	635	1.5
Waterloo–Cedar Falls, IA	725	9.5	0	0.0	125	1.6	20	0.3	100	1.3
Wausau, WI	20	0.2	4	0.0	930	10.9	0	0.0	78	0.9
Wenatchee–East Wenatchee, WA	0	0.0	20	0.8	0	0.0	0	0.0	35	1.4
Wheeling, WV–OH	80	2.6	0	0.0	35	1.1	0	0.0	14	0.5
Wichita, KS	1,795	7.4	170	0.7	2,510	10.3	4	0.0	490	2.0
Wichita Falls, TX	395	8.9	25	0.6	300	6.7	0	0.0	70	1.6
Williamsport, PA	180	3.5	30	0.6	25	0.5	0	0.0	8	0.2
Wilmington, NC	2,045	30.9	20	0.3	120	1.8	0	0.0	29	0.4
Winchester, VA–WV	50	1.4	0	0.0	30	0.8	0	0.0	150	4.1
Winston–Salem, NC	3,425	22.6	15	0.1	195	1.3	70	0.5	114	0.8
Worcester, MA	705	3.3	10	0.0	1,425	6.7	0	0.0	295	1.4
Yakima, WA	55	0.7	250	3.2	260	3.3	10	0.1	90	1.1
York–Hanover, PA	660	3.5	10	0.1	360	1.9	0	0.0	240	1.3
Youngstown–Warren–Boardman, OH–PA	2,605	11.9	40	0.2	100	0.5	0	0.0	89	0.4
Yuba City, CA	0	0.0	10	0.3	580	17.2	0	0.0	90	2.7
Yuma, AZ	15	0.5	25	0.8	10	0.3	0	0.0	15	0.5

C-13 Transportation and Material Moving Operative Workers, by Metropolitan Statistical Area, Sex, Race, and Hispanic or Latino Origin, 2006–2010

Metropolitan Statistical Area	Total who worked in the last 5 years	Male Number	Male Percent	Female Number	Female Percent	Hispanic or Latino Number	Hispanic or Latino Percent	White alone, not Hispanic or Latino Number	White alone, not Hispanic or Latino Percent
Abilene, TX	2,830	2,485	87.8	345	12.2	550	19.4	2,125	75.1
Akron, OH	15,955	12,440	78.0	3,515	22.0	110	0.7	13,340	83.6
Albany, GA	5,020	3,665	73.0	1,355	27.0	40	0.8	1,635	32.6
Albany–Schenectady–Troy, NY	17,365	14,955	86.1	2,410	13.9	870	5.0	14,610	84.1
Albuquerque, NM	15,330	12,810	83.6	2,520	16.4	7,700	50.2	6,140	40.1
Alexandria, LA	3,535	3,010	85.1	525	14.9	10	0.3	2,405	68.0
Allentown–Bethlehem–Easton, PA–NJ	22,895	18,555	81.0	4,340	19.0	4,075	17.8	17,220	75.2
Altoona, PA	3,870	3,280	84.8	590	15.2	10	0.3	3,805	98.3
Amarillo, TX	6,250	5,430	86.9	820	13.1	1,320	21.1	4,335	69.4
Ames, IA	1,855	1,645	88.7	210	11.3	50	2.7	1,740	93.8
Anchorage, AK	7,260	6,205	85.5	1,060	14.6	420	5.8	5,130	70.7
Anderson, IN	3,725	3,040	81.6	690	18.5	150	4.0	3,240	87.0
Anderson, SC	5,095	3,940	77.3	1,155	22.7	145	2.8	3,700	72.6
Ann Arbor, MI	5,400	4,330	80.2	1,065	19.7	75	1.4	3,745	69.4
Anniston–Oxford, AL	2,825	2,095	74.2	730	25.8	65	2.3	2,125	75.2
Appleton, WI	6,545	5,140	78.5	1,405	21.5	150	2.3	6,125	93.6
Asheville, NC	8,370	6,920	82.7	1,450	17.3	465	5.6	7,235	86.4
Athens–Clarke County, GA	3,325	2,885	86.8	440	13.2	260	7.8	1,680	50.5
Atlanta–Sandy Springs–Marietta, GA	123,030	97,815	79.5	25,215	20.5	10,275	8.4	48,180	39.2
Atlantic City–Hammonton, NJ	5,470	4,250	77.7	1,215	22.2	910	16.6	3,060	55.9
Auburn–Opelika, AL	3,060	2,360	77.1	705	23.0	74	2.4	1,980	64.7
Augusta–Richmond County, GA–SC	12,735	9,970	78.3	2,770	21.8	310	2.4	6,190	48.6
Austin–Round Rock–San Marcos, TX	25,985	22,220	85.5	3,770	14.5	9,580	36.9	11,330	43.6
Bakersfield–Delano, CA	20,685	16,995	82.2	3,690	17.8	12,040	58.2	6,370	30.8
Baltimore–Towson, MD	55,185	46,115	83.6	9,070	16.4	1,825	3.3	27,470	49.8
Bangor, ME	3,575	3,240	90.6	335	9.4	0	0.0	3,510	98.2
Barnstable Town, MA	3,055	2,570	84.1	485	15.9	0	0.0	2,760	90.3
Baton Rouge, LA	17,725	14,550	82.1	3,170	17.9	190	1.1	8,320	46.9
Battle Creek, MI	3,875	2,995	77.3	880	22.7	170	4.4	3,070	79.2
Bay City, MI	2,560	2,180	85.2	380	14.8	95	3.7	2,410	94.1
Beaumont–Port Arthur, TX	8,720	7,085	81.3	1,635	18.8	775	8.9	4,810	55.2
Bellingham, WA	4,030	3,400	84.4	625	15.5	180	4.5	3,560	88.3
Bend, OR	2,460	1,970	80.1	490	19.9	255	10.4	2,075	84.3
Billings, MT	3,520	3,035	86.2	480	13.6	100	2.8	3,245	92.2
Binghamton, NY	6,530	5,440	83.3	1,090	16.7	100	1.5	5,850	89.6
Birmingham–Hoover, AL	25,545	21,745	85.1	3,800	14.9	445	1.7	15,505	60.7
Bismarck, ND	2,590	2,325	89.8	265	10.2	0	0.0	2,420	93.4
Blacksburg–Christiansburg–Radford, VA	2,705	2,225	82.3	485	17.9	10	0.4	2,605	96.3
Bloomington, IN	4,875	3,890	79.8	985	20.2	195	4.0	4,420	90.7
Bloomington–Normal, IL	3,040	2,620	86.2	420	13.8	180	5.9	2,640	86.8
Boise City–Nampa, ID	12,965	10,570	81.5	2,395	18.5	1,435	11.1	11,055	85.3
Boston–Cambridge–Quincy, MA–NH	74,860	61,075	81.6	13,785	18.4	8,940	11.9	51,715	69.1
Boulder, CO	3,525	2,815	79.9	710	20.1	715	20.3	2,605	73.9
Bowling Green, KY	3,310	2,690	81.3	625	18.9	110	3.3	2,715	82.0
Bremerton–Silverdale, WA	4,430	3,430	77.4	1,005	22.7	225	5.1	3,770	85.1
Bridgeport–Stamford–Norwalk, CT	13,365	10,355	77.5	3,005	22.5	3,135	23.5	6,585	49.3
Brownsville–Harlingen, TX	8,040	6,915	86.0	1,125	14.0	7,395	92.0	610	7.6
Brunswick, GA	2,805	2,180	77.7	625	22.3	130	4.6	2,035	72.5
Buffalo–Niagara Falls, NY	23,610	18,855	79.9	4,755	20.1	1,025	4.3	18,435	78.1
Burlington, NC	4,035	3,165	78.4	875	21.7	920	22.8	2,150	53.3
Burlington–South Burlington, VT	3,685	3,020	82.0	665	18.0	75	2.0	3,430	93.1
Canton–Massillon, OH	11,060	8,750	79.1	2,310	20.9	74	0.7	9,665	87.4
Cape Coral–Fort Myers, FL	11,160	9,390	84.1	1,765	15.8	2,880	25.8	6,800	60.9
Cape Girardeau–Jackson, MO–IL	2,415	2,160	89.4	255	10.6	40	1.7	2,160	89.4
Carson City, NV	855	705	82.5	150	17.5	225	26.3	555	64.9

C-13 Transportation and Material Moving Operative Workers, by Metropolitan Statistical Area, Sex, Race, and Hispanic or Latino Origin, 2006–2010—*Continued*

Metropolitan Statistical Area	Black alone, not Hispanic or Latino Number	Percent	American Indian and Alaska Native alone, not Hispanic or Latino Number	Percent	Asian alone, not Hispanic or Latino Number	Percent	Native Hawaiian and Other Pacific Islander alone, not Hispanic or Latino Number	Percent	Two or more races, not Hispanic or Latino Number	Percent
Abilene, TX	115	4.1	0	0.0	0	0.0	0	0.0	39	1.4
Akron, OH	2,145	13.4	55	0.3	140	0.9	0	0.0	165	1.0
Albany, GA	3,305	65.8	0	0.0	35	0.7	0	0.0	4	0.1
Albany–Schenectady–Troy, NY	1,365	7.9	20	0.1	200	1.2	10	0.1	285	1.6
Albuquerque, NM	520	3.4	555	3.6	255	1.7	0	0.0	160	1.0
Alexandria, LA	1,045	29.6	20	0.6	25	0.7	0	0.0	30	0.8
Allentown–Bethlehem–Easton, PA–NJ	1,035	4.5	0	0.0	410	1.8	0	0.0	160	0.7
Altoona, PA	45	1.2	0	0.0	0	0.0	0	0.0	10	0.3
Amarillo, TX	425	6.8	25	0.4	55	0.9	4	0.1	90	1.4
Ames, IA	25	1.3	4	0.2	20	1.1	0	0.0	20	1.1
Anchorage, AK	420	5.8	410	5.6	445	6.1	165	2.3	269	3.7
Anderson, IN	265	7.1	0	0.0	0	0.0	0	0.0	69	1.9
Anderson, SC	1,220	23.9	0	0.0	0	0.0	0	0.0	25	0.5
Ann Arbor, MI	1,265	23.4	35	0.6	155	2.9	0	0.0	120	2.2
Anniston–Oxford, AL	570	20.2	40	1.4	0	0.0	0	0.0	25	0.9
Appleton, WI	0	0.0	25	0.4	205	3.1	0	0.0	40	0.6
Asheville, NC	515	6.2	10	0.1	45	0.5	0	0.0	90	1.1
Athens–Clarke County, GA	1,320	39.7	0	0.0	50	1.5	0	0.0	15	0.5
Atlanta–Sandy Springs–Marietta, GA	59,945	48.7	95	0.1	3,000	2.4	175	0.1	1,365	1.1
Atlantic City–Hammonton, NJ	1,065	19.5	10	0.2	330	6.0	0	0.0	90	1.6
Auburn–Opelika, AL	940	30.7	15	0.5	4	0.1	0	0.0	45	1.5
Augusta–Richmond County, GA–SC	6,025	47.3	55	0.4	80	0.6	30	0.2	55	0.4
Austin–Round Rock–San Marcos, TX	4,175	16.1	65	0.3	490	1.9	40	0.2	305	1.2
Bakersfield–Delano, CA	855	4.1	125	0.6	865	4.2	4	0.0	425	2.1
Baltimore–Towson, MD	22,915	41.5	185	0.3	1,930	3.5	0	0.0	865	1.6
Bangor, ME	0	0.0	40	1.1	0	0.0	0	0.0	30	0.8
Barnstable Town, MA	105	3.4	90	2.9	0	0.0	0	0.0	105	3.4
Baton Rouge, LA	8,915	50.3	30	0.2	75	0.4	0	0.0	194	1.1
Battle Creek, MI	575	14.8	10	0.3	4	0.1	10	0.3	34	0.9
Bay City, MI	35	1.4	10	0.4	0	0.0	0	0.0	15	0.6
Beaumont–Port Arthur, TX	2,960	33.9	25	0.3	145	1.7	0	0.0	4	0.0
Bellingham, WA	40	1.0	70	1.7	110	2.7	35	0.9	40	1.0
Bend, OR	60	2.4	15	0.6	20	0.8	0	0.0	35	1.4
Billings, MT	20	0.6	125	3.6	0	0.0	0	0.0	29	0.8
Binghamton, NY	280	4.3	0	0.0	120	1.8	0	0.0	170	2.6
Birmingham–Hoover, AL	9,270	36.3	65	0.3	110	0.4	0	0.0	159	0.6
Bismarck, ND	0	0.0	120	4.6	0	0.0	0	0.0	50	1.9
Blacksburg–Christiansburg–Radford, VA	45	1.7	15	0.6	25	0.9	0	0.0	0	0.0
Bloomington, IN	100	2.1	10	0.2	60	1.2	0	0.0	90	1.8
Bloomington–Normal, IL	155	5.1	0	0.0	20	0.7	0	0.0	45	1.5
Boise City–Nampa, ID	105	0.8	55	0.4	60	0.5	0	0.0	250	1.9
Boston–Cambridge–Quincy, MA–NH	9,065	12.1	125	0.2	3,460	4.6	15	0.0	1,535	2.1
Boulder, CO	50	1.4	20	0.6	90	2.6	0	0.0	45	1.3
Bowling Green, KY	280	8.5	30	0.9	160	4.8	4	0.1	10	0.3
Bremerton–Silverdale, WA	195	4.4	45	1.0	45	1.0	40	0.9	114	2.6
Bridgeport–Stamford–Norwalk, CT	2,810	21.0	35	0.3	570	4.3	10	0.1	225	1.7
Brownsville–Harlingen, TX	0	0.0	0	0.0	40	0.5	0	0.0	0	0.0
Brunswick, GA	545	19.4	0	0.0	20	0.7	0	0.0	75	2.7
Buffalo–Niagara Falls, NY	3,480	14.7	150	0.6	250	1.1	0	0.0	280	1.2
Burlington, NC	870	21.6	30	0.7	45	1.1	0	0.0	20	0.5
Burlington–South Burlington, VT	35	0.9	50	1.4	60	1.6	0	0.0	40	1.1
Canton–Massillon, OH	1,155	10.4	0	0.0	30	0.3	0	0.0	135	1.2
Cape Coral–Fort Myers, FL	1,375	12.3	0	0.0	45	0.4	0	0.0	55	0.5
Cape Girardeau–Jackson, MO–IL	175	7.2	0	0.0	25	1.0	0	0.0	15	0.6
Carson City, NV	0	0.0	10	1.2	0	0.0	45	5.3	25	2.9

C-13 Transportation and Material Moving Operative Workers, by Metropolitan Statistical Area, Sex, Race, and Hispanic or Latino Origin, 2006–2010—Continued

Metropolitan Statistical Area	Total who worked in the last 5 years	Male Number	Male Percent	Female Number	Female Percent	Hispanic or Latino Number	Hispanic or Latino Percent	White alone, not Hispanic or Latino Number	White alone, not Hispanic or Latino Percent
Casper, WY	2,015	1,745	86.6	270	13.4	74	3.7	1,860	92.3
Cedar Rapids, IA	5,855	4,930	84.2	930	15.9	145	2.5	5,525	94.4
Champaign–Urbana, IL	4,590	3,935	85.7	655	14.3	145	3.2	3,785	82.5
Charleston, WV	7,105	6,550	92.2	560	7.9	25	0.4	6,750	95.0
Charleston–North Charleston–Summerville, SC	15,090	11,915	79.0	3,175	21.0	525	3.5	7,340	48.6
Charlotte–Gastonia–Rock Hill, NC–SC	41,920	32,495	77.5	9,425	22.5	3,930	9.4	19,830	47.3
Charlottesville, VA	3,100	2,350	75.8	750	24.2	75	2.4	2,095	67.6
Chattanooga, TN–GA	13,815	10,865	78.6	2,945	21.3	285	2.1	10,585	76.6
Cheyenne, WY	2,505	2,255	90.0	250	10.0	210	8.4	2,240	89.4
Chicago–Joliet–Naperville, IL–IN–WI	246,295	196,415	79.7	49,885	20.3	70,810	28.8	111,720	45.4
Chico, CA	4,105	3,330	81.1	775	18.9	660	16.1	3,015	73.4
Cincinnati–Middletown, OH–KY–IN	51,650	41,535	80.4	10,115	19.6	1,065	2.1	41,730	80.8
Clarksville, TN–KY	6,410	4,945	77.1	1,465	22.9	320	5.0	4,410	68.8
Cleveland, TN	3,640	2,815	77.3	825	22.7	95	2.6	3,350	92.0
Cleveland–Elyria–Mentor, OH	47,215	37,250	78.9	9,965	21.1	2,345	5.0	32,975	69.8
Coeur d'Alene, ID	2,595	2,040	78.6	555	21.4	55	2.1	2,375	91.5
College Station–Bryan, TX	3,920	3,400	86.7	525	13.4	910	23.2	2,485	63.4
Colorado Springs, CO	10,090	8,390	83.2	1,700	16.8	1,630	16.2	7,120	70.6
Columbia, MO	2,875	2,270	79.0	605	21.0	40	1.4	2,515	87.5
Columbia, SC	15,635	12,070	77.2	3,565	22.8	545	3.5	7,000	44.8
Columbus, GA–AL	6,510	5,240	80.5	1,270	19.5	295	4.5	2,370	36.4
Columbus, IN	2,020	1,645	81.4	370	18.3	215	10.6	1,750	86.6
Columbus, OH	44,005	34,985	79.5	9,020	20.5	1,250	2.8	32,625	74.1
Corpus Christi, TX	8,710	7,670	88.1	1,040	11.9	5,740	65.9	2,550	29.3
Corvallis, OR	1,110	860	77.5	250	22.5	80	7.2	945	85.1
Crestview–Fort Walton Beach–Destin, FL	2,635	2,170	82.4	465	17.6	230	8.7	2,025	76.9
Cumberland, MD–WV	2,530	2,200	87.0	330	13.0	20	0.8	2,390	94.5
Dallas–Fort Worth–Arlington, TX	142,450	115,765	81.3	26,685	18.7	44,160	31.0	59,515	41.8
Dalton, GA	6,745	5,135	76.1	1,610	23.9	1,515	22.5	4,925	73.0
Danville, IL	2,810	2,185	77.8	620	22.1	100	3.6	2,425	86.3
Danville, VA	3,400	2,535	74.6	860	25.3	15	0.4	1,635	48.1
Davenport–Moline–Rock Island, IA–IL	11,595	9,645	83.2	1,945	16.8	1,030	8.9	9,380	80.9
Dayton, OH	20,800	16,245	78.1	4,555	21.9	280	1.3	16,835	80.9
Decatur, AL	4,470	3,680	82.3	790	17.7	335	7.5	3,545	79.3
Decatur, IL	2,910	2,385	82.0	525	18.0	30	1.0	2,410	82.8
Deltona–Daytona Beach–Ormond Beach, FL	8,505	7,090	83.4	1,410	16.6	755	8.9	6,425	75.5
Denver–Aurora–Broomfield, CO	48,855	41,695	85.3	7,160	14.7	12,645	25.9	29,495	60.4
Des Moines–West Des Moines, IA	11,725	10,030	85.5	1,695	14.5	915	7.8	9,975	85.1
Detroit–Warren–Livonia, MI	95,000	75,150	79.1	19,850	20.9	3,700	3.9	63,800	67.2
Dothan, AL	3,860	3,175	82.3	685	17.7	45	1.2	2,640	68.4
Dover, DE	3,940	2,880	73.1	1,060	26.9	145	3.7	2,635	66.9
Dubuque, IA	2,380	2,030	85.3	350	14.7	15	0.6	2,235	93.9
Duluth, MN–WI	6,940	6,010	86.6	930	13.4	245	3.5	6,375	91.9
Durham–Chapel Hill, NC	8,045	5,880	73.1	2,165	26.9	395	4.9	3,200	39.8
Eau Claire, WI	5,130	4,130	80.5	1,000	19.5	55	1.1	4,895	95.4
El Centro, CA	3,875	3,130	80.8	745	19.2	3,535	91.2	280	7.2
Elizabethtown, KY	2,900	2,415	83.3	485	16.7	55	1.9	2,610	90.0
Elkhart–Goshen, IN	6,670	5,040	75.6	1,630	24.4	985	14.8	5,120	76.8
Elmira, NY	1,980	1,620	81.8	360	18.2	25	1.3	1,775	89.6
El Paso, TX	21,250	17,805	83.8	3,445	16.2	18,530	87.2	2,030	9.6
Erie, PA	6,325	5,200	82.2	1,125	17.8	190	3.0	5,470	86.5
Eugene–Springfield, OR	7,185	6,030	83.9	1,155	16.1	480	6.7	6,315	87.9
Evansville, IN–KY	10,685	8,305	77.7	2,380	22.3	160	1.5	9,560	89.5
Fairbanks, AK	1,865	1,450	77.7	415	22.3	10	0.5	1,645	88.2
Fargo, ND–MN	5,450	4,865	89.3	585	10.7	130	2.4	5,150	94.5

C-13 Transportation and Material Moving Operative Workers, by Metropolitan Statistical Area, Sex, Race, and Hispanic or Latino Origin, 2006–2010—*Continued*

Metropolitan Statistical Area	Black alone, not Hispanic or Latino Number	Percent	American Indian and Alaska Native alone, not Hispanic or Latino Number	Percent	Asian alone, not Hispanic or Latino Number	Percent	Native Hawaiian and Other Pacific Islander alone, not Hispanic or Latino Number	Percent	Two or more races, not Hispanic or Latino Number	Percent
Casper, WY	0	0.0	25	1.2	0	0.0	0	0.0	54	2.7
Cedar Rapids, IA	140	2.4	0	0.0	4	0.1	0	0.0	40	0.7
Champaign–Urbana, IL	480	10.5	45	1.0	90	2.0	0	0.0	40	0.9
Charleston, WV	185	2.6	4	0.1	0	0.0	0	0.0	150	2.1
Charleston–North Charleston–Summerville, SC	6,760	44.8	175	1.2	200	1.3	0	0.0	90	0.6
Charlotte–Gastonia–Rock Hill, NC–SC	16,365	39.0	185	0.4	1,270	3.0	10	0.0	335	0.8
Charlottesville, VA	870	28.1	0	0.0	35	1.1	4	0.1	15	0.5
Chattanooga, TN–GA	2,720	19.7	15	0.1	30	0.2	0	0.0	175	1.3
Cheyenne, WY	20	0.8	10	0.4	20	0.8	0	0.0	0	0.0
Chicago–Joliet–Naperville, IL–IN–WI	52,405	21.3	230	0.1	8,575	3.5	35	0.0	2,520	1.0
Chico, CA	70	1.7	75	1.8	130	3.2	4	0.1	145	3.5
Cincinnati–Middletown, OH–KY–IN	7,705	14.9	100	0.2	605	1.2	45	0.1	410	0.8
Clarksville, TN–KY	1,540	24.0	85	1.3	25	0.4	20	0.3	20	0.3
Cleveland, TN	140	3.8	10	0.3	0	0.0	0	0.0	40	1.1
Cleveland–Elyria–Mentor, OH	11,135	23.6	75	0.2	425	0.9	10	0.0	250	0.5
Coeur d'Alene, ID	10	0.4	80	3.1	0	0.0	25	1.0	55	2.1
College Station–Bryan, TX	460	11.7	10	0.3	30	0.8	0	0.0	20	0.5
Colorado Springs, CO	795	7.9	45	0.4	230	2.3	40	0.4	225	2.2
Columbia, MO	260	9.0	15	0.5	30	1.0	0	0.0	10	0.3
Columbia, SC	7,870	50.3	0	0.0	65	0.4	10	0.1	145	0.9
Columbus, GA–AL	3,665	56.3	0	0.0	25	0.4	0	0.0	150	2.3
Columbus, IN	0	0.0	0	0.0	50	2.5	0	0.0	0	0.0
Columbus, OH	8,750	19.9	50	0.1	740	1.7	0	0.0	590	1.3
Corpus Christi, TX	280	3.2	25	0.3	60	0.7	0	0.0	59	0.7
Corvallis, OR	25	2.3	0	0.0	35	3.2	0	0.0	25	2.3
Crestview–Fort Walton Beach–Destin, FL	290	11.0	10	0.4	20	0.8	0	0.0	60	2.3
Cumberland, MD–WV	90	3.6	10	0.4	0	0.0	0	0.0	20	0.8
Dallas–Fort Worth–Arlington, TX	32,755	23.0	455	0.3	3,610	2.5	360	0.3	1,590	1.1
Dalton, GA	235	3.5	25	0.4	0	0.0	0	0.0	50	0.7
Danville, IL	220	7.8	0	0.0	20	0.7	0	0.0	49	1.7
Danville, VA	1,725	50.7	0	0.0	0	0.0	0	0.0	20	0.6
Davenport–Moline–Rock Island, IA–IL	845	7.3	50	0.4	95	0.8	0	0.0	185	1.6
Dayton, OH	3,185	15.3	10	0.0	205	1.0	4	0.0	269	1.3
Decatur, AL	455	10.2	45	1.0	0	0.0	0	0.0	85	1.9
Decatur, IL	440	15.1	0	0.0	0	0.0	0	0.0	29	1.0
Deltona–Daytona Beach–Ormond Beach, FL	1,130	13.3	0	0.0	80	0.9	0	0.0	110	1.3
Denver–Aurora–Broomfield, CO	4,615	9.4	205	0.4	1,060	2.2	75	0.2	765	1.6
Des Moines–West Des Moines, IA	460	3.9	15	0.1	210	1.8	0	0.0	155	1.3
Detroit–Warren–Livonia, MI	24,630	25.9	250	0.3	1,430	1.5	30	0.0	1,165	1.2
Dothan, AL	1,100	28.5	10	0.3	10	0.3	0	0.0	55	1.4
Dover, DE	1,090	27.7	15	0.4	4	0.1	0	0.0	50	1.3
Dubuque, IA	20	0.8	0	0.0	25	1.1	0	0.0	85	3.6
Duluth, MN–WI	50	0.7	130	1.9	0	0.0	0	0.0	150	2.2
Durham–Chapel Hill, NC	4,200	52.2	4	0.0	130	1.6	0	0.0	110	1.4
Eau Claire, WI	0	0.0	0	0.0	95	1.9	4	0.1	75	1.5
El Centro, CA	30	0.8	20	0.5	0	0.0	0	0.0	10	0.3
Elizabethtown, KY	175	6.0	20	0.7	0	0.0	0	0.0	45	1.6
Elkhart–Goshen, IN	400	6.0	45	0.7	60	0.9	0	0.0	60	0.9
Elmira, NY	145	7.3	0	0.0	20	1.0	0	0.0	25	1.3
El Paso, TX	555	2.6	30	0.1	40	0.2	0	0.0	64	0.3
Erie, PA	460	7.3	20	0.3	135	2.1	35	0.6	19	0.3
Eugene–Springfield, OR	10	0.1	90	1.3	60	0.8	30	0.4	190	2.6
Evansville, IN–KY	715	6.7	10	0.1	155	1.5	0	0.0	89	0.8
Fairbanks, AK	60	3.2	115	6.2	0	0.0	15	0.8	20	1.1
Fargo, ND–MN	75	1.4	50	0.9	20	0.4	0	0.0	19	0.3

C-13 Transportation and Material Moving Operative Workers, by Metropolitan Statistical Area, Sex, Race, and Hispanic or Latino Origin, 2006–2010—Continued

Metropolitan Statistical Area	Total who worked in the last 5 years	Male Number	Male Percent	Female Number	Female Percent	Hispanic or Latino Number	Hispanic or Latino Percent	White alone, not Hispanic or Latino Number	White alone, not Hispanic or Latino Percent
Farmington, NM	3,530	2,930	83.0	600	17.0	720	20.4	2,000	56.7
Fayetteville, NC	7,300	5,800	79.5	1,500	20.5	455	6.2	3,125	42.8
Fayetteville–Springdale–Rogers, AR–MO	10,870	8,485	78.1	2,380	21.9	2,130	19.6	7,635	70.2
Flagstaff, AZ	2,680	2,185	81.5	495	18.5	375	14.0	1,600	59.7
Flint, MI	11,035	8,750	79.3	2,285	20.7	245	2.2	8,445	76.5
Florence, SC	5,590	4,350	77.8	1,240	22.2	120	2.1	2,725	48.7
Florence–Muscle Shoals, AL	3,715	3,115	83.8	600	16.2	100	2.7	3,095	83.3
Fond du Lac, WI	3,575	2,695	75.4	880	24.6	180	5.0	3,275	91.6
Fort Collins–Loveland, CO	4,715	4,070	86.3	640	13.6	450	9.5	4,140	87.8
Fort Smith, AR–OK	9,135	7,735	84.7	1,400	15.3	685	7.5	7,320	80.1
Fort Wayne, IN	11,545	9,265	80.3	2,280	19.7	640	5.5	9,675	83.8
Fresno, CA	23,980	18,670	77.9	5,310	22.1	14,215	59.3	5,925	24.7
Gadsden, AL	2,965	2,555	86.2	410	13.8	95	3.2	2,555	86.2
Gainesville, FL	3,285	2,715	82.6	570	17.4	295	9.0	1,805	54.9
Gainesville, GA	5,310	3,820	71.9	1,495	28.2	1,940	36.5	2,600	49.0
Glens Falls, NY	3,150	2,425	77.0	725	23.0	24	0.8	3,040	96.5
Goldsboro, NC	3,290	2,600	79.0	685	20.8	270	8.2	1,590	48.3
Grand Forks, ND–MN	2,185	1,870	85.6	315	14.4	170	7.8	1,905	87.2
Grand Junction, CO	3,625	3,255	89.8	365	10.1	320	8.8	3,225	89.0
Grand Rapids–Wyoming, MI	20,895	15,830	75.8	5,060	24.2	2,195	10.5	15,955	76.4
Great Falls, MT	1,350	1,195	88.5	155	11.5	10	0.7	1,270	94.1
Greeley, CO	6,520	5,485	84.1	1,030	15.8	1,740	26.7	4,630	71.0
Green Bay, WI	8,390	6,985	83.3	1,405	16.7	600	7.2	7,250	86.4
Greensboro–High Point, NC	20,715	15,840	76.5	4,875	23.5	1,030	5.0	11,815	57.0
Greenville, NC	4,005	3,280	81.9	725	18.1	60	1.5	1,785	44.6
Greenville–Mauldin–Easley, SC	14,005	10,265	73.3	3,740	26.7	770	5.5	8,635	61.7
Gulfport–Biloxi, MS	5,350	4,500	84.1	850	15.9	45	0.8	3,855	72.1
Hagerstown–Martinsburg, MD–WV	8,210	6,515	79.4	1,695	20.6	200	2.4	7,315	89.1
Hanford–Corcoran, CA	4,460	3,525	79.0	930	20.9	2,675	60.0	1,460	32.7
Harrisburg–Carlisle, PA	16,910	13,430	79.4	3,475	20.5	1,245	7.4	13,120	77.6
Harrisonburg, VA	3,460	2,745	79.3	715	20.7	250	7.2	3,030	87.6
Hartford–West Hartford–East Hartford, CT	23,580	18,990	80.5	4,590	19.5	3,465	14.7	15,585	66.1
Hattiesburg, MS	3,590	2,750	76.6	840	23.4	15	0.4	2,340	65.2
Hickory–Lenoir–Morganton, NC	11,790	9,385	79.6	2,405	20.4	790	6.7	9,570	81.2
Hinesville–Fort Stewart, GA	2,265	1,465	64.7	805	35.5	120	5.3	860	38.0
Holland–Grand Haven, MI	6,660	5,175	77.7	1,485	22.3	775	11.6	5,605	84.2
Honolulu, HI	16,510	14,165	85.8	2,345	14.2	1,120	6.8	1,670	10.1
Hot Springs, AR	2,005	1,760	87.8	245	12.2	75	3.7	1,655	82.5
Houma–Bayou Cane–Thibodaux, LA	7,065	5,930	83.9	1,135	16.1	145	2.1	5,230	74.0
Houston–Sugar Land–Baytown, TX	133,645	112,055	83.8	21,590	16.2	50,785	38.0	42,545	31.8
Huntington–Ashland, WV–KY–OH	6,375	5,780	90.7	595	9.3	60	0.9	6,230	97.7
Huntsville, AL	8,515	6,405	75.2	2,115	24.8	720	8.5	5,210	61.2
Idaho Falls, ID	2,890	2,475	85.6	415	14.4	545	18.9	2,260	78.2
Indianapolis–Carmel, IN	42,155	32,510	77.1	9,645	22.9	2,960	7.0	30,270	71.8
Iowa City, IA	3,365	2,720	80.8	645	19.2	355	10.5	2,760	82.0
Ithaca, NY	1,460	1,085	74.3	375	25.7	100	6.8	1,225	83.9
Jackson, MI	4,075	3,155	77.4	920	22.6	75	1.8	3,705	90.9
Jackson, MS	12,435	10,685	85.9	1,750	14.1	85	0.7	4,350	35.0
Jackson, TN	2,970	2,330	78.5	640	21.5	60	2.0	1,595	53.7
Jacksonville, FL	29,185	23,845	81.7	5,340	18.3	1,630	5.6	17,480	59.9
Jacksonville, NC	2,740	2,135	77.9	605	22.1	250	9.1	1,760	64.2
Janesville, WI	5,425	4,425	81.6	1,000	18.4	360	6.6	4,750	87.6
Jefferson City, MO	2,940	2,535	86.2	405	13.8	75	2.6	2,720	92.5
Johnson City, TN	4,135	3,450	83.4	685	16.6	35	0.8	4,020	97.2
Johnstown, PA	3,820	3,405	89.1	415	10.9	0	0.0	3,700	96.9

C-13 **Transportation and Material Moving Operative Workers, by Metropolitan Statistical Area, Sex, Race, and Hispanic or Latino Origin, 2006–2010**—*Continued*

Metropolitan Statistical Area	Black alone, not Hispanic or Latino Number	Percent	American Indian and Alaska Native alone, not Hispanic or Latino Number	Percent	Asian alone, not Hispanic or Latino Number	Percent	Native Hawaiian and Other Pacific Islander alone, not Hispanic or Latino Number	Percent	Two or more races, not Hispanic or Latino Number	Percent
Farmington, NM	0	0.0	755	21.4	20	0.6	0	0.0	25	0.7
Fayetteville, NC	3,240	44.4	165	2.3	70	1.0	20	0.3	220	3.0
Fayetteville–Springdale–Rogers, AR–MO	180	1.7	225	2.1	280	2.6	60	0.6	355	3.3
Flagstaff, AZ	55	2.1	610	22.8	15	0.6	0	0.0	24	0.9
Flint, MI	2,055	18.6	95	0.9	60	0.5	0	0.0	140	1.3
Florence, SC	2,675	47.9	10	0.2	10	0.2	0	0.0	55	1.0
Florence–Muscle Shoals, AL	470	12.7	0	0.0	0	0.0	0	0.0	55	1.5
Fond du Lac, WI	20	0.6	20	0.6	0	0.0	0	0.0	85	2.4
Fort Collins–Loveland, CO	55	1.2	35	0.7	0	0.0	0	0.0	30	0.6
Fort Smith, AR–OK	310	3.4	125	1.4	365	4.0	0	0.0	330	3.6
Fort Wayne, IN	950	8.2	55	0.5	95	0.8	0	0.0	130	1.1
Fresno, CA	1,220	5.1	100	0.4	2,025	8.4	45	0.2	450	1.9
Gadsden, AL	260	8.8	15	0.5	0	0.0	0	0.0	34	1.1
Gainesville, FL	1,045	31.8	0	0.0	75	2.3	0	0.0	60	1.8
Gainesville, GA	715	13.5	10	0.2	30	0.6	0	0.0	20	0.4
Glens Falls, NY	0	0.0	30	1.0	20	0.6	0	0.0	34	1.1
Goldsboro, NC	1,365	41.5	4	0.1	35	1.1	0	0.0	24	0.7
Grand Forks, ND–MN	25	1.1	50	2.3	25	1.1	0	0.0	10	0.5
Grand Junction, CO	30	0.8	20	0.6	25	0.7	0	0.0	4	0.1
Grand Rapids–Wyoming, MI	2,235	10.7	120	0.6	145	0.7	0	0.0	244	1.2
Great Falls, MT	30	2.2	30	2.2	0	0.0	0	0.0	10	0.7
Greeley, CO	50	0.8	30	0.5	15	0.2	0	0.0	55	0.8
Green Bay, WI	140	1.7	115	1.4	180	2.1	0	0.0	110	1.3
Greensboro–High Point, NC	7,280	35.1	75	0.4	405	2.0	0	0.0	110	0.5
Greenville, NC	2,165	54.1	0	0.0	0	0.0	0	0.0	0	0.0
Greenville–Mauldin–Easley, SC	4,355	31.1	50	0.4	100	0.7	30	0.2	60	0.4
Gulfport–Biloxi, MS	1,215	22.7	15	0.3	20	0.4	0	0.0	205	3.8
Hagerstown–Martinsburg, MD–WV	580	7.1	4	0.0	60	0.7	0	0.0	59	0.7
Hanford–Corcoran, CA	265	5.9	15	0.3	15	0.3	0	0.0	30	0.7
Harrisburg–Carlisle, PA	1,995	11.8	15	0.1	225	1.3	0	0.0	300	1.8
Harrisonburg, VA	130	3.8	0	0.0	50	1.4	0	0.0	0	0.0
Hartford–West Hartford–East Hartford, CT	3,695	15.7	20	0.1	510	2.2	0	0.0	305	1.3
Hattiesburg, MS	1,180	32.9	20	0.6	0	0.0	0	0.0	35	1.0
Hickory–Lenoir–Morganton, NC	1,150	9.8	55	0.5	225	1.9	0	0.0	0	0.0
Hinesville–Fort Stewart, GA	1,165	51.4	30	1.3	0	0.0	45	2.0	45	2.0
Holland–Grand Haven, MI	15	0.2	40	0.6	105	1.6	0	0.0	130	2.0
Honolulu, HI	170	1.0	25	0.2	7,490	45.4	2,485	15.1	3,555	21.5
Hot Springs, AR	255	12.7	15	0.7	0	0.0	0	0.0	10	0.5
Houma–Bayou Cane–Thibodaux, LA	1,100	15.6	570	8.1	0	0.0	0	0.0	15	0.2
Houston–Sugar Land–Baytown, TX	36,030	27.0	345	0.3	3,015	2.3	120	0.1	810	0.6
Huntington–Ashland, WV–KY–OH	85	1.3	4	0.1	0	0.0	0	0.0	0	0.0
Huntsville, AL	2,325	27.3	55	0.6	125	1.5	4	0.0	75	0.9
Idaho Falls, ID	0	0.0	80	2.8	0	0.0	0	0.0	4	0.1
Indianapolis–Carmel, IN	7,605	18.0	150	0.4	725	1.7	0	0.0	445	1.1
Iowa City, IA	165	4.9	4	0.1	70	2.1	0	0.0	15	0.4
Ithaca, NY	70	4.8	0	0.0	45	3.1	0	0.0	20	1.4
Jackson, MI	210	5.2	4	0.1	25	0.6	0	0.0	60	1.5
Jackson, MS	7,890	63.4	30	0.2	25	0.2	0	0.0	54	0.4
Jackson, TN	1,310	44.1	0	0.0	4	0.1	0	0.0	0	0.0
Jacksonville, FL	8,955	30.7	80	0.3	565	1.9	35	0.1	435	1.5
Jacksonville, NC	535	19.5	110	4.0	0	0.0	0	0.0	90	3.3
Janesville, WI	145	2.7	25	0.5	30	0.6	4	0.1	113	2.1
Jefferson City, MO	145	4.9	0	0.0	0	0.0	0	0.0	4	0.1
Johnson City, TN	60	1.5	0	0.0	0	0.0	0	0.0	20	0.5
Johnstown, PA	110	2.9	0	0.0	0	0.0	0	0.0	4	0.1

PART C—METROPOLITAN STATISTICAL AREA TABLES

C-13 Transportation and Material Moving Operative Workers, by Metropolitan Statistical Area, Sex, Race, and Hispanic or Latino Origin, 2006–2010—*Continued*

Metropolitan Statistical Area	Total who worked in the last 5 years	Male Number	Male Percent	Female Number	Female Percent	Hispanic or Latino Number	Hispanic or Latino Percent	White alone, not Hispanic or Latino Number	White alone, not Hispanic or Latino Percent
Jonesboro, AR	2,910	2,600	89.3	310	10.7	44	1.5	2,575	88.5
Joplin, MO	5,340	4,405	82.5	940	17.6	295	5.5	4,705	88.1
Kalamazoo–Portage, MI	7,650	5,710	74.6	1,945	25.4	495	6.5	6,055	79.2
Kankakee–Bradley, IL	4,350	3,370	77.5	980	22.5	530	12.2	3,230	74.3
Kansas City, MO–KS	46,840	37,450	80.0	9,390	20.0	3,625	7.7	33,675	71.9
Kennewick–Pasco–Richland, WA	6,175	4,800	77.7	1,380	22.3	2,320	37.6	3,505	56.8
Killeen–Temple–Fort Hood, TX	7,540	6,420	85.1	1,120	14.9	1,190	15.8	4,435	58.8
Kingsport–Bristol–Bristol, TN–VA	6,910	5,680	82.2	1,230	17.8	70	1.0	6,665	96.5
Kingston, NY	4,250	3,570	84.0	680	16.0	295	6.9	3,735	87.9
Knoxville, TN	13,625	11,420	83.8	2,205	16.2	410	3.0	11,980	87.9
Kokomo, IN	2,325	1,760	75.7	565	24.3	20	0.9	2,150	92.5
La Crosse, WI–MN	3,920	3,280	83.7	645	16.5	35	0.9	3,720	94.9
Lafayette, IN	4,320	3,625	83.9	695	16.1	365	8.4	3,730	86.3
Lafayette, LA	6,100	4,990	81.8	1,110	18.2	120	2.0	3,680	60.3
Lake Charles, LA	5,105	4,440	87.0	660	12.9	90	1.8	3,465	67.9
Lake Havasu City–Kingman, AZ	4,025	3,455	85.8	565	14.0	185	4.6	3,695	91.8
Lakeland–Winter Haven, FL	14,735	12,280	83.3	2,455	16.7	2,695	18.3	9,525	64.6
Lancaster, PA	15,555	11,855	76.2	3,700	23.8	1,430	9.2	13,200	84.9
Lansing–East Lansing, MI	9,815	7,835	79.8	1,980	20.2	630	6.4	8,130	82.8
Laredo, TX	7,895	7,150	90.6	745	9.4	7,715	97.7	155	2.0
Las Cruces, NM	3,450	2,790	80.9	655	19.0	2,540	73.6	840	24.3
Las Vegas–Paradise, NV	40,285	34,710	86.2	5,575	13.8	9,775	24.3	20,645	51.2
Lawrence, KS	1,420	1,065	75.0	355	25.0	90	6.3	1,185	83.5
Lawton, OK	2,275	1,760	77.4	515	22.6	140	6.2	1,360	59.8
Lebanon, PA	4,680	3,960	84.6	720	15.4	610	13.0	3,945	84.3
Lewiston, ID–WA	1,545	1,260	81.6	285	18.4	30	1.9	1,415	91.6
Lewiston–Auburn, ME	2,535	2,095	82.6	435	17.2	4	0.2	2,430	95.9
Lexington–Fayette, KY	9,770	7,705	78.9	2,065	21.1	310	3.2	7,910	81.0
Lima, OH	3,320	2,570	77.4	755	22.7	30	0.9	2,900	87.3
Lincoln, NE	6,530	5,395	82.6	1,135	17.4	210	3.2	5,780	88.5
Little Rock–North Little Rock–Conway, AR	14,985	11,900	79.4	3,085	20.6	560	3.7	9,345	62.4
Logan, UT–ID	2,355	1,915	81.3	435	18.5	180	7.6	2,115	89.8
Longview, TX	5,540	4,925	88.9	615	11.1	460	8.3	3,880	70.0
Longview, WA	2,565	2,205	86.0	360	14.0	205	8.0	2,275	88.7
Los Angeles–Long Beach–Santa Ana, CA	283,090	226,290	79.9	56,800	20.1	183,160	64.7	51,585	18.2
Louisville/Jefferson County, KY–IN	34,460	27,545	79.9	6,915	20.1	1,090	3.2	27,260	79.1
Lubbock, TX	5,360	4,410	82.3	955	17.8	2,265	42.3	2,660	49.6
Lynchburg, VA	6,420	4,835	75.3	1,585	24.7	90	1.4	4,535	70.6
Macon, GA	5,810	4,915	84.6	900	15.5	25	0.4	2,420	41.7
Madera–Chowchilla, CA	3,065	2,575	84.0	495	16.2	1,645	53.7	1,210	39.5
Madison, WI	11,195	9,385	83.8	1,815	16.2	520	4.6	9,825	87.8
Manchester–Nashua, NH	8,630	6,770	78.4	1,860	21.6	475	5.5	7,745	89.7
Manhattan, KS	2,135	1,840	86.2	295	13.8	265	12.4	1,475	69.1
Mankato–North Mankato, MN	2,665	2,240	84.1	425	15.9	170	6.4	2,450	91.9
Mansfield, OH	3,625	2,870	79.2	755	20.8	15	0.4	3,255	89.8
McAllen–Edinburg–Mission, TX	15,235	13,240	86.9	1,995	13.1	14,530	95.4	585	3.8
Medford, OR	4,315	3,065	71.0	1,250	29.0	455	10.5	3,700	85.7
Memphis, TN–MS–AR	40,710	31,755	78.0	8,955	22.0	1,995	4.9	12,770	31.4
Merced, CA	8,835	7,100	80.4	1,735	19.6	5,380	60.9	2,485	28.1
Miami–Fort Lauderdale–Pompano Beach, FL	106,110	89,180	84.0	16,930	16.0	56,355	53.1	20,120	19.0
Michigan City–La Porte, IN	3,335	2,690	80.7	645	19.3	140	4.2	3,015	90.4
Midland, TX	3,185	2,905	91.2	280	8.8	1,340	42.1	1,475	46.3
Milwaukee–Waukesha–West Allis, WI	34,995	27,735	79.3	7,265	20.8	3,945	11.3	22,555	64.5
Minneapolis–St. Paul–Bloomington, MN–WI	64,975	53,725	82.7	11,245	17.3	3,440	5.3	50,550	77.8
Missoula, MT	1,920	1,745	90.9	175	9.1	80	4.2	1,775	92.4

C-13 Transportation and Material Moving Operative Workers, by Metropolitan Statistical Area, Sex, Race, and Hispanic or Latino Origin, 2006–2010—*Continued*

Metropolitan Statistical Area	Black alone, not Hispanic or Latino Number	Percent	American Indian and Alaska Native alone, not Hispanic or Latino Number	Percent	Asian alone, not Hispanic or Latino Number	Percent	Native Hawaiian and Other Pacific Islander alone, not Hispanic or Latino Number	Percent	Two or more races, not Hispanic or Latino Number	Percent
Jonesboro, AR	240	8.2	20	0.7	20	0.7	0	0.0	15	0.5
Joplin, MO	70	1.3	60	1.1	15	0.3	70	1.3	129	2.4
Kalamazoo–Portage, MI	805	10.5	40	0.5	60	0.8	0	0.0	199	2.6
Kankakee–Bradley, IL	575	13.2	0	0.0	0	0.0	0	0.0	10	0.2
Kansas City, MO–KS	7,910	16.9	190	0.4	550	1.2	0	0.0	880	1.9
Kennewick–Pasco–Richland, WA	145	2.3	40	0.6	65	1.1	25	0.4	79	1.3
Killeen–Temple–Fort Hood, TX	1,600	21.2	25	0.3	70	0.9	40	0.5	179	2.4
Kingsport–Bristol–Bristol, TN–VA	135	2.0	0	0.0	0	0.0	0	0.0	39	0.6
Kingston, NY	190	4.5	0	0.0	30	0.7	0	0.0	4	0.1
Knoxville, TN	1,070	7.9	50	0.4	60	0.4	0	0.0	55	0.4
Kokomo, IN	130	5.6	0	0.0	0	0.0	0	0.0	25	1.1
La Crosse, WI–MN	10	0.3	15	0.4	75	1.9	0	0.0	59	1.5
Lafayette, IN	100	2.3	20	0.5	60	1.4	0	0.0	39	0.9
Lafayette, LA	2,220	36.4	30	0.5	0	0.0	0	0.0	49	0.8
Lake Charles, LA	1,425	27.9	20	0.4	0	0.0	0	0.0	105	2.1
Lake Havasu City–Kingman, AZ	45	1.1	20	0.5	0	0.0	0	0.0	80	2.0
Lakeland–Winter Haven, FL	2,230	15.1	65	0.4	105	0.7	0	0.0	115	0.8
Lancaster, PA	480	3.1	25	0.2	260	1.7	0	0.0	155	1.0
Lansing–East Lansing, MI	855	8.7	10	0.1	25	0.3	0	0.0	175	1.8
Laredo, TX	0	0.0	0	0.0	15	0.2	0	0.0	0	0.0
Las Cruces, NM	55	1.6	10	0.3	0	0.0	0	0.0	10	0.3
Las Vegas–Paradise, NV	6,450	16.0	190	0.5	2,180	5.4	505	1.3	545	1.4
Lawrence, KS	75	5.3	30	2.1	20	1.4	0	0.0	19	1.3
Lawton, OK	515	22.6	125	5.5	0	0.0	20	0.9	115	5.1
Lebanon, PA	85	1.8	15	0.3	15	0.3	0	0.0	15	0.3
Lewiston, ID–WA	0	0.0	20	1.3	0	0.0	0	0.0	80	5.2
Lewiston–Auburn, ME	15	0.6	0	0.0	0	0.0	0	0.0	84	3.3
Lexington–Fayette, KY	1,465	15.0	0	0.0	15	0.2	0	0.0	70	0.7
Lima, OH	350	10.5	4	0.1	20	0.6	0	0.0	10	0.3
Lincoln, NE	305	4.7	45	0.7	170	2.6	4	0.1	14	0.2
Little Rock–North Little Rock–Conway, AR	4,810	32.1	35	0.2	80	0.5	0	0.0	150	1.0
Logan, UT–ID	25	1.1	25	1.1	4	0.2	0	0.0	0	0.0
Longview, TX	1,135	20.5	20	0.4	25	0.5	0	0.0	20	0.4
Longview, WA	10	0.4	25	1.0	10	0.4	0	0.0	40	1.6
Los Angeles–Long Beach–Santa Ana, CA	20,885	7.4	495	0.2	22,590	8.0	1,170	0.4	3,210	1.1
Louisville/Jefferson County, KY–IN	5,415	15.7	90	0.3	205	0.6	10	0.0	390	1.1
Lubbock, TX	335	6.3	0	0.0	35	0.7	0	0.0	60	1.1
Lynchburg, VA	1,710	26.6	0	0.0	75	1.2	0	0.0	10	0.2
Macon, GA	3,310	57.0	0	0.0	50	0.9	0	0.0	4	0.1
Madera–Chowchilla, CA	85	2.8	4	0.1	75	2.4	0	0.0	45	1.5
Madison, WI	580	5.2	30	0.3	190	1.7	0	0.0	60	0.5
Manchester–Nashua, NH	215	2.5	30	0.3	65	0.8	0	0.0	105	1.2
Manhattan, KS	300	14.1	4	0.2	25	1.2	10	0.5	49	2.3
Mankato–North Mankato, MN	40	1.5	0	0.0	10	0.4	0	0.0	0	0.0
Mansfield, OH	285	7.9	30	0.8	10	0.3	0	0.0	25	0.7
McAllen–Edinburg–Mission, TX	40	0.3	10	0.1	55	0.4	0	0.0	15	0.1
Medford, OR	10	0.2	50	1.2	25	0.6	0	0.0	70	1.6
Memphis, TN–MS–AR	25,355	62.3	75	0.2	250	0.6	15	0.0	250	0.6
Merced, CA	315	3.6	40	0.5	450	5.1	0	0.0	170	1.9
Miami–Fort Lauderdale–Pompano Beach, FL	27,600	26.0	240	0.2	1,000	0.9	20	0.0	765	0.7
Michigan City–La Porte, IN	150	4.5	15	0.4	0	0.0	0	0.0	8	0.2
Midland, TX	345	10.8	0	0.0	30	0.9	0	0.0	0	0.0
Milwaukee–Waukesha–West Allis, WI	7,310	20.9	210	0.6	655	1.9	0	0.0	325	0.9
Minneapolis–St. Paul–Bloomington, MN–WI	7,015	10.8	315	0.5	2,710	4.2	0	0.0	945	1.5
Missoula, MT	0	0.0	55	2.9	0	0.0	0	0.0	10	0.5

C-13 Transportation and Material Moving Operative Workers, by Metropolitan Statistical Area, Sex, Race, and Hispanic or Latino Origin, 2006–2010—Continued

Metropolitan Statistical Area	Total who worked in the last 5 years	Male Number	Male Percent	Female Number	Female Percent	Hispanic or Latino Number	Hispanic or Latino Percent	White alone, not Hispanic or Latino Number	White alone, not Hispanic or Latino Percent
Mobile, AL	10,005	8,380	83.8	1,625	16.2	80	0.8	5,830	58.3
Modesto, CA	16,055	12,880	80.2	3,175	19.8	7,680	47.8	6,250	38.9
Monroe, LA	3,895	3,380	86.8	515	13.2	120	3.1	2,255	57.9
Monroe, MI	4,930	3,975	80.6	955	19.4	255	5.2	4,550	92.3
Montgomery, AL	8,240	6,350	77.1	1,890	22.9	160	1.9	3,605	43.8
Morgantown, WV	2,375	2,050	86.3	325	13.7	64	2.7	2,275	95.8
Morristown, TN	4,605	3,570	77.5	1,035	22.5	355	7.7	4,110	89.3
Mount Vernon–Anacortes, WA	3,005	2,425	80.7	580	19.3	390	13.0	2,485	82.7
Muncie, IN	2,320	1,915	82.5	405	17.5	25	1.1	2,115	91.2
Muskegon–Norton Shores, MI	4,225	3,010	71.2	1,215	28.8	175	4.1	3,405	80.6
Myrtle Beach–North Myrtle Beach–Conway, SC	4,355	3,450	79.2	900	20.7	40	0.9	3,155	72.4
Napa, CA	2,435	2,075	85.2	360	14.8	1,250	51.3	1,060	43.5
Naples–Marco Island, FL	4,810	4,055	84.3	760	15.8	2,375	49.4	1,830	38.0
Nashville-Davidson–Murfreesboro–Franklin, TN	37,205	30,660	82.4	6,540	17.6	2,135	5.7	26,385	70.9
New Haven–Milford, CT	18,720	14,255	76.1	4,465	23.9	3,200	17.1	11,730	62.7
New Orleans–Metairie–Kenner, LA	24,600	21,215	86.2	3,385	13.8	1,570	6.4	11,110	45.2
New York–Northern New Jersey–Long Island, NY–NJ–PA	418,325	351,420	84.0	66,905	16.0	146,135	34.9	139,015	33.2
Niles–Benton Harbor, MI	3,840	3,030	78.9	810	21.1	235	6.1	3,060	79.7
North Port–Bradenton–Sarasota, FL	10,430	8,750	83.9	1,680	16.1	1,245	11.9	7,930	76.0
Norwich–New London, CT	4,910	3,965	80.8	945	19.2	365	7.4	4,095	83.4
Ocala, FL	6,695	5,400	80.7	1,295	19.3	645	9.6	4,360	65.1
Ocean City, NJ	1,650	1,405	85.2	245	14.8	55	3.3	1,405	85.2
Odessa, TX	4,170	3,765	90.3	400	9.6	2,385	57.2	1,560	37.4
Ogden–Clearfield, UT	11,150	9,075	81.4	2,070	18.6	1,560	14.0	8,930	80.1
Oklahoma City, OK	25,975	22,180	85.4	3,795	14.6	2,425	9.3	18,115	69.7
Olympia, WA	4,115	3,505	85.2	610	14.8	205	5.0	3,400	82.6
Omaha–Council Bluffs, NE–IA	19,060	15,830	83.1	3,230	16.9	1,795	9.4	14,805	77.7
Orlando–Kissimmee–Sanford, FL	41,815	35,495	84.9	6,320	15.1	13,630	32.6	17,480	41.8
Oshkosh–Neenah, WI	4,575	3,605	78.8	970	21.2	175	3.8	4,250	92.9
Owensboro, KY	3,095	2,450	79.2	645	20.8	95	3.1	2,865	92.6
Oxnard–Thousand Oaks–Ventura, CA	15,465	12,435	80.4	3,030	19.6	9,300	60.1	4,970	32.1
Palm Bay–Melbourne–Titusville, FL	9,530	7,860	82.5	1,675	17.6	755	7.9	6,875	72.1
Palm Coast, FL	1,125	945	84.0	180	16.0	90	8.0	835	74.2
Panama City–Lynn Haven–Panama City Beach, FL	2,850	2,330	81.8	520	18.2	80	2.8	2,450	86.0
Parkersburg–Marietta–Vienna, WV–OH	4,475	4,040	90.3	435	9.7	0	0.0	4,295	96.0
Pascagoula, MS	3,135	2,710	86.4	420	13.4	10	0.3	2,510	80.1
Pensacola–Ferry Pass–Brent, FL	8,190	6,765	82.6	1,425	17.4	210	2.6	5,820	71.1
Peoria, IL	9,735	8,330	85.6	1,405	14.4	170	1.7	8,685	89.2
Philadelphia–Camden–Wilmington, PA–NJ–DE–MD	127,885	103,950	81.3	23,930	18.7	12,505	9.8	76,170	59.6
Phoenix–Mesa–Glendale, AZ	74,055	61,740	83.4	12,320	16.6	23,525	31.8	41,305	55.8
Pine Bluff, AR	2,875	2,365	82.3	510	17.7	4	0.1	1,470	51.1
Pittsburgh, PA	52,460	43,770	83.4	8,690	16.6	455	0.9	47,050	89.7
Pittsfield, MA	2,355	1,945	82.6	410	17.4	60	2.5	2,090	88.7
Pocatello, ID	2,515	2,140	85.1	375	14.9	180	7.2	2,160	85.9
Portland–South Portland–Biddeford, ME	9,765	8,290	84.9	1,475	15.1	60	0.6	9,265	94.9
Portland–Vancouver–Hillsboro, OR–WA	48,095	39,170	81.4	8,925	18.6	4,660	9.7	37,915	78.8
Port St. Lucie, FL	6,725	5,770	85.8	955	14.2	1,380	20.5	3,735	55.5
Poughkeepsie–Newburgh–Middletown, NY	13,520	11,040	81.7	2,480	18.3	2,070	15.3	9,825	72.7
Prescott, AZ	3,260	2,560	78.5	700	21.5	175	5.4	2,960	90.8
Providence–New Bedford–Fall River, RI–MA	37,845	29,895	79.0	7,950	21.0	5,690	15.0	28,870	76.3

C-13 Transportation and Material Moving Operative Workers, by Metropolitan Statistical Area, Sex, Race, and Hispanic or Latino Origin, 2006–2010—*Continued*

Metropolitan Statistical Area	Black alone, not Hispanic or Latino Number	Percent	American Indian and Alaska Native alone, not Hispanic or Latino Number	Percent	Asian alone, not Hispanic or Latino Number	Percent	Native Hawaiian and Other Pacific Islander alone, not Hispanic or Latino Number	Percent	Two or more races, not Hispanic or Latino Number	Percent
Mobile, AL	3,785	37.8	100	1.0	95	0.9	0	0.0	114	1.1
Modesto, CA	810	5.0	85	0.5	805	5.0	140	0.9	290	1.8
Monroe, LA	1,460	37.5	4	0.1	10	0.3	0	0.0	45	1.2
Monroe, MI	85	1.7	15	0.3	0	0.0	0	0.0	20	0.4
Montgomery, AL	4,355	52.9	4	0.0	95	1.2	0	0.0	24	0.3
Morgantown, WV	0	0.0	0	0.0	15	0.6	0	0.0	20	0.8
Morristown, TN	115	2.5	0	0.0	20	0.4	0	0.0	4	0.1
Mount Vernon–Anacortes, WA	15	0.5	50	1.7	15	0.5	4	0.1	45	1.5
Muncie, IN	130	5.6	0	0.0	40	1.7	0	0.0	10	0.4
Muskegon–Norton Shores, MI	480	11.4	50	1.2	30	0.7	0	0.0	94	2.2
Myrtle Beach–North Myrtle Beach–Conway, SC	1,000	23.0	95	2.2	35	0.8	0	0.0	30	0.7
Napa, CA	30	1.2	4	0.2	50	2.1	25	1.0	15	0.6
Naples–Marco Island, FL	610	12.7	0	0.0	0	0.0	0	0.0	0	0.0
Nashville-Davidson–Murfreesboro–Franklin, TN	7,515	20.2	75	0.2	720	1.9	30	0.1	340	0.9
New Haven–Milford, CT	3,225	17.2	85	0.5	190	1.0	0	0.0	290	1.5
New Orleans–Metairie–Kenner, LA	11,210	45.6	120	0.5	440	1.8	0	0.0	150	0.6
New York–Northern New Jersey–Long Island, NY–NJ–PA	84,685	20.2	480	0.1	41,450	9.9	95	0.0	6,465	1.5
Niles–Benton Harbor, MI	470	12.2	15	0.4	35	0.9	0	0.0	20	0.5
North Port–Bradenton–Sarasota, FL	1,030	9.9	10	0.1	55	0.5	15	0.1	145	1.4
Norwich–New London, CT	245	5.0	10	0.2	50	1.0	0	0.0	145	3.0
Ocala, FL	1,490	22.3	80	1.2	50	0.7	0	0.0	64	1.0
Ocean City, NJ	140	8.5	0	0.0	0	0.0	0	0.0	50	3.0
Odessa, TX	195	4.7	4	0.1	0	0.0	0	0.0	20	0.5
Ogden–Clearfield, UT	165	1.5	45	0.4	150	1.3	165	1.5	129	1.2
Oklahoma City, OK	3,070	11.8	875	3.4	580	2.2	4	0.0	895	3.4
Olympia, WA	145	3.5	70	1.7	60	1.5	105	2.6	120	2.9
Omaha–Council Bluffs, NE–IA	1,850	9.7	30	0.2	170	0.9	0	0.0	400	2.1
Orlando–Kissimmee–Sanford, FL	8,945	21.4	125	0.3	980	2.3	30	0.1	635	1.5
Oshkosh–Neenah, WI	25	0.5	4	0.1	110	2.4	0	0.0	10	0.2
Owensboro, KY	115	3.7	10	0.3	0	0.0	0	0.0	15	0.5
Oxnard–Thousand Oaks–Ventura, CA	245	1.6	40	0.3	700	4.5	40	0.3	170	1.1
Palm Bay–Melbourne–Titusville, FL	1,650	17.3	40	0.4	135	1.4	0	0.0	75	0.8
Palm Coast, FL	145	12.9	0	0.0	55	4.9	0	0.0	0	0.0
Panama City–Lynn Haven–Panama City Beach, FL	235	8.2	15	0.5	15	0.5	0	0.0	55	1.9
Parkersburg–Marietta–Vienna, WV–OH	25	0.6	0	0.0	0	0.0	0	0.0	155	3.5
Pascagoula, MS	540	17.2	10	0.3	20	0.6	0	0.0	40	1.3
Pensacola–Ferry Pass–Brent, FL	1,705	20.8	30	0.4	195	2.4	50	0.6	179	2.2
Peoria, IL	755	7.8	10	0.1	20	0.2	0	0.0	90	0.9
Philadelphia–Camden–Wilmington, PA–NJ–DE–MD	32,100	25.1	250	0.2	5,230	4.1	85	0.1	1,540	1.2
Phoenix–Mesa–Glendale, AZ	5,365	7.2	1,685	2.3	1,045	1.4	185	0.2	955	1.3
Pine Bluff, AR	1,390	48.3	15	0.5	0	0.0	0	0.0	4	0.1
Pittsburgh, PA	4,185	8.0	55	0.1	225	0.4	15	0.0	475	0.9
Pittsfield, MA	140	5.9	0	0.0	65	2.8	0	0.0	0	0.0
Pocatello, ID	4	0.2	60	2.4	15	0.6	0	0.0	90	3.6
Portland–South Portland–Biddeford, ME	255	2.6	4	0.0	120	1.2	0	0.0	60	0.6
Portland–Vancouver–Hillsboro, OR–WA	2,150	4.5	350	0.7	1,585	3.3	240	0.5	1,195	2.5
Port St. Lucie, FL	1,515	22.5	15	0.2	0	0.0	0	0.0	75	1.1
Poughkeepsie–Newburgh–Middletown, NY	1,190	8.8	25	0.2	135	1.0	0	0.0	275	2.0
Prescott, AZ	30	0.9	35	1.1	10	0.3	15	0.5	40	1.2
Providence–New Bedford–Fall River, RI–MA	1,765	4.7	105	0.3	695	1.8	0	0.0	715	1.9

PART C—METROPOLITAN STATISTICAL AREA TABLES

C-13 Transportation and Material Moving Operative Workers, by Metropolitan Statistical Area, Sex, Race, and Hispanic or Latino Origin, 2006–2010—Continued

Metropolitan Statistical Area	Total who worked in the last 5 years	Male Number	Male Percent	Female Number	Female Percent	Hispanic or Latino Number	Hispanic or Latino Percent	White alone, not Hispanic or Latino Number	White alone, not Hispanic or Latino Percent
Provo–Orem, UT	6,880	5,370	78.1	1,515	22.0	960	14.0	5,660	82.3
Pueblo, CO	2,415	1,995	82.6	415	17.2	1,060	43.9	1,305	54.0
Punta Gorda, FL	2,635	2,155	81.8	480	18.2	265	10.1	2,165	82.2
Racine, WI	5,675	4,525	79.7	1,150	20.3	610	10.7	4,290	75.6
Raleigh–Cary, NC	18,285	14,370	78.6	3,915	21.4	1,380	7.5	8,980	49.1
Rapid City, SD	2,580	2,210	85.7	365	14.1	85	3.3	2,285	88.6
Reading, PA	11,560	8,830	76.4	2,730	23.6	2,120	18.3	8,630	74.7
Redding, CA	3,140	2,640	84.1	495	15.8	145	4.6	2,795	89.0
Reno–Sparks, NV	10,685	8,485	79.4	2,200	20.6	2,685	25.1	6,930	64.9
Richmond, VA	26,060	21,175	81.3	4,890	18.8	880	3.4	12,795	49.1
Riverside–San Bernardino–Ontario, CA	114,505	93,705	81.8	20,800	18.2	67,420	58.9	31,755	27.7
Roanoke, VA	8,220	6,710	81.6	1,510	18.4	225	2.7	6,445	78.4
Rochester, MN	3,825	3,325	86.9	500	13.1	295	7.7	3,225	84.3
Rochester, NY	22,220	17,320	77.9	4,895	22.0	1,785	8.0	17,130	77.1
Rockford, IL	10,665	7,895	74.0	2,770	26.0	1,400	13.1	8,285	77.7
Rocky Mount, NC	5,935	4,505	75.9	1,425	24.0	205	3.5	2,095	35.3
Rome, GA	2,030	1,675	82.5	355	17.5	200	9.9	1,485	73.2
Sacramento–Arden-Arcade–Roseville, CA	37,040	30,925	83.5	6,115	16.5	8,790	23.7	19,805	53.5
Saginaw–Saginaw Township North, MI	4,165	3,230	77.6	935	22.4	280	6.7	3,280	78.8
St. Cloud, MN	5,690	4,695	82.5	995	17.5	80	1.4	5,305	93.2
St. George, UT	2,680	2,180	81.3	505	18.8	135	5.0	2,365	88.2
St. Joseph, MO–KS	3,490	2,875	82.4	610	17.5	135	3.9	3,240	92.8
St. Louis, MO–IL	61,510	49,910	81.1	11,600	18.9	1,505	2.4	44,420	72.2
Salem, OR	9,110	6,880	75.5	2,230	24.5	2,460	27.0	5,910	64.9
Salinas, CA	10,260	7,760	75.6	2,500	24.4	8,100	78.9	1,560	15.2
Salisbury, MD	3,335	2,815	84.4	525	15.7	120	3.6	1,965	58.9
Salt Lake City, UT	23,435	19,470	83.1	3,965	16.9	4,055	17.3	17,100	73.0
San Angelo, TX	2,040	1,680	82.4	360	17.6	665	32.6	1,200	58.8
San Antonio–New Braunfels, TX	40,065	34,410	85.9	5,655	14.1	23,855	59.5	12,115	30.2
San Diego–Carlsbad–San Marcos, CA	44,830	36,220	80.8	8,605	19.2	17,000	37.9	19,410	43.3
Sandusky, OH	2,000	1,470	73.5	530	26.5	60	3.0	1,680	84.0
San Francisco–Oakland–Fremont, CA	72,425	60,010	82.9	12,420	17.1	22,370	30.9	21,325	29.4
San Jose–Sunnyvale–Santa Clara, CA	28,290	22,035	77.9	6,250	22.1	11,360	40.2	7,310	25.8
San Luis Obispo–Paso Robles, CA	2,985	2,420	81.1	565	18.9	715	24.0	2,170	72.7
Santa Barbara–Santa Maria–Goleta, CA	7,475	6,130	82.0	1,345	18.0	4,520	60.5	2,390	32.0
Santa Cruz–Watsonville, CA	4,090	2,950	72.1	1,135	27.8	2,080	50.9	1,765	43.2
Santa Fe, NM	1,660	1,400	84.3	255	15.4	880	53.0	695	41.9
Santa Rosa–Petaluma, CA	8,360	6,740	80.6	1,615	19.3	2,835	33.9	4,830	57.8
Savannah, GA	8,920	7,650	85.8	1,270	14.2	340	3.8	4,525	50.7
Scranton–Wilkes-Barre, PA	17,010	13,905	81.7	3,105	18.3	1,330	7.8	15,060	88.5
Seattle–Tacoma–Bellevue, WA	72,090	58,245	80.8	13,845	19.2	5,355	7.4	49,650	68.9
Sebastian–Vero Beach, FL	2,045	1,555	76.0	490	24.0	435	21.3	1,260	61.6
Sheboygan, WI	3,650	2,655	72.7	995	27.3	220	6.0	3,195	87.5
Sherman–Denison, TX	3,090	2,550	82.5	540	17.5	330	10.7	2,455	79.4
Shreveport–Bossier City, LA	9,310	7,450	80.0	1,860	20.0	290	3.1	4,410	47.4
Sioux City, IA–NE–SD	4,135	3,410	82.5	730	17.7	645	15.6	3,390	82.0
Sioux Falls, SD	5,595	4,815	86.1	780	13.9	260	4.6	5,060	90.4
South Bend–Mishawaka, IN–MI	8,585	6,610	77.0	1,975	23.0	550	6.4	6,960	81.1
Spartanburg, SC	8,910	6,655	74.7	2,255	25.3	395	4.4	5,370	60.3
Spokane, WA	9,155	8,005	87.4	1,150	12.6	385	4.2	8,355	91.3
Springfield, IL	3,535	3,110	88.0	425	12.0	4	0.1	3,030	85.7
Springfield, MA	14,985	12,020	80.2	2,965	19.8	1,845	12.3	12,115	80.8
Springfield, MO	11,135	9,455	84.9	1,680	15.1	140	1.3	10,470	94.0
Springfield, OH	4,095	3,410	83.3	685	16.7	80	2.0	3,800	92.8
State College, PA	2,380	1,870	78.6	515	21.6	44	1.8	2,315	97.3

C-13 Transportation and Material Moving Operative Workers, by Metropolitan Statistical Area, Sex, Race, and Hispanic or Latino Origin, 2006–2010—*Continued*

Metropolitan Statistical Area	Black alone, not Hispanic or Latino Number	Percent	American Indian and Alaska Native alone, not Hispanic or Latino Number	Percent	Asian alone, not Hispanic or Latino Number	Percent	Native Hawaiian and Other Pacific Islander alone, not Hispanic or Latino Number	Percent	Two or more races, not Hispanic or Latino Number	Percent
Provo–Orem, UT	40	0.6	35	0.5	80	1.2	45	0.7	65	0.9
Pueblo, CO	10	0.4	0	0.0	0	0.0	0	0.0	35	1.4
Punta Gorda, FL	145	5.5	4	0.2	0	0.0	0	0.0	55	2.1
Racine, WI	625	11.0	4	0.1	50	0.9	0	0.0	90	1.6
Raleigh–Cary, NC	7,445	40.7	50	0.3	270	1.5	0	0.0	164	0.9
Rapid City, SD	0	0.0	45	1.7	20	0.8	0	0.0	140	5.4
Reading, PA	600	5.2	0	0.0	55	0.5	0	0.0	154	1.3
Redding, CA	45	1.4	20	0.6	90	2.9	4	0.1	40	1.3
Reno–Sparks, NV	530	5.0	125	1.2	215	2.0	30	0.3	175	1.6
Richmond, VA	11,650	44.7	90	0.3	395	1.5	0	0.0	250	1.0
Riverside–San Bernardino–Ontario, CA	9,375	8.2	510	0.4	3,655	3.2	275	0.2	1,505	1.3
Roanoke, VA	1,345	16.4	0	0.0	130	1.6	0	0.0	80	1.0
Rochester, MN	135	3.5	40	1.0	80	2.1	0	0.0	45	1.2
Rochester, NY	2,720	12.2	80	0.4	285	1.3	4	0.0	205	0.9
Rockford, IL	830	7.8	15	0.1	110	1.0	0	0.0	25	0.2
Rocky Mount, NC	3,560	60.0	0	0.0	0	0.0	0	0.0	79	1.3
Rome, GA	295	14.5	0	0.0	0	0.0	0	0.0	55	2.7
Sacramento–Arden-Arcade–Roseville, CA	3,040	8.2	210	0.6	3,750	10.1	755	2.0	690	1.9
Saginaw–Saginaw Township North, MI	590	14.2	10	0.2	4	0.1	0	0.0	4	0.1
St. Cloud, MN	185	3.3	10	0.2	80	1.4	4	0.1	23	0.4
St. George, UT	50	1.9	10	0.4	25	0.9	95	3.5	0	0.0
St. Joseph, MO–KS	60	1.7	10	0.3	0	0.0	0	0.0	49	1.4
St. Louis, MO–IL	14,365	23.4	85	0.1	670	1.1	0	0.0	470	0.8
Salem, OR	90	1.0	60	0.7	200	2.2	170	1.9	220	2.4
Salinas, CA	275	2.7	0	0.0	235	2.3	4	0.0	85	0.8
Salisbury, MD	1,175	35.2	0	0.0	40	1.2	0	0.0	34	1.0
Salt Lake City, UT	670	2.9	355	1.5	485	2.1	610	2.6	160	0.7
San Angelo, TX	95	4.7	40	2.0	0	0.0	0	0.0	40	2.0
San Antonio–New Braunfels, TX	3,165	7.9	60	0.1	325	0.8	80	0.2	465	1.2
San Diego–Carlsbad–San Marcos, CA	3,735	8.3	180	0.4	3,410	7.6	280	0.6	815	1.8
Sandusky, OH	255	12.8	0	0.0	0	0.0	0	0.0	0	0.0
San Francisco–Oakland–Fremont, CA	10,065	13.9	255	0.4	15,160	20.9	975	1.3	2,275	3.1
San Jose–Sunnyvale–Santa Clara, CA	1,235	4.4	85	0.3	7,615	26.9	160	0.6	520	1.8
San Luis Obispo–Paso Robles, CA	10	0.3	15	0.5	4	0.1	0	0.0	65	2.2
Santa Barbara–Santa Maria–Goleta, CA	200	2.7	25	0.3	240	3.2	0	0.0	105	1.4
Santa Cruz–Watsonville, CA	155	3.8	0	0.0	70	1.7	0	0.0	20	0.5
Santa Fe, NM	60	3.6	20	1.2	4	0.2	0	0.0	0	0.0
Santa Rosa–Petaluma, CA	170	2.0	130	1.6	270	3.2	0	0.0	119	1.4
Savannah, GA	3,935	44.1	4	0.0	30	0.3	0	0.0	81	0.9
Scranton–Wilkes-Barre, PA	330	1.9	10	0.1	190	1.1	0	0.0	95	0.6
Seattle–Tacoma–Bellevue, WA	6,990	9.7	555	0.8	5,515	7.7	1,385	1.9	2,640	3.7
Sebastian–Vero Beach, FL	315	15.4	30	1.5	0	0.0	0	0.0	0	0.0
Sheboygan, WI	4	0.1	25	0.7	190	5.2	0	0.0	19	0.5
Sherman–Denison, TX	195	6.3	45	1.5	15	0.5	0	0.0	55	1.8
Shreveport–Bossier City, LA	4,455	47.9	20	0.2	0	0.0	20	0.2	120	1.3
Sioux City, IA–NE–SD	25	0.6	0	0.0	50	1.2	0	0.0	25	0.6
Sioux Falls, SD	105	1.9	120	2.1	30	0.5	0	0.0	18	0.3
South Bend–Mishawaka, IN–MI	920	10.7	15	0.2	55	0.6	0	0.0	85	1.0
Spartanburg, SC	2,905	32.6	0	0.0	210	2.4	0	0.0	30	0.3
Spokane, WA	130	1.4	80	0.9	70	0.8	0	0.0	140	1.5
Springfield, IL	430	12.2	0	0.0	10	0.3	0	0.0	50	1.4
Springfield, MA	790	5.3	4	0.0	135	0.9	0	0.0	100	0.7
Springfield, MO	190	1.7	40	0.4	45	0.4	0	0.0	250	2.2
Springfield, OH	200	4.9	0	0.0	0	0.0	0	0.0	19	0.5
State College, PA	4	0.2	10	0.4	0	0.0	0	0.0	8	0.3

PART C—METROPOLITAN STATISTICAL AREA TABLES

C-13 **Transportation and Material Moving Operative Workers, by Metropolitan Statistical Area, Sex, Race, and Hispanic or Latino Origin, 2006–2010**—*Continued*

Metropolitan Statistical Area	Total who worked in the last 5 years	Male Number	Male Percent	Female Number	Female Percent	Hispanic or Latino Number	Hispanic or Latino Percent	White alone, not Hispanic or Latino Number	White alone, not Hispanic or Latino Percent
Steubenville–Weirton, OH–WV	3,390	2,970	87.6	415	12.2	0	0.0	3,245	95.7
Stockton, CA	20,300	16,655	82.0	3,645	18.0	8,745	43.1	6,425	31.7
Sumter, SC	3,095	2,500	80.8	600	19.4	15	0.5	910	29.4
Syracuse, NY	13,770	11,585	84.1	2,185	15.9	380	2.8	12,120	88.0
Tallahassee, FL	5,025	4,060	80.8	970	19.3	215	4.3	2,300	45.8
Tampa–St. Petersburg–Clearwater, FL	48,485	40,105	82.7	8,385	17.3	8,885	18.3	30,185	62.3
Terre Haute, IN	4,660	3,600	77.3	1,060	22.7	90	1.9	4,345	93.2
Texarkana, TX–Texarkana, AR	3,205	2,740	85.5	465	14.5	305	9.5	1,995	62.2
Toledo, OH	20,480	16,275	79.5	4,205	20.5	1,125	5.5	16,420	80.2
Topeka, KS	5,175	4,195	81.1	980	18.9	620	12.0	4,065	78.6
Trenton–Ewing, NJ	7,665	5,665	73.9	2,005	26.2	2,125	27.7	3,045	39.7
Tucson, AZ	14,770	12,050	81.6	2,720	18.4	5,980	40.5	7,370	49.9
Tulsa, OK	19,790	16,745	84.6	3,045	15.4	1,155	5.8	14,310	72.3
Tuscaloosa, AL	5,245	4,150	79.1	1,095	20.9	100	1.9	2,470	47.1
Tyler, TX	4,930	4,200	85.2	730	14.8	720	14.6	2,850	57.8
Utica–Rome, NY	6,440	5,320	82.6	1,115	17.3	195	3.0	5,815	90.3
Valdosta, GA	3,915	3,270	83.5	645	16.5	194	5.0	2,005	51.2
Vallejo–Fairfield, CA	9,250	6,890	74.5	2,360	25.5	2,225	24.1	3,420	37.0
Victoria, TX	2,895	2,460	85.0	440	15.2	1,345	46.5	1,205	41.6
Vineland–Millville–Bridgeton, NJ	5,375	3,765	70.0	1,610	30.0	1,885	35.1	2,620	48.7
Virginia Beach–Norfolk–Newport News, VA–NC	31,935	24,480	76.7	7,460	23.4	765	2.4	15,255	47.8
Visalia–Porterville, CA	12,115	8,980	74.1	3,135	25.9	7,860	64.9	3,755	31.0
Waco, TX	5,855	4,745	81.0	1,110	19.0	1,490	25.4	3,295	56.3
Warner Robins, GA	2,390	1,660	69.5	730	30.5	210	8.8	1,395	58.4
Washington–Arlington–Alexandria, DC–VA–MD–WV	84,890	70,330	82.8	14,560	17.2	12,695	15.0	25,690	30.3
Waterloo–Cedar Falls, IA	4,650	4,085	87.8	565	12.2	120	2.6	4,245	91.3
Wausau, WI	3,720	3,130	84.1	595	16.0	49	1.3	3,545	95.3
Wenatchee–East Wenatchee, WA	2,990	1,955	65.4	1,035	34.6	1,195	40.0	1,770	59.2
Wheeling, WV–OH	3,565	3,130	87.8	435	12.2	0	0.0	3,470	97.3
Wichita, KS	12,375	10,010	80.9	2,365	19.1	995	8.0	9,940	80.3
Wichita Falls, TX	3,585	3,035	84.7	550	15.3	485	13.5	2,635	73.5
Williamsport, PA	3,075	2,440	79.3	635	20.7	60	2.0	2,765	89.9
Wilmington, NC	7,150	5,545	77.6	1,605	22.4	205	2.9	5,080	71.0
Winchester, VA–WV	3,585	2,910	81.2	675	18.8	170	4.7	3,170	88.4
Winston–Salem, NC	12,020	9,130	76.0	2,890	24.0	1,280	10.6	7,350	61.1
Worcester, MA	16,975	13,675	80.6	3,300	19.4	2,005	11.8	13,540	79.8
Yakima, WA	8,460	5,585	66.0	2,875	34.0	4,810	56.9	3,195	37.8
York–Hanover, PA	12,625	9,670	76.6	2,955	23.4	875	6.9	10,715	84.9
Youngstown–Warren–Boardman, OH–PA	15,535	12,350	79.5	3,185	20.5	275	1.8	13,660	87.9
Yuba City, CA	4,315	3,495	81.0	820	19.0	1,340	31.1	1,875	43.5
Yuma, AZ	4,535	3,440	75.9	1,090	24.0	3,275	72.2	1,005	22.2

C-13 Transportation and Material Moving Operative Workers, by Metropolitan Statistical Area, Sex, Race, and Hispanic or Latino Origin, 2006–2010—*Continued*

Metropolitan Statistical Area	Black alone, not Hispanic or Latino Number	Percent	American Indian and Alaska Native alone, not Hispanic or Latino Number	Percent	Asian alone, not Hispanic or Latino Number	Percent	Native Hawaiian and Other Pacific Islander alone, not Hispanic or Latino Number	Percent	Two or more races, not Hispanic or Latino Number	Percent
Steubenville–Weirton, OH–WV	100	2.9	30	0.9	0	0.0	0	0.0	12	0.4
Stockton, CA	1,620	8.0	45	0.2	2,910	14.3	100	0.5	455	2.2
Sumter, SC	2,150	69.5	0	0.0	0	0.0	0	0.0	20	0.6
Syracuse, NY	775	5.6	170	1.2	160	1.2	15	0.1	149	1.1
Tallahassee, FL	2,345	46.7	70	1.4	20	0.4	0	0.0	75	1.5
Tampa–St. Petersburg–Clearwater, FL	7,850	16.2	95	0.2	955	2.0	50	0.1	465	1.0
Terre Haute, IN	180	3.9	30	0.6	0	0.0	0	0.0	15	0.3
Texarkana, TX–Texarkana, AR	885	27.6	15	0.5	0	0.0	0	0.0	10	0.3
Toledo, OH	2,660	13.0	10	0.0	110	0.5	20	0.1	145	0.7
Topeka, KS	215	4.2	90	1.7	45	0.9	0	0.0	139	2.7
Trenton–Ewing, NJ	2,220	29.0	35	0.5	220	2.9	0	0.0	20	0.3
Tucson, AZ	750	5.1	235	1.6	150	1.0	0	0.00	290	2.0
Tulsa, OK	1,585	8.0	1,505	7.6	240	1.2	0	0.0	990	5.0
Tuscaloosa, AL	2,555	48.7	40	0.8	20	0.4	0	0.0	65	1.2
Tyler, TX	1,250	25.4	20	0.4	35	0.7	0	0.0	60	1.2
Utica–Rome, NY	205	3.2	10	0.2	125	1.9	0	0.0	84	1.3
Valdosta, GA	1,670	42.7	20	0.5	20	0.5	0	0.0	4	0.1
Vallejo–Fairfield, CA	1,780	19.2	35	0.4	1,360	14.7	45	0.5	385	4.2
Victoria, TX	330	11.4	0	0.0	0	0.0	0	0.0	15	0.5
Vineland–Millville–Bridgeton, NJ	785	14.6	15	0.3	10	0.2	0	0.0	50	0.9
Virginia Beach–Norfolk–Newport News, VA–NC	14,445	45.2	125	0.4	610	1.9	0	0.0	730	2.3
Visalia–Porterville, CA	60	0.5	105	0.9	170	1.4	0	0.0	160	1.3
Waco, TX	950	16.2	4	0.1	30	0.5	0	0.0	90	1.5
Warner Robins, GA	740	31.0	25	1.0	20	0.8	0	0.0	0	0.0
Washington–Arlington–Alexandria, DC–VA–MD–WV	38,925	45.9	165	0.2	6,085	7.2	35	0.0	1,300	1.5
Waterloo–Cedar Falls, IA	235	5.1	4	0.1	20	0.4	0	0.0	24	0.5
Wausau, WI	25	0.7	4	0.1	90	2.4	0	0.0	4	0.1
Wenatchee–East Wenatchee, WA	0	0.0	0	0.0	0	0.0	0	0.0	25	0.8
Wheeling, WV–OH	40	1.1	0	0.0	10	0.3	0	0.0	45	1.3
Wichita, KS	755	6.1	170	1.4	200	1.6	0	0.0	315	2.5
Wichita Falls, TX	350	9.8	20	0.6	85	2.4	0	0.0	14	0.4
Williamsport, PA	185	6.0	0	0.0	0	0.0	0	0.0	65	2.1
Wilmington, NC	1,755	24.5	35	0.5	0	0.0	0	0.0	74	1.0
Winchester, VA–WV	175	4.9	0	0.0	30	0.8	0	0.0	35	1.0
Winston–Salem, NC	3,240	27.0	25	0.2	50	0.4	0	0.0	74	0.6
Worcester, MA	790	4.7	15	0.1	395	2.3	0	0.0	225	1.3
Yakima, WA	150	1.8	190	2.2	20	0.2	0	0.0	95	1.1
York–Hanover, PA	885	7.0	0	0.0	120	1.0	0	0.0	25	0.2
Youngstown–Warren–Boardman, OH–PA	1,470	9.5	30	0.2	50	0.3	0	0.0	55	0.4
Yuba City, CA	65	1.5	35	0.8	740	17.1	0	0.0	260	6.0
Yuma, AZ	90	2.0	35	0.8	105	2.3	0	0.0	25	0.6

PART C—METROPOLITAN STATISTICAL AREA TABLES

C-14 **Laborers and Helpers, by Metropolitan Statistical Area, Sex, Race, and Hispanic or Latino Origin, 2006–2010**

Metropolitan Statistical Area	Total who worked in the last 5 years	Male Number	Male Percent	Female Number	Female Percent	Hispanic or Latino Number	Hispanic or Latino Percent	White alone, not Hispanic or Latino Number	White alone, not Hispanic or Latino Percent
Abilene, TX	3,380	3,050	90.2	330	9.8	985	29.1	2,180	64.5
Akron, OH	12,675	10,680	84.3	1,995	15.7	230	1.8	11,040	87.1
Albany, GA	3,685	3,065	83.2	620	16.8	260	7.1	920	25.0
Albany–Schenectady–Troy, NY	12,750	10,805	84.7	1,950	15.3	745	5.8	10,715	84.0
Albuquerque, NM	12,175	10,240	84.1	1,935	15.9	6,945	57.0	3,780	31.0
Alexandria, LA	2,535	2,215	87.4	320	12.6	430	17.0	1,135	44.8
Allentown–Bethlehem–Easton, PA–NJ	15,835	13,215	83.5	2,620	16.5	2,785	17.6	12,295	77.6
Altoona, PA	2,780	2,225	80.0	555	20.0	115	4.1	2,600	93.5
Amarillo, TX	5,380	4,830	89.8	550	10.2	1,835	34.1	2,710	50.4
Ames, IA	2,210	1,875	84.8	335	15.2	145	6.6	1,855	83.9
Anchorage, AK	6,590	5,535	84.0	1,055	16.0	730	11.1	3,985	60.5
Anderson, IN	2,625	2,230	85.0	395	15.0	200	7.6	2,165	82.5
Anderson, SC	3,460	2,920	84.4	535	15.5	115	3.3	2,645	76.4
Ann Arbor, MI	4,095	3,265	79.7	830	20.3	200	4.9	3,230	78.9
Anniston–Oxford, AL	2,750	2,305	83.8	445	16.2	80	2.9	1,905	69.3
Appleton, WI	5,010	3,885	77.5	1,125	22.5	450	9.0	4,315	86.1
Asheville, NC	8,325	6,950	83.5	1,375	16.5	1,150	13.8	6,615	79.5
Athens–Clarke County, GA	3,805	3,020	79.4	785	20.6	745	19.6	2,205	58.0
Atlanta–Sandy Springs–Marietta, GA	87,085	73,520	84.4	13,565	15.6	20,475	23.5	31,940	36.7
Atlantic City–Hammonton, NJ	4,250	3,685	86.7	565	13.3	1,365	32.1	2,210	52.0
Auburn–Opelika, AL	2,215	1,755	79.2	460	20.8	95	4.3	1,415	63.9
Augusta–Richmond County, GA–SC	10,480	8,815	84.1	1,665	15.9	1,160	11.1	4,925	47.0
Austin–Round Rock–San Marcos, TX	24,345	20,865	85.7	3,485	14.3	13,290	54.6	7,965	32.7
Bakersfield–Delano, CA	42,700	31,915	74.7	10,785	25.3	35,790	83.8	4,630	10.8
Baltimore–Towson, MD	35,950	30,605	85.1	5,345	14.9	4,600	12.8	18,725	52.1
Bangor, ME	3,330	2,875	86.3	455	13.7	0	0.0	3,275	98.3
Barnstable Town, MA	4,715	4,090	86.7	625	13.3	95	2.0	4,320	91.6
Baton Rouge, LA	12,615	11,470	90.9	1,140	9.0	785	6.2	5,530	43.8
Battle Creek, MI	3,090	2,260	73.1	830	26.9	260	8.4	2,490	80.6
Bay City, MI	2,160	1,840	85.2	320	14.8	255	11.8	1,785	82.6
Beaumont–Port Arthur, TX	7,085	6,460	91.2	625	8.8	1,555	21.9	2,915	41.1
Bellingham, WA	5,245	4,225	80.6	1,020	19.4	1,530	29.2	3,150	60.1
Bend, OR	3,295	2,610	79.2	685	20.8	390	11.8	2,810	85.3
Billings, MT	3,190	2,670	83.7	525	16.5	230	7.2	2,665	83.5
Binghamton, NY	3,850	3,140	81.6	710	18.4	100	2.6	3,605	93.6
Birmingham–Hoover, AL	20,700	18,040	87.1	2,660	12.9	2,465	11.9	10,955	52.9
Bismarck, ND	1,800	1,600	88.9	200	11.1	30	1.7	1,705	94.7
Blacksburg–Christiansburg–Radford, VA	3,020	2,550	84.4	475	15.7	145	4.8	2,610	86.4
Bloomington, IN	3,305	2,720	82.3	585	17.7	155	4.7	2,855	86.4
Bloomington–Normal, IL	2,785	2,435	87.4	345	12.4	285	10.2	2,305	82.8
Boise City–Nampa, ID	12,890	10,660	82.7	2,230	17.3	4,710	36.5	7,835	60.8
Boston–Cambridge–Quincy, MA–NH	57,890	48,690	84.1	9,200	15.9	9,840	17.0	40,720	70.3
Boulder, CO	3,935	3,195	81.2	740	18.8	1,420	36.1	2,335	59.3
Bowling Green, KY	2,525	2,155	85.3	370	14.7	240	9.5	2,005	79.4
Bremerton–Silverdale, WA	4,495	3,525	78.4	965	21.5	830	18.5	2,975	66.2
Bridgeport–Stamford–Norwalk, CT	14,550	12,715	87.4	1,835	12.6	6,165	42.4	6,335	43.5
Brownsville–Harlingen, TX	7,685	6,930	90.2	750	9.8	7,160	93.2	430	5.6
Brunswick, GA	2,605	2,290	87.9	310	11.9	310	11.9	1,620	62.2
Buffalo–Niagara Falls, NY	16,790	14,270	85.0	2,520	15.0	555	3.3	13,825	82.3
Burlington, NC	2,665	2,265	85.0	405	15.2	375	14.1	1,475	55.3
Burlington–South Burlington, VT	4,235	3,325	78.5	915	21.6	220	5.2	3,715	87.7
Canton–Massillon, OH	9,435	7,685	81.5	1,755	18.6	160	1.7	8,445	89.5
Cape Coral–Fort Myers, FL	11,565	9,500	82.1	2,065	17.9	4,360	37.7	6,005	51.9
Cape Girardeau–Jackson, MO–IL	1,915	1,620	84.6	295	15.4	54	2.8	1,785	93.2
Carson City, NV	1,090	940	86.2	155	14.2	410	37.6	640	58.7

C-14 **Laborers and Helpers, by Metropolitan Statistical Area, Sex, Race, and Hispanic or Latino Origin, 2006–2010**—*Continued*

Metropolitan Statistical Area	Black alone, not Hispanic or Latino Number	Percent	American Indian and Alaska Native alone, not Hispanic or Latino Number	Percent	Asian alone, not Hispanic or Latino Number	Percent	Native Hawaiian and Other Pacific Islander alone, not Hispanic or Latino Number	Percent	Two or more races, not Hispanic or Latino Number	Percent
Abilene, TX	130	3.8	0	0.0	45	1.3	0	0.0	34	1.0
Akron, OH	1,120	8.8	115	0.9	145	1.1	0	0.0	20	0.2
Albany, GA	2,455	66.6	0	0.0	0	0.0	0	0.0	55	1.5
Albany–Schenectady–Troy, NY	660	5.2	30	0.2	170	1.3	4	0.0	425	3.3
Albuquerque, NM	465	3.8	725	6.0	90	0.7	0	0.0	180	1.5
Alexandria, LA	880	34.7	30	1.2	45	1.8	0	0.0	14	0.6
Allentown–Bethlehem–Easton, PA–NJ	490	3.1	30	0.2	165	1.0	0	0.0	65	0.4
Altoona, PA	45	1.6	0	0.0	0	0.0	0	0.0	20	0.7
Amarillo, TX	490	9.1	35	0.7	170	3.2	4	0.1	135	2.5
Ames, IA	90	4.1	0	0.0	115	5.2	0	0.0	0	0.0
Anchorage, AK	220	3.3	560	8.5	460	7.0	215	3.3	424	6.4
Anderson, IN	150	5.7	0	0.0	4	0.2	0	0.0	100	3.8
Anderson, SC	625	18.1	4	0.1	0	0.0	0	0.0	65	1.9
Ann Arbor, MI	490	12.0	30	0.7	65	1.6	0	0.0	79	1.9
Anniston–Oxford, AL	705	25.6	0	0.0	40	1.5	0	0.0	14	0.5
Appleton, WI	35	0.7	105	2.1	60	1.2	0	0.0	40	0.8
Asheville, NC	440	5.3	40	0.5	0	0.0	10	0.1	75	0.9
Athens–Clarke County, GA	735	19.3	10	0.3	0	0.0	0	0.0	110	2.9
Atlanta–Sandy Springs–Marietta, GA	31,445	36.1	270	0.3	2,020	2.3	85	0.1	850	1.0
Atlantic City–Hammonton, NJ	465	10.9	0	0.0	175	4.1	0	0.0	35	0.8
Auburn–Opelika, AL	665	30.0	20	0.9	0	0.0	0	0.0	19	0.9
Augusta–Richmond County, GA–SC	4,290	40.9	4	0.0	55	0.5	0	0.0	35	0.3
Austin–Round Rock–San Marcos, TX	2,260	9.3	10	0.0	280	1.2	75	0.3	465	1.9
Bakersfield–Delano, CA	530	1.2	80	0.2	1,270	3.0	20	0.0	385	0.9
Baltimore–Towson, MD	11,770	32.7	100	0.3	400	1.1	0	0.0	350	1.0
Bangor, ME	15	0.5	4	0.1	4	0.1	0	0.0	25	0.8
Barnstable Town, MA	140	3.0	25	0.5	20	0.4	0	0.0	115	2.4
Baton Rouge, LA	6,000	47.6	45	0.4	65	0.5	0	0.0	185	1.5
Battle Creek, MI	220	7.1	0	0.0	40	1.3	0	0.0	74	2.4
Bay City, MI	15	0.7	4	0.2	0	0.0	0	0.0	105	4.9
Beaumont–Port Arthur, TX	2,410	34.0	25	0.4	110	1.6	0	0.0	65	0.9
Bellingham, WA	30	0.6	270	5.1	220	4.2	4	0.1	40	0.8
Bend, OR	0	0.0	40	1.2	4	0.1	15	0.5	40	1.2
Billings, MT	25	0.8	230	7.2	4	0.1	0	0.0	35	1.1
Binghamton, NY	60	1.6	0	0.0	15	0.4	0	0.0	65	1.7
Birmingham–Hoover, AL	6,940	33.5	45	0.2	70	0.3	0	0.0	230	1.1
Bismarck, ND	0	0.0	25	1.4	10	0.6	0	0.0	30	1.7
Blacksburg–Christiansburg–Radford, VA	150	5.0	0	0.0	65	2.2	0	0.0	50	1.7
Bloomington, IN	170	5.1	0	0.0	110	3.3	0	0.0	15	0.5
Bloomington–Normal, IL	160	5.7	0	0.0	4	0.1	0	0.0	30	1.1
Boise City–Nampa, ID	60	0.5	40	0.3	80	0.6	25	0.2	135	1.0
Boston–Cambridge–Quincy, MA–NH	3,815	6.6	80	0.1	1,680	2.9	15	0.0	1,745	3.0
Boulder, CO	4	0.1	20	0.5	115	2.9	0	0.0	29	0.7
Bowling Green, KY	245	9.7	0	0.0	0	0.0	0	0.0	30	1.2
Bremerton–Silverdale, WA	110	2.4	100	2.2	190	4.2	55	1.2	230	5.1
Bridgeport–Stamford–Norwalk, CT	1,435	9.9	4	0.0	360	2.5	0	0.0	255	1.8
Brownsville–Harlingen, TX	15	0.2	30	0.4	15	0.2	0	0.0	30	0.4
Brunswick, GA	655	25.1	0	0.0	25	1.0	0	0.0	0	0.0
Buffalo–Niagara Falls, NY	1,815	10.8	135	0.8	130	0.8	0	0.0	340	2.0
Burlington, NC	700	26.3	40	1.5	15	0.6	50	1.9	10	0.4
Burlington–South Burlington, VT	200	4.7	15	0.4	25	0.6	0	0.0	55	1.3
Canton–Massillon, OH	770	8.2	25	0.3	4	0.0	0	0.0	34	0.4
Cape Coral–Fort Myers, FL	1,000	8.6	65	0.6	75	0.6	0	0.0	60	0.5
Cape Girardeau–Jackson, MO–IL	45	2.3	0	0.0	20	1.0	0	0.0	10	0.5
Carson City, NV	0	0.0	10	0.9	30	2.8	0	0.0	4	0.4

C-14 Laborers and Helpers, by Metropolitan Statistical Area, Sex, Race, and Hispanic or Latino Origin, 2006–2010—Continued

Metropolitan Statistical Area	Total who worked in the last 5 years	Male Number	Male Percent	Female Number	Female Percent	Hispanic or Latino Number	Hispanic or Latino Percent	White alone, not Hispanic or Latino Number	White alone, not Hispanic or Latino Percent
Casper, WY	1,400	1,125	80.4	275	19.6	115	8.2	1,195	85.4
Cedar Rapids, IA	5,010	4,110	82.0	900	18.0	230	4.6	4,615	92.1
Champaign–Urbana, IL	4,750	4,000	84.2	750	15.8	465	9.8	3,525	74.2
Charleston, WV	4,165	3,530	84.8	635	15.2	30	0.7	3,920	94.1
Charleston–North Charleston–Summerville, SC	11,120	9,335	83.9	1,785	16.1	1,275	11.5	5,260	47.3
Charlotte–Gastonia–Rock Hill, NC–SC	30,035	25,225	84.0	4,805	16.0	6,385	21.3	13,755	45.8
Charlottesville, VA	3,350	3,015	90.0	335	10.0	650	19.4	2,185	65.2
Chattanooga, TN–GA	9,300	7,930	85.3	1,370	14.7	785	8.4	6,545	70.4
Cheyenne, WY	2,020	1,690	83.7	330	16.3	325	16.1	1,595	79.0
Chicago–Joliet–Naperville, IL–IN–WI	156,110	129,510	83.0	26,600	17.0	65,200	41.8	61,530	39.4
Chico, CA	5,595	4,825	86.2	770	13.8	1,570	28.1	3,445	61.6
Cincinnati–Middletown, OH–KY–IN	37,120	30,255	81.5	6,865	18.5	2,325	6.3	28,670	77.2
Clarksville, TN–KY	4,295	3,290	76.6	1,005	23.4	505	11.8	2,785	64.8
Cleveland, TN	2,615	2,185	83.6	430	16.4	355	13.6	2,135	81.6
Cleveland–Elyria–Mentor, OH	35,835	29,930	83.5	5,910	16.5	3,590	10.0	24,635	68.7
Coeur d'Alene, ID	2,245	1,815	80.8	430	19.2	55	2.4	2,100	93.5
College Station–Bryan, TX	4,420	3,780	85.5	640	14.5	1,790	40.5	1,950	44.1
Colorado Springs, CO	8,730	7,165	82.1	1,560	17.9	1,680	19.2	6,095	69.8
Columbia, MO	2,460	2,070	84.1	390	15.9	145	5.9	2,025	82.3
Columbia, SC	13,970	12,050	86.3	1,920	13.7	1,745	12.5	6,750	48.3
Columbus, GA–AL	4,250	3,680	86.6	575	13.5	495	11.6	1,640	38.6
Columbus, IN	1,300	1,045	80.4	260	20.0	250	19.2	1,005	77.3
Columbus, OH	33,070	26,185	79.2	6,885	20.8	2,020	6.1	24,280	73.4
Corpus Christi, TX	8,220	7,180	87.3	1,040	12.7	5,425	66.0	2,120	25.8
Corvallis, OR	2,340	1,915	81.8	425	18.2	470	20.1	1,845	78.8
Crestview–Fort Walton Beach–Destin, FL	3,180	2,720	85.5	460	14.5	340	10.7	2,240	70.4
Cumberland, MD–WV	1,855	1,695	91.4	160	8.6	40	2.2	1,670	90.0
Dallas–Fort Worth–Arlington, TX	106,520	91,290	85.7	15,230	14.3	51,780	48.6	34,025	31.9
Dalton, GA	2,470	2,070	83.8	400	16.2	620	25.1	1,700	68.8
Danville, IL	2,250	2,015	89.6	235	10.4	80	3.6	1,590	70.7
Danville, VA	2,580	2,310	89.5	270	10.5	455	17.6	1,140	44.2
Davenport–Moline–Rock Island, IA–IL	7,370	5,995	81.3	1,375	18.7	905	12.3	5,870	79.6
Dayton, OH	14,690	11,855	80.7	2,840	19.3	525	3.6	11,575	78.8
Decatur, AL	3,400	2,870	84.4	535	15.7	410	12.1	2,235	65.7
Decatur, IL	2,410	1,905	79.0	505	21.0	25	1.0	1,820	75.5
Deltona–Daytona Beach–Ormond Beach, FL	10,525	8,690	82.6	1,835	17.4	2,555	24.3	6,600	62.7
Denver–Aurora–Broomfield, CO	41,540	34,105	82.1	7,435	17.9	15,950	38.4	20,755	50.0
Des Moines–West Des Moines, IA	10,070	8,500	84.4	1,570	15.6	1,180	11.7	8,065	80.1
Detroit–Warren–Livonia, MI	68,360	55,455	81.1	12,905	18.9	6,340	9.3	44,640	65.3
Dothan, AL	3,040	2,600	85.5	440	14.5	410	13.5	1,830	60.2
Dover, DE	2,805	2,285	81.5	515	18.4	300	10.7	1,860	66.3
Dubuque, IA	2,280	1,885	82.7	400	17.5	25	1.1	2,165	95.0
Duluth, MN–WI	4,455	3,700	83.1	755	16.9	85	1.9	4,110	92.3
Durham–Chapel Hill, NC	8,020	6,925	86.3	1,095	13.7	2,920	36.4	3,100	38.7
Eau Claire, WI	4,065	3,095	76.1	970	23.9	200	4.9	3,645	89.7
El Centro, CA	6,645	5,120	77.1	1,530	23.0	6,100	91.8	385	5.8
Elizabethtown, KY	1,780	1,280	71.9	500	28.1	190	10.7	1,400	78.7
Elkhart–Goshen, IN	4,650	3,410	73.3	1,240	26.7	1,025	22.0	3,260	70.1
Elmira, NY	1,450	1,250	86.2	200	13.8	0	0.0	1,310	90.3
El Paso, TX	11,260	9,930	88.2	1,330	11.8	10,255	91.1	660	5.9
Erie, PA	5,135	4,175	81.3	960	18.7	285	5.6	4,435	86.4
Eugene–Springfield, OR	8,835	7,440	84.2	1,390	15.7	1,300	14.7	6,980	79.0
Evansville, IN–KY	7,365	6,040	82.0	1,325	18.0	480	6.5	6,380	86.6
Fairbanks, AK	1,765	1,390	78.8	375	21.2	70	4.0	1,285	72.8
Fargo, ND–MN	4,920	4,350	88.4	575	11.7	150	3.0	4,350	88.4

C-14 **Laborers and Helpers, by Metropolitan Statistical Area, Sex, Race, and Hispanic or Latino Origin, 2006–2010**—*Continued*

Metropolitan Statistical Area	Black alone, not Hispanic or Latino Number	Percent	American Indian and Alaska Native alone, not Hispanic or Latino Number	Percent	Asian alone, not Hispanic or Latino Number	Percent	Native Hawaiian and Other Pacific Islander alone, not Hispanic or Latino Number	Percent	Two or more races, not Hispanic or Latino Number	Percent
Casper, WY	30	2.1	0	0.0	20	1.4	0	0.0	35	2.5
Cedar Rapids, IA	100	2.0	10	0.2	15	0.3	0	0.0	39	0.8
Champaign–Urbana, IL	610	12.8	4	0.1	50	1.1	0	0.0	88	1.9
Charleston, WV	55	1.3	0	0.0	0	0.0	0	0.0	159	3.8
Charleston–North Charleston–Summerville, SC	4,165	37.5	75	0.7	165	1.5	0	0.0	179	1.6
Charlotte–Gastonia–Rock Hill, NC–SC	9,040	30.1	65	0.2	420	1.4	15	0.0	355	1.2
Charlottesville, VA	405	12.1	0	0.0	0	0.0	0	0.0	110	3.3
Chattanooga, TN–GA	1,765	19.0	20	0.2	15	0.2	0	0.0	165	1.8
Cheyenne, WY	15	0.7	0	0.0	15	0.7	0	0.0	70	3.5
Chicago–Joliet–Naperville, IL–IN–WI	24,790	15.9	235	0.2	2,835	1.8	45	0.0	1,470	0.9
Chico, CA	105	1.9	15	0.3	120	2.1	15	0.3	330	5.9
Cincinnati–Middletown, OH–KY–IN	5,345	14.4	90	0.2	245	0.7	0	0.0	435	1.2
Clarksville, TN–KY	835	19.4	80	1.9	50	1.2	0	0.0	45	1.0
Cleveland, TN	110	4.2	0	0.0	0	0.0	0	0.0	15	0.6
Cleveland–Elyria–Mentor, OH	6,940	19.4	30	0.1	315	0.9	0	0.0	320	0.9
Coeur d'Alene, ID	4	0.2	0	0.0	35	1.6	0	0.0	49	2.2
College Station–Bryan, TX	610	13.8	10	0.2	15	0.3	10	0.2	35	0.8
Colorado Springs, CO	570	6.5	55	0.6	140	1.6	0	0.0	190	2.2
Columbia, MO	260	10.6	10	0.4	4	0.2	0	0.0	20	0.8
Columbia, SC	5,295	37.9	4	0.0	30	0.2	0	0.0	145	1.0
Columbus, GA–AL	1,995	46.9	0	0.0	75	1.8	0	0.0	55	1.3
Columbus, IN	10	0.8	4	0.3	0	0.0	0	0.0	34	2.6
Columbus, OH	5,685	17.2	40	0.1	405	1.2	0	0.0	640	1.9
Corpus Christi, TX	510	6.2	4	0.0	105	1.3	0	0.0	50	0.6
Corvallis, OR	0	0.0	25	1.1	0	0.0	0	0.0	0	0.0
Crestview–Fort Walton Beach–Destin, FL	480	15.1	10	0.3	35	1.1	0	0.0	70	2.2
Cumberland, MD–WV	105	5.7	4	0.2	25	1.3	0	0.0	10	0.5
Dallas–Fort Worth–Arlington, TX	17,220	16.2	300	0.3	1,690	1.6	170	0.2	1,330	1.2
Dalton, GA	105	4.3	15	0.6	10	0.4	15	0.6	10	0.4
Danville, IL	550	24.4	0	0.0	0	0.0	0	0.0	30	1.3
Danville, VA	965	37.4	0	0.0	20	0.8	0	0.0	0	0.0
Davenport–Moline–Rock Island, IA–IL	350	4.7	20	0.3	85	1.2	0	0.0	140	1.9
Dayton, OH	2,135	14.5	105	0.7	145	1.0	0	0.0	215	1.5
Decatur, AL	670	19.7	10	0.3	0	0.0	0	0.0	80	2.4
Decatur, IL	445	18.5	0	0.0	15	0.6	0	0.0	104	4.3
Deltona–Daytona Beach–Ormond Beach, FL	1,180	11.2	10	0.1	60	0.6	30	0.3	100	1.0
Denver–Aurora–Broomfield, CO	2,935	7.1	170	0.4	1,050	2.5	70	0.2	610	1.5
Des Moines–West Des Moines, IA	455	4.5	55	0.5	250	2.5	0	0.0	70	0.7
Detroit–Warren–Livonia, MI	15,460	22.6	265	0.4	610	0.9	20	0.0	1,025	1.5
Dothan, AL	770	25.3	15	0.5	4	0.1	0	0.0	12	0.4
Dover, DE	595	21.2	15	0.5	30	1.1	0	0.0	4	0.1
Dubuque, IA	30	1.3	10	0.4	15	0.7	10	0.4	25	1.1
Duluth, MN–WI	55	1.2	155	3.5	25	0.6	0	0.0	23	0.5
Durham–Chapel Hill, NC	1,865	23.3	30	0.4	30	0.4	0	0.0	80	1.0
Eau Claire, WI	115	2.8	20	0.5	60	1.5	0	0.0	25	0.6
El Centro, CA	95	1.4	4	0.1	4	0.1	0	0.0	50	0.8
Elizabethtown, KY	155	8.7	20	1.1	0	0.0	0	0.0	15	0.8
Elkhart–Goshen, IN	210	4.5	15	0.3	70	1.5	4	0.1	60	1.3
Elmira, NY	120	8.3	0	0.0	0	0.0	0	0.0	20	1.4
El Paso, TX	230	2.0	4	0.0	50	0.4	0	0.0	65	0.6
Erie, PA	320	6.2	4	0.1	25	0.5	0	0.0	65	1.3
Eugene–Springfield, OR	50	0.6	210	2.4	60	0.7	65	0.7	164	1.9
Evansville, IN–KY	330	4.5	40	0.5	25	0.3	0	0.0	104	1.4
Fairbanks, AK	80	4.5	245	13.9	0	0.0	0	0.0	79	4.5
Fargo, ND–MN	305	6.2	40	0.8	25	0.5	0	0.0	50	1.0

PART C—METROPOLITAN STATISTICAL AREA TABLES

C-14 Laborers and Helpers, by Metropolitan Statistical Area, Sex, Race, and Hispanic or Latino Origin, 2006–2010—Continued

Metropolitan Statistical Area	Total who worked in the last 5 years	Male Number	Male Percent	Female Number	Female Percent	Hispanic or Latino Number	Hispanic or Latino Percent	White alone, not Hispanic or Latino Number	White alone, not Hispanic or Latino Percent
Farmington, NM	2,430	1,940	79.8	490	20.2	660	27.2	820	33.7
Fayetteville, NC	5,745	4,855	84.5	890	15.5	1,070	18.6	2,025	35.2
Fayetteville–Springdale–Rogers, AR–MO	9,275	7,140	77.0	2,135	23.0	2,055	22.2	6,235	67.2
Flagstaff, AZ	2,410	1,835	76.1	570	23.7	465	19.3	1,170	48.5
Flint, MI	7,460	6,230	83.5	1,230	16.5	180	2.4	5,920	79.4
Florence, SC	3,585	3,200	89.3	380	10.6	245	6.8	1,500	41.8
Florence–Muscle Shoals, AL	2,675	2,215	82.8	460	17.2	40	1.5	2,165	80.9
Fond du Lac, WI	2,945	2,335	79.3	610	20.7	275	9.3	2,485	84.4
Fort Collins–Loveland, CO	5,900	4,645	78.7	1,255	21.3	975	16.5	4,735	80.3
Fort Smith, AR–OK	6,870	5,510	80.2	1,360	19.8	1,315	19.1	4,415	64.3
Fort Wayne, IN	8,165	6,755	82.7	1,410	17.3	980	12.0	6,045	74.0
Fresno, CA	46,120	37,110	80.5	9,010	19.5	39,710	86.1	4,085	8.9
Gadsden, AL	2,250	1,835	81.6	415	18.4	135	6.0	1,710	76.0
Gainesville, FL	5,120	4,415	86.2	705	13.8	795	15.5	3,005	58.7
Gainesville, GA	4,875	4,125	84.6	750	15.4	2,480	50.9	2,045	41.9
Glens Falls, NY	3,070	2,540	82.7	530	17.3	20	0.7	3,010	98.0
Goldsboro, NC	3,095	2,500	80.8	595	19.2	1,155	37.3	960	31.0
Grand Forks, ND–MN	2,720	2,320	85.3	405	14.9	160	5.9	2,440	89.7
Grand Junction, CO	2,795	2,300	82.3	495	17.7	780	27.9	1,930	69.1
Grand Rapids–Wyoming, MI	17,800	14,075	79.1	3,725	20.9	3,760	21.1	12,305	69.1
Great Falls, MT	1,700	1,415	83.2	280	16.5	39	2.3	1,540	90.6
Greeley, CO	6,290	5,140	81.7	1,150	18.3	2,955	47.0	3,215	51.1
Green Bay, WI	8,125	6,325	77.8	1,800	22.2	1,270	15.6	6,430	79.1
Greensboro–High Point, NC	14,725	12,470	84.7	2,255	15.3	1,615	11.0	7,400	50.3
Greenville, NC	4,020	3,350	83.3	675	16.8	870	21.6	1,640	40.8
Greenville–Mauldin–Easley, SC	11,720	9,805	83.7	1,915	16.3	1,830	15.6	7,520	64.2
Gulfport–Biloxi, MS	3,935	3,425	87.0	510	13.0	310	7.9	2,430	61.8
Hagerstown–Martinsburg, MD–WV	5,875	4,570	77.8	1,305	22.2	205	3.5	4,660	79.3
Hanford–Corcoran, CA	9,520	8,295	87.1	1,225	12.9	8,030	84.3	1,430	15.0
Harrisburg–Carlisle, PA	13,115	10,825	82.5	2,290	17.5	700	5.3	10,300	78.5
Harrisonburg, VA	4,445	3,445	77.5	1,000	22.5	1,210	27.2	2,875	64.7
Hartford–West Hartford–East Hartford, CT	17,820	14,870	83.4	2,950	16.6	3,590	20.1	11,410	64.0
Hattiesburg, MS	2,350	2,120	90.2	225	9.6	235	10.0	1,200	51.1
Hickory–Lenoir–Morganton, NC	7,890	6,745	85.5	1,150	14.6	945	12.0	5,960	75.5
Hinesville–Fort Stewart, GA	1,245	895	71.9	345	27.7	215	17.3	295	23.7
Holland–Grand Haven, MI	6,715	4,965	73.9	1,750	26.1	1,325	19.7	5,160	76.8
Honolulu, HI	15,165	12,625	83.3	2,540	16.7	1,345	8.9	1,580	10.4
Hot Springs, AR	1,735	1,470	84.7	270	15.6	275	15.9	1,245	71.8
Houma–Bayou Cane–Thibodaux, LA	4,295	3,715	86.5	580	13.5	240	5.6	3,100	72.2
Houston–Sugar Land–Baytown, TX	106,235	93,790	88.3	12,450	11.7	61,280	57.7	22,300	21.0
Huntington–Ashland, WV–KY–OH	4,010	3,565	88.9	445	11.1	10	0.2	3,845	95.9
Huntsville, AL	6,375	5,470	85.8	905	14.2	805	12.6	3,320	52.1
Idaho Falls, ID	2,990	2,510	83.9	480	16.1	750	25.1	2,115	70.7
Indianapolis–Carmel, IN	31,075	24,865	80.0	6,205	20.0	3,805	12.2	20,625	66.4
Iowa City, IA	2,370	1,850	78.1	520	21.9	185	7.8	2,040	86.1
Ithaca, NY	1,590	1,360	85.5	230	14.5	50	3.1	1,510	95.0
Jackson, MI	2,915	2,340	80.3	580	19.9	55	1.9	2,590	88.9
Jackson, MS	9,330	8,260	88.5	1,070	11.5	505	5.4	3,225	34.6
Jackson, TN	1,940	1,685	86.9	255	13.1	150	7.7	1,050	54.1
Jacksonville, FL	23,600	19,975	84.6	3,625	15.4	2,230	9.4	13,445	57.0
Jacksonville, NC	2,445	2,080	85.1	365	14.9	275	11.2	1,790	73.2
Janesville, WI	3,640	3,030	83.2	610	16.8	585	16.1	2,840	78.0
Jefferson City, MO	2,820	2,270	80.5	550	19.5	110	3.9	2,625	93.1
Johnson City, TN	3,275	2,790	85.2	480	14.7	225	6.9	2,930	89.5
Johnstown, PA	2,730	2,295	84.1	435	15.9	54	2.0	2,605	95.4

C-14 **Laborers and Helpers, by Metropolitan Statistical Area, Sex, Race, and Hispanic or Latino Origin, 2006–2010**—*Continued*

Metropolitan Statistical Area	Black alone, not Hispanic or Latino Number	Percent	American Indian and Alaska Native alone, not Hispanic or Latino Number	Percent	Asian alone, not Hispanic or Latino Number	Percent	Native Hawaiian and Other Pacific Islander alone, not Hispanic or Latino Number	Percent	Two or more races, not Hispanic or Latino Number	Percent
Farmington, NM	0	0.0	910	37.4	15	0.6	0	0.0	25	1.0
Fayetteville, NC	2,250	39.2	120	2.1	90	1.6	10	0.2	174	3.0
Fayetteville–Springdale–Rogers, AR–MO	200	2.2	215	2.3	330	3.6	100	1.1	139	1.5
Flagstaff, AZ	30	1.2	695	28.8	0	0.0	0	0.0	45	1.9
Flint, MI	1,205	16.2	60	0.8	4	0.1	0	0.0	85	1.1
Florence, SC	1,805	50.3	0	0.0	0	0.0	0	0.0	30	0.8
Florence–Muscle Shoals, AL	455	17.0	4	0.1	0	0.0	0	0.0	10	0.4
Fond du Lac, WI	150	5.1	10	0.3	20	0.7	0	0.0	4	0.1
Fort Collins–Loveland, CO	125	2.1	4	0.1	0	0.0	0	0.0	60	1.0
Fort Smith, AR–OK	345	5.0	270	3.9	185	2.7	0	0.0	335	4.9
Fort Wayne, IN	920	11.3	10	0.1	100	1.2	0	0.0	110	1.3
Fresno, CA	580	1.3	130	0.3	1,160	2.5	0	0.0	455	1.0
Gadsden, AL	390	17.3	0	0.0	0	0.0	0	0.0	10	0.4
Gainesville, FL	1,225	23.9	0	0.0	20	0.4	10	0.2	60	1.2
Gainesville, GA	325	6.7	15	0.3	0	0.0	0	0.0	10	0.2
Glens Falls, NY	40	1.3	0	0.0	0	0.0	0	0.0	0	0.0
Goldsboro, NC	950	30.7	0	0.0	4	0.1	0	0.0	29	0.9
Grand Forks, ND–MN	65	2.4	4	0.1	20	0.7	0	0.0	35	1.3
Grand Junction, CO	0	0.0	70	2.5	0	0.0	0	0.0	20	0.7
Grand Rapids–Wyoming, MI	1,265	7.1	35	0.2	320	1.8	0	0.0	120	0.7
Great Falls, MT	15	0.9	65	3.8	0	0.0	0	0.0	40	2.4
Greeley, CO	0	0.0	0	0.0	70	1.1	0	0.0	45	0.7
Green Bay, WI	85	1.0	215	2.6	45	0.6	0	0.0	80	1.0
Greensboro–High Point, NC	5,045	34.3	150	1.0	325	2.2	0	0.0	185	1.3
Greenville, NC	1,470	36.6	0	0.0	0	0.0	0	0.0	40	1.0
Greenville–Mauldin–Easley, SC	2,175	18.6	4	0.0	50	0.4	10	0.1	130	1.1
Gulfport–Biloxi, MS	1,125	28.6	0	0.0	70	1.8	0	0.0	0	0.0
Hagerstown–Martinsburg, MD–WV	775	13.2	0	0.0	90	1.5	0	0.0	145	2.5
Hanford–Corcoran, CA	55	0.6	0	0.0	0	0.0	0	0.0	4	0.0
Harrisburg–Carlisle, PA	1,515	11.6	30	0.2	290	2.2	0	0.0	279	2.1
Harrisonburg, VA	310	7.0	4	0.1	40	0.9	0	0.0	4	0.1
Hartford–West Hartford–East Hartford, CT	2,350	13.2	0	0.0	155	0.9	0	0.0	320	1.8
Hattiesburg, MS	825	35.1	0	0.0	45	1.9	0	0.0	40	1.7
Hickory–Lenoir–Morganton, NC	615	7.8	15	0.2	300	3.8	0	0.0	55	0.7
Hinesville–Fort Stewart, GA	670	53.8	0	0.0	25	2.0	0	0.0	40	3.2
Holland–Grand Haven, MI	60	0.9	4	0.1	130	1.9	0	0.0	35	0.5
Honolulu, HI	40	0.3	45	0.3	6,995	46.1	2,420	16.0	2,735	18.0
Hot Springs, AR	155	8.9	10	0.6	15	0.9	0	0.0	40	2.3
Houma–Bayou Cane–Thibodaux, LA	500	11.6	255	5.9	95	2.2	0	0.0	100	2.3
Houston–Sugar Land–Baytown, TX	19,030	17.9	135	0.1	2,650	2.5	0	0.0	840	0.8
Huntington–Ashland, WV–KY–OH	140	3.5	4	0.1	4	0.1	0	0.0	4	0.1
Huntsville, AL	1,945	30.5	130	2.0	0	0.0	0	0.0	180	2.8
Idaho Falls, ID	20	0.7	30	1.0	10	0.3	0	0.0	60	2.0
Indianapolis–Carmel, IN	5,840	18.8	140	0.5	350	1.1	0	0.0	310	1.0
Iowa City, IA	95	4.0	25	1.1	4	0.2	0	0.0	20	0.8
Ithaca, NY	0	0.0	0	0.0	0	0.0	0	0.0	29	1.8
Jackson, MI	225	7.7	0	0.0	4	0.1	0	0.0	39	1.3
Jackson, MS	5,520	59.2	0	0.0	35	0.4	0	0.0	43	0.5
Jackson, TN	705	36.3	0	0.0	15	0.8	0	0.0	20	1.0
Jacksonville, FL	6,790	28.8	245	1.0	460	1.9	0	0.0	430	1.8
Jacksonville, NC	275	11.2	4	0.2	35	1.4	0	0.0	65	2.7
Janesville, WI	170	4.7	0	0.0	25	0.7	0	0.0	20	0.5
Jefferson City, MO	45	1.6	4	0.1	20	0.7	10	0.4	0	0.0
Johnson City, TN	65	2.0	25	0.8	0	0.0	0	0.0	30	0.9
Johnstown, PA	30	1.1	15	0.5	0	0.0	0	0.0	25	0.9

PART C—METROPOLITAN STATISTICAL AREA TABLES

C-14 **Laborers and Helpers, by Metropolitan Statistical Area, Sex, Race, and Hispanic or Latino Origin, 2006–2010**—*Continued*

Metropolitan Statistical Area	Total who worked in the last 5 years	Male Number	Male Percent	Female Number	Female Percent	Hispanic or Latino Number	Hispanic or Latino Percent	White alone, not Hispanic or Latino Number	White alone, not Hispanic or Latino Percent
Jonesboro, AR	3,585	3,115	86.9	470	13.1	315	8.8	3,015	84.1
Joplin, MO	3,795	2,980	78.5	815	21.5	410	10.8	2,945	77.6
Kalamazoo–Portage, MI	7,425	5,500	74.1	1,920	25.9	1,495	20.1	5,310	71.5
Kankakee–Bradley, IL	2,935	2,555	87.1	380	12.9	865	29.5	1,680	57.2
Kansas City, MO–KS	35,295	29,890	84.7	5,405	15.3	5,595	15.9	23,010	65.2
Kennewick–Pasco–Richland, WA	10,025	7,995	79.8	2,025	20.2	7,230	72.1	2,540	25.3
Killeen–Temple–Fort Hood, TX	6,170	5,220	84.6	950	15.4	1,630	26.4	3,065	49.7
Kingsport–Bristol–Bristol, TN–VA	5,430	4,670	86.0	760	14.0	75	1.4	5,285	97.3
Kingston, NY	3,175	2,675	84.3	500	15.7	420	13.2	2,470	77.8
Knoxville, TN	12,210	9,980	81.7	2,230	18.3	965	7.9	10,160	83.2
Kokomo, IN	1,885	1,425	75.6	460	24.4	100	5.3	1,640	87.0
La Crosse, WI–MN	3,270	2,560	78.3	710	21.7	145	4.4	2,885	88.2
Lafayette, IN	4,090	3,145	76.9	950	23.2	780	19.1	3,165	77.4
Lafayette, LA	5,000	4,520	90.4	485	9.7	370	7.4	2,680	53.6
Lake Charles, LA	3,155	2,595	82.3	565	17.9	70	2.2	2,325	73.7
Lake Havasu City–Kingman, AZ	3,210	2,665	83.0	545	17.0	670	20.9	2,365	73.7
Lakeland–Winter Haven, FL	17,480	14,240	81.5	3,240	18.5	6,235	35.7	8,125	46.5
Lancaster, PA	13,175	10,520	79.8	2,660	20.2	1,385	10.5	10,995	83.5
Lansing–East Lansing, MI	9,165	7,375	80.5	1,790	19.5	1,030	11.2	7,070	77.1
Laredo, TX	4,455	4,210	94.5	245	5.5	4,320	97.0	115	2.6
Las Cruces, NM	4,545	3,865	85.0	680	15.0	3,705	81.5	445	9.8
Las Vegas–Paradise, NV	33,635	28,560	84.9	5,075	15.1	16,145	48.0	11,755	34.9
Lawrence, KS	2,170	1,545	71.2	630	29.0	230	10.6	1,675	77.2
Lawton, OK	1,910	1,430	74.9	480	25.1	310	16.2	1,070	56.0
Lebanon, PA	3,190	2,670	83.7	520	16.3	220	6.9	2,805	87.9
Lewiston, ID–WA	1,380	1,240	89.9	135	9.8	69	5.0	1,145	83.0
Lewiston–Auburn, ME	2,180	1,615	74.1	565	25.9	95	4.4	2,000	91.7
Lexington–Fayette, KY	11,600	10,005	86.3	1,595	13.8	3,810	32.8	6,905	59.5
Lima, OH	2,555	2,075	81.2	480	18.8	100	3.9	2,090	81.8
Lincoln, NE	5,535	4,530	81.8	1,005	18.2	370	6.7	4,775	86.3
Little Rock–North Little Rock–Conway, AR	12,120	10,570	87.2	1,550	12.8	925	7.6	7,725	63.7
Logan, UT–ID	2,600	2,190	84.2	410	15.8	545	21.0	1,990	76.5
Longview, TX	4,770	4,285	89.8	480	10.1	1,535	32.2	2,520	52.8
Longview, WA	3,435	2,720	79.2	715	20.8	1,035	30.1	2,295	66.8
Los Angeles–Long Beach–Santa Ana, CA	231,940	200,300	86.4	31,640	13.6	175,855	75.8	30,735	13.3
Louisville/Jefferson County, KY–IN	29,360	23,570	80.3	5,790	19.7	2,830	9.6	21,995	74.9
Lubbock, TX	6,090	5,450	89.5	640	10.5	2,670	43.8	2,750	45.2
Lynchburg, VA	5,125	4,250	82.9	875	17.1	50	1.0	3,820	74.5
Macon, GA	4,120	3,870	93.9	250	6.1	470	11.4	1,660	40.3
Madera–Chowchilla, CA	10,145	8,215	81.0	1,935	19.1	8,905	87.8	1,045	10.3
Madison, WI	10,175	8,050	79.1	2,125	20.9	1,060	10.4	8,460	83.1
Manchester–Nashua, NH	6,615	5,475	82.8	1,140	17.2	655	9.9	5,610	84.8
Manhattan, KS	2,095	1,650	78.8	440	21.0	79	3.8	1,760	84.0
Mankato–North Mankato, MN	2,405	1,990	82.7	415	17.3	60	2.5	2,285	95.0
Mansfield, OH	3,170	2,330	73.5	840	26.5	8	0.3	2,855	90.1
McAllen–Edinburg–Mission, TX	19,670	17,750	90.2	1,925	9.8	19,080	97.0	570	2.9
Medford, OR	5,510	4,820	87.5	695	12.6	1,670	30.3	3,560	64.6
Memphis, TN–MS–AR	29,230	23,010	78.7	6,215	21.3	2,655	9.1	9,025	30.9
Merced, CA	13,835	12,030	87.0	1,805	13.0	10,800	78.1	2,305	16.7
Miami–Fort Lauderdale–Pompano Beach, FL	102,130	88,015	86.2	14,115	13.8	54,730	53.6	20,260	19.8
Michigan City–La Porte, IN	2,495	2,020	81.0	475	19.0	165	6.6	2,165	86.8
Midland, TX	2,695	2,295	85.2	400	14.8	1,285	47.7	1,200	44.5
Milwaukee–Waukesha–West Allis, WI	27,520	22,755	82.7	4,765	17.3	5,740	20.9	16,530	60.1
Minneapolis–St. Paul–Bloomington, MN–WI	48,615	39,635	81.5	8,980	18.5	5,505	11.3	37,330	76.8
Missoula, MT	2,445	2,120	86.7	325	13.3	80	3.3	2,135	87.3

C-14 Laborers and Helpers, by Metropolitan Statistical Area, Sex, Race, and Hispanic or Latino Origin, 2006–2010—*Continued*

Metropolitan Statistical Area	Black alone, not Hispanic or Latino Number	Percent	American Indian and Alaska Native alone, not Hispanic or Latino Number	Percent	Asian alone, not Hispanic or Latino Number	Percent	Native Hawaiian and Other Pacific Islander alone, not Hispanic or Latino Number	Percent	Two or more races, not Hispanic or Latino Number	Percent
Jonesboro, AR	195	5.4	15	0.4	0	0.0	0	0.0	50	1.4
Joplin, MO	210	5.5	45	1.2	65	1.7	35	0.9	79	2.1
Kalamazoo–Portage, MI	455	6.1	40	0.5	15	0.2	0	0.0	110	1.5
Kankakee–Bradley, IL	380	12.9	0	0.0	0	0.0	0	0.0	10	0.3
Kansas City, MO–KS	5,315	15.1	155	0.4	430	1.2	65	0.2	730	2.1
Kennewick–Pasco–Richland, WA	60	0.6	60	0.6	60	0.6	0	0.0	70	0.7
Killeen–Temple–Fort Hood, TX	1,215	19.7	4	0.1	80	1.3	50	0.8	135	2.2
Kingsport–Bristol–Bristol, TN–VA	55	1.0	0	0.0	15	0.3	0	0.0	0	0.0
Kingston, NY	185	5.8	40	1.3	15	0.5	0	0.0	45	1.4
Knoxville, TN	765	6.3	100	0.8	30	0.2	0	0.0	190	1.6
Kokomo, IN	145	7.7	0	0.0	0	0.0	0	0.0	0	0.0
La Crosse, WI–MN	45	1.4	35	1.1	125	3.8	0	0.0	40	1.2
Lafayette, IN	100	2.4	0	0.0	0	0.0	20	0.5	35	0.9
Lafayette, LA	1,900	38.0	25	0.5	4	0.1	0	0.0	25	0.5
Lake Charles, LA	675	21.4	40	1.3	0	0.0	0	0.0	45	1.4
Lake Havasu City–Kingman, AZ	20	0.6	80	2.5	0	0.0	0	0.0	75	2.3
Lakeland–Winter Haven, FL	2,785	15.9	0	0.0	225	1.3	15	0.1	105	0.6
Lancaster, PA	565	4.3	0	0.0	115	0.9	35	0.3	89	0.7
Lansing–East Lansing, MI	645	7.0	10	0.1	200	2.2	0	0.0	205	2.2
Laredo, TX	15	0.3	4	0.1	0	0.0	0	0.0	4	0.1
Las Cruces, NM	190	4.2	90	2.0	20	0.4	0	0.0	100	2.2
Las Vegas–Paradise, NV	3,545	10.5	175	0.5	1,260	3.7	185	0.6	570	1.7
Lawrence, KS	120	5.5	50	2.3	55	2.5	0	0.0	44	2.0
Lawton, OK	220	11.5	160	8.4	85	4.5	35	1.8	35	1.8
Lebanon, PA	160	5.0	0	0.0	4	0.1	0	0.0	0	0.0
Lewiston, ID–WA	0	0.0	70	5.1	65	4.7	20	1.4	8	0.6
Lewiston–Auburn, ME	45	2.1	4	0.2	0	0.0	0	0.0	39	1.8
Lexington–Fayette, KY	775	6.7	45	0.4	20	0.2	0	0.0	45	0.4
Lima, OH	235	9.2	10	0.4	10	0.4	0	0.0	110	4.3
Lincoln, NE	120	2.2	20	0.4	220	4.0	0	0.0	25	0.5
Little Rock–North Little Rock–Conway, AR	3,305	27.3	0	0.0	10	0.1	4	0.0	150	1.2
Logan, UT–ID	55	2.1	0	0.0	4	0.2	0	0.0	10	0.4
Longview, TX	675	14.2	0	0.0	10	0.2	0	0.0	25	0.5
Longview, WA	0	0.0	0	0.0	25	0.7	4	0.1	75	2.2
Los Angeles–Long Beach–Santa Ana, CA	10,885	4.7	370	0.2	11,050	4.8	880	0.4	2,175	0.9
Louisville/Jefferson County, KY–IN	4,025	13.7	95	0.3	170	0.6	0	0.0	245	0.8
Lubbock, TX	510	8.4	20	0.3	30	0.5	0	0.0	105	1.7
Lynchburg, VA	1,135	22.1	40	0.8	30	0.6	0	0.0	50	1.0
Macon, GA	1,920	46.6	65	1.6	0	0.0	0	0.0	0	0.0
Madera–Chowchilla, CA	100	1.0	10	0.1	40	0.4	0	0.0	44	0.4
Madison, WI	480	4.7	20	0.2	115	1.1	0	0.0	42	0.4
Manchester–Nashua, NH	155	2.3	80	1.2	60	0.9	0	0.0	60	0.9
Manhattan, KS	170	8.1	4	0.2	40	1.9	0	0.0	39	1.9
Mankato–North Mankato, MN	10	0.4	0	0.0	20	0.8	0	0.0	24	1.0
Mansfield, OH	280	8.8	0	0.0	0	0.0	0	0.0	25	0.8
McAllen–Edinburg–Mission, TX	0	0.0	0	0.0	0	0.0	0	0.0	14	0.1
Medford, OR	30	0.5	40	0.7	20	0.4	35	0.6	154	2.8
Memphis, TN–MS–AR	16,805	57.5	20	0.1	210	0.7	0	0.0	515	1.8
Merced, CA	175	1.3	0	0.0	405	2.9	35	0.3	110	0.8
Miami–Fort Lauderdale–Pompano Beach, FL	25,080	24.6	125	0.1	975	1.0	0	0.0	960	0.9
Michigan City–La Porte, IN	150	6.0	0	0.0	0	0.0	0	0.0	15	0.6
Midland, TX	200	7.4	0	0.0	10	0.4	0	0.0	0	0.0
Milwaukee–Waukesha–West Allis, WI	4,060	14.8	185	0.7	585	2.1	0	0.0	420	1.5
Minneapolis–St. Paul–Bloomington, MN–WI	2,950	6.1	330	0.7	1,570	3.2	0	0.0	930	1.9
Missoula, MT	0	0.0	150	6.1	30	1.2	0	0.0	50	2.0

PART C—METROPOLITAN STATISTICAL AREA TABLES

C-14 Laborers and Helpers, by Metropolitan Statistical Area, Sex, Race, and Hispanic or Latino Origin, 2006–2010—Continued

Metropolitan Statistical Area	Total who worked in the last 5 years	Male Number	Male Percent	Female Number	Female Percent	Hispanic or Latino Number	Hispanic or Latino Percent	White alone, not Hispanic or Latino Number	White alone, not Hispanic or Latino Percent
Mobile, AL	7,965	6,895	86.6	1,070	13.4	830	10.4	3,735	46.9
Modesto, CA	16,835	13,790	81.9	3,045	18.1	11,775	69.9	4,195	24.9
Monroe, LA	3,630	3,190	87.9	445	12.3	200	5.5	1,760	48.5
Monroe, MI	3,745	2,870	76.6	870	23.2	195	5.2	3,355	89.6
Montgomery, AL	7,190	6,180	86.0	1,010	14.0	600	8.3	2,875	40.0
Morgantown, WV	1,985	1,770	89.2	215	10.8	15	0.8	1,970	99.2
Morristown, TN	3,190	2,495	78.2	695	21.8	490	15.4	2,620	82.1
Mount Vernon–Anacortes, WA	3,730	2,745	73.6	985	26.4	1,665	44.6	1,985	53.2
Muncie, IN	2,580	2,000	77.5	580	22.5	40	1.6	2,245	87.0
Muskegon–Norton Shores, MI	4,125	3,105	75.3	1,020	24.7	705	17.1	2,860	69.3
Myrtle Beach–North Myrtle Beach–Conway, SC	4,435	3,875	87.4	560	12.6	890	20.1	2,925	66.0
Napa, CA	6,405	5,750	89.8	655	10.2	4,870	76.0	1,435	22.4
Naples–Marco Island, FL	10,165	8,675	85.3	1,485	14.6	7,010	69.0	2,625	25.8
Nashville-Davidson–Murfreesboro–Franklin, TN	28,315	23,980	84.7	4,335	15.3	4,530	16.0	17,800	62.9
New Haven–Milford, CT	12,175	10,840	89.0	1,335	11.0	2,725	22.4	7,365	60.5
New Orleans–Metairie–Kenner, LA	18,890	16,590	87.8	2,300	12.2	1,865	9.9	8,200	43.4
New York–Northern New Jersey–Long Island, NY–NJ–PA	220,125	189,250	86.0	30,875	14.0	94,845	43.1	78,330	35.6
Niles–Benton Harbor, MI	3,885	3,095	79.7	790	20.3	765	19.7	2,625	67.6
North Port–Bradenton–Sarasota, FL	13,705	11,660	85.1	2,045	14.9	4,405	32.1	7,800	56.9
Norwich–New London, CT	3,975	3,465	87.2	510	12.8	210	5.3	3,265	82.1
Ocala, FL	7,430	6,035	81.2	1,390	18.7	2,150	28.9	4,400	59.2
Ocean City, NJ	1,820	1,655	90.9	165	9.1	245	13.5	1,340	73.6
Odessa, TX	2,770	2,390	86.3	380	13.7	1,750	63.2	890	32.1
Ogden–Clearfield, UT	7,995	6,520	81.6	1,475	18.4	1,500	18.8	6,115	76.5
Oklahoma City, OK	21,115	18,390	87.1	2,725	12.9	5,170	24.5	11,315	53.6
Olympia, WA	4,135	3,325	80.4	810	19.6	440	10.6	2,950	71.3
Omaha–Council Bluffs, NE–IA	15,750	13,415	85.2	2,330	14.8	2,655	16.9	11,600	73.7
Orlando–Kissimmee–Sanford, FL	40,500	33,440	82.6	7,060	17.4	13,570	33.5	18,515	45.7
Oshkosh–Neenah, WI	3,990	2,945	73.8	1,050	26.3	275	6.9	3,620	90.7
Owensboro, KY	2,440	2,025	83.0	415	17.0	110	4.5	2,180	89.3
Oxnard–Thousand Oaks–Ventura, CA	26,510	21,660	81.7	4,850	18.3	21,730	82.0	3,945	14.9
Palm Bay–Melbourne–Titusville, FL	7,970	6,830	85.7	1,135	14.2	740	9.3	6,205	77.9
Palm Coast, FL	1,605	1,425	88.8	180	11.2	105	6.5	1,295	80.7
Panama City–Lynn Haven–Panama City Beach, FL	2,710	2,345	86.5	365	13.5	145	5.4	2,040	75.3
Parkersburg–Marietta–Vienna, WV–OH	2,830	2,295	81.1	540	19.1	19	0.7	2,685	94.9
Pascagoula, MS	2,480	2,065	83.3	415	16.7	250	10.1	1,350	54.4
Pensacola–Ferry Pass–Brent, FL	7,700	6,110	79.4	1,590	20.6	555	7.2	5,300	68.8
Peoria, IL	6,695	5,515	82.4	1,180	17.6	145	2.2	5,780	86.3
Philadelphia–Camden–Wilmington, PA–NJ–DE–MD	88,105	74,395	84.4	13,710	15.6	18,230	20.7	50,490	57.3
Phoenix–Mesa–Glendale, AZ	75,240	65,150	86.6	10,085	13.4	44,260	58.8	24,615	32.7
Pine Bluff, AR	2,715	2,330	85.8	385	14.2	20	0.7	1,195	44.0
Pittsburgh, PA	39,215	32,710	83.4	6,500	16.6	365	0.9	35,610	90.8
Pittsfield, MA	2,450	2,030	82.9	420	17.1	30	1.2	2,355	96.1
Pocatello, ID	2,290	2,045	89.3	245	10.7	675	29.5	1,545	67.5
Portland–South Portland–Biddeford, ME	10,265	8,750	85.2	1,515	14.8	105	1.0	9,840	95.9
Portland–Vancouver–Hillsboro, OR–WA	47,330	38,910	82.2	8,420	17.8	15,300	32.3	27,525	58.2
Port St. Lucie, FL	10,010	8,525	85.2	1,485	14.8	3,585	35.8	4,650	46.5
Poughkeepsie–Newburgh–Middletown, NY	10,050	8,355	83.1	1,695	16.9	2,980	29.7	6,150	61.2
Prescott, AZ	3,545	2,825	79.7	715	20.2	960	27.1	2,365	66.7
Providence–New Bedford–Fall River, RI–MA	24,260	20,860	86.0	3,400	14.0	3,730	15.4	18,865	77.8

C-14 **Laborers and Helpers, by Metropolitan Statistical Area, Sex, Race, and Hispanic or Latino Origin, 2006–2010**—*Continued*

Metropolitan Statistical Area	Black alone, not Hispanic or Latino Number	Percent	American Indian and Alaska Native alone, not Hispanic or Latino Number	Percent	Asian alone, not Hispanic or Latino Number	Percent	Native Hawaiian and Other Pacific Islander alone, not Hispanic or Latino Number	Percent	Two or more races, not Hispanic or Latino Number	Percent
Mobile, AL	3,055	38.4	40	0.5	205	2.6	15	0.2	85	1.1
Modesto, CA	160	1.0	25	0.1	410	2.4	75	0.4	195	1.2
Monroe, LA	1,605	44.2	0	0.0	0	0.0	10	0.3	60	1.7
Monroe, MI	145	3.9	0	0.0	25	0.7	0	0.0	25	0.7
Montgomery, AL	3,605	50.1	20	0.3	65	0.9	0	0.0	20	0.3
Morgantown, WV	0	0.0	0	0.0	0	0.0	0	0.0	0	0.0
Morristown, TN	45	1.4	0	0.0	0	0.0	0	0.0	30	0.9
Mount Vernon–Anacortes, WA	0	0.0	45	1.2	4	0.1	0	0.0	34	0.9
Muncie, IN	160	6.2	10	0.4	0	0.0	0	0.0	130	5.0
Muskegon–Norton Shores, MI	500	12.1	15	0.4	10	0.2	0	0.0	35	0.8
Myrtle Beach–North Myrtle Beach–Conway, SC	550	12.4	0	0.0	55	1.2	0	0.0	15	0.3
Napa, CA	0	0.0	0	0.0	55	0.9	0	0.0	44	0.7
Naples–Marco Island, FL	380	3.7	15	0.1	90	0.9	0	0.0	49	0.5
Nashville-Davidson–Murfreesboro–Franklin, TN	5,095	18.0	65	0.2	395	1.4	30	0.1	395	1.4
New Haven–Milford, CT	1,675	13.8	0	0.0	150	1.2	0	0.0	264	2.2
New Orleans–Metairie–Kenner, LA	7,760	41.1	155	0.8	790	4.2	0	0.0	120	0.6
New York–Northern New Jersey–Long Island, NY–NJ–PA	34,045	15.5	450	0.2	9,230	4.2	10	0.0	3,215	1.5
Niles–Benton Harbor, MI	440	11.3	10	0.3	35	0.9	0	0.0	15	0.4
North Port–Bradenton–Sarasota, FL	1,225	8.9	95	0.7	100	0.7	0	0.0	85	0.6
Norwich–New London, CT	370	9.3	30	0.8	35	0.9	0	0.0	60	1.5
Ocala, FL	800	10.8	15	0.2	50	0.7	0	0.0	10	0.1
Ocean City, NJ	115	6.3	0	0.0	0	0.0	0	0.0	119	6.5
Odessa, TX	90	3.2	4	0.1	35	1.3	0	0.0	0	0.0
Ogden–Clearfield, UT	115	1.4	90	1.1	95	1.2	10	0.1	65	0.8
Oklahoma City, OK	2,485	11.8	865	4.1	315	1.5	15	0.1	945	4.5
Olympia, WA	80	1.9	85	2.1	285	6.9	105	2.5	180	4.4
Omaha–Council Bluffs, NE–IA	960	6.1	70	0.4	135	0.9	0	0.0	330	2.1
Orlando–Kissimmee–Sanford, FL	6,960	17.2	120	0.3	865	2.1	10	0.0	455	1.1
Oshkosh–Neenah, WI	4	0.1	40	1.0	30	0.8	0	0.0	19	0.5
Owensboro, KY	125	5.1	0	0.0	0	0.0	10	0.4	10	0.4
Oxnard–Thousand Oaks–Ventura, CA	210	0.8	70	0.3	375	1.4	15	0.1	160	0.6
Palm Bay–Melbourne–Titusville, FL	800	10.0	45	0.6	110	1.4	0	0.0	65	0.8
Palm Coast, FL	125	7.8	40	2.5	40	2.5	0	0.0	0	0.0
Panama City–Lynn Haven–Panama City Beach, FL	420	15.5	20	0.7	50	1.8	0	0.0	35	1.3
Parkersburg–Marietta–Vienna, WV–OH	10	0.4	0	0.0	35	1.2	0	0.0	80	2.8
Pascagoula, MS	740	29.8	0	0.0	110	4.4	0	0.0	30	1.2
Pensacola–Ferry Pass–Brent, FL	1,270	16.5	35	0.5	220	2.9	0	0.0	325	4.2
Peoria, IL	645	9.6	4	0.1	30	0.4	0	0.0	94	1.4
Philadelphia–Camden–Wilmington, PA–NJ–DE–MD	16,050	18.2	105	0.1	2,240	2.5	10	0.0	985	1.1
Phoenix–Mesa–Glendale, AZ	2,660	3.5	2,125	2.8	695	0.9	160	0.2	720	1.0
Pine Bluff, AR	1,485	54.7	0	0.0	0	0.0	0	0.0	15	0.6
Pittsburgh, PA	2,635	6.7	25	0.1	270	0.7	0	0.0	303	0.8
Pittsfield, MA	35	1.4	0	0.0	0	0.0	0	0.0	29	1.2
Pocatello, ID	15	0.7	0	0.0	4	0.2	0	0.0	50	2.2
Portland–South Portland–Biddeford, ME	90	0.9	55	0.5	80	0.8	0	0.0	89	0.9
Portland–Vancouver–Hillsboro, OR–WA	1,475	3.1	300	0.6	1,400	3.0	395	0.8	930	2.0
Port St. Lucie, FL	1,585	15.8	80	0.8	65	0.6	0	0.0	50	0.5
Poughkeepsie–Newburgh–Middletown, NY	790	7.9	10	0.1	45	0.4	0	0.0	70	0.7
Prescott, AZ	25	0.7	50	1.4	0	0.0	0	0.0	139	3.9
Providence–New Bedford–Fall River, RI–MA	520	2.1	125	0.5	380	1.6	0	0.0	640	2.6

C-14 Laborers and Helpers, by Metropolitan Statistical Area, Sex, Race, and Hispanic or Latino Origin, 2006–2010—Continued

Metropolitan Statistical Area	Total who worked in the last 5 years	Male Number	Male Percent	Female Number	Female Percent	Hispanic or Latino Number	Hispanic or Latino Percent	White alone, not Hispanic or Latino Number	White alone, not Hispanic or Latino Percent
Provo–Orem, UT	6,740	5,550	82.3	1,190	17.7	1,250	18.5	5,115	75.9
Pueblo, CO	3,015	2,440	80.9	575	19.1	1,265	42.0	1,530	50.7
Punta Gorda, FL	2,470	1,945	78.7	525	21.3	165	6.7	2,220	89.9
Racine, WI	3,765	2,890	76.8	875	23.2	860	22.8	2,485	66.0
Raleigh–Cary, NC	15,275	13,040	85.4	2,230	14.6	4,005	26.2	7,280	47.7
Rapid City, SD	2,395	2,145	89.6	250	10.4	130	5.4	2,065	86.2
Reading, PA	9,965	8,055	80.8	1,910	19.2	2,495	25.0	6,990	70.1
Redding, CA	3,510	3,015	85.9	490	14.0	670	19.1	2,610	74.4
Reno–Sparks, NV	8,530	6,890	80.8	1,640	19.2	3,215	37.7	4,390	51.5
Richmond, VA	20,115	16,940	84.2	3,175	15.8	2,215	11.0	9,885	49.1
Riverside–San Bernardino–Ontario, CA	95,355	78,920	82.8	16,435	17.2	68,715	72.1	18,605	19.5
Roanoke, VA	5,630	4,755	84.5	870	15.5	395	7.0	4,235	75.2
Rochester, MN	2,940	2,445	83.2	495	16.8	210	7.1	2,580	87.8
Rochester, NY	15,850	13,220	83.4	2,625	16.6	1,745	11.0	12,165	76.8
Rockford, IL	6,670	5,130	76.9	1,540	23.1	1,275	19.1	4,225	63.3
Rocky Mount, NC	3,655	3,240	88.6	415	11.4	795	21.8	1,000	27.4
Rome, GA	1,820	1,465	80.5	355	19.5	350	19.2	1,070	58.8
Sacramento–Arden-Arcade–Roseville, CA	36,935	30,380	82.3	6,555	17.7	16,950	45.9	13,835	37.5
Saginaw–Saginaw Township North, MI	3,340	2,850	85.3	495	14.8	450	13.5	2,270	68.0
St. Cloud, MN	4,950	3,950	79.8	1,000	20.2	390	7.9	4,370	88.3
St. George, UT	2,475	2,065	83.4	410	16.6	510	20.6	1,870	75.6
St. Joseph, MO–KS	2,985	2,385	79.9	600	20.1	150	5.0	2,630	88.1
St. Louis, MO–IL	48,040	40,135	83.5	7,905	16.5	2,810	5.8	35,280	73.4
Salem, OR	14,660	11,965	81.6	2,695	18.4	8,610	58.7	5,440	37.1
Salinas, CA	30,715	22,590	73.5	8,125	26.5	28,055	91.3	1,965	6.4
Salisbury, MD	1,950	1,705	87.4	240	12.3	190	9.7	1,265	64.9
Salt Lake City, UT	19,195	15,885	82.8	3,310	17.2	6,100	31.8	11,580	60.3
San Angelo, TX	2,080	1,730	83.2	350	16.8	945	45.4	1,055	50.7
San Antonio–New Braunfels, TX	34,075	29,215	85.7	4,860	14.3	22,230	65.2	8,905	26.1
San Diego–Carlsbad–San Marcos, CA	49,390	42,410	85.9	6,980	14.1	29,880	60.5	13,720	27.8
Sandusky, OH	1,595	1,355	85.0	240	15.0	39	2.4	1,385	86.8
San Francisco–Oakland–Fremont, CA	64,845	54,325	83.8	10,515	16.2	33,915	52.3	16,340	25.2
San Jose–Sunnyvale–Santa Clara, CA	26,760	22,955	85.8	3,805	14.2	17,945	67.1	4,980	18.6
San Luis Obispo–Paso Robles, CA	6,285	5,280	84.0	1,005	16.0	2,745	43.7	3,220	51.2
Santa Barbara–Santa Maria–Goleta, CA	20,860	16,030	76.8	4,830	23.2	18,055	86.6	2,410	11.6
Santa Cruz–Watsonville, CA	10,005	7,260	72.6	2,740	27.4	7,800	78.0	1,885	18.8
Santa Fe, NM	2,695	2,300	85.3	395	14.7	1,720	63.8	815	30.2
Santa Rosa–Petaluma, CA	13,705	12,070	88.1	1,635	11.9	8,300	60.6	4,770	34.8
Savannah, GA	6,140	5,370	87.5	770	12.5	530	8.6	2,545	41.4
Scranton–Wilkes-Barre, PA	11,195	9,220	82.4	1,975	17.6	970	8.7	9,585	85.6
Seattle–Tacoma–Bellevue, WA	57,880	46,680	80.6	11,200	19.4	12,120	20.9	34,415	59.5
Sebastian–Vero Beach, FL	4,300	3,570	83.0	735	17.1	1,555	36.2	1,870	43.5
Sheboygan, WI	3,595	2,900	80.7	695	19.3	280	7.8	3,155	87.8
Sherman–Denison, TX	2,455	2,150	87.6	305	12.4	490	20.0	1,680	68.4
Shreveport–Bossier City, LA	7,945	6,800	85.6	1,145	14.4	615	7.7	3,620	45.6
Sioux City, IA–NE–SD	4,150	3,310	79.8	835	20.1	1,060	25.5	2,580	62.2
Sioux Falls, SD	5,110	4,180	81.8	930	18.2	260	5.1	4,355	85.2
South Bend–Mishawaka, IN–MI	6,395	5,140	80.4	1,255	19.6	875	13.7	4,795	75.0
Spartanburg, SC	5,540	4,725	85.3	815	14.7	850	15.3	2,985	53.9
Spokane, WA	8,145	6,660	81.8	1,485	18.2	525	6.4	7,050	86.6
Springfield, IL	3,015	2,640	87.6	375	12.4	135	4.5	2,650	87.9
Springfield, MA	12,265	10,110	82.4	2,155	17.6	2,330	19.0	9,035	73.7
Springfield, MO	8,680	7,465	86.0	1,210	13.9	360	4.1	7,805	89.9
Springfield, OH	3,085	2,580	83.6	510	16.5	380	12.3	2,440	79.1
State College, PA	2,815	2,390	84.9	425	15.1	10	0.4	2,660	94.5

C-14 **Laborers and Helpers, by Metropolitan Statistical Area, Sex, Race, and Hispanic or Latino Origin, 2006–2010**—Continued

Metropolitan Statistical Area	Black alone, not Hispanic or Latino Number	Percent	American Indian and Alaska Native alone, not Hispanic or Latino Number	Percent	Asian alone, not Hispanic or Latino Number	Percent	Native Hawaiian and Other Pacific Islander alone, not Hispanic or Latino Number	Percent	Two or more races, not Hispanic or Latino Number	Percent
Provo–Orem, UT	15	0.2	55	0.8	60	0.9	130	1.9	115	1.7
Pueblo, CO	110	3.6	25	0.8	0	0.0	20	0.7	70	2.3
Punta Gorda, FL	75	3.0	15	0.6	0	0.0	0	0.0	0	0.0
Racine, WI	310	8.2	0	0.0	25	0.7	0	0.0	85	2.3
Raleigh–Cary, NC	3,530	23.1	15	0.1	340	2.2	0	0.0	105	0.7
Rapid City, SD	0	0.0	130	5.4	30	1.3	0	0.0	40	1.7
Reading, PA	230	2.3	4	0.0	130	1.3	0	0.0	110	1.1
Redding, CA	25	0.7	100	2.8	20	0.6	35	1.0	49	1.4
Reno–Sparks, NV	235	2.8	150	1.8	370	4.3	20	0.2	150	1.8
Richmond, VA	7,475	37.2	85	0.4	260	1.3	0	0.0	190	0.9
Riverside–San Bernardino–Ontario, CA	4,480	4.7	190	0.2	1,420	1.5	170	0.2	1,775	1.9
Roanoke, VA	915	16.3	0	0.0	75	1.3	0	0.0	15	0.3
Rochester, MN	10	0.3	0	0.0	95	3.2	0	0.0	40	1.4
Rochester, NY	1,615	10.2	50	0.3	75	0.5	0	0.0	200	1.3
Rockford, IL	965	14.5	15	0.2	150	2.2	0	0.0	39	0.6
Rocky Mount, NC	1,790	49.0	20	0.5	4	0.1	0	0.0	45	1.2
Rome, GA	320	17.6	4	0.2	55	3.0	0	0.0	19	1.0
Sacramento–Arden-Arcade–Roseville, CA	2,040	5.5	315	0.9	2,565	6.9	340	0.9	885	2.4
Saginaw–Saginaw Township North, MI	590	17.7	0	0.0	15	0.4	0	0.0	19	0.6
St. Cloud, MN	105	2.1	0	0.0	55	1.1	0	0.0	35	0.7
St. George, UT	0	0.0	15	0.6	15	0.6	10	0.4	65	2.6
St. Joseph, MO–KS	155	5.2	0	0.0	0	0.0	20	0.7	24	0.8
St. Louis, MO–IL	9,005	18.7	115	0.2	210	0.4	25	0.1	590	1.2
Salem, OR	40	0.3	95	0.6	100	0.7	0	0.0	365	2.5
Salinas, CA	85	0.3	55	0.2	195	0.6	115	0.4	249	0.8
Salisbury, MD	430	22.1	4	0.2	45	2.3	0	0.0	10	0.5
Salt Lake City, UT	285	1.5	155	0.8	255	1.3	580	3.0	240	1.3
San Angelo, TX	40	1.9	0	0.0	20	1.0	0	0.0	10	0.5
San Antonio–New Braunfels, TX	2,175	6.4	75	0.2	295	0.9	0	0.0	395	1.2
San Diego–Carlsbad–San Marcos, CA	1,870	3.8	315	0.6	2,120	4.3	595	1.2	880	1.8
Sandusky, OH	140	8.8	25	1.6	0	0.0	0	0.0	0	0.0
San Francisco–Oakland–Fremont, CA	5,545	8.6	170	0.3	6,910	10.7	500	0.8	1,465	2.3
San Jose–Sunnyvale–Santa Clara, CA	500	1.9	90	0.3	2,605	9.7	115	0.4	525	2.0
San Luis Obispo–Paso Robles, CA	20	0.3	20	0.3	145	2.3	15	0.2	125	2.0
Santa Barbara–Santa Maria–Goleta, CA	85	0.4	25	0.1	220	1.1	0	0.0	65	0.3
Santa Cruz–Watsonville, CA	85	0.8	20	0.2	55	0.5	0	0.0	155	1.5
Santa Fe, NM	55	2.0	75	2.8	0	0.0	0	0.0	25	0.9
Santa Rosa–Petaluma, CA	95	0.7	35	0.3	260	1.9	45	0.3	205	1.5
Savannah, GA	2,930	47.7	0	0.0	25	0.4	0	0.0	105	1.7
Scranton–Wilkes-Barre, PA	470	4.2	10	0.1	105	0.9	0	0.0	60	0.5
Seattle–Tacoma–Bellevue, WA	3,630	6.3	1,085	1.9	3,835	6.6	750	1.3	2,055	3.6
Sebastian–Vero Beach, FL	840	19.5	0	0.0	25	0.6	0	0.0	15	0.3
Sheboygan, WI	0	0.0	40	1.1	110	3.1	0	0.0	10	0.3
Sherman–Denison, TX	245	10.0	10	0.4	0	0.0	0	0.0	30	1.2
Shreveport–Bossier City, LA	3,600	45.3	15	0.2	30	0.4	0	0.0	65	0.8
Sioux City, IA–NE–SD	155	3.7	30	0.7	210	5.1	50	1.2	60	1.4
Sioux Falls, SD	160	3.1	190	3.7	110	2.2	0	0.0	35	0.7
South Bend–Mishawaka, IN–MI	570	8.9	55	0.9	0	0.0	0	0.0	94	1.5
Spartanburg, SC	1,455	26.3	15	0.3	235	4.2	0	0.0	0	0.0
Spokane, WA	160	2.0	55	0.7	125	1.5	35	0.4	204	2.5
Springfield, IL	230	7.6	0	0.0	0	0.0	0	0.0	0	0.0
Springfield, MA	650	5.3	10	0.1	100	0.8	0	0.0	140	1.1
Springfield, MO	180	2.1	45	0.5	100	1.2	0	0.0	185	2.1
Springfield, OH	130	4.2	25	0.8	0	0.0	0	0.0	110	3.6
State College, PA	125	4.4	4	0.1	15	0.5	0	0.0	4	0.1

PART C—METROPOLITAN STATISTICAL AREA TABLES

C-14 Laborers and Helpers, by Metropolitan Statistical Area, Sex, Race, and Hispanic or Latino Origin, 2006–2010—Continued

Metropolitan Statistical Area	Total who worked in the last 5 years	Male Number	Male Percent	Female Number	Female Percent	Hispanic or Latino Number	Hispanic or Latino Percent	White alone, not Hispanic or Latino Number	White alone, not Hispanic or Latino Percent
Steubenville–Weirton, OH–WV	2,530	2,170	85.8	360	14.2	0	0.0	2,360	93.3
Stockton, CA	22,330	18,240	81.7	4,090	18.3	15,700	70.3	4,110	18.4
Sumter, SC	1,590	1,270	79.9	320	20.1	100	6.3	610	38.4
Syracuse, NY	10,730	8,905	83.0	1,825	17.0	590	5.5	9,375	87.4
Tallahassee, FL	6,115	5,035	82.3	1,080	17.7	535	8.7	3,155	51.6
Tampa–St. Petersburg–Clearwater, FL	48,725	41,045	84.2	7,685	15.8	14,125	29.0	26,770	54.9
Terre Haute, IN	3,410	2,950	86.5	460	13.5	25	0.7	3,200	93.8
Texarkana, TX–Texarkana, AR	2,965	2,680	90.4	285	9.6	745	25.1	1,300	43.8
Toledo, OH	15,195	12,015	79.1	3,180	20.9	1,390	9.1	11,740	77.3
Topeka, KS	4,450	3,820	85.8	630	14.2	580	13.0	3,420	76.9
Trenton–Ewing, NJ	6,885	6,415	93.2	465	6.8	3,265	47.4	2,270	33.0
Tucson, AZ	15,970	13,585	85.1	2,380	14.9	8,980	56.2	5,950	37.3
Tulsa, OK	15,100	12,710	84.2	2,395	15.9	2,515	16.7	8,285	54.9
Tuscaloosa, AL	4,685	4,135	88.3	550	11.7	385	8.2	2,475	52.8
Tyler, TX	4,330	3,595	83.0	735	17.0	1,755	40.5	1,485	34.3
Utica–Rome, NY	5,080	4,360	85.8	725	14.3	190	3.7	4,665	91.8
Valdosta, GA	3,090	2,545	82.4	545	17.6	530	17.2	1,385	44.8
Vallejo–Fairfield, CA	7,815	6,410	82.0	1,405	18.0	3,795	48.6	2,225	28.5
Victoria, TX	2,370	2,105	88.8	265	11.2	1,275	53.8	860	36.3
Vineland–Millville–Bridgeton, NJ	4,135	3,620	87.5	515	12.5	2,355	57.0	1,080	26.1
Virginia Beach–Norfolk–Newport News, VA–NC	25,465	20,865	81.9	4,600	18.1	1,090	4.3	12,820	50.3
Visalia–Porterville, CA	33,275	26,365	79.2	6,910	20.8	29,610	89.0	2,845	8.5
Waco, TX	4,455	3,755	84.3	700	15.7	1,965	44.1	1,710	38.4
Warner Robins, GA	2,145	1,885	87.9	260	12.1	190	8.9	990	46.2
Washington–Arlington–Alexandria, DC–VA–MD–WV	62,455	52,420	83.9	10,035	16.1	20,620	33.0	21,170	33.9
Waterloo–Cedar Falls, IA	4,210	3,430	81.5	780	18.5	125	3.0	3,695	87.8
Wausau, WI	3,970	3,040	76.6	930	23.4	255	6.4	3,465	87.3
Wenatchee–East Wenatchee, WA	5,880	4,800	81.6	1,080	18.4	4,115	70.0	1,660	28.2
Wheeling, WV–OH	3,295	2,640	80.1	655	19.9	35	1.1	3,210	97.4
Wichita, KS	10,000	8,465	84.7	1,535	15.4	1,165	11.7	7,205	72.1
Wichita Falls, TX	2,545	2,150	84.5	400	15.7	800	31.4	1,610	63.3
Williamsport, PA	3,690	2,880	78.0	810	22.0	45	1.2	3,470	94.0
Wilmington, NC	7,390	6,230	84.3	1,160	15.7	1,685	22.8	4,385	59.3
Winchester, VA–WV	4,145	3,280	79.1	865	20.9	685	16.5	2,355	56.8
Winston–Salem, NC	8,205	7,035	85.7	1,170	14.3	1,855	22.6	4,300	52.4
Worcester, MA	12,400	10,175	82.1	2,225	17.9	1,745	14.1	9,935	80.1
Yakima, WA	16,565	13,140	79.3	3,425	20.7	13,585	82.0	2,385	14.4
York–Hanover, PA	10,710	8,425	78.7	2,285	21.3	875	8.2	9,300	86.8
Youngstown–Warren–Boardman, OH–PA	12,330	10,430	84.6	1,900	15.4	670	5.4	10,205	82.8
Yuba City, CA	6,565	5,385	82.0	1,180	18.0	3,865	58.9	1,635	24.9
Yuma, AZ	8,110	5,615	69.2	2,495	30.8	7,320	90.3	645	8.0

C-14 Laborers and Helpers, by Metropolitan Statistical Area, Sex, Race, and Hispanic or Latino Origin, 2006–2010—*Continued*

Metropolitan Statistical Area	Black alone, not Hispanic or Latino Number	Percent	American Indian and Alaska Native alone, not Hispanic or Latino Number	Percent	Asian alone, not Hispanic or Latino Number	Percent	Native Hawaiian and Other Pacific Islander alone, not Hispanic or Latino Number	Percent	Two or more races, not Hispanic or Latino Number	Percent
Steubenville–Weirton, OH–WV	100	4.0	0	0.0	4	0.2	0	0.0	68	2.7
Stockton, CA	840	3.8	85	0.4	1,245	5.6	105	0.5	255	1.1
Sumter, SC	835	52.5	0	0.0	25	1.6	0	0.0	15	0.9
Syracuse, NY	570	5.3	60	0.6	55	0.5	0	0.0	80	0.7
Tallahassee, FL	2,305	37.7	105	1.7	10	0.2	0	0.0	0	0.0
Tampa–St. Petersburg–Clearwater, FL	6,470	13.3	85	0.2	595	1.2	50	0.1	640	1.3
Terre Haute, IN	120	3.5	15	0.4	45	1.3	0	0.0	10	0.3
Texarkana, TX–Texarkana, AR	910	30.7	0	0.0	0	0.0	0	0.0	4	0.1
Toledo, OH	1,820	12.0	30	0.2	110	0.7	15	0.1	94	0.6
Topeka, KS	340	7.6	40	0.9	0	0.0	4	0.1	70	1.6
Trenton–Ewing, NJ	1,190	17.3	0	0.0	90	1.3	0	0.0	70	1.0
Tucson, AZ	250	1.6	425	2.7	45	0.3	40	0.3	275	1.7
Tulsa, OK	1,890	12.5	1,280	8.5	60	0.4	0	0.0	1,070	7.1
Tuscaloosa, AL	1,820	38.8	4	0.1	0	0.0	0	0.0	0	0.0
Tyler, TX	1,040	24.0	10	0.2	0	0.0	0	0.0	45	1.0
Utica–Rome, NY	105	2.1	4	0.1	65	1.3	0	0.0	50	1.0
Valdosta, GA	1,170	37.9	0	0.0	0	0.0	0	0.0	0	0.0
Vallejo–Fairfield, CA	850	10.9	20	0.3	525	6.7	95	1.2	315	4.0
Victoria, TX	200	8.4	0	0.0	0	0.0	0	0.0	35	1.5
Vineland–Millville–Bridgeton, NJ	635	15.4	10	0.2	25	0.6	0	0.0	29	0.7
Virginia Beach–Norfolk–Newport News, VA–NC	10,050	39.5	165	0.6	635	2.5	20	0.1	690	2.7
Visalia–Porterville, CA	100	0.3	85	0.3	505	1.5	0	0.0	130	0.4
Waco, TX	620	13.9	45	1.0	40	0.9	15	0.3	60	1.3
Warner Robins, GA	875	40.8	0	0.0	35	1.6	0	0.0	55	2.6
Washington–Arlington–Alexandria, DC–VA–MD–WV	17,910	28.7	115	0.2	1,765	2.8	10	0.0	865	1.4
Waterloo–Cedar Falls, IA	325	7.7	10	0.2	0	0.0	20	0.5	35	0.8
Wausau, WI	15	0.4	30	0.8	180	4.5	0	0.0	20	0.5
Wenatchee–East Wenatchee, WA	50	0.9	4	0.1	0	0.0	0	0.0	50	0.9
Wheeling, WV–OH	35	1.1	10	0.3	0	0.0	0	0.0	0	0.0
Wichita, KS	1,055	10.6	95	1.0	310	3.1	4	0.0	165	1.7
Wichita Falls, TX	80	3.1	15	0.6	45	1.8	0	0.0	0	0.0
Williamsport, PA	110	3.0	10	0.3	0	0.0	0	0.0	65	1.8
Wilmington, NC	1,095	14.8	70	0.9	15	0.2	0	0.0	149	2.0
Winchester, VA–WV	1,055	25.5	0	0.0	0	0.0	0	0.0	50	1.2
Winston–Salem, NC	1,910	23.3	0	0.0	100	1.2	0	0.0	35	0.4
Worcester, MA	255	2.1	4	0.0	315	2.5	0	0.0	145	1.2
Yakima, WA	0	0.0	405	2.4	30	0.2	0	0.0	160	1.0
York–Hanover, PA	255	2.4	30	0.3	115	1.1	0	0.0	125	1.2
Youngstown–Warren–Boardman, OH–PA	1,345	10.9	25	0.2	10	0.1	0	0.0	70	0.6
Yuba City, CA	50	0.8	85	1.3	720	11.0	0	0.0	205	3.1
Yuma, AZ	70	0.9	50	0.6	20	0.2	0	0.0	4	0.0

PART C—METROPOLITAN STATISTICAL AREA TABLES

C-15 Protective Service Workers, by Metropolitan Statistical Area, Sex, Race, and Hispanic or Latino Origin, 2006–2010

Metropolitan Statistical Area	Total who worked in the last 5 years	Male Number	Male Percent	Female Number	Female Percent	Hispanic or Latino Number	Hispanic or Latino Percent	White alone, not Hispanic or Latino Number	White alone, not Hispanic or Latino Percent
Abilene, TX	2,190	1,580	72.1	610	27.9	350	16.0	1,680	76.7
Akron, OH	5,930	4,735	79.8	1,195	20.2	60	1.0	4,930	83.1
Albany, GA	1,890	1,410	74.6	480	25.4	25	1.3	690	36.5
Albany–Schenectady–Troy, NY	11,085	8,885	80.2	2,200	19.8	340	3.1	9,815	88.5
Albuquerque, NM	11,880	9,175	77.2	2,700	22.7	5,310	44.7	5,170	43.5
Alexandria, LA	2,130	1,825	85.7	305	14.3	4	0.2	1,440	67.6
Allentown–Bethlehem–Easton, PA–NJ	7,425	5,930	79.9	1,495	20.1	570	7.7	6,140	82.7
Altoona, PA	1,160	955	82.3	205	17.7	10	0.9	1,145	98.7
Amarillo, TX	3,615	2,865	79.3	750	20.7	655	18.1	2,730	75.5
Ames, IA	525	395	75.2	130	24.8	20	3.8	465	88.6
Anchorage, AK	4,115	3,445	83.7	670	16.3	170	4.1	3,310	80.4
Anderson, IN	2,010	1,620	80.6	395	19.7	65	3.2	1,675	83.3
Anderson, SC	1,140	940	82.5	200	17.5	15	1.3	970	85.1
Ann Arbor, MI	2,460	1,795	73.0	665	27.0	45	1.8	1,630	66.3
Anniston–Oxford, AL	945	865	91.5	80	8.5	10	1.1	780	82.5
Appleton, WI	1,780	1,295	72.8	485	27.2	10	0.6	1,650	92.7
Asheville, NC	3,135	2,505	79.9	630	20.1	105	3.3	2,710	86.4
Athens–Clarke County, GA	1,640	1,165	71.0	470	28.7	20	1.2	1,150	70.1
Atlanta–Sandy Springs–Marietta, GA	51,745	37,010	71.5	14,735	28.5	1,320	2.6	23,155	44.7
Atlantic City–Hammonton, NJ	5,585	4,480	80.2	1,105	19.8	485	8.7	3,725	66.7
Auburn–Opelika, AL	1,390	1,140	82.0	250	18.0	14	1.0	1,115	80.2
Augusta–Richmond County, GA–SC	6,030	4,685	77.7	1,345	22.3	210	3.5	3,165	52.5
Austin–Round Rock–San Marcos, TX	14,730	11,735	79.7	2,995	20.3	3,675	24.9	8,690	59.0
Bakersfield–Delano, CA	11,095	8,780	79.1	2,315	20.9	3,585	32.3	5,915	53.3
Baltimore–Towson, MD	40,265	28,175	70.0	12,090	30.0	775	1.9	20,720	51.5
Bangor, ME	1,545	1,395	90.3	150	9.7	0	0.0	1,490	96.4
Barnstable Town, MA	2,330	1,920	82.4	410	17.6	120	5.2	2,195	94.2
Baton Rouge, LA	10,175	6,870	67.5	3,305	32.5	94	0.9	5,230	51.4
Battle Creek, MI	1,140	855	75.0	285	25.0	10	0.9	1,040	91.2
Bay City, MI	985	770	78.2	215	21.8	15	1.5	915	92.9
Beaumont–Port Arthur, TX	4,885	3,210	65.7	1,675	34.3	220	4.5	2,390	48.9
Bellingham, WA	1,960	1,500	76.5	460	23.5	120	6.1	1,655	84.4
Bend, OR	1,085	925	85.3	165	15.2	15	1.4	1,005	92.6
Billings, MT	1,145	890	77.7	255	22.3	4	0.3	1,115	97.4
Binghamton, NY	2,440	1,940	79.5	495	20.3	15	0.6	2,325	95.3
Birmingham–Hoover, AL	11,220	8,905	79.4	2,315	20.6	165	1.5	6,810	60.7
Bismarck, ND	1,010	775	76.7	235	23.3	0	0.0	930	92.1
Blacksburg–Christiansburg–Radford, VA	1,500	1,210	80.7	290	19.3	0	0.0	1,315	87.7
Bloomington, IN	1,280	1,085	84.8	195	15.2	4	0.3	1,250	97.7
Bloomington–Normal, IL	1,670	1,165	69.8	500	29.9	15	0.9	1,445	86.5
Boise City–Nampa, ID	5,240	4,205	80.2	1,035	19.8	360	6.9	4,650	88.7
Boston–Cambridge–Quincy, MA–NH	48,795	39,165	80.3	9,630	19.7	3,015	6.2	38,410	78.7
Boulder, CO	1,660	1,115	67.2	545	32.8	175	10.5	1,420	85.5
Bowling Green, KY	885	560	63.3	325	36.7	0	0.0	830	93.8
Bremerton–Silverdale, WA	2,830	2,355	83.2	475	16.8	110	3.9	2,110	74.6
Bridgeport–Stamford–Norwalk, CT	7,370	5,950	80.7	1,420	19.3	1,025	13.9	4,740	64.3
Brownsville–Harlingen, TX	4,890	4,025	82.3	865	17.7	4,425	90.5	395	8.1
Brunswick, GA	1,295	950	73.4	345	26.6	15	1.2	860	66.4
Buffalo–Niagara Falls, NY	13,515	10,535	78.0	2,975	22.0	360	2.7	11,270	83.4
Burlington, NC	1,460	1,145	78.4	315	21.6	135	9.2	1,040	71.2
Burlington–South Burlington, VT	2,250	1,755	78.0	495	22.0	85	3.8	2,045	90.9
Canton–Massillon, OH	3,005	2,620	87.2	385	12.8	55	1.8	2,790	92.8
Cape Coral–Fort Myers, FL	7,150	5,770	80.7	1,380	19.3	775	10.8	5,480	76.6
Cape Girardeau–Jackson, MO–IL	930	835	89.8	95	10.2	20	2.2	775	83.3
Carson City, NV	910	570	62.6	340	37.4	50	5.5	795	87.4

C-15 **Protective Service Workers, by Metropolitan Statistical Area, Sex, Race, and Hispanic or Latino Origin, 2006–2010**—*Continued*

Metropolitan Statistical Area	Black alone, not Hispanic or Latino Number	Percent	American Indian and Alaska Native alone, not Hispanic or Latino Number	Percent	Asian alone, not Hispanic or Latino Number	Percent	Native Hawaiian and Other Pacific Islander alone, not Hispanic or Latino Number	Percent	Two or more races, not Hispanic or Latino Number	Percent
Abilene, TX	115	5.3	10	0.5	25	1.1	0	0.0	4	0.2
Akron, OH	825	13.9	20	0.3	20	0.3	0	0.0	75	1.3
Albany, GA	1,170	61.9	0	0.0	0	0.0	0	0.0	10	0.5
Albany–Schenectady–Troy, NY	610	5.5	40	0.4	80	0.7	0	0.0	205	1.8
Albuquerque, NM	495	4.2	660	5.6	50	0.4	10	0.1	185	1.6
Alexandria, LA	545	25.6	40	1.9	50	2.3	0	0.0	50	2.3
Allentown–Bethlehem–Easton, PA–NJ	645	8.7	0	0.0	20	0.3	0	0.0	55	0.7
Altoona, PA	0	0.0	0	0.0	4	0.3	0	0.0	0	0.0
Amarillo, TX	125	3.5	15	0.4	20	0.6	4	0.1	58	1.6
Ames, IA	0	0.0	0	0.0	0	0.0	0	0.0	35	6.7
Anchorage, AK	255	6.2	120	2.9	45	1.1	60	1.5	160	3.9
Anderson, IN	175	8.7	10	0.5	0	0.0	0	0.0	89	4.4
Anderson, SC	150	13.2	0	0.0	4	0.4	0	0.0	4	0.4
Ann Arbor, MI	605	24.6	20	0.8	50	2.0	0	0.0	110	4.5
Anniston–Oxford, AL	135	14.3	0	0.0	0	0.0	0	0.0	25	2.6
Appleton, WI	0	0.0	75	4.2	30	1.7	0	0.0	10	0.6
Asheville, NC	285	9.1	4	0.1	0	0.0	0	0.0	30	1.0
Athens–Clarke County, GA	385	23.5	65	4.0	0	0.0	0	0.0	20	1.2
Atlanta–Sandy Springs–Marietta, GA	25,685	49.6	150	0.3	445	0.9	40	0.1	950	1.8
Atlantic City–Hammonton, NJ	1,165	20.9	4	0.1	135	2.4	0	0.0	70	1.3
Auburn–Opelika, AL	245	17.6	0	0.0	15	1.1	0	0.0	0	0.0
Augusta–Richmond County, GA–SC	2,550	42.3	25	0.4	0	0.0	0	0.0	80	1.3
Austin–Round Rock–San Marcos, TX	1,975	13.4	45	0.3	90	0.6	25	0.2	225	1.5
Bakersfield–Delano, CA	850	7.7	185	1.7	290	2.6	0	0.0	260	2.3
Baltimore–Towson, MD	17,550	43.6	65	0.2	435	1.1	0	0.0	725	1.8
Bangor, ME	0	0.0	20	1.3	15	1.0	0	0.0	25	1.6
Barnstable Town, MA	15	0.6	0	0.0	0	0.0	0	0.0	0	0.0
Baton Rouge, LA	4,705	46.2	50	0.5	45	0.4	0	0.0	55	0.5
Battle Creek, MI	60	5.3	20	1.8	0	0.0	0	0.0	4	0.4
Bay City, MI	20	2.0	15	1.5	0	0.0	0	0.0	15	1.5
Beaumont–Port Arthur, TX	2,140	43.8	55	1.1	4	0.1	0	0.0	75	1.5
Bellingham, WA	55	2.8	35	1.8	45	2.3	10	0.5	45	2.3
Bend, OR	25	2.3	10	0.9	25	2.3	0	0.0	4	0.4
Billings, MT	0	0.0	15	1.3	10	0.9	0	0.0	0	0.0
Binghamton, NY	65	2.7	0	0.0	15	0.6	0	0.0	19	0.8
Birmingham–Hoover, AL	4,155	37.0	30	0.3	30	0.3	0	0.0	30	0.3
Bismarck, ND	0	0.0	60	5.9	20	2.0	0	0.0	4	0.4
Blacksburg–Christiansburg–Radford, VA	160	10.7	0	0.0	30	2.0	0	0.0	0	0.0
Bloomington, IN	15	1.2	0	0.0	4	0.3	0	0.0	4	0.3
Bloomington–Normal, IL	195	11.7	0	0.0	0	0.0	0	0.0	14	0.8
Boise City–Nampa, ID	80	1.5	60	1.1	15	0.3	0	0.0	70	1.3
Boston–Cambridge–Quincy, MA–NH	5,225	10.7	90	0.2	980	2.0	65	0.1	1,015	2.1
Boulder, CO	40	2.4	0	0.0	10	0.6	0	0.0	20	1.2
Bowling Green, KY	55	6.2	0	0.0	0	0.0	0	0.0	0	0.0
Bremerton–Silverdale, WA	70	2.5	80	2.8	245	8.7	30	1.1	180	6.4
Bridgeport–Stamford–Norwalk, CT	1,360	18.5	4	0.1	45	0.6	30	0.4	165	2.2
Brownsville–Harlingen, TX	40	0.8	25	0.5	10	0.2	0	0.0	0	0.0
Brunswick, GA	405	31.3	0	0.0	0	0.0	0	0.0	15	1.2
Buffalo–Niagara Falls, NY	1,625	12.0	90	0.7	35	0.3	0	0.0	130	1.0
Burlington, NC	275	18.8	0	0.0	0	0.0	0	0.0	4	0.3
Burlington–South Burlington, VT	25	1.1	20	0.9	30	1.3	0	0.0	45	2.0
Canton–Massillon, OH	125	4.2	0	0.0	0	0.0	0	0.0	29	1.0
Cape Coral–Fort Myers, FL	695	9.7	0	0.0	70	1.0	0	0.0	130	1.8
Cape Girardeau–Jackson, MO–IL	115	12.4	0	0.0	0	0.0	0	0.0	25	2.7
Carson City, NV	0	0.0	10	1.1	20	2.2	0	0.0	40	4.4

PART C—METROPOLITAN STATISTICAL AREA TABLES

C-15 Protective Service Workers, by Metropolitan Statistical Area, Sex, Race, and Hispanic or Latino Origin, 2006–2010—Continued

Metropolitan Statistical Area	Total who worked in the last 5 years	Male Number	Male Percent	Female Number	Female Percent	Hispanic or Latino Number	Hispanic or Latino Percent	White alone, not Hispanic or Latino Number	White alone, not Hispanic or Latino Percent
Casper, WY	410	345	84.1	65	15.9	50	12.2	355	86.6
Cedar Rapids, IA	1,955	1,540	78.8	415	21.2	0	0.0	1,910	97.7
Champaign–Urbana, IL	1,925	1,385	71.9	540	28.1	225	11.7	1,465	76.1
Charleston, WV	3,020	2,385	79.0	635	21.0	0	0.0	2,795	92.5
Charleston–North Charleston–Summerville, SC	6,680	5,180	77.5	1,500	22.5	115	1.7	4,315	64.6
Charlotte–Gastonia–Rock Hill, NC–SC	14,455	11,175	77.3	3,280	22.7	420	2.9	9,245	64.0
Charlottesville, VA	1,825	1,335	73.2	490	26.8	0	0.0	1,420	77.8
Chattanooga, TN–GA	4,550	3,765	82.7	790	17.4	85	1.9	3,660	80.4
Cheyenne, WY	1,040	890	85.6	150	14.4	45	4.3	915	88.0
Chicago–Joliet–Naperville, IL–IN–WI	105,705	79,870	75.6	25,835	24.4	12,925	12.2	56,545	53.5
Chico, CA	2,005	1,615	80.5	390	19.5	130	6.5	1,600	79.8
Cincinnati–Middletown, OH–KY–IN	19,485	15,435	79.2	4,055	20.8	145	0.7	16,290	83.6
Clarksville, TN–KY	2,940	2,255	76.7	680	23.1	90	3.1	2,105	71.6
Cleveland, TN	945	700	74.1	245	25.9	10	1.1	900	95.2
Cleveland–Elyria–Mentor, OH	21,765	17,000	78.1	4,765	21.9	780	3.6	15,640	71.9
Coeur d'Alene, ID	1,100	800	72.7	300	27.3	8	0.7	1,060	96.4
College Station–Bryan, TX	1,935	1,445	74.7	490	25.3	125	6.5	1,435	74.2
Colorado Springs, CO	6,785	5,330	78.6	1,460	21.5	845	12.5	4,915	72.4
Columbia, MO	1,630	1,190	73.0	445	27.3	15	0.9	1,420	87.1
Columbia, SC	9,205	6,590	71.6	2,620	28.5	235	2.6	4,515	49.0
Columbus, GA–AL	3,130	2,390	76.4	740	23.6	110	3.5	1,480	47.3
Columbus, IN	630	540	85.7	90	14.3	0	0.0	630	100.0
Columbus, OH	19,250	15,185	78.9	4,065	21.1	260	1.4	15,155	78.7
Corpus Christi, TX	5,290	4,330	81.9	955	18.1	2,880	54.4	2,130	40.3
Corvallis, OR	550	405	73.6	145	26.4	35	6.4	495	90.0
Crestview–Fort Walton Beach–Destin, FL	2,075	1,705	82.2	370	17.8	165	8.0	1,595	76.9
Cumberland, MD–WV	1,365	1,190	87.2	170	12.5	0	0.0	1,330	97.4
Dallas–Fort Worth–Arlington, TX	57,025	43,475	76.2	13,555	23.8	7,270	12.7	33,995	59.6
Dalton, GA	805	695	86.3	110	13.7	75	9.3	675	83.9
Danville, IL	650	545	83.8	105	16.2	0	0.0	595	91.5
Danville, VA	1,250	1,095	87.6	155	12.4	0	0.0	885	70.8
Davenport–Moline–Rock Island, IA–IL	3,050	2,500	82.0	555	18.2	150	4.9	2,715	89.0
Dayton, OH	7,960	6,075	76.3	1,885	23.7	75	0.9	6,355	79.8
Decatur, AL	1,035	810	78.3	220	21.3	25	2.4	875	84.5
Decatur, IL	925	755	81.6	170	18.4	10	1.1	810	87.6
Deltona–Daytona Beach–Ormond Beach, FL	5,540	4,435	80.1	1,100	19.9	445	8.0	4,340	78.3
Denver–Aurora–Broomfield, CO	25,490	19,455	76.3	6,040	23.7	3,480	13.7	18,720	73.4
Des Moines–West Des Moines, IA	3,960	3,340	84.3	620	15.7	180	4.5	3,505	88.5
Detroit–Warren–Livonia, MI	41,370	31,080	75.1	10,285	24.9	835	2.0	24,590	59.4
Dothan, AL	1,305	1,090	83.5	215	16.5	4	0.3	960	73.6
Dover, DE	2,275	1,710	75.2	565	24.8	85	3.7	1,605	70.5
Dubuque, IA	745	605	81.2	145	19.5	4	0.5	715	96.0
Duluth, MN–WI	2,810	2,210	78.6	605	21.5	85	3.0	2,535	90.2
Durham–Chapel Hill, NC	4,020	3,030	75.4	985	24.5	95	2.4	2,555	63.6
Eau Claire, WI	1,465	1,185	80.9	280	19.1	0	0.0	1,420	96.9
El Centro, CA	3,720	3,135	84.3	590	15.9	2,565	69.0	870	23.4
Elizabethtown, KY	1,275	1,035	81.2	240	18.8	10	0.8	1,075	84.3
Elkhart–Goshen, IN	950	760	80.0	190	20.0	40	4.2	710	74.7
Elmira, NY	1,645	1,355	82.4	290	17.6	50	3.0	1,510	91.8
El Paso, TX	12,060	9,725	80.6	2,340	19.4	9,195	76.2	2,395	19.9
Erie, PA	2,400	2,035	84.8	365	15.2	135	5.6	2,180	90.8
Eugene–Springfield, OR	2,575	2,125	82.5	450	17.5	115	4.5	2,195	85.2
Evansville, IN–KY	2,910	2,150	73.9	760	26.1	50	1.7	2,600	89.3
Fairbanks, AK	1,085	765	70.5	315	29.0	30	2.8	800	73.7
Fargo, ND–MN	1,440	1,050	72.9	390	27.1	14	1.0	1,260	87.5

C-15 Protective Service Workers, by Metropolitan Statistical Area, Sex, Race, and Hispanic or Latino Origin, 2006–2010—Continued

Metropolitan Statistical Area	Black alone, not Hispanic or Latino Number	Percent	American Indian and Alaska Native alone, not Hispanic or Latino Number	Percent	Asian alone, not Hispanic or Latino Number	Percent	Native Hawaiian and Other Pacific Islander alone, not Hispanic or Latino Number	Percent	Two or more races, not Hispanic or Latino Number	Percent
Casper, WY	0	0.0	4	1.0	0	0.0	0	0.0	0	0.0
Cedar Rapids, IA	15	0.8	10	0.5	10	0.5	0	0.0	15	0.8
Champaign–Urbana, IL	180	9.4	15	0.8	40	2.1	0	0.0	4	0.2
Charleston, WV	130	4.3	0	0.0	0	0.0	0	0.0	95	3.1
Charleston–North Charleston–Summerville, SC	2,165	32.4	15	0.2	35	0.5	0	0.0	29	0.4
Charlotte–Gastonia–Rock Hill, NC–SC	4,535	31.4	80	0.6	95	0.7	0	0.0	84	0.6
Charlottesville, VA	405	22.2	0	0.0	0	0.0	0	0.0	0	0.0
Chattanooga, TN–GA	745	16.4	0	0.0	0	0.0	0	0.0	60	1.3
Cheyenne, WY	40	3.8	0	0.0	0	0.0	0	0.0	40	3.8
Chicago–Joliet–Naperville, IL–IN–WI	33,025	31.2	230	0.2	1,760	1.7	25	0.0	1,190	1.1
Chico, CA	55	2.7	70	3.5	30	1.5	0	0.0	120	6.0
Cincinnati–Middletown, OH–KY–IN	2,640	13.5	15	0.1	30	0.2	15	0.1	350	1.8
Clarksville, TN–KY	620	21.1	0	0.0	40	1.4	30	1.0	55	1.9
Cleveland, TN	35	3.7	0	0.0	0	0.0	0	0.0	0	0.0
Cleveland–Elyria–Mentor, OH	4,995	22.9	65	0.3	70	0.3	10	0.0	200	0.9
Coeur d'Alene, ID	15	1.4	15	1.4	0	0.0	0	0.0	0	0.0
College Station–Bryan, TX	275	14.2	0	0.0	30	1.6	0	0.0	70	3.6
Colorado Springs, CO	615	9.1	90	1.3	70	1.0	15	0.2	240	3.5
Columbia, MO	145	8.9	4	0.2	0	0.0	0	0.0	50	3.1
Columbia, SC	4,210	45.7	55	0.6	20	0.2	0	0.0	175	1.9
Columbus, GA–AL	1,465	46.8	0	0.0	35	1.1	0	0.0	40	1.3
Columbus, IN	0	0.0	0	0.0	0	0.0	0	0.0	0	0.0
Columbus, OH	3,125	16.2	25	0.1	165	0.9	35	0.2	490	2.5
Corpus Christi, TX	200	3.8	0	0.0	10	0.2	0	0.0	75	1.4
Corvallis, OR	0	0.0	10	1.8	10	1.8	0	0.0	0	0.0
Crestview–Fort Walton Beach–Destin, FL	205	9.9	0	0.0	10	0.5	0	0.0	100	4.8
Cumberland, MD–WV	25	1.8	4	0.3	0	0.0	0	0.0	4	0.3
Dallas–Fort Worth–Arlington, TX	13,945	24.5	205	0.4	605	1.1	110	0.2	895	1.6
Dalton, GA	55	6.8	0	0.0	0	0.0	0	0.0	0	0.0
Danville, IL	45	6.9	0	0.0	0	0.0	0	0.0	10	1.5
Danville, VA	345	27.6	10	0.8	0	0.0	0	0.0	10	0.8
Davenport–Moline–Rock Island, IA–IL	155	5.1	4	0.1	4	0.1	0	0.0	19	0.6
Dayton, OH	1,385	17.4	35	0.4	15	0.2	0	0.0	95	1.2
Decatur, AL	85	8.2	45	4.3	0	0.0	0	0.0	4	0.4
Decatur, IL	100	10.8	0	0.0	0	0.0	0	0.0	4	0.4
Deltona–Daytona Beach–Ormond Beach, FL	690	12.5	25	0.5	0	0.0	15	0.3	30	0.5
Denver–Aurora–Broomfield, CO	2,235	8.8	145	0.6	550	2.2	15	0.1	340	1.3
Des Moines–West Des Moines, IA	170	4.3	40	1.0	10	0.3	0	0.0	55	1.4
Detroit–Warren–Livonia, MI	14,890	36.0	210	0.5	285	0.7	60	0.1	495	1.2
Dothan, AL	315	24.1	4	0.3	0	0.0	0	0.0	14	1.1
Dover, DE	510	22.4	40	1.8	0	0.0	0	0.0	34	1.5
Dubuque, IA	0	0.0	0	0.0	0	0.0	0	0.0	30	4.0
Duluth, MN–WI	0	0.0	145	5.2	15	0.5	0	0.0	34	1.2
Durham–Chapel Hill, NC	1,280	31.8	0	0.0	45	1.1	0	0.0	40	1.0
Eau Claire, WI	20	1.4	0	0.0	10	0.7	0	0.0	15	1.0
El Centro, CA	125	3.4	90	2.4	35	0.9	0	0.0	40	1.1
Elizabethtown, KY	130	10.2	4	0.3	0	0.0	0	0.0	60	4.7
Elkhart–Goshen, IN	140	14.7	10	1.1	25	2.6	0	0.0	25	2.6
Elmira, NY	75	4.6	0	0.0	0	0.0	0	0.0	14	0.9
El Paso, TX	345	2.9	15	0.1	20	0.2	30	0.2	65	0.5
Erie, PA	55	2.3	0	0.0	25	1.0	0	0.0	4	0.2
Eugene–Springfield, OR	75	2.9	40	1.6	20	0.8	10	0.4	115	4.5
Evansville, IN–KY	245	8.4	0	0.0	0	0.0	0	0.0	15	0.5
Fairbanks, AK	80	7.4	90	8.3	40	3.7	0	0.0	40	3.7
Fargo, ND–MN	0	0.0	25	1.7	100	6.9	0	0.0	39	2.7

C-15 Protective Service Workers, by Metropolitan Statistical Area, Sex, Race, and Hispanic or Latino Origin, 2006–2010—Continued

Metropolitan Statistical Area	Total who worked in the last 5 years	Male Number	Male Percent	Female Number	Female Percent	Hispanic or Latino Number	Hispanic or Latino Percent	White alone, not Hispanic or Latino Number	White alone, not Hispanic or Latino Percent
Farmington, NM	1,070	775	72.4	295	27.6	180	16.8	520	48.6
Fayetteville, NC	3,880	3,085	79.5	795	20.5	125	3.2	2,145	55.3
Fayetteville–Springdale–Rogers, AR–MO	3,640	3,205	88.0	435	12.0	180	4.9	3,185	87.5
Flagstaff, AZ	1,910	1,390	72.8	520	27.2	130	6.8	1,455	76.2
Flint, MI	4,190	3,045	72.7	1,145	27.3	125	3.0	2,590	61.8
Florence, SC	1,825	1,415	77.5	410	22.5	25	1.4	1,145	62.7
Florence–Muscle Shoals, AL	1,385	1,115	80.5	270	19.5	4	0.3	1,265	91.3
Fond du Lac, WI	1,290	910	70.5	380	29.5	40	3.1	1,240	96.1
Fort Collins–Loveland, CO	2,755	2,175	78.9	580	21.1	215	7.8	2,400	87.1
Fort Smith, AR–OK	2,065	1,710	82.8	355	17.2	4	0.2	1,735	84.0
Fort Wayne, IN	3,100	2,540	81.9	555	17.9	155	5.0	2,580	83.2
Fresno, CA	9,310	7,760	83.4	1,550	16.6	3,615	38.8	4,010	43.1
Gadsden, AL	990	890	89.9	105	10.6	0	0.0	840	84.8
Gainesville, FL	2,750	2,040	74.2	710	25.8	125	4.5	2,000	72.7
Gainesville, GA	1,065	860	80.8	205	19.2	65	6.1	920	86.4
Glens Falls, NY	1,785	1,345	75.4	440	24.6	8	0.4	1,720	96.4
Goldsboro, NC	1,355	1,110	81.9	250	18.5	65	4.8	650	48.0
Grand Forks, ND–MN	645	450	69.8	190	29.5	39	6.0	605	93.8
Grand Junction, CO	1,295	995	76.8	300	23.2	120	9.3	1,145	88.4
Grand Rapids–Wyoming, MI	5,325	4,335	81.4	990	18.6	120	2.3	4,430	83.2
Great Falls, MT	895	710	79.3	185	20.7	10	1.1	860	96.1
Greeley, CO	2,305	1,755	76.1	545	23.6	350	15.2	1,815	78.7
Green Bay, WI	2,395	1,965	82.0	425	17.7	19	0.8	2,220	92.7
Greensboro–High Point, NC	5,950	4,640	78.0	1,310	22.0	165	2.8	4,330	72.8
Greenville, NC	1,870	1,305	69.8	565	30.2	85	4.5	1,380	73.8
Greenville–Mauldin–Easley, SC	4,515	3,565	79.0	950	21.0	130	2.9	3,660	81.1
Gulfport–Biloxi, MS	3,295	2,555	77.5	740	22.5	65	2.0	2,440	74.1
Hagerstown–Martinsburg, MD–WV	4,065	3,220	79.2	845	20.8	50	1.2	3,635	89.4
Hanford–Corcoran, CA	2,860	2,465	86.2	400	14.0	720	25.2	1,520	53.1
Harrisburg–Carlisle, PA	4,570	3,495	76.5	1,075	23.5	110	2.4	3,790	82.9
Harrisonburg, VA	875	655	74.9	220	25.1	45	5.1	735	84.0
Hartford–West Hartford–East Hartford, CT	12,485	9,825	78.7	2,655	21.3	1,595	12.8	8,805	70.5
Hattiesburg, MS	1,235	960	77.7	275	22.3	20	1.6	760	61.5
Hickory–Lenoir–Morganton, NC	3,465	2,705	78.1	760	21.9	15	0.4	3,240	93.5
Hinesville–Fort Stewart, GA	1,300	855	65.8	445	34.2	70	5.4	590	45.4
Holland–Grand Haven, MI	1,230	1,025	83.3	205	16.7	105	8.5	1,100	89.4
Honolulu, HI	13,925	11,410	81.9	2,510	18.0	1,070	7.7	2,735	19.6
Hot Springs, AR	775	615	79.4	160	20.6	25	3.2	605	78.1
Houma–Bayou Cane–Thibodaux, LA	2,035	1,350	66.3	680	33.4	30	1.5	1,250	61.4
Houston–Sugar Land–Baytown, TX	56,415	41,515	73.6	14,900	26.4	9,715	17.2	25,495	45.2
Huntington–Ashland, WV–KY–OH	2,370	2,005	84.6	365	15.4	20	0.8	2,335	98.5
Huntsville, AL	3,555	2,625	73.8	930	26.2	120	3.4	2,175	61.2
Idaho Falls, ID	1,160	1,010	87.1	145	12.5	45	3.9	1,075	92.7
Indianapolis–Carmel, IN	16,905	12,690	75.1	4,215	24.9	290	1.7	13,105	77.5
Iowa City, IA	1,025	750	73.2	280	27.3	4	0.4	945	92.2
Ithaca, NY	735	515	70.1	220	29.9	0	0.0	675	91.8
Jackson, MI	1,815	1,560	86.0	260	14.3	15	0.8	1,605	88.4
Jackson, MS	6,265	4,860	77.6	1,405	22.4	4	0.1	2,370	37.8
Jackson, TN	1,070	910	85.0	160	15.0	0	0.0	625	58.4
Jacksonville, FL	15,710	11,755	74.8	3,950	25.1	750	4.8	10,595	67.4
Jacksonville, NC	1,335	1,015	76.0	320	24.0	135	10.1	875	65.5
Janesville, WI	1,005	800	79.6	205	20.4	55	5.5	885	88.1
Jefferson City, MO	2,130	1,615	75.8	520	24.4	35	1.6	1,895	89.0
Johnson City, TN	1,660	1,400	84.3	260	15.7	30	1.8	1,555	93.7
Johnstown, PA	1,835	1,620	88.3	215	11.7	8	0.4	1,710	93.2

C-15 **Protective Service Workers, by Metropolitan Statistical Area, Sex, Race, and Hispanic or Latino Origin, 2006–2010**—*Continued*

Metropolitan Statistical Area	Black alone, not Hispanic or Latino		American Indian and Alaska Native alone, not Hispanic or Latino		Asian alone, not Hispanic or Latino		Native Hawaiian and Other Pacific Islander alone, not Hispanic or Latino		Two or more races, not Hispanic or Latino	
	Number	Percent	Number	Percent	Number	Percent	Number	Percent	Number	Percent
Farmington, NM	4	0.4	355	33.2	0	0.0	0	0.0	4	0.4
Fayetteville, NC	1,350	34.8	75	1.9	30	0.8	30	0.8	129	3.3
Fayetteville–Springdale–Rogers, AR–MO	30	0.8	80	2.2	0	0.0	30	0.8	135	3.7
Flagstaff, AZ	0	0.0	300	15.7	0	0.0	0	0.0	24	1.3
Flint, MI	1,315	31.4	40	1.0	0	0.0	0	0.0	125	3.0
Florence, SC	610	33.4	15	0.8	30	1.6	0	0.0	0	0.0
Florence–Muscle Shoals, AL	90	6.5	25	1.8	0	0.0	0	0.0	4	0.3
Fond du Lac, WI	4	0.3	0	0.0	0	0.0	0	0.0	0	0.0
Fort Collins–Loveland, CO	0	0.0	45	1.6	65	2.4	0	0.0	35	1.3
Fort Smith, AR–OK	60	2.9	165	8.0	0	0.0	0	0.0	95	4.6
Fort Wayne, IN	340	11.0	25	0.8	0	0.0	0	0.0	0	0.0
Fresno, CA	795	8.5	40	0.4	625	6.7	55	0.6	164	1.8
Gadsden, AL	95	9.6	25	2.5	0	0.0	0	0.0	30	3.0
Gainesville, FL	515	18.7	0	0.0	60	2.2	0	0.0	50	1.8
Gainesville, GA	75	7.0	0	0.0	0	0.0	0	0.0	4	0.4
Glens Falls, NY	10	0.6	50	2.8	0	0.0	0	0.0	0	0.0
Goldsboro, NC	630	46.5	0	0.0	0	0.0	0	0.0	10	0.7
Grand Forks, ND–MN	0	0.0	0	0.0	0	0.0	0	0.0	0	0.0
Grand Junction, CO	0	0.0	15	1.2	4	0.3	0	0.0	10	0.8
Grand Rapids–Wyoming, MI	620	11.6	45	0.8	15	0.3	0	0.0	90	1.7
Great Falls, MT	10	1.1	15	1.7	0	0.0	0	0.0	0	0.0
Greeley, CO	55	2.4	0	0.0	4	0.2	0	0.0	80	3.5
Green Bay, WI	35	1.5	100	4.2	10	0.4	0	0.0	4	0.2
Greensboro–High Point, NC	1,300	21.8	25	0.4	30	0.5	10	0.2	90	1.5
Greenville, NC	360	19.3	0	0.0	15	0.8	0	0.0	35	1.9
Greenville–Mauldin–Easley, SC	650	14.4	10	0.2	10	0.2	0	0.0	55	1.2
Gulfport–Biloxi, MS	750	22.8	0	0.0	0	0.0	0	0.0	40	1.2
Hagerstown–Martinsburg, MD–WV	370	9.1	0	0.0	0	0.0	0	0.0	14	0.3
Hanford–Corcoran, CA	430	15.0	30	1.0	160	5.6	0	0.0	0	0.0
Harrisburg–Carlisle, PA	595	13.0	15	0.3	20	0.4	0	0.0	39	0.9
Harrisonburg, VA	35	4.0	25	2.9	20	2.3	0	0.0	15	1.7
Hartford–West Hartford–East Hartford, CT	1,835	14.7	35	0.3	65	0.5	0	0.0	150	1.2
Hattiesburg, MS	450	36.4	0	0.0	0	0.0	0	0.0	0	0.0
Hickory–Lenoir–Morganton, NC	165	4.8	10	0.3	10	0.3	0	0.0	30	0.9
Hinesville–Fort Stewart, GA	560	43.1	30	2.3	15	1.2	0	0.0	35	2.7
Holland–Grand Haven, MI	15	1.2	0	0.0	15	1.2	0	0.0	0	0.0
Honolulu, HI	365	2.6	10	0.1	3,950	28.4	2,290	16.4	3,503	25.2
Hot Springs, AR	135	17.4	0	0.0	0	0.0	0	0.0	10	1.3
Houma–Bayou Cane–Thibodaux, LA	635	31.2	65	3.2	35	1.7	0	0.0	20	1.0
Houston–Sugar Land–Baytown, TX	19,280	34.2	145	0.3	1,120	2.0	0	0.0	655	1.2
Huntington–Ashland, WV–KY–OH	0	0.0	0	0.0	0	0.0	15	0.6	0	0.0
Huntsville, AL	1,165	32.8	35	1.0	0	0.0	20	0.6	40	1.1
Idaho Falls, ID	4	0.3	0	0.0	0	0.0	0	0.0	35	3.0
Indianapolis–Carmel, IN	3,140	18.6	40	0.2	70	0.4	0	0.0	270	1.6
Iowa City, IA	50	4.9	0	0.0	30	2.9	0	0.0	0	0.0
Ithaca, NY	35	4.8	0	0.0	15	2.0	0	0.0	15	2.0
Jackson, MI	185	10.2	10	0.6	0	0.0	0	0.0	0	0.0
Jackson, MS	3,840	61.3	10	0.2	35	0.6	0	0.0	10	0.2
Jackson, TN	445	41.6	0	0.0	0	0.0	0	0.0	0	0.0
Jacksonville, FL	3,880	24.7	40	0.3	290	1.8	0	0.0	155	1.0
Jacksonville, NC	290	21.7	20	1.5	0	0.0	0	0.0	15	1.1
Janesville, WI	40	4.0	0	0.0	4	0.4	0	0.0	25	2.5
Jefferson City, MO	140	6.6	20	0.9	10	0.5	0	0.0	39	1.8
Johnson City, TN	75	4.5	0	0.0	0	0.0	4	0.2	0	0.0
Johnstown, PA	100	5.4	0	0.0	0	0.0	0	0.0	20	1.1

C-15 Protective Service Workers, by Metropolitan Statistical Area, Sex, Race, and Hispanic or Latino Origin, 2006–2010—Continued

Metropolitan Statistical Area	Total who worked in the last 5 years	Male Number	Male Percent	Female Number	Female Percent	Hispanic or Latino Number	Hispanic or Latino Percent	White alone, not Hispanic or Latino Number	White alone, not Hispanic or Latino Percent
Jonesboro, AR	685	585	85.4	100	14.6	4	0.6	630	92.0
Joplin, MO	1,140	850	74.6	290	25.4	30	2.6	1,070	93.9
Kalamazoo–Portage, MI	2,570	1,815	70.6	755	29.4	70	2.7	2,140	83.3
Kankakee–Bradley, IL	1,075	935	87.0	140	13.0	80	7.4	825	76.7
Kansas City, MO–KS	20,735	15,965	77.0	4,770	23.0	865	4.2	16,540	79.8
Kennewick–Pasco–Richland, WA	2,170	1,710	78.8	460	21.2	280	12.9	1,765	81.3
Killeen–Temple–Fort Hood, TX	6,560	4,365	66.5	2,195	33.5	915	13.9	3,780	57.6
Kingsport–Bristol–Bristol, TN–VA	2,585	2,085	80.7	500	19.3	25	1.0	2,525	97.7
Kingston, NY	2,510	2,175	86.7	335	13.3	275	11.0	2,090	83.3
Knoxville, TN	5,420	4,420	81.5	1,000	18.5	0	0.0	4,900	90.4
Kokomo, IN	725	515	71.0	210	29.0	0	0.0	685	94.5
La Crosse, WI–MN	840	615	73.2	220	26.2	0	0.0	790	94.0
Lafayette, IN	1,445	1,080	74.7	365	25.3	10	0.7	1,385	95.8
Lafayette, LA	2,800	2,170	77.5	625	22.3	0	0.0	1,680	60.0
Lake Charles, LA	2,750	1,985	72.2	765	27.8	70	2.5	1,855	67.5
Lake Havasu City–Kingman, AZ	2,365	1,960	82.9	405	17.1	190	8.0	2,075	87.7
Lakeland–Winter Haven, FL	6,275	5,020	80.0	1,255	20.0	470	7.5	4,610	73.5
Lancaster, PA	2,805	2,340	83.4	460	16.4	245	8.7	2,415	86.1
Lansing–East Lansing, MI	4,425	3,300	74.6	1,125	25.4	285	6.4	3,365	76.0
Laredo, TX	4,590	3,885	84.6	700	15.3	4,245	92.5	345	7.5
Las Cruces, NM	2,620	1,970	75.2	645	24.6	1,600	61.1	920	35.1
Las Vegas–Paradise, NV	31,420	25,000	79.6	6,420	20.4	4,140	13.2	19,030	60.6
Lawrence, KS	615	490	79.7	125	20.3	10	1.6	530	86.2
Lawton, OK	1,740	1,410	81.0	330	19.0	235	13.5	945	54.3
Lebanon, PA	1,150	1,005	87.4	145	12.6	0	0.0	1,100	95.7
Lewiston, ID–WA	615	520	84.6	95	15.4	15	2.4	495	80.5
Lewiston–Auburn, ME	745	615	82.6	130	17.4	0	0.0	735	98.7
Lexington–Fayette, KY	4,045	3,330	82.3	715	17.7	10	0.2	3,330	82.3
Lima, OH	1,235	930	75.3	305	24.7	0	0.0	1,035	83.8
Lincoln, NE	2,515	2,015	80.1	500	19.9	60	2.4	2,340	93.0
Little Rock–North Little Rock–Conway, AR	6,110	4,775	78.2	1,335	21.8	105	1.7	4,275	70.0
Logan, UT–ID	810	605	74.7	200	24.7	0	0.0	750	92.6
Longview, TX	2,010	1,375	68.4	630	31.3	45	2.2	1,535	76.4
Longview, WA	870	815	93.7	55	6.3	0	0.0	845	97.1
Los Angeles–Long Beach–Santa Ana, CA	118,625	94,460	79.6	24,160	20.4	44,080	37.2	40,895	34.5
Louisville/Jefferson County, KY–IN	11,520	8,425	73.1	3,095	26.9	185	1.6	9,480	82.3
Lubbock, TX	2,820	2,260	80.1	565	20.0	905	32.1	1,650	58.5
Lynchburg, VA	2,305	1,930	83.7	380	16.5	40	1.7	1,930	83.7
Macon, GA	2,815	2,005	71.2	810	28.8	4	0.1	1,230	43.7
Madera–Chowchilla, CA	1,620	1,145	70.7	475	29.3	415	25.6	1,030	63.6
Madison, WI	4,690	3,370	71.9	1,320	28.1	165	3.5	4,245	90.5
Manchester–Nashua, NH	3,095	2,530	81.7	565	18.3	49	1.6	2,920	94.3
Manhattan, KS	1,160	920	79.3	240	20.7	55	4.7	985	84.9
Mankato–North Mankato, MN	995	810	81.4	190	19.1	4	0.4	905	91.0
Mansfield, OH	1,535	1,255	81.8	280	18.2	0	0.0	1,320	86.0
McAllen–Edinburg–Mission, TX	7,125	5,830	81.8	1,295	18.2	6,335	88.9	670	9.4
Medford, OR	1,400	1,180	84.3	220	15.7	95	6.8	1,225	87.5
Memphis, TN–MS–AR	17,560	12,865	73.3	4,690	26.7	195	1.1	7,610	43.3
Merced, CA	1,930	1,630	84.5	300	15.5	595	30.8	1,110	57.5
Miami–Fort Lauderdale–Pompano Beach, FL	76,850	56,545	73.6	20,305	26.4	24,095	31.4	26,020	33.9
Michigan City–La Porte, IN	1,410	1,090	77.3	320	22.7	25	1.8	1,200	85.1
Midland, TX	1,000	680	68.0	320	32.0	275	27.5	635	63.5
Milwaukee–Waukesha–West Allis, WI	15,125	11,565	76.5	3,560	23.5	930	6.1	10,515	69.5
Minneapolis–St. Paul–Bloomington, MN–WI	22,385	16,495	73.7	5,890	26.3	650	2.9	18,490	82.6
Missoula, MT	885	680	76.8	205	23.2	0	0.0	870	98.3

C-15 **Protective Service Workers, by Metropolitan Statistical Area, Sex, Race, and Hispanic or Latino Origin, 2006–2010**—*Continued*

Metropolitan Statistical Area	Black alone, not Hispanic or Latino Number	Percent	American Indian and Alaska Native alone, not Hispanic or Latino Number	Percent	Asian alone, not Hispanic or Latino Number	Percent	Native Hawaiian and Other Pacific Islander alone, not Hispanic or Latino Number	Percent	Two or more races, not Hispanic or Latino Number	Percent
Jonesboro, AR	50	7.3	0	0.0	0	0.0	0	0.0	0	0.0
Joplin, MO	15	1.3	4	0.4	10	0.9	0	0.0	15	1.3
Kalamazoo–Portage, MI	295	11.5	20	0.8	15	0.6	0	0.0	35	1.4
Kankakee–Bradley, IL	150	14.0	0	0.0	0	0.0	10	0.9	4	0.4
Kansas City, MO–KS	2,720	13.1	60	0.3	105	0.5	10	0.0	440	2.1
Kennewick–Pasco–Richland, WA	65	3.0	35	1.6	0	0.0	0	0.0	20	0.9
Killeen–Temple–Fort Hood, TX	1,625	24.8	20	0.3	15	0.2	0	0.0	200	3.0
Kingsport–Bristol–Bristol, TN–VA	10	0.4	10	0.4	0	0.0	0	0.0	15	0.6
Kingston, NY	75	3.0	35	1.4	25	1.0	0	0.0	10	0.4
Knoxville, TN	400	7.4	20	0.4	0	0.0	0	0.0	100	1.8
Kokomo, IN	40	5.5	0	0.0	0	0.0	0	0.0	0	0.0
La Crosse, WI–MN	0	0.0	20	2.4	0	0.0	0	0.0	30	3.6
Lafayette, IN	0	0.0	4	0.3	10	0.7	0	0.0	35	2.4
Lafayette, LA	1,120	40.0	0	0.0	0	0.0	0	0.0	0	0.0
Lake Charles, LA	770	28.0	25	0.9	0	0.0	0	0.0	29	1.1
Lake Havasu City–Kingman, AZ	0	0.0	55	2.3	0	0.0	15	0.6	34	1.4
Lakeland–Winter Haven, FL	1,020	16.3	0	0.0	25	0.4	20	0.3	134	2.1
Lancaster, PA	55	2.0	0	0.0	60	2.1	0	0.0	25	0.9
Lansing–East Lansing, MI	670	15.1	15	0.3	25	0.6	0	0.0	70	1.6
Laredo, TX	0	0.0	0	0.0	0	0.0	0	0.0	0	0.0
Las Cruces, NM	70	2.7	15	0.6	10	0.4	0	0.0	10	0.4
Las Vegas–Paradise, NV	5,025	16.0	270	0.9	1,825	5.8	240	0.8	900	2.9
Lawrence, KS	20	3.3	0	0.0	4	0.7	0	0.0	50	8.1
Lawton, OK	325	18.7	95	5.5	40	2.3	0	0.0	95	5.5
Lebanon, PA	45	3.9	0	0.0	0	0.0	0	0.0	0	0.0
Lewiston, ID–WA	0	0.0	40	6.5	15	2.4	0	0.0	50	8.1
Lewiston–Auburn, ME	0	0.0	0	0.0	0	0.0	0	0.0	10	1.3
Lexington–Fayette, KY	690	17.1	0	0.0	0	0.0	0	0.0	15	0.4
Lima, OH	200	16.2	0	0.0	0	0.0	0	0.0	0	0.0
Lincoln, NE	0	0.0	30	1.2	4	0.2	35	1.4	45	1.8
Little Rock–North Little Rock–Conway, AR	1,565	25.6	15	0.2	10	0.2	0	0.0	145	2.4
Logan, UT–ID	0	0.0	15	1.9	25	3.1	20	2.5	0	0.0
Longview, TX	415	20.6	0	0.0	0	0.0	0	0.0	8	0.4
Longview, WA	0	0.0	0	0.0	0	0.0	0	0.0	25	2.9
Los Angeles–Long Beach–Santa Ana, CA	20,970	17.7	645	0.5	8,835	7.4	630	0.5	2,565	2.2
Louisville/Jefferson County, KY–IN	1,730	15.0	25	0.2	0	0.0	0	0.0	99	0.9
Lubbock, TX	200	7.1	4	0.1	25	0.9	0	0.0	40	1.4
Lynchburg, VA	280	12.1	45	2.0	0	0.0	0	0.0	10	0.4
Macon, GA	1,480	52.6	20	0.7	80	2.8	0	0.0	0	0.0
Madera–Chowchilla, CA	100	6.2	50	3.1	15	0.9	10	0.6	0	0.0
Madison, WI	135	2.9	10	0.2	20	0.4	10	0.2	100	2.1
Manchester–Nashua, NH	95	3.1	4	0.1	0	0.0	0	0.0	20	0.6
Manhattan, KS	45	3.9	0	0.0	0	0.0	0	0.0	70	6.0
Mankato–North Mankato, MN	4	0.4	0	0.0	70	7.0	0	0.0	10	1.0
Mansfield, OH	195	12.7	4	0.3	0	0.0	0	0.0	10	0.7
McAllen–Edinburg–Mission, TX	105	1.5	0	0.0	10	0.1	0	0.0	0	0.0
Medford, OR	4	0.3	10	0.7	10	0.7	0	0.0	55	3.9
Memphis, TN–MS–AR	9,465	53.9	35	0.2	85	0.5	0	0.0	173	1.0
Merced, CA	85	4.4	0	0.0	100	5.2	0	0.0	34	1.8
Miami–Fort Lauderdale–Pompano Beach, FL	25,210	32.8	55	0.1	855	1.1	70	0.1	545	0.7
Michigan City–La Porte, IN	180	12.8	0	0.0	0	0.0	0	0.0	10	0.7
Midland, TX	75	7.5	0	0.0	0	0.0	0	0.0	10	1.0
Milwaukee–Waukesha–West Allis, WI	2,930	19.4	35	0.2	365	2.4	15	0.1	335	2.2
Minneapolis–St. Paul–Bloomington, MN–WI	1,890	8.4	250	1.1	710	3.2	0	0.0	405	1.8
Missoula, MT	4	0.5	0	0.0	0	0.0	0	0.0	15	1.7

C-15. Protective Service Workers, by Metropolitan Statistical Area, Sex, Race, and Hispanic or Latino Origin, 2006–2010—Continued

Metropolitan Statistical Area	Total who worked in the last 5 years	Male Number	Male Percent	Female Number	Female Percent	Hispanic or Latino Number	Hispanic or Latino Percent	White alone, not Hispanic or Latino Number	White alone, not Hispanic or Latino Percent
Mobile, AL	3,950	3,110	78.7	840	21.3	90	2.3	2,145	54.3
Modesto, CA	4,595	3,875	84.3	720	15.7	1,275	27.7	2,845	61.9
Monroe, LA	1,735	1,435	82.7	300	17.3	4	0.2	1,045	60.2
Monroe, MI	1,425	1,055	74.0	370	26.0	10	0.7	1,355	95.1
Montgomery, AL	4,660	3,645	78.2	1,015	21.8	35	0.8	2,115	45.4
Morgantown, WV	1,450	1,120	77.2	330	22.8	0	0.0	1,430	98.6
Morristown, TN	1,140	860	75.4	280	24.6	0	0.0	1,140	100.0
Mount Vernon–Anacortes, WA	1,060	910	85.8	150	14.2	175	16.5	840	79.2
Muncie, IN	1,160	835	72.0	325	28.0	35	3.0	1,005	86.6
Muskegon–Norton Shores, MI	1,545	1,180	76.4	365	23.6	35	2.3	1,180	76.4
Myrtle Beach–North Myrtle Beach–Conway, SC	3,805	3,310	87.0	490	12.9	80	2.1	3,255	85.5
Napa, CA	985	870	88.3	115	11.7	200	20.3	615	62.4
Naples–Marco Island, FL	3,155	2,535	80.3	620	19.7	325	10.3	2,460	78.0
Nashville-Davidson–Murfreesboro–Franklin, TN	14,760	11,235	76.1	3,525	23.9	235	1.6	10,905	73.9
New Haven–Milford, CT	9,635	7,955	82.6	1,680	17.4	920	9.5	6,965	72.3
New Orleans–Metairie–Kenner, LA	14,415	10,315	71.6	4,100	28.4	435	3.0	6,655	46.2
New York–Northern New Jersey–Long Island, NY–NJ–PA	264,370	204,095	77.2	60,275	22.8	51,240	19.4	123,510	46.7
Niles–Benton Harbor, MI	1,160	955	82.3	205	17.7	0	0.0	985	84.9
North Port–Bradenton–Sarasota, FL	5,595	4,515	80.7	1,080	19.3	350	6.3	4,735	84.6
Norwich–New London, CT	4,040	3,205	79.3	835	20.7	140	3.5	3,435	85.0
Ocala, FL	3,785	2,665	70.4	1,120	29.6	175	4.6	2,730	72.1
Ocean City, NJ	1,435	1,185	82.6	250	17.4	60	4.2	1,310	91.3
Odessa, TX	1,005	740	73.6	265	26.4	230	22.9	650	64.7
Ogden–Clearfield, UT	4,525	3,545	78.3	980	21.7	195	4.3	4,115	90.9
Oklahoma City, OK	12,135	9,350	77.0	2,785	23.0	490	4.0	9,445	77.8
Olympia, WA	3,100	2,530	81.6	570	18.4	95	3.1	2,425	78.2
Omaha–Council Bluffs, NE–IA	7,610	5,600	73.6	2,015	26.5	360	4.7	6,330	83.2
Orlando–Kissimmee–Sanford, FL	23,400	16,975	72.5	6,425	27.5	5,315	22.7	12,795	54.7
Oshkosh–Neenah, WI	1,805	1,320	73.1	485	26.9	20	1.1	1,770	98.1
Owensboro, KY	890	590	66.3	305	34.3	0	0.0	840	94.4
Oxnard–Thousand Oaks–Ventura, CA	7,910	6,705	84.8	1,205	15.2	1,725	21.8	5,180	65.5
Palm Bay–Melbourne–Titusville, FL	6,395	4,695	73.4	1,700	26.6	480	7.5	5,190	81.2
Palm Coast, FL	990	770	77.8	220	22.2	145	14.6	740	74.7
Panama City–Lynn Haven–Panama City Beach, FL	2,270	1,865	82.2	405	17.8	185	8.1	1,865	82.2
Parkersburg–Marietta–Vienna, WV–OH	1,245	1,005	80.7	240	19.3	95	7.6	1,140	91.6
Pascagoula, MS	2,070	1,380	66.7	695	33.6	30	1.4	1,605	77.5
Pensacola–Ferry Pass–Brent, FL	4,875	3,970	81.4	905	18.6	210	4.3	3,940	80.8
Peoria, IL	3,095	2,480	80.1	610	19.7	30	1.0	2,515	81.3
Philadelphia–Camden–Wilmington, PA–NJ–DE–MD	68,915	52,055	75.5	16,865	24.5	3,635	5.3	40,380	58.6
Phoenix–Mesa–Glendale, AZ	45,250	34,865	77.0	10,380	22.9	8,860	19.6	30,910	68.3
Pine Bluff, AR	2,155	1,455	67.5	700	32.5	0	0.0	780	36.2
Pittsburgh, PA	21,775	17,025	78.2	4,750	21.8	230	1.1	18,875	86.7
Pittsfield, MA	1,255	1,060	84.5	190	15.1	0	0.0	1,200	95.6
Pocatello, ID	780	590	75.6	190	24.4	95	12.2	625	80.1
Portland–South Portland–Biddeford, ME	4,140	3,490	84.3	645	15.6	24	0.6	3,995	96.5
Portland–Vancouver–Hillsboro, OR–WA	17,575	13,345	75.9	4,225	24.0	690	3.9	14,940	85.0
Port St. Lucie, FL	5,890	4,660	79.1	1,230	20.9	575	9.8	4,300	73.0
Poughkeepsie–Newburgh–Middletown, NY	13,535	11,075	81.8	2,460	18.2	2,125	15.7	9,030	66.7
Prescott, AZ	2,730	2,330	85.3	395	14.5	150	5.5	2,465	90.3
Providence–New Bedford–Fall River, RI–MA	18,620	14,985	80.5	3,635	19.5	885	4.8	16,095	86.4

C-15 Protective Service Workers, by Metropolitan Statistical Area, Sex, Race, and Hispanic or Latino Origin, 2006–2010—Continued

Metropolitan Statistical Area	Black alone, not Hispanic or Latino Number	Percent	American Indian and Alaska Native alone, not Hispanic or Latino Number	Percent	Asian alone, not Hispanic or Latino Number	Percent	Native Hawaiian and Other Pacific Islander alone, not Hispanic or Latino Number	Percent	Two or more races, not Hispanic or Latino Number	Percent
Mobile, AL	1,630	41.3	0	0.0	0	0.0	0	0.0	85	2.2
Modesto, CA	170	3.7	15	0.3	105	2.3	30	0.7	160	3.5
Monroe, LA	590	34.0	10	0.6	0	0.0	0	0.0	85	4.9
Monroe, MI	50	3.5	10	0.7	0	0.0	0	0.0	0	0.0
Montgomery, AL	2,430	52.1	15	0.3	25	0.5	0	0.0	40	0.9
Morgantown, WV	20	1.4	0	0.0	4	0.3	0	0.0	0	0.0
Morristown, TN	0	0.0	0	0.0	0	0.0	0	0.0	0	0.0
Mount Vernon–Anacortes, WA	15	1.4	20	1.9	4	0.4	0	0.0	0	0.0
Muncie, IN	105	9.1	0	0.0	0	0.0	0	0.0	15	1.3
Muskegon–Norton Shores, MI	305	19.7	20	1.3	0	0.0	0	0.0	10	0.6
Myrtle Beach–North Myrtle Beach–Conway, SC	430	11.3	10	0.3	10	0.3	0	0.0	15	0.4
Napa, CA	70	7.1	0	0.0	60	6.1	0	0.0	40	4.1
Naples–Marco Island, FL	325	10.3	0	0.0	45	1.4	0	0.0	0	0.0
Nashville-Davidson–Murfreesboro–Franklin, TN	3,145	21.3	100	0.7	95	0.6	0	0.0	270	1.8
New Haven–Milford, CT	1,500	15.6	10	0.1	80	0.8	0	0.0	165	1.7
New Orleans–Metairie–Kenner, LA	7,105	49.3	95	0.7	25	0.2	10	0.1	95	0.7
New York–Northern New Jersey–Long Island, NY–NJ–PA	75,810	28.7	495	0.2	9,035	3.4	30	0.0	4,250	1.6
Niles–Benton Harbor, MI	160	13.8	0	0.0	0	0.0	0	0.0	14	1.2
North Port–Bradenton–Sarasota, FL	335	6.0	55	1.0	35	0.6	25	0.4	55	1.0
Norwich–New London, CT	260	6.4	50	1.2	30	0.7	0	0.0	125	3.1
Ocala, FL	745	19.7	50	1.3	25	0.7	0	0.0	50	1.3
Ocean City, NJ	65	4.5	0	0.0	0	0.0	0	0.0	0	0.0
Odessa, TX	105	10.4	0	0.0	0	0.0	0	0.0	20	2.0
Ogden–Clearfield, UT	10	0.2	25	0.6	40	0.9	75	1.7	65	1.4
Oklahoma City, OK	1,255	10.3	505	4.2	20	0.2	0	0.0	420	3.5
Olympia, WA	210	6.8	80	2.6	70	2.3	55	1.8	160	5.2
Omaha–Council Bluffs, NE–IA	730	9.6	10	0.1	25	0.3	0	0.0	155	2.0
Orlando–Kissimmee–Sanford, FL	4,280	18.3	35	0.1	495	2.1	10	0.0	480	2.1
Oshkosh–Neenah, WI	0	0.0	10	0.6	0	0.0	0	0.0	4	0.2
Owensboro, KY	45	5.1	0	0.0	10	1.1	0	0.0	0	0.0
Oxnard–Thousand Oaks–Ventura, CA	390	4.9	35	0.4	335	4.2	30	0.4	220	2.8
Palm Bay–Melbourne–Titusville, FL	545	8.5	25	0.4	35	0.5	0	0.0	120	1.9
Palm Coast, FL	100	10.1	0	0.0	0	0.0	0	0.0	0	0.0
Panama City–Lynn Haven–Panama City Beach, FL	205	9.0	15	0.7	0	0.0	0	0.0	0	0.0
Parkersburg–Marietta–Vienna, WV–OH	10	0.8	0	0.0	0	0.0	0	0.0	0	0.0
Pascagoula, MS	415	20.0	4	0.2	0	0.0	0	0.0	14	0.7
Pensacola–Ferry Pass–Brent, FL	580	11.9	0	0.0	50	1.0	15	0.3	80	1.6
Peoria, IL	470	15.2	10	0.3	10	0.3	0	0.0	59	1.9
Philadelphia–Camden–Wilmington, PA–NJ–DE–MD	22,960	33.3	90	0.1	830	1.2	55	0.1	970	1.4
Phoenix–Mesa–Glendale, AZ	3,160	7.0	1,030	2.3	480	1.1	205	0.5	605	1.3
Pine Bluff, AR	1,335	61.9	15	0.7	15	0.7	0	0.0	10	0.5
Pittsburgh, PA	2,220	10.2	40	0.2	90	0.4	0	0.0	325	1.5
Pittsfield, MA	30	2.4	0	0.0	15	1.2	0	0.0	4	0.3
Pocatello, ID	0	0.0	60	7.7	0	0.0	0	0.0	0	0.0
Portland–South Portland–Biddeford, ME	20	0.5	50	1.2	0	0.0	0	0.0	49	1.2
Portland–Vancouver–Hillsboro, OR–WA	715	4.1	85	0.5	400	2.3	165	0.9	575	3.3
Port St. Lucie, FL	890	15.1	15	0.3	90	1.5	0	0.0	20	0.3
Poughkeepsie–Newburgh–Middletown, NY	1,945	14.4	0	0.0	240	1.8	0	0.0	195	1.4
Prescott, AZ	35	1.3	60	2.2	0	0.0	0	0.0	19	0.7
Providence–New Bedford–Fall River, RI–MA	870	4.7	0	0.0	185	1.0	0	0.0	590	3.2

C-15 Protective Service Workers, by Metropolitan Statistical Area, Sex, Race, and Hispanic or Latino Origin, 2006–2010—Continued

Metropolitan Statistical Area	Total who worked in the last 5 years	Male Number	Male Percent	Female Number	Female Percent	Hispanic or Latino Number	Hispanic or Latino Percent	White alone, not Hispanic or Latino Number	White alone, not Hispanic or Latino Percent
Provo–Orem, UT	3,385	2,550	75.3	840	24.8	225	6.6	2,980	88.0
Pueblo, CO	2,600	2,035	78.3	565	21.7	890	34.2	1,640	63.1
Punta Gorda, FL	1,905	1,500	78.7	405	21.3	0	0.0	1,875	98.4
Racine, WI	2,015	1,470	73.0	545	27.0	245	12.2	1,415	70.2
Raleigh–Cary, NC	9,435	6,780	71.9	2,655	28.1	245	2.6	5,920	62.7
Rapid City, SD	1,335	1,035	77.5	300	22.5	35	2.6	1,205	90.3
Reading, PA	3,405	2,775	81.5	630	18.5	360	10.6	2,835	83.3
Redding, CA	1,930	1,635	84.7	295	15.3	80	4.1	1,705	88.3
Reno–Sparks, NV	5,515	4,470	81.1	1,040	18.9	505	9.2	4,325	78.4
Richmond, VA	15,865	11,080	69.8	4,785	30.2	350	2.2	8,875	55.9
Riverside–San Bernardino–Ontario, CA	50,450	40,080	79.4	10,365	20.5	16,915	33.5	23,470	46.5
Roanoke, VA	2,785	2,245	80.6	540	19.4	20	0.7	2,320	83.3
Rochester, MN	1,235	975	78.9	260	21.1	85	6.9	1,095	88.7
Rochester, NY	10,300	8,255	80.1	2,040	19.8	385	3.7	8,040	78.1
Rockford, IL	2,970	2,285	76.9	680	22.9	90	3.0	2,435	82.0
Rocky Mount, NC	1,330	935	70.3	395	29.7	0	0.0	775	58.3
Rome, GA	975	755	77.4	220	22.6	0	0.0	840	86.2
Sacramento–Arden-Arcade–Roseville, CA	24,555	19,550	79.6	5,005	20.4	3,315	13.5	15,270	62.2
Saginaw–Saginaw Township North, MI	1,570	1,190	75.8	380	24.2	110	7.0	1,025	65.3
St. Cloud, MN	1,725	1,315	76.2	410	23.8	80	4.6	1,610	93.3
St. George, UT	620	520	83.9	100	16.1	45	7.3	570	91.9
St. Joseph, MO–KS	1,640	1,145	69.8	500	30.5	10	0.6	1,575	96.0
St. Louis, MO–IL	25,850	20,025	77.5	5,825	22.5	225	0.9	18,325	70.9
Salem, OR	4,125	3,270	79.3	855	20.7	420	10.2	3,510	85.1
Salinas, CA	4,570	3,590	78.6	980	21.4	1,900	41.6	2,060	45.1
Salisbury, MD	1,835	1,370	74.7	465	25.3	39	2.1	1,140	62.1
Salt Lake City, UT	10,165	7,505	73.8	2,655	26.1	625	6.1	8,755	86.1
San Angelo, TX	1,275	935	73.3	340	26.7	260	20.4	905	71.0
San Antonio–New Braunfels, TX	21,080	16,735	79.4	4,345	20.6	10,395	49.3	8,210	38.9
San Diego–Carlsbad–San Marcos, CA	32,855	26,600	81.0	6,255	19.0	8,550	26.0	16,925	51.5
Sandusky, OH	730	615	84.2	115	15.8	14	1.9	625	85.6
San Francisco–Oakland–Fremont, CA	36,800	28,445	77.3	8,355	22.7	5,420	14.7	15,455	42.0
San Jose–Sunnyvale–Santa Clara, CA	13,350	10,275	77.0	3,075	23.0	3,060	22.9	6,100	45.7
San Luis Obispo–Paso Robles, CA	4,240	3,585	84.6	655	15.4	670	15.8	3,325	78.4
Santa Barbara–Santa Maria–Goleta, CA	4,155	3,225	77.6	935	22.5	1,140	27.4	2,355	56.7
Santa Cruz–Watsonville, CA	2,255	1,940	86.0	310	13.7	575	25.5	1,490	66.1
Santa Fe, NM	1,380	1,090	79.0	290	21.0	970	70.3	320	23.2
Santa Rosa–Petaluma, CA	4,450	3,615	81.2	835	18.8	490	11.0	3,260	73.3
Savannah, GA	3,870	2,515	65.0	1,355	35.0	175	4.5	1,655	42.8
Scranton–Wilkes-Barre, PA	6,445	5,560	86.3	885	13.7	85	1.3	6,005	93.2
Seattle–Tacoma–Bellevue, WA	29,570	22,650	76.6	6,925	23.4	1,965	6.6	21,600	73.0
Sebastian–Vero Beach, FL	935	695	74.3	240	25.7	14	1.5	730	78.1
Sheboygan, WI	860	570	66.3	295	34.3	94	10.9	740	86.0
Sherman–Denison, TX	915	720	78.7	190	20.8	60	6.6	785	85.8
Shreveport–Bossier City, LA	5,200	3,570	68.7	1,630	31.3	60	1.2	3,000	57.7
Sioux City, IA–NE–SD	1,020	810	79.4	210	20.6	90	8.8	930	91.2
Sioux Falls, SD	2,135	1,640	76.8	500	23.4	20	0.9	2,035	95.3
South Bend–Mishawaka, IN–MI	2,230	1,775	79.6	455	20.4	40	1.8	1,905	85.4
Spartanburg, SC	1,830	1,425	77.9	405	22.1	30	1.6	1,535	83.9
Spokane, WA	4,435	3,520	79.4	920	20.7	100	2.3	4,095	92.3
Springfield, IL	2,370	1,835	77.4	530	22.4	25	1.1	2,125	89.7
Springfield, MA	7,535	5,580	74.1	1,950	25.9	725	9.6	5,850	77.6
Springfield, MO	3,475	2,725	78.4	745	21.4	95	2.7	3,190	91.8
Springfield, OH	1,430	1,010	70.6	420	29.4	0	0.0	1,320	92.3
State College, PA	1,325	1,160	87.5	160	12.1	0	0.0	1,160	87.5

C-15 **Protective Service Workers, by Metropolitan Statistical Area, Sex, Race, and Hispanic or Latino Origin, 2006–2010**—*Continued*

Metropolitan Statistical Area	Black alone, not Hispanic or Latino Number	Percent	American Indian and Alaska Native alone, not Hispanic or Latino Number	Percent	Asian alone, not Hispanic or Latino Number	Percent	Native Hawaiian and Other Pacific Islander alone, not Hispanic or Latino Number	Percent	Two or more races, not Hispanic or Latino Number	Percent
Provo–Orem, UT	45	1.3	4	0.1	45	1.3	15	0.4	70	2.1
Pueblo, CO	0	0.0	15	0.6	25	1.0	0	0.0	35	1.3
Punta Gorda, FL	15	0.8	0	0.0	0	0.0	0	0.0	15	0.8
Racine, WI	345	17.1	0	0.0	10	0.5	0	0.0	0	0.0
Raleigh–Cary, NC	3,115	33.0	0	0.0	100	1.1	0	0.0	60	0.6
Rapid City, SD	20	1.5	70	5.2	0	0.0	0	0.0	10	0.7
Reading, PA	200	5.9	10	0.3	0	0.0	0	0.0	0	0.0
Redding, CA	0	0.0	55	2.8	10	0.5	10	0.5	75	3.9
Reno–Sparks, NV	190	3.4	75	1.4	170	3.1	55	1.0	195	3.5
Richmond, VA	6,305	39.7	55	0.3	185	1.2	0	0.0	94	0.6
Riverside–San Bernardino–Ontario, CA	6,710	13.3	375	0.7	1,775	3.5	170	0.3	1,035	2.1
Roanoke, VA	380	13.6	0	0.0	10	0.4	0	0.0	55	2.0
Rochester, MN	25	2.0	0	0.0	0	0.0	0	0.0	34	2.8
Rochester, NY	1,655	16.1	30	0.3	30	0.3	0	0.0	160	1.6
Rockford, IL	340	11.4	15	0.5	40	1.3	0	0.0	50	1.7
Rocky Mount, NC	550	41.4	0	0.0	0	0.0	0	0.0	4	0.3
Rome, GA	135	13.8	0	0.0	0	0.0	0	0.0	0	0.0
Sacramento–Arden-Arcade–Roseville, CA	2,600	10.6	220	0.9	1,855	7.6	430	1.8	860	3.5
Saginaw–Saginaw Township North, MI	380	24.2	15	1.0	10	0.6	0	0.0	24	1.5
St. Cloud, MN	4	0.2	20	1.2	0	0.0	0	0.0	10	0.6
St. George, UT	0	0.0	0	0.0	0	0.0	0	0.0	4	0.6
St. Joseph, MO–KS	15	0.9	10	0.6	10	0.6	20	1.2	0	0.0
St. Louis, MO–IL	6,880	26.6	35	0.1	100	0.4	15	0.1	275	1.1
Salem, OR	20	0.5	30	0.7	45	1.1	10	0.2	85	2.1
Salinas, CA	305	6.7	0	0.0	250	5.5	0	0.0	54	1.2
Salisbury, MD	625	34.1	0	0.0	15	0.8	0	0.0	15	0.8
Salt Lake City, UT	155	1.5	75	0.7	220	2.2	235	2.3	100	1.0
San Angelo, TX	80	6.3	15	1.2	0	0.0	0	0.0	15	1.2
San Antonio–New Braunfels, TX	1,905	9.0	45	0.2	180	0.9	20	0.1	320	1.5
San Diego–Carlsbad–San Marcos, CA	3,595	10.9	230	0.7	2,375	7.2	205	0.6	975	3.0
Sandusky, OH	15	2.1	0	0.0	15	2.1	0	0.0	64	8.8
San Francisco–Oakland–Fremont, CA	7,135	19.4	175	0.5	6,370	17.3	715	1.9	1,525	4.1
San Jose–Sunnyvale–Santa Clara, CA	1,190	8.9	95	0.7	2,360	17.7	235	1.8	310	2.3
San Luis Obispo–Paso Robles, CA	40	0.9	10	0.2	60	1.4	0	0.0	135	3.2
Santa Barbara–Santa Maria–Goleta, CA	115	2.8	95	2.3	155	3.7	50	1.2	240	5.8
Santa Cruz–Watsonville, CA	15	0.7	15	0.7	30	1.3	30	1.3	105	4.7
Santa Fe, NM	0	0.0	95	6.9	0	0.0	0	0.0	0	0.0
Santa Rosa–Petaluma, CA	130	2.9	45	1.0	245	5.5	100	2.2	185	4.2
Savannah, GA	1,900	49.1	0	0.0	50	1.3	35	0.9	49	1.3
Scranton–Wilkes-Barre, PA	190	2.9	0	0.0	30	0.5	0	0.0	135	2.1
Seattle–Tacoma–Bellevue, WA	2,460	8.3	485	1.6	1,995	6.7	195	0.7	879	3.0
Sebastian–Vero Beach, FL	95	10.2	0	0.0	15	1.6	0	0.0	85	9.1
Sheboygan, WI	25	2.9	0	0.0	0	0.0	0	0.0	4	0.5
Sherman–Denison, TX	60	6.6	4	0.4	0	0.0	0	0.0	0	0.0
Shreveport–Bossier City, LA	2,000	38.5	10	0.2	60	1.2	0	0.0	70	1.3
Sioux City, IA–NE–SD	0	0.0	0	0.0	0	0.0	0	0.0	0	0.0
Sioux Falls, SD	10	0.5	55	2.6	0	0.0	0	0.0	20	0.9
South Bend–Mishawaka, IN–MI	220	9.9	20	0.9	0	0.0	0	0.0	49	2.2
Spartanburg, SC	215	11.7	4	0.2	30	1.6	0	0.0	15	0.8
Spokane, WA	90	2.0	60	1.4	0	0.0	4	0.1	90	2.0
Springfield, IL	180	7.6	0	0.0	15	0.6	0	0.0	29	1.2
Springfield, MA	810	10.7	15	0.2	70	0.9	0	0.0	65	0.9
Springfield, MO	145	4.2	0	0.0	0	0.0	0	0.0	45	1.3
Springfield, OH	75	5.2	0	0.0	25	1.7	0	0.0	15	1.0
State College, PA	40	3.0	0	0.0	60	4.5	0	0.0	65	4.9

PART C—METROPOLITAN STATISTICAL AREA TABLES

C-15 Protective Service Workers, by Metropolitan Statistical Area, Sex, Race, and Hispanic or Latino Origin, 2006–2010—Continued

Metropolitan Statistical Area	Total who worked in the last 5 years	Male Number	Male Percent	Female Number	Female Percent	Hispanic or Latino Number	Hispanic or Latino Percent	White alone, not Hispanic or Latino Number	White alone, not Hispanic or Latino Percent
Steubenville–Weirton, OH–WV	1,220	980	80.3	240	19.7	4	0.3	1,165	95.5
Stockton, CA	7,405	5,610	75.8	1,795	24.2	1,595	21.5	3,990	53.9
Sumter, SC	1,380	1,090	79.0	290	21.0	70	5.1	610	44.2
Syracuse, NY	6,890	5,250	76.2	1,640	23.8	280	4.1	5,715	82.9
Tallahassee, FL	5,190	3,465	66.8	1,725	33.2	225	4.3	3,095	59.6
Tampa–St. Petersburg–Clearwater, FL	26,100	20,545	78.7	5,555	21.3	3,025	11.6	18,590	71.2
Terre Haute, IN	2,495	1,990	79.8	505	20.2	50	2.0	2,325	93.2
Texarkana, TX–Texarkana, AR	1,555	1,005	64.6	555	35.7	15	1.0	1,065	68.5
Toledo, OH	6,200	4,570	73.7	1,630	26.3	330	5.3	4,720	76.1
Topeka, KS	2,915	2,195	75.3	715	24.5	115	3.9	2,395	82.2
Trenton–Ewing, NJ	4,690	3,750	80.0	940	20.0	415	8.8	2,460	52.5
Tucson, AZ	13,250	10,745	81.1	2,505	18.9	4,020	30.3	8,055	60.8
Tulsa, OK	7,385	5,900	79.9	1,485	20.1	235	3.2	5,210	70.5
Tuscaloosa, AL	1,950	1,510	77.4	440	22.6	4	0.2	1,260	64.6
Tyler, TX	1,800	1,425	79.2	375	20.8	105	5.8	1,350	75.0
Utica–Rome, NY	4,675	4,035	86.3	640	13.7	170	3.6	4,385	93.8
Valdosta, GA	2,130	1,660	77.9	465	21.8	10	0.5	1,340	62.9
Vallejo–Fairfield, CA	6,380	5,005	78.4	1,375	21.6	840	13.2	3,135	49.1
Victoria, TX	1,005	645	64.2	360	35.8	205	20.4	760	75.6
Vineland–Millville–Bridgeton, NJ	3,215	2,625	81.6	585	18.2	295	9.2	2,245	69.8
Virginia Beach–Norfolk–Newport News, VA–NC	21,860	16,300	74.6	5,555	25.4	1,125	5.1	12,765	58.4
Visalia–Porterville, CA	5,880	4,650	79.1	1,230	20.9	2,815	47.9	2,620	44.6
Waco, TX	1,915	1,355	70.8	560	29.2	255	13.3	1,335	69.7
Warner Robins, GA	1,590	1,300	81.8	285	17.9	15	0.9	1,125	70.8
Washington–Arlington–Alexandria, DC–VA–MD–WV	83,110	59,645	71.8	23,465	28.2	5,310	6.4	36,855	44.3
Waterloo–Cedar Falls, IA	1,200	900	75.0	300	25.0	20	1.7	1,135	94.6
Wausau, WI	675	535	79.3	140	20.7	10	1.5	650	96.3
Wenatchee–East Wenatchee, WA	1,005	820	81.6	190	18.9	140	13.9	830	82.6
Wheeling, WV–OH	1,375	1,190	86.5	185	13.5	0	0.0	1,320	96.0
Wichita, KS	5,515	4,310	78.2	1,205	21.8	360	6.5	4,580	83.0
Wichita Falls, TX	2,200	1,715	78.0	485	22.0	160	7.3	1,800	81.8
Williamsport, PA	1,240	1,030	83.1	210	16.9	10	0.8	1,045	84.3
Wilmington, NC	3,505	2,745	78.3	765	21.8	90	2.6	2,920	83.3
Winchester, VA–WV	1,235	1,000	81.0	235	19.0	85	6.9	1,110	89.9
Winston-Salem, NC	4,025	3,035	75.4	990	24.6	119	3.0	2,860	71.1
Worcester, MA	9,375	7,965	85.0	1,415	15.1	710	7.6	8,360	89.2
Yakima, WA	1,620	1,335	82.4	285	17.6	335	20.7	1,175	72.5
York–Hanover, PA	3,905	3,235	82.8	670	17.2	130	3.3	3,500	89.6
Youngstown–Warren–Boardman, OH–PA	5,275	4,115	78.0	1,160	22.0	195	3.7	4,330	82.1
Yuba City, CA	1,525	1,200	78.7	330	21.6	255	16.7	1,150	75.4
Yuma, AZ	3,360	2,920	86.9	440	13.1	2,205	65.6	885	26.3

C-15 Protective Service Workers, by Metropolitan Statistical Area, Sex, Race, and Hispanic or Latino Origin, 2006–2010—Continued

Metropolitan Statistical Area	Black alone, not Hispanic or Latino Number	Percent	American Indian and Alaska Native alone, not Hispanic or Latino Number	Percent	Asian alone, not Hispanic or Latino Number	Percent	Native Hawaiian and Other Pacific Islander alone, not Hispanic or Latino Number	Percent	Two or more races, not Hispanic or Latino Number	Percent
Steubenville–Weirton, OH–WV	30	2.5	10	0.8	0	0.0	0	0.0	10	0.8
Stockton, CA	775	10.5	10	0.1	655	8.8	140	1.9	240	3.2
Sumter, SC	670	48.6	20	1.4	0	0.0	0	0.0	15	1.1
Syracuse, NY	645	9.4	70	1.0	95	1.4	0	0.0	95	1.4
Tallahassee, FL	1,710	32.9	10	0.2	35	0.7	25	0.5	95	1.8
Tampa–St. Petersburg–Clearwater, FL	3,740	14.3	160	0.6	270	1.0	0	0.0	320	1.2
Terre Haute, IN	95	3.8	0	0.0	4	0.2	0	0.0	14	0.6
Texarkana, TX–Texarkana, AR	460	29.6	15	1.0	0	0.0	0	0.0	0	0.0
Toledo, OH	1,045	16.9	45	0.7	25	0.4	0	0.0	30	0.5
Topeka, KS	275	9.4	70	2.4	15	0.5	15	0.5	24	0.8
Trenton–Ewing, NJ	1,685	35.9	20	0.4	15	0.3	0	0.0	90	1.9
Tucson, AZ	380	2.9	220	1.7	200	1.5	20	0.2	355	2.7
Tulsa, OK	710	9.6	730	9.9	20	0.3	30	0.4	460	6.2
Tuscaloosa, AL	685	35.1	4	0.2	0	0.0	0	0.0	0	0.0
Tyler, TX	310	17.2	20	1.1	0	0.0	0	0.0	14	0.8
Utica–Rome, NY	65	1.4	0	0.0	10	0.2	0	0.0	49	1.0
Valdosta, GA	770	36.2	0	0.0	0	0.0	0	0.0	4	0.2
Vallejo–Fairfield, CA	1,185	18.6	45	0.7	675	10.6	115	1.8	385	6.0
Victoria, TX	15	1.5	0	0.0	0	0.0	0	0.0	25	2.5
Vineland–Millville–Bridgeton, NJ	560	17.4	30	0.9	25	0.8	0	0.0	65	2.0
Virginia Beach–Norfolk–Newport News, VA–NC	7,380	33.8	70	0.3	275	1.3	0	0.0	245	1.1
Visalia–Porterville, CA	260	4.4	60	1.0	65	1.1	0	0.0	63	1.1
Waco, TX	285	14.9	0	0.0	0	0.0	0	0.0	39	2.0
Warner Robins, GA	405	25.5	0	0.0	15	0.9	0	0.0	34	2.1
Washington–Arlington–Alexandria, DC–VA–MD–WV	36,925	44.4	205	0.2	2,090	2.5	45	0.1	1,685	2.0
Waterloo–Cedar Falls, IA	30	2.5	0	0.0	0	0.0	0	0.0	10	0.8
Wausau, WI	0	0.0	4	0.6	10	1.5	0	0.0	0	0.0
Wenatchee–East Wenatchee, WA	0	0.0	0	0.0	0	0.0	0	0.0	40	4.0
Wheeling, WV–OH	35	2.5	4	0.3	0	0.0	0	0.0	10	0.7
Wichita, KS	460	8.3	45	0.8	4	0.1	0	0.0	70	1.3
Wichita Falls, TX	170	7.7	15	0.7	15	0.7	0	0.0	45	2.0
Williamsport, PA	180	14.5	0	0.0	0	0.0	0	0.0	0	0.0
Wilmington, NC	470	13.4	20	0.6	0	0.0	0	0.0	0	0.0
Winchester, VA–WV	35	2.8	0	0.0	0	0.0	0	0.0	0	0.0
Winston–Salem, NC	950	23.6	10	0.2	15	0.4	15	0.4	49	1.2
Worcester, MA	235	2.5	20	0.2	4	0.0	0	0.0	39	0.4
Yakima, WA	45	2.8	50	3.1	4	0.2	0	0.0	10	0.6
York–Hanover, PA	265	6.8	0	0.0	0	0.0	0	0.0	8	0.2
Youngstown–Warren–Boardman, OH–PA	630	11.9	25	0.5	0	0.0	0	0.0	95	1.8
Yuba City, CA	15	1.0	4	0.3	65	4.3	10	0.7	25	1.6
Yuma, AZ	190	5.7	4	0.1	0	0.0	0	0.0	75	2.2

PART C—METROPOLITAN STATISTICAL AREA TABLES

C-16 Service Workers, except Protective, by Metropolitan Statistical Area, Sex, Race, and Hispanic or Latino Origin, 2006–2010

Metropolitan Statistical Area	Total who worked in the last 5 years	Male Number	Male Percent	Female Number	Female Percent	Hispanic or Latino Number	Hispanic or Latino Percent	White alone, not Hispanic or Latino Number	White alone, not Hispanic or Latino Percent
Abilene, TX	12,390	3,580	28.9	8,810	71.1	3,560	28.7	7,360	59.4
Akron, OH	53,005	18,285	34.5	34,715	65.5	985	1.9	41,965	79.2
Albany, GA	10,710	3,545	33.1	7,165	66.9	185	1.7	2,770	25.9
Albany–Schenectady–Troy, NY	61,995	23,650	38.1	38,345	61.9	3,750	6.0	46,205	74.5
Albuquerque, NM	60,990	22,230	36.4	38,760	63.6	34,130	56.0	18,360	30.1
Alexandria, LA	10,885	3,410	31.3	7,475	68.7	205	1.9	4,730	43.5
Allentown–Bethlehem–Easton, PA–NJ	55,065	17,865	32.4	37,200	67.6	8,370	15.2	41,700	75.7
Altoona, PA	9,505	3,145	33.1	6,360	66.9	165	1.7	9,120	95.9
Amarillo, TX	18,175	6,420	35.3	11,760	64.7	5,450	30.0	9,795	53.9
Ames, IA	7,820	3,055	39.1	4,765	60.9	310	4.0	6,755	86.4
Anchorage, AK	29,090	10,525	36.2	18,565	63.8	2,850	9.8	15,810	54.3
Anderson, IN	9,000	2,865	31.8	6,135	68.2	210	2.3	7,690	85.4
Anderson, SC	11,695	3,250	27.8	8,445	72.2	510	4.4	8,150	69.7
Ann Arbor, MI	25,850	10,045	38.9	15,800	61.1	1,870	7.2	17,235	66.7
Anniston–Oxford, AL	7,435	2,265	30.5	5,170	69.5	255	3.4	4,330	58.2
Appleton, WI	14,830	4,805	32.4	10,025	67.6	915	6.2	12,850	86.6
Asheville, NC	31,080	10,810	34.8	20,270	65.2	2,270	7.3	25,285	81.4
Athens–Clarke County, GA	13,825	5,370	38.8	8,455	61.2	1,275	9.2	8,260	59.7
Atlanta–Sandy Springs–Marietta, GA	321,715	112,380	34.9	209,335	65.1	48,935	15.2	128,040	39.8
Atlantic City–Hammonton, NJ	36,935	16,515	44.7	20,415	55.3	9,310	25.2	15,630	42.3
Auburn–Opelika, AL	9,025	3,370	37.3	5,655	62.7	365	4.0	5,500	60.9
Augusta–Richmond County, GA–SC	35,290	11,465	32.5	23,825	67.5	1,335	3.8	15,330	43.4
Austin–Round Rock–San Marcos, TX	114,960	43,600	37.9	71,360	62.1	50,795	44.2	48,710	42.4
Bakersfield–Delano, CA	46,295	16,125	34.8	30,170	65.2	23,940	51.7	15,650	33.8
Baltimore–Towson, MD	176,165	60,040	34.1	116,125	65.9	13,840	7.9	83,675	47.5
Bangor, ME	12,805	4,330	33.8	8,480	66.2	130	1.0	12,220	95.4
Barnstable Town, MA	16,590	5,825	35.1	10,765	64.9	550	3.3	14,460	87.2
Baton Rouge, LA	54,450	17,850	32.8	36,600	67.2	1,825	3.4	23,285	42.8
Battle Creek, MI	10,380	3,270	31.5	7,110	68.5	370	3.6	8,290	79.9
Bay City, MI	9,560	3,265	34.2	6,295	65.8	595	6.2	8,470	88.6
Beaumont–Port Arthur, TX	23,520	6,990	29.7	16,530	70.3	3,240	13.8	11,235	47.8
Bellingham, WA	16,595	5,460	32.9	11,135	67.1	1,300	7.8	13,265	79.9
Bend, OR	12,130	3,535	29.1	8,600	70.9	1,880	15.5	9,795	80.8
Billings, MT	12,920	4,295	33.2	8,625	66.8	680	5.3	10,960	84.8
Binghamton, NY	19,195	7,470	38.9	11,725	61.1	825	4.3	16,730	87.2
Birmingham–Hoover, AL	66,290	22,240	33.5	44,045	66.4	5,120	7.7	32,600	49.2
Bismarck, ND	9,195	2,720	29.6	6,475	70.4	75	0.8	8,565	93.1
Blacksburg–Christiansburg–Radford, VA	12,345	4,695	38.0	7,650	62.0	560	4.5	10,375	84.0
Bloomington, IN	15,350	5,900	38.4	9,455	61.6	490	3.2	13,555	88.3
Bloomington–Normal, IL	12,965	5,295	40.8	7,670	59.2	675	5.2	10,460	80.7
Boise City–Nampa, ID	38,230	12,625	33.0	25,605	67.0	5,015	13.1	30,500	79.8
Boston–Cambridge–Quincy, MA–NH	325,180	120,640	37.1	204,540	62.9	51,620	15.9	205,115	63.1
Boulder, CO	21,285	8,070	37.9	13,215	62.1	4,590	21.6	14,990	70.4
Bowling Green, KY	8,880	2,895	32.6	5,985	67.4	350	3.9	7,055	79.4
Bremerton–Silverdale, WA	17,470	5,805	33.2	11,665	66.8	1,405	8.0	12,745	73.0
Bridgeport–Stamford–Norwalk, CT	60,975	20,800	34.1	40,175	65.9	19,090	31.3	26,735	43.8
Brownsville–Harlingen, TX	28,810	8,745	30.4	20,060	69.6	27,255	94.6	1,350	4.7
Brunswick, GA	8,995	3,125	34.7	5,870	65.3	530	5.9	4,815	53.5
Buffalo–Niagara Falls, NY	87,370	33,055	37.8	54,315	62.2	3,760	4.3	66,015	75.6
Burlington, NC	10,400	3,585	34.5	6,815	65.5	1,090	10.5	6,060	58.3
Burlington–South Burlington, VT	16,990	6,260	36.8	10,730	63.2	265	1.6	15,230	89.6
Canton–Massillon, OH	32,770	10,300	31.4	22,470	68.6	585	1.8	28,370	86.6
Cape Coral–Fort Myers, FL	43,680	15,445	35.4	28,235	64.6	9,830	22.5	25,470	58.3
Cape Girardeau–Jackson, MO–IL	7,705	2,290	29.7	5,415	70.3	100	1.3	6,355	82.5
Carson City, NV	4,660	1,775	38.1	2,885	61.9	990	21.2	3,190	68.5

C-16 **Service Workers, except Protective, by Metropolitan Statistical Area, Sex, Race, and Hispanic or Latino Origin, 2006–2010**—*Continued*

Metropolitan Statistical Area	Black alone, not Hispanic or Latino Number	Percent	American Indian and Alaska Native alone, not Hispanic or Latino Number	Percent	Asian alone, not Hispanic or Latino Number	Percent	Native Hawaiian and Other Pacific Islander alone, not Hispanic or Latino Number	Percent	Two or more races, not Hispanic or Latino Number	Percent
Abilene, TX	870	7.0	120	1.0	195	1.6	70	0.6	215	1.7
Akron, OH	8,395	15.8	60	0.1	765	1.4	0	0.0	830	1.6
Albany, GA	7,600	71.0	0	0.0	95	0.9	0	0.0	60	0.6
Albany–Schenectady–Troy, NY	7,815	12.6	375	0.6	1,950	3.1	15	0.0	1,880	3.0
Albuquerque, NM	1,910	3.1	3,860	6.3	1,675	2.7	75	0.1	970	1.6
Alexandria, LA	5,555	51.0	60	0.6	265	2.4	0	0.0	79	0.7
Allentown–Bethlehem–Easton, PA–NJ	3,250	5.9	70	0.1	900	1.6	0	0.0	780	1.4
Altoona, PA	145	1.5	0	0.0	70	0.7	0	0.0	8	0.1
Amarillo, TX	1,785	9.8	80	0.4	730	4.0	4	0.0	335	1.8
Ames, IA	295	3.8	4	0.1	345	4.4	0	0.0	105	1.3
Anchorage, AK	1,685	5.8	1,930	6.6	3,855	13.3	640	2.2	2,320	8.0
Anderson, IN	635	7.1	0	0.0	130	1.4	10	0.1	330	3.7
Anderson, SC	2,780	23.8	15	0.1	165	1.4	0	0.0	79	0.7
Ann Arbor, MI	4,495	17.4	70	0.3	1,215	4.7	0	0.0	965	3.7
Anniston–Oxford, AL	2,725	36.7	60	0.8	35	0.5	0	0.0	30	0.4
Appleton, WI	210	1.4	300	2.0	370	2.5	15	0.1	175	1.2
Asheville, NC	2,530	8.1	140	0.5	390	1.3	10	0.0	470	1.5
Athens–Clarke County, GA	3,830	27.7	4	0.0	190	1.4	0	0.0	265	1.9
Atlanta–Sandy Springs–Marietta, GA	121,575	37.8	570	0.2	18,005	5.6	65	0.0	4,520	1.4
Atlantic City–Hammonton, NJ	6,445	17.4	25	0.1	4,960	13.4	35	0.1	525	1.4
Auburn–Opelika, AL	2,870	31.8	10	0.1	220	2.4	0	0.0	64	0.7
Augusta–Richmond County, GA–SC	17,330	49.1	55	0.2	760	2.2	15	0.0	460	1.3
Austin–Round Rock–San Marcos, TX	9,865	8.6	450	0.4	3,640	3.2	25	0.0	1,470	1.3
Bakersfield–Delano, CA	2,945	6.4	465	1.0	2,285	4.9	35	0.1	970	2.1
Baltimore–Towson, MD	66,510	37.8	350	0.2	8,435	4.8	50	0.0	3,315	1.9
Bangor, ME	45	0.4	120	0.9	145	1.1	0	0.0	144	1.1
Barnstable Town, MA	830	5.0	80	0.5	195	1.2	0	0.0	475	2.9
Baton Rouge, LA	27,335	50.2	15	0.0	1,310	2.4	0	0.0	680	1.2
Battle Creek, MI	1,345	13.0	40	0.4	65	0.6	0	0.0	270	2.6
Bay City, MI	175	1.8	40	0.4	70	0.7	30	0.3	185	1.9
Beaumont–Port Arthur, TX	8,135	34.6	65	0.3	620	2.6	0	0.0	215	0.9
Bellingham, WA	205	1.2	505	3.0	745	4.5	65	0.4	515	3.1
Bend, OR	30	0.2	140	1.2	130	1.1	55	0.5	100	0.8
Billings, MT	145	1.1	690	5.3	165	1.3	10	0.1	275	2.1
Binghamton, NY	830	4.3	35	0.2	545	2.8	0	0.0	225	1.2
Birmingham–Hoover, AL	26,980	40.7	105	0.2	1,000	1.5	20	0.0	460	0.7
Bismarck, ND	105	1.1	275	3.0	25	0.3	0	0.0	155	1.7
Blacksburg–Christiansburg–Radford, VA	665	5.4	0	0.0	535	4.3	15	0.1	200	1.6
Bloomington, IN	540	3.5	70	0.5	320	2.1	0	0.0	375	2.4
Bloomington–Normal, IL	1,495	11.5	0	0.0	195	1.5	4	0.0	139	1.1
Boise City–Nampa, ID	450	1.2	355	0.9	1,165	3.0	25	0.1	720	1.9
Boston–Cambridge–Quincy, MA–NH	38,370	11.8	600	0.2	19,000	5.8	155	0.0	10,320	3.2
Boulder, CO	275	1.3	175	0.8	835	3.9	0	0.0	425	2.0
Bowling Green, KY	995	11.2	0	0.0	245	2.8	75	0.8	155	1.7
Bremerton–Silverdale, WA	715	4.1	215	1.2	1,640	9.4	235	1.3	520	3.0
Bridgeport–Stamford–Norwalk, CT	11,635	19.1	85	0.1	1,735	2.8	15	0.0	1,680	2.8
Brownsville–Harlingen, TX	85	0.3	0	0.0	110	0.4	0	0.0	10	0.0
Brunswick, GA	3,500	38.9	0	0.0	110	1.2	0	0.0	35	0.4
Buffalo–Niagara Falls, NY	14,390	16.5	365	0.4	1,905	2.2	40	0.0	905	1.0
Burlington, NC	2,885	27.7	15	0.1	125	1.2	0	0.0	225	2.2
Burlington–South Burlington, VT	475	2.8	85	0.5	480	2.8	0	0.0	455	2.7
Canton–Massillon, OH	2,945	9.0	50	0.2	250	0.8	0	0.0	570	1.7
Cape Coral–Fort Myers, FL	6,215	14.2	50	0.1	1,410	3.2	15	0.0	700	1.6
Cape Girardeau–Jackson, MO–IL	860	11.2	35	0.5	215	2.8	4	0.1	135	1.8
Carson City, NV	100	2.1	100	2.1	150	3.2	0	0.0	124	2.7

PART C—METROPOLITAN STATISTICAL AREA TABLES

C-16 Service Workers, except Protective, by Metropolitan Statistical Area, Sex, Race, and Hispanic or Latino Origin, 2006–2010—Continued

Metropolitan Statistical Area	Total who worked in the last 5 years	Male Number	Male Percent	Female Number	Female Percent	Hispanic or Latino Number	Hispanic or Latino Percent	White alone, not Hispanic or Latino Number	White alone, not Hispanic or Latino Percent
Casper, WY	5,710	1,745	30.6	3,965	69.4	595	10.4	4,895	85.7
Cedar Rapids, IA	18,635	5,315	28.5	13,320	71.5	415	2.2	16,525	88.7
Champaign–Urbana, IL	18,415	7,440	40.4	10,975	59.6	1,195	6.5	12,840	69.7
Charleston, WV	20,020	7,200	36.0	12,820	64.0	175	0.9	17,230	86.1
Charleston–North Charleston–Summerville, SC	47,305	16,290	34.4	31,020	65.6	2,795	5.9	24,360	51.5
Charlotte–Gastonia–Rock Hill, NC–SC	112,015	39,225	35.0	72,790	65.0	14,495	12.9	55,265	49.3
Charlottesville, VA	13,825	4,505	32.6	9,325	67.5	990	7.2	8,630	62.4
Chattanooga, TN–GA	37,490	13,155	35.1	24,335	64.9	2,245	6.0	25,900	69.1
Cheyenne, WY	6,660	2,230	33.5	4,425	66.4	1,145	17.2	4,915	73.8
Chicago–Joliet–Naperville, IL–IN–WI	631,170	240,160	38.0	391,010	62.0	172,495	27.3	287,340	45.5
Chico, CA	17,750	6,025	33.9	11,725	66.1	3,375	19.0	12,050	67.9
Cincinnati–Middletown, OH–KY–IN	150,395	51,115	34.0	99,280	66.0	4,570	3.0	113,510	75.5
Clarksville, TN–KY	17,595	5,675	32.3	11,925	67.8	1,385	7.9	10,585	60.2
Cleveland, TN	6,720	2,500	37.2	4,225	62.9	240	3.6	5,800	86.3
Cleveland–Elyria–Mentor, OH	155,760	53,505	34.4	102,250	65.6	8,250	5.3	97,055	62.3
Coeur d'Alene, ID	10,120	2,975	29.4	7,145	70.6	560	5.5	9,205	91.0
College Station–Bryan, TX	16,460	6,380	38.8	10,080	61.2	5,130	31.2	7,970	48.4
Colorado Springs, CO	44,300	14,835	33.5	29,470	66.5	8,530	19.3	28,295	63.9
Columbia, MO	14,145	4,995	35.3	9,155	64.7	790	5.6	10,140	71.7
Columbia, SC	49,915	17,490	35.0	32,425	65.0	2,975	6.0	21,285	42.6
Columbus, GA–AL	19,760	5,550	28.1	14,210	71.9	1,035	5.2	7,375	37.3
Columbus, IN	4,515	1,440	31.9	3,075	68.1	220	4.9	4,000	88.6
Columbus, OH	126,435	45,825	36.2	80,610	63.8	7,315	5.8	87,695	69.4
Corpus Christi, TX	32,125	10,215	31.8	21,910	68.2	21,295	66.3	8,335	25.9
Corvallis, OR	5,715	1,990	34.8	3,725	65.2	395	6.9	4,910	85.9
Crestview–Fort Walton Beach–Destin, FL	14,715	5,595	38.0	9,120	62.0	980	6.7	10,680	72.6
Cumberland, MD–WV	7,975	2,275	28.5	5,700	71.5	85	1.1	7,260	91.0
Dallas–Fort Worth–Arlington, TX	393,180	143,145	36.4	250,035	63.6	151,070	38.4	149,255	38.0
Dalton, GA	7,225	2,580	35.7	4,645	64.3	2,115	29.3	4,475	61.9
Danville, IL	5,690	1,900	33.4	3,790	66.6	310	5.4	4,330	76.1
Danville, VA	7,395	2,000	27.0	5,400	73.0	225	3.0	3,495	47.3
Davenport–Moline–Rock Island, IA–IL	28,400	9,170	32.3	19,235	67.7	2,375	8.4	22,175	78.1
Dayton, OH	62,285	21,255	34.1	41,030	65.9	1,350	2.2	46,055	73.9
Decatur, AL	8,960	2,485	27.7	6,475	72.3	270	3.0	6,465	72.2
Decatur, IL	8,495	2,570	30.3	5,925	69.7	135	1.6	5,990	70.5
Deltona–Daytona Beach–Ormond Beach, FL	36,065	12,860	35.7	23,205	64.3	4,100	11.4	24,375	67.6
Denver–Aurora–Broomfield, CO	173,575	63,875	36.8	109,700	63.2	57,175	32.9	92,080	53.0
Des Moines–West Des Moines, IA	40,405	13,985	34.6	26,415	65.4	4,360	10.8	31,570	78.1
Detroit–Warren–Livonia, MI	318,055	109,790	34.5	208,265	65.5	14,210	4.5	196,015	61.6
Dothan, AL	9,135	2,610	28.6	6,525	71.4	230	2.5	5,355	58.6
Dover, DE	10,900	3,435	31.5	7,465	68.5	695	6.4	5,740	52.7
Dubuque, IA	8,480	2,715	32.0	5,770	68.0	250	2.9	7,790	91.9
Duluth, MN–WI	26,330	9,050	34.4	17,280	65.6	480	1.8	23,920	90.8
Durham–Chapel Hill, NC	34,675	13,085	37.7	21,590	62.3	6,095	17.6	12,440	35.9
Eau Claire, WI	13,760	4,260	31.0	9,500	69.0	270	2.0	12,710	92.4
El Centro, CA	9,985	2,670	26.7	7,310	73.2	8,660	86.7	1,025	10.3
Elizabethtown, KY	7,105	2,110	29.7	5,000	70.4	315	4.4	5,210	73.3
Elkhart–Goshen, IN	11,955	3,665	30.7	8,290	69.3	1,480	12.4	9,130	76.4
Elmira, NY	6,120	1,885	30.8	4,230	69.1	65	1.1	5,335	87.2
El Paso, TX	50,675	16,980	33.5	33,695	66.5	44,860	88.5	3,925	7.7
Erie, PA	21,630	7,335	33.9	14,295	66.1	710	3.3	18,790	86.9
Eugene–Springfield, OR	26,830	8,900	33.2	17,930	66.8	2,610	9.7	21,545	80.3
Evansville, IN–KY	26,320	8,970	34.1	17,350	65.9	515	2.0	23,060	87.6
Fairbanks, AK	6,200	2,305	37.2	3,895	62.8	545	8.8	3,980	64.2
Fargo, ND–MN	18,075	5,550	30.7	12,525	69.3	600	3.3	16,010	88.6

C-16 Service Workers, except Protective, by Metropolitan Statistical Area, Sex, Race, and Hispanic or Latino Origin, 2006–2010—Continued

Metropolitan Statistical Area	Black alone, not Hispanic or Latino Number	Percent	American Indian and Alaska Native alone, not Hispanic or Latino Number	Percent	Asian alone, not Hispanic or Latino Number	Percent	Native Hawaiian and Other Pacific Islander alone, not Hispanic or Latino Number	Percent	Two or more races, not Hispanic or Latino Number	Percent
Casper, WY	30	0.5	0	0.0	35	0.6	0	0.0	155	2.7
Cedar Rapids, IA	895	4.8	0	0.0	470	2.5	55	0.3	280	1.5
Champaign–Urbana, IL	3,340	18.1	20	0.1	670	3.6	0	0.0	350	1.9
Charleston, WV	1,490	7.4	55	0.3	260	1.3	0	0.0	820	4.1
Charleston–North Charleston–Summerville, SC	17,705	37.4	125	0.3	1,415	3.0	60	0.1	840	1.8
Charlotte–Gastonia–Rock Hill, NC–SC	36,215	32.3	260	0.2	3,680	3.3	180	0.2	1,920	1.7
Charlottesville, VA	3,640	26.3	10	0.1	275	2.0	0	0.0	280	2.0
Chattanooga, TN–GA	8,280	22.1	80	0.2	510	1.4	0	0.0	480	1.3
Cheyenne, WY	295	4.4	80	1.2	155	2.3	10	0.2	58	0.9
Chicago–Joliet–Naperville, IL–IN–WI	129,440	20.5	605	0.1	33,435	5.3	250	0.0	7,600	1.2
Chico, CA	465	2.6	110	0.6	1,225	6.9	85	0.5	445	2.5
Cincinnati–Middletown, OH–KY–IN	27,340	18.2	265	0.2	2,565	1.7	130	0.1	2,010	1.3
Clarksville, TN–KY	4,740	26.9	55	0.3	435	2.5	0	0.0	400	2.3
Cleveland, TN	515	7.7	10	0.1	95	1.4	20	0.3	40	0.6
Cleveland–Elyria–Mentor, OH	45,585	29.3	220	0.1	2,600	1.7	0	0.0	2,055	1.3
Coeur d'Alene, ID	80	0.8	60	0.6	90	0.9	0	0.0	130	1.3
College Station–Bryan, TX	2,675	16.3	30	0.2	490	3.0	0	0.0	154	0.9
Colorado Springs, CO	3,565	8.0	340	0.8	2,105	4.8	95	0.2	1,365	3.1
Columbia, MO	2,475	17.5	65	0.5	300	2.1	15	0.1	360	2.5
Columbia, SC	23,695	47.5	70	0.1	1,200	2.4	10	0.0	680	1.4
Columbus, GA–AL	10,565	53.5	10	0.1	370	1.9	0	0.0	405	2.0
Columbus, IN	85	1.9	0	0.0	130	2.9	0	0.0	80	1.8
Columbus, OH	25,200	19.9	215	0.2	3,805	3.0	25	0.0	2,185	1.7
Corpus Christi, TX	1,415	4.4	30	0.1	940	2.9	0	0.0	110	0.3
Corvallis, OR	30	0.5	0	0.0	290	5.1	15	0.3	79	1.4
Crestview–Fort Walton Beach–Destin, FL	1,670	11.3	165	1.1	970	6.6	0	0.0	245	1.7
Cumberland, MD–WV	465	5.8	15	0.2	90	1.1	0	0.0	68	0.9
Dallas–Fort Worth–Arlington, TX	66,885	17.0	1,290	0.3	19,365	4.9	335	0.1	4,980	1.3
Dalton, GA	490	6.8	40	0.6	40	0.6	0	0.0	65	0.9
Danville, IL	905	15.9	0	0.0	55	1.0	0	0.0	90	1.6
Danville, VA	3,595	48.6	0	0.0	40	0.5	0	0.0	39	0.5
Davenport–Moline–Rock Island, IA–IL	2,545	9.0	85	0.3	665	2.3	0	0.0	565	2.0
Dayton, OH	12,165	19.5	55	0.1	1,195	1.9	10	0.0	1,455	2.3
Decatur, AL	1,720	19.2	175	2.0	80	0.9	0	0.0	245	2.7
Decatur, IL	2,220	26.1	4	0.0	4	0.0	0	0.0	150	1.8
Deltona–Daytona Beach–Ormond Beach, FL	6,245	17.3	45	0.1	545	1.5	0	0.0	750	2.1
Denver–Aurora–Broomfield, CO	11,155	6.4	1,035	0.6	8,255	4.8	360	0.2	3,520	2.0
Des Moines–West Des Moines, IA	2,415	6.0	40	0.1	1,400	3.5	15	0.0	600	1.5
Detroit–Warren–Livonia, MI	92,430	29.1	1,275	0.4	8,800	2.8	65	0.0	5,260	1.7
Dothan, AL	3,330	36.5	55	0.6	120	1.3	0	0.0	44	0.5
Dover, DE	3,585	32.9	185	1.7	410	3.8	55	0.5	230	2.1
Dubuque, IA	165	1.9	10	0.1	45	0.5	40	0.5	185	2.2
Duluth, MN–WI	305	1.2	930	3.5	365	1.4	4	0.0	325	1.2
Durham–Chapel Hill, NC	13,600	39.2	155	0.4	1,550	4.5	15	0.0	825	2.4
Eau Claire, WI	135	1.0	80	0.6	390	2.8	10	0.1	165	1.2
El Centro, CA	150	1.5	55	0.6	30	0.3	0	0.0	65	0.7
Elizabethtown, KY	1,045	14.7	40	0.6	200	2.8	85	1.2	210	3.0
Elkhart–Goshen, IN	825	6.9	30	0.3	315	2.6	20	0.2	150	1.3
Elmira, NY	445	7.3	20	0.3	70	1.1	25	0.4	165	2.7
El Paso, TX	955	1.9	195	0.4	550	1.1	15	0.0	175	0.3
Erie, PA	1,535	7.1	40	0.2	255	1.2	0	0.0	304	1.4
Eugene–Springfield, OR	415	1.5	425	1.6	915	3.4	100	0.4	825	3.1
Evansville, IN–KY	2,180	8.3	75	0.3	270	1.0	4	0.0	220	0.8
Fairbanks, AK	335	5.4	525	8.5	385	6.2	50	0.8	375	6.0
Fargo, ND–MN	550	3.0	290	1.6	345	1.9	25	0.1	250	1.4

PART C—METROPOLITAN STATISTICAL AREA TABLES

C-16 Service Workers, except Protective, by Metropolitan Statistical Area, Sex, Race, and Hispanic or Latino Origin, 2006–2010—Continued

Metropolitan Statistical Area	Total who worked in the last 5 years	Male Number	Male Percent	Female Number	Female Percent	Hispanic or Latino Number	Hispanic or Latino Percent	White alone, not Hispanic or Latino Number	White alone, not Hispanic or Latino Percent
Farmington, NM	7,745	2,340	30.2	5,405	69.8	1,705	22.0	2,665	34.4
Fayetteville, NC	24,715	7,175	29.0	17,540	71.0	2,055	8.3	8,185	33.1
Fayetteville–Springdale–Rogers, AR–MO	28,900	9,325	32.3	19,575	67.7	4,860	16.8	21,595	74.7
Flagstaff, AZ	12,085	4,520	37.4	7,565	62.6	2,585	21.4	5,775	47.8
Flint, MI	32,435	10,430	32.2	22,005	67.8	925	2.9	22,550	69.5
Florence, SC	14,230	4,230	29.7	10,000	70.3	325	2.3	5,380	37.8
Florence–Muscle Shoals, AL	8,680	2,405	27.7	6,275	72.3	105	1.2	7,010	80.8
Fond du Lac, WI	8,145	2,185	26.8	5,960	73.2	255	3.1	7,540	92.6
Fort Collins–Loveland, CO	23,600	8,285	35.1	15,320	64.9	3,720	15.8	18,675	79.1
Fort Smith, AR–OK	18,670	5,460	29.2	13,210	70.8	1,450	7.8	13,980	74.9
Fort Wayne, IN	29,420	9,805	33.3	19,615	66.7	2,030	6.9	21,925	74.5
Fresno, CA	59,355	20,560	34.6	38,795	65.4	32,380	54.6	15,610	26.3
Gadsden, AL	6,295	2,010	31.9	4,285	68.1	110	1.7	4,435	70.5
Gainesville, FL	21,100	8,475	40.2	12,625	59.8	1,940	9.2	11,905	56.4
Gainesville, GA	9,145	2,820	30.8	6,320	69.1	2,005	21.9	5,490	60.0
Glens Falls, NY	9,675	3,380	34.9	6,295	65.1	190	2.0	9,300	96.1
Goldsboro, NC	8,080	2,180	27.0	5,895	73.0	625	7.7	3,520	43.6
Grand Forks, ND–MN	10,200	3,620	35.5	6,580	64.5	440	4.3	9,160	89.8
Grand Junction, CO	10,445	3,150	30.2	7,295	69.8	1,635	15.7	8,205	78.6
Grand Rapids–Wyoming, MI	56,205	18,505	32.9	37,695	67.1	5,475	9.7	42,025	74.8
Great Falls, MT	5,905	2,000	33.9	3,905	66.1	225	3.8	4,805	81.4
Greeley, CO	16,455	5,035	30.6	11,420	69.4	5,255	31.9	10,465	63.6
Green Bay, WI	22,465	7,495	33.4	14,970	66.6	1,220	5.4	19,125	85.1
Greensboro–High Point, NC	47,290	16,570	35.0	30,720	65.0	4,210	8.9	23,730	50.2
Greenville, NC	15,610	5,715	36.6	9,890	63.4	705	4.5	7,305	46.8
Greenville–Mauldin–Easley, SC	40,530	13,885	34.3	26,645	65.7	3,640	9.0	25,270	62.3
Gulfport–Biloxi, MS	21,310	8,390	39.4	12,920	60.6	1,475	6.9	12,560	58.9
Hagerstown–Martinsburg, MD–WV	18,000	5,385	29.9	12,610	70.1	650	3.6	15,495	86.1
Hanford–Corcoran, CA	8,255	2,995	36.3	5,265	63.8	4,090	49.5	2,670	32.3
Harrisburg–Carlisle, PA	37,595	13,525	36.0	24,070	64.0	2,455	6.5	28,035	74.6
Harrisonburg, VA	8,405	2,440	29.0	5,965	71.0	960	11.4	6,940	82.6
Hartford–West Hartford–East Hartford, CT	87,540	31,905	36.4	55,635	63.6	17,015	19.4	52,530	60.0
Hattiesburg, MS	8,975	3,060	34.1	5,920	66.0	100	1.1	4,715	52.5
Hickory–Lenoir–Morganton, NC	22,555	7,205	31.9	15,350	68.1	1,495	6.6	17,525	77.7
Hinesville–Fort Stewart, GA	4,755	1,400	29.4	3,355	70.6	345	7.3	1,690	35.5
Holland–Grand Haven, MI	18,285	5,210	28.5	13,080	71.5	1,685	9.2	15,680	85.8
Honolulu, HI	76,265	31,755	41.6	44,510	58.4	5,150	6.8	9,645	12.6
Hot Springs, AR	7,145	2,830	39.6	4,315	60.4	305	4.3	5,630	78.8
Houma–Bayou Cane–Thibodaux, LA	11,530	2,980	25.8	8,550	74.2	300	2.6	7,045	61.1
Houston–Sugar Land–Baytown, TX	378,195	122,195	32.3	256,000	67.7	180,640	47.8	94,100	24.9
Huntington–Ashland, WV–KY–OH	20,425	7,105	34.8	13,320	65.2	180	0.9	19,035	93.2
Huntsville, AL	24,130	8,365	34.7	15,765	65.3	1,080	4.5	13,035	54.0
Idaho Falls, ID	7,630	2,260	29.6	5,365	70.3	1,040	13.6	6,195	81.2
Indianapolis–Carmel, IN	117,370	40,675	34.7	76,695	65.3	11,250	9.6	76,545	65.2
Iowa City, IA	14,340	5,425	37.8	8,915	62.2	865	6.0	11,905	83.0
Ithaca, NY	6,605	2,910	44.1	3,695	55.9	400	6.1	5,165	78.2
Jackson, MI	11,565	3,550	30.7	8,020	69.3	425	3.7	9,745	84.3
Jackson, MS	35,250	11,280	32.0	23,970	68.0	900	2.6	10,130	28.7
Jackson, TN	8,670	2,785	32.1	5,890	67.9	365	4.2	4,445	51.3
Jacksonville, FL	90,525	33,180	36.7	57,345	63.3	7,085	7.8	52,035	57.5
Jacksonville, NC	11,145	3,055	27.4	8,090	72.6	1,230	11.0	5,755	51.6
Janesville, WI	12,445	3,855	31.0	8,585	69.0	1,105	8.9	9,950	80.0
Jefferson City, MO	9,290	3,280	35.3	6,010	64.7	340	3.7	7,895	85.0
Johnson City, TN	14,110	5,100	36.1	9,010	63.9	645	4.6	12,415	88.0
Johnstown, PA	11,130	3,160	28.4	7,975	71.7	210	1.9	10,460	94.0

C-16 **Service Workers, except Protective, by Metropolitan Statistical Area, Sex, Race, and Hispanic or Latino Origin, 2006–2010**—*Continued*

Metropolitan Statistical Area	Black alone, not Hispanic or Latino Number	Percent	American Indian and Alaska Native alone, not Hispanic or Latino Number	Percent	Asian alone, not Hispanic or Latino Number	Percent	Native Hawaiian and Other Pacific Islander alone, not Hispanic or Latino Number	Percent	Two or more races, not Hispanic or Latino Number	Percent
Farmington, NM	140	1.8	3,110	40.2	75	1.0	0	0.0	50	0.6
Fayetteville, NC	11,860	48.0	480	1.9	980	4.0	115	0.5	1,040	4.2
Fayetteville–Springdale–Rogers, AR–MO	580	2.0	515	1.8	630	2.2	240	0.8	475	1.6
Flagstaff, AZ	100	0.8	3,055	25.3	185	1.5	0	0.0	380	3.1
Flint, MI	7,595	23.4	150	0.5	470	1.4	4	0.0	740	2.3
Florence, SC	8,230	57.8	30	0.2	165	1.2	0	0.0	98	0.7
Florence–Muscle Shoals, AL	1,360	15.7	60	0.7	115	1.3	0	0.0	24	0.3
Fond du Lac, WI	220	2.7	30	0.4	20	0.2	0	0.0	83	1.0
Fort Collins–Loveland, CO	240	1.0	65	0.3	465	2.0	10	0.0	430	1.8
Fort Smith, AR–OK	1,025	5.5	600	3.2	470	2.5	0	0.0	1,145	6.1
Fort Wayne, IN	4,415	15.0	70	0.2	525	1.8	0	0.0	460	1.6
Fresno, CA	3,910	6.6	310	0.5	5,550	9.4	110	0.2	1,485	2.5
Gadsden, AL	1,510	24.0	20	0.3	100	1.6	0	0.0	115	1.8
Gainesville, FL	6,155	29.2	25	0.1	825	3.9	0	0.0	245	1.2
Gainesville, GA	1,005	11.0	10	0.1	480	5.2	15	0.2	125	1.4
Glens Falls, NY	65	0.7	0	0.0	40	0.4	15	0.2	75	0.8
Goldsboro, NC	3,720	46.0	4	0.0	160	2.0	0	0.0	54	0.7
Grand Forks, ND–MN	175	1.7	250	2.5	100	1.0	0	0.0	80	0.8
Grand Junction, CO	70	0.7	85	0.8	95	0.9	35	0.3	320	3.1
Grand Rapids–Wyoming, MI	6,090	10.8	245	0.4	1,170	2.1	80	0.1	1,115	2.0
Great Falls, MT	65	1.1	490	8.3	175	3.0	0	0.0	155	2.6
Greeley, CO	140	0.9	200	1.2	275	1.7	25	0.2	100	0.6
Green Bay, WI	695	3.1	500	2.2	515	2.3	50	0.2	360	1.6
Greensboro–High Point, NC	16,720	35.4	330	0.7	1,680	3.6	25	0.1	590	1.2
Greenville, NC	7,370	47.2	0	0.0	70	0.4	0	0.0	165	1.1
Greenville–Mauldin–Easley, SC	10,080	24.9	75	0.2	815	2.0	130	0.3	525	1.3
Gulfport–Biloxi, MS	5,685	26.7	115	0.5	1,220	5.7	0	0.0	250	1.2
Hagerstown–Martinsburg, MD–WV	1,305	7.3	35	0.2	330	1.8	15	0.1	180	1.0
Hanford–Corcoran, CA	825	10.0	60	0.7	540	6.5	35	0.4	34	0.4
Harrisburg–Carlisle, PA	4,715	12.5	65	0.2	1,485	3.9	50	0.1	785	2.1
Harrisonburg, VA	330	3.9	0	0.0	160	1.9	0	0.0	15	0.2
Hartford–West Hartford–East Hartford, CT	13,165	15.0	80	0.1	2,930	3.3	110	0.1	1,700	1.9
Hattiesburg, MS	4,040	45.0	0	0.0	70	0.8	0	0.0	50	0.6
Hickory–Lenoir–Morganton, NC	2,510	11.1	70	0.3	705	3.1	0	0.0	255	1.1
Hinesville–Fort Stewart, GA	2,550	53.6	0	0.0	45	0.9	0	0.0	119	2.5
Holland–Grand Haven, MI	410	2.2	15	0.1	240	1.3	30	0.2	230	1.3
Honolulu, HI	945	1.2	70	0.1	41,600	54.5	6,885	9.0	11,970	15.7
Hot Springs, AR	945	13.2	15	0.2	125	1.7	0	0.0	120	1.7
Houma–Bayou Cane–Thibodaux, LA	3,515	30.5	355	3.1	180	1.6	0	0.0	135	1.2
Houston–Sugar Land–Baytown, TX	75,535	20.0	605	0.2	24,170	6.4	200	0.1	2,940	0.8
Huntington–Ashland, WV–KY–OH	815	4.0	50	0.2	85	0.4	0	0.0	255	1.2
Huntsville, AL	8,725	36.2	195	0.8	490	2.0	0	0.0	605	2.5
Idaho Falls, ID	40	0.5	145	1.9	65	0.9	15	0.2	135	1.8
Indianapolis–Carmel, IN	24,555	20.9	210	0.2	2,200	1.9	35	0.0	2,575	2.2
Iowa City, IA	760	5.3	60	0.4	455	3.2	0	0.0	295	2.1
Ithaca, NY	375	5.7	10	0.2	555	8.4	0	0.0	95	1.4
Jackson, MI	1,125	9.7	35	0.3	45	0.4	10	0.1	184	1.6
Jackson, MS	23,460	66.6	25	0.1	570	1.6	0	0.0	170	0.5
Jackson, TN	3,670	42.3	35	0.4	140	1.6	0	0.0	15	0.2
Jacksonville, FL	25,235	27.9	195	0.2	4,395	4.9	90	0.1	1,495	1.7
Jacksonville, NC	3,425	30.7	35	0.3	310	2.8	65	0.6	315	2.8
Janesville, WI	895	7.2	35	0.3	185	1.5	0	0.0	280	2.2
Jefferson City, MO	810	8.7	4	0.0	130	1.4	0	0.0	105	1.1
Johnson City, TN	685	4.9	40	0.3	260	1.8	0	0.0	65	0.5
Johnstown, PA	300	2.7	0	0.0	90	0.8	10	0.1	54	0.5

C-16 Service Workers, except Protective, by Metropolitan Statistical Area, Sex, Race, and Hispanic or Latino Origin, 2006–2010—*Continued*

Metropolitan Statistical Area	Total who worked in the last 5 years	Male Number	Male Percent	Female Number	Female Percent	Hispanic or Latino Number	Hispanic or Latino Percent	White alone, not Hispanic or Latino Number	White alone, not Hispanic or Latino Percent
Jonesboro, AR	7,970	2,420	30.4	5,550	69.6	515	6.5	5,895	74.0
Joplin, MO	13,755	4,915	35.7	8,840	64.3	845	6.1	11,910	86.6
Kalamazoo–Portage, MI	26,695	9,675	36.2	17,025	63.8	1,265	4.7	20,785	77.9
Kankakee–Bradley, IL	8,565	2,805	32.7	5,755	67.2	660	7.7	5,675	66.3
Kansas City, MO–KS	134,205	47,525	35.4	86,675	64.6	16,335	12.2	87,410	65.1
Kennewick–Pasco–Richland, WA	15,760	4,920	31.2	10,840	68.8	4,725	30.0	9,375	59.5
Killeen–Temple–Fort Hood, TX	25,530	7,515	29.4	18,015	70.6	5,670	22.2	11,470	44.9
Kingsport–Bristol–Bristol, TN–VA	20,020	6,210	31.0	13,810	69.0	365	1.8	18,605	92.9
Kingston, NY	13,310	4,875	36.6	8,435	63.4	1,950	14.7	9,640	72.4
Knoxville, TN	46,030	16,270	35.3	29,760	64.7	2,415	5.2	37,510	81.5
Kokomo, IN	7,365	2,335	31.7	5,025	68.2	235	3.2	6,275	85.2
La Crosse, WI–MN	11,685	3,685	31.5	8,000	68.5	155	1.3	10,785	92.3
Lafayette, IN	16,465	6,230	37.8	10,235	62.2	1,680	10.2	13,510	82.1
Lafayette, LA	19,590	6,560	33.5	13,030	66.5	760	3.9	9,900	50.5
Lake Charles, LA	14,330	4,740	33.1	9,590	66.9	420	2.9	7,920	55.3
Lake Havasu City–Kingman, AZ	16,175	6,080	37.6	10,095	62.4	3,950	24.4	11,235	69.5
Lakeland–Winter Haven, FL	40,505	13,130	32.4	27,375	67.6	8,085	20.0	22,940	56.6
Lancaster, PA	33,835	10,000	29.6	23,835	70.4	3,170	9.4	28,130	83.1
Lansing–East Lansing, MI	37,860	13,630	36.0	24,230	64.0	2,550	6.7	28,305	74.8
Laredo, TX	16,450	4,370	26.6	12,080	73.4	16,180	98.4	230	1.4
Las Cruces, NM	16,035	4,955	30.9	11,080	69.1	12,225	76.2	3,155	19.7
Las Vegas–Paradise, NV	230,695	106,705	46.3	123,990	53.7	85,375	37.0	85,980	37.3
Lawrence, KS	9,845	4,120	41.8	5,725	58.2	925	9.4	7,760	78.8
Lawton, OK	8,185	2,740	33.5	5,450	66.6	1,105	13.5	3,615	44.2
Lebanon, PA	10,390	3,005	28.9	7,385	71.1	795	7.7	9,215	88.7
Lewiston, ID–WA	5,135	1,650	32.1	3,485	67.9	285	5.6	4,495	87.5
Lewiston–Auburn, ME	8,150	2,920	35.8	5,230	64.2	130	1.6	7,430	91.2
Lexington–Fayette, KY	34,320	12,460	36.3	21,860	63.7	2,620	7.6	24,395	71.1
Lima, OH	9,060	3,195	35.3	5,870	64.8	175	1.9	7,305	80.6
Lincoln, NE	24,290	8,575	35.3	15,715	64.7	1,980	8.2	20,385	83.9
Little Rock–North Little Rock–Conway, AR	47,220	16,865	35.7	30,355	64.3	3,485	7.4	26,460	56.0
Logan, UT–ID	8,275	2,645	32.0	5,625	68.0	1,215	14.7	6,760	81.7
Longview, TX	13,975	3,385	24.2	10,595	75.8	2,065	14.8	7,180	51.4
Longview, WA	7,340	2,355	32.1	4,985	67.9	410	5.6	6,435	87.7
Los Angeles–Long Beach–Santa Ana, CA	906,025	345,455	38.1	560,570	61.9	523,345	57.8	186,275	20.6
Louisville/Jefferson County, KY–IN	87,525	31,185	35.6	56,340	64.4	4,765	5.4	61,070	69.8
Lubbock, TX	23,580	8,855	37.6	14,725	62.4	9,895	42.0	10,485	44.5
Lynchburg, VA	18,505	5,680	30.7	12,825	69.3	720	3.9	11,835	64.0
Macon, GA	16,250	5,495	33.8	10,760	66.2	665	4.1	5,685	35.0
Madera–Chowchilla, CA	8,130	2,680	33.0	5,450	67.0	4,245	52.2	3,010	37.0
Madison, WI	41,820	15,520	37.1	26,300	62.9	4,580	11.0	32,330	77.3
Manchester–Nashua, NH	26,020	9,165	35.2	16,855	64.8	1,760	6.8	22,390	86.0
Manhattan, KS	9,025	3,010	33.4	6,010	66.6	905	10.0	6,585	73.0
Mankato–North Mankato, MN	9,120	3,120	34.2	6,000	65.8	365	4.0	8,195	89.9
Mansfield, OH	8,060	2,415	30.0	5,640	70.0	110	1.4	6,710	83.3
McAllen–Edinburg–Mission, TX	54,440	14,735	27.1	39,710	72.9	51,930	95.4	2,015	3.7
Medford, OR	15,320	5,365	35.0	9,955	65.0	2,080	13.6	11,910	77.7
Memphis, TN–MS–AR	89,425	31,290	35.0	58,135	65.0	4,820	5.4	31,830	35.6
Merced, CA	15,365	4,480	29.2	10,890	70.9	8,185	53.3	4,720	30.7
Miami–Fort Lauderdale–Pompano Beach, FL	436,730	155,385	35.6	281,345	64.4	192,915	44.2	109,320	25.0
Michigan City–La Porte, IN	7,620	2,440	32.0	5,180	68.0	415	5.4	6,045	79.3
Midland, TX	9,205	2,550	27.7	6,650	72.2	4,485	48.7	3,625	39.4
Milwaukee–Waukesha–West Allis, WI	108,825	36,190	33.3	72,635	66.7	11,795	10.8	66,870	61.4
Minneapolis–St. Paul–Bloomington, MN–WI	234,435	84,450	36.0	149,985	64.0	23,145	9.9	165,590	70.6
Missoula, MT	10,285	4,080	39.7	6,205	60.3	185	1.8	9,200	89.5

C-16 **Service Workers, except Protective, by Metropolitan Statistical Area, Sex, Race, and Hispanic or Latino Origin, 2006–2010**—*Continued*

Metropolitan Statistical Area	Black alone, not Hispanic or Latino Number	Percent	American Indian and Alaska Native alone, not Hispanic or Latino Number	Percent	Asian alone, not Hispanic or Latino Number	Percent	Native Hawaiian and Other Pacific Islander alone, not Hispanic or Latino Number	Percent	Two or more races, not Hispanic or Latino Number	Percent
Jonesboro, AR	1,355	17.0	35	0.4	100	1.3	0	0.0	70	0.9
Joplin, MO	340	2.5	265	1.9	110	0.8	0	0.0	279	2.0
Kalamazoo–Portage, MI	3,420	12.8	115	0.4	500	1.9	25	0.1	595	2.2
Kankakee–Bradley, IL	2,075	24.2	45	0.5	55	0.6	0	0.0	54	0.6
Kansas City, MO–KS	23,055	17.2	585	0.4	3,970	3.0	255	0.2	2,595	1.9
Kennewick–Pasco–Richland, WA	375	2.4	300	1.9	665	4.2	70	0.4	245	1.6
Killeen–Temple–Fort Hood, TX	5,870	23.0	120	0.5	1,390	5.4	385	1.5	635	2.5
Kingsport–Bristol–Bristol, TN–VA	575	2.9	30	0.1	220	1.1	0	0.0	224	1.1
Kingston, NY	1,115	8.4	35	0.3	290	2.2	0	0.0	285	2.1
Knoxville, TN	4,340	9.4	175	0.4	1,120	2.4	0	0.0	470	1.0
Kokomo, IN	570	7.7	0	0.0	175	2.4	10	0.1	100	1.4
La Crosse, WI–MN	255	2.2	55	0.5	380	3.3	0	0.0	55	0.5
Lafayette, IN	695	4.2	25	0.2	385	2.3	0	0.0	170	1.0
Lafayette, LA	8,165	41.7	100	0.5	430	2.2	95	0.5	140	0.7
Lake Charles, LA	5,250	36.6	105	0.7	335	2.3	10	0.1	280	2.0
Lake Havasu City–Kingman, AZ	170	1.1	215	1.3	300	1.9	0	0.0	305	1.9
Lakeland–Winter Haven, FL	7,905	19.5	110	0.3	910	2.2	30	0.1	530	1.3
Lancaster, PA	1,140	3.4	60	0.2	800	2.4	10	0.0	530	1.6
Lansing–East Lansing, MI	4,185	11.1	135	0.4	1,455	3.8	15	0.0	1,220	3.2
Laredo, TX	0	0.0	0	0.0	20	0.1	0	0.0	20	0.1
Las Cruces, NM	295	1.8	160	1.0	165	1.0	0	0.0	34	0.2
Las Vegas–Paradise, NV	21,055	9.1	775	0.3	31,150	13.5	1,440	0.6	4,925	2.1
Lawrence, KS	420	4.3	160	1.6	405	4.1	0	0.0	175	1.8
Lawton, OK	2,075	25.4	515	6.3	205	2.5	85	1.0	595	7.3
Lebanon, PA	180	1.7	0	0.0	60	0.6	0	0.0	145	1.4
Lewiston, ID–WA	50	1.0	120	2.3	60	1.2	25	0.5	100	1.9
Lewiston–Auburn, ME	130	1.6	50	0.6	120	1.5	0	0.0	289	3.5
Lexington–Fayette, KY	6,075	17.7	0	0.0	675	2.0	0	0.0	560	1.6
Lima, OH	1,300	14.3	4	0.0	145	1.6	0	0.0	135	1.5
Lincoln, NE	945	3.9	75	0.3	525	2.2	35	0.1	350	1.4
Little Rock–North Little Rock–Conway, AR	15,575	33.0	290	0.6	860	1.8	4	0.0	540	1.1
Logan, UT–ID	75	0.9	0	0.0	155	1.9	4	0.0	55	0.7
Longview, TX	4,290	30.7	4	0.0	195	1.4	65	0.5	179	1.3
Longview, WA	0	0.0	65	0.9	195	2.7	10	0.1	225	3.1
Los Angeles–Long Beach–Santa Ana, CA	59,435	6.6	1,760	0.2	118,410	13.1	2,085	0.2	14,715	1.6
Louisville/Jefferson County, KY–IN	18,305	20.9	320	0.4	1,610	1.8	30	0.0	1,425	1.6
Lubbock, TX	2,570	10.9	55	0.2	325	1.4	10	0.0	240	1.0
Lynchburg, VA	5,305	28.7	35	0.2	220	1.2	10	0.1	385	2.1
Macon, GA	9,605	59.1	55	0.3	155	1.0	0	0.0	95	0.6
Madera–Chowchilla, CA	215	2.6	175	2.2	210	2.6	10	0.1	270	3.3
Madison, WI	2,580	6.2	165	0.4	1,335	3.2	0	0.0	830	2.0
Manchester–Nashua, NH	845	3.2	10	0.0	700	2.7	10	0.0	310	1.2
Manhattan, KS	755	8.4	120	1.3	310	3.4	0	0.0	345	3.8
Mankato–North Mankato, MN	145	1.6	4	0.0	200	2.2	0	0.0	205	2.2
Mansfield, OH	1,030	12.8	65	0.8	20	0.2	0	0.0	125	1.6
McAllen–Edinburg–Mission, TX	80	0.1	60	0.1	245	0.5	0	0.0	110	0.2
Medford, OR	75	0.5	270	1.8	500	3.3	15	0.1	460	3.0
Memphis, TN–MS–AR	49,465	55.3	260	0.3	1,880	2.1	50	0.1	1,130	1.3
Merced, CA	645	4.2	150	1.0	1,415	9.2	0	0.0	250	1.6
Miami–Fort Lauderdale–Pompano Beach, FL	115,225	26.4	490	0.1	13,870	3.2	150	0.0	4,760	1.1
Michigan City–La Porte, IN	885	11.6	4	0.1	150	2.0	0	0.0	115	1.5
Midland, TX	905	9.8	35	0.4	90	1.0	0	0.0	55	0.6
Milwaukee–Waukesha–West Allis, WI	25,635	23.6	880	0.8	2,000	1.8	100	0.1	1,545	1.4
Minneapolis–St. Paul–Bloomington, MN–WI	26,590	11.3	2,005	0.9	12,430	5.3	145	0.1	4,530	1.9
Missoula, MT	25	0.2	335	3.3	150	1.5	75	0.7	315	3.1

C-16 Service Workers, except Protective, by Metropolitan Statistical Area, Sex, Race, and Hispanic or Latino Origin, 2006–2010—Continued

Metropolitan Statistical Area	Total who worked in the last 5 years	Male Number	Male Percent	Female Number	Female Percent	Hispanic or Latino Number	Hispanic or Latino Percent	White alone, not Hispanic or Latino Number	White alone, not Hispanic or Latino Percent
Mobile, AL	27,225	9,235	33.9	17,990	66.1	625	2.3	12,045	44.2
Modesto, CA	32,345	10,170	31.4	22,175	68.6	13,205	40.8	14,630	45.2
Monroe, LA	11,875	3,455	29.1	8,420	70.9	170	1.4	5,180	43.6
Monroe, MI	11,505	3,005	26.1	8,505	73.9	365	3.2	10,620	92.3
Montgomery, AL	23,280	8,705	37.4	14,580	62.6	690	3.0	7,975	34.3
Morgantown, WV	9,440	3,525	37.3	5,910	62.6	180	1.9	8,570	90.8
Morristown, TN	8,915	3,010	33.8	5,910	66.3	385	4.3	7,825	87.8
Mount Vernon–Anacortes, WA	7,910	2,450	31.0	5,465	69.1	1,445	18.3	5,920	74.8
Muncie, IN	11,110	3,860	34.7	7,250	65.3	260	2.3	9,545	85.9
Muskegon–Norton Shores, MI	12,910	3,490	27.0	9,420	73.0	660	5.1	10,160	78.7
Myrtle Beach–North Myrtle Beach–Conway, SC	24,130	9,270	38.4	14,860	61.6	2,080	8.6	16,295	67.5
Napa, CA	10,055	3,665	36.4	6,390	63.6	4,190	41.7	4,730	47.0
Naples–Marco Island, FL	25,170	9,985	39.7	15,185	60.3	8,365	33.2	12,440	49.4
Nashville-Davidson–Murfreesboro–Franklin, TN	104,125	36,420	35.0	67,705	65.0	9,700	9.3	67,045	64.4
New Haven–Milford, CT	64,500	22,450	34.8	42,045	65.2	11,975	18.6	36,865	57.2
New Orleans–Metairie–Kenner, LA	80,545	27,885	34.6	52,660	65.4	8,210	10.2	33,460	41.5
New York–Northern New Jersey–Long Island, NY–NJ–PA	1,430,770	562,440	39.3	868,330	60.7	514,620	36.0	434,095	30.3
Niles–Benton Harbor, MI	12,355	3,940	31.9	8,415	68.1	505	4.1	8,335	67.5
North Port–Bradenton–Sarasota, FL	48,155	18,975	39.4	29,180	60.6	8,120	16.9	32,680	67.9
Norwich–New London, CT	25,935	10,550	40.7	15,385	59.3	3,730	14.4	16,590	64.0
Ocala, FL	20,575	6,230	30.3	14,340	69.7	2,295	11.2	13,550	65.9
Ocean City, NJ	8,430	3,325	39.4	5,105	60.6	1,010	12.0	6,240	74.0
Odessa, TX	9,645	2,490	25.8	7,155	74.2	5,540	57.4	3,465	35.9
Ogden–Clearfield, UT	29,510	9,895	33.5	19,615	66.5	5,095	17.3	22,575	76.5
Oklahoma City, OK	86,285	30,675	35.6	55,610	64.4	12,635	14.6	49,650	57.5
Olympia, WA	16,465	5,445	33.1	11,020	66.9	1,465	8.9	11,775	71.5
Omaha–Council Bluffs, NE–IA	64,115	22,805	35.6	41,310	64.4	6,650	10.4	46,780	73.0
Orlando–Kissimmee–Sanford, FL	173,275	69,505	40.1	103,770	59.9	48,965	28.3	76,410	44.1
Oshkosh–Neenah, WI	13,470	4,320	32.1	9,150	67.9	660	4.9	12,055	89.5
Owensboro, KY	7,805	2,475	31.7	5,330	68.3	140	1.8	6,815	87.3
Oxnard–Thousand Oaks–Ventura, CA	49,710	17,375	35.0	32,340	65.1	26,255	52.8	18,300	36.8
Palm Bay–Melbourne–Titusville, FL	37,290	12,555	33.7	24,735	66.3	3,805	10.2	26,235	70.4
Palm Coast, FL	5,465	1,925	35.2	3,540	64.8	515	9.4	3,895	71.3
Panama City–Lynn Haven–Panama City Beach, FL	12,720	4,080	32.1	8,640	67.9	445	3.5	9,365	73.6
Parkersburg–Marietta–Vienna, WV–OH	11,320	3,415	30.2	7,905	69.8	210	1.9	10,770	95.1
Pascagoula, MS	11,305	4,180	37.0	7,130	63.1	380	3.4	6,530	57.8
Pensacola–Ferry Pass–Brent, FL	32,355	11,480	35.5	20,875	64.5	1,460	4.5	20,700	64.0
Peoria, IL	27,815	8,915	32.1	18,900	67.9	830	3.0	22,320	80.2
Philadelphia–Camden–Wilmington, PA–NJ–DE–MD	395,150	145,900	36.9	249,250	63.1	40,810	10.3	215,345	54.5
Phoenix–Mesa–Glendale, AZ	263,775	97,650	37.0	166,125	63.0	98,440	37.3	131,605	49.9
Pine Bluff, AR	5,895	1,765	29.9	4,130	70.1	40	0.7	2,185	37.1
Pittsburgh, PA	180,095	63,810	35.4	116,285	64.6	3,145	1.7	149,445	83.0
Pittsfield, MA	12,330	4,400	35.7	7,935	64.4	690	5.6	10,585	85.8
Pocatello, ID	6,540	2,335	35.7	4,205	64.3	495	7.6	5,520	84.4
Portland–South Portland–Biddeford, ME	42,235	13,750	32.6	28,490	67.5	780	1.8	38,755	91.8
Portland–Vancouver–Hillsboro, OR–WA	154,390	51,760	33.5	102,630	66.5	24,750	16.0	107,160	69.4
Port St. Lucie, FL	28,325	9,665	34.1	18,660	65.9	4,455	15.7	16,725	59.0
Poughkeepsie–Newburgh–Middletown, NY	43,860	16,635	37.9	27,225	62.1	8,645	19.7	26,485	60.4
Prescott, AZ	15,250	5,395	35.4	9,855	64.6	3,440	22.6	10,830	71.0
Providence–New Bedford–Fall River, RI–MA	130,165	46,365	35.6	83,800	64.4	16,015	12.3	97,705	75.1

C-16 **Service Workers, except Protective, by Metropolitan Statistical Area, Sex, Race, and Hispanic or Latino Origin, 2006–2010**—*Continued*

Metropolitan Statistical Area	Black alone, not Hispanic or Latino Number	Percent	American Indian and Alaska Native alone, not Hispanic or Latino Number	Percent	Asian alone, not Hispanic or Latino Number	Percent	Native Hawaiian and Other Pacific Islander alone, not Hispanic or Latino Number	Percent	Two or more races, not Hispanic or Latino Number	Percent
Mobile, AL	13,415	49.3	25	0.1	745	2.7	45	0.2	325	1.2
Modesto, CA	910	2.8	350	1.1	2,320	7.2	180	0.6	745	2.3
Monroe, LA	6,305	53.1	55	0.5	110	0.9	0	0.0	60	0.5
Monroe, MI	290	2.5	10	0.1	25	0.2	30	0.3	165	1.4
Montgomery, AL	13,795	59.3	75	0.3	435	1.9	0	0.0	310	1.3
Morgantown, WV	365	3.9	25	0.3	195	2.1	20	0.2	80	0.8
Morristown, TN	465	5.2	4	0.0	4	0.0	40	0.4	195	2.2
Mount Vernon–Anacortes, WA	30	0.4	205	2.6	205	2.6	30	0.4	78	1.0
Muncie, IN	950	8.6	40	0.4	65	0.6	0	0.0	250	2.3
Muskegon–Norton Shores, MI	1,840	14.3	70	0.5	65	0.5	4	0.0	115	0.9
Myrtle Beach–North Myrtle Beach–Conway, SC	4,955	20.5	25	0.1	475	2.0	30	0.1	275	1.1
Napa, CA	140	1.4	45	0.4	755	7.5	50	0.5	139	1.4
Naples–Marco Island, FL	3,420	13.6	120	0.5	705	2.8	0	0.0	125	0.5
Nashville-Davidson–Murfreesboro–Franklin, TN	22,710	21.8	405	0.4	3,190	3.1	115	0.1	950	0.9
New Haven–Milford, CT	12,010	18.6	90	0.1	2,010	3.1	70	0.1	1,480	2.3
New Orleans–Metairie–Kenner, LA	34,455	42.8	400	0.5	3,180	3.9	60	0.1	780	1.0
New York–Northern New Jersey–Long Island, NY-NJ-PA	320,570	22.4	2,075	0.1	136,060	9.5	340	0.0	23,010	1.6
Niles–Benton Harbor, MI	2,935	23.8	100	0.8	315	2.5	0	0.0	174	1.4
North Port–Bradenton–Sarasota, FL	5,405	11.2	90	0.2	1,280	2.7	35	0.1	550	1.1
Norwich–New London, CT	2,460	9.5	110	0.4	2,365	9.1	0	0.0	675	2.6
Ocala, FL	3,875	18.8	60	0.3	460	2.2	50	0.2	295	1.4
Ocean City, NJ	705	8.4	50	0.6	270	3.2	0	0.0	154	1.8
Odessa, TX	445	4.6	20	0.2	85	0.9	0	0.0	100	1.0
Ogden–Clearfield, UT	330	1.1	175	0.6	850	2.9	80	0.3	400	1.4
Oklahoma City, OK	13,575	15.7	2,930	3.4	3,500	4.1	135	0.2	3,860	4.5
Olympia, WA	500	3.0	275	1.7	1,430	8.7	210	1.3	810	4.9
Omaha–Council Bluffs, NE–IA	7,430	11.6	185	0.3	1,480	2.3	70	0.1	1,515	2.4
Orlando–Kissimmee–Sanford, FL	35,550	20.5	370	0.2	8,405	4.9	195	0.1	3,380	2.0
Oshkosh–Neenah, WI	215	1.6	90	0.7	280	2.1	0	0.0	170	1.3
Owensboro, KY	615	7.9	45	0.6	115	1.5	0	0.0	75	1.0
Oxnard–Thousand Oaks–Ventura, CA	610	1.2	130	0.3	3,400	6.8	15	0.0	1,000	2.0
Palm Bay–Melbourne–Titusville, FL	5,215	14.0	235	0.6	1,200	3.2	0	0.0	600	1.6
Palm Coast, FL	755	13.8	10	0.2	190	3.5	0	0.0	100	1.8
Panama City–Lynn Haven–Panama City Beach, FL	1,950	15.3	70	0.6	730	5.7	0	0.0	155	1.2
Parkersburg–Marietta–Vienna, WV–OH	130	1.1	4	0.0	85	0.8	0	0.0	120	1.1
Pascagoula, MS	3,515	31.1	30	0.3	695	6.1	0	0.0	154	1.4
Pensacola–Ferry Pass–Brent, FL	7,200	22.3	175	0.5	1,560	4.8	105	0.3	1,150	3.6
Peoria, IL	3,920	14.1	15	0.1	360	1.3	0	0.0	364	1.3
Philadelphia–Camden–Wilmington, PA-NJ-DE-MD	114,945	29.1	685	0.2	17,745	4.5	120	0.0	5,505	1.4
Phoenix–Mesa–Glendale, AZ	12,495	4.7	6,710	2.5	10,380	3.9	570	0.2	3,580	1.4
Pine Bluff, AR	3,570	60.6	0	0.0	35	0.6	0	0.0	65	1.1
Pittsburgh, PA	22,190	12.3	155	0.1	2,635	1.5	80	0.0	2,440	1.4
Pittsfield, MA	520	4.2	25	0.2	235	1.9	10	0.1	270	2.2
Pocatello, ID	60	0.9	185	2.8	120	1.8	0	0.0	160	2.4
Portland–South Portland–Biddeford, ME	1,085	2.6	130	0.3	895	2.1	4	0.0	585	1.4
Portland–Vancouver–Hillsboro, OR–WA	5,715	3.7	900	0.6	9,885	6.4	830	0.5	5,155	3.3
Port St. Lucie, FL	6,125	21.6	65	0.2	620	2.2	15	0.1	320	1.1
Poughkeepsie–Newburgh–Middletown, NY	6,490	14.8	85	0.2	1,415	3.2	75	0.2	670	1.5
Prescott, AZ	100	0.7	285	1.9	200	1.3	0	0.0	390	2.6
Providence–New Bedford–Fall River, RI–MA	9,255	7.1	460	0.4	3,210	2.5	35	0.0	3,475	2.7

PART C—METROPOLITAN STATISTICAL AREA TABLES

C-16 Service Workers, except Protective, by Metropolitan Statistical Area, Sex, Race, and Hispanic or Latino Origin, 2006-2010—Continued

Metropolitan Statistical Area	Total who worked in the last 5 years	Male Number	Male Percent	Female Number	Female Percent	Hispanic or Latino Number	Hispanic or Latino Percent	White alone, not Hispanic or Latino Number	White alone, not Hispanic or Latino Percent
Provo–Orem, UT	29,055	9,795	33.7	19,260	66.3	4,175	14.4	23,285	80.1
Pueblo, CO	11,585	3,775	32.6	7,810	67.4	5,805	50.1	5,210	45.0
Punta Gorda, FL	9,250	3,365	36.4	5,885	63.6	680	7.4	6,830	73.8
Racine, WI	12,430	4,045	32.5	8,380	67.4	1,365	11.0	8,555	68.8
Raleigh–Cary, NC	60,370	21,290	35.3	39,075	64.7	9,435	15.6	30,340	50.3
Rapid City, SD	9,775	3,435	35.1	6,345	64.9	425	4.3	7,540	77.1
Reading, PA	29,170	9,355	32.1	19,820	67.9	4,400	15.1	21,825	74.8
Redding, CA	12,110	4,520	37.3	7,590	62.7	1,240	10.2	9,610	79.4
Reno–Sparks, NV	36,750	14,800	40.3	21,945	59.7	10,875	29.6	19,710	53.6
Richmond, VA	80,025	27,115	33.9	52,915	66.1	6,650	8.3	35,760	44.7
Riverside–San Bernardino–Ontario, CA	262,680	89,530	34.1	173,150	65.9	136,085	51.8	82,725	31.5
Roanoke, VA	19,600	6,265	32.0	13,330	68.0	920	4.7	13,850	70.7
Rochester, MN	14,785	4,950	33.5	9,835	66.5	875	5.9	12,510	84.6
Rochester, NY	73,035	26,480	36.3	46,555	63.7	5,305	7.3	52,125	71.4
Rockford, IL	23,085	7,380	32.0	15,705	68.0	3,390	14.7	15,675	67.9
Rocky Mount, NC	9,520	3,125	32.8	6,395	67.2	280	2.9	3,085	32.4
Rome, GA	6,755	2,390	35.4	4,365	64.6	620	9.2	4,280	63.4
Sacramento–Arden-Arcade–Roseville, CA	144,360	51,835	35.9	92,530	64.1	36,365	25.2	69,235	48.0
Saginaw–Saginaw Township North, MI	16,795	5,280	31.4	11,520	68.6	1,475	8.8	11,015	65.6
St. Cloud, MN	15,785	4,765	30.2	11,015	69.8	400	2.5	14,430	91.4
St. George, UT	8,535	3,275	38.4	5,260	61.6	1,580	18.5	6,435	75.4
St. Joseph, MO–KS	9,135	2,505	27.4	6,630	72.6	470	5.1	7,990	87.5
St. Louis, MO–IL	213,305	77,880	36.5	135,425	63.5	7,505	3.5	138,845	65.1
Salem, OR	26,685	8,430	31.6	18,260	68.4	5,315	19.9	19,200	72.0
Salinas, CA	29,145	11,480	39.4	17,665	60.6	17,160	58.9	7,000	24.0
Salisbury, MD	9,375	3,010	32.1	6,365	67.9	300	3.2	5,560	59.3
Salt Lake City, UT	68,155	24,725	36.3	43,430	63.7	17,505	25.7	44,670	65.5
San Angelo, TX	9,025	3,110	34.5	5,920	65.6	4,505	49.9	3,675	40.7
San Antonio–New Braunfels, TX	144,095	51,960	36.1	92,135	63.9	92,565	64.2	34,425	23.9
San Diego–Carlsbad–San Marcos, CA	212,950	79,625	37.4	133,325	62.6	93,200	43.8	78,205	36.7
Sandusky, OH	6,380	2,305	36.1	4,075	63.9	190	3.0	5,275	82.7
San Francisco–Oakland–Fremont, CA	304,585	119,310	39.2	185,275	60.8	107,260	35.2	85,385	28.0
San Jose–Sunnyvale–Santa Clara, CA	106,670	41,030	38.5	65,640	61.5	49,625	46.5	24,545	23.0
San Luis Obispo–Paso Robles, CA	19,890	7,085	35.6	12,805	64.4	5,915	29.7	12,285	61.8
Santa Barbara–Santa Maria–Goleta, CA	33,315	12,860	38.6	20,455	61.4	17,560	52.7	12,460	37.4
Santa Cruz–Watsonville, CA	19,445	7,470	38.4	11,975	61.6	7,715	39.7	9,845	50.6
Santa Fe, NM	11,805	4,860	41.2	6,945	58.8	7,685	65.1	3,370	28.5
Santa Rosa–Petaluma, CA	36,385	13,040	35.8	23,345	64.2	12,405	34.1	19,620	53.9
Savannah, GA	24,055	7,915	32.9	16,140	67.1	1,255	5.2	10,825	45.0
Scranton–Wilkes-Barre, PA	41,200	13,405	32.5	27,790	67.5	1,915	4.6	37,230	90.4
Seattle–Tacoma–Bellevue, WA	234,925	80,200	34.1	154,725	65.9	32,635	13.9	138,635	59.0
Sebastian–Vero Beach, FL	9,750	3,165	32.5	6,585	67.5	1,165	11.9	6,530	67.0
Sheboygan, WI	8,920	2,845	31.9	6,075	68.1	585	6.6	7,660	85.9
Sherman–Denison, TX	8,995	2,825	31.4	6,170	68.6	1,445	16.1	6,225	69.2
Shreveport–Bossier City, LA	31,860	10,485	32.9	21,375	67.1	1,025	3.2	10,965	34.4
Sioux City, IA–NE–SD	10,595	3,545	33.5	7,045	66.5	1,415	13.4	8,225	77.6
Sioux Falls, SD	15,785	4,610	29.2	11,175	70.8	560	3.5	14,015	88.8
South Bend–Mishawaka, IN–MI	22,610	7,855	34.7	14,755	65.3	1,775	7.9	16,020	70.9
Spartanburg, SC	17,900	5,265	29.4	12,635	70.6	1,145	6.4	10,785	60.3
Spokane, WA	37,565	12,690	33.8	24,875	66.2	2,000	5.3	31,230	83.1
Springfield, IL	16,600	6,675	40.2	9,925	59.8	415	2.5	12,745	76.8
Springfield, MA	54,925	19,630	35.7	35,295	64.3	9,435	17.2	37,125	67.6
Springfield, MO	32,700	11,710	35.8	20,990	64.2	1,160	3.5	28,940	88.5
Springfield, OH	10,125	3,070	30.3	7,055	69.7	235	2.3	8,065	79.7
State College, PA	11,925	4,910	41.2	7,015	58.8	445	3.7	10,475	87.8

C-16 **Service Workers, except Protective, by Metropolitan Statistical Area, Sex, Race, and Hispanic or Latino Origin, 2006–2010**—*Continued*

Metropolitan Statistical Area	Black alone, not Hispanic or Latino Number	Percent	American Indian and Alaska Native alone, not Hispanic or Latino Number	Percent	Asian alone, not Hispanic or Latino Number	Percent	Native Hawaiian and Other Pacific Islander alone, not Hispanic or Latino Number	Percent	Two or more races, not Hispanic or Latino Number	Percent
Provo–Orem, UT	105	0.4	155	0.5	550	1.9	325	1.1	455	1.6
Pueblo, CO	195	1.7	115	1.0	70	0.6	40	0.3	149	1.3
Punta Gorda, FL	1,125	12.2	95	1.0	255	2.8	0	0.0	265	2.9
Racine, WI	2,085	16.8	15	0.1	100	0.8	0	0.0	310	2.5
Raleigh–Cary, NC	17,015	28.2	145	0.2	2,755	4.6	0	0.0	685	1.1
Rapid City, SD	100	1.0	945	9.7	325	3.3	0	0.0	450	4.6
Reading, PA	1,985	6.8	0	0.0	560	1.9	10	0.0	390	1.3
Redding, CA	155	1.3	90	0.7	580	4.8	30	0.2	405	3.3
Reno–Sparks, NV	695	1.9	430	1.2	3,860	10.5	460	1.3	715	1.9
Richmond, VA	32,970	41.2	225	0.3	3,105	3.9	75	0.1	1,245	1.6
Riverside–San Bernardino–Ontario, CA	19,190	7.3	1,195	0.5	17,200	6.5	780	0.3	5,495	2.1
Roanoke, VA	4,025	20.5	25	0.1	550	2.8	0	0.0	230	1.2
Rochester, MN	500	3.4	15	0.1	740	5.0	0	0.0	140	0.9
Rochester, NY	12,180	16.7	135	0.2	2,150	2.9	30	0.0	1,105	1.5
Rockford, IL	3,070	13.3	30	0.1	595	2.6	0	0.0	325	1.4
Rocky Mount, NC	5,980	62.8	4	0.0	45	0.5	0	0.0	120	1.3
Rome, GA	1,575	23.3	0	0.0	185	2.7	0	0.0	95	1.4
Sacramento–Arden-Arcade–Roseville, CA	11,430	7.9	1,035	0.7	20,610	14.3	1,705	1.2	3,985	2.8
Saginaw–Saginaw Township North, MI	3,870	23.0	40	0.2	170	1.0	0	0.0	225	1.3
St. Cloud, MN	370	2.3	145	0.9	300	1.9	0	0.0	130	0.8
St. George, UT	35	0.4	150	1.8	180	2.1	10	0.1	145	1.7
St. Joseph, MO KS	410	4.5	65	0.7	35	0.4	0	0.0	165	1.8
St. Louis, MO–IL	58,565	27.5	260	0.1	5,140	2.4	30	0.0	2,965	1.4
Salem, OR	285	1.1	425	1.6	700	2.6	235	0.9	520	1.9
Salinas, CA	1,125	3.9	60	0.2	2,620	9.0	385	1.3	795	2.7
Salisbury, MD	3,175	33.9	4	0.0	255	2.7	10	0.1	64	0.7
Salt Lake City, UT	830	1.2	715	1.0	3,030	4.4	760	1.1	649	1.0
San Angelo, TX	635	7.0	40	0.4	105	1.2	0	0.0	75	0.8
San Antonio–New Braunfels, TX	11,220	7.8	405	0.3	3,720	2.6	150	0.1	1,605	1.1
San Diego–Carlsbad–San Marcos, CA	10,620	5.0	635	0.3	24,680	11.6	1,075	0.5	4,535	2.1
Sandusky, OH	630	9.9	60	0.9	40	0.6	0	0.0	180	2.8
San Francisco–Oakland–Fremont, CA	26,110	8.6	915	0.3	75,365	24.7	2,475	0.8	7,070	2.3
San Jose–Sunnyvale–Santa Clara, CA	3,300	3.1	410	0.4	26,105	24.5	585	0.5	2,100	2.0
San Luis Obispo–Paso Robles, CA	195	1.0	165	0.8	795	4.0	0	0.0	535	2.7
Santa Barbara–Santa Maria–Goleta, CA	505	1.5	115	0.3	1,960	5.9	155	0.5	550	1.7
Santa Cruz–Watsonville, CA	195	1.0	15	0.1	1,045	5.4	20	0.1	605	3.1
Santa Fe, NM	25	0.2	410	3.5	220	1.9	4	0.0	100	0.8
Santa Rosa–Petaluma, CA	765	2.1	360	1.0	2,050	5.6	345	0.9	835	2.3
Savannah, GA	11,055	46.0	35	0.1	725	3.0	0	0.0	165	0.7
Scranton–Wilkes-Barre, PA	1,145	2.8	30	0.1	550	1.3	10	0.0	315	0.8
Seattle–Tacoma–Bellevue, WA	17,625	7.5	2,110	0.9	32,855	14.0	1,995	0.8	9,065	3.9
Sebastian–Vero Beach, FL	1,790	18.4	25	0.3	155	1.6	0	0.0	80	0.8
Sheboygan, WI	140	1.6	85	1.0	345	3.9	0	0.0	105	1.2
Sherman–Denison, TX	870	9.7	115	1.3	80	0.9	0	0.0	255	2.8
Shreveport–Bossier City, LA	18,765	58.9	45	0.1	685	2.2	0	0.0	375	1.2
Sioux City, IA–NE–SD	215	2.0	300	2.8	305	2.9	0	0.0	124	1.2
Sioux Falls, SD	485	3.1	365	2.3	195	1.2	0	0.0	165	1.0
South Bend–Mishawaka, IN–MI	3,810	16.9	115	0.5	460	2.0	15	0.1	405	1.8
Spartanburg, SC	5,435	30.4	55	0.3	275	1.5	0	0.0	205	1.1
Spokane, WA	740	2.0	840	2.2	1,200	3.2	210	0.6	1,339	3.6
Springfield, IL	2,800	16.9	20	0.1	235	1.4	40	0.2	344	2.1
Springfield, MA	5,590	10.2	190	0.3	1,690	3.1	15	0.0	870	1.6
Springfield, MO	1,135	3.5	200	0.6	555	1.7	4	0.0	710	2.2
Springfield, OH	1,540	15.2	25	0.2	50	0.5	0	0.0	219	2.2
State College, PA	370	3.1	30	0.3	360	3.0	25	0.2	225	1.9

C-16 Service Workers, except Protective, by Metropolitan Statistical Area, Sex, Race, and Hispanic or Latino Origin, 2006–2010—*Continued*

Metropolitan Statistical Area	Total who worked in the last 5 years	Male Number	Male Percent	Female Number	Female Percent	Hispanic or Latino Number	Hispanic or Latino Percent	White alone, not Hispanic or Latino Number	White alone, not Hispanic or Latino Percent
Steubenville–Weirton, OH–WV	10,225	3,335	32.6	6,890	67.4	34	0.3	9,395	91.9
Stockton, CA	40,355	13,205	32.7	27,150	67.3	16,145	40.0	12,890	31.9
Sumter, SC	7,080	2,125	30.0	4,955	70.0	250	3.5	2,275	32.1
Syracuse, NY	48,675	18,170	37.3	30,505	62.7	1,950	4.0	38,050	78.2
Tallahassee, FL	26,935	10,790	40.1	16,140	59.9	1,320	4.9	13,255	49.2
Tampa–St. Petersburg–Clearwater, FL	190,030	70,900	37.3	119,130	62.7	37,240	19.6	111,105	58.5
Terre Haute, IN	12,370	4,020	32.5	8,350	67.5	280	2.3	11,115	89.9
Texarkana, TX–Texarkana, AR	8,795	2,805	31.9	5,990	68.1	610	6.9	4,935	56.1
Toledo, OH	53,245	17,995	33.8	35,250	66.2	3,075	5.8	37,965	71.3
Topeka, KS	17,445	5,635	32.3	11,810	67.7	2,460	14.1	12,495	71.6
Trenton–Ewing, NJ	23,890	9,710	40.6	14,180	59.4	6,220	26.0	8,845	37.0
Tucson, AZ	70,440	25,430	36.1	45,010	63.9	29,685	42.1	32,255	45.8
Tulsa, OK	63,835	20,850	32.7	42,985	67.3	7,690	12.0	37,940	59.4
Tuscaloosa, AL	14,595	5,060	34.7	9,535	65.3	490	3.4	6,845	46.9
Tyler, TX	15,285	4,825	31.6	10,460	68.4	3,195	20.9	6,955	45.5
Utica–Rome, NY	21,675	7,985	36.8	13,690	63.2	1,115	5.1	18,630	86.0
Valdosta, GA	9,920	3,395	34.2	6,525	65.8	585	5.9	4,225	42.6
Vallejo–Fairfield, CA	28,555	10,215	35.8	18,340	64.2	7,115	24.9	10,130	35.5
Victoria, TX	8,035	2,230	27.8	5,805	72.2	4,305	53.6	2,935	36.5
Vineland–Millville–Bridgeton, NJ	11,670	4,235	36.3	7,435	63.7	2,920	25.0	5,200	44.6
Virginia Beach–Norfolk–Newport News, VA–NC	111,185	36,750	33.1	74,435	66.9	6,365	5.7	50,350	45.3
Visalia–Porterville, CA	24,995	8,555	34.2	16,440	65.8	14,565	58.3	7,905	31.6
Waco, TX	17,365	5,705	32.9	11,660	67.1	4,655	26.8	8,205	47.3
Warner Robins, GA	8,380	2,460	29.4	5,920	70.6	535	6.4	3,760	44.9
Washington–Arlington–Alexandria, DC–VA–MD–WV	352,010	120,485	34.2	231,520	65.8	104,650	29.7	98,580	28.0
Waterloo–Cedar Falls, IA	14,430	4,705	32.6	9,725	67.4	420	2.9	12,185	84.4
Wausau, WI	9,620	3,120	32.4	6,500	67.6	185	1.9	8,860	92.1
Wenatchee–East Wenatchee, WA	8,070	2,450	30.4	5,620	69.6	2,240	27.8	5,400	66.9
Wheeling, WV–OH	11,765	3,565	30.3	8,195	69.7	105	0.9	10,975	93.3
Wichita, KS	43,395	13,455	31.0	29,940	69.0	6,370	14.7	28,655	66.0
Wichita Falls, TX	10,990	3,575	32.5	7,415	67.5	1,915	17.4	6,955	63.3
Williamsport, PA	7,770	2,255	29.0	5,515	71.0	95	1.2	6,985	89.9
Wilmington, NC	28,275	9,765	34.5	18,510	65.5	1,355	4.8	20,025	70.8
Winchester, VA–WV	8,455	2,240	26.5	6,210	73.4	740	8.8	6,870	81.3
Winston–Salem, NC	30,830	10,400	33.7	20,430	66.3	3,920	12.7	16,515	53.6
Worcester, MA	54,865	19,185	35.0	35,680	65.0	6,110	11.1	41,595	75.8
Yakima, WA	15,870	4,870	30.7	11,000	69.3	6,010	37.9	8,565	54.0
York–Hanover, PA	28,880	8,785	30.4	20,095	69.6	1,465	5.1	24,165	83.7
Youngstown–Warren–Boardman, OH–PA	43,280	13,810	31.9	29,470	68.1	1,175	2.7	34,585	79.9
Yuba City, CA	10,315	3,175	30.8	7,140	69.2	2,960	28.7	5,365	52.0
Yuma, AZ	11,430	3,820	33.4	7,610	66.6	8,205	71.8	2,460	21.5

C-16 **Service Workers, except Protective, by Metropolitan Statistical Area, Sex, Race, and Hispanic or Latino Origin, 2006–2010**—*Continued*

Metropolitan Statistical Area	Black alone, not Hispanic or Latino Number	Percent	American Indian and Alaska Native alone, not Hispanic or Latino Number	Percent	Asian alone, not Hispanic or Latino Number	Percent	Native Hawaiian and Other Pacific Islander alone, not Hispanic or Latino Number	Percent	Two or more races, not Hispanic or Latino Number	Percent
Steubenville–Weirton, OH–WV	510	5.0	0	0.0	40	0.4	0	0.0	250	2.4
Stockton, CA	2,895	7.2	155	0.4	7,180	17.8	215	0.5	875	2.2
Sumter, SC	4,310	60.9	65	0.9	150	2.1	0	0.0	24	0.3
Syracuse, NY	6,095	12.5	415	0.9	1,455	3.0	10	0.0	700	1.4
Tallahassee, FL	11,250	41.8	30	0.1	855	3.2	20	0.1	205	0.8
Tampa–St. Petersburg–Clearwater, FL	29,755	15.7	325	0.2	7,975	4.2	300	0.2	3,325	1.7
Terre Haute, IN	595	4.8	20	0.2	180	1.5	0	0.0	180	1.5
Texarkana, TX–Texarkana, AR	2,835	32.2	95	1.1	90	1.0	0	0.0	235	2.7
Toledo, OH	10,690	20.1	65	0.1	770	1.4	10	0.0	660	1.2
Topeka, KS	1,495	8.6	360	2.1	205	1.2	20	0.1	410	2.4
Trenton–Ewing, NJ	7,395	31.0	25	0.1	1,200	5.0	4	0.0	195	0.8
Tucson, AZ	2,930	4.2	2,125	3.0	2,420	3.4	30	0.0	1,000	1.4
Tulsa, OK	7,530	11.8	4,645	7.3	1,665	2.6	55	0.1	4,315	6.8
Tuscaloosa, AL	7,140	48.9	4	0.0	25	0.2	0	0.0	90	0.6
Tyler, TX	4,655	30.5	35	0.2	250	1.6	0	0.0	195	1.3
Utica–Rome, NY	1,075	5.0	20	0.1	570	2.6	0	0.0	265	1.2
Valdosta, GA	4,710	47.5	20	0.2	240	2.4	0	0.0	140	1.4
Vallejo–Fairfield, CA	4,345	15.2	30	0.1	5,600	19.6	135	0.5	1,190	4.2
Victoria, TX	655	8.2	4	0.0	65	0.8	0	0.0	75	0.9
Vineland–Millville–Bridgeton, NJ	3,105	26.6	40	0.3	260	2.2	0	0.0	149	1.3
Virginia Beach–Norfolk–Newport News, VA–NC	46,050	41.4	210	0.2	5,705	5.1	145	0.1	2,360	2.1
Visalia–Porterville, CA	295	1.2	275	1.1	1,525	6.1	65	0.3	359	1.4
Waco, TX	4,020	23.2	55	0.3	330	1.9	0	0.0	100	0.6
Warner Robins, GA	3,665	43.7	0	0.0	345	4.1	0	0.0	75	0.9
Washington–Arlington–Alexandria, DC–VA–MD–WV	104,370	29.6	670	0.2	37,015	10.5	150	0.0	6,575	1.9
Waterloo–Cedar Falls, IA	1,285	8.9	4	0.0	330	2.3	15	0.1	185	1.3
Wausau, WI	45	0.5	80	0.8	350	3.6	0	0.0	100	1.0
Wenatchee–East Wenatchee, WA	25	0.3	75	0.9	80	1.0	35	0.4	209	2.6
Wheeling, WV–OH	360	3.1	10	0.1	95	0.8	0	0.0	215	1.8
Wichita, KS	5,035	11.6	370	0.9	1,555	3.6	105	0.2	1,300	3.0
Wichita Falls, TX	1,640	14.9	130	1.2	220	2.0	0	0.0	140	1.3
Williamsport, PA	420	5.4	15	0.2	60	0.8	0	0.0	200	2.6
Wilmington, NC	5,800	20.5	35	0.1	500	1.8	25	0.1	530	1.9
Winchester, VA–WV	675	8.0	0	0.0	70	0.8	0	0.0	100	1.2
Winston–Salem, NC	9,360	30.4	140	0.5	555	1.8	25	0.1	320	1.0
Worcester, MA	3,830	7.0	75	0.1	1,705	3.1	10	0.0	1,545	2.8
Yakima, WA	195	1.2	570	3.6	235	1.5	30	0.2	265	1.7
York–Hanover, PA	2,065	7.2	35	0.1	525	1.8	0	0.0	620	2.1
Youngstown–Warren–Boardman, OH–PA	6,625	15.3	120	0.3	305	0.7	15	0.0	460	1.1
Yuba City, CA	245	2.4	90	0.9	1,215	11.8	40	0.4	400	3.9
Yuma, AZ	255	2.2	135	1.2	165	1.4	0	0.0	205	1.8

Appendixes

Page

- 479 Notes and Definitions
- 483 Detailed EEO Occupation Groups
- 555 Metropolitan Statistical Areas, Metropolitan Divisions, and Components

APPENDIX A
NOTES AND DEFINITIONS

Race and Ethnicity

The U.S. Census Bureau collects race data in accordance with guidelines provided by the U.S. Office of Management and Budget (OMB). Except for the total, all race and ethnicity (Hispanic origin) categories are mutually exclusive. Black refers to Black or African American; AIAN refers to American Indian and Alaska Native; and NHPI refers to Native Hawaiian and Other Pacific Islander. This book uses a total of seven race and ethnicity (Hispanic origin) categories:

Hispanic or Latino

The Census Bureau categorizes ethnicity into two categories: Hispanic or Latino OR not Hispanic or Latino. The data on the Hispanic or Latino population were derived from answers to a question that was asked of all people. The terms Hispanic, Latino, and Spanish are used interchangeably. Some respondents identify with all three terms while others may identify with only one of these three specific terms. Hispanics or Latinos who identify with the terms Hispanic, Latino, or Spanish are those who classify themselves in one of the specific Hispanic, Latino, or Spanish categories listed on the questionnaire (Mexican, Puerto Rican, or Cuban) as well as those who indicate that they are of another Hispanic, Latino, or Spanish origin. People who do not identify with one of the specific origins listed on the questionnaire but indicate that they are another Hispanic, Latino, or Spanish origin are those whose origins are from Spain, the Spanish-speaking countries of Central or South America, or the Dominican Republic. Up to two write-in responses to the another Hispanic, Latino, or Spanish origin category are coded.

Not Hispanic or Latino:
  White alone
  Black or African American alone
  American Indian and Alaska Native alone
  Asian alone
  Native Hawaiian and Other Pacific Islander alone
  Two or more races

In the EEO tabulation, there are a total of 15 categories:

Hispanic or Latino origin
  1. White alone Hispanic or Latino
  2. All other Hispanic or Latino

Not Hispanic or Latino, one race
  3. White alone
  4. Black or African-American alone
  5. American Indian and Alaska Native alone
  6. Asian alone
  7. Native Hawaiian and Other Pacific Islander alone

Not Hispanic or Latino, two or more races
  8. White and Black
  9. White and AIAN
  10. White and Asian
  11. Black and AIAN
  12. NHPI and White (Hawaii only)
  13. NHPI and Asian (Hawaii only)
  14. NHPI and Asian and White (Hawaii only)
  15. Balance of not Hispanic or Latino

In this book, all Hispanic or Latino persons are combined into one group Hispanic or Latino, and all Not Hispanic or Latino, two or more races are combined into one group, Two or more races, not Hispanic or Latino. Both of these combined groups include persons who marked "some other race."

Race

White. A person having origins in any of the original peoples of Europe, the Middle East, or North Africa; includes people who indicate their race as White or report entries such as Irish, German, Italian, Lebanese, Arab, Moroccan, or Caucasian.

Black or African-American. A person having origins in any of the Black racial groups of Africa. It includes people who indicate their race as Black, African-American, or Negro or report entries such as African, Kenyan, Nigerian, or Haitian.

American Indian or Alaska Native. A person having origins in any of the original peoples of North and South America (including Central America) and who maintains tribal affiliation or community attachment. This category includes people who indicate their race as American Indian or Alaska Native or report entries such as Navajo, Blackfeet, Inupiat, Yup'ik, or Central American Indian groups, or South American Indian groups. Respondents who identified themselves as American Indian or Alaska Native were asked to report their enrolled or principal tribe. Therefore, tribal data in tabulations reflect the written entries reported on the questionnaires. Some of the entries (for example, Metlakatla Indian Community and Umatilla) represent reservations or a confederation of tribes on a reservation. The information on tribes is based on self-identification and therefore does not reflect any designation of federally or state-recognized tribe. The information for the 2010 ACS was derived from the American Indian and Alaska Native Tribal Classification List for Census 2000 and updated from 2002 to 2009 based on the annual *Federal Register* notice entitled "Indian Entities Recognized and Eligible to Receive Services from the United States Bureau of Indian Affairs," Department of the Interior, Bureau of Indian Affairs, issued by the OMB, and through consultation with American Indian and Alaska Native communities and leaders.

Asian. A person having origins in any of the original peoples of the Far East, Southeast Asia, or the Indian subcontinent, including, for example, Cambodia, China, India, Japan, Korea, Malaysia, Pakistan, the Philippine Islands, Thailand, and Vietnam. The term Asian includes people who indicate their race as Asian Indian, Chinese, Filipino, Korean, Japanese, Vietnamese, and Other Asian or provide other detailed Asian responses.

Native Hawaiian or Other Pacific Islander. A person having origins in any of the original peoples of Hawaii, Guam, Samoa, or other Pacific Islands. It includes people who indicate their race as Native Hawaiian, Guamanian or Chamorro, Samoan, and Other Pacific Islander or provide other detailed Pacific Islander responses.

Some Other Race. The category includes all other responses not included in the White, Black, or African-American, American Indian or Alaska Native, Asian, and Native Hawaiian or Other Pacific Islander race categories described above. Respondents reporting entries such as multiracial, mixed, interracial, or a Hispanic, Latino, or Spanish group (for example, Mexican, Puerto Rican, Cuban, or Spanish) in response to the race question are included in this category.

Two or More Races. People may choose to provide two or more races—by checking two or more race response check boxes, by providing multiple responses, or by some combination of check boxes and other responses. The race response categories shown on the questionnaire are collapsed into the five minimum race groups identified by the OMB, and the Census Bureau's Some Other Race category. For data product purposes, Two or More Races refers to combinations of two or more of the following race categories:

1. White
2. Black or African-American
3. American Indian or Alaska Native
4. Asian
5. Native Hawaiian or Other Pacific Islander
6. Some Other Race

Fifty-seven possible combinations exist involving the race categories shown above. Thus, according to this approach, a response of White and Asian was tallied as Two or More Races, although a response of Japanese and Chinese was not because Japanese and Chinese are both Asian responses.

Race Concepts

Given the many possible ways of displaying data on race, data products will provide varying levels of detail. Several concepts are used to display and tabulate race information for the six major race categories (White; Black or African-American; American Indian or Alaska Native; Asian; Native Hawaiian or Other Pacific Islander; and Some Other Race) and the various details within these groups.

The concept "race alone" includes people who reported a single entry (for example, Korean) and no other race, as well as people who reported two or more entries within the same major race group (for example, Asian). Accordingly, respondents who reported Korean and Vietnamese are part of the larger "Asian alone" race group.

The concept "race alone or in combination" includes people who reported a single race alone (for example, Asian) and people who reported that race in combination with one or more of the other major race groups (for example, White, Black or African-American, American Indian and Alaska Native, Native Hawaiian and Other Pacific Islander, and Some Other Race). The "race alone or in combination" concept therefore, represents the maximum number of people who reported as that race group, either alone, or in combination with another race(s). The sum of the six individual race "alone or in combination" categories may add to more than the total population because people who reported more than one race were tallied in each race category.

The EEO tabulations use only the "race alone" concept.

For more information on race and Hispanic origin, see the Subject Definitions at www.census.gov/acs/www/data_documentation/documentation_main/.

Occupation

The occupations in this tabulation are based on the *2010 Standard Occupational Classification (SOC)*, published by the Executive Office of the President, Office of Management and Budget. This classification groups occupations according to the nature of the work performed, and relates these occupations to others of a similar nature. Census occupation codes, based on the 2010 SOC, provide 539 specific occupational categories, for employed people, including military, arranged into 23 major occupational groups. The Census Bureau has adapted the SOC to create the occupation categories used in the American Community Survey (ACS), and shown on the EEO Tabulation 2006–2010 (5-year ACS data). In some cases, the Census categories are groupings of the more detailed SOC categories. As a method of disclosure avoidance, detailed categories are collapsed for occupation. Each category contains at least 10,000 cases nationwide. That is why instead of having the full set of 539 specific occupations, data were published for 488 detailed occupations.

The EEO residence tables (the basis for most of the tables in this book) have 488 occupational categories and the worksite tables have 487 categories. The difference is that residence tables contain a Census occupational category for the unemployed, which includes people who are 16 years old and over who are unemployed, AND have no work experience in the last 5 years; people who have never worked but are looking for work; and people who have worked in the last 5 years but whose last job was in a military-specific occupation and are now looking for work. People in this category have a place of residence but no worksite.

See Appendix B for a complete crosswalk of the ACS occupations, how they are combined from the SOC occupations and how they are combined into the 14 EEO occupation groups.

Educational Attainment

Educational attainment data are tabulated for people 18 years old and over. Respondents are classified according to the highest degree or the highest level of school completed. The question included instructions for persons currently enrolled in school to report the level of the previous grade attended or the highest degree received.

The educational attainment question included a response category that allowed people to report completing the 12th grade without receiving a high school diploma. Respondents who received a regular high school diploma and did not attend college were instructed to report "Regular high school diploma." Respondents who received the equivalent of a high school diploma (for example, passed the test of General Educational Development (G.E.D.), and did not attend college, were instructed to report "GED or alternative credential."

"Some college" is in two categories: "Some college credit, but less than 1 year of college credit" and "1 or more years of college credit, no degree." The category "Associate's degree" included people whose highest degree is an associate's degree, which generally requires 2 years of college level work and is either in an occupational program that prepares them for a specific occupation, or an academic program primarily in the arts and sciences. The course work may or may not be transferable to a bachelor's degree.

Master's degrees include the traditional MA and MS degrees and field-specific degrees, such as MSW, MEd, MBA, MLS, and MEng.

Instructions included in the respondent instruction guide for mail out/mailback respondents only provided the following examples of professional school degrees: medicine, dentistry, chiropractic, optometry, osteopathic medicine, pharmacy, podiatry, veterinary medicine, law, and theology.

The order in which degrees were listed suggested that doctorate degrees were higher than professional school degrees, which were higher than master's degrees. If more than one box was filled, the response was edited to the highest level or degree reported. The instructions further specified that schooling completed in foreign or ungraded school systems should be reported as the equivalent level of schooling in the regular American system. The instructions specified that certificates or diplomas for training in specific trades or from vocational, technical, or business schools were not to be reported. Honorary degrees awarded for a respondent's accomplishments were also not to be reported.

The categories included in this book are the following:

Not a high school graduate: This category includes all persons who have not received a high school diploma. People who reported completing the 12th grade but not receiving a diploma are not high school graduates.

High school graduate (including equivalency): This category includes people whose highest degree was a high school diploma or its equivalent.

Some college or associate's degree. This category includes all persons who have attained any college credits or an associate's degree but have not attained a bachelor's degree.

Bachelor's degree. This category includes people whose highest degree was a bachelor's degree.

Graduate or Professional degree. This category includes persons who have earned a master's, professional, or doctoral degree. Master's degrees include the traditional M.A. and M.S. degrees and field-specific degrees. Some examples of professional degrees include medicine, dentistry, chiropractic, optometry, osteopathic medicine, pharmacy, podiatry, veterinary medicine, law, and theology.

Metropolitan Areas

The tables in Part C present data for 366 metropolitan statistical areas. The metropolitan statistical areas are listed alphabetically.

The U.S. Office of Management and Budget (OMB) defines metropolitan and micropolitan statistical areas according to published standards. The major purpose of defining these areas is to enable all U.S. government agencies to use the same geographic definitions in tabulating and publishing data. The general concept of a metropolitan or micropolitan statistical area is that of a core area containing a substantial population nucleus, together with adjacent communities that have a high degree of economic and social integration with the core. Currently defined metropolitan and micropolitan statistical areas are based on application of the new 2000 standards to 2000 decennial census data. Current metropolitan and micropolitan statistical area definitions were announced by the OMB, effective December 1, 2009.

New delineations based on the 2010 census were released in February 2013. In the next few years, federal agencies will begin to use these new definitions of metropolitan and micropolitan areas, but the tables in this book continue to use the 2009 definitions. Standard definitions of metropolitan areas were first issued in 1949 by the Bureau of the Budget (the predecessor of the OMB), under the designation standard metropolitan area (SMA). The term was changed to *standard metropolitan statistical area* (SMSA) in 1959, and to *metropolitan statistical area* (MSA) in 1983. The term *metropolitan area* (MA) was adopted in 1990 and referred collectively to metropolitan statistical areas (MSAs), consolidated metropolitan statistical areas (CMSAs), and primary metropolitan statistical areas (PMSAs). The term *core based statistical area* (CBSA) became effective in 2000 and refers collectively to metropolitan and micropolitan statistical areas.

The 2000 standards provide that each CBSA must contain at least one urban area of 10,000 or more population. Each metropolitan statistical area must have at least one urbanized area of 50,000 or more inhabitants. Each micropolitan statistical area must have at least one urban cluster of at least 10,000, but less than 50,000 people.

Under the standards, the county (or counties) in which at least 50 percent of the population resides within urban areas of 10,000 or more population, or that contain at least 5,000 people residing within a single urban area of 10,000 or more population, is identified as a central county (counties). Additional outlying counties are included in the CBSA if they meet specified requirements of commuting to or from the central counties. Counties or equivalent entities form the geographic building blocks for metropolitan and micropolitan statistical areas throughout the United States.

If specified criteria are met, a metropolitan statistical area containing a single core with a population of 2.5 million or more may be subdivided to form smaller groupings of counties referred to as metropolitan divisions. Metropolitan divisions are not included in the EEO tabulations.

As of December 1, 2009, there were 366 metropolitan statistical areas and 576 micropolitan statistical areas in the United States. This book includes only the 366 metropolitan statistical areas.

The largest city in each metropolitan or micropolitan statistical area is designated a principal city. Additional cities qualify if specified requirements are met concerning population size and employment. The title of each metropolitan or micropolitan statistical area consists of the names of up to three of its principal cities and the name of each state into which the metropolitan or micropolitan statistical area extends. The principal city need not be an incorporated place if it meets the requirements of population size and employment. Usually such a principal city is a census designated place in decennial census data, but it is not included in most other data sources.

In view of the importance of cities and towns in New England, the 2000 and 2010 standards also provide for a set of geographic areas that are defined using cities and towns in the six New England states. These New England city and town areas (NECTAs) are not included in this edition.

Appendix C lists the 366 metropolitan statistical areas, together with their component metropolitan divisions, where appropriate, the component counties of each area, and their 2010 census populations.

APPENDIX B
DETAILED OCCUPATIONS, BY EEO OCCUPATION GROUPS, 2006–2010

2010 EEO Occupation Title	2010 EEO Occupation Code	2010 SOC Code(s)	EEO Occupation Group (14)	2010 SOC Code	2010 SOC Occcupation Title	SOC Definition
Management, Business, and Financial Workers							
Chief executives and legislators	0010	11-10XX Combines: 11-1011 11-1031	1	11-1011	Chief executives	Determine and formulate policies and provide overall direction of companies or private and public sector organizations within guidelines set by a board of directors or similar governing body. Plan, direct, or coordinate operational activities at the highest level of management with the help of subordinate executives and staff managers.
				11-1031	Legislators	Develop, introduce or enact laws and statutes at the local, tribal, state, or federal level. Includes only workers in elected positions.
General and operations managers	0020	11-1021	1	11-1021	General and operations managers	Plan, direct, or coordinate the operations of public or private sector organizations. Duties and responsibilities include formulating policies, managing daily operations, and planning the use of materials and human resources, but are too diverse and general in nature to be classified in any one functional area of management or administration, such as personnel, purchasing, or administrative services. Excludes First-Line Supervisors.
Advertising and promotions managers	0040	11-2011	1	11-2011	Advertising and promotions managers	Plan, direct, or coordinate advertising policies and programs or produce collateral materials, such as posters, contests, coupons, or give-aways, to create extra interest in the purchase of a product or service for a department, an entire organization, or on an account basis.
Marketing and sales managers	0050	11-2020	1	11-2021	Marketing managers	Plan, direct, or coordinate marketing policies and programs, such as determining the demand for products and services offered by a firm and its competitors, and identify potential customers. Develop pricing strategies with the goal of maximizing the firm's profits or share of the market while ensuring the firm's customers are satisfied. Oversee product development or monitor trends that indicate the need for new products and services.
				11-2022	Sales managers	Plan, direct, or coordinate the actual distribution or movement of a product or service to the customer. Coordinate sales distribution by establishing sales territories, quotas, and goals and establish training programs for sales representatives. Analyze sales statistics gathered by staff to determine sales potential and inventory requirements and monitor the preferences of customers.
Public relations and fundraising managers	0060	11-2031	1	11-2031	Public relations and fundraising managers	Plan, direct, or coordinate activities designed to create or maintain a favorable public image or raise issue awareness for their organization or client; or if engaged in fundraising, plan, direct, or coordinate activities to solicit and maintain funds for special projects or nonprofit organizations.
Administrative services managers	0100	11-3011	1	11-3011	Administrative services managers	Plan, direct, or coordinate one or more administrative services of an organization, such as records and information management, mail distribution, facilities planning and maintenance, custodial operations, and other office support services. Medical records administrators are included in "Medical and health services managers" (11-9111). Excludes "Purchasing managers" (11-3061).
Computer and information systems managers	0110	11-3021	1	11-3021	Computer and information systems managers	Plan, direct, or coordinate activities in such fields as electronic data processing, information systems, systems analysis, and computer programming. Excludes "Computer Occupations" (15-1111 through 15-1199).

DETAILED OCCUPATIONS, BY EEO OCCUPATION GROUPS, 2006–2010—*Continued*

2010 EEO Occupation Title	2010 EEO Occupation Code	2010 SOC Code(s)	EEO Occupation Group (14)	2010 SOC Code	2010 SOC Occupation Title	SOC Definition
Management, Business, and Financial Workers—Continued						
Financial managers	0120	11-3031	1	11-3031	Financial managers	Plan, direct, or coordinate accounting, investing, banking, insurance, securities, and other financial activities of a branch, office, or department of an establishment.
Compensation and benefits managers	0135	11-3111	1	11-3111	Compensation and benefits managers	Plan, direct, or coordinate compensation and benefits activities of an organization. Job analysis and position description managers are included in "Human resource managers" (11-3121).
Human resources managers	0136	11-3121	1	11-3121	Human resources managers	Plan, direct, or coordinate human resources activities and staff of an organization. Excludes managers who primarily focus on compensation and benefits (11-3111) and training and development (11-3131).
Training and development managers	0137	11-3131	1	11-3131	Training and development managers	Plan, direct, or coordinate the training and development activities and staff of an organization.
Industrial production managers	0140	11-3051	1	11-3051	Industrial production managers	Plan, direct, or coordinate the work activities and resources necessary for manufacturing products in accordance with cost, quality, and quantity specifications.
Purchasing managers	0150	11-3061	1	11-3061	Purchasing managers	Plan, direct, or coordinate the activities of buyers, purchasing officers, and related workers involved in purchasing materials, products, and services. Includes wholesale or retail trade merchandising managers and procurement managers.
Transportation, storage, and distribution managers	0160	11-3071	1	11-3071	Transportation, storage, and distribution managers	Plan, direct, or coordinate transportation, storage, or distribution activities in accordance with organizational policies and applicable government laws or regulations. Includes logistics managers.
Farmers, ranchers, and other agricultural managers	0205	11-9013	1	11-9013	Farmers, ranchers, and other agricultural managers	Plan, direct, or coordinate the management or operation of farms, ranches, greenhouses, aquacultural operations, nurseries, timber tracts, or other agricultural establishments. May hire, train, and supervise farm workers or contract for services to carry out the day-to-day activities of the managed operation. May engage in or supervise planting, cultivating, harvesting, and financial and marketing activities. Excludes "First-line supervisors of farming, fishing, and forestry workers" (45-1011).
Construction managers	0220	11-9021	1	11-9021	Construction managers	Plan, direct, or coordinate, usually through subordinate supervisory personnel, activities concerned with the construction and maintenance of structures, facilities, and systems. Participate in the conceptual development of a construction project and oversee its organization, scheduling, budgeting, and implementation. Includes managers in specialized construction fields, such as carpentry or plumbing.
Education administrators	0230	11-9030	1	11-9031	Education administrators, preschool and childcare center/program	Plan, direct, or coordinate the academic and nonacademic activities of preschool and childcare centers or programs. Excludes "Preschool teachers" (25-2011).
				11-9032	Education administrators, elementary and secondary school	Plan, direct, or coordinate the academic, administrative, or auxiliary activities of public or private elementary or secondary level schools.
				11-9033	Education administrators, Postsecondary	Plan, direct, or coordinate research, instructional, student administration and services, and other educational activities at postsecondary institutions, including universities, colleges, and junior and community colleges.
				11-9039	Education administrators, all other	All education administrators not listed separately.

DETAILED OCCUPATIONS, BY EEO OCCUPATION GROUPS, 2006–2010—*Continued*

2010 EEO Occupation Title	2010 EEO Occupation Code	2010 SOC Code(s)	EEO Occupation Group (14)	2010 SOC Code	2010 SOC Occcupation Title	SOC Definition
\multicolumn{7}{c}{**Management, Business, and Financial Workers**—*Continued*}
Architectural and engineering managers	0300	11-9041	1	11-9041	Architectural and engineering managers	Plan, direct, or coordinate activities in such fields as architecture and engineering or research and development in these fields. Excludes "Natural sciences managers" (11-9121).
Food service managers	0310	11-9051	1	11-9051	Food service managers	Plan, direct, or coordinate activities of an organization or department that serves food and beverages. Excludes "Chefs and Head cooks" (35-1011).
Gaming managers	0330	11-9071	1	11-9071	Gaming managers	Plan, direct, or coordinate gaming operations in a casino. May formulate house rules.
Lodging managers	0340	11-9081	1	11-9081	Lodging managers	Plan, direct, or coordinate activities of an organization or department that provides lodging and other accommodations. Excludes "Food service managers" (11-9051) in lodging establishments.
Medical and health services managers	0350	11-9111	1	11-9111	Medical and health services managers	Plan, direct, or coordinate medical and health services in hospitals, clinics, managed care organizations, public health agencies, or similar organizations.
Natural sciences managers	0360	11-9121	1	11-9121	Natural sciences managers	Plan, direct, or coordinate activities in such fields as life sciences, physical sciences, mathematics, statistics, and research and development in these fields. Excludes "Architecture and engineering managers" (11-9041) and "Computer and Information Systems managers" (11-3021).
Property, real estate, and community association managers	0410	11-9141	1	11-9141	Property, real estate, and community association managers	Plan, direct, or coordinate the selling, buying, leasing, or governance activities of commercial, industrial, or residential real estate properties. Includes managers of homeowner and condominium associations, rented or leased housing units, buildings, or land (including rights-of-way).
Social and community service managers	0420	11-9151	1	11-9151	Social and community service managers	Plan, direct, or coordinate the activities of a social service program or community outreach organization. Oversee the program or organization's budget and policies regarding participant involvement, program requirements, and benefits. Work may involve directing social workers, counselors, or probation officers.
Emergency management directors	0425	11-9161	1	11-9161	Emergency management directors	Plan and direct disaster response or crisis management activities, provide disaster preparedness training, and prepare emergency plans and procedures for natural (e.g., hurricanes, floods, earthquakes), wartime, or technological (e.g., nuclear power plant emergencies or hazardous materials spills) disasters or hostage situations.
Miscellaneous managers, including funeral service managers and postmasters and mail superintendents	0430	11-9XXX Combines: 11-9061 11-9131 11-9199	1	11-9061	Funeral service managers	Plan, direct, or coordinate the services or resources of funeral homes. Includes activities such as determining prices for services or merchandise and managing the facilities of funeral homes. Excludes "Morticians, undertakers, and funeral directors" (39-4031).
				11-9131	Postmasters and mail superintendents	Plan, direct, or coordinate operational, administrative, management, and supportive services of a U.S. post office; or coordinate activities of workers engaged in postal and related work in assigned post office.
				11-9199	Managers, all other	All managers not listed separately.
Agents and business managers of artists, performers, and athletes	0500	13-1011	1	13-1011	Agents and business managers of artists, performers, and athletes	Represent and promote artists, performers, and athletes in dealings with current or prospective employers. May handle contract negotiation and other business matters for clients.
Buyers and purchasing agents, farm products	0510	13-1021	1	13-1021	Buyers and purchasing agents, farm products	Purchase farm products either for further processing or resale. Includes tree farm contractors, grain brokers and market operators, grain buyers, and tobacco buyers.

DETAILED OCCUPATIONS, BY EEO OCCUPATION GROUPS, 2006–2010—Continued

2010 EEO Occupation Title	2010 EEO Occupation Code	2010 SOC Code(s)	EEO Occupation Group (14)	2010 SOC Code	2010 SOC Occcupation Title	SOC Definition
\multicolumn{7}{c}{**Management, Business, and Financial Workers**—Continued}
Wholesale and retail buyers, except farm products	0520	13-1022	1	13-1022	Wholesale and retail buyers, except farm products	Buy merchandise or commodities, other than farm products, for resale to consumers at the wholesale or retail level, including both durable and nondurable goods. Analyze past buying trends, sales records, price, and quality of merchandise to determine value and yield. Select, order, and authorize payment for merchandise according to contractual agreements. May conduct meetings with sales personnel and introduce new products. Includes assistant wholesale and retail buyers of nonfarm products.
Purchasing agents, except wholesale, retail, and farm products	0530	13-1023	1	13-1023	Purchasing agents, except wholesale, retail, and farm products	Purchase machinery, equipment, tools, parts, supplies, or services necessary for the operation of an establishment. Purchase raw or semi-finished materials for manufacturing. Excludes "Buyers and purchasing agents, farm products" (13-1021) and "Wholesale and retail buyers, except farm products" (13-1022).
Claims adjusters, appraisers, examiners, and investigators	0540	13-1030	1	13-1031	Claims adjusters, appraisers, examiners, and investigators	Review settled claims to determine that payments and settlements are made in accordance with company practices and procedures. Confer with legal counsel on claims requiring litigation. May also settle insurance claims. Excludes "Fire inspectors and investigators" (33-2021).
				13-1032	Insurance appraisers, auto damage	Appraise automobile or other vehicle damage to determine repair costs for insurance claim settlement. Prepare insurance forms to indicate repair cost or cost estimates and recommendations. May seek agreement with automotive repair shop on repair costs.
Compliance officers	0565	13-1041	1	13-1041	Compliance officers	Examine, evaluate, and investigate eligibility for or conformity with laws and regulations governing contract compliance of licenses and permits, and perform other compliance and enforcement inspection and analysis activities not classified elsewhere. Excludes "Financial examiners" (13-2061), "Tax examiners and collectors, and Revenue agents" (13-2081), "Occupational health and safety specialists" (29-9011), "Occupational health and safety technicians" (29-9012), "Transportation security screeners" (33-9093), "Agricultural inspectors" (45-2011), "Construction and building inspectors" (47-4011), and "Transportation inspectors" (53-6051).
Cost estimators	0600	13-1051	1	13-1051	Cost estimators	Prepare cost estimates for product manufacturing, construction projects, or services to aid management in bidding on or determining price of product or service. May specialize according to particular service performed or type of product manufactured.
Compensation, benefits, and job analysis specialists	0640	13-1141	1	13-1141	Compensation, benefits, and job analysis specialists	Conduct programs of compensation and benefits and job analysis for employer. May specialize in specific areas, such as position classification and pension programs.
Training and development specialists	0650	13-1151	1	13-1151	Training and development specialists	Design and conduct training and development programs to improve individual and organizational performance. May analyze training needs.
Logisticians	0700	13-1081	1	13-1081	Logisticians	Analyze and coordinate the logistical functions of a firm or organization. Responsible for the entire life cycle of a product, including acquisition, distribution, internal allocation, delivery, and final disposal of resources. Excludes "Transportation, storage, and distribution managers" (11-3071).

APPENDIX B

DETAILED OCCUPATIONS, BY EEO OCCUPATION GROUPS, 2006–2010—*Continued*

2010 EEO Occupation Title	2010 EEO Occupation Code	2010 SOC Code(s)	EEO Occupation Group (14)	2010 SOC Code	2010 SOC Occcupation Title	SOC Definition
	Management, Business, and Financial Workers—*Continued*					
Management analysts	0710	13-1111	1	13-1111	Management analysts	Conduct organizational studies and evaluations, design systems and procedures, conduct work simplification and measurement studies, and prepare operations and procedures manuals to assist management in operating more efficiently and effectively. Includes program analysts and management consultants. Excludes "Computer systems analysts" (15-1121) and "Operations research analysts" (15-2031).
Meeting, convention, and event planners	0725	13-1121	1	13-1121	Meeting, convention, and event planners	Coordinate activities of staff, convention personnel, or clients to make arrangements for group meetings, events, or conventions.
Fundraisers	0726	13-1131	1	13-1131	Fundraisers	Organize activities to raise funds or otherwise solicit and gather monetary donations or other gifts for an organization. May design and produce promotional materials. May also raise awareness of the organization's work, goals, and financial needs.
Market research analysts and marketing specialists	0735	13-1161	1	13-1161	Market research analysts and marketing specialists	Research market conditions in local, regional, or national areas, or gather information to determine potential sales of a product or service, or create a marketing campaign. May gather information on competitors, prices, sales, and methods of marketing and distribution.
Business operations specialists, all other	0740	13-1199	1	13-1199	Business operations specialists, all other	All business operations specialists not listed separately.
Appraisers and assessors of real estate	0810	13-2021	1	13-2021	Appraisers and assessors of real estate	Appraise real property and estimate its fair value. May assess taxes in accordance with prescribed schedules.
Budget analysts	0820	13-2031	1	13-2031	Budget analysts	Examine budget estimates for completeness, accuracy, and conformance with procedures and regulations. Analyze budgeting and accounting reports.
Credit analysts	0830	13-2041	1	13-2041	Credit analysts	Analyze credit data and financial statements of individuals or firms to determine the degree of risk involved in extending credit or lending money. Prepare reports with credit information for use in decision making.
Financial analysts	0840	13-2051	1	13-2051	Financial analysts	Conduct quantitative analyses of information affecting investment programs of public or private institutions.
Personal financial advisors	0850	13-2052	1	13-2052	Personal financial advisors	Advise clients on financial plans using knowledge of tax and investment strategies, securities, insurance, pension plans, and real estate. Duties include assessing clients assets, liabilities, cash flow, insurance coverage, tax status, and financial objectives.
Insurance underwriters	0860	13-2053	1	13-2053	Insurance underwriters	Review individual applications for insurance to evaluate degree of risk involved and determine acceptance of applications.
Financial examiners	0900	13-2061	1	13-2061	Financial examiners	Enforce or ensure compliance with laws and regulations governing financial and securities institutions and financial and real estate transactions. May examine, verify, or authenticate records.
Credit counselors and loan officers	0910	13-2070	1	13-2071	Credit counselors and loan officers	Advise and educate individuals or organizations on acquiring and managing debt. May provide guidance in determining the best type of loan and explaining loan requirements or restrictions. May help develop debt management plans, advise on credit issues, or provide budget, mortgage, and bankruptcy counseling.
				13-2072	Loan officers	Evaluate, authorize, or recommend approval of commercial, real estate, or credit loans. Advise borrowers on financial status and payment methods. Includes mortgage loan officers and agents, collection analysts, loan servicing officers, and loan underwriters.

DETAILED OCCUPATIONS, BY EEO OCCUPATION GROUPS, 2006–2010—*Continued*

2010 EEO Occupation Title	2010 EEO Occupation Code	2010 SOC Code(s)	EEO Occupation Group (14)	2010 SOC Code	2010 SOC Occcupation Title	SOC Definition
\multicolumn{7}{c}{*Management, Business, and Financial Workers—Continued*}					
Tax examiners and collectors, and revenue agents	0930	13-2081	1	13-2081	Tax examiners and collectors, and revenue agents	Determine tax liability or collect taxes from individuals or business firms according to prescribed laws and regulations.
Tax preparers	0940	13-2082	1	13-2082	Tax preparers	Prepare tax returns for individuals or small businesses. Excludes "Accountants and auditors" (13-2011).
Financial specialists, all other	0950	13-2099	1	13-2099	Financial specialists, all other	All financial specialists not listed separately.
Morticians, undertakers, and funeral directors	4465	39-4031	1	39-4031	Morticians, undertakers, and funeral directors	Perform various tasks to arrange and direct funeral services, such as coordinating transportation of body to mortuary, interviewing family or other authorized person to arrange details, selecting pallbearers, aiding with the selection of officials for religious rites, and providing transportation for mourners. Excludes "Funeral service managers" (11-9061).
Agricultural inspectors	6010	45-2011	1	45-2011	Agricultural inspectors	Inspect agricultural commodities, processing equipment, and facilities, and fish and logging operations, to ensure compliance with regulations and laws governing health, quality, and safety.
Construction and building inspectors	6660	47-4011	1	47-4011	Construction and building inspectors	Inspect structures using engineering skills to determine structural soundness and compliance with specifications, building codes, and other regulations. Inspections may be general in nature or may be limited to a specific area, such as electrical systems or plumbing.
Transportation inspectors	9410	53-6051	1	53-6051	Transportation inspectors	Inspect equipment or goods in connection with the safe transport of cargo or people. Includes rail transportation inspectors, such as freight inspectors; rail inspectors; and other inspectors of transportation vehicles, not elsewhere classified. Excludes "Transportation security screeners" (33-9093).
\multicolumn{7}{c}{*Science, Engineering, and Computer Professionals*}					
Computer and information research scientists	1005	15-1111	2	15-1111	Computer and information research scientists	Conduct research into fundamental computer and information science as theorists, designers, or inventors. Develop solutions to problems in the field of computer hardware and software.
Computer systems analysts	1006	15-1121	2	15-1121	Computer systems analysts	Analyze science, engineering, business, and other data processing problems to implement and improve computer systems. Analyze user requirements, procedures, and problems to automate or improve existing systems and review computer system capabilities, workflow, and scheduling limitations. May analyze or recommend commercially available software.
Information security analysts	1007	15-1122	2	15-1122	Information security analysts	Plan, implement, upgrade, or monitor security measures for the protection of computer networks and information. May ensure appropriate security controls are in place that will safeguard digital files and vital electronic infrastructure. May respond to computer security breaches and viruses. Excludes "Computer network architects" (15-1143).
Software developers, applications and systems software	1020	15-113X Combines: 15-1132 15-1133	2	15-1132	Software developers, applications	Develop, create, and modify general computer applications software or specialized utility programs. Analyze user needs and develop software solutions. Design software or customize software for client use with the aim of optimizing operational efficiency. May analyze and design databases within an application area, working individually or coordinating database development as part of a team. May supervise computer programmers.

DETAILED OCCUPATIONS, BY EEO OCCUPATION GROUPS, 2006–2010—*Continued*

2010 EEO Occupation Title	2010 EEO Occupation Code	2010 SOC Code(s)	EEO Occupation Group (14)	2010 SOC Code	2010 SOC Occupation Title	SOC Definition
\multicolumn{7}{c}{**Science, Engineering, and Computer Professionals**—*Continued*}
Software developers, applications and systems software—Continued	1020	15-113X Combines: 15-1132 15-1133	2	15-1133	Software developers, systems software	Research, design, develop, and test operating systems-level software, compilers, and network distribution software for medical, industrial, military, communications, aerospace, business, scientific, and general computing applications. Set operational specifications and formulate and analyze software requirements. May design embedded systems software. Apply principles and techniques of computer science, engineering, and mathematical analysis.
Web developers	1030	15-1134	2	15-1134	Web developers	Design, create, and modify Web sites. Analyze user needs to implement Web site content, graphics, performance, and capacity. May integrate Web sites with other computer applications. May convert written, graphic, audio, and video components to compatible Web formats by using software designed to facilitate the creation of Web and multimedia content. Excludes "Multimedia artists and animators" (27-1014).
Computer support specialists	1050	15-1150	2	15-1151	Computer user support specialists	Provide technical assistance to computer users. Answer questions or resolve computer problems for clients in person, or via telephone or electronically. May provide assistance concerning the use of computer hardware and software, including printing, installation, word processing, electronic mail, and operating systems. Excludes "Network and Computer Systems Administrators" (15-1142).
				15-1152	Computer network support specialists	Analyze, test, troubleshoot, and evaluate existing network systems, such as local area network (LAN), wide area network (WAN), and Internet systems or a segment of a network system. Perform network maintenance to ensure networks operate correctly with minimal interruption. Excludes "Network and computer systems administrators" (15-1142) and "Computer network architects" (15-1143).
Database administrators	1060	15-1141	2	15-1141	Database administrators	Administer, test, and implement computer databases, applying knowledge of database management systems. Coordinate changes to computer databases. May plan, coordinate, and implement security measures to safeguard computer databases. Excludes "Information security analysts" (15-1122).
Network and computer systems administrators	1105	15-1142	2	15-1142	Network and computer systems administrators	Install, configure, and support an organization's local area network (LAN), wide area network (WAN), and Internet systems or a segment of a network system. Monitor network to ensure network availability to all system users and may perform necessary maintenance to support network availability. May monitor and test Web site performance to ensure Web sites operate correctly and without interruption. May assist in network modeling, analysis, planning, and coordination between network and data communications hardware and software. May supervise computer user support specialists and computer network support specialists. May administer network security measures. Excludes "Information security analysts"(15-1122), "Computer user support specialists" (15-1151), and "Computer network support specialists" (15-1152).

DETAILED OCCUPATIONS, BY EEO OCCUPATION GROUPS, 2006–2010—*Continued*

2010 EEO Occupation Title	2010 EEO Occupation Code	2010 SOC Code(s)	EEO Occupation Group (14)	2010 SOC Code	2010 SOC Occupation Title	SOC Definition
\multicolumn{7}{c}{**Science, Engineering, and Computer Professionals**—*Continued*}
Computer network architects	1106	15-1143	2	15-1143	Computer network architects	Design and implement computer and information networks, such as local area networks (LAN), wide area networks (WAN), intranets, extranets, and other data communications networks. Perform network modeling, analysis, and planning. May also design network and computer security measures. May research and recommend network and data communications hardware and software. Excludes "Information security analysts" (15-1122), "Network and computer systems administrators" (15-1142), and "Computer network support specialists" (15-1152).
Computer occupations, all other	1107	15-1199	2	15-1199	Computer occupations, all other	All computer occupations not listed separately. Excludes "Computer and information systems managers" (11-3021), "Computer hardware engineers" (17-2061), "Electrical and electronics engineers" (17-2070), "Computer science teachers, postsecondary" (25-1021), "Multimedia artists and animators" (27-1014), "Graphic designers" (27-1024), "Computer operators" (43-9011), and "Computer, automated teller, and Office machine repairs" (49-2011).
Actuaries	1200	15-2011	2	15-2011	Actuaries	Analyze statistical data, such as mortality, accident, sickness, disability, and retirement rates and construct probability tables to forecast risk and liability for payment of future benefits. May ascertain insurance rates required and cash reserves necessary to ensure payment of future benefits.
Operations research analysts	1220	15-2031	2	15-2031	Operations research analysts	Formulate and apply mathematical modeling and other optimizing methods to develop and interpret information that assists management with decision making, policy formulation, or other managerial functions. May collect and analyze data and develop decision support software, service, or products. May develop and supply optimal time, cost, or logistics networks for program evaluation, review, or implementation.
Miscellaneous mathematical science occupations, including mathematicians and statisticians	1240	15-20XX Combines: 15-2021 15-2041 15-2090	2	15-2021	Mathematicians	Conduct research in fundamental mathematics or in application of mathematical techniques to science, management, and other fields. Solve problems in various fields using mathematical methods.
				15-2041	Statisticians	Develop or apply mathematical or statistical theory and methods to collect, organize, interpret, and summarize numerical data to provide usable information. May specialize in fields such as bio-statistics, agricultural statistics, business statistics, or economic statistics. Includes mathematical and survey statisticians. Excludes "Survey researchers" (19-3022).
				15-2091	Mathematical technicians	Apply standardized mathematical formulas, principles, and methodology to technological problems in engineering and physical sciences in relation to specific industrial and research objectives, processes, equipment, and products.
				15-2099	Mathematical science occupations, all other	All mathematical scientists not listed separately.

APPENDIX B

DETAILED OCCUPATIONS, BY EEO OCCUPATION GROUPS, 2006–2010—*Continued*

2010 EEO Occupation Title	2010 EEO Occupation Code	2010 SOC Code(s)	EEO Occupation Group (14)	2010 SOC Code	2010 SOC Occcupation Title	SOC Definition
\multicolumn{7}{c}{**Science, Engineering, and Computer Professionals**—*Continued*}
Architects, except naval	1300	17-1010	2	17-1011	Architects, except landscape and naval	Plan and design structures, such as private residences, office buildings, theaters, factories, and other structural property. Excludes "Landscape architects" (17-1012) and "Marine engineers and naval architects" (17-2121).
				17-1012	Landscape architects	Plan and design land areas for projects such as parks and other recreational facilities, airports, highways, hospitals, schools, land subdivisions, and commercial, industrial, and residential sites.
Surveyors, cartographers, and photogrammetrists	1310	17-1020	2	17-1021	Cartographers and photogrammetrists	Collect, analyze, and interpret geographic information provided by geodetic surveys, aerial photographs, and satellite data. Research, study, and prepare maps and other spatial data in digital or graphic form for legal, social, political, educational, and design purposes. May work with Geographic Information Systems (GIS). May design and evaluate algorithms, data structures, and user interfaces for GIS and mapping systems.
				17-1022	Surveyors	Make exact measurements and determine property boundaries. Provide data relevant to the shape, contour, gravitation, location, elevation, or dimension of land or land features on or near the earth's surface for engineering, mapmaking, mining, land evaluation, construction, and other purposes.
Aerospace engineers	1320	17-2011	2	17-2011	Aerospace engineers	Perform engineering duties in designing, constructing, and testing aircraft, missiles, and spacecraft. May conduct basic and applied research to evaluate adaptability of materials and equipment to aircraft design and manufacture. May recommend improvements in testing equipment and techniques.
Biomedical and agricultural engineers	1340	17-20XX Combines: 17-2021 17-2031	2	17-2021	Agricultural engineers	Apply knowledge of engineering technology and biological science to agricultural problems concerned with power and machinery, electrification, structures, soil and water conservation, and processing of agricultural products.
				17-2031	Biomedical engineers	Apply knowledge of engineering, biology, and biomechanical principles to the design, development, and evaluation of biological and health systems and products, such as artificial organs, prostheses, instrumentation, medical information systems, and health management and care delivery systems.
Chemical engineers	1350	17-2041	2	17-2041	Chemical engineers	Design chemical plant equipment and devise processes for manufacturing chemicals and products, such as gasoline, synthetic rubber, plastics, detergents, cement, paper, and pulp, by applying principles and technology of chemistry, physics, and engineering.
Civil engineers	1360	17-2051	2	17-2051	Civil engineers	Perform engineering duties in planning, designing, and overseeing construction and maintenance of building structures, and facilities, such as roads, railroads, airports, bridges, harbors, channels, dams, irrigation projects, pipelines, power plants, and water and sewage systems. Includes architectural, structural, traffic, ocean, and geo-technical engineers. Excludes "Hydrologists" (19-2043).
Computer hardware engineers	1400	17-2061	2	17-2061	Computer hardware engineers	Research, design, develop, or test computer or computer-related equipment for commercial, industrial, military, or scientific use. May supervise the manufacturing and installation of computer or computer-related equipment and components. Excludes "Software developers, applications" (15-1132) and "Software developers, systems software (15-1133).

DETAILED OCCUPATIONS, BY EEO OCCUPATION GROUPS, 2006–2010—*Continued*

2010 EEO Occupation Title	2010 EEO Occupation Code	2010 SOC Code(s)	EEO Occupation Group (14)	2010 SOC Code	2010 SOC Occcupation Title	SOC Definition
\multicolumn{7}{c}{**Science, Engineering, and Computer Professionals**—*Continued*}
Electrical and electronics engineers	1410	17-2070	2	17-2071	Electrical engineers	Research, design, develop, test, or supervise the manufacturing and installation of electrical equipment, components, or systems for commercial, industrial, military, or scientific use. Excludes "Computer Hardware Engineers" (17-2061).
				17-2072	Electronics engineers, except computer	Research, design, develop, or test electronic components and systems for commercial, industrial, military, or scientific use employing knowledge of electronic theory and materials properties. Design electronic circuits and components for use in fields such as telecommunications, aerospace guidance and propulsion control, acoustics, or instruments and controls. Excludes "Computer hardware engineers" (17-2061).
Environmental engineers	1420	17-2081	2	17-2081	Environmental engineers	Research, design, plan, or perform engineering duties in the prevention, control, and remediation of environmental hazards using various engineering disciplines. Work may include waste treatment, site remediation, or pollution control technology.
Industrial engineers, including health and safety	1430	17-2110	2	17-2111	Health and safety engineers, except mining safety engineers and inspectors	Promote worksite or product safety by applying knowledge of industrial processes, mechanics, chemistry, psychology, and industrial health and safety laws. Includes industrial product safety engineers.
				17-2112	Industrial engineers	Design, develop, test, and evaluate integrated systems for managing industrial production processes, including human work factors, quality control, inventory control, logistics and material flow, cost analysis, and production coordination. Excludes "Health and safety engineers, except Mining safety engineers and inspectors" (17-2111).
Marine engineers and naval architects	1440	17-2121	2	17-2121	Marine engineers and naval architects	Design, develop, and evaluate the operation of marine vessels, ship machinery, and related equipment, such as power supply and propulsion systems.
Materials engineers	1450	17-2131	2	17-2131	Materials engineers	Evaluate materials and develop machinery and processes to manufacture materials for use in products that must meet specialized design and performance specifications. Develop new uses for known materials. Includes those engineers working with composite materials or specializing in one type of material, such as graphite, metal and metal alloys, ceramics and glass, plastics and polymers, and naturally occurring materials. Includes metallurgists and metallurgical engineers, ceramic engineers, and welding engineers.
Mechanical engineers	1460	17-2141	2	17-2141	Mechanical engineers	Perform engineering duties in planning and designing tools, engines, machines, and other mechanically functioning equipment. Oversee installation, operation, maintenance, and repair of equipment such as centralized heat, gas, water, and steam systems.
Petroleum, mining and geological engineers, including mining safety engineers	1520	17-21XX Combines: 17-2151 17-2171	2	17-2151	Mining and geological engineers, including mining safety engineers	Conduct sub-surface surveys to identify the characteristics of potential land or mining development sites. May specify the ground support systems, processes and equipment for safe, economical, and environmentally sound extraction or underground construction activities. May inspect areas for unsafe geological conditions, equipment, and working conditions. May design, implement, and coordinate mine safety programs. Excludes "Petroleum engineers" (17-2171).

DETAILED OCCUPATIONS, BY EEO OCCUPATION GROUPS, 2006–2010—*Continued*

2010 EEO Occupation Title	2010 EEO Occupation Code	2010 SOC Code(s)	EEO Occupation Group (14)	2010 SOC Code	2010 SOC Occupation Title	SOC Definition
Science, Engineering, and Computer Professionals—*Continued*						
Petroleum, mining and geological engineers, including mining safety engineers—Continued	1520	17-21XX Combines: 17-2151 17-2171	2	17-2171	Petroleum engineers	Devise methods to improve oil and gas extraction and production and determine the need for new or modified tool designs. Oversee drilling and offer technical advice.
Miscellaneous engineers, including nuclear engineers	1530	17-21YY Combines: 17-2161 17-2199	2	17-2161	Nuclear engineers	Conduct research on nuclear engineering projects or apply principles and theory of nuclear science to problems concerned with release, control, and use of nuclear energy and nuclear waste disposal.
				17-2199	Engineers, all other	All engineers not listed separately.
Agricultural and food scientists	1600	19-1010	2	19-1011	Animal scientists	Conduct research in the genetics, nutrition, reproduction, growth, and development of domestic farm animals.
				19-1012	Food scientists and technologists	Use chemistry, microbiology, engineering, and other sciences to study the principles underlying the processing and deterioration of foods; analyze food content to determine levels of vitamins, fat, sugar, and protein; discover new food sources; research ways to make processed foods safe, palatable, and healthful; and apply food science knowledge to determine best ways to process, package, preserve, store, and distribute food.
				19-1013	Soil and plant scientists	Conduct research in breeding, physiology, production, yield, and management of crops and agricultural plants or trees, shrubs, and nursery stock, their growth in soils, and control of pests; or study the chemical, physical, biological, and mineralogical composition of soils as they relate to plant or crop growth. May classify and map soils and investigate effects of alternative practices on soil and crop productivity.
Biological scientists	1610	19-1020	2	19-1021	Biochemists and biophysicists	Study the chemical composition or physical principles of living cells and organisms, their electrical and mechanical energy, and related phenomena. May conduct research to further understanding of the complex chemical combinations and reactions involved in metabolism, reproduction, growth, and heredity. May determine the effects of foods, drugs, serums, hormones, and other substances on tissues and vital processes of living organisms.
				19-1022	Microbiologists	Investigate the growth, structure, development, and other characteristics of microscopic organisms, such as bacteria, algae, or fungi. Includes medical microbiologists who study the relationship between organisms and disease or the effects of antibiotics on microorganisms.
				19-1023	Zoologists and wildlife biologists	Study the origins, behavior, diseases, genetics, and life processes of animals and wildlife. May specialize in wildlife research and management. May collect and analyze biological data to determine the environmental effects of present and potential use of land and water habitats.
				19-1029	Biological scientists, all other	All biological scientists not listed separately.
Conservation scientists and foresters	1640	19-1030	2	19-1031	Conservation scientists	Manage, improve, and protect natural resources to maximize their use without damaging the environment. May conduct soil surveys and develop plans to eliminate soil erosion or to protect rangelands. May instruct farmers, agricultural production managers, or ranchers in best ways to use crop rotation, contour plowing, or terracing to conserve soil and water; in the number and kind of livestock and forage plants best suited to particular ranges; and in range and farm improvements, such as fencing and reservoirs for stock watering. Excludes "Zoologists and Wildlife biologists" (19-1023) and "Foresters" (19-1032).

APPENDIX B — 493

DETAILED OCCUPATIONS, BY EEO OCCUPATION GROUPS, 2006–2010—*Continued*

2010 EEO Occupation Title	2010 EEO Occupation Code	2010 SOC Code(s)	EEO Occupation Group (14)	2010 SOC Code	2010 SOC Occcupation Title	SOC Definition
Science, Engineering, and Computer Professionals—*Continued*							
Conservation scientists and foresters—Continued	1640	19-1030	2	19-1032	Foresters	Manage public and private forested lands for economic, recreational, and conservation purposes. May inventory the type, amount, and location of standing timber, appraise the timber's worth, negotiate the purchase, and draw up contracts for procurement. May determine how to conserve wildlife habitats, creek beds, water quality, and soil stability, and how best to comply with environmental regulations. May devise plans for planting and growing new trees, monitor trees for healthy growth, and determine optimal harvesting schedules.
Medical scientists, and life scientists, all other	1650	19-10XX Combines: 19-1040 19-1099	2	19-1041	Epidemiologists	Investigate and describe the determinants and distribution of disease, disability, or health outcomes. May develop the means for prevention and control.
				19-1042	Medical scientists, except epidemiologists	Conduct research dealing with the understanding of human diseases and the improvement of human health. Engage in clinical investigation, research and development, or other related activities. Includes physicians, dentists, public health specialists, pharmacologists, and medical pathologists who primarily conduct research. practitioners who primarily provide medical or dental care or dispense drugs are included in "Health diagnosing and treating practitioners" (29-1000).
				19-1099	Life scientists, all other	All life scientists not listed separately.
Astronomers and physicists	1700	19-2010	2	19-2011	Astronomers	Observe, research, and interpret astronomical phenomena to increase basic knowledge or apply such information to practical problems.
				19-2012	Physicists	Conduct research into physical phenomena, develop theories on the basis of observation and experiments, and devise methods to apply physical laws and theories. Excludes "Biochemists and Biophysicists" (19-1021).
Atmospheric and space scientists	1710	19-2021	2	19-2021	Atmospheric and space scientists	Investigate atmospheric phenomena and interpret meteorological data, gathered by surface and air stations, satellites, and radar to prepare reports and forecasts for public and other uses. Includes weather analysts and forecasters whose functions require the detailed knowledge of meteorology.
Chemists and materials scientists	1720	19-2030	2	19-2031	Chemists	Conduct qualitative and quantitative chemical analyses or experiments in laboratories for quality or process control or to develop new products or knowledge. Excludes "Geoscientists, except Hydrologists and Geographers" (19-2042) and "Biochemists and Biophysicists" (19-1021).
				19-2032	Materials scientists	Research and study the structures and chemical properties of various natural and synthetic or composite materials, including metals, alloys, rubber, ceramics, semiconductors, polymers, and glass. Determine ways to strengthen or combine materials or develop new materials with new or specific properties for use in a variety of products and applications. Includes glass scientists, ceramic scientists, metallurgical scientists, and polymer scientists.

DETAILED OCCUPATIONS, BY EEO OCCUPATION GROUPS, 2006–2010—*Continued*

2010 EEO Occupation Title	2010 EEO Occupation Code	2010 SOC Code(s)	EEO Occupation Group (14)	2010 SOC Code	2010 SOC Occcupation Title	SOC Definition
\multicolumn{7}{c}{**Science, Engineering, and Computer Professionals**—*Continued*}
Environmental scientists and geoscientists	1740	19-2040	2	19-2041	Environmental scientists and specialists, including health	Conduct research or perform investigation for the purpose of identifying, abating, or eliminating sources of pollutants or hazards that affect either the environment or the health of the population. Using knowledge of various scientific disciplines, may collect, synthesize, study, report, and recommend action based on data derived from measurements or observations of air, food, soil, water, and other sources. Excludes "Zoologists and Wildlife biologists" (19-1023), "Conservation scientists" (19-1031), "Forest and conservation technicians" (19-4093), "Fish and game wardens" (33-3031), and "Forest and conservation workers" (45-4011).
				19-2042	Geoscientists, except hydrologists and geographers	Study the composition, structure, and other physical aspects of the Earth. May use geological, physics, and mathematics knowledge in exploration for oil, gas, minerals, or underground water; or in waste disposal, land reclamation, or other environmental problems. May study the Earth's internal composition, atmospheres, oceans, and its magnetic, electrical, and gravitational forces. Includes mineralogists, crystallographers, paleontologists, stratigraphers, geodesists, and seismologists.
				19-2043	Hydrologists	Research the distribution, circulation, and physical properties of underground and surface waters; and study the form and intensity of precipitation, its rate of infiltration into the soil, movement through the earth, and its return to the ocean and atmosphere.
Physical scientists, all other	1760	19-2099	2	19-2099	Physical scientists, all other	All physical scientists not listed separately.
Sales engineers	4930	41-9031	2	41-9031	sales engineers	Sell business goods or services, the selling of which requires a technical background equivalent to a baccalaureate degree in engineering. Excludes "Engineers" (17-2011 through 17-2199) whose primary function is not marketing or sales.
Aircraft pilots and flight engineers	9030	53-2010	2	53-2011	Airline pilots, copilots, and flight engineers	Pilot and navigate the flight of fixed-wing, multi-engine aircraft, usually on scheduled air carrier routes, for the transport of passengers and cargo. Requires Federal Air Transport certificate and rating for specific aircraft type used. Includes regional, national, and international airline pilots and flight instructors of airline pilots.
				53-2012	Commercial pilots	Pilot and navigate the flight of fixed-wing aircraft on nonscheduled air carrier routes, or helicopters. Requires Commercial Pilot certificate. Includes charter pilots with similar certification, and air ambulance and air tour pilots. Excludes regional, national, and international airline pilots.
\multicolumn{7}{c}{**Health Care Practitioner Professionals**}
Chiropractors	3000	29-1011	3	29-1011	Chiropractors	Assess, treat, and care for patients by manipulation of spine and musculoskeletal system. May provide spinal adjustment or address sacral or pelvic misalignment.
Dentists	3010	29-1020	3	29-1021	Dentists, general	Examine, diagnose, and treat diseases, injuries, and malformations of teeth and gums. May treat diseases of nerve, pulp, and other dental tissues affecting oral hygiene and retention of teeth. May fit dental appliances or provide preventive care. Excludes "Prosthodontists" (29-1024), "Orthodontists" (29-1023), "Oral and maxillofacial surgeons" (29-1022) and "Dentists, all other specialists" (29-1029).

DETAILED OCCUPATIONS, BY EEO OCCUPATION GROUPS, 2006–2010—*Continued*

2010 EEO Occupation Title	2010 EEO Occupation Code	2010 SOC Code(s)	EEO Occupation Group (14)	2010 SOC Code	2010 SOC Occcupation Title	SOC Definition
\multicolumn{7}{c}{**Health Care Practitioner Professionals**—*Continued*}
Dentists—Continued	3010	29-1020	3	29-1022	Oral and maxillofacial surgeons	Perform surgery and related procedures on the hard and soft tissues of the oral and maxillofacial regions to treat diseases, injuries, or defects. May diagnose problems of the oral and maxillofacial regions. May perform surgery to improve function or appearance.
				29-1023	Orthodontists	Examine, diagnose, and treat dental malocclusions and oral cavity anomalies. Design and fabricate appliances to realign teeth and jaws to produce and maintain normal function and to improve appearance.
				29-1024	Prosthodontists	Construct oral prostheses to replace missing teeth and other oral structures to correct natural and acquired deformation of mouth and jaws, to restore and maintain oral function, such as chewing and speaking, and to improve appearance.
				29-1029	Dentists, all other specialists	All dentists not listed separately.
Dietitians and nutritionists	3030	29-1031	3	29-1031	Dietitians and nutritionists	Plan and conduct food service or nutritional programs to assist in the promotion of health and control of disease. May supervise activities of a department providing quantity food services, counsel individuals, or conduct nutritional research.
Optometrists	3040	29-1041	3	29-1041	Optometrists	Diagnose, manage, and treat conditions and diseases of the human eye and visual system. Examine eyes and visual system, diagnose problems or impairments, prescribe corrective lenses, and provide treatment. May prescribe therapeutic drugs to treat specific eye conditions. Ophthalmologists are included in "Physicians and surgeons, all other" (29-1069).
Pharmacists	3050	29-1051	3	29-1051	Pharmacists	Dispense drugs prescribed by physicians and other health practitioners and provide information to patients about medications and their use. May advise physicians and other health practitioners on the selection, dosage, interactions, and side effects of medications.
Physicians and surgeons	3060	29-1060	3	29-1061	Anesthesiologists	Physicians who administer anesthetics prior to, during, or after surgery, or other medical procedures.
				29-1062	Family and general practitioners	Physicians who diagnose, treat, and help prevent diseases and injuries that commonly occur in the general population. May refer patients to specialists when needed for further diagnosis or treatment.
				29-1063	Internists, general	Physicians who diagnose and provide non-surgical treatment of diseases and injuries of internal organ systems. Provide care mainly for adults who have a wide range of problems associated with the internal organs. Subspecialists, such as cardiologists and gastroenterologists, are included in "Physicians and Surgeons, all other" (29-1069).
				29-1064	Obstetricians and gynecologists	Physicians who provide medical care related to pregnancy or childbirth and those who diagnose, treat, and help prevent diseases of women, particularly those affecting the reproductive system. May also provide general medical care to women.
				29-1065	Pediatricians, general	Physicians who diagnose, treat, and help prevent children's diseases and injuries.
				29-1066	Psychiatrists	Physicians who diagnose, treat, and help prevent disorders of the mind.

DETAILED OCCUPATIONS, BY EEO OCCUPATION GROUPS, 2006–2010—*Continued*

2010 EEO Occupation Title	2010 EEO Occupation Code	2010 SOC Code(s)	EEO Occupation Group (14)	2010 SOC Code	2010 SOC Occupation Title	SOC Definition
\multicolumn{7}{c}{**Health Care Practitioner Professionals**—*Continued*}
Physicians and surgeons—Continued	3060	29-1060	3	29-1067	Surgeons	Physicians who treat diseases, injuries, and deformities by invasive, minimally-invasive, or non-invasive surgical methods, such as using instruments, appliances, or by manual manipulation. Excludes "Oral and maxillofacial surgeons" (29-1022).
				29-1069	Physicians and surgeons, all other	All physicians and surgeons not listed separately.
Physician assistants	3110	29-1071	3	29-1071	Physician assistants	Provide health care services typically performed by a physician, under the supervision of a physician. Conduct complete physicals, provide treatment, and counsel patients. May, in some cases, prescribe medication. Must graduate from an accredited educational program for physician assistants. Excludes "Emergency medical technicians and paramedics" (29-2041), "Medical assistants" (31-9092), "Registered nurses" (29-1141), "Nurse anesthetists" (29-1151), "Nurse midwives" (29-1161), and "Nurse practitioners" (29-1171).
Podiatrists	3120	29-1081	3	29-1081	Podiatrists	Diagnose and treat diseases and deformities of the human foot.
Audiologists	3140	29-1181	3	29-1181	Audiologists	Assess and treat persons with hearing and related disorders. May fit hearing aids and provide auditory training. May perform research related to hearing problems.
Occupational therapists	3150	29-1122	3	29-1122	Occupational therapists	Assess, plan, organize, and participate in rehabilitative programs that help build or restore vocational, homemaking, and daily living skills, as well as general independence, to persons with disabilities or developmental delays.
Physical therapists	3160	29-1123	3	29-1123	Physical therapists	Assess, plan, organize, and participate in rehabilitative programs that improve mobility, relieve pain, increase strength, and improve or correct disabling conditions resulting from disease or injury.
Radiation therapists	3200	29-1124	3	29-1124	Radiation therapists	Provide radiation therapy to patients as prescribed by a radiologist according to established practices and standards. Duties may include reviewing prescription and diagnosis; acting as liaison with physician and supportive care personnel; preparing equipment, such as immobilization, treatment, and protection devices; and maintaining records, reports, and files. May assist in dosimetry procedures and tumor localization.
Recreational therapists	3210	29-1125	3	29-1125	Recreational therapists	Plan, direct, or coordinate medically-approved recreation programs for patients in hospitals, nursing homes, or other institutions. Activities include sports, trips, dramatics, social activities, and arts and crafts. May assess a patient condition and recommend appropriate recreational activity. Excludes "Recreation workers" (39-9032).
Respiratory therapists	3220	29-1126	3	29-1126	Respiratory therapists	Assess, treat, and care for patients with breathing disorders. Assume primary responsibility for all respiratory care modalities, including the supervision of respiratory therapy technicians. Initiate and conduct therapeutic procedures; maintain patient records; and select, assemble, check, and operate equipment.
Speech-language pathologists	3230	29-1127	3	29-1127	Speech-language pathologists	Assess and treat persons with speech, language, voice, and fluency disorders. May select alternative communication systems and teach their use. May perform research related to speech and language problems.

DETAILED OCCUPATIONS, BY EEO OCCUPATION GROUPS, 2006–2010—*Continued*

2010 EEO Occupation Title	2010 EEO Occupation Code	2010 SOC Code(s)	EEO Occupation Group (14)	2010 SOC Code	2010 SOC Occupation Title	SOC Definition
Health Care Practitioner Professionals—*Continued*							
Other therapists, including exercise physiologists	3245	29-112X Combines: 29-1128 29-1129	3	29-1128	Exercise physiologists	Assess, plan, or implement fitness programs that include exercise or physical activities such as those designed to improve cardiorespiratory function, body composition, muscular strength, muscular endurance, or flexibility. Excludes "Physical therapists" (29-1123), "Athletic trainers" (29-9091), and "Fitness trainers and Aerobic instructors" (39-9031).
				29-1129	Therapists, all other	All therapists not listed separately.
Veterinarians	3250	29-1131	3	29-1131	Veterinarians	Diagnose, treat, or research diseases and injuries of animals. Includes veterinarians who conduct research and development, inspect livestock, or care for pets and companion animals.
Registered nurses	3255	29-1141	3	29-1141	Registered nurses	Assess patient health problems and needs, develop and implement nursing care plans, and maintain medical records. Administer nursing care to ill, injured, convalescent, or disabled patients. May advise patients on health maintenance and disease prevention or provide case management. Licensing or registration required. Includes Clinical Nurse specialists. Excludes "Nurse anesthetists" (29-1151), "Nurse midwives" (29-1161), and "Nurse practitioners" (29-1171).
Nurse anesthetists	3256	29-1151	3	29-1151	Nurse anesthetists	Administer anesthesia, monitor patient's vital signs, and oversee patient recovery from anesthesia. May assist anesthesiologists, surgeons, other physicians, or dentists. Must be registered nurses who have specialized graduate education.
Nurse practitioners and nurse midwives	3258	29-11XX Combines: 29-1161 29-1171	3	29-1161	Nurse midwives	Diagnose and coordinate all aspects of the birthing process, either independently or as part of a health care team. May provide well-woman gynecological care. Must have specialized, graduate nursing education.
				29-1171	Nurse practitioners	Diagnose and treat acute, episodic, or chronic illness, independently or as part of a health care team. May focus on health promotion and disease prevention. May order, perform, or interpret diagnostic tests such as lab work and x-rays. May prescribe medication. Must be registered nurses who have specialized graduate education.
Health diagnosing and treating practitioners, all other	3260	29-1199	3	29-1199	Health diagnosing and treating practitioners, all other	All health diagnosing and treating practitioners not listed separately.
Other Professional Workers							
Human resources workers	0630	13-1070	4	13-1071	Human resources specialists	Perform activities in the human resource area. Includes employment specialists who screen, recruit, interview, and place workers. Excludes "Compensation, benefits, and job analysis specialists" (13-1141) and "Training and development specialists" (13-1151).
				13-1074	Farm labor contractors	Recruit and hire seasonal or temporary agricultural laborers. May transport, house, and provide meals for workers.
				13-1075	Labor relations specialists	Resolve disputes between workers and managers, negotiate collective bargaining agreements, or coordinate grievance procedures to handle employee complaints. Excludes equal employment opportunity (EEO) officers who are included in "Compliance officers" (13-1041).

DETAILED OCCUPATIONS, BY EEO OCCUPATION GROUPS, 2006–2010—*Continued*

2010 EEO Occupation Title	2010 EEO Occupation Code	2010 SOC Code(s)	EEO Occupation Group (14)	2010 SOC Code	2010 SOC Occcupation Title	SOC Definition
\multicolumn{7}{c}{Other Professional Workers—*Continued*}
Accountants and auditors	0800	13-2011	4	13-2011	Accountants and auditors	Examine, analyze, and interpret accounting records to prepare financial statements, give advice, or audit and evaluate statements prepared by others. Install or advise on systems of recording costs or other financial and budgetary data. Excludes "Tax examiners and collectors, and Revenue agents" (13-2081).
Economists	1800	19-3011	4	19-3011	Economists	Conduct research, prepare reports, or formulate plans to address economic problems related to the production and distribution of goods and services or monetary and fiscal policy. May collect and process economic and statistical data using sampling techniques and econometric methods. Excludes "Market research analysts and Marketing specialists" (13-1161).
Psychologists	1820	19-3030	4	19-3031	Clinical, counseling, and school psychologists	Diagnose and treat mental disorders; learning disabilities; and cognitive, behavioral, and emotional problems, using individual, child, family, and group therapies. May design and implement behavior modification programs.
				19-3032	Industrial-organizational psychologists	Apply principles of psychology to human resources, administration, management, sales, and marketing problems. Activities may include policy planning; employee testing and selection, training and development; and organizational development and analysis. May work with management to organize the work setting to improve worker productivity.
				19-3039	Psychologists, all other	All psychologists not listed separately.
Urban and regional planners	1840	19-3051	4	19-3051	Urban and regional planners	Develop comprehensive plans and programs for use of land and physical facilities of jurisdictions, such as towns, cities, counties, and metropolitan areas.
Miscellaneous social scientists, including survey researchers and sociologists	1860	19-30XX Combines: 19-3022 19-3041 19-3090	4	19-3022	Survey researchers	Plan, develop, or conduct surveys. May analyze and interpret the meaning of survey data, determine survey objectives, or suggest or test question wording. Includes social scientists who primarily design questionnaires or supervise survey teams. Excludes "Market research analysts and Marketing specialists" (13-1161) and "Statisticians" (15-2041).
				19-3041	Sociologists	Study human society and social behavior by examining the groups and social institutions that people form, as well as various social, religious, political, and business organizations. May study the behavior and interaction of groups, trace their origin and growth, and analyze the influence of group activities on individual members.
				19-3091	Anthropologists and archeologists	Study the origin, development, and behavior of human beings. May study the way of life, language, or physical characteristics of people in various parts of the world. May engage in systematic recovery and examination of material evidence, such as tools or pottery remaining from past human cultures, to determine the history, customs, and living habits of earlier civilizations.

DETAILED OCCUPATIONS, BY EEO OCCUPATION GROUPS, 2006–2010—*Continued*

2010 EEO Occupation Title	2010 EEO Occupation Code	2010 SOC Code(s)	EEO Occupation Group (14)	2010 SOC Code	2010 SOC Occcupation Title	SOC Definition
\multicolumn{7}{c}{*Other Professional Workers—Continued*}					
Miscellaneous social scientists, including survey researchers and sociologists—Continued	1860	19-30XX Combines: 19-3022 19-3041 19-3090	4	19-3092	Geologists'	Study the nature and use of areas of the Earth's surface, relating and interpreting interactions of physical and cultural phenomena. Conduct research on physical aspects of a region, including land forms, climates, soils, plants, and animals, and conduct research on the spatial implications of human activities within a given area, including social characteristics, economic activities, and political organization, as well as researching interdependence between regions at scales ranging from local to global.
				19-3093	Historians	Research, analyze, record, and interpret the past as recorded in sources, such as government and institutional records, newspapers and other periodicals, photographs, interviews, films, electronic media, and unpublished manuscripts, such as personal diaries and letters.
				19-3094	Political scientists	Study the origin, development, and operation of political systems. May study topics, such as public opinion, political decision-making, and ideology. May analyze the structure and operation of governments, as well as various political entities. May conduct public opinion surveys, analyze election results, or analyze public documents. Excludes "Survey researchers" (19-3022).
				19-3099	Social scientists and related workers, all other	All social scientists and related workers not listed separately.
Counselors	2000	21-1010	4	21-1011	Substance abuse and behavioral disorder counselors	Counsel and advise individuals with alcohol, tobacco, drug, or other problems, such as gambling and eating disorders. May counsel individuals, families, or groups or engage in prevention programs. Excludes "Social workers" (21-1021 through 21-1029), "Psychologists" (19-3031 through 19-3039), and "mental health counselors" (21-1014) providing these services.
				21-1012	Educational, guidance, school, and vocational counselors	Counsel individuals and provide group educational and vocational guidance services.
				21-1013	Marriage and family therapists	Diagnose and treat mental and emotional disorders, whether cognitive, affective, or behavioral, within the context of marriage and family systems. Apply psychotherapeutic and family systems theories and techniques in the delivery of services to individuals, couples, and families for the purpose of treating such diagnosed nervous and mental disorders. Excludes "Social workers" (21-1021 through 21-1029) and "Psychologists" of all types (19-3031 through 19-3039).
				21-1014	Mental health counselors	Counsel with emphasis on prevention. Work with individuals and groups to promote optimum mental and emotional health. May help individuals deal with issues associated with addictions and substance abuse; family, parenting, and marital problems; stress management; self-esteem; and aging. Excludes "Social workers" (21-1021 through 21-1029), "Psychiatrists" (29-1066), and "Psychologists" (19-3031 through 19-3039).

DETAILED OCCUPATIONS, BY EEO OCCUPATION GROUPS, 2006–2010—*Continued*

2010 EEO Occupation Title	2010 EEO Occupation Code	2010 SOC Code(s)	EEO Occupation Group (14)	2010 SOC Code	2010 SOC Occcupation Title	SOC Definition
\multicolumn{7}{c}{**Other Professional Workers**—*Continued*}
Counselors—Continued	2000	21-1010	4	21-1015	Rehabilitation counselors	Counsel individuals to maximize the independence and employability of persons coping with personal, social, and vocational difficulties that result from birth defects, illness, disease, accidents, or the stress of daily life. Coordinate activities for residents of care and treatment facilities. Assess client needs and design and implement rehabilitation programs that may include personal and vocational counseling, training, and job placement.
				21-1019	Counselors, all other	All counselors not listed separately.
Social workers	2010	21-1020	4	21-1021	Child, family, and school social workers	Provide social services and assistance to improve the social and psychological functioning of children and their families and to maximize the family well-being and the academic functioning of children. May assist parents, arrange adoptions, and find foster homes for abandoned or abused children. In schools, they address such problems as teenage pregnancy, misbehavior, and truancy. May also advise teachers.
				21-1022	Health care social workers	Provide individuals, families, and groups with the psychosocial support needed to cope with chronic, acute, or terminal illnesses. Services include advising family care givers, providing patient education and counseling, and making referrals for other services. May also provide care and case management or interventions designed to promote health, prevent disease, and address barriers to access to health care.
				21-1023	Mental health and substance abuse social workers	Assess and treat individuals with mental, emotional, or substance abuse problems, including abuse of alcohol, tobacco, and/or other drugs. Activities may include individual and group therapy, crisis intervention, case management, client advocacy, prevention, and education.
				21-1029	Social workers, all other	All social workers not listed separately.
Probation officers and correctional treatment specialists	2015	21-1092	4	21-1092	Probation officers and correctional treatment specialists	Provide social services to assist in rehabilitation of law offenders in custody or on probation or parole. Make recommendations for actions involving formulation of rehabilitation plan and treatment of offender, including conditional release and education and employment stipulations.
Miscellaneous community and social service specialists, including health educators and community health workers	2025	21-109X Combines: 21-1091 21-1094 21-1099	4	21-1091	Health educators	Provide and manage health education programs that help individuals, families, and their communities maximize and maintain healthy lifestyles. Collect and analyze data to identify community needs prior to planning, implementing, monitoring, and evaluating programs designed to encourage healthy lifestyles, policies, and environments. May serve as resource to assist individuals, other health professionals, or the community, and may administer fiscal resources for health education programs. Excludes "Community health workers" (21-1094).

DETAILED OCCUPATIONS, BY EEO OCCUPATION GROUPS, 2006–2010—*Continued*

2010 EEO Occupation Title	2010 EEO Occupation Code	2010 SOC Code(s)	EEO Occupation Group (14)	2010 SOC Code	2010 SOC Occcupation Title	SOC Definition
Other Professional Workers—Continued							
Miscellaneous community and social service specialists, including health educators and community health workers—Continued	2025	21-109X Combines: 21-1091 21-1094 21-1099	4	21-1094	Community health workers	Assist individuals and communities to adopt healthy behaviors. Conduct outreach for medical personnel or health organizations to implement programs in the community that promote, maintain, and improve individual and community health. May provide information on available resources, provide social support and informal counseling, advocate for individuals and community health needs, and provide services such as first aid and blood pressure screening. May collect data to help identify community health needs. Excludes "Health educators" (21-1091).
				21-1099	Community and social service specialists, all other	All community and social service specialists not listed separately.
Clergy	2040	21-2011	4	21-2011	Clergy	Conduct religious worship and perform other spiritual functions associated with beliefs and practices of religious faith or denomination. Provide spiritual and moral guidance and assistance to members.
Directors, religious activities and education	2050	21-2021	4	21-2021	Directors, religious activities and education	Plan, direct, or coordinate programs designed to promote the religious education or activities of a denominational group. May provide counseling and guidance relative to marital, health, financial, and religious problems.
Religious workers, all other	2060	21-2099	4	21-2099	Religious workers, all other	All religious workers not listed separately.
Lawyers, and judges, magistrates, and other judicial workers	2100	23-10XX Combines: 23-1011 23-1020	4	23-1011	Lawyers	Represent clients in criminal and civil litigation and other legal proceedings, draw up legal documents, or manage or advise clients on legal transactions. May specialize in a single area or may practice broadly in many areas of law.
				23-1021	Administrative law judges, adjudicators, and hearing officers	Conduct hearings to recommend or make decisions on claims concerning government programs or other government-related matters. Determine liability, sanctions, or penalties, or recommend the acceptance or rejection of claims or settlements. Excludes "Arbitrators, mediators, and conciliators" (23-1022).
				23-1022	Arbitrators, mediators, and conciliators	Facilitate negotiation and conflict resolution through dialogue. Resolve conflicts outside of the court system by mutual consent of parties involved.
				23-1023	Judges, magistrate judges, and magistrates	Arbitrate, advise, adjudicate, or administer justice in a court of law. May sentence defendant in criminal cases according to government statutes or sentencing guidelines. May determine liability of defendant in civil cases. May perform wedding ceremonies.
Judicial law clerks	2105	23-1012	4	23-1012	Judicial law clerks	Assist judges in court or by conducting research or preparing legal documents. Excludes "Lawyers" (23-1011) and "Paralegals and Legal assistants" (23-2011).
Postsecondary teachers	2200	25-1000	4	25-1011	Business teachers, postsecondary	Teach courses in business administration and management, such as accounting, finance, human resources, labor and industrial relations, marketing, and operations research. Includes both teachers primarily engaged in teaching and those who do a combination of teaching and research.
				25-1021	Computer science teachers, postsecondary	Teach courses in computer science. May specialize in a field of computer science, such as the design and function of computers or operations and research analysis. Includes both teachers primarily engaged in teaching and those who do a combination of teaching and research.

DETAILED OCCUPATIONS, BY EEO OCCUPATION GROUPS, 2006–2010—*Continued*

2010 EEO Occupation Title	2010 EEO Occupation Code	2010 SOC Code(s)	EEO Occupation Group (14)	2010 SOC Code	2010 SOC Occcupation Title	SOC Definition
\multicolumn{7}{c}{Other Professional Workers—*Continued*}
Postsecondary teachers—Continued	2200	25-1000	4	25-1022	Mathematical science teachers, postsecondary	Teach courses pertaining to mathematical concepts, statistics, and actuarial science and to the application of original and standardized mathematical techniques in solving specific problems and situations. Includes both teachers primarily engaged in teaching and those who do a combination of teaching and research.
				25-1031	Architecture teachers, postsecondary	Teach courses in architecture and architectural design, such as architectural environmental design, interior architecture/design, and landscape architecture. Includes both teachers primarily engaged in teaching and those who do a combination of teaching and research.
				25-1032	Engineering teachers, postsecondary	Teach courses pertaining to the application of physical laws and principles of engineering for the development of machines, materials, instruments, processes, and services. Includes teachers of subjects such as chemical, civil, electrical, industrial, mechanical, mineral, and petroleum engineering. Includes both teachers primarily engaged in teaching and those who do a combination of teaching and research. Excludes "Computer science teachers, postsecondary" (25-1021)
				25-1041	Agricultural sciences teachers, postsecondary	Teach courses in the agricultural sciences. Includes teachers of agronomy, dairy sciences, fisheries management, horticultural sciences, poultry sciences, range management, and agricultural soil conservation. Includes both teachers primarily engaged in teaching and those who do a combination of teaching and research. Excludes "Forestry and conservation science teachers, postsecondary" (25-1043).
				25-1042	Biological science teachers, postsecondary	Teach courses in biological sciences. Includes both teachers primarily engaged in teaching and those who do a combination of teaching and research.
				25-1043	Forestry and conservation science teachers, postsecondary	Teach courses in forestry and conservation science. Includes both teachers primarily engaged in teaching and those who do a combination of teaching and research. Excludes "Agricultural science teachers, postsecondary" (25-1041) and "Environmental science teachers, postsecondary" (25-1053).
				25-1051	Atmospheric, earth, marine, and space sciences teachers, postsecondary	Teach courses in the physical sciences, except chemistry and physics. Includes both teachers primarily engaged in teaching, and those who do a combination of teaching and research.
				25-1052	Chemistry teachers, postsecondary	Teach courses pertaining to the chemical and physical properties and compositional changes of substances. Work may include instruction in the methods of qualitative and quantitative chemical analysis. Includes both teachers primarily engaged in teaching, and those who do a combination of teaching and research. Excludes "Biological science teachers, postsecondary" (25-1042) who teach biochemistry.
				25-1053	Environmental science teachers, postsecondary	Teach courses in environmental science. Includes both teachers primarily engaged in teaching and those who do a combination of teaching and research.
				25-1054	Physics teachers, postsecondary	Teach courses pertaining to the laws of matter and energy. Includes both teachers primarily engaged in teaching and those who do a combination of teaching and research.
				25-1061	Anthropology and archeology teachers, postsecondary	Teach courses in anthropology or archeology. Includes both teachers primarily engaged in teaching and those who do a combination of teaching and research.

DETAILED OCCUPATIONS, BY EEO OCCUPATION GROUPS, 2006–2010—Continued

2010 EEO Occupation Title	2010 EEO Occupation Code	2010 SOC Code(s)	EEO Occupation Group (14)	2010 SOC Code	2010 SOC Occupation Title	SOC Definition
\multicolumn{7}{c}{Other Professional Workers—Continued}
Postsecondary teachers—Continued	2200	25-1000	4	25-1062	Area, ethnic, and cultural studies teachers, postsecondary	Teach courses pertaining to the culture and development of an area, an ethnic group, or any other group, such as Latin American studies, women's studies, or urban affairs. Includes both teachers primarily engaged in teaching and those who do a combination of teaching and research.
				25-1063	Economics teachers, postsecondary	Teach courses in economics. Includes both teachers primarily engaged in teaching and those who do a combination of teaching and research.
				25-1064	Geography teachers, postsecondary	Teach courses in geography. Includes both teachers primarily engaged in teaching and those who do a combination of teaching and research.
				25-1065	Political science teachers, postsecondary	Teach courses in political science, international affairs, and international relations. Includes both teachers primarily engaged in teaching and those who do a combination of teaching and research.
				25-1066	Psychology teachers, postsecondary	Teach courses in psychology, such as child, clinical, and developmental psychology, and psychological counseling. Includes both teachers primarily engaged in teaching and those who do a combination of teaching and research.
				25-1067	Sociology teachers, postsecondary	Teach courses in sociology. Includes both teachers primarily engaged in teaching and those who do a combination of teaching and research.
				25-1069	Social sciences teachers, postsecondary, all other	All postsecondary social sciences teachers not listed separately.
				25-1071	Health specialties teachers, postsecondary	Teach courses in health specialties, in fields such as dentistry, laboratory technology, medicine, pharmacy, public health, therapy, and veterinary medicine. Excludes "Nursing instructors and Teachers, postsecondary" (25-1072) and "Biological science teachers, postsecondary" (25-1042) who teach medical science.
				25-1072	Nursing instructors and teachers, postsecondary	Demonstrate and teach patient care in classroom and clinical units to nursing students. Includes both teachers primarily engaged in teaching and those who do a combination of teaching and research.
				25-1081	Education teachers, postsecondary	Teach courses pertaining to education, such as counseling, curriculum, guidance, instruction, teacher education, and teaching English as a second language. Includes both teachers primarily engaged in teaching and those who do a combination of teaching and research.
				25-1082	Library science teachers, postsecondary	Teach courses in library science. Includes both teachers primarily engaged in teaching and those who do a combination of teaching and research.
				25-1111	Criminal justice and law enforcement teachers, postsecondary	Teach courses in criminal justice, corrections, and law enforcement administration. Includes both teachers primarily engaged in teaching and those who do a combination of teaching and research.
				25-1112	Law teachers, postsecondary	Teach courses in law. Includes both teachers primarily engaged in teaching and those who do a combination of teaching and research.
				25-1113	Social work teachers, postsecondary	Teach courses in social work. Includes both teachers primarily engaged in teaching and those who do a combination of teaching and research.

DETAILED OCCUPATIONS, BY EEO OCCUPATION GROUPS, 2006–2010—*Continued*

2010 EEO Occupation Title	2010 EEO Occupation Code	2010 SOC Code(s)	EEO Occupation Group (14)	2010 SOC Code	2010 SOC Occupation Title	SOC Definition
\multicolumn{7}{c}{Other Professional Workers—*Continued*}
Postsecondary teachers—Continued	2200	25-1000	4	25-1121	Art, drama, and music teachers, postsecondary	Teach courses in drama, music, and the arts including fine and applied art, such as painting and sculpture, or design and crafts. Includes both teachers primarily engaged in teaching and those who do a combination of teaching and research.
				25-1122	Communications teachers, postsecondary	Teach courses in communications, such as organizational communications, public relations, radio/television broadcasting, and journalism. Includes both teachers primarily engaged in teaching and those who do a combination of teaching and research.
				25-1123	English language and literature teachers, postsecondary	Teach courses in English language and literature, including linguistics and comparative literature. Includes both teachers primarily engaged in teaching and those who do a combination of teaching and research.
				25-1124	Foreign language and literature teachers, postsecondary	Teach languages and literature courses in languages other than English. Includes teachers of American Sign Language (ASL). Includes both teachers primarily engaged in teaching and those who do a combination of teaching and research.
				25-1125	History teachers, postsecondary	Teach courses in human history and historiography. Includes both teachers primarily engaged in teaching and those who do a combination of teaching and research.
				25-1126	Philosophy and religion teachers, postsecondary	Teach courses in philosophy, religion, and theology. Includes both teachers primarily engaged in teaching and those who do a combination of teaching and research.
				25-1191	Graduate teaching assistants	Assist faculty or other instructional staff in postsecondary institutions by performing teaching or teaching-related duties, such as teaching lower level courses, developing teaching materials, preparing and giving examinations, and grading examinations or papers. Graduate teaching assistants must be enrolled in a graduate school program. Graduate assistants who primarily perform non-teaching duties, such as research, should be reported in the occupational category related to the work performed. Excludes "Teacher assistants" (25-9041).
				25-1192	Home economics teachers, postsecondary	Teach courses in childcare, family relations, finance, nutrition, and related subjects pertaining to home management. Includes both teachers primarily engaged in teaching and those who do a combination of teaching and research.
				25-1193	Recreation and fitness studies teachers, postsecondary	Teach courses pertaining to recreation, leisure, and fitness studies, including exercise physiology and facilities management. Includes both teachers primarily engaged in teaching and those who do a combination of teaching and research.
				25-1194	Vocational education teachers, postsecondary	Teach or instruct vocational or occupational subjects at the postsecondary level (but at less than the baccalaureate) to students who have graduated or left high school. Includes correspondence school instructors; industrial, commercial, and government training instructors; and adult education teachers and instructors who prepare persons to operate industrial machinery and equipment and transportation and communications equipment. Teaching may take place in public or private schools whose primary business is education or in a school associated with an organization whose primary business is other than education.

DETAILED OCCUPATIONS, BY EEO OCCUPATION GROUPS, 2006–2010—*Continued*

2010 EEO Occupation Title	2010 EEO Occupation Code	2010 SOC Code(s)	EEO Occupation Group (14)	2010 SOC Code	2010 SOC Occupation Title	SOC Definition
Other Professional Workers—Continued							
Postsecondary teachers—Continued	2200	25-1000	4	25-1199	Postsecondary teachers, all other	All postsecondary teachers not listed separately.
Preschool and kindergarten teachers	2300	25-2010	4	25-2011	Preschool teachers, except special education	Instruct preschool-aged children in activities designed to promote social, physical, and intellectual growth needed for primary school in preschool, day care center, or other child development facility. Substitute teachers are included in "Teachers and instructors, all other" (25-3099). May be required to hold state certification. Excludes "Childcare workers" (39-9011) and "Special education teachers" (25-2050).
				25-2012	Kindergarten teachers, except special education	Teach elemental natural and social science, personal hygiene, music, art, and literature to kindergarten students. Promote physical, mental, and social development. May be required to hold state certification. Substitute teachers are included in "Teachers and instructors, all other" (25-3099). Excludes "Special education teachers" (25-2050).
Elementary and middle school teachers	2310	25-2020	4	25-2021	Elementary school teachers, except special education	Teach students basic academic, social, and other formative skills in public or private schools at the elementary level. Substitute teachers are included in "Teachers and instructors, all other" (25-3099). Excludes "Special education teachers" (25-2050).
				25-2022	Middle school teachers, except special and career/technical education	Teach students in one or more subjects in public or private schools at the middle, intermediate, or junior high level, which falls between elementary and senior high school as defined by applicable laws and regulations. Substitute teachers are included in "Teachers and instructors, all other" (25-3099). Excludes "Career/technical education teachers, middle school" (25-2023) and "Special education teachers" (25-2050).
				25-2023	Career/technical education teachers, middle school	Teach occupational, career and technical, or vocational subjects in public or private schools at the middle, intermediate, or junior high level, which falls between elementary and senior high school as defined by applicable laws and regulations. Substitute teachers are included in "Teachers and instructors, all other" (25-3099). Excludes "Special education teachers" (25-2050).
Secondary school teachers	2320	25-2030	4	25-2031	Secondary school teachers, except special and career/technical education	Teach students in one or more subjects, such as English, mathematics, or social studies at the secondary level in public or private schools. May be designated according to subject matter specialty. Substitute teachers are included in "Teachers and instructors, all other" (25-3099). Excludes "Career/technical education teachers, secondary school" (25-2032) and "Special education teachers" (25-2050).
				25-2032	Career/technical education teachers, secondary school	Teach occupational, career and technical, or vocational subjects at the secondary school level in public or private schools. Substitute teachers are included in "Teachers and instructors, all other" (25-3099). Excludes "Special education teachers, secondary school" (25-2054).
Special education teachers	2330	25-2050	4	25-2051	Special education teachers, preschool	Teach preschool school subjects to educationally and physically handicapped students. Includes teachers who specialize and work with audibly and visually handicapped students and those who teach basic academic and life processes skills to the mentally impaired. Substitute teachers are included in "Teachers and instructors, all other" (25-3099).

DETAILED OCCUPATIONS, BY EEO OCCUPATION GROUPS, 2006–2010—*Continued*

2010 EEO Occupation Title	2010 EEO Occupation Code	2010 SOC Code(s)	EEO Occupation Group (14)	2010 SOC Code	2010 SOC Occupation Title	SOC Definition
\multicolumn{7}{c}{*Other Professional Workers—Continued*}
Special education teachers—Continued	2330	25-2050	4	25-2052	Special education teachers, kindergarten and elementary school	Teach elementary school subjects to educationally and physically handicapped students. Includes teachers who specialize and work with audibly and visually handicapped students and those who teach basic academic and life processes skills to the mentally impaired. Substitute teachers are included in "Teachers and instructors, all other" (25-3099).
				25-2053	Special education teachers, middle school	Teach middle school subjects to educationally and physically handicapped students. Includes teachers who specialize and work with audibly and visually handicapped students and those who teach basic academic and life processes skills to the mentally impaired. Substitute teachers are included in "Teachers and instructors, all other" (25-3099).
				25-2054	Special education teachers, secondary school	Teach secondary school subjects to educationally and physically handicapped students. Includes teachers who specialize and work with audibly and visually handicapped students and those who teach basic academic and life processes skills to the mentally impaired. Substitute teachers are included in "Teachers and instructors, all other" (25-3099).
				25-2059	Special education teachers, all other	All special education teachers not listed separately.
Other teachers and instructors	2340	25-3000	4	25-3011	Adult basic and secondary education and literacy teachers and instructors	Teach or instruct out-of-school youths and adults in remedial education classes, preparatory classes for the General educational Development test, literacy, or English as a Second Language. Teaching may or may not take place in a traditional educational institution.
				25-3021	Self-enrichment education teachers	Teach or instruct courses other than those that normally lead to an occupational objective or degree. Courses may include self-improvement, nonvocational, and nonacademic subjects. Teaching may or may not take place in a traditional educational institution. Excludes "Fitness trainers and aerobics instructors" (39-9031). Flight instructors are included with "Aircraft pilots and flight engineers" (53-2010).
				25-3099	Teachers and instructors, all other	All teachers and instructors not listed separately.
Archivists, curators, and museum technicians	2400	25-4010	4	25-4011	Archivists	Appraise, edit, and direct safekeeping of permanent records and historically valuable documents. Participate in research activities based on archival materials.
				25-4012	Curators	Administer collections, such as artwork, collectibles, historic items, or scientific specimens of museums or other institutions. May conduct instructional, research, or public service activities of institution.
				25-4013	Museum technicians and conservators	Restore, maintain, or prepare objects in museum collections for storage, research, or exhibit. May work with specimens such as fossils, skeletal parts, or botanicals; or artifacts, textiles, or art. May identify and record objects or install and arrange them in exhibits. Includes book or document conservators.

DETAILED OCCUPATIONS, BY EEO OCCUPATION GROUPS, 2006–2010—*Continued*

2010 EEO Occupation Title	2010 EEO Occupation Code	2010 SOC Code(s)	EEO Occupation Group (14)	2010 SOC Code	2010 SOC Occupation Title	SOC Definition
Other Professional Workers—Continued						
Librarians	2430	25-4021	4	25-4021	Librarians	Administer libraries and perform related library services. Work in a variety of settings, including public libraries, educational institutions, museums, corporations, government agencies, law firms, nonprofit organizations, and Health care providers. Tasks may include selecting, acquiring, cataloguing, classifying, circulating, and maintaining library materials; and furnishing reference, bibliographical, and readers advisory services. May perform in-depth, strategic research, and synthesize, analyze, edit, and filter information. May set up or work with databases and information systems to catalogue and access information.
Other education, training, and library workers	2550	25-90XX Combines: 25-9011 25-9021 25-9031 25-9099	4	25-9011	Audio-visual and multimedia collections specialists	Prepare, plan, and operate multimedia teaching aids for use in education. May record, catalogue, and file materials.
				25-9021	Farm and home management advisors	Advise, instruct, and assist individuals and families engaged in agriculture, agricultural-related processes, or home economics activities. Demonstrate procedures and apply research findings to solve problems; and instruct and train in product development, sales, and the use of machinery and equipment to promote general welfare. Includes county agricultural agents, feed and farm management advisers, home economists, and extension service advisors.
				25-9031	Instructional coordinators	Develop instructional material, coordinate educational content, and incorporate current technology in specialized fields that provide guidelines to educators and instructors for developing curricula and conducting courses. Includes educational consultants and specialists, and instructional material directors.
				25-9099	Education, training, and library workers, all other	All education, training, and library workers not listed separately.
Artists and related workers	2600	27-1010	4	27-1011	Art directors	Formulate design concepts and presentation approaches for visual communications media, such as print, broadcasting, and advertising. Direct workers engaged in art work or layout design.
				27-1012	Craft artists	Create or reproduce hand-made objects for sale and exhibition using a variety of techniques, such as welding, weaving, pottery, and needlecraft.
				27-1013	Fine artists, including painters, sculptors, and illustrators	Create original artwork using any of a wide variety of media and techniques.
				27-1014	Multimedia artists and animators	Create special effects, animation, or other visual images using film, video, computers, or other electronic tools and media for use in products or creations, such as computer games, movies, music videos, and commercials.
				27-1019	Artists and related workers, all other	All artists and related workers not listed separately.
Designers	2630	27-1020	4	27-1021	Commercial and industrial designers	Develop and design manufactured products, such as cars, home appliances, and children's toys. Combine artistic talent with research on product use, marketing, and materials to create the most functional and appealing product design.
				27-1022	Fashion designers	Design clothing and accessories. Create original designs or adapt fashion trends.
				27-1023	Floral designers	Design, cut, and arrange live, dried, or artificial flowers and foliage.

APPENDIX B

DETAILED OCCUPATIONS, BY EEO OCCUPATION GROUPS, 2006–2010—*Continued*

2010 EEO Occupation Title	2010 EEO Occupation Code	2010 SOC Code(s)	EEO Occupation Group (14)	2010 SOC Code	2010 SOC Occcupation Title	SOC Definition
\multicolumn{7}{c}{Other Professional Workers—*Continued*}
Designers—Continued	2630	27-1020	4	27-1024	Graphic designers	Design or create graphics to meet specific commercial or promotional needs, such as packaging, displays, or logos. May use a variety of mediums to achieve artistic or decorative effects.
				27-1025	Interior designers	Plan, design, and furnish interiors of residential, commercial, or industrial buildings. Formulate design, which is practical, aesthetic, and conducive to intended purposes, such as raising productivity, selling merchandise, or improving life style. May specialize in a particular field, style, or phase of interior design. Excludes "Merchandise displayers and Window trimmers" (27-1026).
				27-1026	Merchandise displayers and window trimmers	Plan and erect commercial displays, such as those in windows and interiors of retail stores and at trade exhibitions.
				27-1027	Set and exhibit designers	Design special exhibits and movie, television, and theater sets. May study scripts, confer with directors, and conduct research to determine appropriate architectural styles.
				27-1029	Designers, all other	All designers not listed separately.
Actors	2700	27-2011	4	27-2011	Actors	Play parts in stage, television, radio, video, motion picture productions, or other settings for entertainment, information, or instruction. Interpret serious or comic role by speech, gesture, and body movement to entertain or inform audience. May dance and sing.
Producers and directors	2710	27-2012	4	27-2012	Producers and directors	Produce or direct stage, television, radio, video, or motion picture productions for entertainment, information, or instruction. Responsible for creative decisions, such as interpretation of script, choice of actors or guests, set design, sound, special effects, and choreography.
Athletes, coaches, umpires, and related workers	2720	27-2020	4	27-2021	Athletes and sports competitors	Compete in athletic events.
				27-2022	Coaches and scouts	Instruct or coach groups or individuals in the fundamentals of sports. Demonstrate techniques and methods of participation. May evaluate athletes strengths and weaknesses as possible recruits or to improve the athletes technique to prepare them for competition. Those required to hold teaching degrees should be reported in the appropriate teaching category. Excludes "Athletic trainers" (29-9091).
				27-2023	Umpires, referees, and other sports officials	Officiate at competitive athletic or sporting events. Detect infractions of rules and decide penalties according to established regulations. Includes all sporting officials, referees, and competition judges.
Dancers and choreographers	2740	27-2030	4	27-2031	Dancers	Perform dances. May perform on stage, for on-air broadcasting, or for video recording.
				27-2032	Choreographers	Create new dance routines. Rehearse performance of routines. May direct and stage presentations.
Musicians, singers, and related workers	2750	27-2040	4	27-2041	Music directors and composers	Conduct, direct, plan, and lead instrumental or vocal performances by musical groups, such as orchestras, bands, choirs, and glee clubs. Includes arrangers, composers, choral directors, and orchestrators.
				27-2042	Musicians and singers	Play one or more musical instruments or sing. May perform on stage, for on-air broadcasting, or for sound or video recording.
Entertainers and performers, sports and related workers, all other	2760	27-2099	4	27-2099	Entertainers and performers, sports and related workers, all other	All entertainers and performers, sports and related workers not listed separately.

DETAILED OCCUPATIONS, BY EEO OCCUPATION GROUPS, 2006–2010—*Continued*

2010 EEO Occupation Title	2010 EEO Occupation Code	2010 SOC Code(s)	EEO Occupation Group (14)	2010 SOC Code	2010 SOC Occcupation Title	SOC Definition
Other Professional Workers—Continued							
Announcers	2800	27-3010	4	27-3011	Radio and television announcers	Speak or read from scripted materials, such as news reports or commercial messages, on radio or television. May announce artist or title of performance, identify station, or interview guests. Excludes "Broadcast News Analysts" (27-3021).
				27-3012	Public address system and other announcers	Make announcements over public address system at sporting or other public events. May act as master of ceremonies or disc jockey at weddings, parties, clubs, or other gathering places.
News analysts, reporters and correspondents	2810	27-3020	4	27-3021	Broadcast news analysts	Analyze, interpret, and broadcast news received from various sources.
				27-3022	Reporters and correspondents	Collect and analyze facts about newsworthy events by interview, investigation, or observation. Report and write stories for newspaper, news magazine, radio, or television. Excludes "Broadcast News Analysts" (27-3021).
Public relations specialists	2825	27-3031	4	27-3031	Public relations specialists	Engage in promoting or creating an intended public image for individuals, groups, or organizations. May write or select material for release to various communications media.
Editors	2830	27-3041	4	27-3041	Editors	Plan, coordinate, or edit content of material for publication. May review proposals and drafts for possible publication. Includes technical editors.
technical writers	2840	27-3042	4	27-3042	Technical writers	Write technical materials, such as equipment manuals, appendixes, or operating and maintenance instructions. May assist in layout work.
Writers and authors	2850	27-3043	4	27-3043	Writers and authors	Originate and prepare written material, such as scripts, stories, advertisements, and other material. Excludes "Public relations specialists" (27-3031) and "Technical Writers" (27-3042).
Miscellaneous media and communication workers	2860	27-3090	4	27-3091	Interpreters and translators	Interpret oral or sign language, or translate written text from one language into another.
				27-3099	Media and communication workers, all other	All media and communication workers not listed separately.
Photographers	2910	27-4021	4	27-4021	Photographers	Photograph people, landscapes, merchandise, or other subjects, using digital or film cameras and equipment. May develop negatives or use computer software to produce finished images and prints. Includes scientific photographers, aerial photographers, and photo journalists.
Television, video, and motion picture camera operators and editors	2920	27-4030	4	27-4031	Camera operators, television, video, and motion picture	Operate television, video, or motion picture camera to record images or scenes for various purposes, such as TV broadcasts, advertising, video production, or motion pictures.
				27-4032	Film and video editors	Edit moving images on film, video, or other media. May edit or synchronize soundtracks with images. Excludes "Sound engineering technicians" (27-4014).
Animal trainers	4340	39-2011	4	39-2011	Animal trainers	Train animals for riding, harness, security, performance, or obedience, or assisting persons with disabilities. Accustom animals to human voice and contact; and condition animals to respond to commands. Train animals according to prescribed standards for show or competition. May train animals to carry pack loads or work as part of pack team.

DETAILED OCCUPATIONS, BY EEO OCCUPATION GROUPS, 2006–2010—*Continued*

2010 EEO Occupation Title	2010 EEO Occupation Code	2010 SOC Code(s)	EEO Occupation Group (14)	2010 SOC Code	2010 SOC Occcupation Title	SOC Definition
					Technicians	
Computer programmers	1010	15-1131	5	15-1131	Computer programmers	Create, modify, and test the code, forms, and script that allow computer applications to run. Work from specifications drawn up by software developers or other individuals. May assist software developers by analyzing user needs and designing software solutions. May develop and write computer programs to store, locate, and retrieve specific documents, data, and information.
Drafters	1540	17-3010	5	17-3011	Architectural and cvil drafters	Prepare detailed drawings of architectural and structural features of buildings or drawings and topographical relief maps used in civil engineering projects, such as highways, bridges, and public works. Use knowledge of building materials, engineering practices, and mathematics to complete drawings.
				17-3012	Electrical and electronics drafters	Prepare wiring diagrams, circuit board assembly diagrams, and layout drawings used for the manufacture, installation, or repair of electrical equipment.
				17-3013	Mechanical drafters	Prepare detailed working diagrams of machinery and mechanical devices, including dimensions, fastening methods, and other engineering information.
				17-3019	Drafters, all other	All drafters not listed separately.
Engineering technicians, except drafters	1550	17-3020	5	17-3021	Aerospace engineering and operations technicians	Operate, install, calibrate, and maintain integrated computer/communications systems, consoles, simulators, and other data acquisition, test, and measurement instruments and equipment, which are used to launch, track, position, and evaluate air and space vehicles. May record and interpret test data.
				17-3022	Civil engineering technicians	Apply theory and principles of civil engineering in planning, designing, and overseeing construction and maintenance of structures and facilities under the direction of engineering staff or physical scientists.
				17-3023	Electrical and electronic engineering technicians	Apply electrical and electronic theory and related knowledge, usually under the direction of engineering staff, to design, build, repair, calibrate, and modify electrical components, circuitry, controls, and machinery for subsequent evaluation and use by engineering staff in making engineering design decisions. Excludes "Broadcast technicians" (27-4012).
				17-3024	Electro-mechanical technicians	Operate, test, maintain, or calibrate unmanned, automated, servo-mechanical, or electromechanical equipment. May operate unmanned submarines, aircraft, or other equipment at worksites, such as oil rigs, deep ocean exploration, or hazardous waste removal. May assist engineers in testing and designing robotics equipment.
				17-3025	Environmental engineering technicians	Apply theory and principles of environmental engineering to modify, test, and operate equipment and devices used in the prevention, control, and remediation of environmental problems, including waste treatment and site remediation, under the direction of engineering staff or scientist. May assist in the development of environmental remediation devices.
				17-3026	Industrial engineering technicians	Apply engineering theory and principles to problems of industrial layout or manufacturing production, usually under the direction of engineering staff. May perform time and motion studies on worker operations in a variety of industries for purposes such as establishing standard production rates or improving efficiency.

DETAILED OCCUPATIONS, BY EEO OCCUPATION GROUPS, 2006–2010—*Continued*

2010 EEO Occupation Title	2010 EEO Occupation Code	2010 SOC Code(s)	EEO Occupation Group (14)	2010 SOC Code	2010 SOC Occupation Title	SOC Definition
	*Technicians—Continued*
Engineering technicians, except drafters— Continued	1550	17-3020	5	17-3027	Mechanical engineering technicians	Apply theory and principles of mechanical engineering to modify, develop, test, or calibrate machinery and equipment under direction of engineering staff or physical scientists.
				17-3029	Engineering technicians, except drafters, all other	All engineering technicians, except drafters, not listed separately.
Surveying and mapping technicians	1560	17-3031	5	17-3031	Surveying and mapping technicians	Perform surveying and mapping duties, usually under the direction of an engineer, surveyor, cartographer, or photogrammetrist to obtain data used for construction, mapmaking, boundary location, mining, or other purposes. May calculate mapmaking information and create maps from source data, such as surveying notes, aerial photography, satellite data, or other maps to show topographical features, political boundaries, and other features. May verify accuracy and completeness of maps. Excludes "Surveyors" (17-1022), "Cartographers and Photogrammetrists" (17-1021), and "Geoscientists, except Hydrologists and Geographers" (19-2042).
Agricultural and food science technicians	1900	19-4011	5	19-4011	Agricultural and food science technicians	Work with agricultural and food scientists in food, fiber, and animal research, production, and processing; and assist with animal breeding and nutrition. Conduct tests and experiments to improve yield and quality of crops or to increase the resistance of plants and animals to disease or insects. Includes technicians who assist food scientists or technologists in the research and development of production technology, quality control, packaging, processing, and use of foods.
Biological technicians	1910	19-4021	5	19-4021	Biological technicians	Assist biological and medical scientists in laboratories. Set up, operate, and maintain laboratory instruments and equipment, monitor experiments, make observations, and calculate and record results. May analyze organic substances, such as blood, food, and drugs.
Chemical technicians	1920	19-4031	5	19-4031	Chemical technicians	Conduct chemical and physical laboratory tests to assist scientists in making qualitative and quantitative analyses of solids, liquids, and gaseous materials for research and development of new products or processes, quality control, maintenance of environmental standards, and other work involving experimental, theoretical, or practical application of chemistry and related sciences.
Geological and petroleum technicians, and nuclear technicians	1930	19-40XX Combines: 19-4041 19-4051	5	19-4041	Geological and petroleum technicians	Assist scientists or engineers in the use of electronic, sonic, or nuclear measuring instruments in both laboratory and production activities to obtain data indicating potential resources such as metallic ore, minerals, gas, coal, or petroleum. Analyze mud and drill cuttings. Chart pressure, temperature, and other characteristics of wells or bore holes. Investigate and collect information leading to the possible discovery of new metallic ore, minerals, gas, coal, or petroleum deposits.
				19-4051	Nuclear technicians	Assist nuclear physicists, nuclear engineers, or other scientists in laboratory or production activities. May operate, maintain, or provide quality control for nuclear testing and research equipment. May monitor radiation.

DETAILED OCCUPATIONS, BY EEO OCCUPATION GROUPS, 2006–2010—*Continued*

2010 EEO Occupation Title	2010 EEO Occupation Code	2010 SOC Code(s)	EEO Occupation Group (14)	2010 SOC Code	2010 SOC Occcupation Title	SOC Definition
\multicolumn{7}{c}{*Technicians—Continued*}
Miscellaneous life, physical, and social science technicians, including social science research assistants	1965	19-40YY Combines: 19-4061 19-4090	5	19-4061	Social science research assistants	Assist social scientists in laboratory, survey, and other social science research. May help prepare findings for publication and assist in laboratory analysis, quality control, or data management. Excludes "Graduate teaching assistants" (25-1191).
				19-4091	Environmental science and protection technicians, including health	Perform laboratory and field tests to monitor the environment and investigate sources of pollution, including those that affect health, under the direction of an environmental scientist, engineer, or other specialist. May collect samples of gases, soil, water, and other materials for testing.
				19-4092	Forensic science technicians	Collect, identify, classify, and analyze physical evidence related to criminal investigations. Perform tests on weapons or substances, such as fiber, hair, and tissue to determine significance to investigation. May testify as expert witnesses on evidence or crime laboratory techniques. May serve as specialists in area of expertise, such as ballistics, fingerprinting, handwriting, or biochemistry.
				19-4093	Forest and conservation technicians	Provide technical assistance regarding the conservation of soil, water, forests, or related natural resources. May compile data pertaining to size, content, condition, and other characteristics of forest tracts, under the direction of foresters; or train and lead forest workers in forest propagation, fire prevention and suppression. May assist conservation scientists in managing, improving, and protecting rangelands and wildlife habitats. Excludes "Conservation Scientists" (19-1031) and "Foresters" (19-1032).
				19-4099	Life, physical, and social science technicians, all other	All life, physical, and social science technicians not listed separately.
Broadcast and sound engineering technicians and radio operators, and media and communication equipment workers, all other	2900	27-40XX Combines: 27-4010 27-4099	5	27-4011	Audio and video equipment technicians	Set up, or set up and operate audio and video equipment including microphones, sound speakers, video screens, projectors, video monitors, recording equipment, connecting wires and cables, sound and mixing boards, and related electronic equipment for concerts, sports events, meetings and conventions, presentations, and news conferences. May also set up and operate associated spotlights and other custom lighting systems. Excludes "Sound engineering technicians" (27-4014).
				27-4012	Broadcast technicians	Set up, operate, and maintain the electronic equipment used to transmit radio and television programs. Control audio equipment to regulate volume level and quality of sound during radio and television broadcasts. Operate transmitter to broadcast radio or television programs.
				27-4013	Radio operators	Receive and transmit communications using radiotelephone equipment in accordance with government regulations. May repair equipment. Excludes "Radio, Cellular, and Tower equipment installers and repairs" (49-2021).
				27-4014	Sound engineering technicians	Operate machines and equipment to record, synchronize, mix, or reproduce music, voices, or sound effects in sporting arenas, theater productions, recording studios, or movie and video productions.
				27-4099	Media and communication equipment workers, all other	All media and communication equipment workers not listed separately.

DETAILED OCCUPATIONS, BY EEO OCCUPATION GROUPS, 2006–2010—*Continued*

2010 EEO Occupation Title	2010 EEO Occupation Code	2010 SOC Code(s)	EEO Occupation Group (14)	2010 SOC Code	2010 SOC Occcupation Title	SOC Definition
Technicians—Continued							
Clinical laboratory technologists and technicians	3300	29-2010	5	29-2011	Medical and clinical laboratory technologists	Perform complex medical laboratory tests for diagnosis, treatment, and prevention of disease. May train or supervise staff.
				29-2012	Medical and clinical laboratory technicians	Perform routine medical laboratory tests for the diagnosis, treatment, and prevention of disease. May work under the supervision of a medical technologist.
Dental hygienists	3310	29-2021	5	29-2021	Dental hygienists	Clean teeth and examine oral areas, head, and neck for signs of oral disease. May educate patients on oral hygiene, take and develop x-rays, or apply fluoride or sealants.
Diagnostic related technologists and technicians	3320	29-2030	5	29-2031	Cardiovascular technologists and technicians	Conduct tests on pulmonary or cardiovascular systems of patients for diagnostic purposes. May conduct or assist in electrocardiograms, cardiac catheterizations, pulmonary functions, lung capacity, and similar tests. Includes vascular technologists.
				29-2032	Diagnostic medical sonographers	Produce ultrasonic recordings of internal organs for use by physicians.
				29-2033	Nuclear medicine technologists	Prepare, administer, and measure radioactive isotopes in therapeutic, diagnostic, and tracer studies using a variety of radioisotope equipment. Prepare stock solutions of radioactive materials and calculate doses to be administered by radiologists. Subject patients to radiation. Execute blood volume, red cell survival, and fat absorption studies following standard laboratory techniques.
				29-2034	Radiologic technologists	Take x-rays and CAT scans or administer nonradioactive materials into patient's blood stream for diagnostic purposes. Includes technologists who specialize in other scanning modalities. Excludes "Diagnostic medical sonographers"(29-2032) and "Magnetic resonance imaging technologists" (29-2035).
				29-2035	Magnetic resonance imaging technologists	Operate Magnetic Resonance Imaging (MRI) scanners. Monitor patient safety and comfort, and view images of area being scanned to ensure quality of pictures. May administer gadolinium contrast dosage intravenously. May interview patient, explain MRI procedures, and position patient on examining table. May enter into the computer data such as patient history, anatomical area to be scanned, orientation specified, and position of entry.
Emergency medical technicians and paramedics	3400	29-2041	5	29-2041	Emergency medical technicians and paramedics	Assess injuries, administer emergency medical care, and extricate trapped individuals. Transport injured or sick persons to medical facilities.
Health practitioner support technologists and technicians	3420	29-2050	5	29-2051	Dietetic technicians	Assist in the provision of food service and nutritional programs, under the supervision of a dietitian. May plan and produce meals based on established guidelines, teach principles of food and nutrition, or counsel individuals.
				29-2052	Pharmacy technicians	Prepare medications under the direction of a pharmacist. May measure, mix, count out, label, and record amounts and dosages of medications according to prescription orders.
				29-2053	Psychiatric technicians	Care for individuals with mental or emotional conditions or disabilities, following the instructions of physicians or other health practitioners. Monitor patients physical and emotional well-being and report to medical staff. May participate in rehabilitation and treatment programs, help with personal hygiene, and administer oral or injectable medications.
				29-2054	Respiratory therapy technicians	Provide respiratory care under the direction of respiratory therapists and physicians.

DETAILED OCCUPATIONS, BY EEO OCCUPATION GROUPS, 2006–2010—Continued

2010 EEO Occupation Title	2010 EEO Occupation Code	2010 SOC Code(s)	EEO Occupation Group (14)	2010 SOC Code	2010 SOC Occcupation Title	SOC Definition
\multicolumn{7}{c}{**Technicians**—Continued}						
Health practitioner support technologists and technicians—Continued	3420	29-2050	5	29-2055	Surgical technologists	Assist in operations, under the supervision of surgeons, registered nurses, or other surgical personnel. May help set up operating room, prepare and transport patients for surgery, adjust lights and equipment, pass instruments and other supplies to surgeons and surgeon's assistants, hold retractors, cut sutures, and help count sponges, needles, supplies, and instruments.
				29-2056	Veterinary technologists and technicians	Perform medical tests in a laboratory environment for use in the treatment and diagnosis of diseases in animals. Prepare vaccines and serums for prevention of diseases. Prepare tissue samples, take blood samples, and execute laboratory tests, such as urinalysis and blood counts. Clean and sterilize instruments and materials and maintain equipment and machines. May assist a veterinarian during surgery.
				29-2057	Ophthalmic medical technicians	Assist ophthalmologists by performing ophthalmic clinical functions. May administer eye exams, administer eye medications, and instruct the patient in care and use of corrective lenses.
Licensed practical and licensed vocational nurses	3500	29-2061	5	29-2061	Licensed practical and licensed vocational nurses	Care for ill, injured, or convalescing patients or persons with disabilities in hospitals, nursing homes, clinics, private homes, group homes, and similar institutions. May work under the supervision of a registered nurse. Licensing required.
Medical records and health information technicians	3510	29-2071	5	29-2071	Medical records and health information technicians	Compile, process, and maintain medical records of hospital and clinic patients in a manner consistent with medical, administrative, ethical, legal, and regulatory requirements of the health care system. Process, maintain, compile, and report patient information for health requirements and standards in a manner consistent with the health care industry's numerical coding system. Excludes "File clerks" (43-4071).
Opticians, dispensing	3520	29-2081	5	29-2081	Opticians, dispensing	Design, measure, fit, and adapt lenses and frames for client according to written optical prescription or specification. Assist client with inserting, removing, and caring for contact lenses. Assist client with selecting frames. Measure customer for size of eyeglasses and coordinate frames with facial and eye measurements and optical prescription. Prepare work order for optical laboratory containing instructions for grinding and mounting lenses in frames. Verify exactness of finished lens spectacles. Adjust frame and lens position to fit client. May shape or reshape frames. Includes contact lens opticians.
Miscellaneous health technologists and technicians	3535	29-2090	5	29-2091	Orthotists and prosthetists	Design, measure, fit, and adapt orthopedic braces, appliances or prostheses, such as limbs or facial parts for patients with disabling conditions.
				29-2092	Hearing aid specialists	Select and fit hearing aids for customers. Administer and interpret tests of hearing. Assess hearing instrument efficacy. Take ear impressions and prepare, design, and modify ear molds. Excludes "Audiologists" (29-1181).
				29-2099	Health technologists and technicians, all other	All health technologists and technicians not listed separately.

DETAILED OCCUPATIONS, BY EEO OCCUPATION GROUPS, 2006–2010—*Continued*

2010 EEO Occupation Title	2010 EEO Occupation Code	2010 SOC Code(s)	EEO Occupation Group (14)	2010 SOC Code	2010 SOC Occupation Title	SOC Definition
Technicians—Continued							
Other Health care practitioners and technical occupations	3540	29-9000	5	29-9011	Occupational health and safety specialists	Review, evaluate, and analyze work environments and design programs and procedures to control, eliminate, and prevent disease or injury caused by chemical, physical, and biological agents or ergonomic factors. May conduct inspections and enforce adherence to laws and regulations governing the health and safety of individuals. May be employed in the public or private sector. Includes environmental protection officers.
				29-9012	Occupational health and safety technicians	Collect data on work environments for analysis by occupational health and safety specialists. Implement and conduct evaluation of programs designed to limit chemical, physical, biological, and ergonomic risks to workers.
				29-9091	Athletic trainers	Evaluate and advise individuals to assist recovery from or avoid athletic-related injuries or illnesses, or maintain peak physical fitness. May provide first aid or emergency care.
				29-9092	Genetic counselors	Assess individual or family risk for a variety of inherited conditions, such as genetic disorders and birth defects. Provide information to other health care providers or to individuals and families concerned with the risk of inherited conditions. Advise individuals and families to support informed decisionmaking and coping methods for those at risk. May help conduct research related to genetic conditions or genetic counseling.
				29-9099	Health care practitioners and technical workers, all other	All health care practitioners and technical workers not listed separately.
Air traffic controllers and airfield operations specialists	9040	53-2020	5	53-2021	Air traffic controllers	Control air traffic on and within vicinity of airport and movement of air traffic between altitude sectors and control centers according to established procedures and policies. Authorize, regulate, and control commercial airline flights according to government or company regulations to expedite and ensure flight safety.
				53-2022	Airfield operations specialists	Ensure the safe takeoff and landing of commercial and military aircraft. Duties include coordination between air-traffic control and maintenance personnel; dispatching; using airfield landing and navigational aids; implementing airfield safety procedures; monitoring and maintaining flight records; and applying knowledge of weather information.
Sales Workers							
First-line supervisors of retail sales workers	4700	41-1011	6	41-1011	First-line supervisors of retail sales workers	Directly supervise and coordinate activities of retail sales workers in an establishment or department. Duties may include management functions, such as purchasing, budgeting, accounting, and personnel work, in addition to supervisory duties.
First-line supervisors of non-retail sales workers	4710	41-1012	6	41-1012	First-line supervisors of non-retail sales workers	Directly supervise and coordinate activities of sales workers other than retail sales workers. May perform duties, such as budgeting, accounting, and personnel work, in addition to supervisory duties.
Cashiers	4720	41-2010	6	41-2011	Cashiers	Receive and disburse money in establishments other than financial institutions. May use electronic scanners, cash registers, or related equipment. May process credit or debit card transactions and validate checks. Excludes "Gaming cage persons and Booth cashiers" (41-2012).

DETAILED OCCUPATIONS, BY EEO OCCUPATION GROUPS, 2006–2010—*Continued*

2010 EEO Occupation Title	2010 EEO Occupation Code	2010 SOC Code(s)	EEO Occupation Group (14)	2010 SOC Code	2010 SOC Occupation Title	SOC Definition
\multicolumn{7}{c}{**Sales Workers**—*Continued*}
Cashiers—Continued	4720	41-2010	6	41-2012	Gaming change persons and booth cashiers	Exchange coins, tokens and chips for patrons money. May issue payoffs and obtain customer's signature on receipt. May operate a booth in the slot machine area and furnish change persons with money bank at the start of the shift, or count and audit money in drawers. Excludes "cashiers" (41-2011).
Counter and rental clerks	4740	41-2021	6	41-2021	Counter and rental clerks	Receive orders, generally in person, for repairs, rentals, and services. May describe available options, compute cost, and accept payment. Excludes "Counter attendants, Cafeteria, Food concession, and Coffee shop" (35-3022), "Hotel, Motel, and Resort desk clerks" (43-4081), "Order clerks" (43-4151), and "Reservation and Transportation ticket agents and Travel clerks" (43-4181).
Parts salespersons	4750	41-2022	6	41-2022	Parts salespersons	Sell spare and replacement parts and equipment in repair shop or parts store.
Retail salespersons	4760	41-2031	6	41-2031	Retail salespersons	Sell merchandise, such as furniture, motor vehicles, appliances, or apparel to consumers. Excludes "cashiers" (41-2011).
Advertising sales agents	4800	41-3011	6	41-3011	Advertising sales agents	Sell or solicit advertising space, time, or media in publications, signage, TV, radio, or Internet establishments or public spaces.
Insurance sales agents	4810	41-3021	6	41-3021	Insurance sales agents	Sell life, property, casualty, health, automotive, or other types of insurance. May refer clients to independent brokers, work as an independent broker, or be employed by an insurance company.
Securities, commodities, and financial services sales agents	4820	41-3031	6	41-3031	Securities, commodities, and financial services sales agents	Buy and sell securities or commodities in investment and trading firms, or provide financial services to businesses and individuals. May advise customers about stocks, bonds, mutual funds, commodities, and market conditions.
Travel agents	4830	41-3041	6	41-3041	Travel agents	Plan and sell transportation and accommodations for travel agency customers. Determine destination, modes of transportation, travel dates, costs, and accommodations required. May also describe, plan, and arrange itineraries and sell tour packages. May assist in resolving clients' travel problems.
Sales representatives, services, all other	4840	41-3099	6	41-3099	Sales representatives, services, all other	All services sales representatives not listed separately.
Sales representatives, wholesale and manufacturing	4850	41-4010	6	41-4011	Sales representatives, wholesale and manufacturing, technical and scientific products	Sell goods for wholesalers or manufacturers where technical or scientific knowledge is required in such areas as biology, engineering, chemistry, and electronics, normally obtained from at least 2 years of post-secondary education. Excludes "Sales engineers" (41-9031).
				41-4012	Sales representatives, wholesale and manufacturing, except technical and scientific products	Sell goods for wholesalers or manufacturers to businesses or groups of individuals. Work requires substantial knowledge of items sold.
Models, demonstrators, and product promoters	4900	41-9010	6	41-9011	Demonstrators and Product promoters	Demonstrate merchandise and answer questions for the purpose of creating public interest in buying the product. May sell demonstrated merchandise.
				41-9012	Models	Model garments or other apparel and accessories for prospective buyers at fashion shows, private showings, or retail establishments. May pose for photos to be used in magazines or advertisements. May pose as subject for paintings, sculptures, and other types of artistic expression.

DETAILED OCCUPATIONS, BY EEO OCCUPATION GROUPS, 2006–2010—*Continued*

2010 EEO Occupation Title	2010 EEO Occupation Code	2010 SOC Code(s)	EEO Occupation Group (14)	2010 SOC Code	2010 SOC Occcupation Title	SOC Definition
Sales Workers—Continued							
Real estate brokers and sales agents	4920	41-9020	6	41-9021	Real estate brokers	Operate real estate office, or work for commercial real estate firm, overseeing real estate transactions. Other duties usually include selling real estate or renting properties and arranging loans.
				41-9022	Real estate sales agents	Rent, buy, or sell property for clients. Perform duties, such as study property listings, interview prospective clients, accompany clients to property site, discuss conditions of sale, and draw up real estate contracts. Includes agents who represent buyer.
Telemarketers	4940	41-9041	6	41-9041	Telemarketers	Solicit donations or orders for goods or services over the telephone.
Door-to-door sales workers, news and street vendors, and related workers	4950	41-9091	6	41-9091	Door-to-door sales workers, news and street vendors, and related workers	Sell goods or services door-to-door or on the street.
Sales and related workers, all other	4965	41-9099	6	41-9099	Sales and related workers, all other	All sales and related workers not listed separately.
Administrative Support Workers							
Social and human service assistants	2016	21-1093	7	21-1093	Social and human service assistants	Assist in providing client services in a wide variety of fields, such as psychology, rehabilitation, or social work, including support for families. May assist clients in identifying and obtaining available benefits and social and community services. May assist social workers with developing, organizing, and conducting programs to prevent and resolve problems relevant to substance abuse, human relationships, rehabilitation, or dependent care. Excludes "Rehabilitation counselors" (21-1015), "Psychiatric technicians" (29-2053), "Personal care aides" (39-9021), and "Eligibility interviewers, government programs" (43-4061).
Paralegals and legal assistants	2145	23-2011	7	23-2011	Paralegals and legal assistants	Assist lawyers by investigating facts, preparing legal documents, or researching legal precedent. Conduct research to support a legal proceeding, to formulate a defense, or to initiate legal action. Excludes "Legal secretaries" (43-6012).
Miscellaneous legal support workers	2160	23-2090	7	23-2091	Court reporters	Use verbatim methods and equipment to capture, store, retrieve, and transcribe pretrial and trial proceedings or other information. Includes stenocaptioners who operate computerized stenographic captioning equipment to provide captions of live or prerecorded broadcasts for hearing-impaired viewers.
				23-2093	Title examiners, abstractors, and searchers	Search real estate records, examine titles, or summarize pertinent legal or insurance documents or details for a variety of purposes. May compile lists of mortgages, contracts, and other instruments pertaining to titles by searching public and private records for law firms, real estate agencies, or title insurance companies.
				23-2099	Legal support workers, all other	All legal support workers not listed separately.
Library technicians	2440	25-4031	7	25-4031	Library technicians	Assist librarians by helping readers in the use of library catalogs, databases, and indexes to locate books and other materials; and by answering questions that require only brief consultation of standard reference. Compile records; sort and shelve books or other media; remove or repair damaged books or other media; register patrons; and check materials in and out of the circulation process. Replace materials in shelving area (stacks) or files. Includes bookmobile drivers who assist with providing services in mobile libraries.

DETAILED OCCUPATIONS, BY EEO OCCUPATION GROUPS, 2006–2010—*Continued*

2010 EEO Occupation Title	2010 EEO Occupation Code	2010 SOC Code(s)	EEO Occupation Group (14)	2010 SOC Code	2010 SOC Occcupation Title	SOC Definition
\multicolumn{7}{c}{**Administrative Support Workers**—*Continued*}					
Teacher assistants	2540	25-9041	7	25-9041	Teacher assistants	Perform duties that are instructional in nature or deliver direct services to students or parents. Serve in a position for which a teacher has ultimate responsibility for the design and implementation of educational programs and services. Excludes "Graduate teaching assistants" (25-1191).
Medical transcriptionists	3646	31-9094	7	31-9094	Medical transcriptionists	Transcribe medical reports recorded by physicians and other health care practitioners using various electronic devices, covering office visits, emergency room visits, diagnostic imaging studies, operations, chart reviews, and final summaries. Transcribe dictated reports and translate abbreviations into fully understandable form. Edit as necessary and return reports in either printed or electronic form for review and signature, or correction.
First-line supervisors of office and administrative support workers	5000	43-1011	7	43-1011	First-line supervisors of office and administrative support workers	Directly supervise and coordinate the activities of clerical and administrative support workers.
Switchboard operators, including answering service	5010	43-2011	7	43-2011	Switchboard operators, including answering service	Operate telephone business systems equipment or switchboards to relay incoming, outgoing, and interoffice calls. May supply information to callers and record messages.
Telephone operators	5020	43-2021	7	43-2021	Telephone operators	Provide information by accessing alphabetical, geographical, or other directories. Assist customers with special billing requests, such as charges to a third party and credits or refunds for incorrectly dialed numbers or bad connections. May handle emergency calls and assist children or people with physical disabilities to make telephone calls.
Communications equipment operators, all other	5030	43-2099	7	43-2099	Communications equipment operators, all other	All communications equipment operators not listed separately.
Bill and account collectors	5100	43-3011	7	43-3011	Bill and account collectors	Locate and notify customers of delinquent accounts by mail, telephone, or personal visit to solicit payment. Duties include receiving payment and posting amount to customer's account; preparing statements to credit department if customer fails to respond; initiating repossession proceedings or service disconnection; and keeping records of collection and status of accounts.
Billing and posting clerks	5110	43-3021	7	43-3021	Billing and posting clerks	Compile, compute, and record billing, accounting, statistical, and other numerical data for billing purposes. Prepare billing invoices for services rendered or for delivery or shipment of goods.
Bookkeeping, accounting, and auditing clerks	5120	43-3031	7	43-3031	Bookkeeping, accounting, and auditing clerks	Compute, classify, and record numerical data to keep financial records complete. Perform any combination of routine calculating, posting, and verifying duties to obtain primary financial data for use in maintaining accounting records. May also check the accuracy of figures, calculations, and postings pertaining to business transactions recorded by other workers. Excludes "Payroll and timekeeping clerks" (43-3051).
Gaming cage workers	5130	43-3041	7	43-3041	Gaming cage workers	In a gaming establishment, conduct financial transactions for patrons. May reconcile daily summaries of transactions to balance books. Accept patron's credit application and verify credit references to provide check-cashing authorization or to establish house credit accounts. May sell gambling chips, tokens, or tickets to patrons, or to other workers for resale to patrons. May convert gaming chips, tokens, or tickets to currency upon patron's request. May use a cash register or computer to record transaction.

DETAILED OCCUPATIONS, BY EEO OCCUPATION GROUPS, 2006–2010—*Continued*

2010 EEO Occupation Title	2010 EEO Occupation Code	2010 SOC Code(s)	EEO Occupation Group (14)	2010 SOC Code	2010 SOC Occupation Title	SOC Definition
Administrative Support Workers—Continued							
Payroll and timekeeping clerks	5140	43-3051	7	43-3051	Payroll and timekeeping clerks	Compile and record employee time and payroll data. May compute employee's time worked, production, and commission. May compute and post wages and deductions, or prepare paychecks. Excludes "Bookkeeping, Accounting, and Auditing clerks" (43-3031).
Procurement clerks	5150	43-3061	7	43-3061	Procurement clerks	Compile information and records to draw up purchase orders for procurement of materials and services.
Tellers	5160	43-3071	7	43-3071	Tellers	Receive and pay out money. Keep records of money and negotiable instruments involved in a financial institution's various transactions.
Financial clerks, all other	5165	43-3099	7	43-3099	Financial clerks, all other	All financial clerks not listed separately.
Brokerage clerks	5200	43-4011	7	43-4011	Brokerage clerks	Perform duties related to the purchase, sale or holding of securities. Duties include writing orders for stock purchases or sales, computing transfer taxes, verifying stock transactions, accepting and delivering securities, tracking stock price fluctuations, computing equity, distributing dividends, and keeping records of daily transactions and holdings.
Court, municipal, and license clerks	5220	43-4031	7	43-4031	Court, municipal, and license clerks	Perform clerical duties for courts of law, municipalities, or governmental licensing agencies and bureaus. May prepare docket of cases to be called; secure information for judges and oourt; prepare draft agendas or bylaws for town or city council; answer official correspondence; keep fiscal records and accounts; issue licenses or permits; and record data, administer tests, or collect fees. Clerks of Court are classified in "Managers, all other" (11-9199).
Credit authorizers, checkers, and clerks	5230	43-4041	7	43-4041	Credit authorizers, checkers, and clerks	Authorize credit charges against customer's accounts. Investigate history and credit standing of individuals or business establishments applying for credit. May interview applicants to obtain personal and financial data; determine credit worthiness; process applications; and notify customers of acceptance or rejection of credit.
Customer service representatives	5240	43-4051	7	43-4051	Customer service representatives	Interact with customers to provide information in response to inquiries about products and services and to handle and resolve complaints. Excludes individuals whose duties are primarily installation, sales, or repair.
Eligibility interviewers, government programs	5250	43-4061	7	43-4061	Eligibility interviewers, government programs	Determine eligibility of persons applying to receive assistance from government programs and agency resources, such as welfare, unemployment benefits, social security, and public housing.
File clerks	5260	43-4071	7	43-4071	File clerks	File correspondence, cards, invoices, receipts, and other records in alphabetical or numerical order or according to the filing system used. Locate and remove material from file when requested.
Hotel, motel, and resort desk clerks	5300	43-4081	7	43-4081	Hotel, motel, and resort desk clerks	Accommodate hotel, motel, and resort patrons by registering and assigning rooms to guests, issuing room keys or cards, transmitting and receiving messages, keeping records of occupied rooms and guests accounts, making and confirming reservations, and presenting statements to and collecting payments from departing guests.
Interviewers, except eligibility and loan	5310	43-4111	7	43-4111	Interviewers, except eligibility and loan	Interview persons by telephone, mail, in person, or by other means for the purpose of completing forms, applications, or questionnaires. Ask specific questions, record answers, and assist persons with completing form. May sort, classify, and file forms.

DETAILED OCCUPATIONS, BY EEO OCCUPATION GROUPS, 2006–2010—*Continued*

2010 EEO Occupation Title	2010 EEO Occupation Code	2010 SOC Code(s)	EEO Occupation Group (14)	2010 SOC Code	2010 SOC Occupation Title	SOC Definition
\multicolumn{7}{c}{**Administrative Support Workers**—*Continued*}
Library assistants, clerical	5320	43-4121	7	43-4121	Library assistants, clerical	Compile records, sort, shelve, issue, and receive library materials such as books, electronic media, pictures, cards, slides and microfilm. Locate library materials for loan and replace material in shelving area, stacks, or files according to identification number and title. Register patrons to permit them to borrow books, periodicals, and other library materials. Excludes "Library technicians" (25-4031).
Loan interviewers and clerks	5330	43-4131	7	43-4131	Loan interviewers and clerks	Interview loan applicants to elicit information; investigate applicant's backgrounds and verify references; prepare loan request papers; and forward findings, reports, and documents to appraisal department. Review loan papers to ensure completeness, and complete transactions between loan establishment, borrowers, and sellers upon approval of loan.
New accounts clerks	5340	43-4141	7	43-4141	New accounts clerks	Interview persons desiring to open accounts in financial institutions. Explain account services available to prospective customers and assist them in preparing applications.
Correspondence clerks and order clerks	5350	43-4XXX Combines: 43-4021 43-4151	7	43-4021	Correspondence clerks	Compose letters or electronic correspondence in reply to requests for merchandise, damage claims, credit and other information, delinquent accounts, incorrect billings, or unsatisfactory services. Duties may include gathering data to formulate reply and preparing correspondence.
				43-4151	Order clerks	Receive and process incoming orders for materials, merchandise, classified ads, or services such as repairs, installations, or rental of facilities. Generally receives orders via mail, phone, fax, or other electronic means. Duties include informing customers of receipt, prices, shipping dates, and delays; preparing contracts; and handling complaints. Excludes "Dispatchers, except Police, Fire, and Ambulance" (43-5032) who both dispatch and take orders for services.
Human resources assistants, except payroll and timekeeping	5360	43-4161	7	43-4161	Human resources assistants, except payroll and timekeeping	Compile and keep personnel records. Record data for each employee, such as address, weekly earnings, absences, amount of sales or production, supervisory reports, and date of and reason for termination. May prepare reports for employment records, file employment records, or search employee files and furnish information to authorized persons.
Receptionists and information clerks	5400	43-4171	7	43-4171	Receptionists and information clerks	Answer inquiries and provide information to the general public, customers, visitors, and other interested parties regarding activities conducted at establishment and location of departments, offices, and employees within the organization. Excludes "Switchboard operators, including answering service" (43-2011).
Reservation and transportation ticket agents and travel clerks	5410	43-4181	7	43-4181	Reservation and transportation ticket agents and travel clerks	Make and confirm reservations for transportation or lodging, or sell transportation tickets. May check baggage and direct passengers to designated concourse, pier, or track; deliver tickets, contact individuals and groups to inform them of package tours; or provide tourists with travel or transportation information. Excludes "Travel agents" (41-3041), "Hotel, motel, and resort desk clerks" (43-4081), and "Cashiers" (41-2011) who sell tickets for local transportation.
Information and record clerks, all other	5420	43-4199	7	43-4199	Information and record clerks, all other	All information and record clerks not listed separately.

DETAILED OCCUPATIONS, BY EEO OCCUPATION GROUPS, 2006–2010—*Continued*

2010 EEO Occupation Title	2010 EEO Occupation Code	2010 SOC Code(s)	EEO Occupation Group (14)	2010 SOC Code	2010 SOC Occcupation Title	SOC Definition
\multicolumn{7}{c}{**Administrative Support Workers**—*Continued*}						
Cargo and freight agents	5500	43-5011	7	43-5011	Cargo and freight agents	Expedite and route movement of incoming and outgoing cargo and freight shipments in airline, train, and trucking terminals, and shipping docks. Take orders from customers and arrange pickup of freight and cargo for delivery to loading platform. Prepare and examine bills of lading to determine shipping charges and tariffs.
Couriers and messengers	5510	43-5021	7	43-5021	Couriers and messengers	Pick up and deliver messages, documents, packages, and other items between offices or departments within an establishment or directly to other business concerns, traveling by foot, bicycle, motorcycle, automobile, or public conveyance. Excludes "Light truck or Delivery services drivers" (53-3033).
Dispatchers	5520	43-5030	7	43-5031	Police, fire, and ambulance dispatchers	Operate radio, telephone, or computer equipment at emergency response centers. Receive reports from the public of crimes, disturbances, fires, and medical or police emergencies. Relay information to law enforcement and emergency response personnel. May maintain contact with caller until responders arrive.
				43-5032	Dispatchers, except police, fire, and ambulance	Schedule and dispatch workers, work crews, equipment, or service vehicles for conveyance of materials, freight, or passengers, or for normal installation, service, or emergency repairs rendered outside the place of business. Duties may include using radio, telephone, or computer to transmit assignments and compiling statistics and reports on work progress.
Meter readers, utilities	5530	43-5041	7	43-5041	Meter readers, utilities	Read meter and record consumption of electricity, gas, water, or steam.
Postal service clerks	5540	43-5051	7	43-5051	Postal service clerks	Perform any combination of tasks in a post office, such as receive letters and parcels; sell postage and revenue stamps, postal cards, and stamped envelopes; fill out and sell money orders; place mail in pigeon holes of mail rack or in bags; and examine mail for correct postage.
Postal service mail carriers	5550	43-5052	7	43-5052	Postal service mail carriers	Sort mail for delivery. Deliver mail on established route by vehicle or on foot.
Postal service mail sorters, processors, and processing machine operators	5560	43-5053	7	43-5053	Postal service mail sorters, processors, and processing machine operators	Prepare incoming and outgoing mail for distribution. Examine, sort, and route mail. Load, operate, and occasionally adjust and repair mail processing, sorting, and canceling machinery. Keep records of shipments, pouches, and sacks; and other duties related to mail handling within the postal service. Excludes "Postal service clerks" (43-5051) and "Postal service mail carriers" (43-5052).
Production, planning, and expediting clerks	5600	43-5061	7	43-5061	Production, planning, and expediting clerks	Coordinate and expedite the flow of work and materials within or between departments of an establishment according to production schedule. Duties include reviewing and distributing production, work, and shipment schedules; conferring with department supervisors to determine progress of work and completion dates; and compiling reports on progress of work, inventory levels, costs, and production problems. Excludes "Weighers, measurers, checkers, and samplers, recordkeeping" (43-5111).
Shipping, receiving, and traffic clerks	5610	43-5071	7	43-5071	Shipping, receiving, and traffic clerks	Verify and maintain records on incoming and outgoing shipments. Prepare items for shipment. Duties include assembling, addressing, stamping, and shipping merchandise or material; receiving, unpacking, verifying and recording incoming merchandise or material; and arranging for the transportation of products. Excludes "Stock clerks and Order Fillers" (43-5081) and "Weighers, measurers, checkers, and samplers, recordkeeping" (43-5111).

APPENDIX B

DETAILED OCCUPATIONS, BY EEO OCCUPATION GROUPS, 2006–2010—*Continued*

2010 EEO Occupation Title	2010 EEO Occupation Code	2010 SOC Code(s)	EEO Occupation Group (14)	2010 SOC Code	2010 SOC Occupation Title	SOC Definition
Administrative Support Workers—*Continued*							
Stock clerks and order fillers	5620	43-5081	7	43-5081	Stock clerks and order fillers	Receive, store, and issue sales floor merchandise, materials, equipment, and other items from stockroom, warehouse, or storage yard to fill shelves, racks, tables, or customer's orders. May mark prices on merchandise and set up sales displays. Excludes "Laborers and Freight, Stock, and Material Movers, Hand" (53-7062), and "Shipping, receiving, and traffic clerks" (43-5071).
Weighers, measurers, checkers, and samplers, recordkeeping	5630	43-5111	7	43-5111	Weighers, measurers, checkers, and samplers, recordkeeping	Weigh, measure, and check materials, supplies, and equipment for the purpose of keeping relevant records. Duties are primarily clerical by nature. Includes workers who collect and keep record of samples of products or materials. Excludes "Inspectors, testers, sorters, samplers, and weighers" (51-9061).
Secretaries and administrative assistants	5700	43-6010	7	43-6011	Executive secretaries and executive administrative assistants	Provide high-level administrative support by conducting research, preparing statistical reports, handling information requests, and performing clerical functions such as preparing correspondence, receiving visitors, arranging conference calls, and scheduling meetings. May also train and supervise lower-level clerical staff. Excludes "secretaries" (43-6012 through 43-6014).
				43-6012	Legal secretaries	Perform secretarial duties using legal terminology, procedures, and documents. Prepare legal papers and correspondence, such as summonses, complaints, motions, and subpoenas. May also assist with legal research.
				43-6013	Medical secretaries	Perform secretarial duties using specific knowledge of medical terminology and hospital, clinic, or laboratory procedures. Duties may include scheduling appointments, billing patients, and compiling and recording medical charts, reports, and correspondence.
				43-6014	Secretaries and administrative assistants, except legal, medical, and executive	Perform routine clerical and administrative functions such as drafting correspondence, scheduling appointments, organizing and maintaining paper and electronic files, or providing information to callers. Excludes Legal, medical, and executive secretaries (43-6011 through 43-6013).
Computer operators	5800	43-9011	7	43-9011	Computer operators	Monitor and control electronic computer and peripheral electronic data processing equipment to process business, scientific, engineering, and other data according to operating instructions. Monitor and respond to operating and error messages. May enter commands at a computer terminal and set controls on computer and peripheral devices. Excludes "Computer occupations" (15-1100) and "Data entry keyers" (43-9021).
Data entry keyers	5810	43-9021	7	43-9021	Data entry keyers	Operate data entry device, such as keyboard or photo composing perforator. Duties may include verifying data and preparing materials for printing. Excludes "Word processors and typists" (43-9022).
Word processors and typists	5820	43-9022	7	43-9022	Word processors and typists	Use word processor, computer or typewriter to type letters, reports, forms, or other material from rough draft, corrected copy, or voice recording. May perform other clerical duties as assigned. Excludes "Data entry keyers" (43-9021), "Secretaries and administrative assistants" (43-6011 through 43-6014), "Court reporters" (23-2091), and "Medical transcriptionists" (31-9094).

DETAILED OCCUPATIONS, BY EEO OCCUPATION GROUPS, 2006–2010—*Continued*

2010 EEO Occupation Title	2010 EEO Occupation Code	2010 SOC Code(s)	EEO Occupation Group (14)	2010 SOC Code	2010 SOC Occupation Title	SOC Definition
\multicolumn{7}{c}{*Administrative Support Workers—Continued*}
Insurance claims and policy processing clerks	5840	43-9041	7	43-9041	Insurance claims and policy processing clerks	Process new insurance policies, modifications to existing policies, and claims forms. Obtain information from policyholders to verify the accuracy and completeness of information on claims forms, applications and related documents, and company records. Update existing policies and company records to reflect changes requested by policyholders and insurance company representatives. Excludes "Claims adjusters, Examiners, and Investigators" (13-1031).
Mail clerks and mail machine operators, except postal service	5850	43-9051	7	43-9051	Mail clerks and mail machine operators, except postal service	Prepare incoming and outgoing mail for distribution. Use hand or mail handling machines to time stamp, open, read, sort, and route incoming mail; and address, seal, stamp, fold, stuff, and affix postage to outgoing mail or packages. Duties may also include keeping necessary records and completed forms.
Office clerks, general	5860	43-9061	7	43-9061	Office clerks, general	Perform duties too varied and diverse to be classified in any specific office clerical occupation, requiring knowledge of office systems and procedures. Clerical duties may be assigned in accordance with the office procedures of individual establishments and may include a combination of answering telephones, bookkeeping, typing or word processing, stenography, office machine operation, and filing.
Office machine operators, except computer	5900	43-9071	7	43-9071	Office machine operators, except Computer	Operate one or more of a variety of office machines, such as photocopying, photographic, and duplicating machines, or other office machines. Excludes "Computer operators" (43-9011), "Mail clerks and Mail machine operators, except Postal Service" (43-9051) and "Billing and Posting clerks" (43-3021).
Proofreaders and copy markers	5910	43-9081	7	43-9081	Proofreaders and copy markers	Read transcript or proof type setup to detect and mark for correction any grammatical, typographical, or compositional errors. Excludes workers whose primary duty is editing copy. Includes proofreaders of Braille.
Statistical assistants	5920	43-9111	7	43-9111	Statistical assistants	Compile and compute data according to statistical formulas for use in statistical studies. May perform actuarial computations and compile charts and graphs for use by actuaries. Includes actuarial clerks.
Miscellaneous office and administrative support workers, including desktop publishers	5940	43-9XXX Combines: 43-9031 43-9199	7	43-9031	Desktop publishers	Format typescript and graphic elements using computer software to produce publication-ready material.
				43-9199	Office and administrative support workers, all other	All office and administrative support workers not listed separately.
\multicolumn{7}{c}{*Construction and Extractive Craft Workers*}
First-line supervisors of construction trades and extraction workers	6200	47-1011	8	47-1011	Supervisors of construction and extraction workers	Directly supervise and coordinate activities of construction or extraction workers.
Boilermakers	6210	47-2011	8	47-2011	Boilermakers	Construct, assemble, maintain, and repair stationary steam boilers and boiler house auxiliaries. Align structures or plate sections to assemble boiler frame tanks or vats, following blueprints. Work involves use of hand and power tools, plumb bobs, levels, wedges, dogs, or turnbuckles. Assist in testing assembled vessels. Direct cleaning of boilers and boiler furnaces. Inspect and repair boiler fittings, such as safety valves, regulators, automatic-control mechanisms, water columns, and auxiliary machines.

APPENDIX B

DETAILED OCCUPATIONS, BY EEO OCCUPATION GROUPS, 2006–2010—*Continued*

2010 EEO Occupation Title	2010 EEO Occupation Code	2010 SOC Code(s)	EEO Occupation Group (14)	2010 SOC Code	2010 SOC Occupation Title	SOC Definition
\multicolumn{7}{c}{**Construction and Extractive Craft Workers**—*Continued*}
Brickmasons, blockmasons, and stonemasons	6220	47-2020	8	47-2021	Brickmasons and blockmasons	Lay and bind building materials, such as brick, structural tile, concrete block, cinder block, glass block, and terra-cotta block, with mortar and other substances to construct or repair walls, partitions, arches, sewers, and other structures. Excludes "Stonemasons" (47-2022). Installers of mortarless segmental concrete masonry wall units are classified in "Landscaping and groundskeeping workers" (37-3011).
				47-2022	Stonemasons	Build stone structures, such as piers, walls, and abutments. Lay walks, curbstones, or special types of masonry for vats, tanks, and floors.
Carpenters	6230	47-2031	8	47-2031	Carpenters	Construct, erect, install, or repair structures and fixtures made of wood, such as concrete forms; building frameworks, including partitions, joists, studding, and rafters; and wood stairways, window and door frames, and hardwood floors. May also install cabinets, siding, drywall and batt or roll insulation. Includes brattice builders who build doors or brattices (ventilation walls or partitions) in underground passageways.
Carpet, floor, and tile installers and finishers	6240	47-2040	8	47-2041	Carpet installers	Lay and install carpet from rolls or blocks on floors. Install padding and trim flooring materials. Excludes "Floor layers, except carpet, wood, and hard tiles" (47-2042).
				47-2042	Floor layers, except carpet, wood, and hard tiles	Apply blocks, strips, or sheets of shock-absorbing, sound-deadening, or decorative coverings to floors.
				47-2043	Floor sanders and finishers	Scrape and sand wooden floors to smooth surfaces using floor scraper and floor sanding machine, and apply coats of finish.
				47-2044	Tile and marble setters	Apply hard tile, marble, and wood tile to walls, floors, ceilings, and roof decks.
Cement masons, concrete finishers, and terrazzo workers	6250	47-2050	8	47-2051	Cement masons and concrete finishers	Smooth and finish surfaces of poured concrete, such as floors, walks, sidewalks, roads, or curbs using a variety of hand and power tools. Align forms for sidewalks, curbs, or gutters; patch voids; and use saws to cut expansion joints. Installers of mortarless segmental concrete masonry wall units are classified in "Landscaping and groundskeeping workers" (37- 3011).
				47-2053	Terrazzo workers and finishers	Apply a mixture of cement, sand, pigment, or marble chips to floors, stairways, and cabinet fixtures to fashion durable and decorative surfaces.
Construction laborers	6260	47-2061	8	47-2061	Construction laborers	Perform tasks involving physical labor at construction sites. May operate hand and power tools of all types: air hammers, earth tampers, cement mixers, small mechanical hoists, surveying and measuring equipment, and a variety of other equipment and instruments. May clean and prepare sites, dig trenches, set braces to support the sides of excavations, erect scaffolding, and clean up rubble, debris and other waste materials. May assist other craft workers. Construction laborers who primarily assist a particular craft worker are classified under "Helpers, construction trades" (47-3010). Excludes "Hazardous materials removal workers" (47-4041).
Paving, surfacing, and tamping equipment operators	6300	47-2071	8	47-2071	Paving, surfacing, and tamping equipment operators	Operate equipment used for applying concrete, asphalt, or other materials to road beds, parking lots, or airport runways and taxiways, or equipment used for tamping gravel, dirt, or other materials. Includes concrete and asphalt paving machine operators, form tampers, tamping machine operators, and stone spreader operators.

DETAILED OCCUPATIONS, BY EEO OCCUPATION GROUPS, 2006–2010—*Continued*

2010 EEO Occupation Title	2010 EEO Occupation Code	2010 SOC Code(s)	EEO Occupation Group (14)	2010 SOC Code	2010 SOC Occcupation Title	SOC Definition
Construction and Extractive Craft Workers—*Continued*							
Construction equipment operators except paving, surfacing, and tamping equipment operators	6320	47-207X Combines: 47-2072 47-2073	8	47-2072	Pile-driver operators	Operate pile drivers mounted on skids, barges, crawler treads, or locomotive cranes to drive pilings for retaining walls, bulkheads, and foundations of structures, such as buildings, bridges, and piers.
				47-2073	Operating engineers and other construction equipment operators	Operate one or several types of power construction equipment, such as motor graders, bulldozers, scrapers, compressors, pumps, derricks, shovels, tractors, or front-end loaders to excavate, move, and grade earth, erect structures, or pour concrete or other hard surface pavement. May repair and maintain equipment in addition to other duties. Excludes "Crane and tower operators" (53-7021) and "Extraction workers" (47-5000).
Drywall installers, ceiling tile installers, and tapers	6330	47-2080	8	47-2081	Drywall and ceiling tile installers	Apply plasterboard or other wallboard to ceilings or interior walls of buildings. Apply or mount acoustical tiles or blocks, strips, or sheets of shock-absorbing materials to ceilings and walls of buildings to reduce or reflect sound. Materials may be of decorative quality. Includes lathers who fasten wooden, metal, or rockboard lath to walls, ceilings or partitions of buildings to provide support base for plaster, fire-proofing, or acoustical material. Excludes "Carpet installers" (47-2041), "Carpenters" (47-2031), and "Tile and Marble setters" (47-2044).
				47-2082	Tapers	Seal joints between plasterboard or other wallboard to prepare wall surface for painting or papering.
Electricians	6355	47-2111	8	47-2111	Electricians	Install, maintain, and repair electrical wiring, equipment, and fixtures. Ensure that work is in accordance with relevant codes. May install or service street lights, intercom systems, or electrical control systems. Excludes "Security and Fire Alarm Systems Installers" (49-2098).
Glaziers	6360	47-2121	8	47-2121	Glaziers	Install glass in windows, skylights, store fronts, and display cases, or on surfaces, such as building fronts, interior walls, ceilings, and tabletops.
Insulation workers	6400	47-2130	8	47-2131	Insulation workers, floor, ceiling, and wall	Line and cover structures with insulating materials. May work with batt, roll, or blown insulation materials.
				47-2132	Insulation workers, mechanical	Apply insulating materials to pipes or ductwork, or other mechanical systems in order to help control and maintain temperature.
Painters, construction and maintenance	6420	47-2141	8	47-2141	Painters, construction and maintenance	Paint walls, equipment, buildings, bridges, and other structural surfaces, using brushes, rollers, and spray guns. May remove old paint to prepare surface prior to painting. May mix colors or oils to obtain desired color or consistency. Excludes "Paperhangers" (47-2142).
Paperhangers	6430	47-2142	8	47-2142	Paperhangers	Cover interior walls or ceilings of rooms with decorative wallpaper or fabric, or attach advertising posters on surfaces such as walls and billboards. May remove old materials or prepare surfaces to be papered.
Pipelayers, plumbers, pipefitters, and steamfitters	6440	47-2150	8	47-2151	Pipelayers	Lay pipe for storm or sanitation sewers, drains, and water mains. Perform any combination of the following tasks: grade trenches or culverts, position pipe, or seal joints. Excludes "Welders, cutters, solderers, and brazers" (51-4121).
				47-2152	Plumbers, pipefitters, and steamfitters	Assemble, install, alter, and repair pipelines or pipe systems that carry water, steam, air, or other liquids or gases. May install heating and cooling equipment and mechanical control systems. Includes sprinkler fitters.
Plasterers and stucco masons	6460	47-2161	8	47-2161	Plasterers and stucco masons	Apply interior or exterior plaster, cement, stucco, or similar materials. May also set ornamental plaster.

APPENDIX B

DETAILED OCCUPATIONS, BY EEO OCCUPATION GROUPS, 2006–2010—*Continued*

2010 EEO Occupation Title	2010 EEO Occupation Code	2010 SOC Code(s)	EEO Occupation Group (14)	2010 SOC Code	2010 SOC Occcupation Title	SOC Definition
Construction and Extractive Craft Workers—*Continued*							
Reinforcing iron and rebar workers	6500	47-2171	8	47-2171	Reinforcing iron and rebar workers	Position and secure steel bars or mesh in concrete forms in order to reinforce concrete. Use a variety of fasteners, rod-bending machines, blow torches, and hand tools. Includes rod busters.
Roofers	6515	47-2181	8	47-2181	Roofers	Cover roofs of structures with shingles, slate, asphalt, aluminum, wood, or related materials. May spray roofs, sidings, and walls with material to bind, seal, insulate, or soundproof sections of structures.
Sheet metal workers	6520	47-2211	8	47-2211	Sheet metal workers	Fabricate, assemble, install, and repair sheet metal products and equipment, such as ducts, control boxes, drainpipes, and furnace casings. Work may involve any of the following: setting up and operating fabricating machines to cut, bend, and straighten sheet metal; shaping metal over anvils, blocks, or forms using hammer; operating soldering and welding equipment to join sheet metal parts; or inspecting, assembling, and smoothing seams and joints of burred surfaces. Includes sheet metal duct installers who install prefabricated sheet metal ducts used for heating, air conditioning, or other purposes.
Structural iron and steel workers	6530	47-2221	8	47-2221	Structural iron and steel workers	Raise, place, and unite iron or steel girders, columns, and other structural members to form completed structures or structural frameworks. May erect metal storage tanks and assemble prefabricated metal buildings. Excludes "Reinforcing iron and rebar workers" (47-2171).
Elevator installers and repairers	6700	47-4021	8	47-4021	Elevator installers and repairers	Assemble, install, repair, or maintain electric or hydraulic freight or passenger elevators, escalators, or dumbwaiters.
Fence erectors	6710	47-4031	8	47-4031	Fence erectors	Erect and repair fences and fence gates, using hand and power tools.
Hazardous materials removal workers	6720	47-4041	8	47-4041	Hazardous materials removal workers	Identify, remove, pack, transport, or dispose of hazardous materials, including asbestos, lead-based paint, waste oil, fuel, transmission fluid, radioactive materials, or contaminated soil. specialized training and certification in hazardous materials handling or a confined entry permit are generally required. May operate earth-moving equipment or trucks.
Highway maintenance workers	6730	47-4051	8	47-4051	Highway maintenance workers	Maintain highways, municipal and rural roads, airport runways, and rights-of-way. Duties include patching broken or eroded pavement, repairing guard rails, highway markers, and snow fences. May also mow or clear brush from along road or plow snow from roadway. Excludes "Tree trimmers and pruners" (37-3013).
Rail-track laying and maintenance equipment operators	6740	47-4061	8	47-4061	Rail-track laying and maintenance equipment operators	Lay, repair, and maintain track for standard or narrow-gauge railroad equipment used in regular railroad service or in plant yards, quarries, sand and gravel pits, and mines. Includes ballast cleaning machine operators and railroad bed tamping machine operators.
Miscellaneous construction workers, including solar photovoltaic installers, septic tank servicers and sewer pipe cleaners	6765	47-4XXX Combines: 47-2231 47-4071 47-4090	8	47-2231	Solar photovoltaic installers	Assemble, install, or maintain solar photovoltaic (PV) systems on roofs or other structures in compliance with site assessment and schematics. May include measuring, cutting, assembling, and bolting structural framing and solar modules. May perform minor electrical work such as current checks. Excludes solar thermal installers who are included in "Plumbers, pipefitters, and steamfitters" (47-2152). Excludes solar PV electricians who are included in "Electricians" (47-2111).

DETAILED OCCUPATIONS, BY EEO OCCUPATION GROUPS, 2006–2010—*Continued*

2010 EEO Occupation Title	2010 EEO Occupation Code	2010 SOC Code(s)	EEO Occupation Group (14)	2010 SOC Code	2010 SOC Occupation Title	SOC Definition
Construction and Extractive Craft Workers—*Continued*							
Miscellaneous construction workers, including solar photovoltaic installers, septic tank servicers and sewer pipe cleaners—Continued	6765	47-4XXX Combines: 47-2231 47-4071 47-4090	8	47-4071	Septic tank servicers and sewer pipe cleaners	Clean and repair septic tanks, sewer lines, or drains. May patch walls and partitions of tank, replace damaged drain tile, or repair breaks in underground piping.
				47-4091	Segmental pavers	Lay out, cut, and place segmental paving units. Includes installers of bedding and restraining materials for the paving units.
				47-4099	Construction and related workers, all other	All construction and related workers not listed separately.
Derrick, rotary drill, and service unit operators, and roustabouts, oil, gas, and mining	6800	47-50XX Combines: 47-5010 47-5071	8	47-5011	Derrick operators, oil and gas	Rig derrick equipment and operate pumps to circulate mud through drill hole.
				47-5012	Rotary drill operators, oil and gas	Set up or operate a variety of drills to remove underground oil and gas, or remove core samples for testing during oil and gas exploration. Excludes "Earth drillers, except oil and gas" (47-5021).
				47-5013	Service unit operators, oil, gas, and mining	Operate equipment to increase oil flow from producing wells or to remove stuck pipe, casing, tools, or other obstructions from drilling wells. May also perform similar services in mining exploration operations. Includes fishing-tool technicians.
				47-5071	Roustabouts, oil and gas	Assemble or repair oil field equipment using hand and power tools. Perform other tasks as needed.
Earth drillers, except oil and gas	6820	47-5021	8	47-5021	Earth drillers, except oil and gas	Operate a variety of drills such as rotary, churn, and pneumatic to tap sub-surface water and salt deposits, to remove core samples during mineral exploration or soil testing, and to facilitate the use of explosives in mining or construction. May use explosives. Includes horizontal and earth boring machine operators.
Explosives workers, ordnance handling experts, and blasters	6830	47-5031	8	47-5031	Explosives workers, ordnance handling experts, and blasters	Place and detonate explosives to demolish structures or to loosen, remove, or displace earth, rock, or other materials. May perform specialized handling, storage, and accounting procedures. Includes seismograph shooters. Excludes "Earth drillers, except oil and gas" (47-5021) who may also work with explosives.
Mining machine operators	6840	47-5040	8	47-5041	Continuous mining machine operators	Operate self-propelled mining machines that rip coal, metal and nonmetal ores, rock, stone, or sand from the mine face and load it onto conveyors or into shuttle cars in a continuous operation.
				47-5042	Mine cutting and channeling machine operators	Operate machinery such as longwall shears, plows, and cutting machines to cut or channel along the face or seams of coal mines, stone quarries, or other mining surfaces to facilitate blasting, separating, or removing minerals or materials from mines or from the Earth's surface. Includes shale planers.
				47-5049	Mining machine operators, all other	All mining machine operators not listed separately.
Miscellaneous extraction workers, including roof bolters and helpers	6940	47-50XX Combines: 47-5051 47-5061 47-5081 (Note 2) 47-5099	8	47-5051	Rock splitters, quarry	Separate blocks of rough dimension stone from quarry mass using jackhammer and wedges.
				47-5061	Roof bolters, mining	Operate machinery to install roof support bolts in underground mine.

APPENDIX B

DETAILED OCCUPATIONS, BY EEO OCCUPATION GROUPS, 2006–2010—*Continued*

2010 EEO Occupation Title	2010 EEO Occupation Code	2010 SOC Code(s)	EEO Occupation Group (14)	2010 SOC Code	2010 SOC Occcupation Title	SOC Definition
\multicolumn{7}{c}{**Construction and Extractive Craft Workers**—*Continued*}
Miscellaneous extraction workers, including roof bolters and helpers—Continued	6940	47-50XX Combines: 47-5051 47-5061 47-5081 (Note 2) 47-5099	8	47-5081	Helpers\extraction workers	Help extraction craft workers, such as earth drillers, blasters and explosives workers, derrick operators, and mining machine operators, by performing duties requiring less skill. Duties include supplying equipment or cleaning work area. Apprentice workers are classified with the appropriate skilled construction trade occupation (47-2011 through 47-2231).
				47-5099	Extraction workers, all other	All extraction workers not listed separately.
Crane and tower operators	9510	53-7021	8	53-7021	Crane and tower operators	Operate mechanical boom and cable or tower and cable equipment to lift and move materials, machines, or products in many directions. Excludes "Excavating and loading machine and dragline operators" (53-7032).
Dredge, excavating, and loading machine operators	9520	53-7030	8	53-7031	Dredge operators	Operate dredge to remove sand, gravel, or other materials in order to excavate and maintain navigable channels in waterways.
				53-7032	Excavating and loading machine and dragline operators	Operate or tend machinery equipped with scoops, shovels, or buckets, to excavate and load loose materials. Excludes "Dredge operators" (53-7031).
				53-7033	Loading machine operators, underground mining	Operate underground loading machine to load coal, ore, or rock into shuttle or mine car or onto conveyors. Loading equipment may include power shovels, hoisting engines equipped with cable-drawn scraper or scoop, or machines equipped with gathering arms and conveyor.
\multicolumn{7}{c}{**Installation, Maintenance and Repair Craft Workers**}
First-line supervisors of mechanics, installers, and repairers	7000	49-1011	9	49-1011	First-line supervisors of mechanics, installers, and repairers	Directly supervise and coordinate the activities of mechanics, installers, and repairers. Excludes team or work leaders.
Computer, automated teller, and office machine repairers	7010	49-2011	9	49-2011	Computer, automated teller, and office machine repairers	Repair, maintain, or install computers, word processing systems, automated teller machines, and electronic office machines, such as duplicating and fax machines.
Radio and telecommunications equipment installers and repairers	7020	49-2020	9	49-2021	Radio, cellular, and tower equipment installers and repairers	Repair, install or maintain mobile or stationary radio transmitting, broadcasting, and receiving equipment, and two-way radio communications systems used in cellular telecommunications, mobile broadband, ship-to-shore, aircraft-to-ground communications, and radio equipment in service and emergency vehicles. May test and analyze network coverage.
				49-2022	Telecommunications equipment installers and repairers, except line installers	Install, set-up, rearrange, or remove switching, distribution, routing, and dialing equipment used in central offices or headends. Service or repair telephone, cable television, Internet, and other communications equipment on customer's property. May install communications equipment or communications wiring in buildings. Excludes "Telecommunications line installers and repairers" (49-9052).
Avionics technicians	7030	49-2091	9	49-2091	Avionics technicians	Install, inspect, test, adjust, or repair avionics equipment, such as radar, radio, navigation, and missile control systems in aircraft or space vehicles.
Electric motor, power tool, and related repairers	7040	49-2092	9	49-2092	Electric motor, power tool, and related repairers	Repair, maintain, or install electric motors, wiring, or switches.
Electrical and electronics repairers, transportation equipment, and industrial and utility	7100	49-209X Combines: 49-2093 49-2094 49-2095	9	49-2093	Electrical and electronics installers and repairers, transportation equipment	Install, adjust, or maintain mobile electronics communication equipment, including sound, sonar, security, navigation, and surveillance systems on trains, watercraft, or other mobile equipment. Excludes "Avionics technicians" (49-2091) and "Electronic equipment installers and repairers, motor vehicles" (49-2096).

DETAILED OCCUPATIONS, BY EEO OCCUPATION GROUPS, 2006–2010—*Continued*

2010 EEO Occupation Title	2010 EEO Occupation Code	2010 SOC Code(s)	EEO Occupation Group (14)	2010 SOC Code	2010 SOC Occupation Title	SOC Definition
\multicolumn{7}{c}{**Installation, Maintenance and Repair Craft Workers**—*Continued*}
Electrical and electronics repairers, transportation equipment, and industrial and utility—Continued	7100	49-209X Combines: 49-2093 49-2094 49-2095	9	49-2094	Electrical and electronics repairers, commercial and industrial equipment	Repair, test, adjust, or install electronic equipment, such as industrial controls, transmitters, and antennas. Excludes "Avionics technicians" (49-2091), "Electronic equipment installers and repairers, motor vehicles" (49-2096), and "Electrical and electronics installers and repairers, transportation equipment" (49-2093).
				49-2095	Electrical and electronics repairers, powerhouse, substation, and relay	Inspect, test, repair, or maintain electrical equipment in generating stations, substations, and in-service relays.
Electronic equipment installers and repairers, motor vehicles	7110	49-2096	9	49-2096	Electronic equipment installers and repairers, motor vehicles	Install, diagnose, or repair communications, sound, security, or navigation equipment in motor vehicles.
Electronic home entertainment equipment installers and repairers	7120	49-2097	9	49-2097	Electronic home entertainment equipment installers and repairers	Repair, adjust, or install audio or television receivers, stereo systems, camcorders, video systems, or other electronic home entertainment equipment.
Security and fire alarm systems installers	7130	49-2098	9	49-2098	Security and fire alarm systems installers	Install, program, maintain, and repair security and fire alarm wiring and equipment. Ensure that work is in accordance with relevant codes. Excludes "Electricians" (47-2111) who do a broad range of electrical wiring.
Aircraft mechanics and service technicians	7140	49-3011	9	49-3011	Aircraft mechanics and service technicians	Diagnose, adjust, repair, or overhaul aircraft engines and assemblies, such as hydraulic and pneumatic systems. Includes helicopter and aircraft engine specialists. Excludes "Avionics Technician" (49-2091).
Automotive body and related repairers	7150	49-3021	9	49-3021	Automotive body and related repairers	Repair and refinish automotive vehicle bodies and straighten vehicle frames. Excludes "Painters, transportation equipment" (51-9122) and "Automotive glass installers and repairers" (49-3022).
Automotive glass installers and repairers	7160	49-3022	9	49-3022	Automotive glass installers and repairers	Replace or repair broken windshields and window glass in motor vehicles.
Automotive service technicians and mechanics	7200	49-3023	9	49-3023	Automotive service technicians and mechanics	Diagnose, adjust, repair, or overhaul automotive vehicles. Excludes "Automotive body and related repairers" (49-3021), "Bus and truck mechanics and diesel engine specialists" (49-3031), and "Electronic equipment installers and repairers, motor vehicles" (49-2096).
Bus and truck mechanics and diesel engine specialists	7210	49-3031	9	49-3031	Bus and truck mechanics and diesel engine specialists	Diagnose, adjust, repair, or overhaul buses and trucks, or maintain and repair any type of diesel engines. Includes mechanics working primarily with automobile or marine diesel engines.
Heavy vehicle and mobile equipment service technicians and mechanics	7220	49-3040	9	49-3041	Farm equipment mechanics and service technicians	Diagnose, adjust, repair, or overhaul farm machinery and vehicles, such as tractors, harvesters, dairy equipment, and irrigation systems. Excludes "Bus and truck mechanics and Diesel engine specialists" (49-3031).
				49-3042	Mobile heavy equipment mechanics, except engines	Diagnose, adjust, repair, or overhaul mobile mechanical, hydraulic, and pneumatic equipment, such as cranes, bulldozers, graders, and conveyors, used in construction, logging, and surface mining. Excludes "Rail car repairers" (49-3043) and "Bus and truck mechanics and diesel engine specialists" (49-3031).
				49-3043	Rail car repairers	Diagnose, adjust, repair, or overhaul railroad rolling stock, mine cars, or mass transit rail cars. Excludes "Bus and truck mechanics and diesel engine specialists" (49-3031).

DETAILED OCCUPATIONS, BY EEO OCCUPATION GROUPS, 2006–2010—*Continued*

2010 EEO Occupation Title	2010 EEO Occupation Code	2010 SOC Code(s)	EEO Occupation Group (14)	2010 SOC Code	2010 SOC Occcupation Title	SOC Definition
\multicolumn{7}{c}{**Installation, Maintenance and Repair Craft Workers**—*Continued*}
Small engine mechanics	7240	49-3050	9	49-3051	Motorboat mechanics and service technicians	Repair and adjust electrical and mechanical equipment of inboard or inboard-outboard boat engines. Excludes "Bus and truck mechanics and Diesel engine specialists" (49-3031).
				49-3052	Motorcycle mechanics	Diagnose, adjust, repair, or overhaul motorcycles, scooters, mopeds, dirt bikes, or similar motorized vehicles.
				49-3053	Outdoor power equipment and other small engine mechanics	Diagnose, adjust, repair, or overhaul small engines used to power lawn mowers, chain saws, recreational sporting equipment and related equipment.
Miscellaneous vehicle and mobile equipment mechanics, installers, and repairers	7260	49-3090	9	49-3091	Bicycle repairers	Repair and service bicycles.
				49-3092	Recreational vehicle service technicians	Diagnose, inspect, adjust, repair, or overhaul recreational vehicles including travel trailers. May specialize in maintaining gas, electrical, hydraulic, plumbing, or chassis/towing systems as well as repairing generators, appliances, and interior components. Includes workers who perform customized van conversions. Excludes "Automotive service technicians and mechanics" (49-3023) and "Bus and truck mechanics and diesel engine specialists" (49-3031) who also work on recreation vehicles.
				49-3093	Tire repairers and changers	Repair and replace tires.
Control and valve installers and repairers	7300	49-9010	9	49-9011	Mechanical door repairers	Install, service, or repair automatic door mechanisms and hydraulic doors. Includes garage door mechanics.
				49-9012	Control and valve installers and repairers, except mechanical door	Install, repair, and maintain mechanical regulating and controlling devices, such as electric meters, gas regulators, thermostats, safety and flow valves, and other mechanical governors.
Heating, air conditioning, and refrigeration mechanics and installers	7315	49-9021	9	49-9021	Heating, air conditioning, and refrigeration mechanics and installers	Install or repair heating, central air conditioning, or refrigeration systems, including oil burners, hot-air furnaces, and heating stoves.
Home appliance repairers	7320	49-9031	9	49-9031	Home appliance repairers	Repair, adjust, or install all types of electric or gas household appliances, such as refrigerators, washers, dryers, and ovens.
Industrial and refractory machinery mechanics	7330	49-904X Combines: 49-9041 49-9045	9	49-9041	Industrial machinery mechanics	Repair, install, adjust, or maintain industrial production and processing machinery or refinery and pipeline distribution systems. Excludes "Millwrights" (49-9044), "Mobile heavy equipment mechanics, except engines" (49-3042), and "Maintenance workers, machinery" (49-9043).
				49-9045	Refractory materials repairers, except brickmasons	Build or repair equipment such as furnaces, kilns, cupolas, boilers, converters, ladles, soaking pits and ovens, using refractory materials.
Maintenance and repair workers, general	7340	49-9071	9	49-9071	Maintenance and repair workers, general	Perform work involving the skills of two or more maintenance or craft occupations to keep machines, mechanical equipment, or the structure of an establishment in repair. Duties may involve pipe fitting; boiler making; insulating; welding; machining; carpentry; repairing electrical or mechanical equipment; installing, aligning, and balancing new equipment; and repairing buildings, floors, or stairs. Excludes "Maintenance workers, machinery" (49-9043).
Maintenance workers, machinery	7350	49-9043	9	49-9043	Maintenance workers, machinery	Lubricate machinery, change parts, or perform other routine machinery maintenance. Excludes "Maintenance and repair workers, general" (49-9071).

DETAILED OCCUPATIONS, BY EEO OCCUPATION GROUPS, 2006–2010—*Continued*

2010 EEO Occupation Title	2010 EEO Occupation Code	2010 SOC Code(s)	EEO Occupation Group (14)	2010 SOC Code	2010 SOC Occupation Title	SOC Definition
Installation, Maintenance and Repair Craft Workers—*Continued*							
Millwrights	7360	49-9044	9	49-9044	Millwrights	Install, dismantle, or move machinery and heavy equipment according to layout plans, blueprints, or other drawings.
Electrical power-line installers and repairers	7410	49-9051	9	49-9051	Electrical power-line installers and repairers	Install or repair cables or wires used in electrical power or distribution systems. May erect poles and light or heavy duty transmission towers. Excludes "Electrical and electronics repairers, powerhouse, substation, and relay" (49-2095).
Telecommunications line installers and repairers	7420	49-9052	9	49-9052	Telecommunications line installers and repairers	Install and repair telecommunications cable, including fiber optics.
Precision instrument and equipment repairers	7430	49-9060	9	49-9061	Camera and photographic equipment repairers	Repair and adjust cameras and photographic equipment, including commercial video and motion picture camera equipment.
				49-9062	Medical equipment repairers	Test, adjust, or repair biomedical or electromedical equipment.
				49-9063	Musical instrument repairers and tuners	Repair percussion, stringed, reed, or wind instruments. May specialize in one area, such as piano tuning. Excludes "Electronic home entertainment equipment installers and repairers" (49-2097) who repair electrical and electronic musical instruments.
				49-9064	Watch repairers	Repair, clean, and adjust mechanisms of timing instruments, such as watches and clocks. Includes watchmakers, watch technicians, and mechanical timepiece repairers.
				49-9069	Precision instrument and equipment repairers, all other	All precision instrument and equipment repairers not listed separately.
Coin, vending, and amusement machine servicers and repairers	7510	49-9091	9	49-9091	Coin, vending, and amusement machine servicers and repairers	Install, service, adjust, or repair coin, vending, or amusement machines, including video games, juke boxes, pinball machines, or slot machines.
Locksmiths and safe repairers	7540	49-9094	9	49-9094	Locksmiths and safe repairers	Repair and open locks; make keys; change locks and safe combinations; and install and repair safes.
Manufactured building and mobile home installers	7550	49-9095	9	49-9095	Manufactured building and mobile home installers	Move or install mobile homes or prefabricated buildings.
Riggers	7560	49-9096	9	49-9096	Riggers	Set up or repair rigging for construction projects, manufacturing plants, logging yards, ships and shipyards, or for the entertainment industry.
Other installation, maintenance, and repair workers, including wind turbine service technicians, commercial divers, and signal and track switch repairers	7630	49-909X Combines: 49-9081 49-9092 49-9093 49-9097 49-9099	9	49-9081	Wind turbine service technicians	Inspect, diagnose, adjust, or repair wind turbines. Perform maintenance on wind turbine equipment including resolving electrical, mechanical, and hydraulic malfunctions.
				49-9092	Commercial drivers	Work below surface of water, using scuba gear to inspect, repair, remove, or install equipment and structures. May use a variety of power and hand tools, such as drills, sledgehammers, torches, and welding equipment. May conduct tests or experiments, rig explosives, or photograph structures or marine life. Excludes "Fishers and related fishing workers" (45-3011), "Athletes and sports competitors" (27-2021), and "Police and sheriff's patrol officers" (33-3051).
				49-9093	Fabric menders, except garment	Repair tears, holes, and other defects in fabrics, such as draperies, linens, parachutes, and tents.
				49-9097	Signal and track switch repairers	Install, inspect, test, maintain, or repair electric gate crossings, signals, signal equipment, track switches, section lines, or intercommunications systems within a railroad system.
				49-9099	Installation, maintenance, and repair workers, all other	All, installation, maintenance, and repair workers not listed separately.

APPENDIX B

DETAILED OCCUPATIONS, BY EEO OCCUPATION GROUPS, 2006–2010—*Continued*

2010 EEO Occupation Title	2010 EEO Occupation Code	2010 SOC Code(s)	EEO Occupation Group (14)	2010 SOC Code	2010 SOC Occcupation Title	SOC Definition
\multicolumn{7}{c}{**Installation, Maintenance and Repair Craft Workers**—*Continued*}
Structural metal fabricators and fitters	7740	51-2041	9	51-2041	Structural metal fabricators and fitters	Fabricate, position, align, and fit parts of structural metal products. Shipfitters are included in "Layout workers, metal and plastic" (51-4192).
Machinists	8030	51-4041	9	51-4041	Machinists	Set up and operate a variety of machine tools to produce precision parts and instruments. Includes precision instrument makers who fabricate, modify, or repair mechanical instruments. May also fabricate and modify parts to make or repair machine tools or maintain industrial machines, applying knowledge of mechanics, mathematics, metal properties, layout, and machining procedures.
Model makers and patternmakers, metal and plastic	8060	51-4060	9	51-4061	Model makers, metal and plastic	Set up and operate machines, such as lathes, milling and engraving machines, and jig borers to make working models of metal or plastic objects. Includes template makers.
				51-4062	Patternmakers, metal and plastic	Lay out, machine, fit, and assemble castings and parts to metal or plastic foundry patterns, core boxes, or match plates.
Tool and die makers	8130	51-4111	9	51-4111	Tool and die makers	Analyze specifications, lay out metal stock, set up and operate machine tools, and fit and assemble parts to make and repair dies, cutting tools, jigs, fixtures, gauges, and machinist's hand tools.
Prepress technicians and workers	8250	51-5111	9	51-5111	Prepress technicians and workers	Format and proof text and images submitted by designers and clients into finished pages that can be printed. Includes digital and photo typesetting. May produce printing plates.
Print binding and finishing workers	8256	51-5113	9	51-5113	Print binding and finishing workers	Bind books and other publications or finish printed products by hand or machine. May set up binding and finishing machines.
Shoe and leather workers and repairers	8330	51-6041	9	51-6041	Shoe and leather workers and repairers	Construct, decorate, or repair leather and leather-like products, such as luggage, shoes, and saddles.
Tailors, dressmakers, and sewers	8350	51-6050	9	51-6051	Sewers, hand	Sew, join, reinforce, or finish, usually with needle and thread, a variety of manufactured items. Includes weavers and stitchers. Excludes "Fabric menders, except garment" (49-9093).
				51-6052	Tailors, dressmakers, and custom sewers	Design, make, alter, repair, or fit garments.
Upholsterers	8450	51-6093	9	51-6093	Upholsterers	Make, repair, or replace upholstery for household furniture or transportation vehicles.
Cabinetmakers and bench carpenters	8500	51-7011	9	51-7011	Cabinetmakers and bench carpenters	Cut, shape, and assemble wooden articles or set up and operate a variety of woodworking machines, such as power saws, jointers, and mortisers to surface, cut, or shape lumber or to fabricate parts for wood products. Excludes "Woodworking machine setters, operators, and tenders" (51-7040).
Furniture finishers	8510	51-7021	9	51-7021	Furniture finishers	Shape, finish, and refinish damaged, worn, or used furniture or new high-grade furniture to specified color or finish.
Miscellaneous woodworkers, including model makers and patternmakers	8550	51-70XX Combines: 51-7030 51-7099	9	51-7031	Model makers, wood	Construct full-size and scale wooden precision models of products. Includes wood jig builders and loft workers.
				51-7032	Patternmakers, wood	Plan, lay out, and construct wooden unit or sectional patterns used in forming sand molds for castings.
				51-7099	Woodworkers, all other	All woodworkers not listed separately.
Power plant operators, distributors, and dispatchers	8600	51-8010	9	51-8011	Nuclear power reactor operators	Operate or control nuclear reactors. Move control rods, start and stop equipment, monitor and adjust controls, and record data in logs. Implement emergency procedures when needed. May respond to abnormalities, determine cause, and recommend corrective action.

DETAILED OCCUPATIONS, BY EEO OCCUPATION GROUPS, 2006–2010—*Continued*

2010 EEO Occupation Title	2010 EEO Occupation Code	2010 SOC Code(s)	EEO Occupation Group (14)	2010 SOC Code	2010 SOC Occcupation Title	SOC Definition
Installation, Maintenance and Repair Craft Workers—*Continued*							
Power plant operators, distributors, and dispatchers—Continued	8600	51-8010	9	51-8012	Power distributors and dispatchers	Coordinate, regulate, or distribute electricity or steam.
				51-8013	Power plant operators	Control, operate, or maintain machinery to generate electric power. Includes auxiliary equipment operators. Excludes "Nuclear Power Reactor Operators" (51-8011).
Stationary engineers and boiler operators	8610	51-8021	9	51-8021	Stationary engineers and boiler operators	Operate or maintain stationary engines, boilers, or other mechanical equipment to provide utilities for buildings or industrial processes. Operate equipment, such as steam engines, generators, motors, turbines, and steam boilers.
Water and wastewater treatment plant and system operators	8620	51-8031	9	51-8031	Water and wastewater treatment plant and system operators	Operate or control an entire process or system of machines, often through the use of control boards, to transfer or treat water or wastewater.
Jewelers and precious stone and metal workers	8750	51-9071	9	51-9071	Jewelers and precious stone and metal workers	Design, fabricate, adjust, repair, or appraise jewelry, gold, silver, other precious metals, or gems. Includes diamond polishers and gem cutters, and persons who perform precision casting and modeling of molds, casting metal in molds, or setting precious and semi-precious stones for jewelry and related products.
Medical, dental, and ophthalmic laboratory technicians	8760	51-9080	9	51-9081	Dental laboratory technicians	Construct and repair full or partial dentures or dental appliances. Excludes "Dental Assistants" (31-9091).
				51-9082	Medical appliance technicians	Construct, fit, maintain, or repair medical supportive devices, such as braces, orthotics and prosthetic devices, joints, arch supports, and other surgical and medical appliances.
				51-9083	Ophthalmic laboratory technicians	Cut, grind, and polish eyeglasses, contact lenses, or other precision optical elements. Assemble and mount lenses into frames or process other optical elements. Includes precision lens polishers or grinders, centerer-edgers, and lens mounters. Excludes "Opticians, Dispensing" (29-2081).
Etchers and engravers	8910	51-9194	9	51-9194	Etchers and engravers	Engrave or etch metal, wood, rubber, or other materials. Includes such workers as etcher-circuit processors, pantograph engravers, and silk screen etchers. Photoengravers are included in "Prepress Technicians and workers" (51-5111).
Production Operative Workers							
Graders and sorters, agricultural products	6040	45-2041	10	45-2041	Graders and sorters, agricultural products	Grade, sort, or classify unprocessed food and other agricultural products by size, weight, color, or condition. Excludes "Agricultural Inspectors" (45-2011).
First-line supervisors of production and operating workers	7700	51-1011	10	51-1011	First-line supervisors of production and operating workers	Directly supervise and coordinate the activities of production and operating workers, such as inspectors, precision workers, machine setters and operators, assemblers, fabricators, and plant and system operators. Excludes team or work leaders.
Aircraft structure, surfaces, rigging, and systems assemblers	7710	51-2011	10	51-2011	Aircraft structure, surfaces, rigging, and systems assemblers	Assemble, fit, fasten, and install parts of airplanes, space vehicles, or missiles, such as tails, wings, fuselage, bulkheads, stabilizers, landing gear, rigging and control equipment, or heating and ventilating systems.
Electrical, electronics, and electromechanical assemblers	7720	51-2020	10	51-2021	Coil winders, tapers, and finishers	Wind wire coils used in electrical components, such as resistors and transformers, and in electrical equipment and instruments, such as field cores, bobbins, armature cores, electrical motors, generators, and control equipment.
				51-2022	Electrical and electronic equipment assemblers	Assemble or modify electrical or electronic equipment, such as computers, test equipment telemetering systems, electric motors, and batteries.

DETAILED OCCUPATIONS, BY EEO OCCUPATION GROUPS, 2006–2010—*Continued*

2010 EEO Occupation Title	2010 EEO Occupation Code	2010 SOC Code(s)	EEO Occupation Group (14)	2010 SOC Code	2010 SOC Occcupation Title	SOC Definition
Production Operative Workers—*Continued*						
Electrical, electronics, and electromechanical assemblers—Continued	7720	51-2020	10	51-2023	Electromechanical equipment assemblers	Assemble or modify electromechanical equipment or devices, such as servomechanisms, gyros, dynamometers, magnetic drums, tape drives, brakes, control linkage, actuators, and appliances.
Engine and other machine assemblers	7730	51-2031	10	51-2031	Engine and other machine assemblers	Construct, assemble, or rebuild machines, such as engines, turbines, and similar equipment used in such industries as construction, extraction, textiles, and paper manufacturing.
Miscellaneous assemblers and fabricators	7750	51-2090	10	51-2091	Fiberglass laminators and fabricators	Laminate layers of fiberglass on molds to form boat decks and hulls, bodies for golf carts, automobiles, or other products.
				51-2092	Team assemblers	Work as part of a team having responsibility for assembling an entire product or component of a product. Team assemblers can perform all tasks conducted by the team in the assembly process and rotate through all or most of them rather than being assigned to a specific task on a permanent basis. May participate in making management decisions affecting the work. Includes team leaders who work as part of the team. Assemblers who continuously perform the same task are classified elsewhere in 51-2000.
				51-2093	Timing sevice assemblers and Adjusters	Perform precision assembling, adjusting, or calibrating, within narrow tolerances, of timing devices such as digital clocks or timing devices with electrical or electronic components. Excludes watchmakers, which are included in "Watch Repairers" (49-9064).
				51-2099	Assemblers and fabricators, all other	All assemblers and fabricators not listed separately.
Bakers	7800	51-3011	10	51-3011	Bakers	Mix and bake ingredients to produce breads, rolls, cookies, cakes, pies, pastries, or other baked goods. Pastry chefs in restaurants and hotels are included with "Chefs and Head Cooks" (35-1011).
Butchers and other meat, poultry, and fish processing workers	7810	51-3020	10	51-3021	Butchers and meat cutters	Cut, trim, or prepare consumer-sized portions of meat for use or sale in retail establishments.
				51-3022	Meat, poultry, and fish cutters and trimmers	Use hand or hand tools to perform routine cutting and trimming of meat, poultry, and seafood.
				51-3023	Slaughterers and meat packers	Work in slaughtering, meat packing, or wholesale establishments performing precision functions involving the preparation of meat. Work may include specialized slaughtering tasks, cutting standard or premium cuts of meat for marketing, making sausage, or wrapping meats. Excludes "Meat, Poultry, and Fish Cutters and Trimmers" (51-3022) who perform routine meat cutting.
Food and tobacco roasting, baking, and drying machine operators and tenders	7830	51-3091	10	51-3091	Food and tobacco roasting, baking, and drying machine operators and tenders	Operate or tend food or tobacco roasting, baking, or drying equipment, including hearth ovens, kiln driers, roasters, char kilns, and vacuum drying equipment.
Food batchmakers	7840	51-3092	10	51-3092	Food batchmakers	Set up and operate equipment that mixes or blends ingredients used in the manufacturing of food products. Includes candy makers and cheese makers.
Food cooking machine operators and tenders	7850	51-3093	10	51-3093	Food cooking machine operators and tenders	Operate or tend cooking equipment, such as steam cooking vats, deep fry cookers, pressure cookers, kettles, and boilers, to prepare food products. Excludes "Food and Tobacco Roasting, Baking, and Drying Machine Operators and tenders" (51-3091).
Food processing workers, all other	7855	51-3099	10	51-3099	Food processing workers, all other	All food processing workers not listed separately

DETAILED OCCUPATIONS, BY EEO OCCUPATION GROUPS, 2006–2010—*Continued*

2010 EEO Occupation Title	2010 EEO Occupation Code	2010 SOC Code(s)	EEO Occupation Group (14)	2010 SOC Code	2010 SOC Occcupation Title	SOC Definition
\multicolumn{7}{c}{**Production Operative Workers**—*Continued*}					
Computer control programmers and operators	7900	51-4010	10	51-4011	Computer-controlled machine tool operators, metal and plastic	Operate computer-controlled machines or robots to perform one or more machine functions on metal or plastic work pieces.
				51-4012	Computer numerically controlled machine tool programmers, metal and plastic	Develop programs to control machining or processing of metal or plastic parts by automatic machine tools, equipment, or systems.
Extruding and drawing machine setters, operators, and tenders, metal and plastic	7920	51-4021	10	51-4021	Extruding and drawing machine setters, operators, and tenders, metal and plastic	Set up, operate, or tend machines to extrude or draw thermoplastic or metal materials into tubes, rods, hoses, wire, bars, or structural shapes.
Forging machine setters, operators, and tenders, metal and plastic	7930	51-4022	10	51-4022	Forging machine setters, operators, and tenders, metal and plastic	Set up, operate, or tend forging machines to taper, shape, or form metal or plastic parts.
Rolling machine setters, operators, and tenders, metal and plastic	7940	51-4023	10	51-4023	Rolling machine setters, operators, and tenders, metal and plastic	Set up, operate, or tend machines to roll steel or plastic forming bends, beads, knurls, rolls, or plate or to flatten, temper, or reduce gauge of material.
Cutting, punching, and press machine setters, operators, and tenders, metal and plastic	7950	51-4031	10	51-4031	Cutting, punching, and press machine setters, operators, and tenders, metal and plastic	Set up, operate, or tend machines to saw, cut, shear, slit, punch, crimp, notch, bend, or straighten metal or plastic material.
Drilling and boring machine tool setters, operators, and tenders, metal and plastic	7960	51-4032	10	51-4032	Drilling and boring machine tool setters, operators, and tenders, metal and plastic	Set up, operate, or tend drilling machines to drill, bore, ream, mill, or countersink metal or plastic work pieces.
Grinding, lapping, polishing, and buffing machine tool setters, operators, and tenders, metal and plastic	8000	51-4033	10	51-4033	Grinding, lapping, polishing, and buffing machine tool setters, operators, and tenders, metal and plastic	Set up, operate, or tend grinding and related tools that remove excess material or burrs from surfaces, sharpen edges or corners, or buff, hone, or polish metal or plastic work pieces.
Lathe and turning machine tool setters, operators, and tenders, metal and plastic	8010	51-4034	10	51-4034	Lathe and turning machine tool setters, operators, and tenders, metal and plastic	Set up, operate, or tend lathe and turning machines to turn, bore, thread, form, or face metal or plastic materials, such as wire, rod, or bar stock.
Metal furnace operators, tenders, pourers, and casters	8040	51-4050	10	51-4051	Metal-refining furnace operators and tenders	Operate or tend furnaces, such as gas, oil, coal, electric-arc or electric induction, open-hearth, or oxygen furnaces, to melt and refine metal before casting or to produce specified types of steel. Excludes "Heat Treating Equipment Setters, Operators, and tenders, metal and plastic" (51-4191).
				51-4052	Pourers and casters, metal	Operate hand-controlled mechanisms to pour and regulate the flow of molten metal into molds to produce castings or ingots.
Molders and molding machine setters, operators, and tenders, metal and plastic	8100	51-4070	10	51-4071	Foundry mold and coremakers	Make or form wax or sand cores or molds used in the production of metal castings in foundries.
				51-4072	Molding, coremaking, and casting machine setters, operators, and tenders, metal and plastic	Set up, operate, or tend metal or plastic molding, casting, or coremaking machines to mold or cast metal or thermoplastic parts or products.
Welding, soldering, and brazing workers	8140	51-4120	10	51-4121	Welders, cutters, solderers, and brazers	Use hand-welding, flame-cutting, hand soldering, or brazing equipment to weld or join metal components or to fill holes, indentations, or seams of fabricated metal products.

APPENDIX B

DETAILED OCCUPATIONS, BY EEO OCCUPATION GROUPS, 2006–2010—*Continued*

2010 EEO Occupation Title	2010 EEO Occupation Code	2010 SOC Code(s)	EEO Occupation Group (14)	2010 SOC Code	2010 SOC Occcupation Title	SOC Definition
Production Operative Workers—Continued							
Welding, soldering, and brazing workers—Continued	8140	51-4120	10	51-4122	Welding, soldering, and brazing machine setters, operators, and tenders	Set up, operate, or tend welding, soldering, or brazing machines or robots that weld, braze, solder, or heat treat metal products, components, or assemblies. Includes workers who operate laser cutters or laser-beam machines.
Heat treating equipment setters, operators, and tenders, metal and plastic	8150	51-4191	10	51-4191	Heat treating equipment setters, operators, and tenders, metal and plastic	Set up, operate, or tend heating equipment, such as heat-treating furnaces, flame-hardening machines, induction machines, soaking pits, or vacuum equipment to temper, harden, anneal, or heat-treat metal or plastic objects.
Plating and coating machine setters, operators, and tenders, metal and plastic	8200	51-4193	10	51-4193	Plating and coating machine setters, operators, and tenders, metal and plastic	Set up, operate, or tend plating or coating machines to coat metal or plastic products with chromium, zinc, copper, cadmium, nickel, or other metal to protect or decorate surfaces. Includes electrolytic processes.
Tool grinders, filers, and sharpeners	8210	51-4194	10	51-4194	Tool grinders, filers, and sharpeners	Perform precision smoothing, sharpening, polishing, or grinding of metal objects.
Miscellaneous metal workers and plastic workers, including milling and planing machine setters, and multiple machine tool setters, and layout workers	8220	51-4XXX Combines: 51-4035 51-4081 51-4192 (Note 2) 51-4199	10	51-4035	Milling and planing machine setters, operators, and tenders, metal and plastic	Set up, operate, or tend milling or planing machines to mill, plane, shape, groove, or profile metal or plastic work pieces.
				51-4081	Multiple machine tool setters, operators, and tenders, metal and plastic	Set up, operate, or tend more than one type of cutting or forming machine tool or robot.
				51-4192	Layout workers, metal and plastic	Lay out reference points and dimensions on metal or plastic stock or workpieces, such as sheets, plates, tubes, structural shapes, castings, or machine parts, for further processing. Includes shipfitters.
				51-4199	Metal workers and plastic workers, all other	All metal workers and plastic workers not listed separately.
Printing press operators	8255	51-5112	10	51-5112	Printing press operators	Set up and operate digital, letterpress, lithographic, flexographic, gravure, or other printing machines. Includes short-run offset printing presses.
Laundry and dry-cleaning workers	8300	51-6011	10	51-6011	Laundry and dry-cleaning workers	Operate or tend washing or dry-cleaning machines to wash or dry-clean industrial or household articles, such as cloth garments, suede, leather, furs, blankets, draperies, linens, rugs, and carpets. Includes spotters and dyers of these articles.
Pressers, textile, garment, and related materials	8310	51-6021	10	51-6021	Pressers, textile, garment, and related materials	Press or shape articles by hand or machine.
Sewing machine operators	8320	51-6031	10	51-6031	Sewing machine operators	Operate or tend sewing machines to join, reinforce, decorate, or perform related sewing operations in the manufacture of garment or nongarment products.
Shoe machine operators and tenders	8340	51-6042	10	51-6042	Shoe machine operators and tenders	Operate or tend a variety of machines to join, decorate, reinforce, or finish shoes and shoe parts.
Textile bleaching and dyeing, and cutting machine setters, operators, and tenders	8400	51-606X Combines: 51-6061 51-6062	10	51-6061	Textile bleaching and dyeing machine operators and tenders	Operate or tend machines to bleach, shrink, wash, dye, or finish textiles or synthetic or glass fibers.
				51-6062	Textile cutting machine setters, operators, and tenders	Set up, operate, or tend machines that cut textiles.
Textile knitting and weaving machine setters, operators, and tenders	8410	51-6063	10	51-6063	Textile knitting and weaving machine setters, operators, and tenders	Set up, operate, or tend machines that knit, loop, weave, or draw in textiles. Excludes "Sewing Machine Operators" (51-6031).

DETAILED OCCUPATIONS, BY EEO OCCUPATION GROUPS, 2006–2010—*Continued*

2010 EEO Occupation Title	2010 EEO Occupation Code	2010 SOC Code(s)	EEO Occupation Group (14)	2010 SOC Code	2010 SOC Occcupation Title	SOC Definition
Production Operative Workers—Continued							
Textile winding, twisting, and drawing out machine setters, operators, and tenders	8420	51-6064	10	51-6064	Textile winding, twisting, and drawing out machine setters, operators, and tenders	Set up, operate, or tend machines that wind or twist textiles; or draw out and combine sliver, such as wool, hemp, or synthetic fibers. Includes slubber machine and drawing frame operators.
Miscellaneous textile, apparel, and furnishings workers, except upholsterers	8460	51-609X Combines: 51-6091 51-6092 51-6099	10	51-6091	Extruding and forming machine setters, operators, and tenders, synthetic and glass fibers	Set up, operate, or tend machines that extrude and form continuous filaments from synthetic materials, such as liquid polymer, rayon, and fiberglass.
				51-6092	Fabric and apparel patternmakers	Draw and construct sets of precision master fabric patterns or layouts. May also mark and cut fabrics and apparel.
				51-6099	Textile, apparel, and furnishings workers, all other	All textile, apparel, and furnishings workers not listed separately.
Sawing machine setters, operators, and tenders, wood	8530	51-7041	10	51-7041	Sawing machine setters, operators, and tenders, wood	Set up, operate, or tend wood sawing machines. May operate CNC equipment. Includes lead sawyers.
Woodworking machine setters, operators, and tenders, except sawing	8540	51-7042	10	51-7042	Woodworking machine setters, operators, and tenders, except sawing	Set up, operate, or tend woodworking machines, such as drill presses, lathes, shapers, routers, sanders, planers, and wood nailing machines. May operate CNC equipment.
Miscellaneous plant and system operators	8630	51-8090	10	51-8091	Chemical Plant and System operators	Control or operate entire chemical processes or system of machines.
				51-8092	Gas Plant operators	Distribute or process gas for utility companies and others by controlling compressors to maintain specified pressures on main pipelines.
				51-8093	Petroleum Pump System operators, Refinery operators, and Gaugers	Operate or control petroleum refining or processing units. May specialize in controlling manifold and pumping systems, gauging or testing oil in storage tanks, or regulating the flow of oil into pipelines.
				51-8099	Plant and system operators, all other	All plant and system operators not listed separately.
Chemical processing machine setters, operators, and tenders	8640	51-9010	10	51-9011	Chemical equipment operators and tenders	Operate or tend equipment to control chemical changes or reactions in the processing of industrial or consumer products. Equipment used includes devulcanizers, steam-jacketed kettles, and reactor vessels. Excludes "Chemical Plant and System Operators" (51-8091).
				51-9012	Separating, filtering, clarifying, precipitating, and still machine setters, operators, and tenders	Set up, operate, or tend continuous flow or vat-type equipment; filter presses; shaker screens; centrifuges; condenser tubes; precipitating, fermenting, or evaporating tanks; scrubbing towers; or batch stills. These machines extract, sort, or separate liquids, gases, or solids from other materials to recover a refined product. Includes dairy processing equipment operators. Excludes "Chemical Equipment Operators and tenders" (51-9011).
Crushing, grinding, polishing, mixing, and blending workers	8650	51-9020	10	51-9021	Crushing, grinding, and polishing machine setters, operators, and tenders	Set up, operate, or tend machines to crush, grind, or polish materials, such as coal, glass, grain, stone, food, or rubber.
				51-9022	Grinding and polishing workers, hand	Grind, sand, or polish, using hand tools or hand-held power tools, a variety of metal, wood, stone, clay, plastic, or glass objects. Includes chippers, buffers, and finishers.
				51-9023	Mixing and blending machine setters, operators, and tenders	Set up, operate, or tend machines to mix or blend materials, such as chemicals, tobacco, liquids, color pigments, or explosive ingredients. Excludes "Food Batchmakers" (51-3092).

DETAILED OCCUPATIONS, BY EEO OCCUPATION GROUPS, 2006–2010—*Continued*

2010 EEO Occupation Title	2010 EEO Occupation Code	2010 SOC Code(s)	EEO Occupation Group (14)	2010 SOC Code	2010 SOC Occcupation Title	SOC Definition
\multicolumn{7}{c}{**Production Operative Workers**—*Continued*}
Cutting workers	8710	51-9030	10	51-9031	Cutters and trimmers, hand	Use hand tools or hand-held power tools to cut and trim a variety of manufactured items, such as carpet, fabric, stone, glass, or rubber.
				51-9032	Cutting and slicing machine setters, operators, and tenders	Set up, operate, or tend machines that cut or slice materials, such as glass, stone, cork, rubber, tobacco, food, paper, or insulating material. Excludes "Woodworking Machine Setters, Operators, and tenders" (51-7040), "Cutting, Punching, and Press Machine Setters, Operators, and tenders, metal and plastic" (51-4031), and "Textile Cutting Machine Setters, Operators, and tenders" (51-6062).
Extruding, forming, pressing, and compacting machine setters, operators, and tenders	8720	51-9041	10	51-9041	Extruding, forming, pressing, and compacting machine setters, operators, and tenders	Set up, operate, or tend machines, such as glass forming machines, plodder machines, and tuber machines, to shape and form products, such as glassware, food, rubber, soap, brick, tile, clay, wax, tobacco, or cosmetics. Excludes "Paper Goods Machine Setters, Operators, and tenders" (51-9196) and "Shoe Machine Operators and tenders" (51-6042).
Furnace, kiln, oven, drier, and kettle operators and tenders	8730	51-9051	10	51-9051	Furnace, kiln, oven, drier, and kettle operators and tenders	Operate or tend heating equipment other than basic metal, plastic, or food processing equipment. Includes activities, such as annealing glass, drying lumber, curing rubber, removing moisture from materials, or boiling soap.
Packaging and filling machine operators and tenders	8800	51-9111	10	51-9111	Packaging and filling machine operators and tenders	Operate or tend machines to prepare industrial or consumer products for storage or shipment. Includes cannery workers who pack food products.
Painting workers	8810	51-9120	10	51-9121	Coating, painting, and spraying machine setters, operators, and tenders	Set up, operate, or tend machines to coat or paint any of a wide variety of products including, glassware, cloth, ceramics, metal, plastic, paper, or wood, with lacquer, silver, copper, rubber, varnish, glaze, enamel, oil, or rust-proofing materials. Excludes "Plating and Coating Machine Setters, Operators, and tenders, metal and plastic" (51-4193) and "Painters, Transportation Equipment" (51-9122).
				51-9122	Painters, transportation equipment	Operate or tend painting machines to paint surfaces of transportation equipment, such as automobiles, buses, trucks, trains, boats, and airplanes. Includes painters in auto body repair facilities.
				51-9123	Painting, coating, and decorating workers	Paint, coat, or decorate articles, such as furniture, glass, plateware, pottery, jewelry, toys, books, or leather. Excludes "Artists and Related workers" (27-1010), "Designers" (27-1020), "Photographic Process workers and Processing Machine Operators" (51-9151), and "Etchers and Engravers" (51-9194).
Photographic process workers and processing machine operators	8830	51-9151	10	51-9151	Photographic process workers and processing machine operators	Perform work involved in developing and processing photographic images from film or digital media. May perform precision tasks such as editing photographic negatives and prints.
Adhesive bonding machine operators and tenders	8850	51-9191	10	51-9191	Adhesive bonding machine operators and tenders	Operate or tend bonding machines that use adhesives to join items for further processing or to form a completed product. Processes include joining veneer sheets into plywood; gluing paper; or joining rubber and rubberized fabric parts, plastic, simulated leather, or other materials. Excludes "Shoe Machine Operators and tenders" (51-6042).
Cleaning, washing, and metal pickling equipment operators and tenders	8860	51-9192	10	51-9192	Cleaning, washing, and metal pickling equipment operators and tenders	Operate or tend machines to wash or clean products, such as barrels or kegs, glass items, tin plate, food, pulp, coal, plastic, or rubber, to remove impurities.

DETAILED OCCUPATIONS, BY EEO OCCUPATION GROUPS, 2006–2010—*Continued*

2010 EEO Occupation Title	2010 EEO Occupation Code	2010 SOC Code(s)	EEO Occupation Group (14)	2010 SOC Code	2010 SOC Occcupation Title	SOC Definition
Production Operative Workers—Continued							
Molders, shapers, and casters, except metal and plastic	8920	51-9195	10	51-9195	Molders, shapers, and casters, except metal and plastic	Mold, shape, form, cast, or carve products such as food products, figurines, tile, pipes, and candles consisting of clay, glass, plaster, concrete, stone, or combinations of materials.
Paper goods machine setters, operators, and tenders	8930	51-9196	10	51-9196	Paper goods machine setters, operators, and tenders	Set up, operate, or tend paper goods machines that perform a variety of functions, such as converting, sawing, corrugating, banding, wrapping, boxing, stitching, forming, or sealing paper or paperboard sheets into products.
Tire builders	8940	51-9197	10	51-9197	Tire builders	Operate machines to build tires.
Other production workers, including semiconductor processors and cooling and freezing equipment operators	8965	51-91XX Combines: 51-9141 51-9193 51-9199	10	51-9141	Semiconductor processors	Perform any or all of the following functions in the manufacture of electronic semiconductors: load semiconductor material into furnace; saw formed ingots into segments; load individual segment into crystal growing chamber and monitor controls; locate crystal axis in ingot using x-ray equipment and saw ingots into wafers; and clean, polish, and load wafers into series of special purpose furnaces, chemical baths, and equipment used to form circuitry and change conductive properties.
				51-9193	Cooling and freezing equipment operators and tenders	Operate or tend equipment, such as cooling and freezing units, refrigerators, batch freezers, and freezing tunnels, to cool or freeze products, food, blood plasma, and chemicals.
				51-9199	Production workers, all other	All production workers not listed separately.
Transportation and Material Moving Operative Workers							
Inspectors, testers, sorters, samplers, and weighers	8740	51-9061	11	51-9061	Inspectors, testers, sorters, samplers, and weighers	Inspect, test, sort, sample, or weigh nonagricultural raw materials or processed, machined, fabricated, or assembled parts or products for defects, wear, and deviations from specifications. May use precision measuring instruments and complex test equipment.
Supervisors of transportation and material moving workers	9000	53-1000	11	53-1011	Aircraft cargo handling supervisors	Supervise and coordinate the activities of ground crew in the loading, unloading, securing, and staging of aircraft cargo or baggage. May determine the quantity and orientation of cargo and compute aircraft center of gravity. May accompany aircraft as member of flight crew and monitor and handle cargo in flight, and assist and brief passengers on safety and emergency procedures. Includes loadmasters.
				53-1021	First-line supervisors of helpers, laborers, and material movers, hand	Directly supervise and coordinate the activities of helpers, laborers, or material movers.
				53-1031	First-line supervisors of transportation and material-moving machine and vehicle operators	Directly supervise and coordinate activities of transportation and material-moving machine and vehicle operators and helpers.
Ambulance drivers and attendants, except emergency medical technicians	9110	53-3011	11	53-3011	Ambulance drivers and attendants, except emergency medical technicians	Drive ambulance or assist ambulance driver in transporting sick, injured, or convalescent persons. Assist in lifting patients.
Bus drivers	9120	53-3020	11	53-3021	Bus drivers, transit and intercity	Drive bus or motor coach, including regular route operations, charters, and private carriage. May assist passengers with baggage. May collect fares or tickets.
				53-3022	Bus Drivers, school or special Client	Transport students or special clients, such as the elderly or persons with disabilities. Ensure adherence to safety rules. May assist passengers in boarding or exiting.

DETAILED OCCUPATIONS, BY EEO OCCUPATION GROUPS, 2006–2010—*Continued*

2010 EEO Occupation Title	2010 EEO Occupation Code	2010 SOC Code(s)	EEO Occupation Group (14)	2010 SOC Code	2010 SOC Occcupation Title	SOC Definition
\multicolumn{7}{c}{*Transportation and Material Moving Operative Workers—Continued*}
Driver/sales workers and truck drivers	9130	53-3030	11	53-3031	Driver/sales workers	Drive truck or other vehicle over established routes or within an established territory and sell or deliver goods, such as food products, including restaurant take-out items, or pick up or deliver items such as commercial laundry. May also take orders, collect payment, or stock merchandise at point of delivery. Includes newspaper delivery drivers. Excludes "Coin, Vending, and Amusement Machine Servicers and Repairers" (49-9091) and "Light Truck or Delivery Services Drivers" (53-3033).
				53-3032	Heavy and tractor-trailer truck drivers	Drive a tractor-trailer combination or a truck with a capacity of at least 26,000 pounds Gross Vehicle Weight (GVW). May be required to unload truck. Requires commercial driverslicense.
				53-3033	Light truck or delivery services drivers	Drive a light vehicle, such as a truck or van, with a capacity of less than 26,000 pounds Gross Vehicle Weight (GVW), primarily to deliver or pick up merchandise or to deliver packages. May load and unload vehicle. Excludes "Couriers and Messengers" (43-5021) and "Driver/Sales workers" (53-3031).
Taxi drivers and chauffeurs	9140	53-3041	11	53-3041	Taxi drivers and chauffeurs	Drive automobiles, vans, or limousines to transport passengers. May occasionally carry cargo. Includes hearse drivers. Excludes "Ambulance Drivers and Attendants, except Emergency Medical Technicians" (53-3011) and "Bus Drivers" (53-3020).
Motor vehicle operators, all other	9150	53-3099	11	53-3099	Motor vehicle operators, all other	All motor vehicle operators not listed separately.
Locomotive engineers and operators	9200	53-4010	11	53-4011	Locomotive engineers	Drive electric, diesel-electric, steam, or gas-turbine-electric locomotives to transport passengers or freight. Interpret train orders, electronic or manual signals, and railroad rules and regulations.
				53-4012	Locomotive firers	Monitor locomotive instruments and watch for dragging equipment, obstacles on rights-of-way, and train signals during run. Watch for and relay traffic signals from yard workers to yard engineer in railroad yard.
				53-4013	Rail yard engineers, dinkey operators, and hostlers	Drive switching or other locomotive or dinkey engines within railroad yard, industrial plant, quarry, construction project, or similar location.
Railroad brake, signal, and switch operators	9230	53-4021	11	53-4021	Railroad brake, signal, and switch operators	Operate railroad track switches. Couple or uncouple rolling stock to make up or break up trains. Signal engineers by hand or flagging. May inspect couplings, air hoses, journal boxes, and hand brakes.
Railroad conductors and yardmasters	9240	53-4031	11	53-4031	Railroad conductors and yardmasters	Coordinate activities of switch-engine crew within railroad yard, industrial plant, or similar location. Conductors coordinate activities of train crew on passenger or freight trains. Yardmasters review train schedules and switching orders and coordinate activities of workers engaged in railroad traffic operations, such as the makeup or breakup of trains and yard switching.
Subway, streetcar, and other rail transportation workers	9260	53-40XX Combines: 53-4041 53-4099	11	53-4041	Subway and streetcar operators	Operate subway or elevated suburban trains with no separate locomotive, or electric-powered streetcar, to transport passengers. May handle fares.
				53-4099	Rail transportation workers, all other	All rail transportation workers not listed separately.

DETAILED OCCUPATIONS, BY EEO OCCUPATION GROUPS, 2006–2010—*Continued*

2010 EEO Occupation Title	2010 EEO Occupation Code	2010 SOC Code(s)	EEO Occupation Group (14)	2010 SOC Code	2010 SOC Occcupation Title	SOC Definition
\multicolumn{7}{c}{**Transportation and Material Moving Operative Workers**—*Continued*}
Sailors and marine oilers, and ship engineers	9300	53-50XX Combines: 53-5011 53-5031	11	53-5011	Sailors and marine oilers	Stand watch to look for obstructions in path of vessel, measure water depth, turn wheel on bridge, or use emergency equipment as directed by captain, mate, or pilot. Break out, rig, overhaul, and store cargo-handling gear, stationary rigging, and running gear. Perform a variety of maintenance tasks to preserve the painted surface of the ship and to maintain line and ship equipment. Must hold government-issued certification and tankerman certification when working aboard liquid-carrying vessels. Includes able seamen and ordinary seamen.
				53-5031	Ship engineers	Supervise and coordinate activities of crew engaged in operating and maintaining engines, boilers, deck machinery, and electrical, sanitary, and refrigeration equipment aboard ship.
Ship and boat captains and operators	9310	53-5020	11	53-5021	Captains, mates, and pilots of water vessels	Command or supervise operations of ships and water vessels, such as tugboats and ferryboats. Required to hold license issued by U.S. Coast Guard. Excludes "Motorboat Operators" (53-5022).
				53-5022	Motorboat operators	Operate small motor-driven boats. May assist in navigational activities.
Parking lot attendants	9350	53-6021	11	53-6021	Parking lot attendants	Park vehicles or issue tickets for customers in a parking lot or garage. May collect fee.
Miscellaneous transportation workers, including bridge and lock tenders and traffic technicians	9420	53-60XX Combines: 53-6011 53-6041 53-6099	11	53-6011	Bridge and lock tenders	Operate and tend bridges, canal locks, and lighthouses to permit marine passage on inland waterways, near shores, and at danger points in waterway passages. May supervise such operations. Includes drawbridge operators, lock operators, and slip bridge operators.
				53-6041	Traffic technicians	Conduct field studies to determine traffic volume, speed, effectiveness of signals, adequacy of lighting, and other factors influencing traffic conditions, under direction of traffic engineer.
				53-6099	Transportation workers, all other	All transportation workers not listed separately.
Conveyor operators and tenders, and hoist and winch operators	9560	53-70XX Combines: 53-7011 53-7041	11	53-7011	Conveyor operators and tenders	Control or tend conveyors or conveyor systems that move materials or products to and from stockpiles, processing stations, departments, or vehicles. May control speed and routing of materials or products.
				53-7041	Hoist and winch operators	Operate or tend hoists or winches to lift and pull loads using power-operated cable equipment. Excludes "Crane and Tower Operators" (53-7021).
Industrial truck and tractor operators	9600	53-7051	11	53-7051	Industrial truck and tractor operators	Operate industrial trucks or tractors equipped to move materials around a warehouse, storage yard, factory, construction site, or similar location. Excludes "Logging Equipment Operators" (45-4022).
Packers and packagers, hand	9640	53-7064	11	53-7064	Packers and packagers, hand	Pack or package by hand a wide variety of products and materials.
Pumping station operators	9650	53-7070	11	53-7071	Gas compressor and gas pumping station operators	Operate steam, gas, electric motor, or internal combustion engine driven compressors. Transmit, compress, or recover gases, such as butane, nitrogen, hydrogen, and natural gas.
				53-7072	Pump operators, except wellhead pumpers	Tend, control, or operate power-driven, stationary, or portable pumps and manifold systems to transfer gases, oil, other liquids, slurries, or powdered materials to and from various vessels and processes.
				53-7073	Wellhead pumpers	Operate power pumps and auxiliary equipment to produce flow of oil or gas from wells in oil field.
Miscellaneous material moving workers, including mine shuttle car operators, and tank car, truck, and ship loaders	9750	53-71XX Combines: 53-7111 53-7121 53-7199	11	53-7111	Mine shuttle car operators	Operate diesel or electric-powered shuttle car in underground mine to transport materials from working face to mine cars or conveyor.

DETAILED OCCUPATIONS, BY EEO OCCUPATION GROUPS, 2006–2010—*Continued*

2010 EEO Occupation Title	2010 EEO Occupation Code	2010 SOC Code(s)	EEO Occupation Group (14)	2010 SOC Code	2010 SOC Occcupation Title	SOC Definition
\multicolumn{7}{c}{**Transportation and Material Moving Operative Workers**—*Continued*}						
Miscellaneous material moving workers, including mine shuttle car operators, and tank car, truck, and ship loaders—Continued	9750	53-71XX Combines: 53-7111 53-7121 53-7199	11	53-7121	Tank car, truck, and ship loaders	Load and unload chemicals and bulk solids, such as coal, sand, and grain into or from tank cars, trucks, or ships using material moving equipment. May perform a variety of other tasks relating to shipment of products. May gauge or sample shipping tanks and test them for leaks.
				53-7199	Material moving workers, all other	All material moving workers not listed separately.
\multicolumn{7}{c}{**Laborers and Helpers**}						
First-line supervisors of landscaping, lawn service, and groundskeeping workers	4210	37-1012	12	37-1012	First-line supervisors of landscaping, lawn service, and groundskeeping workers	Directly supervise and coordinate activities of workers engaged in landscaping or groundskeeping activities. Work may involve reviewing contracts to ascertain service, machine, and workforce requirements; answering inquiries from potential customers regarding methods, material, and price ranges; and preparing estimates according to labor, material, and machine costs.
Grounds maintenance workers	4250	37-3010	12	37-3011	Landscaping and groundskeeping workers	Landscape or maintain grounds of property using hand or power tools or equipment. workers typically perform a variety of tasks, which may include any combination of the following: sod laying, mowing, trimming, planting, watering, fertilizing, digging, raking, sprinkler installation, and installation of mortarless segmental concrete masonry wall units. Excludes "Farmworkers and Laborers, Crop, Nursery, and Greenhouse" (45-2092).
				37-3012	Pesticide handlers, sprayers, and applicators, vegetation	Mix or apply pesticides, herbicides, fungicides, or insecticides through sprays, dusts, vapors, soil incorporation, or chemical application on trees, shrubs, lawns, or botanical crops. Usually requires specific training and State or Federal certification. Excludes "Commercial Pilots" (53-2012) who dust or spray crops from aircraft.
				37-3013	Tree trimmers and pruners	Using sophisticated climbing and rigging techniques, cut away dead or excess branches from trees or shrubs to maintain right-of-way for roads, sidewalks, or utilities, or to improve appearance, health, and value of tree. Prune or treat trees or shrubs using handsaws, hand pruners, clippers, and power pruners. Works off the ground in the tree canopy and may use truck-mounted lifts. Excludes workers who primarily perform duties of "Pesticide Handlers, Sprayers, and Applicators, Vegetation" (37-3012) and "Landscaping and Groundskeeping workers" (37-3011).
				37-3019	Grounds maintenance workers, all other	All grounds maintenance workers not listed separately.
Nonfarm animal caretakers	4350	39-2021	12	39-2021	Nonfarm animal caretakers	Feed, water, groom, bathe, exercise, or otherwise care for pets and other nonfarm animals, such as dogs, cats, ornamental fish or birds, zoo animals, and mice. Work in settings such as kennels, animal shelters, zoos, circuses, and aquariums. May keep records of feedings, treatments, and animals received or discharged. May clean, disinfect, and repair cages, pens, or fish tanks. Excludes "Veterinary Assistants and Laboratory Animal Caretakers" (31-9096).
First-line supervisors of farming, fishing, and forestry workers	6005	45-1011	12	45-1011	First-line supervisors of farming, fishing, and forestry workers	Directly supervise and coordinate the activities of agricultural, forestry, aquacultural, and related workers. Excludes "First-Line Supervisors of Landscaping, Lawn Service, and Groundskeeping workers" (37-1012).

DETAILED OCCUPATIONS, BY EEO OCCUPATION GROUPS, 2006–2010—*Continued*

2010 EEO Occupation Title	2010 EEO Occupation Code	2010 SOC Code(s)	EEO Occupation Group (14)	2010 SOC Code	2010 SOC Occcupation Title	SOC Definition
\multicolumn{7}{c}{Laborers and Helpers—*Continued*}					
Miscellaneous agricultural workers, including animal breeders	6050	45-20XX Combines: 45-2021 (Note 2) 45-2090	12	45-2021	Animal breeders	Select and breed animals according to their genealogy, characteristics, and offspring. May require knowledge of artificial insemination techniques and equipment use. May involve keeping records on heats, birth intervals, or pedigree. Excludes "Nonfarm Animal Caretakers" (39-2021) who may occasionally breed animals as part of their other caretaking duties. Excludes "Animal Scientists" (19-1011) whose primary function is research.
				45-2091	Agricultural equipment operators	Drive and control farm equipment to till soil and to plant, cultivate, and harvest crops. May perform tasks, such as crop baling or hay bucking. May operate stationary equipment to perform post-harvest tasks, such as husking, shelling, threshing, and ginning.
				45-2092	Farmworkers and laborers, crop, nursery, and greenhouse	Manually plant, cultivate, and harvest vegetables, fruits, nuts, horticultural specialties, and field crops. Use hand tools, such as shovels, trowels, hoes, tampers, pruning hooks, shears, and knives. Duties may include tilling soil and applying fertilizers; transplanting, weeding, thinning, or pruning crops; applying pesticides; or cleaning, grading, sorting, packing, and loading harvested products. May construct trellises, repair fences and farm buildings, or participate in irrigation activities. Excludes "Graders and Sorters, Agricultural Products" (45-2041) and "Forest, Conservation, and Logging workers" (45-4011 through 45-4029).
				45-2093	Farmworkers, farm, ranch, and aquacultural animals	Attend to live farm, ranch, or aquacultural animals that may include cattle, sheep, swine, goats, horses and other equines, poultry, finfish, shellfish, and bees. Attend to animals produced for animal products, such as meat, fur, skins, feathers, eggs, milk, and honey. Duties may include feeding, watering, herding, grazing, castrating, branding, de-beaking, weighing, catching, and loading animals. May maintain records on animals; examine animals to detect diseases and injuries; assist in birth deliveries; and administer medications, vaccinations, or insecticides as appropriate. May clean and maintain animal housing areas. Includes workers who shear wool from sheep, and collect eggs in hatcheries.
				45-2099	Agricultural workers, all other	All agricultural workers not listed separately.
Fishing and hunting workers	6100	45-3000 Combines: 45-3011 45-3021	12	45-3011	Fishers and related fishing workers	Use nets, fishing rods, traps, or other equipment to catch and gather fish or other aquatic animals from rivers, lakes, or oceans, for human consumption or other uses. May haul game onto ship. Aquacultural laborers who work on fish farms are included in "Farmworkers, Farm, Ranch, and Aquacultural Animals" (45-2093).
				45-3021	Hunters and Trappers	Hunt and trap wild animals for human consumption, fur, feed, bait, or other purposes.
Forest and conservation workers	6120	45-4011	12	45-4011	Forest and conservation workers	Under supervision, perform manual labor necessary to develop, maintain, or protect areas such as forests, forested areas, woodlands, wetlands, and rangelands through such activities as raising and transporting seedlings; combating insects, pests, and diseases harmful to plant life; and building structures to control water, erosion, and leaching of soil. Includes forester aides, seedling pullers, and tree planters.

DETAILED OCCUPATIONS, BY EEO OCCUPATION GROUPS, 2006–2010—*Continued*

2010 EEO Occupation Title	2010 EEO Occupation Code	2010 SOC Code(s)	EEO Occupation Group (14)	2010 SOC Code	2010 SOC Occupation Title	SOC Definition
				Laborers and Helpers—*Continued*		
Logging workers	6130	45-4020	12	45-4021	Fallers	Use axes or chainsaws to fell trees using knowledge of tree characteristics and cutting techniques to control direction of fall and minimize tree damage.
				45-4022	Logging equipment operators	Drive logging tractor or wheeled vehicle equipped with one or more accessories, such as bulldozer blade, frontal shear, grapple, logging arch, cable winches, hoisting rack, or crane boom, to fell tree; to skid, load, unload, or stack logs; or to pull stumps or clear brush. Logging truck drivers are included in "Heavy and Tractor Trailer Truck Drivers" (53-3032).
				45-4023	Log graders and scalers	Grade logs or estimate the marketable content or value of logs or pulpwood in sorting yards, millpond, log deck, or similar locations. Inspect logs for defects or measure logs to determine volume. Excludes "Buyers and Purchasing agents, Farm Products" (13-1021).
				45-4029	Logging workers, all other	All logging workers not listed separately.
Helpers, construction trades	6600	47-3010	12	47-3011	Helpers\Brickmasons, blockmasons, stonemasons, and tile and marble setters	Help brickmasons, blockmasons, stonemasons, or tile and marble setters by performing duties requiring less skill. Duties include using, supplying or holding materials or tools, and cleaning work area and equipment. Construction laborers who do not primarily assist brickmasons, blockmasons, and stonemasons or tile and marble setters are classified under "Construction Laborers" (47-2061). Apprentice workers are classified with the appropriate skilled construction trade occupation (47-2011 through 47-2231).
				47-3012	Helpers\Carpenters	Help carpenters by performing duties requiring less skill. Duties include using, supplying or holding materials or tools, and cleaning work area and equipment. Construction laborers who do not primarily assist carpenters are classified under "Construction Laborers" (47-2061). Apprentice workers are classified with the appropriate skilled construction trade occupation (47-2011 through 47-2231).
				47-3013	Helpers\Electricians	Help electricians by performing duties requiring less skill. Duties include using, supplying or holding materials or tools, and cleaning work area and equipment. Construction laborers who do not primarily assist electricians are classified under "Construction Laborers" (47-2061). Apprentice workers are classified with the appropriate skilled construction trade occupation (47-2011 through 47-2231).
				47-3014	Helpers\Painters, paperhangers, plasterers, and stucco masons	Help painters, paperhangers, plasterers, or stucco masons by performing duties requiring less skill. Duties include using, supplying or holding materials or tools, and cleaning work area and equipment. Construction laborers who do not primarily assist painters, paperhangers, plasterers, or stucco masons are classified under "Construction Laborers" (47-2061). Apprentice workers are classified with the appropriate skilled construction trade occupation (47-2011 through 47-2231).

DETAILED OCCUPATIONS, BY EEO OCCUPATION GROUPS, 2006–2010—*Continued*

2010 EEO Occupation Title	2010 EEO Occupation Code	2010 SOC Code(s)	EEO Occupation Group (14)	2010 SOC Code	2010 SOC Occcupation Title	SOC Definition
Laborers and Helpers—Continued						
Helpers, construction trades—Continued	6600	47-3010	12	47-3015	Helpers\Pipelayers, plumbers, pipefitters, and steamfitters	Help plumbers, pipefitters, steamfitters, or pipelayers by performing duties requiring less skill. Duties include using, supplying or holding materials or tools, and cleaning work area and equipment. Construction laborers who do not primarily assist plumbers, pipefitters, steamfitters, or pipelayers are classified under "Construction Laborers" (47-2061). Apprentice workers are classified with the appropriate skilled construction trade occupation (47-2011 through 47-2231).
				47-3016	Helpers\Roofers	Help roofers by performing duties requiring less skill. Duties include using, supplying or holding materials or tools, and cleaning work area and equipment. Construction laborers who do not primarily assist roofers are classified under "Construction Laborers" (47-2061). Apprentice workers are classified with the appropriate skilled construction trade occupation (47-2011 through 47-2231).
				47-3019	Helpers, construction trades, all other	All construction trades helpers not listed separately.
Helpers\installation, maintenance, and repair workers	7610	49-9098	12	49-9098	Helpers\installation, maintenance, and repair workers	Help installation, maintenance, and repair workers in maintenance, parts replacement, and repair of vehicles, industrial machinery, and electrical and electronic equipment. Perform duties such as furnishing tools, materials, and supplies to other workers; cleaning work area, machines, and tools; and holding materials or tools for other workers.
Helpers\production workers	8950	51-9198	12	51-9198	Helpers\production workers	Help production workers by performing duties requiring less skill. Duties include supplying or holding materials or tools, and cleaning work area and equipment. Apprentice workers are classified in the appropriate production occupations (51-0000).
Automotive and watercraft service attendants	9360	53-6031	12	53-6031	Automotive and watercraft service attendants	Service automobiles, buses, trucks, boats, and other automotive or marine vehicles with fuel, lubricants, and accessories. Collect payment for services and supplies. May lubricate vehicle, change motor oil, install antifreeze, or replace lights or other accessories, such as windshield wiper blades or fan belts. May repair or replace tires.
Cleaners of vehicles and equipment	9610	53-7061	12	53-7061	Cleaners of vehicles and equipment	Wash or otherwise clean vehicles, machinery, and other equipment. Use such materials as water, cleaning agents, brushes, cloths, and hoses. Excludes "Janitors and Cleaners, except Maids and Housekeeping Cleaners" (37-2011).
Laborers and freight, stock, and material movers, hand	9620	53-7062	12	53-7062	Laborers and freight, stock, and material movers, hand	Manually move freight, stock, or other materials or perform other general labor. Includes all manual laborers not elsewhere classified. Excludes "Material Moving workers" (53-7011 through 53-7199) who use power equipment. Excludes "Construction Laborers" (47-2061) and "Helpers, Construction Trades (47-3011 through 47-3019).
Machine feeders and offbearers	9630	53-7063	12	53-7063	Machine feeders and offbearers	Feed materials into or remove materials from machines or equipment that is automatic or tended by other workers.
Refuse and recyclable material collectors	9720	53-7081	12	53-7081	Refuse and recyclable material collectors	Collect and dump refuse or recyclable materials from containers into truck. May drive truck.
Protective Service Workers						
First-line supervisors of correctional officers	3700	33-1011	13	33-1011	First-line supervisors of correctional officers	Directly supervise and coordinate activities of correctional officers and jailers.
First-line supervisors of police and detectives	3710	33-1012	13	33-1012	First-line supervisors of police and detectives	Directly supervise and coordinate activities of members of police force.

DETAILED OCCUPATIONS, BY EEO OCCUPATION GROUPS, 2006–2010—*Continued*

2010 EEO Occupation Title	2010 EEO Occupation Code	2010 SOC Code(s)	EEO Occupation Group (14)	2010 SOC Code	2010 SOC Occcupation Title	SOC Definition
\multicolumn{7}{c}{**Protective Service Workers**—*Continued*}
First-line supervisors of fire fighting and prevention workers	3720	33-1021	13	33-1021	First-line supervisors of fire fighting and prevention workers	Directly supervise and coordinate activities of workers engaged in fire fighting and fire prevention and control.
First-line supervisors of protective service workers, all other	3730	33-1099	13	33-1099	First-line supervisors of protective service workers, all other	All protective service supervisors not listed separately above.
Firefighters	3740	33-2011	13	33-2011	Firefighters	Control and extinguish fires or respond to emergency situations where life, property, or the environment is at risk. Duties may include fire prevention, emergency medical service, hazardous material response, search and rescue, and disaster assistance.
Fire inspectors	3750	33-2020	13	33-2021	Fire inspectors and investigators	Inspect buildings to detect fire hazards and enforce local ordinances and State laws, or investigate and gather facts to determine cause of fires and explosions.
				33-2022	Forest fire inspectors and prevention specialists	Enforce fire regulations, inspect forest for fire hazards and recommend forest fire prevention or control measures. May report forest fires and weather conditions.
Bailiffs, correctional officers, and jailers	3800	33-3010	13	33-3011	Bailiffs	Maintain order in courts of law.
				33-3012	Correctional officers and jailers	Guard inmates in penal or rehabilitative institutions in accordance with established regulations and procedures. May guard prisoners in transit between jail, courtroom, prison, or other point. Includes deputy sheriffs and police who spend the majority of their time guarding prisoners in correctional institutions.
Detectives and criminal investigators	3820	33-3021	13	33-3021	Detectives and criminal investigators	Conduct investigations related to suspected violations of Federal, State, or local laws to prevent or solve crimes. Excludes "Private Detectives and Investigators" (33-9021).
Miscellaneous law enforcement workers	3840	33-30XX Combines: 33-3031 33-3041	13	33-3031	Fish and game wardens	Patrol assigned area to prevent fish and game law violations. Investigate reports of damage to crops or property by wildlife. Compile biological data.
				33-3041	Parking enforcement workers	Patrol assigned area, such as public parking lot or city streets to issue tickets to overtime parking violators and illegally parked vehicles.
Police officers	3850	33-3050 Combines: 33-3051 33-3052	13	33-3051	Police and sheriff's patrol officers	Maintain order and protect life and property by enforcing local, tribal, State, or Federal laws and ordinances. Perform a combination of the following duties: patrol a specific area; direct traffic; issue traffic summonses; investigate accidents; apprehend and arrest suspects, or serve legal processes of courts.
				33-3052	Transit and Railroad police	Protect and police railroad and transit property, employees, or passengers.
Animal control workers	3900	33-9011	13	33-9011	Animal control workers	Handle animals for the purpose of investigations of mistreatment, or control of abandoned, dangerous, or unattended animals.
Private detectives and investigators	3910	33-9021	13	33-9021	Private detectives and investigators	Gather, analyze, compile and report information regarding individuals or organizations to clients, or detect occurrences of unlawful acts or infractions of rules in private establishment.
Security guards and gaming surveillance officers	3930	33-9030	13	33-9031	Gaming surveillance officers and gaming investigators	Act as oversight and security agent for management and customers. Observe casino or casino hotel operation for irregular activities such as cheating or theft by either employees or patrons. May use one-way mirrors above the casino floor, cashier's cage, and from desk. Use of audio/video equipment is also common to observe operation of the business. Usually required to provide verbal and written reports of all violations and suspicious behavior to supervisor.

DETAILED OCCUPATIONS, BY EEO OCCUPATION GROUPS, 2006–2010—*Continued*

2010 EEO Occupation Title	2010 EEO Occupation Code	2010 SOC Code(s)	EEO Occupation Group (14)	2010 SOC Code	2010 SOC Occupation Title	SOC Definition
Protective Service Workers—*Continued*							
Security guards and gaming surveillance officers—Continued	3930	33-9030	13	33-9032	Security guards	Guard, patrol, or monitor premises to prevent theft, violence, or infractions of rules. May operate x-ray and metal detector equipment. Excludes "Transportation Security Screeners" (33-9093).
Crossing guards	3940	33-9091	13	33-9091	Crossing guards	Guide or control vehicular or pedestrian traffic at such places as streets, schools, railroad crossings, or construction sites.
Transportation security screeners	3945	33-9093	13	33-9093	Transportation security screeners	Conduct screening of passengers, baggage, or cargo to ensure compliance with Transportation Security Administration (TSA) regulations. May operate basic security equipment such as x-ray machines and hand wands at screening checkpoints.
Lifeguards and other recreational, and all other protective service workers	3955	33-909X Combines: 33-9092 33-9099	13	33-9092	Lifeguards, ski patrol, and other recreational protective service	Monitor recreational areas, such as pools, beaches, or ski slopes to provide assistance and protection to participants.
				33-9099	Protective service workers, all other	All protective service workers not listed separately.
Service Workers, Except Protective							
Nursing, psychiatric, and home health aides	3600	31-1010	14	31-1011	Home health aides	Provide routine individualized Health care such as changing bandages and dressing wounds, and applying topical medications to the elderly, convalescents, or persons with disabilities at the patient's home or in a care facility. Monitor or report changes in health status. May also provide personal care such as bathing, dressing, and grooming of patient.
				31-1013	Psychiatric aides	Assist mentally impaired or emotionally disturbed patients, working under direction of nursing and medical staff. May assist with daily living activities, lead patients in educational and recreational activities, or accompany patients to and from examinations and treatments. May restrain violent patients. Includes psychiatric orderlies.
				31-1014	Nursing assistants	Provide basic patient care under direction of nursing staff. Perform duties such as feed, bathe, dress, groom, or move patients, or change linens. May transfer or transport patients. Includes nursing care attendants, nursing aides, and nursing attendants. Excludes "Home Health Aides" (31-1011), "Orderlies" (31-1015), "Personal Care Aides" (39-9021), and "Psychiatric Aides" (31-1013).
				31-1015	Orderlies	Transport patients to areas such as operating rooms or x-ray rooms using wheelchairs, stretchers, or moveable beds. May maintain stocks of supplies or clean and transport equipment. Psychiatric orderlies are included in "Psychiatric Aides" (31-1013). Excludes "Nursing Assistants" (31-1014).
Occupational therapy assistants and aides	3610	31-2010	14	31-2011	Occupational therapy assistants	Assist occupational therapists in providing occupational therapy treatments and procedures. May, in accordance with State laws, assist in development of treatment plans, carry out routine functions, direct activity programs, and document the progress of treatments. Generally requires formal training.
				31-2012	Occupational therapy aides	Under close supervision of an occupational therapist or occupational therapy assistant, perform only delegated, selected, or routine tasks in specific situations. These duties include preparing patient and treatment room.

APPENDIX B

DETAILED OCCUPATIONS, BY EEO OCCUPATION GROUPS, 2006–2010—*Continued*

2010 EEO Occupation Title	2010 EEO Occupation Code	2010 SOC Code(s)	EEO Occupation Group (14)	2010 SOC Code	2010 SOC Occupation Title	SOC Definition
\multicolumn{7}{c}{**Service Workers, Except Protective**—*Continued*}
Physical therapist assistants and aides	3620	31-2020	14	31-2021	Physical Therapist assistants	Assist physical therapists in providing physical therapy treatments and procedures. May, in accordance with State laws, assist in the development of treatment plans, carry out routine functions, document the progress of treatment, and modify specific treatments in accordance with patient status and within the scope of treatment plans established by a physical therapist. Generally requires formal training.
				31-2022	Physical Therapist Aides	Under close supervision of a physical therapist or physical therapy assistant, perform only delegated, selected, or routine tasks in specific situations. These duties include preparing the patient and the treatment area.
Massage therapists	3630	31-9011	14	31-9011	Massage therapists	Perform therapeutic massages of soft tissues and joints. May assist in the assessment of range of motion and muscle strength, or propose client therapy plans.
Dental assistants	3640	31-9091	14	31-9091	Dental assistants	Assist dentist, set up equipment, prepare patient for treatment, and keep records.
Medical assistants	3645	31-9092	14	31-9092	Medical assistants	Perform administrative and certain clinical duties under the direction of a physician. Administrative duties may include scheduling appointments, maintaining medical records, billing, and coding information for insurance purposes. Clinical duties may include taking and recording vital signs and medical histories, preparing patients for examination, drawing blood, and administering medications as directed by physician. Excludes "Physician Assistants" (29-1071).
Pharmacy aides	3647	31-9095	14	31-9095	Pharmacy aides	Record drugs delivered to the pharmacy, store incoming merchandise, and inform the supervisor of stock needs. May operate cash register and accept prescriptions for filling.
Veterinary assistants and laboratory animal caretakers	3648	31-9096	14	31-9096	Veterinary assistants and laboratory animal caretakers	Feed, water, and examine pets and other nonfarm animals for signs of illness, disease, or injury in laboratories and animal hospitals and clinics. Clean and disinfect cages and work areas, and sterilize laboratory and surgical equipment. May provide routine post-operative care, administer medication orally or topically, or prepare samples for laboratory examination under the supervision of veterinary or laboratory animal technologists or technicians, veterinarians, or scientists. Excludes "Nonfarm Animal Caretakers" (39-2021).
Phlebotomists	3649	31-9097	14	31-9097	Phlebotomists	Draw blood for tests, transfusions, donations, or research. May explain the procedure to patients and assist in the recovery of patients with adverse reactions.
Health care support workers, all other, including medical equipment preparers	3655	31-909X Combines: 31-9093 31-9099	14	31-9093	Medical equipment preparers	Prepare, sterilize, install, or clean laboratory or Health care equipment. May perform routine laboratory tasks and operate or inspect equipment.
				31-9099	Health care support workers, all other	All Health care support workers not listed separately
Chefs and head cooks	4000	35-1011	14	35-1011	Chefs and head cooks	Direct and may participate in the preparation, seasoning, and cooking of salads, soups, fish, meats, vegetables, desserts, or other foods. May plan and price menu items, order supplies, and keep records and accounts.
First-line supervisors of food preparation and serving workers	4010	35-1012	14	35-1012	First-line supervisors of food preparation and serving workers	Directly supervise and coordinate activities of workers engaged in preparing and serving food.

DETAILED OCCUPATIONS, BY EEO OCCUPATION GROUPS, 2006–2010—*Continued*

2010 EEO Occupation Title	2010 EEO Occupation Code	2010 SOC Code(s)	EEO Occupation Group (14)	2010 SOC Code	2010 SOC Occcupation Title	SOC Definition
Service Workers, Except Protective—Continued						
Cooks	4020	35-2010	14	35-2011	Cooks, fast food	Prepare and cook food in a fast food restaurant with a limited menu. Duties of these cooks are limited to preparation of a few basic items and normally involve operating large-volume single-purpose cooking equipment.
				35-2012	Cooks, institution and cafeteria	Prepare and cook large quantities of food for institutions, such as schools, hospitals, or cafeterias.
				35-2013	Cooks, private household	Prepare meals in private homes. Includes personal chefs.
				35-2014	Cooks, restaurant	Prepare, season, and cook dishes such as soups, meats, vegetables, or desserts in restaurants. May order supplies, keep records and accounts, price items on menu, or plan menu.
				35-2015	Cooks, short order	Prepare and cook to order a variety of foods that require only a short preparation time. May take orders from customers and serve patrons at counters or tables. Excludes "Fast Food Cooks" (35-2011).
				35-2019	Cooks, all other	All cooks not listed separately.
Food preparation workers	4030	35-2021	14	35-2021	Food preparation workers	Perform a variety of food preparation duties other than cooking, such as preparing cold foods and shellfish, slicing meat, and brewing coffee or tea.
Bartenders	4040	35-3011	14	35-3011	Bartenders	Mix and serve drinks to patrons, directly or through waitstaff.
Combined food preparation and serving workers, including fast food	4050	35-3021	14	35-3021	Combined food preparation and serving workers, including fast food	Perform duties which combine preparing and serving food and nonalcoholic beverages.
Counter attendants, cafeteria, food concession, and coffee shop	4060	35-3022	14	35-3022	Counter attendants, cafeteria, food concession, and coffee shop	Serve food to diners at counter or from a steam table. Counter attendants who also wait tables are included in "Waiters and Waitresses" (35-3031).
Waiters and waitresses	4110	35-3031	14	35-3031	Waiters and waitresses	Take orders and serve food and beverages to patrons at tables in dining establishment. Excludes "Counter Attendants, Cafeteria, Food Concession, and Coffee Shop" (35-3022).
Food servers, nonrestaurant	4120	35-3041	14	35-3041	Food servers, nonrestaurant	Serve food to individuals outside of a restaurant environment, such as in hotel rooms, hospital rooms, residential care facilities, or cars. Excludes "Door-to-Door Sales workers, News and Street Vendors, and Related workers" (41-9091) and "Counter Attendants, Cafeteria, Food Concession, and Coffee Shop" (35-3022).
Miscellaneous food preparation and serving related workers, including dining room and cafeteria attendants and bartender helpers	4130	35-90XX Combines: 35-9011 35-9099	14	35-9011	Dining room and cafeteria attendants and bartender helpers	Facilitate food service. Clean tables, remove dirty dishes, replace soiled table linens; set tables; replenish supply of clean linens, silverware, glassware, and dishes; supply service bar with food; and serve items such as water, condiments, and coffee to patrons.
				35-9099	Food preparation and serving related workers, all other	All food preparation and serving related workers not listed separately.
Dishwashers	4140	35-9021	14	35-9021	Dishwashers	Clean dishes, kitchen, food preparation equipment, or utensils.
Hosts and hostesses, restaurant, lounge, and coffee shop	4150	35-9031	14	35-9031	Hosts and hostesses, restaurant, lounge, and coffee shop	Welcome patrons, seat them at tables or in lounge, and help ensure quality of facilities and service.
First-line supervisors of housekeeping and janitorial workers	4200	37-1011	14	37-1011	First-line supervisors of housekeeping and janitorial workers	Directly supervise and coordinate work activities of cleaning personnel in hotels, hospitals, offices, and other establishments.

DETAILED OCCUPATIONS, BY EEO OCCUPATION GROUPS, 2006–2010—*Continued*

2010 EEO Occupation Title	2010 EEO Occupation Code	2010 SOC Code(s)	EEO Occupation Group (14)	2010 SOC Code	2010 SOC Occcupation Title	SOC Definition
Service Workers, Except Protective—Continued							
Janitors and building cleaners	4220	37-201X Combines: 37-2011 37-2019	14	37-2011	Janitors and cleaners, except maids and housekeeping cleaners	Keep buildings in clean and orderly condition. Perform heavy cleaning duties, such as cleaning floors, shampooing rugs, washing walls and glass, and removing rubbish. Duties may include tending furnace and boiler, performing routine maintenance activities, notifying management of need for repairs, and cleaning snow or debris from sidewalk.
				37-2019	Building cleaning workers, all other	All building cleaning workers not listed separately.
Maids and housekeeping cleaners	4230	37-2012	14	37-2012	Maids and housekeeping cleaners	Perform any combination of light cleaning duties to maintain private households or commercial establishments, such as hotels and hospitals, in a clean and orderly manner. Duties may include making beds, replenishing linens, cleaning rooms and halls, and vacuuming.
Pest control workers	4240	37-2021	14	37-2021	Pest control workers	Apply or release chemical solutions or toxic gases and set traps to kill or remove pests and vermin that infest buildings and surrounding areas.
First-line supervisors of gaming workers	4300	39-1010	14	39-1011	Gaming supervisors	Supervise and coordinate activities of workers in assigned gaming areas. Circulate among tables and observe operations. Ensure that stations and games are covered for each shift. May explain and interpret operating rules of house to patrons. May plan and organize activities and services for guests in hotels/casinos. May address service complaints. Excludes "Slot Supervisors" (39-1012).
				39-1012	Slot supervisors	Supervise and coordinate activities of slot department workers to provide service to patrons. Handle and settle complaints of players. Verify and pay off jackpots. Reset slot machines after payoffs. Make repairs or adjustments to slot machines or recommend removal of slot machines for repair. Report hazards and enforce safety rules.
First-line supervisors of personal service workers	4320	39-1021	14	39-1021	First-line supervisors of personal service workers	Directly supervise and coordinate activities of personal service workers, such as flight attendants, hairdressers, or caddies.
Gaming services workers	4400	39-3010	14	39-3011	Gaming dealers	Operate table games. Stand or sit behind table and operate games of chance by dispensing the appropriate number of cards or blocks to players, or operating other gaming equipment. Distribute winnings or collect playersmoney or chips. May compare the house's hand against playershands.
				39-3012	Gaming and sports book writers and runners	Post information enabling patrons to wager on various races and sporting events. Assist in the operation of games such as keno and bingo. May operate random number generating equipment and announce the numbers for patrons. Receive, verify, and record patronswagers. Scan and process winning tickets presented by patrons and payout winnings for those wagers.
				39-3019	Gaming service workers, all other	All gaming service workers not listed separately.
Motion picture projectionists	4410	39-3021	14	39-3021	Motion picture projectionists	Set up and operate motion picture projection and related sound reproduction equipment.
Ushers, lobby attendants, and ticket takers	4420	39-3031	14	39-3031	Ushers, lobby attendants, and ticket takers	Assist patrons at entertainment events by performing duties, such as collecting admission tickets and passes from patrons, assisting in finding seats, searching for lost articles, and locating such facilities as rest rooms and telephones.

DETAILED OCCUPATIONS, BY EEO OCCUPATION GROUPS, 2006–2010—*Continued*

2010 EEO Occupation Title	2010 EEO Occupation Code	2010 SOC Code(s)	EEO Occupation Group (14)	2010 SOC Code	2010 SOC Occupation Title	SOC Definition
Service Workers, Except Protective—Continued						
Miscellaneous entertainment attendants and related workers	4430	39-3090	14	39-3091	Amusement and recreation attendants	Perform a variety of attending duties at amusement or recreation facility. May schedule use of recreation facilities, maintain and provide equipment to participants of sporting events or recreational pursuits, or operate amusement concessions and rides.
				39-3092	Costume attendants	Select, fit, and take care of costumes for cast members, and aid entertainers. May assist with multiple costume changes during performances.
				39-3093	Locker room, coatroom, and dressing room attendants	Provide personal items to patrons or customers in locker rooms, dressing rooms, or coatrooms.
				39-3099	Entertainment Attendants and Related workers, all other	All entertainment attendants and related workers not listed separately.
Embalmers and funeral attendants	4460	39-40XX Combines: 39-4011 39-4021	14	39-4011	Embalmers	Prepare bodies for interment in conformity with legal requirements.
				39-4021	Funeral attendants	Perform a variety of tasks during funeral, such as placing casket in parlor or chapel prior to service; arranging floral offerings or lights around casket; directing or escorting mourners; closing casket; and issuing and storing funeral equipment.
Barbers	4500	39-5011	14	39-5011	Barbers	Provide barbering services, such as cutting, trimming, shampooing, and styling hair, trimming beards, or giving shaves.
Hairdressers, hairstylists, and cosmetologists	4510	39-5012	14	39-5012	Hairdressers, hairstylists, and cosmetologists	Provide beauty services, such as shampooing, cutting, coloring, and styling hair, and massaging and treating scalp. May apply makeup, dress wigs, perform hair removal, and provide nail and skin care services. Excludes "Makeup Artists, Theatrical and Performance (39-5091)," "Manicurists and Pedicurists" (39-5092), and "Skincare specialists" (39-5094).
Miscellaneous personal appearance workers	4520	39-5090	14	39-5091	Makeup artists, theatrical and performance	Apply makeup to performers to reflect period, setting, and situation of their role.
				39-5092	Manicurists and pedicurists	Clean and shape customersfingernails and toenails. May polish or decorate nails.
				39-5093	Shampooers	Shampoo and rinse customershair.
				39-5094	Skincare specialists	Provide skincare treatments to face and body to enhance an individual's appearance. Includes electrologists and laser hair removal specialists.
Baggage porters, bellhops, and concierges	4530	39-6010	14	39-6011	Baggage porters and bellhops	Handle baggage for travelers at transportation terminals or for guests at hotels or similar establishments.
				39-6012	Concierges	Assist patrons at hotel, apartment, or office building with personal services. May take messages, arrange or give advice on transportation, business services or entertainment, or monitor guest requests for housekeeping and maintenance.
Tour and travel guides	4540	39-7010	14	39-7011	Tour guides and escorts	Escort individuals or groups on sightseeing tours or through places of interest, such as industrial establishments, public buildings, and art galleries.
				39-7012	Travel guides	Plan, organize, and conduct long distance travel, tours, and expeditions for individuals and groups.
Childcare workers	4600	39-9011	14	39-9011	Childcare workers	Attend to children at schools, businesses, private households, and childcare institutions. Perform a variety of tasks, such as dressing, feeding, bathing, and overseeing play. Excludes "Preschool Teachers, except special education" (25-2011) and "Teacher Assistants" (25-9041).

APPENDIX B

DETAILED OCCUPATIONS, BY EEO OCCUPATION GROUPS, 2006–2010—*Continued*

2010 EEO Occupation Title	2010 EEO Occupation Code	2010 SOC Code(s)	EEO Occupation Group (14)	2010 SOC Code	2010 SOC Occcupation Title	SOC Definition
\multicolumn{7}{c}{**Service Workers, Except Protective**—*Continued*}
Personal care aides	4610	39-9021	14	39-9021	Personal care aides	Assist the elderly, convalescents, or persons with disabilities with daily living activities at the person's home or in a care facility. Duties performed at a place of residence may include keeping house (making beds, doing laundry, washing dishes) and preparing meals. May provide assistance at non-residential care facilities. May advise families, the elderly, convalescents, and persons with disabilities regarding such things as nutrition, cleanliness, and household activities.
Recreation and fitness workers	4620	39-9030	14	39-9031	Fitness trainers and aerobics instructors	Instruct or coach groups or individuals in exercise activities. Demonstrate techniques and form, observe participants, and explain to them corrective measures necessary to improve their skills. Excludes teachers classified in 25-0000 education, Training, and Library Occupations. Excludes "Coaches and Scouts" (27-2022) and "Athletic Trainers" (29-9091).
				39-9032	Recreation workers	Conduct recreation activities with groups in public, private, or volunteer agencies or recreation facilities. Organize and promote activities, such as arts and crafts, sports, games, music, dramatics, social recreation, camping, and hobbies, taking into account the needs and interests of individual members.
Residential advisors	4640	39-9041	14	39-9041	Residential advisors	Coordinate activities in resident facilities in secondary and college dormitories, group homes, or similar establishments. Order supplies and determine need for maintenance, repairs, and furnishings. May maintain household records and assign rooms. May assist residents with problem solving or refer them to counseling resources.
Personal care and service workers, all other	4650	39-9099	14	39-9099	Personal care and service workers, all other	All personal care and service workers not listed separately.
Flight attendants	9050	53-2031	14	53-2031	Flight attendants	Provide personal services to ensure the safety, security, and comfort of airline passengers during flight. Greet passengers, verify tickets, explain use of safety equipment, and serve food or beverages.
Transportation attendants, except flight attendants	9415	53-6061	14	53-6061	Transportation attendants, except flight attendants	Provide services to ensure the safety and comfort of passengers aboard ships, buses, trains, or within the station or terminal. Perform duties such as greeting passengers, explaining the use of safety equipment, serving meals or beverages, or answering questions related to travel. Excludes "Baggage Porters and Bellhops" (39-6011).

Metropolitan Statistical Areas, Metropolitan Divisions, and Components (as defined December 2009)–Continued

Core Based Statistical Area	State/County FIPS Code	Title and Geographic Components	2010 Census Population	Core Based Statistical Area	State/County FIPS Code	Title and Geographic Components	2010 Census Population
10180		Abilene, TX Metro SA	165,252	11500		Anniston-Oxford, AL Metro SA	118,572
10180	48059	Callahan County, TX	13,544	11500	01015	Calhoun County, AL	118,572
10180	48253	Jones County, TX	20,202				
10180	48441	Taylor County, TX	131,506	11540		Appleton, WI Metro SA	225,666
				11540	55015	Calumet County, WI	48,971
10420		Akron, OH Metro SA	703,200	11540	55087	Outagamie County, WI	176,695
10420	39133	Portage County, OH	161,419				
10420	39153	Summit County, OH	541,781	11700		Asheville, NC Metro SA	424,858
				11700	37021	Buncombe County, NC	238,318
10500		Albany, GA Metro SA	157,308	11700	37087	Haywood County, NC	59,036
10500	13007	Baker County, GA	3,451	11700	37089	Henderson County, NC	106,740
10500	13095	Dougherty County, GA	94,565	11700	37115	Madison County, NC	20,764
10500	13177	Lee County, GA	28,298				
10500	13273	Terrell County, GA	9,315	12020		Athens-Clarke County, GA Metro SA	192,541
10500	13321	Worth County, GA	21,679	12020	13059	Clarke County, GA	116,714
				12020	13195	Madison County, GA	28,120
10580		Albany-Schenectady-Troy, NY Metro SA	870,716	12020	13219	Oconee County, GA	32,808
10580	36001	Albany County, NY	304,204	12020	13221	Oglethorpe County, GA	14,899
10580	36083	Rensselaer County, NY	159,429				
10580	36091	Saratoga County, NY	219,607	12060		Atlanta-Sandy Springs-Marietta, GA Metro SA	5,268,860
10580	36093	Schenectady County, NY	154,727				
10580	36095	Schoharie County, NY	32,749	12060	13013	Barrow County, GA	69,367
				12060	13015	Bartow County, GA	100,157
10740		Albuquerque, NM Metro SA	887,077	12060	13035	Butts County, GA	23,655
10740	35001	Bernalillo County, NM	662,564	12060	13045	Carroll County, GA	110,527
10740	35043	Sandoval County, NM	131,561	12060	13057	Cherokee County, GA	214,346
10740	35057	Torrance County, NM	16,383	12060	13063	Clayton County, GA	259,424
10740	35061	Valencia County, NM	76,569	12060	13067	Cobb County, GA	688,078
				12060	13077	Coweta County, GA	127,317
10780		Alexandria, LA Metro SA	153,922	12060	13085	Dawson County, GA	22,330
10780	22043	Grant Parish, LA	22,309				
10780	22079	Rapides Parish, LA	131,613	12060	13089	DeKalb County, GA	691,893
				12060	13097	Douglas County, GA	132,403
10900		Allentown-Bethlehem-Easton, PA-NJ Metro SA	821,173	12060	13113	Fayette County, GA	106,567
				12060	13117	Forsyth County, GA	175,511
10900	34041	Warren County, NJ	108,692	12060	13121	Fulton County, GA	920,581
10900	42025	Carbon County, PA	65,249	12060	13135	Gwinnett County, GA	805,321
10900	42077	Lehigh County, PA	349,497	12060	13143	Haralson County, GA	28,780
10900	42095	Northampton County, PA	297,735	12060	13149	Heard County, GA	11,834
				12060	13151	Henry County, GA	203,922
11020		Altoona, PA Metro SA	127,089	12060	13159	Jasper County, GA	13,900
11020	42013	Blair County, PA	127,089				
				12060	13171	Lamar County, GA	18,317
11100		Amarillo, TX Metro SA	249,881	12060	13199	Meriwether County, GA	21,992
11100	48011	Armstrong County, TX	1,901	12060	13217	Newton County, GA	99,958
11100	48065	Carson County, TX	6,182	12060	13223	Paulding County, GA	142,324
11100	48375	Potter County, TX	121,073	12060	13227	Pickens County, GA	29,431
11100	48381	Randall County, TX	120,725	12060	13231	Pike County, GA	17,869
				12060	13247	Rockdale County, GA	85,215
11180		Ames, IA Metro SA	89,542	12060	13255	Spalding County, GA	64,073
11180	19169	Story County, IA	89,542	12060	13297	Walton County, GA	83,768
11260		Anchorage, AK Metro SA	380,821	12100		Atlantic City-Hammonton, NJ Metro SA	274,549
11260	02020	Anchorage Municipality, AK	291,826	12100	34001	Atlantic County, NJ	274,549
11260	02170	Matanuska-Susitna Borough, AK	88,995				
				12220		Auburn-Opelika, AL Metro SA	140,247
11300		Anderson, IN Metro SA	131,636	12220	01081	Lee County, AL	140,247
11300	18095	Madison County, IN	131,636				
				12260		Augusta-Richmond County, GA-SC Metro SA	556,877
11340		Anderson, SC Metro SA	187,126				
11340	45007	Anderson County, SC	187,126	12260	13033	Burke County, GA	23,316
				12260	13073	Columbia County, GA	124,053
11460		Ann Arbor, MI Metro SA	344,791	12260	13189	McDuffie County, GA	21,875
11460	26161	Washtenaw County, MI	344,791	12260	13245	Richmond County, GA	200,549
				12260	45003	Aiken County, SC	160,099
				12260	45037	Edgefield County, SC	26,985

Metropolitan Statistical Areas, Metropolitan Divisions, and Components
(as defined December 2009)–Continued

Core Based Statistical Area	State/County FIPS Code	Title and Geographic Components	2010 Census Population	Core Based Statistical Area	State/County FIPS Code	Title and Geographic Components	2010 Census Population
12420		Austin-Round Rock-San Marcos, TX Metro SA..................	1,716,289	13820		Birmingham-Hoover, AL Metro SA..............	1,128,047
				13820	01007	Bibb County, AL........................	22,915
12420	48021	Bastrop County, TX..................	74,171	13820	01009	Blount County, AL......................	57,322
12420	48055	Caldwell County, TX..................	38,066	13820	01021	Chilton County, AL......................	43,643
12420	48209	Hays County, TX......................	157,107	13820	01073	Jefferson County, AL..................	658,466
12420	48453	Travis County, TX....................	1,024,266	13820	01115	St. Clair County, AL....................	83,593
12420	48491	Williamson County, TX................	422,679	13820	01117	Shelby County, AL....................	195,085
				13820	01127	Walker County, AL......................	67,023
12540		Bakersfield-Delano, CA Metro SA..............	839,631				
12540	06029	Kern County, CA......................	839,631	13900		Bismarck, ND Metro SA..............	108,779
				13900	38015	Burleigh County, ND..................	81,308
12580		Baltimore-Towson, MD Metro SA..............	2,710,489	13900	38059	Morton County, ND....................	27,471
12580	24003	Anne Arundel County, MD............	537,656				
12580	24005	Baltimore County, MD................	805,029	13980		Blacksburg-Christiansburg-Radford, VA Metro SA............	162,958
12580	24013	Carroll County, MD....................	167,134				
12580	24025	Harford County, MD..................	244,826	13980	51071	Giles County, VA......................	17,286
12580	24027	Howard County, MD..................	287,085	13980	51121	Montgomery County, VA............	94,392
12580	24035	Queen Anne's County, MD..........	47,798	13980	51155	Pulaski County, VA....................	34,872
12580	24510	Baltimore city, MD....................	620,961	13980	51750	Radford city, VA........................	16,408
12620		Bangor, ME Metro SA..................	153,923	14020		Bloomington, IN Metro SA............	192,714
12620	23019	Penobscot County, ME..............	153,923	14020	18055	Greene County, IN....................	33,165
				14020	18105	Monroe County, IN....................	137,974
12700		Barnstable Town, MA Metro SA........	215,888	14020	18119	Owen County, IN......................	21,575
12700	25001	Barnstable County, MA..............	215,888				
				14060		Bloomington-Normal, IL Metro SA............	169,572
12940		Baton Rouge, LA Metro SA............	802,484	14060	17113	McLean County, IL....................	169,572
12940	22005	Ascension Parish, LA................	107,215				
12940	22033	East Baton Rouge Parish, LA......	440,171	14260		Boise City-Nampa, ID Metro SA..............	616,561
12940	22037	East Feliciana Parish, LA............	20,267	14260	16001	Ada County, ID........................	392,365
12940	22047	Iberville Parish, LA....................	33,387	14260	16015	Boise County, ID......................	7,028
12940	22063	Livingston Parish, LA..................	128,026	14260	16027	Canyon County, ID....................	188,923
12940	22077	Pointe Coupee Parish, LA..........	22,802	14260	16045	Gem County, ID......................	16,719
12940	22091	St. Helena Parish, LA................	11,203	14260	16073	Owyhee County, ID..................	11,526
12940	22121	West Baton Rouge Parish, LA......	23,788				
12940	22125	West Feliciana Parish, LA..........	15,625	14460		Boston-Cambridge-Quincy, MA-NH Metro SA..................	4,552,402
12980		Battle Creek, MI Metro SA............	136,146				
12980	26025	Calhoun County, MI..................	136,146	14460		Boston-Quincy, MA Metro Div 14484..........	1,887,792
				14460	25021	Norfolk County, MA..................	670,850
13020		Bay City, MI Metro SA................	107,771	14460	25023	Plymouth County, MA................	494,919
13020	26017	Bay County, MI........................	107,771	14460	25025	Suffolk County, MA....................	722,023
13140		Beaumont-Port Arthur, TX Metro SA..........	388,745	14460		Cambridge-Newton-Framingham, MA Metro Div 15764..........	1,503,085
13140	48199	Hardin County, TX....................	54,635				
13140	48245	Jefferson County, TX................	252,273	14460	25017	Middlesex County, MA..............	1,503,085
13140	48361	Orange County, TX..................	81,837				
				14460		Peabody, MA Metro Div 37764..................	743,159
13380		Bellingham, WA Metro SA............	201,140	14460	25009	Essex County, MA....................	743,159
13380	53073	Whatcom County, WA................	201,140				
				14460		Rockingham County-Strafford County, NH Metro Div 40484..........	418,366
13460		Bend, OR Metro SA..................	157,733				
13460	41017	Deschutes County, OR..............	157,733	14460	33015	Rockingham County, NH............	295,223
				14460	33017	Strafford County, NH................	123,143
13740		Billings, MT Metro SA..................	158,050				
13740	30009	Carbon County, MT..................	10,078	14500		Boulder, CO Metro SA..............	294,567
13740	30111	Yellowstone County, MT............	147,972	14500	08013	Boulder County, CO..................	294,567
13780		Binghamton, NY Metro SA............	251,725	14540		Bowling Green, KY Metro SA........	125,953
13780	36007	Broome County, NY..................	200,600	14540	21061	Edmonson County, KY..............	12,161
13780	36107	Tioga County, NY....................	51,125	14540	21227	Warren County, KY..................	113,792
				14740		Bremerton-Silverdale, WA Metro SA..........	251,133
				14740	53035	Kitsap County, WA....................	251,133
				14860		Bridgeport-Stamford-Norwalk, CT Metro SA..................	916,829
				14860	09001	Fairfield County, CT..................	916,829

APPENDIX C

Metropolitan Statistical Areas, Metropolitan Divisions, and Components
(as defined December 2009)–Continued

Core Based Statistical Area	State/ County FIPS Code	Title and Geographic Components	2010 Census Population	Core Based Statistical Area	State/ County FIPS Code	Title and Geographic Components	2010 Census Population
15180		Brownsville-Harlingen, TX Metro SA	406,220	16740	45091	York County, SC	226,073
15180	48061	Cameron County, TX	406,220	16820		Charlottesville, VA Metro SA	201,559
				16820	51003	Albemarle County, VA	98,970
15260		Brunswick, GA Metro SA	112,370	16820	51065	Fluvanna County, VA	25,691
15260	13025	Brantley County, GA	18,411	16820	51079	Greene County, VA	18,403
15260	13127	Glynn County, GA	79,626	16820	51125	Nelson County, VA	15,020
15260	13191	McIntosh County, GA	14,333	16820	51540	Charlottesville city, VA	43,475
15380		Buffalo-Niagara Falls, NY Metro SA	1,135,509	16860		Chattanooga, TN-GA Metro SA	528,143
15380	36029	Erie County, NY	919,040	16860	13047	Catoosa County, GA	63,942
15380	36063	Niagara County, NY	216,469	16860	13083	Dade County, GA	16,633
				16860	13295	Walker County, GA	68,756
15500		Burlington, NC Metro SA	151,131	16860	47065	Hamilton County, TN	336,463
15500	37001	Alamance County, NC	151,131	16860	47115	Marion County, TN	28,237
				16860	47153	Sequatchie County, TN	14,112
15540		Burlington-South Burlington, VT Metro SA	211,261				
15540	50007	Chittenden County, VT	156,545	16940		Cheyenne, WY Metro SA	91,738
15540	50011	Franklin County, VT	47,746	16940	56021	Laramie County, WY	91,738
15540	50013	Grand Isle County, VT	6,970				
				16980		Chicago-Joliet-Naperville, IL-IN-WI Metro SA	9,461,105
15940		Canton-Massillon, OH Metro SA	404,422				
15940	39019	Carroll County, OH	28,836				
15940	39151	Stark County, OH	375,586	16980		Chicago-Joliet-Naperville, IL Metro Div 16974	7,883,147
15980		Cape Coral-Fort Myers, FL Metro SA	618,754	16980	17031	Cook County, IL	5,194,675
15980	12071	Lee County, FL	618,754	16980	17037	DeKalb County, IL	105,160
				16980	17043	DuPage County, IL	916,924
16020		Cape Girardeau-Jackson, MO-IL Metro SA	96,275	16980	17063	Grundy County, IL	50,063
16020	17003	Alexander County, IL	8,238	16980	17089	Kane County, IL	515,269
16020	29017	Bollinger County, MO	12,363	16980	17093	Kendall County, IL	114,736
16020	29031	Cape Girardeau County, MO	75,674	16980	17111	McHenry County, IL	308,760
				16980	17197	Will County, IL	677,560
16180		Carson City, NV Metro SA	55,274				
16180	32510	Carson City, NV	55,274	16980		Gary, IN Metro Div 23844	708,070
				16980	18073	Jasper County, IN	33,478
16220		Casper, WY Metro SA	75,450	16980	18089	Lake County, IN	496,005
16220	56025	Natrona County, WY	75,450	16980	18111	Newton County, IN	14,244
				16980	18127	Porter County, IN	164,343
16300		Cedar Rapids, IA Metro SA	257,940				
16300	19011	Benton County, IA	26,076	16980		Lake County-Kenosha County, IL-WI Metro Div 29404	869,888
16300	19105	Jones County, IA	20,638				
16300	19113	Linn County, IA	211,226	16980	17097	Lake County, IL	703,462
				16980	55059	Kenosha County, WI	166,426
16580		Champaign-Urbana, IL Metro SA	231,891				
16580	17019	Champaign County, IL	201,081	17020		Chico, CA Metro SA	220,000
16580	17053	Ford County, IL	14,081	17020	06007	Butte County, CA	220,000
16580	17147	Piatt County, IL	16,729				
				17140		Cincinnati-Middletown, OH-KY-IN Metro SA	2,130,151
16620		Charleston, WV Metro SA	304,284				
16620	54005	Boone County, WV	24,629	17140	18029	Dearborn County, IN	50,047
16620	54015	Clay County, WV	9,386	17140	18047	Franklin County, IN	23,087
16620	54039	Kanawha County, WV	193,063	17140	18115	Ohio County, IN	6,128
16620	54043	Lincoln County, WV	21,720	17140	21015	Boone County, KY	118,811
16620	54079	Putnam County, WV	55,486	17140	21023	Bracken County, KY	8,488
				17140	21037	Campbell County, KY	90,336
16700		Charleston-North Charleston-Summerville, SC Metro SA	664,607	17140	21077	Gallatin County, KY	8,589
				17140	21081	Grant County, KY	24,662
16700	45015	Berkeley County, SC	177,843	17140	21117	Kenton County, KY	159,720
16700	45019	Charleston County, SC	350,209				
16700	45035	Dorchester County, SC	136,555	17140	21191	Pendleton County, KY	14,877
				17140	39015	Brown County, OH	44,846
16740		Charlotte-Gastonia-Rock Hill, NC-SC Metro SA	1,758,038	17140	39017	Butler County, OH	368,130
				17140	39025	Clermont County, OH	197,363
16740	37007	Anson County, NC	26,948	17140	39061	Hamilton County, OH	802,374
16740	37025	Cabarrus County, NC	178,011	17140	39165	Warren County, OH	212,693
16740	37071	Gaston County, NC	206,086				
16740	37119	Mecklenburg County, NC	919,628				
16740	37179	Union County, NC	201,292				

Metropolitan Statistical Areas, Metropolitan Divisions, and Components
(as defined December 2009)–Continued

Core Based Statistical Area	State/County FIPS Code	Title and Geographic Components	2010 Census Population	Core Based Statistical Area	State/County FIPS Code	Title and Geographic Components	2010 Census Population
17300		Clarksville, TN-KY Metro SA......	273,949	18880		Crestview-Fort Walton Beach-Destin, FL Metro SA............	180,822
17300	21047	Christian County, KY............	73,955				
17300	21221	Trigg County, KY............	14,339	18880	12091	Okaloosa County, FL............	180,822
17300	47125	Montgomery County, TN............	172,331				
17300	47161	Stewart County, TN............	13,324	19060		Cumberland, MD-WV Metro SA............	103,299
				19060	24001	Allegany County, MD............	75,087
17420		Cleveland, TN Metro SA............	115,788	19060	54057	Mineral County, WV............	28,212
17420	47011	Bradley County, TN............	98,963				
17420	47139	Polk County, TN............	16,825	19100		Dallas-Fort Worth-Arlington, TX Metro SA .	6,371,773
17460		Cleveland-Elyria-Mentor, OH Metro SA......	2,077,240	19100		Dallas-Plano-Irving, TX Metro Div 19124	4,235,751
17460	39035	Cuyahoga County, OH............	1,280,122	19100	48085	Collin County, TX............	782,341
17460	39055	Geauga County, OH............	93,389	19100	48113	Dallas County, TX............	2,368,139
17460	39085	Lake County, OH............	230,041	19100	48119	Delta County, TX............	5,231
17460	39093	Lorain County, OH............	301,356	19100	48121	Denton County, TX............	662,614
17460	39103	Medina County, OH............	172,332	19100	48139	Ellis County, TX............	149,610
				19100	48231	Hunt County, TX............	86,129
17660		Coeur d'Alene, ID Metro SA............	138,494	19100	48257	Kaufman County, TX............	103,350
17660	16055	Kootenai County, ID............	138,494	19100	48397	Rockwall County, TX............	78,337
17780		College Station-Bryan, TX Metro SA............	228,660	19100		Fort Worth-Arlington, TX Metro Div 23104 ..	2,136,022
17780	48041	Brazos County, TX............	194,851	19100	48251	Johnson County, TX............	150,934
17780	48051	Burleson County, TX............	17,187	19100	48367	Parker County, TX............	116,927
17780	48395	Robertson County, TX............	16,622	19100	48439	Tarrant County, TX............	1,809,034
				19100	48497	Wise County, TX............	59,127
17820		Colorado Springs, CO Metro SA............	645,613				
17820	08041	El Paso County, CO............	622,263	19140		Dalton, GA Metro SA............	142,227
17820	08119	Teller County, CO............	23,350	19140	13213	Murray County, GA............	39,628
				19140	13313	Whitfield County, GA............	102,599
17860		Columbia, MO Metro SA............	172,786				
17860	29019	Boone County, MO............	162,642	19180		Danville, IL Metro SA............	81,625
17860	29089	Howard County, MO............	10,144	19180	17183	Vermilion County, IL............	81,625
17900		Columbia, SC Metro SA............	767,598	19260		Danville, VA Metro SA............	106,561
17900	45017	Calhoun County, SC............	15,175	19260	51143	Pittsylvania County, VA............	63,506
17900	45039	Fairfield County, SC............	23,956	19260	51590	Danville city, VA............	43,055
17900	45055	Kershaw County, SC............	61,697				
17900	45063	Lexington County, SC............	262,391	19340		Davenport-Moline-Rock Island, IA-IL Metro SA............	379,690
17900	45079	Richland County, SC............	384,504				
17900	45081	Saluda County, SC............	19,875	19340	17073	Henry County, IL............	50,486
				19340	17131	Mercer County, IL............	16,434
17980		Columbus, GA-AL Metro SA............	294,865	19340	17161	Rock Island County, IL............	147,546
17980	01113	Russell County, AL............	52,947	19340	19163	Scott County, IA............	165,224
17980	13053	Chattahoochee County, GA............	11,267				
17980	13145	Harris County, GA............	32,024	19380		Dayton, OH Metro SA............	841,502
17980	13197	Marion County, GA............	8,742	19380	39057	Greene County, OH............	161,573
17980	13215	Muscogee County, GA............	189,885	19380	39109	Miami County, OH............	102,506
				19380	39113	Montgomery County, OH............	535,153
18020		Columbus, IN Metro SA............	76,794	19380	39135	Preble County, OH............	42,270
18020	18005	Bartholomew County, IN............	76,794				
				19460		Decatur, AL Metro SA............	153,829
18140		Columbus, OH Metro SA............	1,836,536	19460	01079	Lawrence County, AL............	34,339
18140	39041	Delaware County, OH............	174,214	19460	01103	Morgan County, AL............	119,490
18140	39045	Fairfield County, OH............	146,156				
18140	39049	Franklin County, OH............	1,163,414	19500		Decatur, IL Metro SA............	110,768
18140	39089	Licking County, OH............	166,492	19500	17115	Macon County, IL............	110,768
18140	39097	Madison County, OH............	43,435				
18140	39117	Morrow County, OH............	34,827	19660		Deltona-Daytona Beach-Ormond Beach, FL Metro SA............	494,593
18140	39129	Pickaway County, OH............	55,698				
18140	39159	Union County, OH............	52,300	19660	12127	Volusia County, FL............	494,593
18580		Corpus Christi, TX Metro SA............	428,185				
18580	48007	Aransas County, TX............	23,158				
18580	48355	Nueces County, TX............	340,223				
18580	48409	San Patricio County, TX............	64,804				
18700		Corvallis, OR Metro SA............	85,579				
18700	41003	Benton County, OR............	85,579				

Metropolitan Statistical Areas, Metropolitan Divisions, and Components (as defined December 2009)–*Continued*

Core Based Statistical Area	State/County FIPS Code	Title and Geographic Components	2010 Census Population	Core Based Statistical Area	State/County FIPS Code	Title and Geographic Components	2010 Census Population
19740		Denver-Aurora-Broomfield, CO Metro SA ...	2,543,482	21140	18039	Elkhart County, IN	197,559
19740	08001	Adams County, CO	441,603	21300		Elmira, NY Metro SA...............................	88,830
19740	08005	Arapahoe County, CO............................	572,003	21300	36015	Chemung County, NY	88,830
19740	08014	Broomfield County, CO	55,889				
19740	08019	Clear Creek County, CO	9,088	21340		El Paso, TX Metro SA.............................	800,647
19740	08031	Denver County, CO	600,158	21340	48141	El Paso County, TX................................	800,647
19740	08035	Douglas County, CO	285,465				
19740	08039	Elbert County, CO	23,086	21500		Erie, PA Metro SA...................................	280,566
19740	08047	Gilpin County, CO	5,441	21500	42049	Erie County, PA......................................	280,566
19740	08059	Jefferson County, CO	534,543				
19740	08093	Park County, CO	16,206	21660		Eugene-Springfield, OR Metro SA..............	351,715
				21660	41039	Lane County, OR	351,715
19780		Des Moines-West Des Moines, IA Metro SA..	569,633	21780		Evansville, IN-KY Metro SA	358,676
19780	19049	Dallas County, IA	66,135	21780	18051	Gibson County, IN	33,503
19780	19077	Guthrie County, IA	10,954	21780	18129	Posey County, IN	25,910
19780	19121	Madison County, IA	15,679	21780	18163	Vanderburgh County, IN........................	179,703
19780	19153	Polk County, IA	430,640	21780	18173	Warrick County, IN	59,689
19780	19181	Warren County, IA	46,225	21780	21101	Henderson County, KY..........................	46,250
				21780	21233	Webster County, KY..............................	13,621
19820		Detroit-Warren-Livonia, MI Metro SA...........	4,296,250				
				21820		Fairbanks, AK Metro SA	97,581
19820		Detroit-Livonia-Dearborn, MI Metro Div 19804	1,820,584	21820	02090	Fairbanks North Star Borough, AK	97,581
19820	26163	Wayne County, MI..................................	1,820,584	22020		Fargo, ND-MN Metro SA	208,777
				22020	27027	Clay County, MN	58,999
19820		Warren-Troy-Farmington Hills, MI Metro Div 47644	2,475,666	22020	38017	Cass County, ND...................................	149,778
19820	26087	Lapeer County, MI	88,319	22140		Farmington, NM Metro SA	130,044
19820	26093	Livingston County, MI............................	180,967	22140	35045	San Juan County, NM...........................	130,044
19820	26099	Macomb County, MI	840,978				
19820	26125	Oakland County, MI...............................	1,202,362	22180		Fayetteville, NC Metro SA	366,383
19820	26147	St. Clair County, MI	163,040	22180	37051	Cumberland County, NC	319,431
				22180	37093	Hoke County, NC	46,952
20020		Dothan, AL Metro SA	145,639				
20020	01061	Geneva County, AL................................	26,790	22220		Fayetteville-Springdale-Rogers, AR-MO Metro SA	463,204
20020	01067	Henry County, AL...................................	17,302				
20020	01069	Houston County, AL...............................	101,547	22220	05007	Benton County, AR................................	221,339
				22220	05087	Madison County, AR	15,717
20100		Dover, DE Metro SA	162,310	22220	05143	Washington County, AR	203,065
20100	10001	Kent County, DE.....................................	162,310	22220	29119	McDonald County, MO	23,083
20220		Dubuque, IA Metro SA	93,653	22380		Flagstaff, AZ Metro SA	134,421
20220	19061	Dubuque County, IA	93,653	22380	04005	Coconino County, AZ	134,421
20260		Duluth, MN-WI Metro SA	279,771	22420		Flint, MI Metro SA	425,790
20260	27017	Carlton County, MN...............................	35,386	22420	26049	Genesee County, MI	425,790
20260	27137	St. Louis County, MN	200,226				
20260	55031	Douglas County, WI	44,159	22500		Florence, SC Metro SA.............................	205,566
				22500	45031	Darlington County, SC...........................	68,681
20500		Durham-Chaspel Hill, NC Metro SA	504,357	22500	45041	Florence County, SC	136,885
20500	37037	Chatham County, NC	63,505				
20500	37063	Durham County, NC	267,587	22520		Florence-Muscle Shoals, AL Metro SA........	147,137
20500	37135	Orange County, NC...............................	133,801	22520	01033	Colbert County, AL	54,428
20500	37145	Person County, NC	39,464	22520	01077	Lauderdale County, AL..........................	92,709
20740		Eau Claire, WI Metro SA...........................	161,151	22540		Fond du Lac, WI Metro SA	101,633
20740	55017	Chippewa County, WI............................	62,415	22540	55039	Fond du Lac County, WI	101,633
20740	55035	Eau Claire County, WI...........................	98,736				
				22660		Fort Collins-Loveland, CO Metro SA	299,630
20940		El Centro, CA Metro SA............................	174,528	22660	08069	Larimer County, CO	299,630
20940	06025	Imperial County, CA	174,528				
				22900		Fort Smith, AR-OK Metro SA.....................	298,592
21060		Elizabethtown, KY Metro SA......................	119,736	22900	05033	Crawford County, AR	61,948
21060	21093	Hardin County, KY.................................	105,543	22900	05047	Franklin County, AR	18,125
21060	21123	Larue County, KY	14,193	22900	05131	Sebastian County, AR	125,744
				22900	40079	Le Flore County, OK	50,384
21140		Elkhart-Goshen, IN Metro SA	197,559	22900	40135	Sequoyah County, OK...........................	42,391

Metropolitan Statistical Areas, Metropolitan Divisions, and Components
(as defined December 2009)–Continued

Core Based Statistical Area	State/County FIPS Code	Title and Geographic Components	2010 Census Population	Core Based Statistical Area	State/County FIPS Code	Title and Geographic Components	2010 Census Population
23060		Fort Wayne, IN Metro SA	416,257	25180		Hagerstown-Martinsburg, MD-WV Metro SA	269,140
23060	18003	Allen County, IN	355,329				
23060	18179	Wells County, IN	27,636	25180	24043	Washington County, MD	147,430
23060	18183	Whitley County, IN	33,292	25180	54003	Berkeley County, WV	104,169
				25180	54065	Morgan County, WV	17,541
23420		Fresno, CA Metro SA	930,450				
23420	06019	Fresno County, CA	930,450	25260		Hanford-Corcoran, CA Metro SA	152,982
				25260	06031	Kings County, CA	152,982
23460		Gadsden, AL Metro SA	104,430				
23460	01055	Etowah County, AL	104,430	25420		Harrisburg-Carlisle, PA Metro SA	549,475
				25420	42041	Cumberland County, PA	235,406
23540		Gainesville, FL Metro SA	264,275	25420	42043	Dauphin County, PA	268,100
23540	12001	Alachua County, FL	247,336	25420	42099	Perry County, PA	45,969
23540	12041	Gilchrist County, FL	16,939				
				25500		Harrisonburg, VA Metro SA	125,228
23580		Gainesville, GA Metro SA	179,684	25500	51165	Rockingham County, VA	76,314
23580	13139	Hall County, GA	179,684	25500	51660	Harrisonburg city, VA	48,914
24020		Glens Falls, NY Metro SA	128,923	25540		Hartford-West Hartford-East Hartford, CT Metro SA	1,212,381
24020	36113	Warren County, NY	65,707				
24020	36115	Washington County, NY	63,216	25540	09003	Hartford County, CT	894,014
				25540	09007	Middlesex County, CT	165,676
24140		Goldsboro, NC Metro SA	122,623	25540	09013	Tolland County, CT	152,691
24140	37191	Wayne County, NC	122,623				
				25620		Hattiesburg, MS Metro SA	142,842
24220		Grand Forks, ND-MN Metro SA	98,461	25620	28035	Forrest County, MS	74,934
24220	27119	Polk County, MN	31,600	25620	28073	Lamar County, MS	55,658
24220	38035	Grand Forks County, ND	66,861	25620	28111	Perry County, MS	12,250
24300		Grand Junction, CO Metro SA	146,723	25860		Hickory-Lenoir-Morganton, NC Metro SA	365,497
24300	08077	Mesa County, CO	146,723	25860	37003	Alexander County, NC	37,198
				25860	37023	Burke County, NC	90,912
24340		Grand Rapids-Wyoming, MI Metro SA	774,160	25860	37027	Caldwell County, NC	83,029
24340	26015	Barry County, MI	59,173	25860	37035	Catawba County, NC	154,358
24340	26067	Ionia County, MI	63,905				
24340	26081	Kent County, MI	602,622	25980		Hinesville-Fort Stewart, GA Metro SA	77,917
24340	26123	Newaygo County, MI	48,460	25980	13179	Liberty County, GA	63,453
				25980	13183	Long County, GA	14,464
24500		Great Falls, MT Metro SA	81,327				
24500	30013	Cascade County, MT	81,327	26100		Holland-Grand Haven, MI Metro SA	263,801
				26100	26139	Ottawa County, MI	263,801
24540		Greeley, CO Metro SA	252,825				
24540	08123	Weld County, CO	252,825	26180		Honolulu, HI Metro SA	953,207
				26180	15003	Honolulu County, HI	953,207
24580		Green Bay, WI Metro SA	306,241				
24580	55009	Brown County, WI	248,007	26300		Hot Springs, AR Metro SA	96,024
24580	55061	Kewaunee County, WI	20,574	26300	05051	Garland County, AR	96,024
24580	55083	Oconto County, WI	37,660				
				26380		Houma-Bayou Cane-Thibodaux, LA Metro SA	208,178
24660		Greensboro-High Point, NC Metro SA	723,801				
24660	37081	Guilford County, NC	488,406	26380	22057	Lafourche Parish, LA	96,318
24660	37151	Randolph County, NC	141,752	26380	22109	Terrebonne Parish, LA	111,860
24660	37157	Rockingham County, NC	93,643				
				26420		Houston-Sugar Land-Baytown, TX Metro SA	5,946,800
24780		Greenville-Mauldin-Easley, NC Metro SA	189,510				
24780	37079	Greene County, NC	21,362	26420	48015	Austin County, TX	28,417
24780	37147	Pitt County, NC	168,148	26420	48039	Brazoria County, TX	313,166
				26420	48071	Chambers County, TX	35,096
24860		Greenville, SC Metro SA	636,986	26420	48157	Fort Bend County, TX	585,375
24860	45045	Greenville County, SC	451,225	26420	48167	Galveston County, TX	291,309
24860	45059	Laurens County, SC	66,537	26420	48201	Harris County, TX	4,092,459
24860	45077	Pickens County, SC	119,224	26420	48291	Liberty County, TX	75,643
				26420	48339	Montgomery County, TX	455,746
25060		Gulfport-Biloxi, MS Metro SA	248,820	26420	48407	San Jacinto County, TX	26,384
25060	28045	Hancock County, MS	43,929	26420	48473	Waller County, TX	43,205
25060	28047	Harrison County, MS	187,105				
25060	28131	Stone County, MS	17,786				

APPENDIX C

Metropolitan Statistical Areas, Metropolitan Divisions, and Components
(as defined December 2009)–Continued

Core Based Statistical Area	State/ County FIPS Code	Title and Geographic Components	2010 Census Population	Core Based Statistical Area	State/ County FIPS Code	Title and Geographic Components	2010 Census Population
26580		Huntington-Ashland, WV-KY-OH Metro SA.	287,702	27740		Johnson City, TN Metro SA	198,716
26580	21019	Boyd County, KY	49,542	27740	47019	Carter County, TN	57,424
26580	21089	Greenup County, KY	36,910	27740	47171	Unicoi County, TN	18,313
26580	39087	Lawrence County, OH	62,450	27740	47179	Washington County, TN	122,979
26580	54011	Cabell County, WV	96,319				
26580	54099	Wayne County, WV	42,481	27780		Johnstown, PA Metro SA	143,679
				27780	42021	Cambria County, PA	143,679
26620		Huntsville, AL Metro SA	417,593				
26620	01083	Limestone County, AL	82,782	27860		Jonesboro, AR Metro SA	121,026
26620	01089	Madison County, AL	334,811	27860	05031	Craighead County, AR	96,443
				27860	05111	Poinsett County, AR	24,583
26820		Idaho Falls, ID Metro SA	130,374				
26820	16019	Bonneville County, ID	104,234	27900		Joplin, MO Metro SA	175,518
26820	16051	Jefferson County, ID	26,140	27900	29097	Jasper County, MO	117,404
				27900	29145	Newton County, MO	58,114
26900		Indianapolis-Carmel, IN Metro SA	1,756,241				
26900	18011	Boone County, IN	56,640	28020		Kalamazoo-Portage, MI Metro SA	326,589
26900	18013	Brown County, IN	15,242	28020	26077	Kalamazoo County, MI	250,331
26900	18057	Hamilton County, IN	274,569	28020	26159	Van Buren County, MI	76,258
26900	18059	Hancock County, IN	70,002				
26900	18063	Hendricks County, IN	145,448	28100		Kankakee-Bradley, IL Metro SA	113,449
26900	18081	Johnson County, IN	139,654	28100	17091	Kankakee County, IL	113,449
26900	18097	Marion County, IN	903,393				
26900	18109	Morgan County, IN	68,894	28140		Kansas City, MO-KS Metro SA	2,035,334
26900	18133	Putnam County, IN	37,963	28140	20059	Franklin County, KS	25,992
26900	18145	Shelby County, IN	44,436	28140	20091	Johnson County, KS	544,179
				28140	20103	Leavenworth County, KS	76,227
26980		Iowa City, IA Metro SA	152,586	28140	20107	Linn County, KS	9,656
26980	19103	Johnson County, IA	130,882	28140	20121	Miami County, KS	32,787
26980	19183	Washington County, IA	21,704	28140	20209	Wyandotte County, KS	157,505
				28140	29013	Bates County, MO	17,049
27060		Ithaca, NY Metro SA	101,564	28140	29025	Caldwell County, MO	9,424
27060	36109	Tompkins County, NY	101,564	28140	29037	Cass County, MO	99,478
27100		Jackson, MI Metro SA	160,248	28140	29047	Clay County, MO	221,939
27100	26075	Jackson County, MI	160,248	28140	29049	Clinton County, MO	20,743
				28140	29095	Jackson County, MO	674,158
27140		Jackson, MS Metro SA	539,057	28140	29107	Lafayette County, MO	33,381
27140	28029	Copiah County, MS	29,449	28140	29165	Platte County, MO	89,322
27140	28049	Hinds County, MS	245,285	28140	29177	Ray County, MO	23,494
27140	28089	Madison County, MS	95,203				
27140	28121	Rankin County, MS	141,617	28420		Kennewick-Pasco-Richland, WA Metro SA .	253,340
27140	28127	Simpson County, MS	27,503	28420	53005	Benton County, WA	175,177
				28420	53021	Franklin County, WA	78,163
27180		Jackson, TN Metro SA	115,425				
27180	47023	Chester County, TN	17,131	28660		Killeen-Temple-Fort Hood, TX Metro SA	405,300
27180	47113	Madison County, TN	98,294	28660	48027	Bell County, TX	310,235
				28660	48099	Coryell County, TX	75,388
27260		Jacksonville, FL Metro SA	1,345,596	28660	48281	Lampasas County, TX	19,677
27260	12003	Baker County, FL	27,115				
27260	12019	Clay County, FL	190,865	28700		Kingsport-Bristol-Bristol + E313, TN-VA Metro SA	309,544
27260	12031	Duval County, FL	864,263	28700	47073	Hawkins County, TN	56,833
27260	12089	Nassau County, FL	73,314	28700	47163	Sullivan County, TN	156,823
27260	12109	St. Johns County, FL	190,039	28700	51169	Scott County, VA	23,177
				28700	51191	Washington County, VA	54,876
27340		Jacksonville, NC Metro SA	177,772	28700	51520	Bristol city, VA	17,835
27340	37133	Onslow County, NC	177,772				
27500		Janesville, WI Metro SA	160,331	28740		Kingston, NY Metro SA	182,493
27500	55105	Rock County, WI	160,331	28740	36111	Ulster County, NY	182,493
27620		Jefferson City, MO Metro SA	149,807	28940		Knoxville, TN Metro SA	698,030
27620	29027	Callaway County, MO	44,332	28940	47001	Anderson County, TN	75,129
27620	29051	Cole County, MO	75,990	28940	47009	Blount County, TN	123,010
27620	29135	Moniteau County, MO	15,607	28940	47093	Knox County, TN	432,226
27620	29151	Osage County, MO	13,878	28940	47105	Loudon County, TN	48,556
				28940	47173	Union County, TN	19,109

Metropolitan Statistical Areas, Metropolitan Divisions, and Components (as defined December 2009)–Continued

Core Based Statistical Area	State/ County FIPS Code	Title and Geographic Components	2010 Census Population	Core Based Statistical Area	State/ County FIPS Code	Title and Geographic Components	2010 Census Population
29020		Kokomo, IN Metro SA	98,688	30620		Lima, OH Metro SA	106,331
29020	18067	Howard County, IN	82,752	30620	39003	Allen County, OH	106,331
29020	18159	Tipton County, IN	15,936				
				30700		Lincoln, NE Metro SA	302,157
29100		La Crosse, WI-MN Metro SA	133,665	30700	31109	Lancaster County, NE	285,407
29100	27055	Houston County, MN	19,027	30700	31159	Seward County, NE	16,750
29100	55063	La Crosse County, WI	114,638				
				30780		Little Rock-North Little Rock-Conway, AR Metro SA	699,757
29140		Lafayette, IN Metro SA	201,789				
29140	18007	Benton County, IN	8,854	30780	05045	Faulkner County, AR	113,237
29140	18015	Carroll County, IN	20,155	30780	05053	Grant County, AR	17,853
29140	18157	Tippecanoe County, IN	172,780	30780	05085	Lonoke County, AR	68,356
				30780	05105	Perry County, AR	10,445
29180		Lafayette, LA Metro SA	273,738	30780	05119	Pulaski County, AR	382,748
29180	22055	Lafayette Parish, LA	221,578	30780	05125	Saline County, AR	107,118
29180	22099	St. Martin Parish, LA	52,160				
				30860		Logan, UT-ID Metro SA	125,442
29340		Lake Charles, LA Metro SA	199,607	30860	16041	Franklin County, ID	12,786
29340	22019	Calcasieu Parish, LA	192,768	30860	49005	Cache County, UT	112,656
29340	22023	Cameron Parish, LA	6,839	30980		Longview, TX Metro SA	214,369
				30980	48183	Gregg County, TX	121,730
29420		Lake Havasu City-Kingman, AZ Metro SA	200,186	30980	48401	Rusk County, TX	53,330
29420	04015	Mohave County, AZ	200,186	30980	48459	Upshur County, TX	39,309
29460		Lakeland-Winter Haven, FL Metro SA	602,095	31020		Longview, WA Metro SA	102,410
29460	12105	Polk County, FL	602,095	31020	53015	Cowlitz County, WA	102,410
29540		Lancaster, PA Metro SA	519,445	31100		Los Angeles-Long Beach-Santa Ana, CA Metro SA	12,828,837
29540	42071	Lancaster County, PA	519,445				
29620		Lansing-East Lansing, MI Metro SA	464,036	31100		Los Angeles-Long Beach-Glendale, CA Metro Div 31084	9,818,605
29620	26037	Clinton County, MI	75,382				
29620	26045	Eaton County, MI	107,759	31100	06037	Los Angeles County, CA	9,818,605
29620	26065	Ingham County, MI	280,895				
				31100		Santa Ana-Anaheim-Irvine, CA Metro Div 42044	3,010,232
29700		Laredo, TX Metro SA	250,304				
29700	48479	Webb County, TX	250,304	31100	06059	Orange County, CA	3,010,232
29740		Las Cruces, NM Metro SA	209,233	31140		Louisville-Jefferson County, KY-IN Metro SA	1,283,566
29740	35013	Dona Ana County, NM	209,233				
				31140	18019	Clark County, IN	110,232
29820		Las Vegas-Paradise, NV Metro SA	1,951,269	31140	18043	Floyd County, IN	74,578
29820	32003	Clark County, NV	1,951,269	31140	18061	Harrison County, IN	39,364
				31140	18175	Washington County, IN	28,262
29940		Lawrence, KS Metro SA	110,826	31140	21029	Bullitt County, KY	74,319
29940	20045	Douglas County, KS	110,826				
				31140	21103	Henry County, KY	15,416
30020		Lawton, OK Metro SA	124,098	31140	21111	Jefferson County, KY	741,096
30020	40031	Comanche County, OK	124,098	31140	21163	Meade County, KY	28,602
				31140	21179	Nelson County, KY	43,437
30140		Lebanon, PA Metro SA	133,568	31140	21185	Oldham County, KY	60,316
30140	42075	Lebanon County, PA	133,568	31140	21211	Shelby County, KY	42,074
				31140	21215	Spencer County, KY	17,061
30300		Lewiston, ID-WA Metro SA	60,888	31140	21223	Trimble County, KY	8,809
30300	16069	Nez Perce County, ID	39,265				
30300	53003	Asotin County, WA	21,623	31180		Lubbock, TX Metro SA	284,890
				31180	48107	Crosby County, TX	6,059
30340		Lewiston-Auburn, ME Metro SA	107,702	31180	48303	Lubbock County, TX	278,831
30340	23001	Androscoggin County, ME	107,702				
				31340		Lynchburg, VA Metro SA	252,634
30460		Lexington-Fayette, KY Metro SA	472,099	31340	51009	Amherst County, VA	32,353
30460	21017	Bourbon County, KY	19,985	31340	51011	Appomattox County, VA	14,973
30460	21049	Clark County, KY	35,613	31340	51019	Bedford County, VA	68,676
30460	21067	Fayette County, KY	295,803	31340	51031	Campbell County, VA	54,842
30460	21113	Jessamine County, KY	48,586	31340	51515	Bedford city, VA	6,222
30460	21209	Scott County, KY	47,173	31340	51680	Lynchburg city, VA	75,568
30460	21239	Woodford County, KY	24,939				

APPENDIX C

Metropolitan Statistical Areas, Metropolitan Divisions, and Components (as defined December 2009)–*Continued*

Core Based Statistical Area	State/County FIPS Code	Title and Geographic Components	2010 Census Population	Core Based Statistical Area	State/County FIPS Code	Title and Geographic Components	2010 Census Population
31420		Macon, GA Metro SA	232,293	33260	48329	Midland County, TX	136,872
31420	13021	Bibb County, GA	155,547	33340		Milwaukee-Waukesha-West Allis, WI Metro SA	1,555,908
31420	13079	Crawford County, GA	12,630				
31420	13169	Jones County, GA	28,669	33340	55079	Milwaukee County, WI	947,735
31420	13207	Monroe County, GA	26,424	33340	55089	Ozaukee County, WI	86,395
31420	13289	Twiggs County, GA	9,023	33340	55131	Washington County, WI	131,887
				33340	55133	Waukesha County, WI	389,891
31460		Madera-Chowchilla, CA Metro SA	150,865				
31460	06039	Madera County, CA	150,865	33460		Minneapolis-St. Paul-Bloomington, MN-WI Metro SA	3,279,833
31540		Madison, WI Metro SA	568,593	33460	27003	Anoka County, MN	330,844
31540	55021	Columbia County, WI	56,833	33460	27019	Carver County, MN	91,042
31540	55025	Dane County, WI	488,073	33460	27025	Chisago County, MN	53,887
31540	55049	Iowa County, WI	23,687	33460	27037	Dakota County, MN	398,552
				33460	27053	Hennepin County, MN	1,152,425
31700		Manchester-Nashua, NH Metro SA	400,721	33460	27059	Isanti County, MN	37,816
31700	33011	Hillsborough County, NH	400,721				
				33460	27123	Ramsey County, MN	508,640
31740		Manhattan, KS Metro SA	127,081	33460	27139	Scott County, MN	129,928
31740	20061	Geary County, KS	34,362	33460	27141	Sherburne County, MN	88,499
31740	20149	Pottawatomie County, KS	21,604	33460	27163	Washington County, MN	238,136
31740	20161	Riley County, KS	71,115	33460	27171	Wright County, MN	124,700
				33460	55093	Pierce County, WI	41,019
31860		Mankato-North Mankato, MN Metro SA	96,740	33460	55109	St. Croix County, WI	84,345
31860	27013	Blue Earth County, MN	64,013				
31860	27103	Nicollet County, MN	32,727	33540		Missoula, MT Metro SA	109,299
				33540	30063	Missoula County, MT	109,299
31900		Mansfield, OH Metro SA	124,475				
31900	39139	Richland County, OH	124,475	33660		Mobile, AL Metro SA	412,992
				33660	01097	Mobile County, AL	412,992
32580		McAllen-Edinburg-Mission, TX Metro SA	774,769				
32580	48215	Hidalgo County, TX	774,769	33700		Modesto, CA Metro SA	514,453
				33700	06099	Stanislaus County, CA	514,453
32780		Medford, OR Metro SA	203,206				
32780	41029	Jackson County, OR	203,206	33740		Monroe, LA Metro SA	176,441
				33740	22073	Ouachita Parish, LA	153,720
32820		Memphis, TN-MS-AR Metro SA	1,316,100	33740	22111	Union Parish, LA	22,721
32820	05035	Crittenden County, AR	50,902				
32820	28033	DeSoto County, MS	161,252	33780		Monroe, MI Metro SA	152,021
32820	28093	Marshall County, MS	37,144	33780	26115	Monroe County, MI	152,021
32820	28137	Tate County, MS	28,886				
32820	28143	Tunica County, MS	10,778	33860		Montgomery, AL Metro SA	374,536
32820	47047	Fayette County, TN	38,413	33860	01001	Autauga County, AL	54,571
32820	47157	Shelby County, TN	927,644	33860	01051	Elmore County, AL	79,303
32820	47167	Tipton County, TN	61,081	33860	01085	Lowndes County, AL	11,299
				33860	01101	Montgomery County, AL	229,363
32900		Merced, CA Metro SA	255,793				
32900	06047	Merced County, CA	255,793	34060		Morgantown, WV Metro SA	129,709
				34060	54061	Monongalia County, WV	96,189
33100		Miami-Fort Lauderdale-Pompano Beach, FL Metro SA	5,564,635	34060	54077	Preston County, WV	33,520
				34100		Morristown, TN Metro SA	136,608
33100		Fort Lauderdale-Pompano Beach-Deerfield Beach, FL Metro Div 22744	1,748,066	34100	47057	Grainger County, TN	22,657
				34100	47063	Hamblen County, TN	62,544
33100	12011	Broward County, FL	1,748,066	34100	47089	Jefferson County, TN	51,407
33100		Miami-Miami Beach-Kendall, FL Metro Div 33124	2,496,435	34580		Mount Vernon-Anacortes, WA Metro SA	116,901
33100	12086	Miami-Dade County, FL	2,496,435	34580	53057	Skagit County, WA	116,901
				34620		Muncie, IN Metro SA	117,671
33100		West Palm Beach-Boca Raton-Boynton Beach, FL Metro Div 48424	1,320,134	34620	18035	Delaware County, IN	117,671
				34740		Muskegon-Norton Shores, MI Metro SA	172,188
33100	12099	Palm Beach County, FL	1,320,134	34740	26121	Muskegon County, MI	172,188
33140		Michigan City-La Porte, IN Metro SA	111,467				
33140	18091	LaPorte County, IN	111,467	34820		Myrtle Beach-North Myrtle Beach-Conway, SC Metro SA	269,291
33260		Midland, TX Metro SA	136,872	34820	45051	Horry County, SC	269,291

Metropolitan Statistical Areas, Metropolitan Divisions, and Components
(as defined December 2009)–Continued

Core Based Statistical Area	State/County FIPS Code	Title and Geographic Components	2010 Census Population
34900		Napa, CA Metro SA	136,484
34900	06055	Napa County, CA	136,484
34940		Naples-Marco Island, FL Metro SA	321,520
34940	12021	Collier County, FL	321,520
34980		Nashville-Davidson--Murfreesboro--Franklin, TN Metro SA	1,589,934
34980	47015	Cannon County, TN	13,801
34980	47021	Cheatham County, TN	39,105
34980	47037	Davidson County, TN	626,681
34980	47043	Dickson County, TN	49,666
34980	47081	Hickman County, TN	24,690
34980	47111	Macon County, TN	22,248
34980	47147	Robertson County, TN	66,283
34980	47149	Rutherford County, TN	262,604
34980	47159	Smith County, TN	19,166
34980	47165	Sumner County, TN	160,645
34980	47169	Trousdale County, TN	7,870
34980	47187	Williamson County, TN	183,182
34980	47189	Wilson County, TN	113,993
35300		New Haven-Milford, CT Metro SA	862,477
35300	09009	New Haven County, CT	862,477
35380		New Orleans-Metairie-Kenner, LA Metro SA	1,167,764
35380	22051	Jefferson Parish, LA	432,552
35380	22071	Orleans Parish, LA	343,829
35380	22075	Plaquemines Parish, LA	23,042
35380	22087	St. Bernard Parish, LA	35,897
35380	22089	St. Charles Parish, LA	52,780
35380	22095	St. John the Baptist Parish, LA	45,924
35380	22103	St. Tammany Parish, LA	233,740
35620		New York-Northern NJ-Long Island, NY-NJ-PA Metro SA	18,897,109
35620		Edison-New Brunswick, NJ Metro Div 20764	2,340,249
35620	34023	Middlesex County, NJ	809,858
35620	34025	Monmouth County, NJ	630,380
35620	34029	Ocean County, NJ	576,567
35620	34035	Somerset County, NJ	323,444
35620		Nassau-Suffolk, NY Metro Div 35004	2,832,882
35620	36059	Nassau County, NY	1,339,532
35620	36103	Suffolk County, NY	1,493,350
35620		Newark-Union, NJ-PA Metro Div 35084	2,147,727
35620	34013	Essex County, NJ	783,969
35620	34019	Hunterdon County, NJ	128,349
35620	34027	Morris County, NJ	492,276
35620	34037	Sussex County, NJ	149,265
35620	34039	Union County, NJ	536,499
35620	42103	Pike County, PA	57,369
35620		New York-White Plains-Wayne, NY-NJ Metro Div 35644	11,576,251
35620	34003	Bergen County, NJ	905,116
35620	34017	Hudson County, NJ	634,266
35620	34031	Passaic County, NJ	501,226
35620	36005	Bronx County, NY	1,385,108
35620	36047	Kings County, NY	2,504,700
35620	36061	New York County, NY	1,585,873
35620	36079	Putnam County, NY	99,710
35620	36081	Queens County, NY	2,230,722
35620	36085	Richmond County, NY	468,730
35620	36087	Rockland County, NY	311,687
35620	36119	Westchester County, NY	949,113
35660		Niles-Benton Harbor, MI Metro SA	156,813
35660	26021	Berrien County, MI	156,813
35840		North Port-Bradenton-Sarasota, FL Metro SA	702,281
35840	12081	Manatee County, FL	322,833
35840	12115	Sarasota County, FL	379,448
35980		Norwich-New London, CT Metro SA	274,055
35980	09011	New London County, CT	274,055
36100		Ocala, FL Metro SA	331,298
36100	12083	Marion County, FL	331,298
36140		Ocean City, NJ Metro SA	97,265
36140	34009	Cape May County, NJ	97,265
36220		Odessa, TX Metro SA	137,130
36220	48135	Ector County, TX	137,130
36260		Ogden-Clearfield, UT Metro SA	547,184
36260	49011	Davis County, UT	306,479
36260	49029	Morgan County, UT	9,469
36260	49057	Weber County, UT	231,236
36420		Oklahoma City, OK Metro SA	1,252,987
36420	40017	Canadian County, OK	115,541
36420	40027	Cleveland County, OK	255,755
36420	40051	Grady County, OK	52,431
36420	40081	Lincoln County, OK	34,273
36420	40083	Logan County, OK	41,848
36420	40087	McClain County, OK	34,506
36420	40109	Oklahoma County, OK	718,633
36500		Olympia, WA Metro SA	252,264
36500	53067	Thurston County, WA	252,264
36540		Omaha-Council Bluffs, NE-IA Metro SA	865,350
36540	19085	Harrison County, IA	14,928
36540	19129	Mills County, IA	15,059
36540	19155	Pottawattamie County, IA	93,158
36540	31025	Cass County, NE	25,241
36540	31055	Douglas County, NE	517,110
36540	31153	Sarpy County, NE	158,840
36540	31155	Saunders County, NE	20,780
36540	31177	Washington County, NE	20,234
36740		Orlando-Kissimmee-Sanford, FL Metro SA	2,134,411
36740	12069	Lake County, FL	297,052
36740	12095	Orange County, FL	1,145,956
36740	12097	Osceola County, FL	268,685
36740	12117	Seminole County, FL	422,718
36780		Oshkosh-Neenah, WI Metro SA	166,994

Metropolitan Statistical Areas, Metropolitan Divisions, and Components (as defined December 2009)–Continued

Core Based Statistical Area	State/County FIPS Code	Title and Geographic Components	2010 Census Population	Core Based Statistical Area	State/County FIPS Code	Title and Geographic Components	2010 Census Population
36780	55139	Winnebago County, WI	166,994	38220		Pine Bluff, AR Metro SA	100,258
36980		Owensboro, KY Metro SA	114,752	38220	05025	Cleveland County, AR	8,689
36980	21059	Daviess County, KY	96,656	38220	05069	Jefferson County, AR	77,435
36980	21091	Hancock County, KY	8,565	38220	05079	Lincoln County, AR	14,134
36980	21149	McLean County, KY	9,531	38300		Pittsburgh, PA Metro SA	2,356,285
37100		Oxnard-Thousand Oaks-Ventura, CA Metro SA	823,318	38300	42003	Allegheny County, PA	1,223,348
				38300	42005	Armstrong County, PA	68,941
37100	06111	Ventura County, CA	823,318	38300	42007	Beaver County, PA	170,539
				38300	42019	Butler County, PA	183,862
37340		Palm Bay-Melbourne-Titusville, FL Metro SA	543,376	38300	42051	Fayette County, PA	136,606
				38300	42125	Washington County, PA	207,820
37340	12009	Brevard County, FL	543,376	38300	42129	Westmoreland County, PA	365,169
37380		Palm Coast, FL Metro SA	95,696	38340		Pittsfield, MA Metro SA	131,219
37380	12035	Flagler County, FL	95,696	38340	25003	Berkshire County, MA	131,219
37460		Panama City-Lynn Haven-Panama City Beach, FL Metro SA	168,852	38540		Pocatello, ID Metro SA	90,656
				38540	16005	Bannock County, ID	82,839
37460	12005	Bay County, FL	168,852	38540	16077	Power County, ID	7,817
37620		Parkersburg-Marietta-Vienna, WV-OH Metro SA	162,056	38860		Portland-South Portland-Biddeford, ME Metro SA	514,098
37620	39167	Washington County, OH	61,778	38860	23005	Cumberland County, ME	281,674
37620	54073	Pleasants County, WV	7,605	38860	23023	Sagadahoc County, ME	35,293
37620	54105	Wirt County, WV	5,717	38860	23031	York County, ME	197,131
37620	54107	Wood County, WV	86,956	38900		Portland-Vancouver-Hillsboro, OR-WA Metro SA	2,226,009
37700		Pascagoula, MS Metro SA	162,246				
37700	28039	George County, MS	22,578	38900	41005	Clackamas County, OR	375,992
37700	28059	Jackson County, MS	139,668	38900	41009	Columbia County, OR	49,351
				38900	41051	Multnomah County, OR	735,334
37860		Pensacola-Ferry Pass-Brent, FL Metro SA	448,991	38900	41067	Washington County, OR	529,710
37860	12033	Escambia County, FL	297,619	38900	41071	Yamhill County, OR	99,193
37860	12113	Santa Rosa County, FL	151,372	38900	53011	Clark County, WA	425,363
				38900	53059	Skamania County, WA	11,066
37900		Peoria, IL Metro SA	379,186				
37900	17123	Marshall County, IL	12,640	38940		Port St. Lucie, FL Metro SA	424,107
37900	17143	Peoria County, IL	186,494	38940	12085	Martin County, FL	146,318
37900	17175	Stark County, IL	5,994	38940	12111	St. Lucie County, FL	277,789
37900	17179	Tazewell County, IL	135,394				
37900	17203	Woodford County, IL	38,664	39100		Poughkeepsie-Newburgh-Middletown, NY Metro SA	670,301
37980		Philadelphia-Camden-Wilmington, PA-NJ-DE-MD Metro SA	5,965,343	39100	36027	Dutchess County, NY	297,488
				39100	36071	Orange County, NY	372,813
37980		Camden, NJ Metro Div 15804	1,250,679	39140		Prescott, AZ Metro SA	211,033
37980	34005	Burlington County, NJ	448,734	39140	04025	Yavapai County, AZ	211,033
37980	34007	Camden County, NJ	513,657				
37980	34015	Gloucester County, NJ	288,288	39300		Providence-New Bedford-Fall River, RI-MA Metro SA	1,600,852
37980		Philadelphia, PA Metro Div 37964	4,008,994	39300	25005	Bristol County, MA	548,285
37980	42017	Bucks County, PA	625,249	39300	44001	Bristol County, RI	49,875
37980	42029	Chester County, PA	498,886	39300	44003	Kent County, RI	166,158
37980	42045	Delaware County, PA	558,979	39300	44005	Newport County, RI	82,888
37980	42091	Montgomery County, PA	799,874	39300	44007	Providence County, RI	626,667
37980	42101	Philadelphia County, PA	1,526,006	39300	44009	Washington County, RI	126,979
37980		Wilmington, DE-MD-NJ Metro Div 48864	705,670	39340		Provo-Orem, UT Metro SA	526,810
37980	10003	New Castle County, DE	538,479	39340	49023	Juab County, UT	10,246
37980	24015	Cecil County, MD	101,108	39340	49049	Utah County, UT	516,564
37980	34033	Salem County, NJ	66,083	39380		Pueblo, CO Metro SA	159,063
38060		Phoenix-Mesa-Glendale, AZ Metro SA	4,192,887	39380	08101	Pueblo County, CO	159,063
38060	04013	Maricopa County, AZ	3,817,117	39460		Punta Gorda, FL Metro SA	159,978
38060	04021	Pinal County, AZ	375,770	39460	12015	Charlotte County, FL	159,978

Metropolitan Statistical Areas, Metropolitan Divisions, and Components
(as defined December 2009)–Continued

Core Based Statistical Area	State/County FIPS Code	Title and Geographic Components	2010 Census Population	Core Based Statistical Area	State/County FIPS Code	Title and Geographic Components	2010 Census Population
39540		Racine, WI Metro SA	195,408	40380	36117	Wayne County, NY	93,772
39540	55101	Racine County, WI	195,408	40420		Rockford, IL Metro SA	349,431
39580		Raleigh-Cary, NC Metro SA	1,130,490	40420	17007	Boone County, IL	54,165
39580	37069	Franklin County, NC	60,619	40420	17201	Winnebago County, IL	295,266
39580	37101	Johnston County, NC	168,878	40580		Rocky Mount, NC Metro SA	152,392
39580	37183	Wake County, NC	900,993	40580	37065	Edgecombe County, NC	56,552
39660		Rapid City, SD Metro SA	126,382	40580	37127	Nash County, NC	95,840
39660	46093	Meade County, SD	25,434	40660		Rome, GA Metro SA	96,317
39660	46103	Pennington County, SD	100,948	40660	13115	Floyd County, GA	96,317
39740		Reading, PA Metro SA	411,442	40900		Sacramento-Arden-Arcade-Roseville, CA Metro SA	2,149,127
39740	42011	Berks County, PA	411,442	40900	06017	El Dorado County, CA	181,058
39820		Redding, CA Metro SA	177,223	40900	06061	Placer County, CA	348,432
39820	06089	Shasta County, CA	177,223	40900	06067	Sacramento County, CA	1,418,788
39900		Reno-Sparks, NV Metro SA	425,417	40900	06113	Yolo County, CA	200,849
39900	32029	Storey County, NV	4,010	40980		Saginaw-Saginaw Township North, MI Metro SA	200,169
39900	32031	Washoe County, NV	421,407	40980	26145	Saginaw County, MI	200,169
40060		Richmond, VA Metro SA	1,258,251				
40060	51007	Amelia County, VA	12,690	41060		St. Cloud, MN Metro SA	189,093
40060	51033	Caroline County, VA	28,545	41060	27009	Benton County, MN	38,451
40060	51036	Charles City County, VA	7,256	41060	27145	Stearns County, MN	150,642
40060	51041	Chesterfield County, VA	316,236				
40060	51049	Cumberland County, VA	10,052	41100		St. George, UT Metro SA	138,115
40060	51053	Dinwiddie County, VA	28,001	41100	49053	Washington County, UT	138,115
40060	51075	Goochland County, VA	21,717				
40060	51085	Hanover County, VA	99,863	41140		St. Joseph, MO-KS Metro SA	127,329
40060	51087	Henrico County, VA	306,935	41140	20043	Doniphan County, KS	7,945
				41140	29003	Andrew County, MO	17,291
40060	51097	King and Queen County, VA	6,945	41140	29021	Buchanan County, MO	89,201
40060	51101	King William County, VA	15,935	41140	29063	DeKalb County, MO	12,892
40060	51109	Louisa County, VA	33,153				
40060	51127	New Kent County, VA	18,429	41180		St. Louis, MO-IL Metro SA	2,812,896
40060	51145	Powhatan County, VA	28,046	41180	17005	Bond County, IL	17,768
40060	51149	Prince George County, VA	35,725	41180	17013	Calhoun County, IL	5,089
40060	51183	Sussex County, VA	12,087	41180	17027	Clinton County, IL	37,762
40060	51570	Colonial Heights city, VA	17,411	41180	17083	Jersey County, IL	22,985
40060	51670	Hopewell city, VA	22,591	41180	17117	Macoupin County, IL	47,765
40060	51730	Petersburg city, VA	32,420	41180	17119	Madison County, IL	269,282
40060	51760	Richmond city, VA	204,214	41180	17133	Monroe County, IL	32,957
				41180	17163	St. Clair County, IL	270,056
40140		Riverside-San Bernardino-Ontario, CA Metro SA	4,224,851	41180	29071	Franklin County, MO	101,492
40140	06065	Riverside County, CA	2,189,641	41180	29099	Jefferson County, MO	218,733
40140	06071	San Bernardino County, CA	2,035,210	41180	29113	Lincoln County, MO	52,566
				41180	29183	St. Charles County, MO	360,485
40220		Roanoke, VA Metro SA	308,707	41180	29189	St. Louis County, MO	998,954
40220	51023	Botetourt County, VA	33,148	41180	29219	Warren County, MO	32,513
40220	51045	Craig County, VA	5,190	41180	29221	Washington County, MO	25,195
40220	51067	Franklin County, VA	56,159	41180	29510	St. Louis city, MO	319,294
40220	51161	Roanoke County, VA	92,376				
40220	51770	Roanoke city, VA	97,032	41420		Salem, OR Metro SA	390,738
40220	51775	Salem city, VA	24,802	41420	41047	Marion County, OR	315,335
				41420	41053	Polk County, OR	75,403
40340		Rochester, MN Metro SA	186,011				
40340	27039	Dodge County, MN	20,087	41500		Salinas, CA Metro SA	415,057
40340	27109	Olmsted County, MN	144,248	41500	06053	Monterey County, CA	415,057
40340	27157	Wabasha County, MN	21,676				
				41540		Salisbury, MD Metro SA	125,203
40380		Rochester, NY Metro SA	1,054,323	41540	24039	Somerset County, MD	26,470
40380	36051	Livingston County, NY	65,393	41540	24045	Wicomico County, MD	98,733
40380	36055	Monroe County, NY	744,344				
40380	36069	Ontario County, NY	107,931				
40380	36073	Orleans County, NY	42,883				

Metropolitan Statistical Areas, Metropolitan Divisions, and Components (as defined December 2009)–*Continued*

Core Based Statistical Area	State/County FIPS Code	Title and Geographic Components	2010 Census Population	Core Based Statistical Area	State/County FIPS Code	Title and Geographic Components	2010 Census Population
41620		Salt Lake City, UT Metro SA...........	1,124,197	42540		Scranton-Wilkes-Barre, PA Metro SA.......	563,631
41620	49035	Salt Lake County, UT.............	1,029,655	42540	42069	Lackawanna County, PA.............	214,437
41620	49043	Summit County, UT.............	36,324	42540	42079	Luzerne County, PA.............	320,918
41620	49045	Tooele County, UT.............	58,218	42540	42131	Wyoming County, PA.............	28,276
41660		San Angelo, TX Metro SA.............	111,823	42660		Seattle-Tacoma-Bellevue, WA Metro SA.....	3,439,809
41660	48235	Irion County, TX.............	1,599				
41660	48451	Tom Green County, TX.............	110,224	42660		Seattle-Bellevue-Everett, WA Metro Div 42644.............	2,644,584
41700		San Antonio-New Braunfels, TX Metro SA..	2,142,508	42660	53033	King County, WA.............	1,931,249
41700	48013	Atascosa County, TX.............	44,911	42660	53061	Snohomish County, WA.............	713,335
41700	48019	Bandera County, TX.............	20,485				
41700	48029	Bexar County, TX.............	1,714,773	42660		Tacoma, WA Metro Div 45104.............	795,225
41700	48091	Comal County, TX.............	108,472	42660	53053	Pierce County, WA.............	795,225
41700	48187	Guadalupe County, TX.............	131,533				
41700	48259	Kendall County, TX.............	33,410	42680		Sebastian-Vero Beach, FL Metro SA.........	138,028
41700	48325	Medina County, TX.............	46,006	42680	12061	Indian River County, FL.............	138,028
41700	48493	Wilson County, TX.............	42,918				
				43100		Sheboygan, WI Metro SA.............	115,507
41740		San Diego-Carlsbad-San Marcos, CA Metro SA	3,095,313	43100	55117	Sheboygan County, WI.............	115,507
41740	06073	San Diego County, CA.............	3,095,313	43300		Sherman-Denison, TX Metro SA.............	120,877
				43300	48181	Grayson County, TX.............	120,877
41780		Sandusky, OH Metro SA.............	77,079				
41780	39043	Erie County, OH.............	77,079	43340		Shreveport-Bossier City, LA Metro SA........	398,604
				43340	22015	Bossier Parish, LA.............	116,979
41860		San Francisco-Oakland-Fremont, CA Metro SA	4,335,391	43340	22017	Caddo Parish, LA.............	254,969
				43340	22031	De Soto Parish, LA.............	26,656
41860		Oakland-Fremont-Hayward, CA Metro Div 36084	2,559,296	43580		Sioux City, IA-NE-SD Metro SA.............	143,577
				43580	19193	Woodbury County, IA.............	102,172
41860	06001	Alameda County, CA.............	1,510,271	43580	31043	Dakota County, NE.............	21,006
41860	06013	Contra Costa County, CA.............	1,049,025	43580	31051	Dixon County, NE.............	6,000
				43580	46127	Union County, SD.............	14,399
41860		San Francisco-San Mateo-Redwood City, CA Metro Div 41884.............	1,776,095	43620		Sioux Falls, SD Metro SA.............	228,261
41860	06041	Marin County, CA.............	252,409	43620	46083	Lincoln County, SD.............	44,828
41860	06075	San Francisco County, CA.............	805,235	43620	46087	McCook County, SD.............	5,618
41860	06081	San Mateo County, CA.............	718,451	43620	46099	Minnehaha County, SD.............	169,468
				43620	46125	Turner County, SD.............	8,347
41940		San Jose-Sunnyvale-Santa Clara, CA Metro SA	1,836,911	43780		South Bend-Mishawaka, IN-MI Metro SA....	319,224
41940	06069	San Benito County, CA.............	55,269	43780	18141	St. Joseph County, IN.............	266,931
41940	06085	Santa Clara County, CA.............	1,781,642	43780	26027	Cass County, MI.............	52,293
42020		San Luis Obispo-Paso Robles, CA Metro SA	269,637	43900		Spartanburg, SC Metro SA.............	284,307
				43900	45083	Spartanburg County, SC.............	284,307
42020	06079	San Luis Obispo County, CA.............	269,637				
				44060		Spokane, WA Metro SA.............	471,221
42060		Santa Barbara-Santa Maria-Goleta, CA Metro SA	423,895	44060	53063	Spokane County, WA.............	471,221
42060	06083	Santa Barbara County, CA.............	423,895	44100		Springfield, IL Metro SA.............	210,170
				44100	17129	Menard County, IL.............	12,705
42100		Santa Cruz-Watsonville, CA Metro SA........	262,382	44100	17167	Sangamon County, IL.............	197,465
42100	06087	Santa Cruz County, CA.............	262,382				
				44140		Springfield, MA Metro SA.............	692,942
42140		Santa Fe, NM Metro SA.............	144,170	44140	25011	Franklin County, MA.............	71,372
42140	35049	Santa Fe County, NM.............	144,170	44140	25013	Hampden County, MA.............	463,490
				44140	25015	Hampshire County, MA.............	158,080
42220		Santa Rosa-Petaluma, CA Metro SA.........	483,878				
42220	06097	Sonoma County, CA.............	483,878	44180		Springfield, MO Metro SA.............	436,712
				44180	29043	Christian County, MO.............	77,422
42340		Savannah, GA Metro SA.............	347,611	44180	29059	Dallas County, MO.............	16,777
42340	13029	Bryan County, GA.............	30,233	44180	29077	Greene County, MO.............	275,174
42340	13051	Chatham County, GA.............	265,128	44180	29167	Polk County, MO.............	31,137
42340	13103	Effingham County, GA.............	52,250	44180	29225	Webster County, MO.............	36,202

Metropolitan Statistical Areas, Metropolitan Divisions, and Components
(as defined December 2009)–Continued

Core Based Statistical Area	State/County FIPS Code	Title and Geographic Components	2010 Census Population	Core Based Statistical Area	State/County FIPS Code	Title and Geographic Components	2010 Census Population
44220		Springfield, OH Metro SA	138,333	46140		Tulsa, OK Metro SA	937,478
44220	39023	Clark County, OH	138,333	46140	40037	Creek County, OK	69,967
				46140	40111	Okmulgee County, OK	40,069
44300		State College, PA Metro SA	153,990	46140	40113	Osage County, OK	47,472
44300	42027	Centre County, PA	153,990	46140	40117	Pawnee County, OK	16,577
				46140	40131	Rogers County, OK	86,905
44600		Steubenville-Weirton, OH-WV Metro SA	124,454	46140	40143	Tulsa County, OK	603,403
44600	39081	Jefferson County, OH	69,709	46140	40145	Wagoner County, OK	73,085
44600	54009	Brooke County, WV	24,069				
44600	54029	Hancock County, WV	30,676	46220		Tuscaloosa, AL Metro SA	219,461
				46220	01063	Greene County, AL	9,045
44700		Stockton, CA Metro SA	685,306	46220	01065	Hale County, AL	15,760
44700	06077	San Joaquin County, CA	685,306	46220	01125	Tuscaloosa County, AL	194,656
44940		Sumter, SC Metro SA	107,456	46340		Tyler, TX Metro SA	209,714
44940	45085	Sumter County, SC	107,456	46340	48423	Smith County, TX	209,714
45060		Syracuse, NY Metro SA	662,577	46540		Utica-Rome, NY Metro SA	299,397
45060	36053	Madison County, NY	73,442	46540	36043	Herkimer County, NY	64,519
45060	36067	Onondaga County, NY	467,026	46540	36065	Oneida County, NY	234,878
45060	36075	Oswego County, NY	122,109				
				46660		Valdosta, GA Metro SA	139,588
45220		Tallahassee, FL Metro SA	367,413	46660	13027	Brooks County, GA	16,243
45220	12039	Gadsden County, FL	46,389	46660	13101	Echols County, GA	4,034
45220	12065	Jefferson County, FL	14,761	46660	13173	Lanier County, GA	10,078
45220	12073	Leon County, FL	275,487	46660	13185	Lowndes County, GA	109,233
45220	12129	Wakulla County, FL	30,776				
				46700		Vallejo-Fairfield, CA Metro SA	413,344
45300		Tampa-St. Petersburg-Clearwater, FL Metro SA	2,783,243	46700	06095	Solano County, CA	413,344
45300	12053	Hernando County, FL	172,778	47020		Victoria, TX Metro SA	115,384
45300	12057	Hillsborough County, FL	1,229,226	47020	48057	Calhoun County, TX	21,381
45300	12101	Pasco County, FL	464,697	47020	48175	Goliad County, TX	7,210
45300	12103	Pinellas County, FL	916,542	47020	48469	Victoria County, TX	86,793
45460		Terre Haute, IN Metro SA	172,425	47220		Vineland-Millville-Bridgeton, NJ Metro SA	156,898
45460	18021	Clay County, IN	26,890	47220	34011	Cumberland County, NJ	156,898
45460	18153	Sullivan County, IN	21,475				
45460	18165	Vermillion County, IN	16,212	47260		Virginia Beach-Norfolk-Newport News, VA-NC Metro SA	1,671,683
45460	18167	Vigo County, IN	107,848	47260	37053	Currituck County, NC	23,547
45500		Texarkana, TX-Texarkana, AR Metro SA	136,027	47260	51073	Gloucester County, VA	36,858
45500	05091	Miller County, AR	43,462	47260	51093	Isle of Wight County, VA	35,270
45500	48037	Bowie County, TX	92,565	47260	51095	James City County, VA	67,009
				47260	51115	Mathews County, VA	8,978
45780		Toledo, OH Metro SA	651,429	47260	51181	Surry County, VA	7,058
45780	39051	Fulton County, OH	42,698	47260	51199	York County, VA	65,464
45780	39095	Lucas County, OH	441,815	47260	51550	Chesapeake city, VA	222,209
45780	39123	Ottawa County, OH	41,428				
45780	39173	Wood County, OH	125,488	47260	51650	Hampton city, VA	137,436
				47260	51700	Newport News city, VA	180,719
45820		Topeka, KS Metro SA	233,870	47260	51710	Norfolk city, VA	242,803
45820	20085	Jackson County, KS	13,462	47260	51735	Poquoson city, VA	12,150
45820	20087	Jefferson County, KS	19,126	47260	51740	Portsmouth city, VA	95,535
45820	20139	Osage County, KS	16,295	47260	51800	Suffolk city, VA	84,585
45820	20177	Shawnee County, KS	177,934	47260	51810	Virginia Beach city, VA	437,994
45820	20197	Wabaunsee County, KS	7,053	47260	51830	Williamsburg city, VA	14,068
45940		Trenton-Ewing, NJ Metro SA	366,513	47300		Visalia-Porterville, CA Metro SA	442,179
45940	34021	Mercer County, NJ	366,513	47300	06107	Tulare County, CA	442,179
46060		Tucson, AZ Metro SA	980,263	47380		Waco, TX Metro SA	234,906
46060	04019	Pima County, AZ	980,263	47380	48309	McLennan County, TX	234,906
				47580		Warner Robins, GA Metro SA	139,900
				47580	13153	Houston County, GA	139,900

Metropolitan Statistical Areas, Metropolitan Divisions, and Components
(as defined December 2009)–Continued

Core Based Statistical Area	State/County FIPS Code	Title and Geographic Components	2010 Census Population	Core Based Statistical Area	State/County FIPS Code	Title and Geographic Components	2010 Census Population
47900		Washington-Arlington-Alexandria, DC-VA-MD-WV Metro SA	5,582,170	49020		Winchester, VA-WV Metro SA	128,472
				49020	51069	Frederick County, VA	78,305
				49020	51840	Winchester city, VA	26,203
47900		Bethesda-Rockville-Frederick, MD Metro Div 13644	1,205,162	49020	54027	Hampshire County, WV	23,964
47900	24021	Frederick County, MD	233,385	49180		Winston-Salem, NC Metro SA	477,717
47900	24031	Montgomery County, MD	971,777	49180	37059	Davie County, NC	41,240
				49180	37067	Forsyth County, NC	350,670
47900		Washington-Arlington-Alexandria, DC-VA-MD-WV Metro Div 47894	4,377,008	49180	37169	Stokes County, NC	47,401
				49180	37197	Yadkin County, NC	38,406
47900	11001	District of Columbia, DC	601,723				
47900	24009	Calvert County, MD	88,737	49340		Worcester, MA Metro SA	798,552
47900	24017	Charles County, MD	146,551	49340	25027	Worcester County, MA	798,552
47900	24033	Prince George's County, MD	863,420				
47900	51013	Arlington County, VA	207,627	49420		Yakima, WA Metro SA	243,231
47900	51043	Clarke County, VA	14,034	49420	53077	Yakima County, WA	243,231
47900	51059	Fairfax County, VA	1,081,726				
47900	51061	Fauquier County, VA	65,203	49620		York-Hanover, PA Metro SA	434,972
47900	51107	Loudoun County, VA	312,311	49620	42133	York County, PA	434,972
47900	51153	Prince William County, VA	402,002	49660		Youngstown-Warren-Boardman, OH-PA Metro SA	565,773
47900	51177	Spotsylvania County, VA	122,397				
47900	51179	Stafford County, VA	128,961	49660	39099	Mahoning County, OH	238,823
47900	51187	Warren County, VA	37,575	49660	39155	Trumbull County, OH	210,312
47900	51510	Alexandria city, VA	139,966	49660	42085	Mercer County, PA	116,638
47900	51600	Fairfax city, VA	22,565				
47900	51610	Falls Church city, VA	12,332	49700		Yuba City, CA Metro SA	166,892
47900	51630	Fredericksburg city, VA	24,286	49700	06101	Sutter County, CA	94,737
47900	51683	Manassas city, VA	37,821	49700	06115	Yuba County, CA	72,155
47900	51685	Manassas Park city, VA	14,273				
47900	54037	Jefferson County, WV	53,498	49740		Yuma, AZ Metro SA	195,751
				49740	04027	Yuma County, AZ	195,751
47940		Waterloo-Cedar Falls, IA Metro SA	167,819				
47940	19013	Black Hawk County, IA	131,090				
47940	19017	Bremer County, IA	24,276				
47940	19075	Grundy County, IA	12,453				
48140		Wausau, WI Metro SA	134,063				
48140	55073	Marathon County, WI	134,063				
48300		Wenatchee-East Wenatchee, WA Metro SA	110,884				
48300	53007	Chelan County, WA	72,453				
48300	53017	Douglas County, WA	38,431				
48540		Wheeling, WV-OH Metro SA	147,950				
48540	39013	Belmont County, OH	70,400				
48540	54051	Marshall County, WV	33,107				
48540	54069	Ohio County, WV	44,443				
48620		Wichita, KS Metro SA	623,061				
48620	20015	Butler County, KS	65,880				
48620	20079	Harvey County, KS	34,684				
48620	20173	Sedgwick County, KS	498,365				
48620	20191	Sumner County, KS	24,132				
48660		Wichita Falls, TX Metro SA	151,306				
48660	48009	Archer County, TX	9,054				
48660	48077	Clay County, TX	10,752				
48660	48485	Wichita County, TX	131,500				
48700		Williamsport, PA Metro SA	116,111				
48700	42081	Lycoming County, PA	116,111				
48900		Wilmington, NC Metro SA	362,315				
48900	37019	Brunswick County, NC	107,431				
48900	37129	New Hanover County, NC	202,667				
48900	37141	Pender County, NC	52,217				

INDEX

A
ACCOUNTANTS AND AUDITORS
  Detailed occupations by group, 15
  Educational attainment, 51
ACTORS
  Detailed occupations by group, 15
  Educational attainment, 56
ACTUARIES
  Educational attainment, 54
ADMINISTRATIVE SERVICES MANAGERS
  Educational attainment, 52
ADMINISTRATIVE SUPPORT WORKERS
  Detailed occupations by group, 23
  EEO occupation groups, 2
  Hispanic origin, 23
  Metropolitan areas
    workers, by area and group, 365
  Race, 23
  Sexes, 23
  States
    workers, by state and group, 228
ADVERTISING MANAGERS
  Educational attainment, 52
ADVERTISING SALES AGENTS
  Detailed occupations by group, 21
AEROSPACE ENGINEERS
  Educational attainment, 54
AGE
  Educational attainment, selected age groups, 50
AGENTS AND BUSINESS MANAGERS
  Educational attainment, 52
AGRICULTURAL AND FOOD SCIENCE TECHNICIANS
  Detailed occupations by group, 18
AGRICULTURAL GRADERS AND SORTERS
  Detailed occupations by group, 35
AGRICULTURAL WORKERS
  Detailed occupations by group, 43
AIRCRAFT ASSEMBLERS
  Detailed occupations by group, 35
AIRCRAFT MECHANICS
  Detailed occupations by group, 30
AIR TRAFFIC CONTROLLERS
  Detailed occupations by group, 18
AMBULANCE DRIVERS
  Detailed occupations by group, 40
ANIMAL BREEDERS
  Detailed occupations by group, 43
ANIMAL CARETAKERS
  Detailed occupations by group, 43
ANIMAL CONTROL WORKERS
  Detailed occupations by group, 45
  Educational attainment, 58
ANIMAL TRAINERS
  Detailed occupations by group, 15
  Educational attainment, 60
ANNOUNCERS
  Detailed occupations by group, 15
  Educational attainment, 56
APPRAISERS
  Educational attainment, 52
ARCHITECTS
  Educational attainment, 52

ARCHIVISTS AND CURATORS
  Detailed occupations by group, 15
ARTISTS
  Detailed occupations by group, 15
  Educational attainment, 52
ASSOCIATE DEGREES
  Educational attainment
    workers with associate degrees, 130
  Hispanic origin
    workers with associate degrees, 130
  Race
    workers with associate degrees, 130
  Sexes
    workers with associate degrees, 130
  Workers with degrees
    detailed occupations by group, 130
ATHLETES
  Detailed occupations by group, 15
  Educational attainment, 52
AUTOMOTIVE REPAIRERS
  Detailed occupations by group, 30
AVIONIC TECHNICIANS
  Detailed occupations by group, 30

B
BACHELOR'S DEGREES
  Workers with bachelor's degrees detailed occupations by group, 156
BAGGAGE PORTERS
  Detailed occupations by group, 48
BAILIFFS
  Detailed occupations by group, 45
  Educational attainment, 58
BAKERS
  Detailed occupations by group, 35
BANKING OCCUPATIONS
  EEO occupation groups, 2
  Hispanic origin, 6
  Race, 6
  Sexes, 6
BARBERS
  Detailed occupations by group, 48
  Educational attainment, 60
BARTENDERS
  Detailed occupations by group, 48
BILL AND ACCOUNT COLLECTORS
  Detailed occupations by group, 23
BIOLOGICAL SCIENTISTS,
  Educational attainment 54
BIOLOGICAL TECHNICIANS
  Detailed occupations by group, 18
BLACKS
  see **RACE**
BOILERMAKERS
  Detailed occupations by group, 27
BOOKKEEPERS
  Detailed occupations by group, 23
BRICKMASONS AND STONEMASONS
  Detailed occupations by group, 27
BROADCAST AND SOUND ENGINEERS
  Detailed occupations by group, 18
  Educational attainment, 56

BUDGET ANALYSTS
   Educational attainment, 52
BUS DRIVERS
   Detailed occupations by group, 40
BUSINESS WORKERS
   EEO occupation groups, 2
   Hispanic origin, 6
   Metropolitan areas
      management, business, and financial workers, by area and group, 281
   Race, 6
   Sexes, 6
   States
      management, business, and financial workers, by state and group, 216
BUTCHERS
   Detailed occupations by group 35

C
CABINETMAKERS
   Detailed occupations by group, 32
CARGO AND FREIGHT CLERKS
   Detailed occupations by group, 23
CARPENTERS
   Detailed occupations by group, 27
CARPET, FLOOR, AND TILE INSTALLERS
   Detailed occupations by group, 27
CASHIERS
   Detailed occupations by group, 21
CHAUFFEURS
   Detailed occupations by group, 40
CHEFS AND HEAD COOKS
   Detailed occupations by group, 48
CHEMICAL ENGINEERS
   Educational attainment, 54
CHEMICAL TECHNICIANS
   Detailed occupations by group, 18
CHIEF EXECUTIVES
   Educational attainment, 52
CHILDCARE WORKERS
   Detailed occupations by group, 48
CHIROPRACTORS
   Detailed occupations by group, 13
   Educational attainment, 56
CITIES
      see METROPOLITAN AREAS
CIVIL ENGINEERS
   Educational attainment, 54
CLAIMS ADJUSTERS
   Educational attainment, 52
CLERGY
   Detailed occupations by group, 15
   Educational attainment, 56
CLINICAL LABORATORY TECHNOLOGISTS
   Detailed occupations by group, 18
COACHES
   Detailed occupations by group, 15
COLLEGE
   Educational attainment
      workers with bachelor's degrees, 156
      workers with some college, 130
   Hispanic origin
      workers with bachelor's degrees, 156
      workers with some college, 130
   Race
      workers with bachelor's degrees, 156
      workers with some college, 130
   Sexes
      workers with bachelor's degrees, 156
      workers with some college, 130
   Workers with bachelor's degrees
      detailed occupations by group, 156
   Workers with some college
      detailed occupations by group, 130
COMMUNICATION WORKERS
   Detailed occupations by group, 15
COMPLIANCE OFFICERS
   Educational attainment, 52
COMPUTER AND INFORMATION SYSTEMS MANAGERS
   Educational attainment, 52
COMPUTER OPERATORS
   Detailed occupations by group, 25
COMPUTER PROFESSIONALS
   EEO occupation groups, 2
   Hispanic origin, 10
   Metropolitan areas
      science, engineering, and computer professionals, by area and group, 295
   Race, 10
   Sexes, 10
   States
      science, engineering, and computer professionals, by state and group, 218
COMPUTER PROGRAMMERS
   Detailed occupations by group, 18
   Educational attainment, 54
CONSTRUCTION AND EXTRACTIVE WORKERS
   Detailed occupations by group, 27
   EEO occupation groups, 2
   Hispanic origin, 27
   Metropolitan areas
      workers, by area and group, 379
   Race, 27
   Sexes, 27
   States
      workers, by state and group, 230
CONSTRUCTION EQUIPMENT OPERATORS
   Detailed occupations by group, 27
CONSTRUCTION MANAGERS
   Educational attainment, 52
COOKS
   Detailed occupations by group, 48
   Educational attainment, 60
CORRECTIONS OFFICERS
   Detailed occupations by group, 15, 45
COST ESTIMATORS
   Educational attainment, 52
COUNSELORS
   Detailed occupations by group, 15
COURIERS AND MESSENGERS
   Detailed occupations by group, 23
COURT CLERKS
   Detailed occupations by group, 23
CRANE AND TOWER OPERATORS
   Detailed occupations by group, 27
CREDIT ANALYSTS
   Educational attainment, 52

INDEX

CREDIT CLERKS
　Detailed occupations by group, 23
CREDIT COUNSELORS
　Educational attainment, 54
CROSSING GUARDS
　Detailed occupations by group, 45
　Educational attainment, 58

D

DANCERS AND CHOREOGRAPHERS
　Detailed occupations by group, 15
　Educational attainment, 56
DATABASE ADMINISTRATORS
　Educational attainment, 54
DATA ENTRY KEYERS
　Detailed occupations by group, 25
DENTAL ASSISTANTS
　Detailed occupations by group, 48
　Educational attainment, 58
DENTAL HYGIENISTS
　Detailed occupations by group, 18
DENTISTS
　Detailed occupations by group, 13
　Educational attainment, 56
DESIGNERS
　Detailed occupations by group, 15
DETECTIVES
　Detailed occupations by group, 45
　Educational attainment, 58
DETECTIVE SUPERVISORS
　Detailed occupations by group, 45
DIETITIANS AND NUTRITIONISTS
　Detailed occupations by group, 13
　Educational attainment, 56
DISHWASHERS
　Detailed occupations by group, 48
　Educational attainment, 60
DISPATCHERS
　Detailed occupations by group, 23
DOOR-TO-DOOR SALES WORKERS
　Detailed occupations by group, 21
DRAFTERS
　Detailed occupations by group, 18
　Educational attainment, 54
DREDGE OPERATORS
　Detailed occupations by group, 27
DRYWALL INSTALLERS
　Detailed occupations by group, 27

E

ECONOMISTS
　Detailed occupations by group, 15
　Educational attainment 54
EDITORS
　Detailed occupations by group, 15
　Educational attainment, 56
EDUCATION ADMINISTRATORS
　Educational attainment, 52
EDUCATIONAL ATTAINMENT
　see **INDIVIDUAL OCCUPATIONS**
EDUCATION WORKERS
　Detailed occupations by group, 15

EEO OCCUPATION GROUPS
　Administrative support workers, 2
　Banking, 2
　Business workers, 2
　Computer professionals, 2
　Construction and extractive workers, 2
　Engineering professionals, 2
　Financial workers, 2
　Health care professionals, 2
　Hispanic origin, 2
　Installation, maintenance, and repair workers, 2
　Laborers and helpers, 2
　Management workers, 2
　Production workers, 2
　Professional workers, 2
　Protective service workers, 2
　Race, 2
　Sales workers, 2
　Science professionals, 2
　Service workers, 2
　Sexes, 2
　Technicians, 2
　Transportation workers, 2
　Unemployment, 2
ELECTRICAL AND ELECTRONICS ENGINEERS
　Educational attainment, 54
ELECTRICAL AND ELECTRONICS REPAIRERS
　Detailed occupations by group, 30
ELECTRICIANS
　Detailed occupations by group, 27
EMERGENCY MANAGEMENT DIRECTORS
　Educational attainment, 52
EMERGENCY MEDICAL TECHNICIANS
　Detailed occupations by group, 18
　Educational attainment, 58
EMBALMERS
　Detailed occupations by group, 48
ENGINE ASSEMBLERS
　Detailed occupations by group, 35
ENGINEERING PROFESSIONALS
　EEO occupation groups, 2
　Hispanic origin, 10
　Metropolitan areas
　　science, engineering, and computer professionals, by area and group, 295
　Race, 10
　Sexes, 10
　States
　　science, engineering, and computer professionals, by state and group, 218
ENGINEERING TECHNICIANS
　Detailed occupations by group, 18
ENTERTAINERS
　Detailed occupations by group, 15
ENVIRONMENTAL ENGINEERS
　Educational attainment, 54
EXPLOSIVES WORKERS
　Detailed occupations by group, 27

F

FARMERS
　Educational attainment, 52

FEMALES
    see **SEXES**
FINANCIAL ANALYSTS
    Educational attainment, 52
FINANCIAL MANAGERS
    Educational attainment, 52
FINANCIAL WORKERS
    EEO occupation groups, 2
    Hispanic origin, 6
    Metropolitan workers
        management, business, and financial workers, by area and group, 281
    Race, 6
    Sexes, 6
    States
        management, business, and financial workers, by state and group, 216
FIREFIGHTERS
    Detailed occupations by group, 45
    Educational attainment, 58
FIRE INSPECTORS
    Detailed occupations by group, 45
FISHING AND HUNTING WORKERS
    Detailed occupations by group, 43
FLIGHT ATTENDANTS
    Detailed occupations by group, 48
FOOD COOKERS AND TENDERS
    Detailed occupations by group, 35
FOOD PREPARATION SUPERVISORS
    Detailed occupations by group, 48
FOOD SERVICE MANAGERS
    Educational attainment, 52
FUNDRAISERS
    Educational attainment, 52
FURNACE OPERATORS
    Detailed occupations by group, 35

G
GAMING CAGE WORKERS
    Detailed occupations by group, 23
GAMING MANAGERS
    Educational attainment, 52
GAMING WORKERS
    Detailed occupations by group, 48
GEOLOGICAL AND PETROLEUM TECHNICIANS
    Detailed occupations by group, 18
    Educational attainment, 54
GLAZIERS
    Detailed occupations by group, 27
GRADUATE DEGREES
    Educational attainment
        workers with graduate or professional degrees, 182
    Hispanic origin
        workers with graduate or professional degrees, 182
    Race
        workers with graduate or professional degrees, 182
    Sexes
        workers with graduate or professional degrees, 182
    Workers with graduate or professional degrees
        detailed occupations by group, 182
GROUNDS MAINTENANCE WORKERS
    Detailed occupations by group, 43
    Educational attainment, 60

H
HAIRDRESSERS
    Detailed occupations by group, 48
    Educational attainment, 60
HEALTH CARE PROFESSIONALS
    EEO occupation groups, 2
    Hispanic origin, 13
    Metropolitan areas
        health care practitioners, by area and group, 3089
    Race, 13
    Sexes, 13
    States
        health care practitioners, by state and group, 220
HEATING AND AIR CONDITIONING MECHANICS
    Detailed occupations by group, 30
HIGH SCHOOL GRADUATES
    Graduates and equivalents
        by detailed occupation, 52
        in workforce, 52
HISPANICS OR LATINOS
    Administrative support workers, 23
    Associate degrees
        workers with associate degrees, 130
    Banking occupations, 6
    Business workers, 6
    College
        workers with bachelor's degrees, 156
        workers with some college, 130
    Computer professionals, 10
    Construction and extractive workers, 27
    Educational attainment, selected groups, 50
    EEO occupation groups, 2
    Engineering professionals, 10
    Financial workers, 6
    Graduate degrees
        workers with graduate or professional degrees, 182
    Health care professionals, 13
    Installation, maintenance, and repair workers, 30
    Laborers and helpers, 43
    Management workers, 6
    Metropolitan areas
        administrative support workers, 365
        all workers, 267
        construction and extractive workers, 379
        health care practitioners, 309
        installation, maintenance, and repair workers, 393
        laborers and helpers, 435
        management, business, and financial workers, 281
        production workers, 407
        professional workers, 323
        protective service workers, 449
        sales workers, 351
        science, engineering, and computer professionals, 295
        service workers, 463
        technicians, 337
        transportation and moving workers, 421
    Production workers, 35
    Professional degrees
        workers with graduate or professional degrees, 182
    Professional workers, 15
    Protective service workers, 45
    Sales workers, 21
    Science professionals, 10

INDEX

Service workers, 48
States
    administrative support workers, 228
    all workers, by state and Hispanic origin, 214
    construction and extraction workers, 230
    health care practitioners, 220
    installation, maintenance, and repair workers, 232
    laborers and helpers, 238
    management, business, and financial workers, 216
    production workers, 234
    professional workers, 222
    protective service workers, 240
    sales workers, 226
    science, engineering, and computer professionals, 218
    service workers, 242
    technicians, 224
    transportation and moving workers, 236
Technicians, 18
Transportation workers, 40

HOME APPLIANCE REPAIRERS
Detailed occupations by group, 30

HOTEL AND MOTEL CLERKS
Detailed occupations by group, 23
Educational attainment, 62

HUMAN RESOURCES MANAGERS
Educational attainment, 52

HUMAN RESOURCES WORKERS
Detail occupations by group, 15
Educational attainment, 52

I

INDUSTRIAL ENGINEERS
Educational attainment, 54

INDUSTRIAL PRODUCTION MANAGERS
Educational attainment, 52

INFORMATION SECURITY ANALYSTS
Educational attainment, 54

INSTALLATION, MAINTENANCE, AND REPAIR WORKERS
Detailed occupations by group, 30
EEO occupation groups, 2
Hispanic origin, 30
Metropolitan areas
    workers, by area and group, 393
Race, 30
Sexes, 30
States
    workers, by state and group, 232

INSULATION WORKERS
Detailed occupations by group, 27

INSURANCE SALES AGENTS
Detailed occupations by group, 21

INSURANCE UNDERWRITERS
Educational attainment, 54

J

JANITORS AND BUILDING CLEANERS
Detailed occupations by group, 48

JEWELERS
Detailed occupations by group, 32

JUDGES
Detailed occupations by group, 15
Educational attainment, 56

L

LABORERS AND HELPERS
Detailed occupations by group, 43
EEO occupation groups, 2
Hispanic origin, 43
Metropolitan areas
    workers, by area and group, 435
Race, 43
Sexes, 43
States
    workers, by state and group, 238

LATHE OPERATORS
Detailed occupations by group, 35

LATINOS
see HISPANICS OR LATINOS

LAUNDRY AND DRY-CLEANING WORKERS
Detailed occupations by group, 37

LAWYERS
Detailed occupations by group, 15
Educational attainment, 56

LEGISLATORS
Educational attainment, 52

LIBRARIANS
Detailed occupations by group, 15
Educational attainment, 56

LIBRARY TECHNICIANS
Detailed occupations by group, 23

LIFE, PHYSICAL, AND SOCIAL SCIENCE TECHNICIANS
Detailed occupations by group, 18

LIFEGUARDS
Detailed occupations by group, 45

LOCKSMITHS
Detailed occupations by group, 30

LOCOMOTIVE ENGINEERS
Detailed occupations by group, 40

LOGGING WORKERS
Detailed occupations by group, 43

LOGISTICIANS
Educational attainment, 52

M

MACHINISTS
Detailed occupations by group, 30

MAGISTRATES
Detailed occupations by group, 15

MAIDS AND HOUSEKEEPERS
Detailed occupations by group, 48

MALES
see SEXES

MANAGEMENT ANALYSTS
Educational attainment, 52

MANAGEMENT WORKERS
EEO occupation groups, 2
Hispanic origin, 6
Metropolitan areas
    management, business, and financial workers, by area and group, 281
Race, 6
Sexes, 6
States
    management, business, and financial workers, by state and group, 216

MANAGERS
Educational attainment, 52
MANUFACTURED BUILDING AND MOBILE HOME INSTALLERS
Detailed occupations by group, 30
MANUFACTURING REPRESENTATIVES
Detailed occupations by group, 21
MARINE ENGINEERS
Educational attainment, 54
MARKETING AND SALES MANAGERS
Educational attainment, 52
MARKET RESEARCH ANALYSTS
Educational attainment, 52
MASSAGE THERAPISTS
Detailed occupations by group, 48
MECHANICAL ENGINEERS
Educational attainment, 54
MECHANICS
Detailed occupations by group, 30
MEDICAL AND HEALTH SERVICES MANAGERS
Educational attainment, 52
MEDICAL ASSISTANTS
Detailed occupations by group, 48
Educational attainment, 58
MEDICAL RECORDS TECHNICIANS
Detailed occupations by group, 18
MEDICAL TECHNICIANS
Detailed occupations by group, 32
MEDICAL TRANSCRIPTIONISTS
Detailed occupations by group, 23
MEETING, CONVENTION, AND EVENT PLANNERS
Educational attainment, 52
METER READERS
Detailed occupations by group, 23
METROPOLITAN AREAS
Administrative support workers
  workers, by area and group, 365
All workers, by sex, race, and Hispanic origin, 267
All workers, by statistical area and occupation group, 246
Business workers
  management, business, and financial workers, by area and group, 281
Computer professionals
  science, engineering, and computer professionals, by area and group, 295
Construction and extractive workers
  workers, by area and group, 379
Engineering professionals
  science, engineering, and computer professionals, by area and group, 295
Financial workers
  management, business, and financial workers, by area and group, 281
Health care professionals
  health care practitioners, by area and group, 309
Hispanic origin
  administrative support workers, 365
  all workers, 267
  construction and extractive workers, 379
  health care practitioners, 309
  installation, maintenance, and repair workers, 393
  laborers and helpers, 435
  management, business, and financial workers, 281
  production workers, 407
  professional workers, 323
  protective service workers, 449
  sales workers, 351
  science, engineering, and computer professionals, 295
  service workers, 463
  technicians, 337
  transportation and moving workers, 421
Installation, maintenance, and repair workers
  workers, by area and group, 393
Laborers and helpers
  workers, by area and group, 435
Management workers
  management, business, and financial workers, by area and group, 281
Nurses
  health care practitioners, by area and group, 309
Physicians and surgeons
  health care practitioners, by area and group, 309
Police officers
  workers, by area and group, 449
Production workers
  workers, by area and group, 407
Professional workers
  other professional workers, by area and group, 323
Protective service workers
  workers, by area and group, 449
Race
  administrative support workers, 365
  all workers, 267
  construction and extractive workers, 379
  health care practitioners, 309
  installation, maintenance, and repair workers, 393
  laborers and helpers, 435
  management, business, and financial workers, 281
  production workers, 407
  professional workers, 323
  protective service workers, 449
  sales workers, 351
  science, engineering, and computer professionals, 295
  service workers, 463
  technicians, 337
  transportation and moving workers, 421
Sales workers
  workers, by area and group, 351
Science professionals
  science, engineering, and computer professionals, by area and group, 295
Service workers
  service workers, by area and group, 463
Sexes
  administrative support workers, 365
  all workers, 267
  construction and extractive workers, 379
  health care practitioners, 309
  installation, maintenance, and repair workers, 393
  laborers and helpers, 435
  management, business, and financial workers, 281
  production workers, 407
  professional workers, 323
  protective service workers, 449
  sales workers, 351
  science, engineering, and computer professionals, 295

INDEX

  service workers, 463
  technicians, 337
  transportation and moving workers, 421
 Technicians
  workers, by area and group, 337
 Transportation and moving
  workers, by area and group, 421
MINING MACHINE OPERATORS
 Detailed occupations by group, 27
MUSICIANS AND SINGERS
 Detailed occupations by group, 15
 Educational attainment, 56

N
NATURAL SCIENCE MANAGERS
 Educational attainment, 52
NEWS ANALYSTS
 Educational attainment, 56
NURSES
 Detailed occupations by group, 18
 Educational attainment, 58
 Metropolitan areas
  health care practitioners, by area and group, 308
 States
  health care practitioners, by state and group, 218

O
OCCUPATIONAL THERAPISTS
 Education attainment, 58
OFFICE CLERKS
 Detailed occupations by group, 25
OPTICIANS
 Detailed occupations by group, 18
 Educational attainment, 58
OPTOMETRISTS
 Detailed occupations by group, 13
 Educational attainment, 56

P
PAINTERS, CONSTRUCTION AND MAINTENANCE
 Detailed occupations by group, 27
PARALEGALS
 Detailed occupations by group, 23
 Educational attainment, 51
PARKING LOT ATTENDANTS
 Detailed occupations by group, 40
PARTS SALESPERSONS
 Detailed occupations by group, 21
PAVING OPERATORS
 Detailed occupations by group, 27
PAYROLL CLERKS
 Detailed occupations by group, 23
PERSONAL CARE AIDES
 Detailed occupations by group, 48
 Educational attainment, 60
PEST CONTROL WORKERS
 Detailed occupations by group, 48
 Educational attainment, 60
PETROLEUM AND MINING ENGINEERS
 Educational attainment, 54
PHARMACISTS
 Detailed occupations by group, 13
 Educational attainment, 56

PHLEBOTOMISTS
 Detailed occupations by group, 48
 Educational attainment, 58
PHOTOGRAPHERS
 Detailed occupations by group, 15
 Educational attainment, 56
PHYSICAL THERAPISTS
 Detailed occupations by group, 13
PHYSICIAN ASSISTANTS
 Detailed occupations by group, 13
PHYSICIANS AND SURGEONS
 Detailed occupations by group, 13
 Educational attainment, 56
 Metropolitan areas
  health care practitioners, by area and group, 309
 States
  health care practitioners, by state and group, 220
PLASTERERS AND STUCCO MASONS
 Detailed occupations by group, 27
PLUMBERS AND PIPELAYERS
 Detailed occupations by group, 27
POLICE OFFICERS
 Detailed occupations by group, 45
 Educational attainment, 58
 Metropolitan areas
  workers, by area and group, 449
 States
  laborers, by state and group, 238
POLICE SUPERVISORS
 Detailed occupations by group, 45
POSTAL SERVICE CLERKS
 Detailed occupations by group, 23
PRINTING PRESS OPERATORS
 Detailed occupations by group, 37
PROBATION OFFICERS
 Detailed occupations by group, 16
PROCUREMENT CLERKS
 Detailed occupations by group, 23
PRODUCERS AND DIRECTORS
 Detailed occupations by group, 16
 Educational attainment, 56
PRODUCTION WORKERS
 Detailed occupations by group, 37
 EEO occupation groups, 2
 Hispanic origin, 38
 Metropolitan areas
  production workers, by area and group, 407
 Race, 38
 Sexes, 38
 States
  production workers, by state and group, 234
PROFESSIONAL DEGREES
 Educational attainment
  workers with graduate or professional degrees, 182
 Hispanic origin
  with graduate or professional degrees, 182
 Race
  workers with graduate or professional degrees, 182
 Sexes
  workers with graduate or professional degrees, 182
 Workers with graduate or professional degrees
  detailed occupations by group, 182

PROFESSIONAL WORKERS
    EEO occupation groups, 2
    Hispanic origin, 15
    Metropolitan areas
        other professional workers, by area and group, 323
    Race, 15
    Sexes, 15
    States
        other professional workers, by state and group, 222

PROOFREADERS AND COPY MARKERS
    Detailed occupations by group, 25

PROTECTIVE SERVICE WORKERS
    Detailed occupations by group, 45
    EEO occupation groups, 2
    Hispanic origin, 45
    Metropolitan areas
        workers, by area and group, 449
    Race, 45
    Sexes, 45
    States
        workers, by state and group, 240

PSYCHOLOGISTS
    Detailed occupations by group, 15
    Educational attainment, 54

PUBLIC RELATIONS SPECIALISTS
    Detailed occupations by group, 15
    Educational attainment, 56

PURCHASING AGENTS
    Educational attainment, 53

PURCHASING MANAGERS
    Educational attainment, 53

R

RACE
    Administrative support workers, 25
    Associate degrees
        workers with associate degrees, 130
    Banking occupations, 6
    Business workers, 6
    College
        workers with bachelor's degrees, 156
        workers with some college, 130
    Computer professionals, 10
    Construction and extractive workers, 27
    Educational attainment
        selected groups, 50
    EEO occupation groups, 2
    Engineering professionals, 10
    Financial workers, 6
    Graduate degrees
        workers with graduate or professional degrees, 182
    Health care professionals, 13
    High school graduates
        workers who are not high school graduates, 71
        workers with high school diploma or equivalency, 100
    Installation, maintenance, and repair workers, 30
    Laborers and helpers, 43
    Management workers, 6
    Metropolitan areas
        administrative support workers, 365
        all workers, 265
        construction and extractive workers, 379
        health care practitioners, 309
        installation, maintenance, and repair workers, 393
        laborers and helpers, 435
        management, business, and financial workers, 281
        production workers, 407
        professional workers, 323
        protective service workers, 449
        sales workers, 351
        science, engineering, and computer professionals, 295
        service workers, 449
        technicians, 337
        transportation and moving workers, 421
    Production workers, 35
    Professional degrees
        workers with graduate or professional degrees, 182
    Professional workers, 15
    Protective service workers, 45
    Sales workers, 21
    Science professionals, 10
    Service workers, 48
    States
        administrative support workers, 228
        all workers, by state and race, 214
        construction and extraction workers, 230
        health care practitioners, 220
        installation, maintenance, and repair workers, 232
        laborers and helpers, 238
        management, business, and financial workers, 216
        production workers, 234
        professional workers, 222
        protective service workers, 240
        sales workers, 226
        science, engineering, and computer professionals, 218
        service workers, 242
        technicians, 224
        transportation and moving workers, 236
    Technicians, 18
    Transportation workers, 40

RADIATION THERAPISTS
    Detailed occupations by group, 13

RADIO AND TELECOMMUNICATIONS INSTALLERS
    Detailed occupations by group, 30

RAILROAD OPERATORS
    Detailed occupations by group, 40

RANCHERS
    Educational attainment, 51

REAL ESTATE BROKERS AND SALES AGENTS
    Detailed occupations by group, 21

RECEPTIONISTS
    Detailed occupations by group, 23

RECREATIONAL THERAPISTS
    Detailed occupations by group, 13

RECREATION AND FITNESS WORKERS
    Detailed occupations by group, 48
    Educational attainment, 60

REFUSE COLLECTORS
    Detailed occupations by group, 43

RENTAL CLERKS
    Detailed occupations by group, 21

REPORTERS AND NEWS ANALYSTS
    Detailed occupations by group, 15

RESERVATION CLERKS
    Detailed occupations by group, 23

INDEX

RESPIRATORY THERAPISTS
Detailed occupations by group, 13
RETAIL SALES WORKERS
Detailed occupations by group, 21
RIGGERS
Detailed occupations by group, 32
ROOFERS
Detailed occupations by group, 28

S
SAILORS
Detailed occupations by group, 40
SALES WORKERS
Detailed occupations by group, 21
Educational attainment, 60
EEO occupation groups, 2
Hispanic origin, 21
Metropolitan areas
workers, by area and group, 350
Race, 21
Sexes, 21
States
workers, by state and group, 224
SCIENCE PROFESSIONALS
EEO occupation groups, 2
Hispanic origin, 10
Metropolitan areas
science, engineering, and computer professionals, by area and group, 294
Race, 10
Sexes, 10
States
science, engineering, and computer professionals, by state and group, 216
SECRETARIES
Detailed occupations by group, 25
SECURITIES AND COMMODITIES AGENTS
Detailed occupations by group, 21
SECURITY AND ALARM SYSTEMS INSTALLERS
Detailed occupations by group, 31
SECURITY GUARDS
Detailed occupations by group, 45
Educational attainment, 58
SERVICE WORKERS
Detailed occupations by group, 49
EEO occupation groups, 2
Hispanic origin, 49
Metropolitan areas
service workers, by area and group, 462
Race, 49
Sexes, 49
States
service workers, by state and group, 240
SEXES
Administrative support workers, 23
Associate degrees
workers with associate degrees, 129
Banking occupations, 6
Business workers, 6
College
workers with bachelor's degrees, 156
workers with some college, 130
Computer professionals, 10

Construction and extractive workers, 27
Educational attainment
selected groups, 50
EEO occupation groups, 2
Engineering professionals, 10
Financial workers, 6
Graduate degrees
workers with graduate or professional degrees, 182
Health care professionals, 13
High school graduates
workers who are not high school graduates, 71
workers with high school diploma or equivalency, 100
Installation, maintenance, and repair workers, 30
Laborers and helpers, 43
Management workers, 6
Metropolitan areas
administrative support workers, 365
all workers, 267
construction and extractive workers, 379
health care practitioners, 309
installation, maintenance, and repair workers, 393
laborers and helpers, 435
management, business, and financial workers, 281
production workers, 407
professional workers, 323
protective service workers, 449
sales workers, 351
science, engineering, and computer professionals, 295
service workers, 463
technicians, 337
transportation and moving workers, 421
Production workers, 35
Professional degrees
workers with graduate or professional degrees, 182
Professional workers, 15
Protective service workers, 45
Sales workers, 21
Science professionals, 10
Service workers, 48
States
administrative support workers, 228
all workers, by state and sex, 214
construction and extraction workers, 230
health care practitioners, 220
installation, maintenance, and repair workers, 232
laborers and helpers, 238
management, business, and financial workers, 216
production workers, 234
professional workers, 222
protective service workers, 240
sales workers, 226
science, engineering, and computer professionals, 218
service workers, 242
technicians, 224
transportation and moving workers, 236
Technicians, 18
Transportation workers, 40
SHEET METAL WORKERS
Detailed occupations by group, 27
SHIP AND BOAT CAPTAINS
Detailed occupations by group, 40
SHIPPING AND RECEIVING CLERKS
Detailed occupations by group, 23

SHOE REPAIRERS
    Detailed occupations by group, 32
SMALL ENGINE MECHANICS
    Detailed occupations by group, 32
SOCIAL AND HUMAN SERVICE ASSISTANTS
    Detailed occupations by group, 23
SOCIAL SCIENTISTS
    Detailed occupations by group, 15
SOCIAL WORKERS
    Detailed occupations by group, 15
    Educational attainment, 56
SOFTWARE DEVELOPERS
    Educational attainment, 56
SPEECH-LANGUAGE PATHOLOGISTS
    Detailed occupations by group, 13
SPORTS WORKERS
    Detailed occupations by group, 15
STATES
    Administrative support workers
        workers, by state and group, 228
    All workers, by state, sex, race, and Hispanic origin, 214
    All workers, by state and occupation group, 211
    Business workers
        management, business, and financial workers, by state and group, 216
    Computer professionals
        science, engineering, and computer professionals, by state and group, 218
    Construction and extractive workers
        workers, by state and group, 230
    Engineering professionals
        science, engineering, and computer professionals, by state and group, 218
    Financial workers
        management, business, and financial workers, by state and group, 216
    Health care professionals
        health care practitioners, by state and group, 220
    Hispanic origin
        administrative support workers, 228
        all workers, by state and Hispanic origin, 214
        construction and extraction workers, 230
        health care practitioners, 220
        installation, maintenance, and repair workers, 232
        laborers and helpers, 238
        management, business, and financial workers, 216
        production workers, 234
        professional workers, 222
        protective service workers, 240
        sales workers, 226
        science, engineering, and computer professionals, 218
        service workers, 242
        technicians, 224
        transportation and moving workers, 236
    Installation, maintenance, and repair workers
        workers, by state and group, 232
    Laborers and helpers
        workers, by state and group, 238
    Management workers
        management, business, and financial workers, by state and group, 216
    Police officers
        workers, by state and group, 240
    Production workers
        production workers, by state and group, 234
    Professional workers
        other professional workers, by state and group, 222
    Protective service workers
        workers, by state and group, 240
    Race
        administrative support workers, 228
        all workers, by state and race, 214
        construction and extraction workers, 230
        health care practitioners, 220
        installation, maintenance, and repair workers, 232
        laborers and helpers, 238
        management, business, and financial workers, 216
        production workers, 230
        professional workers, 222
        protective service workers, 240
        sales workers, 226
        science, engineering, and computer professionals, 218
        service workers, 242
        technicians, 224
        transportation and moving workers, 236
    Sales workers
        workers, by state and group, 226
    Science professionals
        science, engineering, and computer professionals, by state and group, 218
    Service workers
        workers, by state and group, 242
    Sexes
        administrative support workers, 228
        all workers, by state and sex, 214
        construction and extraction workers, 230
        health care practitioners, 220
        installation, maintenance, and repair workers, 232
        laborers and helpers, 238
        management, business, and financial workers, 216
        production workers, 234
        professional workers, 222
        protective service workers, 240
        sales workers, 226
        science, engineering, and computer professionals, 218
        service workers, 242
        technicians, 224
        transportation and moving workers, 236
    Technicians
        workers, by state and group, 224
    Transportation workers
        transportation and material moving workers, by state and group, 236
SURVEYING AND MAPPING TECHNICIANS
    Detailed occupations by group, 18
SURVEYORS
    Educational attainment, 54
SWITCHBOARD OPERATORS
    Detailed occupations by group, 23

T
TAILORS AND DRESSMAKERS
    Detailed occupations by group, 32
TAXI DRIVERS
    Detailed occupations by group, 40

INDEX

TAX PREPARERS
    Educational attainment, 54
TEACHER ASSISTANTS
    Detailed occupations by group, 23
TEACHERS
    Detailed occupations by group, 15
    Educational attainment, 56
TECHNICAL WRITERS
    Detailed occupations by group, 15
    Educational attainment, 56
TECHNICIANS
    Detailed occupations by group, 18
    EEO occupation groups, 2
    Hispanic origin, 18
    Metropolitan workers
        workers, by area and group, 337
    Race, 18
    Sexes, 18
    States
        workers, by state and group, 224
TELEMARKETERS
    Detailed occupations by group, 21
TELEPHONE OPERATORS
    Detailed occupations by group, 23
TELEVISION AND MOTION PICTURE PROFESSIONALS
    Detailed occupations by group, 15
    Educational attainment, 56
TELLERS
    Detailed occupations by group, 23
TEXTILE WORKERS
    Detailed occupations by group, 38
THERAPISTS
    Detailed occupations by group, 13
TOOL AND DIE MAKERS
    Detailed occupations by group, 32
TOWNS
    see **METROPOLITAN AREAS**
TRAINING AND DEVELOPMENT MANAGERS
    Educational attainment, 53
TRANSPORTATION WORKERS
    Detailed occupations by group, 40
    EEO occupation groups, 2
    Hispanic origin, 40
    Metropolitan areas
        transportation and moving workers, by area and group, 421
    Race, 40
    Sexes, 40
    States
        transportation and material moving workers, by state and group, 236
TRAVEL AGENTS
    Detailed occupations by group, 21
    Educational attainment, 60
TRUCK MECHANICS
    Detailed occupations by group, 30
TYPISTS
    Detailed occupations by group, 23

U

UNEMPLOYMENT
    EEO occupation groups, 2
UPHOLSTERERS
    Detailed occupations by group, 32
URBAN AND REGIONAL PLANNERS
    Detailed occupations by group, 15
    Educational attainment, 55

V

VETERINARIANS
    Educational attainment, 58
VETERINARY ASSISTANTS
    Detailed occupations by group, 49

W

WAITERS AND WAITRESSES
    Detailed occupations by group, 49
    Educational attainment, 60
WATER AND WASTEWATER TREATMENT PLANT OPERATORS
    Detailed occupations by group, 30
WEB DEVELOPERS
    Educational attainment, 54
WEIGHERS AND MEASURERS
    Detailed occupations by group, 24
WELDERS
    Detailed occupations by group, 35
WHITES
    see **RACE**
WHOLESALE AND RETAIL BUYERS
    Educational attainment, 52
WORKERS WITH SOME COLLEGE
    College, Sexes
WRITERS AND AUTHORS
    Detailed occupations by group, 16
    Educational attainment, 56